A MOMENT TO REFLECT

The National Library of Poetry

Diana Zeiger, Editor

A Moment to Reflect

Copyright © 1997 by The National Library of Poetry
as a compilation.

Rights to individual poems reside with the artists themselves.
This collection of poetry contains works submitted to the Publisher by individual authors who confirm that the work is their original creation. Based upon the authors' confirmations and to the Publisher's actual knowledge, these poems were written by the listed poets. The National Library of Poetry does not guarantee or assume responsibility for verifying the authorship of each work.

The views expressed within certain poems contained in this anthology do not necessarily reflect the views of the editors or staff of The National Library of Poetry.

All rights reserved under International and Pan-American copyright conventions. No part of this book may be reproduced, stored in a retrieval system or transmitted in any form, electronic, mechanical, or by other means, without written permission of the publisher. Address all inquiries to Jeffrey Franz, Publisher, P.O. Box 704, Owings Mills, MD 21117.

Library of Congress
Cataloging in Publication Data

ISBN 1-57553-349-9

Proudly manufactured in The United States of America by
Watermark Press
One Poetry Plaza
Owings Mills, MD 21117

Editor's Note

Sometimes a single moment can define an entire generation. How many people can remember what they were doing when the atomic bomb was dropped on Hiroshima? Or when John F. Kennedy was shot? When Neil Armstrong took his historic first steps on the surface of the moon? Or, more recently, when the Federal Building in Oklahoma City was bombed? Each of these defining moments altered the way thousands, even millions, of people viewed themselves and the world around them.

Defining moments such as these also occur on a personal scale — graduations, marriages, giving birth, losing a loved one. Even the act of simply contemplating one's past or actions can produce revelations that will forever alter one's world view. Taking a moment to reflect, then, may seem like a small act, but it is one that can produce enormous repercussions.

Debra Greenfield's "Am I But A Muse" (p. 1) is about just this sort of reflection. The poem's persona wonders whether her sole purpose in life is merely to be a "muse," who inspires and nurtures others, but is unable to create for herself:

> *Am I but a muse, a master('s) inspiration,*
> *With a talent to infuse, a light to light the way?*
> *And am I none but fodder for the blank sheet on the blotter,*
> *A gift for every thief who smiles gladly as I pay.*

She laments that she has allowed herself to be seduced by the blandishments of so many who have come along ("...And so I've sold my soul to every knave...") and leaves the reader with the impression that this has happened to her more times than she cares to remember. The persona also implies that she gained nothing from these relationships: "...was I mere diversion for every dashing jingo / Who never won at Bingo but always took the cash...." These "knaves" would flatter her, take what they could from her (be it artistic inspiration, emotional support, or money) then run off, leaving her alone.

Finally, in the wake of yet another disastrous relationship, she finds herself reflecting upon what has just happened and gains sudden insight:

> *Mourning's darker sky lays claim to thorny revelation;*
> *"Awake, and fie! There never was a poet, silly girl!"*
> *As I, alas, remove Deception's mist and bow to Truth — I wonder,*
> *How I make a poet of a churl...*

She sees the "smarmy sycophants" for what they are and realizes that she can and must be her own inspiration, not one for others.

Ms. Greenfield conveys a powerful message in "Am I But A Muse," and she does it with remarkable poetic skill. Her language is formal, and some of her vocabulary ("knave," "fie," "churl") is almost antiquated in tone — both of these stylistic elements complement the subject well. The poem adheres to a strict rhyme scheme, rhyming the second and fourth lines of each stanza, with an internal rhyme in the third line (or third and fourth line, as in the third stanza). The meter and rhyme are disrupted at times when the persona reaches an important revelation. For example, the third line of the fourth stanza contains no internal rhyme, and its meter does not conform with that of the rest of the poem — it is as if her sudden insight has thrown her off balance, and she momentarily loses the 'feel' of her rhythm. Neither does the final stanza of the poem adhere to the strict structure imposed upon the rest of the poem. The final two lines contain internal rhymes, but the poem's close ("left to amuse myself") rhymes with nothing else and serves to emphasize the persona's decision to break with her past patterns of behavior.

Although the subject of "Am I But A Muse" is rather serious, the poem is not a somber one. The rhythm of the poem is light and almost whimsical, and there are a number of plays on words. The persona calls herself both "a master('s)" and "a comic('s) inspiration," implying that she is both the source of inspiration to "masters" and "comics," and that she is an authoritative, as well as comic, figure. At the conclusion of the poem, the persona is "left to amuse [herself];" that is, she must occupy herself, as well as serve as her own muse.

Debra Greenfield has presented a thought-provoking message with "Am I But A Muse," and she has done so in an inventive and clever manner. For these reasons, the judges and I have awarded her the Grand Prize in the contest held in connection with *A Moment to Reflect*.

On occasion, it is reflection upon a moment captured by another (perhaps in a song, a photograph, or a painting) that helps us to define ourselves. In "Self-Portrait" (p. 98), Hillary Chute describes a persona who is perched on the cusp of womanhood, and uses a description of Gustav Klimt's painting, "The Kiss," to illustrate her feelings of ambivalence. The persona seems to be a typical adolescent girl suffering through the angst so peculiar to teenagers (in addition to the physical changes which occur in those years):

> *My lips are wet and tragic.*
> *My hair is matted.*
> ....
> *My uterus yanks itself out slowly.*
> *It tugs on my body like an anvil*
> *lodged in my cervix.*

She feels dragged down by the realities of becoming a woman and longs for the simplicity of childhood:

> *Sometimes I wish I had a face*
> *like a drawing: two dot eyes*
> *and a circular upturned mouth.*
> *A little penny nose,*
> *two long lines for hair.*
> *Hands like a five-pronged fork.*

In childhood, as in such a childish drawing, things are clearly defined and unembellished.

Though she longs for such simplicity, the persona actually feels entangled in a morass of conflicting feelings. She says:

> *I am the look*
> *of the woman in the Klimt painting.*
> *Eyes closed as if asleep,*
> ....
> *Hands grip the back of her frail neck*
> *with strong fingers*
> *and she smiles*
> *without moving her almond mouth.*

In the painting "The Kiss," the woman appears to be both supported and dominated by her partner. The look on her face is an enigmatic one, reflecting emotions ranging from pleasure to resignation. In comparing herself to such an image, the persona implies that she recognizes she must accept the fact of her own impending adulthood, and may even be able to take some faint pleasure in it eventually. In addition, she is also stating her awareness that real life resembles more a Klimt painting, with its complexities and variations of color and texture, than a childlike stick drawing. The moment captured in "The Kiss" has led the persona to a greater self-understanding and self-awareness.

In "Daff In A Bang-Bang" (p. 357), Christine Ginetti alludes to a moment that many feel defined the entire anti-Vietnam-War movement: the famous photograph that appeared in *Life* magazine which features a young woman placing a flower in the barrel of a National Guardsman's rifle. She captures the dizzying, psychedelic atmosphere of the late 1960's with these lines:

> *Tulips wearing granny glasses as working class heroes—imagine*
> *electric bananas play with mellow yellow flowers in a*
> *strawberry field forever while the carousel spins crazily and*
> *plays backwards music.*

And:

> *limitless undying love shines everywhere with a silver light as midnight does the twist in the sergeant pepper afternoon.*

These references to popular culture, especially to the music of The Beatles, enhance the atmosphere Ms. Ginetti has created. Sadly, this gentle time cannot last — "insane thoughts drive knife that commits evil / star murder" (the assassination of John Lennon by Mark David Chapman). But even though the harshness of reality has intruded and murdered one of the most prominent icons of that peaceful time, the images and music that came from that era ensure that its feelings of hope and love will never die: "Daffodil in a shotgun says peace and daisies declare the / walrus is not dead." It is reassuring to reflect upon such moments.

There are many poems worthy of note within this anthology, including: "Remains" (p. 490), by Francis Connolly-Weinert; "Thinking Man" (p. 355), by Thomas G. Corrigan; "Vespers" (p. 284), by Sarah C. Fry; "Summer on Sanibel" (p. 486), by Ronan McNamara; "An Early Morning" (p. 162), by Christine Meranda; "A Brief Thought" (p. 12), by Jason Pacilli; "adrift" (p. 259), by Mark Power; and "The Ring Of Cicadas" (p. 236), by Forrest Schaefer. I urge you to pay special attention to all of these poems. I also wish to congratulate each of the artists featured in *A Moment to Reflect*: though I cannot present a detailed critique of every work contained in this volume, I must commend all of the poets herein and encourage them to continue their artistic pursuits.

In addition, I would like to thank all the editors, assistant editors, and customer service, administrative, and general services staff who have contributed their hard work and talents to the production of *A Moment to Reflect*. I am sincerely grateful to them all.

Diana Zeiger
Editor

Cover Art: *Tracy Hetzel*

Grand Prize Winner

Debra Greenfield / New York, NY

Second Prize

Hillary Chute / Cambridge, MA
Francis Connolly-Weinert / Jamaica, NY
Thomas Corrigan / Palm Beach Gardens, FL
Sarah Fry / Palo Alto, CA
Christine Ginetti / Matteson, IL
Ronan McNamara / Welcome, MD
Christine Meranda / Vienna, VA
Jason Pacilli / Brooklyn, NY
Mark Power / Easton, IL
Forrest Schaefer / Blue Springs, MO

Third Prize

Robert Arnold III / Charlotte, NC
Sharon Austin / Pasco, WA
Tomas Beauchamp, Bloomington, IN
Rebecca Billings / Marshall, MI
Katie Carlstrom / Manchester, MO
Esequiel Chacon / Lakewood, CO
Mary Lou Connelly / Brighton, MA
Margery Cooper / Detroit, MI
Janet Corley / Twisp, WA
Jonathan Davis / Warrington, PA
Grant Dean / Austin, TX
Karen DiBenedetto / San Jose, CA
John Dorsey / Petaluma, CA
Carla Duffy / Beaverton, OR
Wilbur Farley / Port Jefferson, NY
Erik Fitzpatrick / Wellesley, MA
John Galuska / Bloomington, IN
Ruth Gibb / Miami, FL
Katie Heffernan / Watertown, CT
Malvino Hoffman III / San Francisco, CA
Nell Huddleston / Pittsburg, TX
Nikki Insdorf / Penn Valley, PA
Robert Jones / Hopelohn, NJ
William Jones / Lake San Marcos, CA
Joshua Klein / Houston, TX
Karen Kouril / Hauppauge, NY
John Landis / Weston, MA
Catherine Larsen / Saint Louis, MO
Charlene Lee / Wyomissing, PA
Amy Lekan / Park Ridge, IL
Galina Leybovich / Elmhurst, NY
Laird McNeel / Portage, WI
Vita Mikelevicius / Hometown, IL
Dennis Myers / Redwood Falls, MN
Helen Nichols / Redondo Beach, CA
Sina Nikkhou / San Francisco, CA
Edward Nordan / Jackson, MS
David Palmer / Shirley, MA
Sy Park / Los Angeles, CA
Deborah Preece / Lexington, KY
Aileen Prera / Sun Valley, CA
Shawn Rowan / Saint Paul, MN
Chuck Samsel / Flushing, NY
Mark Scheffer / Coatesville, PA
Brian Schuette / Rockville, MD
Michael Sharpe / New York, NY
Michael Simons / Cleveland Heights, OH
Jane Smith / Virginia Beach, VA
Jolieta Smith / Tujunga, CA
Marian Snyder / Oakland, CA
Gabriel Steinbach / Dublin, NH
Charles Thatcher / Friendswood, TX
Ryan Tilley / Baton Rouge, LA
Patricia Totten / Saratoga Springs, NY
Margaret Vaught / Central City, KY
Thomas Walters / Freehold, NJ
Jeffrey Waters / Las Cruces, NM
Matthew Watson / Pueblo, CO
A. Yakawiak / Chittenango, NY

Congratulations also to our Editor's Choice Winners!

Am I But A Muse

Am I but a muse, a master('s) inspiration,
With a talent to infuse, a light to light the way?
And am I none but fodder for the blank sheet on the blotter,
A gift for every thief who smiles gladly as I pay.

Morning's grayish sky holds uncanny consolation,
And so I've sold my soul to every knave...
When kissed along the midway, it seems the poet did say,
"You are none but Goddess, and I, devout, your slave".

Oh, was I but a muse for any sycophant so smarmy?
He'd steal my pearls, disarm me, and then go off to dance?
And was I mere diversion for every dashing jingo
Who never won at Bingo but always took the cash.

Mourning's darker sky lays claim to thorny revelation;
"Awake, and fie! There never was a poet, silly girl!"
As I, alas, remove Deception's mist and bow to Truth — I wonder,
How I make a poet of a churl...

Am I but a muse, a comic('s) inspiration,
With a talent to approve the perfect beat of Time?
Merely a confection seen oddly as Perfection;
And so disposed when the show has closed — left to amuse myself.

Debra Greenfield

Grand Prize Winner

True Hearts Desire

What is to become of you and me?
Are we both just too blind to see?
What's right before us, we do not see;
Our true heart's desire.

We look right through, but we do not see,
What we're searching for, both thee and me.
It's as if through a looking glass we peer,
We look and stare at each other we are near.
For we are both the same deep down inside,
Still afraid and scared; still wanting to hide.
Yet what's right before us, we do not see,
Our true hearts desire.

Searching, searching; I cannot find.
Wanting, wanting, someone to call mine.
Someone who is gentle and kind,
Yet sometimes we are just to blind,
For what's right before us is our true hearts desire.

Teresa Maria Staczewicz

God

You breathe life into my nostrils.
You make me in the likeness of you.
You care for me, and you give time for me.
You are kind gentle and true.
There is gracefulness in your footsteps,
And beauty in your words.
You are as pure as the snow.
Perfect in every sway.
The color of one's skin makes no difference to you.
Size and shape doesn't matter,
For you look at the soul.
You have three names:
God the father, God the son, and the Holy Ghost.
I can't help but to love you,
And I know that you love me, too.
You are my God, Lord, and Savior,
And for that, and all the love and blessings you have given me,
I will always love you.

Joy Casto

Midwest-Eastern Calamity '94

An earthquake had just rocked the West Coast.
Another calamity was making its boasts.
Deep freeze had come upon the land.
Low temperatures were in great command.

Broken records filled weather reports.
Shut-in citizens were out of sorts.
Car engines would only stop after they whine.
Furnaces broke down in last resign.

Global warming just wasn't there.
Frozen and broken pipes were everywhere.
Energy power was down or completely lost.
Unheated houses could be a perilous cost.

A ninety year old woman without any heat.
Desperation drove her to her basement to retreat.
Her Maker - She knew she must talk to Him.
Time for her was now growing close to dim.

In kneeling stance; she started to freeze to the floor.
All knew what was in store.
A cry of help was uttered there.
There was a rescue — a proof of prayer?

Jean L. McBride

"Song For The Seasons"

Clouds of different shapes
Silver lining around their face
Trees of unusual kind
Colorful leaves will show their sign

The cold is in the air
Winter means long underwear
Another summer has left
Spring is on the shelf

Birds are on their way
To build nest out of leaves and hay
Chicks are born and raised
Hungry for song and praise

This the Mother will bring
At the sound of the falling rain
The chicks were elated
For they knew this would be their new home

A place for feeding
A place for breeding
And also a place for a song.

Charles Don Pressley

The Mixed Narcotic

   Since we met
You've begged my stay; and because you accept
my flavor each day; I'll live to my rep
and bring joy your way. But remember my concept:
Someone has to pay....

   I've seen your future
and time marks your limit, to you I'll torture
though you'll submit I'll write a new chapter
named the mixed narcotic, I've caught you in my rapture
and never will you escape it....

   You've reigned long enough
now I'll take control, you've gotten very tough
and dangerously bold, I'm the one who's famous,
so now I'll treat you cold....

   I'm heroin, yet counterfeit I'm cut with an unknown
I'm mixed with some vital sh** my friend you've just been blown
you had to feed your habit you should have left me alone
I'll find my way to my next addict, and let him taste my tone.

Ray Viveiros

Hope

Hope is a free commodity that can come by
the thousands or not at all.

Only time will tell in our darkest hour
the amount of hope we all possess.

I believe it is in this darkest hour we find
something we thought we knew was there or
what we thought we lost years ago.
Ourselves.

Because, hope is never alone strength and
courage always follow even though it is
unseen and unfelt times, it is there.

And when we no longer think we can afford
to hope we must still believe because
without Hope we are lost.

Susan Abrams

A Verse For Lunch (Oh, What A Sweater!)

The spontaneous realization of green
Washed over me like a provocative wave
Breaking on the impressionable shore of my mind
Captivating my senses and
Rendering me thoroughly intoxicated.

Green begets envy yet for m'eye it's desire
Rapturing the body and
Stealing the soul
As it arrests
All over distractions and influences
To bind with seductive fetters
The lust and opportunity
It so quickly denies,
Mercilessly,
To be replaced by
A kiss to the air and
A glance for I
In a mockery of promise
Overwhelmed by tantalizing possibility.
Jonathan C. Davis

The River Of Life

Ever been down a river on a raft
catching some rays and lots of laughs?
At times it's slow, easy, and relaxing.
Then before you know it, You're crashing!
Racing! Bouncing down the rocky stream!
Not sure to hold your breath or scream!
All of a sudden you are drifting slow
kicking back again going with the flow.
Ann! The sun! The river! The life! The love!
All given to us by great God above!
It's weird how the river changes so much.
But when I drop my hand down to touch
I realize; no matter what, it's still
The same ole river that I feel!

The river is always one river flowing to the sea.
As is your life! Always one life as is your destiny!
Anthony R. Borst

The Cry Of A Babe

As the glass fell upon my cast
  I wish I could have passed this grim ripping blast.
I wish my eyes would deceive me,
  If not my mother had conceived me.
My hearing, though not so well, I think,
  Pounds the sounds of dust upon mine ear.
The taste of blood and fiberglass
  Eludes this babe's tongue.
The weight upon my chest
  Seems to be a pest.
Buried beneath this place,
  The lick of a dog upon my face,
    I only wish it were grace, for hell is this place.
I want to see light, Oh how
  I wish it weren't night.
For if it were light, I'd crawl up
  That flight, to yonder sight.

I only hope that one man's quest
  Has fulfilled his best,
For a terrorist known as McVeigh has taken this life away...
Paul K. Wright

Where I Stand

I stand on the very most outer part of the popular circle, but I stand very close when people are in need.
I stand very far away from my bedroom door, but I stand very close when my house feels hurt.
Sometimes I would like to stand on the very end of a long bridge and just slip off.
Other times, I like to stand on a very short bridge very tall and proud and just sit down.
Sometimes I would like to stand on the tallest sky scraper and scream.
Other times, I like to stand on the smallest building and just be heard with my tears.
Sometimes I would like to stand away from the awfulness in the world.
Other times, I like to stand up to all the crap in my own country.
Sometimes I would like to stand in another galaxy.
Other times, I like to stand in my own world.
Sometimes I would like to stand no more.
Other times, I like to stand forever.
I stand between heaven and hell but no one understands, because
where I stand, I stand alone.
Kristie Julien

Sometimes...

Sometimes I wonder...
If it's my soul you want to drink
If your motives are as pure
As the stuff you say you think
Sometimes I wonder...

Sometimes I say...
What makes you hide your unborn tears
Behind that mask of lies
Showing none of what you fear
Sometimes I say...

Sometimes I hear...
Your soft voice knocking on my door
You want to unveil those thoughts, don't you?
No, instead you'll keep them all in store
But sometimes I hear them
Sometimes I know...
Brittany Marling

Left Behind

They lie all alone, cold and untouched
But others will come, others will come
They leave behind mud, their soles have clutched
But still and unmoving, others will come
Then sun rises high in a scarlet ocean
Dried up and frail, others will come
More left behind in chaos and motion
Still, others will come

Being pressed to the sidewalk, cold but not alone
Others will come in the future unknown
No one caring what they've left behind
A small print left of unconscious minds
Worried to get in, worried to get back
Still, no one notices the uncared track
The track meaning movement across a lawn
Someone's been there, the someone's gone

Not only are the prints being left behind
So is the person watching, standing still in time.
Rebecca Billings

The Welcome Wagon

I came to this land with love in my heart.......
I landed in jail without even a start....
The "statue" I read of with arms so encircling...
Dissolved from my dreaming of life so enriching...

My monies were taken, my clothes torn and tattered....
My whisperings un-noticed....
I just did not matter....

I came to this land with love in my heart.....
To work in a room surrounded by dark...
Rumblings of hunger refusing to leave me...
Flashes of "Home", beginning to grieve me....
I came to this land with love in my heart.....
To study and write with learning so ample....
So, give me a break,....I don't want to take.....
A future I'll make
My body to ache....
Not back in a crate......
Just give me a break......
Matti Lascoe

Before The Expansion Camp

To take this journey,

when green leaves are eaten by industrial caterpillars,
flowers are waiting for rain eternally,
burning bushes have stopped firing clay souls,
and jungles are loosing their children...

when floods go to war on forbidden soil,
blizzards have condensed inside man's ears,
earthquakes smile without fear,
and lava flows in the streets of every city...

when bones shatter under sky's scrappers,
(their bodies longing for some kind of freedom),
spirits dry like ancient paint in a vast desert,
and voices wither to jagged cracks of earth under sun...

to take this journey requires being human.
John D. Galuska

The Spider's Erroneous Hospitality

"Welcome my lace-winged friend, to my humble
abode," rasped the spider to the fly.

"I am so excited to see you, my friend,
for not many enjoy dropping by.

Would you care to stay and chat with me,
while we snack on crumpets and tea?

I often get so lonely here, please stay a long while,"
the spider begged with an erroneous smile.

"My life is so dull and the outlook is bleak.
If you would like, my friend,
spend the night, or better yet, stay the week.

Come, companion, and brighten my life.
If you would prefer, you may ring your wife.

Explain to her you will be late tonight,
for I am having you for supper."
Shenoa Herlinger

"I Love My Children"

If you claim you love your children
why do you deliberately, knowingly, and
intentionally give them poison. I heard
you with my "own" ears, when you told your
children, I love you, then you give to
them freely a poisonous disease called racism.
Leon R. Thomas

America The True

Red,
White,
And blue,
The colors of our nation true.
The stars,
And the Stripes,
That stood through that hell-like night.
Yes,
Red,
White,
And Blue,
The colors of our nation true!
Brandon Prioreschi

Untitled

I came to you desperate
and defeated.
I arrived on your doorstep
hollow and disheveled.
I reported to you
pompous and arrogant.
You met a person
of questionable moral fiber.
You listened
to the twisted version
of my life, my self-pity, my strife.
You told me things, I did not want to hear.
You exposed my naked soul.
You introduced me to honesty.
You handed me a mirror
And coaxed me to look,
You held my hand,
You believed in me.
Barry Godin

I Believe

I believe in God, my Father in Heaven.
He loves me, He protects me, I try to trust Him.
However, sometimes I may think He has failed me.
Yet, He takes me with these doubts and all my questions.
Eventually, I see the way, His way, His plan.

I believe in Jesus Christ, my brother.
He loves me so much He died so I may live.

I believe in the Holy Spirit.
He loves me and He guides me, although I may not always follow.

I believe in the Redemption of souls.
We shall not be lost.
God looks for all that stray.
He finds them, He helps them.
Do we?

If I get lost and I look for God, He is there.
Always.
No matter how long it takes for me to begin looking,
He is there,
Waiting for me to come home.
Kimberly A. Kasprack

Sometimes Actually

Sometimes fire-spurned comets actually streak the sky
Sometimes once-wounded birds actually learn to fly
Sometimes sun-seared deserts actually flood with rain
Sometimes one's best memories actually end in pain
Sometimes stones strike and actually cause a spark
And sometimes Cupid's arrow actually hits its mark
Chance Reynolds

The Closed Door

I look into your eyes, the windows of your soul,
And see a great sadness, a painful hole.
They see you smile; I see you cry.
Day after day, you don't know why.
Life is boring; it's no fun.
With no destination, you continue to run.
Where is the laughter? Where is the love?
All the happiness you're dreaming of?
Decisions become hard to make.
What you can't face, you just try to escape.
Should you stay? Should you go?
That should have been determined long ago.
Which way will you choose?
Pick just one...the other, you lose.
You've been blessed with so very much.
Yet, day by day, you're losing touch.
Try to reach deep down inside
And release the sadness that you must hide.
Please, please don't hesitate.
Open the door...before it's too late.
   Mary Ann Eidem

The Vision

I have a vision - of pain and unrelated sorrow.....
Refuting the machinations of timeless reality,
It strikes forth on the 13th second of the 13th minute of the 13th hour.

Carelessly twisted Deviousness have I envisioned -
Thoroughly doubting the elevations it has sought to aspire to.
Yet, going far beyond that it has ever accomplished before.

The very definition of love is destined to fall prey to evil trickery-
Like an anguished city destroyed by man's thoughtlessness.
From its precarious position on its lofty pedestal,
Love will die promising true vengeance on Grace.

Curious as we are to gain knowledge from the depths of our Souls-
We cannot hope to derive from them the meaning of Truth
In order to escape our personal Labyrinths.

Therefore, the sorrow of which I envision will be our ultimate Destiny-
One we will choose to underestimate and ignore...
Yet, when it reveals itself, it will become our Salvation.
   Rachel P. Villanueva

"Flowers"

   Someone is walking on my grave;
Shuffling feet through the loose soil, dragging
worn shoes uncaring over the rose blooms so long ago
placed by tiny fingers. I must be truly forgotten
to have been left among the tangled weeds that have
overgrown my blossoms. I wish to scream at them,
   "Stop! Move! Don't you remember I am here!",
But no sound can be forced through these lips. Surely
they see my headstone, the monument left of me. And
realize where they tread.
   Silently alone as in life I lie wondering who moves
above. I do not wish to contemplate the idea. It may
be someone I hold dear moving so malevolently upon
my refuge; for my eternal sleep would then be sorrowful.
   So here I lie quiet, accepting, as always, better
unknown who tramples my flowers.
   Sheila Gonzales

This Christmas

Centuries ago the first Christmas came,
A Savior born to bear our blame.
Through the years the Christmas Season has come,
Traditions differing for some.
In modern holidays it seems as if
Forgotten is God's Divine Gift.

As we decorate and anticipate
Our gifts to give and gifts to get,
The Love in Christmas we often forget.
Now once again Christmas is near...
What will we do with our Christmas this year?
   Mary-Alice Wightman

An Insight

The mind
an endless energy which gives me peace.
The heart
the seat of love and patience.
The soul
a heavenly fortress which gives me strength.

All these things make up me.
An individual in our vast society
which lives from day to day.
   Charles M. Boudreau

One Wish

As I wander through the woods
I wonder how you are

I sit down and I look up
to wish upon a star

As I sit and wonder
what my wish should be

I think about how much it would mean
to be the best friends that friends could be
   Kali Schuschke

"Empty Inside"

With each hit you take a thought
escapes your mind, a memory fades away
The more you do, the more you want
Stop now before it's too late
Your brain will vanish, your heart will stop
Think of the precious time you waste, totally gone from reality —
numb
When you're high you enter a new world, a make believe world
Come down to reality and take advantage of the things around you
Enjoy life to its fullest
Think of the money you burn, what do you really get out of it?
Peace of mind? Happiness?

is a state of mind - you don't need any substance
to create it, all you need is a mind
But keep inhaling and you won't have a mind left,
you'll be empty inside
You'll end up with nothing.
   Kelly A. McCreight

Rest In Peace

I don't know where to start,
but I have to let you know,
This poem is from the heart,
I simply haven't let you go.

Even though you're not around
I hope you know I care,
because no matter where I go
you're with me everywhere

You often cross my mind, when I'm around the way,
friends like you are hard to find, it's kind of hard for me to say.

What I'm feeling deep inside
Can you see me? Are you alright?
Have you gone very far? Or do you,
watch me day and night?

These questions shall remain
Since you're gone away for good
Is there anyone to blame?
If there was you know I would.

It's so hard to say goodbye, well to let you go at least,
I send you all my love, my friend, please, rest in peace.

Desserie Richardson

Untitled

Dear James,
The world seems so different now, everyone has changed,
no-one seems to care anymore, why has it been arranged?
We lost you about two months ago, and still things are out of place,
nothing will ever be the same, it's your death we must all face.
Tears continue to fall, down the side of my face,
it's so hard for me to accept it, accept you're in such a beautiful place.
As I sit and stare at your picture, or listen to the songs you
would sing, tears still form within my eyes, with the
memories that I bring.
I want you to know that I love you, for I've always told you so,
know that I pray for you, and I will never let you go.
As I conclude this letter, smile a smile for me,
your best friend here, is what I'll always be.

Melissa Cerrissa Holguin

What I Did Today

I almost didn't think of you today,
but I couldn't help myself.
It's hard to be in this position
with your heart upon a shelf.
I almost didn't think of all the fun we've had,
but the memories kept coming back,
boy—is this bad!
I almost didn't think of things that we've been through,
but believe me, that wasn't hard to do.
I almost didn't sleep tonight
wondering if you were under the same full moon,
but I finally slipped off to slumber
only to be awakened by the sun at noon.
I almost didn't dream of your face last night,
but there it was again.
It seems it's meant to be there until the very end.
I almost didn't think of you today, but I did.
And it made me smile.

Patti A. Johnson

Show Me To My Mountain

I see a beam of light shining in the wind I can hear my name
they are calling me to my mountain where there is no more
  suffering or pain

Please show me to my mountain be patient and give me some time
I'm very slow at climbing you see, I lost my legs in Viet-Nam

My arms are tired, and my fingers bleed my mind gets foggy,
  so I must take heed
The flesh on my fingers is torn to the bone I have to keep
  climbing, I must find my home

After many sunny days I almost lost my sight and there on the
  mountain was a beam of light
My reward was there by what I saw it was all the M.I.A.'s and
  prisoners of war
Now I know my home has been found when they all embraced me
  not uttering a sound

I had seen a beam of light shinning and I had heard them call my name
Now I am home on my mountain where there is no more
  suffering or pain

Fred W. Robinson

Builder Of Castles

Love of adventure should not be enslaved, mountains to climb,
castles to build can only be done by the brave.

No bounds, no bounds have these limitless reaches called space.
new cities, new worlds to build in this wide wide place.

Go build your castles out there my friend, for you are free of
yokes from the world within.

No chains, no laws to hold you down, only the adventure
In your hands unbound.

To build, to build is never a scheme, shelter to live is
a rewarding dream.

Castles you'll build where there is fertile sod, you'll need
only your hands and the hands of God.

And so, we give you our dreams.

Don McEllistrim

Shades Of Madness (One Manic - Depressive's View)

A darkness descends darker than before.
Tears of pain inside can anyone lighten the score?
Crying in anguish against the sky
can't sleep anymore and wondering why.
Remember the good days? Not anymore.
When was it better?
Seems like never before.
Feelings of loss linger;
bitterness for days gone by.
Can't seem to get it together no matter how hard I try.
Tears subside. I see the light.
Am I better now or just getting "high"?
Can't determine how long it
will last, but I try. I try, am I going too fast?
Only a kind of madness that
colors the world too dark, too light.
Seems I've been here in the past.
When will I come down? I'll give it a fight.
I'll keep trying as long as I endure.
Hoping I'm around when they find a cure.

Mary Jo Palka

Untitled

I see a raging beast, ready to bust free
I see a shy boy, persecuted by others
I see hatred and madness
I see love and compassion
The beast and the boy help each other
The beast gives confidence and strength to the boy
The boy gives tolerance and understanding to the beast
Each are separate, each are needed to make the other whole
They are one, they are me!
   Larry McDaniel Jr.

Lord, Walk With Me

Lord, walk with me as I walk life's pathways.
Lord, take my hand lest I stumble and fall.
Lord, guide my feet, keep me on the straight and narrow.
Lord, lead me home to you.

You, oh Lord, are my shelter from the storm.
It is you, oh Lord, that keeps me safe and keeps me warm.
You have always been there, through my yesterdays
  and my tomorrows.

Be with me now I pray.

You, oh Lord, are my rock and Salvation.
You, oh Lord, are everything I'll ever need.
So stay with me now and help me through these
times of darkness.
Lord, guide me to the light.

Lord, walk with me as I take life's journey.
Lord, take my hand, be always at my side.
Lord, guide my feet, may I follow in your footsteps.
Lord, lead me home to you.
   Katrina Lister

Forever Searching

As the soul searches for eternal fulfillment,
So be it true the heart must feel the pain.

It is a feeling like a running stream,
Always rushing and searching, but seldom finding calm waters.

With passion, the soul intimately controls the restlessness,
Having no compassion for forgiveness and always remembering.

The only thriving glimmer of hope is that of contentment,
A state of mind that is not so easily envisioned.

How or when that self being is achieved is not known,
However it is the question that keeps us holding on.

Time may be the only answer, or rather, that it has already passed,
Leaving the soul forever searching.
   Gina R. Drumright

Colors Of The Past

Blue skies.
Green grass.
White clouds.
They are all colors of the past.

But what is in the future?
What color does it have in store for you and I?
Will we live a long time or will we die?

Will the colors all be a blur of black and gray?
Or will the color be as clean and as bright as day?

Listen to the words that I say.
Every man goes his own way.
   Dena Power

Everlasting

Where were you Lord, when I fell that time,
Where were you Lord, when the time just slipped away like water through my fingers.
Where were you when the day changed to night,
where were you when I was crying in the dark,
Where were you when the very sound of my tears was captivating
  my heart,
Where were you when my accusers lay in wait for me,

Wait one minute, let me better understand,
Lord there you were picking me up when I had fallen,
And there you were again in the very day that slipped away
from me.
And in the night you were also there watching by my bedside,
And when I was crying, so that was your shoulder Lord,
And you were the peace within my soul and sweeping into my heart
  that night,
My accusers were scared away from me in silence,

Lord your grace is without end,
Your peace fills my heart with joy,
Your happiness fills my eyes with a light so bright,
my very being is outside of myself when you are near me,
I thank you for the love, that is everlasting.
   Jessica Ann Jones

Kites...

How beautiful!!! You guide them gently
at the first breath of wind...
and you wait and hope... and here they go...
they climb up, they hesitate...
they seem a little lost...
a little wind comes to their rescue pushing them
higher, giving them a little strength! Here, now
they are in place; they have gained confidence...
they can fly.

Look... they are playing with the breeze coming
from the sea... finally, they have met!
How happy! They are dancing with such agility...
they are swerving and swooping... they are making loops...
One, two, three... four... climbing up again,
higher and higher...

And so our lives, our spirits, our hopes...
When we seem to be lost, somehow a friendly wind blowing
gently from somewhere... a smile, a hug, a good word, all
unexpected, come to our rescue lifting us up, to a new life, hopes,
and we are free and happy again.
   Annabella Norris

Wailon

I have never known a man
Who was quite so grand
For me he held my world in his hands
Hands so big and hands so strong
I just can't believe he is really gone
Life without him will be so hard to live
Because there was nothing he could not do
He took care of me and he took care of you
Always with love and always sincere
You could tell God was hovering near
I have no doubt that it was in God's plan
For he too must have needed this man
So I will try to let go as best as I can
And live my life as I know God has planned
I will try to serve God and let him heal my heart
As only he can
Because somehow this was all God's plan
Even though I will never understand
   Virginia Martin Meyer

Truly Alive

I've stepped into the gathering darkness
and faced the winds of fate.
Placed life upon its fickle breeze
and stared beyond the mortal gate.

I danced the swirling clouds
of that gathering storm
and victoriously emerged,
though slightly battered and worn.

I saw the ashen face of death
looming over me.
He smiled his evil smile and said
not yet, but mine you shall be.

Most people are afraid to die.
Even more are afraid to live.
But, you only get out of life
the sum and total of what you give.

Many will never understand
that though I could have died,
how at that very moment
I was never more alive.

Richard Todd Owens

"One Way Window"

Open up the window
Look down toward the street
You feel the wind cut through your face
But you can't feel your feet

You twist and tie the spinning sky
Like thread around your hand
You watch and smile as the sidewalk crumbles
Into a pile of filthy sand

Your blood is drunk on the chill of the wind
It's no longer drunk by your world
You taste the blood burning in your mouth
As your troubled heart unfurls

You see the glass but can't see through it
So you close your eyes and count to ten
And the screaming wind makes you wish
You could close the window up again

Raj Wahi

Mommie

A little old lady sits by the door and wonders
why don't she come and see me no more?
No, Mommie we've got other plans
I can't come see you today.
She's so busy doing this and that with who and who.
I'll go see her some other day.
And the days and weeks and months go by.
And one day she says "I'll go see Mommie today."
She drove up and opened the door
and found her Mommie lying dead on the floor,
She fell to her knees, put her head in her hands.
And the tears began to run
Mommie, oh Mommie, what have I done?
If only I could go back in time.
There'd be no excuses for reason or rhythm
I'll never forget as long as I live
oh, what a horrible fate!
I came to see my Mommie today.
But I waited too late.

Chris Ellis

The Milkweed

So green and stately in the spring;
The milkweeds come to do their thing.
They stand so straight, grand and tall
Beside the other plants so small.

The summer arrives, with sun so hot;
The big green trees notice them not.
They blend with cat-tails and goldenrod;
Their heads in rhythm all do nod.

The Autumn comes. They all turn brown;
They begin to split...so full of down.
Their lives now are nearly over,
As is the wheat, rye and clover.

The seeds burst forth like little men
Attached to parachutes...then when
Tis time, they come floating down
To implant another milkweed in the ground.

Thelma Hunt

In My Dreams

In my dreams...
 Friends long dead are alive and smiling.
I ride horses with no fear of falling,
 The only means of controlling them is with my mind.

 I've seen God smiling, greeting new souls as they enter His kingdom.
I've intruded upon Him as He mapped out the future of our world,
and as I humbly knelt before Him, He laid His hands upon my neck...
 "You are healed."

 It is wonderful to be in a place where everything is beautiful
and good. I am gently led to feel things that I have not felt in
 this world. Fantasies that I dare not mention come to life:

I am hated, I am adored.
I am feared, I am afraid.
I can do anything, I am helpless.

In my dreams...

Carlita J. Miles

Wonders Of Existence

Through the shadows of the world's night,
There comes a beam of sheer delight,
The moon comes forth quietly to shine,
Bringing peace to yours and mine.

Following comes the break of day,
And the brilliance of sun comes our way.
To show the beauty and bring to light,
The many wonders unseen by night.

The drifting winds, and sky so blue,
Bring thoughts in time so very true,
While the birds of nature in their song,
Bring a brilliance of singing all along.

Beauty in the brilliance of night and day,
Bring to us all along the way,
Combined with the creations of land and sea,
A pleasure in life for you and me.

The creation and wonders of life's being,
Bring many questions with answers unseen,
But in our wonders, thanks can be given,
For the peace and pleasures brought to us all.

Edmund C. Bowie

Inhibitions

Embrace the night! The Young One pleads
While the Ancient One ceases to think
Screw democracy, conformity, obedience, duty
Break from the shackles as a child-
   laughing, taunting

Naked and free
Arching your back toward tomorrow

Suffocating by emotions
Space for the body - breath for the soul
Where does the mind appease itself of the
   ongoing chatter-the principles which rule our lives

Complexities...questions
Unknown words
   Allyson Minear

"Sun: Rising"

What pulls you up at this time of day?
Who holds you up all of the way?

What strong hand is taking care of you,
in the changing phases you have to do?

Pink, red, a burnt orange dye,
'What' brush painted you while in the sky?

A wonder, a miracle; do we notice, do we care?
Created for all, a blessing to share.

It is time again, see, the night is past,
may this New Beginning always last....
   Grace E. Oberkircher

Retirement

My body is strong
My mind is not gone
According to corporate world
Age has waved its magic wand

Where do I turn
What do I do
It's time to begin a life anew

I tapped my brain and lo and behold
Brain waves were spinning ideas of gold
I selected one and put it on hold

Then I began a life a new
Empowered, enlightened and moving with ease
Accomplishments and strides that I have made,
Far surpassed what I did to get paid

Peace and contentment without any strife
is now my wonderful world of retirement life
   Mabel Catanzaro

The Mask

  We are delicate shadows, silently whispering sad music into the skies ears. Although our faces shine like red roses newly in bloom we are internally crying. We live only in front of our masks except in dreams. In dreams we are sometimes dragged, screaming, to our deaths where knives rip our delicate shadows to shreds. In one moment we are shown our sad lives behind our masks, clawing at our skin to get out. But the moment is fast and soon the false faces are glued together once again in front of our repulsive souls. And then we awake and put on our masks, oblivious of the talons tearing at our souls.
   Laura Miller

Moment's In The Sun

If you think back; try to remember
A young blonde girl, curvaceous and tender.
We met by the river; the attraction was real.
Our hearts beat strong, your loving I could feel.
You were much older; I was so young
Into each other's arms, our bodies were clung.
You were my hero; you made me forget
In moment's of passion; I'll never regret.
You were my first love; I was your many
A small Indiana town; where others were pretty.
I never forget you and am still in love
Not just the memories; but I feel true love
I carried my feelings for you, all my life
And I am much older and was someone's wife.

I'll never forget you and how I would run;
Down to the river and you.
for our moments in the sun.
   Kathryn Strong

Always Try

You will not always be the best,
but no one will ever be the best.
Work for what you want, try for
what is expected, and do what is told.
Accomplish that and you will not be judged
but you will be praised.
   Tyler Elslager

Spring, 1994

Perhaps thousands dead, it stresses.
Tens of thousands dead.
Rather
braided black bodies piled to borders and back,
a twentieth-century burial rite, a predictable effect;
there forms a place without citizens or homes, more
the unclear echoes of different types of guns.

It's revenge for resisting, it explains;
resistance to revenge.
Better
bombed-out offered still, rotten to fate, above
prisoners against leaders twisting obeisance out of clay;
expect no vacations, swims, or strolls:
tag an unknown or snare one of your own.

Readers sunk by day plead for truth become dull.
Red, green, gray. All force lines in order wished anew.
They flee naked from hands-greedy and legs-full;
children run aimless as I wonder what to do.
   Shana R. Cohen

Sunrise

It used to be night out on the beach.
Now the sun begins to reach
Up and over the sand,
Spilling gold on the land.
Night has left and day has come.
The sun and sky have become
A shimmering sheet of amber and gold,
A touch of purple -
It never grows old.
  Slowly, silently, the splendor fades away.
  But it will come when once again
  The night turns into day.
   Lydia Eckhoff

The Trophy

She smiles.
He nods.
Years of smiles and nods and caresses to follow.
Her beauty is likable, but he does not like her.
To move on is too difficult.
To let go, self-defeating.
Easier to create a masterpiece of lies to satisfy the fragile eyes.
The eyes are filled with disbelief and longing,
   and the lips form words of submission.

He has his trophy.

She hides the tears from his disapproving grin.
He caresses his trophy and puts it to bed - he will take it out
again when its touch seems new
  once more
    Many times more.
But his love is showered on another
   whose foolish eyes are hidden from the pain,
   and who will know the truth once his love
takes on a new name.

Laura Pesin

My Old Home

I'm going back to my old home
where I lived many years ago
I'm going back to Southwest Georgia
where the pines and willows grow.

I would like to go fishing
where I used to go back then
I would like to swing under the old oak tree
In our back yard again

It was just a plain old house
Nothing special to see
But I was so contented there
It was home sweet home to me.

Ozzie B. Glisson

"O Beautiful Tree"

Go to sleep O Beautiful Tree,
Until God wakes you in the spring.
You've displayed your colors
Of red, brown, gold and green.
Now sleep, sleep until the spring.

The air is crisp and turning cold,
As the wind doth shake your colors so bold.
Sleep now tree for winter will come,
And scatter your leaves upon the lawn.

Soon your branches will fill
With a blanket of white,
And once again your beauty
Will fill my heart with delight.

So sleep now tree and take your rest,
I'll see you in the spring
When robin builds her nest.

Then through summer, your
Leaf-filled branches will bring
Shade from the sun, shelter from the rain,
As I rest and thank God for your beauty again.

Gloria Campbell

Primary And Final Diagnosis

And now another disease - Multiple Sclerosis - is coming out of
  the closet
And the silent, soundless sufferers who have kept their symptoms
  secret
You're hearing of them not because of how they've lived their lives
We're learning now about the ways in which they chose to end
  their days

They did not die from their disease, but they died with and of it
They'd been given a Life Sentence - no plea bargains or appealing
Their condition was not terminal, so there were always options
Surviving was a role that they could always choose to play.

MS is not an ailment, it's a certain destination
The travel guide is given with the tour and diagnosis
There is no turning back when one embarks upon this voyage
And where one starts cannot foretell how long it takes to get there.

The road we travel on is one that's steadily declining
There may be turn-offs, twists and turns, and often-times a detour
We cannot plan ahead, we do not know what we'll be needing
We can't learn from other travelers, each of us must go alone.

Carole Henkoff

Our Lovely Earth

Dancing in its wet dew
As the green grass grows

Stripping to your bathing suit
by tossing off your clothes.
Splashing in the warm pond
as several ducks swim by.

I could live in nature
from today until I die.

Drying off upon a hill
in the beautiful sun's rays

Lying on the grassy plains
where the cattle graze.

Colorful is the sunset
as it falls behind the mountainside

Staring at the star's twilight
until my eyeballs hide.

When the birds play their lovely melodies
My eyes smile again...

As I'm carried in the wind's breeze.

Angela D. Rose

The Pain

I hate when I hurt
and I hurt when I hate!
When I see the ugly face of violence,
tearing eyes, a grimace of pain
and I hear a cry
for help and mercy in vain,
I hurt and I hate!
At the sight of endless wars,
of human suffering day and night
and of rivers of blood flooding the fields,
I hurt and fear, and hate!
To this very day, I'm sorry to say,
I'm not a good Christian!
I cannot forget,
I cannot forgive,
when I witness the destruction
Of nature and man!
And I hurt when I hate!

William T. Enders

Untitled

As I walk into the night,
Surrounded by my fear and fright,
I think back to the days before
I knew of fear, hate, and war.
I remember my friends as they once were,
Not as bloody bodies on the shore
of the eternal hell that's coming fast,
Because of their ignorant past.
Jeff Reid

A Brief Thought

Breakfast morning
I sit in my kitchen
Drinking tea,
And it blinks at me
Mistake and confused
About the babies,
I scream with laughter
Tones of grey turn black before me.
It divides my stomach in two
The effects are
Infecting, they call out my name
Caressing me with dangling hands,
Blue fingers and dead eyes.
Floating I sit still unfortunate.
Encrusted my spinal cord tightens
Foreign voices: Soothing and ailing.
Shadows cold, transparent and slender.
Motionless, in a silent background, yellow pamphlets
A call to arms to the windows, a glance it blinks again,
Drinking the same breakfast tea.
Jason Pacilli

The Parting

I'm so filled up with emptiness;
My eyes cried dry from tears.
Today I learned there'll be one less;
You've gone home, after all these years.

While part of me says you're not "gone,"
You're really just "away";
There's part of me - the heart of me -
That cries for one more day.

In time, I know I'll get along;
I'll learn once more to sing;
And treasure memories of you
'Til I fly home on Gabriel's wing.

So, it's God's speed I wish for you,
As your love helps ease my fears;
And in my soul I hear Him say,
"Welcome home, after all these years."
Bette A. Conrad

Travels

As we grow older, and travel through the years,
Ones we used to know so well, are we now simply our peers.
Some of us seem to drift apart.
For others, friendships begin to start.
I look upon the faces that I once thought I knew,
Years ago, it seems, that together so much we would do.
But now we are different, and our paths have split,
But I know that none of you I will ever forget.
It seems when we are together, we don't have much to say,
And as each day passes, our friendships seem farther away.
As I once knew you, I know you no more,
And memories of our friendship are safely stored,
With reflections I once knew of the past,
And I know our friendship had died at last.
Stephanie Savage

A Poem For Two Voices The Lion And The Lioness

We belong together,	We belong together,
And work together,	And work together,
We'd love to explain!	We'd love to explain!
I lounge and clean myself,	
Being a lion.	
	While I, the lioness have to search and salvage for food with help from others.
Then at noon I sit down for lunch and finish it off with a big cat nap.	
	While I eat the scraps from their meal.
We work to help each other	We work to help each other Well, most of the time.
But we still love each other.	But we still love each other.

Heidi Kleister

Wishing On A Water Wall

I hear the whispers of the water wall,
A wily lover's wishing wall,
While standing from afar.
I know the truth of the water wall,
I've heard the stories it has to tell,
While standing from afar.
I call it a wall of tears,
Tears for lovers who never loved,
Tears for dreamers whose dreams ended
While standing from afar.
Reality sets in as he kisses you Again,
I watch the sky fall,
While standing from afar.
Sweet girl, the softness that you feel,
Is not from him, but from the wall,
It is the tear of me whose heart cried out
While standing from afar.
Anjan Choudhury

The Runaway

She's up till dawn and walks till two
She stares across empty streets and ponders what to do

She never meant to leave and never planned to stay
She tried to get out but her habit got in the way

To be portrayed a prostitute just a woman who knows the game
Would be in false pretense and she wished to clear her name

Trapped against her will she feeds an angry flame
Bound by the evil beast she can only call her shame

She quickly bows her head when eyes begin to stare
She sees herself alone but still her hope is there

Someday she will return, believe it to be true
And all the prayers that you have said
Will come right back on you.

Maybe then you'll understand her dream and life and goal
The passion of her tears the wrenching of her soul

The day you open up your ears and listen to her sighs
Hold her deep within your heart and find yourself inside her eyes.
Keri Cornell

Stephen

His eyes were soft, a velvet brown
They laughed, and spoke, and wept
His body lithe, so graceful, tall
He ran, he danced, he slept

His family so close and loved
Lived always in his heart
And friends were near and far and sure
And life a thing of art

Precious, heady, gay or sad
In beauty or in pain
And then the darkness and the still
Came, disappeared again

Oh, how did chilly, misty breeze
Invade this dear warm son?
Close in until the battle's strike
No longer could be won!

Ten years have passed, three decades here
He graced our earth and sky
The leaves, the stars, the songful birds
Still whisper his goodbye.
   Joanne Ott

One Rose

One rose for the love I feel,
One rose is my love's seal,
One rose for what might be,
One rose is my heart's key,
One rose for the one I've always adored,
For one rose is all I could afford.
   Shawn Weeks

Hopeless

When you have very little hope left,
everything you see is something you can't have.
The dreams you wish to come true
are always beyond your reach . . .
Just so close, but so far gone.
Broken mirrors unveil a broken future
and cracked memories of the past.
Everyone seems to be running towards their destiny,
And I'm standing alone in the fog . . .
Without hope.
   Amy Graham

Loss Of Man

Wandering lonely adrift in my mind,
words cannot tell what we never can find,
out there on the edge pulled away from the crowd,
the voice from within is impossibly loud,
wanting and needing but never quite reaching
the silence wraps slowly around.
Time has forgotten forsaken and taken,
the soul of my being has been brutally shaken,
this void in my world I cannot foresee making,
my will bend to that of his own.
Ending beginning it all seems the same,
the loss I shan't mourn of his primitive game,
my angst is no longer fed fuel from the flame
in wisdom I start life anew.
   Kim E. Mathieus

To Our Friend

No matter how dark the day or the night
friends like Elouise makes everything
nice and bright.

Sharing a table morning, noon and night
made all the days wonderful and bright.

Now she is with her savior up above,
surrounded with happiness, joy and love.

We don't wish her back here below,
but where she is we hope to go.
   Kenneth Hendrickson

Homesickness

Emotions come, deep from inside,
I remember them, oh, how I cried.
I hated it here, with my home sickness,
But everything changed, with its quickness.
Time will pass, and time will come,
But no, this place will never be home.
I want to go, but yet cannot,
For now I live here, where I was brought.
I cannot leave, but just can't stay.
But here I'll be, day after day.
   Emily Arnold

'Our Voyage'

Back and forth, in the middle of the sea
We rocked in a boat the color of a pea.
Strange, we may have looked, but not for long
We couldn't scare you, even if we did have a gong.
We landed on an island, not far from the cold.
The island was tropical and looked pretty old.
We built a hut and repaired our ship.
Our ship would take us on a very long trip.
We stayed in our hut for quite a while
It was as long as a quarter of a mile.
It was happy there in our hut
It was happy there, so we bought a mutt.
   Kathleen Adams

The Eye

Through the square of window
To the square of building,
Up from square of building,
To the square of sky,
Geometrically simple,
Always perfectly circled
Through the mazes of squares
Goes curious -
   Eye.

And accepting whatever
Blocked from stone and glass
Through the mazes - amazing
Circle circles for us.
In the circus of city
I am juggling the eyes
Being juggler, magician
Over million "I"s.
In the middle of changing
Square world, after all
I'm having an eyeball, I'm having a ball.
   Galina Leybovich

The Performer

For the girl with black hair
For the man next door
For the doctor in his office
For the traveler on the plane
For my bedfellow
And for my closest companion
I perform
As they see me walking down the street,
I am strutting across my stage
Full of holes that only the performer can see
A precarious moment
I am close to falling in
I dare not, for I know what lies within
The pain of truth I avoid as the stage creaks beneath me
Each performance closer to the end
Some day the stage will crack and the audience will stop clapping
Then I will perform naked within the crowd
My stage will be gone
Until the end
I perform

Diana Marter

The Starlit Sky

Setting outside on a cool breezy night
I watched the stars as they popped into sight.
One by one they appeared,
filling the sky with their glittering glow.
As I watched I felt as though,
I was lost in a dream from long ago
I saw the one so dear to me;
wishing he belonged to me.
As I looked into his eyes
I saw me and the other guy.
I turned my head to avoid the scene
And when I looked back,
All I saw was The Starlit Sky.

Margaret G. Ark

The Sunset

   The colorful sunset rose above the city hills.
Red, orange, blue, and purple that mixed together like
watercolors in the sky. The glazy colors reflected on
rivers, lakes, and oceans. That took my breath away.

Christina Riordan

Songs Of The Seasons

Spring is for learning the songs of living,
   Seeing wondrous sights through awe-wakened eyes
Feeling youthful stirrings, taking, giving,
   Tasting wins and losses, puppy-love ties.

Summer is the season of songs for two,
   Reciprocal feelings for another,
Dreaming, hoping, sharing the best of you,
   Preparing to be father or mother.

Autumn's music is at a slower pace.
   Grown children spread their wings, desert your nest.
Old photos, mementos, new life to face,
   Excluding sadness to savor the best.

Winter echoes the songs of seasons past,
   Yet augurs the music and songs to be.
Enjoy the music to the very last.
   From God the arranger for you and me.

Edward J. McCarthy

Texas Sunflowers

From this handful of seeds, I'm promised
by the package's pictures and the words,
A bed of riotous blooms so strong and tall.
Can the package claims of 10 to 12 feet
Best the onslaught of the fierce summer sun,
The attacks of the nearby desert's rabbits,
The sparrows' and quails' leaf-loving pecks,
And lastly the whitefly and spider-mite nibbles?

The care given, from the special flowerbed soils
to scheduled waterings and spaced fertilizations,
And to chemical protection and mineral additives,
Parallel a child's careful rearing, the education
and health care, the nurturing of the mind and body
To yield an adult, physically and mentally strong.
In those that fully fend off the many travails
Pure beauty rests in the flower and in the face.

Robert F. Parker

Learning How to Love

The emotion of love should not have been bestowed upon man.
It is far too complicated and too hard to understand.
What is love to me is not love to you,
And the ways of expressing love are as different too.
Some people are romantic, like me, and tend to love too much.
We go overboard with flowers, poems, and such.
We seem to drive relationships apart,
When all we are trying to do is to let our lover deeper into our heart.
I am the worst type of romantic,
For I try to make everything perfect.
Good never seems to be enough for me.
I don't understand why I can't just ease up instead of trying to achieve.
A world without love would be so easy to live in,
But since such a world does not exist, I must change to fit in.
I must learn to love, not to smother.
I must understand that good is enough for the sake of my lover.
I need only fulfill my lover's dreams and expectations.
I do not need to go beyond for the sake of personal gratification.
The feelings of my lover should be the only worry in my life,
For without her there would be no life.

Jason L. Pennypacker

How Shalt I Know?

Dost thou see me or through me and how shall I know?
By a word, by a look, by a touch?
Dost thou love me or hate me and how shalt I know
When I yearn for thee so much?
Dost thou know me or someone else, someone thou knew before
Dost thou see me on every street as in those tales of yore?
Dost thou talk to me in thy dreams and however shalt I know?
Wouldst thou tell me or a secret keep?
Dost thou think of me by morning's light-however shalt I know?
When thou doesn't even make a peep.
It breaks mine heart to see, me so far from thee
I need thee so-and how shalt thou know?
Simply reach out to me.

Hilarie Sherman

Alaska

Faithful of course. To them. So mysterious. So new.
Only they know its ways.
Amazing and different to us.
The land so large and beautiful in every way.
Adventurous it may seem to us, but hardly to them.
To us it is land, gorgeous land.
To them it is home, they know no other.
They see us they don't mind us, but their home does.

Megan Nicole Swanby

Forever Yours

She came to him, He came to her, with words meant only for each other.
With promises of eternal love, they became one, legally, forever.
She came to him, he came to her. In a moment of innocence and bliss
Their flesh united, and they became one, consummated beyond a
passionate kiss.

She walked with him, he walked with her, their souls woven with strong
cord. Nothing could ever separate them, no! Not even a sword!
She walked with him, he walked with her, their spirits no longer two,
but one. Can anything ever tear them apart? No! Never! Their
spirits will always be one.

The years pass on, and life takes its toll. Circumstances, children,
jobs, whatever. A wedge is driven so sharp and deep, what was one
soul now becomes two forever. The body which was one now
becomes two. She went her way, he went the other. Not knowing
their spirits were still united, Will this be forever and ever?

I met him, and foolishly I thought I could make him a wonderful wife.
So legally and physically and mentally we became one, looking toward
tomorrow, forgetting the strife. How long did it take for me to
realize He has not wholly given himself to me. In the area that
counts the most, he is still joined to her spiritually!

Patricia Ann Taylor

He Can Work Through A Dove

The Lord's love is so gentle and pure, as pure as the rain that
falls from up above. And as pure as a dove that flies through the
sky. The Lord can work through a dove because through the dove
the Lord sent his love, upon his servant Jesus. It was a dove
that flew when the waters on the earth was deep that the bird
could not find a perch for the soles of its feet. Then one day
the dove returned to the boat that the Lord kept afloat bringing
good news by way of a leaf in its beak, telling the occupants
that there was dry land. It all adds up to the man up above who
had worked through the dove showing us his endless love.

Michael E. Gainer

Kerosene Sandwiches

They married for poverty and loneliness
and were gone
They left the chapel black and blue
He limped with tin cans, tied to naked feet
Cold glass and winter smelled of
her beaten body
Until until he whispered
White bread kerosene sandwiches,
Smoke against her cold
Left her black and blue
Winter thaw found spring
Very shallow shallow grave.

Jeremy W. Aldridge

Clouds Tell The Tale

I look up into the sky and I see more
than colors of galore. I see beautiful clouds
and a bright sun that reassures me
my day will be full of goodness lore.
I see a cloud that tells me there is love on
hot sunny shores. But then I look again and
I see a dark cloud that tells me there are people
starving to death, and their skin is tight as a glove,
and you can see right to their ribs. I look
up again and I see no clouds to be found;
it's like the clouds have no more tales to tell.

Kelly Widener

Untitled

Born naked. Clothed to protect, against the cold cruel world.
Standing before another, naked for them to see, my inner most
fear and anxiety. Made of clay for the world to mold,
into another cruel and cold.
Open your soul, let another in. Lips of an angel, heart of satan.
Empty now. Lost and alone. The world claims one more victim.
Where I am buried, let a rose grow, to blossom and bloom.
Let her thorns protect against the cruelty of man.
Let the sun shine on her, never to fail, for she will wilt and pale.
Roots deep into the soil, sun upon her blossom, dew upon
her petals. A gentle breeze to sway to insect.
Her fragrance to linger, her stem straight and strong.
The sun gleams on her thorns, razor sharp.
As a reminder in the beauty God has given her
clothing to protect against the
cold
  cruel
    world of man!

Sara Schwarz

Untitled

Writing a poem for a contest,
it easy, just write the very best!
O.K., so what'll I write about
The birds the bees,
the sparrow, my knees,
the breeze or politics,
animals or roses, romance or love.
trees or babies or blue sky above.
A drive down route 66 getting my kicks
ok! Get on with it! Think of a subject.
A poem to write: I need to win:
Not next week, tonight!
I just coloured my hair but that not poem material,
I vacuum the floor and dusted my desk.
What do I write about? Lets think of something!
Before the kids become a pest
I drive an oldsmobile, but nothing rhymes with that.
Now the kids are screaming playing with the cat.
So this it, it's the best I can do.
I'll just hope and pray I'm a winner too.

Jennifer Gotts

Forsaken Land

Everything is wrathful in this forsaken land;
Everyone shall know the end is at hand;
For the time draws near when the Lord shall appear;
Even the strong and mighty shall
Cower with desolate fear;
When the trumpets sound from up above;
Everyone will know their time is up;
Now everything's so hectic that no one
Notices the heaven above;
But when that day surely comes,
they'll wish they had looked to God Above;
For the Lord is our savior with
everlasting love.

Donnie E. Stanley Jr.

Cherished Times

I ponder my thoughts of a lady I love,
She keeps me together when times are tough.
The moments are cherished that out shines
The bad no matter where we may end up.
Up and down left or right, I'll follow her
and she follows me just like the night
That turns into day and day turns to night
together forever at each other side.
A love that will never die.

Frank A. Boone

Untitled

I stumble through time and space
Don't know why I exist
Think about If I were gone
Doubt if I'd be missed

I try not to show if I feel hurt
Most of my feelings I can't explain
I'll put on my act just for you
A cheap smile to disguise the pain

A bed of fear every night
In it I go to sleep
Caught in the riptide of the ocean of suffering
Because I went in too deep

Cannot find rest in this world
Lost is my epitome
Could be called a sad clown
Change my name to misery

Chris Loeffler

Heaven Has A Face

Heaven has a face
now I know that's true
I saw it just the other day
when I first saw you.
Walking into the room her beauty filled up my eyes,
she lit up my world with a smile of sweet surprise.
She moves like a woman
with the innocence of a child,
she looks so beautiful, she drives me wild.
Like a breath of fresh air into a cold and tired world,
Who is this angel?
Who is this girl?

I've seen so many faces
in so many different places.
But I've never been touched like this.

Carlos Gutierrez

Untitled

The leaves stir, the grass sways
As the wind whistles through the sky
Shaping, molding, changing
While the movement is at times unseen
The result is ever apparent
What was before may never be again
But how marvelous the creation of the wind

Giving no resistance the trees bend with each gust of wind
Their leaves flittering with joy
As they are detached from the bond once thought eternal
Who knows their destination as they float
   willingly in the breeze
But how marvelous the creation of the wind

Now seeking some direction, I find wisdom in His creation
That speaks not with lips or words
Letting go of the securities I grasp so tightly
To be caught up in the freedom of His spirit
No longer seeking knowledge of my course
But trusting in the ways of our amazing God
And how marvelous the creation of His wind

Melissa L. Deming

My Name Is Kurtie The Martini Man

Now, let me tell you the plan...
Jo Ann was reading the Black Widow Making book...

and I tell you man that's all it took...
to make me want to drink drink and drink...
and I did and it put me on the brink.

I felt good for a while and on my face was a smile...
then my stomach began to rumble...
and to the bath room I did stumble...

on the floor I did mumble,

leave me just five more minutes.

Richard Wilkerson

Exhale

   A child cries in the heat of the night, she searches for love as she grasps onto life. She's the Light that shines from deep within, she's the ache from the pain when a young life ends.....
   Each day that passes, she drifts farther away; how does she store the memories, when it hurts to speak his name? Who can she run to, to chase away her fears? How will she prevail when she fights back the tears? When your world is shattered and your life's a living Hell; How do you let go of the anger? When will you exhale?.....
   The death of her brother, brought her to her knees; a silent prayer broken-hearted with a weeping plea. Such a tiny little soul, reaching out her hands, calling on her Savior begging him: "Please Jesus, help me understand." Her first loss, an ache that was unforeseen; she cried unto the Lord: "God why would you take my Best Friend, and not take me"?.....
   Jesus looked down upon her, as he heard her cry; he wiped her cheeks, and then he lifted her head, as he dried her welling eyes. He sent her an Angel, his smile was as bright as the moon, and as sweet as a summer breeze; the angel he sent, was her brother Sam, freed from his pain, and he was coming to collect his Wings!
   He soothed her mind with the stories that he told, he eased her heart, restored her faith, as her aches and her pain unfold. When his work was done he waved good-bye; heaven smiled, for he had done well. She released her anguish and gave it to the Lord, and as she praised his name, she EXHALED.

Besthines Maria Davis

The Sun Came Up

The sun came up gently today,
Tentatively putting forth fingers of pink
In the December sky.

Through the fog and the mist,
Lingering reminders of yesterday's rain,
She touched the petals of roses
Refusing to bow to the first brief
   blasts of cold,
Reminders of glorious summer.

The mild, moist air
Deceptively lulls the drowsy senses
In comfort and warmth, masking
   a tinge of warning
That winter is near.

Elizabeth C. Potts

Glimmers Of Glass

Wishes may unfold, play with flight, shifting light embracing, frightening away shadows, upon softened walls, which may wander, fires thirsty flame, colors may dance, trials hardily endured, respite in wonder, each thought untold, dreams await fill, escaping spread lines, others seen bearing, becomes spoken past, silence tenses ears, dances upon air, captured running moonlight, searching for answers, shimmers of dust, sparkles where whispers, seek sanctuary until, fleetingly lost within, glimmers of glass.

Larry D. Rader

Like A Clown

Like a clown, I sometimes frown to show the world I've been
around. Through the paint I'm forced to wear, I fool
the world and those who care. That humorous laugh I once
instilled, has gone astray and lost its thrill. My
secret life I choose to live, has cost me more than
love or sin. In hope of a future. I pray out loud, but
through my travels a fallen cloud. I bear the anger
and think of the days, when life was simple and
somewhat plain. Through my tears I create an ocean
I drown my fears with no emotion. Like a clown I
cover my frown, I try to be strong and absorb the wrong.
I turn the page and all I see, are misled words
that have no means. I wonder how this clown survives
when all she has are sadden eyes. My prayer of
prayers will one day be. To grant me life and solid
peace. Be brave my soul for now I see,
that saddened clown is really me...

Francesca D'Angelo

20th Century Paranoia

Wait a minute!

Are those safe toys?
Are they good boys?
What was that noise?

Wait a minute!

If someone says, "It's a nice day."
Should I stay?
Should I run away?

Wait a minute!

Should I jog in the park?
Should I be out after dark?
Who's there?! Why did my dog bark?

Wait just a minute!

I want to look at the moon..
I want to play in the sun...
I don't want to carry a gun!
I want to walk in the park... And say, "Hi", to a stranger
without the feelings that my life's in danger!
Hello life, goodbye Paranoia!

Muriel Morton

Elegy For Age And Time

When you look at me and all you see
  Is someone old and withered and gray,
Remember once I too was young;
  Was it only yesterday?

Time seemed to stretch before me;
  I had plans and dreams and fears.
Like you I thought youth invincible,
  And knew I had many years.

But time has passed by, and yesterday
  Has now become tomorrow.
I know now life is all too short,
  And I am filled with sorrow.

My life is almost at an end,
  And as you now see me,
Shoulders bent by age and time,
  Someday that's how you'll be.

Enjoy life while you can, my friend,
  For all too soon it's gone;
But remember on some distant day,
  That we will all be one.

Paula L. Annino

I Can't Count

I can't count all the ways to tell you
  what you mean to me,
But at least you know my heart beats true.
I don't know what my life would be,
If I didn't have you.
I know you'll always be by my side,
And I shall walk the town with pride.
I can't count half the things I would like
  to say,
I think about you night and day.
I can't count all the ways I know how to
  love you,
But at least you know my love is true.

Tawnya Barron

Baby Blue

Hiding inside, can you come out to play?
We have been waiting, such a long time.
We will keep waiting,
When ever you're ready
  Baby Blue
You seem to have no need to come out, not today
Everything is safe and warm.
Maybe someday
  Baby Blue
Our words can't describe how much we need you.
We see your eyes of the truest blue.
They sometimes dance with joy.
Sometimes they're like windows of pain.
You look out at us......
Maybe someday
  Baby Blue

Gayle Frost

You're Never Alone

Have you ever thought you were all alone
  When you think about it, it chills you to the bone
You try so hard to forget all the things that made you feel this way,
  You hope this will happen some day!
I cried "oh dear Jesus can you help mend my broken spirit?"
  If you can take away and forgive my sins I will sure cheer it
He answered my prayers, wiped away my sins and forgave me.
  I love you dear Jesus for opening up my eyes to see
So now as I go along life's path the bible will be my rule book.
  If you want to be with the Lord, just open up your heart
    and eyes to take a look.
Just fall on your knees, call on the Lord in Prayer
  Any time day or night, call him by name and he'll be there!

Martha Clayton

I See

This big, brilliantly, bright beam makes me see
Never saw the blossoms that were in bloom
Never knew the beauty of open room
Never did I hear the buzz of one bee
This material world's focus blinds me
This world a prison, with its shallow gloom
My lust was like a self-inflected tomb
Bills and mortgage payments were never free
My shades lenses were lifted from my face
After this I truly saw and I knew
Most people read braille, and walk in one place
I read the book of life and smell fresh dew
To lose is to gain, your sight left me blind
I see with one eye now, and she is my mind

Denequia Washington

My Feelings

We have a history together
It will continue forever
Some things are very special between us
I have to tell you again I love you plus

When I am sleeping
I can see you in my dreaming
And I feel much better
You know it will be forever

My mouth is drying
When I am with you
My head is spinning
When I look at you

My hands are sweating
When I see you
My eyes are shining
When I speak with you

And my heart is beating
For you, just for you

Arzu Yazar

What Is The Deal?

Why are you strapped?
Why do you kill?
My young black brother,
How do you feel?

You sing about the fact that you "get around,"
But does that come from killing your brothers just to be 'down?'

What are you going to do with yourself?
What are you going to become?
Do you have any life dreams?
Do you just want to be a bum?

You ride around in your black car with 'tints,' so no one can see,
Just how beautiful you are, and how good you could really be.

With your life you could do something special.
Yet you claim no one will let you.
So you walk around, selling drugs and buying guns.
And you have no concern for the life of anyone.

Why are you strapped?
Why do you kill?
My young black brother,
What is the Deal?

Shaye Brown

Mom

Mom you are my guiding light, through all these darkened days
You are there in all my times of trouble and get me through the haze.
To say I love you is not enough to show you how I care
When chips were down, with no one around, I'd always knew
   you'd be there
Words alone can't tell you how I feel inside
So from my heart I write this, with all my love and pride.
I remember all the times you did without so we could have nice things
and when I think of all your love my heart jumps out and sings.
God don't give us more than we can handle, but he sure gave you your
share — losing Chuck, Dad and Granny, was too much for you to bear
But I was there with you, mostly in a drunken daze
I'm cleaned up now, and I'll show you how, I'll be sober
   for the rest of my days
Don't you ever think, that you'll be left alone.
because where ever I am, that will be your home.

Michael J. Signore

Nightfall

   Within the tainted, and aged abode.
The structure shimmers deathly cold.
Shadows lurk in corners hidden from sight.
Where even the brave die of fright.

   Reflections flash eerily, and creep.
Across the floor denying sleep.
When once thought so securely held at bay.
Phantoms refuse to fade away.

   When beneath the door their vapors have come.
Appear for you, but not for some.
To pilfer your breath, and leave you a gasp.
You struggle with their deadly grasp.

   Lashing out at the twisted assassin.
Drawing for strength, and all passion.
Fighting off death you are reeling with pain.
To live until night falls again.

Edward Sell

Rainbows And Sunbeams

Rainbows and sunbeams come after the rain,
Refreshing the beauty around us again.
They chase from the skies all the rain and the gray,
And fill us with wonder the rest of the day.

They say that there's gold at the rainbow's end,
But just let me say this to you my dear friend.
No riches nor money will ever compare,
With rainbows or sunbeams or skies that are fair.

Sunbeams will shine through a misty haze,
And color the world from the rainbow's blaze.
It gladdens your heart and makes skies of blue,
And makes the birds sing all their sweet songs to you.

Rainbows and sunbeams are wonders to see,
They bring happy days to you and to me.
Rainbows and sunbeams are things that unfold,
And bring joy to our lives that never grows old.

Kathleen Sager

Her Majesty

There she stands, in all her majestic grace
A captive of her children
in a God forsaken race

Her reign now threatened
Her Majesty now cursed

Her clock of redemption
now tolls in reverse

Her morals and standards
steeped in chaos and crime

Her freedoms and liberties
fighting tyranny and time

Her servant soon her master
as her children walk asleep

Stalinism today a charlatan
cloaked as public safety

Will her children awake in time
or will apathy render them prey

As all Her Majesty stands for
by the Reaper taken away

Harvey Peterson Jr.

Late At Night

Late at night, as I sit and write you this note
I can't help but feel how my heart is broke.
I love you more each passing day,
I'm sorry for all the mean things I say.

A lot of the things I said, I did not mean,
But after all, I'm only a human being.
Maybe we'll never have another fight,
Late at night, as I think, maybe we might.

Michael J. Mellas

A Special Gift

God sent a special gift to me
It was a daughter you see.
   A special product of his love and peace
and no other can take her place.
She has a part of my heart filled with love and
encased with flowing ribbons of joy and peace
that she gave to me and I now release
them back to her to retain,
then send them out again to the daughter she will train.
   Although this gift I may not merit,
we are two souls but one in spirit.

Cora Douglas Bass

Forever Dance With Me

Will you dance for me in the moonlight
Under a cloudless sky of a summer's dream
Oh, it would be such a beautiful sight
If you'd dance for me in the moonlight, tonight.

If I could only dance with you, I don't know.
I would not dare spoil your heavenly motion.
But I know it is my destiny, it will be so.
Someday we will join, and with me the wind we will flow.

Like only lovers dream, like only lovers can,
We will become as one, oblivious to the world.
We will dance to places, unknown to man,
With the wind, across the sea, like only lovers can.

In my arms you will forever be.
No power on earth could make me let go.
And you and I, with the wind and the sea
Will be together for all eternity.

Joshua J. West

Puppy Love

Snow stood like dandruff on your hair and jacket
as you entered the kitchen and leaned against the door
until I spied the tiny beagle peeping from your pocket.
"She's not old enough for a puppy," I said, drying my hands,
"we agreed — remember?"
You just grinned and waited for me to touch that downy head;
you knew my protests would melt
faster than the snowflakes on your collar.

Six dogs later, I still recall those sweet-sad eyes,
that graceless slide of paws which ended in a sprawl
beside our darling creeping on the floor
who held her baby face to his and let him
nudge and lap his way into our hearts by loving her.

That gentle time of baby-beagle days has vanished
with the snows of Northern yesteryears; she does not
remember them at all. (She was too young, as I foretold,)
but I grow old remembering that wintry day of long ago
when snowflakes circled your dear face and we embraced:
the pup, and you and I, beside our kitchen door.

Charlotte H. Geyer

1/2 Truths

For Charlene

I tell them your skin shines like the Nile River on a sunny day
It's smooth and infinite.
This I do tell them....
your smile lights up the heavens, I say.
(but I fail to mention how rarely your smile appears)
I say "My sister is the Cleopatra of Anchorage...she is an
African Queen".
I boast of your marriage and pronounce "He is also direct from
the Motherland."
(Somehow his emotional abuse and lack of devotion slips my memory)
I tell them,
she loves me sisterly like no one else, we are the sisters that
others envy.
(The sexual abuse bond that forever ties us together somehow
does not come up)
This I do tell.
She walks defiantly and effortlessly in 4 inch heels. Royalty.
(They never hear of the pain and sadness that your eyes reflect)
She speaks articulately with dignity and grace.
(Yet the uncertainty in your voice I fail to share with them)
This I do tell.
She is my sister, my love, my heart. She is forever part of me.
(The abandonment I feel from the miles which separate us goes
unmentioned)

Wendy Brownlee

In 1863

On a bright moonlight night in 1863
I was standing my guard at my post

Down the road came a soldier riding
A white horse, looking like a ghost.

From the stories I had heard
Around the campfire at night,
I knew in a moment who he could be.

It could only be one person
Our Commander and Chief, General Robert E. Lee.

As he rode up to me, he got off his horse, Traveller

We walked and we talked
He asked about the war and what I thought

When he left, General Lee wished me well

Oh if I make it home
From this awful war, what stories I could tell.

The stories I can tell my
Children and grandchildren to be

That on that bright moonlight night in 1863
My Commander and Chief General Robert E. Lee,
Spoke to me.

Uldean T. Wells

Silent Message

A silent message, here I send
Preserveth thy love, with glorious honor
The majesty of its beauty
Shall fulfill generations for the reign of eternity
Feel the boldness of its power
The brilliance of its grace
Is the harp of salvation, no evil may face
Dance in the fields of the depths of my words
Fly high in the wind
With the beauty of the birds
Let it be known to others, your light
Guide them with grace as they attempt flight
Bring joy and be blessed, shall the waters flow
Let no one, hold no other, on a shelf below

Robert A. Edgar Jr.

Ode To A Grandmother

Oh, for the love of a grandmother;
Never in my heart will there be another.
Hardly a day will pass by,
That for you will I not cry.
Though you had died before I was born,
For your death I will always mourn.

As darkness hovered over your world,
I know you passed through those gates of pearl.
Onto those streets that are paved with gold
A sight to be foreseen, for the eyes to behold.

Faraway from this earth where you paid your price;
A whole new world for you to entice.
And there you are with the King of all Kings,
An angel of God wearing his wings.
Shirley M. Crowe

New Life

Where has the day of leisure gone?
Books read, slow walks, and watching the dawn

Two beautiful children have entered this scene
With a laugh, a dance, such energy unseen

I thought I had known life at its best
But clean clothes, clean noses, these are my quest

Coloring books and crayons and games abound
'Tis joy, 'tis laughter, 'tis a child's sound

His car with big wheels — it wins many races
Her doll with blue eyes — gets loving embraces

A boy — a girl — and a smile, I'll shout
This is life is really about!

I gave up the music and wine and exotic places
To watch the moonlight on these angelic faces

Their dreams full of color, wonder, and delight
As they screen the future all thru the night

Greater than the moon, the sky, and the stars up above
Is my devotion, my life, and my heart full of love!
Aggie Lujan

The Lord Loves You

The Lord loves you in many ways
As he watches his flock
The Lord loves those who care
And those who care not
The sun, moon and stars are his creation
If we had more love
We would have a greater nation
His trees, flowers, rocks and streams
The Lord loves to help fulfill your dreams
From ocean to ocean - it is his formation
If we had more love
We would have a greater nation
He is the guy who loves you
Standing with open hands
He is also the guy that wrote
The first ten laws of the land
He is the guy that loves you
If you are crippled, sick or weak
The Lord is the guy that loves you
Seven days of every week.
Richard E. Jones

One Last Kiss

One last kiss before we say good-bye,
One last kiss between you and I.
Make it soft, make it sweet.
That one last kiss you just can't beat.

I ask of this because I care,
Wondering if you'll always be there!
Please do me a favor and do it with flare,
Because you must know, I won't always be here.

One last kiss, that's the one I'll remember,
One last kiss, that the one I'll miss.
The first one a cold night in December,
Why not the last one on a warm September's Day.

One last kiss it didn't happen,
One last kiss that's the one I'll be trap'n.
In my mind that's where it will stay.

One last kiss forever and a day,
In my mind that's where it will stay.
Joe Hoffman

The Forgotten One

As the knife jabbed my hand I screamed silently.
Beyond all my screaming, the pain was as horrifying as a cat clawing deep into my skin.
As to why she inflicted me with pain, is something I will never grasp.
Over the rivers of blood, a rubbery hand seized me.
In spite of the distress, I thought the pain would halt.

Upon crying for help, the pain stopped.
Underneath all the agony and hate, I saw the love - the love for me!
For this love was like an arrow shot into my breast.
Like a baby kangaroo has to be with its mother, so do I.
For life is a decision, made by her.

Within her heart I will always be remembered as the child she murdered.
Inside her soul is where I'll stay even if I was restricted of the right to break free of my mother's womb - Alive!
Tracy Perez

I Met A Man

I was walking down the street,
and met a man that made me shriek.

His skin was paleish-green,
and he looked real mean.

He held a puppy in one arm,
I decided he could do no harm.

"Who are you?" Asked I.
He didn't answer, but pointed to the sky.

"Who are you?" Asked I again and again.
Finally he answered, "An Alien."

He didn't want to stay,
so he jumped in his spaceship, and flew away.
Kati Leone

Untitled

To my mother, whom I lived with
laughed with, learned from and love.
Every problem seems a little more difficult,
every achievement less exciting without you to share it.
I miss your light heart, smile, hugs.
But most of all, my friend.
I feel you with me still.
I will love you forever.
Patricia A. Sprouse

Changing Of The Guard

In between the two horizons
The last roses of summer my dear.
I tightrope the hairline equinox;
Ashes assemble,
I tremble,
They disappear.
The first days of Autumn
Are as warm as the summer's retreat.
Where the last creature to sing her praise
I claim as my sorrow,
Slow to recede.
And pirates have come, in ragged ships,
To plunder the galleons of the season.
Now my anxious heart must lie in wait,
To expel the beam
From its window of treason.
    James R. Granger

Array Of Souls

Don't tell a soul about the day we died,
Encased in the promises that were once implied,
Already forgotten in the past of our minds,
Remembering slightly when we are inclined.

The days gone by are present now,
Creeping in slowly from denied rebound,
Embracing their warmth with outstretched arms,
Neglecting the knowledge of deceiving charm.

We bask in the glory of love that has faded,
Ignoring the times of feelings debated,
Deny the day whose arrival is feared,
Open instead to the heart that is seared.

Licking my wounds I return to my den,
Embarrassed by thoughts I can't comprehend,
But I will always have them to comfort me,
Leaning on their power of stability.

Sleeping once more, only then I return,
Living the life where scorn does not burn.
But morning will come and I will arise,
Facing the infinity of our lost enterprise.
    Tracy D. Freitag

Your Decision

You need space. You need less responsibilities.
You need space. You need to be alone.
You need space. You need not to make decisions.
You need space. You need freedom for all that's worth —
You need space. You need space.

I sit here all alone. I won't cry.
There will be no tears. I won't cry.
There will be no shouting. I won't cry.
There will be no pounding. I won't cry.
In my heart I'm sad but my face is smiling.
I won't, cry. I won't cry.

Wash the clothes. Life goes on.
Clean the house. Life goes on,
Every day I go to work. Life goes on.
Friends ask, "How you doing?" Life goes on.
Blue is my favorite color - inside and out.
Life goes on. Life goes on.
    Emma Lynn Westin

Memories

Something to be cherished:
Never to be perished.
Always reminding us of the past.
How did it go so fast?
Forever yours to hold,
but sometimes never told.
Some are bad and some are good:
Having meaning like no other could.
They make us who we are,
and shape our lives from near and far.
Many help us during hard times:
Especially when hiding our crimes.
They are always there to reflect upon:
It's too bad those times have gone.
Your future lies ahead quite expectedly,
for your past is just a mere memory.
    R. Michael Vogler

Mea Culpa

Would I have joined that hostile angry crowd
Gathered in Pilate's courtyard shouting loud,
Would I His claim as Son of God deny,
Crying, "He blasphemes and deserves to die?"
  Surely, not I.

Would I with them have called, "Barabbas free,
His blood upon us and our children be,"
Or watched Him scourged with no protesting cry,
Would I in rage have shouted, "Crucify?"
  No, never I.

Rather would I have risen at early morn
And with the loving women spices borne,
Beside the empty tomb with tear-dimmed eye,
Beheld with joy my living Rabboni!
  Gladly, would I.

But - 'twas my sin that nailed Him to the tree,
Redeeming love brought Him to Calvary;
Dying for me beneath the darkened sky,
Yielding His life that I should never die!
  Yes, it was I.
    Emma Ruiter

Pretty Polly

  Pretty Polly was real pretty.
She shone like a star.
All the boys that thought her
witty, she'd pity them with heart.
  Then one day Pretty Polly was
dancing at the ball.
  She was a wonderful dancer,
she would neither slip nor fall.
  Pretty Polly was the highlight
of the ball, she did her most
amazing turns, she was graceful as a swan.
  Then as Pretty Polly was
about to do a leap, she turned
and spied the most handsome
man-to look at him was a treat.
  She asked him to dance
with her, but instead he made retreat.
  For the rest of the ball Pretty Polly
was not herself at all.
For now she knew being rejected was not fun at all.
    Andrea J. Adams

The Gentle Donkey

This is the story of a gentle donkey.
Who carried a mother with child.
They were on the way to Bethlehem,
  and he plodded carefully for miles.
He knew he could not go fast or Jerky
  because her baby was nearly due.
He finally came to Bethlehem and found
  a comfortable stall in a nice warm barn
  with straw and water too.
He stood sturdy and steady while she got off his back,
and watched her make a bed with clean straw.
On the mark of twelve her son was born,
  and the sheep, and cows, and chickens and the donkey
  all watched as the baby was placed gently on the bed.
Oh what a sight they beheld as the baby laughed
  and gurgled, they felt so proud and happy
  that they had played a small part of destiny.
For this was the wonder of the ages,
  "Jesus the Holy son of God was born."
God Bless "Baby Jesus".
Thank you Gentle Donkey.
      Amen.
    Gilda Messina

Childhood Memories

How well I remember my childhood home
With the family together and the joys I have known.
We had no computers or T.V. sets
Yet with so much love there were no regrets.
We would sit in the parlor with our Mom and Dad
As he read us the stories from the Bible he had.
We learned about Jesus and the things He had said
And begged to hear more before going to bed.
Well maybe one more - my father would say
Then it's right off to bed - it's the end of the day.
But first you must kneel for a good night prayer
And give thanks to Jesus for His love and His care.
    Josephine Silano

"The Ambience Of Summer"

The fragrant winds of summertime whisper
softly into my ears,
the Jovial gossip revealing secrets,
as daylight secedes
into strands of golden yarn,
walking barefoot among the dandelions,
their spores like lost satellites,
wandering aimlessly and lethargically on
the audible breeze, a secret rendezvous
with childhood dreams, embracing the past
with a tender kiss, memories of carefree tranquility and
gargantuan pastel ice cream cones dripping, the
sweet taste still on my tongue, the ambience of summer
like dancing light on the surface of a placid blue pond.
    Erik Fitzpatrick

"Ashes To Ashes   Dust To Dust"

It all started with the big bang
Dust and ashes formed the earth
The soil, the water and the air combined to give us birth
Our universe was self sustained in perfect synchrony
A systematic perfect chain of air and land and sea
Then flowers bloomed and fishes swam and man soon came to be
Everything a combination of the air, the land and sea
Recycling is nothing new   it's gone on since time began
The very air that Adam breathe now we breathe once again
But man may soon destroy it all, we will be a star that's burned
And some time later with a bang to dust we will return
    Tillie L. Yocus

Lost In A Wave...

Lost in a wave which lures you under,
into a place invaded with sombre.
Lost in its deepness of a darkness, turning,
longing to find the hope which was burning.
Always it seemed there was never a light,
silently screaming in darkness with might.
Always adrift, no ground in view,
Endlessly searching for that someone you knew.

Lost in a wave that pulls you deeper,
trapped in its darkness, it becomes your keeper.
Lost is the struggle as it comes to an end,
wilting with every inch you descend.
Letting the darkness be your guide,
giving in to its depth of demise.
Letting that someone you once knew.
Disappear in a wave forever, in you.
    Janette Mitchell

Life + Baby = Change

My son is born, my life has changed, a room I have to rearrange.
A body to bathe, a mouth to feed, he depends on me for every need.
My child is crying, for me he'll reach, I wipe the tears from his tender cheek.
My child is napping, in his room I creep, I've only gone to take a peek, (to assure myself he's still asleep).
He's in a bathtub full of bubbles, and in my arms he often snuggles, he'll soon be mobile and into trouble.
My child is smiling a toothless grin, a dimple appears upon his chin.
My child is sitting, on his own, and can no longer be left alone.
My child is crawling, this stage won't last, and only a few short months have passed.
My child is waking, my life — still changing, now every room needs rearranging.
My child is running, and then he falls, I hurry to his anguished calls.
A bandage on a skinned-up knee, next week he's outside climbing trees.
His first day at school, I can't believe how he's grown,
I'm counting the minutes until he's home.
Next a first kiss, and then a first date, he's off to college —
Don't be late!
And then the day comes when he will marry, over his threshold a bride he'll carry.
My little boy has gone away, a man in his place is here to stay,
— and life has changed —
My life I have to rearrange —
    Debbie Ankrom

Mother

There she sat like an angel in the morning sun.
  Why is she so lonely?
    Why is she so sad?
There must be something on her mind.
  Why is there pain surrounding her heart?
Could it be her son?
He left her there all alone.
  He did not even say good bye.
Why does he want to hurt her so?
  He cannot be doing it on purpose.
How could he be so cruel?
  To the woman who gave him life.
Maybe someday he will come back
  And all of her pain will go away.
Maybe, just maybe,
  They will love each other once again.
    Amanda Crimmins

Snooze

I'm a sleepwalker
   (through the kitchen,
    through the state;
hell, I drove to Newark and back)

And I dream in color
   (vivid enough to taste the turkey on Thanksgiving.
   It's one of those recurring dreams...
I always have blonde hair)

Well sir, the tragedy comes in your dreams
   which are in third person.
   once something directly affects you,
open your eyes...

   Blink

Now for real life,
   I'm not awake yet

Julie Ann Drallos

Banshees

What yonder lights are these I see.
Through windy night and naked tree...

A shadow there doth call my name—
Upon that air a Ghostly Train...

Upon their faces I see red tears,
And the bitter taste of long lost years...

And in their souls of cold, white bone
A Death Bell tolls for me, alone..

Kenneth W. Newton

Loyalty And Love

One is dead,
One is alive;
I've had life with both
These two brothers.
I married one,
And stayed by his side;
For loyalty, no other reason.

I kissed his cheek
When he went away;
In walked his brother,
And with me he stayed.
We married, I kissed his cheek that day,
For love, no other reason.

Sharon K. Carter

Untitled

As long as I've had eyes, I can't believe,
That they perceive someone of such beauty.
More beautiful than light on my Death's Eve,
Softer than roses, your love is your beauty.

Roses or diamonds can't tell my love for you,
Brighter than the sun, deeper than oceans.
My heart can't love any, the way it loves you.
I tell you I love you, with devotion.

Though you know how I feel, listen again.
With all my heart I tell you I love you.
As I write this I hope you will begin,
To love me in the way that I love you!

I have written this with all of my heart,
To show you how I love you, with my heart.

James Nero

The Watch

Luna leads her latent bellydancers
Crossing undulating inlet waters—
    waxing,
  Waning,
        Pale precipitation
   Holds in pause,
       as on opinions shared, as
Two who gathered, watched from Manasquan the
  Moon's four fellows: spotlights spanning
Through Point Pleasant hazes, stuttered, wakened
By convection currents: whorls which waft up
  (Hiding her in cheshire pleasure). Luna
   Holds us gravid,
       revelating stories.
  Clouded comments clear cool air, yet fog rings,
  Wrapped around in rapt attention
          bridging
  Gaps between both you and I,
       my brother.

Thomas M. Walters

Black And White

If you look at the world today you
will not see. If you look at the world
tomorrow you will not be able to
see, but if you look as hard has you
can you can see that the world is
falling apart in our hands. When you
look out-side you may not find flowers
but dead ones. When are you coming home
You will not see friends but enemies.
When your at home you may not
see family only shadows, but
if you believe that the world is
peaceful it will be, but if you
believe that it is falling apart it is.
It's your decision.

Casey Marston

God's Sky

When you look up
What do you see?
You see the sky,
with its true meaning.

And within it,
Are fog, rain and ice.
To make our world, a paradise.

Nobody, and nobody knows the cause,
but for one thing,
We know it's not chaos.

When it's summer time,
And you look up,
The sky to you seems a bit blue.
But to me, both the sky and the earth become true.

And then at night,
when you look up high,
The stars will look very bright,
And then you'll know God's meaning for the sky.

David Huang

The Echo

I shouted out loud and louder while in my cell one day.
The sound grew faint and fainter until it went away.
My words went on forever and left no trail or tracks.
But the walls nearby caught up my cry and sent an echo back.
I've betrayed the two I love, my two most important friends.
Like a knife it cut them deeply, a wound that's been hard to mend.
That crime, so thoughtlessly committed, I wish we could all forget.
But its echo lives and memory gives, still yet.
Both their hearts were broken, both my friends are lost.
By that crime I committed, before counting the cost.
I hope my words of kindness will repay a hundred fold,
When it finally reaches their hearts, and echoes in their souls.

Tracy Henson

A Crimson Rose

In the mangled crush of bodies lay a rose of crimson red,
But no one saw the rose as they stared with eyes of dead.
Who were the ones who lay in this anguished heap of death?
The bodies left to tell no tales without a living breath.

Across the space and raging sea to places yet explored,
They do not know what lay behind or choose to ignore
The agony of others' plight who suffered needless death.
Life is good and pleasure much with each and every breath.

One day when cycles go their round and those who walked in mirth,
Will find themselves with blackened pain lying face upon the earth.
In the mangled crush of bodies will lay a rose of crimson red,
But no one will see the rose as they stare with eyes of dead.

Wilma L. Wood

Escape Of A Young Maple

I watch the morning glory growing up the trellis...
She is so beautiful!
Her vines are turning and twisting around and around, up and up.
What is this! She's reaching toward me.
I can feel her wrapping around me, caressing me.
No! She's choking and pulling me.
Where's the gardener? Get her off me!
So this is the beauty and the splendor of the vine of death.
She has the glory in the battle of the summertime garden.
Thank goodness now the frost has loosened her grip on me.
My leaves will turn and I will rest.
The next season I will be taller and stronger.
I will again escape the furry of the beautiful morning glory.

Sharon Hartman

Don't Forget The Tree

Come, Little Hebrews, come unto Me,
Sing the song of Moses, but don't forget the Tree.
Hurry, grab your babies, hold them close;
Avert your eyes from Babylon up from its repose.

Come, Little Hebrews, come stand by Me,
Sing the song of David who tells us of the Tree.
Take the one true cup, and drink from it so pure;
Lift your sword of David, long will it endure.

Come, Little Hebrews, come walk with Me,
Sing the song of Freedom and hold high the Tree.
Curse the children of Babylon, Tree's blood on their hands;
Let Me show you what is yours, your Peace and all it spans.

Come, Little Hebrews, come unto Me,
Sing the song of Moses, but don't forget the Tree.
Come, Little Hebrews, come stand by Me,
Sing the song of David who tells us of the Tree.

Alma G. Stenger

The Ill Dark Corner

Though small and seemingly harmless,
The ill, dark corner beckons.
It calls from above the droll wall.
So calm, serene, so guilt free,
But this corner instills deep melancholy
within my soul.
I can't stop but to stare into its
false abyss.
Never ending, never slowing.
It breeds dark visions,
Which leaves me to lie awake.
Why can't this suckling hunger,
Which came from the ill corner,
Hold mercy? It doesn't.
It holds ash towards me.
Why?

Christopher Bell

Untitled

Oh beautiful morning! God's graces bestowed
Upon our arrival to Mary's abode.
Her gift to the people who praise God and sing:
Our Lord, Jesus, savior, her son and our king.

How joyful her feelings as we gathered there
To pray in her presence and gloriously share
Her blessings and graces as a mother would.
Immaculate virgin made holy and good.

A sense of her presence like perfume we felt
Like Roses, a fragrance, as jointly we knelt:
The love of a mother bestowing her love,
The matron of mortals and heaven above.

A heart-felt elation we felt in her shrine
To strengthen our focus on her son, divine.
We left with a peaceful and sharing of heart.
We prayed that the feeling would never depart.

Raul Paramo

A Flowery Sonnet (Acrostic)

Arranging properly the rose bouquet,
Flowers picked to make life colorful.
Long stemmed roses are placed in the right way.
Ornate lines make the sonnet visual.
With precision, I carefully choose the
Eloquent modulation of my lines.
Red roses mock my conventionality;
Yellow roses express alternating rhymes,
Six of each color for the three quatrains-
Ordered to fit specifications.
Neatly assembled, the arrangement feigns
Nuance to create the right impressions.
Elaborates structure in my sonnet;
Two white roses symbolize the final couplet.

Ryan Tilley

Thinking

I got out of Bed to think about
happy things, and I thought of you.
I hope you can always remember
me, also this poem. When I grow
up I will always think of you.
When I am sleeping,
singing, talking, writing,
dancing, playing and crying. I will
always remember you. Please remember me.

Jordyn Billings

3 Ring Ceremony

We repeated our vows in front of all
I put a ring on his finger, he put one on mine
minister announced us husband and wife
we kissed and everyone thought it was fine.

I brought out ring number three and
snapped it on his nose with great surprise
He knew from that moment on
when I spoke he would shine and rise.

It was a 3 ring ceremony, 3 ring ceremony
I put a ring on his finger, he put one on mine
following the vows, I put a ring in his nose
as I said to him, don't ever step out of line.

After settling down he often asked
how long he had to wear the nose ring.
It all depends on your actions and behavior
but don't think you will ever be a King.

Ray Burleigh

There's Happiness Here

To the Man I Love and Think Of, Jeffrey W. Graves
Of more than friendship I hold to my heart
so dear, you couldn't be more cherished or more
showered with love, you're everything to me everything
I could ever dream of, just look into my eyes there
you will see just how much you mean to me,
if you see a tear roll down my face these are the tears
of love and laughter in my heart you have placed.
You're very very much loved, you're often thought of,
if you had my heart you'd know, you'd feel its glow
that is what I feel when I'm looking at you no one,
no where will pull us apart, no one will ever
get that close to my heart my love for you will last
for all the days and years to come, I am so proud
to say you are the one, there's nothing more special
than to have you here; you're the only one I hold
in my heart so dear.

Tammy L. Graves

Together

I've always wondered what it would be like
To set myself free and ride a bike,

To faraway places I've never seen,
And take along a lover who's faithful and keen.

We could ride through the woods on the brightest of days,
And hold each other close when the skies are gray.

We could build us a house way back in the trees,
Or just stay in caves and make memories.

We would eat the wild berries and fruit of the earth;
Take life to the extreme, for all that it's worth.

The sky is the limits, for me and my lover,
No place is too far, as long as we have each other.

Jeana Burian

Life is Wonderful!

Went to the store just the other day,
got a speeding ticket, along the way,
The car blew a tire, the gas gauge was on "E"
Why does it seem it all happens to me?
These are the days I should have stayed in bed...
These are the days that bring an ache in my head!
But despite all the bad luck, that I have met...
The tougher it goes, the tougher, I get!
And I ain't seen nothing I can't handle yet!!!

Kathy Ketter

"Life"

Life is a very precious thing,
It can leave you as fast as
a bell makes it ring.
While most people realize this, others do not.
They waste their own bodies
not knowing what they've got.
It's a shame to see
so many people die
Imagine their families,
most not being able to say goodbye.
Aids, drugs, and suicide
are some of the ways,
But most commonly are the ones used in these days.
All caused from sadness and hatred within,
Now how is this the answer,
not trying to win?
Why is life so low on this degree,
So much hatred why not just agree?
Life is so precious can't you see,
What would this world be like without you and me?

Tiffany Figel

"Screams"

What is going on? I am boiling inside.
My brain spins in my head with no place to hide.

My life is a dream. I just have to scream.

How can a time machine be?
Where is it going to take me?
When I arrive, who shall I be?

Can it be that I've gone mad?
What the hell happened to the life I once had?

I am afraid, I am in fear.
What will I do the rest of my years?

I feel so happy when I lie dreaming.
I am soon awake and so starts the screaming.

My life is good. I am well.
My life is a screaming hell.

What made me come to this time?
What results will be mine?

You can't get there from here.
That is my greatest fear.

I just have to scream, I just have to scream. I just have to...

Lloyd Tisher

Bill, Sam, And Joe

Way back in '65
We were young and feeling alive.
We danced the limbo into the night
We bought every Beatle album in sight.

But there was a war going on in a place called 'Nam
It robbed boys of their youth.
And made them be damned.

In Ohio there was a school named Kent.
Its students hated war and what war meant.
The Civil War divided our land.
The Vietnam War almost did it again.

Some in the know, just didn't go.
Others were drafted, Bill, Sam, and Joe
Many were killed, many were maimed.
When they returned, they were never the same.

Were we fair to Bill, Sam, and Joe?
I was a girl, I didn't go.

Jackie Mixon

Inhaling My Insanity

Inhaling my insanity like oxygen
deep into the existence of my
non-functioning reality that feels more like an insecure fantasy

The smoke swirls around my head
it quickly fills the room of isolation
consuming it in darkness that hides the emotions and feelings that
carry double edged swords ready to cut me down

My mind is filled with the intoxication of my insanity
my eyes are blinded, I cannot see
my body is numb, I cannot feel

I hear voices inside my head the voices are many
loud and soft at the same time I call out to them I say

Come all you wise men with all your tools of solution
and your power of suggestion
gathered around there is much work to do before we are done

Show me your hand but don't try to pull me out
just hold on so that I will know
that you are there to offer your love and support

When I finally decide to climb out of the shallow
pool of self pity and rejoin the insane searching for sanity

Rocky Davis

The Definition Of A Cat

Cats are graceful creatures that run swiftly in the wind,
but softly and carefully like a prancing deer.

Their frisky little tails wag constantly, like a pendulum on a clock.

In darkness their eyes glow, almost like a ghost, but they look
at you with love and affection.

Whenever you are sad, it's almost like they can read your mind,
they will rub against you to let you know that they are there.

They have fine, shiny, fur that feels like silk if you dare to
touch them.

They will come to the warmth of your cozy bed, and lazily
cuddle against you like a child and her teddy bear.

They will never harm you but protect you from the "ferocious
yarn" and the "spooky" shadows that move quietly all around.

They softly lap up the warm milk that you give them, and in
return they lovingly nuzzle against you.

A dog is man's best friend because it's active and playful, but
a cat is woman's best friend because it's soft and graceful.

In a dictionary's eyes a cat is a small domesticated animal,
but in my eyes a cat is a faithful and loyal friend.

Melissa Teoli

Untitled

As the blood trickled down the old woman's face,
she felt the growing heat of her prideless disgrace.
Though the crowd was roaring with the pleasure of pain,
many knew it was wrong, though none would refrain.

Stones they did throw, accusations did fly,
"she's a n****r", one said, "she has no right to cry".
Yet she stood anchored in position, in that single file line.
Waiting to taste freedom, drink that blessed wine.

Yet as she dreamed of her paradise, through the air flew a stone
which found its place behind the old woman's head,
to whom it belonged, was said unknown,
and as her withered body lay, in that street while she bled.

It made people think, for a simple drink from a fountain.
She ended her day, dead...

Kevin Jurica

Melancholy Memories

I push the computer buttons of my brain,
  not to see if I am sane.
But to view once more the beauty of your smile.
  And to know all the while.
  That the rerun is the most,
  but lesser than the first.
In memory of things that could have been,
  longing that it could be again.
  Why did I let you go?
  I do not know.
My mind was filled with bricks and bats,
  Old love affairs and dirty hats.
as the zip napper says to cause more pain,
In howling wind and pelting rain.
You've gone by your last gas pump,
Its over and back you cannot jump.
I strive and strain with all my might,
But see you drift away into the night.

John William Auten

Flags Of Liberty

Some flags in American history,
Are about the Tree of Liberty.

A flag of Linked Hands hung high,
The Newbury flag shall always fly.

The Taunton flag with cross so bright,
The Bennington flag with stars tonight.

Guilford flag with stars of three,
Culpeper flag "Don't tread on me".

Texel flag all aglow,
Flag of Merchants ready to go.

Stars and Stripes first to be,
Bedford flag with armory.

Then came the Moulters flag with liberty and moon,
With peace to come very soon.

All the flags in America's past proclaim,
To all nations again and again,
America's flag shall always last,
To our independence we hold fast.

Chris M. Yadon

Empathetic Symphony

The lightning illuminates the sky
  with an abrupt flash.
Amidst the blinding fog,
  the rain hammers its ambiguous melody.
The intensity of every drop provokes fear
  while the underlying melody
  simultaneously soothes the spirit.
The symphony pitters fear of separation
  and patters solace in love.

Bearing the very names of these unsuspecting souls,
  nature expresses the tunes of the heart.
The two are fused in consolation
  as trepidation drips from their eyes.
Finding comfort in knowing that
  dividing their bodies
  does not separate their souls.

While the mist begins to rise
  and the sun initiates the dawn
  the vision of the souls has been revitalized.

Kristen Johnson

Crystal Tears
Written in Loving Memory of Mary J. Hale
A crystal tear runs down my face,
Though I know you're in a better place,
The memories of you I'll always hold, It seems so hard to let you go.

I see you walk across the lawn,
In the bright pink light of a brand new dawn,
You give me a long sad look of despair,
Then disappear into the morning air.

I dressed up all in black today, and to the church I made my way.
In a wooden casket did you lay, never another word to say.

The wood on your casket was shiny and new,
Such an odd thing to use to bury you.
Something so bright as a scene so gay,
Why didn't you live one more day?

I never got to say goodbye, so all these crystal tears I cry.
For you are gone, you can't come back,
and the world your company does lack.

Why can't you be here, this earth to see,
Instead, God took you away from me,
and all your friends cry crystal tears,
for all of us still hold you dear.
Marsha Maeby

Keeping The Memories
Though we grieve the loss of that wonderful person
who made life easier to bear,
Our fondest memories of our moments with them
reminds us they will always be there.

All we see is a horrible loss
but little do we see,
Their souls, now thriving in sunlit valleys
happy to be free.

Free of torture, free of pain
and from the struggles in life we must bear,
But we must remember that they're spiritually with us
and that they will always be there.

Memories of loved ones keep us alive
and give us the strength to go on,
To continue our chosen journey in life
remembering them in life's song.

Though their physical self is gone from us
their souls will forever stay,
Next to our hearts so that they may take a part
in our lives with each passing day.
Patricia E. Wootten

All I Could See
Looking down on empty streets
All I could see
Was the thing that I was looking for all of my life-
Silence

Looking forward to distant futures
All I could see
Was hopes and dreams yet one thing that I had never expected-
Living

Looking back at all the mistakes
All I could see
Was the echo of the future beckoning me-
My past
Benjamin Daniel Lawless

Castles In The Sand
When you were a little girl you loved to hold my hand;
When we crossed the street; played a game, or just on command.
Now that you have grown, I want to hold your hand.
I want to keep you here with me, and not let you go as planned.
But I know, I have to let you go to make your own castles
   in the sand.
Perhaps one day, you will have a daughter of your own,
And she will hold our hands,
And we will watch her together,
As she makes her own castles in the sand.
Debra S. Gee

Secret Identity
My life I'm not that certain with, but my name and age I am.
I don't know much about myself,
I've been living a secret life
I'm living a secret identity trying to hide my dark and scary past,
A secret to me that no one shall know, a nightmare that shall one day
   be put to rest,
I'm afraid to tell for I am a shame,
If I tell anyone they'll shut me out like a cold winter storm,
I've been living a lie for so many years,
I the person me doesn't really exist,
One day this lie will destroy me make me bitter and cold,
The day I tell anyone, will be the day I come to peace with me,
Myself and the people who put me through this living hell.
I wish I would of told my secret when I was young now it's too late.
It caught up with me and won the race,
It's destroyed at last, I thought I was strong enough to win
The day it came to rest was when I came to say goodbye.
Paula Marie Bryant Hill

Untitled
I search your eyes and I see pain.
   As I continue to look, I feel your pain.
I don't run away, you don't run away-
   We stay and Be.

Again, I search your eyes and the pain parts.
   Beneath the pain, I see the Spirit.
As I continue to look, I feel Love.
   I don't run away, you don't run away-
   We stay and Be.

I no longer search your eyes.
   I follow your cord of Love and Light to your Christ self.
My Christ self joins you and we are warmed
   In the Light to wholeness.
   We are One.

We return to our bodies to complete our service.
   Our way is clear and our journey lightened—
As we know our true essence resides in another realm
   And in that realm—We are One—
   We are Love—We are Light—
   We are God.
Jane McDonald

The Darkest One
Dark as the inside of a wood troll's belly, concealing my fears,
   my loves, my weaknesses and strengths,
The pitch black of a New Iberian bayou is my eternal shade.

Black can be as peaceful and serene as a warm summer night,
   or as evil and malevolent as a napalm-breathing dragon.

Black is a symbol of a tempestuous emotion, whether it be delirious
   joy, or violent rage.

Black is powerful and majestic, sleek and sophisticated.
It is also a cool facade to present to the rest of the world
   with the real me peeking through to watch you.
Allison C. Cross

Sitting In Front Of A Mirror

Sitting in front of a mirror
Cross winds of warm morning dew
A voice from across, asks for the dealer
52 cards near his left leg, appeared to be miraculously new
Sounds of love, mixed with falling trees
Her voices, crackling through the air
The man is on his knees
Does she burn, or even care
A hand of three queens and two aces
Anger from the mirrored man
He has 5, none are faces
Trembling bass, from the band
Was it them, or is it us
Warmth, a shining sun
Do you stay or take the bus
Shot dead, bang! The gun
New deal, 50 cents the mirror says
Knives and rocks, no man, luck in faith
As the glass shatters, death becomes
Then appears a whole new face
Ian Shapiro

"Entranced"

I thought of you throughout my day...
More than a little, along the way.
I saw the sky and thought, "How blue!";
Then I thought, "His eyes are, too!"
I hoped your chores this day were light;
And that you'd had a restful night.
I asked for blessings to come your way
And knew they would without delay.
When you called with words so sweet
I had to smile. We planned to meet.
You need to know that the time we share
Is special to me - beyond compare.
You fill my heart with warmth replete;
Your presence gives me joy complete.
As I ponder bad times gone past,
I pray, please, may good times last!
We both have many lessons learned;
Many times we have both been burned.
Now there are dreams to follow instead;
With peace in our souls let's move ahead!
Marlene S. Richards

Sorrow

The air, thick and damp,
A horse lies still in the distance.
There is no movement, only the, flutter of a bird,
Closer, closer I walk,
Still no movement, but now there is sound
Heavy breathing strained by saliva,
Cold and damp to the touch,
Pale are the gums,
Response is only in the eyes,
Pain and sadness darken the morning light.
The brush is matted; all expressions dim,
A blanket is laid on an old friend.
Time creeps as help is beckoned,
Help comes with death laughing.
Efforts are made, hope shows its face,
An old friend goes to sleep.
Todd W. Bosworth

Mom's Tears

I don't know your name, but I do know your pain.
Days and nights you watch your
child, you pray for your baby, (no matter what age.)
You cry for them and with them.
The doctors and nurses do their job.
Endless needles and tests and expect us MOMS to sit by
and comply to all the pain ...voiceless.
But that's not their child. They
don't feel the pain of their tears.
Of course. They care for our children.
or they wouldn't do what they do.
But they are just not MOM!
We, as moms, don't want to be, selfish, mean, or uncaring.
But the endless hours of sleeplessness
the waking of a sleeping child, who's only peace is sleep.
and the numbness you start to feel.
becomes a part of your heart. And you wish someone, anyone
could understand, your pain and your tears.
Each night I say a silent prayer for you, MOM.
because, I know your pain.

Love and improving health
to your child.
and a caring heart to you!
Cammy Harper

Li*e

Waking from a deep silent rest, only to bring death one hour closer.
Debating the very question whose answer is found in the realm of eternal life, eternal nothing...
My mind escaping like a bullet that is hurled from its womb completing its destiny without question nor timidness.
Relaxing, like the yellow rose which grows on top of a forgotten grave, whose roots tickle the nose of the deceased.
Visions of the church bell hanging above the city, dead.
Just as we all grow and mature does God not too?
The human race, a side show, costing only pennies to observe and laugh at.
Civilized drunk bums talking, "Rest and wonder, write and ponder, die and live again."
Life and the 20th century coming to an end. Concluding in another beginning of lost religion, forgotten frontier, and more time consuming products which save more time, giving us more time slots to fill as we have more time on our hands. Ending in a mass hysteria of insane maniacs, who have no time at all...
Life another forbidden 4 letter word.
Grant Dean

A Parent's Prayer

The miracle of our children, the way they live and grow,
They're with us such a short time, before their time to go,
They leave to seek their fortunes, their lives, and their loves,
We pray they find your guidance, Lord, from heaven up above,
Keep them safe, keep them warm, our future ladies and men,
Make them strong enough to resist, the evil ways of sin,
Help them to be better people, to show in their hearts they care,
Their lives, and love and wisdom, give them a special one to share,
Make their lives grow stronger, and deeper in every way,
Make their lives grow happier and more brighter everyday,
Give them roses and sunshine, on a day that looks like rain,
Give them courage to speak their mind, without any fear or pain,
The evils in the world today Lord, can make them quiver in fear,
But they fold their hands, and bow their heads and your soothing
  voice they hear,
In the name of the Father, Son and Holy Ghost, their trembling voices
say, God please help me be the best person, that I can today,
Amen
Charles E. Johnson

In the Wilderness

The woods are abundantly full of animals that cannot be seen.
Lions trailing behind the Caribou, as the Eagle observes lunch
  from his perch.
Everything is silent;
Only the music of the birds, hidden in the trees, can be heard.
Many animals are quenching their thirst at the waterhole,
In peace they drink, until the game of survival resumes again.
The elephants raise their heads and listen to the sounds around them.
They hear a very strange, yet familiar noise.
All the animals sense it.
It is the vibration of man, coming to consume the tranquility of life.
The animals run, but not all of them escape the hands of death.
A shot is heard, then another and another.
Three animals have faced their destiny,
All the others have disappeared,
They have been replaced by what is conceived to be civilization.
No longer is there peace,
In the wilderness.
Kathleen R. Howze

Fallen Star

Once I saw a falling star
fall among the hills afar
I went to reassemble it
piece by piece and bit by bit

I found it there, where it lie
fallen there, from the sky
I tried to put it together right
So I could view its awesome might

But its light was, completely dead
Its bright soul, had completely fled
nothing was left of that empowering might
Just lying there, such a pitiful sight

But then like a Phoenix, from the ashes
It rose up, and grabbed the lashes
A new beginning, was given life
And allowed to grow, from this chaotic strife

It took its place as the new star
So very close, and yet so very far
Binding all together like a powerful mortar
Commanding peace, prosperity, and solemn order
Casey Bennett

The Truth

Evil owns the world like a wet sheet around a man that doesn't care,
like a knife in the victims back with a scorpion wrath, but the world
doesn't see it or feel it.
People go about life not being smart and not thinking of death when
that's what they are when they have giving in. Evil is so horrible
that it kills you day after day. When you're sleeping, when you're
talking and even when you're thinking. The world doesn't fight back
as the family we are supposed to be.
We are supposed to be in one love with God together, but we don't
realize that evil is all around us. When a teacher talks of God being
fake or when you see a bum on the street and when you notice a
marriage gone to waste, this is how the devil and his Evil works, he
wants you to think these things are ok.
I try to notice all this before it penetrates me and God has shown me
how to notice these things, but we all must learn to fight these
happenings.

Don't be foolish for God is not the God of the dead but the
God of the living, and if you resist the Evil and stay true to God's
love, you will live for eternity.
Tim Maguder

Bubbles

I hate this bottle, there's no room in here
For me to move around.
The little girl is all grown up,
And she has gone away
I remember very well, how she couldn't wait to play.
She'd run home from school every day,
And come into the room,
She'd pick us up and run outside,
Ignoring the screams from her mother.
I could hear her unscrew the lid slowly,
Then I'd see her eye peek in,
Seeing me inside.
She'd take the wand in her fingers,
And mix us up real good,
Pulling the wand out ever so slowly,
She'd blow as hard as she could.
That little girl would laugh and scream
As she danced among my friends,
Until they would float down to the ground,
And she'd have to start again.
Karin Kinkel

"Alone"

At night I would tuck our children in bed alone,
Wondering when and if you would come home.

The lights would burn soft and low,
Setting my heart and love aglow.

The empty hours would come and go,
Still I am alone,
Wondering when and if you would come home.

Alone as the soaring eagle,
Looking for its mate,
I ask myself, why do I wait?

I wait all alone,
Waiting, waiting for you to come home.
Marilyn H. Curtis

Steven's Sigh

Tell a leukemia patient's mother or a cancer patient's father,
Tell a terminally ill patient's sister a car fatality's brother,
Why, oh yes, tell them why their loved one had to die.

Love your children well for what are they but our legacy?
And what are they when they're gone by a faded memory.
The reaper is not our friend, so make the reaper wait.
From when we're born and the first breath we take
until death takes us by the hand, we are governed by destiny
  and fate.

Suicide is ignorance don't give into the sadness or the pain
Born of woman, sin of man, don't give the reaper what others have
  fought for and lost
Make him forcefully take it from you

Though your life be black and cold, and despair makes your life
  a living hell.
Give to him which no one living has seen
Your respect maybe, your contempt definitely, but never worship.
Life is the most precious thing you own, so make the reaper pay
  a high price.
Grab and hold on to that which is like a crystal hammer
That which with one sharp blow will gone
The darkest night isn't anything like the darkness of death,
  death is forever.
Ray A. Metzgar

Wide Stretch

Deep in caverns of your soul
Eyes with power, they draw your goal
You feel your spirit rise, as your chest cries

The sign says wide stretch
Do you care?
Or do you dare?

Misconception, misunderstand, ability to conceive reality,
A feeling no one knows
Joyful depression in a dark world
Sensitive caring shows

People in a frightening land
They need a helping hand
People with nowhere to hide
No one is there; but you tried

You must make a wide stretch!
You may be surprised what you can catch!
A helping hand, a caring man
For that there is no ban
Just do all you can
   James Thue

"Pages Of Life"

Life's like a book, that opens one day,
All different stories along the way.
Some are happy, others are sad.
Some sweet as poetry, while others are bad.

Each day of our life is like turning a page
in a new chapter changing with age.

If you like happy endings, as all of us do.
Hunt for the good books, and read them all through.

Look at the titles and learn them by heart,
if you don't like a mystery, be sure
you know them apart.
   Maryann White

A Message Of Hope

Out of this present darkness, one brilliant beacon of light
A star shining out of sheer midnight.
A permanence of hope, a glimmer so slight.

A chance to dream, to harness our thoughts,
And anchor them on shimmering moon beams.

To summons courage and strength, to field precious seed
To birth into being, a brand new breed.
To believe it can happen and recognize the need.

To seize this moment and clutch it tight
Holding onto it with all of our might.

To our dearth of wisdom, a clarion of truth
This glorious message to our old and to our youth:
Ours is the challenge, in this present hour
Unto His people, God has granted grace and power.

We must arise — though sometimes from ashes
While often our hopes with despair make bitter clashes.

We will arise, take courage and stand strong
Doing what he's called us to do, all "our" day long.
Withstanding much, victory is our final song.
   Janet L. Kenion

The Two Of Us

Here we are, the two of us,
Hunched from time and experience.
Looking forward to find our place,
Longingly back to measure our space.
Feeling each others presence,
Knowing each other's pace.
Red eyes searching, wary of the unknown.
It is our reason. It is our rhyme.
It tethers our existence.
It tempers our time.
It is our obsession,
Blending our moments with its needs in mind.
It becomes our future, it is our past.
We watch, we care, we touch,
Covering, uncovering, turning softly with fluted plume.
Nestled is our ontogeny, where the common becomes uncommon,
For the two of us, the common loon.
   Thurman D. Noblet

For Now I Am In The Light Of Eternity

Oh Lord,
Many are crying
But yet, I sing.
The dove of everlasting life has swooped down;
And now,
My soul to God it brings.

Weep not,
Because a long life I have lived,
And to this world God knew
A gift of two children I would give.
Be strong my family, though I lie still,
Because God will bless you all
And along will come many generations to fill.

I've seen times so hard 'till life seemed too hard to bear,
But I kept fighting for the family I love
Cause God I knew was there.

So pick up your heads and don't cry for me,
For now I am in the light of eternity.
   Dwaine Mouton

Deception

Daring, dashing, devastating are written on his brow.
Hate, grievance, shame are the words upon my breast.
A cry for help breaks at a closed ear and no one hears my pain.

Such beauty from his lips but hatred in the tone.
To be deceived by his mask left me unguarded from the meaning.
I wanted love and nothing less but I ended with so much more.

To see the shadows now I want to hide behind my wall.
This wall I have built around my aching, crumbling heart.
A longing for revenge draws too much darkness to my soul.

He thinks nothing of this burning bridge of mine.
Wallowing in his own self-pity and pride I had to crush.
Never again will he have his way with another innocent heart.
   Leigh Thomas

Spring

Spring is like a birth to most living creatures;
Flowers bloom and grass grows
It's all a part of nature.
If you look around you'll see it's just like magic
When winter comes it's almost tragic;
If you think in your mind a little ahead
Next year you'll see the beauty of spring again.
   Angelina Marie Pargoff

Ode To An Incestuous Father

I was only three when you came to me
  and took me for your own.
In the deep of night - you had no right,
  but then the deed was done.
No reason, no rhyme, no sense of time
  A fractured brain resulted.
  You took my sex, my innocence.
  for yourself - to feel exalted.
Some manly thing, crowned yourself King
A little girl was shattered.
Tortured by fear, but you didn't hear
Feeling the power was all that mattered.

Now I'm all grown and out on my own
But your presence is with me yet.
You sneak into my bed, you mess with my head,
How can I ever forget?
You filthy touch, yet I loved you so much
You were my earth and sky.
Ignoring the screams you destroyed a
child's dreams, and all I can ask is...Why?

Cheryl Yelek

If All I Believed......?

Could there have been a connection between me and you
If all I have believed, could have been true?

I believed I could have a perfect life
If always I live as honest as I might.
Follow the rules, obey the laws.
Try always to do what I know is right.

If I love all God's creatures,
without judgement or fear.
Reach out to everyone with respect and care.
Then, the same for me will always be there.

After all these years of sowing beliefs like seeds;
crops of disappointments, despair, and tears
Seems all I am able to achieve.

If all I believed had been revered.
The world might still be peaceful and dear.
So sad it is, but, it is all too clear.
A world ever changing, progressive, severe.

And nothing I have believed has ever been true.
If all I believed can never be real.

Virginia D. Melton

Stars

As I look up to the stars,
this is what I see;
Someone is crying shedding tears on me.

So I put my arm around them
and tell them it's O.K.
"Just hold your head up high and the pain will go away."

I tell a little joke
'cause I love to see them smile
even if the laughter lasts only for a while.

But the comfort that I give them,
I cannot give myself.
And when I am hurting who is there to give me help?

Who is there? It is no one!
No one lends a tender hand.
I am left to be alone in a cold and heartless land.

So when you look up to the stars,
this is what you see;
someone is crying, and that someone is me!

Heather Robertson

My Hero

The same one that delivered Israel
From Pharaoh by parting the sea,
Is the same one that delivered Daniel
By clenching the lion's teeth!

The same one that came down from heaven
Died on the cross of Calvary,
Is the same one that saved my soul
Blood washed and made me free!

I know it's one thing to say it
And another thing to realize it,
But when God gives his word
He's going to stand by it!

He opened up all the windows
And poured out all these blessings,
He's awesome, and his marvelous works
Still astound and keep the world guessing!

His name is called wonderful counselor,
He blesses as we kneel and nod,
"Jesus" the Prince of Peace,
My hero, Almighty God!

Harriet Lipscomb

Here I Stand

Here I stand, not knowing, not seeing,
Here I stand, reflexing God's promise.
Here I stand, the sun shining down.
Here I stand, on the cross road of life.

Here I stand, not knowing, not seeing.
Here I stand, reflexing God's promise.
Here I stand, the after glow of God's grace.
Here I stand, thou toss with trials of life.

Here I stand, not knowing, not seeing the way.
Here I stand, reflexing God's promise.
Here I stand, changing time, places, spaces and things.
Here I stand, thou I may fail, I'll have tried.

Here I stand, with new insight and specific focus.
Here I stand, with colors showing
Here I stand, with a prayer for integrity and contentment.
Here I stand, reflexing God's promise.

Barbara Benice Miles Jackson

Forever In My Heart

I will always love you even though we are apart,
Because I have you in my heart.

I catch a glimpse of you in the wind,
I can only set and imagine how it could have been.

You choose the arms of a stranger,
As you now live your life with danger.

Hoping he will never figure out,
What your love for him is all about.

For someone who will never know,
My love for you will forever grow.

My days are getting shorter,
As my nights are getting longer.

I set and cry in sorrow,
For I know there is no tomorrow.

As the great love I had for you, comes to an end.
A new life I now begin.

Brian Halloway

Pain

Pain is the common thread of life
weaving and tying us together as one.
Struggle
is the norm of each passing day.
From the womb of life
to death and the grave.
It ain't black, white, yellow, or red.
It ain't napped up, curly, resistant, straight, or easy laid.
It's what little girls and women are made of.
Not sugar and spice and everything nice - but pain.
Thick, heavy, crusted, sagg'in, bitter, burnt pain
Stinging through our mindsssss.
Pppulsing through our veinzzzzzz, and ohhhhhhhh
hhhhhhhhhhhow it flows
to the Depth of our souls.
My sisters
to the Depth of our soulsss.
Seprenia Whitaker

Love Everlasting

To there a think curtain between us?
Like the mist in scarves on the moor.
Are you watching me, caring each moment
Hurt by the pain I endure.

I love you, my darling, I love you,
Death cannot take you away.
Our love is more real and more lasting
Than the earth or the light of this day

I remember the first time you kissed me,
Your lips brushed my brow as we danced.
Your love lit my life like a sunbeam
Your magic enfolded, entranced.

You must be still there through the curtain,
I feel you are close to me here.
I will never leave you while memory lasts
I hold you eternally dear!
Sheila Brooks

What To Write

Wanted to write something that could only be from me
because words sometimes heal.
They sometimes inspire.
They sometimes warm the heart to tears
and challenge the mind to transcendent thoughts.
But what would I write?
Something blue... or something to make someone smile?
Maybe I'll write a song,
maybe something long... no, no that's all wrong.
Something short and intense to make great minds ponder
while my emotions wander..., wander on to another mood.
Moods, humph... now there's a good subject too.
I could write about many things, but
I really want to write about something that will make a difference.
Take away someone's pain.
But what could I write?
What words could take that dare?
Maybe I'll just write something and send it somewhere.
Send something, to somewhere, to someone.
That is, if you know anyone who cares... about what I write.
Yolanda N. Clark

Mother

When I think about you, mother
   A smile comes across my face
I remember all the love you gave
   And that no one could take your place

I think of all you did without
   All the places you could not go
Just so I could have the things
   I thought I needed so

I know that being a Mom
   Is a difficult and thankless chore
But you were the greatest mother
   I could not have ask for more

You're my teacher and my preacher
   My counselor and my friend
So on this day that's just for you
   My thanks and love I send.
Joy Moody

Losing My Lover

As you lay on your death bed,
As I hold your hand in mine,
I stare deep into your eyes
And I tell you, I love you.

A tear trickles down my cheek
I try to speak, but you silence me,
You look at me, and me at you
And I see the fear in your eyes.

The times gone by, the times we spent
Will never, ever, be forgotten,
The love we shared will live on
The joy, will always be in my heart.

As we sit there, alone, in silence
I move closer, but I stop, as your trembling
   hand sweeps through my hair,
We have one final kiss, one final goodbye
Then, your head falls, and then I cry.
Maria Onest

Cinnamon

An adorable puppy's head
Nudged my hand
And a baby soft paw
Begged for attention.

Pudgy baby Cinnamon
Rolling in the grass
His tongue hanging out
As he barked with joy.

His lovable crawl
As I bent down to pet him
His tail wagged happily
A glint of content shone in his lovable brown eyes.

Then one night before Christmas eve
The tree stood bright in the corner
Glistening with hope,
To good to be true.

A rapid knock sounded on the door
The hushed voices
Our poor baby Cinnamon
Was gone, up to Heaven.
Lisa A. Fearon

If I Were Running The Show

If I were running the show I would say all systems go.
But my Father says he will supply all my needs.
I don't mean to be a greed.
His word is true so therefore I don't need to be blue.
I don't worry, I don't fret cause my God hasn't failed
me yet. He's just a prayer away. So I can call him
anytime of day. He's won the battle for you and me.
So don't you worry you see.
We have all the riches in glory, so let's just shout
Holy! Holy! Satan you have no dominion, let me tell
you my opinion. You rot in hell and I'm going to tell
everybody that you're a nobody. I'm going to wear my
armour for when you attack, so I can throw you back.
The battle has been fought the victory won. Satan you
ain't nothing but a little crumb.
Praise the Lord let's be on one accord.
Jesus is the answer for the world today!!!

Pamela S. Wise

Winter Picnic

A flurry and fluttering
Of acrobatic feathered wings that
Brave and waft the chilly winter air.

Long pyracantha branches
Weighted berry clusters, full and red
Picked till they are still and brown and bare.

How do they know—those flocks
Of bright-eyed circling missile beings
The hour, the day, the sweetest time to come
With wondering earth to share

Such beauty as a winter picnic spread
Just waiting for us there.

Flora M. Workman

The Enchanted Unicorn

People say that unicorns are fairy tales,
Nonsense... they exist in far away worlds;
Worlds of enchantment,
Where beauty is unfurled.

The unicorn is as white as an April cloud,
With gleaming stars for its eyes;
The mane and tail are long golden tresses,
A horn of pure gold and truth... no lies.

It frolics in the sunshine,
In a beautiful meadow carpeted with flowers,
With its brothers and sisters gathered together,
And the trees overhead like towers.

At night it tosses its mane from side to side,
Then lowers its golden horn to the earth,
The dark sky opens up,
And the stars begin to birth.

Next time the stars begin to appear,
Remember the light in the eyes of the unicorn,
And picture that far away world,
Where dreams are frequently born.

Chandra Xeloures

The Idyll Fisherman...

See him snoozing there, afloat,
Rocking in his slumber boat...
Rod, reel, and line at the ready,
Why then stays the boat so steady?...
I'll tell you why dear...should you look —
You'll find no bait upon the hook...

Susan L. Droste

Goodbye Mama

It is time for me to say goodbye
As I sit here with tears overflowing my eyes

I feel this tremendous aching
Deep within my heart...
For I am going to miss you mom,
This time we are apart

Sometimes I think you were taken from me;
In a malicious sort of way
Life can seem unfair at times.
But in all reality, it really is ok.

To know that you're in a better place
makes this goodbye a little easier you see...
for this is only temporary mama
we will meet again someday
happy, joyous, and free

Lidia Quintin

The Begotten Son Of God - Jesus Christ

To him we should give all the praise
For all the beautiful things in this place
He sends us his undying love, from heaven above
Some don't know this man that came to teach
He did all he could, this man to preach
Some people hated him, but he said
that he loved them
They nailed this man to a cross
all they could do was stand and applaud
On that third and glorious day
this man arose from the grave
In this life he is the only way
What a wonderful life to have
with him to stay

Kathy Steelman

My Friend Vic

Vic sits across from me
And we type till our fingers are numb
With every tap on every key
Vicki chomps her chewing gum!
She chomps and chews and pops and cracks" . . .
(This helps her brain react)
And before we know, it's time to go
To "feed the face" and "hit the sack!"
After working all day, we're dead for sleep
But morning comes soon and we're back on the heap!
The key's in the lock . . .we stumble on in . . .
There's the telephone !! — our head's in a spin.
Turn on the xerox, switch on the light
On mark, get ready for the present day's plight.
We're all settled down, the computers hum
And there's old "Vic" — a Chompin' her gum!

Mimi Reed

The Demon Gate

Night time begins as day time fades,
the shadows of life drift away,
as the last bit of sunlight disappears,
the demon gate gives away.

They scramble through just in time,
as the gates slide back into place,
They scream and they moan for this isn't a game,
to the demons of death it's a race.

It's the souls of young humans they crave,
for them they rant and they rave,
Keep away from them if you hold your life dearly,
And your soul and your body you'll save.

Matthew Kocourek

The Knight I Dream Of

   I walked through the darkest night only
to approach the largest crack in the earth.
   No place to go. No where to turn. Suddenly
the sidewalks are illuminated with light and the
macadam is electrified with fluorescence, that only
he can produce from his presence.
   I feel him lift me from danger. I slowly
turn. Tall dark; his eyes like stars that brighten
the darkest night. Lips soft, crimson. The curve
of his smile reflects across his teeth; like white
powdered virgin snow.
   Surrounded by the distance between his shoulders,
miles of safety. His torso, sleek and erect. Legs like
the kentucky derby winner.
   I reach for him only to touch cold, hard metal.
He disappears into the darkness. Was it really him?
The man, the knight, I searched for all my life!
Will I ever know him? Will he ever love me again?
The knight I dream of.
   Adrienne Periandi

Untitled

Relentless, remorseless it seeks through the heavens.
Homing to ears, listening and attentive
Gathering force it is relayed onward
To the well springs of source fundamental

Back again bonding in blinding speed
Guided to hands with authority to lead
a soft spoken word, a gentle command,
and the cloak of the heavens descend on this man

Fear not this cloak, oh murderous one
It is rendered invisible by what you have done

The hand that placed it is a trusted son,
Who will not destroy for destruction done.
   Dean D. Boatright Jr.

World Of Me

In my wonderful world of me
I feast on raspberry moonbeams
And drink of the Chocolate Sea

My hair is blue, with eyes to match,
The grass is red, the trees are black

My marshmallow palace sits on turtle shell clouds
Where I rule the stars and sing to the crowds

In the Cellophane City that sits on the marsh
Awaits a music box princess with eyes that are harsh

I shun her though, for the psychedelic maiden in the
blueberry house,
With the seven black cats and the strawberry mouse

We will ride on the wind of a thousand good-byes,
Seek and destroy the little white lies

That plague and infect the city of Hope,
Hang the corrupted heroes on a justified rope

We will carry forth Truth on a silver plate,
Served to the people to destroy the Hate.

All this and more in my world of me,
But somehow I locked the door and lost the key.
   Zach MacKenzie

Get Out And Vote

When the day comes for you to vote,
Don't sit back and clear your throat.
Adorn your hat and your coat,
Go to the polls and cast that vote.

We like to give a bit of advice,
Some give it without thinking twice.
If you haven't voted let's break the ice,
Go to the polls and advocate that right.

We sit back and grumble, what should have been,
A lot of who shot John and who went in.
Come on now and bring your friends,
So you can be sure your man will win.

To cast your vote doesn't take much time,
You stand longer in a coffee line.
Just to spend one thin dime,
Cast that vote and you'll feel just fine.

Whether you be young or old,
Living in or out of doors,
Swing into action, be on your toes,
So Long, my friends I'll be seeing you at the polls,.
   E. M. Horne

Just Daydreams

As I lay on the grass, as a child,
Watching the clouds as they piled,
My mind was a daze
I enjoyed the sun's rays
And the breeze that was ever so mild.

I would dream about faraway places,
Sandy beaches, palm trees, and new faces.
As I let my mind race
I didn't notice the pace
Of the clouds, and their dark threatening traces.

I'd think about life and how it would be
As a grownup, would poor follow me?
Or would I be wealthy?
Would I be healthy?
And I'd wish the future was for us to see.

As my mind wandered off to some tropical place.
I could actually feel the ocean's spray on my face.
SPRAY? .... That's not spray!
Soaking me where I lay,
And the rain brought me back to home base.
   Bonnie Parker

So Long To Find

You're so gentle,
  Warm and kind;
The one it took me
  So long to find.

You've given me the strength
  To want to go on;
Because I know you're there for me
  When I come home.

Your eyes are so beautiful
  With love showing through;
Each time I look at them,
  So clear and blue.

You've stolen my heart,
  My soul and mind;
The one it took me
  So long to find.
   Marie Lee Thomason

The Farmer And The Siren

She beckons, the siren alluring.
   Entrapped, he follows her call.
Thoroughly fooled by promises made
   She leads him on to the fall.

A promise of better tomorrows,
   Each yesterday passes away.
The glimmering dreams of life's precious schemes
   She dangles, then dances away.

So fast the decades have hastened.
   The limbs and body grow weak.
But the siren calls on, relentless, cold, stern.
   No pity for the strong or the meek.

His family, so long forgotten,
   Have drifted, or darted, away.
Yet lonely he waits for next seasons plate;
   Whatever she offers, he'll take.

At long last she mercifully lets him
   Rest. No more will he toil.
He's finally there where he wanted to be,
   Permanently part of the soil.

   Nanci Crone

Lost Love

I don't know just where to start,
It must be somewhere in my heart,
I don't know who or what to blame
For all my sins that I'm ashamed.

As a child, I went to Sunday School
and learned about the golden rule.
Respect, loyalty and trust my parents taught,
But love is something they forgot.

In my own backward and sinful way
I kept on living from day to day
Doing things wrong and later thought
Of how to cover up the plot.

My friends, family and children too,
Paid for my sins the same as you.
Oh! How I paid for what it cost
For the love that I must have lost,
Dear God some day before I part
Please put it somewhere in my heart.

   Mamie L. Medrano

What Is "It"

Some people live or at best they exist
Not even aware of the joy they have missed
For it isn't a thing that you buy at a store
Or hastily borrow from the house next door
It's not something you plant in the early spring
And wait for the rain and warm weather to bring
And yet it can grow and become very strong
Or if the fates will it, not last very long
It's not found in a pot on a window sill
Or something you leave, or bequeath in a will
You can't hold it to see in the palm of your hand
Nor will it appear upon your command
And yet you can take it wherever you go
It can be right there with you and not even show
If you have it you've guessed by now what it is
It's a bond we call friendship
And it's all ours to give

   Dianna Mount

Poison Love

You stared at me with passion in your eyes
But I could see so well through your disguise
You had in your mind so much more than a good time
And even though I knew the score, I didn't mind
And poison love was all around you

As if I were in a trance, I had no will
And though I was filled with fear, I kept it concealed
For to let you know that I was would ruin the game
And we both know, no matter what, it will end the same
And poison love was all around you

You wove your magic spell, throughout the night
A feeling I knew too well, a feeling of fright
You're closing in on my heart, I feel the pain
Loving to you is an art, with nothing to gain
And poison love was all around you

Now I'm just a memory in your mind
Another one of your prey, one who was blind
And now outside on the street you still remain
Looking for somebody else to feel your pain
And poison love was all around you

   Ron Haynie

Just Joe

How I love you, no one will ever know
The most wonderful one in the world is you, Joe
I think of you each night and day
When your car goes you seem so far away
Till at night when I dream of you in my arms
And there you are so wonderful with all your charms
I think if you ever loved me, I would be flying on a cloud
In a faint memory I see you as my prince who has just bowed
Will we ever get together now and then
Or will it be just my yen
Someday soon I am hoping you will be my beau
Or will you forever be just Joe

   Margaret Rodgers

David

The man leaves me breathless.
He is just too damn bright!
I'm endlessly surprised—no
shocked
That he knows me—God,
He knows me!
How did he learn to read people like that?
I don't know me the way he knows me!
The man wins every round—no—
But he thinks he does!
But I have learned
to hear
and
I can read a little too!
And I have chapters he'll never see...
Unless he learns to read me by heart
and
not by intellect.

   Sandi Murchison

Untitled

Do not lecture me about Loyalty,
I am young and beautiful and wish to be free.
You can not own me honestly,
For I as a bee have sucked the nectar from another tree.

   Elisa Mercedes Melendez

Understanding

Look deep into one's inner self
Look past the physical and see within
Past all pain, strife and emotions
Look into the very heart

See what very few see
See what one truly is
The beauty of the true and loyal heart
The very soul

Then look into one's spirit
See the freedom and the love there
For only the pure of mind, heart and soul can do this
For only the children of God can be so sensitive,
caring and loving in this world that can be so cold
   Joanne Carlstedt

Papa Knows

Down underneath that old willow tree...
That's where my papa used to fish with me...
In the morning when the light was dim...
That's where you'd find us...
Just me and him...
He'd bait the hook on my old cane pole...
Then we'd sit until the day got old...
"You know"...
Sometimes I wish I could go back in time...
Go back and hug that papa of mine...
Tell him I love him, and how much it meant...
The time together that we had spent..
But in my heart I know...
  Papa knows...
   Michael L. Snow

Ode To My Ex

Why does my heart beat so fast, with just the thought of you.
Why does your presence make me sweat,
when the wind outside is cool.
Why after all the things you've done,
I still have good thoughts of you. About your silly smile.
About your lies, I sometimes wish were true.

I can't remember how it ended,
what words were last or said.
I only know the hurt I felt and the loneliness in my self.

If I could turn back the hands of time,
I don't think I would meet you.

They say from each experience, there is a lesson learnt.
But yet I search myself,
for that knowledge I have gained.

They say for you to find happiness,
you must circum some pain.
But how long must we travel, this road again and again.

I don't know what to call it.
I don't know what it was.
I only know I did it, because it felt like love.
   Coreen Lee

Remembering When

Remembering when we were together
Like two peas in a pod and a birds of a feather
Loving each other day after day
We knew what we felt nothing needed to say
Walking the shores of a sandy beach
Sharing a kiss or a moment of peace
Remembering when is always a pleasure
Our love affair though just didn't measure
   Debra Rosario

Masquerade

Whirling like a dervish,
Unnerving chatter from
Monkey's throats
Without regard for substances or necessity
Halting only for the iron hand of manners
Gold plated...Agitated
Belles and their stress-pot men
Hung on wire of snaps and suspensions

Everyone trying as hard as they can
Without anyone thinking about the others
Masquerade continues with the mechanical ring of trinkets and music

That no one really enjoys
But everyone claims adore
And so hidden are we from the specter of wallflowers
And the fear of behind-the-back laughter

But I prefer the rose that blooms 2-D
Without any pretentious need for
Saffron masks and glass beads.
No, I enjoy the portly man in the corner
Who whispers over the din of hollow cacophony.
   John David Thompson

Mother's Day

President Wilson said
The second Sunday in May
From this time forward
Will be called Mother's Day

But, just stop and think
What your mother has done
Think of all she's taught you...
How to laugh, and play, and have fun

She stands by you in the worst of times
With the strength of a thousand men
She'll smile and step to the background
When she's sure you're going to win

Her love has never faltered
Her pride will never waver
We know that she has done her best
And God will surely save her

So remember your mother everyday
Not just once a year
Because all the love she's given you
Will surely bring a tear
   Steve Heslep

The Beauty Of It All

   When I think of beauty, I think of an
inward process - that takes its own special time
   before it manifests.
   There is a lot of inner work, that may not be understood
Some may not think it is worth while. Or appreciate it
if they could.
   Beauty is like the fine wine, it refuses to be rushed
it has its own time capsule - in every grape that is crushed.
   You cannot see the beauty of the wine - when first
you see the grape - but in fermenting. After sugar is added.
It takes its own sweet time.
   So when beauty has its perfect work,
it is a work of art - and really doesn't matter
if one is dumb or smart.
   An attribute of beauty - can be quite unique
within itself -
When one truly possesses it
it is rarely kept.
   Edna J. Martin

Less Than Perfect

Though you have toiled, with all of your might,
to do things the best, and ever so right,
when your imagination lifts you, to the highest sect,
be wise to remember, you're still less than perfect.

When the others around you, applaud what you do,
dare to fight the temptation, of thinking you're through.
'Cause, there's room for improvement that you haven't met,
be wise to remember, you're still less than perfect.

There may be those present, whose talents may pale,
when they're compared to yours, on an even scale,
flee from your pride and then learn to suspect,
be wise to remember, you're still less than perfect.

Those you meet, as you reach for your crown,
you will see again, on your way back down.
Strive to bridle your Ego, and always practice respect,
be wise to remember, you're still less than perfect.

A final message if you still care to hear,
cling to its meaning, hold it ever so near,
you're still only human, with many flaws and frets,
be wise to remember, you will never be perfect.
Steven J. Nelson Sr.

Planting Shade Trees That You Don't Sit Under

God has many shade trees in His garden of love,
   Free for the asking from above.
The species are noted for their beauty and shade.
   They grow very well in the everglades.
There is no time to sit in the shade,
   Because of the problems man has made.

Children are yearning for love in all lands,
   To make them happy and to feel grand.
Some are suffering from criminal acts.
   Some are abused, but fear to state facts.
Some are hungry and malnourished, you know,
   Many discern it, and their bodies do show.

What about the elderly who are thrown in rest homes
   Wondering where their children are, who roam?
These problems exist among all races of men,
   Black, white, yellow, and red skin.
Let's all band together who are physically fit,
   In the shade, we have no time to sit.
Ruth Golson

Our Son's Daddy

To the father of our child
On his special day of the year.
I know these words cannot express it true;
The love you have for your son of almost two.
The tenderness of heart,
The strongness of your hands.
The loving way you play
With him throughout the day.
The sadful way you discipline
When he needs a corrective hand.
You are to him,
As you are to his mother...
Our very best friend.
So I wish for you
On this Father's Day
All the happiness and joy
This precious one can give you;
And the memories of the love
That glows in the blue eyes
Of your little boy.
C. L. Jenot

Tornado

I'm eight years old
Cradled in a hall
Protection from my hold
Hearing the ghost's call

I lift my head
A noise in the hall
Wishing to be home in bed
Remembering the ghosts call

I look around
A desk sucked down the hall
Out the doors and into town
Into the ghosts call

I hear a scream
Somewhere down the hall
We're all in this together, we're all a team
Ignoring the ghost's call

Outside a tornado blows
Rage and fury heard in the hall
We did something wrong the tornado knows
That's why the ghosts call
Julie Swaney

Unanswered Questions

As I sit here thinking today,
Have I really gone astray?
And though I haven't served him in a while,
Does he still love me as his child?

Oh, how I try to live in this world
With all the circumstances that are whirled
At me through the winds that come my way
Lord, help me to take time even to pray.

How many more storms do I have to go through
Before I can serve him like I want to?
I hope that someday I can find the answer
To these questions that are in my mind.
I'll serve the Lord with all my heart
And from him, never part.
Hazel Wilson

Untitled

K is for King, Martin Luther
What manner of man is this
Who was from Montgomery
What manner of man is this
Who walked for all to see
What manner of man is this
Who dreamed for you and me
Who saw peace from sea to sea
What manner of man is this who won a war without guns
What manner of man was this
Why he was Dr. King, one of America's brightest sons
Delores Antoine

Animotion

A power in the midst of spring,
feelings that are shared by two only once in a lifetime.
Building on what is known in the unknown.
Here time is but a masterpiece waiting to occur.
Hours sail by on the rippling sea,
while others seem to stand still.
Is there not enough for everyone?
Only the honest, trustworthy fool can tell.
He is omnipotent in the ways of the world.
But we are egotistical and vain,
searching for things that are not there.
Melissa S. Lessick

Memory's Closet

Shoes and hats. One frayed glove. An
old silk scarf. Out of vogue.
Some ribbon, and wrap - no bows.
Looking for that box, you know?
It holds 17 years of her life, and
often spills its contents. Pain
and sorrow, the remnants...
like factory seconds
Of an impassioned heart. Do not
despair. She's buried the box,
In here. Somewhere.

The belly of the closet imparts its
holdings - the search is done.
Chits and chunks of paper. Bits and
scraps of poems. Secrets and energy.
Neatly etched into the fabrics of
The closet. A quilting of stories
illuminates her life. How she kept safe
those three small years. Her struggle done.
She can remember them - now.

Carol E. Budzinski

Your Gracious Love

Timid as the morning breeze.
Beautiful than the midnight star.
Stronger than an oceans roar.

   Your Gracious Love!

Bonded together with inseparable hearts.
Never to be broken or torn apart.
Taking the time to show you care.
Always near when I need you there.

   Your Gracious Love!

Glad to be given the chance to feel your grace.
Moments of pleasure when seeing your face.
Sweet thoughts come to mind when thinking of you.
Realizing just how much your love pulls me through.

Thankful to have you as my Aunt.
Thankful to be your Nephew.
Joy and happiness - kindness and love
Remembering the times with

   Your Gracious Love!

Marcel Washington

Met A Master

Met a master along my way
Sitting in Samadhi for one full day.
His eyes were shut tight
But he could still see the light. He levitated into the air
The wind blew his long matted hair.
I stood in awe - at such a sight full of wonderment and delight.
As he descended back to the ground
I couldn't help but gather around.
He spoke these words so plain so clear
"Be not afraid, nor have no fear.
The power of God is ever so near.
Be open to love, let love flow through your heart
Come to realize that you and God shall never part.
You are his child he is your father
Stand as one and you shall never falter.
May the lovely Godly grace Shine forever on your face"
He stopped talking and gave a sigh
He went back into Samadhi as quick as a wink of an eye.
Met a master along my way
So I made up my mind and decided to stay.

Andre Alvin Moore

A Child Untold

Looking back yesterday, when you said goodbye,
I searched myself, for the reason I cried.
Was it because, you'd left me alone?
Or was it because of our child untold?

I know the child, is the reason I cried,
And thinking about it, I understand why.
For what do you have, to offer this child?
When you've always treated me, so very wild.

Will it be like you, or take after me?
This is the question I'll wait and see.
Will it succeed, or do as we've done,
Just run around looking for fun?

I guess you do, have the right to know.
But if I tell you, will you still go?
Maybe you'd change, but that would be new,
For your deepest cares, have always been you.

Now that you've left me, for someone new.
Not knowing or caring, that I'm really 'two'.
I really don't know what will become of this mess.
I hope for this child's sake, it'll turn out the best.

Karen Fletcher

Homeless

On the streets, people lay their head,
the big city is their bed

If one was killed, no one would care,
one less homeless is out there

Trying to live while on the street,
being nice to people they meet

They have feelings that no one seen
people don't care because they're mean

They are people like you and me,
they are human and can see.

The looks and laughs people make,
their jokes are cruel and hard to take

People should look at what's inside,
and let the outside pass on by

(They live their lives and don't bother you,
so just live your life to the fullest too.)

Tanya Hicks

Library Labyrinth's, Home To The Poet

Here in a home
There are no closed doors
To focus a phobia
To be lost in the floors
All roofs of glass
All faces pose drowned
All crowded in one mask
The actors have found
Some places for captions
Speak of near and far
Some caught in action
Never flexing their heart
I seek the cup on the shelves of the wall
A maze to some, to me thirst calls
From the chords of upstairs high with an angel
Her wings are familiar with the architect's angle
The beds are maskless
So I lie here alone
Onto the stairs, I crawl
Here in a home

Mike Roberts

A Faded Love

It all seems too long ago
The day we made a promise to each other
It seemed like nothing would stand in our way

But through the years
It seemed like everything had changed
It's not what it use to be

The love I thought I had found
Has slowly drifted by, like a fall leaf in the wind
Going and going until it disappears somewhere

The feelings inside are no more, like a cold winter day
Nothing matters anymore

There's always hope
That things will get back to the way they use to be
But it seems like they only get worse
Nothing seems to change

I have to hope for the future
Things will get better
Someday I will find a special someone
Who will warm me inside, like the sun on a cool autumn day

Cindy Benner

Tacky Threads

There was a bright purple shirt and ugly brown pants,
That were on the body of a guy named Lance.
He wore an orange headband and navy blue socks,
He looked like one of those paint smeared smocks.
He wore a neon belt and pea green shoes,
With that outfit you will always lose.
He went to a party with his girl named Fran,
But she looked as tacky as her main man.
She wore white from her head to her toe,
She looked like a really big flake of snow.
At the party they were the best,
Don't judge a book by its cover, look at the rest.

Meta David

The Moors

Of dragons and damsels and wicked white froth
   Come clouds and bangdingles all elated with cloth.
To the moor to the highlands up cursors with swords
   Down the valleys of kings, queens and their Lords.

Fire doth soak the battle here they do volley
   The shrieking tall tales of fate in the molley.
All clansman arise to the whimper of fate
   Kill the chastle of many knowing its weight.

Sing aloud of the millers grinding sour grain
   Hear the tooth of voices who cry out in great pain.
Over hedges and briars sound pipes in the mist
   Of those who have fallen like the wheat and its grist.

Lift up the proud banner and then dash it in shame
   Through the smoke and the embers of the dragons flame.
Court to hamper the journey into this great realm
   Let captains and sailors go to sleep at the helm.

Then soon there is silence it abounds on the moors
   And ships lie shattered on far distant shores
And dragons and damsels will have a new court
   Then live in a peace of a life of a sort.

Dennis A. Myers

Just So You'll Know

Dedicated to my Grandchildren Joanna, J.P. and Jennifer

Life is really funny, but not the ha! ha! kind.
It can be peaceful, or confusing, depending on your state of mind.

When you are young your life is sunny, with very few rainy days.
Teenage years are adventurous, and their energy abounds.
Nothing seems to frighten them, as their world goes round and round.

Parenting can be such joy, with your little girls and boys.
The old saying goes, they can step on your toes, they can step on your heart.
This all goes with the parenting part.

As a Senior Citizen, I feel this is the hardest part of life.
Everybody seems to be too busy to notice your cares or strife.

I don't question the good Lord's planning, I wouldn't be so bold.
But I think life should be better as you come to the end of the road.
For many years you've carried your burdens, now is when he should lighten the load.

In old age your teeth, hair, strength and patience is so much less.
A few years of happiness, comfort and laughter would show us we've passed life's test.

Dorothy Valeska

Endless Haze

Thick fog below, haze in my eye.
Nothing around to find.
The colorless sky surrounds my soul
And lives in my mind.

Every night my soul returns.
Coming back to this dark place.
Days of torture and sleep without rest.
This dream will not erase.

I trudge through the dream, searching for help.
Just someone to understand.
Is there anyone to save me now?
Anyone to take my hand?

I look forward, expecting haze.
But something shines through the grey.
A great light blinding to all but myself.
Shining straight through the dismay.

Someone steps out of the blinding light.
And reaches out his hands.
And at that moment, all fear is erased.
For I realize, God understands.

Narrissa Gouldsbrough

Death

For all those special people that touch our lives

We live our lives from day to day.
When it comes to this - what is it that we say.
We come together in life's end.
For our dear special friend.

The Lord needed you in his call.
You will be at peace now that's the best of all.
You touched many peoples' lives
with your caring heart.
Will we try to cope with life's toughest part.
For those who worked with you side by side.
We can say you did it with great pride.
For we must live to love before we each die.
My dear friend we all came to say
Goodbye...

William Copley

Untitled

Abortions and births fill the news
Head lines abound with smiles and death
Free speech and religion are topics today
This seems to be the only way
We're starting to grow I can see the light
Someone must save us from this plight
Politicians, bankers write your senators too
Send all your mail to you know who
Who's running this country into the ground
Poverty destruction, killing abound
Let's pull out while the gettin's good
Fly to the moon we all understood
Shot down from the sky they won't let us go
We're here to say no one runs away
Prisoners of this world that's what we are
This other world dis just too far we can't fly we're
out of gas no minerals or fossils can save our ass
There's too much pollution that's what the headlines say
We'll all die in the same way breathe now
for there will be no tomorrow
   Joseph A. Halenar

Potter's Field Equipoise

Beneath the turf of Potter's field,
   Lie those of ignoble means.
Shadows once their ambiance,
   Mock presence cruelly deemed.
Ignored upon life's passing, petrified as stone.
   Evaporated memories - tale of loss now prone.
Trifling and pathetic cast, to all, except to God.
   Reduced to tags and numbers, rotting casket's cryptic sod.
Fleeced of pride and dignity, discarded pauper waste.
   Incarcerated relics, left for darkness to embrace.
Bequest of thee thou holy grail, its legacy they reap.
   No longer restless slumber, but blest delightful sleep.
Sentiments thus recognized, in accordance too thy will.
   Futile casements open wide, no longer visions still.
It's now their time for glory, repressive energy now past.
   Divinity engulfed by grace - justice theirs at last!
Who's not to say the humblest ones, the poorest souls on earth.
   In heaven rein as richest, dire poverty their mirth?
As for those endued who feel that wealth, is all that life should yield
   Come meditate upon the turf of hallowed potter's field.
   Edward A. Nicholson

Yes I'm Fine

Time seems endless as I sit alone
Thoughts seem endless, into my world I'm thrown
I've tried to fight but the windows of the past expand
They are larger than I remember, that's all I can stand
The hurt and pain come on and attack relentlessly
Only promises can I make to insure that I'm still me
Sorrow begins to flow like the tears running down my cheek
Taking away my soul and forcing my will to be weak
I hope that they can't tell what my condition might be
I've disguised my feelings so they won't worry about me
I'm beginning to understand as the tears come falling down
That there's healing inside though my face is still a frown
The night is almost over and my weeping begins to cease
To my puzzle I've just added one more piece
But the affliction will strike again, my face will start off dry
And the misery will pour out as I ask myself why
Time seems endless in this world of mine
Then someone breaks in...

"yes I'm fine."
   Russel Hamm

Hidden Sunshine

It's raining out, the weather's cold
A winter storm rolls in so bold
And soon the rain will turn to snow
With temperatures of 10 below

Inside the house we're warm and dry
And still a tear falls from my eye
We're far apart but I can see
That all alone I'll never be

Because things you taught me long ago
Have helped more than you'll ever know
I learned what's right and what is wrong
By watching as you stood so strong

And now I'm grown and far away
I think about you every day
I really wish that you could see
Me and my little family

I know at times I did my part
So many times I've hurt your heart
And though the sky is grey with clouds
I think I've finally made you proud.
   Allen L. Scudder

Poetry Contest

Am a poet, you wish to know?
What I prepared in poem limit?
I bring to you but twenty lines,
And I prepared a poem lyric.

A table (is) set in front of me,
Eight persons ready for verdict.
What can I say? Some love poets!
But others hate them, stop the strands.

What they will say about my work?
They will like it? Or hope in hog?
In any case my food is good
Is excellence strength not doom!!

I know what to prepare in poetry
As in your honor or your majesty,
And to combine the line as you can see
So, number one my table, yes! Should be!!

Please taste! Be satisfied! And you will see!
How best of best or number one should be!
About you eight? You have a word to say?
My line are twenty in contest today!
   Irina Rosca

Memories

Even if present, past and future
Stood aside on a fixed line,
I could not select at will
A point in time to explain
The thoughts and doings of my life.

There's no sequence in time
When memory reaches back
To capture life from events passed
Between birth and death,
The dreamy fixed moments of existence;

So, it takes some cutting-off of memories
To find out the brief moments
When my soul was entrapped,
For I'm not merely the dreamt images
That I often forget,
I'm also the remembrance of my past.
   Maria Luz Anguiano

The Marigold Man

He had worked in a nursery
wheeling around petunias in rusty old carts
and neatening the endless rows of seed packets
He liked to do the displays, arranging peonies and
zinnias like pretty girls in a pageant
He talked little to the customers, preferring to sit in the
back and pot flowers, which he did with such careful attention
that his hands shook
In a free moment, he would wander the aisles, breathing
the colors and grasping the way the fragile petals rustled ever
so slightly in a summer breeze
He touched their leaves often, to check moisture and also,
to run his fingers along the smooth undersides where the
veins were so distinct you could almost feel a pulse
Each day before closing, he swept the floor meticulously
making a neat pile in the corner
A perfect tower of stems and leaf cuttings and crispy dead flowers.
He would bag up this pile carefully and place it reluctantly
in the dumpster
Then, he would take a final look around at the flowers,
stopping always in front of his favorites, the marigolds
And it was marigolds they had at the funeral
Bright red and orange and yellow, almost a roomful

Morgan Hilpert

"Evil Spirit"

Who will save your soul???
The lies you tell, the lives you stole??
You've possessed so many innocent teens,
pressuring them to do Evil.
One by one, you fill their souls with anger,
hatred, and frustration.
In a state of depression,
someone young has taken his life.
You Laugh... We Cry
You Win... We Try
Your goal is to kill God,
So everyone will worship you
in a Wold of hatred.
Tell me, who will save your soul????

Caroline Sharone Hamm

Unhuman

Struck down a rod of lighting, piercing through the summer's sky
Brisk the horizon; take inside the beauty of the sea's currents
As the shadow of the earth shuns its light below
A beast appears: Ripping and roaring with delight
I need release
From worlds of permanency
Constructed within the atmosphere's boundaries
You can never take my forsaken thoughts away
As you march along the perimeter of the rocky mountains
Torch in your hand, back to your forbidden land
(Marchers of the Night)
The planets unite, as they get ready for twilight
Communication is made as the chain is tied
My body starts to rest under many life forms
Of no human perception
You are what you make of this mysterious world
Human knowledge was meant to be sealed to minimal understanding
The sand of one thousand specks under my human uniform,
warms my senses
As my human mind constructs unhuman thoughts

Danielle A. Douglass

Foliage Of Faith

When the leaves display their brilliance
In the crisp autumnal air,
They resemble stained glass windows
In a church peaceful and fair;

Resplendent in their colors,
Lifting boughs to pray,
Dressed up in their Sunday best,
They celebrate each day.

God's handiwork is everywhere,
A magnificent display.
I'm thankful for the beauty
God gives to us each day.

Arlene Rudyk

Love

It can be seen in your caring face.
It can be felt in your warm embrace.

It can be heard in what you say.
It's always with us, day after day.

It can even span a thousand miles.
I think of you and it makes me smile.

It's always with us, no matter where.
Wherever love is, we'll always be there.

I love you more than anything.
Will you do me the honor of accepting this ring

And spend with me the rest of your life;
Me as your husband and you as my wife?

Kevin Keitch

Mama

Just one year has past since you've been gone,
yet, in our hearts it seems so long.
We've missed you, oh so very much,
your jolly laugh, your gentle touch.
There's not one day passes by
that we don't gaze on heavenly skies.
What are you doing, Mama, in your home up above?
Are you singing? Are you dancing? Are you sharing with
　those you loved?
Did you bring them up to date on all that had gone on?
Did you give them all the scoop on your daughters and your son?
Did you give our love to Daddy—Nana and Papa too?
And tell them that we missed them just like we now miss you?
I know that if we could have our choice to have you back again,
We wouldn't ask a loving God back to this earth to send.
In our hearts and minds we know we joy you now possess
Your life on earth is over-you've entered heaven's blessed.
How could we even think to ask our Lord for your return
Instead our hearts watch and wait for Heaven is what we yearn.

Brenda Knight

An Old School House

Alone in the meadow, near the rise of a hill,
　is an old school house, abandoned and still.
Weeds have overgrown the path to her door.
　The bell tower has fallen, and beckons no more.
A gnarled tree with wisps of frayed strands,
　which once held a swing, dangles empty hands.
Some desks are still standing, but ink wells long dry.
　Windows are boarded, blackboards awry.
Years have taken their toll, the children long gone.
　But the school house keeps waiting, from sunset to dawn,
remembering cheery faces and laughter shrill.
　She is now lonely, forgotten, keeping vigil still.

Melba E. Van Camp

The Ladies In White

The ladies in white have their jobs to do;
taking care of me and you,
they are as sweet as they can be;
and when I talk to them I feel free,
they have devoted themselves, taking care of us;
and not causing a fuss,
there is no one earth;
sweeter than a nurse,
they will greet you with a sincere smile;
and it will be worth your while,
their love and affection, will always show;
and within their heart is a glow;
they help the sick and poor;
trying to find a cure,
they are your friend indeed;
and will help when in need,
speak to them with a voice of cheer;
and let them know you do care.

Joseph Ralph Williams

A Mother's Love

I want to tell a true story for all to hear,
About an unselfish woman whom I hold dear.

It seems like yesterday when we met face to face,
With infant eyes I saw I was in the right place.

Diapers changed, bottles warmed, and baby rocked to sleep,
Formula mixed, prayers said, "...I pray my soul to keep."

When sick or hurt you lovingly nursed me to health,
Your concern for me, I consider my greatest wealth.

On my first day of school, anticipations were high,
You masked your tears with a smile as you kissed me goodbye.

Throughout my school days, projects would stimulate my mind,
But, if needed, your generous help I would find.

You are not known for your cooking, sewing, and cleaning,
But more for a life that is worth emulating.

Of all memories, the most important would be,
Your morning's private prayers to God about me.

Words cannot express what all you've done means to me,
I've become the whole person I had hoped to be.

One of the greatest blessings given from above,
Is the blessing of a mother like you to love.

Bill Spencer

Untitled

Rake in hand.
Eyes not seen under rounded cap.
Arms like cord and black.

Green soldier of fortune he is.
The prize? Tomatoes and corn.
He is also magician, turning earth to food.

His hard labor nourishes fall thieves.
Depleted of food he smiles, with replenished soul.

Old man in the garden has died.
Plot neglected and torn.
Union with God, he is reborn.

Anthony Slauson

Untitled

Dear Son,

The day is waking
The rooster crows his hello
I am tired and I haven't even moved an eyelid...
I lie thinking of you, son, my once healthy child,
With an ache in my heart and tears finding a path down my cheek,
I now lie here wondering why
Why are you now confined to a hospital bed
With tubes and I.V.'s tangled about your frail body
Needles piercing your flesh
Pain ravaging your every breath...
Too weak to resist.
I lie here exhausted, by my instincts are awakened and I know...
As when you were in my womb, using my energy to grow
Now, too, by some phenomenon;
God is giving you strength through me...
I'll stay strong for you
My baby, my son,
My Brett.
Love, Mom

Carolyn L. Johnson

A Fool

A fool I was
To think that you really did care
A fool I was
To think that you'd always be there

A fool I was
To fall for each and every lie
A fool I was
To think that you were a nice guy

A fool I was
To let you control me all the time
A fool I was
To be ready for you at the drop of a dime

A fool I was
To have you lead me on
A fool I was
To have you play me from dusk till dawn

A fool I was
To think that you were mine
A fool I am
Till the end of time.

Renee Petersen

Flying

  Oh I feel so free
when I'm flying just the birds and me.
  It's like you can feel his presence in the air
you can't see him, but you know he's there.
  I go high in my plane.
Sometimes sunny, sometimes rain.
  I can't tell you how it feels
having wings instead of wheels.
  I go soaring like the eagle when he flies so high
periwinkle blue, that's the color of our sky.
  For a long time it was a man's pleasure to take to the sky.
But I'm a woman and I gave it a try.
  So now I think it doesn't matter who you are,
you can seek the sun or chase a falling star.
  So sometimes I look at the sky,
and thank God I have learned how to fly.

Laura Annadale

Insanity

Hate and destruction;
Death and fear,
All in one little tear.

Love and hate;
Death by your mate,
What a strange fate to fall on a date.

Mother and son;
Father and daughter,
This is the incest from the east to west.

Adultery, anger, child abuse;
Insanity,
The killers excuse.

Criminal minds;
The killing kinds,
This is what you find when hatreds combined.

Morality dropping fast;
Each generation a little worst that the last.
An eternal repetition of a never ending past.
Jessica DeAnn Soto

Your Child

Your child's not a gift to you, only a loan
Jesus can at anytime take his dear Child home
While he's in your tender care tell him about the hate out there
But show him, show him of our savior's love

Show him that you're honest, that's it wrong to cheat
Teach him to be humble, Jesus washed his disciple's feet
Gently show him kindness, let him hear you pray
Tell him about forgiveness, an example be today

Tell him how our savior, hung on Calvary's tree
With all our sins upon him, he died to set us free
Tell him Christ is coming back, although you don't know when
Tell him that you love him, read the Bible to him

Tell him about old Satan, the prince of this world
He offers sweet temptations to every boy and girl
Mom and Dad please warn them, of this world full of sin
Pray to God for guidance, be both parent and friend

Some sweet day when Jesus calls, they'll be at heaven's gate.
The Bible tells us, they'll not depart from the faith
Mom and Dad you'll know you've raised quite a daughter or son
What a reunion in heaven when Jesus says "A job well done"
Sylvia A. Munsey

The Stacked Deck

From the dealer a card is played,
As to be expected the ace is spade.
From white knuckles your card is laid,
High as it is you still lie frayed.

Continuously dealt only "farmer's" hands,
You stay in the game, for you must stand.

Anxious for your card, adrenaline pumps...
But one again the dealer has trump.
Uneasily you pray for the "stop".
Fair? These meager cards are not from the top.

Yes, it's true the deck is stacked,
And against you the world is packed,
But stand tall and don't give in -
For those who stand long stand to win.
Heidi J. Tarwacki

Possibility

So oft you hear of the "Good Old Days"
The way things used to be
And of the younger generation being influenced
By video games and T.V.

I was then, when things were good
Or so they claimed to say
It really wasn't that much different
We had the same struggle day by day

Where did things go wrong?
It's hard to say, many things stand out alone
Like the way they teach, the way they preach
The runaway kids left on the streets to roam
And the lack of respect for each others rights
The homeless sleeping on the streets at night
Most of these things could have been eliminated
In an understanding and loving home
Everett D. Kimble

Saving A Seat For You

Thirteen years old
In a teenage trance.
My heart searching, soaring,
learning to dance.
My final wish as a child was
not to come true.
Only silence sat in the seat
I saved for you.

Sixteen years old
And still you are gone.
Sixteen years, I've known the
truth all along.
No tender kiss upon my brow.
No "My little boy is a grown man, now,"
and still my heart hopes somehow.
Oh, soul, forgive me, but this I must do:
Clasp my chest and wish anew,
And you can bet,
and never forget,
I'm saving a seat for you.
Nathan Conrad

A Cry From The Land - Intro Retreat....

Out relaxing in my huge garden
Thus a thunderous cry...

I stand among creatures and people
Like a shadow
They see me and do all sorts nonsense
On my back
As if am not a living creature
As if am not any purpose to you
still you strike, wound and kick harder
on my back.

Agriculture, engineers destroy me with their tools
wounding and using me carelessly
I pretend as if I don't know anything
Armies trample, invade and destroy me
With their bombs and dangerous weapons
Still I kept quiet
Agriculturists work on every minute of the day on me
Just for search of minerals
All these things I see
Made me to cry.
Chukwuemeka Ezejiofor

The Plastic Box

It sat there,
The plastic box of imitation life.
Silent, undaunting, and innocent,
But it comes to life with a twitch of a muscle.
How easy it is fall prey.
Its paralyzed victims
With fixed stares.
Victims of imaginary life and reality,
Adventure and romance.
How easy to the idealist it can be defeated.
Simply twitch that same muscle,
The opposite way and
Send the evil specter of imitation life
Back into the black void.
Behind the glass.

Scot D. Friesen

Seasons

Seasons may come, and seasons may go,
Changes taken place, as we all know.

Spring holds the magic, that never dies away,
As strong bond of love, began in the month of May.

Summer tightens the hold, the heat is never to hot.
The risk is worth all, for the remaining time we sought.

Fall blows into our lives, we become best of friends.
Never losing sight, our dreams carry with the winds.

Winter cares in quickly, freezing the dead of night,
Ice forms into happy tears, from the warmth of a fire light.

The laughter and tears give us endless is reasons,
To hold onto the future, to hold on to all seasons.

Ed Swatkowski III

I Didn't Quite Dare

I had fear, I wanted to run.
I didn't quite dare, so I walked with strength.

I had shame, I wanted to walk with my head down.
I didn't quite dare, so I walked with pride.

I had anger, I wanted to destroy.
I didn't quite dare, so I walked with respect.

I had sadness, I wanted to cry.
I didn't quite dare, so I walked with joy.

I had hate, I wanted to kill.
I didn't quite dare, so I walked with love.

Of all the feelings I had,
I chose to walk with strength, pride,
Respect, joy, and love.
Then I saw that I walked with God.

Julia Cranford

My Angel

One day I was laying in bed thinking and it just hit me, God sent me an Angel
I have always felt special when my Angel was around
I would get that butterfly feeling in my stomach
I look at my friend differently now that I see that special sparkle of Angel inside
Angels aren't perfect and neither is mine, but mine is close enough
Angels have wings and halos, my angel has wings and halos, but only that I can see
My Angel is as real as can be, but he has a special Angel way about him
My Angel is very special to me
Every night I thank God for sending me my dear Angel

Laura A. Hieber

Untitled

To my Grandfather on your special day
I thank you for all the love and wisdom you have graciously sent my way.
For the days of pretending to be a tree,
playing cards, taking walks, and most of all listening to me.
I thank you for the letters you write each week,
the voice you give, and the prayers you speak.
For making me feel special and so loved
and for teaching me about the man up above.
As you can see I am your biggest fan,
because you are the greatest Grandpa known to man.
So on your 90th Birthday I wish you a happy day
and a wonderful year,
and remember that I think of you all the time even though I am not near.
You will always have a spacial place in my heart,
And no one but you Grandpa will ever fit the part.
Happy Birthday!
I Love You,

Heather Young Cooper

My Poetry Contest Entry

With pen in hand, I sat to write, a poem to win a prize;
  It's easy so I thought at first, but came to realize-
"What shall my subject be" I thought, and thought, and thought in vain;
  It's not too easy, now I've learned, I'm feeling mental strain!

Then finally as the hours ticked by, an idea occurred to me;
  Why think about a subject, when it's clear and plain to see.
I'll write about the contest and the prize that I may win;
  I'll tax my brain enough to let, the words come from within.

And so I matched some sentences, and lined them up just so;
  They had to fall in place to rhyme, be metered too, to flow.
Although some poems don't always rhyme, and meter can be nil;
  Writing verse and using both, requires a bit of skill!

A poem, unless a ballad, should be short and not too long;
  Its rhythm can be any style, its topic light or strong.
But most of all be interesting, to hold its reader's eye;
  And strike a place in memory, as the years go by.

So though I'm just an amateur, my poems are not well known;
  I hope they hold some promise, for the effort I have shown.
And should this poem show merit, I ask that you advise;
  You need not send me money, recognition's the best prize!

Ruth L. Gibb

Untitled

The boy lives in fear
  of his heartless parent's fists
All of the punches that were thrown,
  there were few that missed.
At night he'd lie on his stomach,
  and not on bruised back
still cut and bleeding from
  that painful whack.
The times they were mad,
  the child would get the belt.
But the pain didn't effect this body,
  it was in his heart where it was felt.
He would dream of places he'd love to go -
  He would read of a special land
Being deathly afraid of their striking hand.
Now the boy's grown older,
  More tolerant to pain
But from all those repeated blows,
  there was nothing he gained.

Justin Bernosky

Blind

Dark,
   Can't see.
     Can't find reality.
Locked away in the chambers of your world.
   You are there but yet unheard.

Though you hear the noise around you.
   Shouting, talking, and joyful laughter..

Feeling lost but you might find, that when you touch
   you're not blind...

Cause so you see that with your hands you'll find your way
   and so you'll stand...

Stumble trip, as time goes on, you may slip
   but please stay strong...

Those around you in the light, may put you down,
   ask why you fight...

So they say that you can't see, but now you've found
   reality...

And reality to this day.
   Is that they are blind..
     and you can see!...

Carolyn Taylor

A Truthful Execution

Where ya' goin' with that life in your hands?
You toss it and throw it to unknown lands.
You sigh at the world, but grin at this place,
You stare in the mirror to find your face.
You're hiding in a cave where many have died,
You find the town where those people have lied.
A rocking chair sways, but no ones' around, you look to the left,
then hear a sound. You drift unwillingly around this eery street,
You want to run, but have no feet. You scamper on stumps and
You hide from my eyes, you hear the sounds, you hear the lies.
The lies you hear are the ones you've said,
You feel something cold on the temple of your head.
You hear a 'click', and begin to shake,
You hope it's a dream, want to wake.
Your time is short, your life is hell, you lie and you scream
off the cliff you fell. You want to live, your temple's still cold,
The gun to your head, you can not hold.
Although no one's around the gun's still there, up to your head,
I can not stare. You flinch and you struggle through your lying self,
The ashes were yours that I blew off the self.

David R. Ryszewski

A Father's Fear

Why, my Daddy, when I'm asleep
Do you worry all night long?
We're tucked safely in our beds,
But you want to be alone.

You tip-toe through our room near dawn,
Wide-eyed, your face is lined,
From battling demons all night long
Until the morning light.

But if you knew how much we loved you,
And lived to play inside your eyes,
You'd laugh at all your fears,
And throw away your fright.

But it's hard to say 'Goodbye' to ghosts,
Bad friends though they might be;
For as you twist and turn at night,
They're your only company

Pat Tamarkin

Would I — Could I

Would I climb the highest mountain, swim the deepest ocean just to get to you?
   I would

Would I be there for you in good times, bad times, sickness, poor health?
   I would

Would I sew buttons on your shirt, when you had a dozen other shirts to choose from?
   I would

Would I love you so much, it would seem, there would be no more love left to give?
   I could

Would I be your friend, someone to share your secrets, your concerns, doubts, problems with?
   I would

Would I cradle your head in my arms, and hum a familiar tune, so as to calm your restless spirit?
   I would

Would you be there for me?
Could you be there for me?

Sylvia Browne

Basketball

Down by two with three seconds to go.
I see competition, my eyes aglow.

The coach wants the ball to go to me,
And I wonder should I go for two or three.

I'm the star of the team, and I have to come through.
If I fail I don't know what I'll do.

As I sit on the bench, I hear the crowd's cry.
They're yelling, "go for the win, not the tie."

The timeout is over and we step on the floor.
I'm telling myself that I have to score.

The ball is inbounded, and it goes to me.
I turn around and square up for three.

The shot is up then it starts to fall,
And every eye in the building is on that ball.

The ball starts to fall through the net,
And the other team starts to get depressed.

I just knew that the shot would fall.
No wonder I just love basketball.

Carl Williams

A Special Love

A rose in full bloom is my true love to me,
A light in the darkness when my eyes cannot see;
A smile for my sad heart and a port for my tears,
A love that's grown more precious in these our golden years.

When our love was new there was no guarantee,
That through all our days you would still be with me;
You brought special meaning to a dark empty space,
With the light of you sweet love for a life with no place.

Through both good and bad times we stood side by side,
And assurance was felt with each tear that we cried;
With true love our anchor, we enjoy a calm rest,
In knowing that with our love we've been most richly blessed.

Now I can sing a new song of the peace I have found,
And of the joy all these years, dear, since you've been around;
To tell you I love you seems so easy to say,
So I'll continue to prove it with each passing day.

Betty Jean Pierce

To Wish Upon A Star

The night air brings to me a calming effect
As I gaze upon the heavens, I try to reflect
My life is a maze, confused and distraught
Caught up in a web of pain, nothing else could be lost
Married once, then married twice
The anguish they caused turned my heart cold as ice
I would not leave any room to feel
For I had nothing more for anyone to steal
I gave my baby, I gave my mind
I even walked the men's narrow line
I took the beatings and verbal abuse
I even tried to make a trues
I have nothing to offer from deep inside
It is only time I need to abide
I need a meaning for life itself
Then maybe I can put the pain upon a shelf
The night air is cool and the stars shine bright
My wish is for a good friend tonight
Someone to take away this frown
To give me Hope instead of tearing me down
Amelia E. Richmond

A Day of Promise

A day of promise
A day of hope
A day of gladness
A day to cope

A week of sunshine
A week of growth
A week of challenge
A week of note

A month of victory
A month of care
A month of learning
A month so rare

A year of conflict
A year of concern
A day - a week - a month
a year to learn

These are the days - weeks
months years for which
we yearn
They come - they go- they mold our concern.
Danny Liddell

A Garden In The Mind

Peace of mind is found in the heart.
It's a wonderful feeling, it's a work of art!
Your mind and your heart belong together.
For they lift the soul in all kinds of weather.
Treat negative thoughts like weeds, pull them out!
Plant a garden of flowers in your mind, don't sit and pout!
Plant roses and violets and watch them grow.
Think of people as flowers you know.
Yes, a garden of love is what we all need.
To our loved ones it brings happiness indeed.
So plant that garden in your mind and heart.
With beautiful flowers a new life will start!
Thinking well of others gives you a glow.
People around you will see the difference, they'll know,
Yes, they'll know! They'll know by the garden you grow.
Always be happy, always be kind!
And the Lord will bless you with peace of mind.
P. Meily

Forgotten

Kill me hate me tear my feelings down
Punish me rip at me make sure no one's around

Crush me tear me go ahead and laugh
Pull me tug me but take only half

All my life I've been trying to win
But no one remembers my name I feel like Rumplestiltskin

Everything I've done I've never had a break
All anybody's ever done is take, take, take

I'm outside of myself I'm really distant now
I really want to hide will someone show me how?

Somebody help me the light is fading fast
I always knew it was too good to last
I'm looking down on me lying on the floor
I hear sirens and pounding on the door

There went living right down the drain
There's angels everywhere I think I've gone insane

Look inside my heart there's really nothing left
I've gone away from this world cold and bereft

They rush me to the ambulance that's out in the street
Little do they know I never had a heartbeat
Shauna Benton

Take Me There

I believe the sun will shine again
I can see the poetry in the sky above
The glory in the air fills my lungs.

Take Me There

Call out to the empty fields
Send a message through the hills
There's a storm raging in our soul.
A flood of emotions; tears of joy.

Take Me There

The time has come for everyone to take part in a journey
Stand together, holding hands—the gift of love
Child, Woman, and Man.

Take Me There

Build a bridge across the tide
Stand together; serve with pride
We are brothers
We are sisters
We are one.

Take Me There.
Kevin Michael Navin

My Parents

A twinkle in my little eyes gave them one in theirs,
A smile made them laugh, and bundle me up with their cares.

Even though they didn't plant the seed,
They nourished it with care,
A touch as soft as a rose, my finger wrapped around theirs.

Once they had me in their arms,
The cold upon me, now was warm.
They knew they were special,
And God would keep them far from harm.
Claire Elise Parker

Children

Children are ours to love to hold,
Not for sex,
Or lust,
Or even sold.

Children want us to hear,
When they have troubles,
And when they have fears.

When children do wrong and then we scold,
We should not spank,
Or hit,
Or even throw.

Children may ask us how and why,
Or even ask us how high is the sky,
We may know or we may not know the answers to all the why's,
But we can show them why a cow cannot fly.

Children are our loves and our joys,
So be glad not sad,
For the children that we have,
Are ours to love and to enjoy.

John Kessler

Who's Heart

When they first started going together,
Her head became as light as a feather.
They were together all the time,
He even wrote her words that rhyme.
Trying to make everything better,
He made it sound bad in a letter.
She tried to write poetry for him,
But did not know where to begin.
To him it came natural,
And to her it was wonderful.
If things ever start to fall apart,
Who will be the one with the broken heart?

Nicole Helminiak

Spring

As the wind blows so do the trees
and the clouds in the sky and the waves on the sea,

Everything grows the grass and the flowers
the drizzling rains become thunder showers,

All shines bright the sun and the moon
Jupiter, Pluto, and Mars
last but not the least when we look up at night
the twinkling of thousands of stars,

The birds come back from the south
with wings that fly so free
to start all over and build their nest
high up in some old tree,

And then we hear the young ones
as they flutter to the ground
tweeting here and everywhere
it's such a lovely sound,

These are all signs
that spring is now here
and the flowers will bloom
in the fields that are near.

Robert C. Howe

Living,

Compromising feelings, trying to find a way out
trying to find reason, logic
feeling the space, environment, (changing (.) it.)
trying to feel the hard points
trying to find the beneath
(make-believing a journey) treeing
beginning to see the path to insanity

getting tired, finding a new day to start again
taking photographs, exploring of external
neutralizing
trying to find the hard points
trying to feel the beneath
   breathing
     wanting, feeling, counting, remembering, analyzing, solving,
   finding
     wondering, loving, hating, arguing, building, growing,
unseeing
     connecting, dreaming, learning, correcting, wronging, creating
     touching, saying, being, trying, thinking, hoping, unknowing,
   non-believing, ceasing,
   blanketing.
non-existent comforting
limited.   [infinity x zero] = circle

Matthew Kreuter

Seasons Of The Heart

The rain comes down like tears against the window pane,
I feel such emptiness, and I going insane?

I stare into the dark night, hoping to see your face,
To hear your laughter, and feel your warm embrace.

The empty house echoes the emptiness I feel.
I look to heaven, bow my head, and kneel.

The rain, will it ever go away?
Will we ever see another sunny day?

I ask God to surround you with his love
My little angel, I know you are in heaven above.

You had to leave too soon, so much you had to give,
Can it be that in dying you taught us all how to live.

Brenda O'Quin

Sand

I float through life,
going wherever the wind takes me.
Laid back I float down the river,
leaving a mark wherever I stop.

Never truly belonging, never wanting to.
Root take time to grow, but I never try.
What is the use if they all get ripped away.

I watch the world as an outsider,
with back to the wall the world goes by.
When I leave nothing changes,
life in the small stream still flows.

I float to a new home,
but Sand is all I can see.
And all know,
roots don't grow in Sand.

When I know roots won't grow,
time in the garden of Sand bears no fruit.
Each garden better then the last,
but still all filled with Sand.

Zachary Graham

Foreign Land

A praise I'll sing for you tonight
As your Guardian angel is sent in flight
She'll come to you and help you through
A situation which weakens you.
   A miracle she'll work and shine your light
   Upon a path which is blind by sight
   Prepare yourself for a long strange journey
   Into a place of no misery or mourning.
Relax your body and you'll feel no pain
Control yourself and yourself you shall regain
But might I warn you, you shan't leave the path
For upon you, you shall receive a miserable wrath.
   Your soul has not yet been put to rest
   But complete your journey and you shall be blessed
   You shall see things which have been questioned
   And realize your life was preserved by His resurrection.
Your angel will lead you as far as she can
By then you shall know of this foreign land
So don't lose hope and follow this road
And soon it will lead you to riches untold....

Jason E. Rhian

I Believe

I have to believe that all of us have a
   destiny to fulfill.
I have to believe that you and I have a
   principle in life.
I have to believe that each of us has an
   intelligent path to follow.
I have to believe that each of us knows
   what is right and what is wrong.
I have to believe that all of us are created equal.
I have to believe that all of us have a grandeur of beauty.
I have to believe that life is so precious we must treasure it.
I have to believe that life itself is love.
I have to believe that each of us has a strong faith in God.
I have to believe that each of us has our
   own shortcomings, let us forgive and forget.
I have to believe that each of us is honest in our own way.
I have to believe that when we give "Love" you get "Love"
I have to believe that no matter what everything is due to "Love".
I have to believe that you "Love Me," because "I Love You."

Josefina S. Quitoriano

First Touch

Our first touch one moonlit night
Has scorched my soul beyond delight
The sweet sensation still is tingling
Passionately it still is lingering
The special memories never die
Though life goes on and time flies by
The tender moments never fade
The gentle heart be not betrayed
For truly in your arms I've found
A peace in your strength does abound
Yet who's to say where we shall be
Together or not eternally
And worlds away from understanding
Or farther even than demanding
The facts will be the same, the questions still remain
Are we in love or just insane
Insanely bound by lust
To a world adverse to trust
In each other we must find the rhyme
And only then we'll conquer time

Teresa Warwick

I Loved You Before

I loved you before you were who you are,
and I became what I am.

I have been loved by others, and I've loved them back,
as far as I'm able.

There should be a word that is stronger than love
and deeper than adore.

There should be a way to say that I loved you before
even our mothers were born.

But words are poor, fragile, flimsy things to use to explain the
heart or the soul of people like us.

I could say that you are my life but everyone says that,
in every silly love song.

I'll say that I would die for you but what does that prove?
Children have said the same.

I might say that my love is an all-consuming flame;
but, that isn't nearly enough.

I guess I must be content with the words, I love you, I adore you.
Always. Forever. Until and beyond.

I loved you before you were who you are,
and I became what I am.

Shela Thornburg

Summer Moon

I was born a true moon child on a summer's night
but ages before memory you shone bright
Through ritual and mystery and every child's first day
and dead souls that passed by you on their way

Young lovers dance, how they sway and swoon
Young mothers sing a lullaby
All hypnotized by the light of the watchful eye and no one's immune...
to the summer moon

Reflecting first love's glow by the garden wall
the knowing orb tells nothing but sees all
But new love, like the new moon, disappears
then comes around full-cycle to light your tears

When heartstrings play a familiar tune enough to make a grown man cry
And he's not sure of the reason why the song ends too soon...
like the summer moon

As we all move toward autumn's colder climes we wistfully
embrace the warmer times
As we grow older and closer to the truth in our memories, hearts
and minds we cling to our youth

I'll see your face again in early June or maybe not 'til the end of July
My ancient, August friend, hung in the sky like a big balloon...
the summer moon

Brian Colgan

Remember Me Not

Remember Me not with tears and sorrow
But with laughter and a smile
For I have not meant for you to cry.

Remember Me not by my achievements or accomplishments
But also by my faults and failures
For no one can survive as a God with clay feet.

Remember Me not as you wished me to be
But as I was, full of mischief, error and idiosyncrasy
For I was a human being.

Remember Me not with just your head
But also with your Heart
For if you do this I will live forever.

Penny E. Roberts

Strange Event

The strangest things can happen...like just the other day
As my horse was pulling my dog and me down along the way.
He came to a screeching halt... He just wouldn't go.
I climbed down from the wagon and called him a "So and So."
I begged and I pleaded I even gave him a pinch,
But nothing seemed to work... He wouldn't budge an inch.
The strangest thing then happened for when he turned his head,
He looked at me and raised one brow, and this is what he said;
"I've worked for you for a real long time and I've never made a dime
Now here I sit, so have your fit. I'll move on in time."
I stood there in amazement...I couldn't blink an eye.
I said, "I've never heard of a talking horse". My dog said, "Nor have I."

Robbie L. Horton

Untitled

They say toss in a penny - And your wish will be granted
A lifetime spent tossing pennies - With three cents in my pocket
Today I will make another trip to that well

They say if you're a strong man - Work hard and never stray
All your dreams will come true - With two cents in my pocket
Today I will make another trip to that well

They say to love your neighbor - And never love in vain
You'll find the one you're looking for - One cent left in my pocket
Today I will make another trip to that well

They say go to church and pray - Stand up for what you believe
Your prayers will all be answered - Nothing left in my pocket
Today I will make another trip to that well

I've tossed my last penny - And tried to be strong
I have loved my neighbor - Gone to church and prayed
I've made my wish - Worked hard and never strayed
I haven't loved in vain - And stood up for what I believe

I will never make another trip to that well
My wish was granted - All my dreams came true
I found what I was looking for - And my prayers were answered
The day I met you

Paul Rulla

Journey Of Heart And Soul

Our hearts; did not begin the walk together.
Yet our souls met up along the way.
Then for an instant in time our hearts and souls joined.
We shared; we cared; we created; we became one.
Earth holds no bounds for our love; even in death.
Our hearts; did not begin the walk together.
Our hearts; did not end the walk together.
Yet our souls shall meet again.
We're in endless time; our hearts and souls shall walk together;
altogether with our everlasting love.

Gertrude LaTanya Jones McCorkle

Love

Love is a beautiful dove
Who flies in the sky above.
Then love backfires and you wish
There wasn't such a thing.
The little thing in your head soon dings
And you realize it was just
All a dream gone bad.
What you had is now gone
And the feeling of love turn drear.

Ladeana Guilliams

I Am

I am a beautiful African American
I wonder if I will survive in the world
I hear my people's prayers at night
I see their guardian angels watching over them
I want them to be free
I am a beautiful African American
I pretend that there is peace in the world
I feel that all their hopes are being put in my hands
I touch their dreams as they sleep
I worry because they are killing each other
I cry because they are hurting
I am a beautiful African American
I understand that there will never be peace
I say that all people should be equal and free
I dream that one day we will walk hand in hand
I try to really help my people
I hope that one day there will be no hate in the world
I am a beautiful African American

Courtney Anderson Jones

A Mother's Love

A Mother's love is something that no one can explain.
 It is made of deep devotion and of sacrifice and pain.
It is endless and unselfish and enduring, come what may,
 For nothing can destroy it or take that love away.
It is patient and forgiving
 When all others are forsaking,
And it never fails or falters
 Even though the heart is breaking.
It believes beyond believing
 When the world around condemns
And it glories with all the beauty
 Of the rarest, brightest gems.
It is far beyond defining,
 It defies all explanation,
And it still remains a secret
 Like the mysteries of creation.
A many splendored miracle
 Man cannot understand
And another wondrous evidence
 Of God's tender guiding hand.

Beatrice M. Chavier

In Pursuit Of A Dream

On a Nebraska farm with wheat fields of gold
A young boy had a dream to hold.
My dream, he quietly said, as he looked to the blue sky
Is to get my wings and learn how to fly.

So the pursuit of the dream in earnest began
I'll study and work hard to grow into a fine young man.
Graduation from high school came around so fast
Air Force ROTC in college prepared him, his future was cast.

Finally one day in July 91, the Air Force called and the voice said,
Report to Columbus, Mississippi in August, the orders were read.
A T-37 was the plane he first flew
He began to touch the Mississippi sky of blue.

On to the T-38's in February he went
Across the country he'd fly and strange places he was sent.
The day finally arrived for him to get his wings
Family and friends were on hand to celebrate what hard work brings.

A dream that began in the wheat fields of gold
A young man now has the dream to hold.
My dream, he quietly said, as he looked at the blue sky
Was to get my wings and I did learn to fly.

Linda Morgan

Seasonal Emotions

Fall and winter are not seasons
but emotions
filled with beauty, happiness, and seclusions.

In fall,
all trees, all leaves turn yellow, orange, and red,
and animals all go to bed.

Fall is a time of whooshes and flutters not stutters,
when wind blows and howls all leaves go whoosh,
when birds all go fluttering none stuttering, all fluttering.

The death and denial of some trees
die turning brown and bare
still live some green all year.

Winter though all the trees have gone before
still I implore
is there no beauty in trees that have gone before?

White with snow is the world,
everything is covered - trees, houses, and roads
everything calm and peaceful
nothing to break the silence,
and the peaceful silence is lifted nevermore.

Matthew Schafer

Dream Fields

In the Fields of Iniquity
Where the Shaft and the Plow no longer heed to Conformity
But where now stands the Heightened Harvest of Dreams
The yield exempts frustrated Constraints formerly experienced
on the High Plains of Life

Illusionary Life is portrayed through vistas of Pastels
and Hoofs of Grain
Through Black Soil that moistens the Soul beneath the rubble
of Conscience
The Stones of Aggravation are thrust aloft to offer fertile Exuberance
The Plain is set for enhanced perceived Demeanor

Release the flow of energy that minds create only
Disintegrate thoughts of Contemporary Contravention
Allow free will to take hold of Euphemistic Restraints
Reach for the Infinite Menu of Indefinite Choices

Never Contend for the Ordinary or Mundane
Seek only the Ultimate path with no Bounds
Iniquity is the Catalyst of Conformity
Avoid the snare of Reality and relish in Non-conformity

Plow trials into the earth with Horses of Vengeance
Release former shackles driving your existence
Ferment your soul with fruits of this Harvest
Reaping decisions yielded till life's end

Ken Arnold

Young Mother To Be

A fragile life conceived in love
Watched over by doctors and the Lord above
Growing inside this young mother to be
Not yet ready for the world to see
Her boyfriend said "So, I don't care"
Four words this girl couldn't bear
Not wanting to abort but unable to keep
An adoption agency she sets out to seek
She's only got love to give
One of many products for her child to live.
The time has come, the baby is here
At three minutes old she holds it near
The time with her child goes by fast
But the memories will always last.

Lauren Famigletti

We Are Gems

We are gems. Well-organized, self-controlled, sparkling gems. Highly intelligent, magnetic, radiant gems. Piercing the outer limits, we soothe the beast with a song, passionate feelings and whispering dreams.

Brilliant, glistening gems. Born in the rich earth, we are not afraid. We build aspirations, we electrify the mind. Sapphires and diamonds, we are multi-faceted oceans of luxury. Healthy, psychological sustenance. Sprinkled with rubies, sipping topaz tea, gazing into emerald eyes.

Working, arguing, loving, we are gems. Hungry, yet satisfied. Suspicious, yet trusting. And each one of us is flawless, proud and dazzling. Oozing with tranquility, delivering the promise. Ecstasy by the flaming fireplace. Music, narcissus, lilacs, cinnamon, pleasure and happiness. Surrounded by gardens of fragrance and rivers of cream. We live in ivory, gold and platinum castles.

We are the beauty, the glory and the power. The cautions, cunning and the quiet. The Crown Jewels. The aristocratic taste. The fervent motion of the waves, the lightning and the reign. The grand piano and the limousine. The victorious, gleaming gems!

Joseph Rockefeller

Dreams

When I was young and in my teens
I often had so many dreams
Some were realized and some were not
Because of time I simply forgot

But now I am old and no longer do I dream,
I spend my time doing other things
By being kind to others in every way
and helping them to find their way

In this life of constant stream
Where everyone has a dream
Of doing things so very well
When only time will really tell

But continue on with full esteem
And never give up on your many dreams

Larry L. Jones

Tomorrow

A golden edge, around a mist of white,
Sun beams not failing to show rays of light
The hush of the darkness, has faded,
This is the beauty for which me have waited.
It is morning.

Marian L. Malone

Untitled

A child sleeps,
Unaware of the beast in the next room.
A child dreams,
The peaceful dreams of gumdrops and teddy bears.
A child wakes,
Screams split the night.
A child cries out,
A mother sobs into her pillow.
A child lies silent,
A mother soothes herself.
A child shakes,
Shots ring out and a mother is no longer hurting.
A child screams,
A mother dies,
A child cries,
A child sleeps,
Unaware of the pain he will endure,
A child sleeps.

Lani Yvonne Simon

He Is Always Here

When I'm feeling lonely
When I feel like no one cares
I raise my voice to heaven
Since I know my Lord is there
When those I know forsake me
When they stab me in the back
I will not fear nor fret
For my Lord will save me yet
In essence he has saved me
Truly I am free
My Lord my savior Jesus is always here for me.

Adrean Chavira

Acrostic To My Hope

"Holy Mother of God" that was my reflection
Observing this beauty standing three steps across
Proving to me again; God is the only boss,
Ending my solemn vow to stop all affection.

For when I saw you there standing and so lovely
Longing to come alive, I thought "She'd be the best
Of creature the Lord in His almightiness
Returned on earth would have for my salvage only".
Entering in my heart and in such a sudden,
Not leaving me a chance, not a thought, not even.

Oh! Sometimes I wonder to deserve this have I
Refused to be humble and in my heart be shy?
Because to win your love-sweeter reward there's none
Exams after exams I will have undergone.
To pass these tests, Oh Lord, my teacher You will be
And in the final end our love will be free.

Jean-Rene Pierre-Pierre

Realization

Out of the blue and longingly awaited,
Was time, an hour or two.
And was more than really anticipated,
Time well spent, with a touch, only a few.

Feelings well articulated, none ever lost,
A closeness, yet creeping.
With a reluctance yet to bare, with no frost,
All with a touch of warmth, hopefully revealing.

The beginnings of a new awakening,
The realm of the creator, with peace and calm.
One can't but go believing.
The smile, the heart, the touch of the palm.

Yet to go with what one is given,
Is the rule of both heart and head.
The rule of the past has only driven.
Hurt into pain, already instead.

Only to live the present as is our wont,
Not judge all from the past.
The true nectar of the fount,
In finding the new, is our true repast.

Jerry L. Duren

Fear Befalls Us All...

Were sheltered as children by our mother's wings.
We know not the pains of life.
Then were pushed out of the nest.
The fall instills great fears in our hearts,
but if we choose to fly we must overcome
those fears and try again.
If we allow our fears from the fall to keep
us on the ground we will never learn to fly.

Steven Monger

The Lamp Of Knowledge

T - is for teaching the world to sing.
H - is for happiness the joy it brings
E - is for eagerness to make your own plans.

L - is for love to make a child become a man
A - is for action a quest to reach; to find different methods
    you use to teach.
M - is for mastery, you strive for each day,
P - is for patience that prevails in its own way.

O - is for obligation, you always perform with a smile.
F - is for keeping the faith, that made you worthwhile

K - is for kindness in each child you instill,
N - is for the needs you strive to fill.
O - is for opinion in speaking your mind, to help others
    achieve a pleasure to find.
W - is for willingness that proves your aggression
L - is for loyalty you have for your profession.
E - is for etching for everyone's success,
D - is for doing - and giving your best.
G - is for Gratitude - for grateful you are,
E - is for Endurance that makes you a star.

Birdie B. McClellan

Innocence

Hello my name is Carole Lee.
I'm watching the clock as you can see.
The school bell will ring at half past three.
Dear God what will happen to her and me?

Sister may I erase the boards?
I'll even stay and sweep the floors.
I don't want to go home because I know he is there.
He was supposed to love us. Supposed to take care.

Why can't he just leave us alone?
So we could be happy to be going home.

Incest they call it. Never heard of that word.
And my pleas for help have not been heard.

I am just a child and I do what I'm told.
But I'm awfully tired of carrying this load.

Bless us all the meek and the mild.
Hear the cries of the children who can't cry out loud.
Please Jesus, reach down and hold Carole Lee tight.
Help us get through each long endless night.

We lost self respect and all of our pride.
Where does a child go when there is no place to hide?
I know what mine did. She curled up and died.

Carole Lee Blankenship

How Is Death

How is death, may ask some people,
and when it does come, with its long sickle.
How will it feel...with it even tickle?
But the certainty ends there,
for to ponder beyond that people don't dare.
They may follow blindly the words of prophets,
they may believe in fate and wait for what comes.
But some may find they've been played like trumpets,
and been blown down by their tones.
But to the subject people are still blind and deaf,
so thru time the question still lingers.
How is death...
And what will be when you finally feel its cold fingers.

Carlos-Andres Payàn-Agudelo

Flight Of Death

Above the thick mist I ride on a wave
My gripping fear is gone, I now will be saved.
All darkness fades away to die,
Sunlight suddenly steals this sky.
Though blackened shadows wish my soul to take,
I am securely protected by heaven's sake.
Endlessly floating I am riding so deep,
Finally reaching the stars I've always wanted to keep.
The fierce blows of wind have long left my face,
Sweet delicate wisps of air have filled in their place.
Exhilarating joy is forever swept into my open heart,
Each soft sound of silence has taken on its own part.
Lost in such extreme wonder of my overwhelming flight,
I can't get enough of this bright powerful light.
Refusing to ever fall back to such unwanted ground,
I bravely promise myself to never turn around.
Curious of what secrets this great light will hold out for me,
I patiently fly forward to watch what will be.
As my peaceful journey gently leads to an end,
I realize yet another is about to begin.

Stefanie Caudill

Lady Liberty

Here's to our Lady on the fourth of July
She must be important, for so many to die

She stands tall for freedom and liberty
And she means as much as the flag to me

And if America ever comes under the gun,
I'm sure when it's over, she will say
That's one more freedom fight won.

For when one fights for freedom, country and God
Never on America's soil shall enemies trod

So in this great country in which we live
All Americans are ready their life to give.

So one hundred years from now our children can say
Let's clean this Lady up, give her a face lift
on this glorious day

Robert Bedore

Visions Through My Ghost

I found myself walking late into the night among the wild midst of ridiculous thoughts. Carefully and cautiously I proceeded. In a feeble attempt at grasping reality, I was instantly lost in a burst of vibrant and boundless thoughts. Flowers, colors, music, animals, lost souls, all floating around me as if carried by the wind howling In a midsummer night storm. Suddenly I felt the spirit of everything around me. Flowing through me like an electric shock. Stimulating all of senses to the point of arousal, as if my heart had skipped a beat. Suddenly running through my mind was my own soul, as if lost with the others. Gone, gone to the wind, gone to the mist of my had slipped away even more. In a half hearted voyage in search of sanity, I became even more lost was being sucked right out of me. All good nature and rational thinking was lost to the wayside torn apart and thrown wildly to the souls around me. My soul split from its very own thoughts. My thoughts cascading into the realm of confusion around me, my soul split from its very own thoughts. My thoughts cascading into the realm of confusion around me. Were they being turned against me? Was my own soul joining the other lost souls around it, attacking what was left of its former existence? Without a moment notice, I had been broken down to my very beginning. My soul, my thoughts, my rational and irrational ways of being. I had surrendered, or had been surrendered to the Kingdom of lost souls and thoughts. But in the last few visions through my ghost, I saw that I had not surrendered to my surroundings, but rather, I had surrendered my surroundings strength to my soul.

Benjamin J. Manning

Without You

Trying to live without you,
Is as hard as you being there.
  Feelings grow colder,
In the heart held in your hands.
  I hate to think,
  you would stay;
But, I could never let you go away.
  The troubles are weighing
  Down on my mind,
  Can't think of nothing,
  But the feelings I hide.
If you could only see what I'm
  trying to say,
It would be that this game,
  Is a game I can't play.
  Too many chances.
  Too many risks to take;
  Not enough laughter,
  To stop the pain and the ache
Of knowing this love, is a love I can't take.

Christy Blake

Sonnet: Looking Out Over Cook Inlet

The tide rolls out, then surges in again.
  A melody played since time's beginning,
  When some deity, probably grinning,
Unleashed on shore some fury held within.
The waves' power doubtless causes chagrin
  To those people who are always pinning
  The earth beneath them, but never winning
  The fight against the sea, who is their kin.
This same cadence has gone on forever —
  Part of everything which remains unchanged,
  Reliably fed by its streams and brooks.
The end of its reign? Something that never,
  No matter how far history has ranged,
  Will find its place in the history books.

Gavin Kentch

A Scorned Child's Plea

I have a dad and yet I don't.
I wonder why it is, he acts as if I'm not really his.
A stranger to me he has become because of another wife.
I hope he won't be the same for the rest of his life.
I'd like to visit dad for a little while.
Have him hold me, see him smile
But his wife says he doesn't care,
And I can't go over there.
I thought a dad's love would always be there,
Now I'm so lonesome and so blue.
I think I'll die of a broken heart,
If we have to stay apart.
Will his wife ever go to heaven when it's her time to die?
Making a daddy hate his own kids, making them cry
Dear God make him find the way he lost
Lead him from the path he crossed.
Help me find the way to his heart.

Gertie Witherspoon

My Ocean

The waves crash like thunder against the rocks. The sea is a deep blue-green and shines like diamonds as the sun sets in the horizon. The gulls caw to each other while swooping and diving for food almost as gracefully as an eagle would. The hot sand on the beach scorches my bare feet. The salt in the air tickles my nose as the salty breeze blows the hair back from my face. So powerful yet so beautiful this is my ocean.

Christine Marie Horgan

Don't Nothin' Mean What It Once Did

Don't nothin' mean what it once did
  ain't nothin' left from when we were kids
  don't nothin' mean what it once did -
  don't say "I love you" unless there's room in your heart for it.

Don't tell me nothin' 'cause I'll just forget
  don't hold me any closer and then go
  don't need no pictures to tell me where I've been
  don't need no tears to know I had regrets -
  life's measured on a second-hand and you're a second slow.

Don't nothin' mean what it once did
  the places I've seen - the faces we knew as kids
  hold on to me as we search for a new tomorrow
  laced with the echoes of yesterday
  face to face with the roots of our sorrow as the
  sunlight flickers away on yet another day.

We learned the facts of life as kids
  the cold-hard facts left us feeling cheated
  we soon found out one chance is all that some of us get -
  I knew somethin' but I kept it hid -
  Father did I ever tell you of the love I had for you
  six years old and all alone...
Don't nothin' mean what it once did...
    Tim Ciocco

The Illness

On a dark, cloudy night, for my family, was a fright,
For it was then when we were told,
Something awful, something cold,
A sickness was in sight, like a tunnel with no light.

A hospital bed was my dread, with scary thoughts in my head,
A poisonous liquid in my heart, I knew then, it was just a start,
Skinny, skinny you will be, those are the words they said to me,
I'd be in every once and again, for fevers and sickness my friend.

Before all this, I needed to say,
I called the church for them to pray,
For God he listened on that morn, he helped me out, I was not torn,
It was a hard battle not only for me,
But also for my friends and family.

The sickness I had, cancer, so sad,
I was healed by God, it was no fraud,
A joyous day for one and all,
With God as my fighter I could not fall,
Testimonies I have for you to hear,
Testimonies that will shed a tear,
Now a tunnel of light I see, God will bless you, 'cause he blessed me.
    Jason Perrigan

Living In The '50s

I'm living in the '50s, or so it seems.
Flying solo for now, reviving my dreams.
My plan is survival, I rock and I roll,
My burdens are changing, there emerges a soul.

I'm living in the '50s, it's my time to use.
They tell me it's prime time, I've paid all the "dues,"
An ocean and continent took our boys out of sight
—We counted their bodies in bags every night.

I'm living in the '50s, not just getting by.
Perhaps I can quiet a hungry child's cry
If I open my eyes to the yearning I see
In a warrior nation, where hope seems to flee.

I'm living in the '50s, heed my mothering call
Not the son of my womb, but the child of us all.
If I help just one child see hope in each day
Then I'm living in my '50s, and making it pay.
    Judith B. Paquet

When Love Speaks

When Love speaks,
Let it not be like the cry that gets lost
in the gale of indecency.
Let it not be like the burden that weighs
so heavily on the children of disobedience.
Let it not be like the soul's mirror,
shattered by the inveterate rages of sin.
Or an holy temple, wasted by the perpetual battle of will.
When Love speaks,
Let it be the cry that awakens the soul
that has slumbered in darkness.
Let it be the burden being lifted off the
shoulders of a heart beleaguered by evil.
Open your heart, oh sightless man, to be lit
by the candle of Light.
Hear the joyous shout of the Father, whose
love transcends the crimson tides of transgression.
When Love speaks,
In silence, there is truth, peace, and unending joy,
In the Great I Am.
    L. Samms

His Table, That Table, The Table

I liked sitting across the table from you
Radio plays the mood for two
You were a well-kept secret
Who keeps secrets so well
My quiet thought 'round mid-night, I'll never tell
I seem to be alone
Odd, I'm almost always home
Somehow I missed that opportune knock
Seems I didn't stop
Now I sit alone, in the silence of indecision
Could it have to do with religion?
Time to wind down and leave the fantasy, to see
If you don't mind
Or perhaps you're so inclined
You might call me, and I'll come,
Out in the sun
Letting all of life's inherited flaw show thru
Secretly kept,
Across the table from you
    Antonette Mims

"My Life"

  During my life, I've never been a stranger to the rain
and I've been a survivor through the floods of life
  I've seen the sorrow and the most unbearable pain
that has pierced my heart like a cut from a knife

  I've lost the loved ones that we really close to me
and had my heart broken into by a girl
  I've drank so much to where I couldn't see
and remember many a times where I was ready to leave this 'ole world

  I've had to fight many a battle in my life time
and there is a story behind every one of my scars
  I have no one to blame cause the fault is mine
and I guess I'm the only reason why this ole world is hard

  Everyone better believe me when I say I know what they're goin'
through cause I managed to survive every one of life's ups and downs
  There is no one in this world that has been able to walk in my shoes
cause the common man would just give up and drown
    Jeromy Ovens

"My Beloved Wife"

She carries herself like the fragrance
of a rose and the grace of a dove,
Her lips and eyes have set my heart
and soul soaring through the heavens above,
She understands and forgives my every flaw,
Her love for our daughter and our
marriage will never fall,
She gives her patience and strength
to bring us closer together again,
For there's no doubt she's not only my
"best friend" but also "My Beloved Wife"
to the end...

David Alan Pritchard

I Believe

On a beautiful fall day, I walked into my garden and sat down to rest. I looked up at the restless leaves as they began to fall so freely to the ground, my eyes took to a certain leaf between my feet that floated down. I gazed at that leaf with peaceful thoughts, noticing that leaf begin to move. At that moment a little caterpillar crawled out from beneath that leaf, curling up beside my feet. With a glance that little caterpillar looked up at me with a tear in his eye, he began to cry. I asked him what was wrong little friend? He looked at me and said, I am so tired as I travel through each day of my life, worrying about my loved ones and all my friends, and knowing one day I'll have to leave, wondering if I'll ever see them again. I told that little caterpillar not to fear as the wisdom of life is always near. That learning process from life to life, you will always perceive, for one day all thy loved ones will re-unite once again, so Believe, Believe. That little caterpillar thanked me for those kind wonderful words, and said I will never forget them. As I watched that little caterpillar crawl away beneath those warm leaves of fall, he kept repeating the words, I believe, I believe. As he moved so gently away, I felt sad that day, wondering if I would ever see him again. As time rolled by and Spring came in, I walked into my garden once again, quietly listening to the wind. I noticed the buds and flowers blooming with a scent so fair, I caught a glimpse of a radiant butterfly soaring through the air. That wonderful creation that God perceived, swirled down upon my shoulder, with a tear in its eye, smiled and said to me...I BELIEVE.I...BELIEVE.

Herbert A. Isaacs

A Beautiful Sunset

I think that I shall never see
A sunset like the one I saw in Nitorie
The beautiful colors gray, red, blue, and gold
All of God's love did unfold.

The big tall buildings to the right
And the little cars coming horns at night,
The cruising ships on the ocean near
Were all a part of that picture so dear.

As I saw the colors changing in the sky;
I thought "We can't do that if we try."
A beautiful red sunset forecasts a good day.
God can change our lives in the same way.

Marybelle Owen

Oh Jesus

Oh Jesus a friend of mine, he walks
and talks with me all the time, and whenever
I'm feeling low no one else can cheer me
so. Oh Jesus he's a friend of mine, a friend
when you're friendless, a father when you're
fatherless, a heart fixer and mind regulator
with you whenever you need him, a
cool glass of water when you're thirsty
oh! Oh Jesus he's a friend of mine

Micah L. Shears

A Gem

Walk along wending paths
That descend, vanishing abruptly,
That end before a gaping black maw,
A jagged tear across the craggy mountain's face.

With stone and flint, a fitful spark
A cheerful orange flame crackling
Beneath painted ceilings that hide the sky,
Living rocks that rise like stunted bushes.

Perhaps a stone shall catch your eye
Attractive and pleasing, well-carved by nature's chisel,
Cracking it open, one finds
A stunted life, a hidden emptiness, a blackened crystal,
Crestfallen, you cast it aside.

Perhaps a stone of ordinary, dull appearance
May you find and behold
A clear, brilliant gem,
Worthy of adorning the Queen of Sheba,
A gem so rare among the many cast away.

Janet Wang

In This World

In this world you came to be,
Born as the daughter of my sister Emily.
You are her sunshine, her sunflower;
Born with her knowledge, her power.

In this world you learned how to walk,
And you started to talk.
In this world you came to be;
And in this world you came to me,
To me, a niece of mine,
Whose smile is like the sunshine.

You gave me joy and happiness,
Which I accepted with gratefulness.
Then came the day,
In which you went away.

So cruelly taken from us,
By a man, whose hand, provided no love.
So, sadly, in this world, your last lesson learned
Was the heat of man's cruelty, and how much it burned.
That was the heat that took you;
Oh Skye, I miss you.

Robert Anderson

The Difference

A rose is but a rose;
And unless nurtured it will not bloom.
A love is much the same;
For without a caring hand and warm words,
It will cease to grow.

Yet once a single rose has bloomed;
Naught matter the nurturing the precious flower receives;
For soon it will wither and die.
Luscious petals fade and fall away;
Nature's way of completing the cycle of growth.

Whereas a rose is real and tangible,
Love is an intense emotion between two people;
And once grown to its fullest extent,
Cannot be smothered as a weed may choke a rose.
For love is an ongoing cycle,
Ever-changing,
Ever-growing,
And never ceasing to bloom.

Karen Bieri

Cowboy Coffee

It's important how a cowboy
Learns to start his busy day

Usually making his decisions
In a very special way

It all begins with coffee
As the aroma fills the air

It helps a cowboy's thinking
To be awakened by this fare

Sometimes it takes a cup or two
To make his senses right

But all his decisions come much quicker
It's like turning on the lights

Oh, what magic does this coffee bring
As the aroma filters through the air

It's as powerful as the nudging
That his partner wants to share

She doesn't ask for much at all
Just wants to share some time

So she makes my coffee magic
Cause she knows it stirs my mind
Robert J. Jantzen

End Of The Road

When you've come to the end of the road
just remember you were told that you're
loved and also cared for never a time that
you were shoved.

There are times you may say what the hell
but just remember when you fell I am not
trying to cuss or fuss I just want you to
know we love you very much.

You've been bad but mostly good just
remember you done the best you could
sometimes sad and also mad but what
the hell we had lots of laughs you're
my man and my friend hey big boy it's
not to end!
Beatrice Williams

I Am A Child

I am a child
Barefoot in the soft lush grass.
Adventures, curious and courageous.

I am trusting
I am naive
I am impetuous

I like to touch and feel all seasons
I am attuned to the nature around me.

I run through the heather
I dance in the rain
I marvel at the beauty of the dandelion.

I laugh spontaneously
I cry when I'm hurt
I sing out of tune.

Won't you give me a chance to touch your life?
Won't you take my hand in yours?
Diane Robinette

Earning What A Body Is Worth

Astonished by the ways and means,
poisoning my life, and yet it cleans.
The circulating medium, which once was blood,
travel through my soul,
then discharged like a flood.
The outstretched arm of nature's gift to air,
could do more than just be fair.
The strongest branch on the tree, is the one that hung low,
and motivated me.

I reached as high as I could,
without breaking the rules,
but I have lost the edge,
I didn't have the tools.
I misplaced my life.
I cannot remember my birth.
It seems I have failed to earn what a body is worth.
Ty S. Lifeset

Why The Crack In The Bell?

Can you tell why the crack in the bell, the bell
Of world renown and Philadelphia fame
The Liberty Bell that people's freedom did knell
So well, yet break! 'Twas never the same, the same
Although the bell still sounded loud with deep intention
As it rang robustly: "Free — we want to be free!"
Could fateful crack be sign of need to question
Abounding power? Or perhaps foresee
More hearts outpouring of dreamed reality?
Was this metallic might too weak to hold
So heavy a hope, so strong a human plea
That broke the bounds of its own inspired mould?
   Oh, symbol of responsibility,
   You remind us every right has its duty!
Stephanie Cedervall

Confused

I just don't know what to think anymore
'Cause my heart is breaking on me again
I just don't know what to say anymore
All I do is stumble over my words
Feel like drowning in a sea of nonsense
All my world has been tossed in the air
And I don't have anyone to catch me
Leaving me very confused in the head
Don't know what's going on; I have no clue
My life is so topsy turvy right now
It is just spinning out of my control
And I can just barely hang on to it
Without flying off into sweet oblivion
Don't know what in the world I'm going to do
Guess I'll just hang in there and hold on tight
And I try to make sense out of this crazy world
Ryan Yung Rominger

Untitled

I grew in a world of shadows and fears,
That no one else could see behind my tears,
And as I grew from year to year,
Those shadows and fears began to clear,
But still I could not see
That love that lives inside of me,
Was what I needed to set me free.

Now I know, I must hold on tight,
To all that love inside of me,
So I will never have to fight
Those shadows and fears behind my tears,
That bothered me throughout the years.
Margaret Schaffert

Willow Tree

Somberly the willow tree's curtains fall.
Shielding the wanting lust of two.
Together acting out Cupid's song.
A kiss igniting the coals to flames.
Flesh upon flesh, skin like silk.
The hungry touch moved deeper inside.
A yearning cry, desiring more.
Moaning pleasures, spoken soft.
Striving closer, pulling nearer.
Magic absorbed in each other.
Whispering breeze on our bodies;
Bringing cool chills of life.
Caressing with velocity.
Quenching our inner thirst.
Upon nature's blanket of earth;
Beneath the willow's lashes;
We had sweetly danced as lovers.

Jena Kennedy

Victimized

Caught with in a dream, where the wild wind is calling
oh how it seems, deep in love is where I'm falling, so
don't let me go, I'm a victim of your touch, desire, you
set my world a flame.
Night winds calling out your name, deep down inside
I know, I'll never feel the same. So where are you now, I
need to feel your touch somehow. Because I see your fire
burning through the night, and it seems to be my guiding light.
Last time I saw you, love was flowing through your eyes.
Yes I could see through your disguise. I know we can never
release the ties, and it hurt so much to say, our last good-byes.
Sometimes I feel so lost without your love, as I pray
for salvation from a kingdom high above. Once your love
so sweetly beckoned me, somehow I felt you held my destiny
Crying in the dark, alone I sooth the fire, extinguishing the sparks,
I've seen the truth transpire
and now I know
I've been victimized
by love's desire!

Joseph G. Vera

New World

Up ahead there is a new world to explore, up ahead at
the end of the night. Let go of my hand, be free.
Go now and explore in the distant fading darkness. Look,
I see you, do you? I see how you smile, I see fairies
dancing in your eyes. The fairies have constructed a
dam to keep the flood of joy from over spilling your
mind. Break down the dam, break down the one wall
which holds you inside yourself...let yourself go!
Succumb to your fate, let your fate be changed, let the
fairies swim. Fish in the newly created stream, use
only the bait of knowledge, catch only the fish of pride.

Eric Allen Martin

Rainbows

Rainbows are like friends,
You wish that they would never end.
Very rarely you find a friend,
Just a rainbow soon to end.
Now I've searched 'bout seven years,
and all I found was myself in tears.
At the end of the rainbow behold,
A treasure worth more than glisten and gold,
For at the end of the rainbow worth all the
wealth in the world,
I found a friend,
I found myself.

Tamira Butler

You Have No Edges

Ode to a chocolate Easter Egg
You have no edges
You're smooth like the foam sneaking up on a sandy ocean shore
You do have a tiny ridge
Where the machine at the factory united your two halves into a
 beautiful whole
Your shiny jacket of thin pastel-colored foil
Beckons me to pull it away and melt you on my tongue

Chocolate kisses aren't the same
There's nothing quite like you
You're so smooth and inviting
You have no edges

Chocolate: I can take it or leave it
But I'd rather take it
Far away from here to a cool place on the green lawn under a shady
 tree and let it slowly melt away over my tongue
That is, if I can keep from chewing it up quickly

But you won't mind if I do
You accept me as I am
You're so smooth
You have no edges

Laura Chester

The Dream

I stood in one place and looked,
Not knowing what I would see.
Finally, I spotted something in the woods,
I looked but nothing was there,
Except my imagination.
All of a sudden it started to move,
I moved slowly toward the sound,
But, again there was silence all around.
I started to leave the woods,
When it ran right past me.
I stood there in complete shock,
Until I realized what it was.
I ran after the sound,
I could practically hear its heart pound.
At last the sound ceased.
I turned around to see it staring at me,
With pretty blue eyes,
It smiled at me.
Finally, all I heard,
Was the sound of my alarm clock.

Julie Shura

Who Am I

Racing against the times of time
Electricity that keeps us alive with in
Dreams that make a reality
Needing things that tear us apart at the seams
Endlessly waiting so it deems
Believing in devotions with quiet screams
Never ending motions
Intellect towards every relocation
Eternal misery and commotions
Wonderment on chivalry
Entirely respecting evolution
Envelopes in holding
Learning the emotions that are concerning
Together replaying the wording
Retorting the memory alerting flirtation
Evaluating the right from the wrong
Bizarre reasoning to hold on strong and tight
Optimism reviving like a dove in flight
Rhythm of love with in the writing that is left questioning

Silvana K. Navarro

The Egret And I

Again today I saw
a lone, brown egret,
covered with oil,
walking slowly on the beach,
asking nothing,
accepting the toxic coat
that keeps her from taking flight.

What weighs me down
and keeps me from soaring to my heights,
while I wash a load of clothes,
empty a wastebasket,
or answer the telephone,
thus siphoning off my juice
in countless ways?

I called Animal Control
to rescue the egret.
What will I do with me?

Jane Dreifus Smith

The Price

Is life so precious to be bought
   at any price; for fear of death?
Well, I think not!
I'll risk my life and fight, and die,
And hope not be forgot.

Is "love" so precious to be sought
   at any price; the price of virtue?
Well, I think not!
I'll risk your boos and jeers to say it,
For so the Savior taught.

What is so precious to be got
   at any price; of life itself;
Its worth unfraught?
My own clean soul on Judgement Day...
That can't be bought.

Larry Kelly

Loneliness

How lonely I feel.
Everything around me seems gray
with a haze of depression covering the room.
I sit in my chair and my dog comes up and rubs his nose against
   my hand as if to say, "Cheer up ya old fool."
I can feel the clutch of death in my lonely house.
Since my wife died I haven't had much to do or talk about.
Slowly I close my eyes and my eighty year old body quickly
   falls into deep slumber.
I dream of how my childhood was - so sad and lonely;
   only a few people lighting up my life.
Then all is black.
Total darkness surrounding me.
I wonder.
Have I died - will I go to Heaven to see my friends once again.
A nudge, my dog wakes me, and I realize I was just dreaming.
So I sit in my little room,
   Still,
     Silent,
       Lonely...

Eric A. Fischer

Fulfillment - The Ponies Of Chincoteague

Across the wide expanse of sea and sand
Comes the thunder of a thousand hooves,
The awesome power of a mighty herd-
Driven by the fires that burn within

Long before the town stirred and flourished there
They roamed the peaceful land that promised life,
The offspring of a noble line, yearning to be free.

What rapture on the faces of children
Enthralled by these magnificent ponies
   hurtling towards the shore,
A cacophony that stirs the very core of their being.

Guided by those who would shelter them from harm,
They welcome the safe harbor that loving mortals bestow-
Their grateful hearts at rest, a journey fulfilled.

Blanche H. Fiora

The Homeless

You poor old man, you have no home
You walk the streets, you're all alone.
What meals are there to feed to you?
And clothes to fit are very few.
There's a little old lady, that just walked by,
She's short and sweet and oh, so shy.
Around the corner is her home,
She sleeps on any cobblestone.
Their families - God, where did they go?
Or were there any, some time ago?
This shouldn't be in this day and age,
It looks like animals out of a cage.
For there are so many, in the street,
I'm sure deep inside, they're very sweet.
I wish there was something, that I could do,
Perhaps some clothes, some food and shoes.
But when they're dressed, where do they go?
Back on the street and no place to go.
We take in dogs and cats as well,
But! Here are humans, that live like hell.

Audrey Reynolds

Angels With Broken Wings

Hand touched flowers, forms, a halo's golden ring
Into this world, God did bring
Beauty, love, and children to sing
Until mistakes, makes them one of God's angels with broken wings.

Houses of God, being burned to the ground
Two hundred lives lost, when a plane goes down
Bomb blast hurts many, in an olympic, Atlantic town
I guess satan is doing his job, all around.

Lost loves, lost lives, loss of dignity and grace
The rich, the poor, all of a different race
We are all the same, in our heavenly father's face
Listen to his prayers and hear his heavenly choir sing
Help him mend his Angels with broken wings.

We all wear the golden halo's ring
sometimes it's bent, or given a fling
But when mended, it is with God's love, touched by his hands
from somewhere above
And with the sound of love, his choir does sing
when he has healed his Angels with broken wings.

Nicole M. Aldrich

Take My Fears Away

Watching every fear in my life that I cannot tame,
Letting every fear take its perfect point to aim,
Turning and returning to find perfect peace of mind,
Watching every fear as it takes my faith away.

Lord take my fears away, take my fears away.

Feeling so scared to the point that I can hardly move,
Letting Satan scare me so that my eyes are off of You,
Learning and praying for You to be right by my side,
Knowing that You'll never leave me very far behind.

There were times I know I felt You,
When you took my fears away,
When the fears came back I called You,
You turned to me to say,
"Don't you be afraid, I'm here to stay."

Watching every fear in my life that I cannot tame,
Haunted by the feeling,
That my fears will keep me the same,
Turning and returning, to find perfect peace of mind,
Believing that you have taken my fears away.

Marcella Lopez-Lavalle

My Son

I looked into the attic.
My eyes filled with tears.
There the boxes stood
Where he put them those last years.
The football pants he wore at ten,
Mickey Mouse ears at twenty.
A duffle bag of navy blue,
Around the world it flew.
The rock collection grandpa gave him when he retired
Crutches only three feet tall
Away on those he scared us all,
His games, his books, his treasures many
Are covered with dust of the years already.
He has gone, my son unto his maker who will
only ask of him - "what did you do with the soul I
gave you, my son!"

Dorothy J. Gorman

Description Of Myself

I am the sun that wakes up in the morning
I am a star that dazzles at nocturnal
At night I take my body and my sparkling
  soul to my daydreams.
When I am in my room it feels, though,
  I were in a cloud of freedom.
My ideas move so firm and it seems that
  my mind is a twister of concepts.
This is what I am a delicate spirit in
  an extensive wave of conceits.

This is what I am... I am what I say!!

Blanca Ines Valencia

Solitary

As I sit here in my chair, my eyes fill up with tears
Cause days are passing by me, and the days turn into years
I've been inside these four walls, for such a long long time
With nothing to look forward to, and it's no one's fault but mine
I wish someone could help me, help me see the light
Lay their hands upon my heart, and make all things alright
But there is no such person, no one to ease the pain
No one to make me happy, no one to stop the rain
The rain that's always falling, falling from my eyes
While I just sit here in my chair, and watch life pass me by.

Sara Gail

Curse

An ember of hope, a bastion of faith
A guiding light reaching through my veil of mistakes
Anathema of wisdom, a symbol of pain
A quest never ending, all done in vain
Strength born from weakness, courage wrought in despair
All of life striving to take breath from the air
Searing the lungs of the world we know
Endeavor to change the course of the show
Conquering fear, intimidation, and shame
Consequential evasion, shifting the blame
See the guilt burning deep in your eyes
Depicting a picture above all the lies
Pre-ordained nature, the will of the one
Caught up in the truth of what we've become
Trapped in the web, spun out of control
The dark woven spell begins to take hold
Poisons the body, the spirit, and mind
Relentless and cunning, leaves nothing behind
Victimized innocence? Claim what you will
The cups in your hands and you've drank your fill

Dan Bliss

A Wrinkle In Time

A tick, a tock, a wrinkle in time
I fell in love and made you mine.
Through all of time we would pass
Knowing well our love would last.
Around, around, til the clock ran down.

I left you there all alone.
I left you there without a home.
Push on my love, push on forever.
Though my body is gone; my spirit is nearer.

Think of me, now and again.
Remember how our lives were then.
When it's time for your life to pass,
We will be together again, at last.

C. R. Burkley

My Mom

  I love my mom with all my heart;
She is as sweet as a candy tart.
My mom took care of me since the day I was born,
She sews up my clothes when they get torn.
  I love my mom, she loves me too,
She cheers me up when I'm blue.
My mom fixes our house all nice and clean,
She is hardly ever mean.
  My mom will skip, hop and run with me,
Then I shout out with glee.
My mom is there for me all the time,
That's how I thought of my little rhyme.

Lindsey Holder

God's Love

The fruit of the spirit is a testimony for you two,
For God's love is reflected in all that you do.
You're always so willing to take people in,
Regardless of circumstance or how great the sin.
The person writing this poem came to you,
Was out in the cold like the "Wandering Jew."
You made me a part of your household that day,
I was not told to go and be on my way,
I've lived in your home now for over a year,
My days have been happy and you've grown so dear.
I want to thank you from the bottom of my heart,
For all you have done and the love you impart.

Ked Brady

Peace In This World

This world would be a perfect place
if everyone would do a simple thing!
pray to God and stop hiding from the world.

This world would be perfect place
if criminals would stop doing crime

This world would be a perfect place
if people didn't kill!
Why Why Why——

This world would be a perfect place
if Adam and Eve didn't get persuaded
by satan into eating the fruit of good and evil.

All I'm trying to say is try to do God's
will and it least try to make this world
a better place.
Belita A. Lee

This Little Room

Bless this little room O Lord
And those who come to stay
It's filled with lots of memories
Children's lives of yesterday.

They played and sang and brought their friends,
who slept upon its floor.
Tents and forts built herein
Created new worlds to explore.

We read your holy scripture here,
and taught the kids to pray.
Seeds of faith and trust in you,
were nurtured day to day.

Now they have grown and left this place
That's the way its supposed to be.
For time goes on and changes come,
New generations we want to see.

Bless their little room, O Lord.
Guard our greatest treasures.
Grandchildren who come and stay the night,
to add to life's sweet pleasures.
Saundra T. Higbe

Reflection

Was in the time of winter,
The snow was on the ground,
The glistening, sparkling snowflakes
Were everywhere around.
It was like a fairy's forest,
Shining crystals in the trees,
The twinkling, tiny crystals
Made soft music in the breeze
That blew a mystic melody,
So plaintive and serene,
Through all the air, for one to hear,
My listening was keen.
I longed to grasp its beauty,
I tried, in vain, to capture
That time in winter's past
Which gave me such a rapture.
A magic moment, glimpsed, then gone,
Yet, in the depths of memory, lingers on.
Ramona F. Fisher

Awaiting The Dawn

Cloudy nights fog my thoughts
As the darkness possesses my mind.
I see only what I have lost;
Yet, I cannot find what is mine.
My world was snatched away
As my heart was, from right under me.
The heavens took my father
When the bullets went thundering.
The love of my life disappeared
Leaving my side all hateful;
For I ruined my good thing
Because I could not remain faithful.
My only gain has been honesty,
My only gift, appreciation.
I only yearn for one love,
And that love's my destination.
Loneliness attacks my soul and eats away at my emotions,
Wondering if I will see the day to once again know devotion.
My only friend is the silence as my all and all is gone.
Living through this darkness as I await the dawn.
Deon Edwards

Sands Of Time

The tide is rising - the soul is grieved
   Overwhelming - stealing strength
Unbearable pain - relentless it seems
   Crippling tide - comes crashing in...

Thundering waves - emotions at sea
   Washed ashore memories - the constant breeze
Scattering fragments - shells of my soul
   Treasures to ponder - as I walk along

The sun is now rising - oh spirit do sing!
   The waves receding - reflections...serene
Gentle breeze, constant - restoring strength
   On glistening horizon - the promise of peace

Many miles later - once distant shore
   New memories made - hope restored
The secret in Christ - Restorer of souls
   Giver of life - treasures of gold

He knows exactly - what the tide brings in
   Omnipotent touch - broken hearts mend
Great is this mystery - Christ's healing hand
   What once just existed - now lives again!
Theresa Gossett

Untitled

How pretty the stars are as they lay in the sky
Always wondering how they don't fall, but never knowing why
Always wondering why the sun is hot, and the snow is cold
Always asking for some kind of answers, but never being told
How can some people have so much, while others have nothing at all
Why must some people be ashamed, while others stand proud and tall
Some people have talents that are so very easy to see
But other's talents are hidden like a singing sparrow in a tree
Let no one take away from you all the beauty you were meant to give
Because a talent you may think useless may give someone
else the strength to live
There are some questions that the answer for is hidden deep
inside of you
So always follow your heart and believe in yourself and in your life
be true
Angel Horne

Empty Years

As all the days before me, each pass in idle thought. In thinking of the empty years, the dreams I've often sought. The times I wished for better things, always wanting what's not in reach. Wandering down lonely and treacherous roads, and searching a moral to teach. Sadness has followed that road to its end, forever onward it stretches in length to suck from within us all mortal strength. The road now has opened, its pathway anew, the sky spreads its majesty in all shades of blue. Let your untrusting heart open, let it always be known, that sadness means nothing, when love can be shown.

Sandra M. Barthlein

Wind Of The Spirit

The wind blows where it will, and so the Spirit goes.
The wind blows where it will, and only Jesus knows.
It swoops against the mountains, covered with sparkling ice,
it sails across the valleys, with ever-knowing eyes.
So is the Holy Spirit, Who lives with-in, with-out,
Who takes us 'cross the rivers, Who carries us through the drought.
Oh, thank you, Holy Spirit, for being there at all,
for knowing when we need you, for coming when we call.
There isn't any mountain, that is too hard to climb,
when you walk beside me, or boost me from behind.
There isn't any river, though raging or ice-cold,
that I can't somehow cross it, with your unfailing hold.
You come from out of nowhere, you go to ends of earth,
You gently lead the masses, into the second birth.
You are the knowing part of Him, Who hung upon the tree.
You are the one Who teaches us, Who helps us all to see,
that were it not for God's great love, that tree would not have been,
man would have walked in darkness, man would have died in sin.
Oh wandering Spirit of the Lord, Oh Wind from heavenly places,
touch us as You gently blow, across earth's many races.

Margaret E. Reed

Precious Time

Time is precious but yet it is a waste.
People are trying to do things in a haste.
Time is waste but yet it is precious.
People want to savor a moment that's delicious.
   A moment in the sun, a moment in the rain.
People think that life is nothing but loss and gain.
There are wonderful things that aren't just made of money.
Think about the way the honey bees make honey.
   What about the way the sun shines on a flower?
And what about the way the earth moves every hour?
Think about how the sun sets at night.
And think about how the birds take flight.
   Do not these all take time?
Is having to wait for something such a crime?
God made everything for a purpose.
The flowers, the trees, that's just how the
   earth is. It's Precious.

Amber Fawn Boisse

"Being In Love Is A Splendid Thing"

Being in love is such a splendid thing,
everyone wants to experience it at least once in their lives.

Being in love makes you feel young and alive,
and has a way of making you feel beautiful no
matter what you look like.

Looking into someone's eyes and feeling that
special excitement when you are first in love isn't
comparable to anything else in a person's life.

Once you lose the "in love" feeling with someone,
it feels like a part of you has died, this is probably
why some people go from relationship to relationship
looking for that forever splendid feeling of being in love.

Cheryl A. Smith

Ask Of God

Life has been very kind to me
Why do I ask for more?
God knows what's good for me
Why then do I ask for more?

Life is more to give than the joy we take
Give life a hug and a kiss, it's such a bliss
God feeds the birds
He makes the lilies bloom
What more could we ask for
Mankind in His Image we are all made.

If God's kingdom we first seek
He will give us the very best
We need not ask for more
In His Hands our fortunes rest.

But ask of God I will
For peace and harmony where confusion reign
That He may cast light to dark places in this realm
For warmth in the cold winter nights across the seas
And when our ship reaches the shores at journey's end
To send His Son to welcome us home.

Maria Evangelina Leviste delos Reyes

Missing You

   As the birds fly overhead,
and the sun begins to shine;
   we cherish what was said,
by our loved one who left us behind.
   As we walk along our paths,
the paths that God intended;
   our memories of you will always last,
although our hearts shall never be mended.
   Life consists of ups and downs,
the future never clear,
   your voice is still a sound,
our ears will always hear.
   As the fish swim below,
and the doves soar above,
   hearing our prayers you shall know,
that our hearts will always ache with love.
   We have prayed, mourned and said good-bye,
and time can never tell,
   when again we shall cry,
wishing you were alive and well.

Melissa Renzoni

If

If - a tiny word
   for all the weight that it might hold.
If only you could see
   that part of me which lies untold.

Wish current roles, in certain lives
   allowed for being free.
Then oh the unrestrained
   and happy feelings there would be!

For now there is the sunshine
   your company brings.
It is never taken lightly.
   Don't be fooled by outward things.

Your words and thoughts are safe with me,
   considered true treasures.
Knowing you, it's plain to see
   could offer matchless pleasures.

Evelyn I. Harriger

The Time

Flow, flow, flow
The time flows today, tomorrow and beyond
The time flew yesterday and before
It was just yesterday
I dreamed and felt my future
Oh, it was brilliant, beautiful
Today, my dream is gone
I feel nothing but emptiness
Yet I am alive, breathing
Flow of time made me old and ugly
With broken dreams and entangled thoughts
That never flow
Oh, my God, where I have been?
Where I will be going
Nobody knows but you above
   Emmy L. Hartwick

Step Aside

   Step aside cause we're coming
through with pride and to the top we
go, and no one can keep us down.
   We took your insulting and abuse
now it's time for you to step aside
and let us through the top and make
our way up where we belong.
   We had our share of pain, got
robbed of our own land, and with
pleasure you'd like changing our names
   We're not afraid of your harassments
anymore and never will be again, we'll
raise our heads up high and with our
flags let every one know that we're
proud Mexicanas with dignity so step aside.
   We'll never give up our respect nor
justice for the pleasure of other people so
step aside cause we're coming through
and no one's gonna hold us down.
   MariSol Balderas

Wolf Hunt

Walking softly on padded feet they come,
Through the forests they run for prey,
The wind through the trees hum,
They will succeeded by day.

The weakest they take as a team,
One body, one mind, and one soul,
Tracking through the dark stream,
They run into the darkness like a hole.

Their prey was nearing,
Food they shall have soon,
The tension searing,
In the light of the full moon.

They surround it one by one,
The creature in the center,
The pack soon will have won,
The adoration of their mentor.

Luna guides them for the kill,
Then all was over as lightning flashed,
The battle won not for ill,
Four lives were saved another smashed.
   Erik Clippard

Concentration Camp H.U.D., August 7, 1996, Loneliness

Loneliness.
It crawls inside you,
Eating, gnawing.
It crawls around until you,
Victim, cry out in pain.
It's like a terrible monster who,
No matter how hard you try, won't let go.
Loneliness is a terrible disease.
Perhaps the most terrible of them all.
There is a cure; but it's not easy.
Companionship, friendship.
These are the only things that cure
Loneliness.
Solitude, isolation, seclusion, alienation
Battling
Intimacy, comradeship, friendship, love
Which will win?
With battles each day, and the way the world is,
Who knows?
   Sarah Fox

Untitled

I didn't seek change or adventures
I needed no place to hide,
But here it is - creation of nature -
a beautiful vision, the view of an isle.

The silk of my sails filled with freshness,
I floated enjoying the depth and the breeze...
How come? Am I doomed or blessed?
Who's willing to help me decide what it is?

Decide between passing or landing?
I wouldn't be stopped by no means anyhow!
I'm diving, I'm swimming, I'm running
to reach it, to have is important right now.

"Control the temptation! Beware of dangers!
Do think once again if the beauty's for you!"
I'll do that, relying on God and my Angel,
Since now I accept them and this isle of view.
   Voitik Tanya

"Spring"

Summer is nice
with her heat and spice
Winter is bold
with her blizzards and cold
Autumn is glorious
with her colors uproarious
But Spring is the jewel
not too hot, not too cool
Vivid with colors of every hue
making our world bright and new
Fresh leaves of green are displayed
with flowers abundantly arrayed
Warm, soft and gentle her sun gleams
renewing in us our hopes and dreams
Radiating the brilliance of a gem
Spring wears her royal diadem
Summer, Winter and Autumn we shant demean
but of the four seasons Spring is the queen.
   Jessie A. Scott

Lost Love

Lost Love - Where did it go
What did I do
Was it me or was it you
somehow, someway, our love has slipped away
Lost, that's what our love is
Can it be found
Would you stick around
To find that lost love and bring it around
How could it be
It slipped away so easily
Is lost love meant to be
Say to me it isn't so
Did we lose that soulful glow
Lost love, where did it go
I know it's not here nor there
I can't find it anywhere
Lost love, where did it go
Cause in my heart, I just don't know
   Carla J. Salter

Weathered Hands

I see them now after many years,
Those weathered hands that calmed my fears,
My shining knight, my hero in play,
Fairytale lands traveled much of the day.

A scratched up hand, a bruised up knee,
One hundred times he'd patch for me,
Those weathered hands would braid my hair,
The tenderness, the adoration, the loving care.

Eyes full of love and pride so grand,
As he held my face in weathered hands,
Darling Angel treasured child,
Tomboy really, scrapping and wild.

When the day is tedious and I'm most dismayed,
I gather my thoughts and let drift away,
To once upon a time life bittersweet,
I played so securely at my shining knight's feet.

I have known him far longer than any person on earth,
Weathered hands have held me through laughter and hurt,
My memories I will savor, my life will be such,
As to have lived with my father and loved him so much.
   Margie C. Tracy

The Wind Followed Me...

The Wind followed me to the ends of the earth,
Always an encouraging force at my back.
The Wind followed me to the very edge of Hell,
Always pushing me away from the brink.
The Wind followed me to the deep blue sea,
Always blowing toward a safe and comforting harbor.
The Wind followed me to tame the perilous skies.
Always giving an upward gust when it was needed.
The Wind followed me out of darkness and into the light,
Always ready to give support when I was weary.
The Wind followed me home,
Always ready whenever I am ready to journey again.
   Lawrence R. Kenyon

Mermaid's Song

Silver mist iridescent upon the dusky blue,
Twilight softened torch beams sever the ghostly hue.

From the depths of Titan
a haunting lyric does arise.
Like mellow, dancing and distant cries.
Across the shoreline and over sea the melody plays forever free.
   Sarah Kathleen Seaman

The World Of No Good-Byes

When the room is spinning and flowers emitting
The softest, sweetest scent,

When the candle light is warm and true
And every poem meant,

When your gaze is locked and tears of joy
Are running from your eyes,

Your wondrous journey will begin
To the world of no good-byes.
   Jennifer Granite

Walking On Water

When the sun sets,
and the tide comes in,
that's when I met,
my soul with in,

When the moon is shining,
and I morn for my daughter,
when the animals are whining,
that's when I walk on water,

I remember the day when I thought,
all my dreams had come true,
I remember laying her down to sleep,
until that night when I became very down and blue,
for I had found my baby daughter dead.
   Jessica Wieczorek

Being Thirteen

Emotions run rampant, tears flow free, anger is deep seated, and love
is a misplaced seed. Parents are tyrants, who boss you around,
giving advice always with a frown.
No one understands you like your radio, no one loves you like your
stuffed toy of old. A closed door, in a music filled room,
all that's familiar in your world filled with gloom.
You no longer wish to do any chores, dishes and mowing are fun
no more.
And still, you are asked to do even more; when all you want is your
day dreams to soar. You wonder day after day, what it
would be like to be a grown-up with all the say.
You have no idea the responsibilities that lie with that title,
you see only the fun things your parents do without bridles.
Nor do you hear the whispered dreams and wishes, for a thirteen year
old that's too big for her britches. This beautiful daughter who was
such a happy child, is now sullen and angry and has forgotten how
to smile. All the time that you wondered where your parents' love went,
you'll find it was always there, as strong as cement.
It was never on hold, or waiting for some kind of exchange, it just
grew slowly each and every day.
And daughter, when some day you look back on this time,
you will know that we did our best to let you know
that love surrounded you,
even when you were almost...but not quite...in tune.
   April A. Westrup

"Navigating Rattlesnake"

Below are the brilliant October trees
In shades of yellow, orange, and red.
Ahead appears a crystal glass lake, parted
By foliage covered islands. The breeze
makes the trees sing the melody of peace.

Vibrant oaks and maples permeated my view
As across the sky a robin flew.
Time no longer had meaning to me
As I watched the leaves gracefully
Falling to the ground, aureate and scarlet
Dancers elegantly performing a ballet.
   Matt Khoury

Lost

I close my eyes and still see your face
Engraved in my mind that three years can't erase
I can remember everything so clear
Your rage and anger, my pain and fear
After a while I just went numb
Now I wonder how could I'd been so dumb
To trust you enough and get in your car
I just never thought you'd go that far
Since there was always someone to hold you back
But I should have been able to see you'd crack
I didn't think anyone could be so cruel and mean
Then I remember, I was only 16
I was so young, just a baby
Did I do anything wrong, I still think maybe
There had to have been something I could've done or said
But I just let it happen to me instead
The memories of those times won't let me live
Now there's so much to others I just can't give
You took so much, there's so much I lack
Now I wonder if I'll ever get it back.

Amy Easley

The Hummingbird

Lord... at my window today
I stood in awe,
While the tiny hummingbird
Drank so carefree from my feeder.
Darting... back and forth
So swiftly... between brief drinks,
I thought of all the world
You have made,
And... knew in my heart,
There is nothing any sweeter.

The speed, the quickness,
The perseverance of one so flighty,
Announces to all Your creation
The Faithful Designer.
And... through every creature you have made,
Reveals our intimate God,
So loving, so giving,
And... Almighty.

Peggy Norwood

Yellow Balloon

The beautiful yellow balloon I chose
To be my friend at the zoo
Bounced along just over my head and tugged
At the button I'd tied him to.

He parked on the ceiling overnight
And bounced a good morning to me.
"Why must all my balloons go limp and die?"
Said I as I set him free.

Oh, my beautiful bouncing bright yellow balloon
Was soon just a speck in the sky
And I ran to my bed where I covered my head
For I'm really too old now to cry.

Dorothy Dowling

Different Strokes

I've many personas I will admit,
Some difficult and hard to bear.
My first husband just upped and quit -
But a second husband still seems to care.
His eyes and smile say I'm a hit!

Barbara B. Warren

Youth Dew

Outdoors, like a false paradise, snow teases.
It shoulders against the mysterious winds.
Spreading across their surface it penetrates,
In this moment between reality and fantasy.

This holding back, I can hear it whistling
   the slow memory of childhood.
And I, like a child, begin to dance, to sing,
   and to move outward beyond.
Beyond the paradise, the winds, the fantasy
   beyond at last, reality.

Into a deeper sense of meaning.....
Thought, soul and conscience.
Now motionless, fantasy is absent.

Keri Seasock

Forever In My Heart

I didn't even know it was coming. How could I know what you were about to do? Everything seemed just about right to me, but I guess it wasn't the same for you. I thought that we were great together and that you were the one for me, but I never really thought that you'd break my heart so selfishly. Our love for each other felt so strong, but day by day it has weakened and it has now all faded away. I thought we'd be together forever, but that dream is now lost for good, and can never be brought back to me. Because you never loved me the way you should. We were the blossoming rose in the Spring, then unexpectedly our beautiful rose died. Our love grew in a spectrum of light, until one day when the shadow filtered through us. Your beautiful smile enlightened me, your handsome eyes fulfilled me. You were my pride and you were my joy, we were the ones who were meant to be. My love for you is never ending, like the circle of life around our hearts, and with love together we can make it, even though we've grown apart.

Andrea Peda

Grim Reaper

The Grim Reaper stopped by the other day
   to have a talk with me
Said he had suffered a case of amnesia
   and somehow had lost his way.

He seemed not harsh, fierce or foreboding
   but rather very old, confused and gray
Chitchatted over a glass of old burgundy
   then departed, feebly staggering away.

I found a scroll he had left behind
   and a sigh of relief came over me
There were lots of names listed on it
   most of them seventy, eighty and ninety.

Telephone numbers were also listed
   so I called each one to say
The Grim Reaper had amnesia
   but lock their doors in case, anyway.

I found the Grim Reaper sometime later
   in a cemetery not far away
The feeble old Grim Reaper had reaped himself
   grateful were those on his scroll, one might say.

William Henry Jones

The Symphony

Standing alone on the mountain so free,
Stillness has become a tangible thing.
Pines standing tall, with focused attention,
Aspens suspended, not daring to breathe.

Birds of all feather silence their song,
All familiar critters have scurried on home.
Holding the railing, I gaze from my porch,
Jubilantly awaiting the approaching storm.

At the outset there is scarcely a sound;
Leaves rustle slightly with an uneasy calm.
Sensing its nearness they radiate the alarm:
"Hold on, it is here, it's about to begin."

The manifestation is begun by the tallest of trees,
Swaying to and fro, the tempo gradually increases,
Oscillations and vibrations of seemingly seismic proportions
The forest comes alive with grand reverberation.

Releasing the railing, my arms spread wide,
Leaning back on the wind, I eagerly close my eyes.
With childlike abandon I join in its rhythm,
Rejoicing...I've become one with the composition.
Marilyn Daniels

A Simple Pathway On The Road To Life

There are many, many times when life seems so unfair
You have so many problems and no one seems to care

You try to find the answers but nothing seems to fit
It's hard to cope and focus and you just want to quit

That would be the easy thing for anyone to do
But you are very special and will see your problems through

You're capable of reaching all your lofty goals
For there is little doubt that you have all the tools

But there will surely be some things that make you mad
And even worse than that some things will make you sad

So just keep thinking positive in everything you do
And through those darkened clouds the sun will soon shine through

Keep in mind the golden rule for every one you meet
And don't forget to have a smile for everyone you greet

And never fail to honor God, He will help along the way
If only you will ask as you go from day to day
David P. Corey

Urban Renaissance

City crushed in abuse,
   outnumbered by its people's neglect.
Transit transforms its lost beauty
   It's all passed by and over looked.
Trees that once stood alone,
   steadfast in their natural form,
Are now forced by fence and concrete
   to kiss these buildings unwillingly.
Beware of those that inhabit,
   now locked in by their own greed,
Their anger is now inherent.
   Have a care of those now doomed to dwell,
Their noise pollutes,
   Sewers churn any chance.
Now its tears may be swept away
   every Tuesday 7-9 a.m.
Beware of its children now choked by challenges
   They learn too swiftly.
Abandon this monster they've created,
   Escape, their only prayer.
Eileen M. Titchnell

"I Truly Believe"

In everyone's life there are times when things go awry,
accidents happen and life seems to pass us by;
But in our world today there are no sure things nor are
there guarantees; only God knows the plan for our lives,
and this, I Truly Believe:

We try our best not to cry or complain, never letting others
know the full extent of our pain;
Because there are some things they could never conceive, only God
knows all, and this, I Truly Believe:

So when you have one of those days when nothing goes right,
He's always there to be our guiding light,
You see, when we're in turmoil we should never doubt,
There's one person who knows what our trouble is all about:

He will never forsake you or cast you aside, there's never
anything you can't tell him, you have nothing to hide;
So when you look within yourself, I know you'll truly see,
Only God knows what's best for us, and this, I Truly Believe.
Stacey D. Andrus

Blind Am I....

Blind am I to what I see, dumb am I to what I know
trying to push aside, forgive, forget things that hurt me so.

You must be aware that the trust in you will have eventually
been stripped bare, it as if it doesn't matter, as if you don't
even care. "What love" is that you speak of, for I've shown you
in so many ways but with that bad habit you've become a cheat
and shortened our days.

Sometimes I feel as though my heart has been frozen, only to slip
through your hands and shatter into a million pieces.
If it is destined to be, only the warmth of your honesty, faith
and sincerity could thaw our love again with strength and
prosperity.

Our conversations are so such accusations on my behalf, but
if only there was no deception there would be no disillusionment,
no destructive paths.

My love for one is not because of, but in spite of everything
"blind I am to what I see, dumb I am to what I know, deaf I am
to what I hear". Trying to push aside all the hurt and pain
and all the I fear, praying soon that your view will be clear.
Isabel Stanley

This Old House

This old house has seen lots of loving
This old house has seen many woes.
But this is just a part of living
That's how life comes goes.

Children's voices raised in conflict
Children's voices full of laughter
What other place could we have picked
That would resound with joy forever after.

Sure, it's old and worn and seedy
It's housed moneyed and the needy
It's housed the generous and the greedy
But never let it be said
That this old house is ever dead.

When you pass our house with a snowy glisten
If you will stop and really listen
You will hear the coo of a grandson
And you will say "yeah, this is the one -

The one where people come and go
with freedom and love - May it always be home."
Shirley T. Tarver

Untitled

I love you, but you do not know this
when I smile at you, you do not
  know what lies behind my smile
I dream of you holding and kissing
  me, but yet you do not know
you do not know of my love for you
And I have little time left to show
To show you all the love I have for you
For you I would do anything and everything
For you I would give my love and all of my passion
My passion that burns so hot
So hot for you like my heart is on fire
My fire is in my desire
My desire for you to know how
  I love you so, but you'll
    never know

Amber Bennett

Things Remembered

A touch, a whisper, a kiss, a hug: What do all these have in common. They don't exist without you in my life. A touch because the very thought of you touching me brings my body to a quick hot fever. A whisper because the soft, sensuous sound of your voice brings peace to my soul. A kiss because your lips taste of honey freshly made by the purest of bees. A hug because caressing you is like holding my dreams in my arms and never letting go.

Shereada Minniefield

Autumn Scent

The wind blows gently upon my face
As leaves begin to dance,
The scent of Autumn strong enough to taste
Forest creatures start to prance.

I stop to breathe deeply and take it all in
The scents, the sights, the feel,
The passing of summer to Autumn is nigh
Like a blanket around me, it's real.

It warms my body, my heart, my soul
As sun rays illuminate the sky,
It carries a promise of things yet to come
And memories of things gone by.

Sandra Hoover

Potatoes Kill Me!

One potato, two potato, three potato, four.
My father is a coach potato, and I tell you I implore...
My mother makes mash potatoes, and throws them on the floor.
My brother digs 'em out of his ears
and the potato skin head yells for more.
My dog has potato hush puppies,
that won't even bark at the door.
They run under the coach instead
where they join the mash potato floor.
Now I'm not a picky eater, now
I'm not keepin' score, but if you
had to eat potatoes all the time I tell you life's a bore.
What's for dinner mom I'd say; she 'de say, "Potato pie".
What's for breakfast mom I'd beg;
"Hash potato on rye"
What's for lunch, oh mother dear,
I pray "one more potato I'd die!"
One potato two potato, no potatoes any more!

Susan Burgess

Alienation

It is alien to me that parents allow kids to watch TV.
Do they have any idea what the children will grow up to be?
Innocence? It is just a pretense. Demi strips. Nolte kicks.
Oh Lord, I miss those Cleaver hicks.
Who are these strange creatures we call children today?
Nintendo, Genesis, Sega they play.
Star fighter, True Lies, Demon Crest
Please tell me these aliens are just a guest.
Roy Rogers' toy pistol
Is now a Smith and Wesson that really whistles.
Whistles you say?
They have become a can of paint to spray!
Chat rooms, e-mail, cybersex?
What ever happened to Oedipus Rex?
With piercing, tattooing and colors displayed,
These aliens would just as soon shoot you as say, "Have a good day."
Oh woe is me what have we done
Allowing children to have such fun?
Aliens are not UFO's and space creatures I fear,
They are simply the children we hold so dear!

Jacqueline L. Rios

Vision

The cool autumn evening sent a chill through me.
I wandered looking for a prince.
He had no face in my dream, but to my heart he was real.
That night I looked for hope, yet I found the truth.
My prince was not rich, not overly romantic, and yet...
He possessed true beauty.
Eyes the color of emeralds, the beauty of Adonis,
Hair the color of wheat, and a heart more precious than diamonds.
Our eyes met and a shot went through me.
I knew he was to be my destiny.
I reached for him to hold, and to behold his beauty.
But my fingers went through the air,
And he was gone.
Leaving me to ponder this vision,
Until I see him again.

Sandi M. Kell

Wonder

Wonder what makes the sky blue
  The sun yellow, the morning dew

Wonder what makes the milky way
  The grass green, another day

Wonder what makes men fight each other
  Scorn their father, curse their mother

Wonder what makes these things to be,
  And why man is too blind to see.

Wonder.

Kirk L. Benson

Love

Love makes us all seem perfect,
in every aspect.
It makes the least of us great,
And dispels hate.
This is the time when you discover,
that a multitude of sins does it cover.
It is what we have all been waiting for,
That we may joy in its splendor.
Yes, Love makes the world go round,
This is what we have found.

Moriah Carella

Daddy

If my Daddy were here today,
There'd be so much for me to say.

"Look at me Daddy, I'm all grown-up,
I drink my coffee from a china cup.

Look at me Daddy, I'm the mother of two,
I went through feelings that were so new.

Look at me Daddy, I'm a woman in satin and lace,
I live and work in a whole new place.

Look at me Daddy, see what you've done,
You showed me from love I should run.

Look at me Daddy, please tell me why
You were never here when I needed to cry?

"Look at me Daddy, I'm really still your little girl,
Just wanting to play and give life a whirl."

But if my Daddy were here today
There'd be really nothing for me to say.
For the Daddy I see is of my own making;
And I'm too grown for pretending or faking.

Rosemarie Lewis-Pavlock

Taxes

It's time our problem's been addressed.
You've made your renovations and regulations on taxes — for rich and poor
But what about us?
"Who are you?" says the politicians,
"You aren't the rich; you aren't the poor."
"We're the middle class."
"The hitch," says one.
"The flaw," says another.
"The middle class - they just must go," and they kicked us from the door.
"I know," says one, "We'll make them poor.
Take off some taxes from rich and poor,
And give the middle class more and more."
And so our fate does seem to be
To become the middle class no more.
They want it to be divided — the rich and the poor.
And soon the middle class will be no more.
So as April 15 comes and goes by
And the amount of taxes blows your mind
As you sit there, contemplate, and sigh —
Think of all the nice things those politicians will buy.

Tara Gianoulis

The Way Of The World

I remember when I was young,
Living in this world was so much fun.
Through the week Daddy would go to work,
And on Sunday all twelve kids would go to church.
We could go and serve God all day,
And never worry about our house while we were away.
But now I've grown up, the world has changed,
All you see now is drugs, guns and gangs.
Through the week, I go to work,
And on Sunday me and my family go to church.
I pray to God that this world would change,
And I mean it from my heart in Jesus name.
That people would stop fighting and killing each other,
And kids would mind their fathers and mothers.
That all people would walk hand in hand,
And turn from drugs to Jesus he'll understand.
Every night I pray for each boy and girl,
   But sometimes I wonder;
Is that just the way of the world?

Murray Mungro

A Lone Rose

I watched a lone rose today as it floated out to sea
where loved ones had gathered to pay their last respects you see

The rose was so beautiful and so full of life
just as your loved ones were on TWA flight 800 that night

Each petal represented the love that you had shared
what a lonely feeling in your heart
when you found out the plane had disappeared

The rose represents the lasting bond you hide
no one can describe your hurt
or how you feel inside

God knows your grief
and the sorrow that you bear
with prayer and faith in God
he will not leave you in despair

When the roses bloom in spring
and then will you know
the rose will shine much brighter
when the sun puts it aglow

Keep your eyes on Jesus don't forget to pray
God will send you a comforter to help you every day

Eva Thompson

That Beautiful Young Woman In The Photograph

A vision of innocence and beauty,
seemingly oblivious to what life had in store.
What fantasies were woven into her dreams.
That beautiful young woman in the photograph.

She became my mother all those years ago.
Memories of her dance gingerly in my mind.
Memories that summon a tear - memories that beckon a smile.
If I could go back for just a little while.

My heart grows heavy at the thought of her,
and how she offered herself to life ever in silence.
She never had very much and asked for so little.
That beautiful young woman in the photograph.

It touched me deeply when she confided,
her only treasures were her children.
These treasures are her greatest gift to me...
My beloved sisters and brothers.

Fantasies and unfulfilled dreams remain elusive,
her tomorrows have faded into yesterday.
But, for today and always she'll ever be in my heart.
That beautiful young woman in the photograph.

Aline J. Drapeau

It's Me Again, Lord

Remember me, Lord? I come every day,
Just to talk with you, Lord, and to learn how to pray.

I come to you frightened, and burdened with care,
So lonely and lost, and filled with despair.

You make me feel welcome, you reach out your hand,
I need never to explain, for you understand.

Now since I know you, Lord, I'm no longer afraid
My burdens are lighter, and the dark shadows fade.

Oh Lord, what a comfort, to know that you care,
And to know when I seek you, you'll always be there.

So remember me, Lord, when you come face to face,
That the faults you might find, won't be a disgrace.

Annabelle Reedy

You Don't Say

You don't tell a girl you
Love her
When she's driving in Big D
She's liable to wreck the car dear
And then where would you be

She wants to say the same to you
And it's raining cats and dogs
The cars are piling up—backlogged
Oh what a day for love

She'd rather just be loving you
Instead of a steering wheel
She looked at you in the rear view
And almost crashed into a BMW

The love in her eyes Forever yours
There's no mistake
There's nothing more to surmise

When their feet touched the ground
He had to be on his way
Oh Lord, please let him know she loves him too

Every moment of each day

Pearl A. Southam

Grandpa

When I was young we all had fun,
We would laugh and joke even when
there was something to be done.

You have a little gray hair and you're kinda old,
But your sweet little heart was never cold.

You were there when I needed to cry,
But God it's going to be hard to say that last goodbye.

You always had something to say,
even if was "Have a good day".

Grandpa I love you with all of my heart,
and a lot of tears will fall when we have to part.

I will always remember the times we had,
Even if they were good or even if they were bad.

Why you have to go I doubt I'll ever know,
But Grandpa I hope you always remember
I love you so.

Crystal Fehmer

Whistling

Live near an army fort as we did
  And you knew there was a war on.
Saw the boys come marching, marching by.
  Rows of khaki or blue dungarees.

From the distance come their voices,
  Resound the shuffle of their feet.
Know that they are marching, marching by
  In rows of khaki or of blue.

Hear them laughing, singing,
  Air-bourne voices reach the ear.
Hear them shouting, calling,
  Whistling when a girl goes by.

Then when summer heat is pressing,
  See them stagger, panting, falter;
Don't hear them laughing, singing,
  Yet, whistling when a girl goes by.

Oh, we knew there was a War on.
  Watched the boys marching, marching by.
Viewed with trust their youthful vigor
  Whistling when a girl goes by.

Trudy McCafferty

Don't Blink

Don't blink,
Don't close your eyes,
Because someone you love might die.
As silent as the wind,
As fast as the tide,
Death takes toll; there's nowhere to hide.
Don't run,
Don't fear,
Because death is always near.
There won't be a reason,
There is no need,
Just like the flower that blooms from the seed.
He lived for the moment,
That's what you'll learn,
There was no explanation,
Only that it was his turn.
So don't be saddened,
When death does arise,
For in that single moment,
We must have closed our eyes.

Leah C. Graham

Untitled

As if in some self-inflicted
mania

A horrid craving
and traces of gold electric
wiring

Unpure
bloodied and in
denial

Let me frighten you
and release you from
your ignorance

Breathe me in and dance
you fool!

I will allow no more disloyalty
I will allow no more reality

Only slight disturbance above the sweet, enticing
chaos

Do Not Disturb

Taletha Maricle-Fitzpatrick

One Grand, Sweet Song

My eyes catch the glittering light
Traveling upon the pastures covered in dew.
The sweet smell of newly-mowed hay
Drifts lazily through the air.
In the distance, a cow calls for her calf,
Pleading with him to come closer.
The clouds float through the sky,
Keeping their watch on nature's gifts.
The farmer guides his tractor in the field,
Prodding the small plants to flourish and grow.
Man's best friend is waiting patiently
For his master to finish in the field today.
The butterflies appear to hop in the garden,
From one flower to another.
The faint aroma of roses
Mixes with the scent of freshly baked bread.
Children laugh and giggle without a care,
As they play on the swings and in the sand.
I remember these days of youth, so long ago-
Forever imprinted in my mind as one grand, sweet song.

Judy K. Rosenthal

In A Dog's Eye

Soft flecked brown rimming limpid pool of black,
Glistening reflections of the outside world,
Intimations of the fleeting thoughts within.

Eagerly beseeching, steadfastly appraising,
Guileless, gentle and warm.
Wondrous structure procreated by eons of life.

What intricate history has engendered such beauty?
What workings of nature such appeal?
What balm erases the brutish glare of its prototype?

Perhaps in this living mirror we see
A noble effect of man's presence on earth:
Conversion from savage beast to faithful friend.
   John W. Landis

From the Grindstone to the Milestone

No one can meet the demand,
of today's workforce and ultimate command
without making a commitment, once it is permitted,
it is the necessity of every man and woman.

Slowly go the moments of each work day,
as you struggle to accomplish your ultimate goal
giving it all you got, heart and soul.
You may start with a yawn and say to yourself,
  it's just a few more days 'til pay.

You work with sentiment,
in spite of disturbing interruptions
striving to make an accomplishment,
then you know the day has been well spent.

As days go by, weeks and months too
you become master of your profession
and can tell others what to do.
It is then when you realize that you are appreciated,
  for being faithful and dedicated.

Your dreams of enrichment and courage of endurance is rewarding,
and it is revealed to you and celebrated on your departing.
   Alice M. Bausley

A Friend

A friend is someone special, understanding dear and kind,
who never ask a lot, and never seems to mine.
Their someone to protect, and to love the whole year through,
at least that's what a friend is, if they're anything like you.
   Tony Carroll

Momma

You held me and loved me when I was sad.
You brought me into this world so I could live.
You cheered me up when I was down and mad;
Momma you are the best that life could give.

You helped me a lot through hard and bad times.
You were my friend, my mother and father.
You taught me how to be loving and kind.
Momma I am proud to be your daughter.

Momma I'm going to buy you a ring.
Cause you deserve the best that life could give.
I'm going to buy you a bird that sings.
Because without you I would not have lived.

I know about all the pain you've been through.
Momma I just wanna say I love you.
   Tiffany Smith

The Newspaper

The newspaper sits on the table awaiting attention;
It sits folded neatly beckoning someone to select it.

A colored photograph reaches out trying to grab a glimpse
from a passerby;
Members of the household rush around cantering something
about being too overwhelmed to sit and read it.

Mention of an article sparks an interest;
The spark extinguishes rapidly overshadowing any thought of
reading it.

There is just too much to be done.
   Christine Brings

Parents

Parents are God's helpers
  For our children so dear
To provide the guidance
  Needed throughout the year
A road map, a lamplight, a torch
  For the wisdom they need
  Only a few of the everyday deeds

Parents are loving, caring, and kind
  Blest with love from almighty divine
  Smiles of sunshine, kisses, and hugs
Little things to deter children from drugs

Parents give of their time...
  What a wonderful priceless gift
Costing absolutely nothing but
  Children reap great benefits

Please take the time beginning today
  To lift up a head and cheer a sad heart
For one who is loved will never depart

Parents are teachers leading the way
  For our children who will one day repay
   Janice Davis Palmer

Untitled

There is a place, in everyone's heart.
There is always light, and never dark.
A place where people can get away.
A place where the inner child can come out to play.
This place is magical in every way
Everyone listens to you,
  Everyone has something nice to say.
A quiet place, with lots to do
A very special place for only you
And when you find this special place
  you will never want to leave
  your only happy space.
So always believe that it is there,
And there is a place,
  where everyone cares.
   Marie Larsen

The Final Judgement

As I sit here inner hatred run through every vein in my body,
my anger compulses weakening my faith in all of the spiritual works.
As my heart pounds in fear of the things to come, my soul
quivers in darkness.
Why does the world fear the truth of a way to a new beginning?
The past is the past and the future lives in torment of the battle
that has occurred.
With a ray of hope I look upon my fellow worshipers,
and with each movement and cry for the peace that once was,
I await for "The Final Judgement"
   Amy Smith

One More Day In Life

Dawn has come,
With pinks and blues,
The world is cast over with soft grey hues;

Morning has come,
The sky is clear,
The birds are singing with unusual cheer;

Noon has come,
The day is fair,
The sun is shining like long golden hair;

Dusk has come,
The world is fading,
Time stops as if it were waiting;

Night has come,
Not a sound to be heard,
Except the good-night call of a far away bird.

Margot Laporte

Untitled

I have a daddy, my mom say it's so.
Though I've never met him, I guess she would know.
I've never seen a picture, or even gotten a call.
I wonder if he even knows that I exist at all.
How can a man have a child,
and not be by his side?
How can a man have a child,
then run away and hide?
It's hard looking in a mirror and not seeing mom's face.
It's like I came from some place else,
maybe outer space.
I wonder if I have his hair, or maybe even his eyes.
I wonder if when mom looks at me,
she thinks of dad with spite.
I have a daddy, my mom says it's so.
But as far as I'm concerned,
Mom's my hero.

Colette Hawkins Holley

Searching

Can we ever, will we never
Find what were looking for
Think about it if you doubt it
A surprise could be in store

A dog as a pet to fuss over and fret
Can be what you desire
Some people need, just a book to read
To kindle inside them a fire

It takes work, you can't shirk
A bother and sometimes a bore
Find it, it's there, you can if you care
It is at your front door

The simplest things to many bring
fulfillment and happiness untold
then there are some, who never come
Even close to their pot of gold

If you're content, your time well spent
and you've learned how to feed your soul,
get on with your living, your loving, and giving
you have reached the ultimate goal

Joyce Dressler

Lima Beans

Lima beans, lima beans
yuk, yuk, yuk,
this is the kind of food,
you feed to a duck.
Those little beans,
that I despise,
I think I'll go have some cherry pie.
Mom said no and I sat back down
but I sure gave her a frown.
Oh, I sat there a very long time,
to feed it to the dog,
that would be fine!
I get my plate,
give it to the dog,
then I say good pup.
But guess who saw — my sister Janine,
she told Mom and Dad,
boy is she mean.
Then I stood up and said no more of this goop,
but Mom still gave me another big scoop!

Meghan Daly

The Pedestal Of Love

Love stands upon its pedestal this day
for Cupid hath cast his magical spell
which forms a bond between lovers and friends
and maketh hate no longer linger or dwell.

God hovers above this world with his love
blessing one and all in a special way.
He fills our hearts with wonder and awe
and cleanses our souls from sin each day.

Now we must not take for granted his love
but shine this amour that he has given us
to each and every person, black or white
and brighten each life with joy without fuss.

Love stands upon its pedestal this day
for God has shed his love for us always
which forms a bond between lovers and friends
each day, especially Valentine's Day.

Jennifer Anne Dionne

Untitled

My brothers, my brothers
We are bonded by our
Touch times and childhood dreams

We grew a little
Drew apart a little

We grew up some more
Drew apart some more
Bonded only by blood

Now we are grown men
Reminiscing our
Touch times and dreams
Bonded only by blood

So let us ride into
The dying day
Before our dreams
Die with it

Bonded only by blood
Which is all we need
To make our dreams a reality, my brothers

Orlando Samarrippas

Memories Of You

Memories are heartbeats,
I recall the sound throughout the years.
Echoes never failing,
Our smiles and then our tears.

Moments that we captured,
You were so unaware.
Pictures in our special album,
With a special lock of hair.

These memories do linger,
Tucked away within my mind.
That special lullaby we cherished,
Of once upon a time....

Memories are like roses,
Blooming forth evermore.
Filling my mind with sweetness,
Of your life once before.

Your life held so much reason,
Growing each day to strive.
But my memories are candles that burn,
To keep my mind alive.

James R. Osborne

Minister's Vacation

An old old man limps up the lane
Footsore, tired and weary with pain,
Stops, lays down his crutches
Sits down upon the church steps to wait in vain.

Not a soul upon the sidewalks,
Not a sound of bell nor hymn,
Dimly wonders, what has happened.
He can't seem to comprehend.

Spies a notice on the church door,
Hobbles closer, mutters "never heard the like afore."
"Him a taking his vacation,"
Church has closed its very doors.

Wonder if when I get to heaven,
And I totter up those golden stairs,
And I reach the pearly gates,
Will St. Peter be awaiting there?

Will the angels be a watchin'?
Or will I find a notice on the pearly gates?,
The Lord is taking His Vacation
Heaven Closed 'Til A Later Date!

Vivian I. Lord

More Than A Friend

   He was a good friend, I always knew,
He would cheer me up when I was blue.
   We played basketball almost every day,
I loved him like a brother, in every way.
   But one day I found out he liked me so.
Hey, I thought, it's the way to go.
   I didn't know how to act or what to do,
I absolutely had no clue.
   I liked him a lot, yet he couldn't tell,
His voice was like a wonderful bell,
   He liked me before, but does he still?
I can't wait like a cup waiting to fill.
   I'd tell him someday I like him so much
Is he real to the touch?
   I want him all to myself somehow,
He is a Babe, so fine, wow!!!
   Does he like me, I want to know?
Which way should I go?
   I'll find my love to tell him well,
   If only I knew how to tell!

Kimberly A. Gudlin

"I Sit Beside Myself"

I sit beside myself.
Treacherous with life's path.
I sit beside myself.
How can others channel their wrath?
Filled with jealousy and greed,
All heightened with remorse,
The fool I made myself to be,
Can ne'er retrace her course.

At my side burns love and trust that has given security.
Forever our souls are locked and remain so for eternity.
Whims of evil dissipate with love's lofty flurry.
Sometimes filled with tender passion,
Sometimes weighted down with worry,

When gentle hands caress, and sweet lips taste of wine,
Troubling essences lift, to the one that is so fine.
Suddenly cold doors lock, away has gone my bliss,
Bolts created by my soul have led me back to this:

I sit beside myself,
In the gloom, so melancholy,
I sit beside myself, staring in at me.

Danielle Guarracino

Breathe

. . . and dad,
I just wanted to let you know how your funeral went
because you weren't there.
Dad,
when are you coming to see my new house?
We need to get the boat out this summer,
dad.
And dad,
you can't fool me.
I can tell you're still alive.
And dad,
I just wanted to let you know how your funeral went
because you weren't there.
And dad,
I love you.
Breathe, dad. Get here.
Jesus . . .

Chad Zawol

Lest We Forget

Lest we forget those years of yore
When our country was first being found
No one really knew what was in store
But determined in mind to own some ground
Our forefathers had to fight for their rights
To settle and build in a life of fear
But often disappeared in darkness of night
How can we thank our forefathers with only a tear?
To make our country such a high level plight
Lest we forget their courage is now our fight.

Anna L. Johnson

Serenity

The sound of a fountain
containing a deep pool of water,
and a deep pool of serenity.
Green plants refresh the eye and soothe the soul.
Planted in deep orange urns they grow,
undisturbed by the activity around them.
It occurs to me that I should grow —
undisturbed by the activity around me,
listening only to the voice of the Heart of God within.

Kit Leamy

Our Best Friend Was Like A Brother

He wandered into our lives one day.
It must have been twenty-five years past.
We thought his friendship would always stay.
One that had a family member's last.

He accompanied by brother and I,
From our teenage years to our family start.
Although he had premarital eye,
He had not yet met his Maker's mark.

Throughout the years of our endeavour,
At times he left the grasp of our persuasion.
Once was to accept the Savior.
Others we lack knowledge of the occasion.

When his life appeared to be making way,
He began to show a physical fiend.
It was unknown of the problem that lay.
But there came a day, we lost our best friend.

David J. Marc

In Life When You Face Struggles

In life when you face struggles,
may they be few and far between.
When you are faced with tough decisions,
may your final goal be seen.

When you are met with questions,
may you find answers in the end.
When heart-felt love proves untrue,
may you always have a friend.

When others disappoint you,
may forgiveness be employed.
When your life is filled with sorrow,
may you still find inner joy.

When your pathway appears blocked,
may you find an open door.
When all you have is the love of God,
may you treasure nothing more.

Andrew H. Smith

Biting The Fireflies

Falling through dreams
Which become no more than chasing fireflies as a child at dusk.
Sitting. Waiting for a faint hint of light to flicker
Against a paint brushed pink and grey sky.
Yet I write this as I'm growing up
Still biting the fireflies.
Chasing the glow, reaching out and grabbing only a handful of air.
The firefly isn't there
But it's smiling at you from the corner of your eye.
Spinning 'round, lashing out an open hand
Which grabs at what you do not know.
So you sit in the moist grass, the sun already gone
Only the porch light shines behind you, your mother calls you home
"Just a second, I've got one," Face beaming with hope.
Opening a hand so tightly clenched around this evening long dream,
But you've tried too hard, you've closed too tight.
The glow remains, but the dream has died
Against a now black sky.
And though I write this as I'm growing up
I'm still biting the fireflies.

Christopher K. McLain

Continue To Do Your Work

Continue to do your work Lord.
Allow the Holy Spirit to dwell within this temple.
Refine the fire that shapes me
into what you have called me to be.

Continue to change my character, Jesus.
Build and strengthen that foundation you
have so carefully laid in my heart.
Take control of my life and do with
it as you see fit.

Continue to use me as your vessel, Holy Spirit.
Reach out to those who don't know you,
and fill the emptiness of those who are searching.
Dig deeper into my soul until you
can dig no more.

Purify, cleanse, and purify again.
Continue the process until I can
enter into the Holy of Holies,
without spot or wrinkle, as your true perfection.

Pharistina Bullock

O.J. Simpson Tries Pontius Pilate

And O.J.S. said, to the lawyers on trial,
letters US, then strike to rest a while;
Give me my blood, I'll prove to the flesh,
that white is white, and black is black;
for strength by law, there is much cash,
as drugs become blood, in one world crash;
In a psychol jury, confused language class.

Let's give O.J. Simpson, a Barabbas arrest,
in a utopia libertinism, of Hillary's mess;
or give him health care, or give him death,
before the Pillory Bill, puts us all to rest;
For that law, is limbo' o easter at its best,
as the laws becomes law less, in the west;
when the word knows Plut'US, will not confess;

Now the people said, you are quite a sport,
for being sanctimonious, setting in the court;
a benevolence expression is upon your face,
in a liberal innocence, of your silent pace; thanking the law less,
for winning the race. But where is O.J.; within his days of grace,
is he taking the Barabbas, to his own place???

George Allen

Help Me To See Calvary

O Lord, help me to see Calvary,
In a light as never before,
Help me to look in those tear filled eyes,
And be grateful forever more.

Show me the love that was there in your heart,
That day as you hung there for me.
Show me the pain and anguish, I pray,
Show me the old Rugged Tree.

Help me to feel what you must have felt
As you took a deep breath and sighed;
Help me to see All of my sins,
For which you hung on that cross and died.

Help me to see that you are the Son,
Help me to see that the Victory's been won,
Help me to live now in light of your power,
Help me to trust You each saving hour.

Obedience to you, Lord, will glorify Thee
And bring the same joy you had dying for me.
For all that you've done and all that you'll do,
I'll thank you and praise you all my life through.

Patricia Nodo

Broken

Unfulfilled resentments bleed,
thoughts I had slowly recede.
Youthful dreams have all been shattered,
as sure as the wind will leave us scattered.

Unrestored reserves of strength,
I try to fill at any length.
Lured again by this siren song,
I can't resist for very long.

Strangers coming from every corner,
A funeral holding a single mourner.
Raped, bitter, beaten and tattered,
Our youthful dreams have all been shattered.
Bob Jones

Melted Snowflake

Way up high in the sky I ask the stars why oh why do I love him as I do. They twinkle as they seem to say he is so wonderful, passionate, sensitive, loving, and kind. A better man you shall never find to share love, and friendship too. Next winter if it should snow....In my heart I shall know I was a snowflake drifting by in your Life. You not caring if I lived or died - only a snowflake melted

As the moon shines so bright, in your arms you held me tight. The river flowing by our side, your eyes which twinkled with delight. Magic always filled the air when our arms were entwined. Your kiss, and touch were so divine. Memories which we can share in a bottle of wine. The sun was shinning so bright that last day, sitting by the stream in the black cafe.

Our arms embraced so tight. I sat wishing, hoping, wanting to beg you never to send me away. Then rivers of tears sliding down my face, not knowing if I would ever see you again. Have I really lost my lover, and my very best friend. Never to hold, kiss, or touch, again never to hear your voice again. Memories of you will be locked in my heart, an old, old lady with a bleeding heart. A snowflake melted and gone away...
Maria Lenie

Strength In Love

Death, with or without warning,
   Is such a painful thing to bear.
Yet, when it brings peace to a loved one
   We can sometimes find comfort there.
But when death strikes a man in the prime of his life,
   We say, "Lord, this is just so unfair.
What will we do, how will we cope,
   The sorrow is so much to bear."
Yet the Lord gives us strength in our loved ones and kin,
   So together the burden we can share.
So I say, turn to us in the days that will come
   When your heart is grief stricken and sad,
And together we'll remember the great gift
   That God gave us - Jimmy,
Loving son, husband, and dad.
Susan Jones

The Forest Preserved In The Rain

The lush green trees and deserted tables...
Are a reminder of a once lost fable...
Lonely and forlorn in a down pour of rain,
Maybe a time of joy and pain
The end of summer and the beginning of fall
A closeness to you is plain to all..
Virginia C. Matthew

Tarnished Angel

I felt like an angel
Flying in the sky.
Higher, higher,
I thought I'd hit the ceiling and go
Straight to heaven on the next jump.

No bed ever jumped like my new bed.
Then, suddenly,
Out of the corner of my eye I saw him.

And in the middle of a jump
Fear froze my throat,
Terror ripped my insides,
And remembered commands
Bellowed in my head.
"Don't ever jump on your new bed!"

And as my Father,
With his belt in his hand
Loomed largely in the doorway,
I, the Angel, made one last desperate jump,
Then fell from heaven's heights,
Crashed past earth and straight into hell!
Jerré Carter

I Will Not Yield

Though life may drag me down into its raging
   ravaging currents,
Though troubles thousand fold may block my path,
Though my weary feet may stumble over boulders
   and pebbles alike,
I will not yield.

Blades a hundred may cut the strands binding me here,
Dreams may be within my grasp only to leap back,
All may seem hopeless
               useless
                           futile...
But I will not yield.

I will continue down the weary path,
I will parry the blades that come too near to my heart,
I will calm the stormy waters,
But I will not yield.
Jen Burns

Untitled

The image in the mirror
Such a fragile state
The expression in her eyes
Filled with fear and hate
The heart that beats so rapidly
It's so desperately furious
The mind that allows naivety
Because it's always wondering and curious
Behind that image lies a child
So timid, shy, and meek
The world comes on so strong
But she is just too weak
The image is blurred
Seen through burning eyes and tears
The future is so distant
Foreshadowed by fears
The image is shattered
Emotions go free
Escaping this destiny
That image was me.
Jheri Cabral

Here And Now

I listen to the seconds passing gently,
you and I are Here and Now.
These seconds are like us, and we, like the seconds,
come and go.

Our life has it's span, but the seconds seem endless.
And our life seems to go on.
Each second is different, but yet alike.
Each life is it's own, yet like all the rest.

I will listen, and feel, and remember these seconds
all my life and all my days.
And when it's over, the seconds will still go on.
For me, they will fade away.
But someone else will hear them gently pass,
and then go on each day.

Marie Balonis

The Tree

I saw a tree in the woods; a dead tree.
Its white withered branches
Lie frozen in their last reach for life.
I shouted at the tree, "Why must all life end in death?"
The answer calmed and uplifted me.

During its lifetime, the tree was beautiful;
Its gold and green leaves beamed against the bright blue sky.
Little animals loved the tree and lived in its strong trunk.
Its striking beauty had a strong hold in anyone's heart
Who saw the tree.

But eventually its strong roots could grasp the ground no longer
And so it fell and died.

But as I look closer at the tree, I still see life and beauty.
A rabbit hides under one of the dead branches,
The smooth wood is a smothering smoky grey
That stands out among the other trees.

Even though it is dead, it is wonderful
And I will remember it

Forever.

Trista Linman

Fulfillment

If I can take a son and love him,
Teach him to be a man,
To walk upright, with faith and hope,
To walk with God in hand.

If I can spare the aged, the lonely,
A little of my time,
To love a child, tho dirty face,
To everyone be kind.

If I can aid the hungry man,
The sick, the blind, the old,
Or help the beggar in his rags
With shelter from the cold.

To have a life that's rich and full
Of blessings such as these,
To live and not regret the doing,
To have the strength of trees.

For friends or foe and fellowman,
To sew the seeds of love,
And reap the harvest golden grain,
To chart my course above, ——That's Fulfillment!

Elizabeth O. Moss

Butterfly Wings

If only they looked closer, they'd see;
a girl, a person, a human being,
a friend, a flirt, a kind heart.
If only they'd take a closer look,
   they'd see.
She's hiding behind a mask,
trying hard to fit in but can't.
They tease and they taunt her,
   always.
She's smart and funny, she knows it,
but she is like a caterpillar in its cocoon,
too afraid to emerge a butterfly, to show her true color.
If they only tried to look,
   they'd see.
They'd see her beautiful wings,
colors beyond compare.
All the hues are beautiful,
but they are too blind to see,
her beautiful golden butterfly wings.

Erin Waters

How Deep The Silence

How deep the silence - it reaches
farther down than a well
dug until water is found
How deep the silence - my heart's blood
travels less, even when emotion overflows
and breaks the dams of control
How deep the silence -
to go beyond the known and
reach past all of the stars
that I have ever been shown
How deep the silence -
beneath the noise of life,
at the base of all things,
heedless - making its own rules
How deep the silence - through my soul
it creeps, slowly, through the unfamiliar
path as in waters deep
How deep the silence - my mind, it wanders
anew; the sound roars over me, through me
I turn to watch it leave as only I remain

Mardell Wood

Voice

Found deep below the mind
far within the soul,
lies a cry of only one kind,
a yearning to be whole.

A place one goes, to never be found,
to rise above, or fall below,
listening to the music of one's own sound,
creating a voice only you can know.

Where does it come from?
Where does it go?
Seeking the answers, one by one,
but always remembering, you reap what you sow.

Sonya Rodriguez

Students

Some are serious
Thinkers and others don't
Understand, but all
Dream of equal opportunity and
Enter my classroom knowing that they will
Not be
Treated as just
Students, but as human beings.

Kay Jones

Determination

You mean so much to me.
So much that I cannot just let go.
I wish you could see,
What I try to show.
I saw the way you looked at me when I last saw you,
That look of love.
The look and other reminders have set the cue,
To beat the odds with a shove.
Three realistic dreams of you in my arms,
Memories of us and bliss,
Thoughts of future love and calm,
All of these treasures would be sealed by your soft kiss.
I cannot ignore these emotions,
Nor can I ignore the hope of having you again.
I hope to regain your affections,
As soon as I can.
My love breeds my determination,
And my determination breeds my love.

D. Jayson Schofield

Sweet Dreams Of You...

A moment of silence, a moment of truth,
a vision of innocence, all wrapped up in youth.
The reality fades out, my fantasies fade in,
the hope for you, which has always been;
consumes me with passion, feeling, and bliss,
a strong urge that I beg not to miss.

Sweet dreams of you...these creations in my mind,
these dreams of you...there is no other kind.
Sweet dreams of you...for there is no way to explain,
these dreams of you...alas, fills my heart with glorious pain.

Your image is sketched, its life my creation,
drawn on a canvas, only to change with aspiration.
Your actions, your speech, are subject to my portrayal,
a scene of beauty, a scene of life, however, You unveil.
My eyes have been closed, but I am not blind,
for I can still see, with my heart, soul and mind.

Sweet dreams of you...of these I will not tire,
these dreams of you...fill my nights with desire.
Sweet dreams of you...at last I must say,
these dreams of you...Oh! Why must there be day!

Patrick Ryan

Window Of The Soul

Simplicity holds the answer
to God enormous plan,
the complexity of life
is noted within a grain of sand;

Truth is held in barring
into the test of time
marked upon the soul, of all mankind;

Life is of creating,
miracles can be found;
dark and dingy corners can be opened and rebound;

Give yourselves the power; the power from within
to endure the trials and tribulations
let the light come from within;

The world is a planet
conjured from above,
every piece a part of an all eternal love;

Fitted within the pieces,
the soul of life of man
marked upon the surface by a tiny grain of sand.

Catherine Ligouri

Circus

Step right up, in here, my boy,
For all you see is yours but to enjoy.
The stench of weirdness is in the air,
Come with us and join the fair.
All the freaks are here for you,
The dwarf, and dog-boy, and fat-lady, too.
Fluorescent rainbows enflame the night.
Forget your fears, you'll be alright.
All about are frightening sounds,
Lost amid outlandish clowns.
What wonders lurk in every ride?
Pierce the darkness, come inside.
See the laughter, tears, and all the pain.
Let the weird and wonderful enter your brain.
Caress the thrill, but, ahh...not too close.
For what you see are only ghosts.
And when you too are dead and gone,
Our twilight world will yet live on.

Stephen Lance Brick

Just Too Busy

Today is a lonely day, it's a cool day
Even the reception is cool
No one to join, no one to join me, just for -
I am all alone, so alone, everyone is so busy
I say the words, but there is no one listening
They are all talking so loud and being happy
They can not hear my words, is anybody listening
I am sure they hear me, they just don't have time anymore
But I can hear them, I always hear them
I call them but they are off being busy
I used to be busy, I wish I could be busy again
If I had someone to join, to be by my side
Then maybe I could be too busy again
As it used to be back when -
Then my days would not be lonely again

Phillip C. Hilbert Sr.

What Is A Poem?

What is a poem,
is it a great work of art.
Or a favorite way to pass the time?

Is it someone's way to express a
feeling of Love. Or just send a
message, that happens to rhyme.

Is it the light side of someone's
imagination and wit. Or fears uncorked,
like a bottle of wine.

Is it the beauty seen by innocent
eyes, that's relayed to us all,
by words in a line.

I think, as we read someone's gift
of a poem. The definition belongs,
to the individuals mind.

Myrlene Hughs

Peace

The sun sets over the purple mountains.
When the leaves pick up the breeze.
A bird sings a soft song over the silent trees.
As the wild life beds down for the night.
As the owls fly on silent wings in search of breakfast.
That's when your eyes see the silence of the forest.

Laura Henrie

Beauty In This Light

Sun blazing on water, which is murky brown.
Wind blowing leaves, the early winter sounds.
Thoughts of her are strong, in this blighted mind,
Giving quiet joy, to a heart which slowly pines.

The endless dome of sky, blue and clear and crisp.
Silent tread of feet, hid in gravels lisp.
People are around yet silence is the rule.
And sits a darkened shadow, known only as the fool.

A naming which is apt for he dances on the edge.
With a heart protected, by a tall and thorny hedge.
He knows the hedge is bright, being of damasked rose.
Matching a soul so torn, and rent with bleeding holes.

The bleeding he has need for, without it nothing heals.
But still it is a burden for his iron will.
Stoically he bears it, no complaints pass his lips,
For he knows in truth, it has made him what he is.

The golden light of evening, holds him fast enthralled.
Beauty in this light comes to touch us all.
With people leaving quietly, their memories fading fast;
He reaches out to touch her, with his empty hollow grasp.

Christopher Lee Rhodes

The Time Of Life

I'm probably beyond (at best) the
halfway mark of living this life.
Yet for all the time allowed so far,
I can only remember these last weeks.
I feel renewed in a manner I have
not before, and will (most likely)
never again.
Just when one thinks they have felt
all feelings and emotions - to an
amazed heart comes a new strength
that has never been before.
Keeping in mind man's frailty (always)
accompanying any strength;
I can still say - this is good and honorable.
It's a lovely day tomorrow.

Hendricus Struijk

The Visit

Who did I see by the tree last night?
His clothes were red and his beard was white.
He seemed as busy as he could be.
I strained and looked his efforts to see.

From the long bag on his back he took a toy
And I knew the children would jump with joy.
Then he saw the stockings hanging there,
And with goodies he filled them with much care.

He patted his tummy and laughed with glee.
I tried the twinkle in his eyes to see.
As he stroked his beard long deep in thought
He wondered if each child a gift he'd brought.

Then he looked around at the work he'd done,
And he counted each gift laid one by one,
I heard the sleigh jingle as he went out of sight,
Could that have been Santa who visited last night?

Pauline Kincaid Prentice

The Last Stand

The chirrup of crickets, an occasional bird call,
As a gentle breeze rustles amber stalks.
Warm sun and galleon clouds
Over Montana's endless expanse.
The long slope ends at a river
Hemmed with tall old cottonwoods.
Tranquility!

Why, then, a feeling of dread?
A shiver of chills on my skin?
There are ghosts here, of white men and red.

Dotting the hillside, clustered or alone,
Small white tombstones, in knee-high grass,
Mark where soldiers died.
There are no markers for embittered Indians,
But their spirits claim, once more,
Their ancient tribal land.

Joyce J. Hannon

The Two Of Us

We met late one day
In the most peculiar way
Nothing was thought of it
Until together we became a hit.

Stories we began to share
Telling each other everything we dare
Our talks would last
And time together was a blast.

Now that you are going away
I have to treasure everything in a day
I will always remember you
Because our friendship is true.

Letters we will write
Even if it be by candlelight
Phone calls day and night
To tell of changes we might.

But to forget our time
Would definitely be a crime
For all the laughter in the air
Will still never make you leaving me fair.

Lisa Voit

Faith

Please dear Lord, I ask of thee,
Take my hand and walk with me
Show me Lord how to be kind
For it's love and honesty I wish to find
It's hopes and dreams I pray to fulfill
Teach me Lord, what is thy will.

I do believe I am your child
Though my past is wreckless and purely wild
Talk with me and let me hear
Hold me Lord and take this fear
Let my senses feel the wind and rain
Assure me Lord you'll ease my pain.

Please dear Lord, enlighten my soul
Answer my prayers and make me whole
For I am lost this is true
Guide me Lord closer to you.

I must have faith with each new day
And with each little step I am on my way
Though my purpose in life is not entirely clear
The more I trust the less I fear.

John F. Hasbrouck

Why?

Why did you hurt me so?
Why did you let me go?
Why did you walk away,
When I had so much to say?
Why did you tear my heart in two?
Because I wasn't pleasing you?
I gave you my heart and soul,
I guess you didn't want it though.
You left me out in the cold,
So you could go search for gold.
Some day you'll realize what you had,
And wish you hadn't treated me so bad.
It's too late now. What we had is dead.
All we have to remember is what's already said.
As they say, "There's plenty of fish in the sea."
But you and I know there's not another like me.

Sarah J. Schermerhorn

Addiction The Color Of Nothing

Fire destroys fire
Fission of desire
Passion undenied stifled to aspire

Emptiness its own entity
Self induced reality
Blind to the color of happiness
Loss of youth and immortality

Crossroads void direction
Wounded soul third degree infection
I promise to be always on your side
Regardless your intention

Fear of fear of an unknown enemy
Eclipsed truth obscured visibility
I question only my own sanity
We all share different views of the same reality

A dream colored play act of how it should be
In this absolute existence I cannot see

I'll defend your life
At the expense of mine
Protector of a beloved enemy of mine

David J. Buetemeister

To Ingrid, My Wife, My True Companion

I watched you from across the room,
　limbs taut,
　　sweat glistening,
the shimmering heat of your body
cooled by your liquid blue eyes,
　reflections of your soul within.

Our lives merged with the heat of our
　passions,
tempered by the passing of time
　into a bright,
　　glistening steel,
a mirror of our love.

And in that mirror lies a reflection,
　our son,
growing strong within you,
　and,
　like his father,
nurtured by the strength of your spirit,
nestled securely in the
　warmth of your love.

Kurtis R. Webb

Just Beyond My View....

The sun came up for a moment,
and then it disappeared just beyond my view...
When I looked up,
all I saw was you.
Staring through the window of oblivion,
staring at you.
Then you came closer to me,
and your touch,
I can still feel your breath on me.
You were a fantasy,
You were a dream,
You meant everything to me.
But like the sun,
you came,
and for a moment you brightened my view,
and then as fast as you came,
you disappeared to.
Just beyond my view....

Amanda S. Swallow

Why?

　Why start what you can't finish,
why end what you won't start?
　Why live with lies pretend
it's true?
　Why make believe you live a life
if you just wait for death?
　Why think of stars and lovely moon
when you can't stand the night?
　Why fall in love if love to hate,
and not learn how to love?
　Why tell her lies that she's your life
when you think of the other?
　Why kiss the lips that you don't want,
why make her think she is the one?!

Alena Lysetska

Life

Twists and turns;
Not knowing where the next path will lead,
You put one foot in front of the other,
And look toward the future,
Some days full of sadness;
Some days full of joy;
But to be the one with all the knowledge you must go on.
You must educate yourself to the full extent.
You must always look forward, forget the horrible past.
You must keep your head high.
You must respect yourself.
To stay ahead in life you must live up to your own standards,
And move ahead.

Shauna Babb

Lonely Life

You have been the only man in my life
I have been with you thirty years as your wife

When we sit down to talk, we have nothing to say
But we have been through a lot and I will love you anyway

It is a lonely life we lead
You go your way and I go mine
It is a lonely life indeed
Will it ever change with time

The kids are all grown and there's no one at home
Should I leave and start a new life or should I continue
to be your wife

Phyllis Wright

Dear one
wander this way a little
the light is brighter here
We're worried about you.
Come out of the shadow place and into the house.

If I could touch your flesh just once I know you'd smile.

"Only if just once lasts forever, sir!"

Beautiful broken-winged blackbird laying on asphalt in congestive
 traffic-
the city will hear your last sweet chirp, pet,
when dandelions have gone to fluff.

"Don't blow, please
just don't blow."

I will go yonder, pet: I'll go yonder.

"I only want respect-for you to listen to me - for you to hear me."

Tumble down your own way down saline slopes, wet one.
They did not hear you, pet.
Roll over.
    Michael Sharpe

Nothing to Live For

I have nothing to live for
I've said it before
I run to the edge
Ready to jump
But can't
I tie a rope around my neck
Ready to pull
But won't
I put a gun to my head
But there are no bullets
Life's not worth living
So why go on
I have no friends there to stop me
I have no bed to sit on to pull the trigger
And no roof to hang the rope on
I live in the streets in a cardboard box
I'd probably die anyway
So why not get a head start
I raise the gun to my head
And count 1, 2, 3.
    Kristin Beck

The Philosopher

"Wouldn't it be nice to have everything you want,
And not having to worry or care?-
Just to know that what your needs may be,
Your cupboard will never be bare."

"If a person could enjoy the rest of their life,
To live their old age in good health-
Without bouts of sickness, and, moments of stress,
It would be easier, if one had some wealth."

"There must be a remedy for this, I'm sure,
To start when one is young-
Be true, be helpful, enjoy your life,
Like a happy tune that's sung."

"Plan your life the best you can,
Better days are yet to come-
Be sure to take good care of yourself,
Always remember, where you came from."

"That is my philosophy,
Ones who's been through the mill-
Now that I am up in years,
It's the doctors and the never-ending pill."
    Marty Rollin

Untitled

You dear person are so nice.
You cook us things;
with sugar and spice.
You buy us things;
that ring and ding.
In fact you buy us everything.
You feeds us healthy stuff you know.
You give us milk;
which helps us grow.
You teach us tips on how to clean.
Sometimes we think you're really mean.
You teach us things we need to know;
for when we grow up and live on our own.
The reason you feed us healthy stuff;
is so when we grow up we'll be rough and tough.
Sometimes we do things that make you mad;
but we think inside it makes you sad.
You make us happy all year round.
We're lucky to always have you around.
    Christine Coolbaugh

Truth

Listen, watch;
For it is not with your eyes that you see, 'tis with your heart.
You could walk blind yet see the lighted path leading the way.
Maybe if you followed the path you may see enchanted worlds.
Do not rely on fantasies to make the world better;
Believe in truth and reality.
We all have doubts and fears;
But to believe and live is to be able to die with truth and liberty
in our hearts as we know it, not as we need it.
People told me to stand up for what I believe;
But how can I stand when the world sits in disbelief?
Nothing but truth is what I command;
No need of power is needed to understand.
For I stand here and say fight for your world of reality and honor.
Do not stand for what they say you must.
You are the one of truth.
    Rachel Demase

Cold Hands

As it comes for me...

As the dark, cold hands come closer, the body gets weaker.
Surging for the target, it reaches further down
Into the throat,
Into the veins,
Into the living.

It travels faster and further into the cells as the red fighters die out.
Into the heart,
Into the heart of knowledge,
Into the heart of blood,
Into the heart of life.

The last vein has stopped, the last twitch is made, the last breath
has left.
The last of the last is gone.

Forget-me-nots are placed on the deceased.
Forget-me-nots is how this one will be.
Forget-me-nots is how all of them should be.

Never forget a one, because there is only one of this one.
Never will there be another.

Never forget me.
    Sara Havan

The Child Within Me

It's early in the morning and I'm alone with a broken heart.
I feel betrayed and rejected,
Alone and afraid.
The child within me is crying out in agony.
She is being murdered by a cold blade that gleams in the light
of my own hope.
The blade is held by one hand and one hand alone, and it is being
pushed deeper into her heart.
How can I stop the slaying of this innocent little girl?
With every tear I cry over him,
With every sleepless night I spend thinking about him,
And every time he breaks my heart,
The blade pierces deeper into her.
Help me stop the pain.
Help me heal the wound.
Help me take my hand away from the blade,
For I am the one who's murdering
the child within me...

Jennifer Marie Chase

The Proud Tree of Pontiac High

I was once a little seed lying in the nice warm ground,
And soon I started growing so tall, I could see all around.
In the morning cars would park in the shade I made.
All day long while the kids slaved I would swing and sway.
Year after year as I stood through sun, rain, and snow
Everyone was hurrying somewhere, but no place did I go.
In the summer I held my green boughs up so bold.
I even held my limbs up straight in bitter winter cold.
I soon towered above many trees and those taller were few.
In fact at my last count, there were only two.
One bright summer day when I was looking around.
Some men came with saws to cut me down.
For years I had stood and watched Pontiac grow,
But now just for a bigger parking lot I have to go.
I have shaded lots of people in many years,
But when I was cut down, very few shed tears.
They cut and sawed through my body, my limbs, and hair.
Never again will I hold my proud head so high in the air.

LaVonne O. Cantreil

Once I Saw A Candy Cane

Once I saw a candy cane
Hopping down Sparkle Lane
he said hello and I said hi
And then a car passed by
I asked him if he would
like to have some tea
I'd be delighted said he
We flew along the street of Rain
and bumped against a windowpane
When we got to my house
on the street of Nice
we crept in as
quiet as mice
we had tea and bread and cheese
we ate it all even though the dog had fleas
we bought fish and a dish
and I got a wish
my wish was
that I could be a bee
buzz, buzz

Krista Bland

Resistance (For His Name's Sake)

There's someone that I hope to find
But if I do not pray
And seek him every day
His will slip away
Leading me astray
Like a needle in the hay
With blatant disarray
Temptation will control me if I act a fool...

There's something you are longing for
But fear can find a way
To fill your heart with pain
So never will you gain
Hold on to your faith
Or, give in to the rage
The choice is yours to make
Temptation will control you if you act a fool...

Don E. Thomas

O Soul Come Take Thy Rest

O'soul come and rest from all thy labor
O'soul come lay down and rest, for I know
That you've been battered by the storm.
O'Soul come and rest, for the wilderness is
Painful and hard, a true test of thy strength.
O soul I know that you are tired, come and rest.
Far beyond unreachable skies awaits a
Bright sunshine. To brighten every area of thy tired life.
O soul I know how tired you are, for in
heaven awaits a crown of life for you,
and a garment of all the colors of strength.
Power, love, kindness, peace, that thou hast
earned throughout thy wilderness test.
O soul come and rest from all thy labor.
O soul wont you come lay down and rest.
From all thy suffering and pain. For when
all life around me fails, then will I
given life to the hills and mountains again.

Lena Sapp

Chasing A Memory

Holding on to the memory of your face,
My heart refuses to forget the touch and feel of
your warm embrace,
As I sit by my window and watch the rain
as it spills down,
I am entranced in a labyrinth that is full of despair,
I hear not a word or sound.

A storm has begun to rage within my soul; I
have become enveloped by constant fear,
Praying that one day I will be able to stop my tears.

The constant ache in my heart represents all too
clearly the love I have lost,
For the love and laughter we once shared are forever
in my thoughts,
As I am walking along these desolate streets of despair,
Voices in the wind are whispering your name,
Now the world I used to know will never look or feel the same.

So I will lie in this bed that I have made.
But here I will also embrace the vision of our eternal
love that in my soul will never fade away.

Michelle L. Ryder

Unforgettable

You held my hand through the walks into the sunset
A pair of twinkling eyes sang a song of their own into my heart
I was drawn to you like an anchor to a ship
We were inseparable
Single daisies that you left on my doorstep enlightened my life
Lying together in buttercup and strawberry fields
Was all that I needed to survive
Your mere presence brightened a room
As we watched the moonlight dance over waves
The wind brushed my hair into your face as you said
I finally have found the one that I've been looking for
Our lives together were soon cut short
As your time here on earth just gave way
I still resort to look at the stars so I may see
The twinkle in your eyes before you fled that day
Our times together were simply wonderful
And I will always cherish them as unforgettable.
   Christina Homady

Autumn

Master of the red horse,
Harbinger of death.
Chill finger's caress the world.
Father sets time forward,
Nature sleeps,
leaving her children to survive....
Alone.
Traitorous sun turns,
leaving this one to carry the forest
on his back.
Pestilence gives his amber steed its head.
Rage,
The fire which burns in all of our veins,
A part of the earth, a part of us.
   Orion Justice

Untitled

In the mist of our sorrows, through the troubled times we live.
The birth of a child, is our only hope within.

Though the woman knows the only true feeling.
A woman stands strong knowing that new life is so fulfilling.

Once labor has come and labor has gone.
The focus of birth is only on one.

So, when it's time to say good-bye,
and start the family you both so strive.

It's up to both of you to realize,
that you're the parents in that baby's eyes.
   John J. Taaffe Jr.

Missing You

Ponder not of seeing thy face,
Illuminates thoughts of memories that ache,
All sweet in the purity of love,
Capturing feelings from on high,
Endure, endure, for thine own sake.

Often the rose in remembrance of you,
Not knowing its end or start,

Enduring
All
Remembering
Thine
Heart.
   Jacqueline Gales

Formaldehyde

A child lies on the concrete.
Gunshot to the head.
Heart no longer beats.

Graffiti on the wall
Tells the story to us all.
All this pain.
All this suffering.
Families mourn dead bodies lost to the streets.

Nightmares coming true.
To your son, the one that loved you.
Gang friends leave him behind.
No memory in mind.

Just another deadbeat lost to the killing kind.
   Edward Shumpert

Goin' This Way?

I went this way, a-walkin',
Quiet was my mind, silent was my heart.
Then came along a dear, sweet lass.
Her gentle love washed o'er me in a ragin' storm!
Her demure ways fired the kindlin' in my mind,
My imaginin's were a volcano's surgin' sperm!
The look of her was in my eyes, sayin',
Goin' this way?

We took some time, and spent some time,
Her and I, She and me, We and us!
The lavender of her love
Was the rushing scarlet of my heart.
The pink of her lips, as they opened to me,
The velvet of her shadows,
This passion of our love is her gleamin' crown!
Touch of breast; sweet fragrance of she;
Love takes me!
Goin' this way?

So I went this way, a-walkin',
Full was my heart; lively was my mind!
   James W. More

Daddy's And Their Little Daughters

I see you cry,
I see you smile,
I can always see you from any mile,
Love is within your heart,
And may never God take us apart,
Daddy I love you, just like I always do,
Although my love is in my heart,
My heart will always be with you,
I love you Daddy, I really do,
Although I will leave you,
You're the power of my heart,
I hope we will never be apart.
You see me cry, you see me smile,
I hope I will see you in a little while...
   Jessica Miller

Last Words Of Little People

What would be the last words of you to a loved one? What would be the last words from me to a loved one? The words would be "I love you" "Don't go" and "I'll miss you."
But with the little power we have over the power of Heaven, we become the little people. And with the little power, we can't stop it. It, the doing of leaving the human race. And leaving without a trace to leave behind. Just leaving this place. This place called Earth. This doing we call death. Death for what, and why? That would be the last words of me a little person. Part of the little people's race.
   Erin Elaine Sawden

A Man Had A Dream

A man had a dream, a vision, you see,
Of a learning center, where for a small fee
Many could gather and develop and grow,
A school to learn how to fend off a foe.

Inch by inch, the vision did unfold and reveal
A grand opportunity to share and to feel
The satisfaction of helping others to learn
While working and toiling, a living to earn.

It's been twenty-four years since the man did dream
Of starting a karate school to teach and create a team
Of competent instructors to help water the great tree
That would branch out and reach many and reveal the key.

"The key?" You ask. "What key is this?"
The key to the future no child should miss
To unlock the hidden treasures within each
Heart and mind, to set the values and morals we teach

One step at a time students move up in rank
Each time a new belt is earned and they thank
The man with the dream that made it come true
The answer to a child's prayer, and to be a Power Ranger, too!

Hazel S. Fetz

Chores

The chores that I have are very unfair,
All I could say is this isn't fair.
Clean up the dog's bowl,
And clean up the cat's,
And don't forget to pick up the baseball bats.
Do this and do that is all I hear.
I'm just living in constant fear...
The house was now clean,
Although on their faces,
No smile was seen.
All of a sudden they cried...
Because you see I had died.

Nvdeep Khaira

Haunted

What's that writing on your arm old man, that writing on your arm?
Don't you know my mama says, tattoos can cause you harm.

Why do you look so sad old man, why do you look so sad?
Can you not see the beauty of the world, why can you not be glad?

What causes that haunted look old man, the look that burns your eyes?
Do you not see natures wonders, the earth, the sea, the skies?

What makes life for you so lonely old man, as lonely as could be?
Do you not have loved ones close at hand, where lives your family?

What's that you say to me old man, what is it that you say?
I know not a man named Hitler, or the coming of that day.

I know nothing of that time old man, nothing do I know,
Of the horrors that you speak of, that day by day did grow.

What's that old man? No, I shall not forget the lessons that
  I've learned.
For to keep that look, you hold from mine, in my soul it shall be burned.

Nancy J. Doll

I Saw a Little Squirrel

I saw a little squirrel sitting in a tree
He seemed very happy as far as I could see.
He looked sort of funny his ears were short and brown
I watched very closely as he jumped to the ground
When he got down he ran into a hollow tree
I guess he was just frightened because he saw me.

Shirley McCoy

Gerald's Tree

From way back when an oak tree was planted by a young gentleman.
From years of growth and tender care, on a high branch
  a swing was hung there.
A man named Gerald would sit for hours without a care.
All of his dreams just gliding through the air.
Getting older by the years these two did grow.
Through all types of weather they did fair.
The man is gone now.
The tree no longer holds its branches high but
  lower to the ground in despair.
It misses the man who planted it there.

Lonnette M. Templet

Saying

The wise man once said,
Where there is love, there is hate.
Where there is an ocean, there is a stream.
Where there is knowledge, there is power.
When you think about this wise man, you wonder,
Who is he?
But this saying comes from the heart, and your belief.
It's yours to give, yours to share.
You don't have to take this saying, you can
leave it in the garbage, so you can take it and share.
This wise man has gone through this, he has hate, he
once loved, and he has the power to say anything.
And you can follow this belief, among the
rest of us, we have pride.
Now you can have this opportunity to
think about who you are.
And what you are going to do with
the rest of your life.

Amber Eastes

The World Of Destruction To A World Of Peace

The world to be, is the world in what you see.
Drugs that are used, shall all be refused.
Guns that were fired, must all be retired.
The hate must cease, to a world of peace.
Towns are destroyed, by forces that are deployed.
Streets are all scattered, with the buildings that shattered.
Mankind will die, from thunder out of the sky.
These wars must cease, to a world of peace.
We must control our cities at home, for this is were the pain
starts to roam.
The time is now, for all to be shown how.
That respect is taught, it can not bought.
The love is there, we all must share.
The destruction must cease, to a world of peace.

Richard Earl Longfellow

Final Touch

A beautiful face
lined with age
Hunched shoulders
bent with pain
I stand quietly, biting back tears
realizing he doesn't know I'm here
"Papa?", I whisper
"Papa, I'm here"
It breaks my heart as
he looks up
and love fills his eyes
As he knows he's seen his grand daughter
again before he dies.

Sherrie Reid

Memorial To Fallen Warriors

Memorial
to those
who gave their lives
A fitting acknowledgement
of bravery and fortitude
The simplicity of the Chapel brings quiet reverence
The elegance of the sanctuary whispered messages
Emotions of anger, fear, frustration and sadness

For so many
lives gone forever
What a lesson to those who remain,

Reunited in their memories,
their terrors, their comradeship

Friends from all around come
to share this fitting tribute
to the young and old
to the brave and courageous
to the whole and disabled
Growing, growing, growing

Mary P. Bard

A Mother

If I'd been able to feel the pain of others
As I feel when my child is in pain
I might have been a nurse

If I'd know the eagerness a child has for learning
And known the rewards I had to gain
I might have been a teacher

If the meaning of to protect and to serve
Meant bringing food to the table
And blowing away the steam
I might have joined the police force

Among these three examples of professions are others
I might have been

But instead of becoming one or the other
I proudly became them all
When I became a mother

Patricia Wilson

Reflections Of Love

Hold grandparents dear, whether far, whether near... For kindly words they do say, taking time along the way. Special ways for us they care, during our moments of despair... Seems they're here, a very short time, or did days go too fast, because they rhyme?
   In a photo, in a dream, we recall, just like a theme. It's the order of things, God wants them first, paving our way, preventing our thirst... Toil on this earth, we muddle along, it's heaven's above, where we belong... A part goes, with ones we lose, It's God's will, that will choose... They leave here, brave heart, don't you fear, for, they've gone to a place, with celestial Grace; wouldn't come back, if given the choice, they've seen God now, his majestic voice... Story isn't over, awake in green clover. Souls alive, the spirit does thrive... A promise was made from Calvary's cross, we'll all unite, there's no more loss...
   Someday we'll walk, in radiant light, angels greet us, know us on sight.
   Ever you feel sad, ever feel low, view the peak best, from the valley below...
   Together now, the circle's complete, not one of us did God delete....

Carol Lynn Morris

Mother

My mother is to me like no words there will ever be
She took me as her own into her loving hands
No caring words or approving smile could ever mean as much as hers.

My mother is the light that shows me where to go
In her footsteps I shall follow until I am my own
Even when I do not follow, I will remember what she's told.

My mother is my own like no other there could be
Like a bird without his wings is how I would be,
If I did not have my mother for
My mother is to me like no words there will ever be.

Carolyn V. Treibley

Winter Whimsey

Sometimes I feel that when the summer comes,
Then will I find a way to set in rhyme,
Like gentle music played in perfect time,
The songs my spirit sings; I'll find the sums
And answers to the problems in my heart.
It seems I well know what I'd like to say,
But winter in a freezing, chilling way
Has crystallized the words at every start.
So, prisoner to winter, like the streams,
I wait the summer when I hope to find
A sweeter freedom and a better mind,
To set to music all my idle dreams.
Dull winter locked my fancy; lost the key;
Will summer's inspiration set it free?

Larry Miller

Friends

Life is a heavenly treasure chest
   Filled with rare blessings from above
We need only to reach in and select
   With patience, fore-thought and love.

Moonbeams glistening in the dew
   And starfire playing at midnight
Sunlight dancing on a delicate rose
   And beautiful birds sing with delight.

There are pleasures and treasures galore
   So many they will never end
But the treasure we hold most dear
   Is the good and true, loyal friend.

LaVern O'Connor

After The Sun

And I hear the sweet angels calling me
It makes me feel like I've gone to higher ground
The old rebel in me is buried
Instead a brand new soul is found
I once was blinded by the colors of the world
Now I know those little things
Weren't worth my time
My dreams should be focused
On the higher things
To touch the Messiah
And embrace the sky
So I will give thanks for being blessed
From this moment until my time is done
It's time to stop chasing the hollow stars
And instead go after the sun.

Colleen Lewis

Goddess Of Fire

In my dreams I see her,
Clad in red flaming silk.
Her hair as red as fire,
Her skin as white as milk.

I bowed down before her,
And shut my eyes tight.
For my mortal heart could not take,
Such a heavenly sight.

She spoke to me with a voice of music,
That would bring a siren shame.
Then she placed upon my lips,
A kiss made of the purest flame.

I opened my eyes to meet her gaze,
Then drew her into a tight embrace.
And as her bosom pressed against my chest,
My heart began to race.

As I woke I cursed the sun,
Who took her from me with spite.
But why should I be angry,
After all tomorrow is another night.
Joseph Thompson

"The Last Farewell"

Leave me not alone - I pray,
To face my emptiness in sorrow.
For what can be worse then such a curse
To my heart upon the morrow?

Stray not far from me - I beg,
Thy presence is most assuring.
Thy voice is balm, and in that calm
Life's trail worth enduring.

Turn not your eyes from mine own eyes,
And such is our understanding
That not one word has need be heard
Within that gaze commanding.

But should you depart with the rising sun,
Like dew upon the heather,
Then remember me as I will thee
And the love we shared together.
Fred F. Fisher

Remember

If I were to go away will a memory of me with you forever stay?
Lingering in mind, withstanding the erosion of each passing day.
For it is easy to forget and all too easy to quickly replace
the love we hold for those gone with another face.
And as memories of me begin to wander far and journey away
from that special place where thoughts of me in your mind lay,
I fear that too soon you won't even be able to faintly recall
my touch, my voice - all the uniqueness in me you saw.
And as time slowly, ruthlessly ebbs forward and by
will my presence held within you begin to fade and slowly die?
For time is a martyr, eroding from your remembrance of me;
that intangible part in each of us which grasps at immortality,
searching for eternal life as it burns in an everlasting pyre
which is lit by the light of recollection found in another soul's fire;
A beautiful flame that allows us to forever glow
in the remembered thoughts of those that we know.
So when I am gone will you promise that you'll never forget
to keep this spark of my memory with you always lit?
Giving me the chance to live within your heart and soul forever on,
held deep in your mind even though my body is gone.
Audra K. Rolf

The Deception Of Reflection

Your actions and body seem distant
But your eyes say you are ready for commitment
Your hands are folded tightly and your shoulder is cold
Yet your eyes say that your love is a fiery passion burning uncontrolled
Your mind wonders what is in the future and you wish you knew
While your eyes say "I love you, I care, I need you
I have so much to offer you"
Then your lips tell me maybe we'll meet again somewhere down the line
The feelings in your eyes are merely a reflection of mine
Amy Serr

Escape

Don't you ever feel like you want to escape
Just to go to another world
An escape like taking 15 minutes out of your day to see where
you're going when the judge is knocking at your door
But what if there is no place to go after life
No Heaven or Hell
Death would be as boring as life
There wouldn't an escape
The idea wouldn't even exist
It would just fade away into sand
Dark, black sand, full of secrets
Ugliness may be beauty, beauty may be ugliness
No one knows, not will they ever
Escaping would be so great
Keith Ford

Lost Souls

Under my sheets with my mind astray,
No one hears a word I say,
So, nothing works in my old world of gray,
So, I move on to a new world today,

Life is nothing but souls in a cell,
All just waiting to go to heaven or hell,

If you dare speak part of your mind,
You will find they're not all kind,
So keep your soul over there in the sky,
And keep your body on the ground with mine,

Drowning in your pools of sweat,
You feel the pain crawling down your neck,
Now every time you close your eyes,
Then you will hear a thousand cries,

No one knows just where to go,
Everyone wonders in the valley of lost souls
Desmond Pickard

A Lost Ghost

I am now lost in my own world of sadness.
I used to be in a world full of love.

I never knew how much it was going to hurt.
But I soon learned that it would wound me.

To never how to love again because I lost my only
love and that was life.
My life lies back in Salem only now it's just memories.

I can keep going back but that will never change how much I miss it.
Everyday I remind myself of the good times only to miss them more.

I never knew how lucky I was.
Now that it is taken away from me I understand why
everyday that I woke up was so
important.
Katie Kampstra

It's All About Ball

"Yo, get your team in here!"
"I'm ready, got no fear!"
"You better be ready, because we're the best!"
"Hold on now, you still have the final test!"
"You think you are really hot?"
"You'll see, but I know you're not!"
"For a chump you talk a lot of crap!"
"You can't play ball, you can't even rap!"
"Don't even go there,
and you know how good I ball!"
"Yeah, I've seen you go up against the best,
and then watch them fall.
But you ain't seen me yet,
and you better not forget!
I'm going to pound your ass into the ground,
and all you'll be able to do is cry and frown!"
"But we'll still be best friends?"
"You know it,
until the very end!"
George Robbins

If I Should Never

If I should never see your face again
   please allow me to keep a positive image of you.
If I should never feel your arms again
   please allow me to keep a warm grip of
   you in mind.
If I should never feel your lips again
   please allow me to keep the last
   kiss in my heart.
If I should never feel your body against mine
   please allow me to think of you when
   the afternoon breeze blows me as I stand
   there.
If I should never speak to you again
   please allow me to whisper your name
   in the night.
If I should never touch you again
   please tell me that it was only a
   dream.
Maria L. Heim

"Someone There"

I looked to the left, I looked to the right
no one was there, nowhere in sight.
All alone I walk in the park.
Morning, evening, now it's dark.
I don't want to go home cause there's no one
there, but before I leave I say a silent prayer.
Lord hear me now, is someone there?
Does any one out there give a care?
Why do I feel so down inside?
So sad I could just break down and cry.
Tears fall, rolling down my face. I say to
myself, please Lord give me grace.
I feel so bad, is someone there? Cause I
don't see anyone anywhere. At home now
I look in the mirror and suddenly now
it's starting to be clearer. I had to come to
the fact that someone was there, I felt so
down I thought no one had cared. So if one
day you feel as if no one is there, search
deep in your heart and say a silent prayer.
Landa James

Colored Blind

Always able to distinguish the phenomenon of light
seeing red, blue, and yellow not just black and white
raised to judge a person by character not shade
hired by a large corporation and all that changed

Trying to fit in with all my might
ignoring my heritage to avoid a fight
using humor to mast my shame
laughing at crude jokes to stay in the game

Working harder than all the rest
only to be considered a token at best
should I remain silent, meek, and lame
or should I shout out who's to blame

The cowards way out was not my way
so I fought the hard fight and won the day
raised to believe that telling the truth was right
but by wining the war I lost my sight

My pride is in tact, my ancestors would be proud
made to feel out of place, no that's not allowed
no longer able to distinguished the phenomenon of light
the only colors I can see are black and white
Pamela M. Easton

The Storm

A hidden force of strong desire
Leads me into the storm.
Some unknown consuming fire
Has ruled me since I was born.

Amid flashes of lightning I long to wander,
The sound of my footsteps fall,
The thunder rips the silence asunder
As an organ in an empty hall.

The wind tears past in a raging tempest,
Pushing me with all its force
Commanding me in its wild behest
Into the twisting dizzying course.

And so I walk in sweet contentment
Myself, with none to see
And only the ending brings resentment
For it is the end for me.

There comes a lull in this great drama
As these soul filling noises cease
And once again I am, a
Prisoner of silence without release.
Praxedes Vyborny

Healing

If you opened your eyes and let the sun shine through,
Would there be so much out there just waiting for you?
Your troubles pile up to weigh you down,
And they'll get your best while you're on the ground.
Don't let your mistakes take who you are,
Just take control and reach for the stars.
When it rains, it pours, that's what you've always said,
But don't let discouragement fill your head.
You're bruised inside and mentally torn,
Too sad to smile, too physically worn.
You start to vision your childhood years,
Then you emotionally drain all your tears.
Where did I go wrong? You begin to ask,
Is this me in the mirror or just a mask?
Could you go on living without a bad thought?
Can you hide the battles you've so desperately fought?
Love and romance continues to fill your heart,
While hate and war tear you apart.
The answer is, "yes!" There is so much out there, waiting just for
me, cause I opened my eyes and let the sun shine free
Shirley Ann Cooper

Silver Blood

The moon bled its silver blood
across the land, as the trees
gathered enough moonlight
to last them the night, of light

The wind threw the leaves about
splashing it into the grove of trees,
spitting water from a arch,
from the mist that rises from the brook.

The mist rises into the tree tops,
mixing in with the dew that lives
on the tops of the leaves.
Rising into the blue silver moon,
 in a green radiance.

Mathew Hulett

Shades

Color! Delightful iridescence. Charmer of senses.
Prime nourisher of life's beauty!
How unfortunate, then, to utilize color for segregation, to violate, to demean.

People, many colors, ever so articulated;
White, brown, black, yellow, red?
Sole use of each extols blinded fallacy
Red, black, white, yellow, brown -
All not related? Just like you and me?
What nonsense. Explain the varied brew!
Not nonsense - when described in terms of hue.
Neath a kaleidoscope of iridescent ground
Lies there a basic, all encompassing brown.
Clear determination, a melding of kin.
Neat it all same colors for skin.

Why blinded by barriers, staunch, yet superficial,
When substance gives the greys of browns, so beneficial!
Brothers and sisters just under the skin?
No! Over and under as always we have been.
Color barriers? Not out there as truths we can find
But deep in here. Here! In deluded recesses of polluted minds!

John Paizis

Chris And Darrel

Chris was a friend forever and for real.
He gave me much more than was ever asked.
Resurrected from cancer he found new life's thrill
It's taste he savored, and in its essence he fully basked
Sure of his gift outright, he held on ever so tight.

And so together we spent his precious time,
Never knowing how few were to be the days,
Did he have that information in his mind?

Darrel in his kind friend found such bliss
And life's gift to him is this man called Chris.
Releasing Chris to his final ten days in an I.C.U.
Releasing him finally, God, so he could see you.
Every moment and every day with Chris was life quite bold.
Love's bonus through fire of tears refined in now pure gold.

Darrel F. Crose

What A Mother Means To Me

A mother means someone who cares for other people.
A mother means someone who is always helping others.
A mother means someone who is always there when you need her.
A mother means someone who has loving care for her children.
A mother means someone who will always do something for you
 even if she is busy or tired.
A mother means she will always be there when you are feeling
 down and sick.

Lesley Davis

Life

Life is like the sea, full of ships,
It's full of downs, it's full of lifts.
People are the ships with a set destination,
but so many lack the fuel, we know as motivation.
Minds are the rudders, hearts are the steers,
the only anchor is a person's own fears.
If people would learn to combine the power of their heart and mind,
they would be amazed at the potential they would find.
People are like ships with differences we see,
but all look the same, in the eyes of the deity.
Some people are yachts, who acquire fortune and fame, some are rafts,
who think life is a game, some are tugboats, who push others ahead,
some are battleships, who fight instead, some are patrol boats who
watch and wish, others are submarines, deep down within the abyss.
Listen to your heart, which is the compass of your goal.
Then engrave your ambitions within the depths of your soul.
You're the pilot of your ship, the navigator, the crew, what your
mind dwells upon, will eventually come true. Follow your current,
chart your course, never forget your original source. Brave the
storms and never abort; sooner or later you will reach your port.

Joseph Carlyle Braswell

Grief

Sliding down invisible sands
Rolling in sunlight gone behind the hills
I stop...
And find you pacing the ancient passageways
of my mind.

Stay beautiful now as you were before
Kicking about in rhythm with my heart.

I cannot let you lie so still
Yet...

Till then

You must haunt my hallways deep inside
That hold my sanity in breath

...so easy to blow away.

Apryl Cameron Hamilton

The Fifth Horseman

I fashion out of time a stallion, formed
As in the image of the Four, and ride
Soon at Depression's manic, heaving side.
But reigning back, I halt, and hope is mourned
As with Despair I stand afield, forewarned,
And make my choice, and with my reigns tied
To Addiction's saddle remain in tow
Until such feeble veins corrode. And now
I, riding through Destruction's silent wake
Astride the failing mount, a fading arm
Flung up against the noiseless harrow's storm,
Am Solitude, and my own beast I slay
To murder ircumstance which brought me forth
And lay to rest that cruel, defiant horse.

Jeffrey S. Waters

Untitled

Unsolved problems; finding no way out;
Weeping tears of pain; is this what life's about?
Heart's always broken, from things they've said and done;
Seeing you in sorrow, them feeling like they've won.
Wanting nothing but death to rid away the pain;
To be with God in heaven is what you want to gain.
For only thought of suicide, but doing nothing more;
Trying to find love, that's what you're seeking for.
You've done too much searching, and yet love was there all the time;
It's the love you've kept within yourself, the love you've yet to find.

Tracy Lynn Bulaich

Damn, I'm Bad

When life's experiences bring about discouragements
and situations are more than I care to tolerate;
I go within; pull that special part of me up,
  My Soul!
And my undying, ever courageous strength prevails.
When circumstances trip me up
and I find myself in the valley of complexities;
wallowing in the sewer of despair;
I take pleasure consoling my ego
knowing I have an impregnable trump,
  My Soul!

When hostile forces crucify me
with their petty jealousies and envious hatred...
whispering and inventing illusion about my integrity,
I shall rise up a winner!
My spirit cannot be broken!
And my endless, undying, ever courageous strength prevails,
sustaining my being to rise above the dismal bull!
  Damn, I'm Bad!
    Fannie Thomas

From Failure Comes Success

When I love it's through and through.
I do all I can to give
A love that is strong and true
To the girl for whom I live.

I don't understand what happened.
I feel I have been betrayed.
The promises on which I depend
Became the failures of which I was afraid.

It was difficult to forget at first.
Because my heart was breaking,
What made it even worse
Was your lavish and grand wedding.

I put my all into my work
Seeking happiness and a purpose...
I did not want to be a monarch
Though my hopes for gold became dross.

It did not take long to forget.
The misfortunes I used to confess,
The failures that caused me regret
Have all been changed to success.
    Ron Beltran

A Voice From Above

As I lie here tonight, no rest is in sight.
I toss and I turn, until dawn's early light.
I look out the window, the sky dim and gray.
I fall to my knees, and oh how I pray.
Please help me dear Lord, for I know not what I fear.
I need reassurance, to know you're near.
Trying times are ahead, so the scriptures read.
Strength my dear Lord, you must give to me.
You speak of a Land, that is holy and free.
A place you call heaven, where I want to be.
Salvation I need, for my soul to feed.
Eternity dear Lord, is all that I need.
Then to my surprise, came a voice from above.
Fear not my child, for you are so loved.
This journey you take, you take not alone.
For heaven my child, will be your sweet home.
And as I opened my eyes, the gray sky disappears.
My heart fills with joy, for I have no more fear.
    Patricia Blakeney

Ode To A Modern Hero

Over the freeway and under a bridge,
To O.J.'s house we go,
The cops know the way to follow their prey
If they keep it to 40 or so.

A gun to the head, our hero has said,
Will keep those fellows at bay,
But why don't they love me, think they're above me,
Have they forgot I'm the famous O.J.?

A Ford painted white, heads into the night,
It's a cargo load of despair,
Big birds whirl around, disdaining the ground,
A posse beyond compare.

His fans line the highway, as we enter his byway,
A nice little place in the hills,
But O.J. sits tight at the ominous sight
And longs for the Buffalo Bills.

The cops cool their wheels as they issue appeals
Til O.J. steps down with a shove,
Oh how did it happen, I must have been nappin'
When I lost that bloody brown glove.
    Ida F. Kanne

Just One Friend

It takes "Just One Friend"...
Who'll be there, to guide you from wrong to right,
Who'll make you laugh instead of cry,
Who'll hold you when you need a hug, and care no-matter what.

One friend...shares their secrets, ideas, thoughts and dreams.
Who stands by with encouragement and who doesn't judge,
  You by your ways and means.

A friend is someone, who'll stick by you, no-matter what's the doubt.
When true friends bond together, all the toughest things work out.
Who's there, through good times and bad?
Who'll comfort you, whenever you're sad?
Who can take the black clouds and turn them blue?
A friend knows, what a gentle "smile"...or...a simple "Hi" will do.

There's...

"A promise between two friends"... To be a friend of today and a
friend for the future... To be sincere, honest and trust worthy...
To pick each other up, when we fall...And to walk side by side,
through it all.

...A promise... Just one friend... You and me.
    Beverly Alvarado

Us

I broke your heart and left you, not knowing what to do,
Only to realize I loved you, and would come crawling back to you.
  I saw my life without you, and couldn't bear to look,
  I saw you with another man and seeing was all it took.
So I rushed out and bought you some gifts. I only bought a few.
  Because the gift I was going to give was saying "I Love You"
  I went to you and held you close and told you how I felt,
You looked at me and began to cry and my heart began to melt.
Ever since then we've been together happier than ever known.
And the love for one another is the strongest that's ever grown.
  My love for you grew so strong, I had to change my life.
On that night I got down on my knee, and asked you to be my wife.
  Now you wear my ring and someday we'll be wed.
To think I got all this happiness from three words that I said.
    Michael James Pellettier

Sisters

When we were little we always fought
But by Mom and Dad we always got caught
We hardly talked but when we did
It made me feel like a friend instead of a little kid

You moved away and I hardly saw you
Leaving my heart with emptiness and sorrow
I remember in your car we used to talk
With your one year old son playing with a stuffed hawk

Then one morning we got a call
Saying you were in death-row hall
All because everyone in the car was drunk
My only sister was killed by a punk
Sarah Kincaid

I Am...

I am a day dreamer
I wonder how I will turn out when I am older
I am curious to see if there is a second life
I hear my mother's voice in my head
I see myself growing old
I want to live my own life
I am a daydreamer

I pretend that I am flying in the sky and no one can touch me
I feel trapped
I touch the ocean with my bare feet
I cry if I am alone
I am a daydreamer

I understand death is something that has to happen
I say that we should all just get along
I dream that I have a family
I am a daydreamer
Gina Biondo

Untitled

Meet me barefoot
meet me on the street in front of luxury
   in front of memory lane
meet me barefoot
naked at your feet like a baby
   before your heart knew of pain
meet me somewhere after midnight passes
like a season
   we need no reason
   for the comin' around again
meet me barefoot
meet me on the curb in front of yesterday
   on dirt roads we will play
take my hand in yours and kiss the sky
   with your laughter
   we'll find what we're after
if you meet me barefoot
meet me barefoot on the street
Diane Dunn

The Mountain

I saw a mountain; it seemed so high.
Then I started to climb it.
I felt like I could fly.
But I encountered many obstacles along the way;
And I realized I couldn't do it on my own,
So I began to pray.
"Dear Lord, protect my path until my journey is complete,
And I know with your help
This mountain I will defeat."
And then before my eyes, and I know it was God's will.
That great big mountain
Became a little hill.
Lowry Van Hoozer

One Last Breath

The sea to you, is what you are to me-
I touch you with my fingers, and it sends
quivers down my spire, as if droplets of water
were rolling down my back.
I look at you and I see the calm, with every once
in a while, a ripple comes rolling ashore, as it gently
kisses the sand, I kiss your cheek-how sweet the
two, when the two shall meet.
The sea can be so very deep, as I've often found you,
in thought, not sure in what direction your current flows-
And in the passion of the blue- I have seen it's furry-
As two bodies crash about the rocks, in rage and with
glory-rolling into one-
Drowning in your love, grasping-clutching, as I
sink deeper, yet deeper-
Closing my eyes, taking one last breath.. and sigh.
Denise M. Caruloff

Clear Lake

A coal black loon rides the cool pristine waters,
seeking a meal, she perseveres.
Man-made devices criss-cross her dominion,
slicing her obliging dining table into recurrent ripples.
Confident diver, proficient predator,
she emerges from her aquatic bistro
which time has encircled by satisfied pines and exposed russet rocks,
a graceful symbol of this northern Precambrian territory.
A lilting soliloquy is her rhythmic beacon to the dawn.
Her noble tenure, a bequest, to this Clear Lake.
Karen Lewis

Suddenly Blind

There dwells this giant scream in me.
It knocks and beats and kicks the walls
that separate my angry self
from social and conventional lies.

Accepting fate: "Yes, I feel fine.
Doing just great! Thanks for your care.
It doesn't bother me one bit".
That I can't see your painted smile.

I sit and smile and rock that scream
that wants to shout, to scream about
its loss of freedom, self-respect,
tries to escape constricting walls.

So here I sit, cradling that scream,
a monster child deep in my womb
that one day will be born to me.
We both will scream, that scream and I.

And then we'll die.
Sonja Kershaw

"Alone"

   We can't talk things out anymore
you've hurt me too bad
   It hurts even more to think about
what we once had
   All of the good times
   How happy I used to be
Now are nothing but boxed up memories
   When it comes to loving someone
With you, I never loved anyone more
   You can never understand all of the
pain you've put me through
   So I'll let you be alone
Like you've left me time and time again
   How does it feel to be your only friend?
Michelle Cohn

Mood Swings

Sometimes I'm happy, sometimes I'm mad.
Sometimes I'm gloomy, sometimes I'm sad.

Sometimes I'm cold, sometimes hot.
Sometimes I'm hungry, sometimes I'm not.

Sometimes I'm normal, sometimes I'm crazy.
Sometimes I'm outgoing, sometimes I'm lazy.

Sometimes I mind my own business, sometimes I'm nosey.
Sometimes I can't get comfortable, sometimes I'm cozy.

Sometimes I'm excited, sometimes I'm blue.
Sometimes I'm healthy, sometimes I have the flu.

Allison Bacon

Untitled

Hi dear Lord, it's just me I can't sleep and it's almost three
I can't rest, my body hurts I try my best, but nothing works

I walk the floor the whole night through
And try to figure what to do

I take a pill, lay on the bed,
But things keep running through my head

I pray to you day and night
For you are the one that can make it right

I cry and weep a whole lot
but have no doubt I'm strong as a rock

Even though I get no sleep
You see, dear Lord I'm on my feet

I move, I see and I can talk
I thank you Lord, that I can walk

I have my faith and my hope
I refuse, dear Lord to sit and mope

I will fight this terrible mess
And struggle through the horrible stress

You see, dear Lord, It's no bed of roses
It has a name - called multiple sclerosis

Betty L. Schram

When Love Ends

Our communion has lapsed all too swiftly;
My arms hang void of you again
   In the great abyss you broke into my heart.
To surmount your conquest of my soul
   Is a performance I will surely feign,
While I waste away in my bittersweet memory of you.

I laid upon your bosom, cloaked by your two arms;
Leal and servile to the hold where with you held me.
I was utterly besotted by the feel of your black hair,
   And the way your pleasant features caressed my eyes.
You were a poem made flesh, a tangible song to be sung —
Such worshipful ebullition took I.
I looked at your face and lavished it with tender kisses;
Captivated with the quintessence of love.

If only I could hold your clothing now, to just bury my face
   In the perfume of your being...
The sun has set upon us but in this,
   The twilight of my memory of you,
I will never understand
   Your slavery to this fate which cleaved us asunder.

Marion E. Park

Lost At Sea

What shall people do when a ship is lost at sea
Whose radio connections have come to an end,
And sign of thy ship has not been seen by thee.
While it seems my grandfather's returning is around the bend
It has been days, now weeks, that seem forever
Since the Coast Guards have seen or heard from
The "POET" which was passing through stormy weather
Carrying wheat and corn amounting to a large sum.
Tis feels like fantasy land, though tis is real.
Thy search is the game of hide n' seek.
No crew of bodies to touch or feel,
Only memories like diseases, strong and weak.
The only thing left is to accept the fact
That what's gone is gone and may never be back.

Susan King

Begin At Jerusalem

Begin at Jerusalem and heal the nations,
   Thus echo the centuries down.

Naught in the world are the human idols,
   There's no other God but One.

Haste awaken to the God of your fathers,
   Lo, God walks with you always.

Separate good from that which is sinful,
   Destruction is the fate of sin.

Make quest for good perceived in Spirit,
   Ten Commandments fully obey

Begin at Jerusalem and heal the nations,
   Thus echo the centuries down.

Israel has left the hands of the Father,
   Fallen back a victim of Baal.

Heal death and disease, heal the sinful,
   Bring lost Israel to her God.

Wrong thinking has deceived the nations,
   Erase from the memory of man.

Hear O Israel, if you'd cease from evil,
   Evil would cease to be known!

Jane McCaw

The Tale Of The Baby Pig

Once upon a time, there was a baby pig
Who played so hard, he could not grow big
He did not listen to dad, when he tried to say
If you wish to be a hog, you must do more than play.

The problem became worse, as days went swiftly by
'Til finally dad, just lay worried in his sty
He became concerned, as his only son
Racing and playing, thinking only of having fun.

One thing that upset dad, with his son not growing big
He would never be strong, which is important to a pig
How will he win blue ribbons, how can he root for food
These are the horrible thoughts, keeping dad in such a mood.

Days soon became months, summer turned to fall
Now the farmer shows his pork, with glee to one and all
Then things began to happen, as the farmer and the men
Came over where dad was lying, and entered into his pen.

Then dad realized, it was he the foolish one
For while just lying round, he looked as if he'd weigh a ton
As they led him away, he turned to his son and said
Don't sit and grow fat, enjoy your great life ahead.

Louise Mills

Sometimes I Wonder Why I Wonder

Sometimes I wonder why I wonder,
But then I wonder and wonder again.
I wonder here and I wonder there
and it never seems to end.
Even now I wonder, what it is I'm wondering,
For surely, there must be some answer.
For alas, if I cannot stop this wondering,
It could indeed be more dangerous to me
than the most serious form of cancer.
So now I give up my wondering,
and about my thoughts, I wonder no more.
For no Captain can guide a ship,
If he or she is wondering, if in fact,
there really is a shore.

May the Light of life within you, always
shine more and more brightly
toward the Perfect Day.

Have a nice Day, and Peace be unto you.
Lewis W. Edwards

My Little Girl

Standing there just a little girl
Ready to take on the entire world

Thinking so strong
But not really knowing

Can't keep her long
Too many thoughts flowing

Standing there on top of the world
Insisting she's not a little girl

Fighting for her independence
Attempting it all and knowing it all too

Trying to keep her near
She's drifting so far from here

Standing there on top of the world
Praying for safety of my big little girl

She shows no fear
And feels the need to be gone from here

I love her and try to stay near
So any cries, saying help me Mommy
  I may hear
Dawn Wing

"My People's Mind"

I sat and I thought,
One day not very long ago,
of how one could hold so much rage,
and place someone so low...
of where the rage came from and replaced all the love.
How sad and how hopeless,
Are the minds of our people,
when slowly — yet suddenly —
they are crammed with evil?
Why be so full of hate?
Why feel so angry?
At your sisters and brothers,
Instead of loving each other?
Why not look so deep?
Why only look this far?
Instead of reaching for a tree,
Why not reach for a star?
....I sat and I thought,
One day not very long ago,
Of how one could had so much age and place someone so low....
Sarah V. Bruce

God Bless My Dad With Alzheimer's

"Hello Dad, how are you feeling today?"
He answers in a soft frail voice, "Oh, not bad I guess."
Although, with a confused look on his face,
tries to remember his daughter, the faithful guest.

Dad tries to speak again, but forgets what he wanted to say.
So with a smile, points to a chair to sit with him awhile.

You see, my Dad is in a nursing home because he has gone astray.
A non-existent father and husband we visit on Sunday
  an hour's drive away.

They say it's the "Disease of the Century", the Alzheimer's
  Disease.
A brain deteriorating condition which affects the thinking and
  behavior of elderly.

I read about the dementia and just can't understand,
Why did it have to attack this poor innocent old man?

Such an active and hard working his entire life.
Today he is helpless, and a stranger to his wife.

Visions I have of those summer days in the past,
Dad's tireless hands planting our garden and mowing the grass.

Mom still recalls the sacred marriage vows on their wedding day...
  "Together in sickness and in health, till death do we part".
But God understands the sacrifice mom made for dad,
She made unselfishly from the love for him in her heart.

I'll cherish our visits together, and this forever holds true,
You'll always be my Dad no matter what, and I will always love you.
Sheila I. Potts

The Clown

The clown understands the bottom line
He knows the people don't come to be talked down to

Who wants to be a ringmaster?
Everybody thinks the ringmaster's a prick!

The lion tamers may be brave
But everyone secretly wishes they'd get their heads bit off

The tightrope walkers remind them a little too much of themselves
And cause a look of shame to creep over their faces

But a clown knows how to speak to them on their most basic level
He blithely reassures them
Knowing full well that every pleasant thing
Is only a creation of the mind

The clown never fears to live among common folk
And in times of peace
There's not a man who would betray him

He has known a thousand eternities
And fears for nothing

But sometimes he wishes he could be like them
A clown lives as a God among men
But can a clown win?
Charles Gavan O'Lanahan

Say No To Drugs

   This is my message to the world,
that never spoke to me,
the simple news that drugs are like bees,
they have a song,
they have a sting,
Ah, too they have a wing,
In this short life drugs destroy lives,
You and I have only one thing to do,
Respect our lives, say no to drugs,
And yes to education!
Adriana Garcia

Peace Of Mind

Each day I awaken to this cold world
   Darkness is all that's surrounding my room
I hear a crash from the clock I just hurled
   A very hard trying day for me looms

I think about all the things that occur
   Whenever I wake up feeling this way
During this course if I couldn't touch her
   There's no point of me living through the day

She's soft, she's tender, quiet and soothing
   Her voice, it sounds so wonderful to me
She's black, she's white, ferocious and moving
   Her beautiful voice is never off key

She's pleasant, she's striking, gentle and kind
And each day she gives me my peace of mind
   Christopher Reynolds

The Endless River Of Life

Life seems like an endless river.
A river of love and joy,
And unfortunately pain and sorrow.

Like a river life can be deceiving,
Many times holding secrets,
And memories of past storms.

A river has many withdrawals and turns,
As does a day of life.

During the course of life we change,
As does a river in its lifetime.

As a river flows through different towns,
We flow through different events.

Each little thing we do adds to who we are,
Just as each town adds to the river as it passes through.

The river goes on each day to discover new places it had yet to flow,
Just as we go through life to discover new kinds of love and pain.

As each endless day turns to night and night turns do day,
The river will always continue to flow through each town and city,
And we shall flow through each joyful and painful time in our lives
and shall make it to the next day of this mysterious life in which we live.
   Marcy Rouse

Autumn Rhythms

The peaceful songs of summertide
Subdued by autumn rhythms
Ushered in by swift-rushing breezes
With rustic and brute forces

Muses, graces, fair goddesses all
Guard over the hot springs, cool brooks
Grassy knolls, woodland groves and shady orchards
Dance till their colors become the soil

From an oasis of beauty and peace
She rises gleaming from sparkling water
Quivering with rapture from the bathing
In the shaded elegance of gentle light

The baptismal ritual performed to assure
Kind benevolence from the spirit world
That wards off the dangers
Of the diseases of fall
That impede her healing

Biophilic sensitivity seeking
The beauty of growing things
That lives in autumn rhythms
   Mary Cathleen Brown

In The Midst Of Heartbreak: A Father's Namesake

The sadness in his eyes fills the beholder's vision
The father's shoulders appear to sag within his clothing

He is a person whose happiness seems to have been a stranger
He laughs in despair as if purging himself of his distress

His feelings "ecstatic" with the news of fatherhood
His emotion today, a living catalogue of agonies

His only child brought music into the elder man's heart
His son becoming the father's namesake

The father ponders the imponderables of what might have been
The desires for his son faded into the midst of heartbreak

The father is watching his adult son die by degrees
The father is dying from utter fatigue of soul

There will soon be no tomorrows for this father's namesake
There is no scant ray of hope - his son's diagnoses - AIDS

There are feelings from high expectation to brooding sadness
There can never be complete condolence for his heartbreak

Feeling unbelievingness, ill-prepared for the first shock
Feeling the cloak of desolation settle around his shoulders

The loss of a child being the worst of life's challenges
The deprivation of an heir, a father's namesake
   Kathy Manney

Just

   With love, strength, and courage, to our first pair of skates, to sitting on her lap when she wanted us to eat, to warming our coats, to go out in the cold and swinging on the swing dripping from ice cream. She even made sure we had enough kitties only softly scolding to stay from the piggies. Never minding when we found a new nest or hanging at the pond to see who we'd become.

   They say she wasn't our mother because of the foster part. But that's crazy when you get them as babies! Isn't that the start? She squeezed, hugged and kissed us time after time, brought the little brown sugar babies and read us rhymes tucking us in twilight...

   And from my peers throughout the years heard that blood is always thicker than water.

   She took many children, paved their new paths. She didn't care of their family trees, possessions or wealth, only to steer us to our health. For she was our Mother when ours could not!

   This is Mrs. Ray Mathews, Ercell or what else, but to us she was our Billie more than anything else.

   Today she is gone, but we are all strong, so it's really not a wonder felt by no one other than her three little girls that she took in. Now we have learned more about blood not always being thicker than the water.
   Errill Moore

The Lords

   An underlying force beneath the psychosocial identity of man. Captains of industry, in the shadows. Heads of state, invisible, inherently malicious. Pullers of strings. They attain a type of faceless, formless bureaucracy by using human puppets. Fueled by Greeds, Desires, Lusts. They have infiltrated every strata of society, religion, government, economy, and entertainment. The Lords work in the background secretly driving ambitions and pushing the bounds of sanity. They don't wish to make their presence known, but sometimes reveal themselves for a split second in reflections in mirrors, too long of a stare, or in the chaos of riots. Some people can detect them, but they are quickly snuffed out by the Authorities with cold precision.
   Matt Fruehe

A Day At The Ocean

Touching down on a tropical paradise
Swimming in the warm salty ocean
The cold water on a hot day feels so nice
In Hawaii you can always smell the suntan lotion.

Lovers walking hand in hand
Sea gulls flying across the sky
The children playing in the sand
The waves crashing by and by.

Hawaii or the Beach, the Ocean's where I'll be
Both have sea gulls and the sun
Near the sand, and by the sea
The Ocean's where I have my fun.
Dawn Hamilton

The Runner

Close to death
he hurries on
the end is not in sight

The other racers
are all on his tail
praying for him to fail

His eyes glaze over
he quickens his pace
he won't let go till the end of the race

His feet aren't sore
he's human no more
at last he's one with the track
Ryan Ebenger

A Little Old Lady

Out in the country,
deep in the plains,
a little old lady is out to claim
the mountains, the rocks and the seas,
all the little apple trees.
She takes what is hers
and leaves what is ours;
she is the sun, the moon, and the stars.
We call her nature, that's what
she is to be,
to set the land and sky
full of harmony.
Leslie Bowen

Anchor

I placed three anchors on the wall
amid wild flowers short and tall
to let three golden butterflies
sail carefree, as if beneath blue skies.
They looked so happy, so content,
I failed to hear one sigh sadly
before it crashed to the floor.
I put my hand among the flowers
to find anchor still in place.
Gently I lifted my golden butterfly
to caress its crumpled wing.
I felt its heart begin to sing,
someone did care, someone came by,
to pick me up, to lift me high.
Fly higher, higher, golden butterfly,
never let go, never crash, never sigh.
The anchor will forever hold you
through any storm that passes by.
Nelda Hartman

Blue Eyes

Though you'd never met me
I longed for you to see
how much I must be like you
and you like me.

I was born a free spirit, unlike mom's family,
and that made it hard for me to be me.
So I kept the real me hidden away
till you came along and had the key.

See, I was born in the country, a six pound baby girl,
the only blue eyed wonder in a brown eyed world.
Mama had brown eyes like all the rest,
I never knew other blue eyes could exist.

I tried so hard to make my blue eyes brown,
to fit in and be like everyone else in town.
If only I had known it was o.k. to be me
the world would be dancin' to a blue eyed sound.

So thank you to the greatest family I almost never knew,
my search for me is over since I found you.
And now that you love me, I can love me too,
cause my heart has found a home where the eyes are blue!
Madonna Hartman Price

Passing Time

Old folks like flowers
both wither and die
one goes to seed the other has need
just to be recognized.

Each covered with soil
to be born again
one flourished while one perished
for his earthly sins.

One burst the soil
to reach for the sky
while the other lies dormant
as mourners pass by.

And so it is written
that here man shall lay
in a place I would call hell
until judgement day.
Jack Bingham

"Hope"

Life is difficult; you have to be strong
You must have discipline to carry on
To make it through another day
Keep your spirits up that's what I say
It isn't easy; it always takes time
But in the end things will be fine
Sometimes it helps if you pray
You may not get everything you want today
Just be thankful for what you have
When you're feeling down and blue
Take a look around and you'll see that it's true
Michele Minshall

Inside Looking Out

What is it, Deep down inside? The hurt, the anguish, the fear or love, the urge to seek to find a way, the way of the innermost mind. Why must we from day to day, try to conceive a more righter way. Everyday misconceptions, heartbreaks, and tears, constituting the tensions of fear through the years. The world cruel and dreary, thought it may be, need not be faced alone, as now I can see. For all is vain, except save one thing, love, the key to mutual understanding and trust, for without love, where would I be now?
Ricky L. Porter

Untitled

Alone.
I stand alone.
Above a sea of incompetence, I stand alone.
Under a sky red with blood, under rain that drips with acid, I stand
alone.
I watch my brothers struggle, I watch my sisters succumb to the
rapists, yet I stand alone.

Alone.
I stand alone.
Beneath a flag of lies, I stand alone.
Our country is pillaged, plundered, and cheated, though I stand
alone.
Our leaders veil themselves in deceit and bribery, and I must stand
alone.

Alone.
I stand alone.
Through trials of strength, I stand alone.
Through endeavors of joy, with a faceless smile, I stand alone.
My emotions contort, my mind rips open, and I have no choice but to
stand alone.

Alone.
I stand alone.
Between good and evil, I stand alone.
My savior beckons, my spirit bends, my soul longs.
Alas, I am left alone to stand.

David Lincicum

Fantasy Walker

Come walk with me through my fantasy where dragons and unicorns both roam free.
Where fairies twinkle their dust to stars and elves spin tales of what heroes are,
Where dwarves whirl in dizzying dance and centaurs perform their graceful prance,
Where wood nymphs wither without their trees and sirens sing their souls to the seas,
Where wizards cast their patterned spells and change the destiny of all men's delves,
These are the beings of the Light — All things good - all things bright.

Come walk with me through my fantasy where evil too weaves its tapestry.
Where fiends and demons stalk the night in endless attempts to douse the Light,
Where harpies screech their vile oaths and ogres enjoy all that is loathe,
Where ghouls and goblins darken your dreams and trolls and vampires utter shrill screams,
Where monsters plague us in all shapes and forms and sorcerers conjure up earthshaking storms,
These are the denizens of the dark who desire a land gloomy and stark.

Come walk with me through my fantasy and let us see what is to be.
Hopes and dreams peace and light? Despair and darkness terror and fright?
Come walk with me through my fantasy. I welcome your warmth and company...

Barbara Mantell Schneider

Walt Disney World Resort Design

Born the son of Joesph of the house of Wenger. In the month of Elul.
Under the sign of the Dragon. Nourished by a woman of the light. Raised
in the word of the Lord. Innocent of the world. Trained and taught
the ways of Mars. Taught by his father the ways of Neptune. Learned
of the ways of Satan and his messengers but never forgetting the ways of God.
Able to walk and deal with the world, but never really
straying from God. Just the fruits of youth. Just a little
forgetting. Touched by Venus. Kept by beauty and the angel's good and
bad. Nourished a tree that grew, And set forth five branches. Cared for in love.

The tree has weathered many storms and endured the desolation, But
the angels of the four winds have watched over the Dragon for God.
Then through the desolation the dragon was awakened, and at the same
time enlightened. Forged like a Fine two edged sword in the word of God.
Ready to do battle for Jesus and to bring in his kingdom. God blessed
the dragon through his trials and tribulations by giving him a child
of light. To show him love, peace and hope through her light And he
empowered through Christ Jesus to show her the light he possessed. So
now through love, hope and peace a new destiny will arise.

Jerry Wenger

Untitled

I stand here upon my mountain, and look into the dark sea.
The wind pushes me towards the edge,
my wings open, but I am not ready to fly.
Colors splash across the darkening sky, and melt into the icy waters below me.
Waves crash against the shore, matching the sound of my pounding heart.
My hair whips across my tear streaked face,
blinding me from the moments of my fear.
And then I see you walk out of the shadows, step by step,
slowly towards the sea, your arms outstretched to capture the moon.
I cry out to you, and for a moment, you turn and look into my eyes,
yet you can not see me.
With your back to me, you close your eyes and drown in the light,
the lost moon of your dreams.
And so I fly, like the eagle in my heart, I fly from the sorrow, from the pain.
The blackness of the night is soothing, the darkness my keeper.
And the last sigh, silences the wind.

Aimee L. Coombs

Lost Knowledge Of Ourselves

Man made scars line the curves and tresses of my straight, shapeless deformed shell.
When I view myself in the mirror, I see an old lady's body the small bent feet and toes,
the bony, skinny legs and the tiny deformed hands that resemble a little girl's
yet portray the shape and character of an old woman.
I am a young woman betrayed in the confines of an old woman's body.
I am young in mind, spirit and heart, yet my body lays dormant and silent to this heart pleas.
Only in my imagination can my idealized figure sway, jump and revel to the music.
Here I am free, safe and entitled my forms, flows glides, bends and twists to the music.
Here I am the sweet, sly temptress enraptured by all who so crave her,
or the nymph who solely and tenderly performs for her sole love.
Here, my twisted-free, muse unfolds in light.

A shield of silence coats me from the pain.
Words are weapons, words are armour,
Words are visions forged in the heart.

The multitude of cries from this city, how it differs from 100 years ago.
Shrieking car alarms replace mellow bird calls; engines swoosh over concrete pillars and jungles
drowning out the soothing, sweet wind on the water.
People sit high above their city reclining inside artificial air boxes to escape their natural world.
They view but do not see, preferring to center their vision on mindless,
metal square shape which promises but never fulfills.
Escape to fantasy... seems lonely and pointless.
What happened to imaginative sunsets on long, sweltering summer nights
or dancing and swirling in the hot/cold wind in the approach of a coming storm?
Or reclining by the opal ocean, hearing its subtle wisdom, grasping the knowledge of ourselves.

Shelly Baer

The Person I Call Me

Here I am, all alone in life's ever-changing motion, stealing a moment from
the hustle and bustle of my hazy existence called life, to examine
myself, my health, my wealth, my being, the why's and whose of how I
have come to be the person I call "me."

If I am only a development of molecules and cells, who am I? A mere
product of chance? If I define myself as a collection of memories
meticulously stored in a form of life, would I not be a mechanical invention.

I think not! Nor do I choose to be! Rather the power of one greater
than I breathed into me the freedom to consider myself whom I have
chosen to be. My fate in which I have partially thought out. I have
been a lifelong plan in time made up of intangible virtues and unseen
intelligence, which cannot be touched without my desire nor destroyed
without my permission.

I allow myself to be seen with the eyes of discernment and touched
with the hand of peace. I am vigilant. I am strong. I am the
molding of my own hands, the fingers of my heart, and the palms of my
mind. This is how the person I am has come to be the person I call
"me."

Clare Alvarez-Manilla

Where Are Thee Oh Little Understanding

Thank you O'Lord, for all of thy blessing that thy has give,
for the insight of the thing that we don't understand!
I see thy many wander of beauty of all thing that is around about me,
went woke, "I said, I thank you and your beloved host! For letting
us see thy many beautiful things living around us day and night.

Today as yesterday I said to myself oh how I thank thee for
understanding, thank you for all your help what understanding of all
things we can't change! We didn't know what out your daily and evening help.

O'Lord God how do we think of you as we go on our-way to
somewhere, really going nowhere in life but right back to your
loving understanding of ourself and our-ways of trying to do the things that is right or/and wrong.
Until we remember your understanding of all things that is within
thy truth of once own understanding of our own doing, and coming, and going in life.

O' Understanding, how far is thee from us? When we look into the
heavens do we see thee? When we look into yourself do we see thee?
If we see the wind blowing and the animals in the fields do we see
thee? O' How can we, see, "See each other without you?" I have ask
myself why are thee so far and still be there with us? O'Lord be not
far from us what understanding we have search for thee and without
end, let us hear what an open mine as well! As an open heart. O'
Understanding be not far from us.

Michael Maurice McCarty

Evening Shade

Out of a blue and lonely sky with the fading rays of a setting sun
Comes a bright and lovely star, why tis almost time the day is done
Out of a tall and stately tree with spreading limbs in green arrayed
Comes a blissful soothing melody of a song bird singing to his maid
Yonder at the village square the tolling bell is heard
Its pealing tones roll over the country mead,
They hail the flock to the blessed rail, who will his words of wise to heed
The service ends, the restless flock returns; each bashful maid her lover seeks at last
And hand in hand they break away, from those whose mellow years have passed
Ere long a peaceful silence reigns as lights of love peer through the dark
And lovers free who cannot see walk side by side through a lonely park
Tis time at last to bid goodnight as lovers vow their love to keep
And as the doors the darkness shuts, the village falls into a restful sleep.

Bruno V. Manno

Tender Loving Man

On the morning Paul cried out to Jesus, "Please try and help me
understand. What in your sacrifice and dying will build a tender loving man?"
"Paul, I'm on my way, where all are going. Melt your footsteps in the sand."
Won't walk away from the love you gave me from a total tender loving man.

Still another heart to breaking from the pain of faking love,
And while your lips were lying know what love is dying of.

I pray your loving light forever shining how I love to see a clear
blue sky above, when every unborn child's life not precious try and
find one full neighborhood of love, we need tolerance, love,
understanding were all crying and dying from this modern plan,
Won't walk away from the love that saved me from a totally tender loving man.

Still another heart be breaking from the pain of taking love,
And while your lips were lying you know what love is dying of.

When we make love darling it's magic/magic/magic well let's get
magical say when, but when a lover cries out our love is
over/over/over and your swearing that you'll never try to love again.
Trust in hope and love try a little magic/magic/magic Try To Say I
Love And Not I Am, I won't walk away from the love you gave me you're a total tender loving man.
Still another heart will be breaking from the pain of making love,
And while your lips were lying you know what love's dying of!

Lee B. Smith

Wednesday 92 Degrees...

Air conditioned community room supposedly available when the
weather is beastly; occupied instead by management's activities, avariciously

Cockroaches roam the halls, incubators for them on the walls.
The landscapers come and go, putting in bushes for dog urine to flow.
A walk outside, through the grounds; alas, the dogs have already made their rounds.
We could watch some TV, but cable is not free, five years the antenna
on the roof has given double images, told, the owner only disparages.
Stepping down to the lobby, every chair is in use. Residents?
No, significant others on the loose.
The manager says, "They don't live here, of such doings I would never hear."
Junk cars line the parking lot, legal registration they have not.
Complaints, requests for help, are sent by the Corporate Office to be made pulp.
To be elderly, ill, poor in America; to be stripped of
dignity, worth, succor and hope.

Anne B. Anderson

I'm A Swing And I Swing

To the eye, of a passerby, looking to that branch up high, it might
appear that I, was merely a stick hanging on a string.
No, no, no my friend much more than that, I am a Swing and I swing.
When the wind blows cold down from the North, I swing.
When the breeze blows warm and gently from the South, I swing.
When a squirrel ascends my mighty strands, I swing.
If the day is calm and nothing stirs, I rest and dream that, I swing.
Kids from up the street, stop and jump up in my seat and, I swing.
They push and pull and wrestle and shriek and, I swing.
An occasional big guy puts me to the test, to see what I can do and, I swing.
I am proud of what I can do, the task I can perform,
A hammer hammers, a saw saws and a furnace keeps you warm.
A light lights, a drill drills and sandpaper, it sands.
So plunk your bottom on my seat, grip my rope firmly in your hands,
let's attack the wind and sky, let me show you what is my thing
I'm the best at what I'm meant to do, my friend, what do I do, I swing.

James A. Kring

To My Mother

I tried to find some things to do match up to your deeds.
But every time one came to mind, it seemed so small and free.
Throughout your life you've sacrificed your days and nights for me,
And without your love and happiness, I simply wouldn't be.
On days of joy you've shared my smile; on days of hurt you cared.
When things go wrong you make them right, when others wouldn't dare.
You've raised me well, as you can see I know my rights from wrongs.
You've helped me out in times of need; you've been there all along.
Sometimes I wonder if you know just what a gift you are
You are my light when days are dark - you are my shining star.
I love the way you smile at me. I love the way you laugh
I love the way you've started me upon the perfect path.
I wonder if you meant to be just what you are today -
'Cause if you didn't, don't ever change I love you just this way.

Melanie Eaton

God's Place

I love to walk among the trees. Among God's beautiful plants.
To see the sun rays peeping through as the birds perch upon its branch.
The furry little rabbit down the trail he hops and hurries
The flighty busy little squirrel up the tree he does scurry.
The air is full of the buzz of bees and colorful butterflies.
It soothes my soul to watch them as like a breeze they gently glide.
A truly beautiful sight to behold the majestic deer so tall and slender.
As he leaps through the air, it reminds me of God's love so tender.
The forest is a place of peace and quiet - a haven of tranquillity.
A perfect place to be with God if one has the ability.
To give up one's self to all of God's wonder and his grace
Among the trees of the forest, it must be God's favorite place.

Lorraine Williams

Untitled

Life's pleasant breath
touched my life,
for many a summer's day.
But now winter approaches,
creeping ever so slowly;
Till at last—
time catches up and grips me
ever so tightly.
Life everywhere struggles to survive
but only the strong live,
and the weak die!

Donna McNulty

Letting Go

Why am I out of step?
Can it be that pretenses no longer work
   or is there nowhere left to hide?

Why am I out of step?
Where do you go - what do you do
   to ease the pain inside?

Dare I risk baring my soul to you?
On the other hand
   can I afford not to?

Will you - can you see?
The beauty and sensitivity there
   lying underneath all the debris.

Becky McCoy

10:47 P.M. Theory Of Increased Life Expectancy

Twenty-four hours
to do twenty-five
things. There aren't
enough hours in a

Day. to educate,
radiate, masticate.
hibernate. There aren't
enough hours in a

Day. Whats gets left
undone, ignored? I
ache for chances to
be bored. There aren't

Enough hours in a day.
How will all my tasks
be done. What of death?
It's sure to come. Death
will have to wait

another day.

Matthew P. Frederick

Why

Why do we fight?
Why do we fuss?
What's wrong with us?
Although we are friends,
When will it end,
This war between us?
Sometimes we plan it,
Sometimes we try to can it.
But why do we fuss?
Is it me or you?
Or is it just us?

Amanda Miller

Baby Girl

Dear Baby,
You are so beautiful
Your mother is grieved
You were a memory
Before she could share
Your life and love
Dear baby, your father
wanted a little girl
to cherish and love
He showed his grief
Comforted your mother
Dear Baby, I held you
you are perfect
God loves you
You are a special person
He couldn't part with you
We wish he had.

Helen J. Clark

A Storm Soul

I hear the wind and all the
   lightning
I feel its pain.
For it's to spend rest of its life
   causing destitution
Its yell for help comes to us
   as a roar of thunder
Its tears as floods.
Which only adds to its suffering
If you look at the sky; you'll
   see its pain.
But we only take it as
   lightning.

Jaimi Bradburn

Love

A thing called love
   could stop the hate.
Wars would cease;
   Violence wait.

To see a light
   bright and clear,
While harmony
   filled the air.

Grand land masses
   would unite,
So there would
   not be a fight.

Lending hands
   to those in need
Shows the love
   the world needs.

A thing called love
   is all it takes
To stop the violence
   and the hate.

Marlene Behrmann

The Many Faces Of Stillness

Black nights
Dark days
Deep concentration
Exciting ends
Terrific beginnings
White snow capped mountains
God's voice.

Emma J. Hanson

Captain Kangaroo And Canada

Every afternoon hot cocoa
brought pain of blood
back to our hands.
Peanut butter and banana
sandwiches fueled our
furnaces for the return
journeys as the kangaroo played
with us from his black and
white home on the wobbly
coffee table.

Lunch break ended, our boots
packed down six feet
of white. We walked the
middle path in a field,
a frothy ocean, Israelites
escaping between the parted
Red sea. Hailstones plagued
our heads like millions
of ping pong balls falling
on the moose.

Robert Arnold III

"Nothing, No One, No Place"

There's nothing to do
Nothing to say
No where to go
No place to stay

   No one to talk to
   No one around
   No place to run to
   No place in town

No one to hold you
No one to laugh with
No one to care for you
No one to love you

   Nothing to keep
   Nothing to give away
   Nothing to hold on to
   Nothing to throw away

No place to hide
Nothing to seek
No reason to be strong
No reason to be weak.

Tyrah K. Mosby

"Desire"

Beauty beneath has wonder.
wrong as it is,
for a desire or love.
Its cravings I can't question.
Thought has lost its meaning.
The only advice heard,
Comes from my pounding heart.
A loss for words, dry mouth,
and sweaty palms.
It shouldn't be this way.
It never came on so fast,
like a fever.
Lost emotion returns with fury.
No, it doesn't!
It never left,
but needed to rekindle.

Patrina Kunow

Dreams

Dreams are just shadows in the night
It's scary to see what could be
Whether you dream of that perfect guy
or when you're going to die
Dreams are just shadows in the night
Some fill you full of fright
Some can give you a new sight
But theirs no need to worry
Dreams are just shadows in the night
So when you awake lonely and scared
Just remember you are prepared
Dreams are just shadows in the night

Shannon Szukala

camp fire

sparking emanations of light
concluded death
dancing flames picking a fight
breathe last breath

logs covered with consummation
last being
light flashing its emanation
ashes fleeing

Raven Smith

My Daddy

My Daddy left me long ago,
By the Heavens in the sky,
He was taken so suddenly
I didn't get to say goodbye.

I've cried myself to sleep at night
Lying there thinking of him,
Wondering if he's doing alright
And if I'll see him again.

I miss the quiet times
We used to share together,
And all fun we had
In all the kinds of weather.

I miss him so very much
My best friend I ever had,
The warmth of his loving touch
Oh how I loved my Dad.

I know he's watching over me
I can feel it in my heart,
And that I will always be
My Daddy's little sweetheart.

Diane Richert

The Boulder's Eye

The grayish boulder sits lonely
    or so it seems,
Rushing water creates clouds
    of sparkling steam,
Sounds of voices are drowned out
    by gentle splashes all about,
Will you regard the silent sky,
    where wandering birds do fly?
So gaze upon the sightly brook
    to see on which the boulder looks.

Cami Singer

The Rainbow

Oh look, the rainbow,
So beautiful to me, you see,
Moments before, the sky's were gray,
And it was such a gloomy day,
But now, oh no,
The sky's aren't dark,
And everything doesn't seem so slow,
It's beautiful to me, you see,
Oh look, the rainbow

Rachael Lawson

Soul

Is there anyone out there,
With a soul so dead as mine.
I thought I could be saved by just one.
That one would have a heart so strong,
    so soft, like an angel's.
If there is someone like that
who still breaths, guide him to me.
Living, I shall forfeit
And, dying must go on.
Unless this angel will come
and rescue me.
To the dust from where the angel came
unwept, unhonored, and unsung,
He shall save me and I will surrender
    with strong integrity.

Michelle Ann Barsky

What Is Happiness

To the memory of my sister, Bonnie
Happiness is knowing you are loved
It is knowing someone cares
It is knowing someone's by your side
It's knowing someone's there.

As the days go by and by
Sometimes my happiness subsides
But my happiness I'll regain
When you come home again.

My definition of happiness
And love are one the same
Because my love for you
Gives happiness a new name
I love you, Bonnie, Come Home Soon.

Ginny Pasciuto

When Earth Is Glad

When earth is glad
its sunny side doesn't
hide, but when earth
is sad, people say "go away,
go away, bad, bad day".
Earth is hardly ever mad.
But when his madness
comes around, he almost
always breaks ground.

Rachel Curtis

A Hidden And Mysterious Order

Moving back to square one
Holding the line
Looking beyond,
But not forgetting,
The strife
Too close to see clearly
Too far to fight

Ronald Mitchiner

I Love Nature

I love nature.
It is beautiful
It is calm.
I love nature.
It is big.
It is green
I love nature.
The animals moving around
The water flowing around
The trees growing around
The birds singing around.
I love nature.
It will be beautiful for ever
I love nature.

Priya Varma

Algebra

My head's in a whirl,
My brain won't function,
to think of this subject,
I've little compunction.

The distribution law,
formulas and solutions,
are jumbled with variables,
ordered pairs and substitutions.

While pondering graphing,
and finding the slope,
quadrant and intercept,
make me lose hope.

Now it's Geometry,
with all its terms,
angles innumerable,
I'm destined to learn.

Thanks to the prof,
Whose efforts are laudable,
I may make it through yet,
Anything's possible!

Mary Stephenson

Untitled

Lonely soul
Unfriendly place
Cruel world
Unknown face

No one to see
No one to hold
No one to care
For this lonely soul

Empty streets
Lives untold
Abandoned heart
In this lonely soul

Frequent tears
Fill the rooms
In the house
Of the lonely soul.

Erinn Denaix Ahdel

First Kiss

Knocking knees
Sweating palms
Pounding heart
Shyness

Jaime D. Strohm

Together

Love is beautiful,
Peace is grand,
Why can't the world
just get along
Like my friends and I
who stand hand and hand

The earth is lovely,
The sea never ends,
The world is still at war
But my friends and I
Still stand hand and hand

Courtney Greenwood

The Cry Of A Mother

The cry of a mother,
is really, really sad.
Especially when she's watching,
her son, who's about to be dead.

And if you are wondering,
why is he dying.
It's because of drugs,
that the mothers are crying.

We give to our children,
poison which will kill them.
We do our own stuff,
and then we just trust 'em.

But it doesn't really matter,
how good your child is.
Teenagers are crazy,
the drug is only his.

The mothers keep crying,
tears are falling down.
The children are dying,
putting on the death crown.

Konrad Torzewski

Sunrise For Mature Lovers

To sense the dawn before one wakes
And turning, touch a body next to you
Which stirs with vise-like legs and
Grasps your ankles.

The dawn is just beginning
Younger lovers would remain in bed
Mature lovers know a sunrise
Can't be wasted.

I kiss your morning lips, still sweet
Despite the breath that comes there
In the night. For I love the
Everything of you, as you do of me.

Shall you make toast and I the coffee?
Let's breakfast out of doors and hear
The birds greeting the dawn and see
The changing colors of the sky.

Elizabeth Ramadass

People

Some people talk and talk
and never say a thing,
Some people look at you
and birds began to sing.
Some people laugh and laugh
and yet you want to cry,
Some people touch your heart
and music fills the sky.

Dariana Kamenova

On The Streets

As I open my eyes
 To the brightness of day,
I bow my head
 For a moment to pray.

Searching through garbage
 For my morning meal;
I think to myself,
 "This can't be real."

I wander around
 From bench to bench;
Trying to escape
 The smell of stench.

The nights are cold;
 And the days, too long;
Only prayer and faith
 Keep me going strong.

As I close my eyes
 At the end of the day;
I bow my head
 For a moment to pray.

Pamela E. Ewell

Lover

Lover I want and need you
I'm waiting here by the phone

Lover I care and respect you
I'm dreaming of you all alone

Lover I desire and deserve you
whisper sweet nothings in my ear

Lover hold and caress me
Embracing beneath the pier

Lay me down firmly but gently
our love will last for years

Morning sun brings warmth to us
I hear "nothing-nothing" in my ears

Clifford Mitchell

School Of Hate

I'd wake up every morning
dreading to go to school
a place full of hate
to people that are different
constantly made fun of
those words hurt but
they didn't care
so I'd act different
to fit their expectations
I now have no confidence
I want to be myself again
but the fear builds up
out of my control
I think to myself
did I deserve this

Shauna Faroh

Misery

If I were you and you were me
You'd see why my life is such misery
Bitchin' parents all day long
With their voices so harsh and strong
As they scream and yell at me
My heart dies with such pain and agony
What did I ever do so wrong?,
Why must my pain linger on?

Cheryl Nadeau

Left Out

Only two seats.
With three people for dinner.
One will have to stand
or not come at all.
And the two that come
will have a ball.

But that one lonely person
who is always me.
Will be left out
from the three.

So outside I'll sit.
And through the window
I'll stare.
Just wishing
that I was in there.

So maybe next time
I'll bring a chair.

Grant Asay

Until Now

I never knew my soul.
I never walked with faith.
I never knew that pain,
was just an excuse to sustain.
And now the light is brighter;
my eyes don't see just here.
The fears I thought were real,
were really burdens shared.
The love I sought was just in vain;
I looked in places it didn't remain.
The perfect hand,
the knowing touch,
were at the end,
of confusions crutch.
So free am I, to finally be;
the laughing spirit,
my father in me.

Leonard J. Umhoefer Jr.

Friends

Too many times I heard people say
What good does it do
To live in this world anyway
Why don't people learn to live
When you see a friend in need
Just be a friend in deed
Don't be afraid to share you wealth
When some one needs your help
What good is life if you don't share
Never be afraid to show you care
You see all these things
Are better than Diamonds and Gold
When you do these things
You do right from wrong
Your heart will sing a pretty song
A friend is worth much more to you
Than you will ever know
And make you happy
Much more than riches untold

Jean Hoch

Untitled

I touched a flower,
I touched a bird,
I touched a child,
And I knew, I had touched God.

Louise A. Parks

My Poodle

I have a poodle named
Goofey.

He's black as the
ace of spades

He can roll over and
give me his paw

But I can't teach him
to fetch a ball.

Twyla Dawn Fisher

A Dream

A dream is
a hidden hope,
a secret wish,
that lies deep within your heart.

It's a hopeful smile upon a sullen face
That brings the hope to find that
special place.

It's a heart full of trust that things
will be okay
It's the sun creeping up upon the sea,
bringing a better day.

It's the wish that you've wished for
upon each star
It's the secret little day dream that
once seemed so far.

A dream is
Achieving the one thing you hoped for
all along
And the happiness and joy that will
last for so very long.

Laura Carroll

In God We Trust

There was a time when man loved God;
Our coins still say "In God we Trust".
What happened to that faith of ours?
We must hang on, we must!

What happened to America
To lose a faith so strong?
Few people lift their voice to God
And praise Him with their song.

But there are some who love the Lord
And work for Him each day.
At night they get down on their knees;
"Thank you, God" is what they say.

God sent His Son to die
Because He loves both me and you.
What we should do is praise the Lord
And say, "I love You, too".

Julie M. Miller

Don't Judge Me

Don't judge me by the clothes I wear,
Don't judge me by my skin and hair,
Don't judge me by the way I walk,
Don't judge me by the way I talk,
Judge me by what's inside,
Go on, I have nothing to hide,
So next time when you look at me,
Don't judge me by what you see,
If you look inside, I'll guarantee,
There's a lot more you'll see in me.

Shakyra Greaves

"A Dog's Plight"

You left me by the wayside
That cold and wintry day
You stopped the car and we got out
I thought we stopped to play

I raced and romped so playfully
And hid behind a tree
When I looked up and you had gone
I knew you were leaving me

The days are long, the nights are cold
And I'm too weak to cry
Oh please, come back and take me home
Don't leave me here to die

They say a dog's a man's best friend
If what they say is true
How could you leave me here to die
How could you be so cruel

Marguerite P. Griswold

Phenomenal Man

I'm not just a face; weary from strife.
  I am a person; wrinkled with life.
I'm not just a hand; however strong.
  I am a person; however wrong.
I'm not just a man; testosterone.
  I am a person; I'm not alone.
I'm not just a mind; I'm not a brain.
  I am a person; I'm not insane.
I'm not just a fist; striking at fears.
  I am a person; plenty of tears.
I'm not finished; I am not done.
  I am a person; **You** cannot run.

John William Earl Kerchner III

Self-Portrait

My lips are wet and tragic.
My hair is matted.
"Rat's nest," my dad says.
My uterus yanks itself out slowly.
It tugs on my body like an anvil
lodged in my cervix.
Sometimes I wish I had a face
like a drawing: two dot eyes
and a circular upturned mouth.
A little penny nose,
two long lines for hair.
Hands like a five-pronged fork.

I am the look
of the woman in the Klimt painting.
Eyes closed as if asleep,
knees bent.
Hands grip the back of her frail neck
with strong fingers
and she smiles
without moving her almond mouth.

Hillary L. Chute

My Morning Star

The morning is the first,
Ever fresh is the air.
The early, the moon may see
As the stars disappear.
All but one,
The one called morning.
You are my morning,
You are the early of my life,
You are my morning star.

Jerry N. Bailey

Untitled

I am me
I am not the girl in the magazine
with the pretty face and perfect hair
I am not always right and have trouble
admitting when I am wrong
I can't always be there
even though I'd like to be

I am myself
I am not the woman in the novel
who can hold her tongue forever
I cannot always be friendly
or always be non-judgmental
I have my problems, too, and I must
deal with them the best I can

I am not you
I will always believe him guilty
and I must sometimes be liberal
I will argue for what I believe
I cannot agree with you all the time
I am me

Tara Woolfrom

Whenever

Whenever I see your smile
The rain doesn't pour,
The clouds seem to disappear
And the sunshine begins to soar.

Whenever I see the sparkle
In your light blue eyes,
The dark shadow in my heart
No longer lingers and dies.

Whenever I feel your touch
with your skin so soft and warm.
It somehow becomes summer
And there are no longer storms.

Whenever I hear your voice
So sweet and soft
It warms my whole body
And my head feels aloft.

But the only time
When everything is right and blue,
Is whenever I can see your lips
Whisper to me, "I love you".

Brittany Walter

First Love

Would that I might hold you
So tenderly in my arms,
And whisper soft the night away
Extolling all your charms.

Would that I might kiss you
And listening for your sighs,
My heart within me throbbing
As my soul soars to the skies.

Would that I might hold you
With my face against your hair,
And breathe that soothing fragrance
That surrounds me everywhere.

John R. Evans Sr.

"Materialistic Things"

Our purpose in life is
to love, learn
and to live
for our lives are only a
moment in time
for time will continue
always and forever
our physical bodies
are given to us
to learn a new form
of life,
for as long as the sun rotates
we will experience a
new life form,
So don't worry so much about
the materialistic things
for they will work themselves out
sense our purpose in life
is to live, learn
and to love

Leah L. Vass

Musical Baby Grand Jewelry Box

Lift my lid from the side,
   And a beautiful song will play.
'Tis a popular theme you know
   From a popular picture today.
You see my little red pocket
   It's for your earrings it's
been said,
I'll fit into your decor too
On the table beside your bed.
   So take good care of me,
Don't wind me up too tight,
   And, I'll be a pleasure to you
To lull you to sleep at night.
   When you've had enough of me
Just close my lid with care,
   I'll rest and just look pretty
'Til you want to be cheered up,
   so there.

Dorothy Dauphinee

Understanding

My life is strange,
strange to understand.
From my head to my toe,
my heart to my hand.
Happiness fills my face,
tears fill my eyes.
Loneliness fills my heart.
But the happiness; just lies.
The man I loved,
he took my heart.
Stabbed it, stomped it,
and tore it apart.
To trust another,
that same way.
Will take many tomorrows,
including today.
My life's not so strange,
if you can understand.
My heart and soul,
my body and hand.

Sarah A. Majercak

Untitled

Poetic notions
hopes of forbidden potions
the leaf that blows free
from a dying tree
turning
but never and always learning
dreaded and undeniable hate
all part of lurching fate
a perplexing soul
from too much smoking of a bowl
taken for granted this pain
never wanted to be sane
drive a nail through my head
all I want is to be dead
coming around, the other side
no need to hide
for this is me
truly and undeniably free

Madeleine Burns

"Love's Own Season"

He walked into my life
smiling. He had been
   waiting for me.

Holding my hand,
courting my heart,
   he showed me all that love was.

The storms held only
gentle breezes. The birds sang,
   the sun smiled its warmth.

Rainbows graced our heaven.
We embraced our love as
   time was passing.

He is an angel now,
at peace. He is again
   waiting for me.

Cynthia White

Find Me

I'm confused, but the
confusion excites me.
I want to find the
key to your secret
garden.

The garden is frightening
But the fear excites me
I must find you in
this garden or I will be
lost forever

Once we find each other
in this secret place
Then together we will
be and together is
how we will stay

Jessica Nicole Barbee

Spider Sky

Spider legs
  rolling across
    the earth
      covering everything
        in its path
          this is what
      we call
        "Lightning"

Bryan Puleo

Remembrances

I saw in your eyes the sadness.
The last hope had gone away.
Then I heard from your lips:
"I will love you in my grave."

Nothing could have avoided
Your being so far from me.
I feel you coming back
In every hour and dream.

In spring, with the flowers.
In the winter, with the cold.
Sometimes over the waves
that fluctuate on the sea.

The memories remain
Time lasts longer than things
Or as long as a nest
Stays upon a tree.

No prints of any tear
When my prayers I say.
Then in the wind I hear:
"I will love you in my grave"

Emelina Espinet-Borges

The Judgment

Forever awake,
My destiny now known.
No choice could I make,
Through space and time I roam.

Forever alone,
I wander a dream.
Planets, galaxies, and beings,
All have I seen.

Forever alone,
Though all I have done.
I wish my life over,
For now there is none.

Forever alive,
My sentence decreed.
Forever awake.
Forever alone.
Forever,....I plead.

Scott Dreblow

Successor Man Of Men

At last.
I've made it over the hill.
Too many times, I stumbled.
Once I even fumbled in
My endeavors to reach the top.

There's no need to feel sorrow.
Saddened times will overturn, tomorrow.
By chance, I am a successor
Of multiple traits.
From birth, I have characteristics.
To represent the life, and the
Living, a human being, to obliterate
The hopes of despair.

I represent the many younger
Men in America who can and will
Excel positively to elevations
Unknown, maturely.
   Intelligence, and
   Knowledge are the
Factors.

Raffael N. Lockhart

Reality

The real world
Seems so unfair.
Old times disappear
And the new times
Come charging in
Do you sometimes
Feel things should
Stay the way they
Are? I do.
Fear of what happens
To other people
Might happen to you,
We make mistakes,
We're only human.
This is no dream,
This is reality.

Bobbie Jo Jenkins

Untitled

Ending now and everything
I see a passing chance
To live a breath a whispered thought
That often is the last

An ever turning ray of light
Broken and benign
Crumbling within my dark
Struggling to rise

Alone and lost alive at last
Left to wander on
Searching for sweet empathy
Until a last I'm gone

John Wilson

Beaten

  You hit me once,
and I knew you'd hit me again.
  I tried to get away,
but you held on to me too tight.
  I kicked and screamed,
though you wouldn't let go.
  I told you no,
but it didn't matter.
  I knew it was wrong,
though you thought it was right.
  Why did you do it?

Sarah Statler

A Moment Of Your Time

Tho' your flowers would be welcome
What I'd really like instead,
Is a phone call or a visit
To shorten lonely hours that I dread.
I know your time is precious
And you don't have much to spare,
Just a call to say "how are you"
Would show me that you care.
A few minutes of your time
Is really all I'd ask,
And hope you wouldn't think of it
As "yet another task."
Throw in a kind word
And it will make my day,
So very much more brighter
Than I can ever say.

Connie Martin

Amusement

Higher and higher
Then low
Gravity says it must be
Must it be?
It often is

Round and round
Faster still
I know of these forces
I know of this
So well

Surprising and surprising
Thrilling yes
If it was understood
Would it be as fun?
As at first

Jeffrey D. O'Gorman

Mystic Inscape

Salt-sea silence surrounds me,
   and Mystery sears my soul.

Soft stirrings swell, senses
   soar,
Self recedes and quiets.

Moments of bliss - raptures
   sway,
And the Spirit instills peace.

Swift severance from strings of time:
A taste of grace essential,
   Makes sense of it all.

Joan F. Blindenhofer

The 301

I have lived and driven in many
places, Detroit, New York, Los Angeles,
and then some
   None had the joy, I get
when riding the "strip bus" 301

When riding this bus 301, it's a
pleasure to be in touch.

There are people lonely, troubled, and
Glad, people complaining about riding
This bus to work.

I wrote home and said, if any
one asks, where is Jannie?
The crazy one

Just say somewhere in
Las Vegas riding the 301.

Jannie L. Benn

Mother's At Work

Mother's at work
What shall I do,
If I clean the
house, she will
say, "Wahoo!"
If I make her
a present
she will say,
"This is pleasant!"
Mother's at work
what shall I do

Amanda Stevens

Eclipse

The waves are growing higher
Could you hear
The whisper of a dolphin
In your ocean deep blue eyes,
Calling you.
When the sun is shadowed by the moon
You feel the storm is coming soon
Close your eyes
Listen very hard,
The thunderstorm is
In my heart.

Murat Tunc

The Civil War

The states were divided
The right and the wrong
Each marching blindly
To their own battle song
A paper of freedom
To be signed one and all
The rebels they laughed
The south will not fall
Brother against brother
The blue and the grey
They think of their homes
'Til their last dying day
The division would last
But not very long
Our unity would keep
Under one holy song
The birth of a nation
A death of a war
Let us feel peace
Forever and more.

Kathy Reck

My Irish Wife

Her hair is like the morning sun,
Her eyes so round and blue.
Her lips are like roses red,
And heart so ever true.

This Irish lass with funny ways,
Of which you can't deny.
For she's the sweetest in the land,
And far beyond the sky.

Whene'er she walks down the street,
People will stop and stare.
For they will know that she's been by,
With her beautiful flowing hair.

Now that we are older,
Our lives are passing by.
I know that I will always want
To be with her - until the day I die.

Henry F. Joyner

Paranoid

I think I hear the phone,
but it's not ringing.
I hear voices, but no one's there.
I see things moving around,
but it's just my imagination.
I freak myself out so much
that I pull out a gun and
kill myself.
The paranoid feeling is gone.

Heather Bueneman

Kentucky Friend Chicken

Resonating pulse: The high tone
of the chicken fryer's alarm.
My pale blue manager
lifts the blackened bodies,
licks the thick, yellow grease.

Grease drips like blood
from her swollen lips.
A black tongue flicks
the flesh into her mouth.

The cooks toss headless bodies;
smother the carcasses in flour,
sprinkle black spices,
chant of grease—good, thick grease—
drop the flesh into the fryer.

Resonating pulse: the high tone
of the chicken fryer's alarm.
My pale blue manager
lifts the blackened bodies,
licks the thick, yellow grease.

Aaron Dodd

Your Knights Love

Tis the place in your heart
Where I'll always dwell,
Your kiss cast the demons
Black wizards once held.

My mind says to me
Tis this a fairy tale
Nay says my soul
It's true love you've found,
Like knights once fought for
In realms past bound.

As we walk through life
Shadows nipping at our tail,
Love keeps them afar
Like the once holy grail.

Are passions are legions
Crusades in their quest,
My castle the soft beating
That lays below your breast.

As I lay in your arms
I hear voices telling me, I'm home!

Frank Alanis

Sanctuary

I wear you like a worn warm sweater
grabbed for shelter
from weather too brutal
to face alone.

You smoothed the ragged scars
with long fingers full of grace
and care,
blind to numerous flaws,
and created a sanctuary
for me to grow.

You gave me the choicest bits
and divine moments
of inexhaustible kindness.

Sue Addy

Untitled

Today we sing;
   what will tomorrow bring?
Will we hide;
   too full of pride?
Can we silence
   the love inside?
Things so deep
   only dreams in sleep
Too many fools
   played by rules
How many lives
   lost in strife??

Brenda Frear

July Afternoon At The Park

You have, in your own subtle way
Captured my heart and soul,
Captured my mind today
Your innocence, your smile
Come sit awhile
Come tell me of games
You have yet to play
Your youth is ravishing
The one so old, so tired
Your energy uplifting
I am silently inspired!
I honor that place in you
Which still believes
In magic

Erika A. Friberg

Pause Of Hope

Two souls alone.
Who knew they'd meet,
and fuse two hearts
in a single beat.

The gaze, the touch,
brought tears so sweet.
A promise of Hope,
in those tiny feet.

Days turned to years,
each one to greet,
the treasure found,
a world complete.

Who could have planned
this special treat,
the power of love,
in those four small feet.

Elizabeth Barron

Quiet Time

It's a quiet time
When gathering thoughts
It's the peaceful moments
For deep reflection
Relaxing and thinking
Sorting out the struggles
That wait ahead
Accepting mistakes of the past
Using them for future education
It's a quiet time
When plans fall into place
And ideas become ambition
It's a quiet time
For reasoning
It's a quiet time
For healing.

Albert E. L. Michaud

Winter Dream

Climbing snowflakes
through
naked frozen
birch tree branches.

A child jumps
up
into the flakes,
mouth open wide
to taste
the huge different
white sweet stars.

They singe his
red chapped
face, forehead, cheek,
and drunken nose.

He bounces
up and falls
slips
drowning in white
dream laughter.

Dominick Scarchello

Life

As rivers flow down mountains side
Animals do roam through the trees
As young men sit and time does bide
The pain of life is put at ease
Though life itself is hard to bare
A life with love is one of peace
A love to share
That does not cease
Makes like complete
With total ease
A life of love is true, you see
Nothing else can compete
With the love of the life
That makes all complete
Total ease comes with the time
The time that still does bide
And so the pain of life is put to ease
But only love awakens it
And life begins again.

Julia Wilkins

Surrounded By Darkness

Tick-tock. Tick-tock.
The hour was 7.

In came a boy,
Drenched from the rain:
His little head sagged;
His eyelids lain.

Tick-tock. Tick-tock.
The hour was 8.

No eyes met the boy's.
No smiles were given;
His presence was ignored,
His spirit was riven.

Tick-tock. Tick-tock.
The hour was 9.

There was chitter and chatter,
Playtime and laugh;
Though through their dark eyes,
The boy turned to chaff.

Tick-tock. Tick-tock.
The hour was late.

Siddharth Srivastava

Love Of A Tree

In the light and depth and the meaning
of your ever knowing, God is forever
being. He gives us life, He gives us love,
He gives us choices and chances, he is
forever forgiving and understanding.
  The plants, the trees, the
animals above and below are all
of ours to honor and adore. There
is more to learn from each of
these, the secrets to hold for us
to find, holds in the hands of time.
Their arms their limbs, the
swaying of the leaves, the embrace
of the strength, the goodness of
all the surroundings makes me
thank God for the love of a tree

Jean C. Pierce

What's Happening To Our World?

What's happening to our world?
It's filling up with hate.
We should try a little kindness,
before it is too late.

With all this hatred and fighting,
people are dying by the scores.
Lets drift back to the seventies,
make peace and love, not wars.

Why don't we seem to realize,
that we've all been given the choice.
He gives us all the answers,
it's just not in a voice.

We've been given all the tools,
and this beautiful world to live.
Why is there so much greed?
Nobody wants to give.

He has put here all we need,
to show us that he cares.
And if we weren't so selfish,
we could all have equal shares.

Cheryl Langiewicz

Untitled

Today there would have
been 19 candles on your cake.
Instead, all we have is grief
and heartache.
We miss your smiling face
And your always
busy pace.
We had no chance
to say 'bye.
Now we can't stop asking,
why?
You will always be missed
and loved.
But now we're depending
on you to watch
over us from above.

Pam McClintock

The Bird Who Wouldn't Sing

Little bluebird sing out to me,
Bird of love and happiness,
Sing! Sing! Sing!
The children wait and cry out to you;
Sing to us bluebird for we love you!

Kera Steavenson

Dreaming

What would give me pleasure?
I sit here and think
I can see it briefly
But it's gone with a blink.
Glimpses of the future
And all it could hold
Visions of happiness
As my dream unfolds.
I see children,
Laughing as they run.
Innocent and carefree
Just having fun.
I see a tall figure
Just holding my hand
His face unclear
But wearing my wedding band.
With a sense of serenity
I open up my eyes
A sigh of frustration
For a dream that never dies...

Kerry Wietrzykowski

Victim Of Lust

When you touched me
I begged you to stop
You always refused
And forced your way on top

While you cried out in pleasure
I sobbed in pain
You took my one prized treasure
In a rugged terrain

I can never forgive you
Love I shall never know
I will not accept this torture
I refuse to grow

I will become as a turtle
Locked up in his shell
And I'll never come out
Until you go to hell

Kayyon C. Harley

When You Say I Love You...

When you say I love you,
My world flips upside down.
The ground shakes,
And my knees quake.

When you say I love you,
My thoughts scatter around.
A bird sings,
And my soul clings.

When you say I love you,
All emptiness inside disappears.
A butterfly flies,
And my inner-child cries.

For when you say I love you,
Your words are so sincere
That each word you say,
Makes me love you more each day.

Minnie Horton

I'm Me

I'm a champion; I'm a beginner.
I'm a loser; I'm a winner.
I'm a prisoner; I'm free.
I'm a person; I'm me.

Melissa Betterman

My Obsession

My obsession I will see.
Slit my wrists in front of me.
Do your little dance of death.
Slowly take away my breath.
You have the feel
You've stole my heart.
Rip off my flesh
Tear me apart
For my obsession
I will see...
My demise is done
By Thee...

Joseph Kennedy

1996

War will rage
Time turns another page
Soon will come a
New Renaissance Age

Battles will be of color
We are sure to violate one another
Children will be left
Without their mother.

Out of all that is wrong
A child will raise its voice in song
Other children
Will follow along

Hands will bang on drums
Strings, their fingers will strum
Prevails a glorious
Life to come

Children fear not the cold
Your melodies will make you bold
And dear ones there will be
Peace when you are old

Pamela Davis

Seasons

In summer...
  I sit facing the beautiful
  sun gazing down at me.
In fall...
  I watch the leaves
  changing colors before eyes.
In winter...
  I watch the snow falling
  Slowly sparkling in rainbow colors.
In spring...
  I run thru the high flowers
growing higher and higher.
  seasons.

Jessica Scheetz

The Young Traveler's Prayer

Skies are clear;
Skies are far.
We're going on a trip in our big car.
When we go we'll be off well,
Hope our journey does not fail.
Bring us home;
Bring us safe;
For what I have in you God
Is much faith.

Wayne Schalk

Untitled

Poetry is a way of life, an art form, nature's way of expressing its desires and feelings. Poetry which can be inscribed in one's mind for the rest of their life. We live and love poetry everyday of our lives. We pass poetry on from generation to generation not only because we like it, or believe it to be educational for our children, but because it is the building blocks of life; our way of escaping the stress and disappointment of daily life, and gathering hope for a brighter tomorrow.

Tiffany Marie Wilson

TITANIC

In
Memory
a night stark
in starry light
lisping shadows
melting metals
auburn crying
flower petals
all for vanity
all for pride
a whispered plea
a shrieking ride
to the bottom of eternity
waves beneath a blackened sea
a night
starlight
forever.

S. L. Thomas

A Better Place

Dedicated to Ralph DeMaio
You're gone now and it's hard but,
You're in a better place
   a place without pain
You're better now, you're sick no more
You're missed alot, it's empty here but,
   it feels good to know
   you're suffering no more
Wish you could be here
   and in no pain
     but since you can't
   it's good to know
You're in a better place!!!

Marianne Divenuto

"The Place"

There is a place I like to go,
  it has a sweet gentle breeze
  and is quiet and you can't
   hear anything, except your thoughts.
There is a place I like to go
  where your dreams come
  true and is the most
   beautiful place you could ever think of.
There is a place I like to go,
  where family and friends
  sit together and talk over
  cookies and milk,
  this place is home.

Jennifer Burnham

Love Song

Like a peaceful song,
It soothes the soul.
The tune is unending,
As is the emotion.
The perfect harmony
Can bring you joy.
And the sweet melody
Makes you smile.
Every little note
Paints a pretty picture.
Each little heart-felt measure
Shows a happy scene.
This eternal music
Is the power of love.

Susan Dyer

Tribute

I know a heart that listens
perhaps you know one, too,
absorbs all that is spoken
and holds it safe for you.

A listening heart can free you
to tell your deepest thoughts
to bare your soul, expand your mind
or share what you've been taught.

The listening heart is always there
though others cannot see
to lift you up, to move you on,
give wings to set you free.

The listening heart encourages
it takes away your fears
and answers you with words of love
that fade not with the years.

Though ears no longer hear as well
and time has changed the face
the listening heart remains the same
and cannot be replaced.

Carolyn Caivano Mason

Rendezvous

Somewhere beyond ecstasy,
In the quiet of old age,
When time has healed all of our wounds
And tempered all of our rage,
I'll sit with you in a garden
And we can discuss the past,
For as long as we can remember,
For as long as the light shall last.

Michael K. O'Rourke

A Friend

A friend is there to laugh
A friend is there to cry
A friend is there to listen
  never asking why
A friend is there to love
A friend is there to defend
A friend is there to trust
  on which you can depend
A friend is there to smile
A friend is there to share
A friend is there to mend
  when your heart's in need of care

Amber Morrow

The Cloud Parade

Buttoned up nicely,
And socially placed,
I muttered in silence,
As dawn shone its face.

Scorn like a whisper,
Polishing grace,
The figure yet forming,
Loud rivets; a trace.

Hands darned in heaven,
The crown still ensued,
The mystery of color,
Malevolent a shrewd.

'Tis mornings first call,
Light as a sphere,
For cloud shaped chaos,
Affront distant, dark pier.

Robert K. Neuteboom

Split Personality

When I'm away from you
Old "Father Time creeps and crawls,
Trips on his beard,
Shuffles along at a snail's pace.

But, when I'm with you,
He puts on another face.
He is a soaring pegasus;
A mercury with wings on his heels
He is jealous and doesn't hide it.
Swiftly and quickly he drags me away.

He ignores my cries of appeal
And does not care for the way I feel.
We'd be better friends if he did as
I told;
And occasionally,
Sometimes,
Reverse his roles.

Robbie DeLaney

Untitled

Sometimes words can be obstacles,
as real as any mountain chain,
or raging river running swift;
sometimes words can cause great pain,
and create a lovers rift;
but words can also fix bridges
and heal wounds;
but words can help spirits lift;
and so with this verse, I send
my sincerest lovers gift—
to help the pain you feel to end;
to right the wrong of words untrue;
from my heart-three words to mend;
and they are simply I love you!

I have outlasted all desire,
my dreams and I have grown apart;
my grief alone is left entire,
the gleaming's of an empty heart.

The storms of ruthless dispensation
have struck my flowery garland numb
I live in lonely desolation
and wonder when my freedom will come!

Clarence Heater

Rose

Delicate and ever so fine,
  it is put into a world full of
hatred and misunderstanding.
  It brings peace.
    The Rose will stand.

The wrath of the wind and the force
  of the rain falling down among those
ever so delicate petals
  but... The Rose still stands.

Hard winters and long summers
  bear down and seem
to never relent
  but... The Rose still stands.

At one glorious moment it is
  respected and loved, but then
sometimes it's forgotten and left alone
  but... The Rose still stands.

You, and only you can help yourself.
  Because like the Rose,
    You must stand.

Alicia Kramer

Soul Song

You can beat me at any game,
But you'll never win.
You can rob me of all I own,
But you'll never be richer.
You can try to take my life,
But you'll never kill me.
You can never break my will.
You can never tame my spirit.
You can never defeat me.
My passion to live is undefeatable.
My edge on life is my soul.
Don't push me, I'm too strong for you.

Roger L. Lowther Jr.

Creations

By your hands,
We all were created,
In the likeness of God,
Yet a man full of hatred.

You made us as equals,
You made us the same,
Yet upon this earth,
We all try to blame,
Each other.

You breathe unto us,
The great breathe of life,
You said unto the earth,
Let there be light.

You gave us your righteousness,
Your spirit, your soul,
A perfect world of love,
That was your goal.

But something went wrong,
Where, we don't know,
We've all tried to stop it,
But it refuses to go . . . away.

Alia Mojzisik

Betrayal

The waves are obstreperous,
I cannot hear.
The water is numbing,
I cannot feel.
The sky is sinister,
I cannot see.
The salt is trenchant,
I cannot smell.
The air is spiritless,
I cannot taste.
I surrender.

Aaron Wayne Pietrykowski

Her Kisses Are Rich In Splendor

Her kisses are rich in splendor
Her embrace is gentle and warm
Her love and devotion is more precious
Then all else I adore

With delicate hands and gentle lips
Does she kiss me to great highs
With generous love and tenderness
She moves my heart to rise

With my heart in song
My soul surprised
I am moved beyond belief

My faith so strong
Our love assured
Our bond forever agreed

Joe Loria

Untitled

Butterfly wings a thing of beauty
   butterfly sign of loving life's duty
    fly butterfly fly

Time not stopping
   time not slowing
    fly time fly

Mighty hawk searching by day
   hawk finding its wounded prey
    fly hawk fly

Grave dug deep today
   grave solemn and grey
    fly grave fly

Vivian Bush

The Princess

A child's innocence dreamt away.
If you're not there on judgement day,
I'll know you went the other way.
Nothing left of your angel's wings,
Your heart is silent,
But your soul will sing.
You shut away your only gift.
And that you know,
Sweetly sorrowed,
You left behind the blossomed rose.
Speaking the language of love
Drinking from its veins
Crushing that blossomed rose
Devouring a broken heart's pain
In your own little world,
You were a princess,
Listening to everyone's sorrows.
Clearing away the clouds,
In hopes of new tomorrows.

Shannon Hoppe

Success

Success is speaking words or praise.
Accepting other people's ways
In doing all the best I can
With every task and every plan
It's silence when my words would hurt
Politeness when my neighbor's curt
It's deafness when a scandal flows
And sympathy for other woes.
Not to drive their nails in deeper
But help to be my brother's keeper.
It's loyalty when duty calls.
It's courage when disaster falls.
It's patience when my hours are long.
It's found in laughter and in song.
It's in my silent time of prayer
It's found in happiness and despair
It's all I've lost and all I've won.
It's in my almost adult son.
In all of life and nothing less.
I find the thing I call success.

Cynthia Bland

If Love Was...

If love was but a mountain
With you upon its top
I'd climb so I could hold you
Not until then would I stop

If love was a vast ocean
With you on distant shore
I'd sail my boat through storm and rain
And swim when its sails tore

If love was the blue heavens
With you on lofty whites
I'd fly the quest to find you
I'd soar to endless heights

And if your love were all these things
I'd solemnly pray to the Lord
That I might conquer everything
And have you as reward

But love is not a mountain
Or an ocean nor the sky
It's this feeling deep within us
Mine for you I won't deny

Thomas J. O'Leary

Tears

A tear falls,
Reflecting the sadness,
Of broken hearts,
Lost dreams,
And aching souls.

A tear falls,
Revealing not a soldier,
But a man,
Who feels and understands fears.

A tear falls,
And forgotten promises are remembered,
And wishes are made,
For a second chance at life and love.

A tear falls,
In joy as black polished boots,
Touch the blessed soil of home,
A tear falls in silence.

A tear falls in thanks.

Bentley N. Williams Jr.

Eagles

I love Eagles as they
soar to the sky

Always watching how high
they fly

It's funny how they just
zoom by

They fly around turning
every tide.

They spread their wings
soft and wide

Swooping down like a big
long slide

Always enjoying a free
feeling ride.

They are such beautiful
birds.

In flight, soaring
without words.

Cliff Larson

My Best Friend

He was my furry little
friend and he could send
love just like a dove.

In the yard he would spin,
he would play with you
until you said "let's go in."

Now he is gone from my
life and all that's left
are memories.

Ashley Mayol

Nature's Gem

See the lovely rose
Placed in a vase,
Delicate red petals
Resemble silken lace.

Its petals feel like velvet
So soft to the touch;
Full of vibrant color,
Enough but not too much.

Placed on display,
So that it can be seen,
Upon a strong, firm stem
Of finest emerald green.

Shapely leaves like satin
Compliment the stem,
A high glossy finish
Polished like a gem.

Nature's floral jewelry,
Beauteous to behold,
One long-stemmed rose
More priceless, to me, than gold.

Alicia J. Kosack

Untitled

I fight for the right to be who I am
Because I am who I am,
I must deal with what I must deal with
And sometimes I wonder...
  Is it worth the fight?

Heidie Clark

No Way Out

Standing at the gates of heaven,
Looking back on my life.
I see the things I miss the most,
My children and my wife.
How could it be, I died so soon,
And left them in this plight.
I vowed to never leave them,
Yet I had no chance to fight.
He snuck up from behind me,
And killed me straight away.
What is it with the gangs,
That make them act this way.
To get in is real easy,
To leave their is no hope,
My killer got me out,
My killer was a rope.
It hurt to leave my family,
But now they are safe to stay.
I gave my life for theirs,
But they'll never know my way.

Trevor H. Ross

Viva Mandela

To be jailed for one man's belief.
Is this just cause for a man's grief.
Of only wanting his homeland back.
Freed is this man to fight the plight.
Between blacks and whites.
To unify a world racism and hate.
Stand tall for what is right.
Open their eyes to mankind's plight.
We are both the same you and I.
So let prejudices lie.
One love, one nation.
He has a dream.

Loree Nicholson

Life

Life is a butterfly with wings
Floating through the endless blue sky
Searching but never finding
Where it intends to go
Life is an extremely bumpy ride
On a busy street during a red light
Commencing to change green
Life is like a colorful picture
Being passed around for approval
Life is communication not being
Properly interpreted or expressed
Life is a meandering road that
Goes nowhere but last forever
Life is a venturous expedition
Into the unknown part of the world
Life is a brand new pair of shoes
It hurts at first but you
Soon get used to it
Life is a sunny day
You don't appreciate it until it's gone

Andrea L. Burrell

When Love Locks

Love locks,
Someone knocks.
A heart-felt free-
No need for a key!
No longer a waif,
As strong as a safe.

Dorothy Justesen

Bassic Instinct

Carefree and lively
my fingers on the strings,
playing bass for all my friends
and the wind beneath my wings;
the flute, the sax and the trumpet too,
creating music and memories
especially for all of you.
My friends and fans, lovers and pals,
enjoying fun and laughter,
now, in the present
and forever after.
When the lights go dim
and the party's over,
play the tunes again
and come a little closer
to bassic instinct...

Cynthia L. Gaines

Letting Go

That night you found it difficult
to look into my eyes,
I knew the end was very near
we'd soon be saying good-bye

But thoughts of you still remain
deep inside my heart
holding back my love for you
was the hardest part.

I knew the day was coming
when you would say good-bye
holding back my tears,
and trying not to cry.

But my pain I'll try to hide
each and every day.
When I see you walk with her
I'll look the other way

Now I try to move on
and find someone new
To fall in love all over again
the way that I loved you.

Melissa Scrogin

Dream's Destiny

Dreams of hazy midnight hues
Glide through the mind.
And in slow, perpetual motion,
Rest in the soul awhile.
Then escape into infinity,
Leaving an imprint
Of uncertainty.

Donna Fillie

Intimation Strawberry

I was round, green, and smooth
Perfection in a square world
Square in the shape of a circle
I was the most handsome girl

When I wore all my frills
Of sweat shirt gray and blue
With my singular touch of hue
Trapped inside something, I nothing new

Of the carpets that lay before me
To enhance the crowned one's way
While everyone was looking on
And I had nothing to say

Andrew Daniel Baran

Lost

Where did they go?
Who told them to leave?
No one is sure.
They left our minds,
hearts, dreams.
Everything you can
imagine.
I think they want
to come back.
They have gone too
far.
Better let them drift
away in the breeze.
All of "them."

Samantha Jones

Twilight Skies

Passionate kisses through the air,
I know that you are there.

Soft blowing breezes
Lift tendrils of my hair,
I know
That you are there.

Come to me a solid vision;
Reveal to me your sordid mission.

Hovering heat in the air,
I know that you are always there.

I feel your presence
Wrapped around me,
I feel your power
Overwhelm me.

I hear your words whisper softly
"Trust in me your one and only."

Discarnate being are you
Flesh and bones am I,
Someday soon we will be together
Amidst the Twilight Skies.

Kerrie Revels

Winter Snow

The snow is like a big white blanket,
As it comes down from the sky
It's nice and fluffy and beautiful,
Because it comes for no reason why.

As it covers the trees and grass
On its way down,
It comes down so quietly
Without the slightest sound.

You can throw it at your friends
You can build castles and forts,
It's not a good idea
To play in it in shorts.

Snow is like love
It keeps growing and growing,
But pretty soon
It will need mowing.

It's a coat for a tree
A blanket fort a road,
Aren't you glad
That it snowed.

Marcus A. M. Green

Our Love

Our love has no boundaries
No ties to bind
Our love has no ending
No doors to find
Our love has true meaning
No need to explain
Our love has sincerity
No emotions to feign
Our love bears good truth
No lies to uphold
Our love bears true value
No digging for gold
Our love brings a joy
No burden to bear
Our love is forever
No love is so rare.

Alison J. Dutro

Transience

Sitting around,
guitars strumming everywhere;
floating whispers
casting thoughts through the air.
What will I do?
Where will I go?
Anywhere?
Navigator returns,
laughing his criminal laugh.
Bye-bye —
There they go;
You don't belong here.

Jane E. Gatewood

Small Tea Party

I had a little tea party
This afternoon at three
It was very small
Three guest in all
There was I, myself and me
Myself ate up the tea cup
While I drank up the tea
It was also I who at the pie
So pass the cake to me.

Fern B. Bartholomew

Untitled

The morning light - so clear
the new sun appears!
If as left the moon
to rest for night
Will come soon, once again
And leave, the sun will do.
With such grace and beauty,
the sky will become a
passionate crimson and
slowly the sun will descend
into darkness...
Darkness which is shown
By the Ivory color of
the moon
Then once again, starts over...
  Time goes on

Melinda R. Bindas

Lonely And Sad

As I walk down the streets,
I see the world around me.
Helpless and lonely,
I wish I were dead.
If I could be anything,
I would be happy and glad.
Glad to be me, Glad to be alive.
But I'm not, I'm not happy and glad,
I'm lonely and sad.

Carrie David

A Child's Dream

Close your eyes and come with me
Then my darling you will see
The image of a child's dream
Do we make them what they seem
Fear and fright of a never ending night
Sullen shadows at their bedside
While under covers strange things hide
The sounds of darkness scream and howl
While in the night strange things prowl
You begin to wonder if this is real
And then you feel a scary chill
A clammy hand runs down your spine
You want to turn and run away
But something there makes you stay
Suddenly you start to fall
You long for someone to hear your call
Falling, falling you start to scream
This has got to be a dream
You wake up and you are in your bed
Was this real or all in your head?

Holly Gerhardt

Night, Night...

Night, Night....
filled with fright,
or with great delight.

One may never know,
who goes with such insight,
to see through the Night.

John Champoli

Satire

Nothing has ever happened
  How could it?
There is nothing to happen;
  But it the future, beware.
You have been dreaming;
  And afraid you never wake up.
We cannot allow that much harm
  To exist in our world.
This preview was a dream
  Of what might have been.
Our will has allowed
  Nothing to happen.
The time is not right yet.
  Everything is not lined up,
  But soon, will be.

Bernard J. Kennett

Submission

  Drink human forehead
what exquisite bitter distress; being.
  Only I cannot thereon
have shape wholly ark; art
loves last enclosed simplicity.

S. Stucki

One Day, Tomorrow

I wake to see
The fog resting
Upon the dawn
I arise and yawn
Saying a prayer
To our God in heaven
Asking for another day
Just like yesterday
A wonderful day ends
I thank God
For them all
Look forward to tomorrow
Another wonderful day
Tomorrow comes
I wake to see
The fog resting lazily
On the rosy dawn
I arise and yawn

Brian Pickering

"Serenity"

Look at the star,
Is it serenity?
Or a scar,
Now long healed?
That once was pain,
What if the wound had never healed?
What if the pain and anger had run hot,
While the heart went cold?
What if I had never seen the star
   or found serenity?

Patricia O'Neill

The Kiss

One kissed...
Twice kissed...
Dare let it happen again?

Physical thrill,
Abdomen chill,
Butterflies deep within.

Mere thought,
Enrapture caught,
Let the tingle begin.

Touching lips,
Morality rips,
Surely this is sin!

Spreading fire,
Descending desire,
God, let it happen again!

Stacy L. Luciani

Untitled

I see you in the mirror,
But do you see me.
Can you see inside my heart.
Do you feel what I feel.
Do you sense the pain I feel,
Do you sense the hurt I hold.
Can you answer the questions I ask.
Can you hold my hand.
Can you wipe my tears.
Could we ever be friends.
or are you just an image.

Lesa Galey

Untitled

Intertwine with me
   Confide in me
Your mind is filled
   Indulge it to me.

Be honest with me
   Laugh with me
Your life is young
   Grow with me.

The moon is in me
   The sun is in me
Be the earth
   Shine thru me.

Learn from me
   Teach to me
We are life students
   Walk with me.

Holly Plyman

Us

When life separates us
It is okay because we
know it will not be forever.

When life seems so unfair
It's okay because we
know we are a perfect pair.

No matter what life throws us
We will take it and throw it back
because between us we are strong.

When I see your smiling
face it makes all the
struggles we have encountered
together all the worth while.

Someday we will rise above
all this together hand in hand,
You and I, mother and daughter,
   Us.

Cheryl Ward

Diagnosis: Christianity

What's this insanity
And crazy obsession
With this pestilence "God?"
A manifestation
Of your own perverted
Minds. You continue to
Worship this false power,
Numb in your whore houses
You call "churches." It is
The result of your sad
Inability to
Make sense of your sour
Existence. It's yours and mine.

Sean Cauffiel

Human Hearts

The flicker seen from any flame,
Can burn forever, but not the same.
Not knowing why, I choose to sit,
And wonder how the flame was lit.

The shadows, are they real or not?
It seems as if it's all a plot.
In human hearts, in caverns dark,
What does it take to make the spark?

Helen Ann Dara

Thinking of You

Once I laid awake in bed,
with lots of thoughts running
through my head.

Thoughts of me without you,
Thoughts that would make anyone blue.

There will be no more happy
days, there will be no more
sunshine Mays.

Without you where will I
be, I don't want any other
fish from this sea.

I hope you will always
remain my friend, although
our relationship will never mend.

Amber Sparks

Beauty

Beauty has its own natural place,
It's everywhere,
Even space,
But you have to give it care.

Beauty is in music,
It's in the air,
Even in guys name Mick,
To see his golden brown hair.

Beauty has a way,
To make it through,
Even in a day,
It can get to you,

You don't have to be born gorgeous,
To have a certain beauty deep down,
Just listen to us,
To learn what you haven't known,

Everyone is beautiful in a way,
so you see,
Each and every day
Even me!

Kelly Blinson

You're My Dad!

You're my Dad,
   I am glad.
Though I wear a ring,
   you'll always be my King.
You were the first man in my life,
   now I am a wife.
Though we go through despair,
   we have our memories to share.
Whenever I have fears,
   you wipe away the tears.
When I've been sad,
   you've made me glad,
Because you're my dad!

Love,
   Princess

Martee L. Burke

Baby Jesus

Everyone in town
Made not a sound
Because of the child's birth
Everyone was happy on earth.

Billie L. Rice

The Summer Of The Red-Tailed Hawk

Summer phenomena.
Sunlight glinting, robustly red,
Dancing curves among the clouds.
Senses acute and watching
For the sliver of movement
To snatch its life in its claws.
I, too, hunted that summer...
For nature to give me life,
But my wings seemed clipped.
The hawk showed me,
Only I can let myself explore
The secret of soaring.

Agnes Waltke

Paradise

It's luscious and green.
It's a meadow with trees and
flowers with bees.
It's kind and clean and
perfect and free.

Everything grows and
everything flows.
It has a lot of sunshine
and a perfect rose.

The temperature's just right.
The breeze is gentle and light.
It has the scent of flowers,
and the clear sky night.

It's never cloudy.
It's always just right.

Jessie Lincoln

Every Morning I'm Reborn

Before I go to bed at night
I say a prayer for all my family,
I say a prayer for all my friends,
I say a prayer for all the oppressed,
I say a prayer for the uprighteousness.

And I go to sleep
After I go to sleep, I die a little
In that death I dream
In that death I dream
In that death I dream

And in the morning I'm reborn
Because God has allowed me to wake up
again —
I am Reborn.

Essie Kirkland Hendley

Save the U.S.A.

Pray for our Flag
Pray for our country
We are on a glide
Path - down
To the death of our nation.
Our politicians and U.N.
Are pushing us along
Down - down - down
Until all is gone.
Even our prayers and God
  So long -

Dorothy C. Palmer

Untitled

Searing heart on the eye of a needle
A flame that burns so hot
beyond the temperatures of fire
beyond the flames of the sun.

I feel your fevered breath
deep down upon mine
you melt down into
my pink flesh
which aches for your touch.

We enmesh in a smoldering lava
and immersed as a candle
one as the energy of two
potential to burn for eight days
With our one wick of tantalation
that is ignited with every kiss.

Valerie Ramirez

Aged To Perfection

True friendship should be treasured,
And polished till it shines,
Guarded in a safe place,
Until the dawn of time.
Cultivate and nurture it,
Right from the very start.
Aged to perfection,
Down deep within your heart!
Friendship you can count on,
Through the good times and the bad.
And on the best and worst of days,
That you have ever had.
True friendship is a precious gift
That's given to another.
It really stands the test of time,
True friendship, there's no other!

Carla Lee Ota

The Pain I Feel

The pain I feel down inside
The pain I feel is left to hide
The pain I feel cause I will not tell
The pain I feel it's a living hell
The pain I feel no one will know
The pain I feel and it does not show
The pain I feel is my own
The pain I feel cause I'm all alone
No one to tell about my pain
not telling my pain drives me insane
The pain I feel

Stacy Donaldson

Slowly I Sink

Slowly I sink
deeper and deeper
more than you think
I get weaker and weaker
till I'm no more.

Lonely I fall
my hate is my keeper
slowly I sink
deeper and deeper

Slowly I diminish
almost hit bottom
can I be saved
abandoned
forgotten

Tovah Hardy

Christmas

If it had not been for Jesus,
  Then Christmas would not be
We'd have no lights, no gifts at all
  There would be no Christmas Tree.
No story of Three Wise Men who
  traveled from afar
No shepherd visit, angels singing,
  no bright and shining star.

If it had not been for Jesus
  who came to us from above
We would have had no way of learning
  the true value of love
But it's because of Jesus
  We celebrate this day
And take the time to demonstrate
  our love in every way.

So let us pause to thank Him
  for this most famous birth
His coming gave a second chance
  to everyone on earth.

Denver L. Tuckey

Slow Sadness

Pillows stain of teardrops fall
Cried from happy, not at all.
The evening past when winter ran
The summer sun's not yet began.
Smiles still of powder gold,
A sacred wish still untold.
A breeze,
A shower,
The beginning of death's devour.
Rings of pale, distant light
Lay the head, for ever is the night -
One last cry, good-bye, goodbye.

Lisa Fuller

Walk With Me

Come walk with me,
Though I know not where I go.

Come walk with me,
Through the cold and wintery snow.

Come walk with me,
You can help me carry the load.

Come walk with me,
On this bumpy, dusty road.

Come walk with me
Through the sunshine and the rain.

Come walk with me
You can let me share the pain.

Come walk with me
We'll go down through the years.

Come walk with me.
Help me learn to share my tears.,

Come walk with me,
Until I reach my golden days.

Come walk with me,
Until they lay me in my grave.

Claud D. Yates

The Quarterback

John Elway is the Quarterback
the one who throws the ball
if John is ever off his mark
the Broncos will fall.

A thrill to watch him scramble.
and run to beat his foes
a shuttle pass to Shannon Sharpe,
and up the field Sharpe goes.

He's taken hits to all his joints
he'll bounce back to his feet,
the more they put the pressure on,
the more he applies the heat.

He strains and trains to be the best
he tries to win each game,
this Quarterback is heading
for the Hall of Fame.

Mike McGuinness

Electric Eyes

Electric eyes to guide
me to light above
and beyond.

To seek the truth
and the joy of happiness.

To share the pride of love
and the sharing of others.

For electric eyes
cannot be seen
or heard, but can
always show the
pathway to the
open door.

Dena L. Ramsey

dewdrops

if
our
lives
are so
fruitless,
if the earth
has no need
of us, then why
are we here? if we are
nothing in this universe; if
our lives are but dewdrops
in a vast ocean, one missing
will go unnoticed, yet many
leave it a lake, a pond a
puddle...or a drop
of dew.

Xenia Arrick

Dawn

On an early morning farmyard
Grass and flowers shine with dew.
Petals boast their velvet beauty
To a sky of brilliant blue.
Old cock's crowing on the fence post;
Yonder, Papa milks the cow.
Hear the sparrow sweetly singing
Nesting near the old mule's plow.
Distant treetops kiss the sunlight
Sparkling down to greet the pond.
What great beauty God had given
Bringing forth another dawn!

Linda Prestriedge

Sunrise

Rays of light are beginning
to appear in the sky.
I sit on my porch and patiently wait
for the sun to appear.

All of a sudden, as if by magic,
the whole heaven seems to light up
as the sun peeps out to show its face.
Flowers smile, birds begin to sing,
and the trees nod their heads.

The sun in all its glory
has awakened the world,
another day with all its
hopes and dreams has begun.
A miracle I have truly witnessed.

Flora C. Bagwell

Coin Toss

The spreading plain
Within my mind,
Choices before me
Spool and unwind
What do I do,
To whom do I go?
Fate's spinning wheel
Says "I don't know..."
I've been told
The choice is mine:
To stay with myself
Or cross loneliness' line
Dare I decide to
Join with another,
To choose companionship
Be it friend or lover?
Though I grow old,
I have my time to bide,
To look for that other
To help me decide

Terry Schwall

Dark

It is now Dark,
and all you see is the shining moon.
You think that
the sun will come back real soon.

It is now Dark,
and you are sleeping,
Lying in your cozy, blue bed,
dreaming.

It is now Dark,
And there goes a bright shooting star!,
You close your eyes and make a wish,
thinking about visiting some place far.

It is now partly Dark,
The moon is setting now,
The sun is coming up,
It's the Awakening of the Dawn.

Seema Shah

White

A bunny's tail,
An old man's hair,
It's snowflakes and milkshakes,
Champagne on New Year's Eve,
But how the bubbles make me sneeze!

Shannon Armstrong

Untitled

This is for you-
a notice of my existence
an affirmation of my love
a symbol of my pride;
this is for you-
a word from my heart
a smile from my soul
a look to respect;
this is for you-
the tear that I cry
the sigh that I make
the song of despair;
this is for you-
the truth on a string
the eternity on the page
the past for tomorrow.

Jennifer A. Hyres

North Woods Thaw

Far away in the darkness of forest,
It is a bare whisper.
A single voice, a single drop,
Lit on a numb branch
By an insistent shaft of light.
Awake!
It falls and echoes from the earth,
Follow, follow, follow!
A voice answers and another
Until the earth can hold no more.
Run, run, run!
Streams ring across the forest floor
Come to the creeks, to the rivers,
Sing, sing, sing!
We are one voice
As we strum the breeze
And drum the rocks,
As we call down the hills to the sea,
Spring, spring, spring!

Christine Grogan

Love's Reward

Unrequited love itself,
is not a fruitless thing.
The world can gaze on priceless art
with countless songs to sing.

And love itself its own reward
transcends my darkest bane.
Never am I so alive
as now, in searing pain.

It's love itself that gives me hope
and gets me up each day.
I reach out for the golden ring
forgetting yesterday.

Grover Mundell

Happy Birthday, Dear

Dylan, subjected to a starring role
What a happy little man you are!
Jolly in your innocence
With curiosity allowed
I loved and laughed at the
  things you dared
In proper hands, I see,
Free from fears, as you
  should be —
Always be —

Anna R. Greenberg

Face Value

Crying out in the night
Gathering all of his might
Preparing for a fight
So tomorrow can be a better sight
Is the child without a face.

Angry with everybody
Who treated him wrongly
Making him feel lonely
And damned in this world eternally
Is the child without a face.

Asking questions
Thinking of retaliations
So full of destruction
Out of desperation
Is the child without a face.

Hating all of human race
For struggling all of his days
Losing all hope and faith in Grace
Died in this unfair place
Was the child without a face.

Hendrix Valdeabella

Shame's Sonnet

Hanging my head in embarrassment
From a feeling of total worthlessness,
It is a state of great emotional pain—
A feeling of complete, utter emptiness.

It's a know that tangles the stomach;
The tensing and wiring of nerves.
Waiting for the last, forceful blow,
I one I feel I deserve.

Wishing that I could be buried,
Hidden forgotten, covered.
Wanting and praying to evaporate,
Disappear and never be discovered.

Eliana Capri Dunlap

America the,...It's up to you.

America the beautiful
I wish this were true
But people are murdering it
For me and for you.

Drive by shootings, kidnappings,
murders and abuse,
Are all of the things
Lighting the fuse.

So please stand up
for what you believe
Re-establish the pride
Keep America Free.

Let's nurture and love
the world around
Give our future
Some solid ground.

Our kids will thank you
As they grow up assured
That love is much cooler
Than murder and war.

Bonnie L. Eichler

Friendship

A friend can last forever,
forever and a day.

When trust is in a friendship,
it will never fade away.

A friend can bring you joy,
joy to fill your heart.

Sticking close together,
you'll never have to part.

When problems come up,
as problems always do,

Just take your time,
and work them through.

A friendship can be a treasure,
made of silver and gold.

You can have this friendship,
no matter if you're young or old.

Abigail Faulk

Onion

Bits and pieces scurry
Away in the wind,
Leaving me chilled
It feels as though they are
Ripped from my very existence

It saddens my soul,
That again I feel
The need to let another
Dream go into the
Wild

I may eventually
Catch them and
Put myself back
Together
Once more

Alas, this is neither
The time nor the place,
So I await for
That futuristic point
When I can be reborn

Kristina Fridas

Gangs

Shootings late in the
middle of the night
just another west side
fight.
You see their rags,
and walk away,
silent as you pray.
You hear the gun
shot right behind,
as you ask...
Is this my life.

Crystal Green

Cast

Arts' dimmed remains,
Cultures torn at the seam.

The feast continues,
 To roam,
Beyond the mounds
of dirt and bone.

Sharon Swain

Feelings

I just saw Gwen in the sky
As the clouds passed by,

I saw her put her hands together
As if to say we will be one forever,

I have often looked to heaven
Only to see a passing raven,

Late mid summer's day
Only made me pray,

Brother and son are there
But yet I know not where,

Clouds, sun, and stars
I know they are out there,

I keep searching,
But yet I know not where,

If they could only reach out
And touch me once more time,

That moment would be mine,
My hand is held open to the skies
Still there are tears in my eyes.

Bryan M. Williams I

Untitled

I chanced to look upon the wall
there was no wall; just light.
Shining from a cross on high
Ever showing thru the night.

And toward that light, my husband
whom I have loved so long
was walking straight and tall
he has gone ahead of me
for he has heard the call.

Dear Lord, let not my footsteps drift
but keep them straight, and trim
for some day I shall hear my name
and I can go to him.

Louise Langille

Untitled

In the dark, in the night,
I do what I know is right.
In the light, in the day,
I have no choice, I must obey.

By the moon, by the stars,
I keep friends from bars.
By the sun, by the sky,
I watch them slowly die.

While hidden, and unseen,
I make the world clean.
With no mask, in plain view,
I smile, and give no clue.

Some see night as filled with crime.
I see it as lots of time.
Some see day as many hi's.
I see these as pathetic lies.

Josiah Barber

Swimming

It's cool to go swimming.
This swimming pool has a sign
In the shallow end that says
It's the deep end. (I should tell
them the deep it is not.)

In the deep end there is no sign.
Only swimmers left behind.
Or maybe just noticers looking
For their reflections.

I stand on the edge of the pool.
I'm no better than the swimming.
Only realizing my strokes.

Daniel Albert Volk

Sing A Happy Song

Don't be disillusioned
When everything goes wrong.
God's watching over you,
Just sing a happy song.

A song that echoes words
Of times that brought such joy,
So full of peace and love
That no one can destroy.

Not everyone can say
That life has been so full,
So sing another tune
For those in need and you'll

No longer feel the pain
The dark of night can bring,
Others have worse burdens,
But they too, also sing.

Eleanor Brown

Mistake

The days are pointless,
The nights are too long.
I mourn a love,
That came out all wrong.
I know you were just,
Another mistake.
A pain that will heal.
I just wish I knew,
How long it will take.

I wonder if you regret,
What you did.
Are you aware,
Of the pain I have hid?
Another mistake.
That's all you were.
I cry only because,
I lost you to her.

Michelle Corlett

Cloudy

Deliberate reflection
in a cloudy pool
sometimes leaves
unclear resolutions
ironic
in the stagnation
the shallow
yet purposeful
indication
of change.

Dee Ann Kreutzer

Life Confusing

Focus on time
A second of present
Always tomorrow to make things pleasant

The wind blows time
North, South, East, West
A second is gone
Where once you could claim it

Introduce lottery
So much to choose
One right, two wrong
Will you lose?

Step left and right
Soon the area is tight
Repetition blows
Sand covers all goals

Present to future
No longer to see
Only behind you
An open sea

Shannon M. Biby

God Help Me!

As I stare, deep into
the eyes of my reflection
in the mirror, I see a
reflection of me crying,
thinking why... why me...
why did this have to
happen to me, I didn't
do anything wrong...

... Oh help God, Help me,
my life is ruined just
because of him, him that
evil person. He dragged me
through the a lie and...
and raped me. I yelled NO,
but did he listen. He just
hurt me more. I just...
wish that never came to be.

Sue Auger

The Disappearing Coast Line

As the continent slowly drifts
The water creeps quietly towards me
A wave spills water against my feet
It secretly splashes up on my knees.

My dry sand is hot
The soft wave eases my burn
The thought of being soaked is scary
No heat to me will feel odd.

I've dreamt of being a nice big beach
The sun's rays beating down on me
A cool breeze chills my toes.
The thought of saying goodbye is sad.

The day is coming quickly
I dread the time it arrives
For soon I will be the floor of the sea
And never again the coast line.

Stacie Diane Haines

Untitled

In the presence of the Lord
living on grace,
living on love
from above.

Not living on guilt, or
scars from the past
I'm living on wealth that will last.

Living on grace,
living on love
from above.

When Satan's out to tempt me,
I claim the presence of the Lord,
and I'm filled with grace,
and I'm filled with love
from above.

living on grace,
living on love
from above.

Susan King

The Choice

Once in his lifetime, man
receives from God a special gift
  Given freely, and with love,
to serve mankind and spirits lift.

  Eagerly he opens it to glimpse
the hidden prize;
  Then sadly closes it again,
inside a box of pride.

  He covers it with wrappings
made of apathy and fear;
  Then with ribbons of tradition,
chokes the thing he holds most dear.

  So follow not the widening road
laid out by mortal men;
  But trust your inner man,
and cut the cords that bind you in.

Myrna Ulery

Insight

Insight of my goal
I can reach it,
I can feel it,
I can see it.

Insight of my goal
Barrier,
Barrier,
But, I can still see it.

Insight of my goal
Hurdle it,
Hurdle it,
It's within my reach.

Insight of my goal
Elation,
Frustration,
Disappointment
Pain
I've got it now,
But what do I do with it?

Cathy London

People

People can be many ways
they can hear many things
they can be in the day
or see into the future

People can act
in so very many ways
they can use eloquence and tact
or be thoughtless and live for the day

People can be boisterous
they can be priceless
or quite illustrious
depending upon the day

People can always be
so different in triumph and tragedy
as people can so clearly see
through the eyes of others

Personalities can be in dismay
as they struggle to find
and vehemently pray
that they find themselves.

Steven Greenwald

It's the Words Unspoken

It's the words unspoken that will be
   remembered forever
It's the silent cries for help that
   everyone hears, but nobody answers
It's the invisible nothing that traps
   us all.
It's the wanting to help that only
   ends up hurting
It's the hopeless hope that is so
   unexplainable
It's knowing the only way to ease
   the pain is death, but, it's not
   your life to take

Nicole Wright

Do You...?

My thoughts run wild
As I kneel to watch the moon.
I stare out at the glowing orb
And feel quite the loon.

Do you think about me
On a cool and quiet night?
It lifts my heart and stills the pain
When I think that you might.

Are you lonesome out there
While I am stuck here?
Do you lie awake at nights
Wishing I was near?

I sit and watch the moon
As the lonely wind does blow,
And I wonder if you love me,
But really, I already know.

Brett T. Johnson

Lost Love

I feel like crying,
But I shed no tears.
I have much pain inside,
Pain that will last for years.
I thought we were in love,
But it did not last.
He was everything to me,
But now it's in the past.
I still love him though,
And he loves me too.
He told me so himself.
And I believe it's true.
He was a true love,
But now a friend.
We grew apart,
I had no idea it would end.
Such a short time.
We were together.
But we have a friendship,
That will last forever.

Dionna Robinson

Untitled

'Twas near the dawn
I began to yawn
When through the mist
I saw them kiss
I tried to cry
I wished to die
He was betraying me
For me to see
When around his neck,
I glimpsed the token
I gave to him when our
Vows were spoken
Through the night I ran
Like the wind
To escape the thought that
Our love could end
But morning will come
And one must go on living
Though there's none to love
And no forgiving.

Kelsey Goughnour

Dreams

Dreams...
Seized by some,
Lived by others.
They begin as a drop of water,
Only to grow in size and shape
Until one day
You look around and realize,
The lake around you
Is a world of your own;
Your own to live in...
To learn about...
And discover not only who you are,
But what you've always dreamt of being.

Brian L. Janik

Sextile

Lowering my eyes
They could not help
but to flutter up
and catch his gaze

Holding my breath
My pulse would then
chase its tail
and chew nervously
beneath the atrium

Lately the days had
been enclosing us
This vacuous space between
our bodies diminishing -
Refilling with flesh

An aroma rising
Sickeningly sweet:
The syrup of Lust
dripping heavily from
our fingertips

Aileen M. Prera

Untitled

Your sweet words go unheard,
Your voice isn't listened to.
You hide a wall of sadness,
That smile isn't you.

I can see it all,
I have been there before.
You can come to me,
I'll love you all the more.

Something's changed inside you,
Something I cannot ignore
I am there to listen,
If just that and nothing more.

Jenney Mounsey

You're Still Here

My Wedding Day hug.
  White hair.
Tomato plants.
  A blue chair.

I tan fishing hat.
  The smell of cologne.
Sunday Mass.
  On the porch, alone.

Cans, in the basement.
  Carving the ham.
Salt sticks.
  Calling me "Sam".

A gray suit.
  The day you died.
Loving me.
  My son has your eyes.

Samantha Opferman

The Streets, A Scary Place

The cold dark shadows all lurking around.
While you are lying on the ground.
The gutters are cold, but your blood is warm.
Your head throbs and you remember
how they did warn.
You know they were right and you were wrong.
Now it's too late to go back home.
Your eyes gently close.
Blood runs down your nose.
You begin to drift.
Oh, the wind is so swift.
You go to sleep, you'll never wake.
The streets, your life did take.
I'll haunt you now and forever more.
No-one can see you anymore.
Hollie Garrett

Thoughts In Passing

Autumn's gilded splendor,
Has all but passed aside.
Winter's pristine stillness,
We soon must all abide.

I remember summer.
I shall never forget
Those special moments
With you, and yet
They cannot return.
I can only live, let
My soul yearn;
For soon you'll be gone,
Your time here no more.
I miss you already-
You're special - so for
The time I shall thank you
And I hope you will see
I wish you life's greatness,
This, to you from just,

  ME.
Karen Borrowman

My Wife

The warmth of your smile makes
My everyday. I love you so
that it's hard for me to
say. Your love and
compassion make life
worthwhile. When I look at
your beauty it makes me
smile. For I know I am the
luckiest man that can ever
be. The day you said I do to
me. From that day forth
And for the rest of my life
I know I'll be happy,
because you are my wife.
Wayne Thomas

Longings

Longings...
Wispy clouds,
Gentle breezes,
Lulling heat,
Softly breaking waves,
Chattering birds,
Swaying trees,
Enchanting melodies
Bright swirling skirts,
Lightly dancing feet,
Illuminated star-studded sky,
Tranquil nights,
Sweet, ambrosial caresses,
Consume me! Oh, consume me!
Faith Meckes

Never Knowing

Pain is in her heart
Evil is in her mind
Never knowing what you'll find
Wanting to see a little girl
You look over to the other side
Never knowing where she'll hide
Searching cold alleys
Walking dark halls
Never knowing where she crawls
Seeing a shadow in the distance
After it you will chase
Never knowing if you'll see her face
Time is of the essence
You must find a cure
Never knowing for sure
If you can help her find her way home
Never knowing where she may roam
Praying Dear God please end it all
You see her and do nothing but stare
Never knowing - does she really care
Paige L. Pennybaker

Moribund

My body has betrayed me
Devious and cruel
Life as its accomplice
And time its deadly tool
While I was busy living
They schemed their dreadful plan
Left me mad and moribund
a shadow of a man
Atrophied and shrunken
A dried out husky shell
Powdered bones crumble now
In this my living hell
With yellowed eyes
And reptile claw
Rattlesnake breath
Through slackened jaw
Leathered and weathered
Alligator skin
Hides the soul
Of the boy within
J. Luttman

The Waves Baby

Soft, Sweet, gentle,
In the sand,
Lies a baby,
Small and grand.

Wiggles and wakes,
As waves splash around,
The small little baby,
Laughs out loud.

From far above,
The sun gives away,
To the dawning,
Of a glorious day.

When the moon comes out,
The sun goes down,
And the baby falls asleep,
Without a sound.
Chelsea Bolliger

Nostalgia

Carried along past
blurry fields of
Whitman grass,
I can think like nothing
close to significant
pondering.
The smell of this planet
sometimes haunts my
brain and shows me
visions
of a child,
late for dinner and
running through
September dusk,
attempting to fly
with every
third
step.
Charles Hosier

Is

Is there a God
To make some of us nice?
Is there a devil
To make the rest evil?

Is there a heaven
For some of us?
Is there a hell
For the rest?

Is there any pride
We can show? Or
Is it just shame?

Is there any love
We can give? Or
Is it just hatred?

Is there anything?
Or
Is there nothing?
Jennifer Cunningham

The Portrait

With this picture, I wish for you,
The best of life, in work or pleasure.
Whatever you hope to gain in life,
May this picture be one treasure.

In case you're ever lonesome,
Old friends no more you see.
When you really feel so down and out,
Just take a look at me.

My eyes will say I love you,
My smile will say the rest.
Whenever I wish a wish for you
You know it will be the best.

Maybe someday in the future years,
You really get disgusted.
I'll only ask of you one thing,
Please keep my picture dusted.

Jean Beckham Davis

North Minneapolis 6 P.M.

One, two,
three light steps
and off the craft,
combustion roars
trailing off
slanted light refract
in blue-grey haze
out of exhaust pipe,
hold breath, as always,
for
one, two,
three long seconds,
feel warm pavement
with my soles
and soak the sunlit calm
on an evening's threshold.

Sy Park

Our Loved Ones

Memories are treasures
time can never take away.
Surround yourself with happy ones
as you live each day.

You need not walk alone
when memory's door swing wide.
The memories of your loved ones
places them right by your side.

Our earthly homes are tempera,
we weren't meant to stay here forever.
Heaven is where our permanent home is
and God promise it will be better.

So believe in God's power,
his mercy, and his grace.
You'll see your love ones again soon
in that very special place.

Algie Tillery

The Angry Sea

Her bowels aflame
with quickening sludge
Her womb extant with vile seed
She thrusts her tongue
Against infested shores
Devouring all that offends
And desecrates her sovereignty.

Patricia A. Totten

Full Circle

Days grow short
The air holds a chill
Colors of autumn fade away

Snowflakes fall
Winds start to blow
Life turns over to sleep awhile

Lakes and streams freeze
Drifts grow high
All is still under the snow

Days soon lengthen
The sun warms the air
Movement of life stirs the earth

Sun shines hot
New beginnings grow tall
Harvest time is drawing near

Summer's bounty stored
Falls colors glow bright
Earth is readying for a rest

Days grow short
The air holds a chill

Jo Cheryl Sylvester

Sea Gull

Ah, to soar on wings like thine!
Rest there upon a crest of air
Dispel and space all time
Upon occasion rare

And veer, and deftly glide
Pillowed there on up swept draft
Dart swift among the tempest tide
and sweep through skies with billows
for my raft!

Kenneth R. Hayes

Somewhere, Sometimes, Somehow

Somewhere among the noises
Of chatter and small talk,
Between the laughter
Of the group,
My shadow walks.

Sometimes, while nodding and agreeing
On issues of the world,
My mind goes forth
To meet the breeze,
For it is bored.

Somehow, though still conversing
With giggles and bright eyes,
My thoughts find paths
So very strange,
Yet no one can surmise.

Marianne Bilicki Remishofsky

Ideas

Words escape me,
gone again!
Noisy syllables
left the pen.

Mind-gates opened.
Swish! They're out!
Soft silence of pure concept
runs about!

Carol Kingsley

Life's Little Trip

Here I go,
down I fall
enjoy the ride
can't do it twice
see the sights
take the trip
down I fall
enjoy the ride
can I go on?
Take the plunge
down I fall
enjoy the ride
prepare to die
lie down and sleep
don't ask why
no need to know
why no one cries
take a trip
the bottom I've hit
I sure enjoyed the ride

Robert Anderson

The Time Has Come

The time has come,
there is a pulling in my loins
a warm sensation spelling down my legs,
the time has come.
A flood of doubts, fears, hopes, dreams
no time for that now,
I Yell the time has come.
With each flood of pain
I count the hours, minutes, seconds,
Oh God please make it stop.
The time is not now
the gentle voice tells me.
I'm so tired
the time is close.
I hear that gentle voice say,
the time is Now.
I give it all the strength my body has.
I hear a scream, I look up
the time has come
my son is here, my son has come at last.

M. Eileen Reilly

Another

If she loves me not,
must I find another flower?
If she loves me not,
must I wait another hour?
If she loves me not
can I find in my heart,
if she loves me not,
the courage to part.
If she loves me not,
then what shall I do
I shall find another flower
and pull petals every hour.
She loves me, she loves me not.
She loves me, she loves me not.
She loves me.

Chris Burke

Pursuit of Happiness

The years go by
The years go best
As we go about our everlasting quest
For unending happiness
Marilyn A. Martin

Untitled

Here I am alone again.
No one to talk to, only the shadows.
Looking around I find nothing.

My mind is a blank piece of paper.
Nothing spoken.
Nothing ever.

Can you feel the emptiness?
Can you feel the loneliness?

Locked doors, trapped inside,
Nowhere to go, except for my mind.

Who's good? Who's bad?
What's left from what we had?

I didn't choose you, you chose me.
So...what am I supposed to be?

It doesn't bother me,
If it doesn't bother you.
So...what am I supposed to do?

You chose me, I didn't choose you.
If you had loved me.
I would have loved you.
Laura Hathaway

Miss You

Out into the sea, my eyes did stray,
Looking for someone who has gone away.
Seeking out thoughts and memories of you,
Asking the future, please, what can I do.
Oh, friend of mine, I will not scorn,
It was meant to be, for someone else, you were born.
I'll watch through eternity, for it may be;
That you'll never return, to my side by the sea.
Nicholas Roman

Be Aware My Brother

Be aware my brother
The future is near
Be aware my brother
The picture is very clear
Be aware my brother
Life is too short
Be aware my brother
We need each others support
Be aware my brother
Envision and see
Be aware my brother
You can be whom ever you want to be!
Michelle Hillman

The Jailer

Hate imprisoned many years
longs to seek revenge,
careful planning to escape
makes a living real intense.
Planning oh so carefully
what will hurt the most,
the tongue we choose as a weapon
and we have no remorse.
Cutting deep and mercilessly
the words destroying now,
aiming at its victim
we think brings peace somehow.
Oh tormented foolish mind
The jailer holds the key,
you caused your own imprisonment
when will you set me free.
Hannelore Grantham

The Pain Is Hard

The rain comes down
and hits the window
very hard and runs to
blood deep red blood
that runs down to
the ground and run
it to a deep river of
blood that goes to
my heart that's in
deep hard pain
Christina Fontaine

Compensation

Oh how can I repay you Spring
For all the happiness you bring
To me a creature filled with greed
To gaze upon each bush and weed,
And watch each bud burst out in flower
And feel the trees above me tower,
Or wander through a forest deep
To watch the fuzzy creatures creep,
Or see a tiny squirrel so meek
And feel the rain upon my cheek.
To watch a tiny sparrow try
To make his way up toward the sky.
I love the Spring!
I love the sod,
For they have brought me
Near to God!
Mary J. Reid

The Dream

In my mind I see her near
Every second her voice I hear
Yet I know she's fading fast
I know her words will never last
Her warm embrace I long to feel
My poor heart I know she'll steal
Does she wonder, does she care
Does she long to be with me
Will she share the dream I see.
Christopher Rychlik

Picture

I've heard it's been said before
That friendship lasts forever
And we may count it all joy
Upon knowing this special person

But what of these moments
When emptiness fills my soul
As each goodbye tears you away
And carries you into eternity

I find no solace in forgotten words
Or ramblings of an old acquaintance
Frantically, I search for a token
To keep you closer than you are

From the bottom of a musty box
I hold a solitary vision
It alone provokes my thoughts
Remembering a thousand memories

If only, I guess it is for not
To wish for what I may not have
You and I here together
As I hold tight... this picture
Todd Brickman

Have You Ever...

Have you ever wanted to write?
Have you ever wanted to play?
Have you ever made such a racket,
That you had to be sent away?

Have you ever lived with a stranger,
Because your parents have passed away?
Or have you ever flown to Africa,
To meet your Great-Aunt May?

Have you ever been in a fire?
Or swung on a giant trapeze?
Have you ever met George Washington,
And blew it by making him sneeze?

Some of these things are impossible,
But some are as easy as cheese,
So keep your eyes on the lookout,
Since you might be scared-or pleased!!!
Ellen Mikowychok

Life

Life is bitter
And sometimes sweet
You may wonder
Who you will meet
But if you look to
the stars above,
You will see god Almighty's love.
For if you put your trust in him.
You will know that you can win.
Carolyn Freda

From Whence I Come

To the elements of the earth
I go.
Back to mother nature who
helped create me.
My body will mix with the
soil, and my soul will be
lifted above.
For I will never die or
leave this earth til
God be decided.
F. E. Colmus

Not Forgotten

The years are rolling by dear Dad,
   and I am growing older.
I remember all the years with you,
   and tears upon your shoulder.

You always seemed to understand,
   the things I've said and done.
The heartaches that I've caused you,
   and the many times of fun.

I haven't been a thoughtful child,
   these years I've been away.
Nor even as I was growing up,
   I guess most folks would say.

But there is sure a special spot,
   inside this heart of mine
That overflows with love for you,
   and I'm sure that's a sign

That even though the years roll by,
   and seldom do you hear.
I've not forgotten you at all
   I'll always love you dear.
Edna M. Williams

The Painful Rain

The drenching rain
   with a vengeance came
   and poured upon my heart
   The wrenching pain
   tore life apart
   never again to be the same

A soul was shattered
   and unchained that day
   from the rain that battered
   and washed dreams away
   leaving me grieving
   with eyes not seeing
   the future that was to be
Mary Ellen Rice

My Soldier's Pain

Wet rivers of pain flow
Gently down his face.
They stain his cheeks,
Once perfectly brown.
Now dry and cracked
With frustration,
Betrayal,
Anguish,
...defeat.
June Wright

Pat

I like it when you're near
My love will always be here,
When you need to talk call on me
Hateful to you I'll never be

So flex those big muscles
Come to me and we'll wrestle
Show off that sexy bod,
I'll make you feel like God

Everything about you,
Everything you do,
Makes me love you as you can see,
The way you smile, kiss, and hold me
Stacy Harman

A Mother's Dilemma

The smell of death is in the air.
The pain of waiting, agony, despair.
A mother's cry.
A baby's silence, deafening.
Loneliness.
No words for comfort.
Another death to come.
A mother's cry to be her last one.
The smell of death is in the air.
No one to mourn.
No one to care.
Kathy P. Johnson

Soul Mates

Enter
there is little pain.
Moving
graceful, rhythmical
the pace quickens.
There's a gasp for air,
nails digging into flesh
in mid-air
souls collide, then descend.
Exit
exhausted
overcome by sleep.
Lynn P. Duffy

Trying To Forget

Can I run or can I hide
from the pain and fear I feel inside.
Can I bury it deep down below
and try my best to not let it show,
Should I fight this pain myself,
and try to make it go or will I
only be letting anger build down
inside my soul.
Why can't I just forget it!
And put it out of my mind, or will
all the pain and fear I felt.
Come back to me another time.
And if it does, will I wonder.
Why didn't I
just let go of the pain along time ago,
Instead of putting up a front
and pretending it doesn't show.
Kimberly Burton Crabtree

Angels Of Darkness

The clouds roll over the sun
Darkening the horizon.
A symmetrical angel
dancing in a chlorine dream.
The rain slowly dripping
down my body.
A nearby puddle
with the reflection
of a different face.
The moonlight starts
to shine
A crazed spirit
howls in excitement
finally the creatures
of night awake.
Wendi Alvarado

Sunflowers

Sunflowers have a little touch
of everything. The petals have a
light touch of sun, so they keep
blooming. The center has a big
touch of life. As the sunflower
gets heavier, it gets full of life.
The stem has a touch of proudness.
Proud to hold a sunflower full of life.
Sunflowers have a touch of everything.
Jessica Evans

Seasons

A tree raises its branches
   toward the sky.

Its leaves fall to the ground
   like tears.

The wind blows and blows.
The tree cries and cries,
   till the last tear falls.

Swaying and rocking in the wind.
The tree slowly falls asleep.

Winter comes and the tree
   is in peace.
Peacefully waiting in deep slumber,
   for spring to show its face.
Jennifer Tetirick

Not Far Apart

Days slipped into nights,
minutes seemed like hours;
All I could think of was you,
near but out of my power.
Then something happened
we found a few minutes alone,
I found myself kissing you
whispering in soft tones.
I'll cherish this memory
forever in my heart,
and no matter how far away we are
we're still not far apart.
Cindy Jimenez

Tears Of Rain

Breaths of fire,
hear my calling.
Tears of rain,
taunt me.
Chill of the air,
fills me.
I shudder as the tears of rain,
turn to tears from my eyes.
The emptiness of the world around me,
becomes realized.
Soon I become surrounded by emotions.
I fall to the ground,
hugging my knees to my body.
Tears from the sky,
tears from my eyes,
become more frequent.
Maybe good will come to me.
Maybe dreams will come true.
For now,
only time will tell.
Jill Chouinard

The Future Is Coming Now

The future is coming now
Now problems fill up each day,
Day gives little contentment
Contentment which does not stay

Stay when we are innocent
Innocent, not ever free,
Free to escape our troubles
Troubles that won't let us be

Be someone who is content
Content that good times are here,
Here to provide us with warmth
Warmth from the coldness of fear

Fear now stalks everyone
Everyone knows not how,
How joy can fill the future
The future is coming now.

Roger Pao

Dawn's Day

The dawn was bright and beautiful
Springtime was in the air,
Winter's end had come at last
The day was warm and fair.

The dogwood trees were blooming
Their fragrance sweet and light,
Tulips bending in the breeze
Some hummingbirds in flight.

Now as I stand and look around
His wonders to behold,
I have no doubts within my heart
That God is in control.

Kitty Ramsey

A New Day

Hear the cheers, from mother earth,
without a tear, she gave birth,
To a new and wonderful day.
She likes it that way.
The rain falls, so dainty,
Like in melody, to my ears.
The music is like a painting
which I can see through my tears.

Faye Takamatsu

Gemini

Gemini, who am I
To dwell on your charms?
I can see you're not free
To come to my arms.

You are fair with an air
Of wildness and grace;
And you seem, when I dream,
To join my embrace.

In the morn, quite forlorn,
I awake to the dawn.
Gemini, then I sigh
For my dream lover, gone.

Alfred G. Rockefeller

Summer

School's not fun.
It's kind of a bummer.
But then it's all over,
and along comes Summer.
You awake in the morning
and out comes the sun.
So you run outside,
and begin to have fun.
The days are long
and never seem to end.
While you're playing and jumping,
with your very best friend.
We were very hot
and wanted to get cool.
So we put on our suits,
and jumped in the pool.
Throughout the Summer,
we had a ball.
Time passed quickly,
and suddenly, it's Fall!

Elizabeth Heider

Untitled

Tonka tickles tiny toes together
To torture ticklish tigers
Tonka lives in Toon Town to play
tennis. Tonka Tickles me too.

Kevin Delaughter

What Happened

We were friends
and once even more.
Then something changed,
and we were friends no more,
What happened?

We could laugh
joke and even talk
about anything. Then
like a flash everything
changed for the bad. I once
said our friendship would change.
What happened?

What ever happened
wasn't for the best,
it went to worse. It's in
the past, and happened
really fast. I miss
the way it was.
What happened?

Stacy McTaggart

Stability

Escaping to inward
Stability
While exiting life's
realities
creates in one
humility
Which escalates
ability
Thus causing
mobility

Veronica Elaine Smith

The Church Bell Tolls

The church bell tolls
in my ear
as I see the approaching wave
Dear me, Dear God
My friend's husband's lost
and daddy won't come home again
this sorrow is as never ends
the church bell tolls again.

Rebecca A. Sauve

For My Sister - Doris

For Mother's Day, I wrote this little
  missive just for you,
Cause it is very special and I think
  that you are too.
You're such a special mother, and
  you have been through the years...
So wonderful to everyone, in spite
  of all the tears.
And as a friend and mother too,
  I'm grateful as can be...
To have a sister and a pal,
  who's everything to me!
God blesses you and cares for you,
  in everything you do...
And just remember every day how
  much that I love you!

Barbara J. Watz

"Angie"

There is a girl named Angie,
She is sweet as Candy.
Blue blue eyes, as the sky,
Strawberry hair,
She doesn't care.
10 little toes, and a button nose.
No one knows, how much I love her.
She has chubby cheeks,
  and sometimes streaks.
That's my sweet little Angie.

Diane Showerman

Untitled

Life in the end is worth living
Her days on earth were giving
When I pray at night
I pray she'll be alright
For all her pain and grief
I feel there is full relief
Where I use to think and frown
Now I hear a beautiful sound
From all the world's things
In my heart, she will always sing
I'm glad to finally know
And, at last, can let her go
For now I can sleep through the night
Because I know I'll be alright
There is a lot of love to be giving
For life in the end is worth living

Katherine Fountaine

A New Life

My mind, heart, and soul hang together heavy
with a common thread of confusion and despair.

Time moves through and beyond me
as I patiently await.

One day into the next
draws me closer to my destiny...

Peace — that will shine bright enough to overcome
the shadows thrown by fate upon my soul.
Michele M. Pavlik

The Sun Comes And Goes

It's raining
It's pouring
As I sit at my window
Waiting for morning
Time is going by ever so slow
Soon the rain turns into snow
I look out as far as I can see
Waiting for the sun
To make its first look at me
As I wait hardly a sound is made
Just a tic and a toc
As each second begins to fade
As always though the sun will make its round
It will sneak up on us all
Without the slightest sound
Soon night will become day
And as time passes
The sun will be on its way
It will eventually be out of sight
And like the beginning, there won't be a spec of light
Larry Votruba Jr.

One Made It On Through

The Colorado Avalanche line-up
has proven to all that they are for real
With blood, sweat, and tears....and the Stanley Cup
they're now established as the "AV's of Steel"
They came from Quebec, these former Nordiques
avoiding certain financial shipwreck
Here, they found fortunes with fans a team seeks
all I can say is, we thank you Quebec!
Oh what a treasure! What a dream come true;
a championship team for deserving fans
Deep down in the heart, these ardent fans knew
we'd cheer a world title, given the chance
The Broncos, The Nuggets, and The Rockies
got to see first-hand what 1st place can do
With the best fans here (and who disagrees)
it's only fitting, one made it on through
All in good time, though, I anticipate
such an achievement can be contagious
Our other loved teams now evaluate
this realization a stimulus
Bob G. Martinez

Exotic Flowers

We are but exotic flowers -
Pinks, reds, yellows, greens, blues.
All requiring an intricate necessity.
Petals closed, slowly spreading to uncertainty.
Finding accepting air -
The free thrill of living.
Torn suddenly by pelting droplets.
Folding in once again,
Learning and relearning the wrath of happiness.
Amanda Fields

Old Soldiers

They fought for our freedom-but do we stop and give thanks
for the sacrifices made from our people of every rank.
We live in a free country and it has nothing to do with luck
when it came time to fight the battle they never passed the buck.
They stood tall and held their ground-no matter what the price
Old Glory was at stake-they never rolled the dice.
The gamble would be for America and the right to live in peace
they fought it for you and me-they deserve our respect-at least.
Some fought for other countries-hoping to set them free-
but the wheels of justice turned them back and they were left to flee.
Some battle scars are outside-obvious to the eye
others are buried within the soul where they will forever lie.
Take time to listen to a veteran-if they have a story to tell
find out why you're living free and not a life of hell.
Shake their hand and thank them-look them in the eye-
it took guts and courage to go that extra mile.
Never take for granted this land of the free-
could we call it home of the brave-if left up to you and me.
When you see Old Glory waving-look at it and smile
many Americans lost their lives so we could feel that pride.
Bobbie Lee Harris

Cigarettes!

Cigarettes are a drug,
They control me from above,
I never get enough,
They can call my bluff,
I dream of them,
And do anything for them,
Cigarettes stay on my mind,
They use up most of my time,
Sometimes I feel like it's a crime.
If I had a dollar,
For every time cigarettes made me holler,
Then it wouldn't be a bother.
I need them,
I want them,
I can't live without them.
They've taken over my life,
For the rest of my life,
They are a deadly love,
They call me from above,
And that's why they are a drug.
Misty Bowman

To Feel, To Love, To Share...

It is not that I hate nor that I distrust.
But that I am in pain.
I have been lanced through the heart,
from which blood flows and cannot stop.
My soul weeps.
And yet my mind through blurry eyes
seeks for that special one to heal the flow
and stay the blood.
To feel and not know pain.
To love and not know emptiness.
To share and not be used.
To be one and not be apart.
A desire unfulfilled leaves only need,
to lay asunder even the staunchest heart.
A need that yet brings about hope
to search again.
Robert Terry Sweeney

There Was A Man

A man sang peace as sweet as a lark,
And then one day someone lurks in the dark.

A rifle he carries in his hand,
And with this weapon he kills a man.

The weeping is not heard above the shouts,
Let's riot and seek these white pigs out.

Destroy, destroy, wreck, and kill.
Little do they realize that they destroy his will.

The feelings between these races are great.
The riots and protests we all must face
Are due to a few hot headed thugs,
Who feel they are being stepped on like rugs.

The world is a mess! It is at war
Not only with foreigners, but with the people next door.

When will people grow up and face
That colour is the only difference in the human race.

Now listen people and hear me well,
Both races, forget your colour and try to dwell,
On helping, aiding and loving peace
Follow your heart and soul, not your mouth and your anger.
Karen R. Clarke

Untitled

Trying to fit my dreams into words,
finding no words intense enough;
what was the story I once heard,
the one dealing with the exotic birds?
I have carried my dreams with me,
faded they have not,
to the far off land I am destined;
this story, this story I have sought!
Remind me of why I have continued through these years,
the enigmas of life often distract;
the memory, the more I ponder it nears!
Around myself I have built many fences, like a shield;
that story - I feel it brushing the tips of my senses!
The chances I took, there was always a price,
my dreams have come true;
the peacocks exiled from Paradise!
Michelle Leedy

Here Is My Heart

Here is my heart - to rest in when you will,
 Thrilling beneath the beauty of your eyes!
Beating a lovely ballad, Dear, until
 I see you coming my way, gypsy wise!

Here are my lips to wear upon your hair,
 When stars are twinkling in the sea of night!
Look down love's moonlit highway, I'll be there,
 Calling to you, across the murmuring light!

Days will be wingless birds when I am gone.
 Night will be as sweet song, out of tune!
Dawn will be hard to rise and gaze upon,
 When dawn, and dusk and night were such a boon!

Here is my heart, to do with what you may.
 I will not need it, while I am away.
Margaret S. Wright

The Perfect Love

Our everlasting love is what my memory is made of,
our enticing challenge,
from what our love was never damaged,
your heart warming smile from morning 'till night,
is all I needed to get things right,
your alluring scene that you sent to me,
was all that I needed to finally see,
The touch of your hand against my skin,
was more than enough to take me in,
The affectionate warmth of your embrace,
Was surely more than enough to brighten up my face,
The amiable attraction that you gave to me,
Was truly enough to let my love be,
As I see you come shining through,
I began to see that our love is true,
Now I want you to see that you're my desirable love,
The one that I've always been dreaming of,
you're the one that I have in my heart,
And from now on we'll never part,
So let's love each other like we did from the start.
Emprise S. Lett

Nature's Bounty

The breath, warmth and awakening of spring
The glisten of sun on a pheasant's wing.

The peace and solitude of walks on country roads
The breath that stirs and rustles in the summer woods.

The bending of dry grass in September's breeze
The riot of color on autumn leaves.

The ripple of a stream across a golden plain
The cooling freshness of falling rain.

The love and laughter, the tender bliss
The glory an ecstasy of love's first kiss

As a thirsty doe from the river sips
So I too a brimming cup raise to my lips.

My mind shall ever cherish images of earth and sky
Like a glorious pageant parading by.
Frances Ruth Rhodes

A Rose

There's a rose straight from my heart
unto a rose so dear
and with it is a wish for you
that you might know much cheer
And with this cheer, the many singles
That lights your eyes so bright
For on this earth I can't recall
A more fantastic sight
This teddy bear I also send
That you may surely know
You've ever tender in my heart
No matter where I go
As roses are so beautiful and smell so very sweet

So are you too, a precious thing that makes my life complete
So on your Trojan white horse, lots of joy
I wish you dear in love
And ask the Lord to bless your heart from heaven up above
I also hope with all my heart so tender and so true
That every wish you make today that God would grant to you
For you're the rose of my dear heart and thus you'll always be
A special sweet and beauty true especially to me
Gloria Hayward

The Child

Homes are destroyed by divorce and greed
Little children are pulled on both sides in between
Parents don't care what their children need
Just so everything goes the way they want it to be
When something goes wrong in their child's life
They complain and say it's the child's fault
They can't put the blame where the blame belongs
Because they are the ones who broke up the home.
A child is a gift sent down from above
It was loaned to us to nourish and love
To teach it respect and the ways of our Lord
To make it happy and secure in its home
A child is more precious than silver and gold
In the eyes of God it's a sight to behold.
It is a bud from the Master's Bouquet
So give your child a big hug and kiss today
Let them know about our Lord Jesus Christ
How he hung on the cross and bled and died
Teach them the way that they should be taught
Stay together and raise them in a happy home.

Querita Marvel

A Wonderful Friend Are You

You have been a friend to me
When others refused to see
That all I want is someone
Whose friendship is given
And does not have to be won.

You have always been there
When others seem not to care.
You have come with and open heart
Never trying to pull apart
The relationship that we have formed.

I hope that our friendship never ends.
I hope that we remain forever friends.
Please remember, forever more.
That mine is always an open door.

With these words from my heart
I hope that if our friendship ever starts
To fall down or break apart,
You will remember through it all
My love, in friendship, will never fall.

Joseph W. Fincher

Forgotten Insanities

Lost
Staring through the eyes of the innocent
Fumbling the thoughts of the insane
Remembering what was once forgotten
Looking back after time has consumed what once stood proud
Now frail and crumbled
As a lie told long ago
Forgotten among the many
A nameless face with an endless story
Looked upon and shunned

Whispers in the wind turning to cries of anger inside my head
Coursing through my veins
Never to be spoken beyond the mind
Blinded by ignorance
Unwilling to understand
Fighting to calm the war within
To tame the child inside
Bringing peace to the unknowing
Only to find the innocence that should not be
crying in vain

Heather L. Tefft

I Wonder

I wonder if the angels move the clouds around each day
To cause the rain to fall in the most advantageous way
To help the farmers grow the seed to keep us all from want and need
   I wonder if?
I wonder if they guard our cars as on the road we go.
And keep us from an accident that from the car would throw
Our bodies into wrenching pain or maybe even death
   I wonder if?
I wonder if they nudge us to keep us from harm's way
Or whisper in our ears some words which we should say
And remind us that it matters much when we have gone astray
   I wonder if?
Some day we'll clearly understand just what the angels do
   Till then we'll be most thankful
      That they watch over me and you.

Norma J. Hall

Cedar, Oaks And Pines

A grove of Cedar Oak and Pines
Together stand the test of time
Standing strong against the wind
They burst with life from within
With twisted trunks and barren branches
They'll bloom again when spring advances
Together they stand the test of time
This grove of Cedar, Oak and Pines

Lana Farnum

Her Voice

As when the sun the drowsy eyes of morn
Awakes, and from its cot the new day starts,
And to each being the warmth of light is borne
To set atremble all the yearning arts
That lie therein; as when the absent rain
Has too long left the earth to dry and burn,
Has parched and shrivelled life in ugly pain,
Then falls, and all drinks in its kind return;
So I leap up and eagerly rejoice,
When to my ear in lilting cadence falls
The bubbling melody of such a voice
As must forever sound in joyous halls.

It is Matilda come to share with me
Her charming self, her sweet simplicity.

Kenneth R. Brown

The Smiling Stranger

In the day he is congenial, and always wears a smile,
Graciously he tells me, "come for just a while,
For there is much you've never tried or seen,
Let me assure you, I can still fulfill your dreams,
I shall make you worldly, wealthy, and wise,
You can do great things with me at your side,"
But in the dark of night, he cannot resist,
He grabs my heart with his evil angry fist,
"You are alone now, and will always be,
I am waiting for you and you must come to me,
In your future, lies only pain and tears,
Why go on? There is no one who really cares,"
Then gently, slowly, comes a wondrous mist,
The dreadful, the terror, cannot coexist,
A sight beyond compare fills my lonely room,
"My child," He said, "I heard your prayer and came as soon,
For your commitment unto Me will keep you safe eternally,
And anywhere you may go, I will forever be,
Just turn around, look back and see....,"
The evil one..., and all his threats..., had simply ceased to be.

Laura Knight

Vacation

As I stand here on this porch,
and watch down touch the sky.
I wonder just how very close,
   to God, am I.
Up high on this mountain,
in a cabin in the clouds
down below in the valley,
   among the rushing crowds
In the great Smokey Mountains
on vacation with my brother and his wife
They have helped give me memories,
that I'll carry all my life
I have seen the proud Cherokee,
and watched a small humming bird.
And a stream in the mountains
is among the many things I've heard.
And I write this to thank you,
for memories so very fine,
The Great Smokey Mountains
   and cabin in no. 9
Henrietta Glover

Why

People are running, People are running everywhere, Why?
   The Lord has descended from the sky.
I look up at His brightly glowing and majestic figure
   As He stands on top of the mountain,
   His arms stretched a mile high.

People are running, People are running everywhere, Why?
   I watch the amazement and ah, are you afraid
   because you've told a lie.
I think to myself, don't you run, don't hide, He has come,
   to take you up on high.

People are running, People are running everywhere, Why?
   The air is clean and calm, not a scent to smell,
   Oh my!
People are running, People are running, as the sky dims,
   and it dims, and it dims....it's dark.
   Don't ask Why!?
Virgil A. Long

Falling

Watching the snow fall in mad rushes to the earth, I wonder why it is relaxing.
In reality, it is pure chaos.
Thousands of frozen rain drops, spinning, twirling, plummeting to the ground in relentless motion. I realize it is kind of like life.

I guess I'm staring out the window now to try and find myself in the crowd.
Maybe I was the one that hit the window and exploded apart;
Maybe I was the one over there that fell to the earth softly, unheard.
It is a lot like life...starting out like a roaring storm and ending abruptly, without explanation...in a whisper.
Their dances, sometimes moving in similar fluctuation,
other times in explosive disunity.
Yet altogether beautiful.
Suddenly, a gust of wind comes by and whisks away a pile of snowflakes...all huddled in a corner.
Once together, they are now apart...never to find each other again, unless by chance.
Blown apart by the same forces that brought them together.
Once again I wonder why it is relaxing.
Amanda Leigh Marie Mele

Delicate Beauty

It seems that life can pass us by
As we try to achieve a status of living
The precious freedoms we were taught as children
In these times are unforgiving
To take the time to smell a rose as so often heard in song
Might be seen today as laziness - hurry, hurry move along
I took some time today, though I had much to do
To sit a while on my front porch, and my eyes began to view
The wondrous pleasures of creation, that only God can do
The delicate opening of a flower, the shading of its colors
I imagined God's creative hand, like an artist with his prelate
Stroking here, dabbing there, a wondrous sight to see
A perfect sense of peacefulness soon enveloped me
All the problems that were weighing on my heart and soul today
Soon began to focus, as my tears washed them away
It seem I found some answer, by taking time to see
Such delicate beauty in his work, was freedom just for me.
Yvonne Shook

Joy For The Journey

Once I was enslaved like a prisoner in chains,
In emotional despair and turmoil I was bound;

When God released me from all of my pain,
He offered the Key, and Love was found;

Though I felt I could no longer cope,
And it seemed like there was no solution;

His Word revealed a ray of heavenly hope;
And inspired me and granted eternal resolution;

Through Christ, God provided total forgiveness,
Like a slate wiped clean, I was then set free;

His grace and mercy are pure and timeless;
And are forever offered for you and for me;

So in times of grief, when you seek internal peace;
And need to press on with hope and perseverance;

His wisdom and guidance can yield eternal release;
As you claim God's love and strength for endurance;

And let His wise and all-powerful arms of comfort,
Reach out and direct your paths and grant security;

Then you will know that our Lord is a true Stalwart;
When you experience serenity and joy for the journey.
Jeanne Hart

Angel Eyes

Have you ever looked into the eyes of an angel?
Sure you have.
You looked into them when the doctor handed her to you and said, "It's a Girl!"
You looked into them as you breast fed him for the first time.
You looked into them as you watched them twinkle in awe at the Christmas lights.
You look into an angel's eyes every day they look at you and say, "I love you, Mommy."
You look into an angel's eyes when you do something he finds heroic and he looks up and says, "I was to be just like you, Daddy!"
You look into an angel's eyes every day look at your child, take their little hands in yours and thank God for little miracles.
Take the time every day to look in that angel's eyes and tell them you love 'em.
You can never tell your child enough that they mean the world to you.
Sharon E. Blanton

Sand And Leaves (Chicano Politics)

Sing song of the tree on the hill on the side of a desert flat.

The clouds come to feed the tree and wash the hill.
But I am of the desert, forsaken and lost
but close enough, yes close enough to see what we miss.

Filled with love, with life green leaves and branches plump with water
the face of God shines on.

Heavy and hot, with the unrelenting face of the sun smashing down,
too paranoid to look away for fear that we might go unpunished.

On this side of the hill we do wish to climb
but hand hold after hand hold our sandy fingers fail to grasp.

In hate we wish the lightning to strike the tree
but not even a million pieces of sand can change the world.

No we did not set up the way that the tree grows, or the fall of the
rain, we simply feed off the water that flows down the hill.
Dirty water, almost as thick as mud, we curse the soil, and pray
for clear rain. Drinking what the tree will not have.

None have dreams of climbing the hill anymore.
We only look at the tree in envy, and ask "Why is a tree a tree
and the desert so dry?"
But no, a million pieces of sand cannot be a tree
No, a million pieces of sand can't change the world.
Matthew T. Watson

Season Of My Wanting

Hot, moist wisps of summer's air,
Bathe, soothe me with thy fare.
Cleanse me through, naught to spare,
For this,
The season of my wanting.

Sun, burst white at heaven's door,
At thy rise tis dark no more.
Give to earth sweet warmth to store,
This,
The season of my wanting.

To dust, oh heart, you will endure,
Passing time in life's allure.
Struggling faint to make pure,
This,
The season of my wanting.

Oh, fleeting glimpse of youth's love song,
Until my last, I e'er will long,
To find, to feel one spirit, strong,
In this,
The season of my wanting.
Steve Etheridge

The Love Poem

Love is like a little flower,
It blooms everyday.
When you're feeling lonely,
it always finds your way.
When you think love is gone,
and you're feeling kind of down,
just look inside your heart and love will come around.
Maybe sometimes you feel sad,
but it's not from the lack of love.
Clouds are always hovering over you from the spirits up above.
Love will never leave you,
if you stay aware,
because love is like people,
it comes in different pairs.
Kristina Downing

Big-Al

He greets you with a strong right hand
Then he'll ask you do you know the man!
Then he'll say that God loves you! And he loves me too!
Brother have you've been praying for me today! This is what he'll say
He's a friend, he's a pal, his name is "big Al"!

He'll tell you I'm not afraid of anything or any man!
Because I have an angel and God on my right hand.
While I'm driving my truck along the way Please!
Brother pray for me today.
Keep the hot line open until we meet again,
He's a friend, he's a Pal, his name is "Big Al"!

He'll tell you I love the Lord! I love you, too.
Jesus died for me and you!
He'll tell you I've got a prayer garden at home.
I'll pray for you when I'm alone.
That's where I'll find peace of mind.
And the Lord is with you all the time.
If you've got troubles here or at home.
I've got your name on a stone. He always makes my Day!
This is what he'll say.
I'm a friend, I'm a pal, my name is "Big Al"!
Johnny Welch

"Destiny"

On this untrodden path of destiny I travel alone,
I have no guide, my destination is unknown.
They head down their smooth traveled road,
Enemies, Friends, Strangers, travel their way below.
They travel downstream, the wind at their back,
They travel with the ease that I somehow lack.

I struggle onward, with their voices in my ear,
Traveling forward, through this foreign air.
Temptations to turn back, for ahead there is fear.
What lies ahead, behind me, they do not care.

I fight to finish my journey unknown.
Against the voices, the wind, the inner fear.
For what drives me inside, no one can hear.
For in this journey, this destiny, I must travel...alone.
John A. Bambenek

Journey Of A Moment's Dream

I've sailed a ship into heaven.
Resting only for a moment's dream.
Pale yellow is the sun.
The fading is in blue.
Auburn is the gray.

I've yearned for likely spots poured over my soul.
The gray is blown when life is gone.

I've sailed a sunset in my dreams.
Partly gone and partly seen.
Piped through a velvet song - pretty and clean.
I parted the cleaner.
I'm neater still.

Forgotten was that journey until I saw this hill.
Yonder it beckons me on.
Don't flitter away this time.
Parting will soon appear.

I've craved that time again.
The hope lived on, breathing within my soul.
Carpenters built first this longing, this forgotten shore.
Question it I must, for I am to bare one day less without it.
Loraine S. Reynoso

Please! Congress! Please!

Once upon a time life was land, trees, plants, cows and chickens
Dine and recline with peace of mind if you worked like the dickens
But the leaders, mostly of war, win or lose, grabbed for it all
The others dug-in and tried to fight this awful selfish regal haul

They found power in their crafts, unionized, they had a shaft
They grouped to revere God and shared the dignity of the Lord
With perseverance, Democracy was born to give the World, DAWN

Respect for one and all, common-sense made law, no stinking war
All to Vote, to elect able leaders to run things and get them more

Now upon a time it is elements, energy and the joy of electricity
With wonderful tho perilous advances by and for work more witty
"Scary Witty" a ditty of pity for less security than land's solidity

Advances, niceties, costly products and services become necessities
Gain, reflecting contribution is human nature and sacrosanct
Leaders get theirs as they should, leaders should enjoy their rank
The unable and unmoral with guidance and restraint savor the tank
But Mister and Missis who really make us go, get a Big Big Whoa!

They get it not, we plan it not, but hope that taxes fill this slot
Look to it America, civilization is on the line, let's not shirk
We can swing it, it is only a matter of happy fulfilling work

George K. Marshall

Lonely Night "Holy Night"

As I look out the window,
On this cold and windy night.
I see emptiness and darkness,
But, yet a star still shines bright
Lost for words, and relaxing dreams.
Vanishing, completely before my eyes.
I whisper softly, as I low down to my knees
To pray and ask Jesus, to watch over me.
As the Angels sing loudly, a gentle voice appears,
Saying listen and join in, there is no fear
Where I am near.
I knew it had to be Jesus,
That answered me tonight.
For I felt his presence,
And the song was "Silent Night"....

— Steven Vogel

To The One I Abused

When I had first enticed you,
it was of your will to be with me.

You held me within the dimness of lights,
we danced to the softest of music,
in a place where misery was company.

It was when you had become confident within yourself.
That you like many others had abused my joy.

I allowed for you to think you could get away with it,
meanwhile, your relationship with your loved ones -
was what I had destroyed.

I did not care about your status,
and that your family needed you.

I had assumed that you knew,
what you were getting yourself into.

And once it came to the point that you could not afford me anymore,
you did exactly what I knew you would.

Very few were strong enough to leave me,
I've always doubted that you could.

This is the bottom line,
the truth, that you always knew.

From our beginning to our end, I've never cared for you!

Ronald E. Smith Jr.

When I Can't Go On

The walk seems longer, the back steps seems steeper,
when did I get old and my knees stiff?

Harsh words still hurt, but he usually doesn't remember the next day.
So forgive and forget, every day is new and God's full of mercy and
forever true. Stop and think before you're so quick to speak.
It could be the last things you'll ever say to the one you love.
So my advice is forgive and forget and...
The walk won't seem so long, the back steps not so steep
and the knees will be strengthened.
You'll discover you're not old after all.
You see, a heart that forgives is healthy and full of peace.
Which helps, because you see when I can't go on...
I go on anyway

Sherry Patterson

Treasure

There is a garden that I have known
It has a wonder all its own
From above branches adorned with flowers reach down
Falling below on the garden, glowing leaves shone
Weaving a pattern to behold
Tapestry of foliage and flowers to enfold
Hearts to acclaim a lasting memory
Applauding a cherished story.

Alas, it has gone away.
It was here the other day.
Who took my treasure away?
Why could it not stay?
The tapestry of foliage was a legacy
Descending from above, breath of mercy
Bouquet of green evermore
I will remember my departed splendor.

Lucia McBride

Missing You

What can I say or how do I begin
To say goodbye to the woman I loved and was my best friend?...
It's been five months since you passed away
Since you took your own life on a snowy March Day...
This is the hardest thing I've ever had to do
And that's trying to move on with a life without you...
The anger and pain is so hard to hide
Why didn't you tell me just what you felt inside...
I miss you more than words could ever say
And I wish I could move time back to that snowy March Day.
But what happened that day can never be erased
Just like no one in the world could ever take your place...
I want you to know that I'll be fine
And I'll look after the son you also left behind...
You stole my heart the day we first met
Those beautiful brown eyes I'll never forget...
This poem is from your Richard and dedicated to you
To tell my Tracy Lee I truly love you...
I miss you baby more than you know
And I'll always remember you, especially when it snows...

Rick Salvatore

Addiction

I ride a Tiger!
Laughing crazily, I dance upon a dagger's point,
Then dangle by my finger tips,
Screaming obscenities in the abyss of my own void.
Why am I not afraid!
  Why
   Am
    I
     Afraid?!
Dorothea Munsell

...Of Trumpets And Violins

Pat on the back apple of eye
Yet I see the worm cheap trick!
Perform for the man big Trumpet in hand
You only make real people sick

The good you do kept inside of you
No need for self praise a conscience trip
It's the Violin you choose as your sweet music soothes
Like prayers whispered from a child's lips

All our front, so loud and blunt
Your mouth is your piece and you shoot!
Strange little things, all air and no strings
Unless attached to what you do

Back of the crowd nor open or loud
The life you upheld spoke for you
You play from the heart never faking your part
Only seeking to make sorrows few

So... Listen up Trumpet
Check yourself close don't be a fool
Who needs good to boast for in the end
As we all must face Him...it's the Violin the world loved most.
   Ron Reno

Cocaine

The wheels have started to turn, the gears are set in emotion,
I will change your life from reality to a notion.
Standing on my throne, my crown of vengeance in my hand,
I step down and cast terror into those bleeding in the sand.
I will destroy your life, your dreams, your hope,
creating terror deep down in your soul until you can no longer cope.
I will own the air that you breathe, the blood in your veins,
you can't accuse me, for I am not the one to blame.
For like the grim reaper, your time has come,
you will hate yourself, maybe even take your own life, by
the time I am done.
Life can be so deceitful and full of pain,
while deep inside of you, I have control of your brain.
Weeping, sobbing, crumpled in your corner you beg
to know my name,
"Allow me to introduce myself, I am known as;
Cocaine."
   Sonnie Wade Roebuck

Inertia

Pacing like a tiger in a cage,
Not knowing what tomorrow will bring, and yet,
   still knowing...
Watching others on the outside from within
   your existence...
Waiting and watching is all you seem to know.

"Is this what others of my species experience?"
   you ask yourself. "Perhaps not", you answer.
Ever wondering how it feels to be free to come
   and go as you please.
Ever feeling as though there is more to life,
   "But what is it?"
Hoping to get out of this rut of life,
   "But how do I achieve it?"
Somehow, somewhere, someday.

"Why am I feeling this way?"
Must be inertia.
   Carol A. Socash

Home

I grew up with the wolves on the wild, rolling plains.
No troubles, no worries, no language, no names.
An endless forever of the cycle of life.
They watched me grow up and I watched them die.
There was no sorrow, it was all understood,
die if you must, live if you could.
I loved to read the art of the primitive man.
It taught me to think and to understand.
The walls were alive - animated with color.
I knew I was not wolf, but early man's brother.
Then came the man from the new, production age.
Set in to destroy, and took my home away.
They took me from my prairie - my heaven on this earth.
They tried to make me lady - they found out what that's worth.
They call it progress; I call it death.
My friends are not here, my mind laid them to rest.
Great memories are with me; they are all that remain,
of my life, my friends, my home on the plains.
   Stephanie Conrad

A Peace Of Mind

I try to find myself within me.
Letting my mind run rapidly and spirit run free.
Sometimes when I'm alone
I try to find my most inner thoughts,
My dreams, my goals are not at a halt,
Sometimes I'm captured by emotions
which has my mind explicitly uphold,
Sometimes the chamber of my self-conscious
reach beyond a story untold.
At times I try to render deep into my inner soul,
Embrace, by a moment of clarity, I'm in control.
It's said, "the key to memories is that they never escape".
The immortal value of it all is just that great.
I suppose I find myself at a
content, sensible moment, confined,
I found tranquility within a piece of mind.
   Robert Whitehead Jr.

No Longer Do They Wonder

Once they laid together attracted from the start;
Once they laid together, with a piece of each other's heart;
Once they laid together as man and woman should;
Once they laid together, and wondered if they really could.

People gaze and wonder why, two so different can be found;
Learning, sharing, feeling, and loving, while finding their
   common ground.

The joy has come in varied ways, so rapid, yet so clean;
A waterfall of trust and caring, the sprinkling mist of a couple's dream.

Oh God, if You played a part, then thanks for helping create this pair;
And bless them now and evermore, that life together they may share.

Love has overwhelmed them, and made life what life should be;
The thrill of waking up each day, knowing from unhappiness
   they are free.

For how can one ever suffer sadness and despair again;
When knowing the one so near is truly their best friend?
A lover, a mate, a partner, standing by their side,
There forever - through life's exciting ride.

Now they lay together attracted from the start;
Now they lay together with more than each other's heart;
Now they lay together as man and woman should;
Now, at last they lay together as before they wished they could.
   John Brooks

Silent Tears

The window looks out on the dimming day.
The breeze slowing, blowing the clouds away.
Birds nesting down for the coming dark,
But hearing, still, soft song of a lark.
I sit inside on my window seat.
Soft cushions beneath my tucked up feet.
I'm watching the closing of the day
And pray these tears wash the hurt away.
I mourn for dreams I thought would last.
But distance between us became so vast.
Our hearts forgot, what once we knew,
Once there was a me and you.

Risa Marie Goodwin

I Ask Thee

   As I sit alone thoughts race through my mind.
I wonder if I truly am alone in this place filled only with sorrow and despair.
I know no love, no pride, no joy that fills the soul.
My mind is filled with the thoughts and wonder of what might have been, if only these things I'd known.
I ask you my Lord, where is this love they spoke of upon my birth
The world is yours they said, the sun your light, the moon your guide, your fellow man be thy brother.
The deed is done, the miles I walked. The deed is done the scars I bear.
The horror I've seen, the death I've smelled, the lies I've heard
Your cloth I wear, the years I've given, thy deed is done.
I ask thee, why have you not taken me home yet?
The job is complete.
I ask you again, why have you not taken me home yet?
Please my Lord, heal my soul, tend my wounds.
I ask thee, take this one home and let him rest.

Chris Caviness

The Ocean

The ocean kissed me with foamy lips,
as it gently lapped at my feet
enticing me into its cool blue-green depths.
I came this far for just one glimpse,
a homecoming to this blue expanse.
I came to immerse myself in its peaceful rhythms.
It accepted me a long lost child enfolded me in
its watery womb.
Whispered secrets of the deep that I had
not heard before.
Whispered to me of whales and
sea turtles still roaming free.
Of secret places untouched by man.
It washed me of my
blue world weariness.
The ocean kissed me.
Deep blue-green silk sliding on my shoulders,
reminding me of my oneness with nature.
The ocean kissed me.

Grace Daniel

Angels

The divine winged creature links God to mankind,
  there is always one beside you, though it's hard for one to find.
This guardian will stay with you through your sickness and health,
  and you will feel it's goodness, from within yourself,
It's the eye of the one you loved, but passed away,
  So they can see your actions day by day.
It's there when you love, and there when you pray,
  but can not control what you do, or what you say.
It fights on your side in battles against wrong,
  and is in every graceful, and holy song.
It was with God from his birth, to His Resurrection,
  and it shall follow you in your every direction.

Renee Joannou

Love

You never felt the tears fall down your cheeks every time I cried,
you never felt the emotions that I felt inside.
You'll always have someone. That I have always known.
And I'm here, thinking of you,
In a dark room alone. Where you are,
it's warm 'cause you have someone to hold.
From where I'm standing, it's frightening and cold.
Your love will be loving you-
listening to your dreams.
I'll be patching up my broken heart,
still mending the seams, your arms will be around
someone elses. It's hard knowing it won't be me.
You are the lucky one, I'm alone and free.
Every thought in my mind when I think about you,
Is so hard to face, because I know that they're true.
Whenever you drifted away, I tried to make you come near.
I didn't pay attention to what people told me.
I only listened to what I wanted to hear.
Even though I know you hurt me, I still care about you.
That's all I have done, it's all I know how to do....

Trina Rodriguez

Grandmother

  She lays in her bed sleeping off the days,
The past was a dream that is now just a haze.
Though she cannot see
her bright blue eyes
glow, With the
happy times, the
sad times, and
all her sorrow.
Her youngest
son visits
her everyday, Though she usually
sleeps he goes anyway. Her oldest
son and his family visit her weekly,
They talk about life, while she
sighs meekly. It's sad to watch
her from across the room, When you
think of her future you feel a sudden gloom.
The point of this poem is that there will
never be another, As unique and as loved as
        my Grandmother.

Julie Hamer

The Field

He came upon this field, where once tall grasses and wild flowers grew. But now it was all black, like the raven's wing, no birds in their nests, no robins to sing.

All was black, as far as the eye could see, no butterflies to hover no busy little bees, death had passed over this field this day, trial by fire was the price to pay.

Then in the distance he heard a small sound, he looked all around, but there was nothing to be found. He searched the black earth, his heart was heavy as he took it all in, then in the distance he heard a faint sound, then he saw the black feathers of a bird gathered round, encircling her young, she had spread her wings, she had given her life, so her babies could sing.

Rosalie Adams

Feelings

You are my sun; when the day is bright
You are my rain; when I begin to cry
You are my joy; each day that I smile
You are my pain; when I haven't seen you in a while.

Latricia Mulkey

St. Patrick Church

A quaint old church peering at the skyway,
Structured so firmly with walls of brick,
Numerous steps are rising to the doorway,
Calmly you enter the house of St. Patrick.

High altars so light are picture perfect,
With artful handiwork and detailed crafting,
Life like statues create a graceful effect,
With stations of the cross quietly mourning.

Stained-glass windows reflect the colors,
As the sunshine glistens beyond compare,
Musical notes float down from the choir,
While parishioners assemble for a prayer.

Our celebrant prays and leads the service,
His homily impresses the attentive crowd,
Receiving communion lifts one's office,
A new day begins on a lily-white cloud.

This is the home of our heavenly father,
Where everyone visits for solemn adoration,
Rewards are generous for those who gather,
Reminding us all to express appreciation.

Francis Lesica

Tomorrow In My Hand

If I could hold tomorrow in my hand,
Then oh, how I'd completely understand
The awesome mysteries that await today.
But then I could never stand up and say,

"This life that God has given me
Undoubtedly is a journey!
To experience all His love
Is the greatest gift from above."

He sent His Son to die.
And though we wonder why,
His Son arose for man
To be with God again!

He paid the price.
Our sacrifice.
So seize the day
And follow His way,

For He holds tomorrow in His hand!

Donald Rockwell Jr.

Untitled

There is a disease spreading the land called Loneliness
It strikes both the old and the young
It robs the mind of all happiness
That's when thoughts of despair can be spun

This dreadful disease known as Loneliness
Holds to no geographical lines
It invades all ethnic cultures
And as to colour.... It's blind!

Loneliness has no respect for position or fame
Great wealth gives one no guarantee
It can happen to men and to women
It could happen to you or to me

The onset of this disease named Loneliness
Does not happen in the blink of an eye
It can take years of neglect and thoughtlessness
The disease strikes when self-worth starts to die

But those who are lonely do not always let it be known
For they feel it is a matter of pride
And so we have to observe and watch for the signs
Caring for each other helps keep us alive

Elizabeth McCarthy Ward

The Day Of Darkness

Have you ever had the feeling of darkness
pressed so deeply in your heart?
When you lose that loved one
And your lives get pulled apart.
You wonder why he left the world
In the shocking way he did
His life shouldn't have been over
He was still just a kid.
On the outside he was grown
Man enough to face his fears
But his childlike soul
Could only shed those silent tears.
Those tears he could not share
Or show to anyone
How were we to know
And what could have been done?
Then the day came
That he took his own life away
Never again can we see him
Until our dying day!!

Jennifer Leigh Rhodes

The Olympic Legend

I stand tall among the saints of history,
I reach out far and wide

And set my sights upon the gold
With ancient heroes by my side

I take the wings of pegasus,
And hammer of Thor

I bring alive again the magic
Of the ancient Gods and more

I call upon the winds
And mighty strength of will

To send a message of truth and grace
Upon olympic thrill

Though the heroes of old
Are mythical at best

Any doubts about my legend
Must be put to rest

For I am the champion
The true hero of today

And no one can ever take
My history away

Nancy I. Caverly

Flower Of Love

Be my flower so I can water you with love
Heaven sent to me by the angels up above
Tell me that you love me so my heart can do cartwheels
And tell me that I mean so much I'd fall head-over-heels

Don't tell me that it's over, that you don't love me anymore
Don't shut me out, no baby, don't you dare walk out that door
How do I know that you love me if you don't tell me you do?
And how can you be insincere and still say, "I love you?"

How do we grow things that we don't water with love?
And how can things be heaven - sent if they aren't from up above?
If we take it step-by-step, we'll surely get by fine
Our love can conquer anything, withstand the test of time

Water your flower and love it, don't just let it waste away
You can't ever plant that seed again, you should cherish everyday
Don't ever rush the blossoms, don't ever rush the buds
'Cause there ain't a better feeling than the one when you're in love

Stephanie M. Shepherdson

Seeking Love

In this world passes strangers of all classes,
who only through our heart we must see,
or hear a voice through a inner choice
from reflections of a previous memory.

Then as our soul breaks over passion
and recedes into our life as we are
We try to foresee who is really me,
and who we think we are.

For each in time as he falls into line
must place his fate at someone's feet
and dream that truth can be found
when we hear her speak.

Were searching for a miracle of sorts
with hope true love may be found with its holy seed.
Endlessly seeking that we may sew,
and final love so we may need.

In that person only we make the choice,
and when she is found
the whole total of our being will rejoice.
   Lynn L. Lockenour

Iguana

Human history, relations and progress
reeked from the ancient ruin walls
like the stench of war,
but the beauty of the ruins was still present.

These empty ruins are now the straggling grounds
for hard and angry looking creatures,
whose stony fossilized skin carries the ages.

As we picked the flower blossoms,
he cautiously approached
and demanded feeding.

He showed no fear,
only courage and wisdom.

The setting sun stretched its shadow, lending the appearance
of a giant dinosaur.
   Tiffany Armstrong

The Dawn Of A New Day

I lay in bed still and calm
My eyes are closed but my mind still lingers
My room dark and motionless
The wind's song plays outside my window as
Shadows dance along my wall
My fan rushes a light breeze towards my face
The warmth of the my blanket keeps the chill from running
through my body
I await the morning
For the sun to rise
My eyes to open
and a new day to come forth
   Christy Baker

Secrets Of Nature

Wind through the trees
How I am cold
The secrets they whisper
The secrets they must hold
For we don't know any secrets of the wind
Or the trees
They won't tell us
If we say please
   Ocherie Pantaleon

My Most Treasured Scene

Birds in the sky, grass so green.
Cows in the pasture, what a beautiful scene.
A child chasing a pretty butterfly.
Dandelion seeds gracefully floating by.
A joy to my very tired eyes.
Birds, grass, cows, a child and butterflies,
These are worth painting in my mind.
When the rainy days come into my life.
I can take out my painting and remember,
The sunny days and blue skies,
The things remembered with my eyes.
The enchanting child, the pretty butterfly,
The dandelion seeds floating by,
The birds, the cows and grass so green,
My most beautiful treasured scene!
   Cynthia J. Borden

Ripples In Time

Our friendship started small,
Like a ripple in a pond when a pebble was carelessly tossed in.
But as time went by, our friendship grew stronger and larger,
Not like the ripple.
Have you ever counted the rings in an old oak tree trunk?
Those, like our friendship, took many years of love,
compassion, and strength to form.
When a small seed is planted into the ground,
no one knows what will happen.
Will it not have the strength to grow?
Or will it survive the hardships, and blossom into a majestic,
swaying creature of nature?
No one knows, but still, many do survive,
and it's not unlike our friendship.
When a bird takes flight for the first time,
Its wings are weak, and the creature does not know if
it has the courage to go on. But look into the sky . . .
there are many birds soaring freely in the never-ending space.
And they are not unlike our friendship.
   Lindsey Steele

Anna Ruby Falls

Anna Ruby Falls rushes down the Mountain side,
it cascades through the rocks like a million tears were cried.
Each and every drop travels to its destination,
it by far is one of God's miraculous creations.
Rushing over stone, branch or tree,
the water flows on knowing it is free.
The sounds is like pure thunder as it plummets to the end,
only to be soothed on the river, round the bend.
Colors sparkle like diamond as sun light dances on the falls,
you can hear the splash for miles on the rocky walls.
Never in my life time have I seen such splendor rare,
nor on this earth is there beauty to compare
listening to the sound; like thunder it calls,
to the rushing water of the Anna Ruby Falls.
   Micki Simpson

Loss Of An Angel

She closed her eyes and went to sleep
Many heads did bow and weep
Unselfish, loving and kind
Family and friends always on her mind
Her absence has left a void in life
A loving friend, mother and wife
We have memories of her we will not let go
But they can't stop the tears that flow
A ray of sunshine and angelic beauty
We love and miss you so very much Judy
   James Hubbard

My Little Tommy

Dimple-cheeked and rosy lipped,
was my fair son tipped.
Still in a small face I could see
my little Tommy smile at me.

This dimple-cheeked child as you can see,
is a boy of tenderness to me.
In the verge of a far off land,
he may someday stand.
With dimpled cheeks and devilish smile,
I'll still hear his voice in all his style.

Smoothing back his stylish hair, I can see
heaven's best angel smile at me.
My son - my little Tommy.
My heart smiles as I sit here listening
to the laughter of the rain.
I still hear the voice of my child plain.
Laughing at play and smiling at me.
That's my little Tommy.

Judy Pierce

Alone

Now I walk the road alone,
The pain of leaving was never so deep,
   As that of your absence.
Realizing, and admitting,
   You are really gone.

My arms ache for the feel of you,
My eyes, for the sight of you.
My lips, for the need of yours, a gentle brush,
My face, for the caress of your tender touch.

A tear slowly traces the path on my cheek,
   Where always before, it lay on your chest.
I silently brush it away,
   With the hand you held so tightly,
     I felt you'd never let it go.

All of these things are now just a memory,
   In my heart, as well as my mind.
But, I will hold to them steadfastly,
   Until all my life is gone,
Even though now, with every step,
   I walk the road alone.

Paula Foster West

Reflections Of Life

Like About Ben Adhem; there are things I doubt;
Things within and on this earth, and in the world without.
I only know of things I like, of those that do me naught
Of things I see and touch and hear, and know within my thoughts.
A butterfly floats softly by toward some quiet bower
A splash of colored beauty, like a winged, stem-less flower.
Birds awake and greet the day, and bid the sun to rise,
Then soar and spread their melodies across the azure skies.
Trees burst forth in regal green and blossoms scent the air,
The magic of each growing thing abounding everywhere
These are things I see and hear, and marvel in their splendor
Small but strong to endure life, and yet so soft and tender.
They come and go; each fills a need, a mark in time and space;
Knowing that in days to pass another takes its place.
There are other eggs to hatch, seeds to plant and grow.
Trees will wither, bloom again, as seasons come and go.
For such is life, and life goes on as does joy and sorrow.
Today will soon be yesterday, and yet, there is tomorrow.

Donald H. Peeples Sr.

Profit In Exercise

What profit has mankind in exercise?
Physical exercise builds strength and enhances our health.
Exercising our rights generates and sense of power and control.
Exercise of the mind add knowledge to our soul.
Still—, what profit have we in exercise?
What have we that really benefits?
The fact is nothing! Unless we include Good Judgment.
Without it, we miss the profit, we miss the prize.
The Good Life!
Only gained by doing the Good Judgment Exercise.
Then we become Totally-Truly-Wholesomely
Wonderfully Alive!
And finally, we profit in exercise.

Kelvy Buck

Challenging Newton

It glows.
The retreating light blazes the blue-day sky.
It is like a falling star sent from heaven.
Only this disaster was not heaven-sent.

I knew.
The exploding burst transfixed all of our eyes.
The falling, fated astronauts had themselves risen to heaven-
this day's events challenged Newton.

I know.
Space is limitless,
but our lives are limited.
As falling, fated astronauts we must also challenge Newton.

Timothy E. Bazzle

Veils

She came to me in a veil of white
   On that warm summer day
Our joys and fantasies were a beautiful sight
   As we grew together in every way

The years flew past in a veil of mist
   With memories our future and our past
It started the first time that we kissed
   Those years flew by so fast

She came to me in a veil of black
   With a tear and a kiss upon my cheek
Our lives are the past we can not get back
   Our loving memories are all she can keep

Grace Ellen Wallis

Yesterday

Yesterday, there were golden rays filtering through the trees
   shining warmth upon my head.
Yesterday, was cool and sweet with the steady beat of rain
   to slowly close my eyes.
Yesterday, there were crickets buzzing their summer songs
   as we played just one more game of tag.
Yesterday, we tramped through the snow's perfect beauty
   to see our footprints left behind
Yesterday, we watched fascinated as the sky was painted bright
   by the evening's setting sun.
Yesterday, was swimming in the creek, singing songs by the fire,
   climbing apple trees in bloom.
Yesterday, with its memories, its joys, simple and great,
   brought me to today.
Today, I live in the happiness of youth, the wisdom of age,
   and the pure love of life itself.
Tomorrow, today will not be gone, it will become, as others,
   yesterday.

Michelle Lee

Death Of The Innocent (Oklahoma City Bombing)

Rose are red violets are blue;
I don't understand, how could you....

Rob hundreds of innocent of their lives;
While families watch as a loved one dies.

All the pain and suffering you caused;
How could you put all those lives on pause?

Why, I ask, have you done these things?
The cries of the innocent are deafening.

All those people paid with their lives;
For nothing really except your lies.

Countless victims had no chance;
When trapped in fatal circumstance.

I sit and wonder how you'll pay;
For all the lives you destroyed that day.

Though the devil throws you illusive crumbs;
May God be with you when your fate comes!

Jodi Burgess

Containment

Deny the swift sweet smelling winds
Of all the freedom it holds
Cage it up with bars of steel
Squish it into your strict molds

Do not allow the streams to flow
Or churn and twist in their anger
Hear the weeping cries of anguish
They can sense the danger

Punish the fire for burning bright
Forget the intense heat
Let it burn until it burns itself
Its power will then deplete

Likewise, stop a child from speaking aloud
And therefore shut his mind
He'll be isolated in the world
From the love he'll never find

Nicole Howard

The Child Dreamer

One night I had a dream
it was full of fights
and all I could do was scream

Everyone was so mean
all they wanted to do was hurt themselves
all in my one dream

I would wake up so terrified
screaming, kicking
sometimes I would cry

Than I finally met you
I was so glad
and then I knew

That you were the one for me
but you had to leave
so far I couldn't see

I know that it was meant to be
but you have somebody besides me

I need you to know
that my love for you will only grow

Jennifer Modellas

Innocent Frustration

To the heavens and to the earth I cry, "Why is it me, O'Lord?"
I try and I walk and I say what needs to be said until I can no more.
"Why is it me?" Will the dead rise to praise my deeds?
All the world may attune itself to me, but what does it matter
   if I am not here to receive.
Will any creature raise its head to understand what is going
   through mine?
"Why is it me, who can go for only so long?"
Words are only words, and what actions I am capable of do not seem
   to signify my duty is done.
It is trickery I tell you. One moment you're running down a hill
   and then up you go.
It is circles, while all around I want the highways and byways.
But even they do not go anywhere in particular,
   just around and around.
It is the act of a crayon man mixing. One color Two; Two colors Three,
   and so on until no color is distinguishable from another.
"Why is it I O'Lord?" To plunge the depths of what amounts
   to be nothing.
"Why is it I?" or "Why is it me?" or does it really matter.
Is today any different from yesterday or tomorrow.
Where am I going and do I really matter?

Burt Fisher

The Dream

In the dream, I have found a rainbow,
And I've found the end.

And in the dream, do you know what was waiting for me?
Well, I got a special treasure, that you could not measure.

For in the dream there was no gold,
Nor a material possession . . .

The dream gave me a special thing,
Or actually, no thing was involved.

The dream gave me something that lasts,
It gave me a relationship with him!

The dream is something special, everyone should have
to carry with us forever and to make us all . . .

Joyful and Proud!!

Kelly Duby

Stars

I was just standing there,
My head aimed at those little lights.
They looked like fireflies stuck in the sky.
   Just staring.

My feet were cold inside my warm boots,
The dog whimpering at my leg.
As far as I could see, that blanket covered the earth.
I was happy,
Like the world had stopped for me,
So that I could stare.
I didn't want to move, I just wanted to stand there,
   Just staring.

They were so far away, yet I wanted to reach out,
Bring one inside, and let it sleep with me.
But what if that glimmering dot, took me up in the sky,
And I could sleep in the clouds.
I was waiting for it to take me away, but it didn't.
It just left me there,
   Just staring.

Marielle Damara Fillit

A Determined Black Woman

A Determined Black Woman
A woman who struggles
A Determined Black Woman
One who conquers the insuperable
A Determined Black Woman
One who goes through many obstacles yet remains steadfast,
A Determined Black Woman
Once weak, but now strong
A Determined Black Woman
A woman with a desire
A Determined Black Woman
A woman with a dream
A Determined Black Woman
Determined to succeed.
  Natasha L. Moore

A Baby Was Born A Chris Wells Thought

From the first sound you hear,
to the first problem you fear.

From the first toy you buy,
to the first sound of a sigh.

From the first night without sleep,
to the first night without a "peep".

From the first diaper you changed,
to the first smell that is strange.

From the first glimpse of a smile,
to the first spit up on the tile.

From the first sign of crawling,
to the first tantrum of bawling.

From the first baby step,
to the firsts that were kept.

From the first attempt at speech,
to the first fall and screech.

From all this Dad will realize,
he's been gifted with a most valuable prize.

A baby was born.
  Christopher Wells

Dreaming

Back and forth, side to side,
Their branches were extended, and could not hide.
As I looked out of the window at the pouring rain,
My mind began to clear, and forgot the pain.
Seeing the rhythm of how they swayed,
Caught my eye, and I saw how they were made.
Two big oak trees planted together,
Had grown to be beautiful and love each other.
Thinking and thinking of how this could be,
That they were so free instead of me.
Coming to a conclusion that "life isn't always fair,"
I had to accept that I was here and they were there.
I knew in my heart that sometime soon,
I would be free like them, instead of stuck in this room.
  Julie Healy

Thanksgiving Day

Five ears of corn boiling in the pot
Four pans of dressing, and that's a lot
Cranberry sauce in three little bowls
Two plump turkeys with hot buttered rolls
And best of all; oh me, oh my,
One big tasty pumpkin pie!
  Martha S. Tillotson

Sunset

While I sit here watching the sunset glow.
No happier moments will I ever know.
When Mother Nature paints her colors across the sky.
And day is done and night is nigh.
You sit entranced as though you were dead,
While across the sky, appear streaks of red.
Soon night clouds begin to appear,
And the songs of birds you cease to hear.

The sun has now sunk out of sight,
And patiently we await the signs of night.
Once more we turn and face the west,
To see the color we like the best.
The tall green grass with dew becomes wet,
While we watch the glory of the vivid sunset.
Do you know who's responsible for this sunset gleam?
It's God, and God alone, who made possible, this beautiful scene.
  Billie L. Spratlin

A Magical Night

The full moon rose over the mountain ledge.
Its light shone down upon the lake as I stood at the edge.
Tiny waves lapped at my naked feet,
As I breathed in the night air which smelled so sweet.
The sand on the beach still held the heat from the day,
Making me never want to go away.
As my gaze rose to meet the sky,
The beautiful sight brought a tear to my eye.
Millions of diamonds glittered so bright,
Turning it into a magical night.
With the wind my hair danced around,
And slowly and silently, I sank to the ground.
The sand fell through my fingers like in an hourglass,
Reminding me that the magical moment will pass.
And as I sit in the soft glow of a moonbeam,
My only wish is to live in my dreams...
  Kelly Perotti

Aloft

I wish to soar like a seabird above the land
where shore meets water
and sleek sheets rub against
coarse brown sand.

I wish to free myself from gravity
and coast
on a slip of a breeze of a wind
that takes me
capriciously.

I want to feel my point of view trip
into high wired quaking electric
as I lose my grip on the basic
and transcend into aerial sweeps.

I wish to soar.
  Sandra Kaul

Continuous Arcs

Knowledge for some may spring Minerva-like;
Mine is winnowed from the threshing floor of the hours
Or refined in the crucible of my composite years.
Exultant when loftier heights I gain,
The sight of peaks of knowing yet beyond
Envelops me in swirling mists of ignorance laid bare.
Though all my wisdom be but one iota against that of the ages,
Gladly I share with the young. They, impelled by my joys,
Mount to pinnacles of truth.
Thus old thoughts gain new sheen
And glow with the luster of discovery.
  Zella Mann Lewis

A Poem

A poem is a delicacy of words.
In an arrangement more beautiful
than the stars.
It is a window through which
the mind sees,
and imagination flows;
The spirit of life captured in a
sculpture of thought.
Caressed and pampered to the brink
of perfection; as it all comes together,
the blend of thought simplifies
the most complex labyrinth
of the soul.

Laura Ramirez

Thy Quilted Milkweed Maiden

   Thither lies thy sky that hath not dull colour,
but many a fruitful hue... And many times within thine eyes of
mine milkweed maiden have I seen the splendour of it.
Her ivory name whispered of water to even the thirstiest of travelers
surely a ghost by her unheard of beauty in all the land.
And her lockes bore not a striking lavishness (quilted),
but only caressed the mind with their comforting plainness,
coal by thy loving touch of nature, soft by the gentle breath of God.
The body in which her wonder slept was of a quality, to this point,
only sung about though never seen by any creature I have yet met.

   Her manner, though it seemed to possess a certain shyness,
was still a dream only dreamt of in the swallowing coolness of the
bed. Within me was felt a building sense of loss and became me
weary and sad from mine want of the girl. And upon me drifted a
milkweed to mine hand, still upon a fence post hereby, and took it
up did I with softness that I took from mine heart. Presented from
thee was a wish, so it is said in testaments and songs of olden, sung
by the many timely minstrels upon the lute and lyre. And so a wish
made I upon the rested milkweed. A wish for that beauty, that
quilted milkweed maiden.

Benjamin Cornwell

The Beauty Of The World

Flowers bloom and flowers die.
Everywhere I go, they lie.
As if a magic carpet was cast.
You used to be the beauty in the world,
But now lifeless you lay...
Sad and forgotten.
The river might take you on its path,
The wind might blow you far and near.
As every thing in this world shall come to an end,
Gently...
   Gently...
As you fall to the ground.

I am an old maid,
Who has come to bury you.
Many people think I am foolish to bury fallen flowers,
But when I die who shall bury me?...

Aileen Chen

Dreams.....

   I dream of things I've never done
I dream of battles never won
   I dream of a world where I play a part
I dream of things close to my heart
   I dream of things that will never be
Then, I dream of you - I dream of me.

Keith F. Anderson

A Tribute To Daddy

He was the greatest man I'll ever live to see.
   He was my strength, my comfort, a friend in time of need.
He gave me breath.
   He gave me life.
He was a part of me.
   Without his love and guidance I wonder where I'd be?
He taught me how to smile, to laugh, to love and even cry.
   The code of life he taught me.
He set my standards high.
   He toiled and strived to make life's pathway a little
      easier for me to tread.
He shared my pain and sorrows.
   He gave me less to dread.
My burdens were not so heavy with him to help me bear.
   The load seemed so much lighter with him along to share.
He's not standing by my side now.
   I must stand alone.
He's resting at the end of life's journey in his heavenly home.
   But as I strive to be the daughter he could be proud of,
I know some day when we meet again he will see his labor of love.

Kathryn Kyker Baines

Why Do I Love Him?

Why do I love him? I know not.
Could it be his belly, although gone to pot?

Could it be the way, he comes through the door,
kicks off his shoes and throws clothes on the floor?

Could it be because, he's still a kid,
since he hasn't yet learned, to lower the toilet seat lid?

Could it be his kisses, which set my heart a twitter,
although his breath may smell like he chewed kitty litter?

Could it be the way, he covers my head with the sheets,
so I can share the air of the onion rings he eats?

So many reasons he I adore. I think of them nightly,
as I listen to him snore.

Why do I love him? This answer is a gem.
No one else in the world, would put up with him!!

I hope that this prose makes you laugh 'til you cry,
but I want you to know — It's All A Big Lie!

The man that I married, is kind, gentle and shy.
The man that I married is a wonderful guy.

Yvonne Heckinger

Jade

Questions arise, I know not why
should I live or should I die
life, so fragile, but most things fade
into sadness, the color of Jade

As a marriage crumbles, and withers away
clinging to memories of by-gone days
could we have changed, decision made
bowl of wrath, the color of Jade

Taking the good along with the bad
nothing to cling to, terminally sad
heart once so sweet, cut out with the blade
beating lifeless, the color of Jade

The sound of crimson lines every room
drowning out laughter, feeling of doom
no reprieve, the sentence stayed
an eternity of misery, the color of Jade

Edward S. Walag

The Very Best

When first we met, some time ago -
   it seems even then, I knew.
That thru this world, together we'd go,
   'cause life for me - had began anew.

Oft times I reflect on our yesteryears,
   with such a feeling of bliss.
And many's the time I brush back tears -
   such grateful tears of happiness.

O'er the years, so much we've shared -
   with a love so dear and true.
You've always let me know you cared,
   and I've always loved you too.

You have a very special way -
   of showing your love for me.
This love you give, each passing day -
   that's just your way, you see.

So on this special day, my dear -
   I feel so richly blest...
'Cause on this very day, one year,
   I married you - the very best.

Jack Gibson

O.J. Simpson

During the long, drawn out trial
There was a man sitting still for a while.

He said that he didn't kill his wife
But we all wondered if he did it with a knife.

Through out the trial he had no reaction
For he was hoping they would find it someone
else's actions.

Their children suffer everyday
with the death of their mother and their father
far away.

And we know as we gaze into the night
That Ron and Nicole's stars shine ever so bright.

If O.J. finally took his life
would he again join his ex-wife???

Sara Lynn Desrochers

Charleston, South Carolina

The natives call it "The Holy City"
a town of splendid buildings, old and
new. Steepled churches, cobbled stone
streets. Narrow winding walks.

Phantom gentlemen in high top hats, and
beautiful ladies in wide hoop skirts,
each holding tiny frilly parasols as
they walk together. History being made.

Clippity-clop, horses hooves, like
tap dancers on a stage. The ancient
marketplace, now a giant yard sale
holding glass and stone beads and colorful
straw baskets, made by natives.

Battered sea wall above cold dark
Water protecting stately mansions.
Cannons in the square always pointing toward
the sea. Dim shadows of an ancient fortress
in the distance, where freedom was won!

Margaret Sawyer McCutchen

Alone

Here I am at home
No one around I'm all alone
It's alright
Nothing's wrong
There are times that I sing songs
Watching T.V. is all I can do
I wish I could go outside and play with you
Usually T.V. would be fun
But on this day there is none
Things are so different
And I don't know why
But I could cry
How can this be?
What's wrong with me?
Today is a day
I see no one
I see today
Is no longer fun

Dustin Vitucci

My World

"In my world,
   The sky is always blue,
   The grass is always green.
In my world,
   There's never a storm to be seen.
In my world,
   You've got a companion,
   Who's always understandin'.
In my world,
   You're never in a fight,
   Cause you're always in delight.
In my world,
   You're as rich as you can be.
In my world,
   You're never a snob, cause you always do your job.
In my world,
   You're never in a pity, cause you're always very pretty.
In my world,
   There's always something pretty, here in the town of friendship city,
   In My World!!"

Helen Manes

Where My Seashore Lies

Whispers of the sea
and a thrashing wave
will make music to my ears
that I will always save.
The music echoes off the canyon
sounding just like a mermaid's song
the song that lasts forever
will soon be gone.
Soon all the living things
on the ground, in the air, even in the sea
all begin to dance and sing
dance and sing for me.
Unicorns bathed in the moonlight
and mermaids swimming in the sea
I will treasure this moment
as long as it will be.
Now dawn is near
I see reflecting rays of sun
now my dream is over
my dream is done.

Sarah Romanowsky

This Precious Life

This precious life
Tree leaf, full and green, then golden and gone

  Blowing wind
  Reaching far like the water from an ancient well

Eternities in every moment
Loves and sorrows, bluees and jazz

  A piano dripping notes of possibilities
  It is more than thought

Ye gifts of clay, smiles and mind
Best to mold, beam and think
Write well the cosmic script before the sun sets

In this precious life
  Tyrone H. Netters

The Ocean's Magic

The moon casts its beauty upon the waves in the night,
Their caps reflect a glittering iridescence from its light,
Repetitive motions of the waves soothe and mesmerize the mind,
Preoccupying the observer for a moment caught in time,
If only these moments could be captured and placed within the heart,
Then when loneliness appears we could reach inside and those feelings shall part,
I long for someone to stroll, along the beach hand in hand,
Taking the time to enjoy the beauty, that surrounds us on the land,
I imagine the waves rolling in, softly caressing and touching our feet,
Making life come alive, revealing its reality, yet displaying it can be sweet,
Until the day I find, someone with which the magic I can share,
I'll continue to observe the beauty, of which the ocean has to bear.
  Linda Mae Lopez

Teddy Bears In The Snow

You sit watching the teddy bears dancing in the snow,
You wish to be a part of them, but you cannot,
For you are a prisoner of your own mind, a prisoner of your body.
Your heart cries out fly Eagle fly, dance teddy bear dance.

You watch the teddy bears with amazement and wonder,
There is longing in your eyes no heart could ever deny.

Day after day you watch them dancing in the snow,
And I stand beside you crying frozen tears,
I see your innocence reflected in their faces,
They remind me of you dancing in the snow with their boyish innocence.

I want to lift you up to dance with them, but I see their silent refusal,
I somehow know you do not belong with them,
And I stand there still crying my frozen tears,
While they go on with their silent merrymaking.

Finally the Spring comes and the snow melts,
The teddy bears die, and with them so do you,
But there are some things I will always remember—the ragged,
Old, white teddy bears dancing in the snow, and the little boy
With childlike innocence, wrapped lovingly in His arms to die,
And I know someday, finally, you will dance with the teddy bears in the snow.
  Jennifer L. Low

D.O.A.

Lie still young man and at the ceiling stare
with all your pulses dormant now.
While I with gentle gesture draw the curtain of your eyes
which gaze beyond the scope of life
with quiet questioning surmise
As if the cooling hand of death
had caught your vigor unprepared.

I still live flavoring my drop of time
and relish it. Why should I gaze
with look of frustrated regret
upon your countenance so peaceful now?

Perhaps there was within my power
some small gift I could have offered...
or yet withheld...to strengthen then
your grasp on life so rudely forced.
Now wings of restless time enfold lost cause
and leave me my lament...
Deeds with doers die and we forget,
and we forget!
  Laird McNeel

Words Of Love

A Sonnet

I love you more than life itself, it's true
Though you may find it too hard to believe
Because I don't express my thoughts to you
And keep my feelings deep inside of me.

Please understand how very shy I am
And see that words of love embarrass me,
For more than you, a strong and caring man
Can know, the fear of truly being free.

I want to say the words so that you know
That I do care for you so very dear;
I try, but oh! Those words remain my foe
And still can't say the ones you want to hear.

  With pen in hand, I write these words, though few,
  That show, I hope, how much I do love you.
  Susan Rapisura

Eternally Yours

Every moment we're apart
my soul aches for you
heavy beats tread on my heart
of love forever true.

When you kiss me that way
my spirit sings with glee
and when you hold me and say
that your passion for me will never flee;

My heart bleeds tears,
too much perfection
this erases all my fears
you have given my life direction.

Falling into you
makes my daydreams fly
thinking of you is all I do
I know our love will never die.
  Angela McCullough

Rainbows And Angels

Enduring structures and strictures,
Many not hewn of love or beauty or truth,
Are accorded power by their age alone—
Leaning posts for the lazy, perhaps

While, coming softly and gently,
Disguised as waterfalls and dandelion fluff,
Playing hide-and-seek in love songs,
Impaled on the wry dry barbs of humor's fence

Reality's strength may be so subtle—
Seeming merely to be what it is —
That some embrace forces less simple
Though more easily understood.

But how does one choose between
Rainbows and angels?

It seems not to matter whether
Doubting religiously is an act of faith
Or a faithless act
When the end is a common caring

For what is, and why,
and how we can help.
Maggie Dunaway

Letting Go

After you lose a love the worst part is letting go,
You think about them over and over again in a constant flow.

Having your heart broken is a feeling that makes you realize things,
Letting go is important for you to see what tomorrow brings.

Remembering moments kept inside your head is tearing you apart,
Letting go helps give you a chance at a brand new start.

Friends are here to guide you when your time of need is known,
They don't make you let go, you must proceed with this on your own.

Letting go is a scary thought, but you're not alone in this place,
Losing someone you love is something everyone must face.

Don't give up, the world is not at its end,
Wait because a broken heart takes time to mend.
Christina Vaccaro

There's No Love Greater Than The Love Inside You

To love someone, is to love as you love self.
There is no love greater than the love inside you.
The Creator formed you from love...His.

Let no man, woman, destroy your love by deception,
Or the lack of anything.
If you choose to build a relationship,
Build it on the foundation on what you can give to another,
If one has less, keeps giving less,
Is it worth to give your all for less when you can be of equal?

No need for pre-fabricated dreams,
Visions of separate lifestyles if you have combined your love as one.
Never give your all to a taker who has nothing to give.

Don't base your love on promises,
That only materialize in words,
With no loyalty of its actions.

We all strive to find inner peace inside to live,
According to the only law of life.
The law of love.
If we can't abide by it,
What do we have to offer self or anyone?   Nothing.....
Deborah Lindsay Tillman

Generations

Beginning, a tree peeks out its head
wishing and hoping, longing to be led.
Struggling roots, starting to spread
digging and pulling, closer to the dead.
Reaching branches, their arms to the sky
grasping and searching, wanting to fly.
Bending limbs, flexing to stretch
floating and flowing, the leaves to catch.
Whistling the wind, through the boughs
coughing and shaking, that which endows.
Shivering, the twigs, entangled in each other
twisting and shriveling, fighting one another.
Jaelithe Ingold

The Moon

Lonely orb floating in the sea of night
Forever drifting across the dark sky.
Heavenly guide of weary travelers
And inspirer of romantic ballads.
The light, that reflects, upon each crescent wave
While couples stroll along at twilight.
The solitary soul who weaves our dream
And adds mystery and intrigue to life.

I beseech thee, heavenly maiden,
What caused thee to retreat to the heavens?
By you, young lovers swear their undying love.
You listen whilst others pine for loves lost.
I know of not what that caused your sorrow,
But I, like you, take others pain to heart.
What caused thee to sigh upon the breeze
And caused your tears to fall like the rain?
Tuyetmai Truong

The Song

There was a tree that was a little tree made for a little bird and me.
How it grew, no one knew, except for the little garden.
Sometimes when I had nothing else to do,
I would come to that little garden.
And as the little bird would start to sing, I would sing along.
And as the harmony would flow,
The words were coveted to know,
By all who heard its sweet song.
Then as the chorus ended, everything was hushed,
There wasn't a bit of rush.
Then when all was very dark, down flew the bird that sang like a lark.
So there we slept, just us three, the little tree, the bird, and me.
Luke Potts

Time He Lent

I met a man all withered and worn,
He looked so sad and very forlorn.
I leaned over and gave him my hand,
In hopes that he would understand.
He started to resist, but only at first;
He seemed to have a craving, a terrible thirst.
What could I give him, went through my mind,
The least I could give was part of my time.
So I sat down with him, for a little while,
And he told me of the days when he was a child.
He seemed now happy while talking to me,
I was beginning to see the things, he wanted me to see.
Life had been good to him, he was very content,
I was glad for the time that he had lent.
I hope that someday when I am old,
I will have beautiful memories that can be told.
Mary Charvet

The Wall

The black granite panels
shielded from the street
stand silently, patiently waiting and the names go on

It's gray, gloomy, raining, voices soft when spoken
love in faces, tears in eyes and the names go on

Dead have a diamond, missing a cross
A circle if one returns
No circles and the names go on

Names disappear in the rain
The sun brings them out
It takes your breath away and the names go on

Protectors need to visit
As all Americans should, give respect, long overdue
and the names go on

My husband did not go nor my young son
John and Walter Elam did and their names are on

The nurses stand near by arms outstretches with care
Many of them have fallen and the names go on

Some are buried in Arlington some are buried at home
Some are still in Vietnam and the names go on

Dixie J. Elam

Africa's Children

I cry, I lament for Africa's children.
I see their beautiful ebony eyes full of tears.
I hear the cruel voice of oppression screaming, trying to drown out their songs of triumph, but to no avail.

A bold and courageous lot are they, deeply rooted
   in their native heritage.
Their spirits, unlike their backs, cannot be broken.
Through turmoil, through tribulation, always they grow stronger.
Though their skin is as the night, their sense of vision is
   as the noonday.

There will be a great day, and a Blessed heaven for these brave children, for He who created all men is with them, and has smiled on them, and one day my tears will be no more. God bless Africa's children, and the great mother who gave them life.

Byron Darensburg

My Mom

When we were young, so very small
You made us stand up straight and tall
You taught us manners and showed us poise
Played with our toys, and listened to our noise

As time went by, we grew older
No longer young, but yet much bolder
Make-up, nylons, boyfriends came
And all you said was I was the same

You taught us respect and gave your love
We love you so, only he knows above
The years have come and gone so quick
You were around when we were sick

The time has come that we have grown
As you can see most of us have left home
They're out the door and on there way
And hope to God, I'm sure they pray
That someday they will say
My mom taught us all in each and every way

Barbara M. Myers

Conversation With A Rock

In England, by a limpid pool,
I found a rock mossed over.
Quietly it lay there, mute I thought.
And then I heard a murmur.

Did you know a rock could talk?

From whence did you come? Mayhap we have met.
From cosmic fire was the soft reply.
When was the year? Do you remember?

In the beginning of time, I hear.

And what is your use, what is your sphere?
Will you through eternity quietly lie here?
The answer came. 'Tis not certain, I have yet to choose.

Perhaps an obelisk reaching high
To honor a soldier who had to die
Then there's a stone for David's sling.
Or a tower to hold the bells that ring.
The Stone of Scone for the Royal Scot.
Or a Grecian Urn, it matters not.

At the end of time, what will you be then?

Why cosmic fire was the soft reply.

Annie Laura Worrell

Belladonna

Belladona lives in Belvidere; in a house with a Belvedere feature
Where she retires for hours upon hours gazing out her window

Upon her garden, with the passing of time;
the scene growing more pleasing!

Take me prisoner Belladonna thought to herself, and
release me from my true prison

As my soul blooms into a beautiful flower; the stem
supporting the climax in my garden

I will have experienced the greatest orgasm of life,
being a friend of Mother Nature

But truth soon grips me as fall ushers in winter's death

Purifying the soul of the earth, preparing its bed
for the colorful garden that will reappear in the spring

As I Belladonna patiently sit and await my destiny,
my fate, my death; to be buried among my flowers

Never again to sit in the Belvedere and look out upon
the Garden, like a deadly human nightshade, Belladonna

Jack Masters

My Father's Star

   Another dark and cloudless sky shines brightly tonight. I cannot sleep and relentlessly I walk and talk to the stars that glisten in the heavens.
   As I scan the millions of bright stars, I look and find the one star that shines the brightest and it momentarily holds my thoughts and grasps for my attention.
   I've been watching this beautiful star for the past five years. I know who made that star, and I know that its maker sends it to the heavens to watch over me every night.
   You see, that beautiful and shining star is there in the midnight sky and I know that it is my Dad's star. Just as though God lets me know that all is well in the light of heaven and He loves me enough to send a special star to remind me that Dad is at peace and he and God are waiting for me.
   Realizing that, I am able to find perfect peace and sleep.

Bonny S. Toavs

Yet Is Now

There is a voice in the mirror
it's a vision you can hear
Of secrets whispered by your heart

Can you hear it?

Study the reflection
of your own subconscious

Something is out there
beyond the mirror

You have come here from before
to the tremendous reality of now
as you travel
there which is not yet

Yet is now

Searching for truth
the experience shares ancient wisdom with fresh dreams

The moment expands beyond time
and becomes memory
there in your soul
   Karen Strole

Ravens And Angels

There are ravens in my dreams
Where they come from,
what they seek, is unknown to me,
but they are there.
Flying in the backlit sky
in subtle malice, convincing me
my night will come to visit.

There are angels in my dreams
Where they come from
who they seek, is unknown to me
But they are there,
standing where the shadows threaten
in veiled whispers convincing me
the daylight holds a promise.

There is you in my dreams.
Where you came from,
why you love me, is a mystery
But you are there, lying where my body rests
convincing me of a need for
Ravens and the Angels.
   Steven A. Jones

Someday

I used to wake up to happy hours
I never dreamed I could ever miss you so
But now when I wake up, I just try not to break up
Because you have gone, and now I know
Someday when I wake up, I know I will smile again
There will be no more tears nor heartaches
Just happy memories, of all the hours we shared before
I waited for their call...heard their knock on the door
Now I pick myself up, and paste a smile on my face
There are just no tears to cry anymore
Someday when I wake up, I know I will smile again
I give back the heartaches, all that they gave to me
Although I will always miss you, in so many little ways I miss you
But I will start all over and someday maybe I will learn
To live without you someday.
   Donna B. McGregor

Untitled

The man on the street sits
with his back pressed against the store window.
His dirt packed fingernails
part of his time laden hands
grasp loosely at his cup of life-
full of empty coins

Maybe it will buy me a
bottle of whiskey to bury my face in

A woman with a child passes him,
she pulls her innocent baby tightly
against her bosom as she realizes
the being of the man.
He jiggles the cup, more in sarcastic sorrow
than need for pennies.

I used to be a man.
   Rachel Evans

The First Lesson

While working in the fields one afternoon,
I was taking a break from a tree I'd just pruned.
I glanced to the north and to my surprise,
A mother deer and her fawn caught my eyes.
They were in a small area with a fence around it.
They were running and playing and jumping a bit.
She came back to her fawn and said a few words.
Then ran to the fence she had observed.
They quit their frolicking and stood for a while.
She walked to her fawn and she seemed to smile.
Over the fence she flew with ease
As her fawn followed her mother to please,
Over the fence she went like a pro
With her fawn at her heels wouldn't you know.
Her fawn leaped the fence like it wasn't even there.
O what a sight I do declare.
Then off they flew to a field of trees
As they ran out of sight in the cool breeze.
   Paul E. Smith

I Don't Know Why

I don't know why
The stars shine so bright in the heavens.
I don't know why
The waters flow unceasingly to the seas.
I don't know why
Some think I am so angelic
And others thinks I am the devil's imp
When I am neither.
I don't know why
People judge a book by its cover
Not by the thoughts and ideas held within.
I don't know why
It is so hard to please everyone's high standards
Lord knows I try.
I still don't know why
I try.
   Melanie Wagner

Rooftop

Up on the rooftop is where I long to be,
up on the rooftop something happens to me,
up on the roof I turn and wonder,
what would happen if I could ride thunder,
if I could lasso clouds way up high,
what would happen if I could fly?
up on the rooftop is where I long to be,
up on the rooftop something happens to me.
   Melissa Renee Essinger

Crumpalatwo

I've won a crumpalatwo,
I've won it! I've won it! How about you?
  I don't mean to brag,
but I'm just so glad.
  It required hard thinking.
I stayed up for nights without even blinking!
  But oh! It was worth it! Cause I won
it! I won it! A crumpalatwo!

  I had to be smart,
and use all my heart!
  I don't mean to be loud,
But I'm just so proud.
  'Cause I won it! I won't it! A crumpalatwo.

  I love it so much,
for whoever has won an award of such
  'Though crazy I may seem,
I'm so happy I could scream!
  So you ask me what is a crumpalatwo,
well that... I wish I knew.

Cory Rae Shaw

The Opening Of Eyes

"Help," she screamed, nobody seemed to care,
"Help," she screamed, nobody seemed to be there,
There was no one there to comfort the pain,
There was the darkness, but it wasn't the same.
She decided she needed to rely on herself, so she broke out of her shell,
She freed herself from her own personal hell.
She kicked off the shackles that restrained her mind,
She destroyed the rest of the restraints and good heart was what
  she had to find.
Like a newborn, she opened her eyes for the first time,
A world of beauty she was to find.
From being shielded, from a world of such beauty, and peace,
She never wanted this drunken feeling of ecstasy to cease.
So she opened her eyes wider, and spread her wings of imagination
  to fly,
As she flew, she started to cry.
She realized no one ever stops to appreciate the little things,
  like a flower,
She realized no one ever appreciated every waking hour.
Her own personal mission was clear as could be.
Her goal was to make everyone else see the beauty she was able to see.
So with her mission in mind, and a gleam in her eye.
She spread her wings and set out to make people care, or at least try.

Darin Bresnitz

Memorial Day

Memorial Day,
A tribute to the American Way!
Bullets are flying,
Family members are crying.
Principles are compromised,
Many people are in for a surprise.
My family stays at home to pray,
As I dash into the fray.
So much blood,
It reminds me of a flood.
We are trying to overcome our strife,
But it's hard when I see no sign of life!
So much hate,
This wasn't supposed to be my fate.
I have so many questions,
Life sure has taught me a hard lesson!
Having so much loyalty,
Many people will think of me as royalty.
I'm beginning to think my life is a drag,
But then I see the American Flag!!!

Deanna M. Kamberger

A Dream To Stand On

Weathered soul searching for a new life
May it be blessed with the gift of no strife
Strive hard and find your own identity
Never run from what might be cold reality

Weathered soul looking for a new home
May a flower bloom in the old glory of Rome
Work harder than Jesus to make believers
Don't fall in the fire but be a leader

Let the light of your soul out of suppression
It has always been your hardest concession
Show others a gift of responsibility
Open your heart for all the people to see

Trust in Christ your search will succeed
May your soul see the light and no longer bleed
Hope your dream is strong enough to stand on
I guess for now it's time to say so long...

Gerald Stansbury

Why Me?

Why me? I didn't drink and drive.
I never took drugs because I wanted to stay alive.
Why me? I went to the party with my friends,
I did not want it to be the end.

Why me? I left the party and started to cross the lane.
It was then I got hit by a car and felt great pain.
Why me? I was hit and my best friend was put to rest.
Thanks to her boyfriend, the rest of my life will beat the test.
Why me? I am laying in a hospital bed,
Now I am almost dead.

Why me? This isn't fair.
That guy who hit as just didn't care.
Why me? He drank for some stupid dare.
Now all I can do is lay here in a blank stare.
Why me?

Mindy Woodruff

Untitled

why any emotion comes crashing in,
like the tide inevitably rises,
'tis almost sin,

to whom who pays heed to the injured one,
the forgotten deed, is left undone,

for it is to judge from whence one came,
nothing else matters,
it's only a game,

ask not of his kind ask nothing of him,
he's only in your mind,
the light is so dim,

for when I walk I walk alone,
not in twain,
not carved in stone,

in one's mind brews a thought,
it won't even surface,
'twill only be fought,

the scarlet embers of a fallen sky,
is that all that's left
of a tear-drop eye?

Nathan S. Morehart

My Father's Son

I've made it through the worst of times by holding to His hand.
He's with me in the best of times. He helps me understand
   that though it seems I am alone, He never leaves my side;
   that if I trust and never doubt, with Him I will abide.

He is my strength, He is my joy, I love Him like no other.
He listens when I need to talk, He's closer than my mother.
I call His name both day and night, I know He's always there.
I ask Him to forgive my sins, I know He answers prayer.

I thank Him for the blessings that I know I haven't earned.
He takes good care of me and mine, I know that I have learned
   to put my trust and faith in Him, He is my dearest friend;
   and He will never let me down, He's with me to the end.

If you are sad or feeling down and you don't know this man
It's time you meet the only one who really, truly can
   supply your needs and heal your pain and turn your night to day.
Just put your hand into His hands and He will lead the way
   to light and love and joy and gain, He is the only one
   who'll save you from this world of sin - He is my Father's son...
JESUS!
Johnnie S. Williams

Reunion

my chest runs blacktopped high
way of scars, like a razorslashed
brailletracked route 80
holdin' thunder and memory.

my hands flash "danger ahead" signs
of age: each knuckle, stenciletched
by yards of broken glass or stenopunched
against your cheekbone, always laughs
at the same wornout joke about finally
settlin' somewhere besides these
trainwhistle windchilled canyons of steel.

and the ghosts of regret that steam
and hiss from all the broken
down mouths and retread thighs
are almost enough to assure
me you'll come home again.
Wilbur Farley

Night End

A gossamer of warmth envelops me
as I step into the night air
of August
A chance to walk home after
a long day of work in a factory
a cold sterile factory
my steps fall noiselessly along the slumbering streets
I am alone yet not lonesome
for the night breeze whispers her secrets
in my ears
and the crickets sing their hymn of summer
the trees wave their greetings
while the corn stalks stand at attention
for my arrival
and an umbrella of stars cover me
like an elegant lace quilt
with each step forward
a ribbon of moonlight is my guide
casting a shadowed path and calling out
you are Home...You are Home
Stephanie Krueger

Those Friends Of Mine

Lavender, Rosemary, Tarragon and Thyme are old friends of mine
They sparkle my culinary dishes just like good wine.
There flowers are lavender, blue, red and yellow
Creating a mosaic of color plus delighting the senses of my neighbor
   fellow.
The medicinal properties of each in turn
Helps heal insomnia, coughing, the flu;
If that wasn't enough!
An antiseptic for your burn.
Till and add amendments to your soil
In a sunny location or on a window pane.
You will be delighted with those friends of mine.
Joyce Garrow

"I Thank You Mom And Dad"

"As the moon rises and the sun sets,
The love you've given us
We will never forget."

"As the days turn into years,
and we get older,
The lessons you've taught us
Will always be with us."

"We now have children of our own,
and your lessons will be handed down
From generation to generation.
This is the greatest gift a family could own."

"So, I thank you Mom and Dad for teaching
us a life of love, understanding, Faith,
Patience and most important what it
means to have a Family!"
Maryanne Carey-Foster

The Voice

Although I'm in a distant land
So, far it seems, from any guiding hand
with many faces so strange to me
and building fear whelming up inside of me
I try to think of home, I close my eyes
and I see all that I left behind me
then of course you only feel worse
And tears of homesickness burst
And when I feel I can't go on
A cherished friend whose voice
Travels across the sea
Especially just to speak to me, calls
And when that telephone rings
Her sweet voice seems to sing
Mum, I'm so glad to hear your voice!
Patricia Hamilton

Who I Am

Who am I? I wonder day to day,
Never knowing where, or which way,

Everyone seems to know who they are,
But everything in my life seems so bizarre.

We all need somewhere....somewhere to start,
If you don't know where; just follow your heart,

This little poem should help you on your way,
Just take life's paths day by day.
Kelli M. Lincoln

Two Lights

I recently saw two powerful lights.
The first was very bright and yet soft and gentle as a sleeping child.

Its light I could have curled up into and lived until my end.
It was so warm and it covered my nakedness.

Then I was plummeted into another light.
It was so bright I had to close my eyes.
I first thought it was like the first light but it wasn't at all.

It was harsh and only after a brief second I began to sweat
   and became dysfunctional.

I felt both lights
I felt them around me and
I in the midst of them both.

I then understood that the first light, although softer,
was actually the best, most powerful and kept me safe.

The latter light was a facade of the real.
An imitation of the best;
A dreaded end
I knew would bring damnation.

   Peggy A. Ramey

Best Friends

   The little girl stared out the window as her best friend drove away. They waved to comfort themselves, and to say, "Everything will be OK." She promised she would visit, as they said their good-byes, and yet it didn't make her forget the lump in her throat, and the sting in her eyes. They gave their final hugs, and without words they said, "You're a good friend." And that little girl stood there knowing her friendship had come to an end.
   Years had passed, and that little girl grew up. She had a family and a good job, but she never forgot the pain of that day. She probably will never see that friend again, or even hear her voice, but she is comforted by these words....
   "Best friends are like a heart. They never say die, they never say part. They beat with one beat, but when they must part, always remember what is in your heart."

   Elizabeth A. Brewer

Los Angeles, 2 a.m.

The incredible surge of the plane
forces me high above the city —
Objectivity can only be
reached from above. Beyond the window,
the molten orange glow of the street lights
burns stolidly through the harshness of night
and distance. The city still lives despite
the smog, hovering in mindless heaps,
Infiltrating, unable to destroy
the clean existence of human courage,
the brilliance of bridges built over
flat black pools of water.

Miles and miles of this land,
orange and black like an explosion, a
violent creation of beauty;
the rebellion against death and the lifelong
struggle to glint with clarity through
those dark veils of self-doubt and confusion.

The city is the exaltation of life and reality
and the ability of the human eye to perceive it.

   Sonja R. Tack

With You

Life with you is so grand.
Every time you hold my hand,

The feeling rushes in:
The feeling we get when we win.

You stand there dressed with honor high above;
You walk down the aisle like God's angel dove.

You speak with no uttering,
Your heart always fluttering.

With love wider than the Nile,
You walk by me and smile.

Your eyes tell this wonderful news;
There's no way I will lose.

To hold you thus, near,
Solves all of my fear.

Our love is grand, and held in God's hand!
   Jackie Leigh Baty

The Dream

Last night I had a dream,
   we were lovers instead of friends.
As you held on to me,
   I wished it would never end.
While I gazed into your eyes,
   I thought I was in paradise.
When you whispered my name ever so slowly,
   I knew then and now, I would never be lonely.
Your lips touched mine and I knew,
   our love forever would be true.
The salty taste of your bare, hardened body,
   makes my emotions explode and my thoughts become flighty.
I lose control, my body thrusts wildly as we make love all night
   and you hold me so tightly.
The hot morning sun awakens in me feelings of sadness,
   from my dream I am free.
   Tina M. Quitt

Death Of A Loved One

Your smiling face is what I see;
That cold unsmiling face is not you.
Your warm embrace is what I remember;
Those motionless hands could not be yours.

When I see you stretched so tall,
In that box my brother chose,
I know you are not there
But I know you are somewhere.

Beloved you did not die alone
I died too
You are not there alone
My heart is there too.

Beloved where will you be waiting?
In a garden so beautiful.
Beloved what will you inhale?
All the fragrance there bestow.

Be loved sleep that blessed sleep,
You have long waited for.
Beloved rest that blessed rest,
We will meet to part no more.

   Runa Delisser Brown

Differences

We enter this world
No one of us the same.
Sometimes it is our differences,
that keep us out of the game.
The game where people laugh and stare
at those who are not the same.
Our parents praying a normal
healthy baby is what God will send,
thinking our differences they can mend.
It is because of our differences
that makes each one of us unique.
To ignore these differences would be a
big mistake.
We must look at a person for who they really are,
and realize that we all have the potential
to reach for a star!
For some differences can be seen,
and some can not.
We all must remember that we're all human beings
right from the start.

Christine A. Howard

The Picture Behind The Frames Mind

Sometimes life can offer very painful happenings
Most of which we do not understand
The infliction seems to linger and drip very slowly
Like that of the hour glass sands

Human life seems so precious and fragile
We should be spared so many hurt feelings
We need more time with less worry
Instead of suffering from day to day healings

It is often said that things happen for a reason
Each one of us is dealt separate cards
The physical and emotional turmoil we struggle to survive
Forces us to put up our strongest guards.

Deep within our wounded human hearts
Waiting to be rid of unwanted holes
Lies a burning desire for hurtless freedom
And a scorched seed flaming like ready hot coals

When hardships do arise, find the strength to be consoled
In the powerful palms of our Creators hands
Surely there, you will find the peace within yourself
To overcome the sorrow God had in your life's plans.

Katrina L. Fischer

The Bond

Since the day I first heard the voice whisper sweetly in my ear,
To the precious moment in time when she caressed a fallen tear.
She has taught me well, how to love and to respond
For there is nothing quite like this everlasting bond.

Our relationship has grown to be so much more than friends,
For I know she will always be with me until the very end.
Until I may learn all the secrets to success,
She will always be there to help me do my very best.

Today and tomorrow, and for all the years to come
I can truly say, by all the rules of thumb,
My mother is my shepherd, my strength, and my star,
For I will always admire her helping me come this far.

Shantil Ellison

You Took My Love From Me
(A Thought for Janice, 'Pay')

Oh Bessemer, you have been so cruel to me
You took away my love before we could be free
She was my breath of spring that carried me through the year
I can now only hope she knew to me she was so dear
It was a time in the South when one's color was a burden
Yet she was a Girl Scout and forced to be with the others
A family affair it almost came to be
Our sisters and brothers were paired just as we
We were forced apart, as my family moved North
It broke my heart, hopefully, she knew this of course
We left for the bus, the family walking down the street
I could not believe my eyes, she was approaching me
She was so cute in her Girl Scout suit
As I looked in her eyes I saw that she knew
"Y" all going to Chicago, my love she asked of me
Yes was my reply as I drank of her beauty
Too young to be in love I was told it was not true
But time it yet rolls on, and still I am so blue
She was taken from this world, a great disease I was told
I never tasted of her goodness, but my love will never grow old

Willie Earl Means

Angel Wings Wisps

You are an old soul;
deep, emotional, sensitive -
the eyes tell it all!

Shhh!
Be quiet my friend.
Have faith that God gives us nothing we cannot bear.
Instead, He sends angels who keep you in their care.
So, let the angels take over
and you'll see
that they work to your benefit.

When things seem to be out of control -
their wings will enfold you as they caress and protect you.
They whisper words of encouragement and love to your soul.

Angel wings - what a wonderful place to be.
They hold your heart gently
while they examine the aches
and soon... Very soon,
they will mend your wound without leaving any scars.

For memories sake - the only trace left will be...
Angel wings wisps.

Vernetta M. Skinner

Night Is Done

It is morn; the sun has come.
Look to the east, night is done.
I see the horizon, radiant and bright,
As dawn brings rays full of light.

Hear the birds; they sing their song;
For once nothing ever seems wrong.
I feel the dew beneath my feet,
But soon the sun makes it obsolete.

Smell the flowers, oh how they bloom,
As the birds still sing their merry tune.
I taste an apple from a tree,
And watch the clouds, what could they be?

The heat is comforted by a breeze,
And morning passes by with ease.
I wish that this would never end,
After all, the morn is my best friend.

Daniel Boyer Jr.

The World Can Blend

If you looked at life, with an imaginative eye!
  You'd begin to notice, all the colors you walk by.
    The trees with their dark, to brilliant green,
      Changing to crimpson, a bright sight to be seen.

An artist's view, of the world each day, is an exciting adventure,
  a great game we can play.

There is no real hatred of a color, or a shade.
  They all mix and blend, with new colors to be made.
For me, it's so simple, to have a neon day, I just paint a picture,
  to take me away.
    Entering a fantasy, or world I create, by mixing and matching
The colors on my plate.
  If all could unite and give it a try.
    You'd see color as beauty, through an artist's eye.
      Irene Betzold

Thoughts Of A Dead Man

Green acres mortuary is the place to be
After you've been bit by a killer bee
Toe's up and all laid out
C'mon now, pick my casket out

O' at work is where I was suppose to be
No one knew I had hit a tree.
After an hour or two, I awoke
The sting in my neck, made me choke.

Life has dealt me a shortened hand
This I don't like, but can understand
As I lay here waiting to meet my maker
. . . hope I look good, thank's to my
Undertaker!
    Daniel R. Bjerk

Obligation

Awake to light, engulf the new,
What was once safe, now frightens you.
Be not afraid, kick and cry out
Find what this world is all about.

Softness will stay for just awhile
To be replaced with armored guile,
Purity fades with each daily sun,
Love is too scarce, just meant for some.

No matter what you receive in life
Accept the pleasure and cope with strife.
Continue to grow and seek your place
It changes often, maintain your space.

Pass your knowledge to those you can
It's your debt to help improve man.
You'll meet that goal as long as you try
Failure prevails when you live a lie.

Finally when life comes to an end
Arrived with a rush, left with the wind.
Sad are they in the middle who stay
But not for those who are new today.
    Janice Gale-Howell

The Eye Of The Beholder

She acquired the meditative state of staring;
eyes set upon the pastels of late spring's dusk.
Within a tranced observation, the first
misted twinkle was unveiled to her childlike eyes.

Mind and thought pressed against and lost her in time,
as the aura danced above the trees
like billowing canopies radiating the essence of grace.
Caught in the moment, she smiled, suspended in life and what could be.
    Cynthia Chipman

The Winding Path

As I walk along the winding path of this life
I can see all the pain, sorrow, and strife,
as men in their carefree, haphazard manners,
strive to plan the fate of their countries' banners.
Oh, they love to war and murder and this seems odd
because they always do this in the name of God.
Woe be to us, all creatures great and small
for God almighty on us someday will call,
then great men of wealth and power will cringe in fear,
the day our creator calls - come ye here.
When all the sands of time have come and gone,
there will be no time then to right our wrongs.
And all the crying, the misery and the pain,
will be no less for man, no matter what his fame.
Give up my brothers, this life of shame,
or burn my brothers, in eternal flame.
    Richard A. Dobbins

Praise

Thank thee for my second life
opened my mind to new.
You've saved me from hate and knife
serene in your honest love
others rebel at my positive passion
feelings released in your bliss
blessed in your coming for late strife
care not for me but for all
refuge of security in this earthly life
opened arms. Shadow of thy wing
all others await to be in your mighty light
you grant me children, they're yours
world's beauty is around us and not his.
Humble am I. Tears of joy
your name I speak.
Praise thee Lord my will be thine.
    John S. Young

But Heart Must Be

God will wing you through the sky
If only you implore Him, "Let me fly".
But heart must be where dreams aren't dry
And candle will light all darkness nigh.

God will give you courage straight
If only you implore Him, "Change my state".
But heart must be prepared to wait
His power, in time, will demonstrate.

God will guide you past the rue
If only you implore Him, "Make me new".
But heart must prove solemn and true
If He is to give these things to you.
    Terena Ward

Ultra-Violet

Lift my spirit.
Burn my skin

Lying on equator...drop dead center.
UV poised on landscape
blind void of blinking.

Blotched....blight...
and blistered, is how I feel.

Bronzed is how I look.
Oh, how so worshipped.
My body, bombastically basking in bondage of beams.

Sundown drops to night.
Mountains becomes the eyelids...
Heavy on the range.
    Gary Rintz

Fly Eagle Fly

Embrace me, stroke me, with the feel of a feather across my face
such feelings that surge inside of me I cannot erase
I shall embrace these feelings and will never let them die as I reach
for the sky and resurrect my spirit to heights one cannot believe
with all that I aspire and all that I know I can achieve
flying high, so high, gliding with the wind
like an eagle so powerful I feel deep from within
soaring through the earth's atmosphere and without fear
I suddenly awaken in astonishment, oh God, how far have I come?
With my accomplishments I'd almost forgotten how it was done
why it was encouragement from those who believed in me
a warm embrace, like the stroke of a feather across my face
sent me flying, soaring, like an eagle who breaks all wind barriers
and squawks in a language even I can understand
no matter how loud, or even in the voice of a sparrow
In my mind I see this brave eagle soaring so high with aspirations
soaring a course so directed and smooth it captures my adoration
so I close my eyes and imagine I too have wings
and spread my arms like the eagle as I look towards the sky
I cry out with a loud voice and say Fly Eagle! Fly!

Lorraine Baker

The Gift Of Friendship

As you grow up throughout the years,
There will be many great people among your peers.
A few of them will shine above the rest,
And they will become friends you will call your best.

They will become an important part of your life,
They'll bring you laughter, and help you through the strife.
They'll stick by your side as you both grow older,
Whenever you're upset, they'll lend you a shoulder.

They'll never criticize you when you are wrong,
As you learn from your mistakes, they'll go along.
When you act a little crazy, or even a little strange,
They will not even judge you, or ask you to change.

See, the gift of friendship is the most special thing,
Because you could not exist without that other being.
Friends are friends forever, even when they're apart,
They will always be remembered forever in each other's heart.

Jeri Pace

That Special Someone

As I looked across the table and into his dreamy eyes
I knew at that moment I loved him, but my love was in disguise
I'd rather be his lover but instead I was his friend
I'd give my life for him and fight until the end.
But in the mean time I just flirted and sent the secret signs
Hoping that held notice then I'd ask him to be mine.

The week with was the best
I had so much time but so little rest
But I'd arise early each morning and wait for him
Hoping we'd have as much fun when it was dim.

I still love him to this day
I think he may love me too
I can't wait until I see him again
That's when I'll say I love you!

Melissa Geiser

Heaven's Request

Tranquil breeze, traveling through the open window,
translucent curtains, undulating in the silent whisper,
gradually transforming, defining a figure unknown,
celestial being radiating light, caressing the benevolent elder,
a cherished book, completed with fond memories,
glancing at them, concluding her life,
soul gracefully departing, her body lay still.

Shawnna Knoeppel

Please Shelter Me

Lord as I travel day by day,
Along this long and rocky way,
Even when I kneel to pray.
Please shelter me.

When closest friends forget their role
And tell tales that should not be told
When enemies seem much too bold
Please shelter me.

When distant turmoils come too near,
When darkness brings an ardent fear,
When I succumb to a secret tear,
Please shelter me.

When I'm impatient with the world,
As riots rapidly unfurl,
While in my corner I tightly curl,
Please shelter me.

And when life's bitter race is run,
After laboring from sun,
After battle is fought and victory is won,
Please shelter me.

Frances L. Hooks

Dreams

A dream is something made in your mind,
That tells you which path to take,
And perhaps what you will find.
They are there your whole life,
Through bad and good,
To lead and guide,
To make you follow where you should.
A dream is something you want for your life,
Or something you wish to achieve,
But to accomplish this you only need to try and believe.
For a person without a dream,
Is just like a smile without a gleam.
But a person who follows their dream,
Will be happier and will always have that extra beam.
A dream is like wings that are on a bird,
That takes it along,
And teaches it a pleasant song.
From sky to sky,
Low to high,
You follow without any cry.

Melanie Van Sise

"When Twilight Falls"

When twilight falls upon our town
Then lights go on all around
Children on their skates at play
Hate for bedtime to come their way.
Mothers begin to call them home
Knowing someday they will roam
But for today they are in our hands
We must mold them our little lambs
When they grow up and travel around
They will be prepared for things abound.

As twilight falls then they will know
Their home is the safest place to go
With Mother and Daddy standing by
Ready to love them if they cry
When twilight falls upon the land
We reach out with a helping hand
To those who are lost and forlorn
Who need a friend to guide them on
So - let your light shine upon all
To keep them safe - "When Twilight Falls".

Blanche Dean

Dreams

Imagine entering the gardens of love,
Is it at all what you dreamed of
My intentions of being in love are unexplainable
The intelligence of human is over
Opinioned on the subject love
If I did love you how would I know
Would it be an undescribable feeling
Or a touch with so much meaning behind it
Should I be afraid of falling in love or thankful
Do you think that when you
Love someone so much it turns to hate or...
Do you think you can love and
Hate someone at the same time my questions are endless
So if I am or was in love how would I ever know
Thinking too hard is a magnetic force to insanity
But falling in love, is an imaginable feeling with an
Unexplainable definition, just a
State of mind all to yourself, inner beauty you withhold
A feeling, a touch, an undescribable meaning.
Sherry Lynn Cornell

Until Next Time

For so long now I have treasured my feelings for you,
yet kept them buried deep inside of me.
For so long now I have told myself,
"next time"...
The time has come to announce my affection,
for I so much desire to utter those simple syllables.
The words struggle to escape my lips,
but only silence is spoken.
At each passing glance, my heart skips a beat,
and for that brief moment when our eyes connect,
I melt.
So, until next time, the truth remains hidden within.
Jodi S. Diaz

Shade Me

The inspiration of my loneliness is an angel
The contribution of its wings is a gift the wind brings
I feel helpless when flying high above strangers
So I'm willing to give you a lift and sing the song that I see...
Imagine the beauty to be if you slowed the race to notice
your pace and admire the shade of a tree
If you wish to see and never to sell,
your connection has been sewn.
So take my word and remember it well,
for shade is not sold, it's grown.
David Brewer

Thunderstorm

When dancing in the sunlight
I sometimes see a flash,
as if it meant something
that happened in the past.
I think it means a good thing
or something to remind me of
my birthday or finding my brand new glove.
Flash, bang, crash, is what I like to hear
especially, in a rain storm or something I'd
rather fear.
Adrienne S. Dust

My Special Diamond

I need no diamonds of sparkling jewels, nor glittery flashy trinkets.
I need no fancy finery, only the brilliant sparkle of your eyes and the flash of your smile, so sweet and gentle and full of love. The fleeting touch of your hand and the embrace of your loving arms.
Of all the beauty in this big world there's nothing to outshine the golden moments I've spent with you. The laughter that fills my heart with joy.
The oh so brief moments of one unforgettable night that will forever be guarded and protected in my heart. For those precious moments hold all my love and can never be taken by others, for you're my special diamond set in a band of gold.
Olga Harvey Hamilton

Fantasy

We play hide-and-seek
In the lonely hearts column
Your aftershave must be in the
Ice-blue sky of the early morning
You may be sipping your
Coffee very slowly in a cream overcoat
Like a little boy at the country fair
You may be the guy from
Save me the waltz
Dancing on his toes
In his army boots
You may be the roman soldier
On the chocolate coin
The man in the dirty London street
Listening to the vendors
With outstretched arms like grandma Dietrich

Save me the waltz
Oh save me the waltz
And give me back my tears
Andre Van Vuuren

Jesus

I need a friend, someone who wouldn't mind to hold my hand.
A soul that lives with me everyday.
Whose kindness touches my heart in many ways.
What I want is someone to believe in
Someone who ignores all of my sin.
We all need something to love
Something that doesn't try to push or shove.
Your heart is beating only for him.
His light is the best, and never grows dim.
Jesus loves me.
He died and set me free.
I pray to him at night and today
I am no longer in fright.

I've got a friend who's mine.
With Him as my friend I'm perfectly fine!
Juliet Pack

A Very Special Person

Someone you can talk to about whatever's
  on your mind

Someone you can trust with all your
  feelings you keep inside

Someone who is sweet and caring
  always very understanding

That person is very close to me,
  he's my cousin.
Shanna Gename

Twas The Evening Of Christmas

'Twas the evening of Christmas and all through the city
the homeless were as scattered and I thought what a pity
as a boy I remember seeing homeless men here and there,
and I'd say to myself, "doesn't anyone care?"
Then as a teen I saw my first homeless lady,
lying in a hallway alone, about to have a baby.
As I got older, and started to grow,
I never imagined a person freezing and dying,
left out in the snow.
So I ask, where's the mayor? The Governor?
And all those rich politicians?
Certainly not sleeping in shelters or eating in soup kitchens.
Then all of a sudden in the midst of this plight.
There he was standing on this dull gloomy night.
Good old father Christmas, Saint Nick.
Looking around him, and what he saw, made him sick!
Yet I heard him proclaim, to all of the homeless, as he drove out
 of sight,
all you sad people, continue the struggle, don't give up the fight,
have faith in your country, and someday you'll find,
a home of your own and some peace of mind.
For the bottom line is, as the homeless still roam,
every man, woman, and child in America, should at least have a home.

Phil Skolnick

Color Blind

There are many different cultures and races,
And some judge others by the colors of their faces.
But if we could all just see,
How much better it could be,
If some could judge others by how they are inside,
And their prejudice feelings they could hide.
We could stop this ignorant racial fight,
And not judge people badly for being black,
Hispanic, or white.
If everyone could leave their differences behind,
And look at one another as though we're color blind.

Brianna Cassidy

Heirlooms

When my mother passed away,
Everyone was heard to say,
"Save the heirlooms, save the
Heirlooms."
As I sat alone day after day,
I tried to think, the heirlooms,
What were they?
The jewelry, the chest, the sewing
Machines? The tables, the footstools,
The record machine?
The pictures, the purses, the piano stool?
No, we, my brothers and I, are her heirlooms.
We are her jewels.

Elizabeth Lewis

Class Of '97

Thinking of the days that have past us,
Looking forward to the days in front of us,
We the class of '97 have seen each other grow and mature,
We have seen tears of sorrow and joy throughout the years,
Never will we forget these sweet days together,
But no tears should be shed,
For regardless of the road each one takes,
Our hearts will always be bound with the love we share.
These days will soon be but a memory,
A small speck in the realm of our lives,
But the times we've shared together are times to be remembered,
 forever.

Rhonda Yates

Alzheimers

It takes your loved ones without warning
You can't stop it even with all the mowing
They are gone even though they are still alive
Some just want to die
My heart aches for her to be her own self
She is not rich, her family is her wealth
Thinking about the emptiness she will bring makes my heart
bruised
She does not even know who I am, she is so confused.
I am not sure
If they will ever find a cure
I'm waiting for the news, when will it come?
The tears will start to fall when she is done.
Why did it have to take her, I do not understand
Who will take off of her cold finger, the old wedding band?

Laura Dawson

Time

I wish we could go back in time,
the time with most of memories.
When you gave me a pop sickle
After you bit off the top,
When we pretended to sail the seas.
When you gave me a kiss in the tree house
and you caught me a pet rat.
Although I didn't like rats too much,
I made sure to get rid of the cat.
When you taught me how to play baseball
and gave me your newest mitt.
You never gave up when I couldn't throw
or never really hit.
I wish we could go back in time,
the time with most of memories.
When I was yours and you were mine,
And we someday would sail the seas.

Kristi Bryan

Always now is our time

Is there no one here
who doesn't always think,
"If I could have..."?
Who doesn't think of times long past,
ashamed of past mistakes and regrets,
still envious of past happiness and joy?
Some say it has to be that way,
that all we do is live in the past,
believing we can go there somehow.
We can't go there, we never will.
Why then, do we torture ourselves,
mind and soul,
to try to relive a time long gone?
Our time is, and always will be now!
We can remember it, to know what was,
and what could be yet again.
For this we remember it.
We must remember,
for it is man's curse that he forgets!

Cory Matessino

Rainbow

Arching colors in the sky,
pearly clouds go floating by;
after the rain, through the mist,
in a changing world, this beauty still exists.

Colors, colors, in the light,
the symbol of everything bright;
rain may bring gloom for awhile,
but afterwards, a rainbow brings a smile.

Allison Matthews

A Mother's Love

As fresh as a summer breeze is all but a bit of mother's love.
It hurts a child to prick a finger on a thorn from a rose
but, there is nothing sadder than to see the tears fall.
As a mother watches how a child grows
as the world is going around so quickly.
But when the going gets tough a
mother's love is always there to hug you.
When you fall down and braze your skin, or get a cut
as deep as the cracks in the sidewalk, she's always had a
bandage and even a story to make it feel better.
She makes it seem as if there is no problem.
She even closes her eyes when her children are doing wrong,
for a mother never sees wrong in a child
But she is a class all by herself as she takes on the world.
A mother should never be sad especially when there
is always other things to feel good about
A child has to learn but always remember how
precious a mother's love really is...
And to think moms are always giving and never looking
for anything but love

Lisa De Nuto

Things I Want

To wake up on a sunshine morn,
to walk through the dew on a newly cut lawn.
To see happy children at their play,
to hear rain on the roof
on a stormy day.
To smell the lilacs, hear a robin sing,
Knowing full well he's announcing spring.
To hear the mighty ocean's roar
when it casts its waves upon the shore.
To see the first star at night,
it fills my heart with great delight.
To hear the rustles of the leaves,
when the gentle wind blows through the trees.
To see the sun sink in the west,
to see the birds fly back to their nests,
a twilight when the world is at rest,
the time of day that I like best.

Ruth E. Cartier

A Friend

I have been lucky enough to see, God
has given you to me, to share and enjoy
through eternity. To walk and talk of
old and new, which only are for me
and you. We touch upon hidden thoughts
which only he can see, as being part of
two. Who view the sun, the moon, the stars,
and sand. His mountain tops in the sea, and
on the land. With all his creatures in the sea, and
on the land, he has given you to me. To
love, and hold, and share life's precious
moments good and bad. With all its beauty,
I would never see, if it were just me. So,
thank you Jesus for lending me, someone
very precious, who really knows me.

Marie George

Sometimes...

Sometimes I want to be like the wind,
with its mighty blow.
Sometimes I want to be like the earth,
with its mighty power.
Sometimes I want to be like the sun,
with its sunshiny days.
Sometimes I want to be like myself, with
my happy life!

Beth Leighanne Pittmon

There Was A Time

There was a time, I'm told when you could leave your front door
    unlocked, and be assured that when you got back
    your stuff would still be there
There was a time, where if you saw little boys playing with guns
    you knew they were toys
There was a time, when young girls said they had a baby, they
    were more than likely talking about a doll and
    not the real thing
There was a time, when you didn't have to worry about where
    your child was, cause someone in the neighborhood would know
There was a time, when old men would speak and young men
    would listen, with Respect
There was a time, when in school you were more concerned about
    making the football team, or the cheer leading squad,
    or getting an A in math, not getting shot, stabbed, cut-up,
    or worse, murdered
There was a time, when we cared more about each other, because it
    was the Christian thing to do, not because it
    is the politically correct thing to do
Yeah I'm told, there was a time.

Odessa Shaw Jr.

Joy And Happiness

You've grown so much in this past year
I love you so much and these words are sincere.

You're the light of my life,
you're every breath that I take.
You're the best thing that happened to me
you are far from a mistake.

You are my baby, we will never depart
you're the life that I live, the beating in my heart

You bring me so much happiness
you bring me so much joy, we
have a special bond together
which no one can destroy.

To watch you walk, to hear you talk
is a feeling I'll never forget
It's like the day February 17th
the first day that we met.

I know there's days still to come to have more feelings,
to have more fun (but...) in those days we're sure to part,
But never forget you're in my heart

Shannon McColligan

A Moment In Time

We lie in the grass, my daughter and I
watching and waiting as the clouds rolled by
our imaginations ran wild and to our delight
we saw an array of animals in flight.

They were gone on their way as quick as could be
leaving behind a wonderful memory.
We returned often to that magical place
our haven away from the "old rat race".

We talked, we laughed, we cried, and then
we were ready to take life on again.
Many years have passed and life goes on its way
but, the memory lingers like it was yesterday.

We shared a moment in time -
a wonderful moment that was truly sublime.

Ruth Sorensen

Dedication

'Twas shining morn, with step so young,
She did view the tumultuous hue,
Of eager faces bright with questions
Posed for answers and her graces.

Plaudits rang through ivy halls.
Escutcheons mounted all those walls.
Inviolable was this praise
The pedagogy trail it blazed.

O' thief of time crept on his way,
Her locks that shone, dulled to grey;
And those who peer from lofty places,
Soon removed those loyal places
And took, and took, for younger paces,
The elder's life that youth replaces.

To the victors go the plunder
Who, too, have sewn the seeds they reap.
God, who knows the sun, the thunder,
All that venerate shall come to weep!

Rita V. Flint

Comes The Fall

It's in the air! Hear the brisk winds blow!
The leaves are flying, their colors aglow.
Farmers hustle to gather their crops.
Hail becomes interspersed with chilly raindrops.
Birds fly south - home furnaces are checked.
Folks make sure their wardrobes are correct.

We get out the quilts, preparing for the change.
We move about faster (there's lots to arrange).
Halloween is ahead, then Thanksgiving and Christmas.
Greeting cards come and go - though phoning is less fuss.
Our spirits perk up for the holidays ahead.
Bright colors appear, more gold, green, and red.

So let's join with nature, looking forward, not back.
If we stay optimistic, we're on the right track.
Our doubts and fears can only sap our strength,
While love and caring give our lives joy and length.
We hope you can feel our great love and affection,
Along with many best wishes sent in your direction.

Arnold Brown

Steps In Time

The road we travel seems to bask in the light,
but just up ahead it fades into night.

We see clearly the road that is traveled by friends,
all the ditches and gullies that await round the bends.

We can go cautiously forward with each step prepared,
or stumble and bumble with each step we dare.

We can't know the outcome of each step we take,
but we know we've done right if it's been for Christ's sake.

When we step out each day, let us walk with an edge.
While walking with Christ, we'll avoid every ledge.

The decisions we make, be they bad, be they good,
if made with the Lord, we've done the best that we could.

Trice Meyer

Journey Of Night

My strength is drawn from the night
From the moonlight
Dappling the water, scarring the depth of the grass
Beneath me;
From the stars, quivering pale against the moon,
Yet bright enough to guide those who wish to follow;
From the untamed power and grace of the wind,
Tempering the trees, rustling, whispering,
Yet arresting itself to caress the cheeks of lovers
Walking hand in hand;
From the cricket's chirp, calling others to communion
Or love or war;
And from the dark that surrounds me too short a time,
The dark that shadows, that hides, that holds
Me
As I walk through my soul
In the night
I am whole.

Nicole D. Amendolara

Skydive

Don't call me a fool, because you see,
of the two of us it is I who is free.
I'll sing my songs joyfully
and see your world toyfully.
I won't be deafened by your sounds.
Life for me has no bounds.
Death for us all has no ends,
so, I'll carry my fears into the winds
and feel my spirit awaken from within.
Not knowing life is the only real sin
and life as we know it won't always last,
so, I refuse to let the moments pass.
I'll spread my arms to hold my dreams
and see the world for more than it seems.

Catherine Davis

"Underneath"

Underneath everything I see a dark, dismal place.
Deep in my soul.
I hear a scream.
Underneath everything I find a cold, empty space.
Nobody's there.
I hear a cry.
Underneath everything I meet a sad, lonely face.
Hurting inside
I hear nothing
But the sound of my heart breaking

Wendy Boos

Valentine O Valentine

On the day we did marry
My love for you I so adored
With your hand in mine
Was my sole reward.
As I dream of thee
It is your beauty I see
You have taken my soul not just a part
You seem to be the fiber and core of my heart
You are so tender and so true
I just cherish the whole day through
So on this day of love and wishes
I will end this poem with some kisses.

Martin Hunt

Esther

Her eyes were made of gold.
She dance at the market,
but at night,
where the sea was running against the green cliffs,
the moon painting her body with gold,
there, Esther kissed the enemy.
But Esther's uncle was Mordicai,
who was sitting at the gate of the city,
looking at the cliffs
running by the sea.

And Mordicai said,
"I will take you to the Royal Court
where your body will be soaked in oil, smelling like jasmine."
And Esther said,
"I will let my body be soaked in oil, smelling like jasmine,
but who will pay my price?"
Then the maidens in the market sang the sad song,
"Goodbye Esther,
so long.
Go to the silk-covered room and cry . . . "
After Esther's body smelled of jasmine she wore her dress,
the color of the cliffs.

Mordicai covered his eyes and said,
"You will save Israel,
and Haman will hang."
And Esther said, "Where is the price for me?"
And Moridai said,
"There is no price for you."
and Esther the Queen left for her silk-covered room.

Steven Kelemen

Untitled

Anxiety producing, stress inducing and heart wrenching circumstances:
My lesson plan book was late
Sara had a seizure
Matthew was sent in with no lunch again
John's been in the same clothes for the past three days
Melissa had a cigarette burn on her back.
At last, the day was over and you greeted me at the door
   with a big kiss.
We walked outside for awhile and you stood so close as if you knew
   about my day's happenings.
The exquisiteness of your crystal, ocean-blue eyes and the way
   the sunlight shined on your deep black hair was simply breathtaking.
We walked in perfect unison with one another, sensing each other's
   thoughts and needs, and communicating without a single word
      ever being spoken.
Forgetting the pain I experienced throughout the day, and losing
   myself in your beauty was both magical and therapeutic.
The bond I share with my Siberian is unique, perfect and unshatterable.

Mona V. Corbett

Untitled

I have a little son
And at times he's naughty as he can be.
He'll tease the cat
And he'll tease the dog
Throw toys all over the place.
And when I scold him
He will hang his little head
And put his little hands behind his back
And in a few moments he comes
And puts his little arms around me
And looks up at me with his blue eyes
And says, Mommy, I love you.
Mothers could you stay angry
At a little boy like that?

Zeailer Reid

Succubus

It lives inside her mouth, is borne deep inside the throat
grows from the tongue, and gathers strength from the darkest,
cruelest areas of the brain.
It oozes forth, its tentacles reach outwards
slowly crawling, then creeping towards the helpless victim.
Suddenly, it jumps, it wraps its tentacles around the victim.
The victim is ensnared and bewildered.
Why this bondage, why this cruelty?
The tentacles bore deep inside the victim's brain.
The wounds are invisible, as are the scars that grow to cover them.
The tentacles suckle, the brain matter is absorbed.
The desires for freedom, love, anger towards the beast grow smaller
and smaller, till they are gone.
The tentacles recede, the monster goes back inside its hiding place.
It waits for the next time and there will be a next time.
Each time, the victim grows smaller and smaller
'til all that remains is a dried up husk
minus feelings and thoughts
an overweight, tired, pained form, minus a soul.

Robert Jones

Emergence

Dedicated to My Mother Lorrain
A struggle I've seen
in the blue gray pools of mother
Earnestly searching for a height in sight
to reach our of here and away
A journey of Holy do's and don'ts
look this way not that
being wisped away hidden
Then touching the slippery silver wings
A faith seed planted to draw her strength
The existence of peace finally lies
in the blue gray pools of mother.

Valerie Helms

Designer Genes?

You say that genetic engineering came along in the early 1970's,
That it's new, up-to-date, ultra-modern, 20th Century?
With its artificial replication, broken linkage,
Repair enzymes, new kinds of protein?

But haven't you heard about the early Centaurs?
Half-human, half-horse
(Both mammals, but somewhat different?)
Genetic intervention? Possible gene splicing?
(They didn't know about the double helix, but somehow . . .)

What about Chimera?
Part lion, part goat, part serpent . . .
How's that for chromosome cross-over?
And Polyphemus, the Cyclops, making thunderbolts?
Mutation anxiety?
Pan, with his goat's legs, horns and ears . . .
Recombinant DNA?
And what about Pegasus, the winged horse?
Just genetic drift?
Or gene manipulation?

George Hinshaw

Diamonds In The Sky

I love the sky at night. What a sight!
When I look up in the sky I wonder why
there are diamonds in the sky. Maybe
they're there because the sky has nothing
to wear. Maybe fairies put them there
because they didn't know where to hide
them so no one could get there. Why do I care!?
Because who could bear the dare of them not being up there?

Caitlin Elin Stevens

Mother's Son (Reflections Of Operation Desert Storm)

The Mother of battle has produced the son that may destroy the father.
The child injects fear with multiple projectiles that have no name.
Toys of deception praised as weapons of peace rain down reminders
of hate that only teach once.
Protectant fathers are on the loose leading their children into the
dawn of destruction.
Haze and mist have lost sight of the son who once knew his place.
Misunderstanding has gripped the masses, choking lies from its fists.
The land is barren leaving hate to cover it in slippery blackness.
The sadness being lives lost in search of an idea called prosperity,.
Shackles risen faceward in hopes of prolonged life.
Shrouds of cloth are assembled and worn to hide the unblemished
temple from fatal fragrances.
The grave houses the dead from the sight of the living.
Happiness is now caution.
Others watch while sustaining damage.
Religion has been abandoned.
The end is a dream waiting to come true.

Jeffery R. Dethrow

The Beauty Of You

I see your heartache, your struggle.
You want to be somebody else,
But if God loves you as you are
Why can't you just be yourself?

You can't be your father, your mother,
Your sister, or your brother.
So why don't you just be free?
Become the special person God made you to be.

Can a sparrow grow a peacock tail?
Now wouldn't that be a sight.
Can you imagine a turtle
Growing wings to take flight?

My daughter you're precious you're special,
And I will tell you why.
You know that God doesn't make junk,
And also neither do I.

So just forget your struggle.
Look on what is really true.
If you look through your mother's eyes
You'll see the beauty of you!

Donna Rusk

The Vintage Years — A Spiritual Outlook

Half a century — gone — and more — has past.
The years are behind, but the memories last.
The wisdom of age — it's hard to define,
As better we should be, as it is with wine.
Control we would like, but we have it not,
The journey goes on, and we know not what
The future will hold...

The timing of smiles, the shedding of tears,
All part of the ongoing harvest of years,
Years that love sowed, no measured too great,
The treasure we find, as we continue and wait.

Change is unending, and our lives are unique,
Pressing on until sunset after reaching our peak,
Far more precious than wealth or silver or gold
Is the peace and contentment as we grow old,
And realize, despite disappointments and pain
Our spirit will live and see the reign
Of a brighter world with no struggle or strife
When we leave this world, there will be new life.

Lilian DiSpigna

Breaking Up

I don't know how to tell you this,
But I think our days are through,
I'm really sorry but I guess
I fell out of love with you.

Please don't be mad at me.
But there's nothing left anymore.
The feelings that we used to have
Just went out the door.

I am so sorry for doing this,
I wish I could change how I feel.
I really thought we'd last always
I thought our love was real.

I just don't want you to hate me,
Please try to understand,
I've been feeling like this for a while
Now I've put it off as long as I can.

I wish there was something
For you that I could do or say,
But really you'll be happier with out me
It's just better this way.

Amanda Leann Martin

God's Glorious Rainbows

My eyes have seen God's glorious rainbows.
My ears have heard the cheerful chips of sparrows.
I have smelled different fragrances of roses,
And climbed many mangoes and apple trees.

I have loved vermilion sunsets and bluebonnets
And flaming red and purple maple trees in autumn.
Precious memories of my detours in the deserts,
Re-assure me through dark days before the dawn.

God's glorious rainbows amid his infinite artistry,
And creations divine order of diversity
The endless hues of blues in sky and sea.....
It is obvious to me, God loves colors and variety.

In God's garland of grace
I see His awesome agape love for every race.
We know that there will be strife
In each and every relationship in life.

Which color of the rainbow is love?
What culture is forgiveness and kindness?
What gender is forbearance?
Seeing God's glorious rainbows, is peace part of the simple abundance?

Betty Klee

The Fire Escape Pastor

Oh Pastor! Teach me to live in such a way
that at my death I will escape — "the lake of fire."

It is written: "Do not be afraid of those who kill
the body but cannot kill the soul. Rather be
afraid of the One who can destroy both soul
and body in hell." (Matthew 10:28)

As I descend the steps of the "fire escape of
life," may the cross on which Jesus Christ died
be before me and the world behind me.

May the church's fire escape remind me on
earth that the cross on which Jesus Christ died
is a fire escape and that Jesus Christ came to
earth to teach the way, the truth and the life.
I want my name written in the Lamb's Book Of Life.

Euris M. Bryant

Being A Kid

Being a kid is a very hard job
You got to remember not to be a slob

Like when Aunt Bertha comes to dinner
Your whole family gets thinner

Or when Uncle Jack comes to town
Makes you want to hide underground

You wish you had a bodyguard
Every time you see cousin Bernard

And when Aunt Kathy squeezes you to death
You wiggle and squirm to get your breath

But being a kid isn't so bad
If you have an understanding Mom and Dad
   Sarah Smith

Time

  Days have passed by,
and not a word to say hi.
  Slowly it builds inside,
until your heart grows long and wide.
  The pain hurts more and more,
as the eyes begin to get sore.
  Tears running down your cheek,
while your body goes numb and weak.
  Soon no one can come near,
for they sense the pain and begin to fear.
  One wrong move or word,
will set you off after the world.
  Finally you start to forget,
only to have your wish met.
  The words sting inside your mind,
as everything slowly unwinds.
  Soon you remember the chime,
that all things come with time.
   Michelle Powers

The Knot

When I forget,
or do something wrong,
a little knot,
will come along.
It sits in my stomach,
for what seems like a day.
And until I'm forgiven,
it won't go away.
This happens in school,
when my homework isn't found,
or when I get into trouble,
for being a clown.
The knot makes my stomach,
feel very tight.
My heart starts beating,
like I've had a fright!
Then it goes away till I get, in trouble
and then...and then...
The knot strikes again!!!
   Sarah E. Werner

The First Christmas Gift

Mary wrapped the first Christmas gift
She wrapped it in swaddling cloth,
It was a gift to all the world
Its value of untold worth,

What was this gift she did present
Worth more than silver and gold,
It was the valley's purest Lily
It was Sharon's most beautiful Rose.

It was the gift of comfort,
It was the gift of love
It was the gift of peace and joy,
Sent down from God above.

The gift of light to light the world,
A lamp to guide our way,
Yet, there it was wrapped in swaddling cloth,
All snuggled in the hay.

It's nearing now two thousand years
Since the first Christmas gift was given,
It was the gift of God's own Son
Sent down to us from heaven.
   Audrey B. Porter

Twilight's Touch

In the twilight of the night as we rock to gentle slumber,
I reflect upon the day and I begin to wonder...
"What will this lifetime hold for my sweet, little daughter?"

I gently rub her light brown hair,
so soft and smooth to touch,
and marvel at this little life I've grown to love so much!

Her smile can melt my heart! That sparkle in those blue eyes
Tell me to prepare to answer an ocean full of "why's."

Her zest for life is so strong, it overflows to mine
and I wonder how I ever got along before this special time!

A toddler can bring about so many new gifts - to see the world
through her eyes can really lift my spirit!

So as my day draws to a close, I have to stop and say,
"no matter how hectic it all can be, I wouldn't have it any other way!"
   Renee Hamilton

Abuse Is A Disease

Abuse is the use of pain,
whether mental or physical,
they both will remain

Remain within the mind, body and soul
leaving you alone, helpless and cold...

Abuse is neither manly, nor is it pure
Abuse is a disease that has a proven cure

Curing abuse, helps to cure the pain...
Curing the pain, helps to ensure that we will remain.
   Johnny T. Wilson

Mom

You make us laugh you make us cry you put a certain sparkle in our eyes. I don't know how you do it, how you do these simple things but it makes me feel oh so good as if I had long, beautiful wings. You touch us on our shoulders and tell us "It's Okay" we love you and adore you don't answer us in dismay. I know someday you will die, someday I'll die too, but as long as we're still around, let's spend some time together me and you. I love you so very much, and I know you love me too.
  I love you Mom.
   Jenna Dominguez

My Old Dog

I had to say goodbye to her for she was taken away to join the spirit of the Wolf.
She came to me when just a pup. She loved me and trusted me and always showed it to me even if I was down on my luck.
I will miss her when I awake at dawn. In the evening when I come home I'll never see her wagging tail or see her run to me again.
You were there with me throughout your life. You never asked for much, a few pats on the head, keep you fed and a place for your bed.
Yes, my old dog, you are now free to roam wherever you please. I pray that God takes care of dogs when they leave and the owners that grieve.
Franklyn Lee Miller

The Keys To Achievement

It seems when things are going right
The stresses of life step into dim the light

When you think all troubles have gone astray
Then comes more calamity to make mock of your day

But as long as there's hope in any given situation
The power of that hope can help bring restoration

Things are more easily said then done
Add aching perseverance and the battle is almost won

So then, let's consider what must also take place
A soft, humble prayer seeking God's grace
Gilbert S. Livingston

Wheel Of Time

The tempest storms toss within bitter lye,
Where sin plunders and bleeds the heart to cry.
And since oft searching an unbounding escape,
To burn the bridges transgression creates.
For this; the lowly memoir of times past,
But love's exquisite right may come at last.

Within times present there's freedom to be,
From out of dream's mist, lives our fantasy.
We find delicate rhyme truly inspired,
All life's hopes and wishes we blessed acquired.
In long-suffered patience we yearn to grow,
To share and to love all the dreams we know.

The morrow's day dawning, the future told
Sealed together beyond our death's age old.
In heaven's ecstasy; children we'll bear,
In them we'll live and love the life we share.
Thus in trials and troubles our hearts confide,
In success and laughter all our fears subside.

Even still you inquire, "just how could it be?"
For truth is love—mine is eternity.
David R. Gasper

Undying-Love

I look into his eyes and melt away,
  and in his arms I want to lay.
My love for him is very strong,
  and so to loose him would be wrong.
I think of him each night and day,
  all that I think of I shall not say.
I dream of him each and every night,
  for us being together will someday be right.
I want our time lives to become one,
  but that will not happen if from my fears I run.
The day has come to say goodbye,
  I'll never forget you and that's no lie.
Claudia Szilagyi

Still Life

Shadows of forest and claret, chestnut and hunter peering
through faded tapestries; glints of gold and port and vine
octagonal beds of mahogany,
beautifully carved images of bats and dragons; occidental...oriental
Ornate and gilded; screens of silk and thread, birds and branches
dusty tomes in Latin, Italian; more things in heaven and on earth,
studies of nudes and still-lives and fruit,
(the dining room)
polished banisters, lazily sloping in languid bend
glowing under dusty tallowed sconces,
age and money, so refined, congealing in corners,
lapping at cobwebs and faded squares of wallpaper high above
hardening, filling cracks with antiquities and their revivals
defined by smoking men, speaking of the Amazon and New Deals,
parasoled wives on the veranda, flappers and swingers in the hall;
(in the room the women come and go, talking of Michelangelo)
Brahms on the Victrola, Glen Miller in the hall
times merging, weaving together unacknowledged, ignominious
a young girl and boy sit and play quietly in the giant hall
will they enjoy the splendor of their youth, use their imaginations,
find the magic wardrobe and delight in their ignorance?
Or will they run from their subliminal consciousness,
blame their limited past, assume that they understand more than those before them,
and live in self-important misery?
Deirdre J. Kamber

The Sun

As the sun shines so does your life.
Your teaching, like beams of light,
touches each child in a special way.
In the morning, you rise with excellency.
By Midday, you're radiating with brilliancy.
By evening, your job has been accomplished.
You've spread warmth, love, and kindness
to all who were willing to receive it.
So in you go to prepare for another day in
order to make a difference in some child's life.
Tracey Morgan

To The Past

Let us take a moment to view the past,
To look at things that could not last.
To dream, our hope long since shattered.
To grasp ideals that should have mattered.

That grandfather or aunt that left us here,
Those friends and neighbors who were so dear.
The Christmas that the special gift was given,
The look on mom, so much like heaven.

The fragrance of spring and freedom of summer.
Young friends and places where you would linger.
That first love and broken heart,
That day when friends had to part.

The job and tasks of all degrees,
The shiny car that all must see.
The separation from mom and dad,
The painful maturing that seemed so bad.

The past is sweet, though it makes me cry.
I must keep these thoughts until I die.
Memories of the past are a gift from above,
Wrapped in tears and sealed with love.
Mike Reeves

My True Love

First love, true love, young love. Our hearts high on the wings of a
dove. Me a child of sixteen, young and shy. You a boy of nineteen,
with eyes as blue as the sky. Your heart was filled with sorrow and
hate. That I could see in your eyes on our first date.

Your family was the problem, this I could see. So I asked you to
come live with me. Our love grew strong, as did the bonds between us.
There never was any sadness or distrust. There was only the music
in our hearts. That would sing to keep us happy whenever apart.

We married in late summer of 1980. Twas a hot day, the breeze was as
gentle as a lady. Family and friends gathered from everywhere. For
this happy and very festive affair. The evening was filled with
happiness. That made our hearts sing with gladness.

A year we lived as man and wife. But then! On my 19th birthday, the
Lord took your life. Upon that eve, the birds sang a sad song. That
dreadful night, seemed so, so long. All of a sudden you were gone
from my touch. The tragedy and pain I felt hurt me so much.

I know you will always be in my heart, as a part of me. For the memories
of you will never leave, for only you have the key. We knew our love
was so true, our happy years did number two. Now you're happy
walking the streets of gold, where the angels sing sweet songs of old.
"GOODBYE MY TRUE LOVE, GOODBYE!"

Lori A. Hill

The Eternal Prevailer

From the skies emerge deliverance, the hellions race for war,
In chariots run ablaze, unsheathing fatal swords,
From the firmaments see all so clear, the inferno has begun,
The divine and evil clash at last, the chains of hell undone,
Emerge forth the deliverer, to elicit vengeance from the skies,
Veers forth a breeze of omen, the final hour is nigh,
The hordes of Hades chambers, in arms arise so bold,
A bad moon now is rising, the upheaval now unfolds,
The defiant hordes of hell emerge, to the path of war now run,
To incur their own destruction when Armageddon is then done,
To the valley of Megiddo, the hordes of hell convene,
For a challenge of the titans, a carnage yet unseen,
From the celestial dawns in triumph, the God of Judgement and of Ire,
From the firmaments so ominous, dawns a barrage of hail and fire,
At the foothills of Megiddo, the hellions slain at war,
Over the legions of Mephisto, hast the Lord prevailed once more!

Lorgio Coimbra

Melancholia

Lying there, next to you, your hair curled, matted against
your head as crisp brown leaves...
beat against the window. Words flow from under me
like...milk from my mouth. I tell you the things I would like to
do to you, how sometimes it rains inside my head, and runs down
my lips and thighs. I watch blood slide through
the spider-woven circuitry in your veins, dancing a green parallel
to the deep cambers of skin that will never quite heal as they should.
The room gradually becomes golden warm, reflecting against the fine
flurry of dust spinning amongst each other around your face,
and while you lie cold I tell you how beautiful the death of day can be
as its last breath dissipates in orange fascination. I reach out.

Tiya Gordon

The Olympics

The Olympics shall come every four years,
While the little ones wait to see their favorite appear
The Olympians compete for the medals handed out,
They wait for the gold, silver, or bronze,
They take home the medal to his or her loved ones,
They try to impress their family, country or state,
Some Olympians take home nothing and feel hopeless to anyone,
But you know the Olympics will come again and they give
  second chances!

Jennifer Ketchersid

A Midnight's Glory

Upon my cozy bed at night
I wonder, 'What's outside my lair?'
I take a peek, of small duration
To uncover what the night will spare.

A mystery, the one I tell;
A secret I can't keep:
Beyond the dark and eerie
Lies a wonder that doesn't speak.

I look, I stare, I don't miss a single space
For what I seek is something I don't know;
But sight, it seems, won't find this thing,
Perhaps my hearing is the final blow.

I listen long, I listen hard,
For sounds of things that are not right,
But then, I hear my wonder,
The silence of the night.

Alex Kloth

Reflections

As I look out my window
I see beauty all around,
But my reflection always shows
A man with just a frown.

I think of the love that we share
And the memories began to sail,
What use to be nights of heaven
Have been replaced by nights of hell.

If I never see the pearly gates
I've held heaven in my arms,
I've heard the voice of an angel sing
And witnessed all your beauty and charms.

I yearn for your loving touch
That burns through my heart into my soul,
I crave the taste of your sweet lips
For these desires I can't control.

So while looking out your window
It's my reflection that you'll see,
For my heart I leave with you
And all my love to be.

Tommy Baker

The Way I Feel

The way I felt about you
was like I never felt before. There was just
that look of yours that made me love you even
more. You have the most beautiful eyes to gaze
into. It just hurts to know you don't feel the
same way I do. When I think of you a tear
comes to my eye. Then I wonder why, why did it
end up the way it did I don't talk about my
feelings for you 'cause now they're all hidden,
hidden behind the anger and sadness that I
brought upon myself to forget about you. Sometimes
I wonder why I care. I know why I care because
my feelings for you are still there. It hurts so much
when those feelings of mine get hurt, it feels like my heart is being
torn apart into pieces, just the thought of you is my weakness
but I'm becoming stronger as I live through all this.
Everything we go through together. I feel that we're getting...
closer as friends....
The way you want it!

Angela McFerren

Letter From An Un-Named Soldier

Oh dearest Ma,
The cruel sights my eyes have seen.
Is this what you wanted me to be?
Is this the dream you had in store for me?
The nightmarish dreams,
Still haunt me.
Will they ever leave?
I have watched many friends die,
Some in my own two arms.
Is this how we go bravely into battle?
Afraid that it might be our last.
Is this what hero's are made of?
Do you have to die to be a hero?
In the end,
There is no other army to fight.
There is no other demons to battle against.
The only demon is yourself,
Because you have just killed another man,
In cold blood.
   Sara Lentini

My Gift To You

My gift to you Babe is my undying love
Often we make judgments instead of understanding
Find faults instead of comforting
For you my dear, my love grows with each day
no matter the hurt or confusion I may feel
My thoughts are always with you
With each down side I believe there's an up side
Each step we take together brings us closer
together not farther apart
For you my love is what I live for
To share with you the good times
and to handle the bad and sad times
I'll always stand by you for we are one
So babe, my gift to you is letting go
You choose what makes you happy and I'll be happy for you.
Even if your choice is not me
For this our love will never be in question
My gift to you love, is letting go
   Jo Rhoades

To My Mother

  I received a letter from
my mother today, she says
"She misses me and wonders why?"
I haven't written through these past days.
Where would I begin to tell my mother,
"Not to worry or feel at blame."
"That is I don't know how to write in special and
wouldn't know how to explain!"
A friend of mine translated this letter of mine,
I felt so lonely inside,
as I went back to my side.
Now, find myself writing this poem to my mom,
one day through translation she will know what has yet,
not come.
Which is, "I don't know where or when, I lost my heretic language."
"But know from my heart I love you and miss you."
Through this english language.
   Rolando Camona

A Chance

Never will he know much she cares,
with any other man he'd be counting his blessings in every prayer.
Other men would set her high atop an ivory tower,
forever protecting it with the love that has all the power.
her eternal life's pledge to him was her call,
in return, he laughs, he teases,
he makes her feels so small.

LIke a rich man who squanders his money,
he takes advantage of his wife's true love,
and thinks it's funny.
For I am poor, just a beggar boy,
without someone like her,
my life will never experience joy.

I am bound to a solitary life,
he doesn't know how to appreciate
having such a beautiful, loving wife.
For we compliment each other, always there's a reminder
the ironies of life is just another bother.
How life could be a wonderful dance,
my only prayer is that I be given a chance.
   Michael J. Crosby

Misty Night

Through a misty rain,
we now look back on the day
the moon was taken away.
To close your eyes tight and hold on forever,
to each other when he hits the brakes.
And the car comes to a screaming halt.
And you wake up in a bed, in a place you are not used to.
And now you can't move.
The last thing you remember is him saying I love you.
And for now you are though, because he is buried in two.
Because of that dreadful night,
you now live in fright.
And for now we say good night.
Forever we will hold on tight,
to that dreadful night.
   Crystal Swenson

Old Man

Yesterday an old man spoke
  of things that were no more
Today a child knows not what of
  the things the man spoke for.

Today has passed and so's a year
  The child has seen much more
  the old man's gone but nay his words
One day the child will hold them dear.

And so the child has come to pass
Through grief and joy, by life and death
And yea the old man's long since dead
Will the child heed words that he once said

Now the child's a man grown old
His world has stopped and grown so cold
Old wise eyes now full of tears
He'd laid to waste so many years.
   Amanda E. Johnson

Ode To The Air Force

These folks in blue really aim high,
doing the best to guard our
country's piece of sky,
to thank them, makes common sense,
for their herculean efforts in
our defense,
like me, they have a strong
interest in aviation,
they study diverse subjects
from meteorology to navigation,
who else can fly a Fortress
or a Tom Cat
at speeds like mach 2, each
one really scats,
they fought many types, from a
zero to a Mig,
as skillfully as an Irishman dances a jig,
in summary, let's thank them
clearly or in a code named Morse,
our high flying protectors, the U.S. Air Force.
Allan Morris

A Phreaks Manifesto

The righteous are punished
and the insane set free.
The system can be bought,
and the blind made to see.
The truth will be hidden;
there are lies to be told.
Our government will fall
and anarchy will hold.
Cover-ups left and right.
What really did happen
will never see the light.
You call us criminals,
yet we are not biased.
We live without racism
and wars we do not wage.
You build bombs and murder,
while we seek more knowledge.
If you judge me yourself,
by your own set standards, then yes I am a criminal.
I say "you may stop this individual, but you can not stop us all."
Patrick Buttonow

A Nature Drink

It was the only sound I heard
 amid quaint chirpings of a bird.
Its gushing journey pierced my ear,
 I touched the stream and drew it near.
I stepped into its rhythmic flow
 content I had no place to go.
It quenched dry roots as it rolled by
 and bathe my feet to ankle high.
I edged a pebble with my toe,
 small minnows darted to and fro.
Each ripple spread out playfully
 reminding me that joy is free.
As morning sunlight kissed the dew,
 a silhouette was painted blue.
A tapestry of sky hung low
 reflected in the liquid glow.
I bent to gaze into the deep
 whose shallowness was mine to keep.
My fingers cupped a formless dip;
 I drank in nature, sip by sip.
Audrey Stech

If The Sky Wasn't Grey

 If the sky wasn't grey,
this lonely feeling of mine would leave.
 I know there's a place in
time. When the skies will return
to blue. Until this happens the world
needs to brighten all our days and nights.
We'll encourage the little ones to run
and play and be happy, all the adults
would relax themselves on the beach
and sit below their grey skies
and watch our next generation
change all things we all know
to look a little brighter.
 If our skies weren't grey.
 Tyler L. Simons

A Line Moves

Within the cubical of acceptance, a line moves;
traveling an unproven course,
Straining the limitation of values set.
In the center of this prejudice stance,
a narrow plane of approval,
the predetermined foundation
on which to converse.
And so the line moves, in a contorted dance.
Seeking the course that defines,
the meaning of those values set.
This conquest will alter the circumstance,
old established standards to bruise,
with a thought provoking threat.
This challenger marks the course,
a new perimeter to set,
and forever changes the contour of acceptance,
eroding the old foundation.
Desiring to find balance, on the line moves,
old values and new horizons to transverse.
 Donald Stanley Semler

Imagination

Imagine a water line, like a mountain peak
Hear the surf hit the rocks, like thunder
Imagine small pieces, of sand, in a sand castle
Imagine blue water and a sky blue sky,
 almost like each other
Feel the cool coolness from the water, on your
 feet as you stand there in it
Imagine this place you are imagining
And take yourself there
What is it you are imagining?
But don't forget the "Shhwush" of the surf
 hitting the rocks or you won't be there.
 Sarah Abboud

Black

Black is the death, of someone close to your heart.
Black is the funeral, where mind and body part.
Black is witches, with their magic and cats.
Black is the misery, from living like rats.
Black is the smell, of dust and smoke.
Black is the insanity, that makes people choke.
Black is betrayal, by someone you love.
Black is the sorrow, that smothers like a glove.
Black is the mystery, of what's on the "other side."
Black is your sins, that are impossible to hide.
Black is nothingness, when you look in the sky.
Black is the war, that makes innocent people die.
 Marya Tremain

He

He tells me he loves me,
as he holds the key to my heart.
He made me feel special,
right from the start.

Each time we meet,
I imagine his kisses sweet.
I imagine his embrace,
and my heart starts to race.

He brings me up when I'm down,
He turns my whole world around.
He understands the problems I face,
He helps me put them in their proper place.

Inseparable is what we are,
and I hope to stay that way, near or far.
I love him so much,
him and his special touch.

Renee Rivera

The Beat Lives On

Written in memory of Allan Flatt 1976-1996
Yesterday he played the drums,
but now the tempo's gone.
His drumsticks lie unused, untouched,
and yet, the beat lives on.

Silent drums and saddened hearts
will learn to beat again.
Somehow we must learn to cope
with the loss of our great friend.

I didn't know him all that well,
but I knew him, just the same.
After all, he was a drummer—
"Golden Child" was his name.

Allan helped me learn to like the drums;
he helped me learn to play.
If I could only thank him now—
this is my only way.

His spirit lives inside of us,
even though he's gone.
His drumsticks may lie unused, untouched,
but still, the beat lives on.

Yesterday he played the drums,
and today, the beat lives on.

Barbara Coln

Spirit

There is a spirit that lives in me, that
always loves to set me free. Like
the birds that fly high in the sky,
that always live deep inside,
When I'm crying and feeling low, the
spirit always, takes it flow. It's
a feeling of love, a feeling of hope,
a feeling to keep inside of me.
It flows like a butterfly, it
sting like a bee, to keep me
on track, with the cool in me.
The spirit is lyrics the spirit
is a song, that you can sing
the whole night long. So when in
church, and the spirit comes out,
thank the Lord and sing about. Lift
your hands and give God praise,
for he is the one, who give us
days. The spirit is in me can't you see,
this is the way it should be.

Murless Jones

Gall

Choices made and mistakes forgotten,
Sometimes things are better left unsaid.
On one knee and the other is missing,
I have one grief and a forgetful thread.

Two against one just isn't fair,
And thinking too much is what kills.
Dreams are things you can't let go,
The scar on my hand is all I know.

It's so strange how everything,
Makes so much of what you are.
Trained and bleed turned upside down,
The love you have doesn't make a sound.

Saying what you feel isn't always right,
You were here and now you're gone.
The life it was is nothing now,
And just like me you forget somehow.

It's too late to turn back this time,
It's easier this way you'll see
The feelings I have aren't me,
I need to wake up from an endless dream.

Lance Steiner

Death Distress

I don't understand. Could someone please explain why?
Can it be that I'm the only one who's afraid to die?

People live and die. You're here and then you're gone.
Is anyone else as apprehensive as I about the unknown?

Going through school and job training and building your career,
But what's the use of trying when the end will soon be near?

Enjoying many good times visiting cheerfully with your best friend,
But when you die, it's your funeral that tearfully she'll attend.

Sharing love with your family, secure in the happiness you've found
But where do all the memories go when you're six feet underground?

How does it feel when suddenly your lungs can't breathe air?
When your heart stops beating, doesn't it all seem so unfair?

Sometimes life makes you frown but sometimes life makes you smile.
Is it really worth living? Let me mull over that question a while?

Martha Deloatch

From Ruby - For Carl

I fell in love with my sweetheart
And many, many years have past
Then my dear sweet baby left me
To be with Jesus at rest.

Tears are falling for my baby
I don't know where they come from
There's more than an ocean still flowing
They'll stop when I get home.

I'm still in love with my baby
Alone with my memories of love
I laugh, I cry, I'm never lonely
Some day we'll meet in Heaven above.

He calls "Don't weep for me darling"
I'm happy on Heaven's bright shore
Family, friends and many loved ones all gathered with Jesus above.

The children all gather around me
To love me and share all my sorrow
They say "Mom please don't be crying, Dad's resting,
We'll see him in Heaven tomorrow."
Heaven's just a breath away.

Ruby P. Rose

Questions Upon Learning That You Were Raped At Age Five

I don't understand how one could demand
an innocent boy, whose favorite toy
is not foreplay. That comes at a day
when he's older, stronger, and bolder.
You were just a child, voice so mild,
screaming in the dark. He's left his mark,
or was it a girl who ruined your world?
How do you feel, when you're behind the wheel,
and your girlfriend decides to blend
your driving with a kiss? Do you miss
the nightmares in your sleep, or do you keep
them all blocked out? This, I doubt,
is possible at night. Did you fight,
though you were small? Through it all,
how did you survive when you were only five?
It's cruel and sick what makes people tick,
and do horrible things to other human beings.
Go on now, don't ask me how,
and return to serenity. You can trust me,
though we just met, I'll keep your secret.

Ariell Flood

My Grandma, My Friend

She taught me to fish, and to eat sugar bread.
She painted a dish, and, made sure everyone was fed.
She brought life to two sons, and then they left her alone,
but to me - Grandma's house was always home.

She loved the outdoors and,
could sit there for hours
she'd listen to the trees, and,
look at the flowers.
She loved to hunt and fish,
and always found time, to make a wish.

We would talk for hours, as friends often do
we told stories and laughed,
and sometimes we cried too.

She was there for the good times,
and also the bad; and, Grandma I love you,
and I'm trying not to be sad.

She brought me back home to my family and friends,
now our daughter carries her name, and she will till the end.
I thank the Lord that I had her, My Grandma, My Friend.

Nancy A. Huntley

On Relationships

It seems to me
The trouble lies in one's goals.
A craving for affection alone
Drives relations to destruction.
The waters of love
Are muddied by titles.
Let not a relationship be but a status.
Generic terms drain emotion.
For the young,
There is time - plenty.
Love is a flower
Which grows only when taken care of...respected.
Attempts to speak this natural process
Will only kill and prevent.
The roots of the flower
Must be planted deep
And must be of good seed, -
For germination takes time.
And love's flower will develop healthy,
From the seed of friendship.

Michael Galgano

Flowers

Have you ever seen a flower's face
so full of mercy and grace?

With the warm glow of colors galore
with the breeze twirling them more and more.

They wear so many diamonds and pearls
as they are picked by girls with golden curls.

As the winter wind starts to blow
they are filled with mourn and sorrow.

As their petals start to fall
they know they'll die, one and all.

As the coldness of winter cuts through like a knife
one by one they lay down their life.

When they fall without any sounds
we know they're at the happy hunting grounds.

In the spring the earth will have a shower
again of bright and beautiful flowers.

With the mountains of flowers made of lace
the children have flower fever — just a mild case.

And with a lot of care
the cascades of flowers perfume the air.

Kari Adolf

Goodbye To A Friend

It's time to say goodbye for now
You've chosen something new.
Although I wish you all the best,
Somehow it makes me blue.

We've had so many pleasant times
and laughed and joked so much.
I won't forget the good times
and I hope we stay in touch.

You've helped me out since that first day
when we worked side by side.
I always felt you were a friend
in whom I could confide.

And so as you prepare to leave
I wanted you to know
I wish you luck and happiness
but I hate to see you go.

So think about us now and then
and the good times that we had
because I didn't write these words
to try to make you sad.

Aubrey Ellis

In Your Embrace

The timeless serenity in your embrace
has brought me to this magic place.
Where I can live, where I can stay
where I no longer run away.
Where our true love lives on forever
where what we do we do together.
Where I no longer live in fear
where all my dreams are crystal clear.
Where I no longer push or shove
where we can work it out with love.
Where I don't have to cheat or lie
where happy tears are the tears I cry.
Yes I'm happy in this place
in the timeless serenity of your embrace.

Richard Diaz

Through A Child's Eyes

It's almost as if I can smell the anger in the air,
loud thundering voice crash down on my ears,
and I am caught by the image of my mother's tears.

The sound of this stinging slap still remains, as his hand comes
    down again.
I can taste the fear now, not for myself, yet for my brother.
I cover his eyes of innocence, and feel his soft trembles.

Now the smell changes, for there's fear in us all.
Smack, his hand rises again,
I am shaken by my sibling's fears.

I am overtaken by the bruises that try so hard
    to hide behind my mother's tears.
I feel responsible, it's my fault, so once again the night drowns
    in hatred.

Too young to make a change,
    yet too old to forget the pain.

So I stand and watch the tears,
    too filled with hatred to shed them myself, all that remains is fear.
Ronda Sherrard

The Unknown Soldier

How is it that you lie undisturbed upon this ground?
You lie here alone, a place where so many others fell all around.
How could you go unnoticed after such a fight?
Could it have been that you were a sniper killed up in that tree,
and later fell from that great height?
The war ended such a long time ago.
Whoever you are, your final resting place, someone will surely want
    to know.
No uniform, no clues, all that remains is bone.
Whether you were a Reb or a Yank remains unknown.
I cannot believe that you've been here so long.
To leave you this way would be a shame, just plain wrong.
I don't know who you are, but I'll dig your grave.
It would be unfitting to let a man's bones bleach in the sun,
when he was so brave.
It does not matter whether you were foe or friend.
I will give you a more proper and dignified end.
Goodbye to you Sir, I am sure that you performed your duties well.
I am sure you fully gave yourself to your cause until you fell.
I pray that your pain did quickly cease,
and that now you've come upon God's peace.
Mark Anthony Carosello

Diamonds And Coal

We must look at our lives at large. All twists turns as diamonds...
Stepping stones.....each one filled with the power to lead us
    to the true being that we are.

It is only with a true understanding of ourselves that
We can find peace and the capacity for happiness on this earth.
With this understanding there is also an infinite
Reserve of strength and perseverance

If upon our journey a stone should by chance
Turn from diamond to coal, we must use all
Of our senses to evaluate its transformation,
As honest reflection is paramount to understanding

We must examine the lump of coal.....
Look deep within the structure of the darkness
Find the source of its pigmentation.....then dissolve
It with all of the strength found in knowing ourselves

Then again it shall become a diamond, upon which we may step.
    Find strength and confidence in each and
Every diamond.....no matter the size.....For without them we will
    remain motionless.....
Stephanie A. Coning

The Dream

Oh! The silence of the night
A fire that burns, kept hidden from sight

The memory of your sweet embrace
Long white stockings of soft white lace

Vivid memories haunt my mind
Of candle-cast shadows locked in time

Late night phone calls and talks till dawn
A love struck journey that I'm still on

I shut my eyes and you are there
Standing beside me in the cool night air

My heart starts pounding and goose bumps rise
As your white silk robe falls down your side

I hold you close, eyes fill with tears
I long to hold you through all my years

No love compares with yours and mine
And, I know I'll love you till the end of time

The alarm starts ringing, I must awake
I reach to hold you each daybreak

As I open my eyes, I want to scream
'Cause once again 'twas just a dream
Carl G. Carson

Gypsy Soul

My soul is mine, my soul wanders
through strange lands that don't exist.
Flies over prairies, green and misty
my gypsy soul . . .

   Time to forget! A white stallion
takes my soul on a galloping pace
through white clouds of silky lace . . .
Climbs up mountains, leaps over springs,
heads to the stars on its wings
    of a rainbow . . .

   Time to remember! The stallion is back
always brisk and proud, but now it's black
as anguish veils my gypsy soul . . .
Guitars are mute, my heart is down
waiting impatiently for another stroll . . .

Possessing me goes to your head
like strong wine!
There is no victory in this conquest.
My soul is mine! . . .
Virginia Maria rebello Ribeiro

Pro-Choice

The seeds of man and woman meet
Silence... then a heart's first beat
mother's womb
Which could become its home or tomb
It's her choice - Life or Death?
That will control the child's last breath
Why shouldn't she have the right to take
A life because of one mistake
and just because it's still inside
Does she think it's not alive?
Someday she will cry tears so cold
For the child she may or may not hold
She was the one too hurt or too selfish to give
The child within a chance to live
Brenda L. Klamerus

Touched By An Angel

Forgiveness cannot change what has happened.
Forgiveness cannot change the past;
   But forgiveness can change you.

Forgiveness can change anger into acceptance.
Forgiveness can change the future;
   And forgiveness can let you love yourself.

Forgiveness cannot make what was wrong into right.
Forgiveness cannot make one forget;
   But forgiveness can let you live without guilt.

Forgiveness cannot change what has become history.
Forgiveness can make history not repeat itself;
   And forgiveness can allow you to grow.

Change yourself. Love yourself. Live without guilt. Grow.
Forgive... be touched by an angel;
   And then become one.

Diane Jeane Stillwell

RESPONSIBILITY...Now It's Up To You!!!

Reliability, do what you say you are going to do
Effort, your output is proportional to your input
Self-motivation, you have to get up and do it
Patience, it takes time to get what you want
Organize, and maximize your time
Number, of little things you do make the difference
Set, priorities to attain realistic goals
Intuition, rely on experience and feelings to make decisions
Budget, your finances and be prepared for the unexpected
Individualism, is what makes you special
Listen, and you will learn something every day
Initiative, be proactive not reactive
Truth, the most important personal quality
Years, the next few years will be the most challenging for you.
   There will always be another want or need but life's
   necessities will limit your ability to immediately satisfy
   your desires. Be patient, work hard and you will be
   rewarded with success and happiness.

Jim Earnshaw

The Awesome Love Of God

God's awesome love shown,
As His glory beamed down from the throne.
Upon the earth of sinful men
Who put the nail prints in His hands — in His hands

They hung Him upon the rugged cross
We who believe are never lost.
To possess this love, no man can.
But lay down His life for another man — like the lamb

The time is near for Him to come again,
To take away His children from this world of sin.
We'll go to heaven and be a bride,
We can sit next to Him on His right side — on His right side

God loves me and He loves you,
For between Him and Satan there's a family feud.
They fight for our souls to see who can win.
God fights with love, Satan fights with sin.

God proves his love by providing a way,
We can go to heaven on the rapture day.
We can live in heaven for eternity,
Eat of the prosperous fruit from the tree — of life

Tom Hubler

The Tree

  It started life as just another tree,
nothing to stand out in one's memory.
Through the years it grew straight and tall
until one day the woodsman paid a call.
  With razor-sharp axe and muscles like steel
he chopped and hacked and the great tree reeled.
Finally, with a mighty crash, to the ground it fell;
then came the carpenter with hammer and nail
  To fashion and shape the once lovely bole
into the cruelest instrument the world would know.
Then came the day it was dragged with great pain
as curses and taunts and the whip's blows rained
  On a man whose death paid for all of man's sin
as He hung on that tree our freedom to win.
Yes, this is the tree that is infamous still
because it was the cross on Calvary's hill.

Jack N. Masterson

Thorns

Surrounding the petals of beauty,
  O guardians of the exquisite bloom
Thee painfully prick the unwary.

Entwined on the stems like serpents
  To strike with innocent passion
The worshipers of thy treasure.

O protectors of the colorful spirea,
  with thy bountiful spines, thee bring
Forth blood from the impatient.

Thy fate: to be offensive to the eye.
  With thy spikes; also to the touch. But ever
Zealous is thy vigilance of the Rose.

Alfred Lee Johnson

Porcupine Coat

The coat was made of porcupine quills,
glistening like tears, dyed in colors
of sun on river water,
fire in grass, blood on snow,
clouds and sky
sitting on the shoulders of winter hills.

Surely a woman
in some tent or cave,
back bent, eyes straining,
brushing long, dark hair away from her face,
was whirled by a vision
in her heart, so powerful
she wrenched beauty from the brute and cruel,
birthed art soaring high
above the white man's buffed and stolen jewels.

Margery Cooper

How Would You Like...?

How would you like to be a wild flower growing,
yet locked away from the sunlight; when you should be
running free in a field of daises?

How would you like to see the innocence of childhood fade,
as you watch your hopes and dreams die, when there is no
prospect of a brighter tomorrow. A time so precious, lost in
the dust of despondency, anger, hopelessness...and death.

How would you like to bear the world on shoulders yet have
no one to turn to....no one fight for you...no one to believe in you.
Always a suspect, because of the skin you are born into.
How would you like to be like little black me?

M. Francis-Dunn

The Country Life

When the sun sets over hills of trees,
I begin to feel the rushing of the evening breeze,
And fireflies begin to glow,
The twilight moon starts to show.
I swing on the porch swing spotting a deer,
But it pranced away quickly so not to be near.
The stars you can see with no smog in the way,
No rush hour traffic on this bright day,
For the country is a calm and beautiful place,
The fawn leap with beauty and grace.
I watch a mother bird fly back to her nest,
To feed her young children and take a short rest.
As it starts to get cooler I go back in the house,
The smell of hot chocolate crept up like a mouse.
I peered out the window loving the sight,
The moon and the stars make a wonderful light,
The light shines on the forest and I'm loving it so,
Because I love the country life.

Brittany R. Valdez

The Day I Fell In Love

The breeze blew through the autumn leaves as we rolled along the trail,
I swept my gaze across the park and back to the river rail.

I noticed children playing games, while the gentry strolled along,
saw frisky squirrels climbing trees, and flitting birds caught up in song.

But the finest work of God's own hand that I noticed on that day,
was the gal in the purple shorts, ('specially when she moved that way).

She raced along on rollerblades, coaxing me to do the same,
but all I saw were awesome legs, (man, what a beautiful dame)!

"Please take the lead, I'll watch your form" she said her innocent way,
"No that's fine, I'll stay here behind, I'll learn by watching you" I say.

Later we shared a lazy meal on a windswept patio bar,
I marvelled at the way she talked, I really liked this girl thus far.

Her words portrayed a loving heart, I mused as we ate and talked,
I liked her laugh and gracious air, (and I loved the way she walked).

Later that night when on my knees, I prayed aloud to God above
"Lord, let this be the one for me and fill her heart, for me, with love."

I guess you know the story told is true in every part,
For the lady I describe above, has forever won my heart.

Now in my nightly prayers I pray, "thank you Lord in ev'ry way,"
for when I feel in love with her, in purple shorts, that autumn day.

Wade T. Myers

It Was You

It was you who was there when I took my first step
It was you who sang songs to me while I slept
It was you who bought me dresses, and brushed my hair
It was you who made me eat when I didn't care
It was you who was there on my first day of school
It was you who brought me up when I was feeling blue
It was you who knocked sense into me when "I knew everything"
It was you who comforted me in my time of need
It was you I screamed and yelled at when I couldn't get my way
but you were there to help me get through those bad days
I could never forget school clothes shopping, talk about butting heads
arguing because you wanted "Payless" and I wanted "Keds"
Remember my track competition in the Carnival of Champions when
I slipped on the gravel and got 4th place? And remember the year
after that when I passed up 2 runners and made 1st place?!!
It was you who was there when I rang the Elementary Bell and then
Junior High, my 1st "C" you gave me "H—"
There's so many memories that I could never dream of changing...
it is you Nana, I give all the credit to - you are so wonderful - I Love You

Sommer Michelle Begley

Thank You For...

In so many ways you have touched me
In so many ways I can name;
You have fulfilled my life in so many ways,
Without you my life wouldn't be the same.

Good times you've always made better
And bad times you've always made good;
If there was anything I could not do,
I would only have to ask and you could.

You know my thoughts before they are said
You even know them before they are thought;
You know me better then I know myself,
You're the type of friend everyone has sought.

While many people spend a lifetime in search
 of someone like you,
Most never find what they're looking for,
Thank you - because for me that's not true.
The bond that is between us, a million miles wouldn't keep us apart
My lips do not tell you these words -
They come from my heart.

Rebecca Wilson

Serving The Lord

Always serve the Lord with joy and gladness
And always with love, hope and never sadness
Although we cannot look on his face
We can serve the Lord with dignity and grace
Our prayers may not be answered the way we ask
Sometimes He may be saving us for greater task
For what He's saving us may not be plain
But if we continue to pray we'll find He's always the same
If we will always serve the Lord with zest
We will surely find that He is always passes the test
If on the Lord Jesus we do always depend
We'll know He will help us from committing sin
Even if it's in life or in death
We will decision to serve God is the best

Melba J. Burke

God's Daughter

Did God have a daughter
Did she die for you and me?
Was it in a ghetto, naked for the world to see?
Did God have a daughter;
Is she buried at Wounded Knee?

Did she jump off at Masada
Or get burned in a camp
Did God have a daughter;
Did someone light a lamp?

Did she pop reds or shoot up to get high
Did God have a daughter;
How did she die?

Could she find a job
Or was her color all wrong
Did God have a daughter;
Did she blame her mom?

Did she curse him, run away from home
Did God have a daughter;
Did she die on the run?
Did God have a daughter; Or only a son?

Henry Deutsch

Let Her Die

And they said "Let her die"
And put a wet towel over her face
I wondered who had died and made them god
Of this God forsaken place

She didn't ask to be conceived
She didn't ask to be a girl
She didn't ask to be born
Where the prince of darkness rules the world

I lie in bed at night
And try to fall asleep
But something is eating at my soul
And all I can do is weep

I see a little baby
Just wanting to be loved
But her mother doesn't want her
So she smothers her, this heaven's dove

I see a little baby
Whose only crime was being a girl
Killed like we would swat a fly
For the prince of darkness rules the world

Monica Gutierrez

A Good Man

Beautiful as a golden summer's day
And gentle as the warm and cool breeze
Lovingly with a passion, that melts away
Even the most hardened thoughts.
You are the answer to a man's bewilderment
A vision to be, bringing to view the
Ending of a mystery.
For you, I'm entwined in admiration,
Encompassing with the heart
Thanking you considerably for your
Belief in a good man.

To love and give love, for a woman
With sensitivity, is the heart felt
Compassion for truly being a good man.

Rayna M. Griffin

Anxiety

There's a smooth cellular motion
grappling with my heart
strings
contortionists fever
paneling my gut dome
dancin' the cha cha trampoline
on my inner child springs
come sailing with my
wavy hemoglobin aches you
gutsy guilt diver
worry blizzard maker
are you snowing my torso over?
Play the harpsichord
on my needle nerve endings
sing sweet sultry soprano
down in my marrowless bones
down to my tippy tipsy toes
coo light and long and loud enough so I can hear
through coarse cottony ears.
Repeat. Repeat. Repeat. Repeat. Repeat.

Amy Sondra Lekan

I Can See God

Wherever we go...whatever we do
You can be sure that God is there too
High on the mountain tops...or down deep in the sea
I can see God looking right down at me
I can see God with His arms open wide
He's reaching down...or He's holding my hand
God whispers softly...deep within my soul
Wherever I go in this beautiful land
I can see God in the face of a child
Or the eyes of the man who's wrinkled...but wise
I can see God in the grace of a deer
And the wings of the dove...He created with care
He's gracious...He's good...He's loving and kind
He comforts the broken-hearted
And opens the eyes of the blind...
Yet He's strong and He's mighty
His power has no end....
He's King of Kings...The Rock of All Ages
He's The Lily of the Valley
He's Saviour...and He's Friend

Rachelle L. Felmet

My Little Three Legged Friend

My little three legged friend, how sorrowful
   Am I, you scurried in the street and
Got hit by a car passing by, now you hobble
   Around your loft with only three
Little furry legs, but you are the greatest
   Little dog, that God has ever made, you can
Still jump in my lap, as I sit hear the
   Fire place, you can still fetch my paper,
With the rising sun. You are a furry little
   Three legged wonder, with my heart you
Have won, you can still dig up bones, under the
   Clear blue sky. And chase the mail man,
As he passes by, so don't you weep,
   About that little leg, that will not mend
For you will always remain, man's best friend.

Edward M. Travis

Ode To A Mosquito

You lowdown, hideous sucker of human blood
Sitting there with evil intent upon the wall
Ready to flee at a second's notice from the flood
Of hands that reach out to squash, tear, and maul.

Your light transparent wings carry you far
Beyond the reach of clumsy hands.
Up to the ceiling you fly and reach the bar
On which, unseen, you stand.

You wait patiently and undisturbed
Until the dull-sensed thing below goes to bed.
Then from your heights you drop upon the wall below
And light as a feather upon your victim's head.

The creature turns and swats at you,
But as usual he is too late.
Upon the wall you sit and boo
And watch the juicy pimple on his forehead take shape.

The electric light above you is turned on.
You cannot fly, you're dazzled by the glare.
Smack! A bright red streak is left
For others of your tribe - beware!

Alvin C. Yantiss

Gentle Days

Back through the years I travel the path
to summer and childhood and gentle days.
Where popsicles drip root beer and lime
and Poppa's store is captured in time.

Sun filters through the old screen door
dancing through shadows and across the floor.
Above the door the Coke sign sways
and I return to gentle days.

Lavender lilacs caress the air;
the ancient oak is always there.
Train whistles muted by the river's haze
and I return to gentle days.

The rag sheenie's horse stands quiet and patient
on a dusty road leading to one more station.
Betsy, Tacy and Tibb were friends
as I shared their adventures by the river's edge.

Time stands still in precious ways
as I return to gentle days.
J. L. Yelton

Nature

I am dying, those who kill me don't stop their lying.
My blood flows like a river
    filled with pollution of other people.
Those people who are killing me
    need to go to an institution.
I used to provide,
    but now I don't even exist.
My soul is dry like a desert.
All I desire to know why?
Why do they kill me?
They lacerate my soul leaving a ruptured immedicable soul
    vulgarize in the name of the cycle of life.
I should have given up when I had the occasion to runaway.
How to recompense myself? For my soul is not pure,
    and my pride is gone. People should have save
me, when I told them so. I cry all night long and
do penitence all day prolong. For afraid to
    fall sleep, to save my dreams in celibacy,
and control my nightmare's appetites.
    I am still dying...
Isabel Santa

Ode To The Little Flute

Oh, sing little flute, and never cease your melody.
Nothing is as gentle or as free
As the song that is flowing out of thee.

The children stop to listen when you call
And fall asleep upon the pillowed grass,
Dreaming of the peace that comes to pass.

The birds have yet to sing with your voice,
The river has yet to flow as smoothly,
And people have yet to speak as truly.

I know the life you give to valleys far.
The music through the night is heard so clear,
Ringing o'er the hills to every ear.

I only fear that you won't play for long,
And songs that make the children dream in sleep
Will play no more, leaving them to weep.

Their tears will start the rivers flowing.
Birds will sing as they have learned from thee.
I only hope that people speak as truly.

As the music ceases in the wood,
The trees will bend in sorrow to the wind,
And all will be quiet in the end.
Carrie Denise Tucker

Contrast

Throughout this coastal country the saltwater is apparent,
The light gentle breeze cascades over the ancient landscape
extending the essence of the sea far inland.

A land of contrast is how it is known,
The North containing the elegant portion of this country, with its
massive amount of colors placed upon the vegetation, that glisten as
the sun slowly begins to dissipated beyond the horizon.

The desert South is arid, the hot blaze of the relentless sun beats
upon the rocks as it tries to seep within its pores.

The vicinity between, has several antique and yet modern structures.
Each are an essential piece of the foundation of the country's future.

City life is always active, the clamor is everlasting,
From the intolerant horn of the taxi bellowing at another,
To the soaring seagulls who sing out in rage after losing their prey.

This country of enchantment, one of a kind,
A land of variety that will always be connected throughout time.
Marla Zeiderman

The Voice Of The Wolf

In the tundra far below,
The sun reaches dusk, the grasses glow
Shadows fall both heavy and dark,
Birds soar in their respective ark
Then, from the caves a howl is heard,
It is neither a bear, nor a bird
Wolves enter the chilled night air,
In their packs they emerge from their lair
Their figures mystique, their eyes all bright,
Outlined by the pale moonlight
They look to each other, their gesture clear,
The whistling wind is all they hear
And as they look unto the sky,
With soaring spirits they begin their cry.
Sophie M. Albert

Always There

For you my children dear, I'm always there.
Your first breath of life, I was there.
Your first steps, I was there.
Skinned knees or broken bones, I was there.
All through your trying years, I was there.
I'm glad we are so close, on this I can boast.
If you should ever need me, on this you can count,
I'm always there.
Even when I'm gone, and in heaven with our father,
This you will know, down on you I will be watching.
Because for you I'm,
    Always there.
Julia Clayton

Nosferatu

Here of flesh but not of soul,
Never again shall I be whole.
I crave the darkness, I crave the night.
Free me from my grave, free me from the light.
I drink the nectar of life straight from its source.
As she screams I listen in ecstasy, until her cries become hoarse.
She goes limp, her heart has stopped,
Next time I must not spill a drop.
In red, I am so drenched,
I must cease for my thirst is quenched.
Of this life I once was fond,
Fly off now into the great beyond.
Now I am weary of it and wish to die,
Awaiting God's splinter to fall from the sky.
Trenton Bailey

The Eternal Quest

Life begins as a snug nurturing tranquil envelope of nutrients, peace and love...

Suddenly...a succession of disruptive pushes, heaves and squeezing...
An explosive smack...a long gasp for air followed by an exhaling
scream, tears, insecurity, fear, panic...arms reach out and nestle upon a soft bosom

A transference of love is felt, security and calm ensue...and peaceful healing sleep overcomes...

Life learning begins..hunger, feeding, visions, hearing, holding,
standing, falling, crawling, walking,
speaking...feelings...laughter,
crying, association...disassociation, frustration, fear, courage, elation

Schooling...learning, security, insecurity, triumphs, defeats,
enthusiasm, ego, assertiveness, identity, a steadfast will develops..

Higher learning...an expansive cycle of knowledge and wisdom begins...

A realization looms that questions once answered create a myriad of
questions to be answered, and depending on the complexity may require
an eternal seeking to arrive at just conclusions...but...whose conclusions?

Regroup, return to simplicity...form a flexible base...respect honor
and love oneself and others irrespective of the differences and
rejoice in the wonder of awe of all that is natural and "All That Is"

Frank L. Rodriguez

Fall's Production

Brilliant and restless, Fall scouts the hillside,
looking in canyons and meadows to find her new talent.
Hoping to upstage Winter's spectacular performance,
she dresses herself in a showboat array of colors.
Staging a scene complete with music and dance, Frost will lift her curtain.
Stealing from Winter, she nips noses, spreading a sugar like glaze in the early morning light.
In orchards, crisp apples sell themselves with their mouth-watering scents.
Harvested wheat stands in gleaming shocks, nodding to show the way to late comers.
Lazily pumpkins lie around waiting for Frost to turn them orange,
hoping to match the beauty of the harvest moon.
Getting the show started, the wind adds music. Playing her flutes and oboes,
she moans around trees looking for a dance partner.
Graceful willows start to waltzes, as show stopping leaves whirl in a high stepping chorus.
Twigs and debris tap dance across a chilled ground,
keeping time with the sound, of drums in hollow logs.
In a rage, Winter steps in to stop the show, blasting the scene with an icy breath, he lowers Fall's thermostat.
Fall bows gracefully, removing her flamboyant dress, she steps behind a curtain of ice,
where she lets Winter begin his glacial performance.

E. J. Knight

I Am

Really bothered by this whole f***ing world/
Ending this misery seems easier than watching the pain
Around me/of friends/of family/of Me/I'm
Going crazy waiting for love and never finding
Anything but sh*t/from you/from him/from her/
No one really wants me to be happy/just to

Conform to all the ridiculous
Heresies and rules of being a part of middle class values/
Repugnant smells make my stomach turn/coming from
Inside yr right-winged/sexist/racist/ separatist/homophobic/rotting corpse
She won't care if we take it all away/
The hell she won't!!/One day when yr ploy to put
I against I blows up in yr pudgy, well-fed face and yr
Nobody but MEMEME rules don't work out/my wretched, twisted mouth will
Erupt with crazy laughter/ha!/even though you tried to make this shell of me

Perish/I lived/I f***ing lived/and I might reach out to grab yr hand
Although I know you want to pull me in given a chance/it
Really might be better under the water
Rather than watching everyone drown/you know/I'm not
As happy as my ugly grin led you to believe/I'm
Sick/all I had to do is open my glassy/bloodshot/tired eyes for you to see that.

Reagan Parras

An Early Morning

Black morning dreams of stars gathered like dew
on a sky saturated in deep navy
far under water, my body feels the call of cold, dark day
fantasy candy shatters and flees faster than a deer's shadow,
and I am left to remember strange stolen kisses on my morning skin
and fall in love with the melancholy grimness which has spewed me up and regrets me.
Swimming through rings of awareness until sensitivity is peaked
morning now feels like a box edged with glass sharply cutting each way
I shift
I bleed 6:30 a.m. noises, whispers like rough screams and footsteps
that are earthquakes
bits of disappointment and dew crack my lips and seal them with a lover's promise
of dullness and numbness and heavy sadness behind half-closed lids
the radio explodes into an aberrant cacophony of pain
and I feel the creak through my veins like an old Yugo run on jet fuel
standing on the edge of razor-sharp dawn
with the murder of velvet night and blissful ignorance still wet on my hands
I am afraid morning has found its prey.

Christine Meranda

It's Not You, It's Me

It's not you; it's me was the only audible phrase she remember
hearing calmness that existed now. In spite of a clogged
up nose, tear soaked eyes, and wrinkled handkerchief; she could
only hear one line, It's not you; it's me.

She fought hard to keep her breath steady, not faltering and
unveiling the true pain that such a simple phrase had caused.
Having given what she thought was her all-and-all: earnest love,
enthusiastic support, insatiable desire, enduring empathy,
and comical levity; she just knew that that she was all he needed.

It's not you; it's me. The words rang in her ear again, then as
it takes the mind to process a thought, it hit like a hard fist the
chin in a country brawl: she had given too much; and now, it was too
late to receive. All of the love she flourished upon him, she
denied herself; in all the support she brandished his way, she forgot
that her inner peace sat on a ledge tottering.
Effortlessly, she made him secure, but in the same motion, insecurity
flowed like the Niagara Falls for her.

Suddenly, the tears stopped flowing and a beam of inner strength
shined on her twisted heart and mind as if God himself had appeared.
All of the pain she felt dissolved into a dull throb as a smile
crossed her full, black lips. In that instant, she realized it
wasn't him; it was Her!

Lolita Hendrix

Dead Roses

I walked alone, on a moonlit path, as roses lay dead at my feet,
And by a song, on this moonlit path, my feelings began to weep,
Crying out loud, why betrayed so bad, they wondered on into the night,
But the song sang on through a beaten path, the roses were often too right,
I asked them so kind, would it be too much if I asked for your wisdom again?
But they looked at me, and so silently grin, we can't for we are now dead,
They told me to wait while they opened a gate for which I was to enter,
But the gate was too bright, contrasting with night, for that I could not enter,
The roses spoke gently as light grew softer, my vision began to blur,
The roses did shutter and cold winds did flutter, my life began to stir,
Don't worry they cried, we're right by your side, we'll always be there too,
Nearly forget us, beat and disdain us, tonight we stay with you,
The roses did dance in my eyes that night, I saw them wither encumbered,
And with that glimpse my eyes did slip into my endless slumber,
I'll never forget my roses prospect when they spoke of death in that way,
Not nearly forgetting, too little too many, right there my roses will stay.

Kevin Mulder

The Gift Of Life

Through out my years, I learned to fear and synonymous. I learned to
love, not hate. I learned to accept my fate. I learned to be happy,
and cheerful, not sad no matter what state. I learned these lessons
at an early stage. While I was still a baby in age. How I learned
this was like a curse. It came as some bliss, as I started feeling
my mother's kisses, seeing her beauty, and hearing her speak that's
what I started to see, that she had blessed me with, "The Gift of Life."

I can't forget the first time she weaned me, it felt so good and
stopped my screaming. The formulas of my bottle feedings were so
sweet I didn't ever want to walk or start speaking. Everyday that she
would bathe and rub me all around, I knew I had never let her love for
me down. When she use to hold me by the feet told me to walk I
started to weep. Again and again I enjoyed this "Toy," she had given me called...."The Gift of Life."

When I became of age, wild as a flower in the morning sun, as I begun
to run, have fun and learn I tried never to turn from the love,
dignity, and respect she taught me. You made me your little boy and
man; I will never forget you for that, you will always be cherished.
I grew because of you, shall die too, but before I do, I will see all
your dreams come true. In me is everything a tree of knowledge
wisdom, will, courage, and strength, "A real man" sought of speak.
All this you gave to me, and is mine until you leave, and I leave...
"The gift of life." "Oh ya, and I'll keep this prayer you've given
me; when I lay me down to sleep, I pray the Lord my soul to keep
if I die before I wake I pray the Lord my soul to take...."

Walter King

Living Proof

Slowly for twenty years I slid down the path of evil.
Putting to rest the best of my judgments to not make the right turn.
The booze was for me more than a companion, it was the center of my life.
There was no pain for me that a shot wouldn't cure.
Honesty was for me a senseless vanity.
My fears would dissipate in the darkness of the anesthetic fume.
To rebound the next day in overwhelming power.
In spite of all warnings I never looked back for the longest of time.
I had reached bottom but I still couldn't stop.
My will power was so thin that it would not have survived one day of abstinence.
The flowers lost for me their color and their fragrance.
The sweetest melody could no more reach my soul.
So many times, engulfed by despair, ending it all came rushing through my mind.
Reviving a buried belief that only God could restore my long lost sanity.
I am today climbing back the tenuous ladders of hope and reborn faith.
And when I'll be able to see again the shining sun.
I'll be living proof of God's compassion for our humanity.

Gregoire Eugene

Future's Man

I am a man!

Caught in a time of rapid change and discontent, a man is in the
process of becoming his own future— "Future's Man".

A man is caught in the past's trap of wanting to be tough when
underneath needing to be tender. As rare today as the need to be
common in coming generations, Future's Man is searching.

Man and woman are spiritually separate in today's world as she rides
a wave of growth into her future. Sensing being left behind in the past,
man continues to consciously claim the future. Genius that she is,
woman leads into the future while still acting as though she
follows— balancing the rhythm of her rising and his falling.

Man is responsible for his own spiritual fall.

Woman has become tougher in her tenderness. Man must become
more tender in his toughness. Balancing toughness and tenderness
reunifies spirituality between man and woman.

Future's Man?.....Future's Salvation!

Through the "sounds of silence", man pleads and woman leads:

WALK BESIDE ME AND BE MY FRIEND!

Thomas P. Glanton

"Silent Cry"

The dead of night, with winter air comes
the silent cry of a child, a child to young to
know, to young to share the horrid secret that lies within.
Gone for awhile, back again try to lead
away, but always stays, the silent cry of a child
to young to know the difference, to young to
share the pain in words, only showing in actions,
playing games of kiss and lust, only knowing
what's been done, that cannot be undone
Listen carefully for the silent cry, the
child doesn't know that they are not to young
to share the horrid secret that lies within
There is nothing more precious than a
child, I know of this horrid secret, this silent
cry it happened with mine . . .
Lori Gutierrez

A Scared Life

As I walked into this world,
I thought to myself
what a wonderful place,
a world full of grace
Then as time went on,
things started to change
the people, the places, the mournful sad faces
Everyday on the street, the people I meet
talk about killing, raping, bombing at their feet,
their eyes full of tears,
their mind with all fears, as they move through their lives
with their mace, guns and knives. They too start too see pain,
the things they will not gain, if they continue how they are,
Soon on that life will be a scar
I'd like to help them, teach them, warn them,
but they won't hear me out; the things I say they doubt.
Their days went on, weeks and months
but they kept trying stunt after stunt
Their life is now over, the final ring of the bell
I bet they wished they'd gone to heaven, after seeing life in hell.
Kelli Godshall

My Prayer

God, give me the strength to carry mt load
Over the smooth and sometimes rough road.
Give me the courage to stand alone,
And delight in others, my example shown.
Give me love that I may impart
A reflection of your love and win a heart.
Give me tolerance that I may suffer long,
And still keep fighting, singing a song.
Give me wisdom that I may be
A servant for you, in any capacity.
Strengthen my faith and endurance too,
So that I can hope to be with you.
Of all these gifts I'll treasure the most,
I will be the love you give, my Lord, my host.
Daisy L. Moore

Life Is Like A Flower

Life is like a flower, it has a beginning and an end.
Life is like a flower, it can stay long or short.
Life is like a flower, it needs seeds to grow.
Life is like a flower, it needs water to spurt.
Life is like a flower, it changes colors like a mood.
Life is life a flower, it takes time to develop,
A flower is a window of our lives,
It goes up when it's happy and down when it's sad.
Life is like a flower!
Devynne Stackhouse

A Small Regret

By chance, I came upon a small regret
That found a furrow near my deepest fear.
It sat and smiled and laughed for just a while,
And then it spoke so soft to catch my ear.
"My friend and father, you have given me life.
I'll build a home, and plant my seed up here.
For you have acted wrongly in this case,
And now I mean to hold your questions near
Your deepest fear." With that, the voice was lost,
And I was left to contemplate the tear
That fell upon my face. Can I go back
And change what happened just last year?
Perhaps Alaadin's servant has a cure
For making conscience lighter and more clear.
So now you see my pain and current thoughts.
I trust your heart was sure enough to hear.
My eyes feel heavy hanging from my brow,
But sleep eludes my weary mind right now.
Roger J. Griesmeyer

A Dream Of Spring

On a harsh and cold Winter's day
I dreamed of Spring bright, bold, and gay,
Of birds, flowers, trees, and breeze,
And wondered, "When will I see these?"

I know Spring is not far away
Soon all will be out to play
Baseball, basketball, and volleyball, soon to come
Then we will wait for Summer fun.

But first, we will enjoy the thrill that's near
Rain washed skies, crystal clear
Sweet smelling Jasmine, freshly cut grass
Building memories that will always last.

I will love the spring for all those things.
The Summer will fly away on wings
As Autumn arrives, the school bell will ring
Then I will return to Winter, dreaming of Spring.
Shannon M. Ringer

My Prayer

Lord may I become what You want me to be
And may I walk in the ways of Thee
May I love with my complete heart
Letting Your words dwell in me whole and not in part

May my smile be an expression of peace
And many I give all without ceasing
May my friends be of Thee
And may I help them as an example of Thee

For I want to live a life that's complete
To serve You Lord and sit at Your feet
Be real to me and wash me clean
And bring me to the place where on You I lean
Teresa C. Boggs

Peaceful White

White is a marshmallow and vanilla ice cream,
and the part you can't remember in a dream.
Snowflakes falling in your face,
and little dots from outer space.
White can be a little dove,
or maybe even freshly boiled love.
Sometimes your breath can be white,
when you blow it on a frosty night.
Heba El-Aayi

Till Death Do Us Part

Over 44 years have long passed
I laughed cause they said it would not last
Five children a cat and a dog
Also a horse a beef and a hog
Sure there was laughter, love and some tears
Drugs alcohol and some fears
But we were together through the years
We had each other and God as our guide
We traveled life's highway with pride
My husband's love has always been true
Just look in his soft lovely eyes of blue
He is so loving sweet and kind
And I am forever thankful that he's all mine
We intertwine our bodies and our hearts
And we'll be together until death do us part
  Maggie Brudnok

Come Join The Army!

The soldier sat
in the trench by the hill,
trench foot and gangrene his constant companions.
He is thinking of home
and the ill-fated posters.
"Come see the world," they said;
"Come join the army."
His father was proud
when he volunteered for the service.
His mother cried,
he remembered the tears.
The soldier sat silently
waiting for the end
and, when the spectre of death
held out its hand,
he gave a little sigh
and proudly gave in.
  Lance Kanoa Hao

SantaCarls

A charming, friendly mouse ran all about
While residing in a wondrous castle
Sharing the dwelling for a long, long time
With the owner, a stately and gentle man
Known to everyone as SantaCarls
So great a relationship was theirs.

Kindness was the divine blessing
Possessed by this godly man
He lived his great life always bestowing
His kindnesses upon all that cross his path.

A better man; a greater uncle
One may never meet and know
God broke the mold after creating
His celestial perfect being.

Be kind to people while on this earth
And, when you enter heaven
You will become an elf in Santa's workshop
Are the words always spoken by SantaCarls
To the mouse, his friend, "Mickey."
  Stephen J. Noonan

Time

Time, what is time?
Time is what we try to beat, but often ends in defeat.
Time is what you make it; it can go fast or slow.
Time sometimes heals things; sometimes it makes them grow.
But there is only one sure thing that time always lets us know;
We only have one lifetime, so let the good times show!
  Kathleen Wells

For What Reason

So when did love really matter?
When did the one I cared for...care for me?
When was my life anymore than mindless chatter
And chasing childhood dreams
Tell me, when ever did love matter?

And what rhythm drives this soul so incomplete
To a destiny so distant and obscure
Where the mannequins and mirages all compete
For what reason am I living, I'm not sure

I push my feet through crowded streets with names unknown
And the shackles of strange fortunes greet me there
Halting indecision chills me to the bone
But tell me, if you can, does love care?

Anxiety streams down frames of frosted windows
While cluttered gutters tide with graven fears
Pleasure hints like blinking eyes in distant innuendos
Has love yet cared? Will love care in million years?
Will love exact a worthy measure, should I live a million years?
  D. Sank Smith

Sail Away

Won't you come and sail away with me
Across the floor of this wind swept sea

Just you and me will get
Splashed with so much color
You could never forget

We'll let the glow of the candlelight
Dry us deep into the night

Bring up memories of old
And brush them off so they can be retold

Get them to feel and fit just right
Let me sail and sail with you all night

Because I don't want you to forget
How much I've loved you and I'm still loving you yet
I'll work at it all night
To paint the sky blue and sand so white

That when you see what I've done
Into my arms you will run

Then we'll raise the sail on the mast
And sail and sail for as long
As we can make this feeling last
  Daniel J. Vukas

I Am A Lunatic With A Smile

I am a lunatic with a smile.
I wonder what sanity is? I've searched for miles.
I hear the voices that really aren't there.
I see the president, or is that Fred Astaire?
I want to live with intelligence and style.
I am the lunatic with a smile.

I pretend I'm with it and on the ball.
I feel so lonely and against the wall.
I touch a loved one who's really not there.
I worry they see me and really don't care.
I cry out—I'm named and numbered, tucked in the file.
I am the lunatic with a smile.

I understand how you could be scared.
I say I'm sane, but you really don't care.
I dream of a world that understands and accepts me.
I long for freedom, but you throw away the key.
I hope in time, I walk the streets in style.
I am a lunatic with a smile.
  Thomas S. Bieber

Revolution Of Elegant

The numbness has arrived yet another time
To blush the mind of an innocent life -
It sneaks up as if it were a mime
But yet it returns to cut like a knife.

The candle has nearly flickered off
And pain rises from below the earth.
At last pursues a gentle cough
During the final chiming of the church.

A life that was once filled in love without fear
Still remains a mystery even to this date.
Many hopes that remission draws near
To secure an eternal fate.

The blooming springtime flowers wilt -
Even the laughter of an early child,
The time has come now for the mire of guilt
Each occurrence has become more mild.

Although the tomb is unattended
The soul seems flat and drained.
With all of the voices unmended
A ghostly body stills remains.

Jamie Carlton

Untitled

Though miles have always come between us, little else ever has.
You are one person who knows me completely, accepts me,
   and loves me.
Not because of what I am, but in spite of what I am.
Why is it then, that I cannot bring myself to give my heart to you?
Is it because I am a fool, or because I am still a child?
Or, is it because I have imprisoned myself in my own ideals?
That, though the strangest reasoning, seems to ring most true.
It amazes and bewilders me, how someone that I've shared so little
   time with
Could so fully understand me. But, in understanding, are there answers?
Or only more questions? Who is it that holds the key?
It seems so very odd - the things that makes us such close friends
Have not brought us still closer together. For some, that would
   tear them apart.
But for us, it is the constancy of knowing no matter what the time
   or the distance we are friends;
It is the uncertainty of feeling whether more will ever grow. But
   it is the confidence of heart
That we will always share an unbreakable bond;
Stronger than friendship, less fickle than love, and more sure than death.
Does that make us Kindred spirits, soul mates, friends - or just
Two hearts that understand one another?
Whatever it makes us, the joy is in knowing
We have been, we will be, we are.

Karen R. Stukey

Watching

You're watching me with your eye
Half closed, bathed in ivory light
You're watching me, a haunting shadow
Cast in a coal black night.

I run from you to catch you out
When your attention is less than alert,
As the cobweb clouds brush over your face
And the stars that winkling flirt.

But when I'm alone and my way has gone dark
And I feel like I might die of fright.
You're watching me with your eye half closed
Bathed in ivory light.

Linda Mueller

"My Daughter"

You came into my life like a star
   lighting up the night sky.
And now, you are the sunshine
   that brightens my every day.

Each day I look in your eyes
   to see the sparkle of life, of joy
And the wonders of a child
   learning to live and love

Being your mother is the greatest gift of all
   you make me giggle like a child
   when we're being silly together
When we're apart
   I feel a part of me is missing

You are a small wonder
   who brightens the lives of everyone you meet

You are a part of me.
   My heart, my soul
You are,
   my daughter.

Melissa J. Carr

My Room

My room is filled with things I treasure
That's were I go when I need some pleasure.

My walls are filled with things of delight
These things will never leave my sight.

My dresser holds a pretty smell
Sweet perfume in a blue glass bell.

The tick-tock sound from my clock
Sounds like the ocean hitting the dock.

My friends the stuffed animals are overhead
As I lie here in my soft warm bed.

Katrina Kraus

New Baby Sister

Our only child a little boy, was almost five
When a new baby sister did arrive.

Later when things began to clear
He said, "I wish she wasn't here".

She won him over after awhile
Especially when she began to smile.

When she was just a little tyke
He taught her how to ride a bike.

When days were nice in early spring
They played ball and he pushed her on the swing.

Together they built a tree-house
And pretend to be husband and spouse.

When he was kind of bossy - she didn't mind at all
She was there for his every beck and call.

He was always willing and nice
When she asked him for his advice.

He forgot what he said when she was a new baby
Now she is a beautiful young lady and he loves her dearly.

Pauline Hicks

Love

I love the trees they make me see.
I love the breeze it laughs when I sneeze.
I love love and love loves me,
And most of all I love the sea.
At times it's silly, sometimes it's sad,
Whatever love is, it can't be bad.
We all have love, it's ours to give,
It's up to us, this love to give.
So love one another, no matter who they are,
For giving love so freely simply lends more love to give.
And if you're shunned and spit upon,
Remember to love and you have won.
So if some day you're all alone
And feel like love is gone,
Just jump right up,
Run out-side,
And find someone to love!
Joyce M. White

Some Day

All alone remembering home
Thinking of family, wanting to phone
Sometimes it's so hard to do the right things
To make our life right the way it should have been
We all make some choices some right some wrong
We all hear the words and try to sing along
For some it's real easy for others real hard
I remember myself playing ball in the yard
Those were the days when life was care free
But everything changes for you and for me
I wish to go back and turn it all around
To fly through sky and get off the ground
But that would taking the easy way out
It's only a dream without a doubt.
So we live each day and look to the sky
Until God gives us wings and like eagles we fly.
David Hablewitz

Cheery Tree (Tree Of Life)

Continually growing...
Spring...leaves and the blossoms bud,
Bloom and glow with life,
With the coming of...
Summer...the fruit of the harvest is ready,
And the leaves glisten with a warm sense of accomplishment,
And so this time passes too...
Fall...earning the right of passage,
Each leaf will bear its own colors,
Slowly each leaf will fall until...
Winter...how quiet in the snow and the still,
But the tree is still growing!
Michael R. Callahan

If This Is Love

My heart aches as my eyes struggle to hold back the tears,
My body shakes as my soul cries out its lonely fears,
If this is love I do not need it,
If this is love I don't believe it,
Love is supposed to feel great,
This hurts even more than hate,
If this is love I don't believe it,
If this is love may I repeat it,
I don't want it.
Amanda L. Carter

A Gifted Man

Professor Bell
Your story I tell
From high and low; blow by blow

You are just and kind,
You've touched many a young mind; you've used your wisdom
To help young people make the right decisions
Because you've always had a positive vision
Of how things could be... Of how things should be...
A vision that you've allowed young people to see

You've taken them to the mountain
And let them see the other side
Then you've grasped their hands and taken them for a ride
To places that only the mind could go...
To places many would never, ever know...

You've taught them that from an atom a cell did spring
And from an egg a bird develops wings
And from a mother's love, a child learns to sing

Oh, Professor Bell your knowledge is a wonderful thing!
You are to many, truly a King!
Jimmie Ahmed

Goodbye

I see you there
your eyes are closed,
and I wish so much
that I hadn't been exposed.

It's caused so much pain,
so much anguish and strife;
I wish that you were gone
and out of my life.

I care so much,
more than ever before,
but now I give up
and leave you to walk down the shore.

I leave you to go
to see what you want to see,
I leave you to grow
into who you will someday be.

I feel that I'm a burden
a weight upon your back,
I know that you don't want me
so I'll just take up my pack and go... Good-bye.
Jenna Fair

This Girl's Life

Can you see through the eyes of me,
my pain and anxiety.
Life's uncertainties have taken their toll,
on my heavy unforgiven soul.
Does anyone care what happens to me?
Is a statistic all I'm destined to be?
No one cares that I'm all alone,
without a bit of light being shown.
Can no one see the confusion in my head?
Is life always destine to be something to dread.
What makes it really bad,
is that everyone's so depressed and sad.
Then a small flower grows,
in my vast land of dead meadows.
It brings a small light again to me,
a small light that all can see.
Marika Eldridge

One Last... Goodbye...
Is all I've been left to write.
  Wishing you could know the way
I need you tonight.
  Distant, chance glances is all that remains
In a turmoil mind that cannot abstain
  From thoughts of you - tonight.

One last goodbye.... Is all I can say
On a white sheet of paper,
  Too far away from you - tonight.
Friction, a mixture of hate between heart and mind
  Has led me to find
You no longer care - tonight.

One last goodbye...
  Are the words this pen cries
As it inks black its tears before running dry
  For it's still the one
Without a lie - tonight.
  Promises; vows proudly passed from one to two
Will never again say -
  "I will, I want, I do", - tonight
Jason Pawlowski

A Hillbilly At Heart
If you are looking for a hillbilly, well, I guess I am one.
I was born so far out in the country they had to pipe in the sun.

Our store-bought groceries - a barrel of flour, some soda
  and some salt now and then.
So Mama could make bread, biscuits, or dumplin's to go with an
  old hen.

We raised our own chickens, pork, and beef.
The vegetables we grew, we canned or put in a root cellar to keep.

When company came, Mama always cooked up a spread.
She needed no recipes; they were all in her head.

The preacher came once a month to our country church on the hill.
For all-day preaching and dinner on the ground, everyone eating
  their fill.

Yes, I guess I am a hillbilly at heart,
'cause that is the way I got my start.
Genevieve Lovett

Memories
Each day there are memories that like a book unfold
Memories to be cherished and are more precious than gold.
Loving and being loved is the greatest gift I know
The joy comes from believing that our love will grow.

I wouldn't change anything about you, even if I could
I love you as you are and I hope that is understood.
My love for you is free and I'm glad to give it away
It is my gift to you for which you never have to repay.

The little things you do and say make me feel good inside
The proud feeling I have when I'm with you cannot be denied.
You are more wonderful than I think you understand
And I'm glad to be walking with you and holding your hand.

I look forward to making more memories with each passing day
Memories that are ours forever and can never be taken away.
I am so very grateful to be sharing my time with you
And making those memories that only you and I can do.
Shirley M. Suits

An Expression Of Love
As I see our family slowly falling apart, I hear her
voice telling me to follow my heart.

The voice I've heard for twenty years, the voice I've
heard in times of tears.

The strong voice of a Mother determined, the sad
voice of a Mother despaired, but always the voice of a
Mother who cared.

A woman who thrives on being strong, who deep
in her heart sang a very sad song.

There was only one love that she ever knew, and
only for us her love grew and grew.

I thank God for her every night, her love for me is
something I always keep in sight.

My Mom's best, it's undisputed, I'm sorry for
the times we feuded.

There's only one person on whom my love depends,
not only is she my Mother, but we are very best friends.
Jennifer Harmon

The Silent Angel
I dreamed of an angel wandering by troubled skies
Seeking her passions lost in dark seas of desire
With an empty heart I wait to hear the cries
Of her broken loves, one a dreamer—one a liar
She complicates realities in a past undone
Only an effort to heal the growing shame
A time of fortune darkened by seasons with no sun
In an echo of sadness and rain
From this sight I will never forget her gentle face
Through shadows burning the night
With this essence of her I long to embrace
My angel, find your love in the silence of the light.
Ryan Whitten

Upon A Midnight Dream
As I walk quietly down this long and winding road,
in the darkness, I hear a wolf cry.
  Into the night I go, waiting, wondering, looking for the one that
I saw in my dream the night before.
  I can hear her voice, and I can still smell her perfume,
I feel her lips upon my lips, I tremble then I shake.
  I keep walking, the fog grows dense so the search
for her intensifies.
  I go on, I know I must have her.
I can still see Venus is rising high in the night sky.
  As I look up to the stars and wonder why.
Still the fog becomes thicker, I can feel her growing nearer, closer,
my heart beats stronger, faster. Just when I think I see her,
the wolf cries; she's gone.
  I must dream another dream hoping to find her.
Tim Siela

The Waterway From God
I once walked upon the stones of an Ice River, as I walked upon the
ice it broke.
I fell through the ice faster than the speed of light. As I fell,
my whole life changed.
At the end of the hole I saw God, he said
that I need to treat people the way I want to be treated, he told me
take a little and give a little. He told me to give and forgive.
Then God sent me on my way, back to the Ice River. When I was
on my way back, I thought about what God said.
I've been having a better life ever since.
Andrea Kolarits

One Serene Life

Life is a game of cat and mouse, sometimes you're running for
just another breath, though you're only moments from your death.

In your laid back world, where humans are your body and souls
dependent, crime and power won't make you a defendant.

Through the years, trapsing in the sun, you frolic in the
deserts warm breezes, running hard, playing ball in the winter
when it freezes.

You coming into my life was with a warm welcome, and an instant love.
So sweet you were, as gentle as a dove.

I became yours and you became mine, together till the end, such
a very fine line. Your protection towards me, was like a
soldier to his country land, in my troubled time your presence
was like a helping hand.

Time made its presence, your life must be retired, you had a
perfect life, one I've come to admire.

In my thoughts you shall journey, in my heart, you shall live, I
thank God for the years of love you could give.

William D. Harm

The Landscape (At Night)

The landscape (when the sky tears down its varied blue array)
   Takes off her greens and browns and dons a gown of dappled grey,
Which hides the vivid colorings that decorate her back
   And suffocates their glimmer and transforms them then to black.

The landscape (when the sun its day-long vigil must desert,
   Its constant searching searing gaze dipped down into the dirt)
Is passingly regarded by a dim and winking eye:
   The moon, that opens, closes, sleepy, slinking through the sky.

The landscape (when the night's vast veil of velvet is unfurled,
   Then punctured with a swarm of stars and stretched across the world)
Becomes a maze of scattered stark invisibilities
   That fill the crack with black and splatter among the trees.

The landscape (when her chirping, buzzing choir no longer sings)
   Sits silent while musicians of the nighttime tune their strings;
Then as the wind breathes soft notes to the orchestra he leads,
   New music, smooth and crickety, proceeds from trees and weeds.

The landscape, in the dying light, endures a wondrous change:
   She alters with the birth of night - grows eerie, wild and strange.

Michael Felix

Going Back

As I watched you at your play,
It reminded me of my childhood days.
I gently took you by your hand,
To introduce you to my playland.

We laid down in the soft warm grass,
And looking way up high,
We imagined what the fluffy white clouds,
Had made up in the sky.

We slowly walked to the creek,
Where we had a pebble toss.
I showed you how to make a house,
Of sticks, leaves, and moss.

It thrilled my soul to watch you run,
Squealing with such delight,
As you were catching lightning bugs,
During their night-time flight.

I smiled to myself as I put you to bed,
When I thought of what you had said,
"Tomorrow if I hold your hand,
May we go back to your playland?"

Della Caudle

Now

The leaves fall, broken, on a disused path,
I think I've tallied awhile;
For through the ages the muses tempt
And to the waste of time beguile.

Our youth does pass so solemn swift,
Adulthood does the same;
We squander all the time we have
And seldom play the game.

We think we have eternity
To laugh and play and dance,
Until Death steals us from ourselves
And we've spent our only chance.

So listen carefully, my friend,
To what I'm telling you;
And live today, for surely swift
So will death come to you.

Melissa D. Fetterman

Untitled

Here we are, we're finally together.
Now I know, we will be forever.
You're lying with me, holding me tight,
And I know everything is right.

All I want is to always lie here.
I feel so safe with you so near.
I have never felt this way before,
And I think I'll feel it forevermore.

We're just together, not even talking,
I still feel, like I'm on the air walking.
I feel like my life is now complete,
And I know, you'll never leave me.

Now we're just going to stay in this place,
All I have to do, is reach out and touch your face.
I've started to reach out, but then I realize,
You're beginning to fade, before my eyes.

What is happening, I cannot understand,
I just know, I've found the perfect man.
Then it occurs to me, things aren't as they seem,
Because I just woke up, it was only a dream.

Marci Pernigotti

Lonely Bird

One morning looking into the sun
There was a pheasant, just only one.

He was pretty as he could be
Standing so proud and looking at me.

There were no others by his side
I wondered why he had such pride.

Where is your family? I was about to say out loud
When all of a sudden there was a small crowd.

A mother pheasant and her family so small
No wonder he was proud and stood there so tall.

That morning while looking into the sun
I was glad to know he was not the lonely one.

Herbert Olander

Mind Vs. The Heart

Almost unreachable, but never lost
Trying to understand why such love was tossed

Loving almost to the core
Only to find a hunger for more

How much we've loved, in so little time
Beware of the intensity, almost a crime

Allow yourself to remember
The heart just might surrender

For the mind has the control
But the heart has the soul

For little we know, in letting love go
Is the constant ache intending to grow

The danger of its loss
Is the hindrance of its cost
    Dawn Marie Barger

Tornado

The sun was high over the small wooden house.
In the desert yard every rodent scrambled to find its heart.
The wind rolled the tumbleweed and
carried its dusty friends across the plain.
I saw him out in the buffalo fields.
I called out to him once or twice but
he never heard me.
His hair was scuffled and his tattered cutoffs covered with earth.
His skin shined but the sunny day don't bother him.
There was a sadness to this face, however.
He looked into my eyes with the fear of a frightened child.
I began to walk to him but, I didn't see what he saw.
I did not see the mighty mass of dust and smoke behind me.
I did not notice that the sky had grown darker.
I ran to him, trying to get to his protective arms,
but, it was too late. I met the sky and the ground all at once.
From above I saw him weeping.
I will miss him.
    Lynette Brogdon

Peace So Beautiful

Pride tears away at my mind.
Guilt runs through my soul.
Envy eats at my very being.
I want to find a peace so beautiful.

I am only human,
Born of flesh and blood
And sin.
I long to find a peace so beautiful.

I am traveling the highways of sin;
The road never curving or ending.
There is nowhere to pull over and rest.
I ache for a peace so beautiful.

When I am lost, He finds me.
When I am naked, He clothes me.
When I am hardened, He softens me.
When I am weak, He strengthens me.

He finds me thirsty, and gives me drink.
He finds me aching and soothes my pain.
He finds me sinning, and forgives me.
In Him I find my peace so beautiful.
    Becky Rister

The Missing Piece

Sweet blossoms on the trees,
honey made by the bees.
  Grass, so green, to lie upon;
red light shining as the coming dawn.

  Sky, so blue; the ocean, gentle;
a stirring heart, being sentimental.
  Watching all these active wonders,
hoping to fulfill all human hungers.

  Wanting peace, and love within.
Hearing the harmony of the wind;
  Searching for the missing piece,
waiting for its song to cease.

  Hoping to find a secret clue,
as colors of reason change their hue.
  Knowing of the Maker and his dreams,
craving the wisdom of what it means.

  Man takes part, in all this he abides,
and hopes on a rainbow, to heaven he rides.
  Finding the link, and what he must do,
finding the missing piece, and the secret clue.
    Jeanette King

My Single Hill

If every mountain was but a single hill
on which the snow had melted and flowers grew,
And there were shady elms guarding their home
then no one would know the pain I knew.

All I ever wanted on my single hill
was someone to talk to and friends to see,
My single hill was little and easy to go by,
so why was it for company I had to plea?

Because on my single hill I was alone
and not a single person cared if I lived or died,
Didn't care that my heart was broken in two,
I sat with the ragged pieces and cried.

The flowers on my hill were brown
and wilted like those fragments of my heart's expense,
The bitter snow had drained my flowers
as it left as love once bled me of my innocence.

The shady elms grew lofty and contemptibly
enduring the pain of seclusion from all,
But these soulful valiants remained
to assure me of at least one protective wall.

So if every mountain was but a single hill
on which the snow had melted and flowers grew,
And there were shady elms guarding their home
then no one must know the pain I knew.
    Angela C. Wade

A Sonnet

The love that we once shared is gone,
Leaving nothing but emptiness and pain.
You treated me like some helpless fawn,
Who needed protection from the cold and rain.
You never really cared at all,
Or even really tried to see.
I couldn't help but come every time you'd call,
But now I see what it has done to me.
So now I find myself walking alone,
Meeting the days as they come and go.
I have to keep looking to the future alone,
Never looking back to see what didn't grow.
For once again I am now free,
To laugh, to love, and again be me.
    Darla Everett

I Remember

I remember many years ago
  the first time I saw you my Father cry
I remember many years ago
  for my mother was about to die
I remember many years ago
  for all I felt was fear
I remember many years ago
  because to me, my mother was so dear
I remember many years ago
  she held me close and began to weep
I remember many years ago
  praying, "God, her please let me keep"
I remember many years ago
  In her chest I buried my head
I remember many years ago
  I woke up and my mother was dead
I remember many years ago
  the first time I saw my father cry
I remember many years ago
  for my mother was about to die.
    Mary Scandrick

Perplexed

The last petal of a rose
Struggling to hang on
Knowing soon his eyes will close
Knowing soon his life will be gone

Strong blows the wind
Heavy falls the rain
Wishing he had a friend
One to share his pain

The sun comes out, from behind a large bend
The warmth, seems like a gift
All his wounds the sun will mend
Now his head, he can once again lift

His eyes are now open wide
His leaves are a beautiful green
Grateful that fate was on his side
Now he sees the world, like it's never been seen

"Today is the beginning of a life,
Yet to become."
    Kristene Elaine Schurg

Life

Life is so short and goes by so fast
It's like a movie with us as the cast
We're born, we breathe, we open our eyes
We maybe get spanked and let loose with cries

Life becomes real in a bewildering way
Why are we here? How long will we stay?
We're given a name and told what to do
We're fed, we're diapered and pampered too

Then it's time for our life in school
We go for 12 years because it's the rule
We may go to college or we may go to work
Then we get married and try not to shirk

Our duties as parents and breadwinners too
'Cause this is the life we're committed to
All at once we're suddenly awake
To the startling fact with a double take!!

It's now starting over with these children of ours
They've started a crop of new "movie stars"
The cycle of life is beginning once more
Our "twilight" in life has moved to the fore!!
    John E. Wolf

The Glorious Lady Freedom Quilt

On an island far from here a statue proudly stands,
and though we never her a voice, she speaks of freedom's lands.

Frenchmen designed her towering frame and carved her copper brow,
Frenchmen brought her over here, but American she is now.

Her eyes set in a perpetual gaze, her tablet forever held fast
her arm raised into a spacious sky, her features forever to last.

Behind her are the mountains, behind which is the sky,
behind which hang the cotton-puff clouds which grow
  and sometimes cry.

Behind her stands a nation strong, though some we'll never see.
They're the ones that leave old home in homes of being free.

Before her are unhappy lands not as free as mine.
They're caught up in a civil war or years behind the time.

Her torch can ignite the biggest battle and spark the largest war.
She shows the soldiers and victims alike the freedom
  they're dying for.

We never see a single tear but we know she's saddened when
She sees a soldier go to war and not come home again.

But through the times both good and bad still standing tall she'll be.
She guards our country with her own two hands from sea
  to shining sea.
    Jennifer Corum

River

  Your longness and quickness hold me in awe,
yet you are subtle and calm and sure to be steady.
  Not like the others are you wild and cruel,
You let the animals drink from your only pool.
  You have seen many seasons,
and yet but one more,
until the rain comes you will be but a stream,
and after the rain you'll show the mighty gleam.
The front will then flourish,
as you ride along the eroded banks of the shore,
where the dirt and sand is that you tore.
  Oh river tell me your ways,
You fascinated and delighted me,
from all the past days.
  Do not stop now,
but keep to the path,
for I will be in your aftermath.
    Robbie Caldwell

If

If someone stabbed you, would you cry?
Sure, because it hurt.
If someone took your family away, would you be sad?
Of course, because you'd be alone.
If someone ate all your food, would you be upset?
Yes, because you'd be hungry.
If it was your heart that got broken,
would you still go on laughing with your friends?
Most definitely not, because a broken heart is much worse
than any of the events listed above.
When you're stabbed, the doctor makes you better.
And when your family's taken away, you could always call, write,
  or visit.
If you're hungry, there's always that friend that will feed you.
But when your heart gets broken, it takes more than
what a doctor can do to heal the hurt.
And it takes more than your family's comfort to make you feel better.
That friend is nice to talk to, but that comfort is only temporary.
A broken heart comes without warning and leaves a permanent scar.
Only the love of the person who has broken a heart can heal a heart.
And even then, there will always be a scar.
    Natalia G. Gradick

"A Message Of Love"

In Oklahoma City on that fateful April day,
The angels came to guide me on my way.
With that bomb's terrible blast,
I closed my eyes, and breathed my last.
   Mom and Dad, I wish I could have said good-bye,
But I never knew the moment I would die.
I've left a world filled with turmoil and strife,
And I hold no malice towards those who took my life.
   Do not let your hearts be overwhelmed with grief,
Just because my time with you was very brief.
I saw the tears run down your face,
As my body was laid in its final resting place.
   Now I'm free from all the suffering and the pain,
I hope my death was not in vain.
Thank you Mom and Dad, for the love you have given me,
I'll cherish it for all eternity.
   From Heaven, I send a message of love,
Someday we will meet again in Heaven up above.

James Feldbruegge

The Struggle

There is a struggle in each face I see
A longing and searching for harmony
A desperate need for each to find peace
to find that final ultimate release

There is no one immune to the desire
No one free from the longing or the fire
We are always longing to be
Yet none is ever truly free

In each other we seek the same thing
No one knows just what life will bring
But of one thing all can be sure
If ever love is found...surely it is the cure

The cure for the struggle, longing and desire
the cure for the seemingly unquenchable fire
The answer for all the ills we possess
In love we hope to find success

Success to be all that we can be
The end to the struggle to be free
The final search for that peace
The acquisition and the ultimate release.

Jo Ann Favre

Elysee (For Estella)

I go where Summer suns never set
Upon blue and placid oceans;
Where sandpipers peck at hidden beaches,
My footprints only on the smoothened sand.

I've been to cold and distant places,
Fooled myself into happier times;
Given over my mind to others' thoughts,
Sacrificed my heart for their illusions.

I've bled into frozen snow broken dreams,
A reckless Romantic, vulnerable man
Clinging closely to the Reason of Feeling;
Exiled by circumstance to a barren land.

I wander there no more, willingly—
I stand here, warm breezes on my face
Watching otter pups in the kelp offshore,
Sensing another traveler nears this place.

Robert Humphrey

Mother Love To A Son

A mother looked across the room
To a little boy with big eyes.
That day the little boy was 8 years old
And weighed 48 pounds.
Through the years the little boy grew to be a man.
Mother love to a son is very special.
This mother can love a son without a real mother.
Do you know a mother who can sit down
And talk 'til 1:00 in the morning?
I know a mother who can do that.
If I tried to know about my real mother today,
I will not forget the mother who raised me as a son.
To look across the room as a man,
To a mother who has the right to say, you're my son.
A mother who is wise, a mother who will listen to a son.
I know a very special mom
Who did not give up on a very special kid.
For that I thank you.

Ransom Hyde Spinner

The Drifters

There it is again...
That smile....
The one you wore when you first laid eyes on me.
It's been a long time since I've seen it.
You're happy now, and it shows.
I'm happy for you, even though we're going our separate ways.
You kept telling yourself things would work out between us....
They didn't.
I kept telling myself we would get married one day....
We won't.
We just drifted apart.
In our own way, we were being selfish trying to make ourselves happy
Instead of paying attention to how the other felt.
I knew you weren't happy, I chose not to believe.
You knew we wouldn't be together, but still you lied.
We have drifted.
But I still love you...
You still love me...
We've grown apart, but we shouldn't be sad.
We did the right thing by saying goodbye.

Wytona D. Holt

A Wise Man

Through abandoned rooms and lost hallways,
behind closed doors;
lies a place so secret, so hidden.
No light exists.
Empty space occupies this tomb,
this dying part of me.

Each day that passes, adds to the silence
the dust is the memory of you.
The only remains of this tiny,
this once sacred, dying part of me.

Once locked, it can't be opened,
my room of remembrances of all that was.
There is a window but too small to notice.
It smiles to the outside awaiting a sunrise,
but light will never touch,
this dying part of me.

A wise man once said "love heals all"
but now is silent and all is forgotten
if what this man said was true,
let you heal this once precious, dying part of me.

Mandy K. Mach

My Love For You

Through everything you put me through,
I always came out still loving you.

Through all the hard times we went through,
You were there for me and I was there for you.

I guess that is why my feelings for you grew strong,
But now, today, I see how I was wrong.

I don't know how and I don't know exactly why,
I guess I'm going to love you until I die.

If there was one wish I could make,
It would be when you awake.

You would realize how much you love me,
And happily ever after we would be.

I know this wish will never come true,
So I guess the only thing I can say, is I still love you.
   Laura Aycock

We're The Children Of The World

We're like a flower needing nourishment.
  We're the children of the world.
A child is to a flower like the whisper
  to the wind.
The gentle frailness escaping in the
  distance you can hear their cries again.
We're like a flower needing nourishment.
  We're the children of the world.
A seedling grows into a radiant flower
  when it's filled with nourishment.
A child taught with caring words of love
  and understanding will grow stronger day by day.
We're like a flower needing nourishment,
  We're the Children of the World.
   Lynn Touloumes

God Why

God gave me a large heart
And from this heart I do part
A small portion of Love
Which was sent from above
And this love I shall share
With anyone who needs my care
Although at times we are hurt and know not why
We have no reason to cry
For God is always near
And when we talk he always hears
Though at times the answers we do not understand
God already has for us a plan
And this is only a small part
We have to go through to finish the start
So why, God, am I willing to share
With no one who needs my care?
   Sheila Travis

Summer

"Oh summer where has thy beauty gone,
fall has arrived which I bemoan.
Winter is coming with snow and wind,
and time indoors I regretfully spend.
Wild geese and such to the south must flock,
and cold weather they can mock.
But spring will appear with April showers,
heralding summer's return and nature's flowers."
   John Tilley

Untitled

I was the world's greatest cowboy when I was four,
ridin' them ponies and spittin' on the floor.
I rode real hard and I sure was tough,
got into some fights 'cause I lived real rough.
Had me a saddle for my ol' ropin' horse...
The only one he'd let ride him was cowboy me, of course!
I busted my rose and broke my arm,
but it didn't matter, I still worked my farm.
I won a big buckle 'cuz I was the best around,
and all the women would sigh when I rode into town.
Fought all the bad guys and I sure saved the day,
then I'd go home to bring in my hay
I was the hero and I always won,
in the fights I was last to holster my gun,
I was the world's greatest cowboy,
but when I was five,
they went and made me the best fireman alive!
   Melissa Fritz

If You Have A Dream

If you have a dream
of swimming across the ocean
never let anything stand in your way
always remember never give up on that notion
just keep on believing it will come true today

If you have a dream
of playing in a marching band
never let anyone say you're not good enough
keep remembering you can do anything you want on our land
never let anyone say you don't have the right stuff

If you have a dream
of becoming king or queen
never listen when people say it can't happen to you
always remember royalty or not you fit the scene
keep on having faith someday it will come true

If you have a dream
never give up and cause it to part
no matter how far out it may seem
always remember within time it comes straight to your heart
   Katherine A. Foard

Untitled

In a society of feelings one is often left alone,
No special person to talk to,
No place to call a home.
One might feel deserted, or even feel astray,
But that one person may not know
That all you need to do is pray...

In a society of hardships
One might feel left out,
You try to make them hear you,
No one will listen to you shout. Money is a memory
And luxuries have faded away,
Just remember that God is here,
And all you need to do is pray...

In a society of violence,
You have to do your part,
People don't need money to make them happy,
Beauty is found within the heart.
Yet if a friend gets murdered and you feel dismay,
Don't let all your anger out,
Get down on your knees and pray.
   Sara Alvarado

My Consuming Love

Consumed by your love
My body, heart, and soul long for you

My body longs to be held by your gentle hands
I want to touch your face to memorize every feature so I can picture
   you perfectly in my dreams
I want the arms of comfort to embrace me and never let go
My body is consumed by your love

My heart beats to the rhythm of your name
I want you to know how deep my love is so maybe
then you'll be sure of my forever
I want your heart to hold mine like never before
My heart is consumed by your love

My soul bears the memories we've created
I want you to read the poem that grows ever longer through a song
of commitment deep inside me that bears my true feelings of love
I want you to share your soul with me so I can know you even better
   and share much deeper things with you
My soul is consumed by your love

I want us to hold on not only today but forever
I want us to be forever perfect just as we are now
I want us to be held in each other's passion endlessly

You are my consuming love
   Nicole Freeman

I Am...

Cut me and I bleed, caress me and I purr.
Curse me and I'm scorned, spurn me and I'm hurt.
Dismiss me and I'm lost, trust me and I'm trustworthy.
Respect me and I'm respectful, acknowledge me and I shine.
Inspire me and I flourish, push me and I push back.
Love me and I am love, hate me and I am hate.
I am the sum of all before me,
And the difference of all that follow.
I am the innocence of the first born child,
And the wisdom of all the ages.
I am the back, the blood, the sweat, and the tears,
That this world was built upon.
I am hope for the hopeful,
And dreams for the dreamers.
I am all that I can be,
And none of what I was before.
I am...
   Norris Flagler

Smiling

It may have happened one early morn,
Or during the middle of the day.
For some it may have happened late at night,
When the angels took our loved one away.
Their passing may have left us sad,
Maybe there was something we did not get to say.
We may have made plans that cannot be fulfilled,
It seems...all we can do is pray.
Yet, don't be afraid to talk to them,
Though they are no longer in view.
They are watching us from above,
And will understand what we are trying to do.
They want us to be at peace,
With the fact that they are gone.
Though we must move forward without them,
In our memories they will always live on.
So, when you see a beautiful rainbow,
Or feel the sun shining warm and true.
Remember, that could be their way,
Of "smiling" down on you.
   David D. McDonald

Someday

I know your needs, and I've studied you,
Even when you didn't know I was in this world,
When you look sad, I want to make you
Happy, when you look disgusted, I want
To make things better,
When you look worried, I want to wipe
Your tears away, when you look upset,
I want to see you cheerful,
When you look lonely, I want to tell you,
You're not, when you look like you want to give up,
I want to tell you things will be ok,
When you smile, you brighten up my day,
And I never want your smile to ever go away,
I always wondered what it would be like to
Be your best friend, someday!
   Trisha DeGrave

Creation

Our path is made
The bricks are laid.
No one understands, one's need to be his own man.
No prejudice will remain
When all of the choices are made.
My heart will then be filled by all that is unreal.
Now the time has come,
To question all that has been done.
The end is near.
We must have no fear.
The world is diseased.
Creation has ceased.
Now creation can begin anew, started with a select few.
   Jesse Lee Prescott

High Plateau

I huddle as tufted grasses
Slap their sides together on the high plateau.
Thin air whines against bent bushes.

Tough, woody stems of Bitterbrush
Offer little protection to creatures; but...
Up here, little is a blessing.

When night arrives the tundra view
Of sameness closes down. Starlight
Shows her stories to the lonely.

My eyes widen. In the dark my
Neck prickles as nature screeches
Her ritual and swallows earth's warmth.

High winds barricade human sound.
So too, my mind tries to barricade
The wail and moan of wind sounds. Or...

Are they my sounds? My creatures
Rising, drawn to Earth's whistles,
Poised like mean-spirited dogs.
   Janet Corley

Shape Poem

(Words) - Loving animals. Graceful, furry, creeping,
hissing, pouncing, growling, defending themselves. Meows of
love, paws like scrubs, tails; not stub, fast...special effects.
   Danielle Johnson

"Soul Shadows"

The awe and affirmation of birth, ancient aperitif of youth,
Revitalizing rainbow sanctifying the sanitizing showers,
Love ladened eyes mirroring passion's perception of truth,
Slow motion strolling through waist high wild flowers,
Sensuous summer morsels of savory sun-sweetened fruit
A cherished one's languid fragrance lingering for hours,
Softly falling city snows, streams flowing into spring,
Stars filling July skies like a concert of frantic fireflies,
Harvest hued revelry, full moons on water silently sing,
Waves washing down waiting rocks, then again upward rise,
Trust harboring hope to overcome any insurmountable thing,
Whispers of faith, whiffs of caring, wisps of sharing, surprise!,
Always alone, never alone, in suffering or our fight for right,
Our higher power, a light making the white night bright.
Ronald T. Policare

The Cries Of A Cancer

In this shell I reside, patiently waiting for the tide

Swallowed by the ocean's mass, fighting all the way
Sinking to the deep blue depth, to my world of dismay

Cold and dark, I feel the pain
Memories linger, thoughts remain

My mood is shifting with the sand
Don't know how much more I can stand

My claws are piercing through your heart
Emotions wild from the start

The light is high above my sight
I reach for it with all my might

If I fail I feel I die, if I make it still I cry

Tide now shifting to the shore
Always wishing for something more

Back on this journey I travel again, against my will I can never win

I never want to leave my shell
The place I learned to love so well

This water dark and cold, it fits me well so I'm told

On the shore again I lay, the sun will watch me while I stay

When the tide comes back for me, I'll go without your sympathy
Matthew Rydeen

It Does Me Just Fine

Sitting at home, so very much alone.
Will I? Could I? I hardly think so.
Why? Because I am not one for going out.
Nobody even likes me.
If I would try, my nose would be broken
from all the doors slammed in my face.
People are cruel! Are you that way?
Please say no. I guess I shall go.
My heart will be broken, for you have not spoken.
If you change your mind, write to me,
I don't live in Beverly Hills, but it does me just fine.
My city has a Baseball diamond, a Football field,
a Hockey arena, and a Basketball court.
It's got a place to play Percussion, Keyboard, and so on.
It's also got music stores, and book stores, like any other place.
It's got schools of course, where I'm in 8th grade.
So give me a try. You won't be denied.
Thank you! Thank you!
So very, very, much.
Andrea Moravec

Advice To Politicians

Unpeople jet by others with dubious irradiance.
Reasoning, why pay dues and go by rules?
Instead they plot, with police consent,
smiling to kneeling listeners.
Vote for me so I can get mine, because I deserve more than thine.
Dare the few who drool for power, with a creed for greed, need to read.
Lie but appear to tell the truth for a career of smear.
Drink your beer and let me make clear,
licking politicking goes to the one who out promises the rest.
John Hovanec

Question

I awoke before dawn with a tear in my eye,
not knowing why.

The pain from within sent pins and needles up my spine,
I tried not to whine.

I turned toward the soft glow that would soon be the sun,
knowing I could not run.

My feet found the floor and I slowly stood and turned,
to seek the comfort I yearned.

Across the room the cradle stood without sound,
where once we gathered around.

Joy is gone without our understanding why,
our only hope is to survive.

Day breaks bright and warm to dispel the gloom,
our tears are shed only in this room.

On the surface of our lives we show only a smile,
our heart asks, Where is the child?
Gail C. Bills

Nature's Serenade

Tears rolling down a soft cheek.
Streams of pearls does she weep.
Gray sheets of sadness fill the sky
As beads of anger are hurled from
Way up high.
Looking through, she wishes that once
Again the sun would shine beaming
Happiness into her life.
Ohh, a break in sight?
A flicker of light?
Through this darkness can she see
What lies behind the gloomy screen?
A rainbow, all big and bright!
Precious bands of colored light,
Each unique and precise:
Transcending joy and happiness
Back into her life.
Pure bliss tip toes through her heart
And away runs sadness off into the night.
April J. Bolle

Daydreams

As I sit in my room,
and look out of the window,
I dream of dreams, by sea and by meadow,
Sailors at sea and Horses full of glee,
All dance around in my head.

Never any worries and never any doubts,
There will be so many dreams to dream about.

As I sit in my room and look out of the window
I dream of dreams, by sea,
and by meadow.
Brooke L. Nuoffer

Where Is Love?

Where are the flowers that once grew
  Along my path in spring?
Where are the green leaves
  Which sheltered every feathered thing?

The petals fell and blew away
  Somewhere beyond my sky
To become a dream and a memory
  That seems to be nearby.

Where is the wife that I once had?
  She used to be standing there
Beside the bed of roses red
  With blossoms in her hair.

Where are my children who used to play
  Beside the garden gate?
They have grown up and moved away
  To live and love a mate.

To find the love that I once had,
  I simply have to look
At photos hanging on the wall
  And in my picture book.

James D. Tankersley

Music Of The Birds

Have you ever sat and listened to the birds?
Theirs is the sweetest music that I ever heard.
I could sit for hours and listen to their songs,
And I sometimes wonder to whom it did belong.

I guess I'm full of questions, but I was wondering
About the people that went above and if God heard them sing?
And if He decided their voices to preserve
Through the music of the birds, some famous singer's words.

Yes, could it be? All those famous people who passed on long ago,
The memories of their songs remains with us below.
So the next time you hear the birds, listen with a careful ear
And listen to the voices of singers that we used to hear.

June Griffith

How Do You Spell Love?

She cooks, she cleans, she sews some, too;
She's always baking something good for you.
She's been there since you were born,
To love you and to mend what you have torn
She's always there to share your joys,
And she's picked up many forgotten toys.
She's on the job...morning...moon...and night.
She's settled many childish fights.
No one's as special or as dear,
She's shared sorrows and wiped away tears.
Grandchild, daughter and son,
In your heart she's number one!
So loving and kind, there is no other,
How do you spell love???
I spell it ... Mother!!!

Debra Crawford Prange

Love

Love has no color. It has no shape, nor
does it have a size. It comes unconditionally
within your heart - something that
can't be torn apart. If you don't abuse
it or misuse it, it's something that comes
in handy all the time. From an animal,
parent, spouse or friend, love has no end.

Ebony Delsid-Avery

Aces In The Dirt

In a time of need, aces fill the sky,
And only the horizon knows is to live,
Or who is to die.
The mornings are early, even the sun isn't up,
But the roar of the engines scream to the sky.
The strikes come quick, from no where it seems,
And again the engines leave with that terrible scream.
The bombs that fallow are a deafening sound, and
Another ace hits the ground, unable to jump being
So close to the dirt, another ace fallows the first.
Of the six that were there, only four are still
Known, the other two have found new home.

Jerry Smothers

Majesty

I sit and watch with wonder as mighty trees bend low
Watching in great reverence God's majestic show,
I hear the thunder rolling as I watch the birds fly by
I feel such awed amazement as lightning brights the sky,
There's nothing like a thunderstorm to make God's power known,
As I sit safe inside myself he speaks to me alone,
It puzzles me as I often think of other people's fears
What I consider beautiful as rain falls down like tears,
It washes clean our spirits and opens up our eyes
It cleanses us from sinful ways that we might lead better lives,
If you stop and think about the storm you then can understand,
We're sheltered in its loving heart and in His mighty hands,
Next time you hear the thunder roll and lightning brights the sky,
Remember He is sharing His beauty in disguise.

Dinah Sapp

Shower By Morning-Juan Is Driving

Coal-chalk skin and deformed callous fingertips.
The flutter of the heater fan disrupts the barely audible stereo noise.
Milk white traffic opposes us,
lurching past trailing a metallic crimson glow.
My driver reaches in his shirt pocket,
and ignites another smoke.
A soft red tint rests on his tired silhouette,
outlining thirty five years of discontent.

I smooth the window out for visibility of the endless factories.
Burdens of pasty toxins strafing the flat black abyss of sky.
I lean ahead on the dash.
Truckers overcome us from behind.
Juan has lit another smoke,
and he rubs his crusty eyes with a handkerchief.
He looks over at me,
awake after a long thirty minute respite.
Morning rush hour will be in full swing in New Jersey in two hours.
I have to find us an alternate route.

Gabriel Steinbach

Silently I Drift Away

There comes that part of day called night
When silence drives the chirping birds
and barking dogs
out of hearing - out of sight.
I sit down with book in hand
and music flowing through my heart,
my mind, my soul
And then the book is closed
The music fades
I sleep.

E. M. Schneider

The Fading Whistle

To hear the train whistle blowing,
It's a hollow, shrilling sound.
Not knowing where it's come from,
Nor knowing where it's bound.

Wondering who or what it may carry,
Wanting to go along.
But really sitting and pondering,
About if I would belong.

Watching the smoke rise and curl,
To quickly drift away.
People forgetting the train ever came,
Just like they will me someday.

You can hear it pull off in the distance,
Away goes a part of your heart.
Wanting to go along with it,
But it seems you just can't depart.

So you continue to wonder,
As to what it would be like.
Never getting on the train,
But always saying goodbye.
Susan E. Brown

The Marionette

I can no longer act in this play.
The script is finished and yet I do not know what to say.
I've become a puppet on a string.
Bending this way and that for everything.
Why do I continue to care?
Freedom beckons me on the winds of everywhere.
No longer will I sacrifice my serenity.
As I stand guard at the door of my mind, he becomes a nonentity.
My mind learns detachment with love.
This emotion can only take root with help from above.
Peace and tranquility will flood the portals of my mind.
Turning my back I will joyfully leave all this behind.
Nancy Hummer

Frame By Frame

In loving memory Michael J. Ryan
There isn't time for yesterday
tomorrow's nearly gone
but what remains "Frame by Frame"
are memories and song
like fishing trips and moon light dips
and laughter by the yard
babies smiles and times that's hard and grandma on my arm
friends like you and feelings too
that forever will remain
in hearts of joy and happiness
we'll disregard our pain

To carry on in ways that's grand we reach to lend a helping hand.
To never judge but understand the differences in every man.
To truly give a thought or two to someone we despise
and wonder what a difference to see them through "God's" eyes.
Rose Ryan

Old Mrs. Biddle

I once knew a woman named old Mrs. Biddle.
She liked to eat tacos with bugs in the middle.
She cooked them in grease on an old rusty griddle.
A typical dinner by old Mrs. Biddle.
Rich Wendling

Gray

War is something that is hard to describe,
It's only an expression of the hate inside.
War is a nightmare that flows through the brain
Of the soldiers who fought and now feel the pain.

Our strongest image of a senseless war
Should only be that of a festering sore.
But for most that's not in the least,
Theirs is a vision of a fight for peace.

A description of war could probably be found
If only we would stop and just look around.

The best way that really know
Is to think of a present without a nice bow.
Or think of a playground with no kids in sight,
Or think of a world without any light.

Maybe the only way is to really be there,
And see the bombs fly through the air,
Or see your best friend
Come face to face with the end.

Or just remember the people who live life each day,
And see no joyful colors, just a dim, warlike gray.
Kevin Madden

Not A Choice

Today my father and my mother made me;
Before I left God's side he told me about my life,
He said that I would be a great old man with many kids and that I would be famous too.
I was so happy to be continued that I swam around, and sucked my thumb with joy.

Today my mom found out that she was going to have me;
I heard her crying late last night, I guess she must be happy.
I heard my mom talk to my dad and couldn't believe my ears.
Who's to say that I'm not good? He hasn't seen my tears.
I heard him tell my mom that I was not his child.
Who's to say I am not his child, God told me that I was.
He told my mom not to keep me if she wanted him;
That silly man, I know she must love me.

Today Mom went to see a doctor who hurt me as I swam.
I could not defend myself but he can.
He ripped and pulled me out of mom until I was no more.
Who is he to play our God, he's just a mortal man?

I am no more and don't understand why this would happen to me.
What will happen to my dreams and what I was meant to be?
Greg Lovekamp

Peaceful Midnight

So peaceful is the midnight, a contrast to the day,
Nothing left to ponder on or take your thoughts away.

No noisy telephones to ring, the callers are asleep,
No memories of the day gone by or promises to keep.

The world has settled down to rest when peaceful midnight breaks,
Beasts and birds and creeping things a needed rest do take.

Some folks don't like the midnight or the solitude it brings,
They'd rather be tied up in knots with people, thoughts and things.

I clearly hear at midnight the wisdom of His way,
Untethered by the cares of life that cross my path by day.

I've found that peaceful midnight is glorious you see,
I find the time to talk to God and let Him talk to me!
Joyce M. Brown

Untitled

As he stumbles through the unending labyrinth,
He wonders if that center exists
He tramples through what seems like endless weeds,
Only to find himself mothering wounds from dead thorns
But to find his way to the center,
You must see the labyrinth as a garden
Though rough and hard to see,
there, below the thick brush of decaying blanket of plants,
lies a bed of rose petals,
waiting for a soft rain to nourish the wilted paleness of each pore
Though down-pours come and go
He, who is the one must release his morning dew
upon my lonely body and rest his loving soul
upon my heart of roses
  Sarah Howard

I Love Being The Mother Of The House

I love being the mother of the house
I love God first
I love my husband
I love my children
I love my neighbor
I love myself
I love being the mother of the house
I can give to God
I can give to my husband
I can give to my children
I can give to my neighbor
I can give to myself
I love being the mother of the house
God is a person
My husband is a person
My children are people
My neighbor is a person
I am a person
I love being the mother of the house
I love, I give, I am a person, who is the Mother of the House
  Susan C. Fritz

To Mother With Love

In my heart I have a special place
For someone who is very close to me,
Without her I couldn't face
The problems and dilemmas that come to be.

Although it seems she's miles away
I know deep down she's always there.
No matter what time of night or day
I can call to talk - she really cares.

She's unlike any person I know
A ready smile, and a hand to lend.
I tell my friends, I love her so
She's not only my mom, she's my best friend.

I don't think anyone will ever see
The person who's really inside of me,
Except for that one, that special one
And she's my mom, forever to be, and gratefully.
  Shaun M. Chokreff

Legend Of Tulip

'Tis a legend gone astray,
'tis a legend out to learn, a story all gone by,
and lost always from earth. Now is the chance to discover, to push
and grow like a bloom, as a bud from the tulip falling on the cold
grass and if the tulip bud falls off onto the ground and it is too cold,
let the tulip flower grow, and it will continue to grow warm and
let the tulip flower grow evermore than the year before.
  Dana Reed

Summertime

Summertime is hot and dry,
with spiders, bees, and butterflies.

Summertime has no school,
no pencils, books, or silly rules.

Summertime has lakes and ponds,
with fairy fish and magic wands.

Summertime has crafts and games,
at camp the fire has big flames.

Summertime has comic books,
with neighbors and their friendly looks.

Summertime has laughs and cries,
with stories and our little lies.

Summertime was so much fun,
but now school starts
and summertime's done.
  Nicole P. Soucy

Storm

I was awakened in the still of the night.
  But this night wasn't all that still.
Outside the sky lit up with fright.
  Then over the earth rolled a rumble.
Again, a bolt lit up the night sky.
  But instead of a rumble, a "Boom" was heard!
Then all was silent, so very silent!
  With his hands God turned over the clouds.
This rain was no sprinkle, no shower.
  But a downpour, a gully washer.
The howling wind forced limbs to scrape the window
  Sending chills and shivers down my back.
Another flash disturbed the blackness.
  Another boom excited the silence.
The pouring rain sounded like drums on the roof.
  A gust of wind threw the rain into the house.
All was quiet. God was no longer angry.
  He turned off the "Storm."
One of God's ways of expressing His feelings
  Is through the "Storm."
  Kerri Rhea

Attainable Emotional Intensity

Words can only go so far
My conscious mind can only think so fast
So hard it is to express oneself
Once it is already said, done, and time elapsed
Hear my ravaging rhythms staccato flawlessly
Let pure tribal tones rape you of attention
Open your mind
Let my pulverized soul pour into your emotional comprehension
Let the waves of sound stimulate the murkiness of the mind
Hear the beat pierce cortex as electricity flows thorough your spine
Now I know you understand,
My feelings.....
Are now in you
  Dave Vago

Behind Every Star

They say there's a dream behind every star,
A dream for two people to share,
A dream of a future much brighter than the past,
A dream of a love that will always last.

My dream's behind a faint little star
High in the heavens afar,
And my only dream is that your only dream
Is behind that very same star.
  Clive Caldwell

To Be Able To See You My Love

To be able to see you my love
To be able to see your soft presence
Like the silent flight of the morning dove
On wings of rising sun in its essence.

Yes, to be able to see you my love
Would be to see the end of my long fight,
The end of fear of once I was made of
And the beginning of what I know is so right.

To see you my love would mean joy
My heart to extend beyond my self
To sustain your happiness, my feelings would employ
And in my heart lay a universe of your wealth.

   Wait for me, for soon you will see
   That love will be yours; for it will be me...
   Dean Robledo

Visiting Day

I'm sitting here waiting for the familiar sound
I get so emotional when this time comes around.
A time to see my family and friends
precious moments I wish would never end
so there we sit on opposite sides
as I try to be brave with tears in my eyes
so as I run my hand over the glass and frame
dying inside as you do the same
and I long to hold you in my arms
to keep you safe from every harm.
But the glass doesn't feel the way you did
as over the glass and frame my hands slid.
   Monet Sanchez

Diamonds In The Snow

Diamonds in the snow like stars in the sky,
I've never thought to wonder and ask why,
How did they get there? I guess I'll never know;
How there came to be Diamonds in the snow.

Diamonds in the snow like fish in the sea,
Sparkling as a ray of sun hits on thee.
Is there not a book that lets you know?
How there came to be Diamonds in the snow.

Diamonds in the snow like a leaf on a tree,
How did they ever get this past me?
I guess it's a mystery that is whispered low,
How there came to be Diamonds in the Snow.
   Denise M. Schuster

Reflected Life

Once a body stripped of all worthwhile
  Time has healed my mental wounds
Memories of darkest nights
  Now are lit by shining lights
Compartments of my mind are filled
  Locked with keys of timely steel
Bodies I have seen will pass
  What I choose to view them as
Are the movies of my past
  To be shown at the proper time
When I can clearly process all the things of my life
  I call a mess
  Tammy M. Wells

"My Secret"

My secret would be something that I would share with only me,
myself, and I.
Of course I need to tell someone, someone I could trust.
I know all this sounds kind of strange, I mean about my dream,
but I'll try to tell you where a perfect place for me, would be.

Deep in the woods there would be a place, a place only I would go.
There I would see, between my two eyes, a path where green
grass grows.
There I'd walk a little longer, about a mile down the road.
I would come to a pile of ivy. It laid across a wall of some sort
with tons of splintery edges. Pushing the ivy away, my eye caught
a glimpse, there in the midst of the brush, was a key...covered by
flower petals.

The key felt almost magic when I held it in my hand.
I thought to myself, what if it goes to this wall or what is held inside?
I crept around seeking holes to place the key.
I looked until I saw, could it be, the hole that fits the key?

Slowly I bent down, just enough to look inside, but what it was,
too great to be true.
It was what I've always dreamed for.
I shoved the key into the hole and twisted just a little...

The sound of an opening lock gave chills up through my spine.
Am I really doing this?
I'd think. I couldn't help my burn of excitement, I had to scream
out loud.
What a wonderful thing that would happen to me,
if my perfect place, would be.
   Janel Lee Derrick

Walk With Me

  I think about you night and day
Your warm cheerful smile that brightens my life
  You change the dark into light
You paint a rainbow of hope around us
  I will not give up on our special love
The bond of trust and solitude will never be broken
  If you had but one choice for love
I hope you would sense the admiration of devotion
  But one kiss to place on your lips
To seal our future together
  The path of life awaits
Will you take my hand and walk with me?
   Jodie Pace

Sonnet

Oh, I have seen the stricken heart, though bled
Of every hope, revive to sing again,
And felt the quiet presence of the dead
As sunshine on the floor, as gentle rain.
Tiptoe with wonder have I stood because
A fairy shook her shining wings at me,
And breathless, that in one dark-lucid pause
A shadowed pool could hold eternity.
The mountain gods before me, thunder-gird,
Have stalked in splendor down the earthward span,
And once upon a windy hill I heard
The far-off, strange-sweet pipes of Pan...
Though subtler magic earth and sky may brew,
I shall have known no miracle like you.
   Dorothy Steinbomer Kendall

Refractions

I have to catch you in my peripheral vision,
   because you won't reveal yourself when I look you in the eye.
I must prompt for answers and circle in on what I need to know,
   because you won't come right out and explain yourself,
     nor even give a straight answer.
But I stand in wonder as you mature,
   as you define and redefine who you are and who you are becoming;
Transforming in ways that gladden my heart; confirming what
   I already knew.

Your essence is gleaned in fleeting glimpses;
   So much is below the surface.
But your wit and humor effervesce in an eye-winking,
   bouncing off the contours of your personality.
I view the son-spots inverted as through a telescope,
   because I can't look directly.
But I bask in your warm and gentle nature
   and relish the times I can put my arm around you and you don't slip away.

Lucy Bair Goodell

I Wonder Where You Are

I wonder where you are
I reach out to touch your mind
We're so close, yet so far
As I touch, I see, I cannot find
I wonder where you are

I wonder where you are
I look and hear nothing
Yet we stretch from afar
I hear and see everything
But I still wonder where you are

I wonder . . . where you are, I'm not sure what to say
Will we ever again reach par?
I wander every day . . . and I wonder . . . where you are

I wonder where you are am I dreaming or is it true
I'm pained by the scar for if it weren't, I wouldn't be blue
But I can't stop wondering where you are

I wonder where you are, someday I may find you
If I look at the right star,
Until if and maybe . . . I see your clue!
I will always wonder where you are.

Barry Piornack

Life

When I was young I spent my time to spare
thinking of the one with which my life to share
And now as I grow older and greater burdens I must shoulder
I must spend my time just to make another dime
But more each day I find nothing on earth is quite so grand
as the love that grows between a woman and a man
and so as I travel from here to there, my mind isn't upon the maidens fair, but I think of the joy so sweet
when at the end of the day the one I love, I meet
and now as my hair turns to gray, and my days of youth have passed away
my one main hope which seems so vain and yet is so just
is to have someone, who will love and trust.
But as among the trees and flowers I toil, there comes a call from afar, a distant land, where I've never been,
From which blows a wind, upon this wind I hear a call
Come to me before the fall, and though my heart is heavy with sorrow
yet I must rise again and face tomorrow, if you wish my life to share
help me when we have an idle hour.
Help with your love and trust so kind, peace and joy in this land to find.

TaulBee Abner

Then

I miss the days when you were here
Always by my side.
You were always there to help me through
When tears filled my eyes.
Now no one's there to help me through,
And they begin to fall.
Through the drops I see you then
As you once were.
The caring friend I long to hold
Close by me once again.

The you I knew is no longer there,
Just a stranger passing by,
But in my heart I'll always know
You cared for me back then.
I wasn't only a reminder
Of things you can't forget.
Now time has come between us
And the love that we once shared,
But I'll always hold the memories...
From then.

Tracy Hahn

Kaput

White light slipping between the cracks
The cracks in front of me all else is black
Is black the color of death doom and destruction
And destruction to cause unlikely harm to me
To me and then bring a full life of harmony

White light slipping between the cracks
The cracks in front of me lying on my back
My back flat downward in the dirt
The dirt staining me the flowers growing reminds me
Reminds me of a past love going down

Is this all death is gonna be
Stained with blood I'm gonna bleed
Cut this life off from me
Set me free free free to fly
And set me up to die

White light slipping between the cracks
The cracks are death are they I ask
I ask that in the future may I
May I one thousand times over may die and be laid to rest
To rest is there life even after death

Phillip Schaefer

The Peaceful Evening

The quiet sunset;
The peaceful evening.
Children laughing, playing, yelling in the woods.
Cars on the highway not far away.
An airplane in the sky;
A few ducks and geese shamelessly fly overhead.
The gentle breeze;
The melting snow.
The trees with tiny, delicate, graceful buds.
Gray-blue waves of clouds drifting
   slowly along the light pink ocean of sky.
The squeak of swings;
The streak of sunlight as dark birds
   fly along the rose color.
How else can I describe my peaceful
   evening of thinking and dreaming
Of romance and love I can only share
   with my very best friend?
I cannot; you have to imagine the rest.

Sara Wagenknecht

In Memory - My Dog Pluto

Pluto you're missed tremendously. Out of 15 yrs. 10 mos.
you have given me joy for 14 years.
When the time came it broke my heart to put you to sleep
and you will always be in my heart.
Your pictures tell me much. You were a dog that was loving.
You enjoyed all dogs no matter what size they were.
There was no meanness in you and likewise with human beings.
You're missed at the table for I do not have my Pluto who
would sit and wait for scrappings before touching your own meal.
Playful you were and oh how you performed and with enjoyment.
Your afghan and pillow is a reminder that once upon a
time I owned a beautiful dog namely Pluto who was named
after one of the planets so far away it only can be detected
by photos of the heavens.
Evangeline Katranis

A Frown In The Woodwork

A voice in the grain,
A face in the stain,
There is history in this wood.
Where it once stood,
A servant to many a mighty rain.

Harvested for its flesh,
Gutted of its fibrous mesh,
To be carved by the will of the carpenter's hand.
The one who reseeded the land,
In hopes his livelihood would replenish.

Future demand will overcome supply,
Earth floors will reveal to the sky,
Our home covered with horrid scenes.
Remnants of everyone's broken dreams,
The silent rivers couldn't reply.

Make good use of the craft man's work,
It may have been a desk for a clerk,
Or a house that survived many long winters.
The wear has reduced it to all but splinters,
Yet, sparing the homes where my feral friends lurk.
Reed Bass

Untitled

When you are gone
no aria is as rousing
no note as resounding
as is your cloying presence

When you are gone
despondent birds cease their song
miraculous fables lose mystical flavor
even the sun seems lax

When you are gone
no flower exhales perfume
as giddy
as intoxicating
Thunderous waves are but tears
streaming down the face of the earth

When you are gone
I shrink in upon myself
until the last wisps of me
are carried away by the faceless, indifferent wind

But when you are near
I tower so above the now obscure, bested sun
John Barra

Seasons

Spring is a time of
flowers blooming, birds singing, and
new love found.

Summer is a time of
lemonade and fireworks,
Lovers enjoying picnics and walking
hand in hand in the park.

Fall is a time of
brilliant colors of red, orange, and yellow.
before mother nature's winter sleep.

Winter is a time of
children's laughter, building snowmen
with the crisp new fallen snow.
Holiday lights ablaze and
good cheer abound.

For right around the corner....
Spring can be found.
Cynthia Sutton

A Soul Not Lost

Through life there is always a thread of truth
that is woven through the fabric of your soul.
And though I hold one needle
that seems to be the master weaver,
there are many hands in this cloth,
many designs that do not lie solely within me.

So I am content with knowing that behind me lies
the obvious lace, satin, wool and burlap.
And before me are the strands I have collected
along the way, with some patterns not yet revealed.

At some point, we are knitted together,
you so skilled in art, and me so willing to talk about it.

Beautiful in the raw material but warm in the air
that lies just below the surface, just out of sight,
But well within the realm of touch.
Renee Lynne-Cochran Foley

The Mysterious Shark

The shark, the graceful shark,
Is a mystery to me.
Swimming amongst the coral,
In the oceans and the seas.
The soothing aqua water,
Fills the oceans and the seas,
And its great majestic beauty,
Is for everyone to see.

The shark, it is a loner,
Cruising along at its own speed.
And the sight of its gracefulness,
Is a beautiful sight indeed.
And the eyes, those deep black eyes,
Are things of wonder not of fright,
They sit right there and stare at me,
Like black holes in the night.

The shark, the graceful shark,
Is a mystery to me,
For there is no other, that things,
Both fear and wonder, to the oceans and the seas.
Michael S. Kasuba

The Hand Of Creation

Not by accident, not by chance...
Nor any setting beneath the sun,
Your destiny was in the making,
Fulfilling: 'God's Will Must Be Done.'

You fought your way to worth and fame...
Through your pugilistic power,
To the world you proved yourself a champion -
Creating for Boxing - its finest hour.

More than that, you chronicled 'Manhood' -
To its highest peak,
Setting an historical record of time,
You carved for yourself a niche in life...

But even more than that, another chore awaits you -
Its epilogue is silently written in the wind,
A whole new concept, a whole new world - of Poetry,
A brand new life to begin...

'The pen is mightier than the sword' 'tis said...
And the mind is by far sharper than the tongue,
Its message is swifter than a single blow,
So let the 'challenge'... now begin.

Katie Marie Stillwell

Who Am I To Ask

Who am I to ask, for long enduring peace?
...think that I deserve my burdens to surcease.

Who am I to say, the good outweighed the bad?
...so, render me rewards - those thing I never had.

Who am I to think, you owe me favors now?
...for sacrificial tears, as if they should endow.

Who am I to dream, the end will bring the light?
...and life will find its place, beyond eternal flight.

Who am I to feel, I've done the job at last?
...to earn my rightful wage, for pain and sorrow past.

Who am I to speak, while others have been still?
...embracing every trial, submitting to Your will.

And who am I to pray, for earthly joys denied?
...when greater blessings wait, to place me by Your side.

Jim La Prade

Who Is She

A woman once caressed me in her loving arms,
Only the two of us, She kept me from all harm.
Taught me how to ride a bike; how to tie my shoes.
When we played a card game, She always seemed to lose.
Kissed my cheek each morning as I boarded the bus,
Greeted me each afternoon, always with a hug.
Although She had to take a job to help us get through
She said to me Don't worry there's always time for you.
I guess She must have meant it even to this day,
She's never missed a softball game, concert, or school play.
Mended many broken hearts and dried a lake of tears,
Held my hand to guide me all through the years.
Memories are priceless of the times we share
She can always make me laugh, it's nice to know She's there.
Although sometimes we disagree and angry words are said,
We stop to think things over and compromise instead.
Now I'd like to say thanks for all She's done.
Oh, Just one more thing:
I Love You Forever....Mom

Kristen Olson

In My Room

I sit in a never ending darkness,
covered by a smothering blanket of loneliness.
I look beyond the comforts of my room,
at my self inflicted doom.
Red smeared walls,
blood filled halls.
Empty shell,
another life sent to hell.
Gone and wasted away,
the happiness I felt yesterday.
Friendship lost,
the price is such a heavy cost.
I know this all to well,
as I find it was my life sent to hell.
I am the only one to blame,
it is my emotions and love that I have learned not to tame.
I have put myself here,
I have made true what I fear.
Alone, I find myself thinking... of you,
Alone, I sit here missing you.

Randy Bowley

Time Traveller

I have seen holy wars, the culmination of religious pride.
I have seen the horsemen burning cities they override.
I have seen bloated bodies like driftwood, wash with the tide.
I have seen death's face grinning on a suicide.

I have heard trumpets blare and the warnings of seer's calls.
I have heard the silent crumblings of ancient stone walls.
I have heard lonely footstep's echo, in once crowded halls
I have heard monkeys shriek as the hungry tiger crawls.

I have felt the fear of men, trapped below in a flooding mine.
I have felt the body of Christ and sipped his warm red wine,
I have felt genius and insanity, thereafter walked that fine line
I have felt the breath of the beast and the coming of the 7th sign.

I have spoken with Tzar's and kings and peasants tending fields.
I have spoken with bowmen, lancer's and boy's behind blazon shields
I have spoken with architects and builders who devised the great
   pyramid seals.
Now I speak with a thief on a cross, as the blood in his veins congeals.

   Shades of the Apocalypse.

Peter C. Waterhouse

Between Two Worlds

She dances on a rainbow between two worlds.
Faster and faster she spins in the spotlight of the moon,
   a sky full of stars her only audience.
On and on she dances not daring to close her eyes.
For should she fall from her narrow stage, the stars will weep,
   and the moon will turn off its shine.
The rainbow will collapse shattering the two worlds waiting
   there to catch her.
And she will be suspended there, alone, never to dance again.

Anne M. Robinson

"My Life"

   Unbashing hope of privacy eludes me.
My sole serenity erased. My positivity awakes
on a new journey down narrow dead end
streets alone. I live beneath all
others. Exiled by society. Who am I,
what am I. If I don't know how do
you? My arms lie open and bleeding not
enough though for one's sorrow. On my
knees in despair stone roses embedded
on my soul. My heart lies bare.

Dublin M. Puglia

Uncle

The hatred burning in your eyes,
was that of a raging bull.

The glaring flame in the center of your pupil,
was the reflection of the red cloth, in the eye of the bull,

The heavy puffs of air exit your nostrils,
compares to that of the bull before it charges the matador.

The person who you are,
or have become,
so well hidden
until it came undone.

You had me fooled.
Like the bull tricked the matador;
I thought I was loved
The matador thought he had the bull.

The bull struck the matador down
Your words cut through me like the horn of the bull
forever ending the relationship.

William Selleck Jr.

What Has Become With This World Today?

What has become with this world today?
Our children don't know how to play.

With head phones strapped to
their heads or watching T.V.
It's no wonder what we can't see.

Computers take place of checkers or go fish
Now they can't survive without a satellite dish.

We ask why are our children this way?
Because the parents have to be at work all day!

Autumn Brown

The Lord Above

Footsteps in the darkness from which I hear at night.
Next to mine they follow
A love I feel so true in life
A wonder if it will always stay
Holding my hand wherever I may turn
Walking along in a path of life
Listening to my thoughts and prayers
Healing our spirits with glory
Never seeing the face of the wonderful
Always feeling safe from harm
forgiving from our awful sins
knowing our stress and pain
Carry our souls to your glorious city
Love me, care for me for I'm a part
of you and you're a part of me
The blind will see once more, the hurt
will feel no pain, the sad will soon find
happiness to gain
Heaven will be our home and we'll walk in love
His steps will always follow, for he's the Lord above.

Fawna Watson

When We Say Goodbye

As we say Goodbye, to the ones we love. We may cry. Because it's so hard to say Goodbye. When someone we love passes on. We try to be strong. We know we must go on. That person is never really gone. That person is where they belong. It's hard to let go. It's even harder to watch the ones we love suffer so. The love and laughter that was shared, will always be there. The memories we carry are here to stay. That's something no one can take away. Or the love that was shared, that too will always be there.

Sherryl Herweh

Rapture

Two souls attached at hearts
Stare into Heaven's lamp,
Searching for answers
When all turns to Satan's fire
We are gone... beneath Earth
Life of hell to be discovered awaits,
passing scorching fires and mortifying laughs.
Waiting for victims to fall
to ground of red, rumbling surface,
red skin, eyes, spirit
shine through the souls
demanding operations of sheer hell
and torture for all eternity.
We now are dead.

Kate Cushman

Golden Years Blues

Upon my treadmill now I go
In hopes of losing a pound or so
The parties and social events continue
So much wonderful food, like a glorious menu
Often I wonder why diets exist
Eliminating foods I just can't resist
When friends call and say, it's time to go shopping
I know that for lunch we'll also be stopping
Oh well, we all know in these "golden years"
There are many good reasons for the change in our gear
So we will be kind to ourselves and each other
For the aches and the pains from which we recover
Will return to remind us, on good days and bad
That we still have so much for which to be glad
So if you can still enjoy good tasty vittles
You'll have to accept that bulge round the middle
Let's stop all the fretting, the worry and stress
And strive for the strength to just do our best
Be happy, stay healthy, keep a good disposition
But just don't forget to pick up your prescription!!!

Gladie B. Pettit

Band Of Silver

From the day she wed
Till the day she was dead,
She wore a thin, silver band
On her left hand.

She promised to be true,
No matter what her husband may do.
Raised to concede,
She endured his nightly need.

She bore four; alone no more.
Her husband went off to war.
He returned
In a casket and was burned.

She remained
Sixty years unchained.
Yet wore the band
To deter the masculine hand.

As she died,
A male stranger at her side
Stole her ring;
Raping her for the last time before eternal spring.

H. C. Bowerman

Captains Of Destiny

Our love is like a sailing ship, sailing across the sea
Some days the sails are full and we skip across the waves
Some days the winds are gone and we drift around for days
But we are captains of this mighty ship and we control its ways

Our ship's a living breathing thing, we're its heart, mind and soul
It's our purpose, our reason for living, our existence, our life, our whole
We live to love, no love no life, no plans, no future, only alone
But we're captains of this mighty ship and we control its roam

A normal ship, it leaks but floats, driven by wind it's one of God's boats
Abandon ship and swim away, to search, for another time,
  the holy grail
Greener grass, we know not where, our quest succeed or fail
But we're captains of this mighty ship and we control its ways

David White

Fall

The golden, brown, red, orange, yellow leaves,
Swirling, dancing, and twirling gently down
to the leaf-laden ground.

The crisp, clear, clean fallish scent in the air
Is lighted by the brisk sunshine of autumn
and the plump orange pumpkins from those green thumbs.

The joyful sight of us kids playing in the foliage,
all sizes and all ages, all colors and abilities,
fills the heart with feelings of many qualities.

Breath the air, crisp, with a faint smell of woodsmoke,
from cozy fires inside homes with love inside,
walk along the ground with leaves underfoot.

Lindsay A. Krisher

Goodbye Mom

The furious anguish that rends my
spirit and smashes me to the floor
pales in the presence of this fragile, aching bruise;
my heart,
which beats a cadence of despair inside my breast.

This slow, sad pain
molests my days and wearies the night
'til my senses are
shriveled and molded,
my body,

barren

dry

as the desert for want of joy.
I no longer resist.
Surely, there is refuge in

submission.

Deborah Patton

Recompense

Regret is a beggar with haunted eyes,
Clothed in the rags of reminiscence,
Had I known the future, I would have been wise,
Knowing the briefness of earth's evanesce;
Forsaken before, by the choice of my life,
Fled I from your kindness or any more ties
SWenl, my heart bears the light of our love's luminesce.

Ola Margaret James

My Prayer

Heavenly Father the time has come, to confess to You what we have done. The guilt and shame in our hearts today, told our minds that it's time to pray. Our souls are ready to stop the sin, and with Your help, let a new day begin. We feel you with us, and we can tell, that it's time to leave this awful hell. Let Your light shine down on us please, and fill us with love, for all to see. We love You God, please forgive our sin, and always remain forever within. Stay with us God, and make us strong, and fill our lives with a cheerful song. Thank You God, for helping us through, the only way out, had to be You. You must love us an awful lot, for we didn't die, just slowly rot. We need Your help ever so, please help us all, to Just Say No! Quitting is harder than we ever thought, winning this battle is the best lesson taught. With God and each other as our support, winning is all the counts in this sport. For those who we've hurt, because of our sin, please help us to never do that again. Stay with us God, for the temptations ahead, for if You don't, were as good as dead. We deserve whatever is coming to us, so we live each day, serving our justice. When we die, and leave this place, right or wrong, to You we must face. We ask Your forgiveness, and for strong will power. May Your spirit be with us, through every last hour.

Terri L. Kincaid

Turquoise Shades

As I sit in my chair and look out the window,
nothing's new.
I'm so lonely and there's no one in sight,
cause it's Saturday night.
I could turn on the T.V. or radio,
Someone could talk to me but,
they can't hear, and even if they could
No one would listen.
I'm just old, lonely and blue,
With no one to talk to.
Life is fast for everyone but me, you see.
People say stop and smell the roses,
But I'm sneezing by now.
I need a life, a love, a true,
I'm so sad, a meaning to know someone,
Who is happy to cleanse my blue.
Can you help? Can you?

Barbara Ponsky

Mom and Dad

Ever since I was a little girl,
I always wanted to be big.
I begged my mother to put me in curls,
I even tried wearing a wig.

I remember playing house with my mother,
Pretending I was a guest in her home.
She always played along with me,
She even let me wear her old clothes.

I didn't realize at the time,
But my life was so simple.
Like when I'd give my Dad a dime,
He'd trade me for a nickel.

As I got a little older,
I wanted to stay out late.
Each day my heart would get colder,
And eventually I started to hate.

I didn't appreciate my Mom and Dad,
Even after all they've done for me.
I didn't realize what I had,
I was blind and couldn't see.

Christine A. G. Cathcart-Palmer

If I Could Change The World

If I could change the world all hatred and anger would be gone.
All ignorance and prejudice be inside my head.
No more to be thought of, no war to be gained.
People would look within to find the
goodness and beauty that each person has to give.
No race, or religion would count on this great earth of ours.
Children would really matter, they would be number one.
Children would listen, grown ups will hear.
No more hurt, no more fear, no more cruelish pleasures,
no children cry of hunger or pain.
No bombs would be made, no wars would be started.
There would be nothing to gain.
The world would be a loving place of happiness and caring.
Children would fear nothing because all would be in the name of love.
No diseases would kill, no germs to end the world.
Just growing old together in a world so full of love.
In all the world, that's all I want to say,
That's all I wish of all of us. It's just two steps away.
Throw away anger, throw away fear,
Now we would be almost there.
Paula Geiser

Another December

Melancholy moon in skies of December
Gliding above me, all knowing and distant
Through clouds that scatter, amid the silence
Like parchments of odes to past lovers.
How dare you to wander, how dare to wane,
To leave the sky beaconless, haunted and empty.

How dare you, old lover, to leave me so empty
To bid your farewells in the cold of December.
The hollowness lingers, the years will not fill
A longing for closeness in days that seem distant
From hours that left us the truest of lovers
Till moonlight would find us all tangled in silence.

But life is one's own, to the deepest of lovers,
Life's callings lead passion to wander and wane.

Sad moon of December, there hiding so distant
Do you know the truths in the hearts of old lovers?
Are his thoughts of me kind or is part of him empty?
Have the years and his calling caused memories to fade?
As loud as the soft wind, it's buried in silence
This aching to know, oh sad moon of December.
Anne Ehlen Spoerl

Sun So High

The sun so high, so beautiful and bright
Shining down its warm rays of light
It shines on the land, the sea, the air
The powerful sun is everywhere

It rises in the east and sets in the west
There it sleeps, rejoiced in rest
It shined since the day the earth was made
And will shine till the day this star will fade

The sun gives light to many trees
The trees are homes for the birds and the bees
For life is a circle that holds everyone
But the circle of life starts with the sun
Kimberly Baumgart

Sleep Now, O' My Beautiful Mother

To the Memory of My Beautiful Mother Elouise Escoto,
12/14/32-11/24/95

Sleep now, o' my beautiful Mother
Your pain and suffering are now gone.
A pain that only God's mighty hand could cease,
You look so beautiful, lying there at peace.

Sleep now, o' my beautiful Mother
Your voice, your smile, now a memory.
I will always remember them, with a silent tear,
For no more laughter, will we ever hear.

Sleep now, o' my beautiful Mother
Your lessons are learned, work on Earth done.
You had nine children, my place is seven,
Two went before you, They have You now, in Heaven.

Sleep now, o' my beautiful Mother
I watched you fight each day, you were so brave.
I gave thanks you were my mother, on Thanksgiving Day,
The next day, with God leading, you went away.

Sleep now, o' my beautiful Mother
Your battle was short.
Death came, it took you, very quick,
Of all the Angels on Earth, You, were God's pick.
Anita Morales Geston

Blood Line

For my ancestor
The caption beneath the photo reads:
"Slave, circa 1862, who escaped to Union lines."
He stares through the womb of time
fourteen or fifteen years old / chestnut colored
hands clenched into fists / defiant
wearing rags.

In the second photo / he stands uniformed
in blue / a drum strapped to his shoulder
white gloved / sticks in hand / defiant still
eyes whispering heart song
prodding memory into
battle cries
bullets
bayonets
smoke / fire
hallelujahs
blood line.
Frederick D. Clark

Untitled

Damn you all who tell the lies.
 I hate you all from deep inside
 You piss me off
 you make me mad.
 You love to see me when I'm sad.

Why must you hurt me.
 I loved you all.
 You set me up to take a fall.

You all I say
 I'll never trust,
 You turned my heart from red to rust.

I needed you more than you'll ever know.
 I miss you now.
 why did you go.........
Jeff Bores

Take Courage

Weeping may endure for a night; but joy will come, so don't doubt it might.
Hold on strong, with all your might; stay in the battle, for it's the Lord's fight.

He is our present help, in the time of trouble.
Just say "Jesus!", and He'll be there on the double.
Have not I commanded thee to be strong and of good courage?
Don't listen to the enemy's lies; that's his job:
To make us discouraged.

Satan wanders seeking whom he may devour.
Silly fool! Someone needs to tell him: Jesus died on the cross
defeated him in hell,
and now holds the key with all superior power.

Sitting on the right hand of the throne. Yep! That's where our King is.
Trying our faith to being out the best in us; after all, the glory is His.

Streets paved with gold, angels shouting, "Holy, Holy."
Along with job, who with stood,
How? I don't know; but the good Lord knew we could.

He saved my soul and set me free. It's my obligation, to tell what Jesus has done for me.
Jesus, Jesus, Jesus! That's the man from Galilee.
There's no other name I know, that can set you free.

Want to go to Heaven? We must go through Thee.
For again, there's no other name than Jesus that can set you free.
   Felicia A. Harrell

But The Flag Is Still There

This we hear, year after year:
What's good for the corporations
is good for the Nation, or
What's good for the unions
is good for the Union.

Is one statement true and the other not?
Or are both simply rot:
It was not with greed, but rather with need
that founding fathers planted the seed
for what we now call our Nation.

When corporations exploit,
or when Unions over-demand,
we have a government empowered to command:
A government which, when duty calls,
Must rise to the occasion for one and for all.
   Thomas W. Clarke

Past Through Present

As the sun rolls back and the clouds drift away.
So comes the end of another day.
The evening spent in peaceful repast.
Thinking of long years now gone past.
Lovers long gone and days yet to come.
Things that were said, and things to be done.
Stories to tell our children at night,
To ward off bad dreams and teach what is right.
Quickly comes the end of our time here,
as the next generation draws ever near.
So disappears the life we knew,
as our children take over with new and different things to do.
   Paul Leser

The Planet Mars

A few billion years ago,
there was life on Planet Mars.

A few billion years ago,
there was life on Planet Earth.

Parent birds feeding their young,
all day long, all day long
Flying back and forth, back and forth.

Parents taking their children to school,
picking them up in the afternoon.
Day after day, day after day.

Trees binding the soil, attracting moisture.
Green meadows, reflecting ponds.
Cities, lights, trees.

The tree is chopped down.
The bird is no longer fed.
The child is not picked up from school.

A desert forms.
The seeds are there but lack moisture.
They wait for the parent to water them.
   August Janssen

Silence

Oh glorious silence
sing unto me,
all of your songs of tranquility.
Lull me with whispers
serenade me with tunes
of your sweet, silent, stories
of starlight and moons.
Let me lie down and close my brown eyes,
And imagine your stillness
Is spread through the skies.
Sing me to sleep with your frozen love song,
Lull me till morning,
And stay with me long.
   Tracie Billings

The Golden Years

A year when bread was to cook.
A year when apples were going red.
A year of reading a cozy book
When gently tucked in bed

Dawn came floating through the skies
In her blushing golden beams,
Then I awake with the rooster's cries.
Strange and new to me it seems.

The wheat fields have turned copper gold,
Holding each tender grain,
And through the meadows, like a fold,
In silver streaks, a morning rain.

A rainbow, with its colorful wings,
Forms angels in the skies,
And through the rain the rainbow springs,
Breaking into fluttering butterflies.

O, those years will never be together.
It just seems that only yesterday were they born,
But all those memories disappear forever
With the cow's calling horn.
   Nina Larionova

Through The Window

In the early hours of the morning
You hear the birds sweetly singing
Welcoming you to the day's beginning
And then you hear the clock begin ringing
Time for me to be a showering

As you rise from your sleepy bed
And begin thinking of what's ahead
There's the family to be fed
And today a dentist appointment you dread
Alas a chapter you haven't read.

Looking through the window and I see
A bird on a branch singing a melody
A squirrel playing in the grass alert to flee
Wind through the willow branches blowing free
A big brown rabbit nibbling grass watching me

For now the house is empty and silent
And through the window sun light glint
I can smell the flower's heavenly scent
I see the beautiful roses with ruby tint
And begin to wonder where the day went
Ann Marshall Heath

Freedom

Swimming out into the ocean blue...
   the sea is empty of all but me...

i feel i am at peace...
   floating on feelings...i am free from me...

free of all of life's chains and countless shackles...
   free...free for all to see...

i am happy now...
   i am gone...far from you...

i am gay...
   no longer queer...now that i am without you...

i am free...
   just to be...me...for no one to see...
Michael A. Rios

The Child Is Gone

A child that I saw today,
Has grown up and slipped away.
She was once mine in the past;
From baby to girl, to woman at last.

I played with her in her crib
Wiped her mouth with her bib
Taught her how to tie a shoe,
Made her laugh when she was blue.

Tucked her in every night,
Had one or two pillow fights.
Watched in worry as she walked away;
Off to school every day.

Muddy shoes and dirty clothes,
Scrapes and bruises stubbed toes
Stitches and band aids; a common supply.
Hugs and kisses mandatory when she would cry.

Homework battles and perfume wars,
Makeup stains and boys galore.
Everyday this went on
Now I sit alone, the child is gone.
Wendy Hope Lagrange

Ever Loving Ellen

Love is beautiful love is real
Love is everything that I feel
When I'm with you...

Love is sharing ups and downs
Love is having you around
Love is knowing you alone can ease my sorrow

Love is what you give to me
Flowing from you selflessly
Love is proud the world can see
How glad I am your majesty
To have your love for each and every morrow...
Vincent Donohoe

I Asked The Angels To Paint The Sky For You

Last night I asked the angels to paint the sky for you
I couldn't just settle for a normal azure blue.
You are very special and dear to me,
So I had to think of the right colors the sky should be.

It had to have a touch of gold; not too bright or too bold.
There had to be pink and orange and red;
Not just any colors, but the prettiest instead.

And when I asked they said they'd try - one even started to cry.
"What a beautiful thought," I heard one say - "to
  care about someone that way."
I too thought it special when one said it was free;
Since it was my gift to you, it was also given to me.

The very thought made me light up inside.
My tears of joy I could no longer hide.
A dream of a special present I had for you,
When the angels painted the sky for me too.

They did it because we are one.
That is why that was done.
My heart was so dear and true,
When I asked the angels to paint the sky for you.
Jennifer M. Arnold

Untitled

I sing a song of sadness
because everything has created madness
the words no longer have meanings
and touches are no longer perceived
darkness is all around yet there is one light found
to be true that light is fading for I have but three words left

I love you

We started out oh so strong
but some how something went wrong
time has blown change
and now that change must move on
even though a painful road lies ahead
it seems to have enough endurance for our last tread

If you ever think of me
I hope you will at times
please remember me
by these last three lines

I will always love you
and in my heart you always will be

no matter what, you are so dear and special to me
Kristie Carter

Midsummer Reflections!

The Light is incredibly bright!
The Daytime wonderfully long...
The Robin sings at Peep of Light
A melodious, throaty song!
The busy Morning seems so fleet...
At Noon, the flowers are extra sweet!
Shimmering hours offer spirited Peace...
(Which all wholehearted Beings seek!)
At Dusk, the Robin trills again
To celebrate the Day that's been!
Joyfully limned in his Roundelay:
"Tomorrow is another day!"
  Virginia Pease Ewersen

From Our Hearts It Can Be Heard

Friendship is such a precious word,
and from our mouths it can be heard.
A smile can brighten any day,
and communicates more than we could say.
A hug is special and oh, so dear,
and it warms all around both far and near.
A tear is hurt in a pool of love.
A friend is a piece of heaven sent from above.
And with this friend the world is bright,
and love is the only thing in sight.
Love is the MOST precious word,
and from our hearts it can be heard.
  Alison Marcon

Mother's Life

Conception and birth makes the first,
Child is nurtured abreast.
Mom is expected to be there come what may,
Child and Mom bonded along the way.
Wonderful, precious years, tears coming only from physical pains.

Adolescent years makes the second,
Child gets lost in the world's Guest.
Mom is perceive to be stupid, know-nothing and embarrassing,
Child wishes she's a different being.
Emotionally painful years, tears coming from hurt feelings.

Mature years makes the last,
Child goes out, conquers aghast.
Mother is rarely needed, left waiting and thinking,
Child rarely calls, busy with her thing.
Emotionally empty years tears shed no feeling.

What is left is the trust,
That with mother's love and care,
Child will emulate the life she'd share.
Mother is reassured, that the child she reared
Will be spared from the pains she'd feared.
  Evelina C. Morales

Moonlight

How the shimmering moonlight spreads its light
Like an angel's wing in the darkness of the night.
It spreads itself over the surface of the earth,
And has been doing so since the day of its birth.
As the moonlight approaches every plant and tree,
You know that it was always meant to be.
It streaks the clearing in the cold night's breeze,
And swims through the leafy hands of the old oak tree.
Its glowing mysteriousness and delight
Comes from the one and only source of light.
Its bold beauty shines on every roof of the sleeping town,
Till sunlight comes at the break of dawn.
  Roshani Parekh

Night State

Consciousness leaves to let your nightmares weave.
Stalking and creeping inside your head.
Contorting your mind and soon you will find,
To them you are eternally dead.

Pleasure gets insane to define the meaning of pain.
Poking and plucking at your eyes.
Visions of hate you can no longer sedate,
So you fall to your knees and cry.

Thoughts of the kill take actions to thrill.
Ripping and tearing at your prey.
Taste the blood and feel your emotions flood,
With the love of yesterday.

Quickly begin to dream before the darkness screams.
Grinding and cracking your fragile soul.
Horror has a face that you can not erase,
For you yourself are your most dreaded foe.

Perpetual fear forever getting so near.
Staring and gazing into your heart.
Terror begins as you display your sins,
Soon the nightmare will start.
  Phil Norris

Untitled

Gentle breezes blowing through my window
brushing away stale memories that have
settled in an inch of summer dust
unwanted upon the furniture.

In having a sense of moving on do I
drop the past like out moded ways,
like stone aged thinking.

New chances taken, more of life to be lived.
Tomorrow still evades me,
for upon grasping it, I find it's only today.

So I take it and fill it with more memories
to be preserved from a stale existence.
Memories that are jazz colored and
taste of pungent espresso and a good read.

Ears filled with possible poetry and breaking hearts
smiles and tears, boredom and busy ness.

Thus is the spice in my taste budded hours
that bring curled noses of the rankness or
desired devouring of a glutton.

It is everything set altogether in Pandora's box.
  Amber Dawn M. Germany

Halloween

Halloween's the time of year when ghosts and goblins do appear.
They throw a party every year, whenever October thirty-first is here.

They scream and howl and rattle their chains;
And when they get tired they feed on human brains.

From bats to witches they all come;
And each brings a jack-o-lantern hung round his thumb.

Dracula will be there and so will Frankenstein.
They'll bring their home brew of blood-root wine.

They'll drink and be gruesome till daylight comes.
Then they'll disband and go away until another year comes.
  Jacob Ailer

Brick By Brick

For a dozen years I've watched how quick
You've built the wall brick by brick.
With strength and skill and much precision
But isn't that how you would build a prison?
Now you're finished and it's complete.
You place me in front to test my feat.
I look at each brick and remember it well
Each represents its own private hell.
The base of the wall holds all the strength
As long as it held... It could be any length.
The wall is made of things that mattered
This and all else was long ago shattered.
I can't be angry and I can not hate
You gave me only what I would take.
As I grab ahold and start to climb
There's only one thing that comes to mind...
Each brick I touch reflects the pain
How easy it'd be if I were insane.

Harvest Palmer

Shadow

Shadow is elusive, so it seems
Not solid in shape or form
Neither is it he or she
Only what it wants to be.

Playing hide and seek is fun
Shadow mimics me
But Shadow moves around a lot
Following or leading, sometimes catching up
Walking on the wall beside me.

Without a word Shadow disappears from sight;
Hiding in the darkness where danger lurks
In any case, evil ready for the chase
Changes Shadow to an unknown face.

Sarah I. Ballantyne

Untitled

Dear Lord,
On this the Fourteenth of October
Nineteen Hundred and Ninety-Five,
I call on you to give Tara and John,
What it takes to let their marriage survive;
Guide them with your guiding light,
To do the things that are right;
Let them be aware of each other's feelings
Never let their tempers hit the ceilings;
Teach them to communicate with one another,
Allow them to give each other space
So they don't smother;
Let their love grow stronger with each passing day,
And let them remain together 'til they're
old and gray!

Dotty Spinosi

Bi Polar Edges

The darkness comes pulling me into its depths
The blinding numbness of the heart and soul takes over
Someone speaks but I can not respond
The weight is too heavy
Would death be a comforting relief
No not this time
For tomorrow the sun may shine and I may soar at the other
   end of the pole
Ecstatic joyous with all the sights and sounds of life
But today I can only retreat into the darkness

Helen E. Hepp

"In My Heart You'll Always Be"

In my heart and mind you'll always be; visions of you so
clear that one could see how easy it would be to love you.
Still somewhere in between here and tomorrow; caught up in
the confusion which held us together not so long ago.

Now I'm certain that you are my eternal love; like the
fountain of youth which gently flows; in my mind our love
will never grow old.

Like the rose which is so perfect; it's hard to imagine that
the thorns could only produce tears of understanding, because
love can be perfect if we realize that everyone has faults.

Disappointment never comes to one that keeps an open mind and
heart. So forever this love will remain where it really ought
to be; you see you're always in my thoughts, and in my heart
you'll always be.

Cynthia Ward

Sonnet To A Sage

Your snowy hair is spindrift on the crest
Of breakers surging up to kiss the shore.
Your mind is agile as a matador
Whose graceful motions swiftly pass the test
As bold "veronicas" fulfill his quest.
Exuding love from every giving pore,
You reach as weathered oak and sycamore
Whose sturdy, swaying boughs so rarely rest.

Fresh water to a thirsting world are you,
Drawn from a well whose depths are cool; serene.
You paint the lilac hills with lambent hue
Where land and sea caress the wind between.
Your vintage years are sweet as morning dew,
While jewels of lapis blue meet eyes of green!

Jolieta Constantine Smith

The Flower

A flower, even when unnoticed for some time,
May fade away from one's memory
But its beauty remains unforgotten
For the flower
Although we may loose sight of its youthful appearance
One aspect
Untouched
Unscarred
Remains incarved in the beauty of its creation
Its fragrance

Maria Teresa Lagattolla

Inner Vow

Something is lost inside of me,
I search my soul for what it could be.
O'er night somehow it slipped away,
but I'll search for it till my dying day.

Near the edge of insanity,
Prisoner of my vanity.
This sickness surely shall not stay,
for I will fight its hold till my dying day.

When blindness rules and I cannot see,
when darkness seems an eternity,
I will live my life, work and play
and this way I'll live till my dying day.

Tony Douglas Brown

Search For Pearls

For years he had lived in a cliff shack;
but it was not home, for he had no wife,
no kids NOT ONE who cared.
His life was to hunt for pearls
which would one day make him rich.
Was the time for that now?
Small boats, huge ships, sails, nets,
fish whales, sharks, shells, and salt;
He knew them all so well.

Was he too old now for a such a dive?
Suddenly, parting the water's surface,
he was in full view of familiar sea life,
and, pearl shells?

Why now the lack of air,
and breath, and sight, and strength!
He prayed, for help, and breath, for life!
No, not wealth now, not riches, norrr,
JUST TO LIVE, to be near the sea.

PEACE came to the old man, and
there were still pearls in the sea.
   Therel A. Frei

Purpose

   Watch, Oh Watch, I tell you all for that one space in time
When God has placed you in His hands to influence your kind
   Know that you're just like a drop of gold that He's poured into a mold
More precious among this massive horde
   Know there is a reason why God placed you on this earth
Don't let it catch you unaware, it could be your rebirth
   Know that God will always be there to help you with the job
It may be just a word or deed unnoticed by the mob
   For a small task may save a soul, or yet it may save many
And yes there's a large task for God's love's not lost from any
   It may be just a hunch or a feeling you must do
But know when He made the job, He made it just for you
   And it matters not who or where you be
You're in the mold God made for you and no one else but thee
   Remember God's love to you He sends
For you'll never know when your chance will come
   It could be the last hour
At life's end
   Jeanne Gardner

Where Did Our Love Go

Where did our love go?
Did it burn out like a flame?
I know that I've made mistakes
So I will sadly except the blame.

I will never set your love free.
For my heart just can't let go.
Because you know that I have these feelings
But they're just to strong for me to show

I can't let you slip out of my life
for the pain I just couldn't bear
waking up without you by my side
or just the fact that you're not there

I hope you know now that I still love you
and I can't wait to let it out
But I can tell you it will last forever.
And forever without a doubt.
   Jeff King

The Spaces In Between

On a hill rising our of the scrub-brushed, cactus-free
desert of southern Oregon, with dirt and stones pressing
into my back , I watch the constellations and jet-planes tumble
together across the sky like the closing credits of the millennium.

Far from the lost metal canyons and the despairing,
bleary, neon smears, the spaces here between the ground
and the heavens are clear; the stars fall as numerous as ashes
from a cigarette, and with the grandeur of dying angels.

As the silence of the desert travels outwards into the night and mingles
with the starlight, I'm reminded of a story I heard once about
   the existence of death,
imagined as a woman so beautiful that when you look at her face
She sucks your breathe and soul right out through your eyes.

In the dry heat of the night, returning the gaze of infinity,
I could almost believe the end would be that brutal, as the silence
draw back from the velvet black, beginning in the pale illumination,

To resemble something like paranoia; sounding a little bit like loneliness.
   Stephen K. Spotswood

Untitled

As the music puts thoughts thru your heads,
It slowly proceeds to give you melted
   visions of life in a different view.
Continues to elevate your brain with
   new ideas and new thoughts.
Maybe death. Death doesn't hurt
   yourself, it hurts others.
It could destroy others for years of their lives -
But at this point in time, the last
   thing you're thinking about is how
   others are going to feel.
How about me? I'm the one dying - understand.
My pain cannot heal the hurt of others.
My pain exceeds all over my body.
   Release my pain, let it out.
Cut my brains to release my thoughts,
Cut my heart to release my love,
Cut my eyes to release the sight of myself.
   Rachel Tarango

Heartfault Mem'ries

Thrown my heart in the wind, as both cannot be seen
I feel the love as deep within, the dust in a tumbleweed.
The moon a lamp unto my trail -
As I trudge my boots through dusty hail
I roped and brand, and fixed and mend
The hours like hawks do fly
I wondered to myself at times, neath the prairie sky.

Knowing our time as the coyotes rest
In patient silence of fears suggest
A yearning so felt as the day's chores toil,
Is vengeful as a rattler's coil.
For the daughter I kissed of the man I shot -
'Neath the tree I'll swing when I'm caught.
   Dalace-Skye Duvall

Unskilled Hands

An uneven sun in a sky of blue crayon
From a child's hand wandering across tattered page
A shapeless bird wandering, no branches to lay on
But no lines are drawn in the shape of a cage
Fish on the water have smiles wide
In the two dimensional world of a child's eye
Unskilled hands can see what is seen only by few
A crooked house standing on a hill of brown sand
The walls of which are supported by the strength of unskilled hands
   Steven J. Femenella

Second Generation Proud

I'm oh so very proud of you
   The way you've raised your girls,
It makes my heart go pitter pat
   And my head is all a whirl.

They have the nicest manners..
   They'd be perfect if they could,
They say their "please" and "thank yous"
   And act just like they should.

Just to prove they're normal....
   Sometimes they fuss and fight,
But straighten up and act real good
   When time dictates it's right.

Already you reap the harvest
   Of the hardy crop you've sown,
Where most the parents have to wait
   Till their children are full grown.

So as this day approaches
   To honor Mothers all,
Stand right up and be real proud
   As among them, you stand TALL!

Linda J. Hicks

Luck Of The Draw

The two destroyers, survivors of more than a year
of task force aggression in the western Pacific,
hum through the flat seas off the Kuriles on their
way to San Francisco for refitting and recreation.

On the after deck of the inside ship, two
galley hands appear dragging heavy garbage cans.

The destroyer lays down a straight path that
stretches back to the horizon. It sizzles
into the night as the scullery hands wrestle
the garbage can to the wire railing, one man to each side.

They lift, then momentarily rest the top edge
on the wire barrier. Then, explosively, the
wire breaks and the two men, still gripping
the can with both hands, disappear with their load.

No call for help was heard, and the ship was miles
away before the two men were missed.

A week later the war was over for the rest of the crew.

Donald P. Gooding

Society

A man sits in a dark room,
alone, panting in desperation.
He had been running.
Running, he knew,
from a nightmare.
A nightmare that had lasted all of his life.
From the minute he was born,
to the day when they would kill him;
he will run.
He runs from society,
society that had tried to change him.
Change the way he thinks;
The way he dresses;
and the way he lives.
But he has run.
And will keep on running.
Until the day he dies.

Brylie Stiffler

Forever

Open your eyes
See it, believe it, then recognize
The lies passed down
For thousands of years
Screaming constantly, hearing with bloody ears
Dying of thirst, gasping for air
Accept the darkness if you dare
Waking up in a sea of black
Walk away, he will take you back
Falling in a fire of rage and despair
Never awake, never aware
Crawl back out and fall back down
Never feel the hardness of the ground
Forever angry, forever sad
Come to think of it, you will become quite mad

Adam Stoyer

The Long War

Today, persecution and execution seem to penetrate our life,
Ridicule and malice are always a fight.

Denying the end is drawing near,
Outcries of wails and gestures of disarray encircle the world with fear.

Embracing our shortcomings so we can free the episodes of reality,
Illustrations of obnoxious people wandering
   through the revolving doors, coming face to face with fatality.

People taking heed to the devil as if he is the master,
Not getting on their knees and asking for absolution,
   so there won't be a disaster.

Hours and hours of torment from evil spirits walking the earth,
Protesting all the dominions for their work.

Incessant castigation and sinister moves everyday,
The dark knight laughing at us in every way.

This long war has gone for centuries to come,
Until we walk the righteous path then the devil has won.

Tasha D. Brimmer

Alone In The Shadows

In a space behind spoken words,
where pride is washed with tears,
and teasing kicks accompany empty smiles.
The stinging spark of ridicule
forces spinning clocks to drag in motion.
The only game to play, throws pawn to prisoner
in a battlefield of misunderstood silence.
The hush of thought
becomes mistaken for weakness,
and a soldier retreats to the solitude
of whispering dreams.
Noticed only by footsteps on the floor,
he searches to find a fairness,
denied years ago.
Doubt weakens the quest.
As visions of truth
flow into empty moments
the silent warrior stands,
   alone in the shadows.

Shawn M. Rowan

Love So Great

Love within is so great
The one who helped it form is of the base
The love for them will never go away
Even as others' love decays
That is why I love you in my heart today

Ronald E. Hight

Our Journey

Our journey in life and what it means to thee.
Is to be whom you want to be!
To go through life living a lie,
so society will honor you why.
On our journey we will have known,
pain and sorrow and being alone.
We shall experience happiness and sadness on this earth,
and know the feelings of death and birth.
One part in our journey that we do know,
are material things stay when we go!
But impressions if carved deep in the heart,
Love ones and family will never part.
So be true to yourself and you will see,
your journey will begin just have faith in thee.
For life is short and when we are gone,
Our journey and impressions will carry on!
Veronica L. Dodge

God's Presence: Timeless And Transforming

God can allow the wonderful works and blessings,
which he has accomplished through a believer's life,
to unfold and transcend beyond the chaos
of our human minds.
Within these timeless and inspiring experiences,
God's Spirit imparts
(within the yielding heart)
the revelation of His redemptive and merciful nature,
which is active, alive, and abounding
in His grace through our Savior, Jesus Christ
Instilling within those of us,
who strive to consistently walk in His presence,
an excitement and encouragement
to acknowledge and reflect upon His work
in and through our lives;
So, that we might serve Him in obedient faith.
With submissive hearts,
may we allow our Lord to enlighten and transform us
through His presence within those joyful, unexpected moments
of worshipful acknowledgement of the great things He has done.
Dolores A. Treadway

Brighter Days

For days that have ended
without even a smile,
For nights that have lasted like
a never-ending mile,
Like a heart that is torn from
the right to the scorn,
There is a new day that is ready
to be born.

If ever a thought would pass through the brain
that time would last with nothing but strain,
Let God speak to you - that a new day will come.
For through his great love - he gave up his Son.

We've all made mistakes and all had our sin.
But, with love and forgiveness - we are living in him.
Never forget that a new day will arise.
Because we are all God's children... Shining in his eyes.
Suzanne M. Lanfear

Sweet Mother

This is a poem to my mother, who is a sweet mother,
Whose love for me, remains a source of inspiration.
Oh!, my sweet mother,
When I was hungry, you gave me something to eat.
When I was sick, you prayed that I got well quick,
You spent sleepless nights, taking care of me,
You will not sleep, until you've lulled me to sleep.
All that you did for me, will run pages.
Ebony black, mother you are beautiful,
You are a sweet, sweet mother.
I cannot forget that early January morning,
When the cold hand of death, snatched you away from me,
You died,
When I needed you most,
Unwilling, you went to the world beyond.
So, I write this poem for love, for life, in memory,
As a tribute to you my dear sweet mother,
Who died nine years ago,
Struggling to educate me.
Sweet mother, the struggle continues.
Michael Nnaemeka Okonkwo

"The Inner Child"

When a child cries out from her
prison within, when her souls longs
for freedom and lone with no end, do
we have the power to set her free or do
we have a child within us that longs to be free.
The wind is so mighty it can bend a tree
with a power so great yet we cannot see, it
will take the power of love to set the child
free. In darkness she weeps and longs
to be free, do we have enough love to
set the child free. Can you hear the
child weeping, can you hear the voice
say, I have been here so long I have
lost my way, the child says I love
you but please stay away, I am much
too afraid to face the light of day, don't
try to save me please go away, nothings
forever I heard the child say.
Carolyn A. Sanders

In The Threats Of War

I wonder what he's doing
I wonder if he thinks about the children
I wonder if he eats from a can like me
I wonder if while he showers he thinks about the papers and magazines
the ones exploiting him, calling him insane
inside his body, are their festering worms?
or is there ever reproducting red blood cells. Like me
does he plan his strategies while he makes love to his wife
robing her intimacies
because he thinking of the solid bodies of his troops
instead of hers
does he shy away from the camera because he's afraid its really a gun?
He couldn't possibly have a sweet mother who picks out
only the finest blends of cotton briefs
I wonder if he really has skin
or if he's covered with raw hide
I feel him breath when the ships go down
I feel him cry when he shoots the babies
I see him die on his daughters bed, and I cry
Elizabeth M. Kinn

Nature Mysterious

Among the splendor of this earth
  such beauty to behold,
For eyes to see and ears to hear
  Surpassing understanding of humans so bold.

To watch a tiny seedling grow
  And change with time to hold it's own,
A wonder one can only see
  With a bloom of true finality.

Vision mountains in a calm clear desert
  Magnificent forms for one to grasp
Images been in superior formations
  Knowing some piece of history has passed

Waves oceans weaving with grace
  snow and rain shower crystals on the green,
A roar of thunder light from above,
  Wind winding an uneven pace.

Beauty everywhere just to be found
  Explore it, enjoy it, breath it in deep,
with one's own senses of sight and sound
God has provided this beauty to keep.

Anita Culloon Humphreys

Break-Up

When I first met you. I had not a clue
that my feelings for you could be so true
you were handsome and caring and genuinely nice
we talked and we dated, you know it was all very nice
Please don't look in my eyes for my heart is breaking
You knew it would you've been just waiting
The sound of your voice, the feel of your skin
a meaningful glance and now it may be the end.
I'll tell you I love you, more than anyone I've known
Know my love is with you no matter where you go
Hold me now before we let it go.
Someday you'll wish you never let go
Then it'll be too late, for I'll be with someone new.
He'll do all the things you wouldn't do
He'll give me his heart unconditional and true
It's really too bad, I wanted it to be you.

Donna Matthews

Why?

There is a place not on any map
where dreams mesh into my day,
when wistful thinking merrily strolls
and this reality fervently fades.
It's languid and lazy, yet loud and angry,
I find myself away in the clouds,
soaring through the shapeless sky.
Perfectly placed are the jewels of space.
How can it be that shooting they go
destroying themselves as part of their life?
Breaking apart into brilliantly lit waves,
shattering hearts as they swelter and sway.
In the end there is dust, for from dust they formed,
scattering hopelessly, drifting apart,
never to be heard from again.

TJ Madigan

Ode To A Son

Dear Lord! You gave me a wonderful son,
  At times we played and had such fun.
He is so special in many a way,
  His order of living, nothing astray.
He was always at work, home or at school,
  Never shirked a duty, that's pretty cool.
But growing up took a toll on him,
  The world is degenerate, not neat as a pin.
He had to change and manage to survive,
  Through severe illness, was kept alive.
Our Father in Heaven, your arm is so long,
  Brought us together, where we belong.
Now, we speak kindness, and even pray,
  The spirit of the world now turns away.
Our goals have no glory, self centered delight,
  Even sports, a proper place in our sight.
Perilous times, have purpose indeed,
  They bring us together, each other we need.
Finally we appreciate, and our eyes do see,
  The Lord has plans for him and me.

Richard H. Swanson

"My Grandpa"

I did not have the privilege of being with my Grandpa you see;
as he passed away around the age of sixty-three.

My father told me about "A saying" my Grandpa would repeat;
"That there was more in the man
  than there is in the land."
He would make good crops in spite of the soil;
and he never gave up because of stress or toil.

When only sixteen, he entered military service as did his brothers;
and he came back victorious as well as the others.

His greatest gift was in his wonderful power of exhortation;
to me and to many, Grandpa, has been an inspiration!

Janie B. Carroll

Raju's Apple - an indelible gift of giving

Born untouchable
Raju slept on the Bombay streets.

Spirit bright and durable
In contrast to his habitat.

Enthusiastic for knowledge
Attended a small learning Centre.

Raju and his companions sat on the floor
Remarkably happy children learned wholeheartedly.

A special excursion to Elephanta
To tour the Hindu Temple caves.

Each with Indian bags filled with sandwiches,
cookies, and apples.
Frolicked joyously untainted by the heat.

Back in Bombay in the midst of the crowd
Stood Raju's frail grandmother with arms to welcome.

Raju gave his grandmother his half gnawed,
heat browned apple.
Each embraced she ate the apple.

With a delight and appreciation rarely seen.
A radiating memory to warm the heart forever.

Georgianne E. Matthews

Roses

Roses are red,
And lavender too,
And pink, and yellow and sometimes blue.

Roses are signs of love and affection,
Roses can also make a connection.

Roses are white,
Roses are red,
I just can't get roses out of my head.

The colors of roses are seen everywhere
They're here all around us.,
And those beautiful colors,
I sometimes wear.

A loving rose,
A simple sign,
Can show you care,
In no time.

Stephanie A. Hill

World Genetics

The only hope for the native hand,
is with the look like people
the colour of this land's sand,
band together-together as DNA is surely a band,
strike it up and play your instruments
and put away the shiny objects
with the state and the federal band,
and once and through nine
become a living festival on your ancestors' land.

Universal D. Mitchell

Eagle's Flight

If I could
Soar above the Earth
What would I see

Would I see the beauty of the land
Or would I see its slow destruction

Would I see the harmony between mankind
Or would I only see death and anger

Would I see the peace between nations
Or would I only see war

How much longer will
our world survive
Our ignorance and destructive ways
If only we could
Turn back time
But retain our knowledge
To prevent the slow death
of this world

That I have seen
While soaring over
The Earth

Lori Patten

With Whose Love but Mine

Touch my hand, travel the world twice over.
Reach to touch the stars, down to touch the
depths of the ocean. Only in my arms, only
when you touch me, love lies within the soul,
deep in corners where no one can reach, but
I. I am the spirit of love and passion. I
am the one you want, the one you need. Walk
with me for now, hand in hand, arm in
arm. Watch the world spin. Around us.
The world is to be ours.

Kristal Weatherby

Remember Me

An elderly lady sits quietly in her rocking chair
You can sense her sadness, loneliness and despair
An elderly man sits staring at TV
We do not know what he's thinking, we can't begin to see
The memories they both keep deep within their hearts
Maybe if we sat a while, to us they would impart
Things they have learned along life's way
Listen to them, they have a lot to say
Wisdom, strength, courage, and pride are their gifts for you
All they ask is for a little of your time
That's really not so hard to do
Like them, someday we will be old too
And we'll welcome a warm smile, a kind hand, I know this is true
So when you pass that little elderly man or lady along your way
Stop, and spend five minutes of your time today
A gentle smile, a few words, a lighter heart will be your thank you
And you'll walk away feeling a much better person too
We should never forget the elderly we encounter along our way
Because of them, we are who we are today

Sandra B. Richardson

A Window To My Past

When I was a little girl,
My mom said I was nice.
Now that I'm a young girl,
She says I'm full of spice.
I guess you change as time goes by,
From sun up till mornings nigh.
When I think back years ago,
Memory after memories flow.
I've loved my life from the very beginning
I can't imagine my life ever ending.
When I think of the memories years ago, I have such a blast.
Because I think of the window to my past.

Tina Thrash

Where Have The Years Gone?

You both throw your caps up into the sky of your future, your gowns billow and blow in the warm breeze.
Your once tiny hands grasp those college diplomas like you once tightly held your dolls and trucks.

My band aid box is full. No more "boo boos" to bandage and kiss and make it better. No more bedtime stories to read and kisses goodnight. No more holding those tiny hands in mine.

My bare feet walk across the kitchen floor not sticking as they once did from the apple juice spills. The gooey crumbles of the animal cookies are permanently stained around the knees on my pants from the clutches of those tiny hands.

I bravely stand in the doorway now, my apron strings flapping loosely in the breeze. My tear filled eyes watch you walk away as you reach for your own stars now.

I reluctantly release those once tiny hands waving goodbye.

WHERE HAVE THE YEARS GONE?

Sandra E. Brown

Children

Children, precious, beautiful little ones,
You are the new generation of the universe.
You should be hugged, kissed and loved by everyone.
All children of the universe are mine.
I will hold you while crying and play with you in times of laughter.
So run and play, my little ones.
Don't be unhappy, smile! You are always wanted in one heart:
Mine.

Carol L. Gilblair

Lilacs On A Hillside

I saw them first on a rainy day
Gnarled, though dauntless, sweet
Branches outstretched
Over a crumbling stone
With the legend "My Loved One Sleeps"

Nearby a trace of a house remains
With fields bearing brush and weeds
But a ruined wall
Holds the lilacs close
Over the earth, "Where A Loved One Sleeps"

Now each spring wafts on its April breeze
The perfume of lilacs sweet
Lovingly planted
Long, long ago
Purple guard over "One Who Sleeps"
Ruth Williams

Untitled

All is not lost in the mystical gloom
   when the rousing storm approaches.
Walking through the fog - snapshot views
   appear in the dim light of the hazy lane.
Random raindrops fall.
   Green grass sparkles: a vision of the Emerald Isle.
Birds sing out in a melancholy key
   and ruffle their variegated feather capes.
The cascade, like tears, descends
   as the drops dance off many a tree branch.
The land smells fresh and spicey green
   as the waters drain towards a main rivulet.
A streak of fireworks flashes
   a broiling drum roll of thunder
     tests the foundations of the earth.
The hazel dome is alive with a power display for all to see.
Yet an absence of faces marks those
   who shun the beauty
whose eyes cannot see the sky
from beneath an umbrella.
Amy S. McGowan

Hunter Of Shadows

Warm evening air breathes
over luscious evergreen meadows.
Raven crickets loudly chirp
to fill an empty void.
Moonlight and star dust illuminates
nocturnal animals.
They relish in the elements
of darkness.
An observer in concealing shadows waits
for a moment to strike.
Hunger flares in liquid amber eyes.
He pounces on startled victim.
Taunt muscles rippling under golden flesh.
The helpless cry echoes in the soft breeze.
Night 's creatures scatter into shadows
while he greedily feeds.
Warm meat dulling the painful ache inside.
Amanda Samatowic

Hope

Hope is a little thing with wings,
By its side your soul can ride.

It's an eagles flight, on a search for height,
It soars like a mid night dream.

But hope can fall when it flies too high
(it will make a terrible sound,)

And there it lies   broke and bent,
  A little thing
     Wingless on the ground.
Frances Reynolds

Mother's Loop

My little boys are brown from the sun,
and they're covered with scratches and scrapes,
but they're tall and they're strong, and they're learnin' to love
what the life of a cowboy takes.

They can close a wire gate fast as you please,
and they know scars remain from a brand,
sure their hats are too big, but they tote their own load,
gather stock as good as a man.

They've learned that a rope's not smooth in your hand,
and that barbed wire will rip out your jeans,
they've discovered your horse has to know who's the boss,
and that mother cows darn sure are mean.

Still, they're just little kids and do like to play,
and a rope is their favorite toy,
there's not a creature, person, or thing spared a loop
from a mischievous cowboy.

They rope chickens and dogs, a fence post or two,
but most of the time it's each other,
though the thing that they've really got lassoed and tied,
is the heart of this very proud mother.
Sandra Dragt Logan

Can't You See

I close my eyes and dream about
How it ought to be you and me together, just you wait and see
I want to wrap my arms around you and hold you close to me
Oh can't you see that you're my girl the one who sets me free

I wish that I was next to you so I could hold you tight
And feel your heartbeat next to me
Make everything alright I want to wrap my arms around you
And hold you close to me oh can't you see that you're my girl
The one who sets me free

Sometimes I lay awake at night
Just lost in make believe and in my mind I take your hand
Cause I believe in you I want to wrap my arms around you
And hold you close to me oh can't you see that you're my girl
The one who sets me free.

Someone to share my life with that's what, I see in you
The one who'll stand beside me
No matter what we both go through
I want to wrap my arms around you
And hold you close to me
Oh can't you see that you're my girl the only one for me
Steve Austin

Why?

I lie in bed and start to wonder
Why does it rain? Why does it thunder?
This whole world is a mystery to me.
There's millions of things that I'll never see.

There's things you can read about for an answer.
Just like the cause and cure for cancer.
The emotions and personality of different people.
The way you look at and admire the steeple.

The way a man can kill just for a drug.
Or a child will cry until they get a hug.
Something always makes me wonder why,
God beautified the world with the sun and sky.

Soon there will be nothing at all.
The Earth will just be an overpopulated ball.
We must change and do it fast.
Mankind just might make it at last.

We almost single handedly destroyed a planet.
Mankind did it - God didn't damn it.
Maybe when I die, God will let me know.
The Father of us all won't let His creations go.

Tracey Sean Burgin

Tragic Twist

Such a tragic twist of fate
That bring me past this lonely gate
I see the birds in flight
And yet, I have lost my sight
All I can bring are flowers
   With their aroma so pleasantly sweet
I shall bring them until we again shall meet
A Red passionate Rose for the Love
   that will never die
Yellow for the sorrow I feel and
   Always the question, why?
Peach for the dreams that bring
   you to me and me to you
Pink for the hop that some
   day the dreams will come true
White for the pureness of your heart
   And All the thorns piercing mine
     While we're apart
And as they all wither and blow away
   Know that my Love will forever stay.

Lillian D. Mercado

My Precious Daughter

Is my unborn child a Boy, I thought
As my belly grew taut, a Girl I got
Dresses and bows for you I bought
The joy you brought right straight to my heart
Now you're three, how dear to me
My little princess wanting to climb fences
Dances and glances soon there will be
A heart to be mended, a shoulder you need
Disagreements I'm sure we'll have
But, I tell you now
How proud I am to have you for my Daughter
I give to you my Strength and Determination
   to be all you can be
Please remember then what we say now
"What Are We" I may say
"Best Friends" as you say
O' how I pray forever we'll be
What a beautiful morn the day you were born

Sheila A. Heckman

To Bill Coe

I'm extremely happy and delighted, my friend for you
That God has chosen and favored you with, great love anew.

Love that was dormant and ready to rise
At this time - for you and Arlene - is not a surprise.

For you have done what Christ has asked
Since proving your love for neighbor was your task.

First your own - your wife - who was given
Illness and discomfort for many years of living.

By helping hurting persons you meet whose lot in life
Is mingled with many challenges of trouble and strife.

The secret of happiness you have found in living
You know and practiced it by giving, giving, giving.

God takes care of His own and will desert you never
Since His will is sought by you with each new endeavor.

To the "Girl of your dreams" I add my wishes for joy and love
For "coming home again" is a great blessing from above.

You will leave a terrible void in the hearts of those who revere you
For your warmth, kindness, great heart of gold and good cheer too.

May God always and daily be with you and Arlene and bless
And continue to grant you each much peace and happiness.

Laurice Beaudry

Evolution

What path shall I follow to see the light?
Shall I lean not on my own understanding?
If I believe so faithfully in the omni above
How can I find the justice I love?

A freedom inspired, inherent at birth
God's giving trust, enlightening the earth
His creation of time has led us to think
Has thou evolved so slowly or by an apparent blink?

And these questions sustain
Through time, we stand.
Never defy the law
Of God's loving hand.

Marjorie Vesovski

A Child's Grace

He walks silently alone
And those who watch remain distant - unsure.
The pattern is constant
Straight ahead - undaunted, focused.

He has the innocence and curiosity of a child
And is unsteady yet trusting.
Dreams have been shattered
But hope always present.

He never asks why
Though questioned by others.
The stares and laughter
Cloud his gentle way.

He is filled with love
And gives his heart freely
To all who choose to believe
In the frailty of life.

He is a survivor - scarred but unweary
And searches through the shadows for a friend.
One who accepts and dares to grow
But he walks silently alone.

Trudy Baum

Summer Pleasures

Calming echoes can make a horrible day
into one that can only be found in your dreams.

Perfectly shaped rain drops fall to the ground,
as a rainbow forms in the warm pink sky.

Raging waves splash at my feet
while the glistening sun soothes them.

Rushing waterfalls touch my cheeks as
the breezy night air blows the
cool drops away.

An exotic rainforest says good night,
but only mother nature can put it to sleep.

The sensuous fire warms my heart
and causes all of my fears to fade away.
Kerry Anne Stack

Letting Go

The time has come for us to part
And as you go, so goes my heart.

Alone into the world you go
To spread your wings, to soar and grow.

Upon life's path now you must travel—
Its mysteries, hoping to unravel.

There's such a great big world out there;
I hope and pray that it will care—

To give you shelter from life's storms,
To dry your tears from piercing thorns,

And when at times, your own world's dark
A passerby will light a spark.

Aspire to be all you can be
For dreams come true, as you will see.

Remember, tread gently as you go, forever, treat kindly all you know.

It seems it was only yesterday,
I watched my pony-tailed child at play,

But this is now another day and with mixed emotions, I say,

The time has come to let you go
My dear, I just want you to know, with all my heart, I love you so.
Elaine Smidl

Accelerated Lover

Speeding home to write my accelerated lover a song
words flying in my mind
trying to fling themselves to a waiting pen in hand
he's my silent God and I love him
driving to the edge where my paper is
and his heart's barbed fence waits
got to show him my song
I think he'd be proud to say that he is my accelerated lover
inside the paper words would be the only pleasure though
with safety seeking a goal with a pen
playing out a door with a lock and tossable key
don't tell a soul of my accelerated lover if you never feel
for one's thoughts might go astray missing the point
sought for by the very few who almost die
speeding to the edge of the paper for an accelerated lover
Brandy E. Geiger

The Eagle

You soar through life
like an eagle in flight,
calmly searching for your prey.
You devoured me.
Heart opened in a gushing flood,
body ravaged by your seductive touch,
soul tortured by your sapphire glare;
nothing left.
A shallow carcass of who I once was.
Acting with the desires of woman,
I struggled with the innocence of a child.
Like that very same eagle,
you flew away sated,
while I lay there, flesh torn,
wondering why I didn't sense the eagle coming.
Stephanie McClung

Heart Search

I listen to the sounds of the night...
   the traffic on the distant freeway,
owls hooting at the moon,
   that funny ringing in my ears,
the refrigerator creaking and the
   wonderful space between sounds
   that is you my beloved.
How I miss you
   miss you early in the morning.
Ah, but you're here.
Late at night - oh, but you're here too.
And is that you I see walking toward me,
away from me,
in and out of my life, but all through my
experience?
Yes it is You my Beloved - You - You
You. Forever You.
Never leave me.
I can't my Beloved Child, I can't.
J. K. Boyd

The Flight Of Time A Tribute To My Son

Each man, and woman, and creature on earth
Travels time's flight from the moment of birth.
For some, this voyage is swift and brief;
Others cling as to a lonely reef,
But, the flight of time is a relative thing...
Sometimes short as from spring unto spring...
Longer, perhaps, as we approach winter life
Rutted with failures, sorrows, and strife.
But for you, my son, at twenty one,
The flight of life has barely begun.

It seems only yesterday that I heard
You speak your very first precious word.
I remember well the first step, the first fall,
The first tooth; I remember them all.

You're now a man...a part of life's scheme...
The physical reality of a mother's dream.
As so, on this day, as you become twenty one,
I thank God that you are my son.

May He grant a mother a wish sublime...
That you travel long in the Flight of Time.
Jane Ellen Pretekin

Rambling Thoughts Of A Wandering Man

I'm a man trapped in a world I hate,
I'm a man born many years too late.
Was there ever a time when men were free,
Was there ever a place for a man like me.
My needs in life are simple at best,
The ability to work and a chance to rest.
I want to be around men not scared of work.
The kind of men who don't laugh and smirk.
At those whom are down and need our hand,
I want to know men who will take a stand.
I want to know those whose word is true,
Not these liars around me and you.
Is there a place where a man's word is his creed,
Where you must be honest in thought, word and deed.
Where a man works to get his own,
And men admit to the seeds they have sown.
Maybe it's never been this way.
Maybe it will be someday.
For now I must, just do my best
Influence a few and pray for the rest.

Douglas T. Wells

Parts Of A Woman

Breathe deep and exhale into thee
The creators breath that makes all things be
From Dawn's early light of time, they came to forge this special kind
With God-like gifts he passes his love through her and brings forth a meld of both. A single soul placed inside his second greatest creation to bring forth mankind, our inspiration.
The bearer of life. The giver of hope. The passion of glorious things to come. She smiles....and grins....and sometimes holds her breath and wishes for that special one.
To answer her dreams and give her peace of mind.
So strong, so good, so passionate with life and courage that's kind.
They place her beside, in the earth infant dust. Together they grow and learn and love in trust.
Must I. Should I. If I. Could I, she thinks. Why I am here
With all these gifts of good if our future seems so bleak. They reply, "To continue mankind a species of rare, no where else will you find". She cries with whole heart "Yes," as only this kind can, to answer the call, "I will have love past through me and bring hope to us all." One part love. One part child. One part lady. One part wild.

W. Axxemanne

Believing

It's not in church bells ringing
Or the passing of an offering plate.
But in child like faith believing
that the right way, is a narrow gate.

It's not just a way of living
Or even putting down your sword,
But salvation comes in knowing
that Jesus Christ is Lord.

It's not in hearing a crashing wave
Or the whistle of a gusting wind,
But in the still, small voice by the spirit heard
that comes from deep within.

It's not in creation or its beauty Lord, you made,
But in the cross of Calvary and the life, blood you gave.

It's not in works or favor
Or the gain of wealth or fame.
But the stone rolled away from the tomb.
To show the world an empty grave.

Debra K. Rivera

That's Just Me

My name is Paul
I'm 30 yrs. old and 6'2" tall.
With brown eyes and blond hair
I work as an EMT and provide emergency medical care.

I've studied hard and acquired a lot of education
Even though I'm still not sure of my career destination
Deep down I'm proud of my many achievements and those yet to be
Some are educational and some, due to physical ability

I currently live with my dad, who could be thought of as a roommate
He's extremely independent, considering his physical state
We've been together for a long long time,
In many ways, I scratch his back and he in turn, scratches mine

My interests are many and here are just a few,
Music, dancing, health and fitness, sunsets and pretty girls too!
Others include water sports, photography and sports requiring a team
Still others are lawn care, washing cars, even cleaning house, strange as that may seem.

I try to care and lend a helping hand
From charitable organizations to individuals that society has banned.
At work, I'll go beyond the normal standard of care
Cause I keep thinking, if I ever need help, maybe they'll be there.

Paul Oenbrink

Untitled

Misery loves company
   or that's what they say
and I seem to be the best acquaintance
   why does it choose to pull me into its rut
   I don't deserve it, I don't appreciate it

Help me come raise my head above these clouds
   the stormy tempest does try to beat me to the ground
the rain pours down my tear streaked face
   the salty pain runs down from this facade
my soul tries to free itself
but to no avail
the crying forced to retreat
the hurt remembered
the facade resumes
   the true being cannot escape its chains and
   the lie takes its place
   once again

Erika Roskowinski

I Am

I am the girl across the street.
I wonder if I'll make it through this life.
I hear the sky fall while hearing the cry of help.
I see this world falling apart.
I am the girl across the street.

I pretend to be a doctor,
I feel if I help I will heal the world.
I touch peoples hearts.
I worry that I will die alone.
I cry when I see the faces of the future.
I am the girl across the street.

I understand that I am young,
I say take it one day at a time.
I dream of suicide but yet I don't know why.
I try to forget the unforgotten.
I hope this time I can make the right decisions.
I am the girl across the street.

Amelia Berumen

About Our World

Earth is like a round ball.
Sun and moon come up and go down.
Birds, wind, clouds, lightning, and thunder all make sounds.
Cherry, apple, peach, banana trees grow like weeds.
Beaches, sand, and water all around.
Lakes, oceans, rivers, and ponds all make up the earth.
Teenagers, adults, children, and kids have an image of the world.
Dogs, cats, rabbits, teachers' pets.
Sun, fun, and surfing is all summer time fun.
Policeman, firemen, schoolmen all have a learning education.
Sparkles, jewelry, dazzling lights make up a surface of a fancy face.
Big books, small books, thin, and tiny books all have covering of
   the earth.
Hotels and motels are like a mansion of the sky.
Cows, pigs, and sheep all make up a farm.
Trees, people, animals, birds, water, sun, and moon are
all a part of the earth and you.
   Victoria Gregory

Words

Lately my life is sketched in ragged lines
Like the dry creek bed, carving its way down the
Steep canyon slope. If only these lines hanging
In the air like ripe pears would splash down their goodness
At the twist of a pen. Instead of living like mice
In the attic, scurrying, worrying, and waiting

To come down, sit by the stove, warm their feet,
Tell their stories and not be driven out like
Unwanted relatives. If they can roam,
Their scratchings start to sound like the choruses

You sometimes hear at the edge of a dream
When the words make no sense, but the distant
Whine wakes you up like a foghorn, telling you
To forsake sleep, grab your pen, and listen to
The night slowly making its way into dawn.
   Kathleen Rampton

Where

Where sparrows dare to fly
In space filled with despair,
And man no doubt has a care
For his fellow man in need,
Doesn't take time to think or take heed.

Where man is destined to be
And no other presence is there,
Who are we to defend or care,
For no one else has a right to be
In an area with which to share.

Where life-in general-has reached its greatest height,
In times of darkness and sheer day light
Take full meaning in the presence thereof,
And thank your lucky stars-and God above.
   Grace L. Parsons

Autumn Beauty

Majestically rise the mountains
   on a clear and sunny day.
The breeze is whistling through the trees as
   to and fro they sway.
The leaves of the aspens have turned to gold
   as summer leaves and fall takes hold.
But as fall moves slowly on and the leaves
   of the aspen fall in time,
The green of summer can still be seen on
   the limbs of the evergreen pine.
   Shawn A. Hagan

Ode To The Beautiful Mushroom

Adornment, she has none — clothed in white
   of heavenly light, she grows in silence through the night.
No ear can hear in silence, as an ungainly spore, in
   earth's deep womb begins to rend its darkened tomb.
A gift of God's from ancient time - as
   manna sent from heaven, a phantom of
   delight, or an apparition hid from sight?
She sees no sun - a silvery feathered moon
   does cross the sky - and guided by the
   evening star - she too shall cross the golden bar.
How then shall such a gift be called?
   A name that tells of joy - not gloom.
   Ah yes - my lovely hidden mushroom.
   Charles F. Middleton

Our Child

I could see it from a mile away tethered on the face of a boy
The weight of the world

All the transgressions one could place upon another were there
Marred upon that boy's face

I wondered how it could be that he had gone unnoticed
A mother's caress he had not felt
A father's wisdom, strength had not been his fortune

He was without love
He was alone

Though I played no part in his demise
I could not help but to feel I had somehow failed
That we had failed

His desperation etched forever in my heart
   Shawney Evans

Now...(SPH)...And Forever

I sit on the shore and moon light illuminates the night sky.
Thoughts of you flow through my mind and touch my spirit
As gently as the breakers touch the sand.
Over and over again I see the image of your face,
I feel the warmth of your hand as it has many times reached out for
mine, I feel the strength you give me each time I search your blue
eyes for answers.
Happiness is hard to find in life and you have given me more than
my share. I feel your restless spirit, I feel uncertainty in your
soul when you question where life's road is leading you.
The road ahead is filled with rocks, potholes, and forks
going off into uncharted directions.
But just as you have always been for me, I will be for you,
with my spirit, the smooth and even path cushioning your steps,
with my smile, the soft breeze to stir the leaves of your imagination,
with my hand, the sturdy bridge gives you safe passage over troubled
waters, with my heart, with my love, the light to guide you along
your journey.
Now...and Forever.
   Carol A. Juszkiewicz

Ilet

I am in a cage
Like a cage in a zoo
Everyone stares at me
They all laugh and make fun of me
They taunt and act like I am not there
But they know that I am there listening
The words hurt; the emptiness hurts more
No one is in the cage with me
I am outside looking in
Will someone let me in
I am in a cage
   Ruta Domeika

Inez O. Brown

This charming lady could crochet,
Finish her afghan in a day.
Pattern and snip material at dawn's early light,
Sew and wear the gown that night.

Her magic decorating skill,
Made atmosphere in her home a thrill.
Ms. Inez liked very much to bake
The best ever German Chocolate and pound cake.
Her cakes were so yum-yum,
Of course you ate every crumb.

Ms. Brown also had a dry wit.
Once said to one of us,
"My goodness what is that you have on?
You look like Aunt Sookie."
On hearing one's burst of song, Ms. Inez said,
"I wish I could sing. But after that I heard just now.
I wish you could".

God needs her now.
He could use her talent and expertise.
So we'll see her in Heaven, a sacred and Holy place.
Rae E. Montague

Setting Sun

As we watch the setting sun
I think to myself why we came,
And as we share
A quiet laughter or a serious moment,
I wonder why we didn't come before
As the people pass us and as the time goes by
We stay still and
Enjoy a moment not soon forgotten,
Then I hope
This won't be the last time we come here,
'Cause never have I ever
Been so at peace
Never have I ever loved so much
Never did I know
That you were the one
I would watch the setting sun with,
And as I sit and dangle my feet
Above the sparkling water
And as the sun sets,
I know I will see it here again with you.
Andrea Schuweiler

Homeless Of The World

Homeless is my name
Youth hath taken my pride
Pride of hope, one of joy
Yet unaccomplished.

The serenity of the earth
Hath not fare me
Henceforth
Homeless is my name
Fate hath rechristened me; a name I'll carry
Till help availeth.

The freedom of our solemn environment know I not; labor overtakes me
The toils of my injury weighs
Subjected homelessness.

Grief of anger; grief of despair
Yet street to street passeth I,
The essence of my existence lingereth
Homeless is my name.
Doris Oforiwah Ofori

The Vision

I had a dream, a strange kind of dream,
where things aren't really what they seem.

Strange things have happened in my past,
and now strange dreams have come at last.

Dreams are reflections of what is meant to be,
to see what is happening out there today is a tragedy.

The world is constant with no end or beginning,
people live and die but the earth still keeps spinning.

Around the world, orbits a very grim sadness,
while the core remains filled with chaos and madness.

Life is short so make it the best,
on judgment day don't complain like the rest.

For if you do, it will be fault of your own,
you did not follow the light that shone.

This light that shines comes from God's hands,
it travels across the globe to distant lands.

You can see it reaching out to you if you only open your eyes,
just take a look at the world today the evil is there to realize.

In nature a man's heart is essentially good,
it's the competition out there that makes him do what the devil would.
Antonio Magana

Lady Of My Dreams

Daily I converse with and see
This lovely lady I so want to be.
She is in too many ways,
Unlike me.

She is in meaningful ways,
Attractive.
Kind, sweet, feverishly active.
She is constantly about and doing.

Working, praying, pursuing
Life in diverse paths.
Quick to Love,
Slow to wrath.

She's not always seeking top billing
Rather, always willing
To lend all she has and more
To major tasks or tiny chores.

My dream is that one day we'll merge
Her power and grace up out of me will surge
No more of the me that would be naughty.
Hope the old saying is true "life begins at forty".
Patricia R. Lunsford

For My Wife On Our 4th Anniversary

"You are my Balance for which I live,
Never asking for anything always the first to give.

You gave me your love asking nothing in Return,
that's what makes the light in my Heart always Burn.

We spent too much time living apart,
but that didn't matter you were alwaysdeep in my heart.

Here it is April the 6th once again,
I'm sorry for all the other times, but now our lives can begin.

The love you possess, the strength you
Endure lets me know you're mine for sure.

My Hopes, my dignity, my dreams, my pride
all came together when you became my Bride."
Rodney C. Miller

Change

The winds of times are ever changing
with the rising and falling of the sun.

The soul rises with the sun to keep on striving
to that unknown point where human ecstasy is at its
highest, only to be reminded of the steep and winding road
it takes to reach the dream that soothes the withered soul.

As the sun falls, so does the soul. It rests, for tomorrow
is another day, another challenge, another defeat, another victory.

Heather Bouler

My Window

I sit upon my window sill, looking and crying, for my heart
has been left (only) in a world of great opportunity and loneliness.

I chance to hear a bird sing that would make me very happy.
Alas, I hear nothing, nothing but the silence and cold.
The world stands still.

I wait here for a long time and envision my problems and pain.
Still I hear nothing. The sun shines high but its warmth
does not warm me.

Alas I close my window for the night is here.

Caroline Covington

My Cameos Of Memory

These are my treasures kept apart,
Cradled in velvet in my heart,
Graven profiles, picture clear
Perfect moments, priceless dear,
Etched in ageless time to be
My cameos of memory.

The hours I have spent with you
the tender times the fun times too
The summer roses and the rain,
The laughter and the precious pain
Of loving you- your loving me-
My cameos of memory.

These are my wealth, my warmth, my light,
I keep them dream— close all the night.
With fingertips of heart and mind
I trace each profile there defined—
These treasures none can take from me
My cameos of memory.

Nancy L. Peters

Becoming Me

I have cried my last cry
I have no tears left in me
This is where I pick up the pieces and begin to move on
This is where I realize I can no longer fit in the mold everyone
has made for me
It's time for the person inside to break free
And realize that I'll never know if I can make it on my own
unless I try
This is where I reach deep in my heart and pull out the scared
and battered soul that has been hiding all these years, afraid
to let her light shine
Right now is the moment I begin to love myself
And learn no one can tell me who I am, but me.

Michelle Taylor

Atlanta's Olympic

What about the Olympic Games in Atlanta?
What about all the fame?
What about from Greece the torch carrying a world of flame?

Caring, love, peace, friendship shown for days known,
As we celebrate our own.

Someone tried to dampen the spirit of fame, but
we rose above that shame.

Yellow, black, white all aglow - swimming, running, jumping.
Doing what they do best, all passing the test.

There was a spirit in Atlanta that surpassed all the rest
Medals of Gold, Silver, Bronze, all the people blessed,
For we are known and we have shown that God takes care of his own.

God Bless America

Nannie K. Bridges

Untitled

Enslaved by poverty
Smelling the horrid scents,
The rank garbage left in dumpsters,
The streets reeked of poverty,
The bodies held unbearable odors,
Many unwashed and in a drunken stupor,
The children stare at them in horror,
Pinching their noses shut,
As if to breath the air would make them street urchins, too,
As if poverty and homelessness were contagious.

Christina L. Beighe

M e

Awakening the world,
Turning the tall mountains
Scarlet, red and pink.
Pink as a young girl's cheeks, red as a rose,
Scarlet as the fallen leaves.
Awakening the world.

Warming the world,
Evaporating the dew on rose petals and grass.
Roses hold their heads high and welcome the warmth.
Magnificent music made by the birds, fill the air.
Warming the world.

Showering of light.
I show off my promise that is the day.
And my radiance,
Which keeps many wondering.
I am beautiful and brilliant,
Bold and bright,
Showering of light.

Nicole Lynch

Life

Life exists in a child.
In the laugh, tear, breath, and love
of a child.

Life exists in love.
In the emotions, sacrifice, soul, and heart
of love.

Life exists deep in the heart.
The place most can't find.

Life is love
and living, loving.

Most don't know love.

Rebekah Leah Watkins

Martyr

My anger is like a thousand hammers,
   Driving nails of sadness into my extremities.
Fear is the cross that I must bear,
   For what seems a hundred millions years.
Whips, like razors, slashing my sides,
   Blood running out, carrying my soul.
People crowding around me, some so familiar,
   Yet as foreign as strangers.
Look unto me, in bewilderment,
   At what I've lost, what I can no longer control.
Tears welling in their eyes,
   A crying child, looks to me with hope.
Seeing nothing in return, he looks slowly away,
   Searching for reason in my self-pity.
A flock of bewildered sheep, quietly filing by,
   Is my crown of thorns.
I see myself a lonely martyr,
   With no cause left to defend.

Reuben Kraft

Daily Learning

Another school day, another lesson;
Homeschool is a daily blessing.
An hour for reading, writing, and prayer,
Lookout! Schoolwork! Everywhere!

Papers on the table, books on the floor;
Some I wish would fly out the door!
Now comes history, science, and math.
Oh joy, we're having a blast!

I've heard it said, that it's really sad,
those poor little homeschoolers, they've got it so bad!
What can they learn, staying home for school?
It won't be socialization! Their parents are cruel!

But, homeschoolers learn an enormous amount!
They learn how to read and they learn how to count!
They learn from their fathers, siblings, and mothers.
They learn academics, fine arts, and yes, playing with others!

Homeschool is a routine challenge.
But, daily learning we always manage.
With each new assignment, and every lesson we discover,
Homeschool is great, but we're glad when it's over!

Giselle Ates

Untitled

When I was young everything fell into place
I had not a care in the world
Yesterday was much easier.
I used to smile but not any more
There once was a beauty on the inside and out
Both are now gone.
Everything is a game of attention, but why?
Is there not love,
Lies make me feel better and very much greater
Others do not understand...they see something
But not what is really there.
A deep sleep would be better... but what about my mother?
The rest just might not care.
Pain lies deep in the soul and eats away at character
Soon it will show and what will become of me?
Good, if not for me than for no one
Why must that be a thought of mine?
Where and when will it go?
Someone to say I love you will probably do
Until that day comes I remain unchanged!

Danita Q. McRae

Heaven's Path

I just saw a star fall from the sky
It had a twinkle in its eye.
I know who it was, a sign meant for me.
A signal from you, reassuring me.

That you are o.k., and doing just fine.
Saying "Dry your tears, let your smile shine."
"I'm working in joy for someone you can't see
And everyone's being good to me."

"There's so much here that has to be done.
Like lighting the moon, then shining the sun.
Then planning the rain, you know what that means.
We're watering down, and keeping things clean."

"There are roads to pave way up here too.
To make the way smooth for all of you!
So that you won't stumble or ever fall down.
On your way up this Path of Love I've found."

"So when you look up at the stars and the sky
See that special one winking, just wave and say "Hi!!"

Carole Ann Wilcher

Elysian Fields

A green pasture free from entangled trees,
   caught on the brim of a free existence;
where the whisperings of freed souls are heard,
   entwined with the slightest breeze;
a joy is born, met with no resistance,
   forever tempted by love's present tease,
free from chance and fate's nagging insistence,
   yet a loss exists, despite what I inferred,
for sleep has finally caught fleeting life,
   who can no longer bare to grasp or seize,
sailing on death's raft, unmoored by a knife,
   and lead on its journey by a simple bird.

Walter Scott Lothian

A Poor Little Indian Boy

(My Brother)
The lone wolf howled as the full moon shown,
A poor little Indian boy stands alone,
No tribe to call his family no tee-pee to call his home,
His moccasins are worn thin and his buckskins are worn bare,
Where does a poor little Indian boy go when there is nowhere,
Many moons have passed since he found his tribe,
Now he is accepted and ever by their side,
They call this warrior Silver Tree, his wife they call White Dove,
Now this Indian warrior's heart is oh so full of love,
No more is he without a family, no more is he alone,
The lone wolf still is howling for it is he that has no home.

Marjorie Helen Roop

Love

Love, love is in the air.
As I stand by a pair.
How I watch the two fall in love.
As I stand alone, alone.
I long to fall in love.
To be held in ones arms.
To kiss softly to one's lips.
That's what I miss.
Once I too loved one.
But my love betrayed my heart.
As I ponder to ask, will I fall in love again?

RaYoung Suh

Remember Me?

My love, my world, my life
The memories cut through me like a knife.
I remember how happy we once were,
Then I see you walking with her.
We shared a lot together,
I thought we would last forever.
You put an ear to ear smile on my face
With your sweet talk and fond embrace.
That night you said things I never heard you say,
I never thought you could be that way.
I guess it's time to set you free
I'll always wonder the way it could be.
There will always be a place for you in my heart
That's one thing that will never, ever part
But you walk with her now - I hope you're happy
Still... I wonder, "Do you remember me?"
    Cheryl Vogel

Ernie

Disabled, yes; perhaps. (And yet, what is "disabled?")

Assigned to him am I, his tutor
And pedengine. But assigned just at first, loyal on to later.

His name is Ernie, he says.
To empty classrooms twice weekly, we'll chair,
Notetakehisthesis, and sometimes just talk, casually.

Six years, he says, six years in dis ease.
(With his hands, cannot write. Cannot see. Cannot walk.)
At twenty-eight, he began a new life-colder, crueler, aloner.

he continues his story.

Being smitten by damned dis ease,
He reached high to without and dug deep to within.
And with these two actions-prayer and reflection-he secured
Two mighty allies-God and himself.

Now, a master's student, he is.

I do not pity Ernie, no; hailhimido.

(I) marvel at his strength, feel
dwarfed by his drive. And realize
that this man who cannot write, see, or walk,
is simply not a man who cannot write, see, or walk.
    Scott Marchal

Deep Down Inside

There's a person inside me with so many thoughts
with wishes of things I'd someday like to do, and
fantasies of things that have to do with you.
Inside of me sometimes is someone who cries
now and then and who feels many needs that never quite get
expressed.
Somehow...you know about these times, and you
keep me from getting too depressed about things.
You know me so well...
You have a wonderful knack for calling at just the right time.
Touching just the right place, saying just the right words...
Everyone else only knows the "outside" of me.
It's only from you that I feel I don't need to hide.
It's with love and honesty and gratitude that
I tell you now...
That you're the only one who has ever really known me...
  Deep Down Inside.
    Tammy S. Whitley

My Wife

Most of my days are long and alone
I wait for my wonderful wife to return home
She works hard and dresses in style
And when she walks through the door,
She's wearing a big smile

She greets me in an inquisitive way
Because she wants to know how was my day
The way she loves me with tender care
I can't stay I had a bad day, I wouldn't dare

She does everything, even feeds the dog
While it seems like I'm just a bump on a log
I feel like a burden, just half a man
But my wife is always there with a helping hand

Without my wife I couldn't survive
She's the one person who keeps me alive
She knows exactly when I need love
And for giving her to me I thank God above
    Thomas F. Nairn

360 Degrees Rasta

To understand this poem you first must have the insight to overstand.

The mind has to be receptive enough to receive what the spirit
of the Most High has to offer.

For a Rasta there is two main objectives in this life and that
is to thirst and hunger after righteousness.

Jerusalem is the body, Judah is the pentacle of Zion, which is the
heart of the Rasta, that resides in the Bosom of the Most High, Selah!

When I read my Bible throughout the day, the feeling that comes over
me, makes me kneel and pray, a Rasta is made that way
and I am 360 degree Rasta.

I am not with you in the body but I am face to face with you
in your mind, so keep the spirit Rasta, pray for all mankind.

Always walk in the spirit never looking back, always keep the
tension tight never giving in to slack; don't worry about today,
for tomorrow is already gone, keeping your eyes on sweet Zion,
soon come I will be home.

All praises be to the most high in Jah-sons Holy Name; don't
waste your prayers on the righteous, but pray for the Beast to be tamed.

For I am 360 degree Rasta and that will never change.

    Jah Guide

    Ras Deacon
    Clarence D. Turner

Belief

The birds do sing for I heard them today!
They had been there all along, but not until I met you did they start
to sing their song.
And that song will be with me for
eternity...
God told me so.

You question that I spoke to thee?
How could you be so blind to see only what lays before your eyes,
instead of waking to the surprise
that a dream it could be,
but instead you only see reality.
What a shame for you and me
for fantasy is the key...
that is what the song meant to me!!
    Shana Marie Orum

Trees

Trees are everywhere so green so green,
some with apples some with oranges,
some with bananas short and tall,
no matter what I still like trees,
they give me shade from the sun,
yet so gentle to me,
I'd probably want to be a tree myself,
the wind may blow but I won't go,
with the wind in my face,
I will stay in the shade,
if you stay close to a tree,
you might hear it breathe,
when it gets cold,
the leaves cover me for warmth,
a squirrel is going up and down on a tree,
showing me that life is to be,
so you see a tree is a lot more to me,
some people run some people play,
I like trees every day.

Zikiria Chaudhary

You Mean You Can Feel That

Why do you think someone can only go somewhere once?
If it starts with so you don't want to say it.
You ask me what does this mean?
I don't know about you but I'll think that's me, so say hello.
There once were two people.
One was looking up and the other down.
I got to thinking evil goes higher.
I ask myself, what is this for then I remember I keep getting high.
I don't know really forget something.
You say "a poet."
Once something came over me and said "poo."
I don't know about you but I'll bring up anger,
 a poet for short.
Who am I?
I am the dictionary man and I couldn't say no.
You mean you can feel that?
As long as you don't talk back.
Everybody went to heaven but me.
Don't look up.

Richard Kenneth Burroughs

A Gift

A gift with no monetary value attached
 but
A gift which cost God the price of his precious Son
 given as a ransom for many

A gift without paper or bow
 but
A gift wrapped in swaddling clothes in a robe of flesh
 to redeem mankind from their sins

A gift not temporal that will depreciate
 but
A gift designed to endure eternity

A gift of love given with all in mind...
Jesus
The only begotten of the Father

For all who will believe and receive Him
 into their hearts as their personal Savior

For the final Gift eternal life in heaven...
The gift is waiting on you.

Margaret C. Cullins

My Loved Ones

My loved ones are not all people,
And some of them are not alive,
They are still very dear to me,
Although sometimes I don't show it,
No matter what they do to me,
I still love them deep down inside,
I do get mad at them from time to time,
And even then, I still love them inside,
Roads, trees, waters, and skies,
Even miles and miles of deserts, so dry,
Will ever take their place in my heart,
No matter how many times anyone tries,
No matter what I say or do,
I still love them,
And that will always be true.

Virginia Schmeling

Remembering My Childhood

I remember my childhood everyday I'm alive
the absentee of my parents, on my own to survive.
I remember only being nine and taking care of myself
I stole from the store, took food from the shelf.

I remember my clothes never mine and torn
I started to feel I should not have been born.
I ate a decent meal only once a week
I never had a dad to kiss on the cheek.

My dad was alive, but didn't pay me much mind
my mom was the boss and would smack my behind.
I remember being lonely in my thoughts and my dreams
I felt my young life splitting apart at the seams.

My mom was as cold as any degree you have felt
if it wasn't her way, she would break out the belt.
I remember after a while not feeling the pain
of the belt, the hunger, no clothes or the shame.

I remember the things that happened so clear
now I'm all grown up it seems to appear.
I now have a son who means the world to me
I will show him how much fun life is supposed to be.

Anthony E. Briguglio

To Norman - Leaving For A New Parish

Walk with Thy servant, Lord, that he may know
The comfort that alone Thy presence brings.
Be Thou a never-failing guide; lend wings
To speed him where-so-ever he may go.

Speak to him, Father, through the darkest night
Sustain and strengthen him; that though he fall,
No stone shall do him harm. Oh, be Thou all
To him - the very Way, the Truth, the Light.

Touch him, Eternal Spirit; let Thy Flame
Enkindle such a fire in his soul,
That by the power of Thy Living Name,
The lost may be redeemed; the sick made whole.
Until Thy Love, impatient for its own,
Shall bring him at the last, rejoicing, home.

Dexter B. Blake

Black

Bewitching, bountiful, beauty
Luscious lips like tutti frutti
Assertive, animated, ample
Classically crafted, wanna sample
Knowledge, kissable, keen
Intelligent, illustrious, watch me preen
Soft, silky, sable skin
Melt me, munch me, then mold me again
Exceptional, exotic, experimental cutie.

Felicia Nesbitt

Dreams

Come with me to the place where dreams come true
And the sky is always blue
Where people dance in golden colors
While the band plays their favorite tune
Where people can tame the wild gardens
And sing with the softness of the moon
Where people lie in fields of gold
And listen to stories untold
For this is the place I only see in my
Dreams

Jenny Power

To The Affianced

    Marriage sings a Siren's song of caring, and loving tenderness, and passion, and all Life's wants fulfilled abundantly.

    But listen closely, Lovers, lest you miss the undertones that warn of risks, of rocks, and shoals, and treacherous tides that threaten shipwreck on an alien shore instead of undiluted bliss.

    If pessimistic clucking tongues, and woeful cautions give you pause, turn back. Already it's too late. Your cause is lost. Otherwise, heed the insistent throbbing urge of hearts aflame with passion.

    It is ever thus with brave, daring souls whose courage overshadows caution, whose dreams turn trepidation into triumph, whose faith leads on to victory, or to death, but to glory nonetheless.

    "Nothing ventured, nothing gained." They cry, and cast off upon the Sea of Life well aware of the risks they take, but fearing most of all a fate far worse than death: a life unlived, unloved.

Malcolm R. Watt

One Lonely Thought

You are a thought stuck in my brain,
without your warm loving heart I'm sure to go insane.
Here comes a part I know I can't refuse,
it's the thought of once again making sweet love to you.
You are like a train going through my brain,
car after car, day after day, just for one
little mistake, will you make me forever pay.
I know it was wrong, I know it wasn't right,
but please, give me one more chance just to make things right...
If you choose to do so, please, let it be said,
because at the end of this poem my heart has been painfully read!

Melvin Goodwin

The Ghetto Backstabber

Rise and shine at eleven a.m.
High tops, baggies, and braids on him
Stomach is empty, pockets are, too
The system has put a label on you
Money is funny, jobs are too slow
That's the way in the ghetto
Everyone knows about skid row
Skid row in the ghetto is the way to go
But street hustlers seem to have it made
What do they do to make the grade
Deals of drugs, women, and goods
Produce fast cash for the boys of the hood
Fine pads, shinney cars, and food galore
The fast easy way to open that door
Backstab the system is the word
Ripoff, tipoff, what have you heard
Men, women, children, black and white
Everybody deals day and night
Until it hits home and then he can see
The agony and misery is not for me

Phyllis Bachelor

Waiting Angel

You haunted my dreams for years, big blue eyes, innocence,
    needing me...
You explored my dreams for years, strawberry hair,
    heavenly laugh, heartbreaking tears, needing me...
Oft times I awoke with a start, little girl,
    Who are you? Where are you? What is your message?
For years you disappeared...sleeping dreamlessly.
    Mindless state; my only salvation.
One evening you returned, after years of absence,
    dancing, laughing, needing me...
Now I watch you sleep, push your silken bangs off your eyes.
Filled with such a satisfied sense of knowing..
My beautiful daughter, you waited patiently for your Mom,
    and I thank God he knew you would be needing me.

Kimberly Kukowski

Chelsea's World

I wonder what the world is like outside my mother's womb
It's oh so safe and warm inside, I'm protected from all harm
I sleep and eat and move a lot, I hear my mother say
But what else is there to do in here, but move and swim and sway.

My mother and father already love me, for I often heard them talk
Of all the things that we will share
From birth, to crawling and then I begin to walk.

I know my Mother's beautiful and warm and gentle too
And my Father is handsome, strong and brave
And will provide for me, as all father's do.

For I am a precious gift of life
Sent from heaven above
For both of them to enjoy and cherish and protect and always love.

I love you both already
And one day I will be able to say
Thank you Mom and Thank you Dad
For caring so much and guiding me in the right way.

Peggy Misner

Subliminal

Winged dreams lodged in the cortex and swirls
  of my brain a long time ago.
The wings would never molt.
The dreams were embedded beneath
  the folds, parasitically.

When the wax bonding the feathers melted
        and the joy waned
Beneath the weight of waiting for the pigeons
      to complete their cycle,
I wondered where the wonder had soared or sunk.
I wandered where mud swirled sluggishly.
I dreamt of dead birds, and I cried.

The dream survives the vacuum and the void.
The flapping entrances more than the dove
        appearing
Beneath the magician's silk.
The tissues of my brain are more resilient
    for having hosted the parasites.
The mud is cool when squished between my toes...
Slime can be sublime when fanned by glowing wings.
    John J. Dorsey

Hindsight

I should've visited often.
but there was never time
too tired after work you know
to hear the church bells chime

You showed me so much comfort
magic where the sea meets the sky.
Pot roast dinners at your loving house
I sit, tears streaming, sipping rye.

I should've visited often.
Father time speeds by so fast.
I love you more than ever now
Remembering the past.

As darkness abated the angels came
You soared on the wings of a dove.
Silver tears from the moon illuminated the way
my heart aches for your unconditional love.

I should've visited the nursing home
How I wish I could see you for just a while
for there's nothing worse than being alone
I miss your voice, your face, your smile.
    Michele Mojica

A Wish To

Weeping willow can I be a tree
A tree that cries just like me
She weeps at every aspect of her falling leaves
Leaves that replenish the ground at my feet
Beautiful daisies and weeds grow around to fill up the empty ground
Yet emptiness lingers in my roots below
Still protection transcends through my branches above
Allowing all living things a place to feel loved
Glimmering sun rays blind my translucent leaves that heed out simplicity
Beams of light scatter
Here and there just enough to warm those who she cares
Oh weeping willow
I really want to be a tree
So I can have some peacefulness and security
    Rebecca Sharman

Breaking Heart

The crumbling of a breaking heart sounds through my ears
as time passes and weeks turn into years,
but no one hears the crumbling of a breaking heart.

I look into your eyes and see you slipping away.
I listen for your voice, but all I hear is
the crumbling of a breaking heart, as the days pass.

Day passes into night,
night passes into day
and you drift further and further away.

As you drift away, one more piece of my
heart crumbles to dust.
Soon you'll be gone forever and they'll be nothing left
of my crumbling heart.

As the hours pass, my thoughts are of you
and the last piece of my heart crumbles
and blows away on the wind.
    Nancy Elizabeth Breland

Will You Fall, Like They?

In the garden, of Eden, Adam and Eve were put into
To dress and to keep it was all they had to do,
But Eve listened to the serpent, and Adam harkened to Eve
And on their lives a curse they received.

God told Noah to build an ark of Gopher Wood
"I will destroy the world," God replied and Noah understood
Noah preached to the people but they laughed at him, jeered
but when the floods came they wished they'd never sneered.

Cain and Abel made an offering to God
one from the flock, the other from the sod,
God honored Abel's, because God looks at the heart,
Cain killed Abel and from his land was forced to depart.

In the land of Shinar, the people started to build a Tower
They thought by doing this they'd have more power
but God confounded their language and scattered them to all lands
That's why we have other languages, because against God they
  did band.

To the land of Egypt Moses went
to lead them but of bondage was why he was sent
God gave them water and food, and calmed their fears
but because of their murmuring, they wandered 40 years.
    Elnora Mills

True Thoughts

As I wish upon a star
I hope and dream that you're not far

I'll cry all night and pout all day
If I woke up one morning and you drifted away

I'll try my best to pass my goal
To love you forever with heart and soul

As sensory images cross my mind
Think of our hearts not as two, but as one combined

I'll ask not of your love,
But to give me a chance
I'll show you the way with true love and romance

Now take a few moments while
I'm on my knee

And tell me this once

    Anne will you marry me
    Anthony DiMaio

Memory Lane

I see a little girl
  cowered in a corner-
    mother's little mourner.
She grieves for raised hands,
  loud voices, and empty bottles.
She suffers from the parental destruction
  of her safe, imaginary lands.
Her land away from drunken coos,
  and fearing the sound of her father's shoes.
Away from the knife hidden under her pillow
  to a place where children can safely grow
Into functional adults who don't flinch from waving arms
  and verbal shots aimed low.
But through those fears, and innumerable tears,
She cowers in a corner,
  finally beaten by her eight long years.
    Monika J. Flaschka

War Memories

With bravery and loyal heart
We heard the call and did our part
The prospect never again to see
Our home, our friends, and family

Walk all day in the tropical heat
Break for a rest and something to eat
To have C-rations served in a can
With generous portions of dirt and sand

Write a letter home every day
Thinking of my family far away
Trusting in God's mercy and grace
Once again to see my wife's sweet face

Look and search for Charlie to fight
Dig a hole in the ground to spend the night
In the dark, whisper a prayer to God above
To thank Him for His protection and love

Never a war hero wanted to be
Just to do what was expected of me
To protect my men and stay alive
To do what was necessary to survive
    Jim Perdue

What Is Life?

Life is fast, life is slow!
Ask the old, they will know.
As we are young, the seasons were long.
As we age, the years become a familiar song.
Songs are memories we hear and don't forget,
of times we've had, and daydreams of yet.
Whatever times we spend, Good or bad,
a old song will make you remember that moment had.
life is a smell, new odors for the future,
familiar odors for the past, and just like the odors
we smell, our life is so short to last.
So don't spend life's time, wishing for things you don't have,
this is your life, and not a time to impress, you owe
your children love, but not your neighbor or a quest.
Life was fast, life was slow, life a destiny we most go.
Life is you and you are life,
Live it now and keep up your brow!
    Aaron Jackson

Dad

I never knew,
How much he hurt you.
You tried to hug him and show your love,
But all you got in return was a hard shove.
Every day when he comes home late,
His eyes are always filled with hate.
The pain has stayed with you,
And you never knew,
If your dad really wanted to,
Hurt you as much as he did,
Hitting you since you were a little kid.
You have kept this secret for way too long,
You dad is doing something so very wrong.
Let me take you away,
So he won't be able to hurt you in any way,
I'm here to make him pay.
And when he comes home,
With me by your side,
No more will you have to hide.
    Julie Lademan

Falling From Grace

  Once there was this angel,
I found her on her knees, weeping.
  I asked, "What's wrong, angel,
have you fallen from grace?"
  She replied, "No. My children turned on me
and pulled me from grace, I lost my book
and my torch has been extinguished forever!"
"What is your name?", I asked.
"America," she said.
    Jason Hurt

Spinning 'Round And 'Round

Spinning 'round and 'round without a sound... It's as quiet as can be for they cannot see... The world is toiling and boiling meanwhile I'm only coiling tighter... Can't stretch much more or I'll snap back and that's that... Can't fight and can't talk; losing faith in God and failing to walk... Simmering in the pressure cooker and losing my flavor that once was savored... Spinning, Spinning 'round and 'round... Can't even lift my head up off the ground. It's gotta stop, but it can't — no, it won't... People don't care anymore... I'm so far away that I can't go anywhere... No helping hand so that I can stand... Stop spinning 'round and 'round. Get up off the ground. You can do it! Don't take the step that you'll regret if you don't succeed... Stand proud upon your mound. Life's good and bad so reject your sadness and don't be had. You can be glad. Yes, glad! Just renew your trust... It's a must — an absolute must... Don't return to the dust. Stop spinning 'round and 'round and start making some sort of sound.
    Lori Jean Sherlock

As I Lie Here To Sleep

As I lie here to sleep
I hope the world will keep,
If the sun doesn't shine
There will be nothing for you to call mine,
If the flowers don't grow
there will be none for me to show,
As I lie here to sleep
I hope the world will keep.
    Alan J. Pershing

Sliding Souls

Walking chemical compound
Not talking in the ground
On tracks to a tunnel
Like a fly in a funnel
I teach the worms to cough
My face is falling off
While the plants are clapping
My synapses are zapping
Ending in a cell
Or crawling out a well
Escape the equational curve
Things not needed to serve
Breaking the chains
Loosen yourself from the rains

Joseph McCormack

Soul Self

Smooth, softly silky, so sweet!
  Sassy silver shines,
    savoury.
Seal, sailing south, surrenders,
   suddenly sensing something
   sequestered, soulful, sanctioned,
    sanctified,
She searched still
  smiling,
    safe.

Sally Rayn

Just Us

  Together we are one.
It's not really a family!
Just you and me,
we should be, cause we're gonna be
together forever
just us
well ten years down the road,
I am thrown in with a big load,
two kids and one on the way.
No child support
so we're going to about today!
Hopefully, maybe, probably
I'll get justice!

Stephanie Tolbert

Federal Down

Weeping eyes around this town,
A ragged building going down.
Memoirs of a bloody past,
Broken hearts rest at last.
Rampant cause of one gone wild,
Cursed soul, some mother's child.
Many lives were lost that day,
Voices cry out for someone to pay.
Fingers point the voices scorned,
Want to know, they're so forlorned.
Throughout nation many touched,
Responded as aid was rushed.
Mending time so needed now,
Cease the pain some ask how?
Christ alone can mend this rift,
Praying hands to God they drift.

Rick Hendrickson

Kittens at Play

Kittens
furry, soft
playing, running, jumping
playing around together every day
cuddly, cute, special
purring, sleeping
Kittens

Tasha Giglitto

Since You Said Good-bye

To Kelly Ann, you'll never know how much.
Come to me sweet paramour, so
  we may be together
Rapt in love, like two bright stars,
  shining on forever.
Two wild flowers grow as one,
  nourished by the earth
Living, loving, sharing time.
  Giving life its worth.
But if you have lost faith in me,
  unable to transcend
losing touch would surely mean a
  part of me would end.
For I know now my love is true,
  my heart has made me fall
All I am I give to you, until the
  heaven's call.

Justin Scheuffele

"Range Pollution"

Home-Home on the Range
Where you and I used to play,
There's so many cars, we'd get hurt,
So where can we play?

Home-Home on the Range
It went when the parking lots came.
There's no Trees or little Bumble Bees,
So where can we stay?

Home-Home on the Range,
Where the water isn't the same.
We hold our noses to get a drink
And be sick the rest of the day!

Home-Home on the Range,
Where it once was, it's not the same.
We wear our mask so we can breath,
And get sicker and sicker each day!

Home-Home on the Range,
Where you and I can't go out to play.
There's so many cars we'd get hurt,
So—Please—Where can we go to play?

Wilma Richardson

Dance Of Love

One learns a lot from a dance
how to move, to take a chance
One learns how to trust
and that working together is a must

One learns how to have fun
and true friendship is often won
To learn the dance takes much time
and one learns to compromise

One learns to go with the beat
and to try and avoid stepping on feet
I thank the Lord above
for teaching us - The Dance of Love

Carrie E. Johnson

Blue

Blue is the color
of the clear sky,
the color of the bluejay
that flies up high.

Blue is easy-going
delightful and free,
the 5th arch of the rainbow
the color of the sea.

Blue is the raindrops
hitting the ground,
the color of the earth
spinning around.

Blue is the ocean
and always will be,
the blue whale swimming
deep down in the sea.

Blue makes me smile
especially for you,
the color of magic
yes, wonderful blue!

Annie M. Swerkstrom

Untitled

Perhaps we have found,
our images we've bound,
with lies to form our union.
The smell of solitude,
embedded with fear, in
which we've deceived ourselves again.
This edge of fine dirt, we
balance upon, between hope
and the thoughts we can't fathom.
To the sound and the eyes
of our wishful intent, I follow
near behind.
To the end, if I see the
distance so near, be it fear
that I will find.
Sleepless in the realms of
content, we wallow in our wake.
Perhaps we have found, our
images we've bound, in the
fear ourselves we make.

Rebecca Wehrman

The Dream

You are the dreamer
You are the dream
You see with eyes
You see with scenes.
One outward
One within
Which is real
Which is veil.
Thoughts will come
Thoughts will go
Inside out
Outside in.
The dream is there
The dream is gone
The dream forgotten
The dream forlorn.
Reclaim your dream
Don't let it wane
You are the dreamer
With much to gain!

Helena R. Zambonis

Like A Rose

You are like a rose
that blossoms in the morning,
and looks up at the bright
sun all day, and closes when
the sun goes behind the trees.

You seem so kind and
gentle that's why everyone
likes you so. Because you are
like a beautiful rose that everyone
who walks by has to stop and stare
at, because you are like a rose.

Corrie Pankhurst

Soul Search

Looking inward
Searching out
Seek to find
What you're about
Shaping image
In your mind
Begin to see
What you will find
Sharing secrets
Of your soul
Fading fears
Found mythical
Eyes become
Clear looking glass
Reflecting joy
Beyond the mask
The moment comes
As time drifts past
Two hearts as one
Commune at last

Robyn M. Roberts

Ode To A Butterfly

Sitting silent among the trees,
Butterfly dancing on summer breeze.
Fluttering, swaying, light of ease,
Exquisite life, given to please.

Where do you go, short is your stay,
Fluffy light beauty, floating away.
Bringing quiet joy, day by day,
Gentle its peace, 'tis God's way.

Terri Loughlin

I Love You

What can you say
What can you do
If that special friend
Says "I love you"

I love you
Three simple words to say
But understanding the meaning
Could take you a lifetime plus a day

Why are they so confusing
Why can they hurt you so
For some, it's an easy question
For others, they'll never know

But to be truly loved
By that special friend
Is a feeling you'll take with you
Clear up to the end

Pamela L. Hazen

Bored

I am bored,
  I am tired.
There is nothing to do.
  I am lonely,
but Yet I am not.
  I am alone,
cause I am bored.
  I am in
a boring place.
  I have nothing
to do,
  nothing but this,
that is,
  for I am bored.

Doug Frase

The Fog

Ever been so engulfed by the fog
  that you saw
    no way out

Ever been so enraged in your heart
  that you were too weak
    to scream

Ever been so entangled by love
  that you lose sight
    of your own grip

Every been so ensnared to stay alive
  just as bad
    as you want to die

Ever been so enslaved by your mind
  that you forget
    your own freedom

Adriana Jordan

The Day I Met You

The greatest things can happen,
When you don't expect them to.
For me it was fate,
The day I met you.

I have felt it since then,
And at times quite a few.
Such a sense of completion,
The day I met you.

I feel so alive,
So secure and so true.
A natural feeling of comfort
The day I met you.

You've always been the one,
Just time was overdue.
To bring us together,
On the day I met you.

Michelle Carreth

Existence

Life is a trial
Death is a mystery
I can live,
I will die;
With nothing but my legacy.

And yet I go through life
And bide my time
Step by step,
Day by day;
And I do just fine.

Oleksander A. Stecyk

Front Page

Live up or
live down
make change or stay the same
leave or make roots
grow or die

Anyway you choose to go
will wake with you everyday
and sleep with you at night
it will either make you happy or
miserable
the choice is yours
but I guarantee
misery
will be the chosen state
for human nature
  discourages peace

Sara A. Sanders

Days Forever Lost

The days fly by like minutes,
upon which comes still another day.
The months and years so precious,
seems they come then fade so far away.

May we come and forever live,
with our memories of no cost.
But shall we never forget,
the cherished days forever lost.

Nicole Marie Wells

Who Am I?

Who am I?
I feel so empty,
So lost inside,
I always wonder,
Who am I?
Am I a sheet of snow,
Or a butterfly,
Does anyone know,
Who am I?
Can I fly like a bird,
Can I swim like a fish,
Will someone tell me,
Who am I?

Nicole Morgello

Daddy

You walk by me
I thought I understand.
The memories of all the good times,
good times that are faded.
You walk by me
Pretending to ignore
but it doesn't work,
I know your ways.
Your harsh glance
burns into my heart.
Wishing you would leave
so I can escape your look,
the look that burns into my soul.
You walk by me
I've learned to cope.
Your boiling fury still stings
but I've learned to ignore like you,
when I'm still aware,
aware of you
pretending to ignore me.

Debra Lynnanne McAlary

Memories

Get a little lost inside,
   Laughing.
Your sense, my thought,
   Never!!
The words of a friend,
   Listen.
What I say is said to understand -
   You were there.
     Standing.
Those visions.
What did you feel?
   Cold?
It's gone. I knew.
True colors never distort.
One look. A glance. So quaint.
Get a little lost outside.
   Looking in.

Sharon Hamilton

Remember

He remembered the walks
And holding hands in the park
He remembered the talks
And making sweet love past dark
He remembered smooth skin
And big beautiful brown eyes
He remembered soft lips
And slim legs with tight thighs
He remembered his love
Death's angel from above
Now days seem much longer
Nights are filled with great pain
He can't ignore the hunger
To hold him once again
To love him one more time
Would that be such a crime
He remembers his laughter
Past romantic escapades
He remembers their crying
They are both dying with A.I.D.S

Adrienne Butler Gilmore

Where To Go

Sometimes I stay up late at night,
To think of when it was so right,
I don't see how it went so wrong,
When our love was so very strong.

He used to have a special touch,
And now I miss it very much.
My friends all tell me not to cry,
But all I want is one more try.

I never thought I'd see the day,
Where I would give my heart away.
But then one day he stole my heart,
And now it is all torn apart.

The game of love I cannot play,
Because the pain will always stay.
I don't know where to go from here,
Inside of me is only fear.

Laura Young

Childhood

She was told
a fairy would dance
on the Christmas tree's
limbs. She waited.

Virginia Rothfuss

"At Your Power"

At your power you created
life. You invented man,
you invented woman,
you invented life.
At your command everything
shall croak...
shall rot...
shall dry up like an
old flower.
At your command
everything and everyone
shall obey their death.
And at your great
wisdom you will
forgive their mistakes.

Maytal Zollchian

Jenny's Life

Jenny's parents have ruined a life,
  (the life of their own daughter).
They made her blue eyes black,
  made her lips swollen,
To rid them of (their) stress.

She would hide in her room,
  (where no one knew),
To make them stop (the abuse),
  She failed.
One day at school, she sat next to
  me (me?).
I could tell she was hurt by the
  gash on her arm,
Hurt more inside than outside.

They tore her body apart,
  Tore her heart apart.
She knows the worst is over.
  After all the abuse,
  No matter how hurt,
  She knows that I care.

Heidi B. Rehmer

Dance

Black is strong and beautiful,
Fluid like running water,
Big, bright shining eyes above.
Faster beat in your two feet,
Rhythm, rhythm, rhythm, yes!

White fabric on your body,
Flowing in the air's cool breath.
Oh, my sisters and brothers,
You define dance for me in
every syncopated step!

Clapping hands and bobbing heads,
Familiar yellow excites,
Rock'a my soul with delight.
Thank your brow for its sweet tear,
Giving gifts to dance, dance, dance!

Jennifer N. Wynder

Spring Poem

The grass is so green.
The sky is so blue.
I can't help to see everything is new.
Everything starts all with a new day
and the beginning of a new day
is like the beginning of May.

Alexandrea Mantello

Untitled

This shall be written
To release my thoughts
From pondering the difference
Between my apparent reality
And the things I love most.
To change and mature
Leaving part of me behind
To become integral and
Of aspiring nature
Sends thoughts
And forms questions
Of who I am...
  - shall I be
    or was I -

James Robert Cronin

He Made It Happen

I never see a bird in flight
across the endless sky,
or touch the rough bark
of a tree
Lifting arms to heaven;

I never pick a dandelion
golden in the sun,
or walk barefoot through the
tender young green grass,
but I am filled with awe
and wonder
at the majesty of God!

Dorothy J. MacKenzie

A Friend

A friend: Is a person who cares
and is there to listen, when you
need someone to talk to, I'll be
there. I'll understand and help
you in any way I can.

A friend: Is a person who loves
and will give you understanding when
you need love the most in your life.
Love is all around, your friends and
family who love and care for you.

A friend: Is a person who is there
and your true friends are the ones
who won't tease you, about your
life and looks. You know who are
your true friends. A friend.

Lisa J. Letterle

Untitled

I see
the stars
Shining
So bright.
It looks
like the
Morning
instead
of the
Night.

Shirley Eaton

A Way With Words

Long words may sound pretty,
Impressive and witty,
And even make you sound smart;
But mind what you say,
For words are the way
To reveal what's there in your heart.

Long words may astound you,
Confuse and confound you
Then fall short..... and fail to convey
What's there in your heart,
So if you're truly smart,
Choose words that won't get in the way.

William E. Hyatt III

Dragonfly

I am the dragonfly.
I watch the images
reflected in my eyes.
I am the dragonfly.
My wings beat
the thousands times
of my heart
and my mind whirls
with the scents
blowing 'round my head.
I am the dragonfly.
I glimmer in the sun
and the shadow hides
my dark frame.
I skim the water - my domain.
I race the wind - my companion.
I see the world
reflected in my eyes-
my kingdom.
I am the dragonfly.

Janet Dahlberg

Agony And Ecstasy

Agony and ecstasy,
These feelings - not a mystery
To one who loves but can't
Express the feelings - deep
With one's breast.

To show one's love is not
Excess, if one had words to
Express the deepest feelings
In one's heart, the loved one
Then would ne'er depart.

Agony and ecstasy,
These feelings - not a mystery
To one who loves, but can't
Express the feeling deep
Within one's breast.

Joyce Hope Scholes

The Souls Of Song

From the depths of the stars
　came the souls of song
Seeking those to whom they belong

And in our eternal quest to survive
　we humans with joy
　brought the music alive!

Now all hearts are singing
　all souls on high
So sing to the children
　and the music won't die!

Georg Hadden

Little Girl I Knew

With your blue eyes
Soft brown hair
Your innocence of
Virtual your prize
Warming smile
If you only knew
That you face of
Innocence capture
My heart.

Love in your eyes
Sweetness smile of innocence
If you would see the
Heart of love
Seeing you was a
Victory in my heart
Watching you was my soul.

My eyes glowed
as I seen you running
but my heart ache
of seeing your shadow.

Laura Ferrara

Brian

I have a cousin named Brian,
Who's hair reminds me of a lion.
It's curly and soft,
With tinges of gold,
I hope he doesn't lose it,
When he starts to grow old.
His eyes they do sparkle,
His smile sincere,
I wish he lived closer,
I wish he lived here.
In school he's a brain,
At home he's the little man,
He's a Superstar athlete,
But in real life,
I'm his Biggest fan!

Ashley Anderson

Smile

Will I ever see a smile,
On a child's face today?
Why must they suffer?
Why must they die?

Will I ever see a smile,
On a child's face today?

Please children smile,
Please smile today.
You don't have to cry.
You don't have to die.

Please children smile!
Please smile today!
Please children smile!
Please smile today!

Shelley Kuhlman

Gardenia

Bud
Small, closed
Blooming, developing, thriving
Root, stem, leaf, petal
Flowering, flourishing, inspiring
Large, open
Gardenia

Kalei Lynn Boyle

Honesty

He told me
he felt differently
with other women.
With me... he felt sad.
Sad I had lost a husband
he could never replace.

Blindly, I had felt awakened,
hoping he would decide
to open his arms.
But he sensed the danger,
and led me honestly
back to the door
of my own lonely room.

Stunned, I need to thank his words
for lighting the dark spaces
with a small friendly candle,
so my eye can envision
something other than a ghost.

Shelly F. Williams

Glad And Sad

　Coming up on Thanksgiving
I'm glad and very sad,
　This will be my first year
without my Dad here.
　I'm glad for his sake
That God chose him to take,
　The cancer caused him so much pain
It was better he did not remain.
　I'm very sad and miss his voice,
but he heard another and had no choice,
　God said, "Come home now son,
Your work on earth is done."
　I'm especially glad for
one thing,
　I know my Dad is with The King!

Loren D. Essenburg

On My Pillow

Sometimes I am engulfed.
A kaleidoscope of images,
All of them related,
Woven together in my mind.
Each have their own instant in time.

A ray of memory,
Passing through a prism.
The source is a single
Brilliant light that comes to me,
When I smell you on my pillow.

Throughout my day,
My thoughts are of you,
Present and future.
And I am anxious to get to my bed,
Where I can smell you on my pillow.

I lie in total darkness.
A ray of light shines into my mind.
It warms my heart to think of you,
Of love, of respect, of devotion,
Then I can smell you on my pillow.

Garett Tunison

Rain

　The rain of jewels
The sun makes them sparkle so,
wet diamonds of skies.

Karry L. Smith

Wind

Sometimes rough,
Sometimes soft,
Sometimes not at all.

It usually,
Is much more harsh
In Winter and in Fall.

Sometimes,
It is so, so, rough,
That you think you can see it,

Rushing,
Through the tree branches,
No gracefulness is with it.

I love wind,
Except sometimes,
When it makes me have to stay inside.

Mollie Speiglman

Wind

  Whistlin' and whirlin' and
squirrelling away like a little old
woman with so much to say.

  Cool and clear from a sky
so grey, my hat stayed on but
my head blew away.

  He'll sit and he'll wait,
but things aren't the same
without my head that just blew away.

Jennifer Kamps

Misty Clouds

Misty clouds
rest upon the mountains
their presence
makes me feel safe
cloaked, enveloped
in their cool wetness
it's almost
ethereal, imaginary
a wonderful fantasy to be
lost in the misty clouds
resting upon the mountains.

Donna Hamilton-May

"The Otter"

I walked by a crystal clear stream
the other day.
And saw an otter,
while he was at play.

He seemed as happy
As he could be.
Many miles from the city
and humanity.

Then a year later
I again walked by.
And thought I saw a tear,
In the otters eye.

Man had polluted
his crystal clear stream
Destroying the otters world,
and his dream

A. H. VanDyke

Untitled

When the skies turn grey
With the bitter cast of a winter day
I feel as if I've been left alone
No place left to call my home

The trees are all quiet in hibernation
Long awaiting a spring rejuvenation

Dry withered leaves tossed to and fro
Dead and forgotten
Nowhere in particular to go

All the flowers are gone
Every butterfly has flown
The birds are nestled
In their homes they have sewn

In the shortness of day
And the longness of night
I wonder what is my plight

Is my life to go on like this forever
Will the future hold a new endeavor

Everything looks desolate and bare
Oh, how I wish you were still there

Michael D. Wortman

Home Of Hell

My home is one of heartache,
A place of steel and stone.
A barren cell, my home is hell
And here I sit alone.
For all my crimes, I pay with time
Where lights glare night and day.
And thought I rage and pace my cage,
I still must stay and pay.
Will I spend my life condemned,
A man the world disowns?
I beat and maul the concrete wall;
I pace the cold hard floor.
I damn each day my stupid ways
And pray for one chance more.
I scream and yell within my hell.
My tears of pain like bitter rain
Spill down on cold hard stone.
None can say the price I'll pay
Within my home of hell.

Sean Barry Jollie

Atlanta 1996 Olympics

"The games were good but tragic."
Athletes worked like magic, but
A bombing in a Park one day
Caused some to walk away.

Yet —
"The 1996 Olympics were exceptional,"
Consisting of top professionals.
They honored the victims whose lives,
Although they had strived,
They lost their lives one day,
Leaving many people in dismay.

Fireworks shimmered,
Some folks quivered.
The 100th — Anniversary Summer games,
They came to a close,
Thousands of spectators stood close up.
Earlier, some were singing.
As many others were cheering.
It was almost a perfect fix,
For Atlanta Olympics 1996.

Barbara Dell Hobbs

A Winter Wonder

My winter wonder is
White.
It is magical and cold,
It is pretty and clean,
My winter wonder is snow.

Kate DiGerolamo

Untitled

The colorless sand lay motionless
Upon the vast mountain climbs.
Surrounded by things not living,
And not dead.
All is quiet and nothing is lost-
But you hear the small soundless
Voices of children.

Dark shadows hang over,
Misty skys unable to be seen.
The monster of the soul slowly-
Slowly begins to grow.
The form you see is not human,
But of sand and mystery.

Hands are grabbing
And screams are not heard,
You run unable to move.
And soon the soul is lost to the,
Dark mysterious sand
Which swallows you up into a-
Colorless land.

Nadine Bell

Sun Kiss

Here in this place, while the wind it
warms my face, the moon I want to
chase, here on this hill, my senses
I want to fill, here the stars
heighten my awareness that I'm a
living being and that beauty is so freeing
The night shines as the world
unwinds, colors fade to black
until the day comes back to
welcome the world to the
morning's glow to the sun
we've come to know,
to the kiss she bestows upon us
each day, to the debts we her
I pray that she always shines her
glory upon us as she lites our way.

Pamela Yarborough

Why Did You...

Why did you have to go?
your time wasn't up
you left and didn't say goodbye.
All I felt was pain.
It puts me into pain to think you
didn't say goodbye.
I just want to see you, touch you
one more time.
You left too much unfinished
business here please come
back at least to say goodbye.
Why did you have to go
and leave me here all alone.

Aimee Sanders

"That Smile"

That smile you used to give me,
I really miss it now
It looked so sweet and free,
I wonder why and how.

I know where it has gone,
And I really wish it wouldn't
I knew I could have helped,
but something told me I shouldn't.

Now that your smile is deep under,
I think what might have been
All I can do now is wonder,
and hope I see it again.
Billy Exline

The Dancer

So you think I'm too old
to be dancing around.

You're thinking, who is this
crazy old clown,
with dresses too short,
and hair way too long.

Get in a chair, where you belong!

Phooey on you, you little young twit!

Some day you'll be sorry,
when you just don't fit
into the mold of what we should be.

Because we grow older
and just wish to see
ourselves young again for the moment.
Audrey Goslin

'Tis A Blessing

'Tis a blessing to be Irish
Or at least that's what they say
As we're counting up the numbers
Of the murders in each day

And we all can see the justice
In who's wrong and who is right
So the innocent keep dying
As we struggle in our fight

We claim we are God's people
So to kill is not a sin?
As the battle keeps on raging
Who will lose and who will win?

It's the devil's work we're doing
As the bullets fly today
And 'tis a blessing to be Irish
Or, at least that's what they say.
Mary Ellen Kelliher

Lazy Eyes

Lazy, lazy, lazy eyes.
Watching nothing by-and-by,
Save shifting, drifting shadows,
And swiftly fleeting birds,
Blinking through the sky.

Lazy, lazy, lazy eyes.
Don't even care to wonder why.
Just let it pass. Just let it go.
All the fussing to and fro,
In that busy, dizzy world outside.
Adam Nearon

God's Gift

Everywhere was loneliness,
And weariness that the sound
Of many useless voices,
Had left upon me.

Then your quiet voice came,
Breaking the heavy silence
As the gleam from a distant gypsy fire,
Pierces the purple darkness
Of a windless night.

God had searched the earth,
From end to end, for His best gift
And found for me a friend,
The friend, He found and
Gave to me, was you.
Margaret Ann Rourk

My Love

Do I love thee now
　as I did then,
No my love
　'tis greater now.

Do I see thee now
　as I did then,
Yes my love
　I see thee fine.

Do I know thee now
　as I did then,
I know thee now
　as I never did then.

Do I think of us now
　as I did then,
No my love
　the two are one.

Do I feel thee now
　as I did then,
No my love
　'tis greater now.
Patricia Barnett

A Simple Request

I look into your eyes.
I feel a slight chill.
I hold your hand.
My heart stands still.
I kiss your lips.
You take my breath away.
I hold you close.
It's here I wish to stay.
Look into my eyes.
Can't you see?
Right by your side.
Is where I wish to be.
Hold my hand.
What do you feel?
Can you sense it?
My love for you is real.
So hold me close
Throughout all of time.
And I will be yours
And you can be mine.
Scott Dingle

Drops

Drops of purification
Drift from a clouded sky.
Troops of glistening
Drops trickle upon the land
To run, frolic, and play
Upon the earth below.
Thirsting flowers, plants, and trees
Drink their fill
Of the precious gift sent
From the heavens above.
When they have been satisfied,
The billows of white fluff give way to
The onslaught of the golden
Rays of the majestic sun.
Running from its
Scorching arms of light,
The troops return
To their rightful place
In the clouds above.
Susan M. Hecker

Much More Than A Mom

　You help me through the bad times
You dry all my tears
　You make me feel special, you
calm all my fears.

　I love you so much, you make
my life great
　You're always willing to help
whether it's early or late.

　You are caring and kind
your love could not bend
　And until the end of time
You are my mom and my friend.
I love you!
Robin Yarger

Summer Night

Crimson n' gold.
Periwinkle hue.
From setting sun,
To rising moon.
The day is old,
Night yet young.
For moonlight we are due.
Summer night,
Not afternoon.
Warm n' starry,
Sky like diamond quarry.
To bed? Not yet. Soon.
Navy to black,
Stars on velvet sack.
Sun behind mountain,
Ocean still, like unused fountain.
Half the world to sleep,
While the rest begin to creep.
Mary Segreti

"Memories"

As the years go by,
You have memories of past years...
of good days and bad.
Warm days and cold days
Life and death
You wonder how it went by so fast
So keep hold of your memories
In the end you'll be happy you did.
April L. Nelson

The Moore Parade

A parade is going on,
At the Ocean House
In Watch Hill, Rhode Island,
Right now on the 4th of July,
They are marching outside
Blowing kazoos and waving flags,
They hear waves crashing on the shore,
They smell the salty ocean,
Some are friends
Most are relatives,
Their Grandfather is leading
For it is a parade,
The Moore Parade.

Anna Marie Jane Moore

Hero

Is he my hero,
or is he what I wish I could be?
Or is that just others thinking for me?
For if that's what they think,
and that's how I act.
I think I'm going to sink,
I think I'm going to get fat.
Full of pathetic thinking of what
should I wear, who should I see.
Down to the bottom of what
society thinks I should be.
You know what I think that I'll be me.

Oscar Rodriguez

Rare Ben

Poets stood round
When they came to honor
A bard laid to rest
In Britain's poets' corner
John Milton showed Ben Jonson
Where He preferred
To be interred
When that occasion occurred
Milton soon lay
Where oft he had stood
Among the recumbents
In close brotherhood
Ben Jonson had but one condition
"Bury me", said he
"In an upright position."
Alexander Pope
He's stretched out too
No longer crabby
But Ben Jonson still stands
In Westminster Abbey.

Nell Huddleston

The Beat Poet Forest

I part her
Dreamy
Milky
Smooth
Legs
We moan
as a
Lazy
Pounding
Rain storm
Floods our sexual forest
as a
Cool
Beat music symphony plays

Keros Johnson IV

A Flame In The Darkness

A solitary girl
taller than most
years of change
singing new songs

Shadow horses, blackjack
moonlit nights and black cats
white magic and fire, wishes and stars
lightning and thunder, loyal and strong

No one understands her
but many believe
that howls in the night
are not just of beasts

Corruption and crime
innocents dead
intelligence low
freedom enslaved

The storm is still raging
this girl breathes her last sigh
but hope lives on
in this young woman's eyes

Audra Baker

Just Another Day

I saw your face today
Nothing's really changed
Your eyes still shine like sapphire
Your hair still moves with the wind
Your smile still so charming,
And when you turned and looked my way
I was lost to you in every way
I wanted to follow you back to...
No, no, I must not think that way
I know you would never forgive
We are both where we are to stay
But it still hurts
So I close my eyes
And your vision fades away
And I promise I will always remember
As I sit by your grave.

Melanie M. Dube-Gold

Steady As The Beating Rain

My love for you is strong and deep,
Steady as the beating rain
A secret found is a secret sweet.
Steady as the beating rain

Surprising love with untold bliss,
Steady as the beating rain
Passion deepening with each kiss.
Steady as the beating rain

Slow at first, but don't lose heart,
Steady as the beating rain
One love ends another love starts.
Steady as the beating rain

Strong, and proud; soft and tender,
Steady as the beating rain
Love is just a hearts surrender.
Steady as the beating rain

April Thompson

Untitled

A little bird flew
a dark cloud through
and let the rainbow out.

Mark J. Goodmanson

Pretend Friend

Enough said,
Communication's dead.
Words misread,
This I dread.
Not again,
My pretend friend.
Words that offend,
This message you send.
Non verbals I read,
Have planted the seed.
Growing weeds,
While my heart bleeds.
The vine strangles me,
Can't break free.
Too tall to see,
What's meant to be.
Fighting drones on,
Friendship's gone.
Unhappy song...
So long.

Gary Farnquist

For Christine

The poet smiled
putting his pen down
like a sword upon sand
he is defeated
knowing he has touched
upon the greatest beauty
words that once flowed
like evening rain
now just seem small, futile
in her presence
in a kiss
she breathes my words
and I read her lips
we talk slow and easy
making love to every word left unsaid.

Christopher Dantzig

It Was A Clear Day

It was love on a clear day,
the roses were red the sun was
warm. Our love has changed. It
came and left quickly as the
light shown through on this
sunny day. Even though the love
never left my heart. It came clear
that my life had changed. It was
love on a clear day. The roses
were red, the sun was warm, our
love has changed. Now I'm grown
and each day becomes clear as
I see the sky starts to become blue, again.
It was love on a clear day
the roses were red, the sun
was warm. Our love has changed.

Heidi L. Miller

Sisters, Sisters

Sisters, Sisters can I tell you
they are very kind and gentle.
Until they yell and kick andcry
all the time I'm wondering why.

Sisters, Sisters I have two
One's my twin and the other's not quite two.
But late at night I lay in bed
and thank the Lord when all is said!

Tara Simpson

Dream Of The Midnight Lover

I have a midnight lover
Who comes from out the dark
He cuddles close beside me
And resides within my heart
His form is but a shadow
Protecting me from the night
His touch is but a gentle wind
Pushing reality from sight

His love is but a dream
His words are but a sigh
They sing to me a melody
As the other world passes by

He chases out the darkness
With hopes and love to share
And when I find I need him most
I know he's always there

It's true he's but a fantasy
This midnight lover mine
An alternate reality
Conforming to my design

Lori L. Fritz

Completion

So afraid of dying, so afraid of crying
thoughts of ending flow through you
horrifying impending ending
sudden

Thoughts of today turn to dismay
going to tomorrow, years away
seconds are years as years are seconds
the future beckons

Motivated or dissuaded
either way you feel jaded
are you going to climb or be carried
cremated or buried?

You can sit on the rock
and watch the clock
about your upshot you lament
or continue your ascent

It will not be at the top
that you reach that sudden
If you go now, think not of this
but of joy, happiness, love, and Bliss

Jason Bant

Desolate

Dancing on a moonlit beam
High above the city scene
Social status; dignified
Contemplating suicide

Made it to the top at last
Out-foxed bureaucratic brass
Feeling empty; all alone
Did it all without a home

Which seems to be the missing link
No more hiding in a drink
No one really seems to care
Glory is, only when it is shared

There's no one on this earth to see
Compassion, sensitivity
It's tucked away, within his soul
He gave it up to death...alone

Lawrence James

Crying Out

Her voice is too subtle and soft
to be recognized through the
whistle of the weeping willows.
As she cries out in shame,
the whistling grows louder
and she can feel the
thunder pounding in her heart.
The cry for help so small
that only her mind can hear it.
Someday someone will hear it,
but by that time it will
be too late, her innocence
stripped away by someone untrue,
in the blink of an eye.

Jackie Fox

The Eagle

Lifted on wings of great strength
Stretched to their ultimate length
The eagle is flying alone,
Winging his way toward his home.

A solitary giant upon wing.
Graceful beauty, deeply serene.
He commands this world to be true,
To supply, to protect, to renew.

Wings of metal proudly we fly,
As we conquer the space in the sky
Detached from the privilege to be
In flight with such greatness as he.

We dare in a short span of time
To bring threats to endanger his kind.
We fumble our way, we're unsure
Yet somehow the eagle endures.

Can we learn what the eagle has shown?
A lifetime of love for its own.

Myra J. Block

Michael

A face
met by chance
causing restless responses
draws me into
a stimulating book
like an impressive introduction.
A smile
well written on blank pages.
I skim through carefully
attempting to read.

Phyllis B. Newman

The Bubble

A great big shiny sphere
Floating through the atmosphere.
Higher and higher it goes,
Where it will stop. nobody knows.
Now moving sideways through the air,
Where it goes, nobody cares.
Now coming down to the ground
And then...

POP!!!!

The bubble is nowhere to be found.

Jasmin Islam

My Ideal Of An Angel

Walking high on moon beams,
reaching out for the stars.
Sliding down the milky way,
to get to where you are.

I'd swim the deepest ocean,
and climb the highest peak.
For just a smile from you,
and a tiny kiss on the cheek.

I yearn to reach out and take you,
in my arms and hold you close,
For you're the one I love dear
you're the one I love the most.

You're my ideal of an angel
a bright and shining star.
Stay close by my side dear,
and never drift too far.

Mildred Kimbler

Her Smile

Her smile is all I saw
Whenever I closed my eyes
Now when I picture her face
I feel my heart's demise

She left me all too sudden
It happened all too soon
No chance for any beautiful moments
Like walking under the moon

Hand in hand we would've walked
Under the glow of the moonlit sky
Now she is gone, she's out of my life
And all I can do is ask myself "Why?"

Why did she leave me?
How come she doesn't know
Oh how I loved her
How I loved her so

But all I can do is wait
I've been waiting all this while
And all I can do
Is remember her smile

Eddie Jimenez

You And I Together

You and I together
Somewhere lost in time
A picnic in the hills
As church bells slowly chime
Say only that you love me
It is all I need to hear
Tell me any different
And I will shed a tear
Be my one safe haven
A place where I can hide
Promise me one day
That you will be my bride
There really is no picnic
We are really not a pair
And all I do is sit
And all I do is stare
At a beautiful picture
Deep within my mind
Of you and I together
Somewhere lost in time

Brian L. Davis

The Insomniac

Oh Sleep, where is thine hiding place
   Thine habitual retreat.
The place I seek so often;
   In whose stead I find defeat.

How cunning thine allusiveness;
   How successful thine escape.
And though I've searched for hours,
   To lose thee is my fate.

I find thee so relaxing;
   So good for body, for mind,
Soothing the brow, stilling the heart.
   So much in thee I find.

Ah! Sleep, at last I've found thee;
   In the secret parts thou hid.
Thou anointest my soul with gladness.
   Mine eye has closed its lid.

Please come to me in the quiet night;
   And soothe my tossing frame.
I have great need of thee Oh Sleep.
   I am so glad you came!

Ellen Phillips

Fears

The door of the past is behind me
The door to the future's before
I stand in the hallway between them
Dreading to open either door.

Why can't I just sit in the hallway
Call a halt to the days and the years?
Escape from the past with its memories
And the future with its tears?

Oh, the door to the past is bolted
No light can creep thru its cracks.
There is no light in the darkness
Even if I could go back.

The door to the future is bolted.
No light can creep thru its cracks.
There is no light in the darkness
Even if I could go back.

The door to the future is bolted.
Time places the keys in my hand.
Death is a far strange country
And I'm not a curious man.

K. C. Swart

"Dreams"

Before awakening
Behind closed eyelids
Beyond reality
During the night
Under warm covers
Within a safe place
Among the clouds
Like a floating balloon
Past, present, and future
In back of my mind
Over the years
Since when and why
Because of what
According to whom
In place of this
In spite of that
From hour to hour
Toward morning's dawn
Ahead of a new day
Until tonight!

Erica DeGarmo

No Ordinary Woman

She is no ordinary woman; she's
   very warm and dear.
Even when I've failed her, she's
   always kept me near.

She has taken much abuse from me;
   more than most could take.
And though I've never meant to hurt
   her, I often make mistakes.

She tries to understand me, in
   everything I do.
And never condemns me; instead she
   sees me through.

This woman that I speak of; is
   my mother and my friend.
A very special woman; whose love
   seems to have no end.

I hope when I am older and raise
   children of my own,
That I can give the love she gives
   and make their house a home.

Mary Longo-Roberson

Deep Down Inside

Deep down inside of me
   There's another part.
Deep down in my soul,
   Waiting to be explored.
A hope doesn't have to remain a hope
   and a fantasy a fantasy.
It's all about you and that
   special voice, that says:
Don't take away my hope or
   leave me in despair
Give me a rope and I'll climb
   the highest mountain.
Don't take away my dreams
   and leave me thoughtless
Give me a chance and I'll find
   my own way.

Earline M. Sims Verdin

Suicidal

For Andrew

I want to go,
I have no reason to stay,
but how will I know,
just what they would say.
I don't like it here,
not in this time,
I have shed many a tear,
but, I won't whine.
Maybe it will get better,
but what if it does not,
People will say, "why her,"
maybe I should not.
Life is so mysterious,
Why throw it all away?
I think this is all just subconscious,
and maybe I'll stay.
I now have a reason to go,
but I've many to stay,
and, maybe I now know,
just what they would say.

Shannon Jackson

Temporary

In the eyes of a poet
agony galore
past shadows
creep through
once more
Time floats backward
memories invade
of all that was seen
the difference
it made
the poet is weary
if just for awhile
a dark world
returns
she forgets how to smile....

Jennifer Guterman

The Hand That Feeds

Live my whole damn life
trying to gain your simple faith
but just when I thought I impressed you
you turn your back and look away

What mountain must I climb
to make you proud of me
just a minor compliment
I ask on bended knee

My dreams were not your own
so to me your heart turned cold
instead of moral support
I was wrong is what you told

All I ask is for your praise
and to help me when I fall
for what better motivation
than you beside me standing tall

What is it you expect of me
shall I give in to the rat race
or do I go my own way
and make history save my place

Joel Justyna

Friends

A friendship seems too many,
a hopeful, endless,
dream.

To others, it's reality
buried beneath the
seams.

Then there are the few,
who have searched both
far and wide.

I know I am the lucky one,
to have you by my
side.

Ami E. Weiser

Mirror

Take your bucket to the ocean,
And dip it in the sea.
Gaze deep down in swirling waters,
And tell me what you see.

I see God upon the ocean,
Laughing at eternity.
And in the bucket's swirling waters,
I see me.

Stacy Olney

Noctilucousphilia

Day is done.
Night's begun.
Enter moon reflect the sun.

Day is torn.
Night is born.
See the moon it looks so worn.

Day is gone.
Night has dawned.
See the moon it seems to yawn.

Day withers,
Night slithers,
A full moon brings out killers.

Day's passed by.
Night is nigh.
See the moon it needs to die.

Andrew B. Roberts

Tomorrow

Will tomorrow really come?
We all act as if it's there.
We go about our daily lives,
Like fools without a care.

When we go to bed at night,
We do without a care,
For each of us truly feels,
Tomorrow will be there.

Only our dear Lord above,
Knows what's in his plan.
If we will wake tomorrow
Or beside him we will stand.

Show your friends and family
Your endless love today,
Then should the Lord take you home
The love you shared will stay.

Will tomorrow really come?
I'm sure I can not say.
So give the gift of love
To those you meet today.

Terry L. Wilkinson

Endless Sleep

My lungs respond, but there's no air,
As I struggle to survive,
It hurts to know that they don't care,
Whether or not I stay alive.

The world is growing dark now,
As I drift toward the light,
I want to cry out somehow;
If I had the strength I might.

I feel like I am falling,
Into a great abyss.
I hear past loved ones calling,
As I taste Death's tender kiss.

Finally, I have found some peace,
My soul is God's to keep,
I have finally gained release,
By slipping into endless sleep.

Katherine Grams

What Happened To Spring?

It's supposed to be sunny
It's supposed to be free
But snow and ice is all that I see

You might think it's warm
I tell you it's not!
What if it never, ever gets hot?

The birds are confused
I wonder why
Is it because
Spring is too shy
To come out and play
This very first day?

Lara Nagle

The Rose You Gave Me I Still Have

The rose you gave me I still have
for this is the only rose I have had.

I remember you, you had a big smile
and a warm touch.
I can no longer touch your body.

You're no longer mine, and now that
red rose has died.

I cry 'cause you're no longer mine
Every time I see that red rose I hurt,
I hurt for you.

Please just give me at least another
red rose I promise I won't let it die.

Paula Ward

To Be Known

I would like to be
shaped by the risks
I've taken. I know
that's going to include
wrinkles, and I hope that
the way I appear to
others is shaped by
all the edges I have
come to in my life, and
most of all, by the
faces I have looked
into with love.

Dolores Doyle

"The Sorrow"

A man's mother's illness
caused a sorrow.
but the man thought
there will always
be tomorrow.
Today in the world
there are a lot of
diseases.
When the diseases are
gone everyone is pleased.
maybe the reason why
a lot of people aren't
healthy.
It's because the world
is nasty and filthy.

Eunice Yang

Life

Full and amazing of
empty thoughts,
bearing tree limbs
bound to break.

We have faith to
hold on to,
the limbs have
a trunk.

We have God to
listen to,
they have wind.

We have praises,
they have shade.

Altogether they
fit as one,
altogether we're
losing some.
The tree falls,
we "rise."

Ashley McGee

An Easter Prayer

Dear Lord, I pray forgive me;
my heart's been black as night.
You died for sins of ones gone wrong;
now help me see the light.
You've given me so very much,
why did I pass it by?
Can you condole the hurt I've caused
before my time to die?
What can I do to make things right,
to soothe the ones I love,
to make the world a better place
before I go above?
I thank the Lord for being you
and listening to my prayer;
and on this easter morning
it's nice to know you're there.

Cindy Ann Davis

Grandfather

Grandfather
Father of she who bore me
Father of those who have bore me
taught me
through the life I live

Jason
Apples and crackers
and Tonka toys

Quietly yet so keenly heard
Although, sadly
you have long been gone
Your mark has always, somehow
guided me
Your influence always so dearly
known

Jeff Dobson

Untitled

Hour's sand
trickles from an iridescent sky
I reach out to grasp
it slips through my bloody fingers

All within silver eyes
mornings fade to grey
a numbness clouds
only rain can make it real

Heather Elko

Gettysburg

The battle of battles,
a war of its own,
each side stays together,
no man stands alone.

As shots ring out
and cannons fire,
for each man that falls,
a flag is held higher.

Brother against brother,
Grant against Lee,
One or the other,
who will it be?

As the fire burns down,
The smoke begins to clear,
each man looks around,
in each eye is a tear.

Jessica Cobillas

A Moment Behaves

A moment behaves
In my escape
Away
To a place
Scenic and robust.
Not a shiver of cold
Any crackles of old
Brittles this castle day.
A cheer for bread
And thirst no more
Whales of haste
I see no more
And still further....
This place
Behaves no more.

Darryl Rosenberg

Boston Harbour

The stormy Atlantic churns
The Indians were a history
Before time as we know it, began
This ocean vastness, the shore
Did they ponder across the sea
As I do now,
Thinking of ancestors
From some foreign country
Sinking roots like an oak
Belonging, clinging to shore
To here, to a future
And the hewing trees and forest
And the building of place
Covered the past, what was
Almost without a trace.
They too stood here
Looking at this ocean,
Only to be vaguely
Remembered.

Jeanne Cooper

Loneliness

Loneliness is a rough
Page in one's lifebook
It slowly eats away
At one's mental shake

Loneliness in not a cool thing.
Oh! The sadness it brings.

So cheer up; step out of the rear!
Remember that God always, forever holds
   you dear.

Andrea Wynter

God's Universal Love

These are the things you need to know
As into manhood you will grow,
The Pentateuch, the Decalogue,
The laws sent down to us by God.
The Gospels and their precious story
Of Christ and his eternal glory.
God made us to be as He,
To blend as in a symphony.
All shades of color, races, and creed,
To meet the basic human need
Of understanding and brotherly love,
Of peace on earth, sign of the dove.
These must be taught to everyone
As I teach them to you, my son.

Helen Crews

Untitled

Dawn's pale light gently caresses
each perfectly formed petal.
A velvet rose yawns, stretches,
opens up to the world.
The early light creates an illusion as
the blossom begins to glow from within.
Its aura speaks of warmth, joy,
the innocence of first love

Bessie Denise Harbison

My Time

My past is gone forever and
   The future wears a mask
I can't recapture yesterday
   Tomorrow slips my grasp

I ask of life where is my time?
   The question echoes far
The answer is returned to me
   Bedazzled by a star

Seek not in memories nor in what
   Has yet to brush your brow
Your time is ever happening,
   This moment, called the Now.

Marie G. Coolidge

Snowfate

Frosty minuets
Dancing ever down
Bitter gust blasts
White streaks
Lasers across the night
But on they fall
Only moments of glory
Were all.

Paul Marsh Rice

Life

Oh, reckless life
   why irresponsibility -
The waves of turmoil
   so obvious see -
Time is a mire twinkle
   in eternal space -
Responsibility must be
   in a heavenly place -
Call to the Father
   to help run the race -
An expression for peace
   is on life's face.

Paul Jeter

Feelings Change

My feelings change
you're not alone.
I think it's time
that we should be strong.

Fighting for love
it's hard to do,
try to understand after,
all we've been through.

We had some good times,
and some bad ones too,
we said some things that
weren't always true.

But somehow I knew, I
could always count on you.

We should try just to
be friends,
cause that way it wouldn't
be the end!

Teri Sanford

Renaissance

The wise moon winks
Through the whispers
In a eucalyptus.

What is the meaning
Of this elipsis?

Aroused by Jasmine's
Fragrant kisses,
I think I know
What this is.

Truth and beauty without name,
Become manifest once again.

In the renaissance
Of my poetic refrain,
Measure what I may feign.

In life's tree lined lane,
Be that which keeps me sane.

Michael Stein

The Search

If you seek to find yourself
   beware of limitation
Don't try to be like someone else
   merely imitation
Go deep inside your heart and mind
   and seek your answer there
Let the world know what you find
   some of us still care

Terry J. Neuschafer

Love

I behold every move you make,
and with aspect not one mistake,
never lifting my eyes from yours,
we don't have anytime to sore,
with our love we have to think
we only have it for awhile.
I love you more than life itself.
For my love for you is all my wealth,
I will love you forever until the day
has come for us to part
but until then we will never be apart.

Shila Magsig

Mary Dear

Merry Christmas, Mary dear
the house is quiet now.
And although I know you're gone
I feel you near somehow.

Mary, the children all were here
sharing gifts beneath the tree.
And a coat, hat and gloves
the grand kids brought for me.

Our daughters got the dinner up
just like you used to do.
Complete with all the trimmings
and the flaming pudding, too.

We sang some carols by the fire
and watched the embers glow.
It was like the times we shared
so many years go.

I'm feeling old and tired now,
perhaps my end is near.
Next Christmas I may be with you,
I miss you, Mary dear.

Carl E. Wegner

Untitled

Look at me,
  look at me...
I'm the girl that can't be seen.
the shadows,
  fall
the shadows that fall across me
carry my obscurity
  like a tomb.
I walk.... And I walk
  I walk here every day.
had you noticed?... No?
but - I like to be real.
I'm walking here,
  every day.
I know you don't see,
(that these lost eyes are me)
alone at my table
  in my book in my hurt
You didn't know that, did you.
Look At Me!

Heather Brockman

Snow

The flakes of snow
dance from the sky like
a million white fairies
caught up in the wild swirling
melody of the wind.

Gary W. Farvour

Spring

The robins say cheer-up, cheer-up
We know that Spring is here
But how can we believe it
When the days are dark and drear?
When snow hides in the corners
And the wind blows icy blasts,
When branches creak and moan and grown
An winter lasts and lasts?

Look up and see the blue sky
Peeping through the clouds of gray,
Look down and see the crocus
Pushing timidly away.
Look deep inside yourself
And feel the hope that's taking wing
And listen to the robins
It is really, truly Spring!

C. J. Ashley Jr.

Friends

Knowing her was fun.
Being her friend was nice.
Now, we're best of friends.
We'd play in the warmth of the sun.
But she's sick.
Very sick.
She can't play anymore.
She could die.
They say she won't live to
The next year.
I'm gonna cry.
I've known her all my life,
And now she might lose hers.
She's my grandma.

Shannon Longenecker

Hitler Victorious

If the world was white,
bland, empty palette,
no shades, no hues,
If the world was white
dull, repetitious eyes,
No colors, except blues,
If the world was white,
pale, blonde hair,
No kinks, just straight,
If the world was white,
ask yourself, whom,
whom shall I hate?

Stephanie H. Williams

Admire

Smooth as velvet, a poet.
In my mind, you are like a
flowers protective leaves,
induced to nurture the
existence of a beautiful
revelation.
I admire you so, and I
want you to know,
that I am heavily effected
by your range and exterior
for the blessings of euthenics.

A composer you are, and
I, am overwhelmed with
your measure.

Keeshawn C. Matthews

I Am For Real

Each day I enter to triumph,
A new outlook takes place.
My endurance is immense
As the shadows overtake a days end.
Tomorrows are to no sorrows,
Then promises become the token
Of a way to get by.
Today is existent.
Unfolding instinct to mislead.
Questions arise. Influenced are
Progressive, while showing worthiness
To be profitable.
Another to grant bestows euthenics.
In a degree unbelievable.
Faith is to persevere.
Are you for real?
I am for real!
Do you pursue aiming ambitiously,
Rotation in a mass of apathy,
Or is the strength at worry
Unleashing multiple desires
To average "I shall prevail".
Are you for real?
I am for real!

Kathy G. Smith

Peace

Peace is love and joy
Collected through the years
That's in your heart forever
Through happiness and tears.

Peace is true harmony
Found only in your heart
It makes you feel so special
When the magic begins to start.

Peace is caring for each other
That truly is sincere
So it will ring out happiness
Throughout the coming year.

Peace is togetherness
Always with your friends
And peace means so much to me
I hope it never ends.

Joe Gizzi

Untitled

Mother's Day is a time to
share and let you know how
much I care.
  You treat me like a flower so
small and very sweet the
feelings that you give me never
will be beat!
  You treat me like a rose as
red as it can be. Roses if you
didn't know mean love from
you to me.
  You treat me like a orchid so
thoughtful and so kind whenever,
you are far away, you're
always on my mind.
  You treat me like an iris
your promises you will keep
and even when it's not
Mother's Day, my love for
you is deep.

Natalie Gabhart

The Homeless

We see them in the bed that they
sleep in, a cold wooden bench.
Where will they go tomorrow?
When their children are cold,
where will they go?

In front of shelters they stand,
empty plates in their hands.
Where will they go tomorrow?
When they are hungry,
where will they go?

We hold our ears and deny,
the problem and reply;
where will they go tomorrow?
When their children are crying,
where will they go?

I think it's time for an answer
to the question we ponder.
Where will they go tomorrow?
When we pass them by,
where will they go?

Amanda Kennedy

Dreams

All my dreams are changing every day,
  in every possible way.

Sometimes I wonder why,
  but all the time just passes by.

Nightmares never visited me,
  but now I have to pay their fee.

Now my dreams are full of fears,
  and I always wake up with tears.

I never want to go to sleep,
  because my mind always goes so deep.

I hope my dreams don't get me lost,
  because my life would be the cost.

Danielle Bulzomi

Me

These changing times I'm glad to see
Them making a great change in me.
One where I feel that I can be
The hidden self I've longed to free.
The person that did cry and plea
Has gone away to ever free.
Just hoping he will let me be
The woman now that is the me.

And if he does not try to do
Reverse the me to old from new,
We may just make it if the clue
Rubs off of me and onto you.
Because a change would make the blue
Spread through my body like a flu.
Resentment sticks and does like glue
So don't change me to just suit you.

Linda C. Grass

Kitten

Once my sisters found a kitten.
At first he didn't feel like sittin'.
He is the cutest thing I ever saw,
It's a good thing he won't be a ma.

Jessica Handy

Midwest Sorrow - National Shame

On a day like today
Yesterday or tomorrow
It started quite normal
But ended with sorrow
On a day like today
With the sun in the sky
By ten in the morning
We would all wonder why
On a day like today
From here on to forever
No one could forget
Not a soul, not ever
On a day like today
As we ask ourselves why
Those women, children
And men had to die
We must stand as a Nation
and as a Nation we'll say
We will bury no more
On a day like today

Randy Michaud

Untitled

Let go of the bitterness, if
just for a day...
Let the Lord take your pain
away.

Turn that frown into a smile
If not just for awhile.

Try picking out the good
in the face of bad
try to laugh when you're
feeling sad.

The love you shared will always
be there...
To go doesn't mean
You didn't care

Tina Levasseur

Michele's Blessing

There's a time
When there's no room
No one to grab onto
To listen, to share, to laugh

So many bring you down
Touched by their cruel words
Poisoned by their selfishness
Left alone to hurt

Take a look in the mirror
That face is loved
A cherished remembrance
A welcomed sight

Know that you are acknowledged
That you are missed
Your presence is blessed
Your words are heard

Hold on to your wishes
Enjoy the person you are
A moment away
Someone wants to hear your voice.

Joy Nicole Pendola

Together Forever

In the morning when I rise
My thoughts turn first to you
I made it safely through the night
The morning sky is blue
Then through the day you're by my side
I share my thoughts with you
You're ever there, you'll always be
Though sometimes I can't really see
Then evening comes and we're apart
I yearn for you with all my heart
I cannot sleep, alone and blue
I toss and turn and long for you
When suddenly it dawns on me
I love you so, we'll always be
Together, forever in my heart

Marilyn G. Delehanty

Alaina

I have a question,
I want to know.
When did you get big?
When did you grow?
It makes me happy,
yet I could weep,
when I get a chance,
to watch you sleep.
First I saw your eyes
all bright and blue,
your skin was lovely,
soft, pink and new.
That wasn't long ago,
it seems like yesterday
Tomorrow you'll be grown
and going your own way.
They say you get out of life,
what you put in it.
I will remember this
and enjoy every minute

Pam Thomas

I Am

I am one with the sky,
I am on the bird's wing.
I am the ocean and all that's in it,
I am the trees and grass.
I feel all the pain and struggle,
The anguish and the destruction.
I feel the happiness, and joy,
The pride, triumph and the love.
I see the colors of emotion,
I see the music as if fills the air.
I know all the fact and fiction,
I see bits and pieces of ahead.
I am the world.

Naomi L. Hatfield

Alone

Here I stand, all alone,
with no one beside me,
no one to comfort me
in times of need,
no one to say "I love you!"
When I am sad,
no one to laugh with,
no one to share my
joys, tears, or triumphs.
No one at all.
Here I stand, all alone.

Jehae Kim

On The Sunset

Having seen so many
Few come to mind
Yet all seem so graceful
Each meaning sublime
A showing of fine, cutting grace
As a lifetime slips away
A burning, blazing marvel
But only a day
It just seems so pointless
A mechanical charade
Then again behind me
And already it starts to fade
What dreams it must concoct there
While cloistered in its room
Perhaps the answer lies
Swimming with the moon
Andrew A. Blacker

Edges

Confusion, indecision.
My life and others.
It's the same old song.
Moving, twisting, changing,
towards our own humanity.
We knife the attack of life,
and fight for a fleeting edge.
Yet the edge will crumble.
falling to the shore below.
It's not bad, not really,
at least the way it sounds.
It's just the way the ball bounces.
So keep going,
keep pushing,
and finding new edges of security.
They'll crumble,
but you'll keep going.
Because we're human,
we have to, must to,
or else we'll stop living.
Andrew Auton

Footsteps

One night I find myself
walking alone
I hear footsteps other than
my own,
I look and see but there is
no one behind me,
What should I do? What
should I do?
Should I scream?
Am I scared or not?
If I am scared then
can I run? The thought
passes on and on through
my mind, I can't see if there
is someone behind me.
Rachel Pearl

The Pinwheels's Color

Red, orange, yellow, blue
There are other colors, too.
Green, purple, black, and brown
Can be seen all over town.

Spinning round and round
Bouncing up and down.
Colors fly everywhere
Making people feel the air.
Patricia Dembro

I Wish That Life Was Again Simple

I wish that life was again simple
  As when I was just a child
Thinking the world could be mine
  Bought with just a smile

No worries about bills or work
  Just playing from dawn to dusk
No problems that Mom could not solve
  No harsh realities for us

But as I grew and come to know
  The games were drawing to an end
From grammar school to Jr. High
  High School and college to begin

All at once here am I
  A wife, two kids and a dog
A house, a car and taxes due
  Wondering what happened to it all

I wish that life was again simple
  As when I was just a child
Thinking the world could be mine
  Bought with just a smile
Jesse T. Craft

Lost Hope

Darkness fades to light
White object so bright
Straying from my cage
I am free
Pen to paper, one more page
Float above the pain
I am able to fly

Light fades to night
Struck down
I am unable to fight
A false sense of hope
Brings reality crashing to my feet
The sadness overwhelms
Another fight, I am beat
Erica McAnally

Life...

  The sun shines upon the
glistening lake, awakening all
that lives within the lake:
fish, bears, birds, deer...
  Life each day begins with
the rising of the sun, and one's
thinking process awakens with
one's self, leaving behind the
dreams of their sleep.
  Life does not necessarily end
with death — but will only,
really end, with the permanent
set of the sun...
Donna M. Walker

Italian Garden

Moonlight kisses
cold marmor cheek-
did you see
its lonely marmor tear?
Brigitte Christine Caperton

Untitled

I think
Day in - day out
Numbers and words
Slang and jargon
Stampedes of thoughts and ideas
A traffic jam of thought
Noisy and impatient
Bumper to bumper
Ideas
All I do is think
and think
and think
and...
One of these days
I will think too much
I will think too long
And in my desperation
I will give myself away
And feel.
Mary F. Rudloff

Once In Life

Sometimes we talk, makes me cry
Sometimes I wish the memories will die
Sometimes I wanna do it again
Sometimes it just depends
Sometimes I wish I was there
Sometimes I think I'm going insane
Sometimes you say it ain't fair
Sometimes I think I get the blame
I saw a lot of pain
I felt a lot of pain
If I stayed would it be the same
Would it make it easier
I'm sick of this life
I'm sick of this town
If I said 'I love you'
It's because I loved you
When I said I need you
It's because I needed you.
Steve M. Mazur

Consorts

You are my consort
I received your solidarity
You are an unique individual
I've learned a lot from your solidarity.
I am remorseful for all the
  unintelligent things I've done in the past.
Please reprieve me for all the
  ludicrous things I have done.

I hope our solidarity matures
  through out the narrow
  hairbreadth future.
We are consorts forever.
Kristian Hoffman

Little Brothers

Dedicated to my brother Lawrence
Sometimes they can be a bug
And they'll quarrel and fight with you all night
But when you see those lights go out
You know there's a special
  little brother standing at the door
With a pillow under one arm
And teddy in the other waiting for you
  to flap back the covers and say
  "There's room for two"!!!
Larissa J. Alarcon

Help Me Find My Way

Will I ever find my way.
What road will I take.
Left, right or straight ahead.
I feel so lost without your hand.
Without your arms to hold me.
Without your strength and wisdom.
You're here but you're not.
How do I find you?
If I reach out my hand will you care?
Ore will you be too busy to see it?
Please help me find my way
Along this journey of life
I need to know you care
That I count I am here
Which road do I take?
Pat Williams

God Gave Me A Gift

God gave me a gift
he made it sweet and gave it a kind heart.

He gave it a beautiful smile
and a gentle touch.

He gave it more love to share
then you can imagine.

Every time I hold my gift in my arms.
I thank God for giving
me a gift as loving as you.

Margaret Ann Ready

Black

Shadows
Blurred, twisted shadows
Memories you don't want to remember
Crying from
within
Feeling alone in a crowd
Shattered glass — why?
Nightmares again
Even though you're innocent
Of course
But
aren't we all?
Irene Yen

Rainbow Dreams

There's a rainbow just around the bend.
Many colors does it hold,
Also many dreams at its golden end.
So I've been, many times, told.

But as the days grow old
And the years pass you by,
Are they really worth the gold
That's never been seen by you or I?

You have to have faith and love,
Keep hoping dreams will come true.
For many things happen from above.
That none can explain, not even you!

Jody Tanner

Life

(Love wins romance and scorn;
adventurers cheat death;
birth brings joy and pain;
Heaven and hell. Mind and body.)
Is poetry.
Tamatha A. Anthony

Vulnerable

You reached out your hand
Promised to set me free,
I took it in good faith
But only got misery.

I thought that you loved me
Everything would be alright,
So I tore down the shield
That I had built during life.

I opened my heart to you
Gave you everything I could give,
I built a foundation of love around you
You were my reason to live.

Then you left me in desolation
Just walked out of my life,
You left my heart bleeding
As if pierced with a knife.

Will I ever get over you?
I sit and wonder this now,
It's so hard to forget
But I'll make it somehow.
Barbara Gray

Drugs Are Dangerous

Drugs are dangerous as can be.
It changes your life,
can destroy a family.
So when you take your first try,
you better learn to steal and lie.
It's what will happen
when you use.
No matter the substance
you will lose.
Not only yourself
but everything that's close.
Your family will hurt,
you'll not even know.
You won't understand.
You won't even care.
Even when you land in jail.
Larenna Houser

Passion Flow

Listen to the thunder roar
See the lightning flashing bright
I sit alone and wonder
If you are remembering too
Another time not so long ago
When I would hold you
You would kiss me
And the passion would flow
They sky darkens
I think about our love
And how it darkened, too
Could there ever be a time
We could chase away the storm
Look deep into each other's eyes
And let the passion flow
Shelby Mae

Loneliness

Loneliness is a frightening state
Cold and black and full of wait
I try to think of other things
But all that comes is emptiness
I feel so alone and in despair
Why won't God let me be part of a pair?
Kathleen A. Miller

The Moon

The moon is, on a starless
  night
Shining as a beacon, a wondrous
  light
Her glory from the darkness
  descends
Seeking to heal the earth, it
  mends
Broken souls and broken
  wings
Through the darkness, she to us
  sings,
Tales of warmth and hope
  and love
All come to us from above.
Misty M. Thompson

One Hundred Years of Glory

Six continents they come from
Thousands of athletes 'round the world,
One flame will unite them
And their common goal of gold.

One city has its glory
Three winners take home pride,
One motto tells their story
Of "Stronger, faster, higher."

One chance at golden victory
Or four more years they'll wait,
One hundred years have gone past
The Olympic's brazen gates.
Mike Strong II

Meaningless Victory

I'll never forget
Our day of victory -
I'll remember always and always

I'll never forget
When we laid down our guns -
I'll remember always and always

I'll never forget
How ecstatic we were -
I'll remember always and always

But most of all
I'll never forget
Those who died - our side and theirs -
I'll remember always and always

Was it worth it?

P.S. May they all rest in peace.
Loredana Luisi

Softer Petals

Flowers, nature's natural blooms.
Makes me smile, the colors so blessed!
Petals so silky, Oh! so soft!!!
Leaves of moisten - filled with dew!
They have freedom, to grow.
No matter where they go!
Flowers show freedom to me,
And wisdom beyond enlightening!
Carla S. Pampain

Berkana (Rebirth)

I dreamt I gave birth
the baby's heart was
outside her body.

To save her little life
I returned her heart
to her body.

Then I gave birth
to my heart
it was scared

I opened it up
inside was a small
black spot.

I cherished my
new baby with her
pure heart.

Awakened I found
my arms were empty.
No baby, no heart.
   Cindy L. Kittelson

Where Are You

Where are you,
tonight my love
Are you under the stars
or with them above
Haven't heard,
from you in a while
Was hoping to see you
and give you a smile
But now only tears,
fall down my face
Since you said good-bye
I lost the race
Leaving you behind
to me was so tough
But turning your back
was pain enough
Walking away
was so easy for you
Now heartache and anger
was never so true
   Lauren N. Vicidomini

If I Can Fly

If I can fly
I will fly over the tallest mountain
If I can
If I can fly
I will fly over the biggest ocean
If I can
If I can fly
I will fly over North America
If I can
If I can fly
I will fly with the birds
If I can
If I can fly
I will fly into your arms
If I can
I would
   LeeRoy Lucas

To Frances

What can I say
I can say
I love thee
But then - alas
I am shackled
By limitations
Of mere expression
How meaningless
The spoken word
How incompetent the pen
Rather it be
A divine tacitness
Extolled by only my kiss
Felt by only my heart.
   Michael D. Arietano

Life On Edge

Taste of salt in my mouth,
From the sweat dripping down.
 The heat of fear coming close,
No stopping now, can't lose hope.
 Seeing through the eyes of a child,
Growing up amongst the wild.
 This pathetic society wanting peace,
Can't get it, too much greed.
 Falling down with religious fakes,
Standing up on unstable legs.
 Future leaders, they're very weak.
Correcting others no room to speak.
 Trusting God to end this disgrace,
Finding peace in heaven's place.
   Marie Christine Lister

Monsters

They're under your bed.
They hide in your closet.
They're under your skin.
They hide in your heart.
Monsters, Monsters Everywhere!
They keep you from sleeping.
They keep you from dreaming.
They keep you from loving.
They keep you from living.
Monsters, Monsters Everywhere!
You can't run from them.
You can't hide from them.
You can't forget them.
You can't avoid them.
Monsters, Monsters Everywhere!
You must turn on the light.
You must get out of the dark.
You must learn to live.
But first,
You have to get out of bed.
   Marina Silva

"An Ode To My Wife Who Abides With Me"

My little dolinka
My little turtle dove
My little dove of the desert
Whooooo I love very much
Now and forever
   Mick Chetterton

Crazy

Running in circles,
wasting my time.
Following foot steps,
I seem to lose mine.

Cheerfully laughing,
With nothing to say.
Being self-conscious
again today.

Chattering lightly,
floating on air.
Sliding down rainbows,
that aren't even there.

Bumping into walls,
not feeling the pain.
Hearing the patter,
not seeing the rain.

My only excuse,
for the things I do,
is simply because,
I'm crazy about you.
   Kari Springer

The Sunday Exodus

There we eat raw
stoning your Christ
chanting the hymn
soaking in life

Deeper than action
pleasure in feasting
rest of reflection
rape of perversion

Heavier than nature
passion without being
fiction of sentiment
death in the origin

Puzzle of the ages gone
lost in the enormity
infinity with windows
truth of nothing and despair
   Northon Arbelaez Jr.

Once

Once as I was walking
 on a path through the trees
A flower with all its beauty
 brought me to my knees
I wanted so dearly to pluck it
 but no matter how I tried
I couldn't bring myself to ruin
 this flower that I spied
So I sat there and watched
 as it tottered in the breeze
Then looking up to Heaven
 I got up from my knees
I gave a smile and thanked my God
 for pleasures such as these
Then sighed a sigh and turned my back
 and walked on through the trees.
   Joe Sarkies

Look At A Puddle

Look at a puddle,
What do you see?
Do you see rose petals,
Looking at me?

Do you see the moon,
And the darkest night?
Or a picket fence,
All covered in white?

Do you see the night,
When the night is green?
Don't try to wake up,
Because it is not a dream.

Do you see waves,
From the puddle's floor?
Yes I see this,
And so much more.

But when the puddle dries up,
What do you see?
All I know is,
I used to see me.

Brittany O'Quinn

Untitled

I walk alone on unsteady ground
   The black night surrounds me
I reach out blindly
   unsure of myself
I choke on silence
   I stumble over nothing
Still I press on
   knowing there is an answer
I know I'll find it
   and with it — light
Nothing will stop me
   Victory shall be mine
I walk on through the mist
   Determination guides me
     The sun begins to rise

Candi Mathews

You're Not The One With The Broken Heart

Today I was sitting on my porch
and I wondered how you were?
And, I also thought you should
be great cause,

You're Not The One With The
  Broken Heart!

As I listen to sad music and
my eyes fill up with tears
you're probably off somewhere
else laughing cause,

You're Not The One With The
  Broken Heart!

It'll probably take me awhile
to date again
but for you, you'll probably
have a girlfriend every weekend cause,

You're Not The One With The
  Broken Heart!

C. Yourish

Where Pansies Grow

Long ago, and far away,
beneath a summer sky,
sheltered by a canopy
of proud woods standing high.

Amid acorns and mosses,
soft forest floorings find,
a child's small foot upon it,
I see it in my mind

I seek a fond desire,
a daylong hide-away,
a place known by no other,
where wild, the pansies play,

There a long crow calls me,
cows low, and clouds float by,
there a stream speaks softly,
where forest fairies play.

I often go there in my mind,
and press the soft earth low,
my childhood room is waiting there,
where still, the pansies grow.

Mary Caruso

My Secret Harbors

A secret, an unfulfilled dream.
I feel a great beginning,
A tremendous soaring within my veins.
Powerful, raging ambitions
swell within my deepest inner chamber.
What can bring my dreams to fruition.
Are my struggles in vain?
Can I appease the dramatic
forces which urge me forward?
I face the sternest of trials.
My courage is strengthened by
my resolve to succeed.
My final prize is the realization
that I have conquered my fears
and overcome my past.

Janice M. Goetz

Tears

The tree outside the window
was crying after the rain.
Its diamond tears were clinging to the
Blue spruce needles
as if it would never rain again.

The long limbs hung down
with the weight of tears, a burden
to bear in quiet shame.

When would the sunshine come
to dry our tears?
When would our sorrow end?
We looked at each other
in rain - washed air,
and tears washed pain.

Vera Brantley

Mate

Beneath the touch of tender skin,
A hunger for love burns deep within.
I pray my heart and give my soul
to find the one that makes me whole.

Antoine E. Modica

Nurses - Unsung Heroes

Theirs is a lifetime of giving,
Always in action,
In good or stormy weather,
All hours of the day.
Giving hope to complete strangers,
Help brighten days for many.
It takes love to help,
Ease pain and sorrow.
They are "Unsung Heroes",
True "Angels of Mercy",
With their gift of giving
Their work a precious gift to all.

Helen Elodora Harlow

Hunger Pains

The little people,
tearing at my stomach,
make it hard for me
to be in reality.
I try to show them that I care
by feeding their greedy mouths.
But they don't understand.
They think it's a joke
when I give them a poke.
I wish they would realize
that I'm in charge,
and they just have to wait.

Shelley Bowers

The Lonely

The lonely know
The painful condition,
A bilious woe,
With a bitter prediction.

Sleep comes poorly,
Can't concentrate;
Disposition's surly,
For appointments, you're late.

You look in the mirror,
And see someone - no good.
You'd like to escape,
If you believed that you could.

Walls close around you,
You're cold and afraid;
As the dark night enfolds you,
In the cloister you've made.

No one wants to be lonely,
It's hard to break out
Of the tightening knot,
That crushes life out.

Marshall Kline

Gypsy

A gypsy lady, strong and true
Is this one a part of you?
Standing tall but feeling low
Letting others tell you so
much of just how you should act
Not keeping on your own straight track.
Who am I? you wonder after while
wishing, yourself, to be a child.

Deborah L. Wildes

The Clouds

The clouds are blue,
Sort of like you.
You have to agree,
It's mostly like me.
But you don't know,
That clouds can grow.
The clouds are up high,
Up way in the sky.
The clouds are blue or white,
It's next to the sun's light.
I wonder how they stay up there,
Way up, up there in the air.
I can't believe it,
That I can see them move a bit.
Clouds are full of fluff,
But the clouds are not buff.
Can't be more wrong,
But clouds are strong.
It's nice to see clouds now,
Go now, see the clouds.

Teresa Nunez

Life

To feel the pain of loss of life.
To never feel or have a thought.

To think of only times in past.
And feel the strife of life that last.

To never know what love can
touch, a tear, a smile, a sigh, a glow.

But when it's done it's said it's past.
I wonder how it went so fast.

William R. Hallman

Still With You

The loved one who
has passed away
is always with you
night and day.

His arms are wrapped around you
with a summer breeze,
Hear him softly whisper
with the swaying of the trees.

The day begins
with the singing of the bird.
Listen with your heart
and you will often hear his word.

The cold winter days
will make you shiver.
Don't worry none
it's just a kiss he can't deliver.

The night begins
with the shining of the moon.
You will feel his warmth again
sometime real soon.

Tamera Hause

Wind Ghosts

Empty schoolyard swings
Move in the wind,
Carrying tiny ghosts
Of long ago.
If we listen, we can hear
Children's voices laughing;
Swing me, swing me higher...
Higher......higher.

Carol Johnson Bye

Untitled

As I sit within these dingy walls
and dream of things to be
A voice—so sweet and gentle calls
and talks of wanting me.
Never had I heard such things
No one had ever dared
to speak of love and hearts that sing
No man had ever cared.
His words, so precious, made me cry
and wiped away my pain.
I love this man who made me sigh—
My heart is his domain.
So every night I sit within
the walls I once thought grim,
just waiting for my lover's calls
and sit
   and dream
      of him.

Kellie M. Figueiredo

The Metamorphosis Of A Butterfly

When I asked a butterfly
How did it feel when it
Was changing the
Butterfly told me,
When I was in my egg
I could not wait to get
Out of my egg. So when I got
Out I said, I am breathing
The air of life but I still
Have a long way to go.
When spring comes the
Butterfly says, I wrap
Myself up and wait,
When I emerge I would
Say, I am breathing the air
Of life again, but still the
Time has not come,
Now I am an adult butterfly,
I may lay eggs and go away
Knowing I soon might die.

Xavier E. Chavez

It Is With Fear I Come To Love

It is with fear I come to love,
Not knowing what love will be,
For once I've pledged all things to you
Will you be true to me?

Or will you break the heart I give?
Tell me, what shall I gain?
For the gift love gives is tears, love
And the vow it vows is pain.

If I were strong I'd run from you
To some strange and distant land
Where no one knows the heart of me
And no one takes my hand.

Then far from you I'd never know
Of the sadness love can be.
I'd only know that tender time
When my love was true to me.

Tobi Roberts

I Touched A Rainbow

I touched a rainbow.
The moist vapors gently....
Blanketed me...
Setting my body aglow.
And time hid its face...
Then: Flew away.
And my emotions soared...
And raced out of control.
And I laughed...
Then: Cried,
I wanted to stay; then run..
But my feet wouldn't let me go.
And the awesome magnificent rays,
Ignited a passion within my soul...
And it burned...awe...so...so...
Warm and wonderful.
When I touched you...
Darling, It was as if....
I touched....
A rainbow.

Myrna Doig

Backward Foresight

As I look,
while streaking forward,
the summer-rich grass
spins away beside me
beneath the far-reaching clouds
that lead the race away from me.
As I look,
a finch skitters
across the air in my wake.
As I look,
yellow darts below on this county road
perforate the path I've traveled,
dividing the farms that slide by
on their way behind me.
Such a narrow panorama
before me
of the wide view moving away
behind me,
as I look forward
in my rearview mirror.

Janelle R. Finke

Through Valleys And Over Streams

Through valleys and over streams,
We ride comparing our dreams.
Some we can share,
Others we do not dare.
How far must we ride,
To show are dreaming side.
Through valleys and over streams,
We talk and discover our dreams.
Searching and knowing,
God has made that perfect one.
It could feel like years,
But one day we will see.
That match for life before me,
My lover and I it will be.
Riding and comparing dreams,
Through valleys and over streams

Missy K. Mraz

Act Of Terrorism

Paranoia rampant
Babies dead

For "Freedom's Sake"

Failed security
Innocence gone

In "Freedom's Name"

Abrupt shock
Orphaned children

To "Save our Land"

Stupid swine
Bombing at random....

and
Our freedom....
Gone forever.
Mary Beran

What If?

What if there were
  no birds to sing?
What if there were
  no bells to ring?

What if there were
  no roses to smell?
What if there were
  no jokes to tell?

What if there were
  no games to play?
What if there were
  no prayers to say?

What if there were
  no clouds above?
What if there were
  no one to love?

Life would be
  sheer monotony
And would sure bore
  the hell out of me.
Helen M. Kerecz

Nobody's Wife

The day is gone, the night is here
down her face trickles one last tear.
Not caring where he might be,
wanting to give him the third degree.

All those working late nights
doesn't give him any right.
He went and slept around,
but now she's standing her ground.

She opens the door
not crying anymore.
She throws his stuff out in the yard,
changing the locks wasn't so hard.

She doesn't want to know why
all the times he had to lie.
She's taking back her own life.
She's now nobody's wife.
Patricia Hunter

A Carpenter

A carpenter is a person
who stays quite busy.
He climbs upon places
that make me dizzy.

His saw buzzes as he
cuts a piece of plywood
Then he checks to see
that it is smooth and good.

He measures here then
finally measures there.
Making sure it is straight,
by using a metal square.

He looks like he is trying
to run a big race.
As he nails each rafter
and tall board in place.

He needs to be someone,
who is good and smart.
Who knows a lot about
the framing and building art.
Glenda Ellis

Written By The Wind:

Wander in high meadows
or lie beneath a pine
watch the river flow
and disregard the time.
Hear the singing firs
their long and supple limbs
written by the wind
into nature's ancient hymns.

Feel the warmth of summer
or winter's icy chill
through the waters of the river
and the trees upon the hill.
Softly walk the river's course
leaving only footprints in the sand
as fleeting signatures of passing
in a lovely, living land.
Randy Stoltmann

Dream Land

Lollipops,
Jelly beans,
Magical things,
And and angels wings.
  Silly rides,
Funny rides,
Fantastic rides and others,
And beaches with beautiful tides.
  Lollipops,
Jelly beans,
Magical things,
And angels wings.
  Favorite past times,
Time flies,
Then you wake up,
And your still there.
  Lollipops,
Jelly beans,
Magical things,
And angels wings.
Courtney Kelso

An Angel From My Mother

There is an angel on my shoulder
that was given to me in love

It was given by my mother
who is now with God above

The gentleness and kindness
she showed to me when here

Has given me heart warming memories
I walk in hope not fear

I know she is with the Father
and surrounded by the arms

Of my Savior, Lord and Master
protect and abounds

In peace, love and happiness
eternal blissful joy

The angel on my shoulder has replaced
all childish toys

It is symbol of her caring
God's protection from above

The angel on my shoulder
she gave to me in love.
Sharon E. McCann

A New Home

Time was when I was
Fully rich,
When life seemed safe
To roam,
For I had treasures
All my own...
A friend, a babe,
And a home.

But then I knew that
I should be,
Like reaching for the stars,
For when the
Second world war passed,
The friend, the babe,
And the dream home crushed.

Now, by and by Someone came,
Swiftly, thriftling passing by,
New life to me He spread
And promise of a new home.
Cornelia Brown Domondon

Soular Undoings

Where in the world
Is that untold proverb
Which dries the desert
While destroying our soul?

As she wakes in the east
With the shimmer of silk,
Smooth synthetic rock
Dances through the air!

A dark violet ball
Begins the deflation.
Habitat crouches,
Leaps like a thousand cats.

Every pupil must contract,
So do not fear!
God's destruction
And renewal are near.
William E. Beach

Space, Time (Perception)

When time began what space was it in?
When space was not
What time was it then?

If there is not time without space
and no space without time
what is it?

Except that perceived
in your mind and mine!

Why so difficult to believe
there was no beginning
and will be no end

Only transformations
over and over again

As this we read
our time is now

For this space are we in!!!
    John E. Gray

Barrio

Hung in Languor, inert,
Among Hell's cartel,
In this district of disrepute-
I breathe the odor of carrion,
the aroma of blood,
Of bone, tooth, and daw.
In this ward,
of lascivious commodity,
of urine and wrought iron,
there lay a festering corpse-
In the gutter of America,
Buried in this barrio,
Above the ground,
Below the sea.
    Timothy McNulty

Fear Of Death

The fear of death
Is constantly around
Yet you go through life
Barely making a sound

You start each day
Expectations a new
Wonder if life will end
Before the day is through

At a certain time of year
To the woods people run
They end a beautiful life
Through the scope of a gun

All I can say is:

If the situation was different
I'm sure this is true,
You'd damn every hunter
If the hunted was you!
    Linda Diane Johnson

Phantom

In the dark shadows of my room
A phantom appears before me
He watches over me
Looking with his evil eyes
I try to close my eyes
I can feel him get closer
Closer
Closer
My body stiffens
He knows I fear him
He feeds off my fear
I feel his icy claws
Wrapping around my neck
slowly digging into me
I open my eyes
All I see is darkness
The phantom had disappeared
Back in the depths of my imagination
    Angela Dardini

Love Hurts

Every time you try
you began to cry.
Can't be with
can't be without.
People try to keep us apart
but our love won't let us depart.
You ask yourself why love hurts
but you will never know why you
   have that thirst.
    Deatrice Halley

"If"

If dreams could be fulfilled,
would they still be dreams?

If wishes could come true,
would goals still exists?

If life was forever,
would we treasure it the same?

If there was no illness,
would we still cherish health?

If there was no pain,
would we still have feelings?

If there was no death,
would there still be new life?

If there was no hater,
would there still be love?

If we had no enemies,
would we still have friends?

If there were no lies,
would there still be truth?

"IF" so small.
But yet, so big.
    Maria C. De La Sota

Divine Mission

I'm on a divine mission
I told myself today
I have a plan, I know my goals
I'm already on my way.

I'm on a divine mission
I know just where to start
I turn within and praise my God
It's coming from the heart.

The road seems long and winding
The stairs seem high and steep
But I'm heading in an upward trend
My mission is mine to keep.

No matter how hard it seems
I know that I can do it.
I'm on a divine mission
I'll complete it, if I will it.

My mission is now complete
What is to be, must be
Everything is possible
Determination is the key.
    Alethea St. Bernard-Marshall

A Sticky Situation

She sticks like glue
Her name's not Elmer

Her crazy glue eyed stare
Followed my every step

Even into the glue pot
Where she shares my life

And her words are binding
But mine are non cohesive

Two different glues
With two different views

We're stuck to each other
Like gum on shoes

So now she's a keeper
Every day of the year

There's no way she can leave
Cause her chemistry's right

To stick, to stay, forever
She has a grip on me.
    Steve Gerchak

My Life Without You

   My life is so cold
without your warmth
love affection pass on.
Every time I see you, give
me goodwill strong feeling
and compassion. You will
always be my baby. And you will
always be my love like
heart and my soulmate
    Lori Williams

Of My Dreams

I've often dreamed,
A thousand dreams
of hills and dales and heather.

Breathed the air,
Inhaled the scents
of wood and grass and leather.

The past still shines
'Round every bend,
So rich with History

Of knights and kings,
Dark deeds and such,
No end to mystery.

I dream of spending
All my days
In the Land of Regal Queens

That Enchanted Place
which holds my heart,
That England Of My Dreams.

Phyllis D'Ambrosio Nichols

Untitled

Time and time again,
The words will spin and spin
Until at last
There comes forth

A filament of truth
　And love
　　And life.
(What quality web will it create?)

Carolyn Kight

Finding Him

His eyes met mine
I stood there frozen
He said Hi
I couldn't speak
He touched my hand
I couldn't move
He kissed me gently
He says he loves me now
I know I love him
Now we're together
I hope it's forever

Ilene Zimmer

Untitled

Could anyone
ever stop me
from destroying myself
I don't know.
No one's ever tried
look me in the eye
and try to convince me
that there's a reason
for my existence.
My parents never could.
C'mon Ryan just talk about it.
take their pills to calm you down
an easy fix
to a hard problem
don't get too close
my presence brings death.
When it's too late
you'll realize
you should have listened to forewarning.

Ryan Cleary

An Annulling Thought......

I've been beaten,
　bruised and battered
　　both inside and out

I've struggled,
　salvaged and survived
　　by being both strong and devout

I've been faithful,
　fundamental and falsely led
　　towards a saving light

I've been hurt,
　harassed and hastily
　　stripped of my sacred rights

I've reflected,
　repented and respectfully
　　submitted all my beliefs

I've been angered,
　anxious and anguished
　　while seeking some relief

My church, why have you forsaken me?
　my Lord, have you?

Gayle Roberts

The Odd Duck's Prized Waddle

　The odd duck
Spun a cocoon wrap of
armor against pellets
hitting with odd duckling
taunts, but there's dent making
pins waking her hurt.
She digs and they laugh
　hit her
　　strange waddles.

　But she
　　digs
out a robust gift of
talent, all hers, spurring
her to ascend blooming,
shocking the blind stunted
groups pride as she rose.
They tried but could not
　rub her
　　prized waddle.

Dorothy Randle Clinton

I Am A Tree

Slowly growing,
stronger each day,
to withstand the wind and storms
that will come and go my way.
Losing pieces of me,
along the way.
Never to regain,
what I have lost.
Perhaps growing is my cost.

Full of beauty,
hidden inside.
Living in darkness,
hoping for sunshine.
To blossom and bloom,
again one day.
For this is me,
I am a Tree.

Nanci-Ann Ashman

Transformation

Neural paths of pleasure, play
With wings of passing prayer
Heaven's Holy Harps resound
As mystic memories stare

Sparks of primal purity
Fly through in pristine grace
Wounds from ancient legacies
In bursts of peace erase

Wisdom from a winter freeze
Rains colors in the sky
Transformations taking hold
As tattered traces die

Walls of ice come crashing down
To melt within the sea
Love unfolds its tender arms
To nurture what's to be

Smell of spring rain air abound
And light of early dawn
Assures this peaceful pilgrim
My webs of pain are gone

David Palmer

The Foxhunt

Out into the cool, crisp morning
we followed the hunters,
my horse and I.

Galloping now at a steady pace
in search of our elusive prey.
My horse and I,
the wind caressing our faces,
the smell of pine hanging
heavily in the air.

The sly fox
running for his life now.
The hounds
barking and chasing.
Is this what it was meant to be?
Oh, run
you beautiful animal.
Escape and be free!

Barbara S. Ruppert

The Bull Rider

I went to a dance
just last night,
I met a guy who fit
his Wranglers just right.

A real tall good-looking guy
by the name of Blane,
After he called me Lisa,
I should have called him Wayne.

I knew a few marbles were loose
when I found out he rode bulls,
Throughout your life,
you know you'll meet some fools.

Even after a couple beers
he wasn't such a bad guy,
If he had not been drinking,
he could have had my heart to buy.

Christy Anderson

When We Can't Be Together

Love is so hard,
When we can't be together.
It hurts so much inside,
When we can't be together.
It hurts when he says "I love you,"
When we can't be together.
I am so lost,
When we can't be together.
But if that's the way it should be,
We shouldn't be together.

Heather King

You Were Mine

I know I hurt you
When I had to say good-bye
and I would like to be in
your heart again, but
this time
you're the one who has to decide
to let me in
I don't know
the reason why I
left you so cold
I was too blind to see
when you were mine
I would do anything
only if you were mine

Linda Rivera

Love Is

Love is giving
Love is mending
Love is understanding
Love is undemanding
Love is forgiving
Love is compassion
Love is without ration
Love is soothing
Love is sweet
Love is cheer
Love is not fear
Love is faithful
Love is not hateful
Love is everlasting

Erma E. Nielsen

The City

It seems like such a pity
that the people of this great city
can't see the beauty of this place,
defacing it is a disgrace.
Why must we mess up the land
that gives us all a helping hand?
Why can't we just plant tree
and thank the Lord for making us free?
Free to wander, free to roam,
don't we know this place is home?

Look upon this land so grand,
Come on people take a stand
and clean up our perfect land.
Show the world it can be done
and band together one by one.
If each of us can do a part,
that would be a perfect start
to show the world we have a heart.
So stand upon this land so grand
with peace and freedom in our hands.

Peggy Martucci

My Walk With Jesus

Today, I walked with Jesus
along the sandy shore.
No footprints could be seen,
as they washed away from shore.
The sun shown brightly and
the wind caressed my cheeks.
I felt the spray of the oceans
waves open my face and feet.
My heart was filled with
joyful praise, as I knew my
Lord was here.
I knelt to pray and felt
his hand upon my head,
I knew my Lord was here.

Lois Jean Switzer

Hespera

I am a moon child
I wake when the sun sleeps
And I sleep while the sunlight
   creeps
I am the lunar child

I am a nocturnal lover
Kissing when all are snoring
Moaning while dreams are
   soaring
I am the twilight lover

I am Hesperus
Shepherding the lost and lonely
Guarding the obscurity only
I am the evening star.

Lillian Pittman

Expressions

Shock, tears, disbelief
Alone, hate, anger
You had to leave with
Questions unanswered
Unfairness, hurt, denial
Unspoken words, no tomorrows
No more first times
College, car, home
Wife, child, growing old
Called by God to be an angel
Human words cannot fathom
The beauty, grace, unfailing love
Would you come back, if you could?
To this cold, unfeeling world
That could not protect you.
Peace, hope, faith are what I have.
Laughing, loving, always together
Until that precious day Dear Brother
Know that I miss and love you
Forever in my mortal heart.

Florence Keller

Babbling Brook

Have you ever seen a babbling brook
where fish and tadpoles play?
Sometimes you can see them
on a bright and sunny day.
While birds are singing,
and children reading,
from a story book.
And grown ups making
food for taking
to a picnic near the brook.

James Lorkowski

Loneliness

Time escapes,
the laughter dies,
Shadows disappear—
blending together
in the darkness,
as the spirits
dissipate into the
mist,
The lone man
left standing
wonders why the music
ceased,
and—
in bewilderment—
allows the baton
to slip to the floor.

Mariah P. Adin

Give

In the land of the living
that's the time for giving
And then I can say, that in this day
an angel shall surely come my way

As God's Holy Spirit
compasses me about it is with praise
and joy will I begin to shout
thank you God for ridding me of doubt

So now instead of hurting people
with words, guns or even a knife
It is me being blessed by
helping someone else life.

Harold Younger

Untitled

No one can
truly define love,
and yet within our
hearts are its words.
Love can be completely
beyond our grasp,
or right in front of
us. It lives somewhere
between calm and passion,
between clarity
and obscurity, and
between music
and silence

Misty Vernon

Why?

Why don't I love all people?
   I have been carefully taught,
   So I don't love as I ought.

Why don't we work together?
   Why are we not forgiving?
   Why lose out - on fulfilled living?

God gives us moments of grace,
   For all life's problems to face,
   Why are we such a disgrace?

"All of us" - are God's children
   Living in His holy will.
   Can we then fulfill this bill?!

It's in understanding "We are one"
Reconciliation has begun.

Eloise King Shaw

Dearest Granddaughter My Life's Inspiration

"Hi Mammy, can we go shopping today?"
"Oh, I'll see if we can arrange that into our schedule."
Suddenly, thoughts of being busy diminished away.

"And Mammy, can we eat at McDonald's after?"
"Yes dear, if you are a good girl"... I replied in silent laughter.

"Hey Mammy, know what?... I really love you."
"And I really love you too, sweetheart."

Baby sitting can be an adventure with this vibrant granddaughter of mine.
She's such a happy-go-lucky little child who's smiling all the time.

Her mother "revisited," I believe you could say.
Amazing how generations tend to repeat in some ways.

A contented busy-body around the house, always wanting to help with the chores.
My dearest daughter, you can be proud of this pleasant lass of yours.

Gosh, how the time flew by during those child-rearing years.
The pressures of being a young mother have turned joy out of tears.

Often I wish I'd taken the time to relax and play back then,
As I enjoy these precious moments that were spread so very thin.

Reliving the past or making amends is what I'm doing now I guess.
When I stop and face reality.... Lord how I have been blessed.

If I should die before she is grown,
I'll rest in peace grateful for the granddaughter I had known.
    Sheila I. Potts

This World

As it has been written, all things of this world will come to be past,
Everything except the people holding on to the Lord's words and standing steadfast.
There will be brother against brother, Nation will rise against Nation,
This has all been written in the Bible's own book of the Revelation.
There is but one way to get through these times, it's by faith in one up above,
If you receive Him into your heart, and accept his patient, undying love.
There will be pain and suffering of the innocent as well as the guilty in times of tribulation,
To get through the hard times, put your heart in God's hands to help you build a strong and solid foundation.
On your way be charitable, love everyone as yourself, let all anger go,
In the end you will see that you will be rewarded for your deeds as the good Lord commanded it to be so.
By falling on your knees and accepting the Lord as your personal Saviour, you will be ready to fight against the flame,
And when the precious Book of Life is opened on that day, it will reveal your name.
    Carlisa J. McCauley

Once In A Lifetime

Once in a lifetime, if we are very lucky, someone special comes into our lives.
Not a parent or a sister or spouse, but someone that we did not expect.
Someone who is there to help us through the every day grind.

Once in a lifetime, if we are very lucky, there will be someone there to understand who we are.
Someone who will not judge, but is there to guide.
Someone who will be there to pick us up when we fall -
or bring us down when we are flying a little too high.

Once in a lifetime, if we are very lucky,
there will be someone to put us on the right path when we lose our way -
help us to find the right direction.

Once in a lifetime, if we are very lucky, we will find someone to take us under their wing -
to nurture us, to teach us - not about unusual things, but everyday life.
They will show us that life can be tough sometimes tougher than we can handle -
but we can succeed if we believe in who we are.

Once in a lifetime, if we are very lucky,
we will find someone who we feel we have known all our lives, even when we first met.
Someone who we don't argue with.
Even when times are tense, we step back and take a deep breath and realize
that nothing is worth the risk of losing this friendship.

Once in a lifetime, if we are very lucky, we will find a mentor -
a teacher, someone to help us - even when we feel that we don't need help.

Once in a lifetime, if we are very lucky, we will realize just how lucky we are.
    Carol A. Dunkel

The Change In Seasons

We say "Good-bye" to summer on Labor Day, and a bang up barbecue and
song fest usually "does the trick"

We say "Hello" to fall by returning to school, and fixing up the house.

Fall comes in October with Halloween, ghosts and goblins.

Thanksgiving comes in November, when it may be rainy and blustery.

After the turkey's been devoured, we turn our thoughts to getting
Christmas gifts for our loved ones and friends,
   For it's the holiest of all seasons.

Many times, on December 25th, the snow starts to fall signifying winter time.

The season of spring begins in March, when our Irish neighbors parade
down Fifth Avenue, in celebration of St. Patrick's Day.

With the coming of April, we celebrate Easter (unless it falls in March),
and we still have to wear winter clothing to ward off the wind.

Then with spring recess from college, we look towards summer, in
search of summer jobs, to pay the bills at school.
   Thus the seasons come and go!
   Gretchen L. Shultz

Spiritual Nature

When I am looking up and the sky is just right, the sun peeking
through the clouds send a ray of hope, this reminds me of my mother.

When I wake up on a beautiful Saturday morning and the sun hits my
face, I feel the energy of my mother's spirit stirring inside me.

When Sunday evening settles in, I feel the calm that always let me
know I was safe when mom was around.

When my spirit is burdened and I wish to be able to speak with my
mother, the sound of the rain on my window sill is a welcomed visit.
I let the tears roll.

When a Spring windstorm comes I welcome the breeze on my face. I
know that God is cleaning the earth, as well as my soul just like
my mother would do when it was time for me to pick myself up and start all over again.

When I look across a body of water clean and blue, I can feel the
Depth of the love she had for me and that I continue to have for her.

When I look at the moon on a star-filled night, I look toward the
Future without her, distant but right. I know that God has a way
for me to feel what I can no longer touch, like the beauty of the moon
I loved my mother that much.

When I think of my mother I know that an eternal spirit will always
Live just like Jesus. May her spirit surround me and live through
me for the rest of my earthly existence.

When the air blows open the doorway to heaven, I liken it to the
need I will have to rejoice when I am welcomed home and reunited
with the Spiritual Nature that is my mother.
   April Smith Coley

Death's Awakening

Awakened from our sleep, we are thrust into this life from pitch black to blinding light.
Blurred shapes and sounds surrounds us instilling our first emotions of fear and fright.
As our vision becomes focused and the haze finally clears,
Our parents raise us as best they know throughout our learning years.
We learn of God and the power of faith to wrestle our temptations in dark times.
And dream the promise of eternal life in the end for all mankind.
As we grow stronger in mind and body and our perception to our existence becomes clear.
We search and find our significant other to love in our living years.
In a blink of an eye and disbelief we are grasped in sorrow's hold.
Our reflection reveals in the mirror of time we have finally grown old.
As our final days spent on this earth atrophy our physical existence.
The mind will haze and visions blur as our skin offers gravity no resistance.
And like a new automobile weathers to rust, we are given back to
This earth . . . fire to ashes and dirt to dust.
And once again we sleep to await life's final awakening.
   R. J. Martino Jr.

When...

When everything you think is wrong,
When everything you do turns bad,
When life just doesn't go your way,
Hold your head high, because tomorrow will be a better day.

When friends are mad,
And boyfriends, too,
When parents gripe,
As they sometimes do,
Just wait it out; it'll be okay.
Wait awhile and you'll find the way.

When your confidence is gone,
And your patience, too,
When you want to just hide in your room,
Take a look at the world, and you will see,
Pretty soon things will be like they should be.

Jennifer Lee

Love Hath A Stranger's Face

   Thine eyes hath never seen the face of Love, nor hath thy heart ever felt its gentle caress. Love hath never visited thee, never spoken softly in thine ear, never fondly held thy hand, or rocked thee slowly in his arms.
   Love is a stranger I have never met, yet I find myself missing him. Night comes and dreams of longing invade upon thy already restless sleep. These dreams which hath become the only companion I know hath filled many a gloomy eve but left the days devoid of expectation.
   Wilst thy destiny someday lead to Love's door? Wilst thy knock be welcome? Wilst Love know thine essence and quench thy thirst with its sweet nectar, and cherish thy being with the kisses of a thousand butterflies, and satisfy thy desire with a burning blaze of passion? Wilst Love then become thine and infinitely embrace thy soul?
   I pray for the dawn of such glorious days where I shall delight in Love's joyous presence. Till then there are always thy dreams...

Rachel Keith

The Other Way

This is no longer love's residence
   memories are shadows and voices have blown away
as all the earth's discarded litter on the wind
gangs guns graffiti-bloated, our punishment is there is no cure
AIDS
there is no solution
not really
and there is no pain anymore - at least not for Me
I've learned to look the other way, I think I may be on a one way
street though a dead end
no outlet - for the pain
darkness descending over the alley, home sweet home
that's okay
I can turn My bruised cheeks and scarred ego
The Other Way
there is no other way, My weary, bleary eyes can no longer make
contact except with the street beneath My aching feet
because My heart evicted love long ago

Rhonda K. Baughman

Oscar

Evenings of tears with glasses of wine,
Dancing with thoughts of you on my mind...
Imagining you, instead of another,
Never looking at them, only seeing my brother...
Illusions of you and the evil gun,
Knowing you're gone, but remembering the fun...
Nightmares and dreams confused as one...
Waking up one morning, hoping to see,
The way we were together, my brother and me...

Alexis L. F. Vandergaag

Birth Of Love

Love is like having a newborn baby.
It is conceived thru moments together,
Then carried within one's body until it
grows so deep that you feel if you
hold it any longer it would die.
You release that love so you both can
enjoy helping to make it grow.
The knot that binds two people together is like
the umbilical cord that feeds life into
the baby; it feeds love into each other.
Just like a newborn baby needs tender,
loving care, so does the love between two lovers.
Remember, to be able to
have love you must conceive it, carry
it within; and then deliver it to the
one you love. Then together you can watch it grow.

Donna M. Riedel

My Child...Always

She sat, she played, all day...today.
Nary a word did she say.

She cares, she shares, all day...each day.
Helping others is her way.

She plans, she dreams, all day...one day.
A teacher of children she will be some day.

She's pampered, she's spoiled, all day...all day.
For she's my child, all day...always!

Darlene Gardner Vaughn

Waves Of Love

My love for you is like an ocean
The waves come in but never out
They are always full with motion
Never without any hesitation or doubt.

As a storm comes about the waters
It causes them to toss about the deep blue,
Making the world think of them as uncontrollable and mean.
But then the storm passes by to take away the cruel
And the waters return out to the sea.

Never under estimate one's love for you
Because you can be like the ocean
Your love so calm and gentle
And then turn into a dim blue.

William Hildreth IV

Love

Love can soothe a lonely heart,
If we are kind and gentle and smart.
Love is what holds us together.
It can last on and on forever.
We must open our eyes and our hearts as well,
For on that love, we all may dwell.
I was lost in my dreams and torn apart,
'Till you picked up the pieces of my lonely heart.
Love is what brought you and I together,
We can make it last forever and ever.
Now that we're together, everything is clear.
Together we have love, but apart we both have fear.

Tara M. Troccia

The Angel Of The Morning

There she stands,
   The Angel of the morning.
The sun captured in her waving hair.
Her eyes, like the cloudless blue sky,
   gaze upon the earth.
As I sit and stare at this beautiful creature,
   I feel that I understand,
I understand her hopes, fears, worries and dreams.
She walks gently upon the earth,
   As a dove that glides swiftly through the air.
Her face, like the moon, shines brightly in the dawn.
As she turns from me, to continue her endless journey,
I know in my heart, she will not forget me.
She will return every morning,
   bringing joy to all the world.
Even though I may not see her,
   I know she is there in spirit.
I will never forget my Angel of the Morning,
   No matter how far life may lead her from me.
She will always have a special place in my heart.

Karen Hyde

The Magic Of Love

She came by night toward the sea
and fell in step with time.
The soft waves lapping at her feet
caressed her weary mind.

Her heartache soon would disappear
as peace transformed her soul,
into a lovely secret place
where only she could go.

To feel the beauty of life's art,
the magic deep within
that lie within the silent realms
between the now and then.

Eyes opened wide with wonder
soon fell upon the girl
who smiled and laughed with utmost glee
as her mother she did see.

Into the night they both did run and hugged so joyfully
until the magic disappeared and it was time to leave.

Descending on her upward flight back to heaven's gate
she waved goodbye as God's love did silently await.

Debra Joy Gonzales

Michelle

When my dreams came true
I look around seeing you
Our love has brought us here today
Our joy could never wash away

I'm trying not to make a mistake or try too hard
I'll do nothing but be myself, for we'll never be apart

Before we met time seemed to just go on
Now time doesn't exist, it seems to be all but gone
My love for you will never die
While we share our lives, side by my side

For years, I was dreaming of my one true love
Then heaven answered, by sending me you my love
I didn't believe dreams could be so right
That dreams could last all of the day as in the night

Now, I live my dream each time we're together
Or hold each other tight in good or stormy weather
You know this is not a mistake, for we don't try
Together we'll be as one, until all time had gone by

Kevin P. Mooney

Patience

When your patience wears thin,
And no matter how hard you try,
You can't manage a grin.
Try sticking out your chin
And counting to ten, and
If necessary, repeat over and over again.
Life has its woes,
But there is the promise that goes,
"As a new day begins,
There is hope for a new perspective."
So relax your chagrin and start over again
And take a deep breath,
Throw your shoulders back
And begin a fresh attack.

Harold B. Fuller

A Shining Star

You're the first star I've seen so bright
May I make a wish tonight?

I wish to be you
If I should die before my love
I wish to be you
A shining star high above

I want to shine brightly
I will guide him through life ahead
Let me shine nightly
I would watch him sleep in bed

Have you seen?
He's been by my side
Always there for me
Through laughter and tears from my eyes

It's this faithfulness I must return
For he has been so kind
His love I'll always yearn
I'll shine so bright that it's me he'll find

So, you see? It's for him, not for me
A shining star I wish to be

Eileen M. Wallenta

The Crashing Waves Of The Crystal Diamond Path

The glowing fire ball sun lit a crystal diamond path heralding the dancing wavy waters surrounding it. There we witnessed the billowy sails of the sailboat stately as it glided across the ocean.

Directly underneath our window front dining table the waves churned and thrashed with mighty, crushing, rhythmic power against the mute sandy shore.

Scaled layered mountains barricade the shore and the smoky hued orange layered whipped parfait sky blends against the deepening powers of the night coming to take the ocean captive from its day time demeanor.

It is a deep, dramatic comforting twinkling splashy night time sky. The translucent orange layered sky against the pitch midnight black ocean and the smoky grey atmosphere added dash and drama like the opening of a great bed time story.

The promise of tomorrow and another day of love and joy and sharing heightens our senses for all that can be. As the seagull wings across the sky and the lights twinkle along the shoreline we say aloha until we meet again.

Lynda Cobden

I Am

I am unique and ambitious
I wonder what my future will hold
I hear the voices of people I will meet
I see my father encouraging me to do what I love
I want to travel and see the sights of the world
I am unique and ambitious

I pretend to not let anything bother me
I feel the ambitions and goals of people who do not try
I touch the souls of long ago who made even the slightest difference
   in the world
I worry that I will not live up to the standards I have set for myself
I cry when I think that I did not try hard enough
I am unique and ambitious

I understand I cannot do everything
I say that if you want it badly enough, you will one day achieve it
I dream that someday I will make a difference in the world
I try to live up to my full potential
I hope to accomplish all that I say
I am unique and ambitious
   Honey L. Samuelson

Untitled

She used to have a lot of friends
They used to play truth or dare
They all used to know her name
Now they don't even care.
She used to have a family
It was all love and respect
Now they all have their own lives
What can you expect.
She used to wish for a better life
Now she wishes for any life at all
She was naive and took it for granted
She set herself up for the fall.
I'm not talking about myself
Or anyone close to me
I'm talking about an outcast
Who longs to be set free.
So if the "she" in this poem sounds like someone you know
Take a look in the mirror and be a friend instead of a foe.
   Violet Garrison

God Took The Dawn

One sunny spring morning all at once it was gone.
The clouds came and filled the sky as God took the dawn.

This dawn was 22 when God made his call.
It all seemed too soon to have her taken from us all.

We had plans as friends to go out on the town.
To stay out late, live it up and be the last to shut it down.

Now I don't have that chance and she's not here to see
How I still miss the dance and the friend she was to me.

Why did she leaves us, I guess heaven only knows.
One thing I believe, is for me her spirit always grows.

Somewhere up there I hope that dawn can see.
There are still those who care and forever friends we'll always be.

Even though God took the dawn that brightened up our days.
She's not completely gone, every morning she has her place.
   Norman L. Abshere Jr.

Soul Mates

Give me a moment, I'll write you a poem,
Give me a year, for no other do I hear,
Such words, sweet words of love.

Give me a chance to let you see,
How wonderful and beautiful life can be,
When two people are joined by the same destiny.

Give me a lifetime of hope and of dreams,
Our faith is tested beyond fair means,
And doubt and disbelief is all that is seems.

But out of the storm, the sun shines so bright,
All of the doubts will be out of sight,
And we will see what we were meant to be.

In love, one true love, one heart,
One soul, one life,
God's greatest gift, to each the other.
   Katherine Rotola

Wasted

It's late in my life Lord and there are things
I regret, things I can not undo.
The one thing I seem to regret most of
All, is the time that I've spent without you.

There's hearts I can't mend, hurts that
won't heal, memories that don't seem to fade.
Seeds I can't dig up, words I can't take back,
and years that were wasted away.

If only I'd given you first place in my life,
I wouldn't be looking back now,
and wishing that somehow I could do it all over...
but time just will not allow.
   Pam Guskie

"Growing Up Too Fast"

One year ago today I gave birth to you,
   Tiny toes, tiny fingers and a button nose too.
So warm, so cuddly, so precious, so sweet.
   I kissed you all over-from your head to your feet.
I had so much to learn in such a short time
   And wouldn't you know - it all worked out fine.
Happiness to you was: dry diapers and being fed
   So happiness to me was staying one step ahead.
From smiling - to crawling - to waving goodbye
   It all happens within one blink of an eye.
It's been a pleasure to watch each day that you grow
   I cannot believe the things you already know.
It feels like yesterday our life as a family had begun
   And now my little angel has just turned one
Congratulations my baby and best wishes all year through
   And before I know it - you'll be turning two.
Each day that goes by is considered the past
   My little girl is just growing up too fast.
   Elisa Holden

I Am

I am a royal blue carpet in a castle ball room.
I am apple juice sitting by an orchard waiting for somebody.
I am lost in a crowd with millions of people.
I am beautiful as the sunset setting down over the mountains.
I am a soft velvet chair waiting for the right person to come along.
I am an evening when the moon and stars shine down brightly
   on the calmest sea.
I am a clarinet softly playing in the evening's sunset.
   Laura Atkielski

His Amazing Love

Our Lord was so amazing, as He hung upon that tree.
Having mercy on sinners everywhere, including you and me.
His love was overpowering as He let out that last cry.
For he knew that through his death, sinners would never die.
His love for us is wonderful, as you can truly see.
For as he hung upon that cross, he hung for you and me.
His blood was shed for you and me through all eternity.
That we might show through our lives a little of him you see.
So as we make our journey through a very perilous life.
We should always keep our vision on our Savior,
  for it was for us He died.
So now we live our lives in trials of what is right and wrong,
But if you'll keep your eyes on Him, He'll carry you along.
David E. Knight

Bad Dream

My worst thoughts and greatest fears,
are presented in most of my nightmares.

They come in visions...visions of shame,
that curse, and mumble, and ruin my name.

But in my sweet bed, in my mind I cry;
begging, and pleading, and wanting to die.

For the shadow of whom ignore all my pleas,
torment and torture, and know no boundaries.

They hurt me; I'm bleeding; but it's all in my head,
(I toss and I turn, lying in my sweet bed).

They are laughing because of the secrets they know,
like the seed of a plant that refuses to grow.

They destroy all these secrets with anguish and pain,
Then down pours the blood as if it were rain.

With a shutter of panic, they pierce through my mind,
I was the last one; last one of my kind.

I was the last dreamer; happy not sad,
but now it's all over as my good dreams turn bad.

And I scream in the night, with sweat on my head,
and with a sigh of relief, I damn my sweet bed.
Peter Hernandez

Unending Love

Unearthly, radiant, the stars shine above,
Silently speaking of unending love.
Souls are tempestuous, seeking their rest,
Longing to arise, doing their best.

Sighs unbidden, calling from afar,
Traveling the distance to every star.
Finally finding the one that they seek.
Unending love is that which I speak.

The cry of the soul has untold power,
Resting only when it finds its bower.
The power of love is stronger than death,
Lasting beyond the last human breath.

Transcending the obstacles life throws its way,
To the very end, it has its say.
Shattering the wicked, winning the fray,
Triumphing o'er night, making it day.

Shudder you weak ones, fear if you will,
But I will not hesitate, no, not until—
I drink of the dregs of love's sweet cup,
Unsatisfied until I'm filled up.
Belinda Brown

College

She learned that hair didn't always
have to be the same color (dye)
and that people sometimes went away (died)
and didn't come back
except maybe in dreams and
English class (dying),
dying in the latticework of light
that dances in the window that she
looks at when she's bored.
He learned that he could sing out loud (Loud)
and that sometimes they came back - LOUDER
than before
in the smile in the eyes
of the girl with the pumpkin-colored hair (dyed)
or in the perfect quiet of a bothered mind
that's only quiet when he looks at friends
or sits alone to think of
words to write, released.
Maria Chi

In Their Eyes

My hot salty tears fall as the pouring rain
My heart bleeds in anguish and pain
Though I know his heart belongs solely to me
The world sees him as hers, forever to be
Before God and man that day he will stand
Looking at him, she will take his hand
The love and passion roar to life, you see
When his smiling eyes look down at me
A cheating heart they all will say
But if truth be known in the hearts of one and all
My heart and soul hears his needful call
A sin, or adultery they all may say
But true love and destiny shall prevail one day.
Cindi Kaderli

The Production

Flowing gracefully
Across the dance floor,
Twirling 'round and 'round,
The ballerina performs

Her over-worked feet
Leap in front of her
Rushing to escape the difficult steps ahead

Filled with excitement,
The crowd sits awaiting
Each elegant movement,
Without a strain

Drawing close to the finish
Each ballerina grows nervous,
Each spectator grows tense
In hopes of a perfect production
Jennifer Flanagan

Like Life

A sudden springtime snow storm, is not always what it seems,
Icicle teardrops and broken, frozen dreams.
Sometimes it's a cover of warmth upon the earth,
A white blanket of love, to herald spring's rebirth.
As the springtime flowers from the ground start to sprout,
Remember that this cycle, is what life is all about.
So when the crystal snowflakes from the sky, start to fall,
Each will be different, like love and us all.
Deborah D. Hoyt

Little Shorty-Smally

One day when we working out in our yard;
There came a stray dog whose life had been so hard.
He was so dirty and covered up with ticks;
It looked as if he'd been beaten by someone with sticks.

He was so afraid, when we tried to pet him he'd always run away;
We tried to be nice, to show we wanted him to stay.
He was so frail and thin you could count every bone;
It looked as if he'd spent his whole life scared and alone.

We wanted to take him and give him a home;
To be his friends so he would no longer have to roam.
We put out food and water in a large bowl;
Then we fixed a bed for him, in out of the cold.

His ears are long and floppy, they almost touch the ground;
He's some sort of a hunting dog, a beagle or a hound.
My husband named him "Shorty" because he's not very tall;
Grandson called him "Smally," as he is kinda small.

He likes to hunt down at the creek or up and down the field;
We love to hear his special howl, it gives us all a thrill.
He guards our home both day and night;
When strangers come, he barks and fills them with fright.
A wounded pup he came to us, almost two years ago;
To win his love we have had to take it slow.
We were determined to love him no matter what;
Now he is the best friend that we've got.

Lois Rogers

Tortured Love

Clinging to her hope alone
she falls further into the abyss
terrified, yet holding on
she melts away into his kiss.

The heat she feels burns her soul
and as their bodies entwine
she hungers, she begs for more
of the pain she feels from deep inside.

And in her mind, she yearns for peace
to calm her tortured lonely cries
of a heart that wants nothing but to see
the love that burned within his eyes.

And as her heart drifts away
carried on the wings of seraphim
the demons in her mind compose
an everlasting requiem.

The fire inside her body grows
her whole being soon becomes immersed
knowing his kiss is the only thing
that will ever quench her undying thirst.

Melissa Fischer

Love Grows On...

You and I had such good times.
I don't know how long you're willing be mine...
The stars will always shine in our fantasy,
Honey, can't you see??
We're like Romeo and Juliet,
I know I fell in love with no regret.
As time goes along,
My love for you grows strong,
Many thoughts that you weren't wrong.
But, when I look into your lovely eyes...
Other guys I see is no surprise.
Even though we were special friends,
The love I feel for you will never end...

Phonsy Heuangsavath

The Ring Of Cicadas

Since the speech of night is couched in silence
the cicadas lend it their language,
dialect honed between the gaps of houses,
and the summer air which hugs my skin.

I sit on the porch where my bones learned their wisdom,
staring at the house I went to
when my Father unlocked his fists from their cages.

It mirrors my own.
A lighter coat of paint perhaps, and a statue of a child,
its shadow grown adult-like from the glow of lawn lights.

I would watch my father wait on these steps;
his hands combing shame from his scalp,
isolated, remote, forlorn as a footnote,
growing monumentally smaller
as the police car crept down the cul-de-sac.

I found forbidden words as they handcuffed him,
shrill pleas, and an army of tears,
Then the husband would hold me back,
his wedding band tapping on my collar bone
and when I turned around, I saw his mustache cloaked a smile.

Forrest Schaefer

Peaceful Wishes

Peace is like the kiss of a summer's breeze
reading a book as the leaves fall from the trees
little bare feet running across the grass
lovebirds singing the chorus at God's mass

Looking into the big brown eyes of cherished friends
the security of closeness that your heart depends
the sound of a storm as you sleep
long-ago memories that you will always keep

The distant sound of a familiar car
reminds you that love is not far
the nervous feeling before a race
is almost the same when that someone quickens your heart pace

The first tear when the movie's deep
the last thought before you drift to sleep
the sudden closeness of a friend
the fear that someday it may end

Wishing on the night's first star
the healing of the heart's first scar
the bees buzzing upon a flower
Peace is the greatest power

Amber Apel

What Am I Fighting For?

For a cause unknown to man
For dignity and respect
For the opportunity and the Divine Right to live my life in the manner that is best suited for me
For the heritage of myself and my ancestors who have lived before, are living with, and will be living after me
For my family who would like to have a secure future just like the next man
For all of the animals who are being destroyed because of mundane beliefs by selfish men
For me, myself, and I because no one else will defend my morals, beliefs, and standards if I do not, and
For the Love Of God—the One Being who loves me the most regardless of who I am, how I look, or what I have and have not...

This, my friends, is what I am fighting for.

Faith S. Redwine

"Childhood Rare"

Oh, I have lived a childhood rare,
Growing up with two brothers,
Taking each step in life, like it's stairs,
Never knowing when to depend on others.

Progressing slowly, seeing what's ahead,
Knowing I have to go on,
Wondering if I'll make it out of bed,
While missing my brother Shawn.

Now getting good grades is a must,
My hobbies are pushed aside,
No time in my life for much love or lust,
To their rules I must abide.

Oh, yes I have lived a childhood rare,
Now tell me, do you care?
Jeanne Spellman

I Am Just Rhoda Long

She has made the shoes and cleaned the tubs,
washed the walls and at times she scrubs.
No job has she that's been easy to do,
but from year to year, she pushed on through.
I ask, who is this person so strong?
   She answers, I am just Rhoda Long.

She does for herself as much as she can,
she papers and paints and puts things on the mend.
She cuts her own grass and plants her own seed,
my God, that woman must be one of a breed.
I ask, who is this woman so strong?
   She answers, I am just Rhoda Long.

Four daughters with eighteen grandchildren has she,
add four little great ones to complete the family tree.
To all the little children, it's a special treat,
to see their favorite "Maw Maw" up and on her feet.
I ask, who is this person who never seems to fall?
   She answers, I am just Rhoda Long.
   I Am Maw Maw!
George D. Malone

Common Sense

Thanks to this Great Country
United States, to all the wonderful people
Many thanks for the hospitality,
Land of peace, jobs and opportunities.

I never blame anyone about my choices
I'm stress-free of any negative worries
I love my life, health and people.
I don't ask questions, why or who
I just love everybody, including you.
I'm very happy, love my job
I enjoy doing it, I'm lucky and healthy
I'm always smiling, simple and sincere
I can go anytime, anywhere.
About the money? Is some, how much is enough, takes a long time
Patience and dedication to save it
Vulnerable things come and go.
But my love for you is forever
Who am I? Never try to think to find me
I belong to God, time, and destiny
Someday I'll not be here, for sure, I don't worry about it.
Lamberto Diaz Cardenas

Life Is A Flower

Life is a flower
Blooming in the breath of each new morning
Life is a flower
Opening in each new experience
The warmth of love nor the chill of sadness can break its process
Life is a flower
Growing within the soil of a fertile heart
Life is a flower
Life can not be thrown by the wayside to simply rot in despair
Life in all is a blessing not to be taken for granted
For life brings happiness and despair but in both...
Life is a flower
Ever blooming, ever beautiful
Heather Hollen

"Oh! My Love"

To find true love is hard to do
That special bond between two
Those moments are to be shared
Never to be openly spared
Two hearts beat as one
Cupid's job must be done
Who is that man of mine?
Love has no concept of time
Just to hold him close to me
That is all I wish to see
A single stroke of his gentle hand
Slowly moving across my wanton land
To gaze into his cooing eyes
I see his need to my surprise
Every man longs for his lost queen
My eyes and ears are sharp and keen
Looking for my dearest friend
My lover, my keeper, my king till the end
I hope to grow with my prince of love,
And ride afar on the wings of a dove!
Ongela Nitra Garza

Good Intentions

No credibility goes to good intentions,
No validity to the benefit of the doubt.
Just plain ole truth and honesty,
Is what love is all about.
When there are no boundaries,
No feelings to compare,
It's open season for the emotionally impaired.
Dangling carrots,
A psychological hook,
From chapter 1 in the "Users Handbook".
One foot in, one foot out,
Running with the choice,
Build a wall, ace another,
Temporarily rejoice,
In non-committal shut-down,
The tools atop the crown.
Erect a shrine to "do-good" efforts,
A payoff down the line,
To the well-intended users,
The unsuspecting beget the crime.
Diane S. McKinney

The Close Of The Day

Behold due west,
A fountain, a sky at rest.

Crimson, orange, children together play a game.
Dance hand in hand, a flickering flame.

And like a fire, yes it warms.
Beauty so full, so void...of form.
Quinn Dirks

Critically Poised

Critically Poised
Synaptic
The blade edge rush the brightly lit desires
of your life go past
Burdened in step with the weight of choice
Arm in arm with expectations,
obligations, benefactions.

Critically Poised
Hesitant
The shriek of decision
The sacrifice of wants
to work with a net
Or celebrate the risk and reach uncompromising
to find that once courageous step,
moving, deciding

Critically Poised
Relentless the inconsiderate balance
The search for quiet
before it goes by to settle in and see - Just. See.
To focus on your pursuit and in the throbbing silence...step.
Marc Giroux

The Bluejay

Morning glory vines, dried since fall
Fragments of tenacious greenness, and now
A queer twisted mass crumples from the wall,
So easily; and still determines how
Spirited tendrils, extending will fare.

It rained madness, lively pods, a shattering spray.

Bare to bluejays, hopeless mass scattering,
The wall denied its new earth spun weaving.
More pods burst with showier shattering,
More for the bluejay, always deceiving
Frustrated sparrows collecting what's left.

New growth blocked from sunlight by summer's past design.
Seeds in flurried hurry devoured before their time.

The bluejay returns, alights on the gate.
Glittering eyes peruse the lifeless vine.
Whiteblack feathers, shrieking thief, his first trait;
Joys in procurement of leaves intertwined.
Spirited tendrils began to breathe free.

The bluejay untangling the last interference,
While brightening daybreak's own flower's reappearance...
Haylie Doner

Untitled

The moon beams in the sky
The shadow darkens on the Earth
The sun sulks in the sky
it waves its heavy head upon the horizon
Its gloomy eyes shadow in the darkness
The moon is happy up above the Earth
It's laughing at the sun - up high
Emily N. Huntley

A Place

I know of a place
That's just right for me.
I know of a place where I'd love to be.

There's no fighting, no stealing,
No death, no disease —
No booze and no drugs,
They're not good for me.

There's no smog, no pollution,
No tires in lakes —
No hurricanes, no volcanoes, and no earthquakes.
I know of this place,
It's a great place to be.
But we're screwing it up for ourselves,
As you can probably see.

But it is not too late,
We can still make it better —
But we have to love this planet,
Care for it, and cherish it forever.

I know of a place that once was and can be.
But for it to survive it depends on you and me.
Jack Radford

Mother Earth (Makakin)

She is awaking from her deep sleep,
in all places, even those I may never seek.
She shows her colors,
rebirth in all that we see.
But She is fragile
and calls to thee.
Listen close,
you will hear her cries,
I ask her forgiveness
Is it too late to try.
Sandy Stephens

After Our Finest Hour

Dedicated to my Grandfather, Jospeh J. Kowalski and the 173rd FA Group

The guns are silent, the bodies still.
The bombs have fallen, the air is chill.
The hills have been taken, the rivers run red
From the fallen heroes, no more will be said.
Fathers, brothers, and sons gave their lives,
From different countries their forces allied,
To fight for freedom their weapons were raised
Now they lie honorably inside their graves.
A grim reminder of the evil men do,
But also a tribute to the passion they knew;
Like a Great Man long before them did,
They gave their lives so that others might live
To grow up strong, and proud, and free,
But never to forget the astronomical fee.
More than half a century now has passed,
Since the air raid sirens sounded last.
It's a little late, but greatly true
The message that I now give to you;
From the bottom of my heart and soul I do
Offer this simple and humble phrase: Thank You.
Rebecca Ann Mitchell

Loneliness

I am all alone in the dark,
loneliness is filling my soul.
My piercing cry drifts through
the air - but it falls on no one's ears.
Amy Dyke

Your New Home

It was hard for me to see your face,
the day I took you to your "new place."
Are you frightened and confused?
I realize everything is different and new,
but this is what is best for you.
I feel sad, but I'm glad.
I laugh, but I cry deep inside.
I put my hands up high, and then again I cry,
"Lord, how can I leave him here all alone?"
My Heavenly Father then replies,
"My child, he'll never be alone.
This is just another stepping stone.
Trust in Me... I'll show him the way to his final home."

Joan Harris

Close Of Day

I sit alone in the evening haze
   The heavens unfolded to my gaze.
Stars like flowers of the night
   Dance and sparkle by the light
Of a moon so old and so wise
   That it brings a mellow glow
To the night time skies.
   A pale reflection of the noon time sun
Which brings to light things yet un-done.
   With break of day the morning sun
Wakes and warms us one by one.
   Take up your burdens, be on your way
God has given us this day.
   We love and labor by His will
He fill our cup, we drink our fill.
   How wonderful to know, He gives us Grace
And knowledge that when we have run our race
   We can sit at His feet and see His face.

Thresea Mitchell

Reality

To let go of the pain in my heart would mean...
That I'd have to let go of you.

The bond of unconditional love...
Appears to be structured around shared glances, fantasies.

Turbulent vastness of my ID is longing for the pain to become real...
Perhaps then you would really be with me.

Love makes all losses possible...
my Ego makes all the losses of life, acceptable.

Jo Anne Templar

A Mother's Love

Seeing her as a child,
did it ever occur to you that she could be different
(a hyper-active tomboy and four broken arms?)
No one may have known at that point and time
(she didn't)
She wasn't willing to admit it
until she was far away from the town she grew up in,
and far away from the kids she grew up with
That's when she discovered those intimidated feelings,
that (until then)
were not yet ready to be noticed
Although, after the accident
you knew she was different, but did you mind?
I don't believe so...
even though your families share no blood
but, all because of a mother's love.

Dee Dee Brinkman

A Mother With Nature

We all know that inside our mourning never stops. A daughter's loss is too much, but is her mother really gone? There are still echoes inside, that symbolize the sweet and unforgettable laughter and tears of our beloved one. We fear that darkness will overtake us forever. Our needs for them will never be lost. And if we think about it: Listen to the wind whistle through the swaying branches and leaves of the old, forgotten oak tree. Is it she? Could it really be her whistling that unforgettable tune she used to sing when you were a child? Tears trickle down and stay in our mouths, and taste salty and bitter. You wonder why raindrops taste and feel so refreshing. You mother always had a way of cleansing fears away. It's her. You look down at the fresh new puddle at your feet, that was made within minutes from the fallen rain. The water ripples as your tears fall helplessly into the distorted reflection of yourself. Funny for a moment, your reflection changes. As you stare down, you can visualize the prettiest face in all the world. Hers. As dusk fades, night begins to fall. The clouds scatter just to reveal the silver moon, that gleams in your wide and anticipated eyes. As the softened moon is released, millions of twinkling stars appear. You wonder if the glory of your mother will ever die.

Sarah Blaylock

An Ideal

Just an outline of its former promise of gorgeous, green,
   glossy leaves,
Like a palm held open cupping the rain.
Come and drink my beauty.
I give this to you to quench your sadness.
It will restore joy
Just an outline of its former promise of splendid, scented
   blossoms coming one at a time,
Existing fully in their individual moment.
Sublime and temporal like the wind-born surf.
Come and breathe my beauty.
I give this to you to satisfy your longing.
It will nurture love.
Just an outline of its former promise, dry and brittle, bare
   and without scent,
Existing in silence,
A silhouette of what once was.
I give this to you to harbor courage.
You can not dig it out.
It exists in the memory of lush foliage, sweet fragrance,
   budding beauty.
My heart cries out at what could have been.
As the tree stands tall in all its failure
To endure.

Gail Lebowitz Shell

Words Of The Heart

"True words of the heart say the way you make me feel", to have a sexy lady love only me is a thrill, so don't you ever worry, don't you ever be sad. Our love will always be strong and our kids will always call me Dad!...letters come to me behind the walls and bars of steel and stone, my heart is full of love for you so we never have to be alone, the day's go slowly by, it hurts so bad, I could cry. I stay strong and pray for the release day, to hold you in my arms and take away your tears fear, and harms, like the words I have told you oh so many times Jill I love you there is no other lover. I wish to be a part, because there is only room to love but one. In my heart... So Jill don't you worry I see this as another test. If I make it to the other side I get you the very best! But if I fail, for I have not sinned,...all that bad, I can say, I will see you in heaven for this I will pray,...here on the last of this page is what I see each day, looking in the mirror. I see your man the Daddy of our babies your lover and best friend...

Elvis Dwayne Presley

Birth Mother's Lament

I searched the card and gift shops
and I searched the grocery stores too
for a card that said what I
wanted to say as a Mother's Day wish for you.

There were pretty ones and cute
ones and ugly ones and such.
They all talked of daughters and
how memories meant so much...

About when you were young and you lost your first tooth
or you fell and skinned up both knees.
And even about your first day at school
and of learning your ABC's.

About the night in the park-way
after dark - and that boy and your very first kiss.
And of all of those times, the hundreds of
times, and the millions of times that I missed.

Well, I read them all one by one
and put them back on the shelf,
and I decided right then to take out my pen
and write you something myself.
And I did. Love, Mom.
Bludworth

Ode To A Farm Truck

Every patch needs one and that's a
fact. To save the owies we get in our backs.
It roars and snorts and gets more
than just flats. But where would
we be without the old wide bed and broken racks.
From the mini to the Maxi they
are on the road everyday. They get
their share of fun, work and play.
With names like "Old Betsy," "Little Red,"
and "Putt Putt." They make many a run
through grass, gravel and rut.
Ann K. Kelso

Memories

No sound of children at play anymore
No shouts of laughter of kids at our door
Bats, balls, and gloves are all stored away
The yard now is silent and empty where he played
His favorite old teddy bear is covered with dust
His bicycle with flats is beginning to rust
His stereo quietly sits on the station he played
The pictures on his wall are beginning to fade
There's never a mess in his room anymore
No clothes or toys to clutter the floor
His room now is dark and still at night
No reason to burn his little night light
The loss of a child is so hard to bear
You hold to the memories of the love that you shared
And relive different moments of that wonderful time
When they were at home and life was divine
They grow up so fast then one day they are gone
And all you have left are memories to hold on.
Billy J. Nivens

Untitled

After one look, I knew you were mine
Though we'd never met, you were always close to my heart
This day forever imprinted in memory
The day you entered my world
The day my life is changed for all eternity
No other love can compare to that that is yours
You have broken the barriers that surround my heart
Not with a word, a touch or a look, but because you are
Freely you have given me the greatest gift, unconditional love
Not in increments like a reward for a good deed done
Not as loan to be repaid, but in generous portions for all time
You are the reminder of the purpose of my mortal days
Untainted, you are the image of complete innocence
You are filled with the purity of sweetness
You are the perfection of God's creation
I pray your spirit remains as it is today
That harm never seeks you out
That you meet all things good
For this, my beautiful child, is your born right
Jennifer I. Hagood

I Have Reached Ninety Three

And everything I see
seems more distinct, more colorful.
Cloud formations at sunset, sunrise
Spectacularly beautiful
The soft glow of the full moon more appealing
And the glitter of the evening star brighter
Even blue jays friendlier, bluer
All flowers intensely lovely
Has my vision cleared?
Or my sensibility deepened?
Or have I finally realized that
life is precious?
And nature lavishes gifts on humanity
Perhaps the environmentalists
Are the true modern prophets?
Viola Q. Seligo

You Have Me In You

You've seen what I've seen, you've done what I've done,
You know what I know.
You have given joy and happiness. I have taken pain and sorrow.
I try to do what you've done and you try to do what I've done
I think you are better than I for I take pain and give it to myself
All the grief is in my mind.
You have cried yourself to sleep for what you have heard.
I cried myself to sleep for what I have felt.
I give warning to all not to give up what you have
For that is what I've done
I got this life because I hated my life so they gave me a new one.
I wished everyone I meet to live a happy life.
I wished you weren't the one. The one they gave it to.
But it is not my decision.
You don't know it's me. But I know it's you.
For what I have seen you act.
How I've heard you speak. And what I see in your eyes
I know what you went through. (But I wish you didn't have to).
I know a lot and learned a lot from you.
I hope you get a better life because silence was my death.
Bambi Rivas

Freedoms

A free land,
Remove the mask.
Our freedoms
Cut short.

Free speech is controlled,
Don't sing this or that.
It is not an infringement,
It is for our own good.

Hey don't burn that flag
As an expression of disagreement.
Or your freedom will be removed,
It is good for the stamina of the country.

Watch who you love,
It will cause great pain
To defend a country that refuses you marriage
It is good for the morals of the country.

By keeping quiet we can keep our freedoms,
But speak out and they could be lost,
So defend these freedoms
That exist only for a few
   Rhonda Wise

My Parents' Undying Love

You are the greatest parents and it's plain to see,
Your love and understanding is the best for me.
Nothing is more precious than my parent undying love,
It will stay with you when they're gone up above.

Your undying love will last forever so I keep it in my heart,
Your love and caring in my life is a real big part.
Your hard work and value are now a part of me,
You taught us well and to be the best that we can be.

My Parents' undying love is always showing that you care,
It's everlasting love that parents and children will always share.
You're always there whenever we've needed you,
If we're sick or in trouble, we know you'll do what you can do.

Thank you for your undying love, it means a lot to me,
You're the greatest parents and I feel it's the way it should be.
It will always stay with us, when you're gone up above,
Cause nothing is more precious than a Parent's Undying love.
   Tracey Miracle

They Don't Know What They Missed

Life is confused and very complicated
And hard to understand, so they say
But isn't true (though poetically stated)
That we have made it this way?
Life is what we make it, can't you see?
And though now it seems it has always been
Long ago it wasn't this race for the money
Nor was it what, who, and when.
Nor cars or clocks, but they didn't fuss
They didn't worry about jobs, bills, and inflation
They lived with nature, but it's too late for us
Because now we're a civilized nation.
Of the things they didn't have, we could make a huge list
But the truth is we don't know what we missed.
   Rhonda McFall

Mother's Day

Put on your corsage, shine your shoes,
Today is the day you're paid your dues.

Stand tall and proud, you're like no other,
You're the queen of queens, you are a mother.

You've wiped a brow and brushed a tear,
You've held a hand and calmed a fear.

When no one cared or could be found,
I knew you'd always be around.

You've loved me sad, you've loved me true,
You've loved me when I didn't love you.

As days turned years, your children grew,
They bore their own and then they knew.

They knew the love, the tender care,
They knew that you were very rare.

Who else could love without condition,
When kids were sick and Dad went fishin'.

You've given love from dusk to dawn,
And how I dread the day you're gone.

And so I'll tell you now my mother,
I love you, Mom, you're like no other.
   Mary O'Neill

Untitled

When I was very young
I thought that life fit some dead poet's dream
Of easy contentment and perpetual hope.
Oh, many years have passed since then.
And now I realize that life is like
A vibrant, fluctuating string,
Sounding and resounding tones of
Solemn sorrow, bitter mockery,
Sweet acclamation and exuberant joy!
Is it whatever was hoped for?
Or is it what we made it seem?
Of one thing I am certain and that is this:
With my hand in the hand of God I do awaken
Ev'ry morning ready to explore a new page of time.
   M. R. Johnson

The Melodies Of Life

A lullaby, a nursery rhyme,
a love song sweet and low,
A march majestic, loud and strong
to help keep step where'er you go,
A waltz, a polka, jazz or blues,
to brighten life - forget the news!

The wedding march; two lives unite;
The sacred hymns to spread God's Light;
The Carols sung at Christmas time,
And New Years Eve brings Auld Lang Syne.
"Happy Birthday to You" on your special day.
Then the solemn peaceful chords of the organ as they play
in reverent retrospect of a life just passed away...
... The Melodies of Life.
   Jeanette Tindula

Numerology Of The Hostages

January 20, 1981
"Spread His word over all the earth,"
That's what the Bible said.
52 Hostages, one for every week in the year,
52 Hostage families and friends pray for their dear,
52 Hostages, a miracle from heaven that they survive,
All came home to their loved ones alive!
52 Hostages, one for the Atlantic, the Pacific and each State,
444 days they suffered, yet they do not hate.
Into Numerology for a moment, let us delve.
444 days equal three fours or four times three equals twelve.
12 Disciples of God, as in days gone by,
but now, our Disciples must multiply,
As the world today has gone astray,
And for all people, we must pray,
That we spread love and peace, and cease our evil ways,
Because God promised to return one of these days.
52 Hostages, each one very brave.
Welcomed home, America and the world, to save.
   Marian Waufle Flannery

A Fond Remembrance - Flight 800 - 17th July 1996

A fond remembrance with tears
Could only be thought of with painful fears,
Of why this should have ever been,

Over the atlantic with the stars
So bright, as well as the hopes
And dreams with them tonight,
With all their thoughts so far away,
Who could ever think of this disaster today!
Oh Lord we cry why should this
Be, such hatred for such humanity.
We must remember all aboard
And we must pray to the bereaved Lord.
For peace and rest eternal,
For in this land of turmoil
Something must be said of this
God bless you all in your eternal rest.
   Linda M. Michael

What Is A Mother?

A mother is someone who holds you close to her heart.
Always ready to guide you with gentle words of encouragement
Yet setting you free to find out for yourself
Just who you are and who you won't to be
and who you won't to be in your life

A mother is someone who dreams great dreams for you.
Yet accepts the dreams that you decide to follow,
and will always love you just the way you are

Mom, your love means so much to me it always has.
It always will.
   Dorshire Thomas

Cousins

   I have a bunch of little cousins,
Who I baby sit every summer,
They scream, yell, and all they talk
about is using #2.
   I love them very dearly,
even though they never mind me,
and when the time comes for them to leave,
I just take a vacation, and that spells my
relief for the week.
   After a few months,
I begin to miss them so,
and then after the next summer,
I'm ready for them to go!!!
   Leslie Byrd

May This Happen! Just For You!

May the grass keep getting greener
   as you travel life's pathway.
May the sun shine bright and early
   at the start of each new day.
May the flowers bloom profusely
   in their splendorous array.
May the gentle breezes sooth you
   on each hot summer day.

As the clouds begin to darken and the rain begins to fall,
   May the warm and tiny droplets feel cleansing to your face.
As you climb the stairs to heaven
   May the moon glow brightly at your feet.
And once you reach the summit — and lie down to sleep!
   May the clouds and stars surround you
      in your eternal peace!
   Paul Annin

Earth Mother Cries

Men raped the land,
   money to fill their hand.
      Earth mother groaned.
Business poison the river,
   and ruin our vigor.
      Earth Mother moaned.
Rain forest stripped for corporate gain,
   but all we get is acid rain.
      Earth Mother sobbed.
Oil is spilt on the seas,
   OPEC says it's nothing see.
      Earth Mother wept.
Man takes in waste,
   Soon it will be too late.
      Through it all Earth Mother cries.
   David M. Coleman

My Passion

You are so very special!
I have hidden desires I wish to explore with you.
Your sensuality turns me on!
When you touch me, I tremble and adore it.
My lips ache to brush ever so gently across your entire body.
When you look at me my fantasies begin and
When you hold my hand, I'm on fire!
I want to do things I've never done before with you!
I want to learn to love and I want to teach,
I'm in love with romance,
Am I then strange for telling you how I feel?
   Eileen O'Marra

Bless You Mommy!

"Mom" was something I always thought I'd be
But as time went on, it just wasn't meant for me
When one summer's day, we got the call
A baby girl waited and we felt 100 feet tall!
In a matter of minutes, after such a long wait
Our lives changed forever, due to someone else's fate.

In two short years, our daughter has grown
She crawled and she scooted and finally walked alone.
While driving one day, I happened to sneeze
When this little voice, who likes to please
Said "Bless You Mommy", my heart skipped a beat
My eyes filled with tears and I knew I could meet
All that was expected of me, for I am a "Mommy" now, you see.
   Susan Montgomery

Just Knowing Someone Cares

The dawn arrives each day with a wake up call from you,
And starts my heart to flutter and soar, though you're not aware of what you do
Just a simple "Good morning and" Have a good day.
Is all it takes to chase any blues away.
The morning goes much smoother, knowing someone cares.

All morning thoughts of you drift in and out of my mind.
I often wonder if you're thinking of me at the same time.
Lunch time doesn't come fast enough, for I begin to watch the clock
For I know that soon the phone will ring, and once again you're Joey on the spot.
And I feel good, knowing someone cares.

As my work day comes to an end, I know your call will come.
To speed me on my way and send me safely home.

The day's come and gone, time for rest is her.
But not before the final call, the one that is most dear.
The one that wishes me, "Have a good night," and Sleep well.
I close my eyes with this thought, someone really cares.
Pat Champ

You Are My Child

I didn't carry you inside of my womb,
but my heart has plenty of room,
I wasn't the one to feel the joy at the
birth of a new baby boy.
I wasn't so privileged to hear your first
cries or gaze in amazement at your
beautiful blue eyes.
I wasn't there to hug you so tight and
chase the scaries away in the night.
I came into play a little late in the
game but I had big dreams when I took
your Dad's name.
Time passes quickly, days become years.
I don't want to push you so I choke down my tears.
If I had one wish guaranteed to come true,
I'd wish that you felt the way that I do.
That you are my child.
Debbie Shifflett

A Witch's Flight

When the Moon is high and shining bright
You can see the bats flying thru the night
If you look real close you just might
See a Witch in full flight
Not many get to see this for she is fast
Only there for an instant but her image will last
And on a future night when the Moon is high
You will lift your eyes up to the sky
You will wish you could and hope you might
Again see a witch in full flight...
Nina S. Robinson

Special People

A virtuous woman is one to behold
But on this special occasion
it's our mothers we uphold.
For they are the ones who took time to care;
Who bowed the knee to say a prayer.
They stayed up at night
When we had the flu;
And their work was never done
With things to do
They are special people
Who need our love,
And they are gifts of God
Sent from above.
Kerry W. Nonnenmocher

Dear Daddy

So many things I wish I could ask you face to face,
where we could be together for a short time in our special place.

I remember your name was the first thing I spoke,
remembering your smile and your funny little jokes.

I remember you calling me daddy's little girl,
your little princess on top of the world.

But now you're gone and in the past,
and the thought of having a dad didn't really last.

Months have gone by since I've heard your voice,
hoping and waiting for you to call since I have no other choice.

I try to hate you so the pain I feel will ease,
but the love I feel comes flushing back like a gentle breeze.

I remember the day that we had to part,
I laid down my head and my heart broke apart.

But I just like to tell you from the start,
that I'll always love you in my heart.
Evelyn Janet Maldonado

A Mother's Gift

Lord, I've asked you in my prayers
"What do I have that I could share?
My talents are so small and few,
What could I give to honor you?"

At last my answer comes to heart.
I should've known it from the start.
No other beautiful or precious gift,
Than my own children to you I lift.

If I should give them back to you,
Your love and aid will see them through.
If they should roam in satan's sin,
I know you'll bring them home again.

They'll honor you and ne'er will sin,
You'll lead them, and make them win.
So God, I give this gift to thee,
You use their lives to set them free.

And if I give them back to God,
To guide the paths that they will trod,
I know when eternity comes around
They will with your great grace abound.
Joan Gross

Presently

Too much blood drawn in anger
So little peace made in love
Too many lives left shattered in hatred
So few good things to dream of

Too many wars with no meaning
So few chances to build in caring
Too many things dark and with constant evil
So little time is spent in sharing
Stephen Geerdes

Freedom

People come in many different sizes, shapes, colors
We should not try to sell the other
It is crazy and so are you
to think this deal just might go through
Aren't you glad that we are free
Freedom means a lot to me.
Rachel Kick

The Reluctance Of Youth To The Passing Of Time

I sit at my window and look out upon the changing landscape, and wonder where all the birds have gone. Have they flown south already, so soon?

No, no it's much too early, much too soon,
Come back Summer, come back birds, you're passing my years so fast, too early.
Let's let Summer last forever, I don't want to grow older.
I'm afraid of the world, of trying new things. Scared am I of leaving my protective womb.
No, no it's much too early, much too soon,
Come back, you crickets who sang such sweet melodies in the night.
Don't collect those acorns, you silly squirrels; if you leave them be,
Summer . . . will come back, you'll see.

Where are all the green leaves that danced so merrily in the breeze?
Don't tell me, they have all gone too!

How did I fail, where did I go wrong, I thought I commanded you all to stay, but instead you've gone . . .

Kimberly L. Runner

Poet's Life

Through the eyes of a poet, life is not the same,
it becomes a mirage of words mystified in pain.
The words are my breath and air,
and the pain is thriving but never fair.
I write my sorrows in darkness and in light,
I ponder over thoughts in my plight.
I write my fears not in blood, but in ink,
the smoothness persuades me to think.
I think not about people and things,
but about the heartaches that life brings.
I haven't conquered much at my age,
but I know that as I turn each page,
I will face another struggle in my life,
but I will take it with strife,
because I know that it is a test,
and ignorance will not allow me to see the rest.

Antoinette Palermo

The Music of the River

   Take a lesson from the river when
obstructions try to block;
   It just keeps on flowing over or around
each stone and rock
   When a mountain looms unnoticed and is
suddenly ahead,
   The river meets the challenge, finds
another course instead.
   Oh the music of the river is a sweeter song by far
Than if there were no obstructions that would try its path to mar.
For the boulders add their beauty to the foamy rhythmic beat.
It inspires the birds to singing and the travelers to retreat.
Can a life be like a river? Can it sing through strife and pain?
Can a person go on living through each sorrow, stress, and strain?
We can find a richer channel round each problem hard to solve.
With a faith and trust in Jesus, walking hand in hand with God.
He can make the music sweeter and more beautiful to sing
And each mile growing stronger with deeper love it brings.
For the pebbles make the music as the river flows along
Each obstruction adds its key notes to the music of the song.

June Doris Huffman

Ready, Or Not?

Fingers wrap themselves very carefully
around the instrument.
Muscles begin to dance.
The hand at the ready,
the instrument prepared...

But, no words flow,
muscles halt their dance.
Only stillness.
Was the preparation in vain?

A flicker, then a flash,
revelation? Much pain.

From whence comes the flash and twitch
to drive the dance.
Must pain or delight be the music to ignite
the light?

Gary Pope

"Why A Golf Ball Doesn't Grow Hair"

A golf ball doesn't have or grow hair,
   because if it did it wouldn't be bare.
It wouldn't be able to roll on the ground,
   and be hit with a golf club up onto a mound.
When it rolls on the golf course it collects dirt and mud,
   causing it to be shampooed with plenty of sud.
Next would come brushing the long tangled hair,
   which had gotten worn out from being hurdled through the air.
When its hair becomes long and needs to be cut,
   it's out of luck, for no one has the gut,
   to give a golf ball a hair cut.
So its hair keeps on growing, until it's so long,
   that it reaches all the way to Mars—and so on.

A golf ball with hair would be such a scare,
   that you would want to display it at the state or country fair.
People would come from everywhere just to stare,
   at the weird looking golf ball that has and grows hair.
So now you all know why a golf ball doesn't grow hair,
   because if it did it wouldn't be bare.

Catherine Zatarski

Mother Of Mankind

This wondrous world that we call earth,
   Mother of mankind, since our birth,
We are we doing? What we have done?
   Are we fighting a battle that cannot be won?
We all agree that we're destroying this land,
   Still it continues and by our own hand.
Do the futuristic movies, correctly portray.
   The life that our children will inherit someday?
A world that is shattered, a world torn apart.
   By lust and greed, without a heart?
Is man so shallow, that he cannot see,
   The pain and the suffering of this legacy?
We don't need a prophet, to see the end of time.
   We need only to look, at the violence and crime.
The moment has come for us to stand and unite.
   For our children and future, for which we must fight.
To falter or fail, a high price we will pay.
   The highest mountain yet to climb, but still the only way.

Cherie Hobbs

Spoiled Harvest

It takes a community to raise a child
An admonition perceived not mild
Violence becomes the way of the son
Father resembled Attila the Hun.
An innocent heart did tear and burn
Where, oh where, could he turn?
His mother stood so coldly by
Silently ignoring the desperate cry.
Now we wonder 'why' at the teenage fun
Exhibiting power brandishing a gun.
The paralyzing fear he felt so young
Remains inside, seeking a voice and a tongue.
Society pays for the parents' sin
Revenge for the terror does finally begin.
To start on a path even close to straight
Focus now, before it's too late.
The child has needs but he's not aware
He's learned to hate, for himself not care.
We must understand the searing pain
His parents' love he could never attain.

Eileen A. Hayes

Look, I'm Important Too

I saw the child in the family, cared for, protected and loved.
There was no doubt this child was important "Sent from God above".
Yet with all the love and understanding from me and you,
I can still hear him say, LOOK, I'M IMPORTANT TOO....

I see the mother, working, caring for everyone around...
She is not to express her feelings, no not even a sound.
After all, this is what mothers are for, and this is very true.
But sometimes she wants to scream, LOOK, I'M IMPORTANT TOO....

What about dad, working day after day...
All the family responsibility seems to come his way.
There must be money earned for food, shelter and clothes,
  to name a few.
Do we think of his feelings, LOOK, HE'S IMPORTANT TOO...

I look at grandparents, sure some are growing old.
Why listen to them? They should do what they are told.
But grandparents are important, and not once but quite a few.
Say with conviction, LOOK, WE ARE IMPORTANT TOO...

As we approach the family then, it was ordained by God, We know...
Take a good look, give an important place as our love we show.
Yes "our" family and God's family all have dreams.
LOOK, WE ARE IMPORTANT TOO,
No matter how small our duty seems...

Clara Vines

Lost In The Fog

What's a world in black and white?
It's a hopeful dream that'll never be seen
Because when you're awake
It's always something in a shade of gray
Or something in between
And the textures and hues of the color
Are our only guide to right and wrong
But the normality of its shade
With its oh so mistakable tint
Leaves us a casualty
Of conscience
And confusion
Judging for ourselves
What's bad
And what's worse
This indecisive tone
Clouds our minds
And covers our eyes
Leaving us dazed
And lost in the fog

Michael Peter

From Within

Look into my eyes if you're so bold,
into my world of secrets untold.
If you go where most don't dare,
you'll unleash the soul deep down in there,
though many loving hearts have tried,
it's hard to open what I try to hide.
But let me give you a little clue,
so listen close here's what you do.
No key, no locks, no doors to open
there's been quite a few who have tried so often
it's nothing material that you're thinking of,
all you need is plain old love.

Terry W. Early

"Housewife's Fantasy"

Oh! I was meant for gentle times
in a golden age - not now;
I wasn't meant to cook and scrub,
but - curtsy - flirt and bow.

I could have been a countess,
no doubt, the mistress of the king.
Who else would I choose as lover-
perhaps a duke - for an occasional fling.

Yes, I was meant for gentler times,
not duty above and beyond,
I'll finish this dream when I have the time-
right now - I gotta go clean the "John".

Doris Snyder

Untitled

Laughing smiles, playing children, happy families, warm feelings
do not penetrate to where I stand.
I place my hand upon the cold musty glass of the window
yet I cannot feel that sense of...
that sense of feeling wanted.
My hand slowly closes into a fist
I beat and I beat, but I cannot break it.
With my bruised hand at my side
my head falls forward, the coolness feels soothing upon my
  burning forehead.
With closed eyes I stand erect once more
and place my trembling hand on the smooth glass.
But the coolness is gone
replaced with... Warmth?
My eye-lids rise to where my hand rests.
A hand much smaller than mine is placed opposite my own.
My glower glides down
down to a young girl
a young girl with smiling eyes
who mouths the word
hi

Hilary Merina

The Untitled

What is! What's to be sitting on the
  banks over looking trees —.
What's to be! Seeing the truth,
  feeling the pain, no one to share
happiness or the gain —?
What is, what's to be! Clear as minds
  are, clear as skies above shall be.
Faith in love not meant to be as for me.
  What is, what's to be!

Richard G. Salas

Building Life's Bridges

When we enter this world of complication
As a parent we try to intercept the pain
Giving our children a life of expectation
Never knowing when or who's to blame.

Life is a bridge that leads to nowhere
Unless you build it strong enough to last
Take each step that leads to somewhere
Make it count but not so very fast.

We've all been tested many times
Through disappointments and aggravation
Recognizing and accepting the signs
To rectify and change your destination

The future holds more than it ever seems
Parents hearts ease when they've done their best
Seeing a child starting to build their dreams
Knowing that they've passed the final test.

Take each day with love and be content
Some get one chance to make their life complete
Knowing the lessons learned have been well spent
The second one is the bridge beneath your feet.

Barbara J. Noel

Illusions

Illusions would be best
If sometimes they would last
And not be torn apart
  by stark reality.

A case in point is my mother
who loved her sister and nephews
much more than she would ever
care for her own husband and daughter.

She and her sister were
forever two little girls, frozen in time

They played violins together
and my mother was always
second fiddle in this
as she was in everything else.

This family's love evaporated
when the sister died
and the nephews never visited.

The daughter she had abandoned emotionally,
she and her husband cared for
the mother in her hour of deepest need, her true family.

Beverly Rowe

Untitled

Two souls as one joined beyond the grave
A breeze of darkness breaks them away
Lost love lost love spread throughout
lost souls two souls with hearts full of doubt
He sees she sees in the deep blue
A dream it seems to good to be true
My love my love
  I'll always
    Love U

LaMuk Makins

Prayer For Positivity

How passionate I look for what I don't want to see;
How negativity brings out the worst in me;
I'm a spiritual wanna be, so close to reality;
Oh higher-power, please help my positiveness show through;
I don't want to just think it, I want it to be true!

Fran G. Merritt

A Mother's Love

When I was a baby, you bounced me on your knee,
When I cried, you held me in your arms.
You rocked me to sleep in your rocking chair,
You were always there!

Ever so proud were you when I took that first step,
Ready to catch me in case I fell.
You were always there!

Your hugs and kisses were ever so dear,
I felt I had nothing to fear.
You were always there!

When I was happy or when I was sad, you would be there
with heart and with hand, to guide me, to help me,
to laugh or cry with me.
You were always there!

As I grew older, it was plain to see,
you gave up so much just to give to me.
You were always there!

Now you are gone, and I miss you so,
but in my heart, I know,
You are still there!

Kathleen M. Pacholke

At The End

When my life comes to an end
I know I will always have a friend
When my family has reached their goal
The all mighty God will rest their souls.

So I cry and cry to see the light
Because in my eyes and others it's so bright
So rise, rise to your destiny
And you'll see your life could be infinity.

'Til the end of the Earth, the day I die
If there is peace on this Earth I will not cry
Those with good lives, the ones that don't sin
Will have a good life at the end.

Joseph L. Hogan

Imagination

  Imagination is a place inside your head,
The place that makes you think you see that monster under the bed,
  In your imagination, just let your thoughts run wild,
Nothing's ever dull or boring, nothing's ever mild.
  Fight a monster late at night, or a dragon in the spring,
You never can quite be sure of the adventures it will bring.
  You could soar up through the clouds on paper wings,
Or even join the happy bluebird as he sings.
  You could own a castle, or win the lottery,
Or be positively right when you think "the most important
  person is me."
You never can be sure of the adventures it will bring,
  Now you see, finally, imagination does all these things.

Ashly Raiti

Sleep Time

I lie in my bed
With a soft pillow under my head

Trying to fall asleep
With my thoughts getting soft and deep

I reminisce about the warm summer's days
Oh, how I played so happy and gay

But now it's time to turn out the light
And say "Goodbye world, have a good night!"

Maryann DiLuglio

Sundown

As I stand alone atop these jagged rocks,
The icy wind screaming in my ears,
I can see the water rushing below,
violently smashing against the cold earth.
Darkness is slowly creeping upon me
like a wicked virus invading my blood,
the wind in freezing my bruised tender
skin like a forest fire eating raw flesh,
now it's raining heavily on my weary head
Sounds like autumn thunder,
my body is drenched and my tears
taste like the bitter sea water,
Deep black clouds are rushing by,
As if to say good-bye
In the distance I can see that
beautiful star slowly disappearing
into the darkness that will soon engulf me.

DeAnna Johnson

I Love You Auntie

Just sitting here, thinking of my aunt
Who raised me from the age of four.
I know she's sitting and waiting for me
  to walk through that door.

My heart is filled with gloom, sadness, pain and woe
I know she's feeling the same, but she'll never let me know.
I often think of how different things would've been
If I hadn't left from home, to go live with my kin.
I know I would be there to help her a little more
There's no doubt about it, I would be there for sure.

But life has a way of things working out
While I'm here thinking of her
Her sisters are taking her about.
She's going out today for a little while
For a few hours and I'm sure that will make her smile.
I love you Auntie, hope to see you soon across the long miles.

Shirley Dargan

The Rain

If I was a drop of water, would you catch me?
If so, what would become of me?
Would you part your lips to the clouds to drink me?
Or would you cup your hands firmly together to catch more of
  me and relentlessly pound me against your naked person to
  feel me drip slowly with your nature until you're lost
  amidst a shower of contentment?
Or would you, without hesitation, step out of the rain?

John P. Byrd Jr.

Quiet Poem

An unopened can of spam collecting dust
while waiting to be bought and opened

A black cat creeping across the window
sill on a calm, dark night.

A snake in the dessert slithering towards
its prey with utmost determination.

A child studying in class, yet daydreaming
about taking a trip to a fluffy cloud.

A hush over a crowd of a critical
moment in the game.

And me
As a mouse creeping through the house
looking for a crumb of food.

Andrea Williams

Untitled

I lie in bed awake.
Cold. Shivering with fear.
I look outside my window. Darkness... Black... Midnight.
Tapping. Tapping against my window.
The skinny branch like the grim reaper beckoning me to walk his path.
Shadows stretch against the wall and fall onto the floor.
My feet. Just out of the reach of death.
Tapping stops. Sweat rolls down my forehead
  Silence!
The hoot of an owl pierces the deadly silence.
I jump. Shadows reach out more. Clawing my legs. Ice cold.
I run off my bed and into the corner. Far away from shadows.
Shadows reach out more. Tapping starts again.
Nowhere to run. Nowhere to hide.
Shadows grip my body with their icy fingers.
I scream. No one can hear.
For I am all alone.
I walk the path of grim reaper.
I Am All Alone. All Alone.

Hannah Thomas

Tragedy Of A Hero

To the many of you who are still in a "fight"
Memories that never fade from your sight
Bombs that still explode in midair
No gratitude shown by those who don't care
Walk down the street with your head held high
For there's still some who care, still some who cry
You fought for your country, you fought for me
If only we could make everyone see
They take you for granted, they live in peace
But in your mind the memories don't cease
All the friends you lost killed in the war
You sometimes question why? What for?
For an ungrateful nation who shows no love
To their fellow man or their Lord above
Thank you so much for all that you've done
The blood that was shed, the wars that were won
Because of you our country has come far
You've given us the right to be who we are
We have not forgotten you, do not fret
You are in my honor, I am in your debt

Lorraine Telfer

"Evening Shades"

Like the moving gray expanse
across the sky this afternoon
the evening shades, so rapidly changing
like my mind, the thick and heavy motions,
one minute clear, the next clouded
without mercy, a relentless unending ache
covering my soul.

The sky producing many moods this afternoon,
details clear memories, forever repeating stories,
the dark covering, begs to remind me
moving close for a moment, then retreating
afraid to linger too long, for fear the day be ruined.

Occasional rumbling, heard at a distance
flickering lights, the forces screaming the eventual reality
bright flashes like rare moments of understanding
beautiful, yet lasting no longer,
the colors now silent, a darkness at last,
envelopes while quieting my restless mind.

Sheryl N. Bolling

The Pretender

Questions asked with answers unknown
feelings felt with fear to be shown
emotions trapped within the soul
reality's blind to the drunken fool.

Faking smiles while knowing your pain
acting normal while feeling insane
The cautious ones will live to tell
that reality turned out worse than hell.

Apathy proves to kill the mind
Ignorance shows to be less than kind.
Belligerent fools will learn to see
There's no suppressing what was meant to be.

Expecting others to tell your lies
Hiding away from the truth outside
You will only live to pretend
finding yourself alone in the end.

Melissa Heiry

Life

Life is only but a dream,
a story book in which every ream,
contains events that were good and bad,
and things that we wished we could of had.

We watch days go by and by,
and find that time does fly,
special moments we hold so dear,
and must keep our family very near.

Each day begins in a different way,
and changes happen every day,
we live and learn and grow through the years,
and find out we cry many tears.

Our time here is very short,
we rely on friends and family for support,
to give us strength to make it through,
and keep each other in mind in whatever we do.

Amy Curry

Traveling To Self

Well, I'm on the way again. I am en route! By the way, thanks for the experiences...the helpful hints...the words of encouragement. In need of rest and relaxation, I travel out of the world to a specific place that is unique to me - my temple. In my temple, I listen to my spirit. I mean the Spirit. Each time I visit, I search for peace and hope to experience joy along the way. I've noticed that the road signs may change, but the route remains the same. Spirit was, spirit is, and spirit will always be. Although I often dream of what a joy it will be to someday travel the world, my travels out of the world bring me abundant joy. There, I find peace in the midst of the journey of life. Greater insight to do what is considered to be "right"... both day and night. My spirit is my road map. It is specific and unique to every human being and every living creature. To me, it's the best teacher. A good map will guide your path. You should know that. Next time you plan a trip that you feel will be "out of this world," look at your map. Travel to your temple. The only cost is time. Simply take time to travel to self. The journey is all that! ...many times more, thanks you, God.

Valerie D. Opher

To Be

Out of the dark halls of youth, in twos they came to lay their claim.
Circling, edging, isolating into the blackness of their bowels,
Satan's den has a James Dean poster.
Freckled faced, thin strowed hormones reaching out with
blood red eyes and their lies. He too young to know lies.
Pushed, pulled and striped of innocence,
pulled to the four quarters of the world.
No savior or God, no where to hide.
Less a being, more a creature.
And the hard earth comes slapping you in the face, and the sound crushes the ears.
Hell becomes a reality. Innocence forever lost.
Not once but twice the point was made, and like those before me,
I too am Hell. Yet life rages, and will not be still.
No Dark Night could he have ever imagined as this, yet the soul is not redeemed?
No contemplation achieved, and St. John ponders - "Why?"
To survive — "To be or not to be..." Shakespeare was much more the dreamer than the actor...Thank God for that.
To create and recreate, is the question.
For in that act of creation what forms will evolve
can only makes up ponder...Why?..." Ah, there's the rub."

Edward Young

Tightrope

Every day I make the trip,
back and forth, I've yet to slip,
I just can't seem to get a grip,
this is my life on the tightrope.

I see your face,
hear your silent scream,
in slow motion,
like a dream,
how much further can you lean?
Believe me it's farther than it seems,
this is my life on the tightrope.

If I slip I'll fall and die,
I think my friends would probably cry,
my family would always wonder why,
and breathing relief in a heavy sigh,
I could finally spread my wings and fly.
This...
Is my life on the tightrope.

Lisa J. Fox

Philosophically Polish

Captured in my eyes while I was dreaming
I gazed upon a star that was revealing
my own image reflecting against my soul

And then I realized these feelings as I was kneeling
as you they had fallen in the air as you I sought them so
appealing then again I lived them as a dare
racing against my God my spirit was captured in the light

Now if you can look through the windows of your soul
and speak with the heavens by a language that you know
then there is a man within whom is trying to find his way
will you answer him he is starving upon what they say

What happened to the light that shivering light
that gave insight into the mind of life
you used to carry me with laughter on your shoulder

James Thomas Miles

Mama's Ring

I have a ring my mother gave me, the day I turned sixteen.
It's not much, really...a bit of gold (I think it's plated),
A chip of a diamond that's hardly even there,
But it belongs to me.

At first I didn't like it, I said to Mama, "It's chipped and old."
But Mama only smiled...knowledge was in that smile,
A thing I was greatly afraid of then,
But I didn't dare to let her know it.

I wore it on my wedding day, just to please my mama.
She talked about tradition...a ring from the bride's mama first,
A ring from the bride's husband second,
But I was never much for tradition.

Mama died two weeks ago, quietly, in her sleep.
My ring became more precious then...a remembrance of Mama,
A remembrance of her mama, too,
But I of course had never seen that part before.

My daughter turns sixteen soon, three months to be exact.
I'll give her my ring on that day...a memory of her ancestors,
A hope she'll think of me sometimes,
But just like me, she won't realize its value now.

Nicole Broussard

Summer

Ice cream cones, picnics, swimming pools,
All of these things make you happy and cool.
Ninety degree temperatures are boiling hot,
Away from school where you are taught.

Vacationing in places from California to Spain,
Doing exciting things without using your brain.
Sunny days, cloudy days, really don't matter,
Raindrops from storm clouds land with a splatter.

Amusement parks are fun and fine,
The thing I don't like is waiting in line.
Soon school starts and you are sad,
But always remember, the joyful summer that
    you have had.

Autumn Rae Kuzmkowski

Michael's Poem

Always remember this dear loved ones,
The many ways he speaks to you
From far above the trees.

The gentle rain upon your cheeks are his tears,
They say, "I miss you."

The warm sun upon your shoulders are his hugs,
They say, "I love you."

The wind that whispers in your ears is his voice,
He says, "I'm safe here."

The diamond glint upon the snow is the sparkle in his eyes,
It says, "I'm happy."

So always remember
The many ways he speaks to you
From far above the trees.

Melissa L. Shepard

Destiny

How can mankind be so insane
To send a missile to down a plane;
To pollute our water, food and mind;
Always trying to kill mankind?
Are greed and power the most important gains?
Who will you control if no one remains?
Open your eyes and see what's real
And maybe you'll learn to love and feel.
Become aware we are all the same
Stop playing the race and religion war-game.
When stripped of skin, bones and faiths
We find the same destiny awaits.
Judgement day is what is in the end;
So change your ways so that you will blend.

Mary Louise Robichaud

Theresa And Mary

I know of two angels, that live in this world!
They have brown eyes and blue eyes, they're wonderful girls!
They're loving and caring, they're pretty and clean!
They're the most precious angels that I've ever seen!
They make your heart feel warm and your soul clean and happy!
I know this is true, because I am their daddy!
I love my angels with all my heart.
They have made my life the best to live, right from their start!

Charles Raymond Carpenter

Creation Of Beauty

The butterfly is a beautiful thing
as it swoops and flies and flutters its wings,
it seems to just ride on the waves in the air
a thing of beauty with never a care.

As we look upon it we know it to be
a beautiful creation of God that we see,
then we know we are included you and I,
a creation of God like the butterfly.

So look around you and know it's a great God we serve,
see the mountains, the oceans and all that we love,
the trees as they blossom, the jasmine at night,
all created for us, what a beautiful sight.

Evelyn L. Alvey

Growth

Such as a raindrop kisses the flowers
So will these roses grow from the silent touch
Even the star that glitters in the sky
Will send those soft rays to gently sooth the human spirit.
The thorns are no longer sharp but are
    gently smoothed with the breath of God
The Western wind will not uproot these flowers,
For the Eastern breeze will shield and uplift their stems
Gently the sun's rays mold the flower's beauty
Nurturing and protecting each other's essence.
The weeds will not smother them,
For these flowers are planted in fertile ground
What is unspoken can be heard
Even as the seed quietly splits to bring upon life
    So can this friendship flourish in the garden of God.

Christine E. Six

Tides Of Passion

My mind runs deep to the ocean depths of my soul.
Trying to find a place to hide where the current of life will pass me by.
Scared of the day I will be pulled free to swim with love again.

I once swam with the tide caressed by each wave and tantalized by the shore.
I heard cries beckoning me to see where the ocean and earth become one.
There I felt your touch.

Your solid grip held me while your passion seduced me and we became one.
A swirling mass of water and sand moving in a pattern that would never survive the ocean tide.
There I felt your love.

I reached out to pull you close but swirling grains of sand was all I felt.
Each one so different than the last so hard to keep together
so easy to let it sift through your hand.
The ocean receded and you were gone.

Michael J. Jacksic

Remorse

The lonesome creatures crawl in the dark midnight of dismay,
Over the lands shadows fall, into the blackness creatures stray,
You have opened your arms to fear, the creatures feed upon fright,
With each second they are coming near, but they diminish in daylight.

You must now escape your fate, so run-run from your past.
For the creatures shall await wherever the shadows are cast.

Lauren Kamlet

Where Is The Sunshine?

Where is the sunshine
To turn my night into day;
Where is the sunshine
To make things go my way.

Why do the gray skies lurk above,
Where are the blue skies, where is the dove;
I'm eaten up by loneliness,
And am longing for some happiness.

So where is the sunshine
To take away the rain;
Where is the sunshine
To take away the pain.

I keep hoping one day
The skies'll no longer be gray,
But break and become blue
Letting the sun shine through.

Where is the sunshine
To heal my broken heart;
Where is the sunshine
To keep me from falling apart.

Scott Awalt

Hate

As I stand, I see hate.
He has a brawny body that flexes with each step.
Trying to mad-dog me, sweat pours from his forehead.
His dark suit looks drab against the red handkerchief
   sticking out of his coat pocket.
Dark and dingy describes his hair,
And his countenance is pale.
When hate speaks, he utters a low, sinister, snarl.
There is a frigid feeling in the air when he is around.
It's like staring the Prince of Darkness,
   Straight in the eyes.

Christopher Stanton

The Hidden Room (A Prison Within)

Is there a place deep within your soul
Where feelings go when they need to grow.
A place so protected from the outside world
That no one gets in against your will.

We build our walls to protect our heart,
And hide within them so as not to hurt.
A prison we've built one stone at a time.
A place where we escape from time to time.

I hear a knock outside that door.
Is this a friend, or something more.
Is it time to reach beyond the door,
And risk hurt and disappointment once more.

A hug and a kiss, what is this.
Is this the opportunity I don't dare miss.
A friendship is being offered with a smile.
And arms reach out in loving style.

Can I trust myself to see what's real.
And trust these things that I feel.
I accept the friendship and the smile.
And dream for more all the while.

Jeanne Marie Lee

Young Love

Just walking in the rain
   Easing young love's pain
Raindrops blending with the tears
   Heart and mind so full of fears.

The wildness of the storm without
   Matches not the turbulent storm within,
High hope crushed to nothingness, you shout, -
   "It cannot be the end of life before life can begin!"

Walking, walking, walking in the rain
   Little white fists clenched with pain,
Your convictions soaring high,
   "This first love can never die!"

The raindrops cannot speak to you
   But, somehow, ease the pain they do,
Lessening young love's turbulence;
   Growth, an unseen recompense.

Martha Day

It's Not Halftime Yet

When I was young and in my prime,
I saw no need to keep track of time.
The summers were long and full of enjoyment,
and I had yet to discover words like "employment."

The years go by one day, then another.
"I" becomes "We" and wife becomes mother.
Weeks are now shorter and time is a commodity;
We hardly notice, as we're busy as we want to be.

The children are growing now, as I look around;
I notice my teens are not to be found -
As much as they were when they were younger;
They always came home when food was their hunger.

Now as adults they see us as Dad, Mom, and friends;
But questions come up like "Where are the ends?"
At 50 years old and constantly thinning;
We respond, there are no ends - only beginnings.

George E. Mark

Christmas Eve

Look at the holly and the mistletoe.
Catch the feeling of the first fallen snow.
The Christmas tree glowing with ornaments bright!
The soft, sweet carols sung all through the night.

Silver and gold! Red and green!
Let's light the lights to let them be seen!
It's the season to be happy and joyous!
So strike up the band and join the chorus!

Silver packages with red ribbon and a Christmas bell.
Let's tell the story of the First Noel.
Stockings with candy, they're such treats!
Tomorrow we'll open presents and then we'll feast.

Tomorrow will be jolly and gay!
We're all looking forward to Christmas Day!
Santa and Rudolph will bring us toys,
And to all the little girls and boys!

Rachel Killebrew

Mom

There is so much I owe to you
And payment in full will never come due.
I'll try to express in this poem of mine
But really to tell all, there isn't much time.

You brought Janet and I up to love everyone
To be honest, and brave when the time did come.
You were always there in all our troubles
To guide us through we'll ever be so humble.

Most of all you gave us your bountiful love
And taught us about our heavenly Father above.
I thank the Lord for you Mom each day
For you were the one who taught me to pray.

You and Daddy have been a blessing to us all
You served your purpose in the parenthood call.
And God had in mind when he sent us to you
And planned not to have a boy in a blanket of blue.

I owe you for so much, you see
To my heart you'll always have the key.
When I think of you I'll never be blue
For Mom, you see, I Love You.

Patty Morrow

The Light Of A Dream

The light of a dream always shines brightly
In your mind, heart, and soul.
It is a symbol of faith, belief, and hope.
Having faith in your dream.
Believing that you can accomplish anything.
And hoping and praying that you will succeed.
It shines far much brighter than any star could ever shine.
The light of a dream can take you anywhere your heart desires
Soaring up high in the bright sky
Or swimming deep down in the ocean
Wherever you want to go
Whatever you want to see
The Light of a Dream will take you there.

Mandy Gendon

Actuality

I often stand alone on a bleak mountain peak;
  Striving to give voice to troubling fallow thoughts;
    Attempting to recall an event that never occurred;
      Reaching to feel a new the touch never felt;
        Seeking to ease the hurt and pain never inflicted;
          And yearning to re-experience a life never lived.

James S. Arellano

Cry Of An Insane Man

Perplexing communication; Hatred
leeching from pipes of fear that pump from his heart.

"Mind's racing; Time's a wasting"
Thoughts that came across his weak mind.

Pacing back and forth; Watching:
Shadows lurk from around the corners of his room.

He shuts his eyes, tilting his dark head back.
He sighs loudly, scaring himself.

He fears being alone in the darkness.
His heart was broken; He's losing it.

"Why?, why?, why?" Questions repeated.
Over and over. "I'll never understand."

He sits back down, leaning against the white padded walls.
"I've been betrayed."

He peers out the window of the door.
The window is small and dauntingly possessive.

His eyes plead, "This isn't me."
"I've been deprived of the freedom I deserve."

He will be there, forever, it seems.
Crying out, "This isn't Me."

Carrie M. McClung

A Legend Of Old

Higher, higher than a star
Rests my heart within you
Took me ages to find out, you were never in doubt
I was the one you had in mind.
Stripped of all my facade.
Undo me, like you would a box of fancy candy
And reminisce, in what you'd choose.
If there were more than one, to choose from.
Then you'd see, what a difficult time I had
Saying "Dear you're the chosen one."
For, from where I sit up on high above the clouds
I see them all; with their glitter and gold
But yours was silver, like my own.
God forbid; I'd choose one, not of my own
To represent me as my messenger, below.
To tell all those, that yell aloud from the crowd
Of one hundred and forty four thousand to one.
You'd already begun, a story to be told!
To prophesy; "The year two thousand, has already begun"

Virginia Mair

It Wasn't Much

It wasn't much.
Just an array of dust swirling in an unseen wind.
Over time it coalesced into a divine string of pearls,
Following their Mama through the heavens.

It wasn't much.
Just a medley of amino acids swimming in a briny soup.
Over time they coalesced into microscopic sparks of life,
Following their instincts through the seas.

It wasn't much.
Just a pair of DNA strands hiding in a warm dark room.
Over time they coalesced and grew into an infant,
Following its instincts into the world.

It wasn't much.
Just a swarm of humanity crawling over the Earth.
Over time they coalesced into a single harmonious fleet,
Following their Mama to the stars.

It wasn't much.

Ann Hall

I Have Thoughts

Thoughts...

    I have many thoughts. Before them, there were dreams, and after them will probably be memories, but for now I have thoughts. I don't know how many I have, I just have them. I have thoughts about friends, family, life and where I live. Sometimes I have thoughts about my three closest friends and I going out one night of the summer. We leave the house at eleven o'clock and we all just walk through the dark streets. The streets that are rarely traveled. The ones that nobody even bothers to put on the map because no one cares for them. We're talking, we're laughing, we're clownin' around,...we're walking. Sometimes we walk for miles, sometimes up and down the streets, and sometimes around the corner. We don't ever know where we're going but we always remember the way back. We know it's time to return at dawn. We always return at dawn. Sometimes it seems like we're not walking but gliding. We glide past houses, with faces looking at the window wondering what all the commotion is, past street lights, with bugs flying around them like they're the source of all life, past stores, with people buying magazines, slushies, frozen dinners, and sometimes even stealing little things like gum or candy, they're all kids. The light from the store was now the light that guided us, since the street lights were behind us. We have fun all night long. We only care about ourselves when we're walking, nothing else. A bomb could go off and we wouldn't notice it because the only thing that matters is what we're talking about and where we're going. We're walking.

    I have many thoughts. Before them there were dreams, and after them will probably be memories, but for <u>now</u>... I have thoughts.

    Nile H. Russell

"The Walls"

I see you lying there,
Not knowing that I watch you...
Oblivious to the pain you're causing.
I long to reach out and hold you while you sleep,
But I can't.
The walls are building up between us and I can't stop them.
We share so much love,
Why can't it stop the walls?
You're not to blame,
Only the insecurity in my heart.
So many disappointments have made my heart weary.
It's so hard to believe...
Believe that someone like you could love me.
I want to believe it's true.
I know it's true;
In my mind.
But my heart doubts—and the walls are getting higher.
Make me believe;
Show me you care;
Help me tear down the walls.

    Stephanie Tugwell

Crazy Dreams

As your mind slowly drifts away
at the end of a very long day
and you begin to dream those crazy dreams
where everything isn't always as it seems.
You see warmth in the cold,
You see youth in the old,
You see smiling thru the crying.
You see life in the dying.
There is always confusion and madness;
Scared people and lots of sadness.
You wake up with a heartache,
Realizing what you saw wasn't fake.
It wasn't what you saw all the day through,
That craziness always surrounds you.

    Angela Finn

Why I Love You

It is the biggest question in the world,
and probably the hardest one too.
But when answering this question about you,
it becomes the simplest thing to do.

It is all the things that you do,
but especially the little things,
which cause me to love you.

The dedication of your love, to care for your man.
The continuous support and backing,
whenever trouble is attacking.
The silent looks, that are forever attaching.

But the most outstanding feature you possess,
is a tremendous deal of understanding and sense.
Forever knowing just what needs to be said and done,
irregardless of what may come.

These are not all, just some of the reasons I love you.
To tell you them completely, would take several lifetimes to do.

So just to let you know,
no matter what may happen or may come our way,
I will love you for always, forever, and a day.

    Charlie M. Carpenter

Melody Of The Swan

An elegant swan glides gracefully across the mirrored surface of the stream.
The motion is effortless as she merges as one with the silver flowing water.
The snow white of her feathers glisten with beads of clear cool water as she emerges from the depths of the stream.
Her beauty adds a mystical presence to the secluded meadow and the crystal brook that envelopes her world.
A soft mist parts around her lithe body as she drifts with the lazy current of the stream.
The waterfalls talk incessantly of their love for her penetrating, awe-inspiring beauty.
She holds her head high, unknowingly flaunting her radiant, glowing ethereal beauty.
The breeze whispers through the willow branches singing softly her glorious name.
The birds, awed by her beauty, sing melodious songs to her, cherishing the beauty placed before them.
This is the magical world of the swan, Queen of all that is eternally beautiful.

    Jennifer Monroe

The Bend In The Road

Death should remain beyond the bend
Not here where I can see.
I want him to take me by surprise
Not walk down the road with me.

Tell old Death I'm not ready yet
To meet him face to face
I know my hour is surely comin'
But, this ain't the time nor is this the place.

So tell that old dude to just be patient
While I take this road to the end.
'Cause he knows and I know it won't be long
Before I come around that bend.

    John F. Harris

My Daughter's Pain

For years I watched her struggle,
just to have a child.
The news would be good, we counted
the days.
Dreading the nights, afraid to sleep.
What would it bring?
I watched her go through this for years
hoping the next would be the one.
I never saw her envy a parent, only
hold the child tightly.
When a child would be lost through an uncaring deed.
She would turn her face toward me, with unshed tears.
As a mother, I had no bandaid for this.
Don't ask me not to cry, for I can see a
brown-eyed child
then God directed her feet to a nurse,
who knew of a doctor.
Well wonders never cease, my daughter
now has three healthy children.
But you know we know who to give the glory.

Ruth C. Dept

River's Heart

My love for you runs like a river
Too deep to measure
Too wide to contain
As warm as the sun on a summers eve
As delightful as the first snowflake of winter
But don't look to hard for it
or you may drown in it.

Stephanie Devorak

Barriers

Trying to pronounce unpronounceable words
on a fancy schmancy menu
is next to impossible, so I just point
and say, that's it - that's what I want.

It's hard to find your way home
when you're jumbled into a fast stream
of people, moving every direction-
but the one you're going in,
until you click your ruby slippers
three times in Kansas.

A mouse scimpers and scampers
through a maze of twisted glass walls.
At first, the mouse grinds his nose
against false pathways and exits,
until at last, the mouse figures out
what evil trick the guy in the white
coat is playing on him, so the mouse runs
the maze cleanly through, and the madman leaves.

Leigh Smith

Listen To The Wind

Listen to the Wind,
It whispers sweet nothings in your ear,
It forgives you if you have sinned,
It is the voice of an angel for the world to hear.

You must listen hard to try and understand,
It whispers to every woman, child, and man.
The wind follows you wherever you go,
Making the trees and bushes put on a show,
In encourages you if you are determined.

The wind whispers all and so much more,
It will tell you the stories by the shore.
Listen to the Wind.

Jennifer Kelly

The Bald Eagle March

For thee I hold all trust and hope within
With freedom to protect me from iniquity
Thee I honor

For thee I give my strength
And seek for understanding mind
To shape, to mold, to show one
Where the roads within thee lie

Thee I serve for thee I sacrifice myself
And pledge anew my faith
To maintain it for thy will

In thee I search for the truth
And pray for fresh new insight
Into instability and unrest
That plagues thee from the fall of all mankind

Thee I love
For thee I pride myself with thoughts to hold
And cherish the symbols and beauties of our land

To thee I look once again
And there the great Bald Eagle stands
Rejoice I now in proclamation America thee by mine

Susan Smeltzer

"Everything Is Silent"

Voices and whispers are heard.
Whispers unclean.
Words that are absurd.
Everything is silent.

Nothing is making a sound.
Yet someone is crying.
Where can this person found?
Everything is silent.

Yet mysteries,
Squeaking noises are near,
How can that be.
There is no one here.
Everything is silent.

So from where are these noises being sent?
For I can only wonder, because
I have no idea what any of them meant.
Everything is silent.

Now I hear something growing
Growing, spreading like thick black clouds
In a perfect blue sky.
The darkness is thickening.

Everything is now silent.

Stephanie Molnar

Only You

Only you can make my life worth while
Only you can make me smile
Only you can create a love so good and true
A love so precious and so new
Only can help our love grow so divine
That is why I have taken you to be only mine
Only you can help me enjoy the things in life
And that is why I have made you my wife.

Gregory Steven Bloom

A Journey Into Despair

Walking through the paths of my mind,
looking up front, to the side and behind.
Looking to see what I can find
on the road to endless foreverness.

It goes around in circles that never end.
Thought I could stop it only to begin again.
Always wanting to know what's on the other end
of the road to endless foreverness.

Doctors give me medicine to help me see
what they want me to see.
But the circle still continues and it's frightening me
on the road to endless foreverness.

Somebody would you please help me?
I'm here begging on bended knee.
Help me get off this terrible ride
on the road to endless foreverness.

Can't anyone hear my cries?
I'm screaming it to the top of the skies.
I wish I could get of this ride,
on the road to endless foreverness.
Juanita Minch

The Wish

One night I made a wish on the brightest star,
And my wish came true 'cause here you are.
I finally found my "Mr. Right",
Just because of something I said one night.
I never thought my wish would come true,
But that's before I met you.
I often wonder if I'm in a dream,
Cause when I think of you I seem to gleam.
I thank the Lord each night and day,
For granting my wish and sending you my way.
Heather Stokes

The Natural - Villanelle

I go to school because I want to learn
And make my presence in class to grow
I made a right decision and a right turn

Students study hard so they can earn
Knowledge from teacher's explaining lessons to show
I go to school because I want to learn

Going to school is like journey
Traveling on a subway every minute of the hour
I made a right decision and a right turn

A beautiful campus is the university, I attend
As I walk into this large, stone tower
I go to school because I want to learn

Passing a course us my major concern
In length of time to prepare, study, and score high on my tests
Now, I know I made a right decision and a right turn

Sunlight is my wake-up call with concern
To raise me from my bed to catch the subway on my journey
I made a right decision and a right turn
Kwan D. Miller

In The Eyes Of A Custodian

Some people ask "How do I find pride in my work?"
I say "Well, look here! I sanitize as in sterilize
I kill living matter, as in germs
For I am safety, as in freedom
from danger, picking up debris,
For I am the custodian!
The caretaker of your sustaining life!"
Bruce Wilson

Speculation

Silently the great ship sails by
As I stand alone upon the shore of the great sea,
Watching the waves roll off the moon's light.
Silently, tenderly, they speak to the shoreline
Whispering tales of their comings and goings.
Moving swiftly back out to sea
Pushing the massive ship toward its destiny.
Soon only the white sails are reflected on the water
Muddled shapes of sparkling light distorted by the water's movement.
How tall and proud those masts seem to stand in the sun's bright light!
As I turn to leave, I wonder;
Just where is that ship headed?
To sail away and reach new lands escapes me.
To roll like the waves continuously from one shore to another
    is incredulous.
Can life itself ever be so easy?
Kim Eldred

The Guider

The guider guides me everywhere
I know that he is mine, he's the one that cheers you
And makes the bright sun shine.
He takes me every where I want
Without leaving my own home
He lets me stay in one place
Or leaves me free to roam.
He guides me through my mind
And tells me the right things
And if I am real quiet
I can always hear him sing.
He takes good care of me
And keeps me in good health, and even if I go broke
If he's still there I'll have the wealth.
Everyone has the guider
If they really care, if you look way deep inside
You'll find that he is there.
He isn't hiding from you
So he will never part, he is the guide of guides
That guide, he is your heart.
Lindsay E. Good

Fugitive Or Miniature Death

   Soon they will come with a death that fits in the palm of the hand that's cold as ice. Soon they will come driven by the will to get me because I relieved others of their guilty conscience, their evil inhuman organic computers.

   Bloody hands, soon they will come loaded with miniature death, because they think me evil and a vicious animal filled with rage. When they touch they will be scared but when that door comes flying off its hinges they will take reassurance from the miniature messengers that spit from their hands and silently laugh, as if gutted by an almost invisible enemy.

   My limbs drop my breathing ceases and I travel beyond the minds eye.
Jaime Binns

To Our Grandparents With Love
(Thank You For Your Inspiration)

Grandparents give love while parents are doing their chores.
Grandchildren say, "Give us your time and love us some more."
Grandparents teach us nice things to know and take us places.
They are the reason why we have happy looks upon our faces.
They buy us books and other gifts to make our lives more carefree.
We are glad to be your grandchildren, branches of the family tree.
We are the third generation from which future greatness may stem.
Grandparents seldom scold us and we try to be good and please them.
Saint Erose

Untitled

My life is like a river,
without any name.
My body is full of twists and turns,
going by as fast as it came.
My mind is like a flowing stream
always going off track.
My hopes and dreams are like a twig,
and never coming back.
My thoughts are full of rocks, mud and stuff,
cans, bottles, pollution, crap.
I'm sailing off course
without any map.
Jessie Fuller

It Disappears

The light goes out, the wind comes crashing in
The smoke comes out, the truth circles in the mind
Thoughts of the past, things left behind

The muffled sounds approach from the distance
Sounds of creatures entertaining the intelligent
A thousand wishes that no one possesses

Stars shine a light upon faith
They whisper an answer no one has heard
They are bold, they know what lies beyond them
They are quiet, they're not understood

The noise is of a lesser nature
The screams of suppressed emotion
Emotion brought on by another
Another cry weakens belief
Belief of nature, belief of faith

Time continues without a fear
Remembering the truth of the past
Controlling the thought of the future
Creating the answers in everyone's mind
Destroying them before they're known
Troy Knudson

The Time Has Come For Me To Grow

The time has come for me to grow,
And venture to places I feared to go.
I've left the pond and swam to the sea.
The others are bigger and have little concern for me.
This water is dark and current strong,
But here is where I now belong.
Many will live, but some will die,
That is why I must try.
To succeed I need to be brave,
Knowing it's my life that I will save.
It's full-speed ahead down this one way road,
Traveling on until I grow old.
Ryan Avery

Ode to Joy

Symphony in Iambic Pentameter
In springtime, there's a fragrant smell.
Yes, I love you very well.

Ishmael went to sea - his place.
Captain Ahab lost his face.

Roland, with his mighty horn.
Blew it, sure as you were born.

Romeo his girl did troth.
Equanimity for both.

Parents bicker, children nap.
Here's to duty. Clap, clap, clap!
Barnet Frommer

The Window

I look out the window
And see the window sill
I see the window pane
But isn't it a shame

As I look out the window
Wish the glass was clean
So I could see my flowers
Trees, shrubs, butterflies and bees

Looking out my window
I see the green, green grass
I see the cobalt blue sky
See the clouds, a cumulus mass

Looking out my window and see
My children playing in the yard
I decide I must wash the glass
Remove the ozone grime

Now looking out my window
Through the glass that is washed shiny and bright
I can see all my blessings
But most important, I have my sight
Joan F. Keever

Trying To Please

Who is this girl in the mirror looking back to me?
Tears in her eyes not knowing why anyone would be so mean
Her mind was full of hope,
Her heart was full of pride,
To be lost by a man who was thought to be the light.
Why did he have to shoot her hopes in the head?
"It's not good enough" was all that needed to be said.
She tried to make him happy, but didn't succeed
She was at a loss for ideas that would make him pleased.
Everything she did or tried to do could not keep him satisfied
and she knew.
Why couldn't he just say something positive
Without saying something negative?
He thinks he is helping,
But he is only hurting the one who thought he cared.
He has no right to cut down her plans
Now all she was left with was a lot of dead ends.
Who is this girl in the mirror looking back at me?
Tears in her eyes, finally realizing why
Her father just did not seem to care.
Kinsey Pascoe

Simon Says

What if Simon doesn't say?
Who is Simon any way?
Someone nice or someone mean,
someone fat or a string bean.
Why can't it be Marvin says, or Melvin says, or Calvin says?
Why bend down low, jump up high, jump up so you touch the sky?
What's the point of all of this?
Now whoever Simon is...
Simon says to say goodbye,
we better listen to this guy!!!
Mindi Mathus

Special Angel

Here is a special angel to hang above your bed,
and after you have kneeled and your prayers have said -
then you can lay and rest your sleepy head,
and your special angel will watch the whole night through.
And when you awake and go to school or even out to play.
Your special angel will go with you and watch you all the day.
For God chose this special angel especially for you -
to walk with you and stay with you all your whole life through.
Lynda Williams

Lisa

If a name can tell a story
Paint a picture, write a song
Then the name we gave our baby
Is the name that sure belongs

When you say the name of Lisa
It brings joy into your heart
Cause it rings with joy and laughter
Which to her is so much a part

She's the gayest, she's the sweetest
The most precious jewel you see
It makes me burst when people say
That she looks just like me

Cause I'm so proud and world is alright.
Cause our lovely Lisa arrived just tonight
  William Dixon

Immortality, Mythology Or Reality?

Can it be, as I see,
Or is it just mythology,
Ambrosia with nectar to be consumed.
The two of us in that remote room.
How could I know when I walked through the portal,
You had the power to make all immortal,
And those who were there,
Knew it is real
You had this purpose a plan a scheme,
Please wake me now,
Perhaps 'twas a dream.
  Jack De Young

Breach Of Faith

Betrayal, treason, sedition, most have their giving point,
Men, Women, Friends, Mates, Countrymen.
One's breaking point is buried deep within,
The unfortunate have it found and used against them.
Of these, some feel guilt and sorrow - feelings that aren't
Revealed or apparent unless looking into another's heart.
Others feel nothing, numb, complacent.
One may take their life and feel pride for the act,
But self-disgust for surrendering to the urge.
The guiltless take many lives, homes, men's honor,
But do not feel quenched.
They may feel that they are living fully, yet they are not.
Deep withing the hearts of all men, there lies a semblance of truth.
This truth is what makes the commoners truly wealthy.
This make their hearts free and their dreams virtuous.
These are the one's who live, love, and
Obtain what life has to offer.
Every man dies, but not every man really lives.
And one that betrays, retains a guilt upon their soul,
Which will never be expelled.
  Steve Rose

"Everything Is Red"

Everything is red.
Some things are dark pink.
Things in shadows I can barely see.
I strain my eyes to better recognize objects.
It is a tree I look at,
with many a leaf on its branches.
It is red and pink splotches instead of
rich green and dark and creamy brown.
I can make out no details;
I need more light and a clear window.
For it is a red one I peer from,
that causes me to see nothing
  like it should be seen.
  Cynthia R. Fulton

I Thought I Knew You

I wait for you. Rain comes. Hours pass,
  still no you. But this is not you,
    This is someone else.

I lend you my stereo for one week.
Two pass, yes still no you. But this is not you,
    this is someone else.

You never keep you word, you never show,
   You never call to say hello.
 I thought I knew you, but yet I knew her.

  She's there when good times are not.
  She's there for me when you are not.

   She keeps her word, she calls a lot—
  She gives me hugs when you do not.

    She is my friend, my best friend,
   And I'm hers too, We are friends
        Not me and you
     This friend I talk of knows you,
        She was you.
    Cathy Freeman, age 10

Waltz With Beloved Earth

I hear the song that I belong
My heart is swept up by the wind
The way that its breeze has opened....

The silence at ease as the branches and leaves
twist and bend to reach my hands
I listen to its beckoning calls
poised to dance in an Earthly Waltz

The air it breathes and softly
leaves you enraptured as twilight falls

Come let us dance with what was
wrought in God's hands
All human beings, plant life and animals
spilling blessings like moonbeams and waterfalls
like the glint of rainbows in grassy knolls

Come be romanced by the joy that's enhanced
by the mirth of an earthly waltz
All existence enchants and calls
Abound and dance in an Earthly Waltz.
  Katherine Scorzo

"Love Letters To Napoleon"

  Dear Napoleon, I never thought I
would be sitting outside in the rain writing
you this letter with beloved. I never
noticed how pretty the pink blossoms
were until a few days ago, but somehow
they appear more beautiful. I love you so
much, remember that all the time. I
see how you smile at me. It is
so hard for me not to feel the
same way. You give me no reason to
not forever treasure you in my heart
I love you Napoleon. See how those
words seem to stand out "Love and Napoleon."
I had to get out in the storm, right
in the middle, maybe you can hear
my heart beating...steady now.
  Josette A. Smith

True Love

They tell us how to feel about the situation,
that it can't really be love,
that the feelings we feel are only infatuation.
But the feelings I feel are like a free flying dove,

No limits there can be,
it goes higher than the highest sky,
it is wider than the widest sea.
And this that I say is not a lie,

Cloud 9? No, that I am far above,
you are everything that I could need or want,
for you, only, are my true love.
So withdraw me from the hunt,

I need not look anymore,
except for the one I truly care about,
your love I will cherish and store.
So please have no doubt,
that you are the one I can't live without.
   Kathryn N. Bowers

I Know

I know that what you're going through makes you feel really blue,
I know that you feel like everyone has abandoned you.
I know that you feel like there's no end in sight,
I know that you feel like everything's wrong and nothing is right.

I know that your belief structure makes this all true,
I also know that this is just from one point of view.
It's during these times we feel alone and lost,
But I know where help can come at no special cost.

What I know is not for just a chosen few,
It's here for all, especially you.
Close your eyes and open your heart,
Then take a few deep breaths as a start.

Ask God to aid you in this time of need,
And your wishes will be granted in the greatest of speed.
Remember to thank God for taking care of you,
I know that He still loves us even when we forget to.

I know this sounds like I know so many things,
But really all it takes is trust, belief, and gratitude for what God brings.
   Cheryl Abdullah

The Crush

You sat beside me
Your hair wet with the moisture
from your shower and the dew
from your morning walk,
the muscles tightening in your arm
as you adjust your pile of books
You clear your throat and twirl
your well sharpened pencil as I
inhale your manly scent of
soap and musk hidden under an addictive scent
that is uniquely you
I lean over to ask you if
you had been smoking
You look up, your bright green
eyes twinkling, a smile
tugging at the corners
of your lips
And with a breath that smelled
like an April fresh breeze you whisper,
'Good morning'
   Michelle Campbell

The Sea

Flowing soft and smooth.
Playing with the rocks and sand.
Your color of blue grows lighter,
   as you reach the shore.

The mountains behind you hide,
   because of your beauty.
You touch the sky and become one,
But you never really touch, do you?

You have many friends within you.
Who travel with your currents and waves.
But no one thing will ever match you strength.

So flow strong and smooth.
Allow us passage into your world.
So we can enjoy your beauty.
And play with your friends.
   Denise Nelson

The Faithful Rose

Dawn's hue breaks gently darkness' cool sleep,
Perpetually vivid its image we reap.

Sweet fragrant harvest fragility its plight,
Surrendering graceful beauty in purity's majestic light.

Charaded illusion no shadow cast at noon,
Hauntingly brilliant beaconing beams from the moon.

Strong stalks climb skyward briery thorns guard nature's gate,
leaves shimmer joyously anticipating crescendo's wait.

Deep roots drink charitably, quenching famine's parched thirst,
nurturing continuous floral spirit, uniting nature's climactic burst.

Blossoming abundantly, fruits from seeds sown,
velvety soft petals crown jewels of its throne.

Exalted true servant I rejoice in your might,
craving strength but sorrow as you dance from my sight.

Sole passage on your journey winging windfully as it blows,
praise thee for my gift, the faithful rose.
   Dave Kenerson

Young Bride's Dream

Here I am in our little flat
Picking up this and cleaning that
Thinking about all the things others do
I can't knit, sew, draw or doodle-de-do
Writing poetry isn't my thing
But I'm going to try - and do something.

Everyone asks, what do you do all day?
Clean, watch TV and prepare a meal is all I can say.
Nothing exciting, no hobby have I
But all I can say, I'm still going to try.

Everyone else is busy as can be
So someday I hope I can see
That I can have a hobby that will be
As interesting to them as it will be to me.
Someday, somehow, you wait and see
I'm going to make folks proud of me.
   Edna Hubbard

Graduation

Who would have thought that this is where I would be
Not long ago I was a toddling tot
Not wanting to go to school
Now I am a graduating senior
Ready for that next step in life
So long a time it seems
That I have already lived
But compare it to what is left
It is extremely short
My past is now a fond memory
One I keep close to my heart
It is all I have left of yesterday
To carry with me day to day
Now I am ready to make new memories
Start a new life full and prosperous
Who knows where I will go?
   Melissa Elsasser

I Love, I Laugh, I Lift

I love the good things of life
Family Friends and Foes alike,
Nature's handiwork is a joy to see
The birds, the bees, and lots of trees.
Travel opens up doors to various places,
That expand the mind as we meet new faces.

I love the good things of life
Family is precious and such a joy,
You glory in the success of each girl and boy.
Your life fulfilled when others achieve,
Through encouragement and example plus a strong belief.
In perseverance, preparation and focus on a goal
Keep your eyes on the prize and humbleness in your soul.

I love the good things in life
I can laugh at my mistakes along the way,
It makes me stronger from day to day.
I lift as I climb and share with others,
My talents, my aspirations with my sisters and brothers.
Be strong, Be brave and love, laugh, and lift;
As you celebrate your life which is a precious gift.
   Ruth D. Harper Ph.D

God Made Man And Woman The Man He Called Adam, The Woman He Called Eve

Long, long ago, so very long
ago that no one can think
how long it was, there was no
beautiful word. No twinkling stars
there was no round yellow moon.
There was only God there was
no bright shining sun. There was only God.
Long long ago,
So very long ago that no one can
think how long it was, there
were no birds and bees, there
were no fish. There were no
animals of any kind. There was
only God. Long long ago so very
long ago that it was, there were no people.
There were no mother and fathers.
There were no brothers and sisters.
There were no children. There was only God.
He gathered the waters
together and called them seas.
   Jesse Dewberry

My Song To You

Should you show someone, the way that you feel
If you know there's no chance for it becoming real.

Should you pass my way, each minute of the day
When you know you'll never come to stay.

Such a peaceful feeling, when being loved by someone
Knowing a gentle touch calms the both of us.
Seems I have such a good time just being with you
The love shared between us is so true
This is my song to you.

My song to you can mend a broken heart
Even when we seem so far apart
The times so short for us to be alone
But still I leave you this song.
   Marie H. Webb

Untitled

Our thoughts have become a burden to everyone
mental illness ain't no fun - crazy is the word
They used to describe what they have heard
Take your pill twice a day - and maybe it will go away
And if it don't we have a place when your voices become absurd
Where from your bed you can't be heard
Tell me again what's that word - restraints for those who will not comply
They're out of their minds and don't know why
Doctors on call if you're off the wall
And if you're already there you don't really care
About color-place-or-hair - for who will see but the doctors there
Writing scripts and reading charts - the dirty square goes home
   before it starts
The nurses there who fix their hair and don't really care
That cigarette break just isn't fair
one for breakfast - one for lunch - they don't understand
We need a whole bunch - it's time for bed
they fill our heads with drugs to smooth out the bugs
Let's face it they're no more than thugs
And as I lie here wide awake - shock therapy my friend
Will take - the funny farm where all will break
   Aaron Simmons

Do You Wonder

How does God select a rain?
The drops are always just the same.
He never sends assorted sizes
From His storehouse of surprises.

Does He pour them through a sieve
When He decides the clouds will give
A rain of pearl-like drops for hours
To water trees and grass and flowers?

Does He in a mood of whimsy
Send rains in temperament so flimsy?
The sun breaks through and shines victoriously
And rainbows show in colors gloriously.

King-sized drops are often speeded
to send a drink when it is needed
To fill the lakes and ponds and rivers
So they in turn can be the givers.

A certain swift decided shower
May give as much in just an hour
As gentler rains may yield in days;
We're struck with wonder of His ways.
   Ressie Jung

A Life of Laundry

It seems my life is in a quandary, all I ever do is laundry.
Put it in the wash and watch it spin, only to get it dirty again.
Wash in cold, then line dry, its enough to make you want to cry.
But if you think laundry is a chore, when you get married,
 you have even more.
Hot or cold, dark or white, in the morning, noon, or night.
My husband will help wash the dishes, he'll feed the dog
 and the fishes.
But when it comes to the laundry, my husband knows, he is forbidden
 to wash the clothes.
It keeps the laundry nice and bright, the reds stay red,
 the whites stay white.
Although he is the age of thirty, how does a husband get so dirty?
Grease and grime from head to toes, in goes the bleach
 with the husband's clothes.
As long as I'm married to this guy, I'll have more to wash, more to dry.
More to fold and to put away, for him to wear another day.
Yes, laundry is the perpetual task, I really shouldn't brood,
For everyone knows we must wear clothes,
We can't just run around nude!
 Mindy Harding

Lone Women Walking

their badge is solitude
their faces wind-whipped visors
lowered on their inner selves the eyes the only truth
and back and forth they walk the shoreline
constant as the tide

at wane of day they come
as sisters in their need
when sated hordes have left their litter of indifference
persistent wash of wavelets lapping
lulls their sorrowing

averted faces when they pass
avoids the mirrored self
the twofold pain of unquenched dream the double desolation
while faint the swish of waters murmuring
sings their sanity

the sea will weep for them
the gulls will screech frustrations
the wind will carry discontent beyond the reach of caring
and they lone women walking
will receive the ocean's peace
 S. Stapleton

Naked Splendor

As sly as a fox, ne'r making a sound,
They appear without trace or a doubt.
Their slender bodies rise up from the ground.
In the wind, they go swaying about.

While driving, you spy them; heads in the air,
Stripped as bare as the bark off a tree.
If you're not careful, you'll be caught in a stare,
At the beauty and radiance you see.

They are met with a lot of onlookers.
They're a wonder; quite stunning unique.
They don't tarry around; they're like hookers.
They're teasers and pleasers, so to speak.

Surprises in splendor; they are revealing.
These flowers flaunt like magic in the night.
They blossom as quick as a bright shooting star
"Naked Ladies" oh, what a gorgeous sight!
 Eva Butler

Prayers In The Night

Down a dark musty alley amongst the rats and the trash.
Digging through rubbish he looked for his stash.
A lame old man, lived in the back room of a bar.
Washed dishes for rent, made his wine in a jar.
Limping and stumbling needing relief for his pain.
When it came to drinking, the man had no shame.
Frantically searching, the man fell to his knees.
He bowed his head crying and begged "Lord Please."
With the filth and the garbage the man wasn't alone.
There was another soul crying and chilled to the bone
In a window well shivering barely alive
Laid the last of six puppies five which had died.
With his last bit of strength and a will to survive.
Gave one final "yip" then silently cried.
 Paul Knispel

adrift

thumbing the pages of your well worn bible
i watch them pack out your life in boxes
and scream inside at your leaving
but selfishly i try to shrug off history
among the rickety ghosts of old farm lives
drifting throughout the barns sinking to
dust in graveyards of prairie grass and wildflowers
where tonight snow falls soft as the down of
angels feathers shed crossing heaven and darkness
moves slowly across the lavender cheek of sunset
against a pillow of blue black clouds that enthrall
the countryside with winter's first cold kiss which
moves me grudgingly toward the house held frozen in
the amber wash of the lamplight and surrounded by
skeleton trees that scrape the roof with leafless fingers
 Mark Power

Walking To Meet The Dawn

Footsteps crunching along the black, gravelly road,
Soon are silenced by the croak of a distant toad.

Passing by trees with dark, brooding branches aloft,
Awakening mourning doves murmur coos so soft.

Then crossing a bridge with water rippling below,
Where an alligator's nose is making a show.

The heron's silhouette is perched high on a palm,
Down below on the ground, all is quiet and calm.

As dawn's arrival lightens the sky,
Sparkling dewdrops shrivel up and dry.

Voices of the crows herald's a glimpse of the sun,
On this wonderful land, a new day has begun.
 Beverly H. Sawyer

Messy Messy!

Red, yellow and green scrawled along the hallway wall.
Who would ever think the artist could be so small?

Look Mommy, look Daddy I did it for you,
screamed the artist who had just turned two.

Although Mom and Dad with their eyes so bright
Just might have hated the sight.

But instead, they said "how pretty" and patted my head.
Because I was such a sensitive child so my parents said.
 Rachel Grove

Midnight Gardens

Midnight garden, midnight garden, how sweet the flowers smell,
calling you, possessing you, with sweet enchanting sounds,
softly, they whisper, "please come and join our dance,"
for no one knows the secret, of the magic we enhance,
let all your dreams, let all your hopes,
escape to midnight showers,
seeing them float above on high,
until, midnight's last hour,
only then, can time tell,
the sweetness of the flowers,
that hold your fears,
that hold your dreams,
when will they bring more showers?
So late at night, no stars in sight,
when will you go to the night?
To behold, the sweetness of the flowers,
and the beauty of their right,
their right to hold the innocence,
of every dream in mind,
the comfortness, will you know, where midnight gardens lie.

Heidi Alcantar

Silent Storms

A hush falls upon the land, the earth falls silent
The time is at hand
The people stop their work and stare
At something lurking in the air.
The sky turns yellow before our eyes
The silence is broken as the peace dies
The world becomes a roaring sea
As thunder cracks and the sky turns green
A wind to end all winds has come
Its mournful song has just begun
It howls and shrieks as it rips through the night
A horrid song filled with fright
The thunder cracks, the lightning shines
This storms has come to end all times
And just when all hope is lost
And the world seems gripped by a wintry frost
The sun shines bright before our eyes
And all receives a big surprise
The world still shines a sea of glass
A world of beauty, hope, and chance

Megan Crouch

To Jenny, From T.B.

Jenny, I guess you won't ever know
For my feelings for you never show
You'll be my friend forever
So sweet, so kind and very clever
You've shot through my heart
With your arrow and bow
It'll hurt me to hear the sound
That you have another guy to hang around
But no one will ever know or tell
If maybe one day you'll be my girl

Kristen Wong

Autumn

A crisp, cool, invigorating breeze, filled with romantic memories.
Days seem shorter, while trees shed their dress of red,
  yellow, orange, and green.
Reminiscence of football games, school days, and Halloween.
This change of season can only be given to us as a gift from
  a God who exemplifies His love for us...

  Through Autumn.

Bobbie A. Schutz

Inner Fear

The darkness holds an image of fear
The way I feel when you're not here
The fear that's hard to be defined
That exists only inside your mind
The fear of hurt. The fear of hate
The fear I opened up too late
The fear I've lost. The fear I've won
The inner fear has just begun
The darkness releases and lets fear out
The cold, dark fear that lingers about
The fear you're gone. The fear we're done
From inner fear you just can't run.

Jennifer Marie Vincent

About Grandmothers

About Grandmothers - I did have one. She was sweet and jolly, so much fun. I loved to visit and sometimes I'd stay overnight, 'stead the day. On these visits she had stories to tell - about morality and sisters, they were really swell.

She had this porch from her bedroom 'twas neat - you could see below onto the street. And when the bus stopped, just about ten, that's when her stories would surely begin.

She'd pick a person on the street and tell a story of love or defeat. And when she'd see a drunk staggering home she'd take this moment to make it known, that perhaps he had a problem bigger than life and taking to drink was like taking the knife. Solve your problems with your mind you should think. Do it before you take that first drink.

And when a couple passed so sullen and sad. She'd sigh and say - one said something very bad. But when they get home they'll make it right, and they'll do it before they each say good night.

Now all this she did telling stories so late - I loved her so much but couldn't stay awake - so before the next person she could take a peek her little granddaughter fell asleep.

Alberta E. Higgins

Bunches

Bad things happen in bunches joined like the plump red grapes,
Death and pain and dying-lies, mistrust, and rape.
The horror of disease the loss of a special friend,
The problems of relationships that seem so hard to mend.
The questions of tomorrow and what the future holds,
Will this sadness change me and turn my heart ice cold?
I never know what evil lurks around the bend,
I'm forced to ask the question "when will all this end?"

A light, a glimmer, a ray of hope I see it far away,
Perhaps I am mistaken, this glimmer is today?
I now have found the answer, to why the songbird sings.
It is because of life and love, and other simple things.
I count up all my blessings, and begin this day anew.
And start with the gentle flower, fresh with morning dew.

Now I make this promise, to myself and all mankind.
To love the good things in my life, and to beauty be less blind.
I will overcome these hardships, and pluck them from the vine.
And with this joy I celebrate, and turn those grapes to wine.

Geoffrey Putt

Goodness

One character of a good man is kindness.
When one has an excellent character, one has goodness.

When one has goodness he has generosity.
Generosity can mean a man can have prosperity.

The man with goodness, is a man that's true.
He's a man with a good virtue.

Chari Lynn Rinkel

The Classroom

When I was 7 or less
With a maple twig for chalk
And the Michigan flat land
For the blackboard
My father A.F. Stegenga
Taught me how to write poetry.

And
He always said that
When the time would be ripe for me
To harvest the fields
I must honor my heritage
With 2 arts:
Poetry would be one, I could select the other one.

So I did what I was supposed to do.
   D. A. Lawn Stegenga

The Awakening

Awake! Arise to your feet!

We must dance, and see the moon shining through the trees.
It's looking for someone to play with through the short night.

Look, my darling, in that pool of water. See your reflection and
the moon's silver light twinkling through your hair.

I am glad we are free of the world, which held us so close.
Now that we are no longer mortals, we can skip across the meadows,
and dance through the night as often and as long as we like.

There is no time. Forever is ours.

The moon, the stars, the night, and meadows, so open and free.

They belong to no one, but you and me.
   Robert B. Boettcher

The Door To Nowhere

Enter all who dares, the door that leads to nowhere
You'll be on your own, wishing that you were home
Memories will fade away, there will be no more sunny days
You raise your hands to the sky, hoping for a sign
No one seems to care, no one seems to be there
Enter at your will, once you're in, you will always be there
It doesn't have to be this way, it doesn't have to be this way
Enter all who dares, the door that leads to nowhere
No one will listen, no one will give you loving
You're feeling very low, that is not the way to go
You'll be giving up all your pride, if you think that this is place to hide
Think about all those who you left behind, that thought you were
   the sweetest kind
You gave me all you had, now all the roses are dead
You feel all alone, you only lived for being stoned
It doesn't have to be this way, if you would only stay
Enter all who dares, the door that leads to nowhere
Tomorrow will be a better day, only if you live past today
It's not as bad as it seems, if you believe in a higher being
There are people who understand, you know that I can comprehend
If you have faith and devotion, you can have something believe in
   Ryan Van Houten

Untitled

Safe is the sound of your voices
Safe is the smell of your clothing
Safe is the yawns of Mom's evenings ending
Safe is the limericks of Dad's songs
Safe is the welcome unbridled
Safe is the beauty of your souls
Safe is the love you give
And safe is my life
   Colleen Murray

Untitled

I stand above many things, I am tall and proud, I'm a
beautiful thing of nature, look at me I am a sight to
behold. I can do many things, I am used as a shield
against the rain, I am used as shade against the blazing
sun. Little children play with me, one, two, three, are
you ready. I can change my colors, to browns and golds,
most times I am green, I stand above many things,
sometimes I suffer pain, I am sawed, hacked, carved, and
chopped, but I survive, I am strong, I will never die, I
stand above many things. As I stand naked in the winter
cold I'm still a thing of beauty, then spring arrives,
and I am given new life, I'm a sight to behold. I stand
above many things, sometimes I stand alone, sometimes
there are others, I can bend with the wind. I am
graceful as a ballet dancer, my leaves are tears for all
the wrong I see, please look at me, I'm a tree, I'm a
thing of beauty, I stand above my things,
"God I stand beneath thee."
   Lois Wilson

From the Heart

A poem is words that come from the heart
But sometimes it's hard to know where to start,
The feelings just start flowing through yourself
Picking and selecting in your own mind's shelf.

It could be from a fantasy where you would like to go
Or from a time in your life that only you know,
Maybe you and your love could go there together
No one ever knows, it could be forever.

So just remember all the good times out weigh the bad
You'll find out it's the best time you ever had,
Just when you think you've finally had enough
Stop and think; are things really that rough.

And when January 1st starts a new year
Make sure your special person is there to hear,
The words and feelings to make you both feel right
Because the rest of the year will surely turn out bright.
   Christopher S. Armes

Kings No More

On breeze above the cypress sang,
towering from water black.
And in the days before they came
Kings of the realm, the heron and the cormorant.

The water swirls, the duck weed parts
beneath the oaken boards.
Like lightening's scar across time's expanse
the paddles are but swords.

And in the boats, alas have come
the makers of all pain.
So in death's embrace can be found
the realm of sun and rain.

The nets now kiss the bottom's silt
and caress the air unsprung.
Yearning to touch their quarry's fin
then venom's bite has stung.

With tearful eye and wind's sweet kiss
they their lofty throne depart,
and stalk and dive among the reeds
Kings no more, the heron and the cormorant.
   David Ashley Godfrey

Untitled

Mezzanine in the sky
   And the movie shall begin at half past tomorrow
Saw the colors of blindness in a vaguely remembered photograph
   A canvas with no colors you could see
Rain reduces to a breezeful mist in Montevideo
   As another swallow lands on a parking meter
Putting on the Alexandrian face that is fiercely repulsive
   But the clues never reveal themselves soon enough for an answer
Mother, may I let myself drown in their hypocrisy?
   Temples keep going up in the rural outskirts of disbelief
And just whatever happened to smiling Pop Haynes?
   Rocking chair, big jeans, the A-minor harmonica, and apple tobacco
The glue-gun fantasy hits at 8:30 every morning
   Love to spew out gray in your black and white world
The most amazing mystery is hidden behind her dress
   But the depth and the moans don't even add up to a prologue
Somewhere in the bars of Palermo, someone must've had the vision
   Ecstasy lies in your fingertips and has always been there
Goddamn it, nothing surprises me anymore
   'Cause the golden speech from afar is a mere whisper in a wanderer's ear

Sina Nikkhou

A Promise

I was brought to you on the wings of a dove,
Nurtured by the tenderness of your love.
My heart was broken and bleeding,
Your touch ever so gentle and healing.

I stood and gazed in your loving eyes,
Our hearts in tune with the strongest of ties.
Yours spoke true happiness and the ability to cherish,
Mine of faith, trust and a love that will not perish.

In you, I have found a love too magnificent for words,
The most delicate note from the prettiest bird.
A love so strong it erased any other,
Forever and ever, we must be together.

We will stand beside the stream of life,
Hand in hand, heart to heart, husband and wife.
For you have made my life complete,
Our hearts as one shall sound an everlasting beat.

Amen

Tally Pruett

Earth

Red, orange, purple, blue,
What do these colors mean to you?

Penguin, bear, and fish galore,
These are animals,
Will there be much more?

Grass and flowers that live on the plain,
Which will survive when down comes the rain?

The water feeds the trees,
And trees clean the air,
Will the trees be so plentiful,
If so, then where?

For the earth is our mother,
And we must help with the cleaning,
But we can't do a thing if we don't know the meaning.

Red, orange, purple, blue;
What do these colors mean to you?

Jason Lee Mitchel Shockley

A Mother's Love

From the time you are born she nurtures and cares
No other love can quite compare
To a mother's love when you're in despair
When you are small with all those childhood diseases
She makes it all better, those sniffles and sneezes
A skinned up knee, you fell today
Mother will make it better and the pain goes away
With a kiss on the cheek and a great big hug
She makes you feel all safe and snug
There is nothing quite like a mother's love
When you are in your teens and have pressure from peers
A mothers caring advice helps to dry all those tears
Now you're a woman, how quickly the years do go by
Married, with a husband and singing your own lullaby
To a child of your very own
As with your child you sit alone
Rocking in that old rocking chair
Remembering back when you were there
In your mother's arms as she sang those songs to you before
Only a mother's love is precious and pure

Linda L. Windsor

Paradise

I saw seven pigeons
Tied up in an old gunny sack
And carried through the heat in the trunk of a car.
Carried to a valley that was paradise,
A small blue lake with yellow flowers blowing.

And the pigeons were taken out,
Out of the bag, one at a time,
Each one dazed and almost dead
Set free - free in paradise.

Each flew over the pond, circled the trees,
Free.

But a man stood on the bank,
Strong and proud, with a rifle in his hands.
And as each bird flew, there was one sharp crack
And the bird fell, floundering in the water.

And the well-taught dog retrieved them,
Brought them back to his master
Who put them back in the sack.
Back in the sack, back in the car, and back to town.
And into the garbage to be thrown away the next day.

Gracia Harper

Keep Smiling!

Keep on smiling baby
cause you look so pretty that way,
no matter what people do to you
don't ever let them take that away

Even though we're not together
even though we're miles apart,
I'll always carry the memory of your smile
deep inside my heart.

So keep on smiling baby
while I take some time to pray,
that you and your beautiful smile
will be beside me again someday.

Barry Jamison

Farewell To Poppy

Our pain has come, but has not went.
The feeling of great loss, the overwhelming pain.
Only God's great comfort which he has sent.
Helps to restore me as my sufferings wane.

God has plans for us we are often told.
It's not our place to ask Him where or why.
His will isn't quiet or small, but great and bold.
Therefore for God must we live if only to try.

He knows we're not perfect, no not nearly.
Poppy had shortcomings, but he came very close.
For people like him God holds them dearly.
Poppy's with them now, God's heavenly host.

He is surely with them this I do know.
As for me, I miss him, but yet am glad.
For he helped me with patience, here I must grow.
He taught me a lot in this short time I have had.

So bye for now and someday I will see,
Him in heaven with that beautiful smile,
Sitting there with my Lord and Savior he will be.
Bye for now, which in God's time is but a short while.

Charles T. Dever

Before They Killed The Buffalo

I had a dream of long ago
Before they killed the buffalo.
I dreamed the air was clear and sweet.
And the trail was soft beneath my feet.
Through the forest cool and green.
Where the bear, the deer, and the fox are seen.
The dove, the lark, and the mocking bird.
Made the sweetest music ever heard
And the red man rode proud and free
And the grass was like an endless sea.
Oh how I wish it were again
The way it was way back then
To have one true and faithful friend
And walk the trail that has no end.
Go back, go back my poor heart cries
To clean sweet water and clear blue skies
To those shining times so long ago
Before they killed the buffalo.

A. P. Schwiger

Acres Of Diamonds

Rising from bed on a cold winter day
Visions of ice greet my eyes on my way,
Signs of pure beauty now brighten the scene
As I glance at the trees which look serene.

Acres of diamonds on field and on tree,
God sent these beauties for you and for me.
Each one is sending a message of love,
Good will and caring, all sent from above.

Acres of diamonds wherever you look,
Sparkle and glimmer in cranny and nook
To brighten our world with beauties galore
And help us each day spread love more and more.

Acres of diamonds with values untold,
These are the things that are made of pure gold.
Nothing is ever more pleasing to see
Than God's gifts of love for you and for me.

Sue Myers Dietz

A Time Of Change

A time of change, when families at home are being torn apart.
A time of change, when youths in the inner city dying by violence.
A time of change, when the elderly are being mistreated.
A time of change, when people are being left homeless.
A time if change, when famine, disease and pollution is on
  an all time high.
A time of change, when hate is still in existence.
A time of change, when capitol punishment is a big failure.
A time of change, when the unborn have no night to be born.
A time of change, when nations are at each others throats.
"Change for better will never be, unless the hearts of men change".

Joseph Manning

Death Of A Sinner

He sits upon his pale, black horse,
  patiently, expectantly.
His newest specimen was slow to arrive.
The ghastly apparition that came forth was
  nothing out of ordinary.
His proud, massive, wings struck fear into the unwary soul,
  as he was carried from his journey to the Pearled Gate.
His form altered from that of a blessed angels to a thing of
  pure terror.
The hapless soul screamed in dismay as his path was actualized,
  and he peered into the gaping maw of the place
  of demons and agony.
And he looked at this soul and laughed as he did when all souls were
  taken from their path, for this place was his home,
  and will remain so until the end of time.
Thus was the death of Cassius.

Matthew Robinson

Love's Flame

It began as just a spark...then two...and soon a flame burned
Brightly in my life.

And I felt myself drawn to the flame...for it was warm and
Exciting, and I was fascinated by its glow.

As I lingered there, I felt its warmth melt the chill that had held
My feelings captive for so long.

But the winds of passion came and fanned the flame...and it
Became a raging fire.

I must draw back, lest it consume me and all that I hold dear.

As I sadly turn away, I reach in and take a tiny flame, to keep it
Ever burning in my heart. It will brighten life's grey days, and
Comfort lonely nights.

I will fan it with whispers of love,
And stoke it with memories of days gone by,
And I will never, never let the flame go out.

Toni Johns

Untitled

One of my very best friends has black matted hair,
One of my very best friends has a short stubby tail,
One of my very best friends has long furry ears,
One of my very best friends has big brown eyes you just can't
  say no to,
One of my very best friends has a very wet nose,
One of my very best friends gets me my slippers every morning,
Can you guess who my very best friend can be????

Melissa McCarthy

The Adventures Of Rover The Dog

Hi, I'm Rover the dog,
did I ever tell you when I got trapped in a log?
Oh, that can wait,
let me tell you when I was Alien bait.
It was a beautiful night inside the house,
not a shadow, not a soul, not even a tiny little mouse.
Then I saw it, an alien space ship, with a very bright beam,
I saw an unusual alien pop out from smoke and steam.
It then saw me through the window,
and then I hid under my chewed up pillow.
I started to bark and bark,
the alien grabbed me through the window, out of the dark.
It pulled out a laser object and aimed it at me,
I had to find out a way to be free.
The alien had turned me into a big hog,
and that's the story of me, Rover the dog.
Jason Ruiz

Revelation

I search stars at night to understand light in darkness.
I listen to fire and hear symphonies in silence.
I touch the mountain to feel the earth move in stillness.
I breathe fresh waters for scents of moisture in dry air.
I savor the winds to taste the seasoning of calm.

I query and reflect on the enigma of truths.
Still, one sense embraces a known imbued in the soul.
An omniscient aura cradles the psyche and chi,
Enlightens mystery and excites the energies.

The sight sheer beauty
The sound enchanting
The caress so soft
The smell mere fragrance
The taste very sweet

And the perception eternal.
Surely, through eons of myth woven into mortals,
Comes revelation from the spells of Aphrodite.
What cosmic pulse is absorbed in this phenomenon?
The essence of love.
Joseph J. Bloyder

The Iceman

Arriving early in his horse-drawn cart,
With a pick splitting the ice block apart;
Lifting gunny sacks o'er the sawdust-covered boulder;
Hoisting it with tongs to his leather-covered shoulder.
Mounting back steps to deliver the rock
To the upper section of an old oaken box;
No need to chisel — 'twas a perfect fit;
There'll be a better use for that ice pick!
On the wall above the storage crate
Was a magical map of the 48 states.
The pick was pointed at places he'd been
And spots he would like to have seen,
Making time for us kids to cry, "Let's go!"
As we raided his unguarded cart below.
How cool on the tongue were those chilly chips;
And how soothing when rubbed o'er parched lips;
A "blizzard" or "breeze" today isn't half so good
As those ice pellets dripping on splintered wood;
But then it's a well-accepted fact
That all things improve when looking back.
Virginia H. Hansen

Lessons

I've made the mistakes that life had to give
Some selfish, some stupid, but through it I lived

I've found that what matters, when you sift through it all
Is the strength that you gain from surviving the fall

So some of this wisdom, I'd like to share
It may give someone a reason to care

To that someone out there, whose heart has been broken
Yesterday's over, your past has just spoken

That person you loved, it's not the end
Just stay on the road and take the next bend

The good times and bad times, they all come together
In your search for that one love, you'll have forever

We all learned a lesson from yesterdays pain
Just make that experience your personal gain

So hold out your hand, don't shy away
This is just the beginning of a wonderful day
Michael F. Paty

This Old Carpenter

This old man was a Carpenter,
so proud of what he was.
He had a lot of hammers,
And also a lot of saws.

He had scars to show you,
He could tell you about everyone.
There wasn't just a few you know,
And none were any fun.

He worked hard all his life,
All the buildings that he built.
Now he sits on his front porch,
And thinks about what life has dealt.

The old carpenter is tired now,
He thinks he will turn his hammer in.
For he knows he can still build a house,
For God will help with his hands.
Carolyn Robinson

A Cycle

The shovel is thrown aside,
The Earth overturned to its place,
The scythe is stilled
The grain is heaped into stacks.

  'Tis Sunset
The birds hush their singing
The crickets begin
The fireflies flit from branch to branch
The owl hoots gently through the leaves.

  'Tis Nighttime
The sun's first rays display the sky,
The awakening lark soars high overhead,
The magpie chatters a lilting sonnet
The bees are kissing the flowers.

  'Tis Morning
The smoke curls lazily from the chimney,
The smells of food fill the valley.
The farmer hastens to the field
The reaper wields the scythe once more.

  'Tis Day.
Candace Samuelson

Storm's Conquest

Have you not blown on me enough
an ordinary tree not very tall and stately
to make my body ache and arch
with restless and relentless bending
and moaning from your wounding wild
but longing for you still
to come again
with all the fierceness of your moving
for nothing else can move me so
only bending my body
the soft body
under the sweet and bitter bark
bending in loving what I love
surrender to your pulse and power
and playing
of my open body your instrument
and you the one
who finally unleashed my music.

Gabriele Mayes

Huna Song

I'm a Hunatic from Onion Creek, Living the Huna way.
I'm a Hunatic from Onion Creek, Leading a helpful hurtless day.
With song and dance, I'll keep you entranced, Learning quite easily,
The Huna basics, its ABC's All quite readily.

My Body Self and Middle Self, Along with my high self,
Live in harmony... In this body, All quite easily.
My Body Self runs the big body, And remembers very well,
It carries our prayers, with mana to tell, Our High Self what we want.

My Middle Self just thinks and does, Whatever it needs to do,
To carry on... Our daily work, Without any hurt or two.
My High Self there... Up in the air, Watches, guides and heals all three.
High energy... Mana loa you see, Lets High Self do its wonders for me.

The energy I use... To get things done, Is mana from food I eat,
We three need it and we use it, In company quite neat.
Middle energy... Is mana mana, To think, decide and do.
Low energy... Is body mana, To eat and work and move.

And so we have... Three energies, To do our work each day.
To round this off, we have bodies three, Aka that you can't see
Complete Huna... Is three by three: Selves, bodies and energy,
With physical body as the extra one, That make us ten, and now
   we're done.

Don Schuster

We, Lost Our Best Friend

   My two sisters and I.
We lost our best friend . . .
Will never finding again . . .
We wore black, for twelve years. With laugh, and cry.
Thus "we, did know why!"
With empty feelings, also plenty of tears.
   Our life stile grow,
From small, day by day to old.
Our smile and pain, No one was there, to talk or say.
We did not have someone to play!
Or to love us, with open mind, or heart.
   This was from the day,
We lost our best friend.
Thus we wore black, until then! . . .
   "This friend," it was our mother,
We will never see her again!
"We" miss her love, and hugging arms.
She went to heaven, with the stars.
And pray for her all of us!

Pota L. Stylos

A Worldly View Not Taken

   The billows of wadded white cotton balls in a crystal blue sky...A poodle stands smiling at the heavens, drifting into a mirage of small staggering strays... Monstrous mountains crumble into moderate plateaus slowly separating into several stones... Clouds are silently full of vitality. The entire sky appears as a pastel painting, dangerously dominant to Picasso.
   Nightfall scatters twinkling stars while chilling the hemisphere... Space and atmosphere are deeply more vibrant than all of the oceans... Hanging lonesome is the moon with his withered and scared face; revolving ever so patiently across the horizon as a pendulum of an enormous clock... As hours and minutes slowly pass, the earth comes back to consciousness...
   Dew drops drip from the trees resembling an elderly man opening his eyes as he wakes early in the morning, tired and worn from the many years before this hour yet still fresh from the nights rest. Time passes... The atmosphere gleams and stands tall through millions of moments of day. Wishing for a wonderful world of wheat fields wavering in the wind.

Brian C. Dunagin

A Beginning

Love in a heart
is like the breath of life in a body;
before it comes into existence
one has no conception
of what it is.

Looking back each seems to be a beginning.
You can watch a love grow
as you can watch a life grow.
You can experience it as it happens.
You can look back and understand how it happened.
Yet you can never cause it to happen
nor will it not to happen.

If one did not live
one would never feel pain.
And if one did not love
one might never hurt.
But who would wish to forfeit life or love
in order to avoid hurt and pain?

Not I, my love,
not I.

Deborah K. Grove

America

"America the beautiful", what happened to our claim?
A country started long ago, based on Jesus' name

Our founding fathers set a course of how our life should be
It started out on the principles of Christianity

A nation that prospered so, until the election of some fools
The ones that wrote the law that took "Jesus out of schools"

While we were on Jesus' side, we strongly faced our foes
Through him we had victory, without him we have woes

I wonder where it all will end, when will our leaders see
With Jesus we were standing tall, now we're on our knees

Greed, hate and violence are some reasons for our strife
Did we forget the reason why, Jesus gave his life

Once we stood strong and proud for all the world to see
That was when we had our eyes on the man from Galilee

Jesus is our only way to prevent this country's loss
We must give it back to him, let's take it to the cross

"America the beautiful," it's not too late to keep that claim
Jesus is the only way to take this country out of shame

Richard C. Jewell

Point Lookout

Down at Point Lookout
There is a nightly cast
Of spirits from
The Civil War's past.
The old camp sleeps
As spirits weep.
The wounds they suffered
Still pain them,
Every night you can hear the cries
Of wounded men left to die.
You can hear them weep
As the guard sleep.
The hospital reeks;
You can smell it where you stand.
The screams of the sick, wounded, and dying
Haunt your head like you were there
With the smell of pain in the air.
If you ever go down,
Please beware of the spirits
Floating in the air.

Melissa Cameron

Tears Of Darkness

I have this friend, you see.
In the serene blackness, I can faintly hear her cry.
I attempt to reach out; no one is there.
When I call out; no one answers.
Do my fingers not feel?... Does my voice not carry?
Constant tears of darkness echo as they fall.
They've become louder and louder, almost deafening.
I cannot break through the barrier of stone.
Panic intercedes all I know.
Horror renders my soul helpless.
Someone, please help her!... The cries do not surrender.
Then, sudden hush.
In a mirror across the eerie room, a silhouette appears.
I can see it, I can hear it, I can feel it.
I ponder curiously at the reflected image.
I recognize the endless cries, however; the face is unknown.
Droplets of water cascade down her sunken cheeks.
I reach out and wipe them all away, for now.
I hear no more sadness, until another day.

I have this friend, you see.

Jodi E. Kinsey

Hoist The Teacups, Matey
Or Burma Used To Be A Place But...

He has roamed the wide world over, he has sailed the seven seas,
And he talks about his travels now at literary teas.

He has eaten poi and mangoes, he has drunk okolehau.
Now they feed him little sandwiches, he's drinking Lipton's now.

With a scorn of things commercial and a sneer for ways routine,
He abandoned home and fireside for the far, exotic scene.

But now he's earning lecture fees (Who said that money irked)
From fascinated wives of men who stayed at home and worked.

He has wooed a maiden yellow, two or three in brown and black.
(But he fled in craven terror from the girl in Hackensack).

His face is lined by desert wind and burned by tropic skies,
And the silver at his temples is a charm for women's eyes.

But his chin's a little double and his waist's a little fat,
His eyes a little bleary now, his feet a little flat.

Oh, alas for gay adventure, and farewell to distant shores—
For now he's autographing books in swank department stores.

Marian Snyder

"Who Am I?"

When I walk across the room, what do you see?
You see a strong Black Woman, and that woman is me.

Whether I'm dressed in blue jeans or in a suit;
My goals and achievements are always in pursuit.

I have been the anchor and backbone for so many years;
During that time, I have been tired and shed several tears.

My strength is determined and my mind is strong;
With my head on my shoulders, what could possibly go wrong?

The tools that I've used can be acquired by anyone;
Education, Confidence and Determination are just to name some.

I consider myself a role model for those to see;
One look at me and this is what they can one day be.

Women like me have paved the road for others to follow;
Despite the prejudices that they had to swallow.

Let my legacy continue on for years to come;
'Cause being a Black Woman, my work is never done.

I will always proceed to follow my dreams;
After all, success isn't as hard as it seems.

So, the next time you ask yourself "Who Am I?";
You're that beautiful, strong Black Woman reaching for the sky!

Lynette Lobo

Open the Door to My Soul

I am alone, inside my empty shell.
It is not that I want to be here;
If only you wanted to share my company.
I am scared to enter into a world with a thousand faces;
If only you could lend me a tenth of your courage
I might be able to befriend the world.
Each day I wait for you to approach me.
Each day I wait for a friendly smile.
It seems that you look at my clothes and frown;
While you never look into my eyes, the door to my soul.
These tattered jeans symbolize my broken home.
The worn-down shoes are from miles of endless journeys.
My shirt, though faded,
Came from a man too ashamed to be called my dad.
These tear stains below my eyes are here,
Because all I needed was a friend.

Brandy Nichols

Fare Thee Well

Farewell my love to all we've known
I've felt your love as we've grown
All we know, all we feel
Is leaving now, a broken seal
The vow we've kept is up to you
Stay with me, or leave me too
From here - you and I must part
But we can stay - within our hearts
The crescent beckons, to draw us near
Will I lose you? This I fear.
In the darkness I clasp your hand
A greater purpose my love demands
But through the tunnel of unknown fears
Don't forget me and don't shed tears
For without each other our love will die
Look to the heavens, look to the skies
Cause beneath the moon's bright rays
You'll feel my love and remember my ways
Dwell on a plane of reminiscence,
And say farewell under the orb's luminescence.

Nathan Bethea

Thanksgiving Day In The Henhouse

Hello, Hen-Rietta, have you heard about Tom?
I just picked it up on my floppy-comb-rom.

He was given high honors upon his demise;
And he's lying there now stuffed with chestnuts and rice.

Remembering him then, the way that he looked,
It's hard to imagine him now that he's cooked.

When the word first went out, feathers shook with alarm.
Tom thought he was the best stud on the farm.

Remember how Cocky he was in a crowd,
Strutting and crowing, conceited and proud?

Had all the other Cox-Combing his hair,
While he checked the Chicks with a come-hither stare!

He was a stuffed shirt, and now, I suppose
That he is still stuffed - with no head and no toes!

Remember how lazy and plump he became?
He was slow on the track, so he was fair game.

Now his "goose has been cooked", and along with mince pie,
Right there on the platter in pieces he'll lie.

If there's a heaven for Turkeys, and if he's up there,
Tom's feelings must be that he's no longer "rare"!

Doreen Coco

Rachel

Before I met you, I was so lost inside
sorting my thoughts as I took long drives.
When I met you my life really changed
the thoughts on my mind became very strange.
The feelings you brought me on the day that we met
these feelings inside I have never had yet
you made it so clear, as time went on
your feelings for me would always be strong
I see brighter days with you by my side
through the laughter we've shared and the tears that we've cried
you brought out the best in me every day
the love for you in my heart shall stay
The fun we've had, the times we've shared
my life could shatter, and I would not care
Some people would die to have a friend like you
I know I've been blessed, and you know by who
They say best friends should never say never
the closeness we share will last forever.

William J. Walter

Clouds

How very deep in love, am I
That as I watched the clouds go by,
I thought I saw a ship, upon a sea.
Your ship, I thought, sailing back to me.
Then as the ship took flight,
I thought I saw a bird of white.
Then as I watched the bird was gone,
And I thought I heard a song.
How very deep in love am I
That as I watched the clouds go by,
I felt a stir of happiness untold,
And all the clouds were turned to gold.

Roberta M. Wilcox

Awakening

When I woke up I smelled your coffee,
And without opening my eyes, I knew I was happy.
For I was restful, contented and glad.
I did not know what my feelings were caused by,
And yet I knew I was glad in my heart.
And I swear by the sun, that shone so brightly that morning,
That I heard your morning paper rustle.
Then with new-morning eyes I looked at the world,
Not doubting a minute, what they would show me.
Then with new-morning eyes I saw-
A chair - book - a shoe,
All in the wrong order, wrong place.
And that is when, I truly awoke.

Mara Gustafson

Where Did The Time Go?

Where did the time go my two little boys?
Wasn't it yesterday you played with your toys?
Running and laughing and oh so carefree,
I hope you both know what you mean to me.

I've watched you both grow into fine young men,
My heart filled with pride as it was then,
You are both loved, wished nothing but joy,
Where did the time go my two little boys?

You'll experience life, know its ups and downs,
You'll know gladness, have heartaches,
  you'll laugh, you'll frown;
You'll know sorrow, feel love, comfort and joy,
Where did the time go my two little boys?

And as the years pass and your children grown,
You'll see them through eyes much like my own,
No more children's games, away put the toys,
Where did the time go my two little boys?

Lorraine Chiarello

Wantagh Senior Center Of The Town Of Hempstead

Are you a senior, who's not on the run?
Then join the Wantagh center and have some fun.
It's open to us five or six days a week,
So trot on down and give us a peek.

You can enjoy yourself in a game of pool,
Just be sociable and stick to the rules.
Do you want some exercise with movement per chance?
Then come on down and learn how to dance.

Do you have a good voice and you like to sing?
Join the Wantagh Mighty Arts Players, and sing like Bing.
We play canasta, pinochle, bridge, and rummy, too.
And also have bingo; there's so much to do.

We have bowling leagues and shuffleboard teams.
We'll fulfill your days and lighten your dreams.
What more can I say, you really want more?
Go on trips and vacations and make new friends galore.

So get off your butt, from in front of the T.V.
Join he Wantagh center, see how happy you'll be.
So come Wantagh seniors, come one and come all,
The admission is free, and you'll have a ball.

Anthony F. Tommasulo

Onset

The darkness looms so silent and still
And morning's light seems too far away
And slowly, so slowly I start to feel
My control of my fear slipping away

The darkness looms so silent and still
Cloaking the room in an eerie glow
Normal objects look like something unreal
While shadows gather around me slow

The darkness looms so silent and still
For me there seems to be no escape
Hysteria grips me against my will
As before my eyes something takes shape

The darkness is no longer silent and still
As colors and noises explode in my head
Can this be imagined or is it real?
Can I still be alive when I feel dead?
The darkness looms so silent and still...
   Lora Shouse

In The Pink

Feeling in the pink.
Pink is what I feel when I think of being brand new
New, like the bottom of a newborn baby's kicking feet.
Kicking. Kicking and cooing on its back
But kicking with all its little might.
Kicking when content - kicking when angry
But kicking just the same.
Kicking to be held next to a warm body
Maybe grasping just a finger,
Knowing it's stronger than its own.
I'm like that newborn baby - when I'm lying next to you.
   Rovenna Harden

A Revisit To The Heart

Sweat streams down his wrinkled forehead
   and he whispers to me one solemn word
Why? Flows from his lips to my ears
   and the only response I can utter is "love"
But that isn't what he hears
He hears his screams echoing through the small house
He feels the pain from the mother who once loved him
He sinks back into his world of fear and memories
   leaving why? To linger on
   in the blackened, stale room-once filled with passion
My mouth trembles and my blood runs cold from
   the silence, but I love him
I turn to look at him,
   but his eyes show that he is no longer with me
The tears he sheds have taken him back home.
   Melanie Austin

The Touch

I long to feel that special touch,
that sends a chill throughout your soul.
I long to feel that special touch,
that makes life seem not such a toll.

I long to feel that special touch,
that gives insight to your hopes and dreams.
I long to feel that special touch,
that sends laughter and joy throughout each being.

I long to feel that special touch,
that only one person can give.
Oh how I long to be touched by God,
so he can show me how to live.
   Florence A. Kilby

A Long Time

As the days turn into years
And the years into tears. As long as you are away.
My life has never been sane.
Along the narrow path of life.
Dreaming, hoping someday to be your wife.
Even though that's never to be true.
Always remember, I hate you.
You made me lose all hope of love.
Looking up at the night above.
You made my dreams fall.
All you have to do is call.
Or if you're really sorry you can write.
It doesn't take all night
Give me what is mine,
Everything will turn out fine. You're always on my mind.
Even though your heart was never kind. Let me go.
Please don't say 'no'.
I hope what I tell you stays in your head.
Lying down thinking of me in your bed.
You promised me.
How could this be.
I'm so blind, how can you see?
Maybe in time I will let you go.
But deep down I will always know.
And always remember what you broke.
You must think of me as a joke.
   Shanna Latham

Mama's Boy

   All throughout my life -
There were things I had to find
And one of them was a love,
That would be as strong as mine.

She had to have a heart
That was to me as pure as gold
Even though I wanted beauty
I wanted mostly a beautiful soul.

And then all of a sudden
everything seemed to explode into a lovely
kaleidoscope for all to see
There you were before my face
a woman that God created,
proving that God makes no mistakes

You are the yellow rose of all my senses
and I am stripped of all pretenses
you are all I ever needed
and you fulfill my heart within
I must thank you for being my love
and from my heart, for being my friend,

I love you Mama!
   Melvin C. Williams

Help

Sky of wonder and awe, come
Succulent sun, enlighten me
Worthy winds, send me a breath of wisdom
Worldly wren, sing a song to me
Sluggish snake, lead me into your kingdom
Raven, allow me to exult like a nation
Willow tree, may your branches protect me
Clustered clouds, send me good dreams
Divine dove, encourage me to love
Fragrant flower, help me to find faith
Brilliant bittern, enable me to learn
Naked night, be near me
Nature I am lost;
Come find me.
   Natalie Watkins

A Bright Star

My precious little Jesus had no crib for a bed
A manger was all they had to rest his head
A big bright star shined as a light
Oh that was a glorious sight
Angels came where shepherds laid
Told them thou be not afraid
They went to the baby the angels told them about
It was all they could do to keep from a shout
Jesus grew an grew until he reached that awful day
When his Father would carry him away
A crown of thorns was put on his head
Pain and suffering was among him and his people
They thought he was dead until he said
Forgive them Lord they know not what they do
A chill came upon them as blood came from the wound
Put a stone there not to be removed but removed it was
By angels of God and Jesus arose
To his kingdom above
   Samantha Swiney

Love Within

Love, is like a turtle dove,
It can come from within,
Or from above.

Love is more than just a feeling,
It's like a magic power,
That grows with every hour.

Love, is more than giving life
The warmth spreads through-out the soul,
And touches each one we know.

Love, is more than finding someone,
And give's us the life of giving.
For, love is life, and worth loving.
   Karen C. Campbell

In The Hands Of Jesus

Everything I have, he gone to me.
I can not count the blessings
He gives so much you see
Here beside me, guides me day by day
When they are problems, he is there
His voice soft, and sweetly talks to me.
And shows me the right way
In the hands of Jesus
Is where I want to be
for everything I have, Jesus gone to me
Earth, Heaven, all in between
he die for me, I am set free
In the hands of Jesus
Is the only place to be
So please came, to Jesus.
Take his hands, salvation it is free.
   Thelma Dupert

Untitled

Ever notice
'bout chess
Nestles
Chocolate
don't always mix well
though, one whose learned
in the game
can concentrate his
players places to win
(Which is what the game is all about in the long run.)
   Nancy Durnell

Untitled

As I walked along the road
I saw dead flowers
Squashed, as if a Mac truck had run over them,
As if they had tragically committed suicide.

And I began to wonder
What horrible event led to this mass suicide
The death of beauty, grace, innocence, gaiety.
Has the world become so corrupt, as to make the flowers want to die?

It was a tragic loss today,
As the flowers forfeited their lives.
They did not leave notes like common society.
But now, they lay squashed, on asphalt.

Who will bury these tragic martyrs?
Who will pull their dead bodies from the road and eulogize them?
What will be done the next time
A flower wants to die?
   Melissa J. Boynton

A Baby Step Closer To The Rainbow

Safe inside, small as can be
I feel my mother's love me
I'm only a seed preparing to grow
Within her womb indeed I know
Her wish for me is that I live,
Free from AIDS, willing to forgive
Her now for what she did not know
My right to life and chance to grow.

A baby step closer to the rainbow will be,
When once I'm delivered, my momma will see
We were blessed by the people empowered and skilled
With the knowledge and desire to do God's will
To keep me safe from danger and harm,
To know while inside you I am safe and warm
Along with my mom by my side we will know
One day at a time is
A baby step closer to the rainbow.
   V. Bob

An Infatuation

Don't seek a cure for loneliness,
out of desperation.
Don't mistake a newfound love,
for mere infatuation.

I suggest you think it over,
talk things out with your lover.
Study the relationship before it goes any further,
or you'll find yourself in real trouble.

Don't expect the unexpected,
don't take things for granted.
Don't settle for a fictionalized story,
then watch then leave in a hurry.

Be careful and as cautious as you can,
anxiety is not the solution.
Patience is the rule to virtue.
don't do something you can't undo.

It's just an ego trip I see,
an ego personality.
Take heed to your situation,
it's only an infatuation.
   Ronda Louise White

If...

If I can trust you
With my secrets and feelings and be sure they are safe from
Gossips and rumor mongers,

If you could listen to my words
And give ear to my soul understanding its sweetness
And never afraid of its pains.

If we could go on spending sprees
And my wallet is empty leaving us with nothing to buy ice cream,
And you are still there for me,

Then you are my friend
And you will always be my friend and I will always be there for you
Until death says otherwise.

You can always trust me with your secrets
And I can always be there to listen to you
To give an ear to your soul to understand its sweetness
And try to find a cure for its pains;

Believe me, I will always be your friend
And you will always be my friend
And we shall always be there for each other
Until death says otherwise.

Marisol Pena

Light

At days end, the dark shades of night settle over all
Windows glow from within, burning campfires stretch out with a
  luminous glow.

The dark of night comes to life with the flip of a switch
  cutting a path to lead us on.
Heavy, though it may be, night cannot resist this switch.

The dark clouds roll in as a storm begins
With a fierce determination, lightening comes
  leaving a thunderous closing as a storm begins.

When the dark of glum pursues my soul
A gentle breath of graceful light fills my heart from God above
Now my burden is light, my heart hath wings
Dark cannot hide the light that fills my heart and soul
For He lighteth my passage as I go.

Barbara Groseclose

"My Last Name is Smith"

My last name is Smith,
But, it could have been Jones.
So, do you get my drift,
My dead beat dad left me all alone.
But, I love him still
Because I know it's God's will.
My mom, I heard her cry,
Then I heard her sigh.
God I am too young for so much pain
That is why I cry and wish they were in love again.

When I am eighteen, I will try to find my dad,
Then I will ask him about all the good times we could of had.
Dead beat dad, no he's not,
My mom says his secret love is all I got.

I miss you dad,
For the love I never had.
Dad, I am happy just the same,
And, I am proud Smith is such a wonderful name.

Loretta Goode

"RESPONSIBLE ICONOCLAST AT LAST!"

mindbodysoulspiritworkenvironment
one word, one purpose, rejecting comparison and pointless competition
May you never harm anyone
finding any judgmental complaints to be more like compliments
Oscillating and contributing between these idiosyncratic
creative outlets
being both sides of my camera's camera
and even "expecting" you to accept this as actually unique
(clear throat) "um... Excuse me?"
Defining OUR OWN subjective "success"
I traditionally defy traditions!
Humbly suggesting that you question any "expert"
"I AM THE BEST!" .... me.
"WE'RE ALL ALREADY DEAD!"
Because we follow! We swallow! We beLIEve all the attractive LIEs!
As Society tries to condition us to become nothing more than
good consumers and respectable abusers.
Is this "worry free" sacrilegious fine-writing at its worst?
Absolutely!.... Absolutely not
It's time that we spend time listening to OUR OWN thoughts
"Please Pardon me.... I've ranted"

ERAMO

The Perfect Time

Let's have some tea,
  It's the perfect time,
No one's around,
  Just you and I.
We'll set a pretty table,
  And choose our favorite cup,
We'll get the tea a brewin',
  Oh please hurry up!
The napkins are lacy,
  Petite fours in a row,
I'm so glad you're here,
  'Cause it pleases me so!
We'll talk of new things,
  And share secrets too,
And when we're all done,
  We'll have cup number two.
Then I'll wash up the pot and put it away,
  "How good it was of you to come," I'll say!
Next time we have this chance, you know it will be,
The perfect time, for us to have tea!

Pamela Nycz Kratzer

Look Through These Eyes...

The sky is a playground where the clouds laugh all day,
The air is the place where the butterflies stay,
The trees are strong men that are good to climb on,
The grass is the carpet they tumble upon.

The hills are the things that are meant to be climbed,
Under rocks is the place where the bugs like to hide,
The sun warms their skin and lights up their day,
The rain makes huge puddles in which they like to play.

Dandelions and weeds are great flowers to them,
The small and unnoticed to them all seem grand,
Their happiness glows like the sun does in the morning,
Even lying on the ground to them is never boring.

This view I have shown you is through different eyes,
They're closer to the ground but they look to the skies,
They shine like a star in the dead of the night,
This is the view of a child... what a beautiful sight.

Rachel Miriah Roslund

In All Due Time The Presence Will Be Clear

Don't cry my love,
Don't be glum or sad,
For the one who seeks your happiness will always be near,
In all due time that presence will be clear.
His heart may be crushed by an external pressure
Or his mind filled with foolish thoughts.
His eyes may seem to have no love
And his voice without a subtle word, but
In all due time the presence will be clear.
The ugly head of disappointment may have risen up
And tried to cloud his feelings for you,
In all due time the presence will be clear.
The emotions once present are still there flowing strong,
Hate will not nor could not shadow over him,
In all due time the presence will be clear.
An image of you danced in the night sky.
On every thought he pondered why!, Oh why!,
Can he not be with you, but
When that time comes everyone will know of his love, and
In all due time his presence will be there.

Lemuel Jackson

The Great American Cowboy

Across the vast open range, towards the setting of the sun,
Rides the great American cowboy - proud 'n tall, his work all done.
He hasn't always been a cowboy, though many things he's been.
We find him now - from the range, towards the bunkhouse, riding in.

You'd recognize this cowboy by the regal way he stands,
by the neatness of his bunk, and love for his fellow man.
He came from foremost education, in a land distinguished and elite.
He humbled himself to be a cowboy - not willing to admit defeat.

He knows life's not easy and weathered for himself -
  as others would not.
He opened massive gates and did his job - non-stop.
He counted each and every cow 'n even learned to ride.
He's worked real hard, accomplished this with unassumin' pride.

He is a man to be appreciated, recognized and understood.
Full of compassion 'n caring. You'd say, "He's just plain good".
He is underestimated by most. His knowledge abounds.
He comes from another country, another place, another town.

His mind drifts to his homeland, his family, the man he's become.
No matter what others may say - He will govern the final outcome.
And when all is said and done - we'll have the last laugh in the end.
The Great American cowboy is a Russian chemist, and my friend.

Sharron Hanson

Lovers

We drove along the coast and watched the sunset over the
Sea and there was a quiet harmony between us

We sat in the grass by a stream and listened to the water
Falling over the rocks and a tower bell ringing in the
Distance and there was a peace within us

We walked through the forest on a winding path hand in hand
Listening to the sounds of quiet solitude around us and we
Felt the comfort of just being together

We sat by a warm cozy fireplace on a cold winter night and
Watched the snowflakes tap lightly against the window panes
And talked for hours about hopes and dreams yet to conquer

I knew at those moments that our love and friendship would
Blossom and grow

Linda Dragone

Love Is Blind

You rode on a donkey into my fortified heart,
And I covered your path with the best palms I could give.
They were brown and dying and quickly fell apart,
But you happily remained in my heart to live.

You were mocked by many for loving me.
You were stoned and whipped and spat upon.
They gave you a crown of thorns so heavy,
And your bowed head they placed it on.

They taunted you by calling you a queen,
And nailed you to the cross of my ugliness.
Yet all the while you let it be seen
That you still loved me nonetheless.

Blood gushed forth, pouring from your side,
In testimony to your endless love.
And I stood for hours and cried and cried,
And prayed out loud to God above.

For you had redeemed my ugly being,
Now forgiven in your eyes.
And now your eyes were only seeing
A greater essence which herein lies.

Andrew P. Marra

The War

Why must we always go to war?
Is there no love left anymore?
Why does no one ever try negotiation?
Do the people that fight really fight for their nation?
Or is it for the praise they might receive?
Why must every soldiers family cry and grieve?
Do people like the blood and gore?
Do they crave more and more?
This world we see, it can't be real.
It kind of makes you wonder, will I live to have another meal?
And every day I hope and pray that this madness will stop.
But by the time we realize what were doing it will be too late.
Most of us will already be headed for the golden gate.
So, in consideration for our whole entire nation I
ask this, why must we go to war?

Faith Finholm

Wedding Day Blues

My wedding is here, this is finally my day
My dad cried a tear as he gave me away

My heart burst with love for this man at my side
He kissed me and called me his beautiful bride

When the minister said we were husband and wife
It was then that I knew we had started our life

Well, the wedding is over, the lights are turned low
All that remains are some left over bows

All the planning that took many months to get right
And the bills for these things that were so out of sight

There was music, flowers, cake, wine and beer
All to share happiness, joy and good cheer

Now the laughter, the dancing and songs have all stopped
The party is over, the last guest dropped off

We're alone now, just us, in this big empty room
No more announcements for us, for the bride and the groom

You hold me, we dance, as you sing me your song
You whisper the words of how much we belong

Together forever, we'll always be true
My life has begun and it started with you

Jacqueline M. Carfi

My Gift

You are my difference, you are my same.
You make me who I am.
You are who I was.
Because of me you will be better than I.

You are my Gift from God.
You were sent to teach me.
No one can give me the gift you have,
and no one can give you what I feel.

You are my Daughter, and no matter what becomes of you or I,
this cannot be changed.
We are bonded by God specially, no man can alter this.
We belong to each other, maybe not in body, but always in Soul.

Laura Bedford

Dreamer

If dreams are a haven for happiness,
I don't want to be awake.
I'd rather righteously be called a dreamer
Then wrongfully pegged a fake.

I'd rather dream about the future things
Then lie about those present;
Live within a dreamer's realm
Among those things most pleasant.

I picture the world as a wonderful place,
Then make myself a believer.
If it is wrong to wish for things better,
I don't want to be a dreamer.

Jamie Belanger

Arizona Storm

The aroma drifts on the breath of a divine wind.
With its gallant descent from heaven,
I inhale it throughout my body.
The moonless night plots revenge on the sun.
The thirsty soil seduces the rain.
The desert whimpers for consideration,
While the saguaro raises its arms,
As if to beg of its maker.

Thunder explodes!
Lighting lights the way.
Peace, now just a memory, rips open
Wildly into madness.

Holding myself, spellbound, while I observe
God's musical theater.
Nature's rejoicing has begun.
I hear its cry,
As the washes become desert highways,
Conquering and tearing bits of the land from home.

It swallows me;
Enraptures my soul.

Elizabeth Ashley Reynolds

My Fright

Sometimes at night I have a little fright,
That only happens when mom shuts off the light,
But when my mom is in my room,
My face will never be in gloom,
But will that fright come back tonight,
It may not come or it might,
All I can say is I hope it doesn't,
So my night can be quite pleasant.

Nicole Dornbusch

The Game

The pieces
of my life are in disarray
from pawns to king they are scattered across the board
with little rhyme
and less reason;
other than perhaps to fend off,
with ever less effectiveness,
the incessant attacks
of my relentless opponent.

The clock ticks
with ever increasing urgency
and seemingly, with ever increasing speed.
The end of the game is near,
and I?
I wish only to be able to end this game and start a new one.
"Set up the pieces again" I cry,
"this time I'll show you a game of utter virtuosity!"
But that can never be.
For this is the only game,
and soon it will be over.

C. Kerry Nemovicher

Silent Heart

It is sad....
  They talk of abortion - making it legal to destroy
  a part of the future, a possible miracle - a child.

  Women - young and old, having children, yet not
  wanting them - to care for - to nourish - to lead the way.

It is sad....
  The hopes of tomorrow - given up for adoption,
  "legally" disposed of by those who created them.

  They put a high price on children no one wants...
  Adoption - how can you put a price on the right to
  give love and happiness to a child without.......

It hurts.....
  There are so many silent hearts in the world crying
  out for a child to love and care for - women who can
  never have one- though it be their greatest desire in
  life - the "cost" of their love is too high........

Adoption - Abortion....
Is it God's will - or his dismay...
I don't understand.................
How can I?

T.C.'s Silent Heart

I Just Want To Be Free

I walk around the town and people wonder what I'm doing
I go into a store not one but everybody wonders if I'm going to steal
People ask me if I worship the devil just because of the music I
  listen to, I just want to be free
I can't stand the way people think about me, I just want to be free
People shouldn't judge people by the way they look
I just want to be free
I don't want to dress different just because someone wants me to
I just want to end it here and now
But no that will just prove I am what they think I am
No I will prove I am not that way I am better than what they think I am
I walk around with my girlfriend we're laughing and smiling and
people think we're stoned or we just had sex
I can't stand it I can't take it anymore
I just want to be free, they look at me like I'm a criminal
I just want to be free, they don't know me they shouldn't judge me
I just want to be free, they were all my age once they should know
Maybe they were worse maybe they judge me the way they were
  at my age
But they shouldn't each generation is different each person is
different everyone is equal

Joshua Galindo

Looking Out My Window

Here I sit, alone in the dark, all by myself once more.
These lonely nights seem to never end, they just go on and on.
Sometimes I wonder if there really is a clear picture in life,
Or is the picture so old and faded do I have to look twice?
What exactly am I missing? I have not a clue!
I need that special something, something I cannot see.
Looking out my window.
My mind turns inside out; it tortures me; it leaves me in despair.
I find myself asking the same old question; does anybody really care?
Twisted and tormented, I might be,
But only because of something I cannot see.
Looking out my window.
I seek so hard for peace, for joy, for the security of perfection.
But, while searching to find these things, I totally lose my direction.
In my world of heartache; no solutions, all pain.
I hang my head and cry for myself; I hide my face in shame.
I hope someday I can overcome this thing that dwells so deep inside;
To wipe away what is preventing from seeing
Through the window of my mind.
   Frank W. Fisher Jr.

Regardless Love

At times I thought I lost you forever
But I realize in our hearts we'll always be together
At times I thought I'd never hear from you again
Yet I also realized you'll always be a friend
I know now I must move on
And carry these memories with you along
Each step I take, I'll take with pride
Knowing you'll always be here by my side
Never will I forget the times we had
The laughter, the tears, the pain hurt so bad
With such little time you taught me so much
Every single word had a gentle touch
You brought me out from the life of pain
Showing me the world and all I can gain
I want to thank you for all you did
Especially for teaching me not to keep my feelings hid
Now I will be able to move on with my life, to forgive and forget
And what we once shared, not to regret
   Michelle Bellissimo

The Woman In The Moon

I have seen many joyful sights, in my life
but nothing is a greater sight
than the sun setting...
and the moon rising

The moon draws upon me a deep glaze
that I can not shake or even hope to break
maybe I glaze upon the moon, because I want to...
or maybe...I have to

But here I stand on this solid land,
staring at the man in the moon
who comforted me, many a night...
in sickness...in health...and because of love

Not near, not close, and not even far, but here in my mind...
I stand as tall as this man
but it's not with my height or size, I out do him with,
but with my imagination and eyes

And I say unto you, that this man in the moon, is indeed not a man
but a women, has we all know as...Mama

And touching the moon with my imagination and eyes is all I need
to enjoy this joyful sight...The Woman In The Moon!
   Tommy P. Winters

Curled In A Corner

A delicate finger presses against a shimmering window pane.
The heat of the sun paused;
For only a split second.
Connecting with one soul
Overflow
Fresh faced color comes to life and dances with her
Pure heat surges have found their way through a
Frightened hand
And passion is born
Born out of the stillness of this peace.
Glowing beauty reinvented in this time withered woman
Rising up her tattered spirit
Stretching to meet the sun with her eyes
For the first time
Her body feels reborn
   A. Yakawiak

Death

Oh death, oh death, please do be delated!
I have some things that must be terminated;
My cousins, sister, friends don't know Him.
And without... their fate is dim.
O, give me time to tell them.
Before, their lives, must you condemn.

Any time now they will be here,
Oh, please, please let them hear.
Oh! Friends come in,
come in, my kin.
Let me tell you of a son,
a fate that must be done.

He gave His life for you and me.
And now must you do the same, you see.
Give Jesus Christ your soul.
Then, only, shall your life be whole
He suffered on a wooden cross.
But did not stay on the cruel cross,

But rose again, and you can be with Him in Heaven.
O, death. You may come now, my patron.
   Deborah E. Fulton

An Old Man's Lament

Take me back to my old home.
Take me back, the hills to roam.
Take me back to the age of propriety.
Take me back to a drug-free society.
Take me back where the waters ran clear.
Take me back, ere I shed a tear.
Take me back for a life's replay.
Take me back to a better day.
Take me back for a look at my life.
Take me back to when I met my wife.
Take me back that I may recapture.
Take me back for love's pure rapture.
Take me back to the time of my youth.
Take me back to when I lost my first tooth.
Take me back to my mother's arms.
Take me back to when I had no alarms
Take me back and let me lie 'neath an unpolluted sky.
Take me back before I cry.
Take me back, oh Lord I pray
Take me back and let me stay.
   Joseph B. Swope Jr.

"People Are Different"

People are different
they're different than you
they may have different colored skin
or different colored eyes
but deep down inside, they're a lot like you

People are different
they're different than you
they may wear different clothes
or smell different than you
they may speak a different language
that seems strange to you
but deep down inside, they're a lot like you

People are different
they're different than you
many are homeless
or look strange to you
they may wear glasses
or walk with a limp
but deep down inside, you find
they're a lot like you

Jennifer Shamp

Be Judged

May my final trial be held in the courthouse of the universe
   and may the stars be my jury as God stand to judge.
May my only defense be the truth that runs through my heart
   like a traveling river and may all that I am
      stand to ridicule, and not all that I have been.
May my trial be fair and undaunted by the weight of
   gold in the pockets of my prosecutors.
And when judgement befalls upon my head
   like a sharp and shiny Guillotine may I smile,
For surely my heart shall bow
   humbling at the feet of my judge
For there and only there shall I be showered in the
   warm and glowing light of truth
For only in truth shall a man, good or bad ever romance lady
   happiness.

Tim Wells

It's All Our Fault

The wind nips at your feet,
The sun hidden behind the clouds.
And there's no one around to see you crying.

And there's nothing to do
But sit down and look
And you realize that everything is dying.

Most things are dead
Or they probably will be soon
As you think about it you are dying too.

It doesn't matter anyway
For you'd live the life of hell
And, besides, there is nothing you can do.

"But why did it happen?",
You scream for no one to hear
Although you answer quickly "One thing is pollution."

And it's so sad to think
That it took a short time
To destroy what took more than a revolution.

It's all our fault.
But it's not too late.

Jennifer Williams

"The Universal Genius"

Who is the renowned author of beauty?
No one has reason to doubt or ask;
His incomparable measure in perfection
To match the hand of a miraculous task!

Splashes of colors on earthly skies,
The spread of greenery on hills and dales,
Massive arrays of delicate petals,
Sparkling waters and winds for sails.

Endowments in patches of earthly grounds,
Humanity to express their maker's wares;
Motions and fixtures to attend their creation
To utilize the gifts of his kindly cares.

His provisions in energy and skills,
Talents, technology, music and arts
The inevitable proof of our Master's touch
Who left his heirs with minds and hearts.

Surely, no reason to question or doubt
The greatest of mind, heart and hand;
Has spread his superior worth in riches
Across the threshold of our beauteous land!

Wilhelmina Bevacqua

Wind And Tree

He blows hard
on the once quiet street corner
standing alone she fights, ready to throw a punch
he blows harder screaming in her face
still harder she tries
not to fall, not to give in
this time...instantly...surprisingly
with all his might
he lets loose and roars so fiercely
testing her will to stay calm
but she lets loose the same
thrashing at him violently
then he hits, hits so hard, so hard
fighting, yelling, threatening, painfully
finally with the calmest voices
they talk, agree, make up
quietly tell each other they're sorry
more peacefully and peacefully
they take each other's hands
and walk off together

Jeanette Morscher

My Angel Was Called Home

Written for Carol Barrs (5/5/64 - 1/13/96)
God gave me a beautiful Angel years ago...
She was so tiny, but had a brilliant glow.
As she grew, she touched out hearts...
So beautiful and loving from the start.
Her life was hard with the cross she had to bear...
But throughout it all she said "God will be there."
Our lives she touched for a while
With her love and her smile.
My heart broke when she went away
I ask God "Why couldn't she stay?"
As I grow older and my time draws near...
I will be ready and show no fear.
For I know "God's" Angel" will be there.
She'll guide me and take my hand...
And together we will travel to the Promised Land.

Sharron T. Jackson

Dear Sherina

Dear Sherina,
Working for over a year, we still haven't been fired
and serving all those chickens has made my hands so darn tired.
But having you around has made it all worth the while,
even if we could only talk when washing the dirty tray pile.
As bad as they smelled they still managed to giggle,
have you ever noticed that the baked beans wiggle?
Yeah me neither I just made that up,
and next time you make lemonade please save me a cup.
Well in case you didn't know, I like you a lot
and I hope we stay friends until we are old and rot!
But now for the words you've been waiting to hear,
Have a very Merry Christmas and a Happy New Year!!!
Daniel C. Johnson

Heart Of America: And They All Fell Down"

And they all fell down

The building intact, the children were there
The government employees, without a care

The coffee was brewing, their countenance high
The weather was promising, revealed in the sky!

The usual banter, the regular routine
The desks were work ready, set was the scene

Around 9 in the morning, the heartland was crushed
An explosion was heard, adrenalin rushed

And they all fell down

The death and debris stopped the world in its tracks
For a moment in time, our souls felt attacked

In the midst of the death and despair of it all
Somehow the measure of men, came to all

And those lacking power, and those unknown to most
Came to grips with devastation, came from coast to coast

They sifted through rubble, they cried with the grieving
Our country united, led us to believing

These unsung heroes with a mission to perform
Gave America hope, its spirit reborn! And, we all looked up!
Mary Jane Bagwell

Why'd You Have To Go?

Why'd you have to go?
For what reason I don't know.
I wish we could be together again,
You're more than just a friend.

Why'd you have to leave?
Love is what we both received.
We were made for each other
Not any other.
You shared your feelings,
I shared mine,
We always had a good time.
Just to hear your voice again,
Is something that my heart would love to comprehend.

Why don't you come back to me?
Make it so we always will be.
All those times together we had,
Both good and bad makes me sad.
If you hear the words that I'm saying you know what to do —
Please come back because I love you.
Marquita Bell

Looking

I'm looking up to see,
Everyone looking down on me.
Women say they want love,
But they really just fake love.
I won't be a one night stand,
And I'm not gonna play in your band.
If you stay with me tonight,
It'll be you and me for life.
I don't care if you call me a fool,
I know what you are, and it ain't cool.
You could be a surgeon,
With your heavy knife and your deadly burden.
Daniel L. Snyder

Untitled

Water, as pure as the day earth began, may now be muddied. Trees forever high, may fall. Beauty once cherished, preserved, now forgotten by yesterday's sunset, will one day return.

Sun, with praising light may wave good-bye.
Sky, calamity clear, may one day crash down.
Those who fear this, will wait to see its rebirth.

Little by little, it will grow, in place of the world before. The exotic difference is wisdom, of its broken past. Learned lessons will sure newborn trees, knowledge, the illuminating match of life.

As before, everything is beautiful, life is beautiful but if is treasured, helped to grow, one day words won't describe it. Love will lift the sky, to laughter, birds sing, and then forever will be now.

In this world, there is love if you want it, hate if you need it, and if you give it in this world there are colors as beautiful as blue and angry as red and in this world there is forgiveness for the deserving; in this world there is life.

In this world, if there are two people, who want to live, they will walk the unmarked path with careful footsteps, leaving behind all the evil for in these two people there is trust, equality, friendship, and forgiveness; but most importantly in their world there is love.
Christine Alana

Seasons Of Love

Where winds once blew warm and sweet
There stood a girl and a boy
Giving sharing loving all life's things
Beautiful pure and full of joy

Where spring rains washed the earth at last
These two stood hand in hand
Giving life, taking life at its very best
Like lovely flowers in desert sand

Where summer sun brought its bounty
They stood stronger than before
Amid the waves their ship rose proud
Always on the crest and safe to shore

Where falls rich colors ablaze and full
Still clinging they stood still yet
With wonder at the storms they braved
Though tossed about together and wet

Now winter winds blow fierce and cold
The two are one, shaken and worn
Beauty has faded the flowers are gone
Neither without the other stands forlorn
Judy Ledford

Road To Nowhere

The road to nowhere I follow
Stumbling along not knowing
The trees and grass fly by
In a blur I hardly notice
People and towns come and leave again
Not caring I ignore the memories
Caring left me long before I began
On the journey down this road
I want to turn around
I want to care and walk towards something,
Something better than where I'm headed
I don't know how
Maybe the way will come
A way I can get off this road to nowhere

Sean Ketcherside

Humpty Dumpty Revisited

Humpty Dumpty sat on a wall;
Humpty Dumpty had a great fall;
All the king's horses, and all the king's men
Cannot set Humpty D. up again.

They tried and they tried without much success;
Finally they called 911 to clean up the mess.
An ambulance came after considerable delay;
And loaded Humpty Dup and sped him away.

And so to a big hospital they took him,
Where an army of doctors examined shell, yolk, and limb.
They easily patched the crack in his shell,
But still Humpty's health was far from well;

For tests of his albumin, fluid, and yolk
Showed his cholesterol would lead to a stroke!
So they pumped him with drugs, serums, and pills
And sent him home with a mountain of bills.

Now Humpty D is still around,
But he has to stay on solid ground.
No more sitting high on the wall,
And a low-fat diet to lower his cholesterol.

Edward R. Lipinski

Wake Up To Jesus

You can have this whole world, with material goods galore;
But if you died today or tonight, would you go with joy to the Lord?
The clock didn't wake you, you didn't wake you
Only Jesus Christ;
So the best part of waking up, is Jesus in your life.

You say you love the Lord, but you give Him so little time,
You go about from day to day, with evil thoughts in your mind.
You forget to pray for the brand new day
You don't take God at His Word,
But you ought to Him thanks for life;
You'd better "wake up to Jesus Christ".

There are times when we forget about the goodness of the Lord,
There are times when we neglect to read in God's Holy Word;
We fret and complain about every-thing,
We don't give Him all the praise,
But you ought to give Him thanks for life,
You'd better thank Him for every day.

Oh, the best part of waking up is Jesus in your life,
Oh, the best part of waking up is Jesus in your life.

Harriet Marie Robinson

A Rose

And once, in passing by, I stopped to watch
 a rosebud life-ing itself to life.
Wrapped within were color, shape and form,
 fragrance, too, and energy;
What energy? The only energy, the Ruah, the
 breath of God
Breathing everything into being since everything
 is because God is.
(And so I am and so you are)

And as I watched I listened and I could hear the
 purr of God purring in divine contentment,
For there before Him stood another masterpiece,
 a rose, resplendent to behold,
Growing lovelier with each moment, more unique,
 more itself;
For God does not repeat Himself; He creates
 in endless creativity.

Johanna Leahy

My Innocence

Pink wiggly sweetness soft and warm
Fresh powder scent dances around a halo of wispy golden hair
Happy smiles and giggles bubbling over little pink lips
Eyes filled with wonder bright and trusting
Little arms with tiny fingers reaching out for love

Pink now muddied in blackness
Wiggling, bitter trying to escape
Hot and rigid with fear
Smell of sweat clings to tangles of baby blonde hair
Tense little lips quivering, trying to stifle a cry
Eyes filled with instant age
An opened window to a pained heart
Breaking with secrets of innocence lost
Little arms with tiny fingers clutched around a tiny body
Still rocking naked
In a dark little room
Hidden in my mind...

Kay Montgomery

Gifts

The gifts you gave to me
I'll cherish the rest of my life
The gift of love, so pure, so true
A touch, a smile, a kiss, I love you.

The joy of finding a new place to eat
But I so enjoyed the meals your hands fixed
Your patience and gentleness amazed me
A joy to learn of earth and flowers.

Roses you loved, now I love them too
Your love of tulips, daffodils all
A man can be a man and be gentle
He can cry, hurt, love, laugh, do it all.

A love of going or staying home
A real home we had not just a house
I loved to see your face when something
Would excite you and see it come to be.

I learned to trust, to love and depend
I learned to talk about everything
Not always agreeing, but loved your ideas
One day again I'll find these and you.

Joan C. Frederick

Untitled

Since I was seven I've been here,
Trapped in these walls they call home.
Feeding me thoughts of conformity,
they want me to be alone.
Rejection is common in this small place,
you can't find a way to escape.
The walls that are here lock you in your place,
No Escape, no escape, no escape.
I will break the wall one day,
the sun will shine down on me.
When I am away from this crazy town,
then I can say I am free.
I'll pack up my things I'll leave just like that,
saying good-bye to a few,
and hope that I'll never come back.
-Staying away is impossible though,
there is too much to hold me here.
Crazy dreams and insane lies,
mixed in with a little fear.

Tanya Lampron

Ageless Time

I sit, while the woman next to me, babbles.
Not incoherently, she knows what she's talking about all too well.
She is talking about the end of a lifetime, for her.
Even though mine has just begun, I listen.
Her words bounce off the concrete walls as if she was sitting in a tomb.
The nursing home people have heard her stories time and time again.
Her life is at an end, so she has no new stories about her life.
They were sent here to wait, for their last hour, which seems
   to never come.
But they hope that the stories of their lives will live on in the youth.
The youth of this time think they are untouchable, as these people
   once did.
Time. The thing these people curse in their prayers, lives on,
   untouched, unworn, unhurt.
When they die, it's as if they are released from a living hell.
I will never reach this point, being forgotten by the world.
My experiences will live on in the youth.
I will be made immortal.

Allison Ido

Three Little Words

Dedicated to the Love of my Life: Keith W. Shifes

I've paced my heart for hours,
trying to find a way.
To tell you three little words,
that seem so hard to say.

It's amazing how three little words,
Can actually mean so much;
And how those words get stronger,
With every single touch.

I know that we're just friends,
but my heart is unaware.
It's blinded by emotions,
That will always be there.

I guess now is the best time,
To do what I need to do.
I'm going to say those three little words,
And the rest is up to you.

Amy Michelle Yelton

Untitled

...And there he stood
   with half a soul.
And she, hers too
   in half was torn.
Monotony from days of old
   had overcome, and left all worn.
Yet in the distance overhead
   she felt the warmth of Younger Days.
And he, as well, had felt the Sun
   as Angels bowed to sing their Praise.
Such Beauty never seemed to live
   as the Breeze, it hymned their Grace.
The Heavens opened up to them
   and gently kissed upon their face.
Within this vast and gracious world;
   across the thundering oceans deep,
Their Souls had met and taken flight
   together, for the Skies to keep.

Amy L. Christopherson

For Eternity

As endless waves roll on the beaches.
As sunlight passes over mountains.
As star lit skies shine far above us.
As God's green earth has turned to sin.

The passing days to soon forgotten.
The gift of life ungratefully received.
The sacrifice God's son had given, to save
a world from the devil's greed.

Through God's mighty powers in Jesus,
our souls can be set free.
Christ our strong hold, our key, to eternity.

Venus M. Keith

Untitled

As I lie here in this cold, dreary dungeon of life
I pray for God All-Mighty to spear a bolt of lightning down
   towards earth
In hope that this bold of electricity may shed some light onto
   all of this darkness which is imprisoning me

Shadows creeping back from the past to the present
Thinking about all of the mistakes and trying to learn from them

Tossing and turning completely wide-eyed
I am once again unable to rest

Part of me wants to experience eternal rest
But this consummation requires more courage than attainable
For only God can create and destroy

The rest of me prays for the bold of lightning
To come towards our horror-filled planet
To shed some light upon my body and soul

If I shall never love again
If I shall never be love again
Then I shall pray for God to take me away

But I believe that all hope is not lost
I believe that a bolt of lightning will light up the sky - and my heart
I believe that you are near me, even when we're miles apart

Vitaliano Sicilia

Shadows

I was walking in the sun one day, enjoying God's warm glow,
upset because my circumstances brought me to a low.
"Why can't I rise above these things? Why do they clutch my heart?"
"Why does it seem that at their peak, God's grace seems to depart?"
I looked upon the ground just then, and saw my shadow fall,
upon the concrete steps I trod, and upward to the wall.
It suddenly occurred to me the answer to my plight,
I knew what I must do now, how to change my wrong to right.
Just as I prove an obstacle when in the sun I stand,
my flesh a hindrance to the sun, when its warmth should bless the land.
My sinful flesh and worldliness does, too, stand in the way,
when God would wish to bless my soul with warmth and care today.
The darkness on my heart, I feel, is not God's lack of grace,
but just a shadow cast below, when on His throne I took His place.
   Anne Elisabeth Grimes

Just And Fair

Tell me the things that's just, and fair.
This world is round, and not a square.

I can fly like the birds if I wanted to,
and swim in the ocean like most fish do.

Tell me there's not a thing I should worry about.
That there's brotherly love without a doubt.

The politicians work just for us,
and the police, and courts are really just.

That women, and men are equal throughout our land.
There is no racial differences that exist you understand.

There is peace on earth, and good will towards man.
These are not just words, and thoughts,
it can be done, we could take a stand.

With such little effort for each to share.
Then we would know the love for God was everywhere.
   William C. O'Neill

My Puppy Dog

Annie, oh, Annie, my puppy dog,
Little at first, big and growing now,
You swim, you run, you play all day,
Are you sure you're a dog?
You're my friend always,
You listen to Barney, have tons of toys and have a binky that
Looks more like Swiss cheese,
I'll love you always,
You'll always be mine,
My bed is full of goodies,
Little trees, a puppy and me crunched up on my wee little bed,
You're the only Annie that I know,
No one can replace you,
So Anne, just be yourself and don't ever change!
   Emily Carle

To My Wife

This morning I woke up in a world I didn't know.
Where I trust what I wouldn't have never before
I find myself hoping for things I would
never have dreamed
That fate or good luck would have turned out to be
I find myself happy and content with my life.
And wonder and excitement fill up my life.
The dull and the boredom that I had
Before leave me when I come in my door.
For I've found the best thing that could ever be.
The Relationship between you and me.
   Jimmy Johnson

Surrender

Surrender is what the autumn does
when winter arrives undaunted in her land
and all of nature can be heard sighing the word "relinquish"

Mountain peaks raise up like hands surrendering
when time comes to etch her fine lines
upon their faces

The song the river sings is surrender
as it hurries to lose itself in the vastness of the ocean

The circle of surrender
but endless cycles of death and birth
doing the dance of honor around the sacred hoop of life

Worn out people pressed against walls of extinction
trading in culture for survival's regalia of shame
surrender's inhuman price
seen somehow not quite as noble as nature's compromise
   Candy Wilson

Muir Woods

To Todd, Elizabeth and Andy, who shared this memory with me and encourage me in my poetry.
Forests of ferns and redwood trees so tall,
Branches meet branches 'till there's no sky at all;
Glades of lacy green and ferns of soft moss
And climbing ivy that creeps up and across
Trunks of trees, then hangs from branch to branch
Creating a beautiful stillness, my soul is enhanced.
This gift of beautiful woods poses a paradise scene
As soil, so moist, drifts through the air sweet and clean.
Quiet, seclusion, no noise around
Except for a brook that makes a babbling sound.
So cool, so refreshing, such a beautiful retreat,
A place of respite from the sun's shining heat.
As I circle the pathway and linger to feel
The embrace of Nature, my trembling heart it does heal.
Caressed by the tender breeze brings me such bliss
While streaming sunlight gives to all that it touches a gentle kiss.
My attention is lost as my mind wanders away
And stores in my imagination the magic of this day,
Longing to dwell in these woods vast and deep,
But knowing these memories are always mine to keep.
   Jo Jaimeson

The Shadow

From the darkness came a flash of light
and soon a shadow was born.
Alone roaming the streets at night
until it found this thing called man.
Now man doesn't have to be lonely anymore
since he now has a faithful companion.
Sometimes it walks way out in front
to search the night ahead.
Or showing no fear it stays at the rear
to protect the back it's said.
Someone to talk to as you walk along,
perhaps a buddy to run with.
None-the-less the shadow is there
remaining close by your side.
"Come my little shadow," the man remarked.
"We have a long, long way to travel".
The figure on the wall then said to him
"When it's, light just remember, I'm free!"
   Cleveland P. C. Lynn

Untitled

Do not remember me and weep
I'm free of pain, I now can sleep
I'm with the balmy winds that blow
I'll share the suns prisms on the snow
I'll ride the golden waves of grain
I'll join the murmur of summer's rain.
Look for me in the morning's quiet hush
I'll be there singing with the thrush.
I'll join the geese in their migration flight
I'll be nestled amid the stars on a full moon's night
I'm all these things, now I am free
I'll watch for you, you look for me
You'll hear me in the ocean's sigh
So forget me not, I did not die.
Aimee T. Sparrow

Why Is All The Hurt Stay With Me

Why is all the hurt stay with me:
Why all the hurt I may have inside stay within me.
I've tried to let the hurt out. But it
seems to come right back to me. I've tried
to let everyone I know how I felt, I was hurt.

Why is all the hurt stay with me: Everyone
said they don't know me. It's because I'm
afraid to let anyone know me. Because I've been
hurt so many times. That I never want to
show my true feelings to anyone. I want
everyone to see me for what I've been through
and what I am today. I want to feel love
from my heart, not my mind. Why is all
the hurt stay with me.
Lisa J. Letterle

"Spring"

The robins are hopping again
From a long adventurous winter flight
A sign that spring is in the air
Hopping on green turfs of grass
In search for a grub with an inward eye
Nothing to fear to hop on grass so green
So happy with merry twitter
Free from the long hungry quest
That winter came and left at last
For them to put on an emphatic call
And let their matins raise (with delight)
To pierce the air with songs of praise
And give thanks to the one who cares
To fluff their feathers and fly about
To find a place to haven and still for the night
And be enveloped in silent sleep.
Gladys Cooper

A Summer's Morn

I stand alone on the big white porch
On this summer's morn in July

And gaze at the view through a soft gray mist
That hangs like a veil from the sky

The grass is wet from the morning's rain
And the roses wear pearls of dew

Creating a fragrance so pungently sweet
Awakening memories of you

I stand alone, where we both once stood
On another summer's morn

When you disappeared in that soft gray mist
Leaving not the rose, but the thorn
Marie Hahn

Hope, The Heart Of Survival

I'm past the years of a young girl's life
Spent many hollow hours alone at night

I've worked and cried and hated and loved
And felt all of life was controlled from above

Emotions controlled all my deeds and my actions
Fell constantly victim to my self imposed passions

I've looked at my life through rose colored glasses
And cried if I wasn't loved by the masses

I've given and loved and tenaciously clung
To lovers who could not give in return

Naivete now gone with my youthful fears
Yet somehow I've grown, a sum total of my years

Looking back at my past, I've managed to learn
That I won't always have all that I yearn

But pleased now I am, for I've learned from my life
From moments of love, of hate and of strife

That a woman I am, with honor and pride
Who was once so sure that all love had died
Can still give and receive with hope as my guide
And always have space for that "little girl's" side.
Linda Adele Russo

Humanity's Collage

The hairless man, striped shirt and white shoes, reads Wall Street.
Sitting and chatting, three women long past middle age
Strangers yesterday thrown together, sharing confidences, meet.
The golden haired girl reads of love and passion and rage.
Snow capped brows, piercing eyes stare, he sits chin on hand.
Plump, short gray cropped hair, a woman ample and soft like jello,
Her body couch shaped, lightly sleeps quiet, smiling and tanned.
Reading TIME, moustache trimmed, sits a long past handsome fellow.

Sofa draped, eyelids fluttering, the Asian woman cuddles her purse.
Four women facing each other, around a table behind the glass,
Fill theirs and each other's lungs with smoke while they converse.
Bearded, pony tailed; old, dark, two men puff cigarettes to make
  time pass.

Sorting cards, the once retired, officious badged and uniformed man
Produces unfamiliar name sounds of those whose names are called.
The toupee adjuster, the panty hose tugger, the capped Bulls fan,
They line up and march to justice — the perfumed, the tall, the bald
Leaving a hundred of random's chosen in the ample room waiting.
Today's new friends totally unique and different. Each of whom
By posture, possessions, appearance, his or her own self stating
A new pieced collage of humanity, time stopped, in the jury room.
Jim Johnson

How Come I Can't Ease The Pain?

There was nothing I could say or do, to ease the pain you were going through. How could people say God was there, when he took her without a care. Then to bury her in the cold, with no chance of growing old. I wanted to tell all who would listen, didn't God know what you would be missing. There would be no ribbons or bows in her hair, just the memory in your heart that she isn't there. I wish I could do something to ease your pain, and wash it away with the rain. I know that when things are beyond control, most people find strength deep inside their soul. The tiny baby that grew from within, is now one with the wind. Her tiny angel wings will take her high in the sky, and leave her family on earth to cry. Your difficult journey maybe slow my friend, keep your faith and in heaven you can hold her again.
The great Lord above, needed one small Angel to love.
Carol Dunlavy

Passing

The passing of time an eternal thing;
A couple bound by a wedding ring.
Living and loving with time ever passing,
Children and grandchildren love ever lasting.
Sixty-three years of wedded bliss;
Sorely they will both be missed.
He was ninety she eighty-seven;
Reunited they hold hands in heaven.

Loretta McBeath

I Am Mother

I am mother to the child who was born to me today.
The Lord and I together, will start him on his way.
He will need a lot of tender care, and disciplining too.
Oh Lord, I hope that you can help see me through!

I am mother to the son who has started in to school.
His teachers and his friends will help him learn the rule.
We will be the thread that helps to weave his soul.
Oh Lord, you gave me such a goal!

I am mother to the man who stands on his own.
With you and me beside him we now have him grown.
It is his turn to give, what we gave to him,
Lord, these tears of joy make my eyes a little dim.

You were there in the beginning and we will see you at the end.
I am mother for your children, and we make a perfect blend!

Delores Jane Kane

Magic Places And Magic Times

Perhaps your magic place in time was a mountain top white with snow,
   Or maybe the glow of a summer morn in your youth of long ago;

Could it be a love that was lost in the spring time of your years?
   A love so sweet that even now, you can see her through your tears,

Maybe it was that summer night as you walked on a sandy beach,
   A very magic moment in time, that now lies beyond your reach;

Or maybe it was that autumn day with the wind blowing through
   your hair
It was long ago and far away but oh how you wish you were there;

Maybe it was a Mother's day, even now you can see her smile;
   In looking back it seems so real that your lost in time for a while;

Maybe it was an Easter day with that magic little bunny,
   You called it many special names but your favorite name was honey;

Could it be that cute little pup that Dad placed on your tiny knee,?
   You grew up, the puppy grew old, but that day's locked in memory;

How about that playground where children's voices could always
   be heard?
Only ghosts play there now and they utter not a word.

These places and moments are locked in time there as endless
   as the past
They lie somewhere beyond the stars, but in our heart will forever last.

James J. Goi

A Place Called Heaven

There is a place called Heaven, would you like to come along.
Where the Saviour will take you by the hand and lead you through the land, where no sorrow, or pain will be, He alone guides and walk on streets of gold.
Heaven is where all the saints have gathered and stand around giving praises and singing to His great name, the One who saved us from hell.
There is no need for the sun, because He shines far above it, there are no tears and love abounds so great, why not come along it is so easy to do, simply say came into my heart and make me new ready to serve the great King of all, the maker of this world.
Please come along.

Ruby D. Casseday

A Midsummer's Night

As I sit here on the river bank
And look at the sky, with blue
Yellow and even pink,
I see the tall grass and wild
Flowers sway, in a breezy way
on a midsummer's day.
I see the first star of night
And say, "I wish I may or even
Might get this wish on a midsummer's night."
The tree above me sways as if saying,
"Go home it's late."
I stand up and gather my books,
And say good night to anything
That saw me,
And I walked home.

Emily Ann Fulghum

Requiem

Every day a yesterday becomes
   When Time in headsman's hood lets loose the blade
Of midnight's guillotine. The muffled drums
   Of history reverberate and fade
Unheard; no monument is raised to mark
   The passing of each present day from life
To grayed oblivion of the past. The dark
   Enshrouds both sight and sound of falling knife.

Not so today or, rather, yesterday;
   From close at hand I mourned its death and pled
In vain for moments more to do and say
   So many things now left undone, unsaid.
Thus came today, and I must onward press
Before it, too, is cut to nothingness.

Charles M. Thatcher

Women

Women are special, unique in a way.
Women are happy and sad everyday.
Women are fun.
Women are different in all different ways.

Different races, different hair,
Different hands, different feet,
Different family and friends.

Women stand barricaded at the wall of freedom.
No work, no feeling.
Destruction, discrimination, stand at the door.
Women can't get away.
Going into the 21st century, still barricaded, still sad, women stand.

Women can't see, but women can hear.
The questions, the answers, they're not right, they're not true.
Women are heroes like you and me.

Women are the ones that can always tell.
When you're sad, when you're mad, all women can tell.
Mothers can, sisters can, aunts, grandmothers, all women of the world.

Women are special, unique in a way.
Women are happy and sad everyday.

Whitney Leader-Picone

Creepy Little Crawly Bugs

Creepy little crawly bugs in a great big creek,
Creepy little crawly bugs crawling up my feet.
Creepy little crawly bugs crawling in my hair,
Creepy little crawly bugs everywhere, but wait, I
See them, they're even in my underwear!

Jasmine Saxton-Mariah

Stony Lawns

Good fortune crosses paths with them too seldomly to know.
I see them, hear them, feel their hearts on stony lawns below.
They bounce about with dusted knees, nails torturing their feet,
Pretending war on rough terrain with bravery replete.
The playful struggle of their sport continues through the day
Devouring heat and sticky skin cannot divert their play.
Convictions for the barren rocks have never given way.
And yet, I watch them laughing, recreating life below.
My face affixed to panes of glass as my compassions grow.
Embroidered pillows, rare cuisine, and warmth from cozy flame
I shun my everyday complaints with disappointed shame.
My daily inconveniences of transitory worth
Trigger rushes of remorse and shrinking sense of mirth.
Still...pondering my status yields a flourishing of pride
For the nameless children down below with nowhere to reside.
'Til I depart my cushioned days this face I won't forget.
My anxieties were trivial (but those I now regret).
For in pessimistic times I turn to those life has beguiled
And am comforted completely by the smile of the child.

Joshua Herschel Klein

Swallows Of My Heart

For All the Children in My Life

Once again the swallows have gathered
   Nestled close to my heart,
So softly, so sweetly they meld
   Never to be torn apart

For once my heart finds a swallow
   It nurtures with loving care,
And holds it up high to the heavens
   A prize both wondrous and fair

Too soon comes the hardest part
   For swallows are born to fly,
My heart takes a great big gulp of joy
   And releases them all to the sky!

But, no matter how far they wander
   Or what paths they may find to roam,
They know they can always wing right back
   And nestle in my heart's home.

Jacquelyn Lee Cox

Rivermount

Above the world; amongst the clouds in the pale
blue sky. I feel the earth's beating melody inside my
body. As high as the mountains stretch, does my
spirit grow in peace. The tranquility of heaven's
serene breath fills my heart. The river water
ripples above the stones, and it runs down through
the soul of the cliffs. Pure and cleansed is my soul
with the warmth of God's light. His compassion
and mercy forgives me of my sin. A path of stones
leads me to my father. This place of joy I find
myself; I here announce it the rivermount of high esteem.

Janice Thompson

Thinking Alone

As I look around the room today,
I see my dreams burn away.
The thoughts of my future,
The essence of my life,
Now disappear before my eyes.
My mind wonders in mysterious ways.
The things I loved, I thought would stay.
Are we all just placed here as a game?
Maybe the winner will play again.

Bruce Stevens

The Dance Of Depression

Oh heart of mine stands still inside
For it's been broken time for time
Whence comes the agony I now endure
Please Lord come capture me from this present darkness

To get on with life I know I can do
You will heal me from my heart broken in two
So when I sink in dark and deep despair
I know you will be there, you will always care
Situations happen in our lives which we have no control
But you are always amongst them; through this I can grow
Oh how ecstatic I'll be when I learn to let go

So forge ahead for my strong will I have encased
My faith is a passion which cannot be erased
My prayer is this healer divine; Enable me to see the beauty
in the nature of all obstacles
Lift the pressures from my shoulders
for you said my burdens you would bear
I know you have done so, now I am free
You are the lamp at my feet that lights the pathway, now I can see
So take me and mold me into what you want, I am yours to eternity

Toni Shew Coker

Sunday Morning

Sunday morning in mid summer time,
   As the sun bathes the earth, the church bells chime;
Ones heart is filled with wonder and peace;
   As we ponder God's love that will never cease.

Then a hymn of praise seems to arise
   As the beauty fills out heart, our eyes;
The birds are singing a joyful song
   That fills the air of the whole day long.

Please take time for a moment to look
   The scene revealing, like opening a book.
Look now, tomorrow will be too late,
   Sunday morning beauty is here and it will not wait.

Beulah Freeman

Husband and Wife

Two strong trees standing side by side
   One does not outgrow the other
Both stand firm and straight
   One does not shade the sunlight from the other
They grow as individuals, together
   Sharing the nutrients of the earth
They will survive many harsh winters and many gentle springs
   Each helping the other to grow
They cannot be separated by ax or by saw
   Because their roots are intertwined
Each is a part of the other

Selina M. Seel

Our Father

Life and years have taken their toll.
His hair has grown thin and white you know.
His face is not as plump as it used to be.
His memory comes and goes, you see.

A locked mind filled to capacity,
A lengthy poem he recites with a single clue.

From his heart he says it through.
With eyes full of tears, he finally gets through.
Saying a poem from yesteryear.

How little we know of what's stored,
Inside such a brilliant mind.
For only a clue releases the mind that fills,
Our hearts with words of yesteryear.

Judy Coffman

Alone

What goes through your mind when you're alone
Do you Think
Do you Pray
Do you Reflect on words to say

It is late you are alone what is going on

Someone is Sleeping
Someone is Reading
Someone is saying Goodbye

Listen to the Echoes of the Night outside

Hear the Rhythm of your Heart inside

Allow yourself to See
Let yourself Hear
You're not alone

Are You Lonely
    Beverly A. Simpson

Retirement Is Freedom

Retirement is freedom earned by an employee.
Who does what it takes to get where she aspires to be.
It is not easy to make it to the number of retirement years,
Because there are so many obstacles that bring on unwanted fears.

Mrs. T, you have given 23 quality years in Food Service
  at Fort Eustis' CDC,
And we want you to remember the number of meals
that you have prepared since February 1973.
After the meals have been calculated and hours are assessed,
You will find it hard to believe that you were CDC possessed.

You have worked eight hours a day oh so many, many times.
Now you should take it easy, relax and listen to the wind chimes.
There is no need to be forced into rejoining a group of workabees,
Because it is certainly time for you to take a trip to Florida,
  or go overseas.

Go forth now, and enjoy your hard earned freedom for retirement,
We know that you need a break because your time was spent.
You have worked with hundreds of children, parents, us,
  and the community, too.
And that is why we wish the very, very best for you.
    Azzie Lee Stroble

A Lonely Forest

   A brown waterfall of silk dripping
over a perfect hill. Two circles of brown
stones sitting so still on a mountain.
A perfect smooth river flowing over two
mounds of sand. Following down to the
mouth of it, onto straight pearl stones.
By the two circles of brown stones are
caves, one on each side of the stones.
In these caves echo hard moving sounds
and sweet sounds of whispers. These sweet
sounds of whispers become lust and passion.
Deep into the depth of those caves
and lost in the roaring of the silk waterfall.
The river flows down a large tree trunk
into the heart of the forest. Yet where it's
lonely, hungering for love and doesn't know
how to find it. It is the forest that doesn't
know how to use its seeds to get to, to the
boundaries. The boundaries of nature's foggy
magic to find the forbidden fruit of the jungle.
    Kirsten Nau

Little Megan!

It all started when I held her in my arms.
A little girl, with all her parents' charms.
With big blue eyes and lashes so long.
I love to hold her and sing her a song.

She's my grand-daughter, who lives far away.
But she's in my heart when I pray each day.
The world sometimes gets hard and cold.
And grand-parents tend to get sick and old.
But God is so wonderful to send us gifts of love.
Like little Megan, who must have came
From above, in her pigtails, with her pretty
pug nose. She begs for a cookie, then off she goes.

Parents have the hard job of raising up kids.
They take things for granted, I know I did.
But a grand-parent's life is touched by a
Little girl or boy, like my little Megan,
My love and my joy!
    Janet R. Hill

Angels Unaware

V is for VALUABLE
O is for OUTGOING
L is for LEADER
U is for UNSELFISH
N is for NEEDED
T is for TREASURE
E is for EARNEST
E is for ENDLESS
R is for RELIABLE

As the letters in the word explain,
you see your work is not in vain.

No one can fully understand, just how much you do.
But we want you to know, we couldn't do it without you.

You do so much for everyone, and still you offer more.
At times I'm sure you wonder, "Is this what my life is for?"

You may not be told often enough
but surely you have guessed,

To have such wonderful volunteers,
any organization would be truly blessed.
    Mary Ann Zilko

Untitled

We all have things to hide, things no one can ever know
Thoughts, actions and the demands we make on other souls

We push away all that is there so no one will see
The person we are and what we will be

It's not this minute or second it's all in the past
The months and years they build you, this is what last

It doesn't matter now, not those things or those times
Have it with you everyday or ever other
Keep it close, keep it tight, those things those times

Tomorrow will come leaving today in the past
One more thing to add, another shadow is cast

When someone has seen the darkness that you hide.
Will you run away, and keep it deep inside.

Twice you've stopped now, can't you say what you feel
If an image can tear, then speaking would kill

It doesn't matter now, not those things or those times
Have it with you everyday or ever other
Keep it close, keep it tight, those things those times
    Alisa D. Rupert

Andy

Where are you tonight, Andy Warhol, now that I really need you?
Where are you tonight, Andy Warhol, now that I really need you?

Sitting out back, back in my room
Covered with a cloud of thickening gloom
Suicidal thoughts come into bloom
You said you'd always be there for me-so where are you...

A hovering life, blown out like a candle
Hanging on to a life that doesn't have a handle
Living like a rumor, like a Hollywood scandal
Oh Andy, can't you save me? My life is just a ramble...

   I'm a frightened little child
   I'm an outcast, Oscar Wilde
   I'm a frightened, I'm a frightened,
   I'm an angry little child

Where are you Andy Warhol? Where are you Andy Warhol?
I trusted you! I trusted you!
  Andy Warhol
    Andy Warhol
      Andy Warhol...
   Natalie Rodgers

The Hourglass

The hourglass is running low.
Death is nearing, this I know.
I sit with my family holding hands.
We say no words. We make no demands.
I think of all the things I didn't do.
Oh how I feel so terribly blue.
Why can't I live longer?
Why can't I be stronger?
There has to be a way,
To get to live just one more day.
But I know there's not.
I start to remember things that I had once forgot.
My family and I talk about old times.
I hear the distant ringing of the wind chimes.
I lay back on my bed.
I feel as if everything has been said.
My life is now ending.
My family's faces are descending.
The hourglass is empty.
   Tiffany Catherine Kelley

Love's Time

You walked away from me and without a word
  you said, "Goodbye."
 I, too, was saying the same word in my heart.
For so long we loved, laughed,
  lingered in each others eyes.
But mists of time dimmed the laughter
  and the moments of touching,
  til only thoughts of touching remained.
  Only pictures of sand, waves, running
  holding each other so tight
  time stopped for a moment
  just for us.
We tried to bring it back again,
  to fill our senses with passion once more.
But no, it said, "No more.
I gave you a moment in time
  your moment your precious portion.
Now your hearts must hold that portion so tight,
  that each time remembered will stop time again
  for a moment."
   Jo Ann West

"Some Body Cares"

Somebody knows when your heart aches and everything seems
  to go wrong;
Somebody knows the shadows need chasing away with a song.
Somebody knows when you are lonely, tired, discouraged, and blue;
Somebody wants you to know you are dearly loved and held so true.

Somebody cares when you are tempted and your mind
  goes dizzy and dim;
Somebody cares when you are slim.
Somebody cares when you have fallen and when you are lost;
Somebody waits for you, because his love will drive
  gloom away at all cost.
God is the somebody, who;
Cares for you!
   Travis Neil Schell

Voice Of The World

I watched as the Silence crept - old
  and arthritic
  and beast-like
  into his chamber.

I watched as the Knight roared with his thousand voices -
  Triumph!
  Victory!
  Defeat!
(He, splendid all around me -
  banners snapping, horse rearing,
  eyes and mouth and spirit all aflame.)

I watched and was enchanted
  (For what Maiden could resist?)
I watched...
  And lost myself
  In the roaring of a thousand voices;
  In the snapping of a thousand banners;
In the triumph of a thousand Heroes.
   Kerri Snead

Just A Sigh

Two hundred gone, without a cry,
A moment's flash, the angels fly.
Lives in motion, stopped in place,
Loves behind, faint memories taste.
Last words in mind, their meanings lost,
Linger timeless, through mental frost.
No more sharing, lost future plans,
Should have, could have, fallen sand.
Thoughtless sunshine, up on que,
Unaware, without a clue,
of missing Mother, Fathers, Sons,
Sisters, Brothers, lives undone.
The ones behind, with answers not,
hold tight whats left, still questions sought
To all but these, time breezes by,
To all but those, now just a sigh.
   Harry L. Plunkett Jr.

Falls Magical Showing

Fall is upon us with its magical showing,
Pay close attention because it won't be long going.

Colors fill the trees in great array,
Assuring us of a gorgeous display.
Oranges, browns, and golds of delight,
Burgundy, red, greens add to the sight.

If you miss it, all is not lost,
Next magical show is called Jack Frost!
   Hoyte Phifer Jr.

Vespers

Somewhere there was lost a foreign token—
at what we called our vespers, when we prayed
kneeling before Roman mirrors, some one of us mislaid
a silence among all fractures which were spoken,
and we cried. Tearless, we wandered in the frayed
stone streets, lying to the men, whose faces stayed
and lingered, refusing to be broken.

And what of sadness, when all around us grew
great etched fountains ripped with lines
of age, and trouble, where painted water would spew
and bubble, like blackened widows whose spines
buckled discontent, frothy spittle.   Who
could have foreseen ancient empires' signs
in guises of wicked foreplay, of too
much frost around the glass, and wines
too delicate to drink?   /I think
                        there is one who pines
to return there, trust me. Wearing blanched ecru
like a pontific robe, she doubles, falls, is you.

    Sarah C. Fry

Key Hole

Passing through the hotel corridor on the way to my room
The passageway light flickers then succumbs to impending gloom
A piercing white light emanates from one of the wooden doors
I poise myself facing the keyhole not knowing what's in store
I peek attentively into this room to check out the scene
My body becomes paralyzed, it becomes harder to breathe
In wonder, one eye is overcome by the celestial glow
The other eye swims in darkness to the likes I'd never known
Clinging to serene visions and keeping sorrow ones at bay
My flaccid body could not move as I tried to break away
Happiness gives way to sadness as hope struggles with despair
Why has fate beckoned me to stay here - to gape and to stare
Attentiveness imprisons while noncompliance sets me free
My eyelids grow heavier as I raise myself from one knee
The corridor becomes lighter as my mind grows attuned
Realizing the one eye is not enough-you must view with two

    Douglas Swailes

Untitled

Here I am an embryo shell,
growing and growing to become something real.

My heartbeat is fierce like a lions loud roar,
my body is ready for all that's in store.

Here we are in the delivery room,
mother is screaming, dad is upset.
The doctor said PUSH... but I'm not out yet.

"I guess I'll go join them,
I think I'll break free".

Down through the chute oh boy!
Here I come, my mother is crying, my father is proud.
The doctor slaps me and I cry out loud.

Then daddy grabbed me and held me up high,
he pulled me back down and let out a sigh.

My name is Jordan and yes I am proud,
even Dad is yelling out loud.

I am so tired it's time to sleep.
Mother just bent down to whisper to me,
"I love you my angel, my baby girl,
you are the most beautiful one in the world."

    Amy Marie Soden

Who?

When life turns black,
Who will bring the light to my world?
When the tunnel seems too long,
Who will beg me to continue?
When my tears fall,
Who will be there to dry my cheeks?
When the nightmares wake me, screaming,
Who will be there to hold me against the terror?
When my heart is breaking,
Who will ease my pain?
When hope lies dying on the floor of my soul,
Who will be there to put the pieces back together?
When I start to doubt if love exists,
Who will touch my face and reach my soul?
When my soul bleeds from the pain,
Who will hold me and heal my wounds?
When life turns black and I begin to fade away,
Who will call my name and find me?

    Nita Walsh

Love

Love is heaven's finest evening arrayed;
A symphony's enchanting melody played!

Love is the night's star-studded robe;
The moon's silent witness of a story retold!

Love is the earth's precious gem most prized;
The secret smile in a lover's eyes!

Love is a rose's delicate grace;
The journey into a magical place!

Love is the waves in an infinite sea;
Another world where time ceases to be!

Love is the rainbow's every wondrous hue;
Love is the happiness I share with you!

    Karen Hayes

Why

Why did your emerald eyes sweep me off my feet?
Why did your new year's kiss save me from everything?
Why did you love me so much I had to love you back?
Why did you know me better than I knew myself?
Why were you the only one my parents approved of?
Why were you the only one who was a gentleman?
Why did we always have so much fun?
Why did your good night kisses make me so light headed?
Why were you my Valentine for three years?

Why did you have to get in that car?
Why with the driver half drunk?
Why did I have to see the crash?
Why were you the one that hit the hardest?
Why did I hold you in my arms while you slipped away?
Why did your sweet blood pour over your chest onto my lap?
Why did I have to see your emerald eyes slowly close as one
   single tear fell? As you uttered I love you, one last time?
Why did you leave me that cold, cold night on the curb?

My love, I hope you are happy where you are.
Please remember me. I will love you always.

    Sarah Asheraft

Humans

Wild, roaming, free
God's greatest gift

Smart, intelligent are we
Why must we do stupid things

Indians rebel, shocked, and amazed
The balance of life altered

The circle of life beaten, bruised, burned
Soon we wonder why all animals are gone

Too late, too late
Pollution, deforestation, nothing but dust

Too late, too late
In God we trust

Courtnay Oatts

Ballad Of A Sad Heart

There once was a little girl whose heart was as pure as a dove.
The only thing she really wanted was to be loved.
She always walked around with a smile upon her face.
But what she wanted was to leave this place.

The little girl was always in tears.
And there was no one there to erase her fears.
Though she seemed happy from the outside, in the inside
  she was crying.
Sometimes she even felt like dying.

Her life at home was filled with pain and anger.
The little girl's parents felt nothing but rancor.
Her dad was nothing but a drunk.
All her mom did was sleep in her bunk.
She took care of her little brother and sisters.
And her hands and feet were filled with blisters.
Her parents would beat her for no reason.
They even dressed her in clothes that were out of season.

The little girl just wanted to be loved.
She didn't even know how it felt to be hugged.
She always prayed to be free.
Just like a bird who had just flown from a tree.

Charmeika Denise Jackson

This Is The End

Thinking of you,
just makes me want to turn blue.
Your smile used to be,
the one thing I loved to see.
But now it's nothing anymore,
'cause my love will never be the same as it was before.
The smile that used to greed me,
will never be the same,
'cause deep down in my heart,
is filled with burning flames.
Of all those times you've lied to me,
you've never let my soul set free.
You've never thought of how I felt,
and now my desire is being melted.
My chances are up, and this is my way,
and there's nothing more that I have to say.
But, before I go,
I just wanted you to know.
That this is the end,
'cause there's nothing left, not even being friends.

Chau Tat

Believe In Your Dream

I'll always believe in you
Don't be afraid to try something new

J... ust another way of staying alive
E... veryday she works so hard to survive
N... o use complaining, it's a fact of life
N... ow y' know, what's it like working in a city
I... heard that "Cafe Verde" is a place to be
F... resh baked muffins serve with hot coffee
E... veryone knows by now, she's a special girl
R... eady and determined to take on the world

I'll always believe in you
Even when you're sad and blue

D... o you want to share your dream with me
E... ver wonder how it will turn out to be
B... et your dream is a very special kind
O... h, how I wished I could read your mind
C... an you tell me if everything is fine
K... indly take me away from this "waiting line"

I'll always believe in you
Wish there's something else I can do

Yandhi T. Cranddent

Mother Earth

A blue jewel born in a time beyond time.
A fiery beginning did she endure.
Locked in a dance eternal,
With no beginning and never an end,
She travels relentlessly along her well worn path.

Thunder rolls a forbidden warning,
And jagged bolts of death-laden gold strikes Earth.
In awe I watch nature's bright show of majesty.
As I wonder what demon lays beyond those boiling towers,
Might I yet know the secret of Thor's dark realm?

A world of raging oceans and rolling beaches,
Of sun drenched deserts and luscious forests.
Windswept plains and mighty palisades adorn her ever changing face,
And she alone in a universe of shining wonder,
Knows life's true secret...

Leondra James

Darkness Shan't Rule

They live in the shadows
Have never known peace
Our next generation
Nobel Prize winners, doctors and priests

When the sun never rises
In their dark, lonely days
We must ask ourselves
Where have we failed

Bruised little legs, broken little arms
The parents say they are stressed
Fear in little eyes, pain in little souls
The guardians say they are depressed

The circle is vicious and rarely does stop
When will it end and why does it start
As a nation, please, let us stand
Put understanding, patience and love in hearts

Lisa Gibson

I Am Someone

I am no one
Surrounded by the world
Busy lives of important minds pass me by
I am no one
Not loved by the world
They don't see the pain in my eyes
I am no one
Not cared about by the world
Anger, pain and sorrow are my closest friends
I am no one
Not known by the world
My heart isn't even a thought in their lives
I am no one
Not accepted by the world
My ways and attitude do not fit
I am no one
Hiding in the world
No secrets can be revealed for I have none
I am no one, forgotten by many
But loved by one. So I am someone.
  Jessica Diven

Creation By God

When I look outside and see God's creation all around me,
I can see His glory and power in something as gentle as a flower.
I can see His strength and might in the planets just hung so right.
I can see His awe and splendor in the seasons that make me wonder.
The changing of the leaves on a tree, and the beautiful colors
they turn out to be.
The falling of gentle snowflakes; each one of a different make.
The rebirth of new life in the spring; that makes everything
rejoicefully sing.
The hot summer days filled with warm glorious sun rays.
Now who, but God, could change the seasons, and give us
this one logical reason;
It's to show us His power and glory -
-Something I couldn't find in a story.
  Jennifer McCray

Gabriel's Fall

I was he who would be their future, their platinum child,
their first of knights
I brought up pure, with only God's word to corrupt me
forming a bond with those that they had broken
holding it still, when given the two paths
I left... falling as if in a thirsty frenzy
curiosity beats down my sadness
my wings lifted off like shackles
the choices, the ideas, the spirit
I fear I will die in free fall
strange... I fear?
  Paul D. Lentini

A Young Life Without Love

The boy's life had played too many quarters.
The ball had been thrown too many times.
And he had been tackled enough to break his young heart.
He tried so hard until his bones ached
Just to make sure they all would survive with enough love
To carry them through the long game.
He loved them all like a teammate should,
But there was no one to love him back, to care for him.
He knew in his mind that he could win,
But his battered heart couldn't be convinced otherwise,
And eventually he would lose.
The game would be over,
Without the love and care from the coaches
That had left at the half.
  Julie Riley

Zapped!

One Sunday night at half past nine, I saw a
movie that was quite fine.
Of joy, of laughter, and full of wonder.
I watched and watched 'till a trance I was under.
A light did flash and the room did spin.
I'm not quite sure where I may have been.
The room went dim and there I was inside the T.V. screen.
By many eyes had I been seen.
Laughing, crying, and singing with glee, every human is looking at me.
I banged on the screen with all my might, with horror,
terror, and lots of fright.
I suddenly left the T.V. screen.
I ended up in my house unharmed.
But what does all this really mean?
I don't know, it could just be me.
Never again have I watched that T.V.
  Ellenor Brown

The Piper

They woke that day, 'twas a glorious morn,
But it wasn't to the sound of Gabriel's horn.
'Twas a Piper piping, sweet and clear,
Piercing the silence for all to hear.

So all that follow will dance to the death.
Follow they will, follow they will.
Tears of blood and wrath shall be shed,
Many a soldier will end up dead.

Yet the Piper pipes on, dancing with his eyes of scorn.
Laugh you may, laugh you might,
But sometimes during the night

A husband, a brother, a sweetheart or lover,
will not wake up.
Then try to laugh, see if it comes,
Still you think the war is over, but it is just begun.

Many soldiers lie in the dust,
Of many soldiers the earth keeps trust.
Yours is only one, child, only one.
  Brynn Ziegenfuss

Untitled

Doctor, Doctor fix my car
It doesn't travel very far
But sputters, spurts and makes a fuss
And causes me to take the bus.

My carburetor always leaks
The springs in back all have the squeaks.
The grinding noise of my transmission
Exacerbates my nerve's position.

My windshield wipers bang and rub
I'm ready now to sell my tub
To any one who'll buy the mess.
I bet I'll get a "Bill" or less.

My motor mounts are worn and loose.
They simply have no earthly use.
The horn does screech, the brakes do squeal.
The vehicle is quite unreal.

Oh Doctor please do diagnose
Before I lose my water hose.
What change is there of happiness
With such a car in such a mess!
  A. Winfred Levinstone

A Wake Up Dream

May your dreams come true are famous words of hope,
and be careful of what you wish for is not just a joke.

Projecting the imagination is a wonder of the mind,
revealing thoughts in pictures seen even by the blind.

Take care in your wishing and understanding what you do,
life is not just a dream, most things depend on you.

Work on your dreams as if they were another chore,
just stair steps to your wishes waiting at the door.

Dreams lay the foundation where most wishes are built,
but like plucked flowers in time dreams start to wilt.

Now awake sleepy head it's time to work on your plan,
don't dream away the foundation where your wishes stand.

William L. Hardister

The Aura Of A Poet

Words still wrapped in flesh.
A frozen landscape as clear as glass
Melting as we speak.
The handle is in the eyes.
The soft and smoky night, invisible to the wide-eyed.

A palm print in the air knocks a bird off-course.
The quiet shadows cross forbidden paths.
Air born on shallow waters.
The water shakes fastened down.
Grasping for a dangling leaf
The butterfly opens and closes its wings.

Survival in the wilderness is a time factor.
Feeling the blindfolded shake your hands,
Whisper in your ear, caress your breast.
Others blow smoke in your face.
Everyone tries to squeeze a drop of red wine.

Vita Mikelevicius

Goodbye

I found you one day, our meeting not planned.
I carefully lifted and held you in my hand.
I took you home loved you and watched you each day.
The changes you went through, molded like clay.
We'd sit in my bedroom at night for a while;
Your touch in my hand brought to me a smile.
'Til one day you changed, hid from me a spell;
Enclosed in darkened and cold bitter shell.
I pondered what happened and why you would hide.
Had something gone wrong? Were you changing inside?
Then one day I came home and saw you again.
You'd changed far too much, it had come to an end.
I gazed at your beauty and said my goodbye;
Then opened the window, "Farewell butterfly."

Brandon W. Stace

Isolated Rushes

Go sailing in your own mind.
  Don't drown in your own sea.
Remember your realizations,
The sea of reality is here to show we're free.

Sometimes people witness your deep thoughts.
The ones that aren't witnessed are isolated rushes.
Don't go swimming all alone,
  The sea of loneliness crushes.

One reality leads to another.
With this relative system no one should drown.
When we all start realizing together,
  On the sea of answers we will be found.

Frank Schaffner

A Nightmare In Belfast

Peace said the papers! Peace said the news!
Everyone had their own private views.
The people were skeptical and still had fears,
Peace they asked after twenty-five years?

The soldiers were gone, the streets were clear
The man didn't know that danger was near,
It was just before Christmas, he was on his way home
Late at night he was all alone.
Did he see someone he thought he might know?
All too late they struck the first blow.

Keep it quiet said the police to the family next day,
We don't want to cause a riot.
Why asked the family? Our son's death was violent.
What asked the family? Do we have to be silent?

Meanwhile, back in the States
His wife to be sits by the phone
And waits, and waits, and waits...

CarolAnn Donner

Quest Of A Memory

As time moves timelessly through space,
Is it joined by memories that have lost their place
in our thoughts? Does our mind
sort memories, discarding a few
that sail with the clouds out in the blue?
The memories retained, those left behind,
Are they filed deep within our mind?
Do our eyes photograph everything past,
providing mental images that last
a lifetime? Gone forever, or so it seems,
Until they reappear in our dreams.
Can a thought, sound or familiar smell,
A touch or taste sometimes tell
of a day gone by? Our five senses, of their own accord,
Can perceive the treasures our mind has stored.

Betty DiProspero

My Love

I love you so deeply, I love you
so much I love your sweet voice
and your soft gentle touch.
I love your bright smile,
your kind thoughtful ways and the joy
that your bring to my life everyday.
I love you today as I did from the start,
I'll love you forever with all of my heart.

Debbie Williams

How Will They Know?

I felt discouraged and lonely today;
  feeling unimportant, forgotten,
  and blue
When in the mail came a short note that
  said, "I'm thinking of you"
How will you know that I'm thinking of you
  if I don't tell you once in awhile?

It set me to thinking how much those words
  meant to me when they brightened my day.
How much happier others would be if we showed
  them our love and care
With the kind words, showing a warm, friendly smile.
How else will they know that we are thinking of
  them if we don't tell them once in awhile?

Martha D. Wooten

Clocked

Tick, tick,
Goes the clock.
Never will it stop.
Until it does.

Nonchalantly, time slips by.
And it did.

Tock, tock,
What a shock.
And it is.

Now and forever are joined in marriage.
To consume the fires and drinks of yore.
Before it all ends.

And it did.
Tick, tick,
Goes the clock.
Never will it stop...
Until it does.
   Chad Parsley

Three Cheers

Three cheers for you
And only one for me
   Is that not the way it goes?
The spotlight before you
The crowd at attention
While I peek out from behind your shadow
Cast upon the wall you, whose glorious self
Bruised my face tore me down
Retreat sweet princess to the darkness
For the light will not last long
Soon you will hide in someone else's shadow
In the odious den of shame
I can no longer find the light you see
The flicker of a candle
My only guide in this horrid dwelling
The darkness calls you child
It calls your wanton soul
Where your dreams pierce my skin like broken glass
Where hopes are lost in the night so awake sweet child
And fall into darkness for the Sandman is waiting
   Melissa Nason

"The Puddle"

A marvelous thing is a puddle in rain!
It gets no bigger, it just stays the same.
The rain drops keep falling - dimpling its face,
But the water won't stay there, it all goes some place.
Each ripple and bubble does its own thing,
But is soon interrupted by a new growing ring.
A bubble will grow and then it will burst,
Being hit by a new drop, though it wasn't the first,
Forms a sphere of its own, then, it too is gone,
But the process continues - it goes on and on.
Some puddles are brown, some puddles are clear,
Some are black far away and blue when you're near.
The birds and rabbits and squirrels drink their fill
From this lovely new pool that is never quite still.
Then after the rain, it sleeps lying there
Resting calmly and cool in the soft morning air
Till the sun comes out brightly and dries it all up,
Like the residue left in your old coffee cup.
Don't be sad 'cause it's gone or it isn't no more.
You'll see it again in the next good downpour!
   Jack R. Hill

The Rollerskater

It's the weekend before regionals and already I'm excited
Arrangements for travel are made and I'm delighted
I'll do my packing a couple of days before
So when the time comes, I'll fly out the door
Only a skater can appreciate the fun of competition
When you're on that floor you lose all inhibitions
It would be nice to place in the upper half
By doing this, fellow skaters would not laugh
Someday I'd like to be the best
So, I'll keep on practicing and not rest
There always seem to be obstacles that get in the way
But I must keep fighting them if I want to say
First place was my goal and I did it today
   Carol Hutchinson

Mother's Guardian Angel

Your guardian angel is here for you.
She'll watch over you in whatever you may do.
For me she reminds me of you. Her silver color,
reminds me of the silver sparkles in your hair.
Her pink wings, reminds me of the warmth
which you have in your heart for others.
And her golden wings, reminds me that
you watched over me in my childhood years,
she'll watch over you in your golden years.
   Donna Willms

A Prayer Is For You

A prayer is for you, that when you feel small and
   insignificant God will grant you the strength and
   height of the cedars of Lebanon.

A prayer is for you, that when in the valley God will
   grant you the majesty of a mountain top.

A prayer is for you, that when buffeted from all around you
   that you will be held secure in the comes of God.

A prayer is for you that as you tread the waves of a
   mighty sea God will calm the storm.

A prayer is for you that when experiencing sinking sand
   that God will raise you up and once again place you
   upon the solid rock.

A prayer is for you, that for all who come into your path
   will get to know the Lord God who sent you.

A prayer is for you that you will always know
   that there is always a prayer for you!
   Sheila Haynes-McCall

One Afternoon In The Park

For Valerie

One afternoon in the park, I was sitting all alone, wondering just
where life would take me.
I wasn't too sure if the dark cloud enveloping my vision would ever
lift and allow me to see.
Then you came along, and brought your essence of joy
that shines so bright.
Your brilliant mind and exquisite loveliness have truly given me
back my sight.
And now that I know there is hope for heavenly bliss with a woman
in whose shoes I would walk a mile
For you have truly captured my heart, my mind, my soul,
and won me over with that beautiful smile.
   William L. Massey

Paradox Of Affirmity

The pain hurts, hurts like Hell.
It's always there, no matter what,
It cuts my soul like a psychological knife,
Letting my essence bleed away as time passes.

Jim Murphy

"Bending Of Twigs"

Communication is a powerful force without which all relationships in general cannot properly flourish.

Actions, words, and deeds of unselfish motivations mostly generate that which is needful to nourish.

In latter years we may discover that our communications have had effect on someone associated with us, whether for ill or good. We can only hope when they are called upon to make important decisions will recall our most inept attempts and so profit by the course we took.

Our once current intelligence and growth dictated our judgment under then existing circumstances so we shouldn't give lingering tears and a self-regretful look.

Never let your tears become deep enough to drown you and others in your own sorrow, rotting in a pool of regrets.

Remember, as a twig is bent so grows the tree and let teaching others to set sights on the future and facing new challenges be that lesson which from you one begets.

Evelyn Cailey

Snowfall

I think I saw a flake or two,
Fall from the sky with glistening hue.
And as I watched, my heart content,
From the heavens another was sent.
With each new flake, two more did follow.
They covered the ground and lit up the hollow.
The woods grew silent as the flakes come down.
All you could hear was a soft twinkling sound.
A blanket of white covered valley and hill.
And all things around stood silent and still.

Edwin Anthony Richardson

"Life's Twists And Turns"

The road I walk,
As I journey through life,
Has a lot of twists and turns.
I seldom know when to walk-straight
Or, to take a winding curve.
Thank goodness for those people - I meet,
They help me choose my way.
Or, is it they
Grateful to me,
On a particular day.

Diane K. Luster

God's Gift

Something precious from beyond
Last step to complete that certain bond;
Filling life with joy and singing;
Years gone leaving a house with
    laughter ringing;
Wondrous things old and new to see
A wee one means this to me.
Memories to look on through time,
For these things will be mine.
Thanking God for this gift of joy:
My child a darling blue eyed boy!

Martha Sue Downs

"Michelle"

Friendship is a word that means kind,
That everyone in the world should find.

Friendship is a word that means nice,
And if I were president you'd be my vice.

Friendship is a word that means caring,
And to you there is no comparing.

Michelle you're my best friend,
You and I just kinda blend.

And part we shall never,
Cause you're my best friend forever.

Shawnta Robinson

A Song For The Romanticist

A song for the romanticist that no-one cares to know,
To the ones who majored in love, and later became pros,
To those of us who dream of "Happy Ever Afters" and
    wait for the moment to come,
But get pushed away by the lonely people who think love is dumb.

To the many who are alone and dream of fairy tales to come true,
To the Cinderellas and Prince Charmings who are often called fools,
To those of us who believe love can change the world in an amount
    of time,
To all those romanticist who leave the realist behind,

The road will be lonely but I know we can last,
For the time will come when love will be a reality and not a
    thing of the past.

Anna C. Jones

The Me That Used To Be

I used to love and laugh and play
My life, a wondrous gift to me.
But now I feel I've lost my way.
Where is the me that used to be.

What dreams I dreamed so long ago
The things I'd do, the sights I'd see.
I long for change, but I don't know
Where is the me that used to be.

My youth has gone, my dreams went, too.
But in my heart, the memory
Still lingers there, steadfast and true.
Perhaps there still is hope, you see,
To find the me that used to be.

Joy M. Adams

Let God Through

With the sea breeze blowing through my hair
and my thoughts drifting through the air
I realize that I'm surrounded by tranquillity
and I find a distinctive peace within my own air.

Not only have I found myself
I've grown up a lot too
and I found out that the best way
is to let God through!!

He helps you through all of life's tribulations
and He is always there for you.
He gives you the strength to move on
to better and more challenging things.

So let Him be your Rock and foundation
let Him take control.
For He is the potter and you the clay
Let Him mold you in His own special way!

Angela Sorrell

The Fisherman And The Pretty Pebble

He fished all day with little success.
As he packed up his gear, he thought "well I guess
I just wasn't meant to fill a limit today.
They wouldn't bite and some got away."

A pretty pebble in the creek caught his eye,
As the swinging current carried it by.
He picked it up, lifting it in his hand
To his shirt pocket, like a nugget panned.

As he stood watching the creek in the evening light
Deepen and darken, preparing for night,
The gathering gloom matched his hurt pride.
Then a tall mountain man appeared at his side.

He said "at fishing you rate only fair,
But you've found a pebble beyond compare.
More precious by far than diamonds or gold
It's yours forever to have and to hold.

Cherish and guard it from all manner of harm,
And it will become your life's good luck charm."
The fisherman paused and said, "Ah, now I see!"
Then he turned toward the man and saw a tall tree.

Gerald G. Cooper

The Ragged Edge

On the ragged edge of nowhere,
all the suffering still existed.
Where as all the while we
remain beguiled, and term
the events as facts of life

The Ego and the Shadow like
to bicker and argue their chosen points.
Some of these things we discuss,
are without a burden to bear,
for they edge their way in from
the ragged edge of nowhere

I'd like to say I hope, but
how useless that can be, since
the answers always come from
the ragged edge of nowhere.

It is smart to have tolerance,
since we are basically all alike.
And patience always helps, although
very hard to come by, since it
too hails from the ragged edged of nowhere

Edith M. Neal

To The Light Of My Life My Autistic Daughter

From the moment you were born
you've been special to me.
Each and every day I try to
reach inside your world to see
what I can see.
Each and every day I learn a
little more from the special things you do.
With comfort and understanding
I'll build your inner strength.
The inner warmth you give to me
comes from Happy times.
You make me want to smile,
when you do the things you do.
I like what I see, in your eyes,
your voice, your touch — you are
the sparkle in my eye, I hope
you'll always know how much.
As you sparkle each and every day
you'll bring a little light to
everyone you meet.

Joan Labrie

Eighty Years And Sharing

My 80th birthday - the 29th of July.
My first-day-on-Earth day 'neath summer's blue sky.
No stars fell from heaven, no sign marked the way,
Yet I knew in my soul 'twas a heaven-sent day.

A chance to achieve - neither fortune nor fame -
Just a family and friends whose devotion I'll claim.
To share in my pleasures and share in my tears;
Whose loving regards I'll count not in arrears.

O, agony, ecstasy, betrayal, and pain -
Misfortunes and blessings - yes, I've sung that refrain.
With children I managed to keep roof overhead
Tho' silent tears often accompanied me to bed.

Eight decades of living - such a packageful of life!
Some pockets of glory, some pockets of strife.
Now I'm facing a ninth with new scenarios in store
That I'll hopefully confront with a patient, "What more?"

When the Roll Call is sounded, I'll respond, in accord,
"Come get me, new shipmates, and take me aboard.
"Let's sail to the heavens that will welcome me back -
"Transcending inexorable life's Final Act."

Alice I. Lescalleet

Beautiful Nature

Waking to nature's sound,
blooming flowers all around;
the air still cool,
and when it heats up - just jump into the pool!
Watching lives crawl on the ground
to the beat of nature's sound.

Zooming, blooming, dwelling and smelling
up and down, all around.
Caring and sharing amongst those creatures
with their nature adjusted features.
What can change some grouchy moods?
Visiting a beautiful place in the woods!

But people, listen well!
To keep that healthy smell,
the pasture's healing heart and mind,
already they are hard to find!
Respect the nature's trails and ways!
So we all can enjoy, for many more days.

Gabriele Grimenstein

Where?

Where, in the world, have you been hiding Dear?
  I've searched high and low;
  Nowhere else to go
To find the love I long to hold near
  For all of my life -
  With luck or through strife.
Please, come to me, there is nothing to fear;
  With you by my side,
  My heart filled with pride,
Joyfully, I would go anywhere in the world!

Beatrice Driscoll

Lady Night

Night is a graceful lady
Who binds up her hair in the day
And at night the beautiful lady,
Takes the bindings away
Her silken, black hair cascades over her frail shoulders
And gently falls about her neck
And the Earth is enveloped in its raven darkness.

Joy Nahalka

Country Lane

I once strolled down a country lane,
with all the splendor and beauty it possessed.
　As honeysuckles lines the fence post,
I watched a robin build her nest.
　In the top of an oak tree,
that stood the test of time.
　As the wind carries the sounds,
of lovely churchbell's chimes.
　Through the beautiful pine trees,
that line this country lane.
　As a little brook rises and flows,
with the help of the rain.
　The tall wheat seems to roll,
with the direction of the breeze.
　When off to my left a stallion runs,
so wild and free.
　With his gracefulness and his beauty,
all of this is nature's chain.
　And I am but another link,
on this country lane.
Richard Lynn Hodge

Faith In God (Only God Has The Power)

When I have moments of complete anxiety...
Of doubt, fear, or despair...
When I feel depressed, angry or with hate...
When I feel my life and life in general are a vicious circle...
And I feel that everything repeats itself...
The good and the evil; the beautiful and the ugly...
The hard work and the crime; the vice and the violence...
The treason, the hypocrisy and the marble heart...
Feeling sad and angry, rebellious, rancorous, vengeful...
Not knowing why...
When I can do no more...
I just relax and put my life in God's hands and pray...
The Pater Noster or the Act of Faith,
The Hail Mary or the Act of Contrition...
Or I just say, "Oh, Sacred Heart of Jesus, I Confide In Thee..."
Or, "Oh, my God, have mercy on me..."
I just drop everything in God's hands and rest...
And the solutions to my problems begin to appear...
And I, like Jesus Christ, resurrect to a better and happier life...
Maria R. Sueiras

A Mother's Remembrance

From the moment he was born you knew you had
a son. Lying upon your breast, you knew he
was the best. Perhaps he's dreaming in his
nap of climbing a tree or becoming a pirate
sailing away to the south seas.
Time passes so quickly that when he awakes,
he's all grown up and the latter part of his
dream becomes reality. He sailed away but will
always be with you in your heart.
Clara Williams

The River

The river's moving swiftly,
　Like a black cat in the night.
With many twists and turns,
　That soon slip out of sight.

If you follow a river,
　You never know where it might extend.
For a river might be like a rainbow,
　With a pot of gold at the end.
Elizabeth M. Fason

The Games

In the beginning we could not wait,
For the story to unfold.
All we could do was anticipate,
What in two weeks would be told.

Half way through the stories unfolding,
With the competition already extreme.
Amazing vaults with pain filled landings,
That give a team a golden gleam.

But stories have their tragic chapters,
And our games would not be spared.
On a night filled with peace and laughter,
A bomb's explosion filled the air.

Tales of horror, give way to spirits,
Determined to keep our hopes renewed.
Vowing not to bow down to fear,
We refused to let our dreams be subdued.

In this story of love and peace,
Where sportsmanship and teamwork soar.
Fore these games which began in Greece,
Will remain in our hearts forever more.
Peg De Veny

Beautiful You

To be beautiful is not a gift, it's what you earn...
after treating people with respect,
and holding your head up high
with pride and dignity.

When beauty is found you'll definitely know.
You'll walk with your back arched,
and you'll always know exactly what you're
talking about.
As you speak, out your mouth the words will flow.
Telling of nothing but knowledge,
which you have plenty to show.

Beauty is in the eye of the beholder,
once it's found no one can ever take it away.
You'll never brag or boast,
and a real beauty will help those in need,
never asking for things in return...
which is just pure greed.
So follow these steps, and as a result...
you'll be the Beautiful You
that you've always wanted to be!
Patrice K. Bynum

Nail Polish II

The chair is overstuffed
　leg rest out
Eight decades rest there
Polish and remover nearby
Cluttered lamp table
Treasured notes
Crossword depot
Polish and file handy
Five decades of seeing
　only now knowing
　　deep level of awareness
　　the ritual of removal
My mother, my other
Disciplined in her polish
　her Faith, her bridge, her cleaning, her penny purse,
　her bravery, her defiant determination
Passed on to me the courage to
File life down,
Remove the polish,
And, change it if needed.
Nancy Penn

Life

There was a time when life was easy
Peaceful and serene
A Time when I had no worries
As if it were a dream
My childhood days, now they're gone,
Never more to be
What lies ahead? The future's mine
I must wait and see
Sometimes it's hard, sometimes it's not,
Living day to day
Sometimes I steer a steady course
Sometimes I lose my way
With the help of loved ones all around
I'll make it through the years
Without that help I'll run aground
And drown in my own tears
God give me strength to live life through
I do the best I can
God give me love enough to share
And I'll live life like a man
    James M. Morris

A Place My Children Will Never Get To Know

Shaking hands with flowers
Talking to the stream
listening to the birds
I begin to dream
That all the roads cut into you can't undo,
And I wonder how long you'll stay
Sun here's mostly shining
The brook here's mostly cold
And unlike city, delicious
And I'm frightened when I'm told
That plans to cut trees from you, can't undo,
And I wonder how long you'll stay
Though hundreds of acres are taken from you
No one remembers the seeding
And the wounds cut into you will never stop bleeding
And the long life they took from you can't undo
And I wonder how long you'll stay
I hope people will care someday.
    Albert Malo

Abortion Baby

Sun poured! Baby cried!
Tear dropped! Mommy lied!

Nursery rhythms sang to put you to sleep
A mother's trust you give your soul to keep
A mother's womb burnt she had no right
Abortion is death it's time to stand up and fight
Beaten children unite!

Like the death of innocence it came without cause
By the foolish government; in its untrusty laws
The gift of life
A acceptance of death

A swinging noose; a store bought crown
A raving and heartless mom
A stained panel, a looking glass

Watching the world go by with a tear in your eye
Living a falseness, living a lie
    Brian Phillips

Freedom

The screech of an owl
The call of a crow
The smell of coffee on an
old wood stove.
The ring of smoke from the
chimney up top, will let
you know if I'm home or not.

Wind breezing through the trees.
Vines growing high, the nestling
of birds, and fluttering butterflies,
Wild flowers blooming, and the humming of bee's,
These are the sights of spring time for me.

The ocean is nice,
The beaches are grand
But a cabin in the mountains is where
I can be found.
    Belma Lee

Your Love

Your eyes strike hard from up above,
You're a hawk that watches prey.
You kept me through your strong backhand—
You passed it off as love.

You knew when only I was near,
You chose that time to strike—
Unknowing and scared, I was your prey;
You passed it off as love.

You flew away to let me die,
You now look back at me—
Only if your attack had killed me
I may still be by your side.

But you were a hawk,
And I, your prey—
How silly I must have been,
For I believed you every time
The lies tore at my skin.

You nearly killed me and
You passed it off as love.
    Kathleen A. Little

A Tear, A Smile And Most Often A Laugh

Once upon a time there was a story told by a man
And though the story was always long,
It brought a tear or a smile or most often a laugh.
And just when it seemed as though it would never end,
The story was over.

When you hear a story please listen carefully,
For in it lies a person's life.
All his wisdom, joy and sorrow.
When you least expect it, it will end
And when it ends, it ends forever.

Once upon a time there was a man who told a story
And though this man's story was long, it ended.
But this is how he will always be remembered:
A story with a tear and a smile and most often a laugh.
    Noreen P. Browne

U.S. Soldiers Of The Vietnam War

They went out and fought this terrible war;
hoping that death would not come knocking on their door.

They fought in the jungles of horror and hell;
praying that this war, they would soon bid farewell.

They counted each day with no end near;
as they hunted for the enemy they truly feared.

Through the mosquito-infested jungles they roamed;
not knowing the scars some would carry home.

Then there were those who did not come back;
the Bills, the Bobs, the Pauls, and the Jacks.

This war that went on we soon forgot;
except the men who went and fought.

For some you see relive the pain;
of the horror in this war that no one could explain.

So let us remember in our hearts and minds;
The ones who lived, the ones who died,
and all the ones who were left behind.

Jeanette Wright

Listen Within

   Our yesterdays have passed
Left only with unsure tomorrows.

   The spell has been cast
Now our love is in sorrow.

We've paid a big price for the things we've done
Because now we're apart, pretending our love is gone.
All the wrong words were spoken, and tore us apart
All the right words were kept deep down in our hearts.
We should have opened our eyes
To the gift that we had, Because
Deep down we knew how to make our love last.

Instead we were fools
   Thinking our love was untrue
   But, our love hasn't died...
   It's in me...It's in you!

So I hope in our futures
If our hearts meet again,
We will take just a moment...
To Listen Within!

Stephanie A. Duffield

Words Of Life

As I look in the sky, is it a bird or a plane?
No. It's just my life flashing before my eyes.
The wind and clouds are only virtues.
Minor adjustments, I have in my life. Understand why
life has to be like this. It's not always
total bliss. You go through everyday doing the
same routine, but what does it all really mean?
All I ask for is to enjoy being here, and that
I will never have any fears. One minute you're
here, the next, you're just a distant memory.

Sara Stroud

Rich With Precious Jewels!

   My memory of growing up was that Ladies should be refined
and spend their time teaching their children the morals of life.

   As years ago by, it becomes more clear as to what she
was really teaching us...what real love was without strife.

   Now my children have children and they all love to come
to my house and spend some time with me!

   Along with a Great Grandson I'm realizing what my
children are giving me...the best of what jewels were meant to be.

   Although I cherish the memories of a time long ago, when
our mother took the time to teach us proper values, I realize
her teachings would not fit into today's ways, but am very
thankful for the background that was so great with love!
Even as a teenager she would wake us up with a verse from her
memory of childhood - "A birdie with a yellow bill, hopped
upon the window sill, cocked its shining eye and said "Ain't
you ashamed, you sleepy head?"

Dorothy Dosier

Under A Canopy Of Stars

Crackling, hissing of logs
Campfires burning bright
Pungent odors invade our senses
Preparation - symphony of the night.

Laser lights of fireflies flashing
Owl hooting in the hollow tree
Silken touch of a moth's wings
Sights and sounds of the country.

Grasshoppers shuffle, crickets chirp
Cicadas cry long and shrill
Soft whoo-oo-o of the morning dove
Lonesome song of the whippoorwill.

Splash in the lake a hungry bass
Coyote yodeling for his mate
Deep throat ribbett of the bullfrog
The hour is getting late.

Closing the flap of our snug little tent
We are quickly lulled to sleep
Sigh of the wind in the tall pine tree
A soul satisfying retreat. Under a canopy of stars!

Florence Carpenter Janis

A Motherless Daughter

The day you did, dear Mama, you took the part of me that
only you could see.

You took with you, dear Mama, the baby that you rocked to
sleep, you took the toddler reciting prayers to our Lord for
our souls to forever keep.

You took the part of me that was still a little girl, the
part of me that wore pigtails and curls.

You left behind, dear Mama, a young lady needing your
guidance and your caring, walking thru out my life with no
mother daughter sharing.

A motherless daughter I became the day you passed away, all
grown up, never again allowed to play.

Danell L. Hill

Prince Of Forbidden Dreams

Once upon a time, in a land of forbidden dreams, the earth dawned a new day. As the water rushed through the land and the flowers blossomed with the wondrous colors of the rainbow, the dew of the morning frost left a fresh, undisturbed sensation as far as the eye could see.

As life began to awaken from a peaceful dream, a love was also awoken. A love that is exiled by many and understood by few. But yet a love that could last FOREVER.

For many, FOREVER is a forbidden word, but to me, FOREVER has a deep and unforgettable meaning. FOREVER is the eternal commitment of love, honor, cherishment, loyalty, and forgiveness.

Although love may perish for some, I have found love's true form. The purest form of love that has ever touched or will ever touch my heart and soul. To love with all my heart is and everlasting and true commitment. I have never loved so deeply as I love YOU! May we never lose sight of the land of forbidden dreams and eternal peace.

Helen Reneé Hair

"Lamenting"

I feel so adrift in a wide, wide sea;
The memories of our past keep coming back to me.
Who can erase them, make them cease to be?
And do I really want to forget
   all the years we shared?
Forget the tender moments, the ways
   you showed you cared?
The pond'ring of these questions
   perhaps will let me know
Just how much farther I really have to go
Before I come to terms with being so alone,
Of not having found the way yet
   to being on my own.
At times I feel I must not dwell
   on past events and such,
At other times I picture you
   and miss you, oh so much!

Margaret Bunt Wagner

Thank You

Fifty years of wedded bliss;
   had all started with a single kiss.
Dad and Mom were introduced on a blind date;
   to find this to be their soul-mate.
Five children to change their hair to gray;
   "We're glad we had them" is all you'll ever hear them say.
These parents of ours are pretty unique;
   giving us much tender love each day of the week.
Seeing to every bump, bruise, and tear,
   letting us know they'd always be near.
All the times we may have let them down or made them mad;
   they've never turned their backs on us or left us unclad.
A standard and example in life they set;
   hoping in our lives it would be met.
We are thankful that their lives never changed;
   even though time might have aged.
For this, it made us children stronger;
   to have faithful parents to God this much longer.
Now it is our time to thank and let them know;
   that their endless love does forever show!!!

Jodi Steuber

My Person

I'm labeled disabled, retarded, slow,
   autistic, hyperactive, even crazy, you know.
But I'd just like to say - of this box I arrived in,
   it is Not "my person", "My Person" is strivin'.

I'm studying to learn how to eat, dress, and walk;
   how to clean, how to play, how to bathe, cook and talk;
how to shop, how to wait, how to work, laugh, and sleep;
   I'm studying for a chance to compete!

I need coaching and grooming and training, I've thought.
   I need chances to practice the tasks I've been taught.
I need reasons to force myself time and again.
   But, at "showtime" - I need to say "when".

Coach, "my person" Can do it, just Ten Seconds I need;
   let me process that message - your cue;
Let my box tell "my person" what job is at hand,
   and then Watch what "my person" can do!

Linda Woodcock

Baseball Poem

Baseball is cool and it's fun,
And I'll show you how it's done.
Like this you hit the ball,
Like this the ball will land and fall.

The thing that you hit with is called a bat,
Everything you wear is a glove and a hat.
And that's what you know about hitting,
Maybe now it's time for splitting!

Go out on the baseball field to catch and play,
Like you want to do everyday.
Out on the field to catch a flying ball,
Very high ball that will land in your mitt and fall
Eventually you will catch the ball!

I'll show you to catch the ball the way it's done,
Nothing's going to be caught if you don't have fun.
Nothing's bad if you try,
I just want you to catch flies.
Now go out and you have to catch,
Go get flying ball you can snatch.

Jimmy Mai

It Only Matters What Is Within

It doesn't matter about the color of your face,
It doesn't matter about what kind of race,

It doesn't matter about the color of your skin,
It only matters what is within.

It only matters about your personality,
Not your race, not your color, can't you see?

People in this world should be treated right,
Because it matters what's within, and not what you see by sight.

Mindy Frazier

Recaptured Peace

Entangled in the midst of kinetic motion,
I long for the feeling of not being in its center
but, being centered.
Shall this chaos, my reality, loom to take
away my peace?
Is it mine to capture back?
But yes.
My resolve will free the burden that I will not allow
to withhold me
From all that I was meant to be.

Kerin Celeste Salie

Modern Mothering

From you have I been absent in the spring,
And also in the summer and the fall.
In fact, I've hardly been with you at all,
Because I've been so busy making a living.
Therefore, dear chick, when you are busy grieving
That my supposed neglect dooms you like a pall,
Kindly reflect, as you grow hale and tall,
Upon the merits of housing and of eating.
Having a bed in which to do your dreaming,
And a table set with food withal,
Though not a mother who watches you play ball,
May help to dry your tears from streaming.
Please know my hours of paid work were not for me,
But so that you, my dear, could learn and grow and be.

Gaye Follmer Deal

Loud Yet Silent Screams Of Betrayal

She felt so betrayed but didn't speak a word
Afraid what was said might be misheard
Screaming the pain she felt but no one could hear
Her insides were dying tear after tear
She is friendly with anyone but yet so alone
The fake smile she wears how could anyone have known
The pain, hurt, and betrayal that she feels inside
Feelings she can't deal with so she tries to hide
Not knowing what to do, how to feel or were to go
She can't put her guard down, she can't trust a soul
Everyone thinks she is happy with this act she puts on
Yet she cries almost every night til the break of dawn
She is trying to find herself through all this confusion
As soon as she thinks she has found it, it's just an illusion
Trying to understand why people do what they do
It always ends up she hasn't got a clue

Jeni Marquart

Aloha!

How can I ever say goodbye
To one so loved as you
How will I ever let you go
With something so simple as farewell
We've shared a lot of special moments
Things done together as friends
Laughing at our private jokes
Helping each other to get through the day
Who will I turn to for support
When my day is going down the drain
Who shall cheer me up when I am blue
Bring a smile to my lips
Who shall I share my secrets with
Or talk about my problems to
Girl you are going to be sadly missed
Because there is no other that can compare to you
Here's hoping that all your tomorrows
Will be as bright as you've made our days
We will miss you.

Tenia E. Brown

If Tomorrow...

If tomorrow I said I love you, would you care?
If tomorrow a chance to return those three special words,
  would you dare?
If tomorrow I died by your side would you care or even cry?
If tomorrow this happens and me no longer alive, what
  would your last words be before I died?
If tomorrow this all happens and we'd just have to
wait and see, would we be together just you and me?
If tomorrow this all happens I would want to be with
you and knowing of no tomorrow would drive me crazy too.

Nicky Steger

Gray Haired And Wrinkled

I looked in my mirror, I couldn't believe what I saw
For that face in my mirror, didn't look like me at all

Their hair was turning silver, its true color was just a trace
For time had took its toll in each wrinkle on their face

Then I looked into their eyes, they say they're the windows
  to the soul
Then I realized it was me, I was only growing old!

When I get to Heaven, a glorified body I'll find
Who's to say, it might look different than the one I now call mine

When I see my Jesus, it won't matter at all
Whether I'm gray haired and wrinkled, at His feet I'm gonna fall

When I get to Heaven, there'll be treasure untold
Who cares if I'm gray haired and wrinkled, when my Jesus I behold

I looked in my mirror and in my eyes I could see
The light of my Lord shining bright in me

For He'll never forsake me, He'll always dwell in my heart
My Lord will be with me, His Holy Spirit will never part

Friend, please look in your mirror, I pray that you too will see
The Lord is looking back at you, as He was looking back at me

When I see my Jesus, His hand I'm gonna hold
I may not be gray haired and wrinkled, when we walk on those streets
  of gold!

Rita A. Stout

The Journey

Where does my journey lie?
I dreamed that beauty passes, like a gleam.
I hear the sounds of water lapping over streams.
Under the passing stars from the skies.
I feel God's silence, that came to cast.
Dishevelled years gone, that soon past.
Morning to where the birds will sing.
As they rise upon their wings.
The wind awaken by whirls of leaves.
Unbound by old tall trees.
God has laid his hands on me.
Thy tender eyes, will always see.
Beauty grown each day through eternity.
What lies ahead of life's mystery.
Mystery to know, what once I have known.
To see the beauty, God has shown.
The pleasure that comes with sleep.
God has grant me to keep.
I may dine in heaven at journey's end.
But what a lovely place, with God as my friend.

Janice Brooks

Motherhood

Nowhere on earth such Heavenly joy,
as a beautiful smiling baby boy.
The clouds overhead cannot disguise.
The sunbeamed laughter in his eyes.
The soft caress of a loving hand.
stretched forth to discover a brand new land.
And I his mother in wonderment still.
Try my best his life to fulfill.
Oh what sweet joy his life has brought.
A new dream I seem somehow to have caught.
As the sunlight plays across his face.
I know deep within I've found my place.
A soft cry floats now through the stillness of night,
My call to motherhood. My own birthright.

Lisa Kettlewell

Suicide

She looked in the mirror into her bloodshot eyes,
She could see past her pitiful lies,
She knew she was suffering from a thing called depression,
She knew sooner or later she would have to make a confession,
Now since her parents had left her,
Her whole life was a blur; life wasn't worth a thought,
And a fight wasn't worth to be fought,
She was going to help because her parents died,
But all she could think was suicide,
But she could think of was suicide,
But she was wrong she wasn't right,
She should've stood up and be able to fight,
She made a big mistake; But she can't fix it's too late.
Anisha Pai

Body Language

I see the way she walks
In sinuous ballet grooves
To me her body talks
I have a book of her moves

Quiet, powerful linguistics
She speaks without speaking
Wordless, moving poetics
I hear without hearing

I can't describe very well, these
words can't be found in any dictionary
Nouns and verbs pronounced to me
Loud and clear, smooth and free
Her novels fill my library

I have never heard such exquisite words
than I have from her shape
. . . a foreign language I cannot translate

Words are strangers when she's around
Elusive strangers I've never found
Gregory S. Jones

The Best Is Free

Thank you, God, for all that's free,
Countless gifts so rare, so fine
Flowing from your wealthy bounty
For which we never "wait in line".

The sun came up, we pushed no button,
Spring is here, we filled no blank,
Summer will follow, so will autumn,
Yet only God we have to thank.

Birds are singing, no practice needing,
Buds are opening, no experts near,
Soft winds blow without a reading,
Geese fly north and there's no fear.

Our children's love is gift sublime
For which we never pray nor strive,
Our love for them is part of thine,
For these we never "wait in line".
Jennie B. Jaramillo

Virgin Answers

Weep the willowing whisper walks
a near felled pretty
can she bare the dripple drop,
of puffed up ocean me?
Hand me stick,
dear talking cane and glossy boots not dry,
Weep the willowing whisper walks
beside her so may I.
John J. Clark

What Can I Do?

Hatred, violence and drugs
Today the only answer is to sue,
We can't stuff these things under the rug,
What can I do?

Wars, bombs and fears,
We call this the new age?
People are looking into a shattered mirror,
All I can do is gaze.

The ozone layer is thinning because of the Human Race,
Think of the poisons the government is baking,
How can we stand to look at ourselves in the face?
And here I sit - shaking.

Poverty and Gangs - is there any way to peace?
We just sit and let it stew
The children we think of the least
What can I do?

I know I've got to try
I know I've got to care
So I wipe the tears from my eye
And try to help the people out there
Courtney Rowe-Bultinck

Untitled

On the beach
Under a fallacious sky
I sit quietly waiting
As a tear drops from my eye
Reminiscing to myself about all that was good
All the while fearing the bomb that would end manhood
I wipe my tear stained cheek and gaze out at the sea
In awe of the power of the tide
As it laps gently against my feet
With lifeless emotion, I pick up a handful of sand
watching it fall through my fingers and back onto the land
Taking a deep breath, I walk towards the sea
feeling a sense of peace as the water engulfs me
In it, I find sanctuary, my own personal abyss
I hear the water whisper my name
And feel the warm liquid kiss
As I sink to the bottom, I become intoxicated by the sea
Poseidon offers up a cup of his divinity
A golden fountain of liquid revelry
for my eternal sanctity has claimed me
Amy Brown

For My Son

Hallelujah, the angels cry in joy!
singing it's a boy
born on the day the Lord has set to rest
he is the best
He is my son, a gifted one
he holds my heart right from the start
I will give to him....

Asking angels to cover him with prayer
forever I'll be there
sharing, caring and bearing what I must
he has all my trust
He is my life, my strength through strife
sent unto me by Almighty
and I will give to him...

Looking in his eyes I'll conquer any quest
fear I lay to rest
His touch is turning hollowed dreams to such fullness
could I've imagined this
he sets me free, puts faith in me
to be the man I believe I can...and I will give to him.
Nick Nikias

Sitting on a Park Bench

To: My best friend, Tim Carmac; My Godfather, Robert Snell

Sitting on a park bench thinking about a friend of mine he
was only 20 gone before he had his time it came without a
warning didn't want his friends to see him cry he knew the day was
dawning and I didn't have a chance to say goodbye in that life I
loved him most of all. Driving down the boulevard thinking
about a
man I knew he was like a father to me nothing in the world that
he wouldn't do for me he taught me to respect my self said
that we're all made of flesh and blood why should he be
treated differently it shouldn't matter who you choose to love.
People pass by and I wonder who's next who determines,
 who knows best
is there a lesson I'm supposed to learn in this case ignorance
is not bliss have you ever watched your best friend die have you ever
seen a grown man cry some say that life isn't fair I say that
people just don't care they'd rather turn the other way while we
wait for this thing to go away why do we have to pretend some
day I pray it will end.

Teresa Marie Kelly

Swirling, Whirling

My mind full of confusion
stop this roller coaster
stop this mad merry-go-round of illusion
up and down
slamming you around the track
round and round
faster and faster
your life speeds by
things always come back
you can't get off
even if you try
it's not a dream
this is reality
worse than nightmares seem
the twists and turns
make you laugh
but the pain will
always bring you back.

Karen Kessler

Barefoot Country

Down the country lane I roam
Bare feet splashing in the dew
Remembering about the days back home
When the world seemed fresh and new

Many years have come and gone
But life still flashes back once more
To when me and my dog Fawn
Played along the river shore

When in the twilight of the day
We are building bridges of love and peace
Hope reigns forever along the way
With dreams that will never cease

Let the thoughts of tomorrow dwell
No one knows where they will go
Precious memories that we can tell
Of summers rain and winter's snow

Time is passing swiftly by
With new friends and pleasures
With hopes reaching up to the sky
But none can replace my barefoot treasures

L. Gladys Fudge

How Nice

How nice of you all to think of me
In such a wonderful way-
On this my 65th birthday

I was so moved I can't express
My delight and pleasure and
feelings of happiness.

How nice and caring of you all
and to think the surprise was so concealed.
You really had me completely fooled-
I know I'm old, and somewhat grey or white
and feel forlorn and times-
"Ha" who cares? You do of course!
I want you to know that in the days to come
I'll have these memories -
I'm sure will bring a smile or two,
a tear, happy feelings all I'm sure-
this is all that really counts - the
kindness and the hands of friendship-
How great and wonderful you all are
thank you all so much and may God Bless you all

Helen Cole

Growing Old

These are the things, I am told
Why we must never grow too old
There's more for us to do on this earth
To help our children from the time of their birth
To teach them how to show much love
And let them know how much they're loved
Then there are those, who will never know
We reap in this world just about whatever we sow
For this is the way we will get along
With all God's people weak or strong
I know it's not easy for us to do each day
When we have many problems come our way
But we must know if we trust in God
He will show us the way to trod
Then we will never be alone
And God Himself will lead us home

Mary Fitzpatrick

Prince

All a man is waiting for,
is to be important to somebody.
And, I desire to be important to you,
and be there steady.
In my heart,
I want to be a hero to you...
With the hero I must be,
I request a lover out of thee.
If you never forget the reason
to befriend the prince you are with,
He will become the King you want him to be.
If we think alike,
Here again is a big hug from me.
My fragrant breeze of spring,
Our hearts are locked together
with a heavenly string...
This is what He planned,
No one can change a thing.

Ashish Vohra

Wanting To Tell You How Much I Love You

No one really knows what is going on
inside my heart or even what
I am thinking about because there's
so many things I would like to tell you
face to face you're only just a few steps
away from me but it seems like you're
thousands of miles away from me but I
know we both know that you are
too close to me to even think that way I just
keep on sitting here I cannot stand another
second without being near you to touch you
to hear you call my name just out for one
more time it's killing me deeply when you're not
near my sight where I can see your handsome face.
   Phyllis A. Felton

Moon Maids

Sun's thirst quenched in sky's blue waters.
Nightwine stains in starry folds.
Cool pale orb in maidens blossoms -
Gliding high in greys and golds.

Moon Maids cast a joyful tribute;
Vessels brimmed in secret spires.
Future tides form ancient eddies;
Timeless whims or hearts desires.

Supple arms unwinding winsome.
Cascades fall as wondrous beams
Surging past embanked repression
Gathered pools of molten dreams.
   Frost Newton

Garden Of The Mind

As summer's day comes to a close,
beside a field where harvest grows,
strawberries touch her lips of rose
while evening breeze so gently blows.

Now I can savor their sweet taste
tho' time has made their field to waste.
Held within my memory's store-
I keep the fruit which our love bore.
   Herbert M. Bryant Jr.

Whisper Infinity

Flawless time in thoughts unknown
and feelings unshown. In the light
just before night, golden rays seal the
days as they pass before our eyes.
To far is that place we want to be,
spinning ever so greatly toward infinity.
And in our mind the sounds are good,
in this world, under this sky, within
the heavens I may fly, in center
with no feelings of any kind. Like
thoughtless passion in blind design,
pleasure and pain vandalize my mind.
An unheard whisper in a crowd,
like a youthful love kept inside,
and with no destiny in my mind
my heart finds love on this earth
for the first time.
   Michael R. Villella

Full Circle

A slight stirring
  and you speak
as you give way to pushes and pulls.

Groans
  Creaks
    Murmurs
      Whispers heard softly in the
       Heavy velvet so rich with the night.

You bend deeply
  Stretching to become one
with the cool lush life below
  Seeking to meet the moist caresses of the dew.

You drink deeply now
  and replenish mutually
Life to Life...
   Pat Krystosek

Mom

Strange days here, feeling alright.
Vagueness, a veil
between desire and action
helping to create a state
  of dull confusion
Easy to live life like this.
But to lift the veil and intensity
of colour and richness of beauty
becoming closer and faster through
the prism.
My eye picking colors and angles, safer
than white light.
My sense of sight
  even diluted from an excess of perception.
It's all murky and hey! Am I just a fish to you
Or the gift to a soul whose tired times
pass like challenge and adventure...
Beautiful mother, cry for joy!!
   Michael James Connor

Whorizon

Cloud shrouded moon in the dead of night,
A ball of cotton grey-white splintered light.
Pinpoints of yellow speak not of stars,
As these are man-made dot the hills from afar
Another place to build seems to be man's only need,
His quest for more land an insatiable greed.
He's been digging and gouging,
So he must surely see...
...less land...
  Less grass...
    ...nowhere left for the trees...
The earth she is crying,
Wonders "when will it end?"
Then just this side of darkness
A lonely quiet descends,
On this soft shadowy eve the moment is fleeing...
...over this...
  ...man's whorizon...
    ...his end...
      ...of his beginning...
   Don Puppel Jr.

Always and Forever

Always and forever are different.
"I'll always love you", is saying
until I can't remember.

Forever I'll love you,
is telling you until I'm dead
and beyond the grave.

So, forever and always I will love you.
Crystal Hendron

Adjustment

So many things I cannot do!
   I've given up a thing or two.
I can no longer ride a horse;
   It shakes my innards up, of course.
My back complains at golf club swing,
   The hike to greens is no mean thing.
To paddle my canoe, though light,
   The wind and tide I cannot fight.
My shoulders groan when I ring bells;
   My sleepless night that follows tells.

So since resigned, I must invite
   Some new activities to spite
Advancing age. Now I must seek
   A quilting group that meets each week.
A musical saw? A challenge true!
   I just bought one! What will it do?
My painting lags, but I can shop
   For bargain frames whenever I stop,
To matt and frame already done,
   My masterpieces, one by one.
Frances E. Knott

Snowball

You were there when I was tired.
You were there when I was sad.
You were there when I was aching,
And always I was glad!

Your snow white Angora fur,
So soft to the touch!
Your lime colored eyes,
Penetrated me so much.

Bright pink tongue, ears, nose, and pawpads
Make the whole of "my Snowball,"
Loving, communicating; never bad.

You have gone to Kitty heaven,
Leaving behind a void,
Which will soon be full of memories,
All hallowed and gold.
Virginia Nellis

Love Me

May you love me in the beginning,
May you love me in my dreams,
May you love me during the bad
As well as the good times in life,
May you love me through the end of time.
Love Me
Jane Coffee

An Arrow's Plight...Man's Desire

An arrow with great flight was set free toward the sky,
Bound upward with great intent to the heavens it did fly;
As with all birds of wingless power given for depth of sight,
Descend to the earth it would surely go with lack of plight;
Now yielding to where its arc will land, destined, a plot unknown,
However, when the blade met soil, plowing new ground,
It found a place called home;
Is not this, for each man, the humble quest,
A place to lay his soul bequeathed of rest;
His heart and dreams, these are the greatest tools;
In the creative tapestry of life all have been deemed fools;
With shovel in hand the journey begins to develop a home,
Conceived of hope, never looking back for the world to roam;
As with the arrow, your heart, the compass, a single desire,
Breaking new earth gives liberty to the dream and frees the fire.
James Trammel

A Hawk's View

A hawk sees a campfire flickering far away from the big city.
A large tree party shades the fire.
A group of people, maybe children, sit around the fire.
A few off at some tables preparing a meal.
Clusters of tents scattered all over the countryside.
A boy yells, a girl cries.
Down at the river, a boy about to jump.
1,2,3, splash.

His body now submerged in the cold, cold water.
A teacher runs down the shore to a toe pincher that was just caught.
A rattlesnake slithers across the rocky ground under the hot sun.
A tarantula moves slowly across the dirt in front of a yellow
and brown tent.
High atop the ridge five children look down at their camp while
ten more are still down in the canyon called Aliso.
Dust coming up from behind a child's feet.
A teacher waters down the dirt.
Another child at a nearby table weaving the web of a dream catcher
while another, at the stove, brands a pendent.
All from the view of a hawk.
Beaumont Shapiro

The Princess and the Toad

So frequently she wandered to the water's edge;
her situation she surmised.
Then she stared passionately to see what would arise.
If it be a hideous toad or ugly pollywog;
she would make him the most handsome Prince in all this filthy Bog.
He would wear a ring upon his finger and ride a stallion so white;
Ill fortune and her enemies he would smite.
Her Lord would rule a kingdom and conquer monarchies;
he would make vassals of kings and duchies.
He would wear a brilliant crown upon his noble brow;
and receive praise and laud from every knee that bows.
Ruling with royal sceptre in bejeweled hand;
He is awaited in court by Viceroys and Ambassadors
from distant Lands.
What e're fate or fortune may capriciously bring;
Ah! If I were only king.....
Richard C. Ditsch

Knight Song

I don't need the white knight to ride up on his charger.
  I learned to fight my own dragons long ago.

From a distance I have watched while others claimed to have found their white knights,
  only later to notice the dents and rust,
    or worse to find that the white was truly black.

So much for the want of an illusion.

The same illusion captures men.
  In seeking to find the damsel they often wind up with an attractive package, but little else they wanted.
    Then usually too late when they realize that.

Again taken in by illusion of an image.

For true knights are not seated on horseback,
  nor are the true damsel held by dragons,
    they are only the lonely souls needing the chance to meet and see the truth.

Gretchen G. Rowlette

Reflections

A beautiful tree, big and round.
and yet not far, from the ground.

Beautiful stars, that I see.
Remind me, of the tree.

There to see, for those who dare.
Both wondrous, beyond compare.

When all else fails.
Remember, that God leaves trails.

When death and ugly, are about.
Remember the wonders, that leave no doubt.

Lift your eyes, to a tree.
It might be God, that you see.

Daniel Rogers

Deaf

I am deaf but, I am happy.
I can't hear you but, I can see what you are doing.
I am deaf but, I am happy.
I have hands to do the talking.
I am deaf but, I am happy.
I can work the same as you.
Why be sad when I am happy.
I am like you and you are like me.

Cruz Marcano

Existing Time

What is Time, it flies by because it was never here,
it's the future that is only the past recycled.
When was it started, will Time ever end,
If it does do we stand still,
And do we spring back at its only will,
Where has it been, as it ages the world,
What great peoples has it claimed,
What great peoples has it given birth,
When will time claim me,
Will it let me achieve all I dreamed to be,
Or will it claim me before I truly live.
We all dwell in the past,
Striving to touch the future,
But it can never be reached, for once it is it becomes the past.
I am just a fragment of time, already a piece of history,
Waiting to never be part of the future.

Graham Ferrier

Despair

Let me not be as one of the dead; walking about in grief;
always in sorrow; never in joy.
For grief has consumed me.
The pangs of death are upon me.

My soul is poured out;
My life has been drunk up, like water upon parched ground;
My head is scorched;
My breath is taken from me.

Death stalks me and sorrow fills my day;
Sleep flees from me and restlessness fills my night;
Sorrow and grief are my comforts and
Death is my companion.

Yet shall I not be consumed by death nor swallowed up by grief,
for the Lord is with me.
He is my shield and buckler, my hope.
He is the lifter of my head.
He gives life to the lifeless, hope to the hopeless;
He makes the desert to bloom again.

I will rise from my bed, wash my face, comb my hair and
walk among the living, for the joy of the Lord is upon me.

Thomas H. Dorer

Flight Wings

Flight wings.
  Flight wings.
    A wheeling clearness height brings.
Rolling free or soaring round
My spirit never touches ground.

Lifted hood.
  Feeling good.
    Never knew I really could
See the wrinkles of the sea.
So real a King in my Aerie.

Flight wings.
  Sight wings.
    Fed me all the right things.
The moment came to sail aloft;
Spread my wings and lifted off.

Ahhh ohh! Could it blow?
There's no fear,
  Sailing clear

On Kite wings,
My Flight wings.

Tom McAlexander

The Greatest Love

Though I never met you -
  I know you're with me each day,
    To walk hand in hand until the end.
You're happy when I am happy;
You're sad when I am sad.
In my mind I picture you as a powerful young man
But I know you're strong enough to get me through
  any storm.
When I stray with others on my mind,
I know I have not left you behind.

And on the day I die and we finally meet,
I come before you on one knee -
For you are the Master and I am the servant.
When you take my hand and lead the way,
Then I'll know the greatest love finally came.

Pamela Marie Chaney

Untitled

The hooting owl, by the sea
Is about as sad as she can be.
You might not think she has feelings too,
But she is just like me and you.
Why is she sad? I wondered one day.
Why does she often look away?
Then she answers, singing a song,
Telling me all about what went wrong.
Her true love vanished one day.
Maybe he left, just flew away.
He left one day, and why? Who knew?
He broke he heart, so sad but true.
Now he is in a better place.
A bullet caught him, by disgrace.
And then she said through all her tears,
Death hurts, and so do years.
Courtney Anne Ramirez

Andrew And Ceceila Targowski

Andrew and Ceceila Targowski
   Search and find no other
Such as the ones so close to me
   Known as Father and Mother
Andrew and Ceceila Targowski
   Joined in more than matrimony
United together a force
   A bond that their love is the source
Of strength for me to always know
   And feel wherever I go
They gave so much of themselves
   They gave all they had
Their my unseen sentinels
   Thank you Mom and Dad
For being lucky to be your son
   To reflect your way of life
So my own family will always have a reason
   To thank you for becoming man and wife
The way God wanted it to be
   Joined together forever Andrew and Ceceila Targowski.
Francis A. Targowski

Why, That's God

A blue bird singing in a tree,
A red bird popping sunflower seeds,
And a hummingbird sipping honey from a flower,
WHY, THAT'S GOD.

A baby nursing at his/her mother's breast,
A father showing his son/daughter how to catch a fish,
A mother frying it in a pan,
WHY, THAT'S GOD.

A grain of rice, wheat, barley, corn or oat,
Ground into flour and
Made into bread,
WHY, THAT'S GOD.

Meat of sheep, beef, fowl, venison, fish;
Milk of goat or cow processed into cheese that nourish man,
Crawling insects that make honey,
WHY, THAT'S GOD.

Ideally, men and women who love each other and beget children
Whom they train to religious living and to conserve the earth,
All these echo the refrain,
WHY THESE ALSO ARE GOD.
Evelyn B. McCulloh

Dreamer

As I walk through the flowers and trees,
I follow the trail of fragrant perfumes
Emanating from honeysuckle vines and honeybees.

The persimmon tree hangs heavy with fruit,
And the Magnolia blooms with great white flowers.
While in the mist of the morning
The hummingbird looms.

The sun shines through the clouds, casting
a glow, making the dew on the leaves
look like sparkling jewels, as the wind
gently blows.

I stopped and gazed around, all these
amazing things are here for my pleasure.
As I walk through the flowers and trees,
I realize these are the world's greatest treasures.

I awake, smile, and thank God, for another day!
Elvis D. Wells

What's Up??

What's up with our government today?
It seems like our leaders have all gone astray
I remember politicians being noble and proud
Not nearly as arrogant, not nearly as loud

Our children's future should be our concern
What's up with our teachers, will their spirit return?

What's up with our government today?
It's the need for posterity that lead them astray
This frightening dilemma should wake us all up
Rush tries to inform us, but we are stuck in a rut

I'm only one person with opinions and views
What's up with the people, don't their opinions count too?
My voice may not carry the power we need
But, by writing this poem perhaps someone will lead

What's up with our government today?
Let's not give it up, we'll fix it someway.
Cynthia G. Brown

[the world through] IRIS EYES

    red green yellow blue
   colors of the spectrum too
 flying fluttering floating butterfly
    a yolk-yellow sunrise
   and a misty moon sky-high
    are the pupil's prize

 blessed Is she with unaided sight
 surfing the constellations late at night
viewing morning muRky blue tide rIp rocks
  She shan't take sight for granted
   Oh wherE are mY socks?
 These things should not be supplanted

     blindnEss
    is blacknesS
J. Scott Kroeze

Silver Thread

Today I was given a glimmer of hope,
Something to hold onto,
Just a word you whispered on the wind,
That I hold within my heart.
A tiny strand of silver thread
Holding me together for one more day —
While I wait for your love to turn my way.
Dawn Stanzione

Born Into Time, Die Into Eternity

We are entered into time the moment we are born into this life.
A life filled with pleasures and strife.
From the moment we are born, to the hour we die.
On time we must constantly rely.
In our youth we thought we had so much of it.
Only to find in maturity, there is never enough of it.
As the hours of our lifetime drifts away;
We hope time will allow us just another day.
But when we finally run out of time,
Both figuratively and literally,
I pray O Lord to have mercy on me.
For I have done my time here, you see.
So take my hand, Lord, and lead me into eternity.
Patrick C. Lisa

The Masterless Slave

The days pass
Time flows at its usual pace
The world turns around me
Yet a colder world stands still inside
Locked in a windowless, doorless cell of solitude
Serving the one with no name
Serving the one that is feeble on the outside
Serving the one that has dominance over my mind, my soul
How far do I have to run to escape
How strong do I have to be to regain control
Will it end
The stink of freedom is bound with the thought of happiness
Yet lurking in the shadows is the one I serve
Never to leave
Never to go away
Forever a part of me
Forever a part of my world
My world of solitude
James Anderer

James

When God Spoke, He Said:

I thought I told you, he was yours for a very short while,
So you could enjoy his cheerfulness and his sunny, sunny smile.

For, he was just on loan to you as you can plainly see,
For, in actuality, he really belonged to me.

Each moment that he spent with you was a happy time indeed,
But he knew the time was way too short for him to fill your every need

He grew to love the people he was surrounded by,
And, he knew how very quickly his time on earth would fly.

I needed to call him home for there was work that was undone,
And I had to make him return and break the hearts that he had won.

I knew it would be difficult for you to send him home,
But, again I will remind you, he simply was on loan.

When Jim Spoke, He Said:

My soft words to all of you, is do not weep for me,
For I am happy in my own way and I have now been set free.

And each of you should be aware that I look over you,
And, I am cognitive of everything that you do.

For, I am your guardian angel watching from above,
And with each passing day I am sending you my love.

Therefore, I do not wish to have you crying nor should you lament,
For I am now happy and in God's hand and very, very content.
Madeline Miller

I Dream

On a bright and sunny day
while the clouds are white and puffy
I like to lay out by the ocean.
With the sound of the water in my ears
and the rush of the wind in my hair
I dream.
I dream I am a princess
trapped in a mile high tower.
My prince will come to rescue me
just like in all the fairy tales.
But before he can come
I awake.
As I lay amidst the sand
with the suns rays beaming down on me
I gaze up at the bright blue sky
that beautifully outlines the clouds
and while I listen to the waves break against the shore
I dream.
Carrie Smith

Olive Left The Farm

On a cold spring day, Olive left the farm.
By going away, she meant no harm
But all her friends and loved ones should know
That Olive was prepared, and ready to go.

Olive was a good woman and nobody's fool
While young, she enrolled in teacher's school
She earned a certificate as good as gold
And as a teacher, she could the minds of youth mold.

Olive used her knowledge to teach in school
And in church, she taught the golden rule.
She was a woman who did not her talent hide,
And she had scores of friends, far and wide.

Olive lived on the farm, for about twenty-five years,
There were good times, much work, pain and tears.
She bore six children, and all did well
Husband died young and left a good story to tell.

Yes, Olive left the farm, and went to her permanent home,
Life's sun was setting, and she was no more on earth to roam.
Olive was ready and willing to leave this world of strife,
Surely, she believed that in dying, we are born to eternal life.
Curtis D. Watkins

A True Friend

When we have a friend who we can trust
No matter what the situation,
We can count on her to be there for us
In loneliness, joy or utter desolation.
In her we confide our deepest thoughts,
Our hopes, our dreams, our desires:
We know that friend will always love us -
Her unwavering faith in us never tires.
When others in our lives should fail us,
We can count on her to care;
To laugh with us, cry with us, sigh with us
And rescue us from the grip of despair.
Our secrets she will take to her grave,
Our love she will always treasure.
She is a staunch defender, nurturer, confidante -
Her value to us cannot be measured.
Though tested by trials, miles and tribulations,
In our spirits we will always be together;
Other people and places in our lives may come and go,
But remember...a True Friend is Forever.
Nanci Elise Steed

Love

Love is a friendship that has caught fire.
It is quiet understanding, mutual confidence,
sharing and forgiving.
It is a loyalty through good and bad.
It settles for less than perfection and makes allowances
for human weaknesses.
Love is content with the present.
It hopes for the future,
and it doesn't brood over the past.
It's the day-in and day-out chronicle of
irritations, problems, compromises,
small disappointments,
big victories and working toward common goals.
If you have love in your life, it can make up
for a great many things you lack.
If you don't have it, no matter what else
it's not enough.
   Marolyn M. Rondorf

A Hidden World

I'm scared of life and the people in mine.
Looking around a smile on their faces.
I stare and wonder, is it as bad as mine?
We all wear masks, I know now.
Each smile a broken heart, a life in ruins.
No one sees through the smiles and laughter.
A life in misery and total agony.
We suffer so much but drown it in laughter.
It is our laughter that kills us.
How you ask? A burst of misery and sorrow.
I'm scared of life and what it holds.
I suffer not alone but with the rest of the world.
Every one holds their own mask. Which is yours?
Why can't we break the string behind the mask!
You know, I know. That horror! That truth no one can handle.
A truth to bring death.
   Alexandra Linares

The Firefighter Of Today

I am a firefighter of today,
please listen to what I say.

I may be the person who lives next door,
or someone you love and really adore.

Fire and emergencies are my bag,
I'm always in a hurry with no time to lag.

I'm a firefighter willing to risk it all,
I never refuse to answer the call.

From fires to haz mats, to wrecks on the street,
I do my job proudly and never retreat.

I know of this job there is no end,
The firefighter of today is really your friend.

The firefighter of today is a noble breed,
rugged and tough, but we still bleed.

Out in the cold or hot blazing sun,
I won't leave my post till the job is done.

And as the day comes when my life will end,
I pray of the Lord to heaven I'll ascend.

Remember these words as I go on my way,
please God! Protect the firefighter of today!
   Jack W. Simon

A Desire

Fill up the glass of my thirsty heart, O'Saki
by the magical drink from distant Madina
by the crude drink the fiery touch of which
Has redened the eyes of the whole world

The horizon's boundary acquired a new life full of enthusiasm
by the spirit of that drink
the dark and cold life submerged in despair
Get a new look by the brightness of that life

Make me drunk by that irresistible magnetism
Bake my existence by the naked flame of the desert
Spark that spontaneous fire and desire in my eyes
Inject in my blood and insert in my limbs of every joint
All the bounty of life reflecting the dazzling light of yours
May a storm brew to call the light.
   Akhtar Banu Bela

Time Travellers

I've always been intrigued with fascination
of time travel, being transported back hundreds of years or so,
if I could only plot a course to any given destination,
where would I venture? Maybe H.G. Wells would know.

Was Napoleon absorbed with madness? I wonder,
is history's portraying account accurate of Josephine;
nevertheless, they perished in a roar of thunder
and lost their crowns as king and queen.

Entering into another dimension I keep this in mind,
pioneers settled the new frontier, a wilderness not known,
so often I marvel, travelling through the boundaries of time,
picturing the glorious days of Rome.

To catch a glimpse of past scholars and inventors,
freezing time in a bottle, or the figments of one's imagination,
are all time travellers and great pretenders
with fantasy at the controls of navigation.
   Kevin Fisher

"A Golden Valley"

Swirling winds spin as gentle silken threads,
Their power entwines the golden morning mist,
Whistling Springtime winds slowly turn downward,
The winding winds embrace a deep valley so fair,
Springtime mist and somber winds are blessed and joined anew,
With God's blessing, they become a magical morning dew,
Deep Valley animal life forms are touched and slowly awakened,
Rabbits and other life forms are stirred to life by the dew,
A bold Bald Eagle soars above on high winds,
He slowly lifts and glides over the depth of the alley,
The Bald Eagle almost hovers as he travails heavenly winds,
A golden mist protects the creatures in a valley far below.
   Jack E. Kraai

Lonely Road

I have walked that lonely road,
I have carried that heavy load.
I have been and seen and done most everything.
That's not what it seems,
There's just too many dreams.
That's just what a lonely road can bring.
   W. Lovvorn Collins

Timber Harvest

My Land hurts
It's bruised and broken by the falling trees
The chainsaws
Aren't loud enough to cover up the Screams.

We all feel the pain
As Life leaves their Veins.

Slashed like a madman in the night
The Ground quivers with a horrible fright.

The animals run
The birds fly
What has man done
Tell us why.

I'm sad for my Land
Whose fate is in my hands.

Only by desperation
Is this situation.

Some will Live
To forgive.
Some will Die
And I'll always cry and cry.
  Martha Schmoe

Can Angels Cry?

Years of pain are filling my soul,
I am suffocating beneath an overflowing bowl.

I prayed to the heavens for answers and relief.
You have appeared next to me, I blink in disbelief.

Not really knowing why you are here,
I pull away and reject you out of fear.

Then a soft voice speaks to my heart,
Pulling me towards you, prodding to start.

Your arms are pulling me to your chest
Making my pain subside and lie down to rest.

I feel my dying soul begin to feel new life.
As my being eliminates the struggle and strife.

You must be the answer to my prayer,
Only an angel would take such a dare.

If I bare my blackened soul, I have to ask,
First and foremost before you take this task.

Can an angel feel pain?
Do they cry and cause the rain?

It must be so, it rained today,
And last night this angel heard me say...
  Kenneth J. Horton

Nature's Creature

Elegantly through the air,
  the wind blows her.

Splashing with brilliance,
  colors carry her.

Dancing around the world,
  nature has freed her.

Spreading beauty with every movement,
  we all believe in her.

For she is a butterfly,
  representing the magnificence of every woman.
  Bridgett Bonn

Roads Go Ever, Ever On

Roads go ever, ever on...
Through the woods and over snow.
Climbing the highest mountains
And running the farthest distance.
Roads go ever, ever on...

Roads go ever, ever on...
Through the hardest rains
And toughest winds together.
Roads go ever, ever on...

Roads go ever, ever on...
Through the swampiest mud puddle
you've ever seen.
Through the hottest deserts in the United States.
Roads go ever, ever on...

Roads go ever, ever on..
Through the roughest roads
Through the smoothest waters.
To our house where we eat at night
To our bed where we have pleasant dreams.
We know that roads go ever, ever on...
  Courtney M. Hodges

Splash

She meanders aimlessly
No goals to guide
No limits to prevent

She goes where she pleases
No one can divert her
Her aim is true

She gives life to those around her
And death to those who challenge.
In her contentment she is peaceful:
She breeds energy, drowsiness, freedom, and song.
In her anger she is feared:
She breeds craziness, panic, chaos, and horror.

In the end, she plummets
Downward, but not to death.
There, she bounces off the bottom
And lands with a different song.
There she starts anew.
  Rebecca M. Taylor

The Righteous Spirit

I'm here, I can run a mile before you take an inch,
I can please the soul and make the heart feel rich.
I have a voice and my direction will always be,
A straight and narrow road of peace and tranquility.
Behold I have strength, for none can compare to thee,
The riches I have for anyone who believes in me.
I am neither form nor matter, yet I'm very wise
But I come like the wind and will burn like fire.
I bring peace in a storm, erase miseries from all strife,
No harm will come to anyone, not even in your life.
I can comfort the comfortless, bring sight to the blind,
Heal the sick and can remove evil from the mind.
Perfectiveness is my perception, nothing more or less,
But I cannot do it if you have no interest.
I'll never refuse, no matter what my job may be,
My test of endurance I've past many times before ye.
Have faith and believe what this is saying is true,
Try me out and see, I'll guarantee I can please you.
  Sandra L. Heard

And Endless Dream

My heart has aged - into a solid mountain
filled with caves,
made of veins of pain and misery.

Giant boulders of once lovely impression,
now taunted memories,
of anger and rage.

Once silent streams of magic
raised roaring flashings — of a time
that could have been an endless dream.

Though am I dreaming
for where once—two hearts and crystallized
two hearts have torn apart.

As if quaking, sounds of thunder
beneath my feet
have split the ground
we have taken our vows upon.

Kirk L. Ames

Broken Ground

When your heart has lost its believing
And you feel the whole world is deceiving
You can't come to me...
You think no hope can be found
All you know is that sorrows abound
You can't come to me over broken ground

You think there won't come a dawn
You think all your choices are gone
You can't come to me...
Lost beneath a stone and a mound
Where the heart doesn't make any sound
You can't come to me over broken ground

If you wrap your heart up in grief
And deny your spirit relief
You can't come to me...
While the lightning strikes all around
And the thunder continues to pound
You can't come to me...
You can't come to me...
You can't come to me over broken ground

JoAnn Fore

Dreamland

I heard you laugh, I turned around,
  You were as pretty as pretty can be.
Right then and there, we were by ourselves
  In a dreamland you and me.
It was a land of no time,
  No place to be, no place to go.
It was a land of beauty
  Where the gentle breeze blows.
We walked across a bridge
  As a family of swans were shown.
They seemed to stop and look at you,
  A beauty far greater than their own.
As a rainbow stretched across the sky,
  Your smile made it true.
At the end of every rainbow is a pot of gold.
  At the end of this one was you.
The day was almost gone as we sat upon a hill.
  There was a sunset in the sky.
I held you close to me,
  And I wished to never say good-bye.

Chris Owens

Deep, Down Inside

Have you ever, thought about the love,
that somehow was lost, but not to God above.

You wonder, deep, down inside,
what you did, to make your love die.

You wish that he, never would have said,
the words that almost, knocked you over dead.

He did something, that he said he'd never do,
he broke your heart, and broke up with you.

You cried all day, and all that night,
because his love, had left your sight.

Why is love, so hard on you,
and why is it that, you are so confused.

No one can explain, the power of love,
and how much it hurts, when it flies away like a dove

For some reason, deep, down inside,
you just have a wish, to no longer be alive.

That is how I feel, deep, down, inside,
my heart screams for love, while tears fill my eyes.

Heather O'Bryan

Writer's Block

it used to be the emptiness of the white paper
wrapped snugly, smugly
around the smooth black roller
that laughed at me or pitied me
i never knew which.

writer's block knows no bigotry of electronic gender
for now it is the flat green of the screen
the monitor
watching my reflection stare back at me
with nothing to say
only a dare to enter letters
in forms of lexicons
which might come to meaningful expression
of questionable existence.

Salha E. Mishaan

Daughter

As many mistakes as a Daughter makes,
Dad always made sure I made my own,
He let me decide either right or wrong,
He just stood by my side,
To catch me either left or right,
Where I fell, he was there,
To pick me up and set me on my way, to take life day by day.

Daughter, Dad would say,
Either cry or laugh, walk or run,
Dad is here by your side,
In your heart always I'll stay,
Loving thought and memories too, dad will never go away.

Dad is looking down from up above,
Still standing by your side,
To hold you up when you cry,
To find that strength you have from way down inside,
Dad will never go away.

Just look way up above, see the brightest star,
It's me daughter, watching from above,
Dad will never go away.

Peggy McAlpine

Commercials

We have chewing gum with flavors,
Toothpaste with pizzazz
Fabric softeners with clean fresh smells,
C.D.'s of Rock and Jazz.

Mom has her Platex,
Dad has his Fruits of the Loom.
Baby has disposable diapers,
And the maid has an Angler broom.

Your cat has Tender Vittles, the dog's
After the Chuck Wagon Man.
Women can have beautiful eyes, and
Now anyone can get a tan.

You can buy Steel Radial tires that
Help you save on gas, the Glad Man has a
Tuff bag that can hold all your trash.

There will always be commercials,
To fit our every need of what we wear,
See, taste, smell, and even read.
Margaret M. Andersen

She Danced

She danced because the month was May,
And winter'd fled and spring had come—
A circus parading into town.

Two nights before, while she had slept,
Some fellow with a crazy brush
had painted tulips on her lawn.

And there were birds, inebriated
From over-tasting April rains.
That went a spinning bush to bush.

Now everywhere her foot-steps touched
A new green thread popped from the ground
To learn what life was all about.

What happened was an obdurate earth
Could not withstand her impudence
So mellowed finally to her love.

She kissed me once and then I knew
I was not old, and all my thoughts
Chased after hers in fantasy.
Forrest Kilbourn

To The Millions

To the millions who gave their lives away,
Wherever they happened to be that day.
Sent to battle for country or causes,
Most so young to die, among the losses.

What was the reward? A relief from fear,
A certain strip of land they held so dear?
For the dead, a cross, star, or monument,
Was it worth it? That is for argument.

Do not forget the millions who became
A part of the earth, sea, or ocean.
Can we not prevent millions more to come?
Can we not settle by some other game?

Think again! Millions of lives that did yield!
Father, mother, brother, sister, child, one
Forever gone, a memory to become.
Our day might come another battlefield?

We'll join with them in the mystery of death.
Time will fade away most memories that come.
The millions become one thought, one vision, one
That should remain with us till our final breath.
Ken McCambridge

Hear My Dream Arlene

A country field.
Frozen dew melts by noon.
Horses pull a wagon, carrying me and you.

Enough leaves left on trees, shades the angels view.
Warm North East wind, circles a picnic for two.

Magical land, replying canyons delay.
Carving into dust.
Hide en seek we play.

Pure truth is love, heart in heart.
Surrounding crystal rapids flow, over the cliff of rock.

Untold miles, mark ancient trails.
Tears from laughter scream.
After turning veils.

Forever forms, be tween hands.
Time loses value, over again.

A quarter moon. lanterns brightly shine.
Blackness fills the rest of night.

Toward home we glide.
Soon fast asleep.
I have never had, this much needed peace.
Lenie D. Burch

A Working Mother

I grow lonely with you in thought, for in body I am not there.
Can't put in words displeasure I've known for hours we could
   not share.
Together as mother and daughter ought to be, filling your idle time,
A widow, being mother and father, has no reason, has no
rhyme. I've watched you grow, from toddler to teen.
From blankets to levis, all this I've seen.
Baby cries of "Mommy, don't leave me" at the toddler age of three,
Have only changed to "I'm lonesome, Mother" now you're thirteen
   plus that three.
I'd love to give you sunny days, place roses in your path
But to toil, being a Mother & Father, is a widow's aftermath.
Marianne J. Sickle

The Villain In Me

Once in a while, I want to know
Which way to turn, which way to go
My mind starts spinning, shattering my pride
Escape from reality or run and hide

It's hard to discover this Stranger of mine
Outside He's cruel, inside He's kind
In a way I feel frightened, full of fear
And fading from the ones for whom I care

I use a high to elude my feel
But when I come down I know it's real
The pain and agony destroying my soul
Is the Master of Ceremonies, the leading role

To visualize myself or to just get away
I have to decide which way one day
I don't know what's happening although I should
I want to feel strong again if only I could

As I go on waiting for myself to unfold
I'm becoming more apt to be less bold
But remember the times we could have had
If only my soul wasn't feeling so bad
Rick Laney

Caterpillars To Butterflies

Forever more I had set aside my emotions for you, unaware of the fact the sleeping slumbers would be awakened. As the day breaks, the light is bright, my mind is clear, free from negative emotion and unbalanced thought!

A new day, beginning with grace and consciousness, enabling me to apply myself to the vast and important. Life is now elaborate. Time is no factor. Representation of one's self is no longer an issue.

Sharing is of no proclamation, it is understood, accepted, and welcomed. To speak of or to make mention of it is to cherish, for one to cherish one must treasure. The unveiling of the treasure has become a prize of prestige, and high esteem. Happiness and contentment are the rewards of the unveiling.

To say Thank You, is a mere gesture of great importance, said in a silent and bashful manner... Thus making all the truthfulness we know, which is unspoken, to be of such an entrepreneurial value. You searched and you found, and we have both been rewarded.

Belinda G. McConnell

My Cry

As I sit with in the sunshine
Enveloped in its rays
I can hear my lonely soul cry out
Amidst a hazy glaze
There is sorrow in my marrow
That protrudes into my heart
Tis the sorrow of the shy one
Who is set afar apart
I could cry into the breezes
And wail away the night
My emptiness is brutal
An abyss fills my sight
Where the crevices cry for a soul
And the bailing with the wailing only make me more annul
How I long for blessed beauty like the dew upon my lips
I imagine one with buckets filled with courage for my sip
But I have no bounty waiting
Or a beat to sooth my ache
So for all that I am staking
I will peace no more intake

Esther Bilyeu

Charis

You are the sparkle of the dew in the morning sun —
You are the soft wind that rustles the leaves and moves the branches.
You are the warm noon sun and the afternoon tranquility —
You are a sudden warm shower.
You are the brilliance of the colorful glow of the setting sun —
Bells ringing in your laughter at the evening chatter
And your eyes sparkle like the bright stars in the heavens.
You glow with the moonlight in the night, and your footsteps are as soft as feathered down
As you lay your beautiful self, with your head on the soft pillow —
To dream of wonderful things ahead —
Awaking with the energizing light upon you in the new day —
To start the song of your life again —
Leaving the warmth and joy of your presence wherever you go.

Lottie M. Szerlag

Untitled

The bluebird in the sky above,
  Sings songs of sweet celestial love.
But here below where I must live
  My song of love I truly give.
A score of years I count plus seven
  I've lived on earth but been in heaven.
If one should ask the reason true
  The answers is - I married you.

K. G. Van Wynen

Numb

You can look in my eyes but you'll never read my soul.
The stories deep within me are ones I've never told.
They creep up inside, fall out in a tear,
then get sucked back down with the drink of a beer.
I hear the tales of many, all their fears and all their woes,
the ones they always swear no one else will ever know.
They spill out their pain as they grasp their last limb,
and they see that distant light beginning to grow dim.
Life eats their flesh and blood, nothing left but skin and bones,
'til they bruise from a brush, not just the hit of sticks and stones.
You can't kiss away pain stored in a vault
of a child that pretends she's already an adult.
It's in her, it is her, it is who she has become,
But there is no need to worry - she's already become numb...

Kimberly Gronemeyer

The Silence

The wind may not be held in our hands, or stored in a box,
To do so, it would no longer be the wind,
nor may we hold onto or confine the love of another.
Like the wind, its beauty comes from passing over us allowing us to feel,
to feel its freedom
and yet, it can never die,
for in its silence, it is always around us
to stir again at a moment's notice.

James E. Walton Jr.

Why

I made a new friend last year you see,
a kind and gentle person who was special to me.

She was sick as though it seemed,
and what happened to her I never dreamed.

On a morning in July she just happened to die.
Now every night I cry, why oh why did she have to die?

No one knows what she meant to me,
I loved her dearly as can be.

Why she had to leave I do not know,
I just wish she did not have to go.

I wish I would not have to
cry and that she did not have to die.

Again I cry, why oh why did she have to die?
  Why?

Jennifer N. Schooley

Farewell To A Friend

He was loving, faithful, kind and sincere
And he loved every moment of his short lived years
He was loved and gave love with all his heart
To someone who adored him from the very start
My heart was broken when he had to leave
For his absence I shall always grieve
He was strong, beautiful and my best friend
I loved him dearly till the very end.
I know he suffered and he surely had pain
He could not talk, so he could not explain.
He was not a person, but my best friend
Part Boxer, part Dane and his name was Duke
Duke's name was appropriate in every way
He was a joy to me every day.
In my heart he will always remain very dear
And my love for him will never cease
Farewell, my friend, may you rest in peace.

Agnes Maher

Untitled

I'm tired of this "Mothering Thing"
The parent of three!!
Two "shes" and a "he"!!!
And Birds-eye and Curitys!!!

I'm tired of this "Mothering Thing"!!!
When young, it was cool
Kids' books a great tool
Now God!!! Help them all finish school!!

Let's talk... 'bout this "Mothering Thing"
They're "married!!..." All three!!
It's "ecstatic" for me!!
The future looks bright and "rosy."

I'm "loving" this "Mothering Thing!""
"Grand-mother" you see
Three "hes" and two "shes"
Thank God!!...."He" gave them to "me".

Gerry Emery

My Thoughts On Being With You Forever Wherever

Whether near or far,
I want to be where you are!
Like peas in a pod or birds of a feather,
I'm all yours - in foul or fair weather!
Like Heckle and Jekyll and Wile E. And Road Runner,
I know life without you would be a "Real Bummer!"
North or South, East, or West,
Wherever you are, that's the best!
Wherever we wonder, wherever we roam,
May we always be together at a place we call home!

In conclusion:
  If you choose to follow your dream
  I'm with you all the way.
  For without pursuing or trying
  You'll always wonder if you could have had it,
  Because I know with you and your love
  I now have everything I ever dreamed of!

Diane Y. Homan

Untitled

Chilly evening walk
My jacket on her back
Silent thoughts
The petals of a flower
She loves me, she loves me not
It doesn't matter
An old flame
She slowly dwindles
Until she is the flicker of a candle in my wind

Danny Groner

Help Needed

I don't care anymore,
what I want is at the Liquor Store.
Mom, and Dad, why haven't you noticed,
can't you see I've lost my focus,
my grades are down, I don't do
homework anymore.
My only thoughts are at the Liquor Store.
My dad, please rescue me,
I can't think straight,
I can't concentrate.
There's a monkey on my back,
Mom, Dad, that's a fact.
Help me Dad, help me Mom,
don't let me become an alcoholic bum.

Lenora Brockington

Following A New Path To Home

I almost lost my mind at a home for the damaged mentally,
but hugging a Standing Person, a tree in the yard,
helped me cling to some stability,
I almost lost my life at a home for the damaged mentally;
because feeling so trapped; and being treated so badly;
started me thinking that death was the only answer for me;
but I was given inner strength from sacred Spirit Bear;
and the scared Pathfinder, Spirit Wolf,
offered me medicine his courage;
so before I slipped down into dangerous despair;
I was able to follow Spirit Wolf
down a new path to a new home;
where I no longer feel desperate and all alone.
The people at the home for the damaged mentally,
tried hard to take away my spirit and my dignity;
but before that happened, I found a new home
and the friendship of a gentle beagle;
and now I am soaring far away from my tormenters with Sacred Eagle.

Candyce King

Sonnet For My Son

You are gone. Time dulls the searing grief
Of sudden death; but never ever does your absence go
Unnoticed. My hidden ache is not allowed to show:
Concealed, controlled, unspoken. "Gone," the world's belief.
What man would you have been? Death like a thief
Has stolen years of mine to watch you grow,
To hear your voice turned deep, to touch, to know
With pride whatever your success, how great or brief.
No act of mine can alter sorrow's face.
Accept what is. Have hope in what's to be.
Time moves along; its ever even pace
Will not change, nor hurry just for me.
I long to join your spirit: so the grief erase.
But I must wait, for none can rush eternity.

Mildred Sanda

Inside Me

He thought he'd never be
noticed he thought he'd never be heard.
He knows not the power but he knew the pain, the life
of a rock star and years and years of fame!

He screamed and singed for a crowd full of losers.
He touched souls and scared
them for life the light for the
losers and a place to put the pain.

Two shots no more no less he laid down to
die and when he reached his grave his head was high.

His power our strength we felt it all when he sang
we all knew every thing had changed.

The man who stole the
souls of every one who listened would rather
play alone in his own world but it could never happen.

We asked the question that will never be answered,
some say it's in the music but it's really the question.

The taste of the music
he made for this world powerful screaming is
waiting for everyone in the next one.

Anna Kreutzer

Breathe

God, how you must hate me when
I am behaving like
some lost and whimpering child
pinning myself to your coattails
desperately clinging to your every word
searching for some hidden meaning in each metaphor
drowning in my urgency
waiting for you to throw me a life jacket
while you would rather stand on the shore and
watch me die
   Ronda L. Kennedy

Untitled

If I were a snowflake, I'd free fall from the sky
From the heavens above, falling past your eyes

In a world so cold, hovering in the air
Awaiting death, this beauty so rare

Causing no sound, when I land at last
This tender moment, ending so fast

As the memories end, as I melt away
I've found the cold, of the tears as I lay

Turn to see, what I did create
It's crystal clear, if it's not too late

It's already done, it's already true
In my mind, just me and you

Here I go again, as the feelings come back
I get swept up in your eyes, and lose track

You've got to know, everything I do and say
Everything for you, to ensure you get your way

As my dreams fade, that only you can make
I still have my visions, If I were a snowflake.
   Lake Oliver

Memories

That certain place that certain time
Deep inside you you're sure to find

A special moment you hold forever
in your heart you'll always treasure

It's that thought you think of when you look inside
Its value is priceless, its time you'll never hide

It's so clear and real and so ever dear
When you feel those thoughts will never disappear

I guess that's what it's all about
Moments, places, life and time
It's that place in your heart
When you're lost, you will always find

It seems to reach within you
as far and deep as oceans
It makes you try to understand
All those in depth emotions

No matter what you need to feel
They can make you laugh and sometimes cry
They seem to come and go inside you
Although...they'll never say good-bye
   Tracy J. McMahon

Something

If I were to express something, something that said it all;
It would be something I wrote, something I feel,
something I am, something I'm not;
something I expressed in my own way that all writers express
as an interpretation of the many or singular aspects of life.
It would be something being that of just a thought;
Or something in each one of us that personally makes me feel alive;
Something that laughs, something that hurts;
Something that helps my soul to bleed.
It would be whatever a written work could be;
Something universal, something esoteric,
something emotional, something blank.
It would be something I'm capable of expressing,
and perhaps something others can appreciate.
It would be something jovial yet something sad.
With God's blessing it would be something divine.
Without, it would be something humble.
Whatever it would be, everyone who reads it would think of it,
as Something.
   Christopher P. Rogers

Dawn Through The Eyes Of The Blind

As I sit on my porch in the early dawn,
I hear the stillness of the morn.

But I see nothing.

I smell it freshness, a dewey wet smell,
And its bitter taste in my mouth.
I feel the cool breeze against my cheeks.

But I see nothing.

And then, out of nowhere,
A warmth comes over me,
At first, only slight, but then
A blast that awakens the world!
I taste the sunshine,
A warm, fresh taste.
And the smell,
A mix of new grass and other sweet scents.

But I see nothing.

I hear the birds chirping their morning song
And the wind ruffling the leaves
As I sit on my porch, in the early dawn thinking:
Oh, how I wish I could open my eyes and see!
   Jennifer Wanamaker

The Price Of Love

Every time I see him in the halls,
My heart whispers to me,
Telling me what to feel.
My heart tells me I love him,
So my mind feels the same.
I'm afraid of him finding out my feelings,
So I keep them to myself.
A foolish thing for me to do.

I see him at a dance one day
With another girl.
I should have told him about me.
Too late now; my heart is broken.

I'll never love again
All because of one certain male.

The things love does to you...
   Rebecca Zink

An Invitation To A Unicorn's Delight

In the garden in the full moon light
I danced with the Silver Unicorn tonight.
His golden eyes sparkled and I laughed with glee
As we waltzed to the music of a band unseen,
Past the blue roses to a cave of light
Lined with crystals illuminating the night.
From the inside drifted the sweet smell of spice
And we entered to find a Unicorn's delight.
A couple of friends and a warm cup of tea,
A crackling fire and plenty of gossiping.
A Rainbow Dragon, Snow-white Pegasus,
And a small bearded Gnome
Exchanging story after story of far off places known as home.
The night grew tired, and daylight awoke
I found myself in bed, beside me — a note
Inviting me to tea, the company of magical friends,
And a little gossiping
When daylight is done, and the night has come.
  Kelly Robinson

You're All I Need

Seeing you again...was not what I had planned
Until that day you reached out your hand
Your loving face staring at me once again
The true feelings in my heart could not pretend

I wasn't looking for true love
But once again you were looking at me
You're the only one I can think of
You're the only one I can see
Is it all in my mind? Because
It seems so hard to believe
You're all I need

Guess it's true...we've all been hurt before
It may be a chance I'm taking but,
It always comes to this
If it isn't love we're making
I don't know what it is

As I look up to the sky...there aren't any stars out tonight
But we are shining our own bright light
And it's never felt so right for
You're all I need
  Chris DeGuise

My Mother

My mother is known as "Mom"
  to many relatives, friends, and neighbors.
"The neighborhood mom"
  Who was always there for everybody.
All the good times we shared
  the ball games in the back yard.
Teaching us games, spoons, and
  hide-the-thimble was a favorite.
All the Sunday dinners and desserts.
  Whether you came for a visit or a chit-chat
Mom made sure you left with a full stomach.
  The time she spent
Sewing, embroidering, gardening, farming, and being "mom".
  to all the laughter and love she gave.
A wife, mother, and grandmother
  who received the "crown of life."
Gone but not forgotten
  cherished memories last forever.
    We love you and miss you, Mom!
  Linda Lee Ewell

Reflections

While walking along this lonely road
I think of all the times gone past.
  The times of sorrow and often stress
The good and the bad we all have had.
  Life is not perfect - it's not meant to be
But there is someone up there watching over me.
  We must hold our heads high and go on with a sigh.
For life is a game that we all must complete,
  So get on with it, go on down the street.
Fulfill your life and make it complete.
  Dolores Summers

If We Could

If we could only listen with our hearts,
instead of our ears.
I know we'd be surprised at the things we could hear
We would understand emotions never spoken
We could hear the sound of a heart that is broken
I know we'd be surprised to hear sounds of joy
We would understand excitement of a new toy.

If we could only listen with our hearts,
instead of our ears
I know we'd be surprised at the things we could hear
  Marsha Beck-Hathcock

After The Storm

My heart doth pine for summer days,
For pleasant walks o'er rocky ways,
For the burning sun upon the sand,
And the bright green carpet about the land.

For the daisies with their hearts of gold,
Nodding and swaying to the locusts bold,
For the many songbirds overhead,
And the lulling sea as I go to bed.

You like winter and its sport,
And the season seems much too short.
Mother Nature does her share
To make for us all a world so fair.

Her winter glories were bestowed on thee,
But her summer ecstasies were meant for me.
  Phyllis H. Jones

What's Cookin'

Sometimes I wonder if I'm not alone
Or do others have this "cook book syndrome"?
Wouldn't it be great to have a cook book complete,
With all my favorite recipes, oh what I feat!

I have a dozen for main dishes, you know,
At least four more to make only bread dough.
Cookie books galore, will they never stop?
Loaded with calories, forget the dress shop!

As elk season gets near, my son will call,
Are the oatmeal and chocolate chip ready for fall?
Should I look in the card file or in a book,
I'm getting older just deciding where to look.

It was easy for grandma, it was all in her head,
"A little molasses, butter and pinch of salt," she said.
She didn't need a cook book to make apple pie,
Biscuits and gravy or pork chops to fry.

Young people are smart, don't have a card file,
But browse a minute, in the frozen food aisle,
Then on to the deli to get them a cake,
"Don't turn on that oven, cause we don't bake".
  Alice J. Holt

Untitled

Dear soul mate . . .
  Countless stars shine at night
  Giving us their primal light.
They tell me of you . . .
  Come mornings dawn bright daily sun
  Sets too soon the day is done.
Life tells me of you . . .
  To gentle rest as shadows fall
  You are my mind while night winds call.
I tell myself of you . . .
  Alone to dream, to pray, then sleep
  My open heart for you to keep.
You tell me of you . . .
All love . . . Joy . . . And peace.
Donald Bangle

Time

All the leaves have fallen; pairs are some and lone are others.
Time has no place, yet it has touched all.

Hurry and find the end of the Season.
The pairs separate and yet, find each other for no reason.

Has it been long since they separated, or has it been yesterday,
and no one remembers the Season?
Judith A. Departo

Grandfather's Time

With time on my hands and no place to go,
I was able to babysit my Granddaughter
who has such a loving glow.
We sat on the living room floor to learn 1, 2, 3, 4.

At the age of one, I tried to make learning fun.
With flash cards and letters
she learned each one by one.
As time went by and she became two
she was learning more and more while having fun too.

We played at times just for fun.
Jumping was fine, sometimes we would run.
Then a ride on the swing and down the slide
she would get tired then we would go inside.

She was still with me when she became three
she had learned so much I was filled with glee.

Then 1, 2, 3, A, B, C, her Mom and Dad had to take her from me.
No more learning on the living room floor,
because my Granddaughter is now almost four
and nursery school is the place to be.

Oh how I wish she was still with me.

By Sara's Papa
John L. Ward

Love's Lesson

Two people bump into each other.
They were the best of friends and lovers,
Yet they are now strangers.
She asks "Are you happy?"
He replies "I am content."
She smiles a bittersweet smile, understanding.
They turn and walk in opposite directions,
Each in their own thoughts...
"She taught me how to love."
"He taught me how to be alone."
Michele Newcome

Happy Birthday

Dear Dad,
Elephants can act proud and stomp around,
  but they cannot see what's on the ground!

Dogs can bark and chase and chew,
  but they can't say words like, "I love you!"

Sure, kittens can purr and cuddle and play,
  but they can't make a smile to brighten your day!

Birds can chirp and soar in the sky,
  but they'll never be your friend and say "Hi" or "Bye!"

Now, I've got the one that's right for you,
  just close your eyes and don't be blue...

The thing that meets your every need
  is your family (and it's also me!)

So, drop the birds and dogs and cats,
  don't let the elephant make you one of his tracks!

Grab a hand and join the fun,
  for Birthdays are special when you're the one!
Happy birthday!!!
Sasha Runne

"The Heart Of A Lion"

When the sun falls beyond the horizon—
  only a memory of things that happen are left.
Sometimes things that can be destroyed are left unharmed.
Sometimes it is the imagination that defends a coward.
If it is pride that kills a man?
If it is dignity that a man posses?
  Then we are engulfed in it.
There is a man—
a man who has forgotten pity,
a man who feels no pain.
This man fears no one, yet respects all.
He bothers no one, for only God exists.
And so it is that to him the world is but a thing.
He'll live a thousand years and shall have no remorse.
For fate will unwind as it must—
and no more.
Esteban Gone

I Am A Shark

I am a shark swimming along.
I am a shark with no song.

I always wondered what it would be like,
to be up there and see the light.
But, when it comes to dinner time,
I like to feed on any kind.

I always wondered what it would be like,
to walk around on human feet.
Instead of swimming in the deep.
James T. Gilmore

The Lodestar

Somewhere between Cairo and Jupiter,
Beneath the twinkling canopy of twilight,
Beyond the harbors of hyperbole,
Where mortality meets eternity;
I travelled across a Saharan Sea.

Impotently navigated by steed,
I galloped onward, freely:
Upon my Rocinante,
Where I, a gypsy passenger
On a pilgrimage bound for recovery,
Was drawn by the inertia of love's discovery.
Eduardo Alejandro Polon

In The Garden

To speak is to die a little
To reveal is to leave yourself open to the darkness
   that comes in the guise of light
So close your mouth, observe your surroundings
   and don't give in to fright
Silence, the voice of a woman in fear
A woman who has lost count of her tears as she stood waiting
   by the road for her faith
But he never came
Now, only the promise of making things new remains
Just out of sight, but not out of reach
Life has yet some things to learn from her,
   life has yet some things to teach
She will take on the challenge
With only a weakened intuition to depend upon and the Lord's mercy,
   she will prevail
And loudly she prayed
"Lord have mercy on me and on all of these women you have put on
   this earth not for themselves, but for *his* pleasure...
   ...remember *she* did not ask to be in the garden."
Bianca I. Gonzalez

Anticipation

I planted a violet seed in the soil,
A small, round, yellow seed.
It had abundant sunlight and water,
And I took care of it tenderly,
Like one would take care of a baby hamster.
I waited and waited patiently,
But the first leaf did not come out.

Every day I looked hopefully
At the dark, black soil,
Expecting to find a single trace of green.
But days went by,
And the black soil stared back at me blankly.

Then suddenly, one day
When I was observing it again,
There it was, a petite little leaf,
Bright green and delicate,
With tiny white hairs rising from its surface.
T'was the most beautiful thing I've ever seen;
The result of my hard work,
The prize of my attending.
Berachah Lui

My Mother

How can I repay my mother
For the countless things she has done,
To make sure I had all I needed
Plus lots of things just for fun?

How can I repay my mother
For sacrifices she made,
For all the hard work she did through the years
And all of the prayers that she prayed?

My mother has given so much of her life
All I know of is just a small part.
I cannot repay my mother,
But I can thank her with all my heart.
Lisa Norris Jones

The Chat (Boothside Version)

       You there? (stifling a yawn)
       I've been thinking. (rolling her eyes)
Let's quit this nonsense. (a flicker of interest brightens her
       expression, briefly)
       Really. (she smiles, anticipating)
       Don't forget (what? she begs)
We can't have it all (sighing longer than necessary)
    But it'd sure be nice if (arching an eyebrow)
Oh, never mind. (grasping his wrist, shaking gently)
   (pausing to look away) You make everything so
      (what? He wonders) Complicated.
       (outraged) Seriously!
(yanking his wrist free from her hold) I really don't want "it all"
      (grumbling) Whatever "it all" is.
      (nodding, mocking) Can't we just...
      (he stares intently, eagerly) Be together?
(clutching her outstretched palm) I want this to work.
      So do I. (relieved, overjoyed)
(desiring her embrace, moving closer)
         (beaming, reaching arms around him)
     (in the silence they smile)
Maria M. Oberg

A Woman's Miserable Curse

As the door closed behind him - I wept.
In rushing second I feel all promises I kept.
He walks and I cry wondering why enough it never is.
Heated by frustration, hard as coal is his.

Chance after chance he's given, I've done the tour.
Awaiting the few moments he'll reach out, secure.
All the time I dare not ask, just a few in between the sore.
Lashing out mistaking me, pushing the very core.

Small moments meaningful, touches of affection I pray.
Instead my feelings and thoughts alone - and by one I lay.
Very few the times and frail I live off what he tosses down.
Once I never begged, for his attention did abound.

Day by day I wait, meeting his needs and wants.
Hoping that by curing his, he'll heal my heart.
Waiting for his touch, affection sharing a devotion.
Security of loving I crave, lending vouch for attraction.

I give my soul, my heart, my trust and yet feel so small.
And when he needs? I'm there at his beck and call.
Intensely I feel with him, I give myself completely.
Why? Because he looks at me once and then smiles sweetly.
Katrina Payne

Nature's Mad Cry

From lightning came thunder and soon there was rain
Vast and complete, in torrents it came
No water of love came down from the sky
But tears of wrath from Nature's mad cry

Rain, relentless, roaring, enraged
Comes not to make fertile the earth to assuage
It stings and lashes and whips at my eyes
And rolls and claps in contempt of my sighs

Most demonic of nights and malevolent storm
Cares not if I'm dry, in comfort and warm
It rears and hisses then lunges and bites
Drenching me weary and sullen...alone in dark night
Paul Deveau

Night Song

In the silence of the night
I listen for your voice
But darkness is the only sound I hear
Still I feel your presence near.

As the night closes in
I feel a need for Freedom
From the silence that is night.

I need a Night Song
To help my spirit soar
To lift me from the darkness
And feel the warmth of light

A vale of darkness covers me
It chills my heart and soul
So suddenly does the silence break
A ray of light from your soul reaches out to me

As the night gives way to the dawn
I feel my soul give in reaching for the light from your heart

I feel your Night Song reaching out to me
To pull me from the darkness
Into your loves warm light.

LeeAnn MacWilliam

Wood Storks

On the ground,
A few old men
Playing at chess or checkers,
Surrounding the board of the marsh pool,
Black shoulders hunched,
Bespectacled beaks,
Contemplating the next move.

In flight, such beauty!

The day the gold green marsh was Spring;
Massive clouds fringed the perimeter of our horizon,
Deep blue overhead.
The sour sweet essence of the marsh stifled by the motor's fumes.
We sputtered through the channel while, all around,
Flights of white birds rose in flowing, convex lines;
Then, wheeling, turning black against the azure sky; then
turning once again, they showered apple blossoms as they
   sought the ground.

Diane Klingenstein

To Be

To be submerged in serenity.
To be embraced by time.
To be in the waves of water.
To have peace in mind.
To be completely and totally free, for what
I am, I am proud to be.
Contemplating the moments in life,
achieving the goals that I strive.
I am but one of many whose eyes can see
of what is really meant to be.
To feel me for I am the wind.
To hear me for I am the waves.
To smell me for I am the air.
To touch me for wherever you are,
I will also be there.
Walk with me and hold my hand,
letting our feet become subdued in the sands.
Life and love will sometimes come together,
just as eternity was meant to last forever.
What is it that you see, for it is me I am to be.

F. M. Cooper

The Soul In Me

Made from the finest pine,
polished to a bright glow,
and delicately lined
with satin soft as snow.
Very grateful I am to be,
adorned with flowers just for me.

But what is the problem?
I do not understand.
Why do my visitors
approach with trembling hands?
With tear-stained cheeks and feelings unleashed,
they utter moanings like savage beasts.

Carefully lowering
through a long, narrow shaft,
they stand o'er hovering
while dirt creates my mask.
In the darkness now we lie,
damp and cold, a corpse and I.

Melissa Huynh

A Special Lady

She is a special lady,
She is a strong minded woman with a loving heart.
She takes care of business.
She gets the job done.
She is an active person.
She is a mother, a grandmother, and great
grandmother rolled up into one for me.
She cared for a baby who grew up in a wheel chair.
She loves me.
She is always there.
She gave me a happy childhood.
She wiped the tears from my eyes when I was sad.
She spanked me when I was bad.
She is my greatest fan.
I love her so much.
She is a special lady.
This special lady I speak of is my great grandmother.
She is number one.

Jennifer Marie Burns

My Mind Went Blank

I think I'll write a silly poem I said to myself today.
But when I tried to think of one, I didn't know what to say.
I thought and thought and couldn't even come up with a rhyme,
So I sat and pondered about it all, for quite a long, long time.
I tried to think of something funny, but nothing came to mind.
I even looked in magazines, to see what I could find.
Something that would jog my mind, and help me think this through.
But nothing comes into my mind, no matter what I do.
So here I sit, just like the thinker, (except I'm wearing clothes).
Trying to think of something funny, that nobody else knows.
I'm sure you'd laugh at me real hard, if you'd see inside my brain.
The cogs are trying hard to turn, ... My goodness, what a pain!
I guess I'll have to quit and rest, but only for a minute,
And read this over so I can see if there's anything funny in it.
Well, here I am back again, you didn't miss me did you?
I still haven't thought of any jokes,
I'm beginning to get rather blue.
So I guess I'll have to give this up, and try a later time.
Maybe I'd better go to school -
   and learn...
      how to be...
         a Mime.

Charlene Emmerich

Grand Kids

Like a good ole recipe
the many ingredients you'll find
Like a furry kitten engrossed with a soft
Ball of twine.
Like a man of knowledge
thinking with his thoughts he so inclined,
all of these descriptions make up these
grand kids of mine.

Like the recipe they are a mixture of him
and her and us, like the kitten with the
twine, over them I make such a fuss.
Like the thinking man full of knowledge, for
their future we'll save and pray, may our
God bless and keep them my grand kids
forever and always.

Bennie Ruth McFall

An Exceptional Teacher

To the world you maybe just a teacher,
but to me, you are a true hero.
You threw me a life line to hope,
because on my own, I couldn't reach her.

You gave me encouragement.
Then sent me on my way
which planted a seed of confidence,
that grew more and more each day.

I want to say thank you;
for all that you've given to me.
You are one of a special few,
and making a difference you knew the key.

Some teachers are very exceptional
they've been given a special sight,
to be able to show someone the love of knowledge
is like giving the blind the beauty of light.

Jackie Carr

Maple Trees, My Friends

   Maple trees, maple trees everywhere,
help me breathe oxygen through the air.
   Big ones, little ones everywhere,
all of them beautiful, all of them care.
   Red leaves, orange leaves, yellow ones too!
These trees house the animals and the food that they chew
   Maple trees, maple trees everywhere,
they're my friends and I sure do care.

Christopher Cruz

The Jewel

Ya one could search a lifetime for this jewel
I hold within my soul, it's color of the
rainbow and O' they glitter so.

This warmth within is sunshine, and
happiness the glow, for deep within its facets
its magic n'er let me go.

O' hard I try to describe it, I do it justice not,
for this jewel has been with me O' these
many, many years, and n'er, has lost its glow.

I know of not a safer place that I could keep
it tho', than deep within this soul of mine
for now and ever more.

This jewel of which I speak ye now,
Darling wife of mine, I do love you so.

My Jewel of Life

Raymond G. Harnden

One Last Kiss

One last kiss
One last goodbye
Before he disappears into a darkening sky

One last kiss
One last embrace
He carefully studies the lines of her face

Held close in his arms
She never wants to let go
There's so much each wants the other to know

She swallows her pain
He boards his plane

Just one last glimpse
One last good-bye
He won't allow himself to cry

Just one last kiss
One quiet sigh

Just one last time
they say good-bye

Kristin Perrone

Starving

Victim!
They are all victims!
Screaming, bloating, crying, wailing, calling for help!
Tears burn as acid -
falling
falling
streaming from frightened eyes.
Thin arms reach...stretching to grasp
something invisible like hope, life...a drink of water!
Life and death on opposite sides of a thin line.
Cries and screams soften - slowed as a clock
weak on winding power.

Spiraling
down
down
down.
Soon...quickly now, all sound, all ticks
of the heart...the earthly clock will
cease to be heard.
(Time has run out.)

Beverly Morrissey

Someday

Someday I will find,
   all the answers I'm looking for
Someday I will be,
   Exactly what I want to be
Maybe not today or tomorrow, but
Someday there will be an end to my sorrow.

Someday I will find,
   the person I'm looking for
Someday she will come along,
   and I will know
Maybe not today or tomorrow, but
Someday she will show.

Someday I will find,
   all the pieces to my puzzle
Someday I will find,
   all my dreams coming true
Maybe not today or tomorrow, but
Someday they all will follow.

John Murray

Love

Happiness? Pride? Faith?
What is love?
It's a feeling most people think they have.

Pain? Sorrow? Emptiness?
That's true love.
Unlike many people I can describe my feelings.

Love.
This is what I feel.
And it hurts.

For there are those who know they feel love.
Just to let them know,
They're not alone.

Someone will help...
God is
Love.

Gennifer LaVante

Grandmother's Wisdom

The wisdom that lies in my grandmother's eyes
She told me I'd have it only I try.

The world is cruel, she said to me
But open your eyes to see how good it can be.

Take the path very few travel
For life is a weave you cannot unravel.

Life is a mixture of sunshine and rain
In order to have strength you must have pain.

The world owes you nothing I hear her say
She gives to those who earn their own way.

Friends are a gift you cannot buy
To have many you really must try.

Always be grateful for what God has give
Be full of kindness and always forgiving.

Gain all the knowledge the world has to give
For knowledge is the wisdom you see in my eyes.

Danielle Rutter

Like A Rose...

Like a rose, we are born
We grow with each ray of light
Thirsting for more each day
And drooping our heads at night.

Like a rose, we are strong
We stand proud and tall
We are all buds of life
From the big to the very small.

Like a rose, we have beauty
We are admired for who we are
Not one of us is like the other
We are each our own star.

Like a rose, we slowly fade
To end our journey on earth
Yet like a rose, we have more blooms
To continue our traditions at birth.

Like a rose, we die
We are remembered for each hug and kiss
And like the rose, we go away
Yet we know our presence will be missed.

Kimberly Brannan Dixon

Mealtime For An Osprey

High on a perch, way up in the tallest tree,
I sit still and stare, waiting, oh so patiently.

The chirping sound of downy fuzz echoes in the breeze,
I scratch my head, hold on tight, and release a tiny sneeze.

Keeping the waters within my sight,
I remiss how it was on a freedom flight.

A brazen master of the sky, not caring of my fate,
Making dives spontaneously, to show off for my mate.

But I'm now the proud father of young ones nearby,
I must remain here and answer their hungry cry.

Scanning the waters down below, searching for a fish,
Is that a ripple? My target? Yes, it's time to grant my wish.

I keep my prey in view, as he swims with all his might,
I almost taste his flesh, and know we'll dine tonight.

I flap my wings, now make the dive, and soar down through the air,
I take the plunge, pursue the catch, and grip it with such flair.

Ripping my talons into his back, proves that I have won,
He struggles hard to no avail, and knows his day is done.

I ascend up high filled with pride, and the battle has been fought,
Homeward bound I must fly, to triumph what I've caught.

Sharonjeanne Burgess

My Dream

I didn't know about our Savior,
   till I was a teenager you see.
My aunt told me all about Jesus
   and how I could live with him eternity.

I had a dream soon after I was told,
   I was walking down a country road.
It was oh so dark and dreary,
   and I was very weary.
All at once I saw a light,
   it was real bright.
I looked up in my Saviour's
   face, it was all aglow -
He said come, my child, hold
   my hand, I'll show you the way to go-

I wish everyone could have a
   dream like mine, and hold Jesus hand too.
I want to line with our Saviour,
   in that wonderful promise land don't you?

P. Lucille Crigler

Mother's Blessing

We all have a blessed mother,
her heart is filled with a mothers love.
She seems to know just what to do,
that's her gift from God above.
A mother utters many silent prayers
that we know nothing of.
But God hears every one of them
and she's blessed from heaven above.
She's a blessing to her family,
and to everyone she meets.
She has a special role on earth
her love makes her job complete.
Today we honor our mothers,
those here and in heaven above.
Thank God for his wonderful blessing
the gift of a mother's love.

Emma Brown

The Feeling Tree

Quiet.
Non-disruptive.
Inspiring and loved by most.
Sitting motionless under a tree it demonstrates peacefulness.
The leaves on the tree sound as though they are whispering.
A brown jagged tree trunk propped me upright.
The tree is a treasure chest full of life.
People can do many things beneath the shade of a tree.
Talking about emotions and the way people feel.
Loving in such a way people can be mysterious creatures.
The sky and ground make a magnificently painted picture.
Always happy under the tree.
Crying it knows not, whining it doesn't do, only listening and waiting.
Never sleeping, always supporting, the tree will always be there for me.

Lorena April Reynolds

Living Life HIV

Loneliness for children I can't have
Insecure about financial, emotional support
Victory for the day of the Cure!
In need of love, compassion, comfort
Neglect, negativity from complete strangers
Going on with my life.

Living life day to day
Intend to life 4-ever
Fighting to stay alive and well
Eager to be Alive when The Cure is Found.

Helpless but very hopeful
In constant hope and prayer for a Cure
There Will Be A Cure 1-Day.

Dianna James

Animal Magnetism

The Wolf's cry is echoing
From depths within its soul
Searching endless roads of fate
Once was lost, His life's soulmate.
His mournful sound is reaching
For the moon tonight
Joining their two destined lives
Through energy and light.

Survival is their war of truth
The rising sun will lead
Their lost and hungry aching hearts
Upon each other feed.

The ground beneath, they've traveled far
Calling moons above
Weaving thoughts unspoken, their harmony is one.
The day will come, their paths to cross,
innate within their souls, it's in their eyes,
their scent, their breath, their instincts will unfold.

Survival was their guiding path, led by stars beyond,
survival is their war of truth, destined by their bond.

Kortney K. Harwood

Whispers

Sweet as the sound of a soft, gentle heart
Soothing, eternal, as the night is dark
Together as one, when you are near
The tender kisses, your whispers, in my ear

Flowing as stream, on a golden autumn morn
Loving, caring, as when a child is born
Warm and so peaceful, when you are near
Our bodies embraced, your whispers, in my ear

Mark Hanson

A Fine Happy Home

A fine happy home, is the one that shows love,
To all those who live there, to all those who stay.
There's love in the work and there's love in the play.
And when we wake up, just to see the new day,
The great quiet morning unfolds, it's own way.
In sunshine, or fog, or if rain finds the day,
We look at each other with sleep in our eyes,
And quietly speak, of the new day with love.
We know there is breakfast and dressing and such.
We know we will work, and we know we will play.
A fine happy home is the one where I'll stay.

Mary C. Walker

Romancing The Rain

A woman's hair, an apple tree,
Look better now, when nature's free.

The rain comes down, like watery bliss,
Young children play, within the mist.

The thirsty fields,
The empty lakes, their thirst is gone,
The rain did slake.

A flower girl, all full of glee,
With golden hair, approaches me.

She takes my hand, and off we go,
We're dancing here,
within the flow.

And when we stop,
I steal a kiss,
She answers back,
I enter bliss.

The rain clears up,
that wasn't long,
I look around,
the girl is gone.

Lord Laurence E. Rector

Especially For You - Vivian

Dark eyes, kind and shining bright,
Hair reflecting the moon's silver light;
A smile of warmth, God's gift to men
Is this delicate beauty - Vivian.

A very kind and generous heart,
Has this tiny work of art;
Her company enjoyed again and again,
So delightful is little - Vivian.

But, "Who is Vivian?" many ask,
To answer is only a small task;
She is dearer to me than any other,
Little Vivian is my - Mother.

Diana E. Dalton, January 20, 1964

Untitled

Beads of sweat form on my flesh
like the night before when
our souls were intermeshed
two lovers free in spirit
Dancing is eternity
Immortalized forever in a memory
Escaping today's pain in the dim of the night
And so now they're off for a mystical flight
the time has come for them to be together
to be captured in a fragment of
the spirit world forever together

Jhone Hayden

"Broken Heart"

I harbour the angst of my tormented soul.
Love unfulfilled - the one I let go.
Paradise unrecognized 'til the bitter end.
Remorse and a hard life lesson remains.
Can I return to a place once filled with love?
I dare not try lest I fail again.
Outstretched hand untaken.
Open heart boarded up never to see the light of day.
My hope is a wilting rose, dying like love. Only thorns remain.
Oh my bleeding heart doth mourn the forgotten springtime of my
   existence.
No more tears flow, unbefriended by pain which stands alone.
Love is only a word now that had false meaning and empty promises.
A game played with no winners.
A mirage for carefree and unsuspecting fools who know no more
   and learn nothing and everything with a story to fall on deaf ears.
Please pass my way for I have met you before.
The different face of a deceitful enemy shall not deceive me again.

Jereme Benyola

Voices From Heaven

In loving memory of Aunt Lil and Uncle Hurl

Now . . . Please don't be sad, for we are glad
   Filled with eternal glee
Because we are home with our Lord and we are free . . . and
   Please don't shed too many tears
   For our souls are filled with sheer ecstasy
Because we are home with you Lord and we are free . . . and
Please don't ask why He called us home
   For we are never alone . . . we are here with loved ones
Yes, we are home, with our Lord and we are free . . . and
Please don't pity us
For we are free . . . Free of pain . . . Free of despair
Free of all life's burdens that
   Shackled us down there
Because we are home with our Lord and we are free . . . and
   Finally, please don't long for us
   For we are with you
In spirit . . . In memory . . . In soul and song
   We are with you all the days long
Because we are home with our Lord . . . And we are free.

Michele Gaymon

January's End

January's end
   nothing more
      another passing of the world clock
         the third decade faced up square
            the third year turned since the beginning of the end
A kind serenity had seemingly soothed the winds with time
                              with velvet dreams

   until with a kaleidoscope twist
      a nightmare pursued into the sun short hours
         terrorizing waking with walking from shaken pillows
            again love burned on like a waxless candle
               reaching the crystal globe
                  and shattering

   Now left to crying
         crying
            to a crying end quaking in separation
               gone off walking in blizzard snows blowing
                  creeping in crevices of the mind
                     filling in the gaps of January's end
                              nothing more.

Michael J. Simons

A Mother And Son

Come, take my hand; we'll walk together.
Let us speak about forever.
Side-by-side, we'll have nothing to hide,
and what we say from day to day
Will be the truth from deep inside.
And never once will we have lied,
Saying what rests deep inside
As we walk on and on together;
As we speak about forever.

We'll speak of our lives,
And of times good and bad;
Sorrows and joys and dreams that we've had,
Likes and dislikes of times gone past;
We'll speak of the love that holds us fast.

And as we walk we may look back
And see our footsteps left behind.
Then we'll rest our troubled minds;
But, as is the way of our kind, We'll look ahead along the track
and resume our journey, A mother and son;
A journey, together, that shall never be done.

John Richard Baldridge

Judith Of Bethulia

As a child, as a maiden I was beautiful and brave and bold.
Worthy maidservant, you did my bidding always, just as told.
Now our bones are brittle. We are honored but are old.

When the Israelites would not bend
To the will of the Assyrian king, he sent forth
To destroy our beloved Bethulia, his general Holofernes.
Wise, a widow, I devised a plan.
My flashing eyes, my beauty, would destroy the man.
We went where our townsmen feared to go.
With wiles, smiles, we beguiled the foe.
Within the tent of Holofernes I danced
With veils. He drank my wine 'til he slept.
Praying, I gripped his mighty sword, and leapt.
You wrapped the severed head in veils within our bag.
I smiled and drowsy sentries let us pass.
We did not lag. We showed our spoils in our Bethulia.
We rallied our people, who fought and fought.
Victory was ours. We gained what we had sought.

Our deed never leaves my mind. Not ever.
Surely you will remember this forever.

Shailah McEvilley Jones

Sonnet To The Easter Lilies

Through whistling winter winds you sit,
Like hermits in your scaly tents,
Till urgings — aaah, benevolent,
Uplift you from earth's murky pit
To bathe in warm spring days, sunlit.
Your guileless blooms magnificent;
A white robed living testament
To Love that's infinite.

O, lilies, nature's floral priests,
On Easter morn your soft bells ring
With perfumed breath, as you exhale,
"The Lord is risen! Dance and sing."

Sweet blossom bells for heaven's feasts,
Tolling, tolling - Life prevails.

Helen Elizabeth Williamson

Prairie Mate

Warming sun rays, breaking of day
Bring the Prairie Cock to the mating foray
Each spring as the cold still clings at day
Cocks begin their grand Display.

Rigid wings brush the turf, rushing their way
Extended throat, red glands puffed, head held high,
Go rushing, strutting bantering competitively;
Their grand rush their booming magical controversy.

Extended bantering of like cock mates,
Rush to prove their power and grace,
Intimidate, dominate and yes to say;
I am the best cock on the prairie today.

Prairie birds, grouse and display,
That's the ritual each spring day.
Extending, protruding their throaty array.
So here's a portrait this glorious way.

Wilson E. Brant

A Peak Inside

Figuratively speaking:
My life is a white canvas and God - my permanent painter.
Each color is a bold representation of who I really am;
A yellow background displays my sunny sense of humor-
my superior personality feature!

Directly in the middle of my canvas stands a bright red cross.
You see - I have a flaming love for Jesus Christ!
Surrounding the "t" are streaks of many colors,
Free-handedly thrown onto the canvas.

Blue because I'm gentle, orange means that I'm wise.
Purple shows I'm giving, and brown....
Well, that's close to the color of my eyes!

The Creator is my painter; who knows what I shall be.
An ever-changing canvas is all that you might see.
Ordinary, yes, to a common man's eye; but I see something special.

Just knowing that I am made with God's plan in mind,
and that I'm different in his gentle eyes,
allows me to:
dig deep, look harder, be my best; and find a peak inside.
(Hey- maybe that's what those brown streaks were!)

Maria Murphy

A Fleeting Moment

Ah for a fleeting moment
We could but turn back time
To capture those great feelings
We oft leave behind

The happiness, enchantments, sorrows
And yes - even tears
For the past has been a great teacher
Where one learns throughout the years

Some forget the past and erase
Memories from their minds
While others explore the future and
Recall their youth and the passing of time

To look ahead and plot one's course
Day by day - can fulfill one's heart
In many ways

But even more precious it would seem to
me is the person who can weigh the past
And decide their destiny

Richard Enebak

People

They look just like you and I
there are kinds that can love or hate you,
be naughty or affectionate to you
there are kinds that would stand by you when you are
winning and abandon you when you are losing.

There are kinds that can cheer you when you are down
and make you feel great even when you feel like crying
there are kinds that would stand and support you
when you made a mistake
and even forgive you when you hurt them
there are kinds that would be around you
for their own interest and purposes.

So we need all kinds to make the world
"People", love them do not hate them.

Kettly Lilavois

Love

Love is the sun,
Warming the earth,
Drying the rain,
Lighting rebirth,
The sparkle of the moon on the shine of a lake,
The stars at night that twinkle your fate,
A bird flying high in a warm spring breeze,
And a mother that comforts her child's awful sneeze,
The feeling you get when you receive a kiss,
Experiences like these, tell me what love is...

Joseph Flanigan

Huron Soul Mate

I walk...

Michigan sky, colorless, bleak, hangs limp
over sandy terrain, flesh toned, cushioning
the meandering silence.
Distance is of no consequence
The dank palm of the Huron wind sharply pushes and prods
further into the recesses of the shore line, time line, fine line

I walk....

for no reason
Where is the world?
This solitude: Perfection waiting to end
Shapeless body, vast, unsettled, fluid
wallowing in Huron blues
A native,

I walk...

Anne Currie Fitzgerald

The Sunset, Nature, And Beauty

I like to sit outside at night
and watch the sunset. To me it's a
beautiful mix of yellow, orange, and
pink in the night sky. It's like a
painting in which someone has a
handful of sky. I would often love
to be that someone because then I
could feel the nature of the beauty of the
sunset. I could call it mine. There is
no price on nature or beauty, but
if there was, many people would
like to own them when only two
people could buy them and then
they would be controlling life.
Glad God made earth the way
he did? I think the biggest question
of all is "Who made God?"

Jessica Chickering

Mom

Mom was always there to comfort my pain
To hand me an umbrella, when it looked like rain
To cook Christmas dinner and open her arms
To shelter, protect, and keep me from harm
Mom was always there....causing dangers to flee
To help me achieve all I could be
To encourage me on, while obtaining my dreams.
To lie strong for me, she silenced her scream
Mom was always there to keep me together
To help calm the storms in the roughest of weather
To stand up for me, never waiting aside
To see me stand tall, pride tears she cried
Mom was always there, an anchor and a friend
But at times there came pain that even she could not mend
Then it was my time to comfort her pain
To hand her an umbrella when it looked like rain.

Nicole Catherine Villa

"Who Is This Jesus?"

Jesus shed His blood for us - from sin He set us free.
He loved us very, very much - To hang upon that tree.
To be placed in a grave - for sings He didn't do
Shows how much He cares -yes, He ares for me and you.
On the third day, He arose - His work was not quite done.
He came to earth to help us - yes, to help everyone.
Jesus is in heaven now - Preparing us a place,
The people who accepted Him - Whose sins He did erase.
Soon there will come the greatest day - the world has ever known.
When Jesus takes his born again Christians
To their eternal heavenly home.

Natalie McWilliams

Unconditional Love

I love you and there's something you should know,
I'll never leave you and I'll never let go.
You've given me the strength to carry on,
And now I know I'll never be alone.

You're my best friend and will always stay that way.
I will help you no matter what comes your way.
Then you will see just how much you mean to me.
And I will stand by your side constantly.

And when you need me, I will be there.
Now there is nothing to fear!

I know that you feel the same way about me.
I do appreciate your honesty.
We will always be together come what may,
To help each other through our darkest days.

I cannot thank you enough for all you do.
So, I'll just say that I love you!

Eric Bruner

Tomorrow Promising

Tomorrow. What could I possibly ask of you? May I wish for the past, or will that make me grow old? The yesterdays diminish, yet through them I still hear her pleas. These greet me with every morning. The past once felt like ballet, quiet as fawn. Bliss scented vanilla. Time flowing like glaciers. Life welcomed me with dawn's every promising new day. Tomorrow. Take me to softness. I beg! Wake me with enthusiasm that I might have a true friend. Kiss me. Kiss me with tomorrow, that I might leave sadness in bed. Your lips on my eyelids, that I might know more of devotion than that of a newborn's mother. Tomorrow, might you bring back spanning fields? Shall you return forests? Will I ever again behold anything with fascination, with wonder? Tomorrow shall never cease, nor hope or dreams. This is its only promise. This I must make my nature.

E. Abriel Gonzales

Heavy Loads

We see them in our travels
the spring beings with their load,
some filled with rocks, some pebbles, some sand,
some others with heavy stone.

We all are created
not by our own request, as we try to build our own
and anxiously fill in the holes
with the stone we carried from home.

Some of us fit our pebbles in quite nicely
and continue to add as we move along.
Other's — keep breaking and find
that their stone is too jagged
and begin to create a falling wall.

Beware of those who seem crooked,
bent and slightly off.
The foundation of their wall
was created from their unstable past.
So quickly surround yourself with your perfect round rocks
and hand a special stone to your siblings
One — that you know will last.

Debby Tommaso

Untitled

How many times do you have to fall
before you can stand on your own?
How lonely do you have to feel
before you no longer feel alone?

How many times does you heart have to break
before no one breaks it again?
how much hurt do you have to bury
before you no longer feel the pain?

How many tears do you have to cry
so that tears don't fall anymore?
How many times must you stick your foot out
only to get it slammed in the door?

How guilty do you have to be
so that others don't feel to blame?
How insane does this world have to get
before you can consider yourself sane?

How sad do you have to feel
before you know how to really be happy?
How many shoes do you have to walk in
before you know what it's like to be... Yourself!

T. J. Thompson

Off To The Races

They're all in line...flexing their muscles...
on your marks...get set...ready...the shot is fired
   Due to masses some were pushed...or just
fell along the side.
   When the hurdles began the conditioned survived
and the weak tasted the sand.
   The distance became the foe only those really
focused will continue to go
   The finish line is just ahead and much sweat
is pouring off the head. It doesn't matter if
you're not the first. Summon that second wind
and straighten that back...it's the game
of life and we won't come back.

Rosalind Nims

A Deep Dark Sea

What lay in the sea would be unknown, for in the depths, lay two dark blocks.
Two blocks with chains, two cold gray chains, attached to feet, two lonesome feet.
The feet set bare on the cold dark blocks, in the depths down there.
The bitterness ate, it ate away, it ate and stung till the next cold day.
Till the widowed wife came to say. She told of how she found out that day.
The cries, the screams, the angry shouts. The shouts of her love, the screams of his voice
That came from his mouth, how the deal went bad, and they made their choice.
Their choice was cruel, but there was a doubt. A doubt in the scream
of the widows shout. So she was brought, brought to the sea, where her husband lay Motionlessly
She saw, then fell, fell to a knee, and hands in face Smiled with glee.
For she had killed, then arose Happily.
Seabren Patrick Reeves

Midlife Awakening

Each day I sing the same old song, and dance to its bitter sweet melody;
The lyrics a blend of contradictions, the notes a background of harmony.

The words are known only too well to me, the story is vague but familiar;
Its message complex yet so simple to sing, living it seems to come natural.

But oh to sing a different song, to dance a different dance!
Why is it we want what we cannot yet have? If I could, would I want my old song back?

On those days when I want the music off and yearn for the silence of my own thoughts,
I am scared when I can no longer find them, I have become enslaved to the thieves of my heart.

Consumed with guilt for there is surely worse, selfish tears wash away my self pity;
Time is my enemy, time is my friend. I have felt its passage and indignity.

Yet warm sunshine you always seem to prevail, with your smiles, hugs and pictures just for me;
For we are the laughter that rides on the wind and the sun that reflects off the sea.

How can I not sing along?
Renee M. Lorditch

The Notebook

It's been a year since her life ended and I realized mine hadn't
I thought the worst of the memories had been rinsed from my heart like yesteryear's laundry
But I came across an old notebook of hers
   The one she used to write her feelings and thoughts in
I should have thrown it away... I knew what would happen if I opened it
You can't take fifteen years of loving and cleanse your body of it in one year
And yet you can't linger in the memories of thousands of nights shared
All that was written I should have remembered since she had read it to me before
It seemed so easy for her to put down emotions on lined paper
I couldn't and didn't even put them into words (yet she somehow knew)
But she'd write them down, read them to me, and I'd pretend to listen
She knew all along I never heard a word
So today, a year too late, I sit here with her heart on my lap
How thoughtful of her to leave a part of us behind
And oh how I wish she was here to see me listen
Pat Rogers

Fate Of One's Custody

I'm standing in a puddle of gray blood
Torn between the world of light and the world of the dark
On the light side, I see my future living with my father and meeting a girl I'd marry
I'll have kids and work at a nine to five job for the rest of my life
The thought of this bores me
On the dark side I see me living with my mother and brother
My future is undetermined and open
That thought somewhat frightens me and yet there is something
intoxicating and alluring about it
It feels like it'll be one big party where the only thing to do is to get high and laugh at stupid people
These stupid people are the people we see on the light side with families and jobs
The dark side seems as though it would be one huge trip-fest with my brother
I'm standing in a pool of gray blood
When I try to go to one side the other side pulls me in
I spin through this twisted game of yo-yo, ever wary of the lake of gray blood
I'm wondering when it will envelope me
I will die, slowly choking on that rusty, metallic tasting thing that lawyers like to call custody
Ethan Flick

Man In War

Man fights man for material possessions, when will we learn our lessons,
that this land called earth, is only a place for rebirth. It is our minds we must free
from negative thinking, don't we realize it's our own ship we are sinking? -
Constantly at war with friends and foes. Watch out! - when the ship rocks, we may fall below,
fall to depths of darkness and uncertainty caught up in a life of turmoil and misery.

Man starts the war, he says he is fighting persecution, is this the solution?
Man fighting man for money, house and land, secretly planning how to swindle the other.
To cheat, to steal, to lie and to kill not a second thought given even if the other is his brother?
The war goes on, the fight goes on, to constantly be free, man says to himself -
"I want to be free of this entangled mass that surrounds me!", the entangled mass are his thoughts
which are all negative of course.

If man is lucky he may someday come to the realization, that he is not at war with his brothers of the nation
but with himself and his negative thinking and this the true reason that his ship is sinking.
Let us look around us and see what emanates, man is what he thinks and what he thinks is what he creates.
Just as success is failure turned inside out, so too is the power of positive thinking without a doubt.
To clean up our act mentally speaking, is to rid our minds of our negative thinking.
To be in control of the mind, is to leave the baggage of negative thinking behind
So let us gather our thoughts and sift them well, what's useful we keep, the rest can go to hell!
War is Man and Man is War, Man-In-War with himself, does he know what for?
To be at peace the world over, is to first be at peace with oneself.
To control one's thoughts is truly the answer, a controlled mind is a man in control of himself.

   Karin Rudd

Into The Storm

We had little warning of what was to come, the call came so soon from above
A tyrant so mad in a land far away had challenged the country we love

They sent the defenders so swift and so brave, the distance we traveled was great
The shield was put up and bravely held high to seal the barbaric one's fate

A land far away a country so frail, we banded the masses no way could we fail
Countries together alliances formed, armed for the fight we went into the storm

With forces assembled we waited and watched, we knew some would never return
To pay for our losses their leader would watch while his country like hellfire burned

We sent out a warning but it was ignored, they thought they could stand up and fight
We soon were to learn and in so little time their bark was much worse than their bite

A hundred short hours and we were the victors, but not without paying
the cost as long as we live we should never forget the memories of brothers we lost

A land far away a country so frail, we banded the masses no way could we fail
Countries together, alliances formed, armed for the fight we went into the storm

   Albert J. Dias

Your Eyes

I look into your eyes of brown, green, blue and all colors in between.
What do I see?
I look into your eyes and I see wonder, excitement, innocence, and love.
I look into your eyes and I see the beauty of life, new and pure.
I see the future, good or bad.
I see a leader.
I see a follower.
I see an individual, unique and powerful.
I look into your eyes and I see hope.
I see a purpose.
I see a chance, however small, however minute, for a better world.
I look into your eyes and I see the need for a helpful hand and some love.
I look into your eyes and I see you looking back at me;
Standing on your own feet;
Giving of your own love;
Making your own dreams;
Creating your own world;
Believing in your own future.

   Laura Commarota

Stormy Night

The clouds came upon us,
as we waited for the bus.
A low rumble we hear,
letting us know the storm is near.

The lightning flashes before our eyes,
the fear in them we cannot disguise.
Lightning strikes with all it's might,
like a lightbulb burning bright.

Thunder booms to let us know,
in our houses we have to go.
The thunder is so loud,
that it shakes the clouds.

We were shakin' in our skin,
when the bus came and we got in.
We gave the man his pay gladly,
wanting to get home badly.

Shanna Carl

I Could

I could trust my eyes to you
to blindfold and lead my way.
Through heavy rain and tears of pain
I'll not see while you're away.

I could trust my feet to you
to follow where you lead
to massage my pain in time of need
and stand behind you as you succeed.

I could trust my hand to you
to hold, to kiss, to bind.
Forever in eternity
to stay with you for all time.

I will give my heart to you
to have, to hold, to not let go.
To comfort in time of sorrow.
To give heart to your tomorrow.

Nanci L. Hagen

All That You Do

Day after day, week after week
  you move on your two
feet
  keeping the house nice and neat.

Hour after hour, minute after minute
  you handle trouble
  trouble when your children
get in it.

Second after second
  you have loved
  and cared.
    You have even helped
  us when we were scared

So all we need to say
  is thank you for
  all the love and
  happy
    mother's
    day.

David L. Davis

Set Free

If I were free to my desire
I'd sit beside an open fire
And lose myself inside the flames
No hopes no fears no foolish blames
If I were free I'd never die
My soul would be a falcon's cry
I'd sail high upon the wind
No land to touch no love to sin
If I were free I'd be a river
My laugh a splash my breath a shiver
Not a beginning not an end
My journey home my spirit mend

Mark R. Bouchard

Untitled

I thought I'd never get over you
I thought you were number one
Then reality hit me
And my thoughts of you were done
I realized you weren't the best
And I should just move on
I needed to get on with my life
My time with you was gone
But I still think about you
Every once in a while
You were my first love
And I still love you, Kyle

Kristen L. McKeen

As I Think Of You

I look up towards the heavens,
And all I see is blue.
Blue skies, white clouds,
But not one trace of you.

So I look a little deeper,
Looking left and looking right,
I look deeper and deeper-
Into the cold, dark night.

I still haven't seen,
What I wish to see,
So I looked within my heart,
And you appeared to me!

Your smile was so bright,
Your eyes - a lovely blue,
Happy - As always,
The way I remember you!

Lilly Summerall

The Gift

Of all the gifts my father shared,
One stands out.

Being raised color blind,
A precious gift beyond a doubt.

Good and bad in every race,
His words ring clear.

Wisdom from a righteous man,
What was the year?
1950

Patti Jean McLendon

"With Love"

Once every 8 or 9 years
I have cried a million tears
Sometimes I see you
There is nothing I can do
I have a lot of pain
I'm going insane
I miss you a lot
I wish I would have fought
There is nothing that will change
what I'm about to say
I love and miss you big Bro.

Danessa Montgomery

Word Games

Word Games, word games,
crossword puzzles, the like.
Once you start,
it's like riding a bike.
I enjoy the challenge,
of a humorous quip.
To keep the mind crisp,
like the snap of a whip.
Each word is a toy,
for me to play.
Where most people talk,
with nothing to say.

Richard Hart

How Do You Say Good-Bye

  How do you say good-bye
When there is so much hurt inside
  The tears that are cried know
    it is time
But how do you let go
  You let the person, go
Not the times shared
  How do you go on
One day at a time
  Live for tomorrow
Not in the past
  The pain goes away in time
Not the times that were shared

Pamela G. Rehs

"Spirits Of The Sun"

The azure sky above me
Changed to grey billowed clouds,
Blazing sun was behind them
Rays piercing through the gloom.
I saw victims of war there
Ships in throes on the sea,
Battered and broken airplanes
Plunging straight to their doom.

There were prisoners of war
So stalwart in their stands,
Heroes who braved the torments
By hands of fellow man.

The ones left behind, so bold
Think of all the brave loved souls,
The Warriors have been dubbed
Beloved "Spirits of the Sun."

Ilene E. Twitchell

Fibers Of Doubt

Spellbound, I watch
As you weave your web of promises

Mesmerized, I listen
To all that I want to hear

Captivating, this web
Woven tight with hopes and dreams

Soul-searching, is it you or me
Weaving a web of insecurity

Eva J. Banta

A Mother's Prayer

Dear Heavenly Father
Please hear my plea
Please speak to my children
As you've spoken to me.

If they knew you, Sweet Jesus,
They would have to agree
That your saving grace
Can soon set them free.

Free from loneliness, bitterness,
Wrath and despair
Free from the past
From the old devil's lair.

On to the future!!!
If they only dare
To kneel at an altar
With confession and prayer.

Your soul is washed clean child
Like the fresh morning dew
Past sins are forgiven
You can start life anew.

Donna Marlowe

An Armchair Sailor's Epitaph

When I die, bury me
And o'er my grave
Plant the seed
Of an oak.
Let my worth be
To fertilize that seed,
That one day,
A giant oak you'll see
From that tree,
Someday they'll hew
A towering mast
To hold the billowing sails
As o'er the world
The "Wanderer" and I
Our never ending voyages,
We'll freely roam,
Just wind and sea
And my tall tree,
A little bit of me
To hold sheets for thee.

Eleanor Grace Elmerick

Marital Bliss

Breathless wonder
Starry eyed adoration
Romantic tryst
Sensual awareness
Mutual respect
Companionable silence
Marital bliss

Peggy Lynne Power

Silence

The fading hollow shallowness
of nothing that's not there.
It's giving not forgiving and
　caring not to care.
Do you dare listen to its
　foreboding call of none?
Is it there when no one listens?
Is it owned by some or one?
Is it wrapped among the nothing
　or coiled upon the dead?
Is it really out there or
　twisted in my head?

Nichole L. Farmer

The Face Of Me

The water stills
The ripples have gone
I look and see what has become
No longer the face of me.

I stare.
The face I see
So clearly there
A thought of which,
I have no memory.

I want to run.
Be quiet! Be still!
Where could I go?
Would anyone know
The true face of me.

Change the tide
Wash back the past
When the ripples die
Please, let the face I see
Be the face of me.

Julie Sancaster

Meant To Be

Good-bye may seem forever
　but if it's meant to be
Somehow, somewhere we'll find it
　If God will let us see
I cannot explain
　The reason we must part
I'm so sorry I can't change it
　But I'll see you in my heart
If it's in God's plan
　For us to be together
I'll wait for the day
　We can begin forever
Time is just a measurement
　That keeps us far away
Counting every second
　Turning minutes into days
I'll miss you every moment
　And keep searching all I see
Somehow, somewhere we'll find it
　If it's meant to be

Cara C. Ward

Melody

A quite rain a gentle breeze,
Blowing softly through the trees.
They sing a song I wish I knew.
Love and joy. Happiness too.
Beautiful melody soft and sweet.
Warms my heart so cold and bleak.

Jennifer Thompson

Time

The breeze of time
Pats the cheek of youth,
Sweet caressing
At the dawn of bright futures.

So soon a brisk wind,
Time sculpts life's wide middle,
Scouring stark realities
From the sands of dreams.

Roaring at gale force
Through twilight fading,
Time's dark passage
Delivers a fresh, new morn.

Larry F. Matthews

Prisoner of the Mind

Your body rises
And your soul set free
Your mind now takes control
But no one else can see

Your head is now a prisoner
For the mind that lurks within
It fills it up with love and hate
Sometimes even sin

Your own true feelings are released
As fantasies dance around
Images of everything
Even such real sound

But all this action does not last
For the sun's light breaks this chain
And until you find a way to stop
These dreams will come again

Sara Saric

Best Friend

He was so sweet
He was so kind
I couldn't take him
Off my mind

Anything he needed
borrowed or lend
I know I could trust him
he was my best friend

He was with me
in good times and in bad
and he held me close
when I was sad

I knew there were some things
for him to mend
but I'll stick with him
because he's my best friend

Jackie Kirtley

Untitled

Words, wisdom, power,
I touched her and death smiled
Luxury, romance, trance,
Too many play sick mad games
Take inquiries that have no meaning
Love is a game
Death is life
I think I'm playing the game wrong
Again....death smiles

Jason Christensen

With Not A Sound

Willows and wildflowers
Cluttered all around,
Makes you hear a peaceful sound.
Laughter and love,
All bundled in your life,
When you come face to face
With your husband or wife.
But just one look at their face,
Is all you need,
To remind yourself not to
Battle with greed.
Samantha Holda

In My Heart

When we met, I didn't think
That we could be
Then something changed
And all I wanted was you with me.

But now that we
Are both together
How can I know
We'll last forever

I know that we
Must both belong
I hope that what we have
Is strong

I think I felt
This once before
But this is better
There's something more.

You hit the bull's eye
With that dart
And now you'll stay there
In my heart.
Pamula Monique Haynes

Just The Same

I can't run as fast as you
But I will get there
   Just the same.

I can't hear the joke you told
But I can laugh
   Just the same.

I can't see your shiny new toy
But I can play lots of games
   Just the same.

I can't ride a bike
But I can walk for miles
   Just the same.

I can't cook your favorite meal
But I can plan a hearty feast
   Just the same.

You could tease me and break my heart
But I will love you
   Just the same.

I am a rose in your garden of daisies.
We are different and yet we are
   Just the same.
Mary K. Strable

The Choice

Dreams of children,
Entwined around my soul,
With tender touches.
Longingly letting go
As the dreams drift away,
Disentangled one by one
And cut loose,
Leaving me in sadness
In a world of other people's children.
Rain falls around me
Washing away my tears
Renewing my search
For a course to take.
A last chance
To mother another's child,
Or to find my way, childless,
On another unknown path,
Enticing me with freedom
And joy and fear.
Louise Lindsay

Roses

Red rose petals blooming,
   growing
Bloodshot beauty glittering,
   glowing
Sunflowers dancing,
   Petunias swaying in the cool
      breeze
Roses laughing,
   bringing
      beauty and ease.
Lisa Ellen Maiden

Love Newborn

Precious infant, heaven sent,
thou art born into time today,
whispering secrets long forgotten
along life's hardened way.

Newborn soul, priceless treasure
of eternal worth,
before the world had been created,
God knew of thy birth.

Fragile lily, turtle dove,
purity exudes from thee,
entrusted to an angel's care,
the miracle of thy soul.
Mary Jo Galente

I Want To See...

It is so beautiful outside
Imagine the sunshine
as thousands of gold thread look like
Imagination on the field
There are many kinds of flowers
Smiling and dancing in the wind.

Open the door, please, Dad
Let the sunshine get into
Why have we closed the door, Dad?
Bright, fresh-air we need.

Open the door, please, Dad
Let me see the sky
and butterflies how they play.
Tuan Tran

The Joyousness Of Spring

The fields and the hills are awakening
   Winter has had her last fling
And bursting forth on every hand
   Is the miracle of spring.
Within my heart arose the urge
   To write a happy song
To tell the whole world of the joys
   That to spring alone belong.
I found a quiet shady nook
   And bent to the task with a will
But nothing that I could bring to mind
   Could half describe the thrill
Of seeing the leaves all bursting forth
   The wild flowers a'bloom by the wall
Pussy Willows along the creek
   And a blue sky over all
But as I labored there in vain
   A lark rose on the wing
And with exquisite song expressed
   The joyousness of spring.
Florence Bowers

Clear And Crystal

A clear and crystal
Moonlit night
Found two small doves
Close in flight

They soared and dove
Together they flew
Entwined their paths
The whole night through

And as they played
One saw the dawn,
Turned back to find
The other gone

Distraction by change
From night to day
Let happiness
Just slip away
Cheryl J. Leslie

Hate

Hate so true,
But yet so defying.
Untrue to the soul,
True to the evil.

Hate is a deep feeling
longing to be let out.
Waiting to be free.
Wanting to hurt and ruin.
To create all evil.
And yet still even wanting to kill.

Hate is deeper than an ocean.
Stronger than anyone's will.
It will always be there no
matter what... It's there.

No one can stop it.
It's in us all
screaming to be let out.
Killing love creating despair.
Destroying life.
And killing us all.
Kristen Garrott

Look Again

When some people look in the mirror
they're unsatisfied with what they see
they're terrified they're turning
into something they don't want to be.
So they stare at their reflection
hoping to disappear
scared they're turning into one of
their deepest, darkest fear.
Little do they know
they can change their attitude around
so that when it's all over
they'll be standing strong
on solid ground!

LaRobin Starks

Untitled

Perhaps one day,
even if it be far away,
I would be like a leaf on a tree,
At last! Free!
To flutter from the twig's grasp,
Fall has arrived at long last.
This be the new awakening,
I am loose from my bonds!
But as I drift aimlessly,
A stark awareness comes to me.
Am I free? I think not!
From being one slave, now
Another master I've got.
The wind!

John Tabor

Reconciled

I do not know the answers,
But I know the riddles well;
There is no glue for broken hearts,
No passage from this hell.

I do not know the password,
But I've knocked on heaven's door:
The blind man cannot see the light,
But craves it all the more.

I do not know the solvents,
But I see the mysteries;
Behind all truth there lies decay,
Behind all love, disease.

I've yet to find the reason
But the rhyme I've always known;
A severed soul cannot be saved,
And sad hearts can't go home.

I cannot speak the language,
Though I still know all the words:
Misunderstood is not so bad...
It's "all alone" that hurts.

Pamela R. Miles

A Tear Of Feelings

To cry a tear
Does not always mean fear
It can mean sad
It can mean mad
A tear can mean hurt
A tear can mean curt
A tear could mean happy
A tear could mean glad
A tear is anything but bad

Leslie Robbins

My Love

I feel you
my heart burns.
With you I long
to be. Please stay
with me. Never go
our love is sure to
grow. Soon I will
take you.
You will be here
with me forever for all eternity
In love and together
soon again we'll be
I cannot wait to
kiss your sweet lips
to feel your fingertips
on my face, you will make it okay.
You will take my
pain away so happy we will be.
Together again forever someday
for all eternity.

Sarah Martinez

Crowning Glory

The crowning glory of a rose
is the head.
Nothing can be more beautiful
More fragrant to the senses.
But alas that bloom of blood red
so desirable so magnificent
is set upon a barbed stem.
Such is our life's journey
and that crowning glory our reward.

Michael J. Taylor

Woodlands

Vibrant, pulsing microcosm,
quietly changing.
Birds singing, flying.
Silent mouth hearing
life speak,
feeling Earth's strength.

Anne Franks

"My Parents"

What my parents mean to me
It's obvious it's plain to see
They gave me life
each breath I take
They gave me love
with no heartache
They gave me hope
when I was down
They always seem
to be around
They are the parents
we all should have
And I have them
I'm so glad

Deborah Clark

The Star

When a star you see,
Think of me for the
star you see I
might see but
thinking of thee.

Esther Franklin

As Night Falls

As night falls and covers
The words and gestures of the day
A loud hush hovers over all
And brings with it a peaceful display

The trees sway gently as the
Crickets sing their song
While the birds find shelter
till morning comes along.

Even the flowers seem nestled
In their beds, saving their fragrance
And beauty for a new day
As they play at turning heads

While entrenched in this silent wonder
I find I must take pause
As I bathe in the nectar
of another day done
Cleansed, refreshed, as night falls

Bonnye Best

Untitled

Grandmother,
    was a woman who provided every need,
A woman whose love never
    ceased,
A woman whose careness was
    never ending
A woman who I'll never forget

Louie Parkin

Angel

I've always considered you
To be my heaven-sent angel
You mean so very much to me
Much more than words can tell

When I'm down you cheer me up
When I'm sick you make me better
For all these things you do for me
I'll love you now and forever

You touched my heart and made me see
What love is all about
In this uncertain life we live
Of your love I have no doubt

You enrich people's lives everywhere
I'm so happy you're in mine
You're the world's most perfect woman
The one I'd always hoped to find

During the day you keep me smiling
And at night you keep me warm
Come to me, my beautiful angel
Let me take you in my arms

Jeffrey Glenn Ayers

The Rose

The lonely petal falls,
silently to the earth.
It lies there,
soaking up the bright
sun's rays.
The petal shrinks
into a tiny sheet
of pinkness.
It is pulled into
the dark soil,
to feed the flower
from whence it came.

Kirsten Maria Patterson

By My Side

Can you hear the crashing waves
as they slap the sand?
Do you see the people
walking hand in hand?

Can you hear the seagulls cry
and smell the salty air?
The shells you find so beautiful
no others could compare!

Can you hear the western wind
its song, sung just for you?
The blue sky and the sunshine
each day brings something new!

Can you feel this love I feel
for you deep down inside?
You have made this day complete
just being by my side!
Darlene A. Price

First Kiss

Eyes closed
Chin up
Relax and enjoy
The cool savory flavor
Of your lover's lips,
Soft and sensuous.

No,
I don't care
That he was mine
Before you stole him
Away.
Jana Davis

Wasted Time

My time is wasted,
I feel so amid
Of life's petty fears,
I have lost all tears

Now the past is gone,
I know I am wrong
Life passed me by,
Despite all my lies

I lied to just one,
To myself, harm done
Nothing was stolen,
But something broken

I have lost my heart,
My now broken start
I feel very blind,
As I wasted time
Matthew Riddle

Sweet Spirit

There are times we sink or swim
through the school of life.
Sensitive souls are awareness blessed
of a golden friend,
with gentle kindness your eyes send.

If it so happens sweetness stays
or drifts away.
A memory of that rich emotion
is yours to bring to thought any day.
I thank you for being my golden friend.

Happy Sweetest Day
Sally F. Guyot

"In Agony"

My conscious,
 is clear,
I, can start,
 brand new,
it, took,
 a long time,
to, clear it, too!
 your mind,
  is your hell,
if, you, let it, be,
 you keep,
your tortured soul,
 burnin', in agony!
Everyone, can,
 be reborn,
and not, necessarily
 with, baptism,
it, can, be done,
 with, your
inherent wisdom!
John Search

Lake Bonaparte

Oh, the beauty of the lake,
Watching the waves' somber wake,
Laying in the sunlight to bake,
Watching the birds zoom by.

Memories of early childhood,
None bad, all good,
Laying in the huge green wood,
Watching the branches sway.

Waking up in the morning,
To see the sun glowing,
And hear the leaves rustling,
Watching the light on the water dance.
Elizabeth Hennessy

The Artist

What do you see? I often wonder.
What do you see? I say.
Oh...but to be the canvas
watching the Artist eyes,
seeing the light brighten
way deep down inside.

What do you see? I often wonder.
What do you see? I say.
Oh...but to be merely the paint brush
within the Artist hand,
for with each stroke feeling
the power flowing through his vein.

What do you see? I often wonder.
What do you see? I say.
Oh...but to be simply a thought
within the Artist mind,
for in his thoughts there is
a world that truly is divine.

What do you see? I often wonder.
What do you see? I say.
Madeline Donohue

They Say

They say he's sexy,
They say he's hot,
They say he's cool,
But I say you're definitely not!
Michelle Desjardins

Face In The Mirror

I am happy
But yet I am sad
This happy loneliness
Will one day make me go mad

I am afraid to peek out
From my protective shell
Even though one day
It might make me well

If I peek out
They will see
All my vulnerabilities

I am confident
But yet I am not
This stubborn will
Will one day rot

When it does
I hope it is not too late
And be forced to suffer
A self given lonely fate
Christian Wachowiak

Whatever You Need

My love for you just grows and grows,
How strong can it get? Nobody knows,
I'd climb the highest mountains
just for you,
And I'd make your world, full
of happiness, if you want me to,
I'll do anything just for you.
My love will always be true to you.
Whatever you need, I'll get for you,
Do whatever you want, even say 'I Do',
I'd walk on the wild, and cut
through the tallest weeds,
Just to give you whatever you
want and whatever you need.
Marie McIntosh

Silence

The eagle stands high on the hill
As graceful as a swan
He stands with his wings spread
And ready for the kill
As the grace of his body stands
High on the hill
He raises his legs up
To swoop into the air
The boy on the hill watches in awe
He mimics the eagle and raises his arms
He moves as graceful as an eagle
He watches and waits while the eagle swarms
In a moment of silence the eagle is gone
The gracefulness of life fly's
On and on
Karen Salmon

Think

Stop and think
what you are
think ahead
of where you are
never say never
of who you are
just be proud
of what you are
Christina I. Kessler

Loneliness

Have you ever felt
Scared and all alone,
Shaking and soaking wet
Just chilled to the bone???

Have you ever sensed
The rising fear,
Of the darkness and
Shadows crawling near???

Have you ever seen
What my eyes have,
If you had then you'd
Know what to give...

Have you ever longed
To be with someone,
To cherish and to hold
When the day is done???

Have you ever touched
The heart of the lonely,
I'm sure you tried
But then pulled back slowly...

Tina Schultz

People Are People

Some things are bad
Some things are good.
People are people
That's not understood.

People hate People
Because of their race,
That's a discouraging thought
And a total disgrace.

They say you're black or white
Or any other race.
That you're different and bad
Just because of your face.

But what they don't see
What they usually miss,
Is that if you're good inside
The race you should dismiss.

People are people
No matter what race.
People are People
And we all have a place.

Amanda Snodgrass

She Walks Among Her Flowers

She walks among her flowers
Where the butterflies dance on high
And the songs of the birds rejoicing
Echo across the sky

Her feet in bare indulgence
Join with Mother Earth
In sweet embracing harmony
Where nature gave her birth

And this one thing she knows
She walks not alone
Of that she is quite certain
In this place she calls home

Dorothy Louise Carney

Untitled

Forever, I say
is not long at all

In each other's arms
we're not so small

In each other's eyes
we see no time

In each other's sighs
infinite thoughts sublime;

Come now with me
in forever days flight
hand in hand we'll be

Then sleep child, sleep
for tomorrow, another forever
we'll see

Mitchell Vernon Herbert

The Year That Was

The year that was is over
The pain it brought now gone
Only fragments of the pieces
flicker in my mind

The year that was came strongly
to open up my eyes
never once hiding
the agony behind
the purpose of its being
the silence of its home
the love it brought so deeply
into my soul

The year that was is over
the calm after the storm

Sylvie G. Jordan

Silence

Do you hear the Silence?
It haunts me day and night.
It echoes through the house.

My dreams are filled of it.
My days are surrounded by it.
My life is Silence.

Do you feel it?
Does it haunt you?
Like it haunts me?

I think I hear a sound
No, it was just my hopes,
my dreams that the Silence will break.

To be alone in a silent house
is the worst punishment given.
To be completely alone forever,
in silence, is my greatest fear.

Melissa Fisher

Heaven

Heaven is a pile of flowers
they grow as you pray
yellow, pink and a touch of red
prayers are as colorful as God's
rainbow, very beautiful and fragile
God is love he never stops loving
us even when we are bad
I wish I could grow a garden
as beautiful as Heaven.

Ami Hutto

God

God, He is Almighty and
answers to no one,
the new way of life
came from his son,
he wanted us to be like Him,
But the Devils wanted
us to be like them,
He knew we were not
perfect and the Devils
had won,
and this is why he
sent his son.

Tommy J. Smith

Forever

It's true you've gone
with out a word.
I can see your face no longer.

The reasons why
are not clear to me,
so I'm left to sit and ponder.

And yet, you're here,
so close my dear,
I can feel your arms around me.

I look at my bed,
where you rested your head,
and the indentation you left beside me.

Forever you said,
I believed what I read,
in denotation there is no question.

But in your mind it seems
five years full of dreams
was the forever in your connotation.

K. C. King

The Dance Of The Clouds

Swirling around, high spirited,
The clouds begin their dance,
first slowly like a waltz,
then into a twist.
They form into a deadly mass.
On what small communities will
they wreak havoc.
What churches will they wipe out.
Will they dance all night,
while twirling about.
Using the earth as a dance floor.
How many towns will be left
in disaster,
and lives with extra chores.
Will it ever be their last dance,
or will there always be more.

Mary Anne Crowe

Story Of The Eyes

What did the eyes show?
Unbearable pain and sorrow.

What feelings did the eyes present?
Very much hate and resentment.

What did the eyes undisguise?
Overwhelming shock and surprise.

What do the eyes read?
Many stories of heartbreak and need.

Melanie Sentz

A Fairy Wind

There's a Fairy Wind a blown'
Tis sure it has me heart beguiled
There's been an arrow sent
From a lovely Rainbow Child

She tells me that she loves me
And sure I know tis true
For the Fairy Wind it whispers
As it blows so gently through

It says: "Come out! Let's Play!"
For nothing matters more
Than to hold this precious day
And create "days of yore"

"Come on! Join in!
Throw away those fears
Take my hand and love me
For days will soon be years

There's Fairy Wind a blowin'
I'll grab hold with all me might
And love this Rainbow Child
Morning, day, and night

Ben Mallory

"My Thanksgiving Prayer"

Thank you Lord for life
Beneath all of its strife
For you are the light
In all of my night

Thank you Lord for your love
That always holds me near
Thank you for every tear
And for friendship very dear

Thank you for patience
When things are going wrong
For it's all my trials
That help me stand strong

Help me to help others
As I go along life's way
thank you for my blessings
I fail to mention when I pray

In all that I do
Lord help me to see
the way you have chosen
is the best for me

Nancy Butler

Dare To Be Great

Remember - be humble
No matter how great
You finally become
With God's given Fate.

The world's yours for the taking
So fly with the birds,
Or if to your liking
You roam with the herds.

Don't veer from your goals,
Be the best that you can.
Don't "follow" your "buddies",
Be a leader of Man.

But if down life's journey
Things don't go as you plan
The thing that counts most
Is that you've done all you can.

Carolyn C. Metcalf

I Will, I Will Never

I will love you
  till eternity
I will care for you
  till I can no longer
I will think of you
  till the day I die
I will be with you
  till the end of time

I will never let you go
   even when we say goodbye
I will never be without you
   even if you're not by my side
I will never be alone
   even if it's in my mind
I will never stop loving you
   even till the end of time

Korrinna Matteson

Guilty Of Loving You

You know that I have loved you
right from the start,
and I really do feel
that I have done my part.

I have done the things
that I thought you wanted
but it's never enough
and you seem so disappointed

Disappointed in me?
I don't understand why
I'm only guilty of loving you more
as each passing day goes by.

You don't know how I ache
for your warm embrace
or to see a simple smile
upon your beautiful face.

But time has a way
of working things out
and one day you will know
what I'm talking about

Shelia Abernathy

God Erases Lonely Faces

I see so many lonely faces
In the world every day
Some have been abandoned
By someone they love, today.
Some have been rejected
By those whom they admire.
Lord, help them to see that you
Have a plan and a desire
To fill that void within
That can never be satisfied
Except with your love
Which will never leave their side.

Dianne Schryer

Now

The past is gone
Let the future take care of itself
Your moment is now
So
Release the past
Make the future
The now 'til eternity.

Rosa C. Johnson

Mother

Walking with skeletons
in the graveyard
the only light shone
was the full moon on the stone marked
"Mother"

Ignoring laughter
from the dead
I cleared the veil
of web she wove
for me

Tearing my wrists on thorns
from the crimson
rose I planted
the night
before

Blood watered the rose
darkness some slow
and the man in
the moon made faces at me

James Ross Orr

Time

Time on my hands
allows me to think.
It is dangerous for me.
My obsessive mind wanders
into depths of despair.
Wondering where I went wrong?
A childhood so sweet
parental love not withheld.
Somewhere I changed
though I know not where.
The dramatic times of my life
I can remember
as well as yesterday.
None betray a point
that is well defined
so, not to dwell
on my thoughts today
I keep my hands busy
and dream of tomorrow.

D. L. Walbrecht

From Her

Take small steps, daughter,
and always face the oneness
of the sun:

(Morning grows only
into longer shadows
that draw the heels
down)

Walk to that noon
where the shadows drown
in light,
where none
so much as tread
upon your walking
shadow past:

Small steps,
small steps, daughter,
  that noon will live,
  will last.

Caroline Wallace

Untitled

Driving on a bus, nowhere to go,
this is the bus to nowhere,
it symbolizes my life,
like a long twisty road uphill,
downhill, twists and turns as far
as the eye can see infinite,
I will never die.

Jason Wagner

Still Alone

I sit alone within my room.
Outside the sky is full of gloom.
The clouds are black,
The sky is grey,
This is a gloomy, gloomy day.

I sit alone within my room,
Just waiting for my endless doom.
The walls are stones,
Where is the sky?
A constant drift is going by.

I sit alone within my room.
The dusty walls feel like a tomb.
There is no noise,
No light is shone,
And I still sit there all alone.

Kary Coleman

The Star Glory

The star glories the night
Carpentry's shelter pure light
the sheep pasture of flocks
Evening time on the clocks

My native home of the holy home
the herds the donkey has come
Holy family aside
Night of good tide

Born Holy manager
Holy Jungfru Virgin mother
Angels Jesus Son of God
Shining star adobe of God.

Alice B. Norman

Leave It To The Future

Leave it to the future
Our sons and daughters,
To live in a world so bad.
Why do we take for granted,
For all that we have?

It is up to us,
To change this world,
Try to promote peace through the land,
Make life better for the common man.

Because if we don't change,
And stop all the pollution,
All the crime and pain,

Leave it to the future,
Our loving, trusting children,
To have only sorrow and
Suffering to gain.

Lisa M. Thacker

Changing

The space in your heart is changing
for me it is getting bigger I can
see I appreciate the feelings you have
for me I have the same for you I
hope our feelings and love will never
fade away in this insane world of
hatred and killings our feelings are
getting stronger they are to now that
they may never break and leave us
hanging on a line a line so thin
that if you try to change your position
you will fall fall forever in pain
depression hatred killing drugs and
suicide but if we can
keep this love none of this will
happen so please never leave me or
hurt me and I will do the same for you.

Brandy L. Price

Young Love

They walked along
   with arms entwined
She said I'm yours
   and you are mine
They spread a blanket
   on the ground
Indulged in passion
   newly found
Their lips were close
   their hearts a flutter
But ne'er a word
   did either utter
And as their passion
   reached its peak
They knew no words
   they need to speak

Ardith M. Baker

Why?

Why are flies called flies?
Why do we only have two eyes?
Why aren't 'mooses' called meese?
Why if just for a second there's
Never any world peace?
Why do we have a middle name?
Why do some people want
Others to be the same?
Why do some people have dimples?
Why is it hard for some,
But for others, simple?
Why are there four different seasons?
Why prejudice, what's the reason?
There are so many unknowns in the world
And in our hearts,
I'm surprised everything doesn't
Just fall apart!

Lindsay Pritts

Time Is Forever

The summertime of life
was a joy to behold.
I winged my way through age
to let the years unfold
and bring forth unto me
the marvel of posterity.

Gladys M. Pollard

Memories

Memories of people
you never forget,
some you may cherish,
some you regret.
My grandfather's a memory
I hold in my heart,
I cared for him always
till death did up part.
My family will miss him,
of course so will I.
He'll always be loved,
that I can't deny.
Last Father's Day
I'd run and I'd wave,
This Father's Day
I'll walk to his grave.
I'll always remember
the good times and bad,
He'll live in my heart,
will I always be sad?

Heather L. Sharp

Untitled

To live but never love
To love but never live
To hear but never listen
To know but never understand
These are gifts only we
Can give ourselves

If I had one last wish
I would wish to see life
Through the eyes of my fellow man

Janette Low

Gemini

What's that I hear
A soft voice in my ear
I try to listen... What does it say?
I see things I've never seen
I see worlds I've never been
I ask for help... I've lost my way

I am Gemini, Two in One
I am here, and I am gone

I have a mission, the voice says to me
What? I ask, for I cannot see
But the voice is gone... And I'm alone
Alone to face the both of Me

I am Gemini, and I see
Not only one, but Two of Me

Where am I, I do not know
I have a feeling I've been here before
But how can that be unless it's true
I am not One, but Two

It is true, know this I
I am the Gemini

Keith M. Shaw

A Very Short Fish Story

"Bite me!" said the rude-dude swimmer
To mama shark who wanted dinner.
Bite she did and it was gory;
End of swimmer, end of story.

Robert Bartlett

Still Dreaming

Looking out on a world
that never looks in
Looking out for mine
And looking out for the end
Seizing the moment
Knowing they are numbered and few
Living in the here and now
-or at least trying to
Occasionally, stepping back
-from my shoes
To get a better view
To see more clearly
Without so much to look through
Yet, still seeking out the answers
I don't even have the questions to
Searching aimlessly, without a clue
Too often wondering what to do
Though, still, dreaming and believing
That my dreams can come true.

Catrina L. Johnson

The Dancing Lord

The sad dancer is dead.
The joyful dancer is living.
He lives on forever.
Never to parish.
He is Lord of the dance
The dancing Lord.

He dances where he pleases.
Never to stop. Never.
To those who except
He gives a great gift
The gift of dance.

"Now dance for me," he says
In his deep, strong voice.
"Show me what you know."

The dancers try, and fail
For they aren't good enough for he.
Then he leaves, leaving them
With the gift of nothing.

With the gift of death.

Michaela Duggins

Forever In Time

There is a place that I see,
Where things are so free.
There are so many thrills,
And there are never any chills.
Somewhere, Forever in Time

Where birds fly,
And children will always try.
Where there is no sorrow,
Nor a worry about tomorrow.
Somewhere, Forever in Time

Where tears are never shed,
And fears are never spread.
Where secrets are shared,
But feelings are always spared.
Somewhere, Forever in Time

Where skies are never gray,
We will never go away.
Where you and I will stay,
And we will always pray.
Somewhere, Forever in Time

Angela Peters

Dearest Dad

I'm sorry that I didn't listen
When I was still at home
It really doesn't matter now
'cause soon I will be gone

Would you take care of Andy
My one and only son
I don't know who his daddy is
Only God knows who's the one

Please tell him of his Momma
Don't let him do like me
He will soon forget me
'cause he is not quite three

I've wrecked my life, because of that
I'm going to my rest
Please take my son and guide him well
To choose what's for the best

I wanted to run my own life
I wanted to have fun
I'm dying now with aids
and I'm barely twenty-one

William D. Bickerstaff

The Dreamer

I sometimes sit and dream,
Of places I would like to be,
Things I would like to do,
And sights I would like to see,

I like to dream of you,
Of your eyes that shine so bright,
Of lips that haunt me,
Far into the night.

I like to dream of days gone by,
Of songs we used to sing,
Days we spent together,
And of the happiness you did bring.

And in my lonely heart,
Your name will always be,
Part of three little words,
That are always dear to me.

At heart I'm not a dreamer,
But with you so far away,
What else can I do,
But sit and dream all day?

Jeff Truett Tucker

Sometimes

Like footsteps in the sand
love sometimes washes
away.

Like water in a lake
love sometimes
freezes.

Like a dead seed in the ground
love sometimes never grows.

Like a piece of paper, love
sometimes gets thrown away.

Meghan Jennings

My Friend

I wake in the morning,
 knowing the night is gone.
But you're always there, my friend!
The sun goes down,
 And the day is done.
But you're always there, my friend!
I can travel through mountains,
 'Till they turn to sand.
But you're always there, my friend!
I sail the vast ocean,
 When appears, the land.
But you're always there, my friend!
In a crowd of people,
 I can feel alone.
But you're always there, my friend!

Lou Gehringer

"Sometimes"

Sometimes I find myself wandering
Lost and alone in my dreams
Cherishing moments of laughter
Each day used to bring

Sometimes I find myself crying
Confused and sad in my room
Waiting for the prince of darkness
To come and rescue me soon

I've searched so long in silence
To find myself a true friend
Someone to love and care for me
Our friendship would never end

I used to find myself searching
But now my search is through
The friend that I've been looking for
I've found right here in you.

Allison Cremo

Running Scared

Frightened by a dream
Not knowing
What tomorrow will bring.
Living
Moment to moment.
Restless nights
Scared to wake.
Wanting and needing
Yet receiving so little.
Hanging on
Like a butterfly in the wind.
Wanting to be touched
And loved.

Lady, lady
What do you do now?
Run?
Run - like a rabbit in the snow.
Or, hang on?
Hang on - for all life can bring
At least, in your dreams.

Sue Julsen

You And You

Learning to do, learning to don't,
Learning you will and that you won't.
Train the you that trades with others,
Know the you, trading covers.

Wayne E. Newton

Citadel

Sheltered by walls, pale lemon
undulating curtains
eyelet lace
morning's breath cushions me
supple and smooth

I wallow in sunlight
aurous
gathering in pools, deep but safe
veiled by dancing dust

Miles away from you, "Daddy"
your probing hands and piercing glances
separated by
oceans
mountains
fences
anything to keep you from me

Comforted by chimerical arms
in the refuge of my head.
Erin K. Marsten

The Straw Hat

In the corner by the cradle
Stands a shelf
On which
There are photographs
And paintings
Dried flowers
A letter
And sitting beside the letter
Is a hat
A straw hat
It has seen the wind
And prairie flowers in bloom
It has seen love
And death
It has also seen dreams
Dreams come true
Because of hope
And love
Gabrielle Blossom

Trying

Laugh or cry
Life or death
Dream and reach for the sky
Courage or fear
Pleasure or pain
Can you cry without a tear?
Live or exist
Fun or boredom
Temptation, can you resist?
Success or failure
Win or lose
One chance for amore, you choose.
All of these opposite make up
  our lives
So why then is someone so
  unhappy who tries and tries!!
Francine DiLucia

Untitled

If you want to
change my life,
Get out of it
Or be my wife!
Frank Palmisano

Untitled

Roses are red violets are blue,
We all are in love and we are all sad,
The love we show is not always true,
When we are sad it is usually true,
Any feelings in between are those
that hurt the most,
for we are the emotional, loving, and
caring people of the 90's for we are
the new generation and no one can
conquer us!
Josh Mulberry

Loves Nuclear Winter

Like the winters she has endured,
harsh and unforgiving,
there comes another season.
No stress or strife
no judgement and no reason,
devoid of the words
"among the living."
June E. Pierson

"Sad Love"

I met him
and we didn't get along
we fought and fought
and everything went wrong

we would yell and scream
and didn't make a good team
then finally one day
we both got our way

We began to learn
how to love
as we were blessed
by the angel up above

He then asked me to marry
and I didn't know what to say
then when I went to say yes
he had passed on away
Deema Tabbara

One Shining Star

One shining star
Standing bright and far
All alone in the dark sky
  Looking so lonesome,
That it caught my eye.

It was not moonlight.
It was not candlelight.
It was at midnight
When I saw the starlight.

It was the only star insight,
  That night,
So I knew the moment was right
To make my wish,
At the sparkling light.
Melissa Chen

Ginsberg In The Walmart

Wandering the blue collared aisles
Corn fed faces in the video section
Drunk cowgirls and their faithful dogs
And Ginsberg tilts his head upwards
To see the infinite fluorescent
Adam Harry Rose

A Mother's Plea

I held her in my arms
Oh, what joy when she came
Oh, God! What I would give
To hold her once again

That pretty little girl
Skipping down the street
Oh, God! What I would give
If once more we could meet

That happy, smiling girl
Laughing at her play
Oh God! What I would give
To hear her voice today

That beautiful young girl
Sixteen! How time does fly
Oh God! What I would give
To just have said good-bye

Please hold her in your arms
And kiss her once for me.
Oh God! What I would give
If I could only see.
Marion B. Snyder

A Million Dollar Lesson

I held the letter in my hand
Wondering how I could win
A million-dollar contest
I had not entered.

They said if I would send five bucks
That I was sure to win
Since I was now a millionaire
I decide to send them ten.

I checked my mailbox daily
Much of my money was spent
Then I found to my horror
The check would not be sent.

I guess I learned a lesson
Though it was late indeed!
I may believe half of what I hear,
But none of what I read.
Nellie Beaty

Brother

With wings so large they
capsized my eyes,
so bright with vivid color,
like no other as we have known.
Off to the heavens is where
you have traveled, in search for
freedom in all that your life
has took in, devoured.
No answers have I been told
why it was that you have been chose.
As my tears shall never cease,
neither shall my prayers
for you and your quest for peace.
My loving brother I'll
cherish your style as you'll remain
in my arms as well as all of my
thoughts; forever, oh forever.
Kristi Gamble

Winter Wind

I wander through eternity,
Like a never ending song.
A journey of monotony,
It seems so very long.

Why? I ask, is this my fate,
What is it I have done?
This loneliness I do so hate,
It weighs a million tons.

It doesn't matter, night or day,
Regardless of the hour.
As I go by folks turn away,
I see them cringe and cower.

I aim no harm and claim no debt,
So why do they shun me?
When next I come, I'll lay a bet,
They'll beckon me to flee.

Days grow longer and I must go,
Yes, soon it will be spring.
And still my loneliness will grow,
'Cause I'm the winter wind.

Peter Twist Lopez

So Wonderful

The way you walk
The way you stride
The way you look into my eyes
It's oh, so wonderful
And I believe it's true
That in this short time
I've fallen for you
You make me laugh
You make me smile
You make me feel special
And worth your while
So, thank you, baby
For all you share
Your sweetness and kindness
And most of all
Your loving care . . .

Dana Carter

Life

Life is a long,
but narrow path
Yet seems short and straight
Full of challenges, curves, and hills
You've had your fill
of ups and downs
Now you're ready to settle down,
at a smooth street.
Life is a long,
but narrow path
That you will never forget.

Sabrina Wise 12 yrs. old

Morning Mist

The wispy mist is an elusive fawn,
Dappled silver
And is golden from the morning sun.
She is a timid creature,
For when you try to draw near
She fades into the pine and fir,
Only to reappear.

Sarah Locke

Cold

And as I watched his teardrops fall
And as I listened to him call
Amazed at the coldness that I felt
After giving the blows I'd dealt
Sat there watching him shed his tears
Felt nothing after all these years
But anger at the way he lied
Then stood before me and cried
One by one his teardrops came
I listened to him call my name
Stood right there and like a knife
Said the words that pierced his life
He looked so sad standing there
But I didn't really care
All I remembered was the pain
The lies that he couldn't explain
All the hurt was getting old
And all I felt inside was cold
And as I listened to him cry
Turned around and said goodbye.

Amanda Roser

Man's Common Destiny

Every moment
   Of time eternal,
A minute fragment
   From the glacier of life
Breaks away, unwilling, and plummets
Into the abyss of forever.
   There to melt and merge
With the ocean of eternity.
And it is as though it never was.

Where the fragment
   Once clung, on the face
Of the escarpment,
   There lingers in its place,
Half-remembered and half-imagined,
A frail perception of its facade.
   But, then, all too soon,
Those remaining fragments break away
And even dim remembrance is gone.

Margaret Peach Vaught

Bamboo Rapture

Golden green
Wave paper wings
Of butterflies.
Bamboo!
Deeply bend your head
Expose your easy nature
Swaying to
Giving forth
Rustling in response
Embrace the wind's caress.

Fuzzy brown
Hide pointed sheaths
Enfolding culms.
Bamboo!
Deeply shade your young
Reveal your inner nature
Yielding to
Bringing forth
Submitting in response
Embrace the wind's caress.

Kara Billingsley-Riordan

My Dream

I built a church
High up in the mountain
With logs from the big pine tree
Its steeple standing
Straight and tall
For everyone to see

My altar was of adobe
Built by willing hands
My seats were gifts
Of missionaries
From here and foreign lands

My windows were not painted
Just big and shiny and clean
Looking out on our savior's miracles
His lakes and beautiful trees

And when my church was finished
The people gathered there
Of every creed and color
To kneel and humbly
Bow their heads in prayer

Frances D. Cheshek

When We First Met...

I remember our first date
Which was in October of 84,
You were 15 minutes late
When you came knocking at my door.

My past was not too pleasant
   and I was tired of being hurt,
When you looked at me and said,
   "That you cared!"
Just because of the other guys
   that treated me like dirt,
I said to you, "I'm sorry, but don't
   even go there!"

You stood by my side
To show me you were not the same,
You even opened up my eyes
To prove this wasn't a game.

Now I know you did understand
When you asked me to be your wife,
Now I can say I found the man
Whom I will be with the rest of my life!

Kathy Sothen

Before You Wake

I love the feelings
you stir in me,
when I wake up early
and watch you sleep.
My beautiful lady
all wrapped in peace.
I love the feel
of your feminine form,
as I wrap you in my arms
to keep you warm.
To see you smile
when I caress your hair,
your eyes slightly flutter
as if you know I am there.
I wonder what thoughts
your morning dreams hide,
and pray they include me
as I close my eyes...

Kevin M. Overy

Winters

Winter night the moon is bright!
Children making snow angels.
Making snowmen out of white snow
Making forts out of ice.
Skating on ice perfectly.
Not making one mistake.
Falling down but getting back up.
Slipping, falling, never giving up!

Gabriel Swords

Escape!

I shut my eyes and go to sleep,
I close the door on light.
I dream of things unknown to me,
I soar the sky in flight.

Just once, I feel I'm in control,
My life's on even ground!
Dare is whisper "Freedom's" name,
For fear I make a sound?

Gliding through the air so still,
I'm peaceful as a dove.
No turbulence or thunderstorm
To alarm me up above.

The darkness of my slumber's rest
brightens now and then.
I toss., I turn., I readjust.,
Then I escape again.

Fran Gammicchia

Little Brown Thing

I found a little brown thing.
About the size of a ring.
Not every high and not very low.
Not like a hand not like a toe.
I put it in a jar.
So it could not go far.
I will keep it today.
And maybe sell it for pay.
And maybe I will let it grow
I think I will put it in the snow
Oh, little brown thing.
Mother said, to put you on a string.

June Fields

Hate Isn't Always It's Just Constant

Who hate sorry to hate
inevitably late always hate
constantly hate and no letting up
leaving this world and going it alone
no one to talk to
no one to relate to; but always
hate
To hate is to love but love
does not always make sense
because the fence around
us does not allow us to flee
into another dimension of the
life of love
So above the fence amongst
the sky
lies the realm of life
in the midst of all hate.

Diz Rigatoni

Tell Me

Time;
You thieving culprit!
Wait.

An eon, more or less, I need;
To shore up Eden's balustrades,
And cogitate her fate.

Mankind has gone a hobbling
Somewhere in outer space.
Mystic moon rings circle;
A comet whizzes by;
A universe of unnamed stars
Gleam in jet black sky.

In awe, we pause and ponder.
We hear a small owl's cry.
See elephants rampage in fear
Against a spearman's try.

So much to know, old father;
So many reasons.

Beulah P. Robbins

The Eichmann Trial

Before the bar of Justice
Humanity stood trial,
Before the court of Heaven
Justice donned her veil;
All of us must shudder now
and weep with those who lived
Through tortured depths of horror
The mind can scarce conceive.

Lillian Kahn

A New Love

I've waited so long
To meet you
And the time
Is finally here

As you already know
I'm a widow
And I've been
All alone for a year

So, it's only fair
that I warn you
Of my one
And greatest fear

I've dreamed of us
being together
and you holding me
so near

But, what if you
don't want me
that's my one
and greatest fear.

Rose Marie Jackson

Giraffe

Seeing to eternity
Tallest of the tall
Pattern of complexity
Puzzling over all.

Head held high with tongue-in-cheek
Listening to my voice
Valentine of lofty heights
Gentleness your choice.

Ann Daigle

J. D. Long Lake

Algae suspended about their faces
as air bubbles rise to the surface.
Buckled up
cause it's the law
Buckled in
to secure her sin.
Momma stumbles up the shore
conjuring up car-jack confabulations
to secure the relations
with her estranged lover.
Seems she didn't want to bother
with tinker toys
or hugs from her boys
who only wanted a little love
Not a shove
into a lake.

Patrick A. Brandimore Jr.

Tomb Of Aphrodite (Prayer For The Exiled)

I'll bring you primitive fire,
Lick your skin
With a serpent's wet desire.
Our thighs will dance to drums
From a pagan past,
Bringing us to screaming savage songs
That last forever.
If,
When we're through,
You'll hold me for a moment.
Or two.
Embrace this child of lost love,
Under the dove's dark wings.
Then,
I'll vanish into the night,
Going home to the desert,
Weeping with, sleeping with
The black Shulamite.

Marilyn Mick

Education

Mix sounds of children's laughter
With the silence of the snow
And whisper an honest word
Where devils fear to go

Kindness of a scent-filled breeze
Amidst all the howls of rain
Added to a wise man's thoughts
Gives joy to an eager brain

Stir in open sunlight with
The main answer to the young
Of life's strange meanderings
Where our history is hung

Tell flowers filled with honey
To spread all the words around
That hope is mixed up in life
With feet solid on the ground

Barbara Hyten

Love Obsession

The river is wide I can't
step it I have you and
I can't help it.

As sure as the vines go round the
well I'll have you in spite of hell.

Dennis Wright

You Proved Me Wrong

I really thought you like me
I actually thought you cared
But still you managed to hurt me
After all the feelings I shared
I thought our love could never end
But it didn't even start
All you did was make me cry
And break my powerless heart
I thought that you were different
But you really proved to me
Friends are just acquaintances
And lovers only dreams

Dawn McPherson

Splendor

Strong threads of diamonds
Woven along a summer fence
Are spread amid the glistening
Leaves of an August morning.
Time is caught on spun
Webs of spider silk
And tipped with dewdrops
Among the filaments so delicate.
A pattern wonderful emerges
To hang in infinite beauty.
This instant is sublime.
It holds one spellbound as
Reality drifts into oblivion.

Jane S. Nichols

Love Flows Like A River

I inhabit on the upper-stream
   of the Pearl River,

While you dwell on the lower-stream
   of the same river.

Everyday I don't see your visage,

But I dream of your image;

And but we drink the same water
   from the same river.

When could this water be exhausted?

When could it come to a pause?

Only would I wish your heart
   being identical as my heart.

So it would never stop
   the ever-flowing love into us.

Hor-ming Lee

Never Meant To Be

You are my true love,
My first love,
Nothing can; Nothing will,
Stop me from thinking about you,
Although it's never meant to be,
And you will never love me,
I will always love you,
This is the truth,
Plain as can be;
For as I said before,
It was never meant to be.

Katie Jo Reynolds

My Mother, My Friend

You have always been there for me,
When I needed you to be.
You made me feel so happy inside,
Just by saying you love me.

Of all the times we argued,
and the times we sat and cried;
When all the odds were against me,
You were always be my side.

You were the first friend I had,
and as a friend, you're the best.
As far as being a mother goes,
you're better than the rest.

I wouldn't change anything,
even the times we fought.
You taught me more than anyone,
more than you ever thought.

Now that I'm a mother I see,
how hard it was for you,
You did the best anyone could
and I want to say, "I Love You"

Wendy L. Leighton

Dream

My hands are shadows and I
Wash them of you.

The gleaming Ginsu grasped in your
Semi-permeable fingers
Like a lollipop.

I'd try to stop you,
But you'd kill me, too.

As if you would.
The unthinkable
Becomes a genocidal
Walk in
-no-
Float above
The many cornered, shadowy Park.

Cindene Pezzell

Untitled

Each night they will greet me,
When I come through the door,
Hug me, please feed me,
Then hug me some more.

They guide me along
All the way to the kitchen,
Whinin', and cryin',
And general bitchin'

They tell me their day
As I listen with pleasure
These two little cats
Are life's greatest treasure.

I hug them, I feed them
Then hug them some more
And know that they'll be there
When I come through the door.

Nicki M. Vitale

Our Love

As we sit here watching the
sunset with many vibrant colors,
   In my mind I think I love
you much more than any other.
   And as the sweet breeze blows
I smell it in your hair, I look
around and see that love is everywhere!
   And as I gaze into those big,
dark, beautiful eyes, I think of how
our love will fall and then will rise.
   Rise, like the sun rising in
the west, rise with many colors
upon the robin's breast.
   Rise upon the hilltop, then
watch the sunset fall and we will
be together, forever, all in all.

Amanda Grigsby

Center

Far off from the center
   So high I've fallen
   Beckoning for help
   I can't get back
   Just the words themselves
Have built the walls
Far off the center
I can't get back
   With swift brilliance
   And a quick Beat
   The heart conned the mind
   I will get back
   The desire appears
   Followed by sweat
   Back to the center
   The heart won the bet

Eric L. McGilloway

Hope

Through the darkness
brightly shining,
a window into the heart of love
calls the weary traveler.

Life-giving water
shimmers in the desert sun
beckoning the parched voyager.

Simple friendship
frankly offered
lifts a lonely one from despair.

True love given
and true love returned
a beautiful gift.

Carmen Ruiz-Castaneda

The Lord

The Lord is the giver of time
   Our life is in His hand
He has it all figured out for us
   Each one a special plan
He knew us before our first breath
   He knows the minute of our last
He is if we believe or not
   Our life's already cast
From this day on we give our thanks
   Our love, our heart, our soul
To the Lord who created us so well
   Then threw away the mold

Dave Long

The Cowboy

Away out on the prairie
Midst the mesquite and the sage
Rides the jolly, sun-burned cowboy
With his horse he draws his wage

Sombrero shields his thick black hair
Red neckerchief does blow
His buckskin vest and flannel shirt
Are fancy and cost "doe".

Riding cuffs around his wrists
Six gun round his waist
White curly chaps protect his legs
And with lariat, has raced.

High heeled boots and jingling spurs
Oh the cowboy life for me
Long may they live and rule the range
By their carefree liberty.

Evelyn Kuper Bushman Lather

Look At Me

Look at me Mommy,
I am getting taller now,
my hands can reach all the things
I never could before.
Look at me Mommy,
I can read by myself,
and understand what you say.
Look at me Mommy,
I have so much to learn
and be thankful to all whom
have shared their lives with me.
Look at me Mommy,
What a beautiful life I can
make for myself and enjoy our
time as the Lord guides me
and protects those I love.
Look at me Mommy,
Smile, love me always.

Jamie Johnston

Daydream

Desire
Ocean wave
Blue blue water
Seaside cave

Captivate
Can't you see
Is it fate
Lament with me

Confuse
Rainbow world
Shatters, scatters
Truth unfurled

Enchant
My breath away
Consume me
Every way

Dominate
Starry night
I wish I may
I wish I might

Jolyn Miller

Rising Moon

Shreds of twilight's cloth
hang from the outstretched limbs
of the hollow oak.
　Fallen memories
crumble in my footsteps
Leaving the forgotten shards
of their death.
　Purple hyacinths
in twisting water
are recognized by their sweet perfume.
　And newborn blossoms
on young trees' fingertips
comb back my windswept hair.
　A trail of honeysuckle
litters the ground behind me
and the sticky nectar
still clings to my lips.
　But as the golden sun falls,
the white moon raises its head
to see me to my door.

Carrie DeHaven

A Summer's Night

The stars drip their honey
　Onto the river
While a thousand and one
Fairies dance above the wheat.

Listen...
　The crickets sing their love songs.
Listen...
　A frog courts his princess.
Hush...
　And you can hear the corn grow.

Sandra A. Stapler

Lost

I'm lost,
but losing more...
I'm losing people,
I'm losing life,
I'm losing things,
I'm lost in the inside of me.
And soon it will be the outside also.

Aimee Rose Wood

Memories

Life's for sale,
And time is cheap.
History flies in
While the future creeps.

We have no flavor,
Unless we await.
We don't miss the present
Until it's too late.

We're always continuing,
Pressing ahead.
We'll never stop
Until we are dead.

We live for "what's next",
It's our way, you see.
And all we'll have left
Is the memories.

Cassie Allen

Waiting

If I should go before you
On the other shore I'll be
Hands outstretched, I will be waiting

I will watch over you in the night
And throughout the days, waiting

Look up into the sky
And you will see the sunlight
Of my smile

Feel the wind against your face
It will be my touch
I will be waiting

Smell the fresh scents of spring
It will be me, waiting

Look out at the stars on a dark
And lonely night
I will be waiting

Moonlight and rainbows
Will remind you, that I will be waiting

Thunder will be my voice
Lightning my eyes, waiting

Charlene L. Holland

Will To Shine

Tragedies in our life
could destroy one's will to live,
our happiness no longer shines
our emotions are not free to give.
You awaken every morning
wanting it to end,
you just exist, lost somewhere
hoping soon your heart will mend.
Then one day, given time
you awaken and can see,
your strength has truly shone for you
you've gotten through this tragedy.
What triggered my emotions?
I feel alive again,
Did I forget or just accept?
Have I moved on, but when?
It's not that you forget
you simply let it fade,
accept what you can't change
this too is what God has made.

Lisa Roy

Ruffles Wrinkles And Roses

The two are for beauty and sweetness
too, but Dod-oh-Dod what's a
wrinkle to do but stay right in
there and shine right through.
　Someone once said that a
wrinkle was a smile turned
up side down, if that be true,
I'm the smilingest wrinkle in
this whole town.
　I was dismayed when I first
took a look at the creases and
crevices and funny nooks; but
I've earned the right to wear
them all, so we'll keeps on
smiling one and all.

Lila Bingham

Roll Call

"Here, Sir!" the voices call,
as the names were read;
"Here, Sir!" came the reply,
from the roll call of the dead.

Names chiseled in the stone,
hard, black and cold;
names of men who are now gone,
but somehow warm my soul.

The names of men who gave so much,
got nothing in return;
the sacred souls listed here,
never in hell will burn.

Give us this day our daily bread,
from the heavens above;
and to those on that cold, dark wall,
my unrelenting love.

"Here, Sir!" the voices call,
as the names were read;
"Here, Sir!" came the reply,
from the roll call of the dead.

Bradley A. Stephens

Secrets

The mind has many secrets.
Some remain unknown.
If you ask me I think
The secrets are not at home.

They travel mind to mind,
Mixing things as they go.
They have a certain technique,
That we just don't know.

Now that little secret,
Has turned upside down.
Now you hope and wish
The secret can be found.

Why can't we learn
Secrets we don't know?
Maybe they were left to be
A mystery and the unknown.

Richard Keithley

Love's Temptation

For the love of God,
For the snares of Christ,
For happiness and peace,
You need avoid my vice.
For the sun to shine,
For the birds to sing,
You must not fall,
For the corruption I bring.
A rose is not smelt,
When surrounded by manure.
Of its own smell,
It becomes unsure.
Love is a concept,
Often misunderstood.
It's pain and anguish,
Mistaken for good.
A simple decision
Is yours to be made,
Of me and my ways,
Should you be afraid?

Dexter Markwood

Difference

A heart can be soft and gentle
  loving in everyway
A heart can be cold and cruel
  deteriorating everyday
A dream can be warm and friendly
  with nothing else to matter
A dream can be harsh and lonely
  cracking until it shatters
A soul can be free and lively
  soaring through the sky
A soul can be trapped and deserted
  left behind to cry
A friend can be true and trusting
  with sun shining each day
A friend can be cruel and helpless
  walking a different way

Gidget Nickle

Time Passes By

One day you are a little girl,
growing up with Mama and Daddy.

Before you know it,
you are a teenager
looking at all the boys,
falling in love for the first time.

then you are grown and married
raising your children,
living life the best you can,,
with this fine, wonderful man.

So many things you meant to do,
but never got around to,
My, how time passes by.

Frances N. Ruff

Deja Vu'

Mirror, mirror
what do I see,
in this bundle of joy
lying in front of me.

Pale blue eyes
a smile so sweet,
long slender fingers
and tiny, long feet.

Time passing slowly
speeds instantly back,
to many years hence
a daughter on my lap.

A grandbaby new
a daughter of mine,
remarkably different
yet twins out of time.

My life's all aglow
no longer apart,
flowing tears of joy
with an overflowing heart.

John F. Negri

A Blind Man's Dream

A blind man's dream
May be to fly
Fly way up high
High in the sky;
A blind man's dream
May be to soar
Soar with the birds
Too speechless for words;
A blind man's dream
May be to see
To see the world
The beautiful world;
But the world may not
Be as nice
As what he would hope;
It may be better
Not to see
The world as it really is,
Because a blind man
Can only have his dream.

Lindsay-Ann Brown

I'm Irritated

I know how an oyster feels
being annoyed by a
grain of sand
only to be killed when
the pearl forms...

I know how a horse
feels being infested
by flies
with only a tail to
reach its unreachable ears...

I know how a dog feels
that's over run with
fleas and no matter
how much it scratches
the fleas don't flee.

I know all these creatures
have one thing in
common with me...

I'm irritated.

Cordelia Vieira

"The Accident"

One lonely eyeball
laying on the ground
looking at
the glass on the ground,
the blood all over the road,
an arm of someone,
an ear laying next to the eye.

The eye sees the
men, women, and children
scream and cry.
The red and blue bubbles on
the police car.

Slowly it gets darker and darker
until it sees no more.

April Lynn Knetter

A Yesterday Remembered

Down friendship's golden pathway,
Memory has planted there;
The shiny tint of a by gone day,
'Tis only a yesterday past.

The days have seemed like ages,
Weeks pass one by one;
Months are turning the pages,
Since the yesterday that's done.

I've pictured many a sunset,
In colors of red, blue and gold;
But never a one can quite surpass,
The memory a yesterday holds.

I'll always keep a secret place,
In the garden where friendship gleams;
To keep for us one perfect trace,
Of a yesterday that dreams.

And now at the close of each long day,
I long for twilight at last;
So I can pause in Dreamland Bay,
Remembering a yesterday past.

Virginia W. Wrenn

The Feel Of Being Here

I like the feel of being here
A part of the wind and sea.
I even think the great big moon
Is some sort of kin to me.

Oh, I like the feel of being here,
A part of the happy crowd.
In a parade I love to march,
Because you just feel so proud.

On frosty days I feel the sun
As warm as a kiss of love.
I climb the highest hill
And feel protected from above.

On summer days I find a big old tree
Full of singing birds,
And read a stirring book
Or make up songs to my own words.

Just any old thing to know I'm here,
And that's why I feel so proud.
Along with heaven, earth and you!
I was allowed.

Alice Spohn Newton

What Is Love?

Love is like the snow-capped mountains
And the rainforest so green,
It's being kind and nice,
Not being mean

It's fluffy, white clouds of the sky
And sun sweet berries
Sweet and dry.

It's rain to a desert
And sand to a beach
A soft sweet voice
And not a screech

A colorful flower
And a milk-white dove
That is to me
The beauty of love

Poonam Basu

The One

He came to me
The words he spoke?
One look at those dimples,
My words he took.

Engulfing eyes,
That single look.
With a soft, soft kiss
My mind he took.

Late talks, slow dances-
I'll always remember
To him, my best friend,
My heart I surrendered.

His peculiar walk,
His laugh, his style
But what I miss most
Across the miles?...

His touch, his feel
His caring ways.
To see him again-
I'll count the days.

Emily Mustafa

We Three Derelicts

We three derelicts
For humbly we are told
We go walking, come this way
Who tobble us with gold.

We swiftly see an early sight
We struggle to bequeathed
A mighty tug surrounds us then
We come up underneath.

We scrabble down the ocean view
We tabble in the night
What else is there; can't you see?
We grabble, oh so right.

We three derelicts
We dig the early sod
We rattle men that won or lost
And drink their fine egg nod!

Brian A. Ford

Free As A Bird

To be as free as a bird, is a dream
I often dream.
To be able to fly over hills and
Gently running streams;
Would be more than just a common
Everyday thing.

With wings that glide on air and
Slice through the wind;
I could fly almost anywhere and
Never wonder where I've been.

Catherine Honan

Untitled

Shower me with kisses
Bathe me in your love
You're my true desire-
The one I hold above
others all around
who want a part of me
Please just say you'll
love me
until eternity

Sandra G. Smith

Goddess Of Impression

She is serene and sublime.
With the taste of one divine.

Subtle sounds of her tears.
Creates curiosity and need.

I interpret what appears,
Difficult to believe.

My thought was pricked,
By a thorn that bled.

Sweet taste was thick,
With roses on my bed.

Hearing laughs through my blindness,
Feeling cries for what I see.

Trusting hints of kindness,
Grasping hopes of glee.

Choosing courage to lie,
While my patience turns red.

Wanting insight to try,
With pictures in my head.

Longing a vision to be replaced,
With physical passion of embrace!

Scott M. Kirtley

Dreams Of Nature

Nature ran to me in my dreams,
The water swallowed up the fish.
The sun came down in wavy beams.
If I had only one wish.

I would go back to the place,
Where my dreams come true.
The grass and trees waved like lace.
The water was warm and blue.

The place was full of quietness.
Just one sound floated unaware.
I never noticed life's sweet caress,
To awake and never see it there.

Kerrynn Waters

Untitled

Two people entered my heart
Both at the same time
One with a smile so true
The other, piercing eyes of blue
One showed interest
The other stayed aloof
One was wild and crazy
The other, kind and gentle
One wanted me
The other, not
One has now gone their way
The other, I have not forgot.

B. J. Mitchell

Spirits

The spirits are here,
They know where you are;
They're coming for you,
From near or from far.

So hide in the cellar,
Just shut the door;
Run for your life,
Or you'll be no more.

Meghan Hunt

Memories Past

If you still know the memories past
You will have great memories to last
But if those memories
have past away let
a tear, fall my way
But if those memories
let you say this was a
happy day let a laugh come
my way
If its too hard to remember
let your self come down and
think how was that day
was it a snowy day in December
or a warm day in May
can all those memories
really last till today
If they last all the way
you may have a special day
Emmy Scelsi

The Place Where Baseball Lives

The Village of Cooperstown
Her streets do we roam,
A feeling of yesteryear
It's like going home,

The treasures of baseball
Reside in this shrine,
On an exploring journey
You go back into time.

A childhood reborn
In shops and the hall,
of yesterday's memories
Of a kid playing ball.

So dream of your heroes
Of baseball's past,
And wonder aloud
Why it's gone by so fast.

Tho' the game has changed
With bright looks and new parks,
That feeling of baseball
Forever lives in our hearts.
James Kozlowski

Kids

Kids are cute
Kids are funny
Kids will laugh
If you give them money
They will roll their eyes
And pucker their lips
Just so you'll take them
With you on that trip
They run in the grass
And play in the water
They mess in their pants
And say they don't wanna
When their tired they like
only your lap
So they can lay down and
take a nap
Yes kids are cute
Yes kids are funny
But I think that parents
Deserve all the money
Lyle Rueckert

Dream

It's early spring
we were running through a
field of wild flowers
your hand in mine
as we fell to the ground
you held me tight
Later
we danced to the silent
song in our head
peacefully...
together
Candyce Fabela

What Happiness Was

Happiness was my hand in yours
The way my heart filled with
    joy when ever you were near
Happiness was the sound of your voice
The way your hug never faded
    away and stayed with me for hours
My happiness was you
Everything about you was my happiness
But my happiness is gone
Because you are gone
You were my happiness
Kimberly Faye Hegwood

"Worried Love"

You hold me in your arms,
and I forget about life's alarms,
I love you.
You never make me blue.

Will you always be there?
Will you always care?
That is what I ask, is
loving me a big task?

You say I love you, is that true?
Is that what I should believe?
Please, I beg of you, don't leave!

We were about to say I do!
Is that she?
Is that who's replacing me?
How can this be?!
You said you loved me!
Laura DeHart

Painted Pony

Take off your silver bridle,
shake your flaxen mane -
throw your head, paw the earth,
your spirit will never tame.

Let your golden hooves guide you
painted pony of the earth,
for you've been set free -
run, embrace new birth.

Step high and proud across the land
as you canter into the plains.
Don't come back or turn around
in the direction in which you came.

And when you see the Golden Gate,
gently turn and wave farewell.
And with it you'll leave a legacy -
we'll miss you carousel.
Kristi Minietta

To A Mystical Place

You always called me
Your bright and shining star

Our love carried us
To a mystical place afar.

Oh, we struggled too,
We were friend and foe

I just never suspected
The other woman, lady snow.

We loved so hard
Until the bottom fell out,

I was left wondering
Full of hurt and doubt.

I've been replaced now
Your bright and shining star,

Lady snow carried you
To a mystical place afar.
Cheryl Mangin

Why I Flew Old Glory On May 14th

'Was a sleepless torrid night,
My brain was racked with pain.
Body dripping beads of sweat,
As if lying in the rain.

The moon sailed waxing 'cross the sky,
In endless rendezvous.
Full of beaming paling light,
It cast a ghostly blue.

Why were dogs so restless?
Countless sirens pealed.
The need for rest eluded me,
Eyelids would not yield.

It ever slowly dawned on me,
The essences of this malaise.
A kamikaze crashed my ship,
Fifty years ago, today.

It wrecked my ship and killed my mates,
Gallant lives were lost that day.
To see us now, the way we are,
'Twas a bloody price to pay.
A. R. Jack Banks

Pardon Me But...

I have been around some
and I think I know the score
I'm tired of being walked on
and I won't be anymore.

I'm tired of saying yes
when no is what I mean,
I'm tired of agreeing with everyone
about every little thing.

This old gal has had it
that's what this is all about,
I'm just sorry it took so damn long
for me to find it out.
Barbara R. Thurston

Would You Hear Me

If I thought, "I love you,"
Would you hear me
As if I spoke out loud,
As if somebody told it,
Or you read it on my brow?

If I whispered, "I love you,"
Would you hear me
Though soft as a raindrop
On a rose petal in May,
Or a snowflake on the ground?

If I said, "I love you,"
Would you hear me?
Would it sink into your soul?
Would it warm your heart or sadden,
Because I told you so?

If I never said, "I love you,"
Would you hear it anyway?
Would you feel it in my eyes?
Would you see it in my face?
Do you hear me?

Andrea Clark

Mothers Are Like Rainbows

Mothers are like rainbows,
After a dark dreary day.
Mothers will cheer you,
And brighten your way.
Her arms will enfold you,
Close to her heart,
At times when you're sad,
Oft the teardrops start.
E'en tho' the rainbows fade away,
Mother's love is constant,
And is here to stay,
Our dear heavenly Father made,
Mothers and rainbows galore.
So their beauty like a master piece,
May be enjoyed o'er and o'er.

Jane Nance

Have You Ever Noticed...

When times are going good,
and everything seems as it should.
We seem to forget to say..
Thank you Lord for it being this way
But when times are sad
And things seem to be going bad
We remember always then to pray
Lord please help me through this day.
How sad it would really be.
For the Lord to do the same to me
But like always, to my surprise
His love for his children never dies
So when I feel I'm at the end of my rope
I'll fall to my knees and know there is hope.
I'll pray to the Lord once again with a plea.
Dear Lord I thank you for being there for me...

Monica O. Granado

Show Me

Show me you love me
Show me you care
Show me I exist to you
Show me I'm there
Show me we can communicate
Show me some understanding
  Show me

Candice Crespin

Alone In Darkness Soon

I've watched my last sunset
I've heard the last dove cry
No more rock-n-roll nights
Just the loneliness of goodbye
No more walks in the dark
Underneath the stars
Just me all alone
Me by myself - life gone by afar
No more Mommy, I love you
Just a deep dark place
I guess this time I've done it
I'll never show my face
No husband to say I love you
No family to hold onto
Just me in the darkness
Dear God, what do I do
Life is too precious
To send yourself to hell
But, everyone's out to get you
This time I've really failed

Lena Wright-Baswell

One Of Those Days

Have you ever had one of "those days,"
where nothing seems to go your way?
Outside the weather's rainy and wet,
and you didn't get your promised pet.
Your dog chewed up your favorite
autographed baseball that was on
the floor, and you slammed your
finger in the door.
You just got grounded for back talking
to your dad, boy are you ever mad.
Be patient and let the day pass
by, and while you're waiting you
might as well eat a piece of pie!

Valerie Van Gundy

A Friend In Need

We may walk alone today
We may walk alone tomorrow
But we all need a friend
To share our joy and sorrow

We can never give too little
Yet we never seem to have enough
To share with that someone
Who really needs our love

Somehow I wish I could take back
Or maybe it's good I feel the pain
Cause this will make me a better person
Then Charles' passing won't be in vain

Arthur Gurlly Jr

The Eagle Lives

The eagle is a graceful bird...
Dancing upon breezes.
His keen eyes stare down at the world,
Searching for his prey.

He spies the rabbit...
The eagle plunges down,
His talons ready!
The rabbit dives into his burrow,
The eagle flies away.

Anna Wieschowski

But In The Still Of The Night...

But in the still of the night
When the quiet was bright
I hung my head low
And cried.

In the morning the sun
Caressed my cheek
And lightly kissed
My forehead.

The clouds billowed round
Creating a clown
Who danced hand in hand
With the wind

Playing hide and go seek
Amid lofty peaks
And I raised my head up
And smiled.

Nadine V. L. Thomas

Shadow In The Night

As she lay dying with death
the moon dared not disturb her
her air blew with the breeze
and the unheard breath —
The eyes stared in open space
no movement, speechless.
Wonder her heart has stopped
or her desire has worn out?
For the last hour of her life
the wrinkles disappeared
the hollow cheeks deepened
the fists clenched —
But the body lay still
forever countless time
until the tear drained out of her eyes.

Alexandria Huynh

Primal Desire

A full moon howls tonight
I feel an ancient primate stir my blood
a little bit restless, a lot wild!
Danger flares my emotions
want it, need it, almost feel it
call of the wild, roots of my soul
scream for attention
demand action.
Slowly grey, blue, purple clouds
fill the sky and my mind.
Soon the fullness will show no more
smothered with gray matter
the essence of our lives.
Too many necessities, responsibilities
life should be lived—
not longed for.
I crave a primal existence:
Food, water, love, and family.

Mary White

"The Kids Of Today"

They are the kids of today,
But tomorrow they will be
  the kids of days long past.
All alone in the world,
Striving to live,
Yearning to love.
With only the hopes
  of the kids of today

Kendra Short

Hold On

Hold on - to your dreams
Hold on - to your heart
Don't ever let go
Because you'll need it so.
Hold on - to the love inside
Hold on - to the one you love
Who knows?
They might leave you tomorrow
So Hold On - to your dreams
They might fly away, high away
Stay with your dreams
Don't let them wander
I will be there to comfort you
To hold you near
To never give up
Even if you do.
Run to me, Come to me
Tell me all your problems
And I'll set you free
So please come back to me.
Eric Ward

The Call Of Solitude

I am sitting in the dark,
   momentarily blinded,
As the arms of darkness
   quickly surround me
I hear a crow caw loudly
   around me
Like a spoiled child that
   hasn't minded
It reaches me through
   the wind
   and plays on my mind
Then the arms let go
   gently.
I fall asleep in total
   solitude and awake with
   it still lingering on
My mind.
Elizabeth Chase

A Sinner's Prayer

Oh Lord, help me in my time of need.
Help me to conquer the greed
That I have within my soul.
Make me once more, whole.

I drifted away just like before.
Once again, my life was a bore.
Surprisingly, you stayed around.
You brought my feet back to the ground.

I was a sinner, but you forgave.
You're my leader, and I am your slave,
But like a friend you treat me.
I'll stay with you throughout eternity.

Teach me what to do,
Tell me where to go.
I will gladly learn.
All my idols I will burn.

Then, when I get the Holy place,
I will see your grace,
No one will ever shed any tears
Like we've done over earthly years.
Gina Helms

Lost Love

The sky is blue and so am I,
Cuz my love said goodbye,
If I could get back just one day,
That would be the day he said he
   would stay,
My life is empty now that you're gone,
The day is long,
The night is too,
My life is empty without you,
I hope you will come back and say
   you will stay,
And not ever go away,
Please come back.
Tiffini Holtmeier

A Picture Of You

I'll paint a picture of you
A lovely moon beam
A star or two
But where will I put little me?

I'll smear a cloud across the sky
Like fresh dipped ice cream
And then I'll close my eyes to look
And dream and dream and dream.

I'll paint a picture of you
A lovely moon beam
A star or two
But where will I put little me?
John M. Altman Sr.

Summer's Prayer

In her heart
Summer knows the answers
to the questions in her mind
In her soul
Summer cries for the endings
to the sadness in her life
in her head
Summer laughs at the daisies
that engulf her dreams
out loud
Summer screams at you
for being her pain
her ache and worry
but also
her pride and passion
this is Summer's prayer.
Angelina Ramirez

Tiffani

You're beautiful as can be
you mean the world to me
I know you will be special
It's very plain to see.
You have dark hair, dark
eyes and a little button
nose, you even have your
mom's cute little toes, you
have your dad's ears
a round little face, your
smile it seems to brighten
the place you were blessed
with wonderful parents as
they were blessed with you,
now you're a happy family,
the Lord has blessed it's true.
Pat Adams

Sunday Sonata

Like earth's vapors we co-mingle,
pausing to savor nature's rhapsody,
in peaceful retreat from noise,
traffic, oppressive heat.

The breeze caresses my cheek,
tousles my hair, whispers assurances
that You are there.

Precious moments alone, You and I
lovers probing, caring,
desiring, yearning.
Closer we draw, old friends
on the road to becoming one.

Time held captive,
we talk things over,
hand in hand,
in step together.

Surrounded by sounds
in perfect harmony,
a Sunday sonata composed
by Thee for me.
Patty Sposato

Untitled

We're getting closer
Suffocate by compaction
I can feel you getting closer
I can feel you start to steal my breath
And are we that much closer?

We're growing older
Older still I'm younger now
I can feel you growing older
I can feel you change beneath my mouth
And are we that much older?

We're going further
Distances can separate
I can feel you getting further
I can feel your distance on my skin
And are we that much further?

And I wear my seatbelt when I...
Thomas Barlow

Teardrop

A teardrop fell last night,
It dropped with a crash.
I tried with all my might,
But it still made a big splash.

A teardrop fell last night,
I hardly noticed it at all,
To remember, because of my plight
It fell, but the puddle was small.

A cheer drop fell last night,
It tumbled and became a pool.
So now my future look bright.
My new friend is a jewel.
Forest Moore

My Friend

I've got a friend who loves me,
who will all my needs supply and I know
yes, I know I'll love him until the day I die.

When I'm feeling blue and don't
know what to do the Lord says
unto me, I will see you through.
Ima Jean Pitts

Star Light...

Star light,
Star bright,
I see your face in the stars tonight.
I wish I may,
I wish I might,
have you here to hold me tight.
Wishes come from far and near,
Some are often followed by tears.
Wishes come and wishes go
Just as rivers flow.
I wonder why these wishes I have
always seem to disappear
As one leaves another just appear.
Star light,
Star bright,
I want this as my wish tonight
I wish this I may,
I wish I might,
Have you come true tonight.

Jamie Sims

Olympics Poem

Reach for the Stars,
Reach for the Gold!
Always be proud.
Always be bold.
Team USA,
We are the best!
Lead all the World,
Give them the test!
Give them your all,
Give them your most!
Need not to brag,
Need not to boast!
Team USA,
Olympics, your call.
Never give up,
Forever stand tall!

Caleigh Epolito

Thought-Leaves

Blowing leafly,
my thoughts scatter
to the four corners of my mind,
sometimes settling on flowers
of light-shivering rainbows,
sometimes lofted
to the blue-echoing halls
of spiralling space,
sometimes carried on winds
of bright promise,
after bending with the rain.

Seymour Pulver

Why

Every night I lay in bed,
  but all I do is cry.
You left me alone in this
  world, all I want to
  know is why?
Why did you leave me here
  to cry these tears I hold?
Why did you leave me here
  alone, to me you never told
Now, I'm sitting here wondering
  what did I do so wrong.
When you left you took my
  heart, and the love I
thought was strong.

Apryl Rhinehart

Please Forgive Me

Lord, please forgive me,
I know not what I do.
I ask for forgiveness from Thee
For I have been untrue.

Please don't judge me Lord
I have made many mistakes.
My sins I've tried to ignore,
My life I've tried to take.

I thought it needed to end,
My life was filled with haze.
I need you to help my heart mend
I need help getting out of this maze.

Lord, please forgive me,
I know exactly what I do.
I asked for forgiveness from Thee
And you have seen me through.

Becky Joseph

My Parents

They were there for me
  Right from the start,
They loved me and cared for me
  Even when I fell apart.

They praised me when good,
  Punished me when bad.
They made me feel better
  When I felt real sad.

When I had the flu
  They knew just what to do.
I owe my life to them,
  I know this is true.

When I get old,
  My turn's just begun,
And I'll take care of them
  'cause the cycle's not done.

Heather Bjorndahl

My Son

Oh Lord! Shed Thee light
Upon my son,
For he is my only one

Tho He is, but a little man,
He surely is his Dad's right hand

Running, playing, fighting too
Is what little boys were made to do

He always had a helping hand,
For anyone, woman or man.

So dear Lord, I know you can
Completely heal my little man

Michael Sharik I

Bedtime

Tired, sleepy,
Last goodbyes of
the day.
A beginning of
a new world.
Close your eyes,
Feel the mist come
over you.
Hear the rustle
of the sandman
Goodnight.

Joanna Klose

Patricia

Morning sunset
A petal sere
A puppy blind
A baby blue
An angel shorn
Patricia pained

Why, God?

And God wondered

Thus

The sun corrects
The petal breathes
The puppy sees
The baby pinks
The angel soars
Patricia heals

Because, God explained

Vincent A. Malito

My Thanks

I climbed up high upon a hill,
  one warm and sunny day,
I felt as tho all time stood still,
  as I began to pray.

I raised my head toward the sky
  it looked so calm and blue.
I thanked the Lord in heaven on high
  and asked for guidance too.

I thanked him for each bright new day.
  end for the rising sun
I thanked him for the flowers in May,
  and the little streams that run.

I thanked him for the birds that sing,
  their songs so sweet and clear,
I just thanked God for every thing
  and oh! he seemed so near.

Elsie Simms

Absence

Fantasies of you cloud
my burden.
The sound of your voice
holds my sweat.
Memories of us kills
my loneliness.
Compromising my movement
for your face.
Although I'm still, I'm
in a million places.
Breathing the scent of
your strength.
With every thought I think of more.
Remembering things
that meant nothing.
With every word you speak, I smile.
Planning a million things to say,
But upon your arrival,
words escape my mind.
Then breaking silence with our eyes.

Crissy L. Moll

Dreams Fulfilled

Thoughts of silver, bronze and gold
Will keep your spirits high.
Within your heart those dreams you hold
Will lift you to the sky.
There is a light that shines above
Not dimmed by things unseen.
Your quest for what you truly love
Will hold you to that dream.
No trial or tribulation
Or unseen potential jinx.
Can dim the awesome spirit
Of Olympics '96.

Beverly Anderson

I Like Spring

I like summer's life style,
Its slow and easy pace,
The long bright days all shimmery hot,
The evening's cool embrace.

I like autumn's color show,
Its golden fields of wheat,
Its empty beaches, frosty morns,
Its festive turkey treat!

I like the crunch my footsteps make
On a winter's walk.
The little puffs of frozen breath
I see when people talk.

But all of these diminish
In the glory that is spring
When new beginnings start to stir
In every living thing!

Lois J. Thut

Haiku's

The cold, silver moon
bright, with the stars in the sky
lights the winter night

Quiet dawn is rising
the morning stillness shattered
by a waking soul

Snowflakes fall gently
covering like a blanket of snow
beautiful and pure

Alyson Terry

The Wolf

His eyes are cold
He instills fright
Beware my friend
The wolf is out tonight

Be careful my friend
As you walk the street
Because his eyes are sharp
And swift are his feet

His fangs are sharp
And big is he
Be careful my friend
And try not to be seen

I warned you my friend
His eyes give a gleam
It's too late my friend
you have already been seen

Tommy George

As You Wed

Your wedding day is special
A day that is so grand
It's the day you pledge eternity
In front of all the land.
A day that's filled with magic
A bond that's made to last
The vows are said, rings exchanged
The sacred spell is cast.
Your families join together
They becomes as one
To love and care for both of you
When all is said and done.
Keep all of your promises
Always cherish your love
Share together all the things
You always have dreamed of.
Together you will live a life
In which you can't go wrong
'Cause with your love and devotion
You both will stand so strong.

Rachele Lynn Peterson

Surprise!

Seeing the need
to lighten things up,
a child
in a fit of spontaneous abandon
flung a bevy of bubbles
out the car window
touching grimy trucks
and sweaty workers
with momentary pristineness
and beauty.
My heart was glad
for this great excuse
to recapture
the absolute care-freeness
of childhood
to feel lifted
innocent
full of joy
amid the clamor
   of progress.

Margaret R. Zuber

Delete

Soul sucking ebon
Drains life energy
Dark bleak scapes
Beckon harshly
Abandoned horizons
Lost sick dreams
Fast frozen aura
Brainwave synapse
Heartbeat paralysis
Electric life freeze
Icy hard plains
Stark bleached bones
Skull hollow need
Barren desolation
Stark absence
Complete

Stan Ross

Tornado Watcher

Tornado watcher
Where are you.

Tornado watcher
What can I do.

Tornado watcher
You watch it spin,

Tornado watcher
Spin again, and again.

Tornado watcher
Why don't you let me in.

The tornado winds blow,
It moves nice and slow.

Tornado watcher
Let me in, let me in

Jamie Gomez

Maybe Later

"Birds of a feather flock together."
That adage is as old as the hill.
They flocked together in Arkansas,
and then migrated with Bill.
Hillary happily hustled health.
Bill pretends to be Presidential.
Foster felt the final fate,
and Hubble became non-essential.
Elders expanded her eloquence,
and returned to Arkansas.
Special Prosecutors are assigned
to find out who broke the law.
Whitewater is awash in Washington,
and the flotsam continues to pass.
Bill Clinton is stranded in midstream,
and Whitewater is up to his knees.
The poem as written doesn't rhyme,
but it does contain a sleeper.
The deficiency will disappear
if Whitewater gets any deeper.

Arnold A. Puckett

Poetry Notebook

Thoughts
strung out on a line
threading through life
Thoughts
hidden in your mind
folded by gentle hands
tucked away
Thoughts
from a notebook
poems from another day.

Elaine D. Snively

The Innocence Of Death

Warm red blood
Down her cold white face
As she lay with flowers
She died in grace
She gazed upon
With one last look
I could read her soul
Like an open book
I felt her pain
I saw her cry
Said I love you
And watched her die

Catherine Fisher

My People

My people old and wise young
and free we do believe yes we do
in spirits that give us powers
of both land and water we
all do not own the Earth she
owns us for she gives us fruit
as well as water my people
know this yes they do my
people strong in spirit carry
stories of not just entertainment
but of our ways
but you yes you have
come and think you own the earth
but my friend you are wrong
the earth owns all of us
you have taken our stories and
changed them but you my
friend can never take my
people's Indian spirit.

Alissa Horent

Sacrifices

Wether of the mind or body
Or of flesh or soul
We all make sacrifices

To let a piece be taken away
Only to leave a hole
We all make sacrifices

Bloody palms and tears
Giving it all, forgetting the fears
We all make sacrifices

To keep that loved one at hand
To count the tiny grains of sand
We all make sacrifices

Frederick Lee Carter Jr.

Striptease

She watches his eyes striptease,
slowing revealing what seems to be
the body of his thought.
As he flexes with tears
she knows that her struggle
with the moment is over.
Her anger subsides to the lover
she met only last week.
She forgives him for the print
on her face, the mark on her mind.
She surrenders
to the fleck of skin on his nose
and skims it with her hand.
She surrenders
to the stale scent of his breath
and covers him with kisses.
She does not see him snicker
as he holds her.
He believes that he has earned
this payment and shows no remorse.

Martha Wall

A Flutterby

A flippy floppy flutterby
Came soaring at me from the sky.
He did a loop and floated off.
At such maneuvers I fain to scoff,
He might have busted his little head
Upon the sidewalk upon which I tread.

Barbara Rosenthaler

To See The Invisible!!

Eyes to see, but such.
A brain to comprehend
only so much. On I go,
to see things I cannot
see. I wish to gaze at
the invisible; only
because the invisible
can see me. Oh!
Thing I can not see-
I do not look at you with
eyes or brain. I have
reached my goal: I
stare at you, with my
heart. I stare at you
with my soul!!

Harold D. Nell

Memories Of Mother

"Oh, how I love Jesus",
As we sang that sweet song
It brought memories to my mind
Of my Mother, who is gone

Gone, but not forgotten,
Nor will she ever be
For as long as I shall live
Mother will be a part of me

"Precious name, O how sweet",
Words of another favorite song
I can almost hear Mother singing
As these lyrics linger on.

My dear Mother is in Heaven
With her pretty face aglow
Singing praises now to Jesus,
Her Savior whom she loved so

Precious memories of Mother
In my heart, I will keep
Until I join her one day
To worship at our Savior's feet.

Jeanne B. Whetzel

Prisoner

Years of despair and agony
Heaviness of the heart
The heart that was stomped on
But now the cord is broken
The shackles removed
It has been coming for me
Now it is done, the game is over
Good bye, farewell, the end.
Relief, closure, You're gone
No more agonizing about you
It is done forever
It was my choice this time
Freedom is here
This is the final page
I can see the light.

Jan Everts Duffy

Friends Going Through Time

As our lives move far apart,
You will make new friends who
are dear to your heart.

But when friends come to mind,
None will love you more
Than those you left behind!

Cora McKenna

A Friend

I thought that I could relate
to feelings not my own
but I can't seem to concentrate
'cause I'd rather be alone

The idea of seeking friendship
seems all too foreign to me
to find a soul who's willing
just to let me be

Many times I've tried to find a soul
not so unlike my own
but it seems I have to pay a toll
just to be left alone

Someday I'll find that partner
that I won't have to defend
but that makes them an acquaintance
and certainly not a friend

Thomas J. Serwan

Sunlit Shadows

Sitting on a rock
My feet dangling over
The mountainside,
Waiting,
Watching,
As the clouds separated,
And the sun's light poured
Down on the mountain,
Highlighting the colors of
Red,
Orange,
Yellow,
And green,
The rock cold beneath my fingers,
As I sit there watching,
The clouds and
The sun,
Create,
Sunlit shadows.

Helen Fox

My Son

If I wake up tomorrow and you are gone
Sweet child pray that I will carry on
Mashed potatoes in your hair
Popsicle dripping down your chin
Wish we could go there again
A blanket I will sew.
And tears will flow.
My memories of you low.
Make haste do not waste
The sun in your eyes.
Time slipping away day by day
To this terrible disease called aids

Vanda Southerland

One Day

I will awake — shining like
    the sun — beaming down
on the face of a sunflower, with
    the gentle breeze flowing past.
The sky will be soft but blue
    with white fluffy clouds floating
so gracefully.

This day, is coming, one day!

Tammy LeAnn Nipper

A Sailing To

A sailing to,
  a sailing from
    adventures here and there.
Where dreams can weave
  a misty tale
    that spirals
      in the air.
A dream is a great mystery
  to those who try to dream,
But push imagination
    far
      to where dreams are
        not seen.
But when those who believe in dreams
    just let the mind afloat,
      unleashing veils of magic
        that others
          can not see,
Discovering the answer to the
  unsolved mystery.
    Elizabeth Quigley

I'll Miss You

The day God called my sister home
I did not want to grieve,
But oh, the pain I felt that day
when my sister had to leave.

I know God called her home
to take away her pain,
my heart will feel an emptiness
Until we meet again.

I'll relive all our memories
That we made throughout the years,
In hopes the many memories
Will take away the tears.

She suffered long and silently
Carrying her cross right to the end,
God not only took my sister
He took my dearest friend.
    Charlotte, I'll miss you!
    Anita G. Sowers

The Ghoul

The night is my home,
the sight of my jungle,
my wondering prey,
dining on sundering carcasses
of the decaying life.
Hunger for the hunt,
trying newer stunts
to catch my meal.
The city is
my table.
I eat from it,
I drink from it.
The city is,
my jungle
and mine alone.
Beware nightfall for
I rule here,
and you are
my prey.
    Larry Mason

The Little Things

A summer cool breeze,
A moonlit walk to the sea,
Is what heaven is to thee.

A sunset on the bay,
A little child at play,
Is what heaven is to thee.

A wonderful land,
A man's caring hand,
Is what heaven is to thee.

A loving soft touch,
A warm gentle brush,
Is what heaven is to thee.

As time will tell,
As it does so well,

Will not pass thee by,
Without life's beautiful eye.

It is always heaven to thee.....
    Dana Longtine

His Eulogy

A visit with great grandpa
Whether morning, noon or night
Begins at his front door
With a memory of delight.

Games of cribbage, some chit chat
Or perhaps some dominoes
Gramp's intelligence and quick wit
Would keep us on our toes.

We'd leave his house with smiles
And lessons that we'd learned
And eagerly awaited
For a day we could return.

Our memories of great grandpa
Are the sweetest, and quite fond
His laughter, personality
And his love will carry on.
    Cheri White

Revisiting Nations Past

Impressive recollections
extraordinary success.
Stars, and stripes, and independence
  some interval
approximate solutions
integration, rational functions
Reflections of faith
   -deliverance-
Strategic, cross linking reaction
   -assassination's
   -the unknown soldier
   -the unborn child
Carbon monoxide - formaldehyde
  terminal components
  One Nation Under God
    Let's not forget it.
    Susan Burnham

Companions

Happy, playful, cute,
Adorable, loving you,
Kittens and puppies.
    Sara Zuniga

Time

There is a time for everything
Some time not at all.
The saying always bring us up
When in time we fall.

Time is of the essence,
What does that mean?
Time is running away
We need all time to be.

Forever is a time we know.
We say it all the time.
Forever is the love they share,
When they drink their wine.

Time is everything
In our simple lives.
Why not sit back and relax
And just let time fly?
    Jessica Hull

My Friend

I have this pug
He is so sweet,
Every time I walk
He chews on my feet.

When I go to sleep
He climbs in my bed,
And curls up
Right beside my head.

He wakes up quickly
When he hears a sound,
He jumps out of bed
And starts running around.

He protects me from danger
Wherever I'm at,
He loves to pester
My black cat.

He's everything to me
Even my best friend,
He'll be right by my side
Until the end.
    Jimmie H. Parsons

What Do You Fear?

What do you fear is a question
often faced in the world today,
But it's a good question
some people say the night,
Some say animals.
Some people even say life,
But most say death.
What most people don't know
Is that they're not afraid of the night
or even animals. They're afraid of Themselves.
Afraid of what they can and can't do.
    Stefanie Camp

Image

As I look into a pool of water
Crystal clear as it can be
I saw an image of myself
I saw an image of me

An image of a face so frail
Of a child that was grown
One wipe of a hand
The image, it was gone
    Elaine Byers

Was It Because Of Me?

Eyes filled with tears, she started my way.
What could I say when she came that day?

Her papa had lived and never counted the cost.
What if I had told him of Jesus, would he now be lost?

He looked at life with an attitude so careless and free.
Not once had I mentioned his named to Christ on bended knee.

He always seemed so big, mean, and tough.
I knew if I spoke of Christ, things would surely get rough.

I had had the chance to tell him that Jesus loved him so.
Why had I let the opportunity so quickly come and go?

With Christ in my heart and a great treasure to share,
I looked upon a girl whose father had only hell to bare.

She looked up at me with eyes upper cast.
"Will the angels come for Daddy?", she eagerly asked.

My eyes filled with tears and I quietly held my tongue.
How could I tell a little girl, what I had so selfishly done?!

Tammy Stevenson

Night

At Night, lying in bed, vision despite darkness,
tranquillity displaces sound, day-time seclusion.
Fatigue estopped...wonderment restored,
no worry, nor hurry for days to come.

This restful mind harbours copious calmness,
a serendipity serenades through an open window,
pleasant thoughts pierce inimical truths,
images - aspirations, free from harbingers of sin or despair.

Sunrise, doubtless, to push aside trouble before,
asleep at last...will come more.

P. Svensson Couch

A Small Ship Sails

A small ship sails in a lonely sea,
And that ship, it carries me.
It carries me to a land that is free...
Free from strife and war and poverty.

Alas, could that be land I see?
A refuge, a shelter for someone like me?
O Lord, I pray to thee,
Let there be peace on the land I see.

Nancy Jane Bowman

A Higher Strength

Take all the problems that life hands you
and give them to the power above;
Fear, hate, prejudice, and envy,
they'll all be replaced with love.

Never doubt that you are cared for,
no near doubt it at all.
Because with God all things are possible,
you just have to believe, that's all.

It is written that in the beginning God created it all.
If this be so, and I believe it to be, what is man after all?

Our little concerns that cause us worry
aren't so important after all.
For the only concern that we should have is with the power
that's over all.

Brian K. Shade

An Old Photograph

Her gaze slants up to her brother, new, in wonder and in curiosity;
He's cradled in her smiling father's arms, a bundle to see and muse about.
Age seven - a footnote to that picture - so she feels.

The years speed by, she grows and plays and startles with her wit and voice,
Her singing voice, in operatic style, in quality and range,
Portending her to fame if that she so desires,
But feels unloved.

"Had I but known" her father says (that's me) "but what should I have done?"
I swelled with pride
To be her sire
But something lacked in me, I guess.

All this I learn when it's far too late,
She lies in bed, in pain, waiting with courage whatever fate and faith
May have in store, but faith in God, not me

And now she's gone.
I have that faded photograph
And wish I'd held her, too.

Von Allan Carlisle

Niagara Falls

Your waters crash against rocks like
thunder in the sky, your mist rises high.
Your beauty is deceiving but seeing is also believing.
Your beauty is shone graceful and
fast like a old bird once young in the past.
Your water will always shine like
the sun in a blue summer sky.

Brittany Carey

Twilight And Future Tense

Orange fire burned through the clouds as the suns rays touched the skyline.
Circling birds were guided by wind in their search for food.
In sharp white, the trails from airplanes arched across a purple atmosphere.

A world pulling back a cape of color.
In prelude to its pulling over
an opaque shroud of darkness.

In the distance a dog barks.
And a baby cries.
In the distance a car is slamming breaks.
As a woman sighs.

Streetlights click on.
An empty day clicks off.
And an ever turning world moves one more notch
into tomorrow.

Christopher Baia

Once Upon This Hill

This hill filled memories of ours.
  This hill is filled with memories of weddings and
   picnics of cool summer days,
   of the winter nights, of children's laughing voices.
The years go on and as we bend down or grow up taller
  the hill still stays the same, tall, proud, and forever staying our hill.
The wind rustling through the trees reminding me of my memories
   that happened once, upon this hill.

Elisabeth Gibson-Mueller

Times

There are times of unwanted sorrow,
when tears are just not enough,
There are times of fearful loneliness
that makes the week become tough.

Regrets and thoughts of what we would have done.
If we had only one more chance,
to make what seemed right, wrong;
and seek forgiveness in advance.

God! Are you waiting for me to ask?
Am I too proud to tell.
Heal my heart from this terrible blast,
free my soul from this hell.

I've just lost a part of me,
that will never be replaced,
I live a time of empty agony,
fill me with your holy grace.

There are times I feel scared,
please hold me in your gentle arms.
Help me through this time of despair,
bring my stormy life to calm.

Aurea E. Ortiz

Dad

Written in loving memory of Dr. Bobby G. Derrick
Even though you have been gone for five years,
We still feel the emptiness and sorrow and tears.

You were the rock that we all leaned on, so sturdy and strong,
Always there to guide and direct us, teaching right from wrong.

You were my coach, counselor, mentor, protector, and my buddy -
truly the best dad in the world,
I was so proud to be your little girl.

You would always be there for me, of that I was sure,
Until that dreaded day when cancer claimed your body; why oh why could there not have been a cure?

We believe that God knows best, but we dearly miss you,
Some days we simply wonder what we will do.

I know our faith in the Lord will keep us going and lead us
in what we do and say,
Until we join you and our Heavenly Father on that blessed and glorious day.

I will always love you and forever keep you in my heart.

Linda Derrick Conley

No One Smells Roses Anymore

   That's right, no one smells roses anymore
Instead people would rather cult then down because they
attract June bugs and bees, or because they have thorns.
Some people would rather step on them because they don't care,
are too lazy to walk somewhere else, say it's fun.
What kind of fun is killing a creation, a creation made
for the enjoyment of its beauty and fragrance.
   Now people stop to smell incense, perfume for $80 an ounce.
We stop to smell the garbage thrown out of a car
because it is easier than finding a trash can
Smell the sh*t we call air, full of toxins, destroying
ourselves and our planet. The skies are no longer blue and clear
but black and cloudy with acid rain.
We smell the homeless and starving people in the alley ways,
"I would help you if I could but the light just turned green."
We speed off in....
This is our manufactured substitute for roses.

Joshua Carl Eubanks

Destiny Of The Damned

You've fallen in the sea of muck, good luck
raking is a hazard, below are the sharks

   Sweaty to the core, and coated like a morsel
   lost sense of hope when you see the first dorsal

   Fin to the chin, and chin to the wind
   horrifying sights induce shrieks from within

      Conjuring Dark tales with subconscious foresight
      children of the night, villains of the light

         Houses offer safety, some shelter, and some spirit
         an atmospheric shroud looms above, Can You Hear it

Nowhere to hide because the night breeds the truth
don't think it's a fluke, who you mix in the soup

   Bowls for the people, eating starts the creep show
   service to Your Conscience with a flavored hint of repo

   Session chains connect, your descent, level I
   cradled by the force, dark tales have begun

      Comatose silence interrupt, dead rest
      big, dark-eyed mystery face express

      Shun, with no more sun for your con
      science on the Run, the Damned now is done.

Anthony McDavid

The Full Moon Talks

If I could care
I'd care for you
If I could love
I'd love you
If I could protect
I'd protect you for the rest of my life
If I could hurt
I'd never allow you to hurt
If I could talk
I'd talk to you
If you would listen
You would hear all I had to say
I am your inner light
The double stars
I am your protector
The full moon
If you understood me, we would be one as it is meant to be
Since you've not heard me
I pray the mighty spirit will watch over you until
The time comes that you hear that which I have to say

Sue Ellen Brooks

Autumn Leaves

As I wander 'round my rain-drenched yard
Amid the brilliant leaves of fall.
I think of those we love and miss,
and 'bout the place that they have gone.

They miss the matchless beauty
of autumn's unique display;
The cool crisp air...the country fair,
Piles of leaves with kids at play.

With this vision vivid in my mind
While rain pelts on my back
I stop and pick these pretty leaves
To enjoy what you sorely lack.

I have pressed each leaf with tender care
And beg you, for goodness sake,
Forget the many times you cursed
The leaves you had to rake.

Charles S. Babcock

Were You There Black Butterfly?

Were you there Black Butterfly; did she say good-bye?
Did you see her spirit rise?
Did you hear her cry?

I wish I would have been there, to hear the final sigh.
To kiss away the tears of death, empty in her eyes.
Were you there Black Butterfly; did she say good-bye?

Crushed in an instant, life became a lie.
Did you feel the broken ties?
Did you hear her cry?

Twisted steel and shattered souls - no faith could ere comply.
Blood red stones, smashed sparkling glass will never leave my eyes.
Were you there Black Butterfly; did she say good-bye?

Settled in an empty grave, with flowers she did lie.
Did you know how screaming "why's"?
Did you hear her cry?

Seething stench of death malign my breath, but never to deny.
Wrenched hearts, contempt, love, peace - what is it to be wise?
Were you there Black Butterfly; did she say good-bye?
Were you there Black Butterfly; did you hear her cry?

Eileen J. Crystal

My Loving Wife

Yesterday has come and gone
And I with hope was left alone
The memories of the past were great
But why did I receive such fate
I had much hope in God's good will
To me seemed like a bitter pill
In prayer I looked to God above
To send me someone I could love
My desire he lovingly heard but still my hope was somewhat blurred
Time it seemed went slowly by and in my thoughts I wondered why
So I prayed for a happy life even though I had no wife
But God heard me in my distress and blessed me with some happiness
A sudden thought came at last of one I knew back in the past
With love and hope I made a call hoping for an answer after all
The call was pleasant and so sublime
For she said "Come and see me sometime"
This all solved my lonely plight
Her pretty name is Ivy White
From here I'm sure you all can guess
We plan for love and happiness

Al Schmidt

A Grandmother's Love

I pass these blankets on to my first grandchild,
They were made for me for my first born child.
Made by the hands of a Grandmother,
Who gave unconditional love.
Sat and crocheted each loop one by one.
Although this Grandmother has passed on,
She is sadly missed but her love carries on.
As her love shines down on you,
From the heavens above.
So that these blankets may be passed on,
As each Grandchild comes along
Know that they were made with love,
As she crocheted each loop one by one.
So hush my little one stay warm and sleep tight.
Grandma is here and everything will be alright.

Anita Fancher

Help! I Need A Credit Card!

One day I went to the mall,
And there were no sales at all.

I went into my favorite store,
And when I came up short I was thrown out the door!

My hair stood on end and my eyes grew round,
Pretty soon I became the laughing stock of the town.

Every store I went to the door was slammed in my face,
Don't think I didn't hear them when they said, "That girl's a disgrace!"

Soon I decided I was ready to eat,
So headed over to the food court to pick up a treat.

I saw the ice cream the pizza shop too,
Everything looked so delicious I didn't know what to do!

That was enough I left the store,
I hopped in the car and slammed the door!

So here's a lesson to remember,
Ask your father this December if he'll give you a special treat
 - his credit card
And tell him you'll massage his feet.

Makenzi Sims Landrum

In The Midst

In the midst of the wind I cry for help, but no one seems to hear me. Why do I yearn for a peace I cannot find? Is it not to be found by mankind? If only I could breathe amongst the evil that smothers me, O'Lord lift the heavy burdens from my aching soul and grant me eternal freedom from this world of wretchedness.

In the midst of the fire I ask forgiveness, but no one listens. My suffering delights in the wicked heat of cruelty and, I know not where to turn. If only I could see through this dark haze which threatens to consume me, O'Lord lift the haze and grant me vision so that I may see through the facades of this creation and heed the brilliancy of my pain.

In the midst of the storm I question my destiny, but no one answers. Why can't I recognize the chaos of joy? If only I could feel the heart clutch of laughter rapping at the brink of my sanity, O'Lord give me an answer and grant me the courage to withstand strong winds of fear, take my hand and pull me from this fiery tunnel of forbidden ecstasy - please, sensitize my flesh so that I may feel the heat which radiates from the flames of passion, the cool silkiness of neglect and the tepid lucidity of my tears.

In the midst of the earth I continue my search, but no one guides me. I agonize over my convictions, and I know not where to turn. If only I possessed the knowledge of where my choices would lead, O'Lord give me your hand and grant me the true path to righteousness.

Sonya Jill White

In Love

The heart wanders from a place of humanity,
to the inhabitance of a place unknown.
The feeling inside is like a burning fire,
waiting to explode.
The warmth of a touch.
The ache of a smile.
The feeling of a lifetime home.
Or the wanting to die if it is lost.
Every waking moment is spent to please,
And the rest is spent on your knees,
praying and hoping.
It is something never to be explained,
but just fell with knowledge from above.
Oh, to be in love!

Summer Stover

House Plant

Oh forgiving one, who asks so little of me,
whose loyalty is unwavering
despite the constant neglected I inflict upon thee,
when I see you looking sad,
bent over as if conserving any vestige of life,
I think not of your fate but rather how I am late for work,
and once again I leave you, desiccated and infertile.
Yet you, who remain faithful and trusting despite this cruel sentence,
upon receiving the smallest drop of nourishment,
will rise graciously, and extend your emerald arms
in a gesture of absolution, as yellowed, brittle reminders of
indifference fall slowly to the floor.
And I, sanctimoniously, ask for your forgiveness,
while making promises I never seem to keep.
Nikki Insdorf

This Must Be....

This must be love
My feelings inside I just can't hide
I'm giving you my heart
100% percent of me
I can only tell you how I feel
because what I feel is oh so real
I just know this is a dream
but I hope I'll never have to wake
You are the biggest part of me
Your my best friend and also my mate
Only you make me happy and
you'll always be just what I need
You know I'll always be here for you
I could never just leave you be
We'll always be together always and forever....
Marissa Davenport

Untitled

You... are my sunshine
  that once I'd seen as rain
  You... are the happiness
that once was known as pain
  You... are the only one
and that you'll always be
  You are the one I've waited for...
the one who's meant for me
  You replace the chaos...
with meaning and a certain peace
  The pressure that had been crushing me...
now has been released
  Words alone cannot describe...
just exactly what you've done
  The only words that come to mind...
you've got to be the one
  I'd been told I'd know...
there would truly be no doubt
  I see now what they must have meant...
your love I can't live without!
Dale J. Hillman

Spring...To Fall

A tender bud hides the beauty
  that man may never see
A blossoming flower waiting to be picked
  naive to the ways of man
The upturned face begs to be noticed
  craving appreciation
But the flower withers and dies
  while its beauty fades away
Never to be seen
  by the eyes of men
Diana Wall

Friendship

Oh, the Heart of a friend is a marvelous place
Where one finds contentment and peace
Where the grasp of a hand shows that you understand
As the blessings of friendship increase.
For the Heart of a friend
Never wonders or doubts
No matter if years intervene
The old faith is there
And none can compare
With the comfort it gives the unseen.
Oh, the Heart of a friend
Is a place sweet and rare
To love to enrich to enjoy
Respond if you will
To its charm and its thrill
While forgetting the cares that annoy.
Yes the Heart of a friend is the one thing I prize
As life lengthens and twilight descends
The last thing I ask
As I finish my task is to remain in the heart of a friend.......
JoAnn M. LaLonde

Marina

I can't believe I'm going, but I must
Leaving this world of destruction, war, and violence
The time of murder, rape, racism, and prejudice
The world sucks
And now I must leave it
I'm hurting too badly
Sickness is eating me alive, and I can't stand the pain
My body has turned against me
Farewell universe of molesters, murders, and dope pushers
I'm leaving you forever——
I don't want to go, I haven't lived long enough
What about the places and things I haven't seen or done?
I'll never see a sunrise, a sunset, or beautiful color again
Trees, flowers, green grass, blue skies, big fluffy clouds
I can barely see them from where I lie
Once more I wish I could feel a breeze blowing through my hair
I never realized how precious life was, until I knew I was dying
I can't believe my life is almost over
The world is bad, but for all the bad it is also good
I know that now——too late
Yolanda A. M. Guile

Silent Whimpers

Little sunflower,
How you look so innocent and calm,
Never caring, oh just whatever may come.
Also in laughter, the heart is sad,
And thus the end of joy comes grief.
You must search, search until the heart is filled with fruit,
Let the petals caress your soul.
And like mighty wings they shall fly,
No longer will you feel the need to cry.
Donna M. Morris

Untitled

Raindrop crystals still are clinging
To the branches of a leafless tree,
And the sky is low and pale.
Fall has painted everything in muted colors.
Letting puddles mirror all the grey.
There - a dot of bright vermilion
In the circle of a beret
On a woman's greying head.
Defiance on display.
Anne Kawato

Untitled

Our love for each other has been divine;
And through the years it will stand the test of time.

Even when we fight, we know it's not in vain;
Since through the tears and sad times we've surpassed all the pain.

Someday we'll look back on the years gone by;
And know our love will still exist 'til the day we die.

But death is just a beginning, a new unopened door;
And someday we will meet again and watch our spirits soar.

Please allow our love to be through life and after too;
Because you'll never know how good it feels so share my love with you.

I Love You....
Dawn M. Turner

Untitled

Little girl
hiding all the time
sometimes she cries
when no one's around
go away inside myself
the cocoon used to be so warm and snug
now it's too big
And the chill enters through the cracks

Where does she go now?
Where can she go?

Sweet sweet scent
bright bright flame

And the world isn't so cruel
for just a little while

Hibernating
Struggling through each tortured sunrise
Crawling on a circular highway
littered with broken glass

Sobbing for the end
Reaching for his hand
Shaana Baluch

Thank You Mom

Did you ever think about how much you owe,
To your mother for bringing you up?
With all the things she's done for us,
She's helped us overflow our cup.

She was there when we needed her,
She would never turn us away.
Because if she did, you couldn't call her a mother,
Well really, what else can I say?

Between taking care of us when we're sick,
And looking after us when we're not.
That's a lot of responsibility,
But when you had us, that's what you got.

I know it's not an easy thing to do,
And I know you had a rough time doing it,
I know there were times when you said, "Let me out of here!"
But the point is, you didn't quit.

I know we didn't treat you the greatest,
But no kid's perfect, you know.
We could never repay you for all you've done,
And we'd never want you to go.
Sandi Ploof

A Feeling Of A Man

It is happiness sadness and madness in a mix,
It is a feeling of rage and a feeling of zeal.
It is a feeling of wanting to become something more,
To do something that has never been done,
To be someone that you were not before.
It is the feeling of a zealous man.
The feeling of great zeal,
A thing that can get you somewhere for once!
It is a feeling of wanting to try to do something
That others say can not be done,
And when not done the first time
is tried again.
That is an awesome feeling.
Micah Seiler

Serious Thinking At 69

I've often sat and wondered
what the last years hold for me,
When it comes to really
being thought about by
those whom I cherish but
so very seldom see.
There are children, grand -
and great grand which I was
their very first face to see as
they entire into this world
And I wept with joy so prayerfully.

There are cousins who say auntie,
nieces and nephews respectfully,
but the names ma, mom, grandma and nanny
oh how much they mean to me.
Growing older is a blessing from
above I clearly see and I do look forward to that great
reunion with my other family.
Lenora A. Brownlee

Oh Why, Oh Why

As I look to the sky I can see many things;
I can see bits of purple-green and periwinkle.
Oh why oh why are things this way?
Oh why must people say the things they say?
If I were a bird I could fly far away;
Away from the troubles I must face everyday.
Oh why must they see the color of my face?
I thought we were all of the same race,
The Human Race.
It is time for us to realize.
I know what most strangely despise.
If only they would take enough time to just look
in my eyes;
They would see love never dies.
Yasmeen Watson

"Memories Of The Heart"

I've known South Dakota.
I've known apple trees and fields of wheat and corn.
The sound of horses in a distant pasture.
I've known South Dakota.

I skipped rocks across the blue waters of Lake Poinsett.
I walked the Indian trails and saw the beautiful sunsets.
I looked across this barren land and imagined it full of buffalo.
I've known South Dakota.

The emptiness of its vast plains.
I've known South Dakota.
Mandi Lund

The Year Of The Golden Harvest

I drink to the glory of a past
toasting the year of the golden harvest

To the buffalo, that were as a flock of geese roaming the plain

To a heritage, as ancient as the river, as proud as the wind

To the cry of brave warriors that is routed in generations
to the valor of a people

It is not in anger I cry out to the conquest of a land
but, to the captive of a free spirit, the castration of my soul

I live, but yet, I live not
I lay prisoner within the den of the jackal
But I wait, with the patience and endurance of the sun
and as the teeth of the jackal grows weak with the trouble of ages
And his jaws no longer hold with the straight of steel
I will set forth, back into the land of my fathers
and in the season of the falling leaves
I will return, to the feast of autumn
and the year of the golden harvest

Doris Robinson

What A Strong Mother

What a strong mother. Raising four kids out of
the blue. What a strong women can do.
What a strong mother. Losing a son, only having
one three daughters left fears for the life but
what can she do she only a wife.
What a strong mother. Raising one not her own.
Wishing to have her only son. But what can she do she not a nun.
What a strong mother putting her daughters through school.
Helping them in Math and Science and English too.
What a strong mother. Helping us through thick and
thin hot and cold. We should treat her like a pot
of gold. What a strong mother. We love you forever
number one the best. A women named Lillian better far
than all the rest. You've seen them all but I got the
Best!

Gloriann Vazquetelles

So Many Faces!

Happy, excited, sad, and angry people, along with the lost and
disappointed faces fill this world.
Many faces with so many expressions. So many unforgiving faces.
Why Did God Put faces On The Front And Not The Back Of
His People?
Sad and angry along with the lost and disappointed faces, always
turning around to see where they've been. Looking back at the past
and wondering how they could have done what they did and
thinking how they can change where they are now.
Happy and excited faces always looking forward to see the sun
rise. Always looking ahead at the future and planning a fresh new
day. Not looking back and knowing God has forgotten the
yesterdays of mistakes. With the quick repentance at heart.
God puts faces on the front of all His people. So we can look
forward and not behind to see where we begin our day!
God forgives us of our past mistakes and if we can forgive
ourselves. What a world this would be with the expression of love
shining through so many faces.
Which Way Are You Facing With So Many Faces?

Jacqueline L. Greek

Untitled

Oh you with eager eyes to see and know
the world, its beauty find.
Look deep within yourself and see
life's greatest miracle abounds.
No sight or sound in all the earth however true,
cannot within yourself be found.

Ethel M. Crum

All That Is Evil

Darkness
In the night
A shadow filled something.
A beating.
Growing,
Turning,
Raging darkness.
A shapeless,
Unnameable terror.
A masked
Villain
A demon,
A devil,
All that is evil in my mind;
Twisting together in a tapestry of hate,
Of loathsome unpure hate,
my soul.

Dannie Smith

Illusions

As I focus to find you;
My eyes catch only a glimpse.

As I strain to listen to you;
I hear nothing but the slightest whisper of your voice.

As I attempt to wrap my arms around you;
I can't seem to hold you in my grasp.

As I bask in your aroma;
I am still unaware of the direction of your presence.

As I try to devour all that you have to offer;
I am seemingly never fulfilled.

As I struggle with whom you are;
I find your identity more obscure.

How can I want what is you;
When you are so much of a mystery to me, an illusion?

Lisa Gayle Allen

Knock, Knock

I came to see you, I knocked upon your door
there was no answer, so I knocked once more
now panic struck and full of doubt
what could this be all about
you're not here and here I stand
hands on hips and hips in hand
What should I do? Should I stay to try once more
and knock knock upon your door
so I made my way to the back
just to calm my panic attack
much more worried than before
I knocked again upon your door
this time harder than before
As suddenly I heard you call
but not from within no not at all
I turned quickly. And there you stand
with a bag of groceries in your hand.

Jenny M. Pounds

Love Is...

Love is soft and as sweet as the air.
Love is found when people really care.
Love is a dream that reaches the sky.
Love is a wonder with a kiss and a sigh.
Love is when people love one another.
Love is when one caresses their lover.
Love is a gift and never a lie.
Love is love if love never dies.

Pamela Shropshire

Sweet Salvation

Not far from yesterday, was so blinded.
Kept from reality, kept from myself.
Filled with anxious paranoia and arrogant discontent.
Never had a strong hold, kept slipping behind the wheel.
Pulled harder - climbed faster.
The rope slipped farther, quicker.
Remaining in the same spot,
I became tired.
Tired of pulling, tired of climbing,
Tired of being meaningless to someone who had meant so much to me.
She cut the rope with the sharp scissor of her disinterest,
Releasing the tension of a nauseous worthlessness.
And so I climbed and climbed until I realized that the rope had run out. I fell into the black nothing, until I was caught by the Angel.
The peaceful Angel, ethereal both physically and mentally,
Guarded me, saved me from an almost inevitably evil fate.
Nurtured me with understanding,
nurtured me back to myself, back to Paradise.
Satan scorned in jealousy of the possession of my soul,
but it was no use, for the Angel had saved me.
     HEAVEN CAN BE FOUND ON EARTH.

Joseph Guza

I Left You

I left you.
But don't think
That I don't love you,
Because no one is able
To love you better than I.

I left you, but don't think
That I don't remember you.
Would be impossible for me
To forget all that you did
To help me when I needed help.

I left you. And you know
That I can't return to you,
Or return to the life that I had with you.
I did what I needed to do, and I have no regrets.
But I am sorry that I can't see you,
Or talk with you.

I left you, but don't worry.
I always loved you
And I always will love you. And please
Forgive me if I ever hurt you.

Shawn Michael McClure

Sometimes A Total Stranger

She lay there asleep
suspended in the shaft
of a frozen half light
so precious, so willing, so true...
I think back to yesterday
and struggle to remember
what it was she said
that gave me such a chill. Mercy.

So I wander out
into another rain
thinking I should quit this town
for the hundredth time or more
but the road still ends
at the beginning.
Baby, what's wrong?
My silhouette on the wall
turns aside as I stand and watch
perfectly still, and suddenly I see....
You rub your sleepy eyes
and answer innocently, everything. Nothing.

Stephen Corbell

With Love

Here is to you while you were here, from those you were
close to and from those you loved. You gave us your
laughter and showed us your tears. You gave us your
happiness and showed us your fears. You showed us joy
and gave us our hopes. But most of all, you gave us your
love when we needed it most. As time grew near for you
to go, we held on tight and said we loved you. We took
our time, for it was hard to say good-bye to someone so loved.

Now here's to you now that you're gone, from those you love
and left behind. Rest your head among God's pillow, for
He'll take care of you from now and tomorrow. Rest your
eyes and rest assured you'll have no more suffering,
that's for sure. Share your peace with those who are
there and those who may follow, then take only a moment
to think of us, for not a day will go by that you will
not be missed.

Karen Nill

Crayons

When you open a fresh box of crayons they are all separated nicely into like shades. Separated by color. Dark ones in the back, light ones up front. Brown, Black - Peach, Apricot. You pick out a crayon, blue and draw the sky. You pick out green and color the ground and yellow for the sun. Then you pick up peach, the skin color, and you draw in the person. Another person picks up his box of crayons and also picks out the blue for the sky, green for the ground, and yellow for the sun. But what's different about his picture is that when he picks up the skin color he takes brown. As others pick up their crayons and color, they mix up the once supposedly organized crayon box. The browns and the peaches sit right next to each other. The greens, blues, and yellows also mix. Nobody minds that the once color coded box is now all mixed up. Nobody notices. The only thing that stays the same is that you pick up the peach and the next guy picks up brown. That never changes, even though the crayons may get mixed up, you never see in your mind the browns and peaches together in that box. In your mind you still see your box of crayons all color coded. No unlike colors near each other, ever.

Katie Vander Velde

Welcome Home

My mother went to heaven, the Lord was waiting there
He beckoned her to come inside, T'was really naught to fear
You have been a wondrous person, I have watched you from above
As you helped so many people, with a heart so full of love
And never once did you request, a favor in return
Tho' a resting place in heaven, Tis a blessing you have earned
You never once complained or let on, how ill you really were
You'd just say AH' it's a bad day, and let it go at that
You kept the pain inside, to save your children that
So welcome home my child, is what the good Lord said
As he handed my Mom a halo, to wear upon her head
Then he added silver wings, and pointing to a door he said
Inside you'll find some other folk, that entered here before
Look yonder, there's your Mom and Dad, over there's your
     husband Wally
And over there's your brother Gene, Brother Walter's by his side
And on and on the roster goes
And down the road a little bit, you'll find your little friends
In a place called Doggie Heaven
It's where this story ends.

Brian Wallace

Time

God smiles as He looks 'pon the newborn babe
   as he lay, so small, in his hospital bed.
One wink in the future, God looks again.
   The babe, now an old man, is dead.

Nancy E. Dreyer Graziani

New York

Granite, Granite in deep Granite has stepped
in the ocean - like a Hercules - New York!
And unforgotten - from eternal times
heroic fights, he fought, with him - the Great, Atlantic!
But, New York, was standing, solemn, majestic, and invincible
in the midst of outraged, salty Blue Giant!
I also hear, how, as a last request, he pleased the God
"I want a present, the only one —
New York, and then forever, I'll rest!"
One by one, the years are passing,
chasing in unwise madness, the centuries!...
But New York is still solemn,, majestic invincible
for eternal times, the pride and -
P-E-R-S-O-N-I-F-I-C-A-T-I-O-N, Of the God!

Ludmi

Waterfalls

Glistening water falls drop
From melting snow-packed mountain tops
Like strands of glassy white pearls
Falling to the ground
At the bottom creating crystal clear blue ponds
With thundering loud crashing sounds
Surrounded by wild flowers all around
While the bright yellow sunshine
Forms a rainbow through the falls
Stretching across the mountain walls
If you were here
We would share it all
Together in our eyes
We would live in paradise

Mark Hill

Dancing Hearts

Out to the dance floor, we fly hand in hand
In a river of music, you guide my direction
People, specks of color, whirl around me like wind
I surrender to the tide
Out, out carried by your confident hands
My screams of delight muffled underwater
The bass crawls inside me and becomes my heartbeat
Thumping so loud we're one
A short black dress spins up with the wind
My head flies back, as you throw me away
Only to catch my hand and yank me back to you
Leaving me with a drunken dizziness
Collapsing in your arms, my head of curls
    splashing over your polished suit
Lights flicker, draping themselves on our bodies
    the dance floor spinning around us
I catch your eyes as they scan the room,
    locking us together and the moment freezes
All is silent and still except for the dancing of my heart

Carolyn Rohrbach

Heart Of Gold

Some people wear their heart on their sleeve,
With their arms outstretched for the world to see,
And then they wonder why it gets smashed and broken,
After all they paid the price, gave up their token.

Others hold it tight, wrapped up in wire,
Afraid to get too close to the burning fire,
And then they wonder why it feels so sad and lonely,
In the end they whisper to themselves, "If only".

I think I'll keep mine here inside my chest,
I've tried both ways, I must confess,
I'll treat it with care, like a piece of gold,
And if I can't handle it, I'll give it to God to hold.

Elizabeth Davis

Truth As It Lies

You know you have lied to me,
And now I can surely see.
I knew deep down something was wrong,
But I tried to fight it, and pretended to be strong.
Life is a mystery, with much to debate,
But I took it in stride for it was my own fate.
All this time has passed us by,
"For what" I asked, for you had only lied.
Well as we both should truly know,
It's our time to wake up and let go.
This is something we must really face,
And take this step as a whole new embrace.
Now this is it, open your eyes,
See all this truth as it lies.
For in our hearts it will always last,
The pain of one another, just being in the past.
As we sit here with our broken hearts,
From this relationship we must part.

Karen Lee Bonneville

Strolling Down Memory Lane

   Vivid autumn leaves crawl to the corner of the
street where they make one vast pile.
   As everything settles in place an elderly woman quietly walks
straight ahead, eyes fixed on the pile of leaves as her goal.
   When she approaches, she kneels down, picks up
a leaf, and slowly turns it over in her ivory, wrinkled hand.
   Her eyes glaze over and she is carried away,
back into cherished days.
   Gently coming out of her reverie, a smile plays
on her lips as she puts four leaves into her battered purse.
   One for sadness, one for happiness, one for
tears, and one for laughter.
   Before she leaves the woman thinks, "This is
not just another street, but my memory lane."

Sarita S. Bakhru

Sprinkle Me With Sugar

The whirling air settling Down.
The geese jetting out of the lake.
The desert sands shifting out on a Cloud.
Friends moving on to a beat beyond the Hill.
Our hearts are oscillating steady Together.
Smiling wildly in the rowing boat with Strawberries.
Inching up the endless trails of Life.
Refresh the constant waving of the Flower.
Sprinkle me with Sugar.
I can't hear the clock, wind it Up.
Hurry up bring a large bowl of Cherries.
Sprinkle me with Sugar.
Does the drops of water hit the part of the Lake?
How many different turns do the river Flow?
Does the spice burns everyday in your Life?

Arnaz Hammond

I Said Goodbye

I said goodbye to my child as I left her there.
She ran and played, not a moment to spare.
I said goodbye to my child, such an angel on earth
I did not realize her true value and worth.
I said goodbye to my child with a twinkle in her eye.
As I left her there my heart was filled with pride.
I said goodbye to my child so playful, yet bold.
I did not know her life story soon would be told.
I said goodbye to my child as the building came down
Her mangled body was finally found.
I said goodbye to my child for one last time.
God took her to heaven and said, "Now she is mine".

Phyllis J. Davis

Leaves! Leaves! Leaves!

Scimper scamper all around
   across the yards across the roads.
You look as if you must hurry
   flying to and fro!

You spin and dance and ride the winds.
   Your life seems so care-free.
And all the colors you bring
   to us are quite a sight to see.
Fiery red, golden yellow, burnt orange,
   brown and even green.
You have more colors than any rainbow
   I have ever seen!

And before it is time to say good-bye,
   you do put on a show,
by covering the yards, hiding the streets
   and flying to and fro!

Sheri Johnson

Little Mark

Soon our school days will come to an end
And we will be missing our little friend
His name is Mark and he's a wonderful boy
And having him in our home was a pleasure and joy
Just to watch him play and to see his big smile
Helped me to know that life is worthwhile.
We became pals from the very first day
And it will really hurt when Mark goes away
Everywhere I went Mark wanted to go
And that is one reason I will miss him so

We worked in the garden, we played on the bed
And when I went to town
Mark said, "I want to go Fwed."
And sometimes I would let him go
It was just too hard to tell him "no".
Soon he will be going away
And with us he will no longer stay,
I think I might just break down and cry
When the little fellow says his last goodbye.
Days, months, years will soon be gone
But the memory of Mark will linger on.

Fred Dunford

Exaltation

Oh Almighty God!
How Magnificent is the splendor
of thy Universe —
Awesome is the Cosmos —
A sea of varied Planets
   And thy beloved Earth an
   Aqueous jewel amongst them.
Pre-ponderous spheres —
   All held in space by thy
   Infinite will —
Brilliant are thy stars —
   Quasars — and Nebulae.
Mega-Colossal detonations of
   Galactic matter —
     fragments to be recreated
Into new Galaxies and Constellations
   Known only unto thee —
Oh Creator of all things
   Visible and invisible —
Most Universal God — Known in all Names
Jehovah — Yahweh — Abba —
Most Infinite... Invincible most profound God.
The Alpha and Omega of all creation —
For thou art The Great "I AM" of all ETERNITY.

Elizabeth Busch

Intentions...

My beautiful son passes away, innocent in his own intentions
Eyes blue like the oceans...
Rivers touched with sympathy and turmoil
False illusions brush the hands of time with every ticking second
Never have I bled so much, shed so many tears, for my entity
My true love has finally found me...
Yet the heart aches and bitter tears still wallow inside
All I ask before death is to lay admits his caressing arms
My hair brushed by his breath escaping onto me
Listening softly to the sound of the heart I love more than myself
Comfort...
I wish this happiness, making me ill with joy, to last forever
I shall always sacrifice myself for him
In hopes that the world can see inside him
The innocence entwined with brilliance that I do
I love him more than anything the world could ever give me.
My heart still yearning for his love
To exist in such indifference is non-existence for my beautiful son.

Jennifer J. Abraham

Starting Over

When your life's been filled
with sorrow, heartache, and pain,
and you've tried to wash it all away
with the tears you've cried like rain.

When you think your heart's been broken
and it's never going to mend,
just pick yourself up, dust yourself off
and start all over again.

When you think you'll never make it
through another day,
with patience, love, and understanding
you will find a way.

Just when you think you can't take it anymore
I'll tell you one thing for sure,
Some things happen for reasons unknown
but you'll be blessed for kindness you've shown.

You'll get over the sorrow, heartache and pain
your tears will no longer fall like rain,
you'll be stronger in the end
you'll be happy to start life again.

Jane Blevins

Flight Of Reason

Once it soared on the wings of rationalism
The epitome of achievement
Carrying the nest egg of empiricism
All prayers answered, heaven sent.
Now, we see it bent and twisted in its flight
Logic skewed, analysis not right
Ready for a fall.
Better to bail out now
Rather than to crash and burn
And so we flee.
But, reason flies on straight and true
Toward dreams we can't remember.
It's our perceptions which are skewed
Brains poisoned, damage rendered
No longer capable of flight.

Alice G. Moore

Listen

Listen to wind wail, endeavoring to find its way,
Listen to the grain, shambling and pondering,
Listen to the tree give direction to the misguided wind,
Listen to the moon bidding to shine the way,
Listen to the clouds beckoning the wind to follow.

Cortney M. Hoek

Loving Is Not Easy

He was so little, smiling up at them
   While holding Sister's hand
There in the orphanage
   Of that distant third world land.

His health problems could be fixed
With love and prayers and medical tricks.

He was a delightful, adopted, loving lad
Before his teens when all went bad.

Loving parents he couldn't hear,
As drugs and "friends" drew him near.

Mom and Dad, no matter what, will always love me,
Keeping friends was harder work, he soon began to see.

The tug between them broke ties he could not mend.
Hearts were broken, but not of "friends."

Sadness replaced the smiling face,
   Handcuffs the Sister's hand.
The bars of prison blurred the view
   Of their adopted, beloved lad.
   Yvonne V. Gehring

The Picture

The picture on the wall was made by me
When heard Poetry Contest I wrote a poem
Don't care it doesn't win or rhyme
as long as I can join
I hope I can win
But hopes are low,
cause I had no improvement
since I wrote "The Faraway Sea"
   Kristin Lee

Everlasting Light

   When day becomes dark and in comes the night,
may your candle burn with everlasting light.
   As the troubles of the day come to an end,
the troubles of the night are soon to begin.
   Please don't worry, they will all be out of sight,
if you let your candle burn with everlasting light.
   The light is the Lord, to show you he's always there,
to wash away your worries and the devil's stare.
   Exercise faith it'll keep you going strong,
the candle will burn all day and night long.
   So when trouble seems hard to fight,
just look for the answer in the everlasting light.
   Deirdre Reese

Gray

I walk this world
to a world awaiting me
with a cool embrace
or a cold heat thrust of fire.
My Lord, he preached to me
to fear the insincerity of shades of gray.

I fly this voyage
(where a Roman traveler lost his sight)
with his destination at his fingertips...

...A cold unworthy way to die,
tortured like a crucified scarecrow
to warn the black birds of vanity, of foolishness.
   John Cross Mossaad

"Home Sick"

There's just one place, I want to be,
But in this flesh, I'll never see.
Where all is grand and so complete,
My loved ones dear, again I'll meet.

My Father's there and all His friends,
And till I'm there, His love He sends.
But there I'll be, one day real soon,
I'll fly on high and shoot the moon.

But till I'm there, my spirit cries,
My soul is burdened, for that I sigh.
This place is such a dreary mess,
Chin up, nose straight, for this He'll bless.

So often, I do write to Him,
And tell Him of, my every whim.
He then writes back, so sweet, so dear,
Can't wait to see you, wish you where here.

Here is where, you do belong,
I've saved your place, I hum your song.
It won't be long, the angels say,
For you've been gone, for just a day.
   Joseph Romano

Way Down

Sometimes, when music is good,
just close your eyes, and imagine
imagine yourself on a beach

You're all alone, it's a private beach
and you're in a sun dress, solid white

You're twirling down the beach
but you feel no dizziness

There's a pier in the background
So you start walking toward it and see
Nothing but gently rolling ocean,
the dolphins playing and jumping,
and the far-off boats, back in the distance

That's how you know if music is
really good. You feel it, Way Down.
   Jessica N. Williamson

Untitled

Here is the joy of the first kiss
the air of love like a peaceful mist
Here is the excitement of our lives to unfold
Like a new horizon so beautiful and bold

Here is the anguish of everyday life
Full of heartache, anxiety and strife
Here is resentment, rejection and pain
So much to accomplish, so little is gained

Here is the tear of a lost love
Here is the feather of a fleeting dove
Here is the pain that we both feel
To fear that our love cannot be healed

Here is a star twinkling bright
A glimmer of hope on a dark night
Here is a song, a wish, and a prayer
Hoping that God will hear me up there

Bring back the joy of the first kiss
The air of love like a peaceful mist
Bring back the excitement of our lives to unfold
Like a brand new horizon so beautiful and bold
   Laura P. Shenkle

The Last Rose

The last rose of summer stands mute witness to the tragedy of
   nature's irony.
For here this thing of beauty grows, only to struggle against forces
   with which it cannot compete.
It strives to do its purpose, to bloom and to shine, but cold and
   dark impede it progress
If it were but chosen to bloom a month, a week, or even a day
   earlier, it would fulfill its promise.
Yet of those who do, few of those who are there to see the dew
   roll down the tender petals.
Or see its glory as first light caresses this flower's tender beauty
   in the mist of early morning.
Even so, the last rose struggles on, the journey incomplete,
   only to die in the cold of winter come.
No one to know the beauty hid within those withered petals.
No one, save the One for Whom all things exist, and from whom
   no beauty lies hidden.
     Frank P. Wilcox Jr.

Mystic Thoughts

Withers within out heart wastelands, and dies:
The rose to soften all our days of rage,
The dream upon which consonance relies,
The light that guides the wisdom of the sage.
Infernal fires sear this world's holy ties,
And demons haunt the times, while princely courage

Withers within our hearts wastelands, and dies.
The spires that mock the loftiness of skies
Loom from the dark cathedrals of an age
Doomed to ignite on History's last page
When, at long last, our dread-kingdom of lies
Withers within our heart wastelands, and dies.
     Robert Betts

Thinking Man

In the way of homo sapiens, pondering
   my situations,
I call to mind the endless quarrel: Instinct
   blind - or reason moral
Joined by doctors anthropological, whose specialty
   is psychological.

Is it meat; or is it magic?
Are we keen or are we tragic victims of a misconception
   that sees us soaring with our reason?
Are we animals, in season?

Are we like our "lesser" brothers:
Bird or fish or ape or lizard; spider, yet, or
   maybe fly, with billions of homunculi
Blindly trained to leap synapses,
Saving us from mental lapses?

Leave the answer to those giants skilled in their
   demanding science,
While I, like other mental hackers, sleep on it
   with milk and crackers.
     Thomas G. Corrigan

Over The CB Air

Some will never know the best friend I once had
or the heart that was full of gold and the wisdom he once had.

He will never know of the loved we once shared,
he will never know how much I really cared.

He touched my heart, my soul, and mind
I pushed him away not knowing the time.

I will never know how much he really cared,
I pushed him away because of the fear.

Like a giant teddy bear he was loved so dear
And now he's gone but not the fear.

It was not fair, he was a good man
the one they called "Desperado" over the CB air.
     Peggy Blattner

The Storm

   Step to the other side,
where the truth can't hide.
   Looking down from above,
I see all the lost love.
   A mother cries as her child dies,
and the press gains glory off another mother's story.
   She keeps asking herself why only eighteen years,
strangers will never know what's behind those dried up tears.
   A boy's life was taken just the other day, was it for love?
Was it for hate? Well it's hard to say.
   May his soul be set free to fly with the birds,
and may the beast burn without any last words.
   The boy has come to me and told me he's okay,
but I have many more questions that must wait for another day.
   So to his mother and friends may our love keep him warm,
'til we all meet again after the storm.
     Larry Narkievich

Nipped In The Bud

There must be a way of enduring
all the hassles that nip at our feet;
the problems that seem overwhelming
may be all in the way that we see.

So positive, happy, and loving,
while creative, successful, and kind,
that's how we would like to be living.
can we turn it around in our minds?

Can we bite in, chew it, and swallow,
and digest the whole thing lying down?
Must we tear it and thrash it about,
and still fight all the while with a frown?

Perhaps the best way to get through is
to ignore the sad feelings and pain,
and put on that broad smile for the world,
and shake off all the woes down the drain.

All we need is the strength we can find
from within, with some love from a friend.
That sharing and caring will soothe us,
and make peace in our soul in the end.
     Linley J. Willsie

The Joy And Sorrow Of Olympics 1996

It was the year of Ninety Six
   The Olympics came to play,
In the city of Atlanta Georgia
   In the good old U.S.A

Multitudes of people gathered
   From many nations, far and near.
You could feel the great excitement
   When you heard the people cheer.

There was basketball and tennis,
   Swimming, racing and jumping too.
There was boxing and gymnastics -
   And many other games to view.

It was a time of great precaution,
   Police and guards were in the crowd -
It seemed security was everywhere,
   And America was proud.

Then some evil minded rebel
   Placed a bomb upon the ground -
Some were killed, and many wounded.
   I pray, that rebel will be found.

     Edwyna E. Boyington

The Night Of The White Dragon

Anger and frustration
Surge through my veins
Like the blood of the white Dragon

My life's degradations
Course through my brain
Like the tears of the white dragon

Confusion and aggravation
Add to my strains
On the night of the white dragon

I must lead the assassination
of the constant pains
Wrought by the fires of the white dragon

     Makesha Loder

Julie

I didn't know I could hurt someone
Someone so near, someone so dear

I didn't know she felt that way
So close to say, You hurt me today

She seemed so tough, she seemed so rough
Inside she feels, She cares a great deal

I missed her actions, I missed her reactions
I thought she was fine, she was with her own kind

She felt alone, Discredited and shown
That I didn't care, or see her there

I need her so much, I owe her too much
My life has changed since she crossed my way

"Is it always this hot?" she said
When we first met she said

I couldn't have known that day
That she'd change my life this way

Never can I repay, The gifts she gives each day
I can only hope and pray

That she'll be there each and every day

     Sarah D. Fraser

Merciful God

Thank you Lord for having mercy on me
For when the devil took over
I'd lost my will to see.
I knew not of the things I did,
I wanted to please you but hurt you instead.
You knew my desire to get to you,
But to pray for your mercy was all I could do.
I had fallen behind and lost sight of your word.
So you allowed me to hit bottom and then it
was your voice I heard.
You said, "Arise my child,
for I have heard your cry unto me,
And now I say to you, I have forgiven thee."

     Valerie Esparza

Those Of No Bond

They would be born of wombs,

That would keep no maker,
But for the whores that lie awake
In the night, kept by a mask of false lovers,

That would steal quietly in,
From the dark bowels of night
Silently. Silently

Sons that would be born, and sent away,
While the weight of mother would linger,
Their minds could not know such sin as this.

The old man smiles, and says to me,
Indeed, sin. Sin. But it was what people do.

I cannot help but to feel a pain, when I hear their muffled sobs in the gutter,
Quiet, and high pitched; for they are not so very old.
Those sobs, from the eyes of so miserable a night.

     James Lee

This Is Me

There below a winding path
lies a reflecting lake
Exposing its beauty only on the outside
hiding away from what builds inside
On the outside of this lake
scenery is beautiful and bright
The sun shines its rays from behind
letting mountains mirror from the light
The beauty that you see
makes you feel the lake lives in peace
But if you know what swims inside
the thought of beauty will soon cease
You'll look through its reflecting waters
and learn its shallow pain
The view you knew is growing old
everything you knew just isn't the same
The reflecting lake you now know
is drying up from what lurks within
Leaving its stones just like a memory
waiting for some peace to begin

     Brian Graham

Life Above The Stars

Life is a race towards a better star.
Life can rise and fall.
Life is a wild dandelion with blooming colors.

Life is a circle of things beyond the imagination.

Life goes through time
and ends with the silence of the wind.

     Elisia Bates

Nanny's

As I walk up the short, gravel drive, I see specks of
bright color beckoning me towards them.
I slowly bend and touch a small, soft, pale pink rose
just opening in the late morning light.
I advance and reach the black wrought iron accented
porch of the small, white doll house.

As I open the slightly squeaking front door, the aroma
of melted butter mixed with cooked apples and cinnamon
tickles my nose.
I walk through the door and the melody of "How are you?"
greets my ear.
I feel secure as if I am small and wrapped in my mother's arms.

This is my haven.
A place where I know I am safe and welcome.

Julie Hutcherson

Voice Of Serenity

On a dark gloomy night, I sit in amazement
as I watch the rain fall from the sky.
I notice the sound of thunder. Its voice
is loud and full of energy with each
word it has spoken. Now, silent, I stare
in the dark, puzzled at the shapes the
trees make. Wind blowing in my face,
I hear a crackling voice. Who's there?,
I cry out but no one answers. I listen
for a minute, and hear the crackling
voice again. Once more I cry out, who's
there? Only I, said the thunder with
its quiet voice of serenity.

Reba Lewis

Be Thankful

We sometimes forget just how blessed we are,
WE should be glad to be alive and come this far.
Instead we just sit and complain.
Even on days when it just rains.
So, look up to the sky above.
Give a kiss and a hug to the one you love.
Be thankful for what you've got,
Even if it's not a lot.
When you rise each and every day just say
    "Thank you!"
And he will know.
In return his love will show.
So, be thankful each day in every way.

Shavia Anderson

Traveler's End

I think so oft' of death and me
And what it truly means
'Tis home again, my spirit free
A place I visit in my dreams.

Beyond the veil, I'm blessed to see
Scenes from life enjoyed before
To see the friends who've gone ahead
Who've stepped beyond the mortal shore.

Our home is there, and I rejoice
To light the lamps along the way
So mortal friends may hear, the voice
Which answers them, when e'er they pray.

Oh Father God, and Mother earth
I hasten home to Thee
'Twas from thy souls, I had my birth
When first I journeyed to find me.

Linda E. Madsen

I Am....

I am always there for you, even at the worst of times.
I wonder if you've ever noticed me.
I hear all your thoughts and cries...
I see your life flying by with happiness.
I want you to notice me and see what I've seen.
I am always there for you, even at the worst of times.

I pretend to be alone and invisible to you.
I feel you regret that I'm there.
I touch your heart every time you dream.
I worry that you've come so far, and you
    still don't see me.
I cry about your sad look and your hopeless act.
I am always there for you, even at the worst of times.
I understand why you don't notice me.

I say "I love you", and you push me away.
I dream until the day you'll love me.
I try to make you want me.
I hope you'll notice and want me.
I am always there for you, even at
    the worst of times.....

Leslie Unzueta

Daff In A Bang-Bang

Tulips wearing granny glasses as working class heroes - imagine
electric bananas play with mellow yellow flowers in a
    strawberry field forever while the carousel spins crazily and
    plays backwards music

An FBI agent, high because of opium, wrapped in a Unionjack,
    sails over a yogurt sea under a marmalade sky
limitless undying love shines everywhere with a silver light as
    midnight does the twist in the sergeant pepper afternoon.

Nine penny Volkswagens come together
the four walk across the abbey road, over black and white
    stripes, one sans sandals
John holds the hand of the eggman as George plays the sitar

All of a sudden, insane thoughts drive knife that commits evil
    star murder, starts riot - a cranberry revolution
blue penguins in handcuffs waltz through an umbrella pub

Daffodil in a shotgun says peace and daisies declare the
    walrus is not dead.

Christine Ginetti

Fruit Age

Dying, the winedusk sun fades
over the western horizon. . .
birthing, the opal moon rises
towards the eastern skies

Ebony clouds of darkness cover hope,
fear, strife, pain, love, hate, joy, peace,
as empty quiet fills the nightwomb of this
worn, this abused, this aged space

The people celebrate, some meditate,
as midnight chimes this message late:
"Ring out the old-ring in the new!"
Still others sleep this last night through

Then suddenly, like the pangs of birth,
a newborn sun arises, scattering morning clouds,
unveiling hope, mystery, change, shock, love,
delusions, war, pain, peace. . . Prince of peace?

Or what pother, what solace will it bring,
this new time, this new millennium?
And traveller. . . what spirit, what wisdom,
what nurture will you bring. . . to it?

John A. Alston

A Vision

Since the dawn of time,
when the Earth was young,
Man made his way through a barren, soulless wasteland.
Under darkened skies,
through streets of ash,
a mountain stands tall.
Climbing higher and higher,
man finally reached the top.
Over yonder man sees light,
in the distant sky, over the horizon.
Man can only smile, for a new day is dawning.

Richard Corbett

My Hawaii

As I look through the clouds from high above
A vision of land appears that I soon would love
Eight beautiful Islands alone in the sea
One only for the Hawaiian, untouchable to me
The beauty of the Islands grows deep within the sea
Created by a force of near disbelief
Surrounded by water so blue and warm
A piece of heaven is beautifully born
Black crystal beaches shimmer so bright
Mysteriously in time turns heavenly white
Gentle sunsets of yellow and orange embrace the soul
Mahalo for the beauty you graciously show
The voice of love speaks through the motion of hands
So softly they flow throughout the land
A gentle voice sings lyrics of love
Created by the beauty of the Islands I see from above
A moment in time that will never end
These are the memories I hold within

Gina Hodges

These Hollow Grounds

As I walk these hollow grounds, white tombstones were all I found. Underneath lay men, young and old. So many men, brave and bold.

In fighting a war, they gave their best. Now here is the place their souls can rest. So many tombstones white and cold, did they all know what they were dying for?

These men and women, some un-named, fought for their country, they weren't ashamed. They fought for Freedom. They fought with Pride. Now look at these tombstones, so many died.

For this they were given a white tombstone and a piece of earth to hold their bones. But who will remember their dying faces. Only the ones who took their places.

As I walk through this field of death, I thank each one that it's here I don't rest. We had no idea how the cards would fall, and now I walk among them all.

As I walk these hollow grounds, white tombstones were all I found.

Michael P. Hudgins

The Art Of Giving

Giving is such a special thing
You give your love and friendship to
people you love and like
God gave His only Son for us
Let's give ourselves to the art of giving!

Don't expect something back
When giving something to someone else
Just give from your heart
Just like one of the Ten Commandments
Just give yourself to the art of giving!

Jessica Ferris

Untitled

I've now concluded, it's okay if you don't like me
   For I am independent
Though if you want my heart
I have left yet a remnant.
To dream is my world, those pastures in my head
   I will not keel and die
I will live instead.
   If you want my love, my world does not stop
Take what you can get
For what's left is a drop.
My sanity has diminished
Remaining quite numb
Shouldn't desist until I'm finished,
   My last, little crumb.
I would volunteer my soul, while being shyly inept.
No one deserves that much control
   To endure with what is kept.
To stay is to remain, to seek is to find
To smile is to move my mouth,
   And convince my mind.

Lindsey Pinner

A Child Alone

I'm a child alone, no one hear's my
plea, an empty face, I don't want to be,
most people think it's silly to say,
their lives aren't in danger every day.

I'm a child alone, in this empty room,
I'd gladly trade it for a cold dark tomb.
A silent voice, an urgent call, lies to
convince, no help comes at all.

I'm a child alone, no dreams to
sustain me. Angel of death, please come and
set me free. No more words to hurt, or
beatings that cripple. Dark waters of life
never again do ripple.

I'm a child alone, with no hope left.
dying for me would be God's
greatest gift.
Please no one shed a tear
for me, especially those who
pretend not to see.

Mary L. Henson

Paradise Lost To Paradise Regain

To myself I ask the question
Why the earth goes round and round
To this there are many answers
Some so simple some profound
When I was young life was so worry free
Now as I grow older it's closing in on me
Friends are few, and they come and go
But the love of God is the constant that I know
So through time I watch it all slip by
Always wondering to myself and asking why
Sometimes my eyes well up with tears
I can't stop crying because nobody really hears
Alone we stand against the world
Hoping to find love with the quality of pearls
Promises are made but they're never really kept
To God alone we owe, a very great debt
For truth to be found it's hard to believe
No matter what happens we have to leave
And when that time comes were all afraid
But into God's hands our trust is laid

David Bardessono

Gibraltar

Sparkling nymphs dance and splash
Their way o'er azure blue seas
Clear and cool like a glacial gash,
Lulling all wayfarers with an ease
Not unlike that formerly likened only
To sirens.

Jutting and arching high o'ertop
Is a majestic embattlement
A tribute to past glories, a stop
For travelers who wished enrichment,
Glory and title, a solitude for the lonely
And rest for ravens.

What better place to mark entrance
To a laughing, easy going way
Of life, fun on the med; a chance
For hope, love, and beautiful whey
A giant pond for the helens and the homily;
Birthplace of empires.
    Matt Fulton

Writhing, Rising, Falling, Twisting, Turning

Hear the cries of the bald eagle as he flies, swooping;
He cannot help it, it is nature. He flies, spreading his wings,
Higher, higher, to the ends of the sky, touching the sun!
Too far now, he is burnt. No one can hear his cries now.
He is losing his green - tipped wings, the center of the universe
cannot hold him; he longs for, his nest is gone.
Vultures loom, an anarchy of the sky, the river of blood
below him, its ebb flowing, which he falls into, drowning in the
innocence of a future gone.
The best of him lacks endurance, strength.
The worst full of passionate intensity.
In the distance, a peep is heard.
    Jeff Fryer

My Garden

I till the rich warm soil
With loving thoughts and not much toil
I mound her sides, for a good watering through and
Packed the dirt tight so there would be no run off
I carefully chose were each seed would go and
With loving care placed them there
I tenderly watered each one, so they could grow and
Put forth their bounty for me, you know
Now with the sun high in the sky
I eat from my garden, as the birds fly by
Almost without my knowing
My garden gave me much love
From my tender caring
She gave back ten fold
From just one sowing
My garden gave me a bountiful showing
    Jackie Reynolds

Peace

Can we have peace once more?
Must we have war?
When we can learn to forgive,
and make it a peaceful place to live
so then we all can live in harmony
then learn to face reality,
because peace can make the world a better place.
If we show it to every face.
    Crystal Beale

Thanking My Fathers

I thank God for creating the earth
And giving me life for what it's worth
I thank my mom and dad for conceiving me
But I give thanks to myself for what I'll be
My dad left us all alone
My mom raised me on her own
My dad walked right out of my life
He made it hard he made it strife
My dad walked out when I was three
I wonder why! Was it because of me?
Sometimes I feel like I was a mistake
I wish to God I could be erased
I wish I could tell my dad how I feel
These feelings within me are so, so real
If he wasn't going to stay by my side
He never should have come inside
I wish I was never born
And if I died would he mourn.
    Monique Billings

Untitled

A gentle breeze tosses the leaves around.
The sweet smell of goodness fills the air,
As the sun-kissed earth glows.
Our world is bright, and healthy, filled with lush greens.
It is radiant with extraordinary colored flowers,
The colors of the soft, velvety petals are hues not yet thought of.
Then, before our very eyes, our world goes gray.
Black, evil clouds obstruct our vast sun, and blanket us in darkness.
Colossal gales of wind thrash about, eradicating all we created.
A venomous odor is all around, and a black rain falls, staining
  our Flowers.
Deafening thunder rumbles, and thin, jagged bolts of lightning
Scorches all objects that it touches, after it rips through the
  Somber sky.
The same sky that had once been a beautiful sapphire.
The sun no longer shines, and the vegetation no longer grows.
It is a gray, and dismal world with no way out.
We should never take what we have today for granted,
For tomorrow it might all be just a dream,
Just a wonderful fabrication of the imagination.
    Sarah A. Holmes

One With The Earth

Galloping through the pasture green,
The mighty stallion was to be seen.
He had black hair, mane and tail,
Black all around, not a speck that was pale.
He stretched his legs, graceful and strong,
Beautifully taken care of, and long.
His mane reached his back, halfway down,
And his tail was always dragging the ground.
With dark black eyes, he's a creature wild,
Easily angered, easily riled.
No one dares ride him, for fear of being thrown,
He is a master all his own.
He runs through the forest and tears through the field,
To no boundaries does he yield.
From early in the morning to late at night,
He's here, the next minute, he's gone out of sight.
Gliding across the ground with ease,
With his freedom he seems to be pleased.
He's a creature from nature, a spirit, so fine,
How majestic he looks, and he will for all time.
    Catherine Fitzsimmons

Country Meadow

I walked out in a country meadow in the
early morning light. I saw a
red bird leave an oak branch, and take
to flight.

Rabbits were whistling, and thumping their
feet, as if keeping time, to mother
nature's musical beat.

Heard a frog calling down by the pond,
he was croaking so loudly it woke
everyone.

The grass in the meadow was swaying in a
soft breeze, that sang a song as it passed
through the trees.

Couldn't see the breeze as it went past,
only felt the softness of its touch, as long
as it would last.

Butterflies and flowers of all colors and shades,
pressed down grass where a deer had lain.
Raccoons, squirrels, crows, and foxes, too,
all in the meadow to enjoy its view.

Melvin Stewart

Why Does Love

Why does love seem so vague, so unpredictable
   and why does every heart chase love
Is it really that imperious of an emotion that
   every life must strive for it
Yet how can one go wrong with it once they were so
   sure, or had they been at all
What is divorce and what is unwavering unity
Is the difference intellectual or plain emotional
How come love destroys some lives yet enriches others,
   and why does it ebb and flow
Or does it
What is love
How come it seems to bring every other emotion with it
Is it really the foundation of all feelings
And if it is, why does it take a lifetime to find it
If it is so vexatious, why is it that people, all people, put forth
   the effort to find it
How do they know it's really worth it when they've never had it before
Why does love seem so vague

Brandy Vander Dussen

"Tribulation"

When life seems to turn its back on you, you blame yourself for what you have done wrong. You have taken every measure to keep in touch with yourself, then you re-evaluate why am I blaming myself for things I can't control. You stop and look at a different perspective, the present situation comes to view, you are causing your own discomfort, face it you have done the best you can do. Why go beyond the fibers of your soul to find a better solution, when there isn't any more you can do, just strive on and hue, you will make it.

Ruth Brandon

No Longer Grapes

Grapes start out juicy, fresh and plump.
They are sometimes red and green, sometimes purple.
They all come in a hand size lump.
As they get old, they begin to wrinkle.

Times ages them, whether red, green, or purple.
When they are left out in the bright sun, that's no sin.
For the older they become, just add another wrinkle.
The grape is no longer a grape, but a raisin.

Nellie Rinkel

Silent Partner

You wanted to give him everything,
So you slipped on the wedding ring.
He said he'd never hurt you, you believed,
Then all he did was make you grieve.
He always wanted a partner who's silent.
Someone to be there when he felt violent.
He'd never know what love was about,
So you found your only way out.
You took some pills, to sleep awhile,
Closed your eyes, you had a smile.
He came to wake you, you weren't asleep
He shook you hard, there wasn't a peep
He didn't understand your reason for this.
With a tear in his eye, he gave you a kiss,
The only time he had shown love for you.
A love, we all knew, had never been true.
You gave almost everything, still he was violent.
Your final gift to him, a partner who's silent.

Lois Ann Cleveland

Hidden

The night hides many things.
   The angry a-creeping about,
   The sad huddled in a corner,
   The frightened trembling in the dark,
   And the lonely in the shadows.
All are alone.

If others knew they might change.
If others cared it might not happen.
   The angry will soon become calm.
   The sad will soon be happy.
   The frightened will soon be sure.
But the lonely...
   if we only knew.
But the lonely...
   if we had cared sooner.
But the lonely will soon be dead.

Vicki Sharp

View Of Life

When you are a child you see
all around the world
there is violence
you wonder how the world could love to hate.
When you are a teenager you feel
the effects of hate
you are judged
not for what you do
or who you are
but how you look.
When you are an adult you are
still wondering why
the world is full of hate
but yet without knowing
you have become the judge
and cause of violence.
When you are old you see
once again the world is full of violence
but now know it was you who helped it thrive.

Laura Elizabeth Dement

I Am

Good, evil and in between,
all things with him are seen.
Live your life within his will,
things will get better still.
Trust in the All in All,
and the largest problems will grow small.

Jon Wickre

Self-Improvement

Silly girl! So lazy and dumb
you have but one emotion; numb
and everything you strive to have
you'd give away in a single flash

getting used? You don't stand alone.
I've been there before and it's not fun
Thinking of letting go? Giving it all up?
life has nothing to do with luck.

Think now! What is real and what is fake
decide now, before it gets too late
find a standing point and hold your ground
take your life and turn it all around.

Holly Ankrom

A House That's Not A Home

Those who live within the confines
of a "House That's Not A Home",
be it a modest abode or mansion
will, in time, begin to roam.

What's embedded in the dwelling
of the place where you reside
will bring out sad and happy tears,
if love and sharing are inside.

Quality time for each of you
could be a family's way of life;
instilling virtues and self-confidence...
the tools to handle strife.

If your child feels they can't come to you,
when and if a problem should arise;
in time, they'll find someone else...
which could lead to their demise!

If you sold your mansion,
and bought a house with a magical dome;
unless you know of love's dimension...
you bought "A House That's Not A Home"!

Patricia A. Wessel

Angels Talking

Sitting alone wondering why,
Why do people have to die?
At night when everyone's fast asleep,
Angels talk with me in their gentle weeps.
When I'm with them I'm not scared,
They're warning me, saying be prepared.
Do they die so others can live?
This answer I cannot give.
One day my time will come,
Maybe I won't be so down in the dumps.
As long as my kids are okay,
I wouldn't mind if I died today.
I've come close to death not long ago,
My temp was so high I'm surprised my head didn't blow.
But it doesn't matter now,
I lost the one I loved, so now I just sit and pout.
But the Angels, they still care,
For me and my kids they bow and say a prayer.

Briana Michelle Warren

Without You

As I look outside the starry sky that hangs above the sea,
I whisper softly to the moon how bright and beautiful you are to me.
And in the morning, to the rising sun, that peers beneath my shade,
I call to God and thank Him for each day that He has made.
Each day that He has made is always bright, beautiful, and new,
Unless of course, my darling dear, it is a day spent alone without you.

Tabitha Jean Huffman

Modern Day Love

I lost my head and bought a diamond ring.
And then I married the pretty thing.

Shortly after we were married I thought I died and went to heaven.
Five years later I thought I would have to take out chapter eleven.

Now I didn't really know what to do.
So I said honey I don't think I can afford you.

Now with all my money done spent. She left town with half of
my retirement. I thought a lot of the pretty thing. But, my monthly
payments remind me I don't want to buy another diamond ring.

Besides I don't think being married is so hot.
Since I've fallen in love with my crock-pot.

It never gets the blues, and it doesn't need 44 pairs of shoes.

My food is always hot and who can ask for more,
now that I don't have any stress at night
I can go to bed and really snore.

That's the end of my poem and there's no more.
It helps to have a sense of humor so you don't stay sore.

So years later I'm still not married and I'm not gay.
I'm divorced and going to stay that way.

Once was plenty and two was enough I can't afford any more
of the stuff.

Gary Buttice

Letter To Michelle

Where have you gone?
I can't hear you.
Little girl voice, rough with pain.
I can't hear you.
Where have you gone?

What are you looking for?
I want to help you.
Baby blue eyes, shining too bright.
I want to help you.
What are you looking for?

You left me. No goodbye...
I feel you drifting away.
Baby with angel hair. Have you seen her?
I feel you drifting away.
You left me. No goodbye...

I know you're not coming back.
My heart is cold as stone.
Is it worth more than love; worth than life?
My heart is cold as stone.
I know you're not coming back...

Carol A. Nolan

Eyes Watching Me

50 million eyes watching me,
as they look upon my face.
I know not what they are
only that they are watching me.
As my heart becomes quicker in beat
I see the eyes, as they get redder, right behind me.
I start to run looking to get away
but it seems like every where's I run, they are right behind me.
As I look back, they are closer than before,
and see the faces of forgotten people I once had known.
But now I realize
a life I once had, is no more,
and I'm here forever,
until the ends of time.

Jason Reil

The Love Of A Mother

The first time you held me close to you heart,
I felt the love you did impart.

It helped me grow day by day,
no one could ever take it away.

We grew very close as years went by,
two special friends, you and I.

I remember the tears we cried, but most of all the joys,
as you guided me through life's glories.

All too soon it was time to go off on my own,
I had to leave this place I called home.

It was so hard to leave you behind,
you told me a new life I must find.

To take everything I had learned at your knee,
and start my own family.

As I held my babies for the first time,
I remember how your love did shine.

All through my life your love so bright,
like the stars that light up in the night.

There will be no other,
like the love of a Mother.

Gail Castro

When Does The Worship Stop?

The pedestal has crumbled, the master is in the dirt!
He left me, in my golden years, for a stupid flirt.

It should have happened years ago, the signs were there to see.
I carefully hid them from the world but, oops, they hid from me.

It's time for me to build a life, it's time to just go on...
I see him now for what he was and I'm better off alone.

His hygiene was atrocious, his attitude was rude.
A self centered ego maniac and often he was lewd.

Lies were not his second nature — to him they were first;
And when it came to taking blame, well, he was sure to shirk.

Life with him was very hard, there was seldom any bliss.
He always seemed to stir the pot and leave me to clean the mess.

So tell me why I think of him, tell me why I grieve?
I didn't ask him not to go when he said he had to leave!

I'm sure I don't still love him, I wouldn't have him if I could.
Why does he still haunt my dreams? This makes me fear I would!

My life is great without him, like a movie's happy ending!
But when I catch a glimpse of him, my emotions are overwhelming

The love is gone, the dreams are lost, my life has changed a lot.
So tell me, if you think you can, when does the worship stop???

B. C. Medford

Who May I Be

If I were to write a poem about me
Heavens dear Lord what would it be
No springtime blooms or summer days
Only times passing in a blinding haze

Loves are never won, only lost
And for this what was the cost,
Time spent alone, not to relax
My life, a figurine molded from wax

This life of mine could never be a poem!
For as I write my mind would roam
Thoughts so hard, who could I be?
No, never will I write a poem about me.

Rebecca Souza

Can You Hear

Can you hear the breeze blow through the trees?
The trees of the deserted battle field.
   Can you hear their cries?
Can you hear the crying child?
The cry of the motherless child.
   Can you hear their cries?
Can you hear the gunshot?
The gunshot used to kill the innocent man.
   Can you hear their cries?
Can you hear the whispering wind?
The wind that carries the stories of our past.
   Can you hear their cries?
Can you hear our freedom?
Freedom while others lie cold in the streets.
   Can you hear their cries?
Can you hear the song of death?
Death of our brothers, sisters, and children.
   I can hear their cries.

Meagan E. Doty

Promises

   You once promised that my
heart would never be broken again,
   But like all the others, that promise
wasn't kept and my life without you must begin.
   No matter how much I might wish
to still be with you forever,
   I'm afraid if I do ask you
back you would smart-off "never."
   And if that were to happen I
would feel pain I haven't felt before,
   I'm sorry but I just can't
take all of this anymore.
   But I better get on with my
life, to try and find someone new,
   And maybe, this time, that
person's promises will be true.

Charity Jones

Life Indeed

Time slipping by; like sand through a glass.
Unknown seconds, and hours will pass.
Is life a future?
Or living a past?
Present nonexistent; inside this frame.
Life is the painting the artist controls the game.
Don't lose symmetry.
Colors, though different; when blended, the same.
If the lines are too heavy, and hues too few.
Think back.
The canvas was fresh.
The artist was you.

Philip Desautel Jr.

Untitled

A Christmas tree, A Christmas tree
to be is fun.
I like to run under the sun
under the Christmas tree.
It is fun to run under the sun.

I like a Christmas tree
'cause Santa comes at night
when it's Christmas night.
Isn't it fun for you to have Santa come?
Is it fun for Santa to come?
Yes it is.

Allison E. Prucnal

Sons

When men would send our boys to war
as mothers we send them to their rooms,
for while they come from God above
we nurture them inside our wombs.

If God intended war for them
he'd plan a different start,
for creatures meant for the likes of war
don't grow neath a woman's heart.

So hold them near and hush their fears
and talk to them of peace.
Our sons will be "those men" someday,
Lord help us to make them see.

They all are sons of woman born,
all sent from God above:
created and born and raised in love;
it is their duty to pass it on!

Joyce Rivers-Fritch

Friendship

A relationship grows from the seed of friendship.
Friendship is nurtured by the rains of
Honesty,
   Sharing,
     and Trust.
Honesty has no boundaries;
   Sharing holds no price; and
     Trust knows no limitations.
Without these rains,
Friendship and Love would just
wither
   and
     die.
And life nothing more
   than the ticking of time;
     repetitive breaths; and
       meaningless heart beats...

Jim Rafferty

Oh, These Changing Times

Life began mysteriously as an exciting adventure,
Time has passed, the natural innocence is now a blur r r r,
Overcrowded cities, drugs, crime, the sheer desperation for money and
   power, too much   too fast
Pollution in the air and water,
The gradual destruction of our ozone,
Oh, these changing times
God's earth a gift so beautiful, so tranquil to us all,
How did we allow ourselves to fall, into abusing the laws of nature,
This may be our downfall,
The disasters of nature throughout this land, the lack of love by man
towards one another,
It was not the ultimate plan.
Must we begin again with the dust of the earth,
Will there be a rebirth?????
Oh, these changing times

Beverly L. Tucker

Untitled

The road is shortened day by day
although its length is the same always.
It's my beating heart that quickens the pace
and my blood that boils to finish the race.
Please wait, my love, I'll be there soon
and sing a poem into a lover's tune.
It will all be worth it in the end
the time on the road I have to spend.

John E. Threat III

"Gina"

Twelve months and some before she walks
She sits and thinks before she talks.
She tries so hard and strives for more
Her frailties make her so unsure.
Encouragement builds her character true
Until she has strength that will see her through.
The toughest times yet in a world full of grief
Not far away comes the family thief.
A home that is broken and full of despair
What happened?
No questions!
Just sorrow was there.
Time to move on and seek her own life
No time for a man, she won't be a wife.
She travels cross country, her needs very few
She holds her head up and thinks often of you.
She asks for your help and of course you are there
Reassure her she's needed and hardly to spare.
She peers in a window her face in full view
She shares how she sees not herself but you.

Agatha Landon

The End

I sit on my bed looking around,
A couple of matches lay on the ground,
The music playing in my ear takes away most of the fear,
The fear comes near,
The end is here,
The music stops,
I shed a tear,
I fall asleep and when I awake,
I look out my window and see day break,
I pick up a book,
That's when I found,
The story of life,
Simple and sound,
As I read on,
The story is clear,
I point my finger and say right here,
The story reads simple and clear,
They lived happily ever after,
The end it says,
And so do I...

Drew Kersey

Answers From A Six Year Old

As I watched my little brother play,
   A question was inspired.
I saw the simplicity of his day,
   And curiously I inquired:

"What do you think of all the hate?"
   I asked the insightful lad.
He looked at me and shook his head
   And responded, "Hate is bad."
"What about violence and killing?"
   I questioned little Billy.
He looked up from his trucks and made a face,
   And told me I was silly.
"But what about fighting and the wars?"
   I asked him, six years young.
He left his trucks and sat on my lap,
   Responding, "They're all dumb."
I cradled my brother, amazed that a boy
   Who still the darkness fears,
Had answered questions that full grown men
   Have struggled with for years.

Charlotte Childs

Gothic Mansion

Gothic mansion with Doric columns
windows stare with looks so solemn
years eroding such stately presence
till time is finally of the essence.

Spirit of life within remains
though sagging frame shows signs of strain.
Backward flow the sands of time
and bring me back to what was mine.

A place of mystery and intrigue
where romance novels often speak
gallant hero of Victorian era
rescue me from unknown terror.

Gas lamps light up cobblestone streets
where horses clop out rhythmic beats
and midnight journey's in moonlit carriages
often brings forth the promise of marriage.

Bonny Branch

Angels

With shining hair, from a summer sun's glimmer
And dewy eyes, from a baby's tear shimmer
With ivory skin, that never grows dimmer

With eyes as blue, as heaven's very sky
And ropes as white, heaven's very light
They walk the clouds, way up high

They look down upon us
They are all around us
They protect us and
Keep us safe

They are, the summer's sun
They are, the baby's tear
They are, the heaven's light
They are, heaven
They are Angels

Christina Newbill

Shyness

It is only around at certain places,
It knows all the faces
who to talk too,
who to leave alone,
It can speak and is mean and cruel,
It has its own little kingdom
that traps you within,
It holds you back from everyone,
It stops you from having fun,
It is really sneaky and doesn't let you through,
It always wants to hold you on to you,
It doesn't let you pass,
It puts up a border,
People think you're weird,
They don't know you well,
and they never did,
You begin to think they never will.

Elias Saba

To My Love

Roses are red. My ring is gold.
My love for you will never be sold.
It is so great! It is so bold!
With you around... I'll never be cold.
And now the truth can finally be told...
When they made you Dear...
They broke the mold!!!

Karen L. Dellapenta

A Mere Nightmare

I hear the angry wind blowing, as it whistles throughout the night. I feel a chill run down my spine, as I sense a bit of fright! As I peer through the shutters, I see aghast scores of many bats take flight. I ponder deeply an erie thought, is there a reason for this plight? I hear the howling of a wolf or jackal, whichever it may be. I pinch myself to ensure I am awake, or is my imagination playing tricks on me? There is someone at my doorstep, I move cautiously to see it's only rustling leaves and branches falling against my door from the mighty old oak tree. Temporarily I find myself relieved, as being startled, my heart does race! I look again, and swear I see in the dark a lifeless face! I'm not sure just what to do, as this all seems like a nightmare at this sudden point of view! Where can I go? What can I do? As it seems there's no escape from what I'm going through! Once again, I hear a knocking, this time by a hand upon my door. I know I must face my destiny regardless to reveal what this visit is for. My knees are weak, my heart is pounding, as it skips every other beat, I fling open the door, and I am faced with two hobgoblins, who in unison say, "trick or treat!"

Jimmy Dan Barthlein

Untitled

Crushed in his embrace
I inhale the scent of hidden things lost upon me
The release is always so abrupt
Always when I need more
I'll let him breathe without me
Until he flashes in the distance
And I hear the echoes calling me
To join the dance of the illusive dream
That horrifies, glorifies my waking sleeping
I turn and spin dazzled by what I see
His rough hands hover but never touch me
I feel myself adapting to what is never quite free
Once it comes to the release in escaping
The empty cries of empty memories
Distort and deteriorate the boundaries
Of shrunken, compromised fantasy
There is too much trust in reality
And all he doesn't know is what I refuse to believe

Kelly Krug

Yesterday's Rose

See, yesterday's rose is faded away
That beautiful rose wasn't put here to stay

The rose can be pink, yellow or red
The pedals will drop because they are dead.

The petals will fall to the ground so slow
And be caught up in the wind, as it blows

Age doesn't suppress or change the odor they had.
The savor was never, never bad
It was such a sweet, sweet smelling scent
Are you, like yesterday's rose as your life is spent?

Will you leave behind a lasting scent,
Or should you this day humbly repent?

And be remembered long after you leave
As a sweet smelling rose who, really believed.

Tressie Ours

The Bird Of Freedom

The bird flies free from unseen grasps
   -how joyous this time is
Fly, Fly, Fly - no concerns, how solemn that can be
You will find an answer
   -you will
and you will know the truth

Richard Wheeler

Where But I

Empty husk of the man once I,
Lifeless and listless and too sad to cry,
Why can I but feel sorrow,
Can't I believe alone, believe for tomorrow.
Breathless of solitude, loss of sensation,
I am numb and cannot rest, my slumber
Is lost to what could, what should, what is, what was,
Help me escape the fathom of despair, the trench of one;
Don't ask for surprise but understand by my far off stare.

Andrew T. Barbe

My Mother Eva

'Tis said there's nothing so lovely as a tree
But, God did greater, when he made Mother for me.
Her tender love has nourished my soul,
When in descending stress, my anguish told.
Her kindly words gave strength and courage
Where lack of discipline, childish anger emerged.
Her secret, silent prayers, so humbly prayed
Often righted the wrong where trouble laid.
Her loving hands though weary and worn,
Never ceased to care for me, her first born,
Her children came and grew and left
But, Mother still thinks of us before herself.
Seventy three years have now graced her frame,
So, please God keep her well and bless her name.

Grace Walston Daughtry

Lost Paradise

There are so many lost and confused souls
some haven't any faith to hold
others don't believe in the 'high supreme' anymore
these are the ones who mistakenly stepped through the door
the entrance to the forgotten universe
where violent demons tell them how much their lives aren't worth
a world where sorrow and pain dominates with so many lies
these tortured souls forever trapped in the lost paradise
now there are faithful ones like you do not want to think of a place
like that but we must remember the weary ones who will never
    come back
we must close our eyes and pray
that they live their eternal lives in color, not in the shades of
gray and if, "it's not my fault", is what you say
then you are the ones who are not compassionate 'cause we must show
the way for there are still so many who get lost
in that world where time forgot
we must show them the door to Christ
and not the door that will close and lock them up forever
    in the lost paradise.

John Lowe

Untitled

Love mad angry bitter, confusion and despair
Are all among the feelings... not showing but are there
Even though you and your loved one may have had your ups
    and downs
He is resting very quiet, with his spirit homeward bound
Look for God to answer questions of confusion you may feel
Deep inside he knows your heart, and knows your troubles are for real
So fear not that what you're feeling, whether guilty or disbelief
God has heard all of your prayers, and will help you through your grief

Angela Washington

Loving Memories

I remember how we ran
around the neighborhood bend
holding each other's hand
to catch the ice cream man.

I remember the popcorn we shared
while sitting in the theater chairs
with tears running everywhere,
and how we didn't care.

I remember another time
when we sang out of rhyme,
then we fought over a crazy dime
whether it was yours or mine.

I remember your beautiful smile
full of brightness with a warming style,
even when we were apart many a mile
I could feel your sunshine a long while.

I remember and may
the memories forever stay
of my sister's loving way
each and every day.

Linda Hudson

"Love Of Love"

If not for the love of the children,
if not for the love of fellow man.
If not for the love of the shining stars,
if not for the love of the sands.

Means to be justified for worlds to believe,
if not for the love of life.
Tortured and tormented, capture and destroy,
eyes refusing to see.

Minds of the intelligent, diligently at work,
planning strategy of the day.
Courses are charted, troops are deployed,
all for the love of peace.

Bare arms, lock hands, steadfast and almighty,
nothing shall penetrate the Godly force.
No Presidents, No Kings, No Queens, No Man,
when nations decide to join hands.

If not for the love of the children,
God; For the love of love.

Maynard Lumbra

Rusted Memories

Remembrance of a summer's day
Folded away and packed like clay
To take a step that did not belong to me
I set my heart upon the sea

Of worthless and worth I would cry
For I dare not bother to say goodbye
What good is tears when crying never ends
My innocence I seek to defend

Wings that are weak like a fallen sparrow
Edges rough and ragged penetrating like an arrow
It's horror that seeps into my very thoughts
Dishonor that misfortune is what it bought

Break these chains that restrain my soul
Precious freedom on which I have no hold
Count for me for I can no longer count alone
Do not discard me I only want to go home

Annie R. Rountree

Words Cannot Describe

With my future bright
and all fears gone,
I brought a friend into the light
where together we sang a song.
The lyrics were so pure
no one could have known,
his selfishness would have no cure
and soon the seeds of politics were sown.
A new type friend he came to be,
with knife in hand
As he talked to me.
Yet, still I had no inkling of his plan.
Too late it was when it was found
the knife it had begun to turn;
to create a pain without a sound.
Soon within it began to burn
and almost with pride, the deed was done.
No longer to myself could I lie
only to gaze into darkness
as I watched a friendship die.
  Stephen M. Lewis

Seashell

You have become an echo in my mind
A nagging question that must be answered
Emotions collide in confusion
I want to hold you close in my arms
And at the same time
Run and hide from your searching gaze
I am afraid
That I will lose myself in your eyes
And you will turn away
Leaving an empty shell
Lying along the ocean of her tears
A seashell
Put to the ears of laughing children
Playing along the sandy shore
How they marvel
At the sound of crashing waves that remain
  Shirley Hixson

The Stranger By The Side Of The Road

My mind on many things as I drive along,
Miles slipping by as my car travels on.

Passing up a stranger by the side of the road,
A pack on his back. Oh My! What a load!

Several days I'm sure his clothes have been worn,
So very dirty and probably torn.

Tired and hot as the sun shines down.
How do we know he's not homeward bound?

To see loved ones whom we'll never know,
I'm sure there's family waiting, don't you think so?

To give of ourselves isn't always easy,
We just pass up this stranger, who to us looks sleazy.

We think we do good, and we do what we can
But we're afraid to stop and pick up this man.

Strange things happen nearly every day,
And too many times, we drivers pay!

But I feel so little as I travel along,
And the image of this stranger is very soon gone.

Dear God in Heaven as You look down from above
Forgive us our weakness and show this stranger your love.
  Margie M. Myers

Mind's Eye

What will it take to get you to see;
that your eyes do not behold the key.
Faith moves mountains and opens eyes,
and love is an answer that saves lives.

I use my mind's eye when all else fails,
and it shows me the cross with the nails.
The eye can make me see and believe,
that many died for Him on bended knee.

I will tell you this again and again,
of His willingness to forgive all sin.
If it is hard for you to believe;
in things that you can't feel and see;
then remember Thomas and his doubt,
and go to a mountain and shout it out;
that Jesus died for you and me,
and that faith beholds the true key.
  Kim Hoggatt

His Eyes

In his eyes all I see,
Is what he really means to me.
I don't see a man at all,
I see a friend and a companion.
He is only a person to others.
But to me, he is warm, caring, and kind.
No matter how cruel his eyes look to anyone else,
They are loving and warm.
They are his eyes.
  Emily

Missing You Beloved Son

Many a day we think of you,
In our hearts we love you too.
Somehow we know we will meet again,
Son you will be to us more than a friend.
Innocent you were when you left that day,
Never having a chance to run and play.
God took you so quick, back to his fold,
You never had a chance to be a man, to grow old.
Only with us a very short while,
Undying is our love for you, and for that we smile.
Because of our love and respect for each other,
Eventually we went on and gave you a brother.
Love in our household grows still to this day,
Over the years, it has proven to stay.
Very blessed are we not to of only had you,
Even went on and gave you three sisters too.
Days turn into months, months into years,
Seems like only yesterday we shed our tears.
Only know this - we will all be together,
Not only for a while, but always and forever.
  Mona Winters

Although We're Apart

Across the miles I write these lines, but to see your
  face would be divine.
Although we're apart we're not alone, while we're
  away our love has grown.
Although we're apart do not despair, my love will be
  with you no matter where.
The road of love isn't always straight, it's the
  winding turns that make it great.
My thoughts of you will always be, thoughts
  of love as you will see.
Emotions of love fill my heart, to help me through
  when we're apart.
Even though I may shed a tear, our love will
  grow throughout the years.
  Joseph Lemons

When I Was Young And 24

When I was young and 24, living fancy free,
I found someone I could adore
who made me laugh with glee.

Did I say she made me laugh?
She made me warm inside,
and soon became my better half,
my life, my hope, my bride.

Now, soon we had a son named John
who filled our lives with joy.
For what could make us prouder than the laugh of a baby boy.

Now John is 25 or so and found his lady fair.
I'm sure they will be happy with all our love and prayer.

We wish them health and wealth and such
throughout their lives together,
or as they way, throughout thick and thin
in any stormy weather.

When John and Tonya take their vows
to last forever more,
I'll know those weren't just dreams I had
when I was young and 24.
Denis A. McManus

The Roses Faith

It hides away
its inner beauty,
closing up a passionate fire
of legendary lust,
when creeps the darkened
dusk of nightfall.
And there in the
radiance of the world,
as the morn breaks way to new hopes,
it opens its delicate petals
to the fingers of new dreams and fantasies,
casting its glow
of love and beauty
on the face of the believer.
And the rose stands,
confined to who believes in this,
being the meaning of life.
Brie Waldkirch

"The Wind Blows"

As the wind blows across the sea, my life means
less and less to me
   Our time is short, the end is near, then our lives
just disappear
   Year by year and day by day, our lives just slip
further away
   The plague is upon us, that we know its killing
our loved ones blow by blow
   After our loved ones have all gone away we sit and
we ponder, is tomorrow my day
   To them they know you're in a better place as they
caress your cold, lifeless face
   We all don't know when our time will come, quicker
for others and longer for some
J. Brandon Smith

"Miss Gracie"

Miss Gracie, laughing, chattering and kind a maze
   With a look of, quite daze
Miss Gracie smiles, as to test
As only a mother can bless
Carol Smithey

People Love To Play

People love to play with words
Writing down everything they hear.

People love to play with memories
Taking pictures of everything without fear.

People love to play games
But not always being fair.

People love to play with loves
But not always with the right gear.

People love to play with times
Until they find there is none left to spare.
John Pipinich

'Flight'

Up! Up! O'er trees, o'er hills and beyond,
Nothing mars its path, either hither or yon.

Oh my! How majestic its flight, as I watched
And watched, till far out of sight.

In memory this sight forever instilled.
This majestic beauty in flight o'er the hills.

Its movements, incredulous grace, what ease.
This body and wings in flight o'er the trees.

Yes! Yes!, it's rapturous, its name is regal.
It could be none other than "The American Bald eagle".

Eagle? Eagle, does heaven to you open its portals?
If so, in your flight, on your wings, take this mortal.

Your flights may they never ever wane.
E'er who of us then could endure the great pain.
Anna A. Vigna

Flight In The Sky

Flight in the sky, swooping down beneath the trees,
Wind beneath their wings, feathers gliding in the breeze.
Lovely as the sun glistens on their heads held high,
If only like a bird, you and I could fly.
Looking down from the heavens upon this earth,
Watching life begin as spring gives new Birth.
Perching on a limb, being careful of its prey,
Searching the elements, deciding to stay.
Wild, free, large and small,
No human eye could capture them all.
From each family, to each nest, protecting their fold,
Spreading their wings, while shaking the cold.
Flying off to catch a ray of the sun,
This is the way living free is done.
As we watch our feathered friends soaring oh, so high,
We watch them disappear to their flight in the sky.
Sheila D. Norris

The Real You

When I look into your eyes,
I don't just see blue,
I see the real you:
Your heart, your soul, your thoughts, your dreams,
What you really mean:
You stand there looking cool,
But you really want someone to love you:
Well I love you,
For who you are,
That great person,
I see from afar.
Melissa Sue Newport

Open Your Eyes And You Will See

Open your eyes and you will see
   Beautiful nature, flowers, and trees.
Open your eyes and behold
   All the stories yet untold.
With every tree, there is a mystery
   Look, and see, but let it be!
In every flower, there is unseen power
   To make a seed become a flower.
Behind every sunset, there are colors galore
   Once you see one, you'll look for more.
The earth is ours to enjoy and share
   But remember, we must always care!

Sarah Marie McGrady

The Stranger

   As I was walking down the road
On a day so bright and clear
   I had a frightful experience
That would later be so dear
   Suddenly a stranger stepped from nowhere
As I went passing by
   He appeared to be so very weak
With deep sadness in his eyes
   Then he approached and kissed my hand
As I just backed away
   But he meekly followed me
No matter what I'd say
   So I slowly turned and started home
But he stayed right by my side
   And not a word was spoken
Of the comforts he'd been denied
   Now he's my constant companion
And I cherish that scary day
   When this loving old dog, the stranger
So hopefully blocked my way

Lulah Clenard

When A Child Cries

Look closely when a child cries
At the pain reflecting in their eyes
Don't turn your back and walk away
Or the pain they feel will always stay
Deep inside their loving hearts
Where eventually the scars will start
To destroy the love and gentleness
To make them feel less and less
As they grow up their hearts grow cold
Emotions gone, they're hard to hold
They trust no one and walk alone
Cry no tears, their hearts are stone
They've learned from us how not to share
How not to feel, how not to care
We've taught them not to cry out loud
We've taught them well, why aren't we proud?
It's our eyes now that reflect the pain
It's our tears now that fall like rain
They remember our lessons, even today
As they turn their backs and walk away.

Thomas G. Mortenson

Highway

The steps have been paved consecutively along the way...
Bumps to be missed to make way for one's proper footing...
The stride is now reinforced and shall not sway...
Lightness of sneaker, sandal, and saunter no sooting...
Smile now with the fancy footwork and be not in dismay...
For now time is the ideal time to put
the strength in the pudding...

Lisa Macklin

Deception

My vacant heart is calling,
Can no one hear its cry?
Is silence all that echoes out,
Into the empty night?

Does no one see beyond the smile,
Enshrouding the endless pain
Can no one see the teas I shed,
Intermingling with the rain?

My deception has fooled the keenest eye,
Impassive through each trial,
Yet one sees beyond this beguiling mask,
Has glimpsed the turmoil behind the smile.

She hears the voice of my vacant heart,
She mocks the unbounded treachery,
She knows the hidden secret,
This reflection in my mirror - me.....

Rebekah L. Burns

The Wonder Of Nature

The sky is a heavenly blue lake,
Reaching down to put a sparkle in my heart.
The rustle of a baby fox in the brush
Echoes the sound of my confidence through the valley.

The early runoff is a flow
Of all my worries being washed away.
The blinding sun
Is my brightly shining spirit.

And the Wonder of Nature carves
An unforgettable memory into my soul.
And it helps me
Down the road to success.

Darren Legge

Ivana Trumps The Ace

   Although it is Bob's Hope that Claude Reigns over all,
one cannot deny that Eddie's Cantor was an influence
making Gene Wilder than Fred March's hare. And then
if Charlie's Chaplain (Jane's Fonda him) hadn't interfered,
Tyrone's Power would not have been a factor and
Robert's Tailor would not have made George Bushed.

   Since it occurred near Nelson's Eddy
adjacent to Jeannette's McDonalds, George Burns
over the fiasco, but in the final analysis,
let's be Sonny and Cher the good news, - Ed Wynns.

Bill Gilmer

The River

Rivers, very similar to all of us.
The river has no way of turning back.
It has only one direction, downstream.
The river has no way of fixing accidents which were upstream,
it only has the choice to work hard for the desired future.
The river divides itself, to the places it can go.
Sometimes to a smaller stream, sometimes to the ocean.
The river may seem like it never changes, the cycle, the volume,
or the content.
But day by day it slowly does, and sometimes greatly.
Some are for the better, but some may hurt the river.
But all through these changes, the river continues flowing.
Sometimes it goes throw smaller problems,
and sometimes experiences the power of the world.
But no matter what, it continues flowing, no way of going back
upstream.
Until one day, when problems are to harsh.
And the river has gone away.

Jackie Jackson

My Friend—My Sister

We must be wrong—it's been since—
At least—the start of time—
It can't have been only—twenty years—
This friendship that binds—your heart with mine.

Too much has happened—too much been shared—
The in's—the out's—the ups the downs—
And—through it all—
We've always cared.

I look back over it now—
Coffee drank and cigarettes smoked—
Laughter, tears, weddings, divorces, children, grown and small—
Even in the worst of times—we still joked.

We're a team—just—you and I—
Pulling together to solve a problem—
Or—playing like children—
And—letting the world—go by.

So my friend—my sister true—
Please always know—
For the next 20 times 20 years—
When I thank God—I'll thank him for you.

Lee Ann Farrior

Distant Memories

Distant memories of days gone by. Locked in the realms
of a private world.
A breath of wind gently glides quietly by one's ear.
Turning quickly, there is no one there.
It's not but a whisper telling one to unlock the door.
To the world of memories so long forgotten.
Desperately found, a turn of the key.
A flood of faces, feeling, and contentment rise in
a mystic swirl of emotions, an escape from one's worn out soul.
The fast and unyielding life is temporarily forgotten.
The precious past is revived and cherished,
Maybe for awhile, or for only an instant.
Then the whisper of wind turns its direction.
The private world slowly fades.
But a smile is still there, knowing the key can be found,
to the realms of distant memories.

Gloria Dee Mazur

Wishing Star

I sit upon my window sill,
Looking out at the sky,
Bathing in the moon so bright,
As planes and jets soar by.

A single star shines bright tonight,
Alone in the sea of blackness,
Putting out the light of a million stars,
Blocking out the dimness.

I wish upon that star this night,
A wish that must come true,
I wish for there to be many more stars,
Just as beautiful as you.

The next few nights I sit on that sill,
And watch the sun go down,
Looking for that wonderful star,
And his companions with him now.

And every night there he sits,
Shining bright and true,
Showering beauty and wonderful gifts,
Of love and kindness too.

Laura College

Without

My heart cries silent whimpers of woe.
I long to shout, but I am mute
Silenced by my own despair.
I opened my soul and it was snatched away,
Gobbled up by a predator in the night
Leaving me without substance — without myself.

The darkness remains
Enveloping what is left of my spirit.
My eyes are opened, yet I can not see.
My arms are outstretched, but my hands cannot feel
Clutching at empty space — void of presence.
My feet are slipping on an icy deck of darkness.

How will I catch myself when I fall
Without my senses?
I pray for light that I might see
And sensitivity that I might feel,
But it doesn't come.
I am without.

Pat Gschwend

A Sort Of Homecoming

I stand on the edge
Look out into time
And wonder
I can only dare to dream
Of what could be
I am transported to a time, a place
I am lost
But fear not
I am one in the darkness
And fear no shadows
Dawn is my awakening
The light my being
I exist with thoughts of love
And walk silently amongst the trees
My insignificance is significance in eternity
Change is my only adversary
But poses no great threat
This endless journey leaves nothing the same
And when I finally arrive
I find peace.

Terrence P. Kinealy

Winter's Song

The faded leaves and crumpled flowers
Call an end to autumn's hours
For winter slams a door on autumn's glory
But sings to all a different story
Of life that's pared so spare and lean
With open spaces in between
Then all is muffled by the snow
And drifted by the winds that blow
Do not follow after autumn's fire
  Stay with me and sing to winter's lyre.

Frances Anne Prince

Sending Pictures To Heaven

No matter where I am, no matter what I do,
I will always think of you.
Not only my mother, but my best friend,
We share a lifetime of memories that will never end.
The memories are like pictures in my mind,
They will travel on with me through time.
The memories of your children at home and at school.
All become pictures you can take with you.
When your time has come and you leave this place,
You will have many pictures to take to heaven's gate.

Kirsten S. Brown

The Light

Light is around us, light is in our
hearts, we see light, we hear light, and
we destroy light. Everybody's light is the
same, each having a purpose to have theirs
brightened and liked. some lights are black,
green, red, brown, yellow, none are different they
all can shine. When somebody's light is destroyed
so are five other lights, just like on a
strand of lights , one goes out they all go
out. So when someone's light is taken
so are all the other lights who know, respect,
and love that one light. Light is around us,
light is in our hearts, we see light, we hear
light, we destroy light, and we love light.

J. C. Leonard

Growing Old

Remember the days when we were young,
holding hands and having fun.

Now we are old and still together,
but our love will last forever.

We have kids who moved away,
the days have passed and they can't stay.

The sky is dark, the stars are bright
we pray to God and wish at night.

A forbidden moment when we will die
the earth in shame at all might cry.

We will miss those loving days
where the sun has shined its glowing rays.

Hold on to your love,
don't let it go,
for now you "are" growing old.

Cydnee Golden

A Child's Wish

A fleeting touch awakens her such beauty to behold
Resemblance of a butterfly she watched his wings unfold
They frolic briefly in the sun and feel the joy of life
She treasures every moment, oblivious to strife
His wings of strength have soared through adventures in the air
Yet gently, they caress her with warmth and peace so rare
Swiftly time will pass them by, it's known all through the land
A transformation must take place, for all had been pre-planned.
She knows no other can replace his beauty pure and fine
For God in all his wisdom gives each one their own design
The child longs to hold him tight, yet knows it can not be
So to make her wishes known she'll profess this final plea
When storm clouds come I'll shelter you to keep away the rain
I need to know that you are safe, and help you bear your pain
Should you feel from me, I fear when your transformations through
Someday we could pass, and I wouldn't realize it's you.
A woman lies in solitude, no tears upon her face
While the child inside her cries no one can take your place.

Peggy McKelvey

Powder

I saw a famous man eating a powdered donut.
It's snowing soft, white powder.
It stains his shirt a chalky white.
His face was plastered all over TV
News, headlines, shows, everywhere.
I hear people mentioning his name in the distance.

When I saw him,
He was perched, wiping powder off his shirt
Struggling to eat his powered donut.

Jeff Hoeksema

Poet's Dream

If my heart were as the sky
And the convolutions of clouds, my dreams
I would have to pray an end
To all my cloudy days.

For clouds are simply colored air
And so made are my dreams
They've no place in reality
They've no place in my life.

Dreams conjure stories
Great stories of untruths
Dreams are the prayers of the foolish
So I must be considered a fool.

Thomas Bret Golson

Treasures Of The Heart

How wonderfully-made are the treasures of the heart.
For they fulfill the needs we so desire . . . may we never part!
What can a smile do for one who's aching inwardly?
It can ease the burden of guilt one suffers for feeling cowardly.
What can a warm handclasp do for one who's shy and often boring?
It can raise one's level of self-esteem and send one's spirits soaring.
What can a helping hand do for one in need of emotional repair?
Why, it can put a grateful smile on the face of one who is in despair.
When offering assistance without expecting payment due,
One fulfills the adage, "Do unto others as you would have them
  do unto you."
These are the wonderful treasures of the heart,
To give aid to others till death do us part.

Maria R. Almonte

The Twinkling

A star and a bird are two different things,
but the star is why the little bird sings.

They know nothing of the world below,
both up high the bird free to go.

So it raises its voice up in song,
hoping the star will sing along.

The star just stares and twinkles back,
A somber voice it seems to lack.

So they just stay the way they are,
A song filled bird and a shining star.

Jamie Rathert

His Journey

He has travelled far and wide,
seeking for what must hide.
Crossed the mountains, through steams,
searching for what never seems.
In his face, he strains, what drives this
man through the rains?
Many leagues he has seen, forever feeling
his dreams.
Though the nights be cold, the stories
of his heart unfold.
What keeps this man from growing old?
In the morning skies well above his eyes.
There is a dove.
What this man sought was love.

Norbert F. Hackl

The Black Jellybean

The black jellybean sat, in the bottom of the bag,
and dreamt of many wonderful things.
Of happy children with awaiting mouths,
and the good times that they'd bring.

Twice before he'd felt the hope,
of leaving his prison there,
but hands always reached for white, or red,
and even the sugar-fused pair.

Mr. Jellybean's time had nearly come,
his colored shell grown hard with age.
He knew it would soon be time to go,
but still the hope remained.

Suddenly, a shadow loomed,
the hand drew ever near,
and from the black jellybean's eye,
fell a silent tear.

He was chewed in exultation.
He drew saliva with great pride.
And with a last, triumphant yell,
He was swallowed then . . . and died.

Morgan Lee

Life

Life can leave its inner circle, never to come back
Or it can stay till eternity
Life teaches lessons needed to be learned
Or it can lead you unknowing, unlearning
Life can let fate take its job
Or life can do it single handed,
Life can be like the red of flame
Life can be like the black of darkness
Life can be quiet and peaceful
Or it can be loud and exciting,
Life can be filled with love
Or filled with hatred.
Life can be short,
Or it can be neverending,
Life can be lenient.
Or it can show no mercy

Laura Gunderson

Thoughts

As waves beat upon the peaceful sand,
I have no thoughts.
As the salt, sand, and sun rub against me,
I have no thoughts.
The colors and images create no pictures
in my mind, I'm so peaceful that
I have no thoughts.

Kelly Denton

"Mary Lou Gansel"

God, thank you for our friend Mary,
    she was always so beautiful, bright and cheery,
    even with all she had to carry.
She's an example for all of us to follow
Her good ways, her smiles,
    carried her for miles.
No matter how sick she may have gotten,
That the dear Lord must have reasons,
    to put her through such treasons.
Her faith she held onto
    with a grip so firm and tight
That the blessed girl has to be
    in heaven,
With you Dear Lord in her sight.

Renee S. Garrison

Matthew's Vacation

I asked God about a year ago or so ago
    If my time was due to take a vacation.
He smiled, and said, "When it's time, I'll let you know—
    And I'll let you pick your own relation."

It seemed like months and months that I looked around.
    God made so many nice people everywhere!
I looked at Moorhead — my Mom and Dad were found!
    Six months ago God said, "Go now - and - take care."

My Mom is Linda - and my Dad's name is Doug.
    Grandmas and grandpas and aunts and uncles too!
And do you know what? Grandma K. sure can hug!
    To make them laugh - all I do is Coo!

I hated to tell them my visit was to end.
    "Come, little Angel Matthew," I heard God say.
Maybe some day I can arrange to help send
    A brother or sister for a longer stay.

Will you tell my sitter I just fell asleep?
    I love you all — I'll miss the whole relation.
The hurt will pass — and you can smile — not weep!
    'Cuz, that was the bestest of all vacations!!!!

Jeanie Brennan

Sometimes I Cry

I knew what I was in for, when I welcomed you in.
Regrets forsaken
This is not a sin.

Feelings abundant
Passion that burns.
The door was open, you only need turn.

Intentions were good, feelings ran strong.
Desire destructive
Something went wrong.

Like a breeze in the night, that you touch and you smell.
Lacking in substance
I should run, but oh well.

Desire takes hold
Fears running high.
Emotions run ramped, sometimes I cry.

Confusion, disbelief
When you shut the door.
I knew what I was in for, still I want more.

Joanna J. NaDell

Memories

Memories are treasures we all hold,
More precious than silver
Worth more than gold.
No one can steal them,
Nor can they be sold,
What one must do,
    is just to be there,
Show others you care,
Here today, gone tomorrow.
Heal with love and heart-filled sorrow,
Enjoy today for what it's worth.
It just may be, one's last day on earth.
Today's time you spend awhile,
Will be tomorrows memories to look back on and smile.
These are treasures of our mind,
You can't walk forward without looking behind.

Alice Lester

"If"

"If" I could feed one starving child, In a strange, but distant land,
"If" I could finally bring world peace, By just the stroke of my hand.
"If" I could cure the incurable disease, And ease the throng of pain,
"If" I could dry the wettest tears, And revive that soul, again!
"If" I could be the friend in need, Be at your beck and call,
   To comfort, guide, to uplift, help, And give my total all.

"If" I could be there, day or night, To the lost and those who strayed,
"If" I could give an encouraging word, And see, a difference made.
"If" I could give strength to the weak, And always, Be right there,
"If" I could offer hope, and faith, and charity, and prayer!
"If" I could fill one's greatest dream, And to achieve its goal,
   To see the "fruits" of excellence, and opportunities, unfold.

"If" I could be the shoulder, To the worn, and the distressed,
   And in some small significant way, to let them know they're blessed!
"If" I could be a beacon, To shed my radiant light;
   Afar to all the merchant's ship
   That sail all through the night.
And only once I pass this way, To touch each life amidst,
   Reflecting on my temporal life,....
And thus... "Fulfilling All the "If's".

   Sharon N. Patrick

Untitled

Water drips down the table from the
place where the flowers stood.
Red roses, fresh roses, every week
then every other week, every month
every special occasion.
The water pours from the vase on the table,
it knows it is no longer needed.
The roses no longer brighten this spot or any
other spot for that matter.
The last petal blew away so long ago that
the water does not remember what color
roses used to set there.
The water knows it is now unless and tries to escape.
To find purer waters, to find a place where water
runs free and is thought of as a thing of beauty.
Because to stay here and be useless is worse
than being nourishment for dead roses.
Who knows what adventures lie beyond the table.
Whether tragic or joyous they will be free
they will all be free.

   Ruth Pepkowski

The Promise

He does not have to talk to me today,
I know what he has to say.
He does not have to touch me today,
I'm still tingling from yesterday.
He does not have to lead me today,
his path I know so well.
For it was here he left me, and showed
me where to dwell.
He does not have to teach me today,
for his lessons I've learned to obey.
For it is he, the Almighty one, whose words
in my heart will stay.
He does not have to see my tears today.
For he has wiped them softly away,
and showed me how to ease my pains,
do I knelt with him to pray.
He does not have to hear me at all today, you see.
For he has promised, no matter what,
he'll always be there for me.

   Virginia L. Boone

Denial Trap

I can do it, I can do it all. I can become all I want
to be through writing, or acting, or teaching.

Never mind that I keep myself locked in my own private
prison; longing, wanting, knowing. Yet reaching

For another way to fix this uneasiness within my soul,
I can't be satisfied until I've realized every goal.

My destiny awaits and I am not even close,
I won't do the footwork required of most.

Give it to me now, I want it all upon demand,
I'm the special case! - yet inflicted with a morbid host of reprimand.

What a frustration to be living less than God's intention,
with all of my dreams forever in suspension.

I guess I'll put on another load of laundry, see what's
on TV, read a book, call a friend;

Go on pretending as I am nearing the end.

   Karen Lavan

A Child's Sorrow

Dry your eyes little one, and wash away the pain.
Forget about your life, and watch, as it goes down the drain.
In the raining of tears, they learn of your fears;
Convincing you to sell,
Your poor, abused, soul, in a world of Hell.

A forgotten smile, you live in denial.
Seeing life painted in shades of gray.
Knowing that they will break you
One day.

   Amanda Jeanette Foss

Across The Water

The moon casts a faint glow across the water.
It appears so close, yet the distance is far.
I hear your voice in my mind, so clear,
Although, you too, are miles across the water.
Out of arms' reach, yet I can feel you in my heart.
Our love is like the light reflecting off the water.
So apparent, yet unable to touch, or to hold to.
Miles away, will you always be?
Almost unreal, so much like a dream.
I fear waking up, I fear the dawn
Will steal the light away.

   Sharon Hightower

Reality

I am now alone, I feel as though you've left me here to die.
So all day long I think of you and then begin to cry.

All my dreams and all my fears in you I did confide.
And all these things you took from me,
My love, my hopes, my pride.

We had our time together, now that the world's a memory.
We laughed, talked, and joked,
But now you won't acknowledge me.

You were my comfort, a shoulder to lean on over the past few years
You were there when I needed you to wipe away my tears.

Where are you now? I thought we would be together for eternity.
I was so blind but now I realize you are not in love with me.

Reality,
That's the bullet in my wounded heart.
Only a word but I can see it's keeping us apart.

   Katherine Williams

Youth

In my youth, I was buffeted and torn,
Too new to the world, too old to be born.
What is this language I think I hear spoken?
And these palpitating hearts; are they broken?

Where lies the evidence to connect me with them?
Is that blood? Whose blood is it, dried on the hem?
How did it get there? Do you know where you were?
But you've always been here! What's that astir?

I'm always at odds! I teeter and twist on the edge
Of the scene, part of nothing, grasping the ledge.
Those faces that stare at me are people unknown,
And wherever I was, I was surely alone.

Youth is not kind; it's an old wicked crone,
Who torments children when she finds them alone.
Where is the sanctuary, the home that was mine?
How find answers to dilemmas? How draw the line?

When I awaken, will I know who I am?
The territory be familiar to this stumbling lamb?
And more importantly, will anyone know me,
Deal with the terror and set me free?

Roberta A. Wood

A Permanent Bond

Time is of no significance
With love there is no need
The imperishable devotion will guide us through with ease
If doubt and worry seem to emerge,
 the remedy is sure to appear — an easy cure
A soft embrace, and we find there is no
 need for fear
No other face can replace the one we
 hold so dear
Although we are among so many,
 our choice is surely clear
Inside of me there is a miracle,
 although we can not see,
 it is a part of the one
 I love not only of me
And in time an obstacle we surely will not see
An immortal love is endless
My love for thee I give for all of eternity

Jeanne Ghirardi

"A Naylien"

The little green man with the gumball head.
The purple sky is bleached to red.

Infested image, hypnotic light.
I now believe but cannot fight.

Glistening blackness, thought process disturbed.
Foreign phrases leaves confusion perturbed.

Awakened in field, crop circles about.
The heavens flash and neighbors shout.

Explain the story again and again.
Uncounted people ask where I have been.

No one listens, no one cares.
Ignore the whispers, return the stares.

Now my white jacket hugs me in my little round room.
I sit in the corner and sing to the gloom.

I speak to no one and no one to me.
With the little green man my lone company.

Teresa Aguilera

A Dance With The Devil

The demons are poking at my soul. Are they hungry? Why do they call me? It tells me lies, promises me gold, treasures, life forever. I tell it to go away and it does sometimes. Sometimes I feel so ugly inside I feel the demons are eating me up. Are they winning my soul, I wonder, will the demons take me. At night, the place where I feel most alone, I feel its dirty claws trapping my soul like a bird in a cage, desperately trying to smother my life. The demons are strong, once in a while I can feel its presence suddenly, as if stocking me. When I feel this way I pray and think of all the good days, this drives the demons away. But they always come back dealing and shouting still promising there gold and internal life. And once again I will tell them to go away.

Carlos Garcia

What Counts

Dedicated to Dana Godorov

As the flame calmly shimmers,
the candle light reflects off her silken skin.
The light is superficial,
revealing only her intense beauty.
The warmth is all that matters,
burning into the soul,
lighting a love with a simple spark,
igniting a passion that does not melt away over time.
An innocence, first revealed by the newly lit wick,
is reduced to embers by the lovers' endless embrace.

Leonard Spangher

Drunk Driving

By the door he paused to stand,
 as he removed his wedding band.
No one who was there could speak,
 as they watched a tear run down his cheek.
And in his head the memories ran,
 as he remembered moments in the sand.
When they laughed and talked,
 when they hugged and walked.
He felt old and strangely cold,
 that he'd never have to hold.
They all watched as he bent near,
 to say "I Love You" in her ear.
As the wind began to blow,
 they lowered the casket in the snow.
Someone chose to drink and drive,
 but if not she'd still be alive.

Amanda Dungan

Hearts

The heart is always understood
for a person who cares,
and a person who could.

If you look within your heart
and you know it will never part,
then it was you who filled it from the start.

The heart is always warm
for the day may be cold,
but the love inside of it will always hold.

David Fukino Jr.

Portals To Infinity

Horrid recollections of one's rasping last breath.
And the striking of doomsday's gong,
The sounds of a ghastly death.
The tattered memories of heart wrenching cries.
And the hollow echoes of empty words and promised lies.
These are the sounds when humanity dies.

The gasping whine of one's first breath. Torn,
From ones mouth, striking ones first note,
The sound when an angel is born.
The blissful cries and the tittering of mirth,
And the echoes of ones roots in the soft fertile earth.
These are the sounds of an angels birth.

Death is a doorway,
Death is a tool,
Diving straight down into a crimson pool.

Are you going my way?
Frank Alexander

Our True Identity

Who are we?
Are we this person,
that we show to the world?
Or are we truly this person,
hidden deep inside,
that's afraid to emerge?
Can you really call this person,
on the outside "me"?
Our true identity,
isn't what it seems
How people see you,
How you see yourself.
This can change us.
Our experiences,
good or bad,
can make you have a different perspective.
As we search for ourselves,
We may become different.
Who we are
Searching for an identity,
Our True Identity.
Vanessa Villa

The Song List

Sonja Marie sings and I Gave My Love To You,
Debbie Gibson sings Out Of The Blue.
Boyz II Men sings On Bended Knee,
Whitney Houston and CeCe Winans sing Count On Me.
The Village People sing YMCA,
Boyz II Men and Mariah sing One Sweet Day.
Rob Base sings It Takes Two,
Faith Even sings Kissing You.
Amy Grant sings Oh How The Years Go By,
Mary J. Blige sings Not Gonna Cry.
Melissa Etheridge sings If I Wanted To,
TLC sings Diggin On You.
Salt N' Pepa sings Whatta Man,
Sheryl Crow sings We Do What We Can.
Boyz II Men sings Please Don't Go,
Alanis Morissette sings You Oughta Know.
Sheryl Crow sings All I Wanna Do,
Baby Face sings When Can I See You.
Now this is the end of the song list,
Nope, there is one more, Melissa Etheridge sings Resist.
Kelly Hofmann

"Victory"

The time and place we do not know.
When the Lord will let his grace flow.

Sing and pray as often as you can.
Receive the Lord take a stand.

To be with him on that final day.
Will be worth the price that we pay.

To follow him in every way.
So make sure you take time to pray.

Pray to God up above.
Pray to Jesus for the ones you love.

Your prayers are heard both day and night.
So pray to Jesus he's won the fight.

The battles won for you and I.
Victory is our battle cry.
David Bryan Franklin

I Wanta Have Some Fun

Mom, can't you get serious?
You act like second grade.
You really do embarrass me
The way you do behave!
And do you have to wear those shorts?
You look like Mrs. Staten;
John's mom, the one that's fat;
Mom, I honestly hate them!
Take them off. I won't be seen with you.
And, Mom, you really can't sing -
So, don't! Whatever you do!
Just take me and Bill to a show
And please - don't sit with us.
Then can we get a pizza,
The kind with the stuffed crust?
Thanks, Mom, I told Bill
We'd pick him up at one;
And can you drive us to the mall?
I wanta have some fun.
Marie Gross

"Ode To A Minstrel"

   My ode is to a Minstrel, a singer of the times
A picker, a poet, a dreamer, the lover of a rhyme
It's the story of the future's past, of life's little ups and downs
Of trying to start over and watching wheels go 'round
The Minstrel feels the world with a very special vibes
He sings of love and life and fate, just to keep his hopes alive
   The Minstrels gathered slowly, they gathered one by one
They sang their songs for me to hear, from dawn to setting sun
Some who played were full of rage, they'd jam with all their might
They'd Rock and Roll, they'd lust for life, They rocked into the night
   Then I met the Minstrel Man, he helped me see my role
His thoughts were just the same as mine
He reached and touched my soul
He sings of what's around him in a Blues 'E'
He sings of Grandeur Illusions and his Trilogy
Aren't you tired of wasting your time?
A strange question I would say
You know the answers are in your rhymes
And I guess it doesn't matter anyway
James R. Park Sr.

374

"Kelly Dawn"

Kelly I miss you so much because you left me
when you were only nine days old.
　We loved you so much it was hard to depart
with you.
　You will always be in my heart, so I will never
forget you; and I will always love you.
　Your face, your eyes, your nose, your hair, your mouth
was so sweet and so loving.
　I seen and held you the day before you left, the
day of sadness I will never forget.
　You were so young and innocent that every time
I hear your name or see your grave, I cry.
　Sometimes I remember that awful night and cry
myself to sleep thinking of only you.
　The day you were to come home you left me
in a dark hole, but also led me into the light.
　You were my sister, my baby sister, that died that
lonely dark night.
　I only hope one thing. That you remember my face
in heaven with the Lord by your side.
Tressie Meyer

Out Of The Dark Into The Light

Sometimes life is like a storm.
To trials and tribulations, we are born.
The skies get dark and eerie
No one knows what next will be...
After the thunder wind and rain
Things seem shiny and clean again
A rainbow forms above the trees
Reflecting in a lake of blue
Flowers bloom anew
Life has a lot of dark moments
But eventually the sun shines through
Life goes by before you know
When God beckons you, you will go...
When my time comes
And my last breath ends
I will walk through the light
And "Live Again"...
Virginia Ann Flynn

Teenage Years

Remember past years when we were young?
Boys and parties...
Just having fun!
Enjoying life free as can be...
Now were over 33!

This time are young are having the fun!
The boys...
The parties...
A couple of dares!

While we sit home with our gray hairs!
Remember our teenage years?

Most likely we did the same back then...
Thinking our mothers would cackle like hens!
Remember our teenage years?
We need to look back...
Is wasn't that bad!
Just look at the memories we all have...
Remember our teenage years?
Their time will come...
We can say isn't it fun you're on your way...
Annette J. Williams

Metamorphosis

Baby girl...so innocent, your eyes...
　so innocent, your smile...
　so tender, your soul...

Such a child you are afraid of adventuring your 1st steps.
So afraid of reaching new heights...

Such a big girl you are, having taken your steps,
adventure to new heights, yet remaining in the
aura of your innocence.

So you take that further step, and reality's pin
pops your innocence's fragile sack, creating new
innocence, but of a new generation.

You are a woman now...
time to teach metamorphosis to your new pupil...
Your child.
Elizabeth Anne Forbes

egoiste?

naked i stand, with a tear in my eye
as i watch hopelessly
while you walk right on by

and i think to myself, how can one just forget
or just push away...i think i'll forfeit

because i can't play your game anymore
there's taxes to pay on your monopoly board

selfish, i think; is it you, or is it me
am i trying to hold on to what just can't be

and i burn myself up; and i wear myself out
but i cannot fall back; on what i'm without

so i wait patiently; as i've done up till now
each night it gets harder; i don't believe you know how

for if you could see your art of strangulation
you wouldn't deal to me your cards of starvation

i'm sick to myself and i can't go on pleading
reciprocity cries!
i will stop the bleeding
Anne Richardson

Life

Sometimes the roads we travel
don't always end in fame
and if life was to be so easy,
everyone would be the same.

The trouble that we fight through
builds us up inside
so we can help others
in their daily strife.

Dark clouds may roll in
and bring a little rain, but be assured
like in the beginning, so it is in the end
the clouds will roll away again.

Tough times don't last forever
although tough people do,
so keep your head up!
this struggle is almost through.

You are not alone in your fight
we're in this all together
and life can't get the best of us
because together we are better.
David Ritchey

Amy

Amy's a sweetheart,
a cute little girl.
With blond hair, and blue eyes
you're our little pearl.

A tiny baby, you was sweet,
when I got to hold you, what a treat!

Your mom was working at the mall,
when you cried too much, I'd make a call.

Your mom would come home and give you a love
and then you'd coo just like a dove.

I'll always love you very much,
I'll be here for you in a crunch.
    Doris Peterson

Reflections

When I look in the mirror....
Who do I see? Who is it? Could it be me.
When I look in the mirror....
Reflections rise from the past
What really is this vast piece of glass?
When the pain runs,
As deep as it does.
When the colors shine,
As bright as they do.
What can I do, but look to you
For advice, I always have.
But now you are gone, it is so sad.
The anger burns,
Each moment the clock turns.
As I look in the mirror....
I'm fading away.
Please find me,
Though I'm a needle in hay.
As I look in the mirror... It shatters
274 pieces fall to the cold, hard, empty floor.
    Geetika Bhargava

A Man's Friend

Thanks for giving me the bread of life, the purity of water.
Thanks for the love everyone has given me.
And now it is that time when a person must be on his own
to fight for freedom of his choice, to support oneself is not
easy in this human race for freedom.
And to have friends who love you and who will stay by you
in hard times, is the most precious gift a man could ever
want or need.
Soon death stalks the man and his loyal friends are heartbroken.
A man's friend soon forgets the tragedy, but still remembers
the loving memories of a friend.
    Cheryl Wiedeman

Heavy Heart

We shall put our disputes aside and start anew
We shall make our arguments far and few.
It's obvious to me, we both care.
Let us ride with our hearts, as the love is there.
Let us accept one another for who we are.
Our hearts must come closer, not distant and far.
Our love for each other is still the same.
Only you and I are to blame.
We must be able to communicate.
if not, a heart split in half, is our fate.
This comes from my heart and is a plea.
To make things right, for you and me.
    Joan Kurten

"The Beauty Of Life"

"As I look across the sky
I see the beauty of life
As the moon sits in the still of early morning light
I see the light of the world."

"As the stars glow and glitter
I feel spirituality
When the sun sets in the evening
I see the beauty of this world."

"When the wind blows
I feel the calmness of freedom
When I stare into the waters of the sea
I see the rock of salvation."

"As the birds fly across the sky
I see the wings of love
And hope kept alive."

"As I look across the nation
And the sunshines
It shines upon different faces of different races
I see God's grace and his mercy
bestowed upon a little child's face."
    Dorothy King

Untitled

Friends are special people
a gift from God above.
They will always be there for you
to give and care and love.

Friends are there for always
to lend a helping hand.
They'll stick with you through hard times
and always do all that they can.

Friends share special moments
to carry through all the years.
They will share in all the laughter
and comfort through all the tears.

Friends are very precious
always show them you care.
Never take them for granted
and trust that they'll always be there!
    Crystal L. Ford

Look At Me

Look at me. See my color, my face.
Am I not the human race.

Look at me. My beauty, my power,
my shine. Acknowledge me, understand
me, talk with me. Your blood is as
red as mine.

Look at me. See me laugh, see me cry,
see me hurt. Comfort me, pull me from the dirt.

Look at me. I work, I play, I dance.
Sit with me, take my hand and let's
be friends by every chance.

Look at me, I am old, I am gray, I am
weak. Care for me, hold me, believe
the words I speak.

Look at me, and you will see yourself.
We are not that different. See through all
the prejudices and beyond the classes,
then realize that we are all born and
eventually we all shall die.

But please, just look at me.
    Willie E. Lewis

Getting Older

To a child almost every one seems old.
Everyone expects us to do as we are told.

By the time we are school age
we are just stepping on life's wide stage

People of all ages play an important role
and still we are expected to do as we're told.

When we get older we'll do as we want
instead of being in the back we'll be in the front.

Twelve years of school to complete
And still older people for us to meet

What age will we be when we are smart
Old enough to know what's in our heart.

With age comes wisdom so we're told
people who say that are being bold

When we reach a special age
we no longer work for a wage.

Just think, now we have all the time we need
But it is hard to hear and harder to see

Getting older is wondrous we all agree
Now we've outlived our friends but not our memories.
Carol Ann Marsh

Heaven Bound

You gazed on stars and firmament
Your mind on visions with great intent

You traversed skies in sleek machinery
To grasp creations mystery

You sailed the boundless seas amain
Adventure and commerce to sustain

You climbed steep hill or mountain range
To witness signs of ruthless change

Your hands took food from willing soil
Gracious bounty repaid your toil

You entered earth through well-dug mines
Of hidden gems and ore-rich finds

And after all this effort you found
That all the while you were heaven bound
Florence J. Kunicki

Words Of A Flower...

A tender flower...they say
gentle and soft...
You watched me bloom capturing the beauty
you sought after me.

Will you now gingerly preserve me for others
to admire me by your side?

Colorful...they say
A light smell of fragrance...
You came close enough to enjoy my beauty.

Do you leave me now?
A tender flower
Ageless, timeless...to be protected or
exposed to the harsh elements of life...

Petals in the wind...blowing...useless
Senseless...powerless by the hands of one
who once held me with such...love

Words of a flower....if they could speak
Sandra Lynn Tanksley

Friendship

Roses may be red
Violets may be blue,
But friendship is true.

As the sky on cloudless day is clear,
Friendship is dear,
And it is to each a friend near.

Friendship is for us all
To live in peace and in control,
Friendship is the strongest of force
Even as strong as a horse.

Friends are we, if it be strong
And it would last long,
Friendship is for us all
Who live in peace and in control.
Can we be friends, if we be not one at all?
Elia Guarneri

Tree's Sing Song Too

With each little rustle there rests a song,
With each little sway there lays a tune.
But only to a perceptive ear can the melody be heard.
The hymn is that of Mother Nature,
And the words are those of Father Time.
Together with the choir of trees,
They create the sounds of sweet music.
They sing the psalm of life and time.
And every season has its tone.
There are really only two songs,
One of change and one of peace.
Yet their music is that of a colorful symphony,
Playing for all to hear and behold.
You see trees can sing songs too.
Mike Nelson

Death Of A Star

Don't weep for the star
Whose life has gone so far
Twice as bright, half as long
See the light, hear the song
The passage was a joyful one
Lots of laughs and loads of fun
Its ending may have been abrupt
But your life, do not let it disrupt
Though the star may shine no longer
Through the experience, may you grow stronger.
Its memory, never forget
For remembering is your debt.
John Marcel Coutorie Jr.

Symbols Of God's Love

Flowers in the sunshine bloom
Fill the air with sweet perfume,
Some grow short, some grow tall,
Some stay hidden until fall.
Through our lives they cheer our days
Serving man in many ways,
Colors blue, red, pink and yellow,
Spread their blooms like sails that bellows,
Fill the church on wedding days,
Nosegays, bouquets, blanket sprays,
Waving fields of gorgeous blooms,
Potted plants to brighten rooms,
Brought to us from God above
symbols of his lasting love.
Jackie Johnson

The Liberated

In Auschwitz concentration camp
   They lived without hope,
Each day they were driven from their
   slave barracks to pass by their
   Jewish brethren murdered in the cruel black night
Planes flew by high above them, eagles
   of the allied nations in mid-flight,
Creatures of despair, and disbelief
   not knowing if they'd ever be free,
   they forlornly continued to grope,
Was there ever any more noble moment in eternity.
Than when they were returned to humanity,
When the allied warriors rescued them
   from their Nazi captors, and restored their dignity,
When the future of people kind endured,
When human decency triumphed over evil,
When righteousness and freedom on earth were again secured,
When Hitlerism's abominable final plan was defeated and laid still.

Alex Ely Handis

Unclaiming Sorrow

I won't admit I'm sad
But happiness is far from here
Looking outside, I see a world
The world gave me no sense in belonging
Though I couldn't leave
I watched people smile
I once was happy
Lust is gone
Love can't truly be found
I don't live in sadness or true gleeful moments
Lost deep in no thought or world
I am here

Margaret Helen Coffman

A Misunderstanding

When words are spoken, not correctly heard,
A gentle thought of love bursts into flames
The first idea lost, misunderstood
The cause of ill expression and debate
Makes voices raise because a temper stirs
The biggest made mistake by those in fate
What should now happen is a simple task;
Avoid the fire which burns the bond of heart
Just satisfy lost words and learn to ask
The blame will always storm out from its rest
And if the newfound rage is not soon tamed,
Then worse things will begin to manifest
The lesson is just simply this:
(So in your mind allow it set)
A vile emotion turns to sorrow
Misfortune haunts what's left tomorrow

Stacy Plisis

The Way God Talks

Dusk is my favorite time of day
It just seems to waft my cares away
The air is so soft and the silence so profound
When no one else is anywhere around.
I love to walk on a deserted country road
Where wagons made ruts from their heavy load.
Wild flowers everywhere, moss covering the rocks.
I say to myself, "This is the way God talks.
He doesn't need words to express his love.
He just sends us down beauty like this from above."
Then the light starts slowly to fade away
And the after glow streaks red to culminate the day.

Virginia Wilson

Songs Of Night

At night when the water is still,
There are two moons to see.
When warm breezes make dancing frills,
Silver moonlight does its dance for me.

I hear the wind run through the green trees,
Call to the crickets to perform their nightly chorus.
After the wind touches all the leaves,
The nightly orchestra begins to play before us.

The bullfrog harps, his song so low.
The crickets chirp their lively tunes.
Silver moonlight dances while the wind blows.
The masked man sings out to the other raccoons.

The song comes to a stop with perfect clarity,
I thank the night for its gift of charity.

John Kenneth O'Neil

The First Christmas

No Santa, no Rudolph
That first Christmas day.

Just a maid and a man
And a babe in the hay.

No bells and no tinsel
That first Christmas night.

Just shepherds and sheep
And a sky pierced with light.

No yule log, no chocolates,
   No mint candy canes.
No egg nog, no turkey,
   No Lionel trains.

No feasting this eve for Joseph and wife.
Just peace, and the way, the truth, and the life.
No singing and dancing around a glittering tree.
Simply God come to earth for you and for me.

Camille Giancristofaro

Queenie

She sleeps and sleeps and sleeps,
But when she awakes she has a truck load of moods,
From an adorable little kitten,
To a ferocious beast ready to attack at any moment!!

But none the less she is my cat,
Without her love I would cease to exist,
Without her soft fur rubbing against my legs I
wouldn't have any comfort,
If she would never run outside into my backyard
and hide in the thick brush;
I wouldn't have any adventure in my life,
if I would never see her tiny, perfect face every morning;
My emotions for everything would vanish.

Saman Khan

A Child's Voice

Take the time to tell me my worth.
The value of a human being is more than the vocal opinion.
Have faith in my spirit and soul.
My existence is worth more than a belief in your mind.

I know of one thing
that has more insight into my being
than those feelings inside the heart.

I took what was needed for my existence
if it was worth what you gave
you have only gained a life
and freed another voice.

Gail Smith

The Light

Looking for an answer to a question I don't know
Searching for light when the sun has gone low

Being so sad and not knowing why
Waking up happy then wanting to cry

Trying to walk with my head held up high
stopping for a second, then wanting to die

Feeling so angry, just after a good laugh
feelings so filthy right after a good bath

Talking so happy to family or friend
thinking to myself, "can this be the end"

Waking up thinking, "can things be alright
just one click of the trigger
and extinguish the light
   Joe H. Sarinana Jr.

Metamorphosis

I recall sunsets over the sea,
  overwhelmed by splendrous colors,
    each one succeeding the others,
      gradating to darker hues,
        as the sun's form from round to oblong
          was swallowed by Neptune;
            and we, perched on the cold, wind-blown bluffs
            were warmed by the joy within us.

Now its's Autumn, and no ocean near,
  yet spectral metamorphosis is also here—
    brilliant, profound, aflame;
      the blaze is in the leaves
        that, too, set, and settle on head and feet,
          as I stand in awe.

And what say these to me?
  That I, likewise, must?
    If so, let me brighter grow until the dusk,
      instilling hope of new birth and fire in another,
        and as I set from view,
          I'll sing a carol of color.
   Timothy Paul Thorndike

Fahrenheit Collisions

A pollen cooked in a fainting sterner,
with the glow of living gold
into it the evaporation glittered
like moving jewels robbed of breath.

  ...I was spooned up and swelling,
stirring a pond of haze smoke soaked blue...

This is a free sun we're under, olive bruise buttered
and sweat-oiled cordially in a bronze melt. the collision.
Those sun set shades of deepening lows paint numbness
As a moaning monsoon across all thought singed.

Yet, the illumination from an unconscious dream
came like slow motion glitter through life and spirit.
It embraced my past and my twitches, the alphabet
of aneurysms only sleepwalkers can understand.

  To wear the most humid malaria to a white boil...
An ejaculation of festers into the sand...what fate...

I, was dressed in iodine up to the sores out of which I see.
And I saw:
An apocalypse ripening in the plum peels of a twilight cool,
In a deadly accident of willingness crossing light...
   Patricia Silva

A New Blossom

There is new flower in the garden.
It is a precious blossom,
One so sweet,
One so fair.
Delicately scented,
Yet its fragrance lingers still.

It is the color of happiness,
Rainbow hued.
its newness is as laughter
Against a sky of blue.
Its purity is that of newly-fallen snow.
Its freshness is as the first ray
Of morning's light.

This beautiful blossom
Is a new baby, one so unique,
One so dear.
It is a rose without any thorns.

Planted by God's own hands,
First within my heart,
And now within my arms
   Shannon Hale Wrye

Purple To Gold

Wanting to be helpful, healing
instead feeling helpless, kneeling.
His chest grows tight, the pain immense,
static crackling over the line,
seeing tiny beads through the noise
teardrops run outward
crossing a great distance, the miles
that lie between them.

If he were God, he could stretch his hand
brush back the tear and hurt;
change the purpling bruises like skies at dusk,
to something golden, beaming skies at dawn.
Create a new beginning from the ending
of another day.

Instead, he sits —watching, waiting, hoping
for the start of another day.
   Kurtis Joe Stubblefield

Terminal

I really think he loved me
Kinda; sorta
at least that's what I'll tell my friends
to brag
'Cause bragging is like an addiction
an egotistical hole I try to fill
and what's up with holes anyway
as if there wasn't enough emptiness already
and what does it mean to be empty
is it where there's nothing there
or just too much to tell so
we call it empty anyway
just cause we're lazy
and everybody's lazy these days
except for the politician rats
rats drive me crazy
crazy?
but I really think he loved me
at least that's what
I'm gonna tell my friends to brag
   Jennifer Whitten

Mommy?

A little girl kneels by her bed,
Wrapped in last year's clothes.
No light is shed to scare the nightmares away,
For the light bill was never paid.
She shares the tiny room with a couple of mice,
The only friends she has.
Sharing what food she can find,
Which is less than would fill a sparrow.
Mommy said she'd be back,
But that was a month ago.
Listen quietly to her prayers,
As the tears puddle around her bent knees,
She asks, "Dear Lord, when will Mommy be back?"

Nikki Habegger

Nostalgia

Chimes sway in harmony as the glass door hushes the busy sidewalk.
Sunlight quietly touches gold rimmed plates.
Majestic colored linens lie peacefully beside floral tapestries.
A blanket chest holds ivory silk dresses and velvet shoes.
Victorian desks carry letters and notes secreted by sweet satin ribbon.
Mahogany tables with outstretched legs and claw feet await guests
  for parties and tea.
Black and white family photos gather in wood carved rose gardens.
Faded pastel quilts lovingly rest in the arms of a Windsor rocker.
Swiss music boxes fill the air with singing birds.
For a moment, the past embraces me.
Elegant wine glasses kiss in celebration.

Jeanne Cushman

M Is For...

She sits motionless, her vacant eyes staring straight ahead.
Her frail fingers pick at the tiny flowers imprinted on her dress.

A visitor sits down beside her and engages in an animated
conversation which, apparently, requires no response. Bright
red nails flash through the air...bracelets jangle and rings
sparkle, as they capture the sunlight that shines through the
open windows.

After about five minutes the conversation winds down. The
visitor glances at her watch, stands, and keys in hand, looks
for the first time directly into the face of the person seated
in the wheel chair. For a fleeting moment her face mirrors
her distaste, then, her proper expression recaptured, she waves
to the room at large, and departs.

Behind the vacant eyes now, we see the reflection of a child,
cradled in her mother's arms. We hear the rhythmic creak of
the chair as it rocks gently back and forth...and then, ever
so softly, we hear the lullaby.

She sits motionless, her vacant eyes staring straight ahead,
her frail fingers pick at the tiny flowers imprinted on her dress.

Helen Trowbridge Nichols

The Why's

Why do people die?
Why do I like apple pie?
Why do I like to smile?
Why is a mile called a mile?
Why is the Sun so hot,
and how much money do you got?
Why is a group of people called a crowd?
Why do some people talk so loud?
I think I'll sit and wonder why about
the Earth, Sun and Sky, and when I
figure out all these things I'll be in
heaven wearing Angel wings.

Marrie Vetter

Learning To See

I'll bet you've never seen green grass grow on a doorknob.
It will grow, I'll have you know.
All you have to do is look
and you can see a fish write a book.
I'll bet you've never seen green grass grow on a doorknob.
It will grow, then you'll see.
All you have to do is look
and you can see an elephant in a tree.
I'll bet you've never seen green grass grow on a doorknob.
It will grow, then you'll see at last.
Some people grow up too fast,
and some childhoods are too far in the past.
I'll bet you've never seen green grass grow on a doorknob.
Let your mind go and let it be free.
Then, and only then, will you see
that green grass really does grow on a doorknob.

Eric Sawicki

Space

"Space!" he said.
"I need it."
He'd touched my heart,
So many years ago.
"Space!"
Such a huge word with only five letters.
How can
Someone you love change?
"Space!"
To never see the look in the eyes.
Never feel the arms
The love so special.
"Space!"
One moment love.
The next indifference.
"Space!"
The love all gone.
To give a man
"Space!"

Carole D. Hillman

"Rainbow's End"

　Once I had a rainbow, at the end a pot of gold;
behind it lay all of Eden, we used to say.
　My angel, you, were sent to me; for
we know deep in our hearts that it was for written to be.
　Adam for you named me Eve, united together
to take a stand for "Good" over "Evil", to battle hand in hand;
without one another our lives will not be what they should.
　Until the day my Adam returns my skies won't be as blue,
my rainbow does not show.
　As for Eden, well it's just doing as all unattended gardens do;
overgrow and slowly die.

Sherri Flowers

Dark Understanding

her skin could shine through the sky
and swim on petal juice lake
diamond white goddess in winter gown head
screaming symphony forest language
always repulsive, the shadow whispered behind her
the purple vision played like her only friend
beneath the enormous garden moon
a sad sea mist loved the delicious lazy void
like an elaborate flood watch
boiling like rust iron can smell like storm
she was most frantic from delicate power
crush death my sweet luscious peach
why stare under the sleeping ship
do not please them and think less

Sharon Jean Austin

Just A Thought

The thought of losing you
Causes a pain in my chest
A thundering begins from my heart,
To echo into my ears; my soul starts to sing
That old Negro spiritual, "Swing Low, Sweet Chariot".
And a piece of me cracks off
then slowly flutters down to the earth
to slowly dissipate...into nothingness,
I lose all purpose, all will.

But then
  I get that one spurt
    That one new start
      My spirit lifts...my soul lightens.

But only for a second.
Only for a piece of time.

Because then the thought returns.
And I slowly die

I sit and wonder about how it would be
  if you left me?

Because as you can see this is only the thought.

Deborah Pendleton

Africa

A is for her animals, happy, wild and free.
F is for her fairness of land, sky and sea.
R is for her rolling plains of golden hue, and grassy green.
I is for the idiocy of those, who seek to strip her clean!
C is for her cradled valleys sheltering sparkling waterfalls,
  both very large and very small.
A is for her anguish as her soul cries in despair,
  destroy not my life and wild beauty,
  for indeed there is room enough for all.

Phyllis M. Nagle

Birthday

  One year, two, three and four,
Time goes by with an eternal roar.
  A great noise seen by all who dare,
But only heard by those who care.
  Material gifts given, shiny and bright,
Presents valued only by sight.
  Gifts with meaning are hard to find,
Pictures and thoughts stored in the mind.
  Memories of friends, dates and places,
Times of loves changing faces.
  As every birthday passes by,
New times replace those that die.
  Go and enjoy, never regret,
True friends and fun you'll never forget.

Thomas S. Crotti Jr.

Rainbow

  I feel the sun's warm rays upon my face as the storm blows on,
It is tranquil all around with the sweet smell of rain surrounding
the mist seeping up from the ground.
A Rainbow beams its beautiful colors, reaching everything that sees it,
The reds are warm, and make me feel welcome,
The blues are quiet and gentle letting me know that someone's
always listening,
The greens are calm and peaceful showing me that even if I am alone,
I don't need to feel alone.
The winds are changing, giving me more choices in my life,
The shadows that use to frighten me are slowly creeping back
from where they once came, and my wings are free to fly
where ever my imagination wishes to wander.

Autymn Rubal

"Christopher My Son (My Heart Cries For You)"

My heart cries for you my son each day that I awake.
I feel a loss within my soul that's a strong and constant ache.
I'll forever treasure the tender moments we once shared;
But just because you died so soon doesn't mean I did not care.

As I held you close to me, it looked like you were asleep.
I watched you slip into a trance, I knew you were at peace.
Chris, as I gazed into your eyes and touched your gentle face;
I knew that no one in this world could ever take your place.

I feel so sad and lonely, I feel like I have died.
Knowing that you will never ever be by my side.
God has taken care of you and set your spirit free.
I'll never ever forget you son cause your soul lives on in me.

Sometimes I find myself asking the question "why,"
My child was taken from me so soon; oh why did he have to die?
Please God, help me to face the pain that I must bear.
I have so much love to give to my child; taking him just isn't fair!

People tell me to forget about you and face reality;
They don't know what I'm going through, you were a part of me.
I wish I'd had one more day with you to tell you how I feel.
I loved you then and always will and I do love you still!!!

Pamela Faye Yancey

Ancient Intimacy

A lover's dream on an earthly night
Ridged stones shaped by heart
Churning, mixing within the mass
Nestled in an ivy wall
Of the mirror the eyes are sleep
Seeing glass chipped like snow
Beaded in the unknown strings
Your lamps will call, call me home

Water sits in pools of sand
The ancient light stares to us
The colors true and pure as their
Golden glow of your smile
Watchful of thy silent figure
Now I feel, feel you move, every breath, breath is full

Darkness follows her footsteps close
Shadows calling a piercing touch
Where deep in the desert twilight swoons
Clutched by the still of the night
Even the distance feels so near
All for the love, love of you.

Gina Lopez

X-ed

An Attempt To Understand The Death Of Charles H Spiegel 4/25/94
I cry out with a silent voice.
But you, you only see calm.
Signs are there, yes,
but subtlety buries them under day to day rush
can you not hear my plea?
Desperation turns to dullness,
alone I sit in silent despair.
Yet, not silent, for I hear the birds, the breeze, the bees.
All have a purpose do I?
I try to think thru the pain that clouds my view.
Pressure, pushing, make it stop.
I try to think good, I find none.
Pain everywhere, make it stop.
Realization strikes like lighting
I'm holding the solution!
"Don't do it", I feebly protest.
The turmoil and anger push me behind walls of unresistance.
I'm floating in nothingness. The silence is shattered
By the reverberating crack of the dishcharging gun.
There is no one there to hear.

Christina Breckenkamp

Thanksgiving Thoughts

I thank the Lord for the sky above
And all the heavenly blue.
I thank Him for the moon and stars
And for the sunshine too.
I thank Him for the grass that grows
And every brilliant flower.
I thank for Him for the sounds I hear
And for each quiet hour.
I thank him for the clothes we wear
And for the food we eat.
He's given us so many things!
I think that's kind of neat!
I'm glad that we're created
To think and feel and talk
And taste and smell — and eat, as well!—
With legs to help us walk.
I thank Him for His grace toward us
And for His mercy true;
And for the Holy Bible;
For our Lord and Savior too.
   Edna Arbuckle

Go Peacefully, Precious Ones

Go peacefully, precious ones,
Where the pain and suffering are no more,
Although we'll miss you greatly,
Our hearts will not always be sore.

For in the Land of promise,
Love forever abounds,
Nighttime will be whisked away,
When the trumpet of the Lord sounds.

Sleep sweetly, precious ones,
Then awake to your new day,
Put on the wings of triumph,
Go out to fly and play.

For when again we see you,
And all our tears are gone,
Together for eternity,
We love you, precious ones.
   Patrick Farr

That Night

As I write this poem I feel inside
The loss of love I shall never deny

Slowly, the dead red roses fell to the
ground and as quickly as the wave of a
wand I lost my love forever

Teardrops fell into the sand
As he laid my head into his hand
He stood up tall and looked me in the eye
And said "I'm sorry but I don't love you anymore"

At that moment my heart filled with fear
Because I knew that we would never be so near

I ran to the edge of the ocean and threw
Myself into the sand, I sobbed until I realized
My love was gone forever

I stood up slowly and walked on home

I walked on in and they asked "what's wrong?"
I dropped the last rose to the floor
And they knew my love was gone

Yes, I lost my love that night
But the question is "will I ever get him back?"
   Kelley Norton

A Traveler's Tale

On the first part of the journey the beaten path winds
   in the desert heat.
Its unbound gravel makes it rigorous on traveler's feet.
As cactus grow and tumbleweed blow under a cloudless sky,
only the snake survives while the path watches the others die.
In this relentless arid climate which seems to last forever,
the scourged path did not realize it crossed through a playful river.
As the journey continued attention to the waterway grew.
Palm trees flourished bringing shade to vegetation below,
   then the path knew.
The jubilant flow of the stream's currents gave life to the beaten way.
Friendship soon developed as the two intertwined joyfully
   in the hours of the day.
Like two children laughing, playing, and having fun,
their bonding was an oasis under the desert sun.
But just as quickly as the two met the path departed,
much to the dismay of the stream, who was left broken hearted.
As for the lonesome trail, it's been known to have said:
"I went back to the water, only to find a dusty river bed".
   Matthew Beliveau

Soul Mates

I can remember a place and a time,
before you entered that place in my mind.
A time when this man wasn't so strong,
his aching heart and soul didn't belong.

Dreams of an angel, all dressed in leathers.
Afraid of her soul being locked up forever.
She awaits for a man, in his possessions a key.
Is this the one true man, who can set her soul free.

Sometimes he can see her beauty, only in his dreams.
He wants it so badly, everything around him screams.
As he closes his eyes to sleep.
These vision's of her likeness, he struggles to keep.

Her eye's are full of a deep blue/green fashion,
the gaze over powers me with a hint of passion.
Golden red hair of a fiery gemstone quality.
A body of subtle perfection, better not let this one be.

And if I ever find her, somewhere in this time.
How will I really know it's her, if she is to be mine.
It's really sad to think, that some don't understand.
Your soul mate is all around you, even when there's no helping hand.
   Dennis DuPaul Ozenghar

Midnight Meditation

It's one minute until midnight.
Today will soon make its official departure.
Tomorrow's scheduled arrival is anticipated.
A new day has suddenly made a silent breakthrough.
Classical music in the background soothes me,
Softly plucking the strings of my soul like a harpist.
Who really knows what today holds?
The full moon glows with a mysterious ambience,
Like a round crystal ball one peers into for answers.
Stars resemble refined diamonds gleaming in the sapphire sky.
Day slowly overturns night like a silent war of the skies.
Through closed curtains and windows, daylight seeps through.
The clock will make its rounds once again.
For only at noon and midnight are the hands of time together.
Periods of reflection are appropriate during the 12 o'clock hour.
For when half the day is gone, we still have another half.
But when midnight draws near, the day is making a grand exit
Out of a door that automatically locks from behind.
   Asta Corley

Haunted

I'm haunted by your voice
I hear you
I have no choice.
I'm haunted by your eyes
the very ones
I love but despise
they seem so happy
so I'm also haunted by your laughter
knowing we won't live
happily ever after.
So I start to cry
when you talk about your kids
and I wish "I" could be the mother of your children
be the one in your arms
I will cherish those dreams well.
Sandra Waterman

Letter Of Goodbye

To my husband, my lover, my friend...we knew that someday
   it would end.
I know that somehow I must try to go on, even though it makes me cry.
I miss you so, and somehow there must be
A place and time for you to see
How brave and strong I am since we're apart...
But everything I do is with a heavy heart.

Every tree and bush you nurtured with your loving hands
Is like a monument to your spirit, and makes demands
That I must continue helping it to grow,
To make it strong and beautiful - you'd have it so.
But above all, the thing that I most miss
Is your welcoming smile each daybreak, followed by
   your morning kiss.

I tell myself you'd not have wished to live
In a world where you'd not be able to give
Of your loving services to everyone in kind,
Or enjoy your books and delving with your special mind.
For, everyone you touched was truly blessed,
And your spirit will never die, although your body's at rest.

So, goodbye my darling, till we meet again,
As the lyric goes: "Tho we know not where or when."
Jan Peterson

From Time To Time

As the leaves go to and fro, so do my thoughts at times.
The memories, the past, the treasures that could never last,
haunt my spirit from time to time.
My spirit seems to wander like the leaves in the wind, and that
haunting never really settles within, it would be nice to become lost
in that same wind from time to time.
That wind would be a shelter through sadness and pain, the world
would be my spirit's to gain, and to be protected from life's rain,
from time to time, to go to and fro as the leaves do go, from time to time.
Reflecting upon that, our spirits may pass from time to time.
So I will look for yours, and you look for mine, and
maybe then new suns will shine, from time to time.
Teresa Nikoley

In Flight

The ground was a sheet of diamonds
as the full white moon rose higher in the sky.
Sweet, sweet air filled my body,
bringing it back to life.
My legs carry me faster, and it seems
as though I could fly, given the chance...
bass undertones of the lives all around me
fill me with an irresistible urge to dance
a new dance to a new song.
Laura E. Chace

Love's Journey

Two young kids sitting quiet in the sand,
Silently expressing love, barely holding hands
Don't bother them with the future, or say "it's out of reach"
Let them live, let them love, to learn only what time can teach.

Slowly as time passes their souls become as one
Their love is becoming something they say will never come undone.
But as subtle as can be, with their dream house well in view
Each grows a curiosity that cannot be subdued
You see that cunning forest, with all its wistful trees
Will lure them away awhile to live life's mysteries
It's a place perhaps not better, but surely very new
Still I know for certain that their love will pull them through.

So fear not for this young love, no do not fret at all
Soon they'll see the best came first, after only a short fall.
They'll break from their demise and meet with open arms
Having quelled the forest, and all its tempting charms
Back unto the place they left, free of the empty things they sought
Their eyes will say I love you, but neither's voice will peep.

The water warms their feet as they calmly make their way
To their blue dream house upon the hill, where forever they shall stay
Mack L. Flinspach III

The Villa

She spends the night in a cozy villa.
A cup of creamy French Vanilla.
The taste so smooth, a sigh of grief.
The enticing aroma of an attempt for relief.

Small bare feet on the bear skin rug.
Drinking her mocha from a small clay mug.
She decides to walk over to the bookcase and dabble.
While taking a bite of sweet candy-apple.

Drowning her heartache in a sea of treats.
The unfortunate moment of the previous week.
But that's behind her, won't think of it today.
However, the pain made her life fade away.

Flipping through pages next to the fire.
Cracking chestnuts hint desire.
Why would a man do such a thing?
She wonders as she stares at her engagement ring.

She lies with the fur rubbing her soft skin.
Without a thread of clothing, the thought makes her grin.
She throws the ring into the fire and watches it lose its depth.
A tear fell from the eye as she took her last breath.
Jesse J. Davis III

C.P.

The greatest gift ever given to me
was the gift of friendship, given unselfishly.
Friends have come, and friends have gone,
but in my heart lives a special one.
She seems to know when I'm sad or blue,
she always knows just what to do.
She's always there to help and care,
if I just say the word.
In good times or bad,
she makes my heart glad,
and for this angel, I thank the Lord.
She's the best friend I will ever have,
She means the world to me.
Her unselfish giving,
makes my life worth living.
And I will love my friend eternally.
To make her happy is my goal,
For that's when I'm happy, you see.
And if I can somehow bless her life,
then the blessing falls upon me.
Randy L. Prim

The Bewitching Hour (The Hour Of 13)

On this day, beware of night
When the witches and warlocks come into sight

There is no moon for you to see,
  just dark, black night, you'll see

Lock your windows and lock your
  doors...the night is young so don't ignore

The witches and warlocks are out for
  the night...beware of this hour, the hour of 13

Be ye frightened...be ye scared, when
  the clock in the tower strikes 13 to
  the hour...the bewitching hour...the hour of 13
    Eileen R. Sipho

Angelic Friends

Dearest are my friends.
Never a word spoken in anger
Nor a scorn of pain upon
any heart of the four musketeers.

Secrets told, shared, then locked away.
Never to be told or understood again.

Love and kindness are all
these sorrowful ears hear when in pain.
How shall I thank God for my Angelic friends?

Our lives spent together only blocks away;
- But now, states apart.
When death shall find me;
I want them there.
- For together all through life;
why not at the end.

Dearest are my true friends.
    Amy Ziegler

The Fragile Gift

Life should be thought of as a fragile gift.
Life after all is what-you make of it.
It's hard to cope when everything goes wrong.
But life never stops, it continues on.
Unwrap life as if it were a present.
You'd be surprised at the change of events.
Life can be changed simultaneously.
If you can just look at life differently.
Look at life with the same sense of surprise.
Somehow you might be able to realize.
Life should be thought of as a fragile gift.
Life after all is what you make of it.
    Charlene Palecki

My Lord and Savior

At times I may fail and fall,
Though my Lord and savior stands me tall...
Difficulties that come and go,
My faith in you just seems to grow...
As time goes by my problems drift,
I thank you Lord for your lift...
I tell you this all my friends,
Trust in him his love he sends...
Let's not worry or have fear,
For our Lord and savior loves us dear...
To those of you who understand,
Place your trust upon his hand...
I say these words to all of you,
For his love is oh so true...
Let no troubles or worries make you blue,
For our Lord and savior cares for you...
    Eddie Garcia

Uncaged

She reminds me of a beautiful bird
A very rare and untamed bird
One that cannot be caged

If you should try to capture it
It would flap and flutter so loudly
You would have to set it free

You can only hope
That one day it would return
To perch on a limb nearby
Allowing you to see it
Or perhaps even touch it

With great desire to rescue it
You allow it to fly away
Over the ocean
And high above the clouds
To reach new heights

You never forget the bird
And never give up, not entirely
Always keep and window cracked
Even in the dead of winter...just in case
    Mary Boatwright-Britton

A Painted Sky

There never was a little girl, more wanted than me
I had all the love a child could ever want or need
Daddy gave me everything, he could afford to buy
And on the ceiling in my room, he painted me a sky
He told me not to be afraid, when it stormed outside
He said in your room sweetheart, the sun will always shine
And through the years of growing up, if something made me cry,
It didn't seem to hurt so bad beneath a painted sky.
Well, girls grow up and fall in love and that's how it is
Sometimes, the man doesn't love them, like their Daddy did
Sometimes the hurt can hurt so bad, the way it does tonight
It makes me want to go back home beneath my painted sky
Beneath my painted sky, that's where I long to be
A place to go when this old world gets the best of me
A place where dreams come true and no one says good-bye
I wish I could be young again, beneath a painted sky.
    Roberta Phillips

The Rainbow

Today is the first day of the rest of my life,
The decision's been made, I will not be his wife.

He moved out on his own and left the house to me,
An apartment for him, he wanted to be free.

When I came home from work, on the counter I see,
A vase full of roses and a letter for me.

The count was twenty-six, one flower for each year,
He had to remind me, it brought pain and a tear.

He wrote of his feelings, his guilt and his pain,
When I broke down and cried, it started pouring rain.

Before the rain ended, the sun came out once more,
I searched for the rainbow and saw it from the door.

A huge double rainbow crossed my house, what a sight!
A message from God, that it will be all right.

My heavy heart lifted after six years of pain,
The answers seemed to be in the sunshine and rain.

The rain was a symbol of the tears I had shed,
Combined with the sunshine for brighter days ahead.

God sent me this rainbow, to free me of the strife,
Today is the first day of the rest of my life.
    Jacqueline E. Sciotto

Harvester Of Sorrow

An old man dies and a woman cries.
   I await in the shadows.
Someone's love turns to hate.
   I laugh to myself.
Lovers speak words of anger.
   I speak the language of the mad.
A woman hides a secret.
   I can see her tortured soul.
Too late you realize your mistake.
   No longer can you hide from me.
You try to run.
   Then you feel the chill run down your spine.
You feel the fear.
   Where there is sadness, you shall meet me.
I am the HARVESTER OF SORROW.
   Joseph M. Kroll

Overlooked Insect

A tiny creature which God created
Crawls along, not needing aid
An insect the most overlooked of all
As you see it across the hall
In your space you think it's invaded
Now you wish to kill the creature God created
You stomp upon it mercilessly, causing its death
A murderer, a destroyer of life, you now are
As the helpless ant, takes its last breath
Are you proud of your triumph over the helpless
What harm has it done to you
   Joseph M. Scarfone

Friend

One night I bowed down and prayed to the Lord above
I asked him to give me a friend
And put between us a special bond of love
I asked for someone who would accept me
And keep me in mind where ever they may be
One who would stick by me
Through laughter and tears, sorrow and fears,
Good times and bad, all through the years.
One who would lift me up, and, when necessary, bring me down.
I thought surely, with such high standards,
Such a friend could not be found.
But when we were each in our darkest hour,
The Lord worked a beautiful miracle
And I found our friendship blooming
Like a glorious, heavenly flower
When I least expected it, the Lord answered my prayer
And I know where ever I may go, whatever I may do,
I will never find another sweet friend like you.
   Jennifer Lynn Davis

In The Summertime (A Poem About Summer)

In the summertime the sun is so bright,
the temperature is always right.
In the summertime the sun is a scorcher,
it melts my ice cream and leaves me with torture.
In the summertime the water is cool,
I can play all day without the worry of school.
In the summertime my friends and I bear the heat,
by spraying water all over our feet.
In the summertime the days are long,
as the birds sing the pure melody of their song.
In the summertime the days smell so sweet
that sometimes you won't even notice the heat.
   Mallory P. Alexin

Step Lightly

The alarm clock buzzes at 5 am,
Time to get up, get ready for the day ahead...

Step lightly, tread softly, laugh often and see,
The sunrise kissing the morning dew.
Birds taking flight, soaring true.
The wind gently blowing, bringing in the rain.
The sunset telling of another day at end.

Step lightly, tread softly, laugh often and see,
Other faces, other lives, their smiles, their pain.
Children's joyful laughter, running "to" not "from."
Their hearts open, bringing in the sun.

Step lightly, tread softly, laugh often and see,
Memories of words, gestures, promises made.
Dance joyfully in the rain together.
Raise your faces to the stars above.
Each other's heart is in each other's hand.
Remember the joys, the tears, the wind.

Step lightly, tread softly for the day begins...
   K. DeLaine Thompson

Remember When

Remember when you used to laugh and play those silly games?
Remember when the children loved to hear you call their names?
Remember when you used to look for lost treasures in every pocket?
Remember when you checked the door; and even when you locked it?
Remember when the laughter swelled from deep within your soul?
Remember when you saw the world through a heart of gold?
Remember when you were young and life was, oh, so gay?
Remember when all your worries dealt with what games to play?
Remember when your eyes were wide and open to all you saw?
Remember when around your heart there were not any walls?
Remember when your mother called and pulled you from your friends?
Remember all the childhood days? Remember when, remember when?
   Georgette Morse

Choose

Each step you take on the road of life
Is a choice you make on your own
The road less traveled or the well trodden path
Choose - your destiny is unknown

Do not be idle day after day
Or circumstance might choose your way
Do not be hindered by trouble and strife
It's not easy, this walk on the road of life

Do you follow you heart or your soul or your mind
Choose - who's to say what you will find
Try to stand firm on what you say and do
And choose the path that is right for you
   Beverly Everett

Listen To The Quiet

Listen to the gentle peace of the quiet,
   It's as if all is well and everything's right.
In the darkness of night not a sound to be heard,
   Not even the song of one lone bird.

Total calm surrounds you, not even a breeze,
   To drift gently through the stately tall pine trees.
Not a ripple on the lake, like a mirror it does shine,
   As the moonlight caresses our cabin, yours and mine.

In the dense woods you hear not a sound,
   And you know all the little critters are stirring around.
I'm awed by the hush that comes with the night,
   Listen to the gentle peace of the quiet.
   Carol Oehler

Behold, I Stand At The Door, And Knock

I heard a faint knocking today at my heart's door, and I was ashamed
to answer, for I knew it was the Lord. There he stood, looking
humble, and sad. His eyes full of compassion like a concerned,
thoughtful Dad. "Don't you know," he said," I know everything, and
there is nothing hidden, child, that I haven't seen. I've watched you
destroying yourself and my spirit has grieved, and my intention in
visiting you today is to set your soul free". Behold my child; I
stand at the door and knock, and only from your side can that door be
unlocked. I have many treasures awaiting you, but remember that my
path is narrow, and my followers few. I won't force the issue, and
I'll never intrude. I respect your will, and wouldn't dare be rude.
And there is one more thing before I go, you must believe that I love
you so. That alone will be sufficient to meet all your needs, but
the requirement is that you truly believe. My love and truth will set
your soul free, even when your will doesn't want to agree. Reach out
and touch me, call on my name. If you're a true believer you'll know
that is why I came. I came to set the captives free, and beloved
this is your name written down in front of me.
   MerryJo Hooker

They Know Not The Real Me

They think I'm dazed and out of reach - I lie there senseless the floor.
They think it's all too much for me, but I've walked this sacred ground before.
They think emotions are too much; they think that I'm too young to see
They think my words are out of touch, but they know not the real me.
If they knew what incites my soul; if they knew any breath of truth;
If they knew what my sense unfolds, they'd question not this aged youth.
But they choose to look and not to find. I hide nothing from on my knees.
Yet their ignorance impales my mind, for they know not the real me.
They think these things will never end. They think I'm not as strong as they.
They think there's nothing I'll amend, but my separate peace lies far away.
They think I'm young and just naive. They think they know one day I'll see.
They think they know what I believe, but they know not the real me.
If they knew where my prayers arrive, and what my closed eyes see at night,
If they opened up and took the ride, they'd question not my earned rights.
But they choose to think and not to know—they're minds so closed they barely breathe
My open eyes will soon corrode, for they know not the real me.
   Chuck Carlise

If I Had One Question To Ask Him

I was told never to judge someone for who they were on the outside,
For if I did, somehow there would be something they would hide,
I would be looking at how cute they were, or how much money they made,
I would be looking at someone for all the wrong reasons, this kind of love would fade.

Instead I chose to love someone for who they were on the inside,
For how kind and warm they were, and if they had self pride.
When I finally found you I knew I was in love because you made my legs weak.
And when I saw you, it was even hard for me to open up and speak.
It was like I was swept off my feet; it was fate we were destined to meet.

Now my problem is I can't stop loving you, even though you've hurt me deep within and made me blue.
So I ask if you can't love someone from the outside, and the inside isn't always true;
What is love? And how do you know if it is real? That's the one simple answer I wish I knew!
   Jaime Keller

If I Had But A Moment!!!

If I had but a moment to live...oh! What a beautiful, fulfilling moment it would be.
I would stop to smell God's flowers.
I would rush out and slowly embrace the first sign of the morning dew.
I would open my arms, and lift my face to God's morning rain,
and when the rain is gone...I would close my eyes, and receive the warmth of the sun against my cheeks.
If I had but a moment, I would walk along the sea shore, and dig my heels into the sand,
and then patiently sit back and wait for the beautiful sunset.
If I had but a moment, I would stop and hold the hand of God's child,
and turn a frown into a smile, and tears into laughter.
Oh Lord, if I had but a moment...a moment...a moment...
Oh! What an endless moment it would be...
   Isolyn Jones

New Beginnings

Since you - the pure splendor of life has unfolded before my eyes
Since you - the joy of living each day because you are part of them has become sweet pleasure.
Since you - I walk in perpetual sunshine, the sweet intoxication of your nearness enthralls me.
Since you - the darkness no longer frightens me- I welcome it
   because there I can enter the dimension of my dreams where my fantasies become reality.
   Where I can hold and embrace you, where I can make love to you, where our two hearts beat as one,
   where we can be inseperable, unencumbered by the effects of everyday life,
   where all is beauty and warmth- and the essence of our love bathes us in an impermeable aura
   protected from the harsh reality of life.

Since you - the memories of moments together have released emotions
   buried within my being to surface and be be savored for their beauty.
Since you - the challenges of everyday life and its implications are
   suddenly tolerable, the pain of existence alone within myself- has become more bearable.
Since you - I have evolved into what I always knew I would be - and this awakening has refreshed and revitalized my soul.

Since you - the future holds more promise - whether we are destined
   or not the excitement of the possibility enriches my soul - and justifies my mortal existence.
Since you - I am now aware of the frailty of mortality - with only
   a fear of leaving this dimension for another - and finding you do not exist!
Since you - there is so much more...
   Lloyd R. Trina

Whose Life R U Living???

My, My, My, ain't you fittin' in well
Climbed up that corporate ladder, now you King of the hill
I guess all that education and hard work has paid off
But, who reimburses those, who got you where you are?

Haven't seen you in a while, it seems you changed your style a bit
Tell me, if I add a mustache to Washington don't that make my dollar counterfeit?
You say it's not where you're from, but rather where you're at
Let's ask OJ how he felt when he couldn't come back.

I see you traded in Shaniqua and now you hanging with Sue Ann
Was is that she reminded u of the man you ain't or that she don't mix well with your friends?
Nah, brother, this ain't about color, it's about your character
Seems u forgot who you are, from whence you've came and now u serve a new master.

Wasn't too long ago, you used to serve the Lord on Sunday
But now this time is used for rest, so you can serve the man on Monday
You say you got career moves to make, and that you don't have time no more!
I say you losing your soul, and you don't even know what for!

Didn't mean to offend anyone; no I truly didn't mean any harm
But within the life u are living you must live the life you are given
And remember those who have given so that your life may be worth living.
   Whose Life R U Living???
   Kenneth Alexander Brisco

I Remember When

I remember when we first met, you were so sad and blue;
You told me that you needed me and I felt compelled to nurture and comfort you.

I remember when you first looked into my eyes. You told me that I gave you the courage to face another day;
Then why oh why did you hurt me that way?

I remember when you first held my hand. You told me that together we would always remain;
Now you want to leave me and I'll never, ever be the same.

I remember when you first kissed my lips. You told me that you would be my king and I your queen;
Now you tell me that you were not quite yourself and those promises you did not mean.

I remember when you first held me close. You told me that you never wanted to turn me loose;
For all my love and affection is insensitivity the repayment that you choose?

I remember when I was like a wounded animal with nowhere to turn;
What a valuable lesson I did indeed learn.

Some people give, some take; Be aware of the difference and you will avoid a heartache.

Now that I have licked my wound and can carry on,
you have the nerve to ask me to take you back as if you were never gone.

While you were away following your need to be free,
my heart decided that it no longer loved another who did not love me.
   Diane McCray

You And Only You

Your beauty
is like a rose,
your sweet fragrance
captures my nose.
Those beautiful eyes
I see every day,
trembles my body
in a tingly way!
In a tingly way!
That smile of yours
makes me happy to see
that you love me so much,
and wanna be with me!

Chavelle Tihati Galton

The Peacemakers

The people who live
their lives by God's
will, and risk all
chances to make peace
in the world. The
ones who solve fights
by agreeing with both sides,
who trust in everyone
and treat everyone with
respect. They cherish
their lives and help
people to turn away
from violence. To be
a peacemaker is the
greatest job of all.
Be a peacemaker in
your everyday lives,
and God will save a
place for you in
heaven as a hero.

Christine Delaet

Sorrow

I'm sitting here in sorrow
because there may not be a tomorrow.

I'm trying not to be in sorrow.
And hoping that there is a tomorrow.

I'm still blue. But I'm not trying
to get the flu.

I make myself sick when I'm blue.
You may as well call it the flu.

I'm blue with sorrow. And hoping
for a tomorrow without the flu.

Crystal R. Monk

Loss

They peer out the window
and whisper to the night
of dreams that haunt
and give no refuge in the light
they turn their heads
to catch a fleeting glimpse
of a voice heard long ago
and not remembered since
one turns away
and looks deep into her soul
a part of her is missing
never to return

Wendy McDonald

Heaven

A spiritual presence
A devout essence
A ravishing place
The city of grace

Void of sins
A new life always begins
Beatitude and glee
Your whole heart is free

Sweet days in the sun
Knowing forever has just begun
Blessedness in heart, mind, and soul
Living eternity always feeling whole

Kelly Marie Gumb

My Children

I dream of giving birth
To help preserve this Earth
I'll teach them how to plant and plow
I'll teach them how to milk a cow
I'll teach them how to hunt and fish
To find their own main dish
My children will be free
Not like you and me.

Kimberly Gunter

As I Gazed (Into His Eyes)

I thought I saw forever
as I gazed into his eyes
two wells of hope and wonder
a mind so full and wise.
A face just like September
so beautiful and warm
energetic and delightful
a man not of the norm.
Just like the four leaf clover
perfect and hard to find
once you've got it in your grasp
bad luck is left behind.
Love and Joy will follow
every step he takes
a romantic 'til the end
no heart will ever break.
This and more is what I saw
as I gazed into his eyes
love, hope and memories
with him will never die.

Erika D. Lawton

The Triangle

We strive against each other
The yin and the yang
Subconscious forces
Cause us to compete.
The struggle is age-old.
Who is right?
Who best-loved?
Where does this struggle end?
In burnt offering?
Oh, God,
Deliver us
From these, our trespasses,
From this, our rivalry.

Kay E. Johnson

Insanity

Her eyes

Hector Luis Diaz

P.O.W.-M.I.A.

A life of sorrow,
A life of pain,
A life of grief, lives joy again,
A family so long separated,
A family soon to be reunited,
A mother's smile, a father's tears,
A son's embrace after all those years,
A calm day,
A warrior's return,
A happy day,
A man reborn.

William M. Guerette

Our Motor Home

Down the road we travel
My wife and I alone
Over mountains and deserts
In a rig, we call home.

Drifting across the great white plains
Where the windmills stand tall;
There, the cattle are moving,
To where the cowboy calls.

Through the red wood forest,
As we slowly drive along;
We can hear the birds singing,
An enchanting, melodious song.

When we camp by the ocean,
Sunlight beams on the tide;
In the distance, whales and dolphins,
Are swimming side by side.

There's motels and hotels,
From coast to coast,
But being in a motor home,
Is what we love most.

George C. Page

Midnight Devil

When the night is far too quiet
And the dawn is miles away
That's when he comes to visit
and makes his plans to stay

He pulls the darkness all around me
He gives the air a chill
We both choose our weapons
And the battle goes uphill

He raises the fear and anger
to the surface once again
The years of tears comes flooding
There is no way to win

How do you fight the stillness
of the ache inside your soul
When the devil comes to call at night
to burn a brand new hole

Do you hold your breath till morning
Pray an answer soon to come
A miracle to save your mind
and strike the devil numb

Tracy Callahan

Exponent Of Inspiration

Never become disappointed
When progress you cannot find it
And don't accuse Providence
Of being absentminded

When setting realistic goals
One can succeed. That's a fact.
Determination and perseverance
Accomplishes the act

Reaching the pinnacle of success
And entertaining no allusion
If you parachute conceitedly
You're jumping to a conclusion.
Christine M. Jones

Karmic

What strange feelings
shared by Twin souls
that have yet to awaken
from separate goals.

A history forgotten
through choice and decision
Present is past again
and is hidden.

In eyes deep in knowing
but much too afraid
of inner spirit showing
an uncomfortable trade,
from a course set and planned
future seen but not yet made
that ignores the Promises
of us and of fate.

And if time were a friend
we would meet again
but now is Forever
in lessons without end.
Taunya Hannibal

The Leaves Of Spring

Watching intently from my window
As flakes of snow fall softly
On bare branches of the trees
Oh how long before the buds will
Come and the unfurling of the leaves
To fill my heart with joys of spring
And birds singing in the trees

Spring and summer came
And all too soon were gone
Now leaves are dancing on the trees
In colors bright and gay
Once more the leaves are falling
And branches almost bare
Now my heart is filled with sadness
As I sit watching from my window
For the leaves of spring again
Jeanette B. Stump

Although

Although the pain never ends,
Until we die we'll always be friends.
My love for you will never change,
My life for yours I would arrange.
I can't express the way I feel
My heart, my soul no one could steal.
Just remember no matter how it turns,
Like a candle my love still burns...
Jeannie Bartuch

My Friend

I have a friend
A special one
His name is Jesus
he is God's son

He is the best friend
No better could be had
He loves me regardless
Even if I am bad

He died for me
Yet He still lives
And everyone can have
The love that He gives

So if you want His love
All you have to do is pray
And it will be yours
Forever and a day
Joanna Robert

My Pretty Little Girl

The children are gone
and on their own
I gaze outside
to greet the dawn

With little hands folded
as if in prayer
she looks up to say
Yes, I'm here

Up to the window
she makes her climb
her eyes say "hello pops"
it's feeding time

Whether there's sunshine
rain or hail
it warms me to see
her bushy tail

To others she may be
only a squirrel
but to me, she's
my pretty little girl!
Brian Haworth

Always

Though I am gone
I am still here
my spirit in the trees
my soul in the fields.
My memories are the flowers
which blossom in spring
my voice is the wind
whose sweet music will sing
my heart's warmth is the sun
and to make loneliness end
the pale moon in the sky
promises to be your friend.
To protect you from
the blackness of fright
the stars are my smile
which will light up the night.
Although I am gone
I'm all around
Just look with your heart
I'll be found.
Jonell Clevenger

When I Turned On The Light

When I turned on the light,
I had hoped I could see,
all the happiness in the world,
happening around me.

When I turned on the light,
it was such a surprise,
instead of joy, their tears
were all around my eyes.

When I turned on the light,
the horror and despair,
all the world was a big balloon,
the sadness was the air.

When I turned on the light,
my hands froze in their place,
I saw the horrid destruction,
of the whole human race,
when I turned on the light.
Elizabeth Penn Whittenburg

Untitled

The tapestry of our lives
   Yours and mine
Is rough as burlap here and there
With many changing hues and threads
   Woven tightly, strongly knotted,
Or unraveling from wear and time
Changing the patterns and the colors
Becoming smooth with age
Hanging with grace upon the Walls
   We've built
Walls of support and Walls of distance
A weaving of hearts and thoughts
   The warp and woof
   of what we have become
Because of what we have been
   To each other
I have learned much from you, David,
   And I love you dearly,
   Dan
Dorothy Anne Ufford

Flowers

   Flowers are things you
think of, things that
bloom and grow.

   Flowers are things I
think of when it's hot
sunny or snow.

   I love to smell the
daisies, hidden in the
grass.

   When the sun is out
or when it's cold.

   Remember the flower
that still grows.
Laura Lopez

Pain

Flickering fire
Licks over the crashed plane.
A man crawls out of the
Mangled metal.
Eerie sirens are heard in the distance.
Screams ring out from his pain.
Andrea Gatschet

Living To Do Right

Yes! I'm young and restless but,
thank God he made me bold and beautiful.
You know! As the world turns,
I must follow God's guiding light,
because the days of our lives
is not leading us to another world.
Now look at me in general hospital
that's where I had all my children,
truly thank God we only have one life to live
and that life, that I live is only for Him!
   Shirley Wilson

To Gabrielle With Love

You can't be afraid of love
It's all around you.
Running away will not do any good.
Forget the past and the bad memories
It holds, think of the future and all
The happiness it can unfold.
It's the bad times that make you
Wonder why, it's the good times that
Bring you the reply. Love can be
The scariest thing.
It can also be your most fulfilled
Dream.
   Michael Doyle

The Beauty of A Rose

The beauty of a rose
pink is for the passion
between two people.
Yellow is for the joy
and happiness.
White is for the peace
in one's spirit
red is for the love
one has to offer another.
   Michael Leo Wilson

Missing You

I thought that I was over you,
But now I know it's not true

The times that we were together,
Thought it would last forever

Now I look back on those days,
And I can't forget your wonderful ways

You were thoughtful and you cared,
You were open and you shared

I thought that together we would stay,
But now we are going our own way

I try to convince myself and say,
You will come back my way some day

I know I will miss you,
But will you miss me?

I know in my heart,
you will always be with me

So please forgive me for loving you,
You don't know how much I really do
   Jody Zenkus

Malfunction

Living in tune with the smoke
Or a haze with a light at the end
Now the passage well lit
We inhale the cloud of righteousness

My mind no longer cluttered
Thoughts pass with ease
With a vision of my family at heart
The thoughts of one thing, our fruits

Fruits which the path was lit with
Have now come to an end
Yet the memory of our journey
Will last until the none
   Gabriel R. Laguna

In Another World

Where all things go my way.
I would live so happily,
Luck never having to stray.
Life is not perfect,

And never will be.
Lucking to try,
Waiting to see.
A change in the world,
Yesterday to today.
Standing aside.

Determined not to play.
Reality won't stop and,
Evolution will change.
And knowing that,
My life I'll rearrange.
   Stacy Wyant

Sweet Song

I've been longing for my song-bird
To cheer me up somehow;
Waiting patiently at sun-down
But, he hasn't come - 'till now!

I searched and listened eagerly,
Hoping to hear that voice;
Languishing 'till springtime
Did I really have a choice?

But, then, today, while out-of-doors
To tend the flowers and such,
I thought I heard the songster
Seemed closed enough to touch!

He came to me at even-tide
His song - so long unheard;
'Twas a harmony of whistles
At last, my mocking - bird!
   William Allen Newsom

Untitled

Today I think of you again,
So close in mind, though body gone.
Your generous way, your patient heart,
Lives on in all who hold you dear.
Though body gone, you leave us not,
We together will survive.
The love you showed will carry on,
by your example you have taught;
To live, to laugh, to love, to learn.
Today I think of you again.
   Mary J. Shafer

The Waterball

On the tails of a dream
Trails the whisper of a child
Who sails on a stream
Through nightmares wild

In a dome this magic child
Know not of day or night
But the kingdom of the waterball
A waterfall of sight

From the eyes sacred tears
Crystal mirrors of ancient truth
Strike the heart as if spears
With the wisdom of his youth

"I am a child of magic in
The caverns of the deep,
Stardust flies with windswept sighs
That carry you through sleep"

"To other worlds for boys and girls
Of china dolls and kings
Of ribbons, bows and tiny curls
Of castles, frogs and wings"
   Jan Stephens

Each Other's Love

I waited around,
All that I could,
then I moved on,
But every time I wanted,
to fall in love,
I fell more in love,
with you,
So then I sat dreaming,
you'd come back,
then one bright day,
you returned,
with a smile on your face,
and love in your heart,
so now we sit,
always content,
with each other's love.
   Melonee Harrison

The Horse

Sea horse,
Saw horse,
Every day horse.
Thought I saw a blue and gray horse!

Sea horse,
Saw horse,
Every night horse.
Thought I saw a blue and white horse.

Sea horse,
Saw horse,
Afternoon horse.
Thought I saw a great baboon horse!

Sea horse,
Saw horse,
Morning light horse.
Thought I saw a snoring bright horse!

Hey! Wake up!
It's in the morning,
So stop snoring!
Wake up!
   Kristen Kushner

Ashes In The Wind

Today I let you go, with
ash as white as snow.
I let them blow in the
wind, so now you're
free and on mind.

I miss you now as I
see you fly, but I can't
say goodbye.
As the wind blows away
the only mother I had
today, please take heart.
That you will always be
mom to me.

John F. Newberger

Waterlily Castle

All around me,
All I see,
Beautifully colored waterlilies.
Purple, yellow, white, and red,
The day I'll have to leave I dread,
For when I leave I now know
That waterlilies my mind will show,
In my dreams of happiness and glory.
My paintings shall tell my story.

Samantha L. Milne

Little Princess

Our brightly shining star,
An angel in our Heaven,
Who gave us all such joy.

Oh, how much we dearly miss you
And long for your embrace
But we can't take comfort in knowing
You're in a better place.

God gave you to us
For only a short while.
But, oh, how much you taught us
To love, to laugh, to smile.

You had a way of touching hearts
Of all whom you have met.
Our love for you we promise
Never to forget.

So rest, our "Little Princess"
Your work on Earth is done.
And we are all now waiting
For the day we'll all be one.

Evelyn R. Werkau

Life And Death

Death! Ah what is death?
For me I see deliverance
From things of clay
Time passed away
I stand a new creation
In the land of living day.

Life! Ah what is life?
To be to see to understand
What God has planned.
He in His grace
Through time and space
Prepared this place.
We live by His command.

Margaret Decker

Hold My Hand

Come hold my hand
And walk with me,
Beside the strand
Beside the sea.

Think with me
Of ages past,
Beside the sea

Alone at last.
Just us two,
No one but we,
Hand in hand

Beside the sea.
Cares of the years
Will pass away.
Gone are the tears
Of the yesterdays.

Come hold my hand
And walk with me
Beside the strand
Beside the sea.

Elizabeth D. Soderstrom

Our World

People look around
you the signs are everywhere.
No one seems to care if what
they do is fair.
   The seasons they go round
the ponies they go up and down.
   But if the people
don't stop what they're doing
the only place the world
will be going is down.

Carmoneda J. Lindsey

Solitary

The rose stands alone
waiting peacefully
yearning to take the first step
unable
nature does not think it is so
its beauty fills the room
but no one is there
so it does not matter
the world doesn't notice
how painfully the rose dies
for it is only a thorn
in your side.

Nora Siewiorek

Winter

Slippery-sliding,
  Kids a-riding;
On their sleds
  Down
   the
    hill

Through the trees;
Watch the weeds
  Oh No!
The sled won't go.
Better go home.
To rest for
The next day of
  Winter.

Rhonda J. Tuttle

A Rose

Slowly from the black earth
one green finger emerges.
Day by day the fingers grows
into a long, narrow stem
and the leaves slowly unfold
to capture the warmth
of the sun
and the cool spring rain.
At the very top of the stem
three small leaves
surround the delicate pink bud.
Soon the bud emerges
from the protection of the leaves.
One by one the petals unfold
and shower me with
their scent and beauty
until it has grown
to full maturity
where its full beauty
and majesty are revealed.

Jennifer Hasslinger

Abandoned Mansion

The past is always with us,
Surviving in the present.
A style of living, once alive
With vigor, strength, and purpose
Falls into abandon and decay.
Durability, once fashioned,
Still stands in testimony;
Disuse and desertion,
A once-proud mansion grieves.
Nostalgia, fascination,
Faint hopes of restoration,
Spark thoughts of brief reprieve.
It lingers on and on, it seems,
Rebuilt in never ending dreams.

William F. Wambsganss

My Now Transparent Renee

I should say,
That it was so unreal...
A mourn...
With no appeal...
So far, but yet so near,
I felt her...
As elusive as a soft breeze,
I could barely hear her sneeze.
I knew that it was her.
Because of the scent of Georgio Red...
She wore before bed.
As she rests there,
So peaceful and gay...
I felt in my heart,
Her soul, was here to stay..
My Now Transparent Renee!

Tiffany S. Grant

Colors

Red is for the passion I feel inside
Blue is for the sadness I can't hide
Pink is for the love you gave to me
Green is for the anger that came to be
White is for those warm, sunny days
Black is for the time the sky was gray
Yellow is for the day you set me free
Purple is the color of your
knees when you crawl back to me

Jennifer Ferrell

Dark Days Of The Past, Brighter Days To Come

We have had many dark days
In the Month of July.
Surely happy days will return
Let us not look behind
Brighter days are to come.

We are a family divided
Let us keep the faith.
Bring us back together
Let us not look behind
Brighter days are to come.

We will survive,
This nightmare will all go away.
We will be a family once again.
Surely happy days will return
Let us not look behind.
Brighter days are yet to come.

Beulah G. Dunn

Days Of Yesteryear

As I walk down the busy streets,
I picture the days of yesteryear,
of darkened forests and wooded swamp,
and many animals to fear.

I see the bold frontiersman,
so dark and yet so sleek,
I learn of all the hardships
the people had to meet.

They were mighty,
they were bold,
and around the campfire,
old legends would be told.

I saw them hunt, I saw them kill,
I saw them dressed alike,
but most of all it was peaceful here,
a place to live and die.

Mary Ann Dominiak

Naked Truth

He sees me,
  I am afraid

What will he think of me,
  I am exposed;
  breathless,

What is it he sees
  weakness? No, strength
  cowardice? No, bravery
  insecurities? No, confidence

What is it,
  I am so afraid

Can I trust him,
  is he honest?
  is he sincere?
  is he caring?

I am so afraid
  who is he?
  Myself

Patricia Ann Labbate

My Haiku

Black baby is born
In spring, his breath of life is
a deep sigh in winter years.

Felicia A. Easterling

A Reasonable Course Of Thought

For every tear I cry
There is justification
For every sigh I sigh
There is an explanation
For every thought in my head
There is cause for remembrance
For every expression I've read
There is reason for conformance
For my confusion
There is consequence
For my pain and affliction
Is taken in a wrong sense
For the wish I desire
There is omission of mention
For my mind is tired
There's no more room for decimation

Jenifer L. Everett

Perfection

Your hair
the yellow rays of the sun,
the curls of perfection,
I love to twirl my fingers in it.

Your eyes,
blue,
clear,
The start of a summer day.

Your cheeks,
they light my life,
they are warm,
I love to kiss them gently.

Your lips,
forming a wonderful smile,
it lights my life,
kissing them brings me joy.

Tad G. Stephens

A Time And A Place

In the middle of the night
I awake from my sleep
And look to the sky
To ponder and think
Of a time and of a place
Where there isn't any
Destruction or disgrace

I let my mind wander
Back to a land
Where children can run free
And never again have to be
Afraid of whom or what they might meet
Just on the other side of the street

I must confess
That I shall wait
In the still of the night
Though my dream may not come true
It shall always be
In the hearts of me and you

Jessica Kiel

Untitled

Darling, darling, darling
  My heart sang
    all day long
I never knew before
  one world could
    make a song!

Lucile M. Campbell

Black Shadow

Black as the night
Only green eyes showing
You are a mystery
Full of love and anxiety.

Lying on my bed
Eyeing me with wonder
I wonder, too, just
what is on your mind.

I want to be you
Just for a moment
To see what great wisdom
You have stowed away.

Gentle as a baby, but
Vicious as the cornered fox
You went to be near
But never confined.

Loving by nature
But not quite trusting
Just like the wildcats
Alert and cautious.

Marilyn S. Miller

Two Years Old

Two-years-old and in control,
Mom says, "You sit on the pot."
I say, "Really, I think not."
She says, "That's so good,"
When I put myself
Upon her stool.
I don't understand
Dropping my goods
To watch it go down
To where or whom.
"No," I scream.
She says, "You will."
But, I'm two and in control.
I do what I will.

Rose Martin

The Wind Whispering My Name

The softness to the stillness
of the air,
gently breezes through
my eye gazing stare.
The chill of the blur
in the evening sky,
brings an echo of tears
down my ever-lasting eye.
The wind is getting higher
And whistling as time goes by,
the animals grow cooler
and let a mourning cry.
The calling breeze,
the eagerness of air,
the gentle touch of
nature's flaming care.
My name, what
I hear,
the wind is whispering
My name so clear.

Sheena Preheim

Wind

Wind has many moods.
It's sad now. Wind is
Wailing loudly.
Hush! Hear it crying.

Amanda Nelis

The Teacher

His eyes shine like daggers
Crafted from the finest onyx.
Have you learned yet? He whispers,
Amusement coating his icy words.
Life is not a game, dear one,
Have I not shown this to you?
Gleefully, he has raped your soul,
Taken everything from you.
Yet still you cling to him,
To his imagined love,
Imagined comfort.
No! You cry,
Reaching out to him
As he once again fastens
His claws into your heart,
Mercilessly intent on making you learn
A lesson that may very well
Kill what is left of you...
And your soul.

Katrina Kohl

Watcher Of The Night

In the dreary darkness of the night,
Where evil runs rampant in the sky,
Forsaken by the guardian of the day,
Replaced by the watcher of the night.

Though her brilliance not as fierce,
Her tender nature wards off fears,
Until the coming of the day,
As we rest in her tender gaze,
She watches over all of us.

Xin Yang

All Alone

As I sit at home
I listen but hear nothing
I keep listening but hear
nothing at all.
Oh but now I do.
It is a car driving down the road.
It is pulling up my drive way.
The lights have turned off,
but no one gets out,
no one comes to my door.
I hear the car start again.
The lights turn back on.
It backs up and drives away.
This life; where did I get it?
Why did God have to pick me for having
this life? Without my consent.
He made his decision
Now I have to live with it.

Toni Michelle Eubanks

Menorah (Love Of God And Man)

As I gaze on the gentle beauty
of the Menorah.
I think of the might power
in the love of God.
As I light the candles
one by one, day by day
for eight days,
to this magnificent God,
I fold my hands in prayer,
my heart leaps with joy to Hanukkah.

Helen A. Cook

"You Remind Me Of A Rose"

You remind me of a rose
A rose that is however unique
I know I can think of you
Whenever things are bleak.

Your beautiful smell
Is something to be adored
And your wonderful face
It can never be ignored.

Your soft, sensitive touch
As fragile as a rose
Gives me goosebumps on goosebumps
From my head to my toes.

And when picking roses
There's always that special one
That's how I feel about you
Your warmth is like the sun.

You remind me of a rose
A rose that is truly unique
A soft, sweet, beautiful rose
A rose I have always seeked.

Jeffery Anderson

Reality

Mine is past,
    With the present here
The future is not mine to consider.

In my past I dwell,
    With the present here
The future is another tomorrow.

My past is my truth,
    With the present here
I walk backward toward the future.

I try but I can't, to leave my past
I ask the future to hurry by
That it may become mine...

Mine is past
    With the present here
The future is not mine to consider.

Mary Marvel

God's Right

It's always hard
to say goodbye
when someone we love had to die.

God had his reason,
God has his right,
to take him home
and snuggle him tight.

Even though
we don't understand,
God is the one
who is in command.

So don't forget,
God has his reason,
and God has his right!

Canaan Lee Vallejos

Music

Loud, soft
Calms, excites, mellows
It opens people's hearts
People's soul food

Jennie Joana Linn

My Lord

The poem I have
Is about You, Lord.
The soldiers nailed You down
Across a big board.
You did nothing at all
But the people accused You.
I'm sorry I put
All this misery to You.
You died for my soul,
Oh, thank You, my Lord.
I'm sorry I put You
To death across a board.
But fate intervened.
My soul became white.
I think of You, Lord,
Everyday and night.
Lord, have mercy on me!

Stephanie Kolcz, Age 11

I've Never Seen...

I never saw another butterfly
Reality quit the game
Even if the butterfly soars
I'll never be the same.

I never saw another butterfly
Since when does seeing count?
For in my mind I have an image
That plays across my heart.

I never saw another butterfly
With colors true to sight
With freedom free upon the air
As its fragile wings take flight.

I never saw another butterfly
But can I? Just this once?
To open my eyes from the dark
And know there still is life.

I never saw another butterfly
And probably I still won't
But in my mind it's floating there
Against the breeze; a simple hope.

Kamila Bergen

Alone

I stand alone, all alone;
No one wants to listen.
No one really cares.
Where do I turn?

I turn to my parents;
It's just not the same.
They're old and won't understand.
Where do I turn?

I try to talk to a friend;
They don't care or have time.
Too many of their own problems.
Where do I turn?

I turn to a book;
It's all about my problems.
The suggestions just wouldn't work.
Where do I turn?

There is God;
He's been waiting there all along.
Dying to hear my problems.
That's where I need to turn!

Shelley Molleur

I Need A Friend

I need a friend
who listens, I need
a friend who cares.
Someone who is,
sweet and kind,
and that knows
my mind.
Tall or short
it doesn't matter.
As long as they'll
be there before and
after. Maybe it's
impossible, maybe
it's true but I'm
still waiting for a
friend like
You!

April Ryan

Nature's Bower

See the Celtic witch
in Autumn's tree,
her flaming hair
flurrying free.
Hear her scream
in Winter's snow,
her soul forever
in overthrow.
The grace and beauty
in silent death,
and nature's acceptance,
does take my breath.
Though suffering of souls
in freezing hour,
reveals the horror
in nature's bower.

Alan C. O'Leary

Remembering

He took off on one last flight
   his Lord had called him home
No time to say "hello, goodbye"
   no time for him to roam

Up there in the great beyond
   he got his special wings
And as he put them on
   a choir of angels sings

No time for tears or despair
   although we may be sad
Just think about the happy time
   and all the joy he had

Now he's up there with the Lord
   and though we need to cry
For he was taken suddenly
   no time to say, "Goodbye"

We will remember him I know
   he was a special one
A friend, a husband, father too
   and most of all a son

Frances Milkey

Night Noises

I hear the wind in the night
   I can't go to sleep.
The wind "shhhs" in the night
And sometime it says my name.

Michelle L. Jacovino

Of Silver

Now that your hair
Is of silver, Mom
I will carry you
For you
Have carried me long enough

I'll buy a chariot
Made of special gold
We'll ride and ride and ride
Into a wonderland made just for
You and me

The finest of foods
Your favorite perfume
We'll enter upon a world of
Beauty and art

And in return, mom;
Just sing that song to me

You know, the one you always sang
Since I was little
Alone just you and me
I love you, you're my mom

Ann L. DeMasi

Eternity

Where is that golden hair
it belonged to my love, so rare

Quietly, laying underground
that is where he can be found

I shed my tears, I know not why
for someday, I too will die

When they ask where I lay
"By him, by him," they will say

Side by side we will be
my love and me

Then we will be truly free
our souls together for eternity

So cry no tears when I have passed
for now, we are together at last.

Cheri L. Hennerberg

Pieces Of The Puzzle

We drift through narrow alleys
not knowing where we go
A maze of false promises
with nothing yet to show

The pictures of the puzzle
are sometimes hard to see
When you don't have all the pieces
of what is meant to be

My Fall is fast approaching
Spring is far behind
Fear of future memories
and dreams I'll never find

My Heart is often bound
by those without a Key
Or left completely barren
by those who are not free

And so we keep on searching
for that special seed,
To plant in fertile soils
the Love we sorely need.

Brian W. Harvie

A Curse

Cursed with eyes that see too much,
Cursed with hearing ears,
Cursed with hands that cannot touch,
Cursed with never ending tears.

Can you not see? We feel!
We wait for kindness still.

Cursed with ever-thinking mind,
Cursed with passions, ne'er fulfilled,
Cursed with angels that are blind,
Cursed with ground to ne'er be tilled.

We live for you, it's true!
You may shun, but we serve you.

Cursed will as weak as sand,
Cursed to never find the love,
Cursed to roam an empty land,
Cursed to never reach above.

Please understand, we love, we love!

Kenneth Pike

Love Just Given Away

My family gathers round me
For pearls of advice.
But oftentimes I wonder
Will one time do. Or twice?
I harp, I nag. I badger.
Please listen, I fervently say.
For nothing is as vital
As love just given away.
We have one life to savor.
One chance to make it last.
If I can grant one favor.
I'd slow it down and cast
A spell upon my loved-ones.
Forget life's problems. Please.
Just give unto each other.
Your life will pass with ease.
'Cause if we love forever.
No conditions will keep us still.
Regrets cannot contain us.
Contentment surpasses will.

Jill G. Pounders

Eagles

The days are short, the nights are long
With memories so dear
I think upon the eagle's flight
The vision very clear

We flew up long, we flew up high
We soared up through the clouds
With wings unfurled, with all our might
And our hearts beating proud

We locked as one as eagles do
I could not let you go
We feel together through the clouds
Our being all aglow

So little time, so much to love
The time flew by so fast
And when time came to let you go
I tried to hold you past

I'll always hold the memory
Deep within my heart
Of Eagles plunging to the earth
Forever, now, apart

Ernest W. Daniel

Too Young

She's too young
To go through this;
She's only fourteen.
She's just a child.
She's a little queen.
Where are her parents?
And where's the man
That gave her this bundle
Cradled in her hands?

She's too young
To be this;
She's only fourteen.
She's just a child.
She's a little queen.
She's a mother now.
And will always be.

Heidianne L. Thames

Friends

Everyone needs a friend these days
so find a friend today
friends are people who
are there for you
and know what you're going though
everyone should have a friend
to help you through now and then
you help them
they help you
and that's what all friends should do.

Callie Dean

The Gift Of Life

Yes, the gift of life is precious
in God's sight, for only Jesus
can give that we may live.
Traveling near or traveling afar,
Jesus is everywhere we are.
Whether we're good or bad, he'll
give us a helping hand.

Always remember, whatever you put
into life that you will get in return.
So, don't throw away that precious
gift from above for we know
it's a gift of divine love.

Sharon Y. Wilson

Somber Thoughts

Somber thoughts fill the air
Thoughts truly unfair

A man in a suit
He plays his magical flute

The drowning sensation
Not just an infatuation

Softly petals wilt
Falling into silt

The lonesome dove cries
While off her mate flies

Smoke fills the room
He dies a groom

Talia Dispensa

Follow Your Heart

Love is uncatchable
As the aroma in the air
It is gone tomorrow
but for today it is here.

Most times it is here
Right in front of our eyes
But most of us are too blind to see
What there really could be.

If more people let
their heart take the lead
there would be less guessing
And more of what we need.

Love is a true feeling
and must be felt from the heart
Not from what they look like
Or what others thought.

Follow your heart
And it will lead
You to a place
that everybody needs.

Marita Eksevics

I Dropped My Heart

I dropped my heart
to see if it would break again.

I looked at it —
A dent here, a chip there,
and, of course,
there were cracks all through.
But it was still in one piece.

I don't know what to make of it!

Junerwanda Papaeliou

Distance Between Us

I can only fight so long
I am growing weak
I place it in the Lord's hands
Because I am so meek.

I know it is not my will
but the Lord's to be
I want you all to know
it's only temporary.

Someday once again
we will together be
but this time with no suffering
no pain from you or me.

So for awhile
I will part
to our Father's house I go
but I'll leave with you the memories
of how I loved you so.

Susan Lapp

You And I

Until you come into my life,
 I never knew,
That could care about anyone
The way I care about you...
 And little did I realize
How happy I could be
Until I fell in love with you
And fell in love with me!

Jessica A. Hoke

Sean's Song

Close your eyes, my little one
It's time for you to sleep.

Jesus is watching over you,
And there's nothing to fear.
So listen to the falling rain
And rest your weary head.

Dream sweet dreams, my little one
It's time to close your eyes

Jesus is watching over you,
And there's nothing to fear.
So listen to the falling rain
And rest your weary head.

It's getting late, my little one
And it's time for you to sleep
So close your eyes, my little one
And go to sleep

Debbie Brissette

Polar Bear

I have a polar bear
Who lives in the frigadare
He comes out at night
To find miss right
He eats all the food
Which puts my mom in a bad mood
His snow, white fur has a nice touch
He's really gentle
And I love him very much

Sarah Christy

Those Hands

I hate those hands,
I told them to stop,
I screamed and pleaded,
But they would not.

They did what they wanted,
They didn't care about me
The hands scarred me for life,
I wonder, "Did they even see?"

They hurt me inside out,
They made me cry,
He used those hands to rape me,
I wonder why.

Natalie Haynes

Childish Laugher

Their laughter is the
sound of an angel's song,

Smile shining brighter than
the morning sun,

Innocence reflected in every
movement and spoken word.
Time flies changing babies
to adults in the blink of
an eye,
Precious moments like these
are but a few,
So with what time I have been given.

I will always cherish the
sound of childish laughter
and smiles from my babies so dear.

Michelle Patrick

Why Don't You Love Me

I'm in Love
but he doesn't love me
I look up above
just to see stars twinkling at me
I pray every night
that he'll soon come to love me
just in spite
of what can and cannot be
all he says is
baby I care for you
it doesn't take a math whiz
to add two and two
this love is all in my head
it's not goin' to happen
I'd be better off dead
while he's lying there napping
why do I put up with him
why won't I move on
because I love him
sooner or later he'll be gone

Andrea Owens

Dreams

When I was young I had big
dreams, of a ranch and cattle
and a lot of things.
Now I'm in my teens, and I
still have my dreams,
but now they are of cowboys
and other things.
Now I'm in my prime for
dreams I have no time for
now I am old and very
slow, so where did all
those dreams go?
Why! in my heart to keep and hold.

Bonnie Raley

Dragon Of Love

Life to me
As Hell it breathes,
Soon to be
As no one sees.

A dragon roars
His breath of end.
Death to me
He soon will send.

Your living presence
Brings to me
Love, then hate-
Which will I be?

This dragon, so near,
Loved dear by me,
Is you my love.
I'd die for thee.

Shannon C. Clark

Untitled

Whisper;
in a absence of words.
All that is,
a flutter of wingtips
across the soul.
Stained glass still conducts heat.

Paul Ray

A Moment In Time

The vows go unbroken
the promise still true
Wishing only in my mind
what life could be anew
Wondrous was the beginning
with caring, love, and concern
Time has stolen the magic
and left nothing in return
No words can ever change it
the hurt that we both feel
Somehow we must move past that
if we ever are to heal
Life has taught a lesson
though we don't understand the rhyme
It is hard to accept we've lost it...
Our one moment in time.

Vicki Taylor Berry

"I Had A Dream"

I had a dream the other
night. I saw your face
in the mirror. Although,
you didn't smile I could
still see the love in
your eyes. You faded in
and out and as I watched
I felt my heart began
to slow and miss beats!
I tried to grab you
and you faded
completely. My heart
stopped!

Mary Louise Hudspeth

Stay True

Tear drops from the sky,
And if you leave,
I will be living a lie.
A lie you will never believe,
Not to be told,
Forbidden love will never be sold.

So if you love being in love,
And if these words fall from above,
Out of a sky that's baby blue,
Just remember...
Stay True.

Vicki Klein

Rain

The rain softly patters
on the window. All of a
sudden it stops. You run
out of the door. You play on
the wet fresh grass. The
air smells sweet. You go
in. Just as you go through
the door it begins to
rain again. Just as you
think it will never end.
The clouds spread, to
see the sunset once
more again.

Amy Garrick

What Color Am I?

Do you see me,
   What color am I?

Look into my eyes,
   What color am I?

Look into my face,
   What color am I?

Look into my heart,
   What color am I?

Look into my soul,
   What color am I?

I am the color not of my skin,
But of emotions and love.
For love sees no color,
Emotion has no color.

Sarah Kay Ault

I Want A New Life

I want a new life,
this one won't work.
It's cracked and it's scarred
and I'm going berserk.
I want to be royalty
and have my own jet,
with money and power,
a giraffe for a pet.
I'm fed up with average,
I'm tired of normal.
I want fancy dinners,
and a party that's formal.
I want people to ask me
what I have to say
and wonder if I'm
having a good day.
So I'm taking my life in for a refund,
and I'd like an exiting,
adventurous new one.

Meredith Larson

Willow

You stand with your face
to the north wind,
beautiful Lord,
arching under the stars,
mantle of ever-emerald vines,
ribbon of river beside you.

You stand with your back
to the high spires,
you upon your throne,
green green golden-leafed hassock,
tall under the stars,
king who weeps a hundred years,
your eyes beholding everything.

Gerise Francies

Peace Dies

A dove soars in the sky,
   The sign of peace flies in.
The dove crosses the field,
   The sign of peace flies in.
The shots ring out,
   The sign of peace flies in.
The dove falls dead to the ground.
   In a world of violence, peace dies.

Jason Owens

Mother

I remember mother.
She raised me,
She fed me,
She dressed me,
She cared for me,
I remember mother.
I remember mother.
She was a comforter.
She was a doctor.
She was a giver.
She was a friend,
I remember mother.
I remember mother.
She prayed for me,
She watched me,
She guarded me,
She loved me,
I remember mother.

Jenny Smith

Capitalism

I dreamed of the future
of land that was very cold,
where everything there
could be bought or sold.

From the Brooklyn Bridge
to a babes first breath.
To a fake gold watch
from a hubby's foul death.

Nothing there is sacred.
No. Nothing. Not at all.
If you have the money,
someone has the gall.

If you could catch it in a bottle,
or cut it with a knife.
You could but it in this land.
A nation, filled with strife.

With the only moral, greed,
and the only God made of gold,
remember, everything you have
can be bought or sold.

A. B. Altyr

People

Everyone is different,
Everyone is unique,
Everyone is special,
and everyone is great!

You could be white,
or black,
or yellow
or maybe even blue!

Everyone has at least
one thing special about them,
which of course is,
  Being You!

Julie D. Polovina

Untitled

I look, and I see
I listen, and I hear
I sniff, and I smell
I taste, and I taste
I touch, and I feel
  But is it real?

Ross Chamberlain

Janus

Unrelentless charmer of Shylock,
Slithering from 'neath roguery rock;
Ere cometh the dawn of a new day,
With credence for a fresh foray.

You, who practice to deceive,
Come one, come all, take your leave;
Vulnerable and stupid am I
Who falls prey to every lie.

Prince of darkness...entreat me,
With your beguiling repartee.
Alone, all alone, though wary,
So bruised, yet a willing quarry.

Take my love, take my life,
Yes, oh yes, I'll be your wife.
So begins the helpless gyre,
Drowning in brief 'tho fervent desire.

And when that consuming passion dies,
Ere bloometh the trellis of latent lies.
Gone, gone is his guileless glow,
To do, what to do with this male ego?

Catherine M. Larsen

Why?

Au Mee, Au Mee, me,
what a wonderful day.
Puppies playing,
kittens meowing,
yes, it's a wonderful day,
I'm shining.
Beautiful trees and plants.
So, why oh why,
do people want to ruin it?

Agnes P. Baker

The Painter

He loathes
The light
The darkness
The painters domain

The colors of Satan's world:
Blacks sulfurous yellows
Fill his creations

With virgin-blood red
The painter begins another

Pureness
Unmarred whiteness
Lay before him
Asking for his touch

The canvas
Innocent
Unaware
Of evil

He readies
His brush
For the defilement

Jenny Chambers

No Mo'

Past loves.
  Built on old songs.
    Love sings, lost songs.
  Sing to me no more.
    For now, I am the writer.

Vickie J. Oliver

A Poem To You From Me

I can't sing you a song,
  nor bring you the sun.
But you know I would,
  if it could be done.
I can't bring back yesterday,
  and make it tomorrow.
I can't put happiness
  in place of sorrow.
There are so many things
  I can't do.
But what I've done,
  I've done for you.

Brenda Webster

The Earth Is...

Rock, planet floating in space
turning around the sun
A man's home
filled land fills
filthy air
dirty streets
trash everywhere
a summary
you're asking me for a summary
pollution
think about killing
helpless defenseless animals
this is our planet
this is also their planet
what about the next generation
destroying their home
will there be another one
I think not
This is our only home
cherish, protect, respect it

Travis Brooks

Day By Day

Oh, just think of all the things
we do everyday
that affect our lives
day by day.

Some of us have it easy
some of us have it hard
either way, we pray
we have a good day.

Whether it be rain or sunshine
let's make the best of our day
by helping one another
every which way we can...

J. Aldon Fruge

Beyond The Dream

A row of fallen angels
the shadows of the nights
covered my soul
beyond the dream
beyond the veil
my teacher said:
Do not forget
your karmic lesson
beyond the dream
the knights of dawn
are coming back
with empty hands
the rainbow's drawn
by eastern winds
the butterflies in blossom

Magdalena Pop

Untitled

Don't look.
You looked.
Don't look again.
You looked again.
Well then go ahead and look.
Big deal nobody cares.
I Do!
See?
But don't look!

David Fryar

New Day

Under all the hate,
I rise
to see a new day
against all the rage,
all the injustice,
all the province,
I rise
to see a new day
with all the
pressure
of friends,
family, death
gangs, and God
still,
I rise
to make a brand
new day.

Anthony Berzoza

Questions

How fast can you go when you're
going down a ski slope...

How fast can you go when you're
jumping rope?

Are you in a race...
do you have to go at a certain pace?

Do you like what you doing...
do you like what you see?

Are you having fun...
do you feel free?

Are you whooshing by like a fire fly?

Are you bored with my questions?
Well here are some suggestions.
I could say goodbye or sing a lullaby.

Jennifer Vinson

"An Innocent Beauty"

I hear gunshots in a distance,
And my body starts to shudder,
Who could kill something so innocent,
One that adds music to the sky.

I watch them play in the meadow,
And I have to laugh out loud,
They remind me a lot of children,
They need their playtime just as well.

How could anyone kill a bird,
Just to pin their feathers to a wall,
They think it's something macho,
But I think it weakens their soul.

Sara Matayoshi

Auch Das Shone Muss Sterben

I walk through darkness
In the midnight hour,
And creatures that
Do not exist
In the daylight
Walk beside me
And give me solace.
We have no name
But that of night,
And we have no love,
But the love of those
We've lost.

Derrick L. Hassert

For You

Through all the bad,
And along with the good,
I'll be here for you.

With whatever comes,
and whatever goes,
I'll be here for you.

If you need to talk,
or just to cuddle,
I'll be here for you.
All because I want to be with You!

Joshua Eagleson

My Heart

I cry with my tears
  ...not with my eyes.
I listen with my heart
  ...not with my ears.
I answer with my thoughts
  ...not with my lips.
I feel with my emotions
  ...not with hands.
I love from my heart
  ...not from my body.

Kristen Pancio

Last Night

Against the bobbing ship
Waves tap a soft heartbeat
Mingling with the silent breathing
Of the girl. Both embrace me.

Her perfume mixes with salty air
And cuddles with me.
Our Hawaii passes farther away;
Soon we will be apart.

I hold her close, savoring
The sweet moment
And soon that too is gone.
I know I will miss her.

Austin Nichols

Eternity

Like a black fire,
Burning at the end of a tunnel,
Darker than a thousand midnights,
At the bottom of the ocean,
Or the reaches of outer space,
Like a black hole,
Eternity lingers on the edge of forever.

Krista J. D'Amico

Nature

I love the trees
Even the bees

The flowers so pretty
They grow like a city

The grass so tall and green
It can always be seen

Listen to the birds sing
Nature is such a beautiful thing!

Ashley Blanco

Understanding After

Keep your chin up high
  For someday you'll know why
You went through what you did
  Lift your spirits up kid

By looking to "Our Father" above
  For there's no greater love
He will not only stay awhile
  He'll help to keep a smile

On your pretty little face
  'Til we meet at "His Place"
Where there's never anymore pain
  And there we'll finally gain

What we so long waited for
  Answers to all our questions or
Just be glad we make it there
  Remember you are very special dear

Betty J. Dayhoff

Summer

Summer is a time to hear
the birds sing or play in
the rain to sit and watch
the daisies grow and after
that on a rainy-day just
feels good under my hood and
watching the rain say good-bye
then I go upstairs and say
my prayers to the stars and
the moon and I let myself
be put to sleep by the song
of the loon.

Sarah Scire

Sorrows Path

We stand idle, watching,
  as our worlds turn.
Futures are dimming,
  growing harder to cope.
The past is our teacher,
  though we don't seem to learn.
Years sliding by slowly,
  draining our hope.
"What can be done?"
  We ask our souls.
Times so short,
  our twisting minds yearn.
"Government will save us!"
  Shouts unseeing fools.
We sit idle, watching,
  as our worlds burn.

Todd James Root

Stage Life

The stage is set
The lights come on
A hush comes over the crowd
You know your lines and your moves
Sweat collects upon your brow.

The curtains open
The crowd applauds
Then you walk on stage.
You've worked too hard
And rehearsed too long
To forget your lines now.

The show is over
You were a hit!
The crowd roars with delight
They give you a standing ovation
And yell "More! More! More!"
The director smiles at you
And gives you a thumbs up sign.
Your peers come out and bow with you
You've had a really good time.

Amanda Ivey

"Your Pain"

I want to tell you that I always know,
the feelings that you try and hide.
I always feel what you feel,
and the pain hurts me inside.

I wish you would confide in me,
your troubles and your thoughts,
I wish that you felt like you could,
to me that's what you taught.

I love you more than words can say,
and it hurts me to see you sad.
Because for you I care a lot for,
and I feel so very bad.

I hope in the future we'll be honest,
and the truth we'll always tell.
Because everything will be better,
and all is well that ends well.

Nicole Connelly

Emotions

Screaming words of anger,
that burn like a red hot coal!
Can rob you of your dignity,
And crucify your soul!
Lying innuendo,
Reap scars that never heal!
Spawn by tongues of wickedness,
No one dare reveal!
Laughing at the tortured,
And those who do without.
Blackening the pure of heart,
And spreading grief throughout!
Logic based on ignorance,
And having one's own way!
Consumes a heart with evil,
Leaving lives in disarray!

Chris Godbee

Time

Time can be a day
Time can be an hour
Time can be a minute
But the best part of time
Is what you do in it

Rose Ann Ricci

Youth

I am curious.
I wonder about everything.
I hear what I want to hear.
I see what I want to see.
I want to know all the answers,
to all the questions.
I am curious.

I pretend to know everything.
I feel all the pain in the world.
I want to touch all the people
with what I say.
I worry about everything.
I cry when I hurt.
I am curious.

I understand some things.
I say what comes to mind.
I dream of the world being kind.
I try to help others.
I hope to succeed.
I am curious.

Amy Elizabeth Park

Who I See

I see trees, and grass
The flowers in bloom
I see the moon, sky, sun, and stars
As they shine down upon our hearts
I see the oceans of blue
Seas, rivers, and streams
Meadows, fields, with morning dew
All that beauty
I see love
I see you

Susan Zakusylo

Dark Angels

With every thoughtful move,
their wings -
like silver screens
reflect the human
poem.
Art, rhythm, motion, dance
are united
as the dark angels dance
beneath His golden moon.
The secret is revealed
as life's greatest meaning
claims the spirit...
and ushers these children
to their deserved
end.

Karen Elford

Words

Words spoken with sharp
daggers,
feared but often ignored
Lack of frequency,
reason for committal
Degradation, humiliation,
saturation
Deeper and deeper we
believe
Ignorance rules the situation
Moderation does not mean
justification

Amy L. Valvo

Full Moon Rising

Full moon rising, nighttime falling
Death and darkness come a-calling.
Dark wolves howl, night wind blows
Death at night when ravens crow.
Corpses rise up from their graves
Nightmare soldiers raise their staves.

Come forth heroes, death awaits.
Slowly opening blackened gates
Sword in hand, make your stand
against the evil of this land.

Foolish heroes, you shall die!
You know it's futile for you to try
To destroy my army of the dead
'Ere you know, we'll have your heads!

Valiant heroes, take your swords,
Make a stand against the hordes
Strike fast and true, for it is you
Who shall be victorious.
Oh, honor great and glorious
The champions shall be you!

Ricardo Gutierrez

Torn Asunder

Perfect gold rings
eternally
encircling
divided souls
Until death do us part

Angry distant voices
like heavy winds
howling
It's over!

Red orange flames
suffocating
scattering
blue violet black ashes
of dead love

Two heartbeats
dance
out of rhythm purposely

Forever

Deborah Gayton

Wither

You breath I cry, You live and I die.
Alone I sit, alone am I.

Hidden in your private palace our
relationship a deadly malice.
My body breaks as my crumbling soul
lives in ache. Bitter are my memories,
sweet are what they used to be.

Closed my eyes I wished for peace all
my dreams just get beat. So down at
your level I feel so low, only God
can lift me up to glow.

Tears of shame you're to blame, the
life you live is not the way. All day
I'll sit and pray for the strength
to get away.

God knows the one you are, the hell
I've live is not so far for you to
see the death in me for you will
certainly be....

Shannon Conley

If You Will

Listen my friend what I'm trying
to say - forget past hurts - wipe
them away. Forgive every wrong that
been done unto you. Give place to
God's love so he'll forgive too, put
past hurts behind you; yours - and
then others - Cover it all with God's Blood
that gives Grace to all Brothers.
Give away all your rights to what
you think is fair - This Gift known as Life
is a waiting right there. Open your eyes
to the power of Truth; your ears to his Word,
and Love as a youth if you will;
Then no matter what the future holds -
Love holds The Future.

Norma L. Mitchell

For All My Greatest Words

For all my greatest words, however
fancy they dance, are always
naked. To ever mourn the death
of a sentence; why waste your
precious time? I waste because
those are the words spoken so
true to the tee. My biggest
novel has yet to spill its story.
The excess lies in a pond so
dull and cold. The depths of
my paragraphs will write you
into a corner of treachery. Blinded
you are, by the words of shallow
thinkers. Encompassed by the
thoughts of a depth, engulfed
short story.

Erin Gironda

One More Day

Oh Lord help me
to make it one more day. With your
love and grace I know is the only way.

Your strength has carried
me all the way and without your
mercy there's no telling where I would
be today. I know I would have surely
lost my way.

Oh Lord help me
to make it one more day.

You have helped me
climb the highest mountain and picked
me up when I was in the lowest valley;
and when I stumbled you lifted
me up with your Love and Grace as
only you can do. Oh Lord thank you
for helping me along my way.

Your love and grace has
carried me all the way. Oh Lord
help me to make it one more day.

Gale Horner

Execution

The pain I feel is your pain
the pain you feel is my pain
lets pray and hope the future
is brighter for all of us
for the ones that are
left behind.

Richard F. Hall

Where Angels Come

I see a place where angels come
To sing their songs and pray
There is a shining light of love
For all who come that way!

Come that way
Oh, come that way
Come that way, today!

Shining light
Oh, shining light
Shining light of love!

Angels come
Oh, angels come
Angels come and pray!

Sing their songs
Oh, sing their songs
Sing their songs today!

Sieglinde Manns

Shows The Wayward

Lord Byron baron
Love struck pigeon
Beethoven's beautiful
wordlessness
the outcasts are the
caste solace the
surrogate Mothers of man
but to true the element
in believing battery
when the arts collide with stars
a man's mind filled with
shapes of Jazz
solitude in this
bite me sunrise I've
eaten your day (jump).

Thadd Taylor

Tragic Hero

Oh! How I admire you tragic hero.
How you lived with us, I don't know.
You showed me the greatest strength
and courage of all.
You! The son of God, You!

Having all the power to do
Anything you wanted to us.
Yet! You remained so humble,
So peaceful and calm.

We were so cruel to you,
Spitting on you and insulting
Your sweet soul.
Brutalizing, and finally killing you.
And you love us still? Hum!
What love you have.

Jonelle M. Corridon

Trees

Trees are green. Trees
are pretty. Trees can also
help us in our city. Trees
are tall and skinny and there
the rainforest people like to
cut down, and when I think
about that it makes me want
to frown.

Jenny Suttles

Peace Maker

There lives a peace maker
in every town, state, and country.
A person who makes cuts, and
ouches better. A person who
cools down arguments between
two little children. A person
who's always wearing a smile.
A person like this is always
with me day and night, to
comfort me when I'm sad.
You might not call her what
I call her.
But I know I call her "Mom".

Chauniquewvah Thompson

Poems

Poems make up a story
that you could love your whole
life and still write more about
your imagination it could be
believing in Santa, Easter Bunny,
tooth fairy, or fairy tales, your
imagination can take you
anywhere and could land on a
paper, for whatever your heart
believes in a poem could tell
the story.

Jelena Rudela

Rose

Like a
   Rose
Life comes and goes

Like a
   Rose
Love comes and goes

But like that
   Rose
Your presence lingers on
  but unlike that
Rose
You are forever gone

Tenorzelle Sturtevant

Love Song

Hold me close all through the night
Be my love song as the day brings light
Time slips away so quickly
So the love song goes
But time is what it is that sings
As the love song grows.
Together we are a love song
And day by day we grow.
You are the only love song
That I will ever know.
You are the music of this love song
Without you we would not sing
Together we are a love song
A song that has no end
Because time will last forever
And the music will play on
Lets spend our time together
And sing our own love song.

For Louie
Love Leslie

Leslie Bell

Who Am I, Not Knowing

From a baby to a teenager
I was never alone
Then I married and
had children of my own

The children grew up
and went on their way
They didn't need my help
or the advice I had to say

Now as a senior, tired, frail,
old and gray
I wonder who will call
or stop by today

Sitting here with memories
of all the years gone past
will my loneliness cause
my life to fade real fast

When my life started out
I questioned where am I going
Now that my time is running short
I wonder "who am I, not knowing"

Lottie Cox

Mama Left In The Spring

It was an ordinary summer day;
The wind was there, July.

The house was clean and free;
Mama was there, Happy.

She had her hands on her hips;
I was there, Looking.

Then, she was throwing up;
Sickness was there, Visiting.

We went to the doctor;
He was there, Helping.

We came home;
Everyone there, Waiting.

We went to the doctors again;
Cancer was there, Killing.

Fall came quickly, then Winter;
The Sunset was there, March.

She was dying;
I was there, Crying.

She left in the Spring, March 31;
Death was there, Taking.

Coywinna Jones

Anasazi Dream

I wake to find
  my water jug is broken,
    potsherds peppered with dry sand.

I wake to find
  my sandals are brittle,
    braided cord opens in my hand.

I wake to find
  my home has fallen,
    stone blocks ageing where they land.

I sleep to find
  my Anasazi dream.

Jack Vernon Nims

Cosmic Sailor

I'm a lovesick cosmic sailor
The starry sky my stormy sea
My starship, my Spanish galleon
Won't you sail the stars with me?

The universe is full of wonder
Many times I've been amazed
I'd put it all asunder
For your warm and tender gaze

Sails unfurled I sail this ocean
I'm lightyears from my home
Set course then I'll be watchin'
Tomorrow I won't be alone

One day now till I see you
Hope to find you safe and sound
Just now I'm passing Neptune
Time to slow this spacecraft down

I'm a lovesick cosmic sailor
The starry sky my stormy sea
My starship, my Spanish galleon
Won't you sail the stars with me?

Nelson A. Koshuta

Time

Time is so little
Time is not slow
Time has no stop it's on the go
If you're waiting for morning
It'll be here in a jiff
If you're waiting for night
Don't jump off a cliff
One minute you're two
The next you're twenty-four
Please take my advice
Do I need to say more
So use time wisely
Don't use it like a fool
Time is a precious thing
It's definitely at rule

Lindsey Fisher

About Peelin' An Onion

Now I've a great big husband
  with a great big head
who can do anything.
  Or so he said!

So, one day in our little kitchen
  thinkin' 'twould do no harm...
he was a helpin' me with the cookin'
  like I did down on the farm...

I found I needed an onion
  so I asked him very nice
if he would cut one up for me...
  either minced or diced.

Imagine my surprise to see
  when I checked on him...
he had cut up that ole onion
  leavin' on its skin!

He thought 'twas how I did it,
  and after all these years...
the tears I was a' cryin'
  were sure not onion tears!

Eunice Yordy Hoover

Sometimes

Sometimes I wonder,
why do people not care?
Sometimes I wonder,
why is life not fair?

Sometimes I think,
is it really all worth it?
Sometimes I think,
maybe I should just quite.

Sometimes I feel,
like I am alone.
Sometimes I feel,
as if I should leave home.

Sometimes is a word,
that often enters my life.
Sometimes is a word,
that can feel like a knife.

There is no end
to sometimes you see.
Just the end of time
for you and me.

Elizabeth Hensley

Our Togetherness

When we are together
There is a special force
That binds us as one.

It is so strong, so beautiful,
So wonderful and warm
While it lasts.

Our togetherness can be
Felt by each other's tender touch.

It draws us together
By its magic force
And we can't resist its power,
Oh, our togetherness
How sweet and heavenly it is;
It puts our hearts a-fire
As it binds us as one.

Carolyn L. Edgerley

Memorial Day Salute

Out to save their country
They marched through the land
So desperate for freedom
Barely able to stand
With their bloodstained clothes
And their flag raised high
They fought through the war
Which many didn't survive
Thinking back on this tragic
War or despair
We heave a big sigh
And are glad we aren't there
Proud that our country
Is finally free
They won independence!
They fought long you see
So on Memorial Day
Let's all raise a cheer
For those brave soldiers
Who allowed us to be here!

Andrea Speir

Magic Dream

A rainbow is a perfect arc
of colors clear and bright
a mysterious band of beauty
that draws darkness into light.

My fervent wish is to touch a rainbow
and wonder how it would feel
this burst of perfect color
that magically appears unreal.

Where else does beauty loom so regal
as summer rains refresh her beams
I may never get to touch a rainbow
but have done so many times in dreams.

Lizanne Conte

My Special Place

I need to find a special place,
A special place for me.
I need to find a special place,
Where my troubles are wee.

It must be a peaceful place,
Like an autumn tree.
I need to find a special place,
A special place for me.

Brian Arthur

My Summer Afternoon

Reflection of light down on my face
Cool breeze flowing through my clothes
Tanning my yellow skin, golden brown
Sweat drips down my warm face
My freckles on my body turn dark brown
Shorts, and T-shirts worn everyday
Wishing to fit in a bikini someday

Summer is here relax and enjoy
Spunk and energy fill my whole soul
Time flies
Be proud
This season only comes once around

Andrea Moreno

All I Care For

All the money in the world
Could never buy my love,
Even if you promise me
The moon and stars above.
I do not care for diamonds,
I do not care for gold,
All I care for is your love
To warm me in the cold.

Susanna Coronel

Untitled

I always look the other way
Never forgetting that tragic day
The day it was said to be
We are just friends that you and me

Why can't thing be the same
Why must you use my name in vain
You told me it could never be
Now we are foes that you and me

How can I prove to you
What must I say and do
To show that I still love you.

Bryon Derleth

Ginseng

There in the ray of sun,
It stands so bright,
It stands so high,
You look to the North,
You look to the South.
It is here, it is there.
From a seed it is sought.
From there you are caught.
You tell no one, you tell all.
Four prong five prong, little sprouts.
You are here, you are there.
Then there were none.
You took it all.
If it stays from now till then,
You will leave some small.
For if not you'll have to crawl.
Just to find it all.

Charles Crockett

The Beginning

The sun rose above the mountains,
the waves crashed the shores,
A new day was beginning.
The rainbow arched from the mountains,
to the sea.
The kiss from God to his creation.

Amy Michelle Taylor

My Precious Angel

Sent down from heaven,
   Meant just for me.

Helping to heal and mend,
   by love alone.

The worst came out,
   yet the best came in.

And that my dear is you.

When you came in,
   through time has changed,

I found myself,
   and who I became.

Someone special,
   all because of you,
My Precious Angel

Christina Etherington

The Beat Of My Heart

Down a winding rocky trail
You and I walk hand in hand
Beneath a sky of sun-lit beauty
Whose golden rays caress the land

With every loving step that's taken
My tender heart you seem to waken
It beats so hard it seems to shaken
All the earth with its joy

Mab O'Connor

Goodness Streams Forth

Let all your goodness shine
   Like sunbeams streaming forth
To help, guide, and cherish
   All people's minds and hearts.

Susan M. Wysocki

Mariner Health Care

I am a patient of Mariner Health Care
that covers the Palm Bay field.
They offer so many separate things,
the program seems most unreal.

There's the occupational therapist,
The nurses with beepers and smiles.
Two aides that drive from Cocoa.
To me that's many miles.

There's the physical therapist
with heating pads for bones
that are stretched in all directions
in everybody's homes.

There are young and lovely ladies
sent north and west and south,
All trained in different health care
for head to foot and mouth.

There are aides to wash your back,
to groom your hair just right.
The only thing they failed with me,
Just five hours sleep per night.

Bess Huber

Love Is A Rose

A rose withered
Its aroma subtle and sweet
Its likened to our time
So loving and discreet
The past is inflexible
Like a lover's yearn to flirt
And often is fulfilling
As often does one hurt
So my dear friend; don't despair
Over clouds, shadows and scorns
For to love and once be loved
Is as getting roses with their thorns.

Gregory L. Oxidine

One Must Cope

In life one must cope
with problems galore
in one's own life
and in the lives of those
we touch for a moment
or more, presaged by our genes
or circumstances, known or unknown,
accept or not, one must cope!

We are born to accept life.
We are not questioned as to our desire.
We are manipulated forever and ever
And so we live to cope until we tire!

Florence K. Wiener

The Candle

There is a candle in my heart,
   That is burning just for you,
It has been burning for many years
   And my heart shall ever be true.

No matter where our footsteps lead us,
   I never shall forget,
Those many happy, golden hours
   That we as lovers spent.

I never shall forget that I loved you,
   As God meant for us to do,
From now until eternity
   That candle will burn for you.

Ardis M. Morgan

Flowing Friendship

My friend
Remain the ever flowing brook,
Traversing hills and contours.
Still sparkle as
God's rays of sun
Touch you with joy.

Carry the reflections
Of ever strong evergreens,
Of the blue, hopeful sky,
Of the woodland nature,
Of the animals who teach us
Like a gallery for all to see,
With exclamatory ripples.

My friend
Without the beaver's dams,
The torrent floods,
And the storm fallen trees,
To change your direction unexpectedly,
There would be no opportunity to deepen
Your riverly knowledge.

Irene L. Evans

Friendship Garden

We have a Friendship Garden
Where lovely flowers bloom
Some last throughout the season
Others fade away too soon

And, like the flowers which we love
Our friends must leave us, too
When they fulfill life's season
And their time on Earth is through

One such majestic flower
Once did grace our garden wall
And it lent its lovely fragrance
As it stood so straight and tall

But much too soon, a blight did strike
Those gracious petals - Gone!
But, the memory of its fragrance
Will forever linger on

No longer in this garden
But, somewhere up above
Once more it blooms with majesty
In the Garden of God's Love.

Carmela Kostopoulos

Safe Harbor

Twilight bathed,
The mariner's gondola of lace
Sailed over gossamer waves
Into the purple space.

Seraphim and cherubim
A multitude at the helm,
Traveled beyond the luminesce moon
To reach the celestial realm.

Oh, sailor renewed abide.
Gone are your sorrows,
Sad memories of life,
Washed away in eventide.

Come home my beloved,
Child of my ardor.
Rest with me here,
You have reached safe harbor.

Josephine M. McNulty

Dreaming Thunder

I enter a place like no other.
It is called Dreaming Thunder.
Here, "I walk with Spirits
    through murals of mist,
to visit my totem
    in the dreaming place".

Here, I am the truth seeker,
    know me well.
I am the mystery
    from mystic flames.
I am the taw
    that gives birth
to every bard.

Though mortal lifetimes
lie scattered to the fates,
wild winds and storms
    shake and slaughter.
My very presence brings pain,
to the dead who lie
undreaming.

Matissa Whitefeather

Learning

There's more to me than meets the eye,
I'm beginning to understand.
It's what I think and how I feel
That makes me what I am.

Why do I do the things I do
And say the things I say?
What is important, and how do I tell?
I'm learning more each day.

I learn from friends and family,
from work, from play, from school.
I've also learned to take some time
To sit and think things through.

The more I learn, the more I grow,
And then the more I see,
Just how much more I want to know.
The me I'm learning to be!

Melissa Manger

I Am

I feel myself inside of me
I am
I feel my face and arms and toes
I am
I feel my loved one's soft embraces
I am
I feel the pain of soul and body
I am
I feel the seasons by its breezes
I am
I feel and see the trees and plants
I am
I feel within and out from me
I am
One day I'll travel from this world
To what's ahead for all of us
Then I will feel who I was and who
I am

Angelina O. Sanchez

My Friend Jon

He was a dear friend,
A true one indeed.
We laughed and we cried,
And that was all that we needed.

On a hot summer's day
Toward the end of July
An accident killed him
And made me cry.

I sobbed and sobbed,
Thinking my life was all through.
But a friend I did find,
A friend that was new.

We shared all our feelings
Through thickness and thin.
We have so many goals,
Of which we still have yet to begin.

Jon still holds
A place in my heart.
He will always be there;
We will never part.

Robert Lincoln

Dreaming

Every time you spoke, I listened.
Softly your words came out.
Your lips move with every sound
you make. I look into
your stone blue eyes,
which put me in a daze.
Dreaming of you
as I lay in bed.
Always thinking of you; I can't
get you out of my head.
Wishing you were
beside me, I just want
you near. To hold me, love
me, and take away my fears.
I wrote this poem just
for you to know, I love
you, and I will never let you go.

Kristina Memari

The Children

Only the ticking of the clock
seems to break my reverie
of the days of long ago
that again I'll never see

Time was when children's voices
rang loudly out to me
and tiny feet came running
as they played their games with glee

It seems like only yesterday
I calmed their childish fears
held them safety in my arms
cuddled and wiped away their tears

Now the house is quiet
no dolls or toys do I see
or rooms filled with laughter
when the children belonged to me

Norma B. Earl

My Win

The sun rises
the fog rolls in
a turkey gobbles
and sends a chill
up your back
you make a call
he answers back
you know in time
you will have him sacked
you wait in anticipation
listening for him to come in
you call again
he answers back
the time is close
you barely breathe
you see him strutting in
to mate a hen
his error is
my win.

Jacob Crismon

Summer

The clouds float by like
Cotton in the wind.
Birds singing as if they
Were performing just for me.

Warm air blows a cool
Breeze my way sweeping
My hair off my back.

A beautiful summer day
In August, one of many
To come and go.

As Autumn approaches
Summer leaves warm
Memories of days gone by.

Barbara Riley

Grandma Loved Jesus

She labored hard for fifty years.
Not missing a single day.
She serviced her God with love.
Now she's a flower in God's bouquet.

The pain is gone from her body now.
No tears run down her cheeks.
For her smile is lighting up heaven.
While all the angels weep.

She laid upon her bed.
Arms folded across her chest.
With a smile upon her face.
She knew Jesus would bring her rest.

Grandma loved Jesus.
She was picked to be a flower in
God's bouquet.
Grandma loved Jesus and holy is
His name.

Alicia L. Fredrickson

Soccer

Soccer
Outdoor, rough
Kicking, scoring, running
Grass, boundaries, sand, team
Hitting, diving, jumping
Indoor, strenuous
Volleyball

Kara Bymers

Untitled

God give me the courage,
to look into your eyes.
To see what you are feeling.
The hidden thoughts,
you won't share with others
The pains you have felt.
The fear you have met.

God give me the courage,
to say what I see.
To determine what I am to you.
To let you know,
what you are to me.

I see only the person
you truly are.
Warm, sensitive of others' needs,
always forgetting your own.
A child that cries to be seen,
A love that wants to be held.

God give you the strength,
to accept what I've seen.

Cathy Mullins

Death Of A Rose

Once so tall
Now with a tilt
Once so strong
Now left to wilt

Through the seasons
It faltered not
Now with the cold
It starts to rot

As it reflects
On seasons past
And of this one-
Its very last

It is not sad
For as it knows
With the cold
Dies every rose

Maxine Taylor

New York Water

Water is crystal clear
A drop comes from the sky
Then more comes down and it goes in
To each reservoir near by
But then more comes falling down.
The drops look like they are flying.
It looks like a beautiful sight.
As I listen to it flow by.

Kamaldai Ramnauth

My Brother

"Oh", that brother of mine.
He makes me laugh all the time.
He's 15 you see.
And he's so dear to me.
He's not my older brother.
He's 3 years younger, not my mother.
He acts that way you see.
Because he tries to mother me.

Char'i Rinkel

If Only

I have a need
A need for you
A need

An emptiness
Where your love should be
Where

No matter what I do
I am pulled back to my lacking
I am

How could one
Leave such a void
Leave

I long for memories
To fill the emptiness
To fill

Anything to fill the emptiness
If only I could fill the emptiness
If only

P. J. Cetee

So

My body dies
slowly by day
by night

But not the flame
spirit
I am

Leaps
in joy
into eternity

Remember
love
me

I have loved
ever
will ever

Love
you

So
I
live

Herman J. Creary

Untitled

i tried with every grain of my soul
tried to please You.
You made me play it
again and
again
and
again
Until finally
You said i wasn't good enough.

Well I went away
and I learned it.
Now I play it
better than you ever could

And I'm laughing,
Laughing at you

But You can't hear me

Maureen Suhr

If You Were Gone

I would be very sorry
  if you should go away,
I do not know how I would smile
  or live from day to day.
I think that I would cry each night
  until I fell asleep,
And all my dreams would only be
  the memories I keep.
The sun would never really shine
  when darkness turned to dawn,
And nothing would be quite the same
  if you were ever gone.
The friendliness of autumn and
  the beauty of the spring,
Would only add a wishful touch
  to my remembering.
I could not find another joy
  to overcome the ache,
And in my utter loneliness
  I know my heart would break.

William H. Graham

"Power Within My Soul"

Boy I need you by my side.
need you to be here with me.
I have fallen head over heels for you.
You're the inspiration of my life.
You're the reason why I live.
You're the hero within my fairytale.
You're the wind beneath my wings.
You raise my head up when I am down.
You give me faith when I don't believe.
When I am so weak that I can't even speak
you give me strength to go on.
Boy as long as I live,
with every breath that I take,
I swear you are the Power
within my soul.

Summer Strickland

Dream Castles

On a warm summer's day
Two lovers hand in hand
On a beach all alone
Building dream castles in the sand.

Each thinking of the other
With a love pure and rare
Dreaming of the future
And the life that they will share.

As the sun sets in the ocean
And the rays sparkle in their eyes
He tells her that he loves her
With a love that never dies.

They run along the beach
As the stars up above
Sparkle their pleasure
At two people in love.

On a warm summer's night
Both lovers up and find
On a beach all alone
Dream castles in their mind.

Pam Bigge

Absence, Pour Kasumi

Petals of the rose,
lying on the ground,
not a sound.

They are aging,
but they do not seem to.

The many winds move them.
Sometimes closer to
each other,
but usually only farther
apart.
Until eventually they are
no longer in the same garden.

One hundred years pass,
before the winds bring them
together again,
but they have not aged
because they are still as
friends.

Curtis Harris

To Those Who Have Loved Me

I know Mom's down there.
She feels so much pain.
September has brought
her October's rain.

Dad knows that I'm safe.
It's only God's plan.
He can't help but cry.
He's only a man.

The teachers who taught me
what little I know
will look at my desk
and my hand will not show.

The kids that I know
think I'm gone for a week.
They will wait at school
to play hide and seek.

So, to those who have loved me,
dry your eyes if you can.
For I've found Someone special
and He's holding my hand.

Sandy Adolphs

To My Friend

I met you for a reason,
My way was not so clear.
I had not seen this lovely spot,
'Had almost been a year.
My life was in such turmoil,
My mind so cloudy too.
I'd not have started thinking,
Had it not been for you.
You helped me gain reflection,
To see the path to take.
I was so lost and lonely,
A friend was there to make.
While walking by the ocean,
You listened to my thoughts.
At that point I realized
The baggage I had brought.
And at that point I did let go,
And truly turned within.
I doubt I could have done this,
Had you not been my friend.

Patricia Lewis

Grandma, What Is Love?

Love Grandma, What Is love?
Is it passion that's in store?
Not just passion, my sweet child,
Love is so much more,

In the heat of magic,
where love and passion meet,
Endearing words are spoken,
of what makes life complete.

Passion mounts in heated play,
within a blaze of fire so real,
But lust confuses love my child,
and that is just: To feel,

Twilight hour has no power
of truth in love or life,
But common day and common play,
amongst daily joy and strife,

Love is conscious effort.
And a pledge of love that's true,
Must each new day begin again
to pledge its love anew.

JoAnn Dena Cantrell

The Shadow Of Life

We seek to find a point of living a
dangerous world. Destroyed thoughts
of the dead past have already been
found. Wishes to be granted but
never are true. Words to be spoken
without having a clue. Angels fly
amongst us watching every move
we make. Our deepest compassion
burned by our mistakes. Caught up in a
web of confusion although the spider
has not finished. The confusion grows
without thought of words. Poisoned
minds, steaming flesh has just begun
by working its way through the
rising sun. Deep and deported blood
from life's wounds are scarred from
hell. To seek and destroy life
without pain leaves us in the darkness
to dwell.

Leslie House

"What If"

What good is my heart;
  if it can not beat for you.
What good is my Love;
  if it is not undividedly yours.
What good is my touch;
  if it can not be touching you.
What good are my eyes;
  if it can not see you.
What good are my hands;
  if I can not touch you.
What good are my arms;
  if I can not hold you.
What good are my ears;
  if I can not hear you.
What good are my lips;
  if they can not be kissing you.
What good is my mind;
  when all I think about is you.
WHAT GOOD AM I WITHOUT YOU!

Charlene Cintron

Halloween

Witches on broomsticks in their
funny black hats.
Black cats are prowling, scarecrows
and bats.

The man in the moon can't believe
his own eyes,
as the kids trick or treat in
their eerie disguise.

Pumpkins in windows with their
big toothy grins light the
way for the goblins to the
goodies within.

So here comes a clown, a ghost,
and there's a Queen,
all to wish you
a Happy Halloween.
Barbara A. Green

Touched

Love,
Joy,
Laughter,
You're touched.

Fun,
Freedom,
Friends,
You're touched.

Books,
Music,
Paintings,
You're touched.

You're touched by all these things,
use them wisely.
Jessica Wick

E-Mail

Nodding his plastic head
And twitching his wire tail,
A user-friendly mouse
Sends you my Soul
Winging
In binary pulses
Across long distance wires.

Strange, you and I, separated,
Come closer now
Than flesh to flesh:
Each sheds his shame,
Electronically.
In spirit only,
We speak our Truth.
Jane B. Willingham

No Friend Of Mine

Pain surely is no friend of mine.
No friend behaves this badly.
Frequently visiting, for days and days,
Not knowing when to go... sadly.
Unexpectedly showing up,
Interfering with special occasions.
Insisting on all of my attention,
Drowning all other sensations.
Blinding me, controlling me,
Causing me to snap and cry.
No... no friend of mine, this pain.
Just a constant companion, gone awry.
Martha Cummins Fischer

Untitled

My mind wanders
 aimlessly,
Drowning in a sea of
 confusion,
Empty thoughts gnaw at
 my soul,
Like so many hungry
 sharks;

Reality an isle just within
 sight,
Yet infinitely out of
 reach;

Love soars above my
 head,
Inches beyond my
 grasp,
Taunting my heart with
 despair,
And eternal loneliness.
Arundel Hunsaker

The Empty House

In a glen where trees stand swaying
By a river ..waters sparkling,
Stands a house alone and silent
Waiting for its lady.

Days of sunshine, rain and breezes
Seasons it with loving kindness
As if time hangs there suspended
Waiting for its lady.

Little wildlife watch in silence
Saddened by this empty haven
Waiting quietly in their thickets
Waiting for their lady.

Soaring birds explore the rooftop
Stopping short to sing their songs
Looking through the darkened windows
Watching for the lady.

In the sky the moon smiles gently
Joins the sun in patient waiting
Clothes the house in warm embraces
Waiting...watching for its lady.
Erma Lee Rachal

Exercise

He climbed the Adirondak,
He climbed "Old Billy's Knee",
A mountain in Kentucky,
As high as you can see.

He thought the hike exciting,
The view he found was fine,
And even 'tho he's now aground,
He sees it in his mind.

He stretches now those muscles,
That make him feel quite wise,
For there is no pain or soreness,
When he simply shuts his eyes.

He may be old, and feeble,
As all his age should be,
Still he can clearly focus,
On the sight that he did see.
Richard L. Fowler

"Mirror"

Deep dark blueness all around,
Cold within everything found;
Same unchanging fickle view,
Always with the perpetual hue.

Illuminated in a fuzzy glow,
Foggy dimness shadows the snow;
Indistinct silhouettes starkly stare,
Burdened by the weight they bear.

Plodding back to the start -
The end is the means to part;
Heard only in silent solitude,
Souls drift in a bruised mood.
Dria Howlett

Cats

Cats are the kind of animal
that soothes a person when
they are feeling down or feeling sick.

Cats are the sparkle in
a diamond or the glimmer in a ruby.

There are many different kinds of cats.
There are white cats, black cats,
there are so many kinds!

Cats, are very special and that's, that!
Amy Rice

The Viking

The sea the sea
It takes him from me
It runs in his veins
It won't let him be.

Beneath its vast depths
The secrets it holds
It keep him so tightly
In each wave and fold.

He risks it all
To be on the sea
He risks his life
He risks losing me.

Only a mermaid
Could keep up with his hunger
She calls him with her song
From depths down under.

But I keep a candle
To light his returning
My soul waits for him
With passions that are burning.
Veronica Deleo-Hendry

Black Forest

Independent
Alone
Afraid
Strong, yet weak
Anxious, yet stable
Unsure
I know everything
I am Independent
Queen of the Crazies
Mother to the Insane
I rule alone
Afraid
Strong
I am Independent
Lindsay Buttle

Untitled

Why is there always war
What are we fighting for
Men say fight for the right
To sleep soundly at night
But how can I sleep
When lamenting mothers weep
For the sons they have lost
Many nights have I tossed
Wondering if this war is just
But if I must serve I must
This war seems to be futile
The ways of the times are brutal
If it means I must die
I won't ask you why
I'll try to serve this land
No matter what the command
So that others can be free
And not forced to be
In a world of conflict and war

Gary Donald Blinn

Our Flag - Your Sacrifice

There she flies Old Glory
America's Red, White and Blue

And in every stitch there's a story
Of our country tried and true

She's been there when men have died
I've looked at her and cried
on a wind swept day

And if she could speak
I know just what she'd say

Thank you from the bottom
Of my 50 stars

Without your strength and dedication
Victory could not have been ours

I thank you for your courage
And your willingness to die

I thank you for your sacrifice
That's kept me flying high

For America

T. C. Wade

Alana

Radiant as an icon, rare
she dances through
  dim seas of time
azure moments, ocean years
fall before her as she climbs.
Rainbows shimmer in the mist
layered deep and drifting down
where she lingers in my dreams
  and weaves them all
    into a crown.

Magic from a silver moon
she is soft
  and velvet framed
autumn eyes wherein there lies
a paradise as yet unclaimed.
Shining simply like a star
sparkling and crystal white
her beauty etched upon my soul
  like diamonds thrown
    across the night.

Edward West

What's Hope

Hope
thin thread
vapor beyond unknown
unreachable touch by hands
Eternity

Bethalene Finestead

The Search

In my prison
there are no walls
or bars to confine

If only to reach out
to grasp life one time
I would know the world

This prison of hate
built on my own
mocking the essence of my heart

Tempting fate, enraging time
with one wish alone
to be free

Charles B. Barker

"She Came"

  She came into my life,
I was so frightened, I was so scared,
I didn't know if I could love her

Enough

I didn't know I cared.
  I tried to run away,
To hide my feelings, to laugh and play,
  To feel the sunshine
On my face, to let her go away;
    She came too soon;
    She came too fast;
    She came beside the air;
    She came to breathe life
Into me,
  I learned to brush her hair.

Robert Overton

Heavenly

Allow me to equate.
But please, don't rate;
Heart and mind mix,
To equate, with olympics...

Mind and heart jump,
They might even slump,
They twist, they turn,
They burn, they hurt...

They do the summer saults,
They clear the vaults;
Score may be high,
Score may be low...

While, mixing all about,
Just to remain stout;
Tumbling on the rings,
For what life brings...

Between, attempts and success,
There lies much stress...
Lord, bless everyone, divinely,
Lift all spirits, heavenly!

Jose M. Castro

A Girl (That I Have Not Met)!

East winds blowing
Full moon glowing
Trees and grass
River flowing; my heart showing
No more seeing the inside!
I'll just stand a side—
  Jet in my car
Roll a number and take a ride—
Get on a guitar and slide!
And watch the tide waves roll
Just like taking a stroll
Watching you with your
Beautiful hair
Seeing everybody stop and stare
I love not to care!

Derek Costen

Untitled

Silent, evil, baffling, cunning,
Its impact, stunning...
Humiliating man in countless ways,
Embracing sanity in its maze.

Into life it shrewdly blends,
Void of rules, boundaries or ends,
Insidiously near, greedily lurking...
Its infinite energy always working.

Powered by insatiable thirst,
Plundering millions with its curse.
It has no conscience, feels no pain,
Possession its sickly gain.

Spares no sex, no age, or race,
Sets no time, picks no place...
Terror and torment in its wake,
Hearts lanced by its stake.

No honor, no shame, no fear,
Never sheds a tear,
Shattered lives its hall of fame...
Addiction its infamous name.

Tim Schoonover

Aslant The Stony Stream

Aslant the stony stream
The hoary grass grows older,
The weeping willows weep,
The reeds linger for death.

Aslant the stony stream,
Thy knighted colors shed,
The songbirds halt their songs,
The morning turns to dust.

Aslant the stony stream
I sit and sadly imagine
The way it used to be;
The way it soon will be.

Aslant the stony stream
A teardrop falls to the ground,
The silence turns to roar,
And the presence of death awaits.

Danielle Leichliter

Tears From A Tree

The sunset and the autumn
Share the same colors
And the sadness
The sunset precedes
The blackness of the night
The autumn precedes
The whiteness of the winter.

The trees in the autumn
Loosing their beauty
With each falling leaf.
The red and yellow leaves
Are falling, in a slow
Farewell dance
The brown leaves
Are falling,
With a sad resignation
They are the silent tears
Tears from a tree.

Martha Guardado

Unspoken

Days go by without it
Nights are slept through it
Weeks pass with only a few
Months seem to let some through
And years have always had a little too

It's hardly ever said
Just expected to remember in your head
So hold onto your memories
For we're not often reminded
enough of the words
"I Love You"

Angela Mickey

Awakening

As a bubble poised proudly in the blue
I placed them there - my ideals of you.
Haughtily I reviewed them
From my safe strong wall of Self
And marveled at their purity
Their light and strength hard shelled.
But at a chance word spoken
My wall came tumbling down
A mighty roar and crash it made
As it came tumbling down.
And with it came my bubble
My pure ideal of you
Shattered in the sunlight
A blot on the bright, clear blue.

Donna B. Allen

Silence Of The Wolves

At night in the dark woods
owls are always hooting and
wolves are always screaming,
and people are always dreaming.

The power and the honor is inside
of me let there be light
and let there be honesty.
The panthers are roaring and the lions
are soaring, the silence of the
wolves will always be here, don't
be afraid and have no fear.

Be careful what you wish for it
might come true, let the power
that you have stay inside of you.

Dana Rettig

Big Lou

A man so big
he reached the skies
is how he was
in all our eyes.
Someone so loved.
He was so strong.
The love he gave
we felt so long.
He's in our hearts
we see his smile
we'll be with him
in just a while.
So please don't cry,
remember his love
and know he's with
our Lord above.

Patty DeLuna

Body Bag

He died
with no pride.
He died with
much
pain. Bleeding inside,
he died insane. His wife
and his child, would not
see him again. His eyes
were red, and shot with
blood. His sleeves
were torn, as
he lay in the
mud. His face
drowning in a sea
of red. How long
would it be, till
they found he
was dead?

Kasey V. Collier

Beyond Dreamscapes

The sun...
The moon...
The stars broad...

A vast empire of the unknown...
Beyond the galaxies...

So far...
Yet at imagination's reach.

We can leap over moonbeams,
And dance with the cosmos,

And someday find an eternal peace.

Sara Kay Robb

If

If I stare at you without speaking
don't distract me. I'm dreaming.
If I hold my coif before letting
it drops into the fountain...
don't scold me, I'm wishing.

If I stand motionless, looking
up into the darkness, at a star...
don't move me, I'm hoping.

If I hold you, as if you'll
never be free...don't push
me away, just let it be.

Kerrie Greer-Meadows

Afraid

Afraid to live, Afraid to die
Afraid of truth, Afraid to lie

Afraid to give, Afraid to take
Afraid to be real, Afraid to be fake

Afraid of all, I don't know why
Afraid to live, Afraid to die.

Maria Nocera

The Castle

The walls so perfectly made,
Nothing can destroy it.
The builder's hands so delicate,
Careful hands must make it.
No clumsy hands may touch
The tiny bits piled about.
It shall never fall, I doubt,
It might stay till May.
If the wall shall fall,
Then it will be all.
Oh no! Here comes a wave.
Oh my, will the castle be saved?
The castle is flat I'm sorry to say.

Rachel Ann Jacobs

Flame

A flame a burning in my eyes.
A flame a burning in the skies.
Oh sweet child so fair and gentle.
A flame a burning in thine hands.
Yet a candle spare to save you.
Help me now or save me never.
How can I explain my voice is in vain
A flame a burning
Now gone out.
You went in the corner to go pout.
Stop now or cry forever,
Sleep or die but save yourself never.

Nikki Swiderski

That Night

I looked into your eyes that night,
I danced with you that night,
For the very first time, I fell in love
with you that night.
Everyday after that night I wondered
if it really was love or just another
game you play.
We were in love for a while, but then
you left me, I didn't know what to do,
so all I did was weep.
Now I think back to that night and I
wonder how my life would be different
if I never would have looked into your
eyes that night.

Jessica Sheets

Don't Take Drugs!

Drugs are bad
They make me sad
I'll won't take drugs
I'd rather have hugs

Teresa Fain

The Coin

Through depth of human turmoil,
When pleasures go to spoil,
With weariness I move along,
Few frailties, no cheerful song.

Adhering to this course I find
That I can understand the mind,
And even so equipped,
I still feel being gypped.

I just as soon would travel high,
Fly weightlessly into the sky,
Nothing to hold that can depress,
While knowing so much less.
Guenter H. Dittmar

Then And Now

When I was young and life was sweet,
   the years trekked slowly by
there was no need to think ahead
   to times I would one day bide.

For now I look back in disbelief,
   and wonder how I missed
all those years or in between,
   from those years to this

The mirror tells me my hair is white,
   and at times my legs are wobbly
but when I think of then and now
   would I change a thing? Not hardly
   ...well, maybe.
Philo Mena

Reunion

Loneliness and fear
They envelope me
Why, Dear Lord, why
I am alone yet I am not
I have happy memories of warm days
Gentle breezes, the scent of spring flowers
A sweet love waits for me
I have nothing to be afraid of
I take comfort in a love I once knew
I feel his hand brush my cheek
His lips on mine
I am not afraid
I shall rejoice
A sweet love waits for me
He shall wait no more
Sylvia Jones

Looking Back

When life is overwhelming
in every possible way,
I turn and look behind me
to when I used to play.

I miss the days behind me,
the ones that were so bright.
They're full of smiling faces
and spirits that are light.

I wish to be that way again,
so happy and carefree,
But I never slow down long enough
to find the former me.

They say that you are wiser
the older you become,
But children hold true wisdom;
"Be happy and have fun."
Crystal Munsinger

Gone But Never Forgotten

You lived, you loved
you laughed, you cried;
I loved you so much
and then you died.

Together we went
to space and back;
But heaven was calling
on a one way track.

You were always there for me,
but now that cannot be;
You are gone and now I long
to have you back with me.
Fawn Marie Doyle

Today's Kids

The problems us kids face
Are not the guns or knives.
We face much simpler problems
But they still affect our lives.
We worry about the other kids
And what they might say
We worry about the clothes we wear
Every single day.
We wonder if we fit "in"
We wonder if we are "cool"
We wonder why we're not ourselves
We act just like a fool.
Why do kids always worry about
What other kids will say
Why can't we just do things
Our very own way.
Jill Kroll

Love

Love, what is love I ask myself?
is it the feeling of running in a
stream of water on a hot summer
day? Or is it facing the challenges
of life with someone day by day?
Or is love a kiss from the
morning dew? Or is love just
being with you?
Selina Medley

Mexicano Puro

i am mexican
by soul
in pulque dreams
i devour flesh of jaguar Gods
i two step with animal spirits
to my delight
the priests tell
of miracles and fortunes
and ghosts of women
my mexican blood
drips sunsets
those celestial things
in serpent skirts
the flight of the moon
at dawn
peyote cheeks
and drunken stars
i am mexican
by soul
Malvino Jose Hoffman III

Night In The City

Do the stars still exist?
I cannot see them here
Save for a handful,
The brightest,
Who alone can bear
To outshine the street lamps.
Remember that clear winter night
When you
Showed me the stars?
Were they really as bright
Or do I only remember them so
Because we were together?
Sarah Brodeur

In The Moment Of A Color

In the moment of a color
   I can see the splashes of
creation forming,
   I can see colors from
an artist's brush stroke, the
   beauty of nature.
Silently stroking the moment,
   like day turning into night,
Not even the beauty of all
   the sunsets could compare
to a glimpse of heaven,
   captured on a canvas, for one
eternal second of our lives
Taylor Fissel

I Want To Write A Poem

I want to write a poem and,
I guess that it should rhyme;

But, every time I try to think,
I just don't have the time;

Important things get in the way,
Like soccer, fun, and dinner;

So I hope that you like my poem,
And, treat it as a winner.
Mary Gardner Henry

You Shine On (Like The Moon, The Stars, And The Sun)

You were a kiss
from the sunshine itself.
A short spark of light
that penetrated my heart,
my soul.
Your bright smile
that now I can only see in photographs,
tells me
"I lived a happy life.
Don't be sad.
Do not cry."
The eyes that only you own,
The life that only you led
are as precious as
a star shooting across
the night sky
leaving a trail of light
that will forever shine
on and on.
(We will never forget you, John Lennon)
Jennifer Lynne Nowak

Untitled

You paint a rosy sunrise as you wake up;
You think it's wise.
As if you follow the rule of getting up on the right foot.
If it is first to touch the floor,
Your day'll be pink, you'll win the war
With grief and sorrow, and hard work, and pains and sufferings,
 and so forth.
But if you happen to step on your left foot,
If it touched the floor the first,
Your day is gone, you've lost the war;
You have not won the battle with the pains of life:
You are painting a cloudy sky.
As you progress, the stormy clouds begin to form,
The thunder sounds.
You try to hide, you get pink paint but,
Mixed with gray,
It's looking faint.
More like your day,
Or like your life.

You are told you are great,
But it's a lie.
Marina Malamis

A Note To Young Lovers

Love is... something that never dies
Love is always there, never uncertain
Love is not only loving, but being loved
For if you feel you are being loved, your love becomes stronger
In becoming stronger, your love will multiply and grow
True love is always there, never uncertain
If love leaves you with sad memories
If it makes you uncertain of the future
If it seems as if the end of the world is near
You must live each day to its fullest extent
Hoping that the pain goes away
Wishing that the memories will leave you
Praying that your love will feel as strong if not
Stronger in loving you
Love is something that you cannot shut your heart to
For if you shut your heart to love
You shut your eyes to life
And in shutting your heart to love
You become an inadequate object and not the supreme
Creation God intended you to be
Joyce Syce

Your Wedding Day

Yesterday was the day for:
    Tender caring; truth sharing; soul baring.
    What-if scanning; passion fanning; bride's planning.

Today is the day for:

    Vow taking; the earth quaking; the groom shaking.
    Sisters sighing; mothers crying; past-loves dying.

Tomorrow is the day for:
    Welcome mats; neighbor's cats; family spats.
    Pipes leaking; trust seeking; value reaping.

And remember:
  Keep:
    The plans you make.
    The vows you take.

  Bless:
    The hopes you bare.
    The life you share.

  Trust:
    The Lord above.
    Your own true love.
Jack A. Dopler

Ways Of Love

Love is splendor, love is a song
It rings so true, it prances long
It longs to tell, and behold life
It longs to give, and be a light
Love cannot wait, to pay a call
To listen intently, to the call
It runs with swiftness, and hurries long
It loves a lot, it is a song
It is a feeling, that's buried deep
And cannot wait, to escape the heat
Of trials fast, and loving planned
By the great love, of the masters hand
It fills me up, until I break
With love divine, and harvest great.
Patricia A. Kirth

To Gain

I look the day completely off
to talk to you from my heart.
Forgive people for not knowing the right time to say.
Forgive people for not knowing the right way.
Forgive people for causing you pain.
Forgive Yourself for not being able to gain.
Maybe, just maybe, you might be able to,
understand everything that has happened through,
time, patience, forgiveness, experience.
Don't know the reasons, altho
people are brought together to touch heart and soul.
Feel the care, share, and love,
people try to bring your way.
Never accept anything less,
no matter what they say.
Please extinguish the bitterness, hurt, scars and pain.
So time, patience, forgiveness, experience,
you will gain.

In God's Name We Pray.
Joanna Gibson

Time And Beauty Of Two Things In Comparison

A sand painting as we may say it

Thus in comparison the flower thus both
Take patience and extreme care and thought.

Though it seems too long for patience
When a sand painting is finally finished
Or a flower but full grown
Both will be beautiful

But as we know when the fall winds come
They will blow away the sand painting
Like the flower at winter when it wilts.
Alexander M. Lucania

I Am Proud To Be An American

I am proud to be an American,
a true patriot of the USA,
enjoying the fruits of freedom day after day.
Come, you true Americans;
join hands and hearts
with bowed heads to pray
that our great republic
is here to stay.
Listen to what dead heroes have to say,
"Yes, we are proud to be Americans —
true patriots of the USA;
Yesterday's sacrifice was so
you might enjoy
the fruits of freedom today."
George Munyer

God! Why Me!

When it rains in the morning,
I awake - with love in my heart.
The rain is like the sun -
For the love in my heart - is you.
My voice sings out: "Oh what a beautiful day,
For the love in my heart is you."
My heart is sad - to know - how long would I be with you.
I fight with all my being - Oh God - Why Me!
Can't you see this love of mine is real?
Spare me my life - for the love I have for this man.
When it rains in the morning -
The birds are chirping - singing to their heart's content.
For the food of life keeps them going.
Oh God! Listen to me!
Spare me my life,
So I can be with the one I love.
Life is good -
I have the love of my life
Loving me...forever
   Toni Salinetro

Friends

I lost one of my best friends,
A couple of years ago;
He was an extra special sort of guy,
So it was very hard to let go.

He guided me through years of my life,
Some that were good and some bad;
But he was always there when I needed him,
And I was proud to call him Dad.

He gave his life to Jesus Christ,
And served him faithfully for years;
And was there for others as well as me,
In times of trials, temptations, and tears.

I loved my father so very much,
And still find it hard to let go;
But I can find peace in this one fact,
He is now in the arms of Jesus, I know!
   David Hamm

Upon A Star

Please come closer because you're too far
How long do I have to pray,
How many wishes on how many stars?
If you were ever in my arms I would hold you so tight,
My love would flow so long,
Long after the night.
And if we ever part,
I'll just put my heart away.
Because knowing how you'll love me,
No other love could be that way.
So let me have some time,
And let this feeling grow.
Give me a chance to make you mine,
Don't let my love go.
   Richard Brown

Alisa

Across the miles her power grows
As spoken words and whispers show
A desire and passion so hard to hide
Endlessly mounts as a rolling tide.
Amorous days turned sleepless nights
And thoughts of her bring wondrous light
to otherwise cold and shadowed heart
Built friendship and love that shall never part.
   Bradley Adkins

Love's Greatest Treasure

Two people joined with great affection;
too soon torn apart by mistrust and deception.
Yet, from their brief encounter
born the greatest treasure.

A bundle of joy and eternal sunshine
filled the hearts...both his and mine,
with songs of endless love
for their gentle little dove.

Her dark brown hair shimmering in the sun,
eyes that sparkle in joyful fun;
her warm complexion, ever glowing;
infectious laughter, ever flowing.

As time passes ever by,
our little dove, no longer shy,
spreading her wings to leave the nest;
wondering, did we do our best?

Mindful of our lessons we pray and hope;
for in this world 'tis so hard to cope.
So much to fear in daily life,
does she know we are here through all the strife?
   Margo M. Nigo

A Tear Through Time

The single tear paused as if to ponder its path.
Then, once decided, dashed down his cheek to his lips.
He is oblivious to the warm saltiness of it,
His hand shaking, he turns the page and it rips.
His tired fingers stretch out and touch the picture.
The dark-haired beauty that reflects back into his eyes;
Reflecting still further into his memory, his past, his soul
"If only I had said I loved you." He cries.
The picture is decades old, yet her beauty as fresh as today.
His life is one of loneliness and wishes of time long past.
Quietly, he folds up the old school yearbook,
He puts it away noticing that time passes just too fast.
Too fast, indeed, for opportunity comes too swiftly;
Comes and is gone and nothing left but too much regret.
He wonders briefly just what she is doing now.
He wipes the tear away, "Why can I not just forget?"
In time, sleep comes and his sadness wanes,
And some miles away she looks the same book through.
She pauses at his picture, a tears appearing in her eye.
It drips on the page. "If only I had said I loved you!"
   Darryl G. Willaman

Horses

The soft satin feel of a weathered old rope
The smooth worn leather of a seat
The dull sliver around your feet
The tight black rubber on your calves
The soft cotton, lined in cool suede on your legs
The snug leather and knit on your hands
The long dark leather strap that flows through your gloves
The hard plastic that warms your head
The smooth rhythm that puts you at rest
The smallest little nudge that takes you away
Riding on a dream
   Amber Lee Bickers

Blossom

Make someone happy, make someone smile;
Spread some sunshine through every rough mile;
Let your dreams flower, with each passing hour;
Let your life bloom, sing out your own tune.
Show a blind man the light, bring some day to his night.
To give from your heart, may not seem so smart,
but a fool's life you'll live, if you choose not to give.
   William J. Roberts

Reality

East of Eden and West of darkness, a child is born
Cries of a newborn are welcomed by the new mother
So young, so carefree, are the ways of this child
They knoweth not what may lie ahead of them
This world so cruel to the innocent
One can only hope that violence or corruption will not overcome them
We cannot shelter our children, but we can teach them
Shots ring out; cries are heard miles away
No, not my child; this could not be happening
Victim or fate?
Patricia Comeau

Clouds

Fluffy, soft, smooth and clean
They build up pictures, but when
you look back at it, it's gone.
They look like a nice big white
pillow. You can see them in
the sky. Seems like you can
grab a cloud, and eat it like ice cream.
Clouds.
Sandy Green

Untitled

There are many people who believe
That when this world your soul does leave
Up to the stars your soul won't go
Nor to fiery depths below.
They say each soul lives with its past,
Each pain you've caused from first to last.
Each time I've said a hateful word;
Each time these awful words were heard.
Those times I did a thoughtless thing,
And times I caused the day to bring
Pain to one whose only sin
Was opening up to let me in.
The times I saw someone in need
And did not help because of greed.
The times I turned and walked away
When I really should have stayed.
The times I've had enough to share
But did not take the time to care.
If hell is as these people say,
These are the things for which I'll pay.
Elaine Wileman

The Prisoner

A Mexican girl with hair of black,
holds my heart above the clouds.
She keeps me prisoner inside myself,
bound by love and emptiness.
The days are long without her near,
wanting her is my greatest fear.
Will she ever look my way?
This I wonder day by day.
Late at night I see her face,
it's only a dream I realize.
Her power is strong upon my soul,
my heart is trapped, this I know.
I haven't the power to break her spell.
Does she love me? I just can't tell.
What would she want with a man like me?
What would she do if I became free?
Yes, yes, I'm a prisoner behind a fence,
A prisoner of crime, as well as love.
Is she my lover? or just a friend,
my love for her, is my biggest sin.
Gilbert Witt

Untitled

A harsh grave, an early end
a brief but lovely life my friend
I miss you, did you have to go?
But you are happy, somehow I know.
When they told me you had died.
I felt so cold, then I cried.
Where the car wrecked, there is still a stain
as in agony with all the pain.
Still in school, I live each day
there must be a better way.
I will always hurt and cry
when I look into the sky.
I see your picture and try to smile.
I'll be seeing you in a short while.
Cheri Marie Spaulding

Mom And Dad

The little white house on the hill stands alone
I'll always remember it use to be home
The wind's barely blowing, it's quite here today
Mom and dad are gone they both have passed away
As I stand here thinking, what will I do now
I can almost see daddy in his garden as he plowed
Mom worked her garden she was a flower queen
Her flowers were so beautiful she planted in the spring
Mom I'll never forget how you were always there
To ease the pain, mend my clothes, and brush my hair
It's been several years since daddy passed away
I'm feeling pain and hurt, momma's leaving me today
It's time for the funeral, I must be going on
I can almost hear momma say, be brave and strong
As I followed close behind her trying to hold up and be brave
I could not hide my sorrow when they laid her in the grave
My burdens feel much lighter, I must have passed God's test
Mom was buried next to daddy as she laid to rest
I knelt by the grave and told them both goodbye
There's a better home awaiting with Jesus in the sky
Patricia A. Meadows

Birthday Poem For Son

To our son, Bob, on a really big birthday
you're our pride and joy and much more in every way.
There were lots of laughs and, of course, many tears.
But all's been well for oh! So many years.
So thank you, Lord, for all you've done,
especially blessing us with an A number one son.
He's a super hubby, a loving dad
and a caring grandpa, though he looks like a lad.
He sent us a note many years ago
it gave our lives a happy glow.
So take good care of him, dear Lord above
as we say "Happy Birthday, Bob, and all our love."
Eleanor L. Johnson

Reflections Of A Year Gone By

Two bodies pressed hard against each other
one mind nothing was bothered
no one was difficult leaves quicken their decent
separating themselves from the branch; vine of life
death to the living time passed swiftly
droplets of snow wet the browning land beneath us
two bodies linking arms, huddling close in the chill dying air
one mind, differing ideas
two halves becoming distant, closing to the death surrounding them
apart from the other thoughts become scattered, feelings disjointed,
ideas incomplete... Distance takes hold
Fingers once intertwined shiver with coldness, leaping without feeling
into darkness two bodies separate under the pressure of time
Melanie A. Burr

Do You Have A Dream?

Do you have a dream, that dances in your head?
And mingles through your thoughts, before you go to bed?

Then listen to your dream, and do as it commands.
For, if you follow it, you may end up in far-off lands.

Don't keep your dream inside you; it needs room to get about!
And, if you ignore it, you may hear your poor dream shout:

"I can do whatever you want of me; your wish is my command!
You only have to let me out, and I will take a stand!"

If your dream is shouting, don't keep it placed inside.
For if you chosen to let it out, it may take you on a ride.

A ride around the world, or to many far-off lands.
But you must listen to your dream, and do as it commands.

Do you have a dream, that dances in your head?
And mingles through your thoughts, before you go to bed?

Carl S. Sterner

In My Eyes

I see a spider climbing up my wall
I see the spider's rise before its fall
So determined, he just tries and tries
The spider is a hero in my eyes

I see a puppy sniffing at the ground
I see he knows there's something to be found
He finds nothing, but utters no cries
That puppy is so strong in my eyes

I see a little girl all by herself
I see the girl has problems with her health
So she'll make sure she really lives before she dies
This little girl's courageous in my eyes

I tilt my head and look up to the skies
There's just so much to see in my eyes

Gennie Adams

Thinking Of You

When I stop and think of you for a while.
In my heart, my mind and on my face I smile.
Though our time together is brief.
My toils and stresses you give relief.
I give thanks for all you do.
And every moment I'll be thinking of you.

I can picture your body, heart, and face.
My memories no one can ever replace.
My thoughts of you not even gold can compare.
To the joy I feel from the love we share.
I give thanks for all that you do.
And every moment I'll be thinking of you.

Now I lay down and go to sleep.
All comfortable and serene in your thoughts that I keep.
Knowing soon I'll be tight in your arms.
Relishing in the joys of your charms.
I give thanks for all that you do.
And every moment I'll be thinking of you.

Jay Harold Edwards

Dreamers

Some think of us as foolish, like a bird who flies in the rain
to try to reach a rainbow, he sees beyond the plain.
His mighty wings grow weary, as he falters in his flight,
to reach a destination of unending light
He screeches a cry of protest, as the heavens begin to rumble
The rain pounds ever harder as he fights to stay aflight.

It seems as if he'll topple to the loaming ground below,
where his flight will surely end too short to reach his goal
But searching deep inside himself, he finds a hidden strength
a strength that will not weaken, amidst the pouring rain.

So like this bird are dreamers, who continue on their quest
despite the opposition, that will put them to the test
And once they reach their goal, stop dreaming they will not.
For dreams are neverending, like the rainbows they create
that continue on forever, amidst the pouring rain...

Toni Westover

The Blizzard Of '96

The forecast called for a heavy winterstorm
And strike it did in steady form
Fell powdery snow quick and thick on Saturday
And continued through till Monday

A metro train gets stuck as temperature lowers
And frustrated commuters were stranded many hours
While Mid-Atlantic states were bracing for another
A couple of fresh inches to clean why bother

Function the Storm-Desk, Storm-Team, Storm-Center
Day through night all in mid-winter
Going wall to wall till the end of the storm
Is there an end to the storm tunnel in good form?

Then there are the stories of goodwill
Of volunteers helping to shovel and till
The elderly were helped with meals-on-wheels
But the merchants were deprived of their best deals

The blizzard stretched from Boston to Atlanta
And places unaccustomed were getting snow-battered
The snow-plows continued from Saturday to Friday
And TV reporters were diversely scattered.

Elizabeth Kythail

the 73 north

at ten o'clock she's forgotten
the day's sun-dried tapestry
that smothered her in
smoggy city stitches
now she's throwing off her high heels
driving onto the north-bound linen
starry-night-canopy bed
cooled by the highway breeze
that flies through
the rolled down window
with the night
to remind her
she likes the feel of cold air biting her
and the way the darkness looks at 60 mph
how it flows by like a ghost
touching her with its street lamp
lights flickering by and by
and soothes her
till she sighs...

Lamman T. Doan

You Are The Sweetest Thing In My Memories

You are the sweetest thing in my memories,
When I need a friend, you are there,
When I need someone to comfort me
From the stressful things in life,
You hold me close and brush back the
Hair from my face, and kiss my lips, tenderly.
You are the sweetest thing in my memories.
Your voice sounds so familiar, as though I
Have heard it before in another place and time,
Your touch makes me forget all of my troubles,
Your smiles bring me joy, and your beautiful
Eyes, they speak softly to me.
And even when I find myself apart from you,
Sometimes I am upset and lonely, but I
Search my mind to find you, so you can comfort me,
For you are the sweetest thing in my memories.
Tracey Daly

How Long Is Forever

Darling, how long is forever
It really isn't hard to explain
Forever is how long I will love you
In my heart you will always remain

Darling, how long is forever
Is it days or months or years
Forever is made up of all of these things
And brings happiness, sadness and tears

Darling, how long is forever
It's how long with you I'll remain
Through life - in spirit even after
My love for you to acclaim

If we realize all of these things
And enjoy the rest of our lives together
Then we will have answered the question
My darling, how long is forever
Orvan W. Childers

No Death! I Choose My Path

I'm determined to live life till it has
taken my last breath.

No death! You will not succeed at this game.

I choose to have my eyes be the window
into my heart, mind and soul. To absorb
what the world has to offer.

My vigor will not unravel when
encountering misfortunes that carry misery.

No death! I will not partake in this
play. I will not let it be that way.

Hear me death! I will fight you to the
bitter end. To give up on life would
symbolize shaking your hand and
conceding you were correct all along.
Dialid Sanchez

At Peace

For once in my life, my soul is at rest.
My heart beats at ease, clean air fills my chest.
My nerves are not bad, my mind does not cloud.
I try to see clear, not under a shroud.

As cool as water, my acts are down pat.
As smooth as the wind, control is intact.
Now no more anger, it's time to let go.
Stop the dead feelings, and let myself grow.
Elizabeth San Jose

To My Loving Mom, From Her Lucky And Thankful Son

Hey ma, me again, just trying to say
that I respect and love you more every day.

Your heart is so large, it must weigh a ton.
I know there isn't another that big under the sun.

You'd be there for anyone in pain, not just me.
Ask anyone who knows you, you're the greatest, it's easy to see.

Through ups and downs, you've been my guiding light.
Through tear-filled eyes, you've made everything bright.

You've helped this little boy to become a man
with your guidance and love like no one else can.

All that I have, and all I shall ever be,
stems from one branch, and that twig is thee!

I owe you a debt I can't ever hope to repay.
Except maybe to be half as good a parent as you are one day!

Best friend, confidant, teacher and especially mother
I've always known I wouldn't want any other!

I can't express how I feel, as you can see
except to say that I love you - infinity!
Brian Burkum

Tide

He waited.
He longed to see her again, to feel her gentle caress, to breathe
in her very essence.
He wanted to see what she saw, to feel what she felt, to be what
she was - to be a part of her.
She was the means to all of his hopes, all of his fantasies, all of
his dreams.
She was everything.
Then he felt it -
a slight change in the wind, a slight change in his heart and his soul.
And suddenly, she was there -
rushing toward him, arms wide to embrace him,
heart full to engulf him.
"The tide's coming in, Captain."
"Yes, I know."
With a signal, he began to run to her.
He gave quick thanks to the moon that had brought her to him again.
Then they met in crashing waves and roaring foam.
She carried him away,
and they were free.
Kim Ball

Showers On My Way

I walked in darkness o'er the grass
   And felt the dew so damp and sweet.
When light of morn came filtering through,
   Diamonds sparkled at my feet.
As morning radiance caressed my face,
   The dryness felt, and arid breath held sway.
A longing came to feel a cooling rain,
   But only tears poured forth, my soul to lave.
Yet even these could not assuage my emptiness and pain.
   As crushed and heaving in the sun's full heat,
My heart cried out for sustenance and hope
   As I lay my burdens at the Saviour's feet.
Suddenly, from the bounty of His gracious hands,
   Came silver drops, anointing, healing, from above.
Enabled then to travel on my way,
   Awash was I, bathed in His peace and love.
Showers of care, showers of pain,
   Come from my Lord who has it all planned.
Showers of blessing, showers of gain,
   Are all in God's time, and I'm safe in His hand.
Hilda N. Priestley

A Poet

What is it that a poet needs:
On what subjects does he feed?
For what type causes does he bleed;
And pickings are easy 'twixt flowers and weeds?

Is there a spirit, inspiring him;
A nagging ambition, retiring him;
A task too arduous, perspiring him?
Or maybe we read is re-wiring him!?

On what shelves does he glean
For new ideas to fill his bean?
Which are the oldies that he must wean:
Let them die; or, let them be seen?

Up and down in frowns and glances;
Words that wear in passing fancies
Of thoughts that spin like dervish dances
And pepped-up cowboys on far away ranches?

Why, oh why? Did I give a dang
To be a poet they'd rather Not hang?

Earl Varner

Uncivilized Heart

I see no glory in my bitterness today,
I find no pride in weakness I betray,
I find no salvation in the purity of love,
I see no grace in bowing to opinion.

I find no justification in my surroundings,
I see no comfort in silence,
I find my faith is all I have,
To lead me through this valley.

I find that I scare myself,
To think, to dream, to create in such uncharted territory,
Such an uncivilized heart is mine...

Jennifer Flores

Always Young

Once upon a time, there was a man whom lived on planet earth. He was in awe of things to see, to hear, to feel, to be. He knew, he was put on earth as a venture to see, to hear, to feel, to be. He laughed at young birds trying to fly, and always asked himself why can't I! He always loved to watch young babies try to walk and try to talk cause as a man he knew they would have to walk the walk. Because he knew, they were put on earth, to see, to hear, to feel, to be and to talk their talk. Yes life is one big venture with little activities in-between, even viewing can be a pleasant scene. Life is what you make it, they say, so enjoy all the wonders to see, to hear, to feel, to be as you may! For life is a physical one I know, as good as it can be, you can be handed a terrible blow! You can get back up voice your tongue and talk your talk, walk your walk cause you can still see, to hear, to feel and to be always young.

Fred Paliani

Pleasant Memories

The memories that come to mind.
Are pleasant ones and are never hard to find.
When I think back when I was young.
I remember that sweet smile from above.
That day you held me in your lap.
The story books that made me laugh.
The cherished moments we spent together.
And the beautiful days in the sunny weather.
My life is filled with so many joys.
Only because you're in it!

Kellie Lowe

Would You Give Up On God?

Would you give up on God, the one who loved you so much that he sent his only son to die on the cross for your sins?

Would you give up on God, the one who said, just call on His name and he would answer your every prayer?

Would you give up on God, the one who said, He would supply you every need according to his riches in glory?

Would you give up on God? The one who said, nothing shall separate you from His love. Would you give up on God, the one who said, He'd never leave nor forsake you?

Would you give up on God, the one who is your help in the time of trouble? Would you give up on God, the one who gives you strength when you are weak?

Would you give up on God, the one who has never at anytime, no-matter the situation, given up on you???

Nedra Mohammed

The Lifers

We are the Lifers..... we're called the Lifers.
Doing "life without parole," inside of me.
We're doing hard time...to pay for my crime.
Chained and shackled, throughout my eternity.

But I recall when... We stood so tall then.
Our name was Pride! Yes, I remember well.
Our name was Hope too! Then Faith in us grew.
Then Pride and Hope and Faith, went straight to Hell.

Hope left us crying...No sense in trying.
So when Faith and Pride abandoned us, we knew.
'Twas such a pity...Our names were pretty.
But names were not enough to see us through.

So when Belief came... We played the name game.
But believing soon was leaving us with doubt.
So with a new hand... A different game plan.
We changed our name to Lady Luck, until our luck ran out.

And now we're Lifer's... Forever Lifers.
Dead men walk... Lifer's talk.... But we all know.
This time it's real! There's no appeal!
And no "stay of execution", when I go.

Penny J. Huggins

A Midnight Bewitching

Hello my friend of virtue's end,
what brings you forth from secrecy?
I venture toward your bend of light,
or is it black magic and sorcery?
Pale, blank eyes hide your lies and
tricks of evil activity blend,
your bellows of language unknown to most men.
What brings you forth to meet my gaze
beneath the midnight lunar rays?
Your skin so frail and eyes so deep,
are they watching for those in sleep?
Your home among the leaves of trees,
your victims cross below,
your hands of evil triumph seize
before the innocent know.
Slinking, watching, seeing all,
waiting for the victory fall
when blight and right are met this night
beneath the moon's bright call.

Nathan Powers

Forbidden Love

Taken from a love that was never meant to be
I wanted to give you everything; you wanted nothing.
What could I do? The question would never be answered.

Could I forget? No.
I would always remember
My forbidden love.

How did we know it would ever come to be?
The question is, would you stay?
Always a possibility, always a chance
Our love would last in the end.

I always wanted to be more than friends.
How could I have known you wanted it too?
A slight touch, a light kiss
Would bring good dreams to me for evermore

But am I dreaming, or am I awake?
Just thinking about -
Our forbidden love.

Jeff Wood

Dear Crow, Prince Of The Night Sky

Above the somber, mournful techno-jungle it came
Above, in the sorrowful smog, now bright in comparison
(if you can imagine)
Its descent slow...graceful... a mockery of itself
Ebony wings spread magnificently, menacingly in intimidation
Thou art the prince of the night
The sky your palatial kingdom
Those infinitely sinister eyes in watchful concern
And as those roving orbs met mine I was pulled in
So powerfully! Making me seem smaller, weaker with every passing second
Each second lasting painfully long, infinitely long, in time with the beating of its heart
Its cold barren heart
Or maybe that was the sound of my fearful heart—betraying my false mask of calm
Compelled to let it draw me into the inky chasm of its soul
Never have I seen anything so dismal!
And then my human ignorance and concerns were pulled away
Like the veil lifted from a bride's face
And I understood
He is the core of sadness and despair
Come to take his toll.

Phil Toalston

The Dragon Steals

It was all a fairy tale.
I was a princess alone.
And then came the prince -
He was beautiful in my eyes.
Through wars and tribulation we endured.
I slew the dragon that almost engulfed him,
And he loved me more.
But one day the dragon resurrected.
And this time he killed our love story.
But the love itself remained.
Now I long for him and he reaches for me.
But the dragon has him -
And he holds him where I can see him,
  but I can't have him.
I can hear his cry coming from the cave -
  that dark prison on the beautiful shore.
But I can't save him.
He must pick up the sword that I
  left in his heart and slay the devil himself.
And then the fairy tale can live forever.

Shannon Tingle

Days

These repeating days within my life, bore my mind and tire my body,
is there nothing different, is it all the same, where will our lives
lead, will we walk an endless circle, till we all go insane?
Shall we follow many paths, or should we all walk the same.

Week upon week the days appear the same, has life lost its luster,
its brilliance of new, where has the excitement gone, was it ever here,
or was I just a fawn.

The enjoyment in life I hardly find, have I just begun to see, or am
I going blind, these solemn days I walk alone, I wonder of God and
our eternal home, these bitter thoughts within my mind, keep building
stronger with the passing of time.

The faster and faster the days go by, the more I wonder, wonder why,
the miracle of life has become so dull, that it's started piercing,
piercing my skull, trying to chain my thought to a pattern tone,
taking my mental freedom, freedom to roam.
Why must I struggle why must I fight, to keep a life I no longer like.

Jeff K. Wantland

I Dreamt Of You Last Night

Last night as I lay down upon my bed
Endearing thoughts of you filled my head
I remembered the kiss of your lips
The soft, lingering touch of your finger tips
I closed my eyes to leave you behind
My heart skipped a beat and brought you to mind
I thought of whispered words in my ear
The image of you drifted in, becoming clear
I waited for your voice to fill the air
To feel your hands running through my hair
I felt your flesh next to my skin
Feeling the soul you carried within
To feel your cheek against my face
Losing my mind in both time and space
Looking deep into your eyes above
Letting you know that it's you I love
The night carries on in so many ways
The world around us becoming a daze
The dawn approaches and you leave in flight
And I remember how I dreamt of you last night.

Lori K. Davis

Face The Music

Classical movements are true to form,
Symphonies, sonatas, concertos were born
Into traditions which play through the years,
with each generation lending new ears.

Country croons of those down on their luck,
while traveling the road in a pick-up truck.
These twangs tell tales of wounded souls
in amusing words for love that's grown cold.

Rhythm and blues laud over life's lessons,
Through the jam of lead guitar sessions.
The jazzy tempo is meant to entrance
while moving limbs slowly into a dance.

Rock and roll can get under your skin
with phrases and harmonies in melodic din.
It blasts a beat through drum and bass
into mindful tunes which can't be erased.

Face the music on its own scale,
And make note of how it never fails
to compose vocal and instrumental tones
That each listener can make their very own.

Laura Frimer

The Wind

It blows all day it blows all night
The wind will never be in sight.

It's cold, it's hot it brings in rain
But the wind will never bring in pain.

The wind has blew, the wind will blow
The wind can bring in rain or snow.

The wind can sing a little song
But the words are never, ever wrong.

The wind can send a sailing ship
But when it gets mad, it stops the trip.

The wind is here the wind is there
The wind can be almost anywhere.

The wind you see is my good friend
And my friend will blow until the end.
Ashlee Fiske

Success

To whom can it be told
the greatest tragedy of mankind.
The blood, the sweat, the tears,
the anguish are insurmountable,
yet we extend ourselves to the breaking points
for the one true joy,
the one joy that all mankind can agree on.
Success!
From birth, it is embedded in our minds
that our worth as a human being is measured in success.
We all strive for success and somewhere,
no one quite knows where,
we lose our compassion, our ability to love,
our general understanding of what people are,
Human!
Why do we expect more from a
person than he is readily capable of doing?
Why must we hurt to gain the one
true measure of our societal worth?
Success!
Matthew Whiteside

A Wedding Day Prayer

Dear God on this momentous day
We take this time and pause to pray.
As this bride and groom start their lives together,
May Your love abide through all kinds of weather.
On the beautiful days when all is well,
May they praise You, for Your grace is unparalleled.
On the dreary days during storms and strife,
May they realize You are in control of their life.
On the mediocre days of partly sunny without rain,
May they rest in You and not complain.
In every situation and in all kinds of weather,
May Your unconditional love bind them together.
I pray a special blessing on this couple tonight.
May You guide their paths by Your Holy Light.
I pray they may prosper as You look on them with favor.
May they depend on You. May their faith never waver.
Brent Lee

Feelings

A cooling breeze on a hot summer's day caresses me.
The rustling of leaves through shielding trees in a rhapsody.
Salt filled air from a protected sound entices me.
Sunrise and sunset behind mountain ranges are ecstasy.
The beautiful creatures of sea, land and air intrigue me.
The city's boats, buildings, and greenery are artistry.
All the beauty of nature and man sets me free.
Martha L. Kady

Sonhwa The Princess, Exiled

The tree knew the wind well,
its coin-faced leaves turned like a whir of sharp wings,
She was on her exile road
as her feet caressed
the jade hills of Paekche's Kingdom.

Her heart received an unknown beggar escort
she met on this path of unexpected light,
Like a turtle slipping its head out of her shelled home
accepts the saltiness of the sandstone she timidly licks.

The beggar's melodies began,
long-sweet consonants rippling the music water
warmed into breathless tunes of chinese yams unearthed.
It cut her heart, a soft rice cake eaten with
a soldier's spoon.

When he filled her with his secret of Paekche's kingdom,
her storms were ceased
and they were wed on water
with crowns of thin ox bone,
and Celadon flowers growing at their footfalls.
Charlene S. Lee

The Nurturing

"Da, don't, don't," floated through the air
as we drifted off to sleep at night.
A muffled sound - "No, Da."

An early awakening to the wildly whistling
coffee kettle as Papa Da got up for
work in the morning.

The gas heater's blue, orange, yellow flames—
a muted explosion of fire on a cold
morning to engulf our hearts and souls
in a warm embrace.

The heater's soft, hissing sound like
a child's breath pushed out on a cold,
foggy school bus window, trying to
see what shapes would appear.

The constant breath of the heater —
warming, nurturing, loving. The cosy
smell of a spent match as we
cuddled and tossed in cotton quilts,
warmed by several small bodies in a bed.
Kathleen K. Modenbach

Celebration of A Beginning

See the crescent in the early morning sky,
This signals the beginning of a new moon.
Soon after, the light explodes over the horizon
Beckoning in the beginning of a new day.
With each, their brilliance allows us to remember our
Yesterdays and look forward to our tomorrows.
Their message is one of serenity, new life, and hope.
Today we also celebrate a beginning, these whose lives entwine.
One I've known all my life, one I've known but a short time.
Today, their new life will begin. Two people in love,
Searching their hearts and minds, coming together as one soul,
Seeking out that which is genuine.
This brought you together and will be
Built upon by the happiness held by each.
Once expressed outside, this happiness may be shared.
That which is shared, begins as a single piece of a much
Larger puzzle. As that piece from each of you is put in place,
Let the two meld together, let them strengthen the bond
Between you, thus becoming one.
Rosemary C. Schmidt

Barbara

Such a lovely baby, that was beautiful and sweet,
the time that you got so sick it made me feel so weak,
so many times you came to me, just to make some tea,
you used to play and sit, on the kitchen floor, and you
would have a tea party for many hours more,
you grew up all so quickly the time went, oh so fast,
your son was born while you were young, he gave you so much love
and happiness, you meet a man,
that I would say was not the best for you,
he was a man that used his charm to get the best of you,
two beautiful girls he gave to you, so perfect and so sweet,
the man you loved and trusted, put you on the street,
he showed you all the evil only heroin can reap,
you left your beautiful children to go and walk the streets,
the man you loved was nothing but a son of a bitching creep,
your children how they miss you, you must come off the street,
a year has passed since you have gone, the time has slowly passed,
heroin is the love you want, you can't resist the chance,
how I wish you could come back, so we could share some tea.

Rose O. Moran

Nona's Living Room

I sit and eat a plate of Grandma Nona's herring —
she talks loudly and laughs even louder.

My uncle Dennis, the "big" Swede, smiles pinkly
and points out that the dogs are going at it

In the back yard under the forsythia bush where
I once buried a cigar box full of old pictures

And coins — a testimony of a young boy's strength.
Now, I drink whiskey and my great aunt's dricka and

Dance with Nona until her cough consumes her step
and she stops to hug me — hard and slow in tears.

She misses Keith who is three years gone now
and smelled of wool and Copenhagen chewing

Tobacco until his dying day, but she says
I'm a better dancer — much quicker on my feet.

We rest and I finish my herring and watch all
my relatives remember — all bright eyed and fair

And happy on alcohol, but my grandma is crying,
I have dark eyes like Keith.

Jason D. Traviss

Never

I think of the things I'm afraid to say,
And all the things I'd never do.
Sometimes I want to run away,
But I know deep inside that I'd never follow through.
I'm so tired of crying all these wasted tears,
That I know that you don't see,
It's scary to think of the lonely years,
'Cause I know that you don't care about me.
How can I hate you, yet love you so much?
Where are your loving arms, where is your gentle touch?
Where is my cupid, where are my wings?
Don't you understand the pain this love brings?
I feel like my life is some pointless story,
Of hopeless love and daydreamed glory.
So I'm making a list of all the things I'd
never say and cannot do..
I'd tell you that I love you.

Andrea Byron

The Age Of Innocence

All of us, eventually grow up,
But we can never retrieve,
That which we had when we were young.

Some of us, try to retrain it,
But with each passing year,
It gets harder and harder.

We would like to go back
And try it all over again,
That time when we were young.

When we were young,
We did not fully understand,
All that we had at that time.

Life is funny,
When we were young, we wanted to be old.
Now that we are old, we would like to be young.

Though we can never retrieve it,
We will cherish the memories of
Our age of innocence.

Steven M. Uhrich

Gun Control

Society dealt me a large blow the other day
A damage irreparable
I lay dying.
Justice has served no purpose; the squirms of my blood
encompass me.
The freedom of society; constitution of rights
All Vanity.

Today I see death; it stands at my door
The pain of my youth being snatched away, overshadows
My dreams standeth aloof.
The shots still sounds; senseless though
Naught but for a cent my life wastes.
Many, foresee but the same;

Loving rebuke, a touch or jolt of a car, unintentional hit of a core
at a vehicle.
Trigger happy louts
Life means nothing to them...the thugs, hopeless beings
Great atrocity of humanity
Failed wisdom, failed love, failed loyalty
All Tragic.

Joseph Adeola Ogunbiyi

True Friends Are Forever!

True friends go on for life,
they're still friends even after one dies.
Being honest can carry you far,
you'll never have to break your true friend's heart.
When I think of you, I think of someone who cares,
not someone conceited, and just wants to get in my hair.
It's nice to say "I have a true friend,
someone who'll stick with me through thick and thin."
If you have feelings and you're loving your friend, then you know
you have a true friend, and you don't want your friendship to end!
You want to spend time with your true friend, because
you don't want to lose them, and have to start all over again.
You can't just pick someone out of the crowd,
and say "come on you're my true friend now!"
I wish it was that easy, but that's too breezy!
True friends are very fragile, you don't want to break them.
You are my true friend,
and our friendship is never going to end!!!

Laura Jean Clawson

Granny

At a family reunion, one hot July day,
my sister asked if some words I would say.

This is about a lady, who, to you and me
was Grandmother, Granny, or Granny Kea.

Each of us knew her in a different way and light,
but she loved each of us with all her might.

She let us play hard all day
and did her best to keep us out of harm's way.

Every time she would look for us, what did she see?
Every one of us in a great big oak tree!

She was a fantastic cook, who needed no measure
and the food she put before us was a palatable pleasure.

As we grew older and spread our wings,
from her mouth, though unsolicited, was heard the wisest of things.

At the time, we paid no attention,
but as the years pass, we recall some of the things she did mention.

She was a lady, a granny, a friend,
I hope my grandchildren will say the same of me
— when my days have come to an end.

Rox Ann Hodge

Phoenix

As the Phoenix, risen anew,
Hurtling from the ashes of forgotten eternities,
Comes to rest on a rocky mound,
He surveys his panoramic majesty.

Inward, his soul remains distant, troubled.
Outward, he stands undaunted in his quest,
Wheeling high, pitching low,
Equanimity nowhere to be found.

Dead yet undying, this curious little character
Called legend by some,
Though ignored by none,
Still soars onward, unbidden... unbound.

Shattering the boundaries of reality,
Beyond the heavens, this Phoenix soars.
Beyond the sun, moon, comets, and stars.
Earth transcended... ether awaits.

Amin B. Swihart

Thoughts From Within

I can't believe this is happening
my heart is empty, but my mind is full,
I shut my eyes to block the pain,
I close my ears to forget my insanity,
Because all I want is to be remembered.
I really can't explain why I let myself down,
I am lost in the emptiness of my head,
my insecurity stops me from your understanding,
The jealousy stops me from opening my eyes,
and the memories keeps your face fresh in my heart.
I understand that you can't escape from your past
But your past is becoming my future.
I can't conceive why I am holding your presence,
I should let go and become what I am.
But it's hard to let go of something you don't have
because everything is just thoughts from within.....

Jonathan Michael Dolleman

I Am Free Now

I am free now
To take my journey to the highest plane
So I can watch over all that knew me
When I was with them here on earth.
I am free now
To bear no more pain and suffering that I have
Experienced throughout my entire life. I will be able
To rest knowing I took care of every responsibility
That I had to face.
I am free now
To guide you through triumphs and tribulations
That you will have to endure without me
To help you face situations on your own.
I am free now
Where I am at peace, and to embrace others
That have gone on before me. So that I can
Learn to comfort you since I am no longer
With you.

Teresa Waltman

Baby's Thoughts

Although my face is not now the same,
You need not carry any shame.

I'm big and healthy and beautiful, too!
An God brought me here just for you!

With all your love and help and hope,
I know as a family we will cope.

I know you feel angry, hurt, and blue,
But together all our dreams will come true!

I'm a precious bundle of joy,
I'm your beautiful little boy.

I'll grow, laugh, learn, and play,
Along with you and dad each and everyday.

I know that no one is to blame.
An in that answer I find no shame.

I'll go off to college sometime from now.
An you'll look at me and say "Wow!"

I maybe a doctor or layer or such,
But just know I love you both very much!

Lesa Lynette Ramsey

The Rose

At a distance admire its beauty,
too close you will get pricked,
is that the way to think of every relationship?
If you've ever darted through a field,
seeking beautiful flowers,
and bumped into a rose,
then you should know the reason,
for picking flowers slow.
If you find a flower you like,
one you think you can't live without,
approach it slowly and be careful,
if not you may be painfully hurt.
Make sure to look it over carefully,
make sure it's free of thorns,
then gently, clever, careful and smart,
slowly take it and plant it in your heart.

David A. Sweigart

Harvest Dusk

Though the soft wind blows making everything
come to life. As the breezes rustle through the trees
as if it were a wave breaking upon the ocean rocks.
And the wheat field almost ready to harvest, gently lays
on its side as if it where reaching out too some thing,
But not quite reaching it. As a tiny bird struggles to
land upon a swing branch it almost seems worth his struggle
to get there. And in the mist of the night a clam wind
seems to come to a gentle breeze, yet still making every
thing so very much alive.
Traci Owen

Oh, Mister Santa

Oh Mister Santa please bring me some toys
  I've been a very very good boy
I cleaned my room and I took out the trash
  Now you can't ask much more than that
Oh Mister Santa please visit us here
  We'll leave a snack of pretzels and beer
Relax a while and we wish you the best
  You work so hard you deserve a rest
Oh Mister Santa I'll be so annoyed
  If you don't bring me some shiny new toys
I've been real good and I do what I'm told
  So bring some toys before you get too old
Oh Mister Santa fill up your sack
  Be oh so careful and don't hurt your back
Please put some new toys under our tree
  I've been so good so be good to me
Oh Mister Santa Merry Christmas to you
  Mrs. Claus and all the elves too
You've been so nice to bring us these toys
  So Mister Santa we wish you much joy
Edward L. Schultski

Blue

Blue is like her still, cold lips,
like darkness coming to take her down.
It is like her hands which do not
touch my face like they used to.
Like her ears which do not hear me
saying "I love you."
It is like her eyes that do not see the pain,
Which devours my blackened heart.
Like her life being sucked away.
It is like the smell of the perfume
she used to wear,
which at one time, smelled like
fresh, sweet roses, but now, is dull
and without her beauty.
Blue is me being alone, she is dead.
Daniel J. Cooper

Death Takes His Toll

Darkness falls across the land,
He lies down to hold death's hand.
Closes his eyes,
As if he dies.
Pulls the dagger close to his heart,
He can see his whole life fall apart.
When he found out about the death of his friend Kurt,
His whole body started to hurt.
He felt as he didn't want to live,
Also like he had no more to give
When he woke up he made up his mind,
Since no one cared about him he had to die.
Pulled the trigger now he's dead,
Laying 6 feet under in that deep bed.
Brad Reiter

Happy Anniversary

Happy Anniversary, Darrell, the love of my life,
It's been twenty-six years since I became your wife.
With God on our side, we have weathered the storms,
Because, through it all, our love has stayed strong.

We have never had much in material things,
But have always looked for what tomorrow would bring.
Your answer to all is "next month we'll be clear",
For us, though, "Next Month" always fails to appear.

We have had bright days, and new hopes to share,
Because despite it all, we know we both care.
God richly blessed us with three children dear
All grown up now, living both far and near.

And the grandchildren, how they've brought joy and love,
They're our special babies sent from Heaven above.
Though times are still hard for us, even today,
You'll always be my anchor when things go astray.

I love you more today than I ever have before,
You're my friend, my love, the one I adore
Happy Anniversary, dearest one.
Elaine White

"Illusions Of Joy"

Illusions of joy spin 'round your mind,
Things aren't what they used to be,
Spiritual skin has been scarred...
Faith is now hard to come by,
The past that is renewed by nightmares, calls,
You have disposed of the spiritual card...
"If I only had this, if I only had that,
I would discover true happiness..." (so you thought)
The dawn of my fulfillment is just around the corner,
I must look to the future... (but your soul's been bought)
Now you've been left exposed,
Embarrassment grins in the light of your face...
(This seems strangely familiar)
A vision rekindles itself in the tracks of your mind...
A man... naked on a cross...
(Memories whisper in your ear)
You retreat to your first love,
The illusion of joy is no longer an illusion...
Sean C. Robinett

"The Dawning"

An old awakening from years gone by
Are written in tears, I now must cry.
Tattered, torn, bruised, and bent;
My childhood years in pain were spent.

Upon my innocence cold hands were placed,
While in my pillow, I hid my face.
The bitterness of lust I was forced to taste,
As he softly moved with insufferable haste.

In silence I screamed through shallow breath,
As my soul bore witness to my childhood's death.
As unwritten pages of my life he stole,
I vowed his secret would never be told.

Betrayed and broken I cried in pain,
And wondered with doubt if I'd ever be sane.
With welled-up tears I laid aside
The shattered dreams of my world inside.

A new awakening I now must face,
Or forever in darkness be encased.
In suffering shame I dare not stay,
As I face the dawn of a bright new day.
Gracie C. Peters

The Old Maid

She had waited all her life
No one had asked her to be their wife
She still had her virginity
She could hold her head up with dignity

She had never known what love meant
No man had ever given her a hint
She lived in a world all her own
In reality she was all alone

Her whole life rushed through her head
No cure was found as she neared her death bed
All of a sudden she began to cry
She was not yet ready to die

She had never known love
Not even the kind from above
So she began to pray
A few moments later, her spirit left her body that day.

Cindy Brown

Life Lines

As I come to this time in my life,
I look for some rhyme in my life,
And I see shadows...

Soft shadows of things that might have been,
Dark shadows of things that were,
Light shadows of laughter and joy,
And hard shadows filled with tears.

As I come to this time in my life,
I hold on to the dreams of my life,
And I feel Jesus...

In the beginning when all was new,
In the end when it all starts over,
Now as I struggle to grow,
Then when He frees my burdens.

Debbie Moulton

Old Runner

His hair is gray, his youth is gone.
He is standing at the line of a marathon.
The gun is fired, he is on his way.
It could not be a better day on word
he strives just passed mile 5
now at mile 16 can he hold
the pace, can he complete the race?
Now it's a hill. I see can he do 23
he has reached the finish line
the clock over head reads 3:59
his hair is gray, his youth is gone
and he has run a marathon

Gerald Crist

Circle Of Dreams

It takes a lot of love, for Fifty Years
a lot of caring, giving, and tears.
Working and sharing,
with each other — side by side.
Raising a family, makes a couple
fill with pride.
Family and friends make our life complete,
always loving each other —
there will be no defeat.
Devotion and love forever
is what it all means,
That is the completion
of the Circle of Dreams.

Margie Jeffrey

One Silent Snowflake

A solitary crystal, drifting aimlessly...
Undefined, falling helplessly...
Fragile and white, reluctantly earthbound.

Dreading the moment of impact,
Knowing the odds of survival,
The traveler continues in fearful
Anticipation.

Mystical creation...   Unprotected...
Alone.
Feeling despair, having come and gone
Unrecognized.
Left to its own devices...   One last,
Anguished plea for acknowledgment.

Instead...
Unpreserved, this fearful fragile creature
Meets death in silent
Whiteness...   Drifting...
Unnoticed...   Into...
Obscurity.

Kelly McDonnell

Rebirth And Legacy

It is early May
I sit by my window watching the rebirth
I am in my later years,
No longer young, but not old
I realize my rebirth will come with the extensions of me
My grandchildren come into view
Their happy spirits light up my very soul
These are my extensions
Eager to learn
Quick to love and trust
I give them lessons
Faith and tolerance
Giving and sharing
Loving and caring
They will go forth and teach their own
And the roots will spread
I will go on forever through them and theirs
They will be my rebirth, my legacy

Marie Orlando

Untitled

To my greek God
Whose love is like poison
Calling me back time and time again;
Pulling me into a deep dreamy trance
Holding me captive, waiting for more.

Only then. He opens my eyes
And shows my soul a love
So pure and white, that my eyes
Sting from his blinding passion
That explodes from his heart.

But no, he doesn't stop there;
His charisma sets me on fire:
So let me burn! Because it cannot
Be put out by mere oceans.
It engulfs me, and destroys me.

So from my burning ashes
Grows a beautiful daisy
Simple and pure, like the love
I bore for him, that blows in
The wind and whispers in little girl's dreams.

Kelly Herbst

One World, Many People

How can this be one world
When in it are so many people?

How can so many people
Exist in just one world?

One world, many people —
We are all the same.

Many people, one world —
We are all so different.

How do we live together?
How do we live apart?

With one world and so many people,
We have to get along.

With so many people in just one world,
Only peace, love, tolerance and understanding
  will make it work.

Bryon J. Grant

A Mother's Love

A cry and whimper is heard in the night,
She's there in a flash right by your side.

Always willing and able to comfort and soothe,
She's there ready to be your guide.

When days are sad, she looks at your face,
She reads your expression just like a book.

There is comfort again, in just knowing her stare.
Knowing her concern and love are there.

A mother's love is so special and treasured,
Memories remain forever and ever.

Cheryl A. Mercs

The Mystery Of Flight 800

Here behold the battle of the bulls:
Bureau vs. Bureau, when only one can be to blame.
Hung like a game fish, skeletal remains of the fuselage.
"Yes Us, yes TWA— The truth—", reporters asks,
"What happened to flight 800?"
Mike in mouth Bureaucrats
Finger point to other's mistakes
Hiding smiles like Cheshire cats,
While they wanly spin their tales.

Unbelievable, but so consistent.
Yet once the stories are homogenized, pasteurized,
Then blandly cooked in type—lest insurance palates be offended,
Only the eternally gladsome will walk away less furrowed brow
And a cockeyed look of stupefaction that asks,
"What happened to flight 800?"
Perhaps the plane lost its balance
By dint of two perennially right wings.

Dominick Castiglione

Hide the Pain

Hide the pain don't let it show,
  don't ever let anyone know.
Keep it inside show that you're strong,
  don't let them see anything wrong.
Hide all the loneliness hide the fears,
  don't let them ever see your tears
Keep all the pain you feel deep inside,
  don't let it show, remember your pride?
Hide all the nights you can't fall asleep,
  and always remember to hide and keep.

Andrea C. Anderson

The Deer

Approaching through the Autumn light
Upon sleek legs of golden elegance,
Falling leaves of Aspen elevate her stance
As she hunts a dream-filled night.
Oblivious to the stark wood of distraction
My sights remain on her, she is my fascination.

Often I wonder if another Judgment has come
As I raise my bow preparing for a kill,
Just as Cupid to control the lover's will.
Glancing my way she causes all by my heart to numb,
Beautiful eyes gazing round always in fear
Of lions, wolves, and bears which seem so near.

Bow drawn, arrow notched, and ready to fly
(Never has God created on near so fair,
I awe at the auburn sun in her hair)
Thankful am I, for Creator's permiss to try.
Arrived has the point when emotions are put to test,
Will I still the throbbing heart within her breast?

This decision is mine by Holy right,
'Less she senses peril and chooses flight.

Charles A. Dorrel

The Girl Who Got Well

I went to seek help from someone more wounded than I,
Her own sense of unworthiness hidden and veiled behind her Ph.D.
and her analytical skills - all facades and cover ups.
Her mind is tense for battle; my mind seeks peace.
Her spirit is judging and fierce; my spirit seeks tranquillity.
She analyzes; I want to experience.
I decided the hell with all this; my wounds are what make me
human and real; not to be fixed like a carburetor.
I went out and bought roller blades and embraced
my own frailty, my own reality, and my own self
as I skated blissfully down my own path.

Dean Worthington

On Top Of A Hill

On top of a hill, there stood a girl
And in her hand, she held a rose
The flaming red of its blooming petals
The rage and aggression of years gone by

On top of a hill, there stood a girl
And in her hand, she held a rod
The strength of the iron always so near
Yet no one to lean on through sorrow and fear

On top of a hill, there stood a girl
And in her hand, she held a chest
Locked with a key that no one could find
Sheltered and hidden letting nothing escape

Through sadness and sorrow
Through thick and thin
There lived a girl who let nobody in
Through anger and turmoil
And wars of the soul
She fought all alone
Without a friend, only foe

Dana Ledoux

Destiny's Desire

We are a tree with a solid place to stand,
Alone we are leaves wandering with every wind's
Command.

Mindy Huffman

Changing Seasons

The winter is harsh and mean,
And leaves snowflakes on a majestic scene.
The birds are gone and the air is cold,
Now warm summer days seem very old.

In spring the daffodils are in full bloom,
And in the sky the sun does loom.
The hills are green and covered with flowers,
And instead of snow there are now showers.

In the summer the sun is ablaze,
And it's a time of fun-filled days.
The grass is high and the mosquitoes are out,
The only sound is of children's shouts.

In the fall the leaves turn red, yellow, and brown,
After that they fall slowly down.
The air is crisp and cool,
And I will once again have to go back to school.

The seasons change one by one,
Alternating between darkness and sun.

Katie Hale

"Just Smile"

When you remember
  The first glance,
  The first touch of hands,
  And the affection it portrayed, just smile

When you remember
  The first kiss,
  The first embrace,
  And the protection it conveyed, just smile

When you remember
  The heartbreak,
  The sorrow,
  And the years past that helped ease the pain, just smile

When you remember
  The love of past,
  The love of present,
  And all the memories that make them special, just smile

But most of all when you remember
  The feelings we shared for each other so long ago,
  And our lives apart as they are now,
  Keep it in your heart always and... just smile

Harold J. Matroni

If I Ruled The World

I sit under a tree reading
I say to myself
"What if I ruled the world"
I think about it very hard
And I decide

If I ruled the world
There would be no pollution
No countries would be fighting
Everyone would have a home
Everyone would have a job
No laws would be broken
No worries about getting kidnapped,
Robbed or killed.
And color would have never been a problem.

If I ruled the world
There would be free toys
For kids 10 and under
Everyone would be friends
If I ruled the world
It would be a better place.

Valerie Salnave

Earth Year 2000....

Earth year 2000 is fast approaching,
People abound, pushing animals around,
Making room for themselves and paving over the ground.
Balance is coming due - Will mankind be through?
Fossilized bones, decaying stones, oxygen loans, groaning moans,
Karmic pay zones. - Flash - Nuclear holocaust.
"Oh please, let's not go down that path; so sad if we do,
so dark, so bad, makes me mad! Makes Me Mad!"
But I'm glad I know, even if we do, life will still grow,
reaching out of the ash, ebbing and flowing, evermore sowing
  and gradually knowing,
building from cellular to organ and body with sense perception
  and dance expression,
with mental and spiritual cosmic progression.
Hope for the mellow flow, help the "green peace" show.
The choice is ours, a desolation of plastic jars, or a vibrant planet
with the dance flow of life crossing the infinite span.
Sunlight shining, warm and bright....
Earth year 2000 people abound recovering the ground,
bringing the balance that is overdue,
working together spreading the love force, clear and true,
reaching out to you and everyone else on this earth life zoo!

Robert Palmer

Nobody's Home

You have reached the home of obsessiveness and denial. Entering the realm of disbelief and rejection. Say hello to abandonment and befriend sorrow. Encompass solitude and make love to loneliness. Wake up next to yourself and the other personalities that you must take on for survival. And if anyone ever calls you weak, feel sorry for them and their true lack of expression. Move to transcendentalism live alone, as we all do anyway, and comfort the hope that runs through the theme of your life like a drug. Addictive hope, a false illusion of what is real, a daydream in the avoidance of reality.
The drug of hope is one of the many to overdose on and die from. Yet the perseverance of hope is the search for dependency. It is there, it is always there, and when you haven't yet obtained it you go through withdrawal. In the search you disrespect yourself, lose yourself, do things you never thought you would do, only others - but you are an addict, you need hope, you need love and you would die for it. You are beginning your trip. Your destiny for irrationality, your lies and deceit just to find the one that makes you feel the best. And the moment lasts as long as the drug and in essence you are only loved for a short amount of time.

Sabrina A. Singarella

Turtle On My Porch

There was a turtle on my porch this morning.
I don't know why, but he made me want to cry.
So far from home, and all alone.
I pondered, what should I do now?
Should I keep him?
How in the hell do I feed him?
Or maybe I should just leave him be, in hopes that he'll cross over
to my neighbors yard?
Just as I was contemplating what to do with the little bugger, he
looked right up at me, glaring, with those stark beady little
reptilian eyes of his.
God, he looked so tired, old, and very dried up.
Looking at him I was painfully reminded of just how frail life can be.
I wondered, will I be looked upon in the same manner
  some twenty years from now?
Will others be pondering what the hell to do with me?
Keep me, feed me, or just leave me be?
Just the thought made shivers run down my back.
Then lo and behold, a fly flew across my view, he spotted it to, a
swatter was found, a mighty blow came down, now Quasimodo and I
will soon be enjoying dinner for two.

Eileen Dennis Luna

I Cry

I lay down to bed and close my eyes;
Nothing seems right and I cannot surmise,
Why these feelings I feel and wish so to hide;
Are condemning me to sadness and killing me inside.
But no one cares, so deep down I cry.

My friends who I trust are telling me lies;
They tease and they taunt me and want me to die,
The reason unknown to them and to I,
Perhaps they will stop and soon realize;
That I'm only human, and wish for more time,
To find someone to care for me, each day and each night;
But no one loves me so deep down I cry.

K. Jarrett

The Elm Tree!!!

The Elm Tree....young.....not full grown,
  stood by the shed, the shed on the right,
  down the lane to the cane mill.

The tree grew tall and straight, not a single trunk,
  but several.

The shed is gone....the lane has vanished!!!!
  What remains? Remnants of the cane mill
  and the Elm Tree, grown taller...stretching
  upward to the sky!

Now a new lane...the driveway for a granddaughter's house...
  passes the Elm on the other side.

Sundown in March! The sun is low in the western sky...
  the Elm is decked with the awakening blossoms of
  spring. It appears as a display of....
    antique lace, delicate....
    spider web thin.....
    golden bronze in the shadows....
    a priceless moment, gone in an instant,
    Except for she who beheld its beauty!!!

Celeste Ward

A Heart Of Purple

On the dark side of the moon
is a purple rose,
and to physically possess it
you must acknowledge
the mental beauty it imposes.

It is a lonely rose,
filled with a purple light
that is satisfying to the soul.

The light fills the universe
on the other side of the moon
a universe filled with passion and hope.

My heart goes out to my purple rose
on the dark side of the moon...

Micah D. Lacy

The Devil's Air

The air I breathe is sin
Forming a dark cloud that covers my soul
Temptations fill my head
A wicked enters my veins
Slithering its way throughout my body
Regret and sadness invades my innocence
The evil seeps through my pores
Making my body quiver
It evaporates into the air
Only for me to breath again

Paul Roehling

The Explorer Badge

Some people ask what my badge means to me,
I tell them "a lot" but most you cannot see,
It is a symbol of honor from the heart, mind, and soul,
It is the beginning of a teenager's life long goal,
Many others my age laugh and turn away,
I just ignore them and forget what they say,
My badge is a symbol of a service I like,
I may help someone or just fix their bike,
Every once in a while I like it when people say "thanks",
I enjoy my job because of the smiles it makes,
I have learned discipline in how to choose my path,
Although there is work there is always a laugh,
When I look at my badge it reminds me of these things,
It reminds me of the happiness being an explorer brings,
Everyday in explorers I learn something new,
There is nothing quite like it a teenager can do,
This badge is more than something you wear,
So wear it with pride and show them you care.

Thomas S. Church

Come Walk With Me

Please let go, come walk with me.
Just take my hand and have no fear.
The time has come to bring you here.
Valleys of shadows I'll show you through.
Just keep your faith, I'm there with you.

Your eyes were closed, but now they're open.
Through death a door will open wide.
So have no fear, I'll be your guide.
You'll hear my voice as choirs sing.
I'll lift you up on angels' wings.

Though tears are shed when you must go,
I'll comfort them and let them know
You're in good hands so they'll let go.
For when it's time, I'll call their name
And bring them home to see again
You waiting here, and no more pain.

My love, my child, will live forever.
Your soul I'll keep and leave you never.
Your body's tired, we'll let it rest.
Your soul is saved, you passed the test.

Marsha K. Kirby

12 Lentils: A Buddhist Home Meditation

12 Lentils, on a shelf, in a row.
One withers and is sere.
A crow, glittering black beaked thief
Two are gone. Nine lentils.
A cloud passes over the face of the moon.
A beggar comes to the door.
Eight lentils left. Bow to the lotus.
It begins to rain.
Lightning illuminates the room.
Seven now. The roof is leaking.
Six lentils. A dog is barking.
Far away. Look out the window to see.
Come in, sit. 5 lentils.
It is dark. Light a candle
Four lentils. What is the use?
Look out to the sea. Three lentils.
Two lentils. Use them for soup.
Carry water in the broken pitcher.
Come, here is the bowl.
It is full, no, it is empty.

Karen Kouril

go

why am i still here? i should have left long ago.
  why did i stay? anna, why are you so stubborn?
    why did you have to resist? your family is gone
      now. you thought they would be found.
        you did not know, then, the terrible horrors of
          slavery. you were young and beautiful then.
            you were a simple house slave. then you
              began to get older, lost your beauty.
                should have gone with your family.
they sent you to the fields, pickin' cotton. you
were tired, couldn't work hard enough. should
have gone north with your family. the whip, cold
and harsh, unforgiving, unforgetting. should have
gone with your family. the memories all come flooding back, all bad.
except one.
mitchell, brave and true, told you were still beautiful.
he is here, now, by your side.
silently urging you to follow your family.
should have gone with your family.
go with him now. go to the free states. go to your family.
go.
   Scott Martin

Fatherdaddies' Love

So many times I've sat and wondered,
About the man I've met, but never knew.
What wrong have I done to him?
And was what mommy said about him true?

I thought fatherdaddies' love was supposed to be wonderful,
A love so strong that it could warm a world of no light,
Yet fatherdaddy has never shared that love with me,
So many times there were tears, my mommy helped me wipe.

Through the years, I've learned from fatherdaddies' false love,
Now I've grown into a strong, unselfish, young man.
I've bloomed with only momadaddies' love to guide me.
I'll take the world by storm, like only a true man can.

Now my role as a fatherdaddy is presently at hand,
My unselfish love will shine brighter than a world of candles,
Giving new strength and comfort to my family.
And my son shall be a real man, because I lead by example.
   Carlos Wilson

Waiting

I wait watching the horizon.
I wait for the rising of the sun.
I have waited an eternity and I must wait longer still,
But I am assured the sun will rise again.
Still I wait.

I wait.
The darkness surrounds me like a blanket of evil, I am terrified.
I imagine thousands of demonic figures dancing about me in the dark.
I can feel their clawed hands reaching out,
Forever seeking to grasp my souls and rip it from me
But, for some unknown reason they wait.

I wait.
What will it be like, will the sun chase away the demons of the night?
I wait and I begin to despair.
When will the sun rise and take me from the darkness?
I wait.

I wait,
And I feel the kiss of death rest gently upon me.
The sun bursts forth from the clouds and warms my face.
I wait no longer.
   Victoria Ann Neeley

Laxity Of Love

A king once told me that the hardest treasure to find
was the one in your heart,
That the love of a woman could never tear apart,
For I have seen uncertainty, confusion and contradiction,
And I'll I can say that it's a bunch of superstition,
Love isn't found in one but is found in all,
It is so strong that it could sustain my fall,
Does death bring life or does life bring death?
Life brings love and love brings regret,
Once you find desire, tenderness and affection,
Nothing can stop you except fear and rejection,
The building blocks of life were to be created and expansive,
But all we are getting is reprehensive,
We are the ones who construct the lives,
So many souls that will eventually demise,
Love is what brings all of us together,
The only thing that can unite us now and forever.
   John C. Longobardi

Under The Stars

Under the stars I'm dreaming.
I wonder as I gaze above,
Why is it that I'm haunted
by the memory of your face?

Under the stars I'm dreaming.
I hear your voice as you sing,
looking deeply into my eyes,
then softly calling my name.

Under the stars I'm dreaming.
A picture so vividly clear,
I see you dancing in front of me.
Until reality sends you away.

Under the stars I'm dreaming.
Please tell me this is true.
I feel your arms encompass me,
An unspoken promise you'll never leave.

Under the stars I'm dreaming.
Crying softly as I lay flowers upon your grave.
My heart grows colder, my soul slips away,
as I mourn my loss—the day you met your fate.
   Angela Askeland

Pieta

I felt my self sliding down a hill side
My skin a sugar quartz white
A wagon carried me to a studio

In the distance I could hear chipping pounding
Who or what ever was getting closer
To the center that I was confined in
First my hand appeared lying limp
Every vein intact waiting to come to life

Next my head was in view lying on a female arm
The robe that the arm was contained in
Ruffled up into a hood
The face of eternal love and empathy looked at my limp figure

I was not a child but a man
I was the ravaged and empty soul of mankind
Being comforted by the immortal virgin

Who well knows the tragedies of humanity
Birth, death, resurrection
The soul's struggle between heaven, hell
Micheal Anglo sighed at my completion
Slowly he turned and closed the door that was creation.
   Esequiel Chacon

My Shadow

I have a little shadow, who goes with me every day,
He is with me as I go about my work and as I play.
I cannot elude him, so close is he to me,
And occasionally, I sort of wish that he would let me be.

For you see, this little shadow's more unique than all the rest,
He has two attributes that are extreme, to that I can attest!
Now, you may think that shadows are no more than they appear,
So I'll explain just why this one has always been so near.

You see, this little shadow is my very own dear son,
Who has eyes that watch my every move, and all that I have done.
Who has ears that listen closely, to my every tone of voice,
And who thinks that all Dad says and does, is his one and only choice!

That is why I must control myself, in all I say and do,
This little shadow will someday be doing these things, too.
And I must instill in him the morals I was taught,
When I was *my* dad's shadow, learning ways that *my* ears caught.

I pray each night when I have tucked my son into his bed,
That I will not have led him wrong, in things I've done or said.
Because someday my son will have a shadow at *his* side,
And he can teach *his* son with honor, what was taught to *him*
   with pride.

   June Newton

Unaware

Are you afraid of your own reflection?
Are you afraid of what you might see?
Larger than life, walk through the same path
And you don't even notice me.

A secret you are trying to hide,
And inside it multiplies.
You crave for their glances, for them to look your way.
Never feeling any pleasure when you get them anyway.

It's raining inside, puddles of chrome.
Energy wasted, can't find your way home.
And feeling alone, but always I'm there.
Abolish the mind game and acknowledge
the scars in your life if you care.
Too much of a short life to live unaware.

   Ruby Sanchez

How Much Is Too Much?

He looks at her-but she's not the one he sees.
He kisses her-but she's not the one he kisses.
The selfish talk and devious motives lead to a quick downfall.
The second time around makes self the fool.
Another heartache only creates a thicker, taller wall for the next
   to attempt.
But who will dare?
No one will.
Not because danger awaits behind it, but because the territory is
   yet unexplored.
They only see a warm smile that is masked by hurt and
disappointment.
Will there ever be one to attempt the area?
Or will it be forgotten that there is a princess behind the wall
   waiting for her knight to come?
Many dark nights have come and gone.
One by one the princesses are chosen.
Yet one still remains.

   Ashley Leonard

Wings Of My Mind

Tiny feet clad in slippers of softness scurry across my mind
Leaving footprints in the dust of yesterdays,
And my heart smiles.
A blanket of gentleness covers me
and the warmth of happy times envelopes me.
Faint breezes rustle by and mingle with the sounds of night
and touch my face with fingers cool and soothing
and I feel joy.
Pale moonlight reaches down and shadows of sadness slip away.
Tiny dewdrops touch my lips
and I taste the sweetness of my dreams.
Brushing past my ears, the sounds of night caress me
and lull my thoughts to sleep in arms of love.
Contentment overpowers me and I drift away
to become part of breezes, moonlight and timeless eternity
So I may touch some sadness
with these intangible things
and someone will know joy
because of me...

   Jerry Meade

Mr. Misery

The man with the mask
had no where to go
He walked to the edge of the world

Take one more step
into another dimension
Step into the Unknown World.
  Beyond Reality
  Beyond Reality;
  And he says to himself,
  "Where is my destiny?"
  "What am I supposed to be?",
  "My name is Misery."

Then appeared a door very tall
an echoing voice, a thundering call,
  "Mr. Misery, have no fear.
  Open the door, for it will all be clear.
  Inside is truth, which is what you seek.
Return to the hopeless; from there you came, and speak."

  When he returned, the people, they asked
about how he got rid of his revolting mask.

   A. J. Borja

Untitled

Overwhelming frustration throws me to the ground.
Anger and determination pick me up again.
Unknowing of my next obstacles, I begin again my ascent.
Incredible are the odds against reaching my first destination.
Something beyond my comprehension of power desperately
tries to stop me.
What amount of suffering must I endure to appease this force?
Am I as a person not important if not for my monetary status?
What force holds this value, that I might look upon a soul
as wretched as this?
Cowardly enough, no doubt it will remain hidden.
My soul burns!
I must succeed!
I must win!

   Thomas O'Connor

Image In The Mirror

Starring at my reflection in the mirror
The smell of wet grass sneaks though my window
A gust of warm air plays with my hair
Blowing tangled strands of ginger red against my face
Pushing it back emerald eyes stares at me
Starring at the glass of orange juice and vodka on my dresser
It hurts to keep looking at the same image of my mother
Will my mistakes mimic hers
Will I lost a million days and nights to vodka and orange juice
Will times, names and place become a blur
Will my only company be the voices in my head mingling together
    making no sense
Surrounded by people but loneliness overwhelms me
Will my blurred reality lead my daughter to find me wrist slashed
    unconscious on the bathroom floor like I found my mother
Will my life be lost with a million sips
    Crystal Osborne

By A Pond

By a pond there's lots to see animals hustling so happily.
Birds soaring like kites in the sky.
The grass growing enormously high.
Butterflies flutter like dancers in the sky.
Fish of all beautiful colors act as a kaleidoscope in their school.
Chipmunks run around so happily. Their chubby cheeks, filled with
acorns, the rest filled with glee.
Bees are the ones that are truly funny doing all of that work for
just a few drops of honey!
Spring time blooms in the morning filled with dew look like
gemstones in a truly magnificent cave!
Turtles just leave them alone because if they get scared
there's always their mobile home.
Baby animals are so adorable but whatever you do without for mommy!
Look there are some deer coming down for a drink their not
watching you, it is only what you think.
For nature is truly only in the eyes of its beholder!
    Erin Boisvert

A Wedding Toast

Last night as I lay sleeping, King Brian visited my bed. Be
there a mortal here unfamiliar with King Brian, 'Tis the king
of the little people.

It was a silly sight, I was sitting up in bed dressed only
in my underwear, Bonnie was stretched out beside me sound
asleep, and old King Brian was sitting on her nose with a
tankard of ale in his hand.

And with a smile, of the wedding he said, 'tis a grand day
for the Irish, and then he said that on their wedding, the
names of Shawn and Andrea would go out to every Leprechaun
throughout all the land, so that no matter where they go, or
what they do they will be watched over by the little people.

Then he told me that on this day, that every Irishman who
has ever lived will pause at this grand occasion, and lift
their tankards high in joyful celebration.

So I would be neglecting me duty if I did not ask all who
are here to raise your glasses high, and join in with all
the Irishmen who've died.

In wishing good fortune to Shawn Michael and his new bride.
    Joseph D. Martin

Chaos

Behind Empty Reflections
Sits Life's true exceptions
Fire, Ice, Heat, Cold
Mean nothing to a human soul
What sets the dark ones apart
Is forgetting the mind and living the heart
True souls care nothing for green
For they know how life is truly seen
While it's always seen through filtered eyes
It is the caring soul that fears not to die
Living life by the seat of their pants
Through peaceful moments and raving rants
Living life day and night
Experiencing wrong and right
The damn breaks and my heart floods
Feeling anger, sorrow, hate, and love
Chaos, life, death, and birth
Bring me Heaven, Hell and Mirth
Life is not just places you see
Life is something you must Be
    James Michael Spahn

Abandon

Abandon is the worst way to feel when
you have no one to comfort you.
Feeling abandoned sometimes makes you
feel as if you are standing all alone.
Because of abandonment, all kinds of things
runs through the mind.
Feeling abandoned makes the mind think that
No one cares for you.
Feeling abandoned leaves the face with a sad
And unpleasant look.
Sometimes your relatives and friends make you
feel abandoned because of the way they treat you.
Acting cold hearted and funny towards people
makes you feel abandoned.
No one knows how it feels to be abandoned until
they have experienced it.
    Antonio Hodges

A Birthday Prayer

Dear Heavenly Father,

Before you created the heavens and the earth,
you knew me by my name.

You have a purpose for me in your plan,
That is why you created me during this span.

I was so in love with sin and myself
Yet you loved me so much you gave a part of yourself.

There is nothing I can do
That can bring me to you.

That is why you sent Jesus your son
To pay for all my transgressions.

With your Holy Spirit you gave me new life
So only you I may worship and glorify.

Even though I still struggle and sin
Your grace is sufficient to strengthen me within.

Please grant me the passion to pray
To seek your wisdom and face you throughout everyday.

Lord, please don't let me keep you inside
But let me share you with others, so they may not die.
    Thomas G. Jebb

I Can Not Tell A Lie

I can not tell a lie.
We are all the same in my eye.
Whether you're black or white;
Catholic or Jewish;
Boy or girl.
We are all one equal world
No one person is better than the other.
We all should be fair
And impartial to one another.
All of us make mistakes,
But that is all it takes.
For one person to become angry with another.
There is something we can do.
We can look past the color of a person's skin.
Instead we can look deep within.
Because I can not tell a lie.
   Holly Aguirre

Untitled

When we are kids,
we learn to hate, to love, to know, and to use.
We are taught by people,
people we know and respect, or not.
By strangers who can't live without giving advice.
Good, bad, who cares, as long as it's there.
We take it or ignore it, the choice is ours.
But we are still grateful, for it is being given.
People care, if we don't know them, it doesn't matter.
Since our childhood we were raised
with the help of others - needed or not.
From the union of all our "mothers"
we know the art of love, freedom, and even selfishness.
Later that art is going to be a guide
that will lead you through life.
   Flora Serebrennik

My Little Lighthouse

Your light is like a cup of tea
Waiting in the morning for me;

It is there for me all day long
It's helping me to sing a song;

Into the morning and into the night
Into the fog your light will fight;

You lift me up when I am down
Your light is forever going around;

You're not as pretty as the white house
What you are is my little lighthouse.
   Dawn O'Donnell

Star

I want his heart
I want his soul
but he gave them to the game
I want his life
I want his name
but they are his price for fame

You could see it in his face
You could hear it in his voice
You could feel it in his touch by night
He's a bright star light in a crowded sky
He'll take away your breath as he soars so high
He'll steal your heart with loving gifts
Reflecting in his eyes

I stand alone and watch...
him fly
   Charlotte Lee McCobb

My Reality...

   In reality... mine are the faces behind the clouds.
       ... those that can laugh.
       ... those that can sing.
       ... those that can smile.
       ... those that can cry.
   In reality... they are there, but, they are hiding.
   With their fog- the clouds keep the faces features
       undistinguishable and safe.
       No laughs. No songs. No smiles. No tears.
   In reality... the fog that the clouds form, shield my heart
       from the blindingly critical rays that shine
       from the faces outside the shadows.
       The clouds slow the pace.
       The fog makes each step predictable,
       determined and uneventful.
   In reality... the dark only exists where the rays shine
       through to the faces.
   In reality... the faces like the fog.
       I've been told the faces also like the rays.
       The rays feed life.
   Susan C. Munro

Faux Pearls Necklace, A Significant Bond

Often enough I have wondered why
My mother and I hardly got along —
As I have later realized it was my stubbornness.

From my childhood to young adulthood
I loved my mother like any daughter should —
Crying and laughing moments we both actually shared.

Especially there was a string of faux pearls
She gave me to wear with my formal attire —
She often felt happy as I wore it around my little neck.

That string of faux pearls was a significant bond
Which my mother and I once cherished fondly —
Later she had gone and left me alone in this sad world.

The faux pearls necklace was the only thing
My mother and I found a family loving bond —
Oh, how much I wish to have this necklace with me now.
   Kethshara Khlok

My Heart's Treasure Chest

Down life's horizons of mystic dreams,
   All decked in their array;
It's hard to sum the heart's contents,
   And tell it all today.

The things that I count special,
   And hold most dear to me;
Are the untold priceless joys,
   Of my treasured family.

Each have their special image,
   With each face it's hard to part,
But the love of each is treasured,
   And is stored within my heart.

Down memory's lane I stand and look,
   And reflect a lifetime through;
I see no greater joy for me,
   Than the love which was left by you.

So bound with mutual feelings,
   I'll keep filled "Your Place" you left,
With all the joys of life we knew,
   In my "Heart's Treasure Chest."
   Doris Lee Gribble

You Don't Look Deep Enough

I have blue eyes and blond hair,
Rosy cheeks and skin that's fair,
So quiet no one knows I'm there.
If you see nothing but this, you don't look deep enough.

If you saw me, you would find
I'm really quite the "simple" kind.
"Out of sight, out of mind."
If you see nothing but this, you don't look deep enough.

Don't you hear my soft, sweet cry?
Don't you see my teary eye?
Will you know me when I die?
Please look deep enough.
Please look deep enough.
  Sarah Wrede

Untitled

The white clouds look like a river in the distance.
if you look close you can see God in the horizon.
He sits upon His throne in Heaven higher than any other being
He is the Supreme being of all things ever made.
he is the Ruler of earth, sky moon, sun stars, lakes and of people
He is the one and only being that passes judgement of all people.
Like you and me.
He is the only God to be worshiped
Not Idols

God is not dead.
  Kathy Chorpening

Hands Are For...

Hands are for BANDING and linking together
Hands are for SHARING to make life better

Hands are for HOLDING, to show we are friends
Hands are for HIGH FIVES even if we don't win

Hands are for embracing people and pets
And HUGGING to make life its very best

Hands held together are a story that tells
Of friendships not found on grocery shelves

Hands come in all shapes, sizes, and colors
Hands even TALK and work special wonders

Hands can fly through the sky
Hands can scratch bugs out of the eye

Hands are for waving to folks near and far
And for scraping peanut butter from the jar

Hands show pleasure, of course
Hands can measure the height of a horse

Hands are for pizza and everything gooey
Hands are for squeezing cookie dough, oh, so chewy

Hands are for LOVING and SHARING
The world gets better when hands are CARING
  James E. Shaw

Troubled Times

I know right now you have a troubled mind.
But always remember we will stand the test of time.
I am yours and you are mine our hearts will always be intertwined.
I will be here for you anytime to talk to, or just to lean upon.
You will always have a shoulder to cry on.
Just remember no matter how many troubles are on your mind.
I will be waiting any time because I am yours and you are mine.
We will be together till the end of time.
  Dorothy J. Dibble

Oklahoma City Bombing

The innocent are lost. The lives of those we loved.
Never to return, but to remain in heaven above.

Why they had to leave, why they were not spared,
We shall never know. It is a time of great despair.

They were at the mercy of one man.
He did not care if they lived or died.

He considered it an accomplishment,
And all he felt was pride.

The bomb was set, hidden away.
And no one expected the destruction of that day.

When it was all over, there was nothing left
But a pile of rubble. And all around, the horror of death.

So many lost their lives on that tragic day.
Not knowing or expecting that it would end this way.

That day is a constant reminder of the violence in this world.
And I pray each day, "Please help us oh Lord!"
  Amber Stringer

I Am Rushing To My Death

I am rushing to my death
Driven by my many masters
I am the slave of the sun
The whore of the clock
The servant with undying faith
In other people's ever-broken timetables
Ever forgetting that I too
Have the right of slower service
The right and pleasure to let my engines idle...

I will try to make my own new timetable
And to follow it
I will seek the quiet ways
I must remember
That we are all moving closer
To that far place
I must remember not to run
I must remember to walk
  Michael Greenfield

Baggy Pants The Clown

There are those that always find the laughter in the lighter side
  of you.
They think that you are humorous in everything you say and do.
They laughed so hard before they left, you had them rolling
  on the ground,
Oh yes, it's not hard for you, you're "Baggy pants the clown."

Not everyone can make you smile when you're feeling low,
And help you rise above a heartache or a very troubled soul.
It's a gift to lift their spirits and take away their frowns,
It's my privilege to introduce to you, "Baggy pants the clown."

And even tho there are days, when your world doesn't seem
  one bit funny,
The sun is shining bright and bold, but your mind is feeling muddy.
You seem to rise above the darkness that your mind and heart are in,
And find a way to make them smile and laugh, be a clown,
  but most of all a friend.

But of all the people I have known they have given back to me,
A piece of there own spectrum for my rainbow of thoughts to see.
So if you're ever up this way, I'd be glad to show you around,
I'm known to everyone in town as "Baggy pants the clown."
  Linda Kay Good

My Life, My Love

My life is like a glass
It is empty without her love
My love is like a rose
Wilting without the sunshine of her face
Without her, I am nothing
But with her, I am something
Something that she's always dreamed of
My life is like a glass
With her, it is filled with sweet wine
My love is like a rose
It is standing tall, bright and red
With the sunshine of her face
   Todd Pogirnicki

Human Fate

Have you ever stopped to hear the silence
and heard hell scream inside your head.
Voices from the great beyond
say all your thoughts are dead.

Have you ever stopped to hear the music
and heard the sounds of hate.
Satan whispered in your ear
It is your only human fate.
   Paul D. Prince

Searching For My Soul

My soul where is it
I can't seem to find it
I have looked almost everywhere
I walked to the mountain and back
I ran to the ocean and sailed back
I skipped to the country and drove back
No where to find my soul
I would think it would be easy to find it, but so far no luck
why is my soul lost
what did I do to lose my soul
I haven't done anything bad
nothing evil
But I have not been happy
my life seems to be lost
I figure if I can find my soul then I can find myself
But so far no luck
then I figured it out
If I find out who I'm what I stand for
Then I can find my soul
   Marina Followell

Farewell

Here we sit about to cry
Waiting to say our last goodbye

Knowing that now you're with God above
Hurting so much for it's you that we love

You taught us so much along the way
Here I stand a product of you today

You did so much, though you were in pain
You did it with Love, you had nothing to gain

We know you were strong, we know you were tough
The pain you were in, I'm sure it was rough

Remembering the time we all had
Of joy, of Love, of hurt and sad

Now here we sit trying not to cry
As long as you are in our hearts
There will never be a last Goodbye.
   Christopher J. Lemond

Future Thoughts

I wonder,
I think
Of what will happen,
Will I go blind?
Will I go deaf?
Will I lose my speach?
Will I get lost?
Will I lose a friend?
Will I get hurt?
Or will I just go on living forever?
I guess I'll never know, until the future.
   Kerry K. Flynn

For Little Souls

Oh, little souls...just born...just died...
Who could be so cruel to steal your smile...?
Oh, little souls...little hearts...
Who was so cruel to steal your dreams...?

People are strange, they gave the children
Darkness instead of playing and joy...
Who was so cruel to destroy
All that you had in your chests...?

Oh, little souls, I hope
That you will be born, again, in the space...
Maybe like small, beautiful birds...

That sky and stars will give you the kiss
Instead of mothers...
Maybe you will exist again
Like small, beautiful flowers...

Oh no, it's so hard to stand
Oh no, it's so hard to know
That you are here no more,
That you are here no more.
   Bojana Blagojevic

Why Don't We Ask God?

  Guns at school, drugs at home
But no one stops to ask.
  We used to be worried about proper
manners, and our daughters with bikers,
  Now we worry about sex, violence, and
the movement of the new age.
  But no one stops to ask God for help.
  Yet our cry for help is louder each day
as America suffers by its own mistakes.
  Day after day children are abused, raped,
and even killed by their own beloved parents.
And the most innocent are trapped in an
unwinding web, but no one asks for help.
  We all say we are too worried about what
happens in other countries. Well open your eyes
America, it's happening here.
  We sing America the beautiful, and we pledge
our allegiance to the flag. What happened to Jesus
Loves me and I pledge my allegiance to the lamb?
Why don't we America, ask God for help.
   Stephanie Lepien

Untitled

She picked up a rose and to the end she walked alone.
He said goodbye and then on they followed.
The dying of our souls meant nothing to them.
She said not to scream, no one ever listened to her.
Crying silently under the pillows of darkness.
Who knew the end was coming?
If they knew, we knew they weren't going to tell us.
   Stephanie Stewart

Untitled

Can't bear to watch that TV crap
don't understand the thing called Rap
Sitting and thinking all alone
Simply had to write this poem.
"We did build for character, not for fame"
We've had personal victories and private pain.
We've been through the War
Saw prices soar, and building galore.
Went into the working world, married and had kids
saw protests and marches and Government go on skids
Saw the end of horsepower and everything in between
to nuclear power.
Railroads are mostly a thing of the past
now everything's moving - moves far too fast.
G.I.'s used to hitch-hike to get home soon
Now astronauts walk in space and are touching the moon.

We were the age of innocence that moved into the age of space
All in the short span of 50 years.
Like the ad in the magazine states,
"You've come a long way, baby."

Joyce Weber Walters

The Flight Of Life

May we spread our wings and soar for a day,
Experience the sun's beautiful rays!
Give us all a loving heart and to forgive one another.
We must soar above all the dark clouds,
And fill our minds with love and laughter and be proud!
May we glide over all our aggressions,
For hopefully we have learned a valued lesson!
The world has a lot of hate and sorrow,
But we must look at a bright tomorrow!
As we catch a light cool breeze,
Let us float above the trees!
This will help our flight with ease,
But it is within ourselves that we must be pleased!
So as we end this flight today,
Remember life is here to stay!!

Thomas W. Unger

One Day At A Time

Where do you go when you're not sure where
you are When all you want to do
is wish upon the star
that's just out of reach burning and
glowing knowing it's too hot to touch but
not caring much if you get scorched by the fire to
satisfy your desire
the longing you feel so strong
Then you steal just a hint a glimmer if you will of the dreams
you imagine could one day be yours and the pain doesn't
matter like the rain just a splatter
to be wiped away
It never stays just plays and feeds on your
mind on your soul like a beast that lurks
just out of sight. You find you can make
it if only you take it step by step
One day at a time

Beth A. Hartmann

Ethereal Embrace

Trees
clasping branches from the opposite sides of the street
generous blots of yellow, red, and green
come under the bouncing spells of riant racy streaks
and stand glorious
glowing with glee....

Tania Gabrielson

Who Do I Listen To?

Who do I listen to?
They say do what's fun.
He says do what's right.
They say go with the mood.
He says go with what you know.
What's the difference
Between your feelings and your heart, they say.
You know the difference, He says
So many, telling me what to do.
They say so much, yet so little.
How do I know, who do I listen to?
How do I choose between my heart and feelings,
My love or my want, now or later?
What means more to me, my body or my soul?
How do I choose?
How do I know? How will I know?
Who do I listen to?

Michelle Stark

Wish

In the distance the sound of thunder sends a chill down my back.
 I know I should be afraid yet I am not. I feel your
gentle arms around me keeping all fear away.
 I jump as a flash of lightning strikes nearby.
You laugh softly and hold me closer.
 Slowly, all fear melts away as you whisper soothing words in my ear.
The rain falls but I know I'm safe. After all you're with me.
 Content I drift off to sleep only to awake a short time later.
Startled, I look around for you, then I realize it was nothing but a dream.
 I know I'll never experience the feel of your arms around me
no matter how hard or long I wish.

Shannon Grootenboer

Morning Madness

Deeply dreaming as darkness is fading,
 My mind in a whirlwind wanders,
Touching down paths long abandoned,
 It pirouettes and steps me to ponder.

There's a veil of illusion before me.
Phantom forms of wisdom convene.
Wild concepts practicing meanings,
 In a gallery of colors supreme.

Innovative, provocative inventions,
Perceptions too broad to embrace,
Genius abounds and engulfs me,
In this spectacular, mind boggling place.

Unlike daydreams of quiet enjoyment,
 Where tranquil emotions pervade,
This mind performance provokes me,
 To remember the brilliance displayed.

Morning breaks and I slowly awaken.
The scene fades as night meets the day.
 I quickly reach out to hold it,
 It is mine... then it slithers away.

Ernest Hodson

Wild Horse

Free...untamed, never to be tamed;
For if the proud, wild stallion was to be tamed,
His heart would break,
And he could no longer live.
His spirit and pride would die.
Wild, not to mean crazy, but to
Mean free. If a wild horse is captured,
His body may be tamed,
But never his heart.

Kelly Boyea

"Ironic"

The boy dug Debb,
He saw her usually once a day,
Until he knew that he dug her,
He looked and looked but couldn't find her,
Then one day Jenn appeared,
The boy always dug Jenn,
And he saw her usually twice a day,
Until he knew that he dug her,
He looked and looked but couldn't find her,
Then suddenly Debb appeared....

"And isn't it ironic, don't ya think?"
"Lose Your Illusions"...
Love,
    MDR

What God Hath Promised

God hath not promised skies always blue,
Flower-strewn pathways all of life through;
God hath not promised sun without rain,
Joy without sorrow, peace without pain.

God hath not promised we shall not know
Toil and temptation, trouble and woe;
He hath not told us we shall not bear
Many a burden, many a care.

God hath not promised smooth roads and wide,
Swift, easy travel, needing no guide;
Never a mountain, rocky and steep,
Never a river, turbid and deep.

But God hath promised strength for the day,
Rest for the labor, light for the way;
Grace for the trial, help from above,
Unfailing sympathy, undying love.
    Glena M. Jessee King

The Gift

I give you my lips
    To kiss at each feeling.

I give you my hand
    To hold when you're frightened.

I give you my arms
    To caress at each milestone.

I give you my mind
    To challenge your thoughts.

I give you my heart
    To unite with your own.

I give you my soul
    To accompany our hearts.

I give you my body
    To add warmth at each chill.

I give you my strength
    To enable us to face our transgressions.

I give you my life
    As long as it exists for me.

I give you my all
    Through all eternity!!!
    Anita H. Odom

Wolf

Wolf, so lonely in the night,
Why do you howl at the moon so bright?
Why do you sing your mournful song,
That lasts forever, oh so long?

And then when the moon goes to bed,
You too lay down your sleepy head.
But why is it that in my mind's eye,
In sleep your heart doesn't cease to cry?

Baying at the moon all night
The gleam in your eye is filled with fright.
Are you scared because you have no mate,
And do you foresee your horrible fate?

But then one winter with new falling snow
Some love in your heart begins to show.
Because you no longer are alone.
Now, on cold nights your heart no longer
has reason to moan.
    Jeniece Escoto

Listen To The Wind

Listen to the wind calling
Hauntingly familiar spirits carry on
Stirring through the memories
Surfacing the passion and the pain
Wind swept with the memories
Taken to the edge again

Torn between the distance in your eyes
When the moments weren't so tender
And the passion in your eyes
At the gates of the surrender...
Listen to the wind calling

Winding with the river
Winding through the passages of time
Slowing for reflection
Then currents start to flow
Winding through the memories
Winding through the passion and the pain
Guiding the direction
More than we can know
    Eric Hilgeford

The Little Leaves

"Come little leaves," said the wind one day.
"Come over the meadow with me and play.
    Put on your dresses of red and gold,
Summer has gone and the days grow cold."

Soon the little leaves heard the wind's lame call.
    Down they came fluttering one and all.
Over the brown fields they danced and flew.
    Singing the soft little song they knew.

"Cricket, good-bye, we've been friends so long.
    Little brook will sing you a farewell song.
    Say you are sorry to see us go.
Oh, you are sorry, right well we know.

Dear little lambs in your fleecy fold,
Mother will keep you from harm and cold.
Fondly we watch through vale and glade;
Say you will dream of our loving shade.

So dancing and whirling the little leaves went,
Winter had called them and they were content.
Soon fast asleep in their heavenly beds
The snow laid a blanket over their heads.
    Tami Lynne Wolterman

While You Were Sleeping

My brother's into baseball, my sister keeps diving.
I play soccer, and my parents keep driving.

When it's all over they lie down for awhile.
And all of us children have an ear to ear smile.

We tear up the house while our parents sleep.
Now the first floor's done so upstairs we creep.

We jump on our beds and trash our rooms.
We leave the water running in all the bathrooms.

Now up to the attic, there's trunks everywhere.
They're full of old clothes that we try on and tear.

Now that that's done we shall wreck the outside.
We T.P. the clubhouse and put mud on the slide.

We tire out our folks 'til they go to sleep,
Then through the house us monsters do creep.

Daniel Box

Enduring Love

She sits there, our friend (in early stages of Alzheimer's)
   so lovely in her soft blue dress and pearls
   so straight and tall and regal yet.
She flips through a magazine, talking softly to herself about the pictures
Oblivious, it seems, to our excited chattering and laughing in the
   midst of the party celebrating the love of one couple married
   fifty years.
Then, in celebration, we sing "Because" and suddenly we realize
   she is singing with us, every word, every note so clear and
   beautiful!

For a moment we get a glimpse of her as she once was -
   giving us joy with her voice, making us laugh with her humor.
Now only music and songs she remembers -
   remembrance of the past is uncertain, awareness of the present
   unclear
Except for the presence of her husband -
   whose name and nearness are her security -
He who cares so gently for her -
   he who is her life-line to the world -
What caring love to witness!

Lavinia M. Short

A Mother's Love For Her Daughter

When real, Angelic love encaptures the heart
no worldly thing can ever make it depart
Not another, not distance, not even work
Can ever erase this wonderful perk.
Angelic love will always remain
For it is given without selfish gain.

Through the toils and tribulations of life
and though there will be many times of strife
The same Angelic love just leads the way
and before you know it those bad times start to sway
Ever so slowly into a memory of the past
To be shared later as a reminder of how love can last.

When the time comes and we must part for a short while
Remember how much I love you and let it carry you that last mile.
Although your load will be heavy and your heart sad
Always remember my Angelic love and let your heart be glad
For all the years I truly loved you
For soon my dear daughter I must bid you adieu
For the Lord will be calling and I must prepare
To return to him my total love that we were blessed to share.

Dorothy June Holt

The Road Called Life

You Enter the world
With no worries, it's fun,
You're too small to realize
The journey that's begun.

Depending on others is easy
Yielding is not what's tough.
It's when you hit adolescence
That your road becomes crooked and rough.

Warning: Your friends become more important
   Than the "you" that's inside.
   Involved in activities you know are wrong
   It's from the wise that you hide.

At different times, each road is straightened
But for some not at all.
It just depends on your character
Whether you Stop or fall.

You continue on over the hill
And your spouse becomes your best friend.
Each moment is lived to its fullest
Until you reach your Dead End.

Christina Rush

Untitled

We look at the world we live in today,
and wonder which way is the right way.
We don't take the time to stop and rest,
or live our lives to their fullest or their best.
We seek answers where there are none to find,
trying so hard that we become blind,
blind to the truth and to reality,
blind to this point, yet we still try to see.
Hearts become broken,
words are not spoken,
needs are not met,
and we begin to regret,
the things we have done and the things we have not,
and getting the things which we so foolishly sought.
Our lives are unraveled before our own eyes,
and in anger we begin to despise,
those around us,
some we call friends,
and we often wonder, "will it ever end?"

Bobby Hemken

Visions Of Birth, Life, Death...

Infinite white, my eyes do see.
Love, Joy, Peace — befall me.
Thoughts of ever after run through my head,
Never would I expect what lies ahead.

Infinite red, my eyes do see.
Hatred, Hurt, Revenge — befall me.
True, of my terrible fate I did not know,
But fear of the unexpected I will not show.

Infinite gray, my eyes do see.
Numbness, Cloudiness, Weariness befall me.
My senses dull to the things around,
Ever onward my life sinks down.

Infinite black, my eyes do not see.
Sorrow, Death, Nothing — befall me.
The darkness round envelopes me whole.
No longer shall I live to grow old.

Justin Portivent

Analogy Of Life

I'm a great green grape, groping in a group
I'm in shining shape, sweetly sugared
Stuck on a stemmed stalk, freshly fruited
Oh, I look lively and luscious, victorious on the vine

Soaking in the sun, I lay lingering
I become beautifully mature, rapidly ripening
There is an awkward awareness, a death-defying difference
I must still stay, regularly ripening rapidly

I'm courageously compared to man, humanly happy
Growing originally old, graciously grand
I have not long to live, lusciously lingering
I am giving graciously, life's natural knowledge

I didn't fall free, temporarily transformed
I am still stuck, growing gracefully
I'm now originally old, good and gracious
I became a ravishing raisin, radiantly wrinkled.

Carla J. Duffy

Caged

It must have been an ungodly deed,
A whispered warning we did not heed;
To be cast out and forced to dwell,
In a cumbersome body, an earthly hell.

There is no silence here only freakish confusion,
Scrambled and broken condemned to delusion;
Listen carefully and hear the hum, droning sound,
As tormented souls scream, caged and bound.

Porous flesh burdened with addiction and obsessions,
In shame, we isolate with unheard confessions.
Flouting, indignant, they mutilate our souls,
Serving only to widen our secret black holes.

Each breath is squelched as we choke and suffocate,
Smiling masks conceal and thinly placate;
Choosing not to see our impotent desperation,
We kill or are killed without reparation.

Clambering and clutching we seek to escape,
Revolutionized gyration of self imposed rape;
Drowning in misery, a mere toss of the dice,
Plunging into the vortex, a life pays the price.

Mary Lou Connelly

Incarceration Deterioration

Alone in a room,
Prone to emotional doom,
No ceiling, no floors,
Windows or doors,
Where the fog of dementia looms.

To my thoughts, I am prey,
As they circle throughout the day,
Perverting the scheme,
Of a delightful dream,
Illusions old and in the way.

So imprisoned, I choose to believe,
Still breaking the chains and trying to leave,
In hope outside the walls,
To my soul destiny calls,
In search of truths I must retrieve.

I must worship the spirit of life,
Overcome the despair and strife,
Permit my heart to cry,
Transgress these walls and fly,
Yes, live, yet, not die by the knife.

Howard Sparks

Broken Bottle

I wonder what it is that controls you.
The liquid running through your veins.
By itself it seems so harmless.
It turns Jekyll into Hyde,
Jesus into Satan,
Family into enemy.
There's no purpose for its existence,
No benefit that it creates.
It provides courage knowing no bounds.
The mortal become immortal,
The weak become strong,
The hurting stricken with pain.
It's a counselor to millions giving
The worst advice imaginable.
What beast within seeks it out?
It gets its fill only to be starving again.
It rips and shreds with no remorse.
It kills...
It kills...
It kills...

Clay Fuller

Neighbor

I know my neighbors who live this way and that,
but I never take time for a bit of a chat,
Don't know their troubles, their burdens they bear,
Their daily bickering, their crosses, their cares.
I greet some with joy, others I pass right by
With a blank look showing in my eye-
I don't say "Good Morning", 'Good Evening'
and "How do you do."
As the highway of life they go speeding thru.

Then came the torch to the town once burned,
spawning a bursting pipe, causing emotions to churn.
Bringing death, and fear in hearts of Olympic fans.
Threats rattled Olympic Park, bombing victim mourned,
With the media harassment of a jewel of a man.
The flame of the torch never flickered once, but
Beamed bright day and night,
While a million strong, daily walked with might,
Without a touch, without a word, without a sign,
They followed the flame.
Yes, I know my neighbor with no face and no name.

Betty B. Trotter

"Yes And No"

Has there ever been a man who never breathed the air?
Has there ever been a freed one without any care?
Has there ever been a purse nobody'd ever share?
Has there ever been a warmth within a cold stare?

Has there ever been a furnace from which the cold would flee?
Has there ever been a caged bird with no wish to be free?
Has there ever been an animal caged inside me?
Has there ever been a lock for which there was no key?

Has there ever been a speaker without any word?
Has there ever been a wisdom nobody's ever heard?
Has there ever been a statement with principles blurred?
Has there ever been a person nobody's ever stirred?

Has there ever been a rule with no exception ever made?
Has there ever been a sin for which no one ever paid?
Has there ever been a bed where nobody ever laid?
Has there ever been a sunshine which never cast a shade?

Has there ever been a sky without any dove?
Has there ever been a home waiting patiently above?
Has there ever been a push that never came to shove?
Has there ever been a word without any love?

Caleb MacGermany

My Little Girl

My daughter Lanie,
To some is considered quite brainy.

She is someone you'd really adore,
For in our home she's never a bore.

With her personality, wit and charm,
I pray she will never endure any harm.

She's a lovely as can be,
Anyone can look at her and see.

With a pencil in one hand and a tablet in the other,
She's always writing—I love you mother.

Jonie Denmon

Tears For Thoughts

As I miss you quiet ways,
These tears fall down my face.
When I don't see you,
I hope that you are crying too.

It's empty in my soul,
you're not here, so I feel alone.
I want your arms holding me tight
I want you to help me sleep at night.

The last time I saw you is still clear in my mind.
I think about you all the time.
But when I do it brings tears to my eyes,
Because you're not here by my side.

So until we meet again,
remember that I love you from within.
Because you're good at bringing out the best in me
And I know that you'll never leave
and you and I will always be one.

Shannon Ware

The Rainbow

One misty morning, damp with dew,
We drove thru the hills for an hour or two.
Sweet and clean was the air that day,
Smelled fresh as could be along the way.

As we drove down the road enjoying the view,
The rain fell softly, cleansing anew.
At the top of the hill to our amaze,
The sun filtered through in soft array.

And Lo, to our own humble delight,
Tints of soft colors blushed into sight.
Colors that glistened in various hues;
Pinks, oranges, greens, yellows and blues.

God gave to us of His glorious gifts,
Such as the Rainbow that comes thru the mist.
Nothing so grand, I am led to say,
Was 'The Glimmering Rainbow' on that notable day.

Alma Therese Glassford

Silence

I sit and listen quietly as the sound of silence grows
Not a bee buzzes not a crow crows
Not a lonely wind whistles through the trees
As I sit and listen there's not even a breeze
The houses sit silent in their time of rest
The birds all curl up warmly in their warm cozy nest
Now the whole world seems to sleep
Even the gopher burrows down deep
But as I closely listen I hear something tense
It is the sound of silence

Neenu Prasad

Three Precious Stones

I have been blessed with three precious stones
An amethyst, a peridot, and a sapphire.
Each is unique with a beauty all its own
And abundant care they require.

Each gem was obtained through labors of love
Arrived perfect in every way.
They are truly gifts from God above
But with me they will not always stay.

Each day the stones must be polished and shined
Prepared for the world to admire.
They have been taught to be polite and kind
For more inner beauty to acquire.

Sometimes the gems bring about great delight
Other times they cause worry and tears.
Keeping them form harm is an endless fright
They will be in my protection for many years.

The value of these stones is priceless to me
And easy for me to remember.
These gems are really my three daughters born to me
In the months of February, August, and September.

Michelle Kirkpatrick

I Dream of Thee

I dream of thee.
Night and day, and day and night
My heart races, because we are apart.
With skin so fair,
And in the wind your long flowing hair;
As we frolic freely without a care.
As I gaze into your eyes
It truly takes my breath away,
For love's not for us to spare.
With passion so deep
As we drink wine that is pink,
And as I am close to you I become aware,
For your grace, beauty, and charm overwhelms me!
But, alas, do we really care,
For is love like ours not but a dream?

John H. Wigington III

Children, Children

We worked our hardest and did our best,
and left it to God to do the rest.
Thank You God for their big success!
The living proof is posted on my class room door.
There is no doubt, that's for sure.

I've stroked those talents in each one of you.
So you would know just what to do.
With those stroking you come through
Happiness come to the school, to me and to you.
Judges read your essays and said you are qualified
You did your very best no one can deny.

We deserve a standing ovation
For these magnificent, graceful writing creations,
God helped us bring glory and honor to the school
This shows that we are very cool.

I humbly ask everyone of you.
To stand up, stand up and clap for us.
Let's do it without a fuss.
Just do it from the heart
Give it a big start.

Susan Braxton

Love Affair

Every morning, every night
   I listen for the geese in flight.
To hear them calling as they fly,
   stirs within my heart a sigh.
Twice a year they send to me
   a message of what is to be.
Today, it tells a happy one
   of flowers blooming in the sun.
That snows and ice are nearly over
   and bees will dance upon the clover.
I wish so very desperately
   that they, somehow, could pause with me.
I yearn to stroke their feathers grand
   and let them eat out of my hand
But, they must stay up high above
   and be my unrequited love.
     Charlotte Bickerton

The Olympic Torch

As I run down the street
With the torch in my hand
I think to myself "Oh my, what a land."
In some countries I see the hurt, the pain, the sorrow
And wish for their troubles to be gone before tomorrow
I wish for them to be brave and bold
As they cheer on their country while they go for the gold

I am so grateful, so happy, so gay
That our country is not that way
Others need to recognize, they have to, they must
And get a motto like ours, "In God, we trust"
I am so happy, glad and gay
To live in the good old U.S. of A.

I see the happiness, the joy, the glee
Of our nation, so proud and free
Atlanta, Georgia is the site
For the Olympians to show off their might
All eyes are on me, I don't understand
Maybe it's the torch that I carry in my hand.
     Justin D. Short

Whispers Of Nature

Standing upon the chilled soils
of the ground. I hear the wondrous whispers of nature.
Tiptoes of vibrant leaves rustle in the murmuring winds.
Strolling across the forest grounds,
trees say their hello's and begin to whistle in the rough breeze.
Leaves and silky flower petals whirl
in the wind and make echoes of
   crackle, crackle, swish, swish, mumm, mumm.
Clouds darken, and become gloomy, and misty.
Pitter patters of crystal clear raindrops.
Splash onto mother nature's plants, and rich soils.
Vaulting grasshoppers chirp in the
darkening evening, while the rains fall upon them.
Suddenly the dim clouds fade, and
the golden sun sprinkles its warmth onto the lands.
The awakening wildlife makes their
brief yawns, and wildly run around the gigantic, tall green trees.
With feet crashing against the grounds.
As the day fades, I begin to walk outside of this magnificent picture,
but think of the enjoyments left behind me now.
     Katia-Marie Alexander

The Unknown Thoughts

I lay here stunned not believing I have just tripped over your words
and fallen into your kiss.
You're fighting with my mind as if it were a pathetic competition.
Please Darling, chase me now I need some water.
I'm slipping, hurry; close your fingers now while you have a strand
of my hair to hold onto as a memory.
First sell me your hands for a moment, I'm in need of caressing.
Sorry, it was a one-time thought thing.
Lay down boy, let me trace your body.
Stand up boy, wanna play darts?
As I painfully watch you sing My dreams to Her as if it were a song
You made up.
Everybody always giggled at the way my snow-white hand
got swallowed by yours anyway.
I'm starting to remember how convincing you tried to sound by telling
me the bruises just added character.
As you'd try to end the conversation with a whip of wickedness.
Just shut up Darling, and wrap your arms around yourself.
     Katie Carlstrom

Long Lost Legends Of Old

I have my own Pandora's box,
A book from long ago.
With leather bound appearances
Nothing much to show.
But open up the book, a dream is what you'll find,
For all of its chapters have been forgotten with time.
   The Manticor, the Harpy, the white Unicorn,
   The Griffon, the Satyr, the Dragon with the horns,
   The Basilisk, the Chimera, the Pegasus airborne,
   The Iktomi, the Goblin, the Troll who's clothes are torn,
   The Yeti, the Gremlin, the Hobbit's shoes are worn,
   The Minotaur, the Centaur, the Mermaid of the morn,
   The Mid-Guard Serpent, the Sphinx, the Fairy of the thorns,
All of these and some more,
Show us things never seen before.
Of love and life, hopes of gold,
These are the Long Lost Legends of Old!
     Tamara NaCole Minor

Life With You

When I take time to ponder how different my life would be
had our paths never crossed, our lives never touched;
If you had not consented to be my wife
to mother my children, to share my journey,
how empty the journey would be.

How many joys I would have missed
joys, shared only between the two of us;
amidst the struggle of the climb,
the laughter, void but for the trials we endure together,
My life, death, it not shared with you.

Half of what I am I owe to you,
the other half I hide and refuse to let others see
the unpolished, the insensitive; but you see,
and love me anyway, and gradually, ever too slowly,
more of you is revealed in me.

How could I ever thank you for what you have given me?
For your constant love, that never gives up on me,
that reminds me of what I want to be, and keeps me
striving to become what you are.
I love you.
     Mercer

Emancipated Watchman

So if it rains, I'll run jumping in puddles, arms extended.
And it if snows, I'll spin with my head back eating flakes with
  open mouth, arms extended.
And when it is sunny, I'll laugh with my back arched, absorbing
  the rays with my pale chest, arms extended.
If you smile or cry
If you sit or stand
If you talk or listen.
If you watch or don't.
Extended arms looking upward will bring you to me.
I'll be whatever you want because it is you who create me.
I am your product, I am your toy
I am your invention.
I am a part of you.
When you look in the mirror with your eyes closed, is the first time
you will see me.
But when you find me. I am yours for the keeping.
Riding with you on the bus, lying beside you at night
in your job and in your world.
Because I have been watching for so long.

Brian Anthony

Cyclical Image

I love my pain and keep my wound alive
for it warns me from worse follies of mine.
Mysteries resolved and subsumed into experiences..
Alas!... The only way
to explore the unknown intriguing world.

I love my pain and my wound.
Oh God! Let it not be relieved,
let it sting when, groping in the dark,
danger is lurking to cause despair.

I know, I'll never learn...
This is the same erstwhile and recurrent image
of the first Spring,
that was implanted in my heart at the primeval age.

As long as it emerges in a mirror, in a fantasy,
or in reveries of yore,
Let it be known: Eternal youth is mine!

Edwin Alcantara

The Angel I Knew

I once knew an angel,
The only one in the world,
With beauty so remarkable
She must hide it in the form of a girl.
This creature, she is kind and affectionate
And has a heart as pure as gold.
I still have yet to see an equal
To her mild and tranquil soul.
Her smile can bring happiness to anyone
And her laughter is so wonderfully funny.
She has eyes that can capture any man's heart
And her voice is as sweet as honey.
Her little hands are the softest of any touch
With skin as smooth as at birth.
Her hair will blow so freely in a breeze
And her love is the greatest on earth.
For I once knew this angel,
The only one in the world,
And if you ask me of how I knew her
Then I'll tell you that she was once my girl.

Scott Gregory

Kyuquot Sound

At Farewell Bend the road begins to climb
Through sage-clad hills above the windy Snake
Where ponderosas crown the round-topped blues.
We've started down that road each time we take
The trip away from roads to rocky shores
To where the massive cedars, yew, and fir,

Salal about their feet, grow at the road's end.
For five remembered summers as a child
I lived between the forest and the tide,
We dug for clams and fished and picked the wild
Red huckleberries from the mossy log.
And now above Kyuquot Sound the hills

Are stripped of logs from highest ridge to beach.
Among the massive stumps the seedlings fill
Not nurseries, but an orphanage so vast
It stretches from the tropics to the poles.
The salmon and the whale spirits turn their backs,
And mountain lions turn, at bay, to kill.

Ellen Nicholson Walker

Chains Of Steel

Tingling, tantalizing, rushing emotions
Butterflies floating, heart jumping, blood rushing
These are all the things I feel when I'm near you.
I have yet to suffer the damage to my body
That a single touch would produce.
I have yet to feel the power your love would have
Over my mind, my soul.
My body could not handle it, my mind could not control it
Yet, my yearning for you grows stronger
With each glance, each smile.
Guilt, consequence, fear, unbending laws
These are the things that hold me back.
One day my restraints will not hold.
One day my emotions will cut loose.
Then will I have you,
In a night filled with ecstasy, in a night filled with passion.
Until that night,
I can only look your way flirting continuously
Keeping my heart tied up
In chains of steel.

Colleen Kelly

Dreamless

Desperate to find a sense of belonging
they search, only to find themselves more lost than ever.

Alone they cuddle to anything that provides security,
the safest place being their empty, dreamless thoughts.

Although hundreds of people may surround
them they see and hear nothing, but the
pounding of their hearts, and the fear they
hope will someday go away.

They, being the homeless girl that gave
up her last ounce of pride to ask for some
change, only to be forgotten in an endless
crowd, or the little boy that huddles in
dark corners hiding from the cruel world
and the truth hidden within himself.

Under a starless sky and a meaningless dream,
they see nothing but the beginning of the end.

Sandra Ventura

Strangers Among Us

Who are these people we've know so long
As friends and neighbors? We've been so - wrong!

They've always been teachers, helpful and kind.
Yet corruption surfaced through time.

Our children looked up to them as good people;
But even a church can have a rotten steeple.

It's sad to know that we may always be blind
To human nature of this kind.

We learn to trust with our hearts, not our minds;
To wake up one day with alarming finds.

Underhanded, overhanded, and in between
They obtain power utilizing these ways to the extreme.

Laws are suppose to protect the innocent;
Not the guilty who leave a repugnant scent.

Children play games that aren't fair.
Adults are suppose to know how to share.

We work hard for what we have and do
To have it taken away by only a few.

It's sad to think that we can't trust our friends.
Strangers among us always to the end.
Carol M. McCorkle

Tee Time

There's nothing like a Day
for a game of Golf,
When you're all together and on time for Tee-off

When the sun is out and warm and bright,
With just the scent of dew but no rain in sight

When your warm-up swings are loose and strong,
Then you make every putt and your drives are long

Sand traps and roughs
are none to be seen,
You birdie, then eagle
and you make every green

No bogey's double bogeys'
no slices or water,
And each divet you replaced
belonged to another

Then a cold one and lunch with plans to do it again
It's back to work on Monday this day's at an end

But your hard work and labor will again pay-off,
Cause there's nothing like a day
you can afford to play golf
Debbie Bagley

Time Bomb

The mind so crazy, the body so lazy
The brain so dead inside the head
A hand so gentle and the temper will kindle
Building inside starting in the arm
Ready to blow like a time bomb
People say he's lazy which really drives him crazy
The bomb put out and restarted like that
Every time someone turned their back
It hurts inside when he's standing along side
And people act like he's not there which really gets him hot
The wick getting shorter, the bomb getting larger
Inside the heart it's about to start
A chain reaction depicting his action
Ready to go with a great big blow
At home he's alone, then it's blown
Then they fall his every tear one and all.
Kyle Schwemmer

Mystery Of The Mind

A heart is broken. Life stands still. No words are spoken.
No more love to spill. A child lay dying. A tragedy of pain.
No need for lying. No happiness to gain. A baby lay sleeping.
Curled up in fear. Love is for her keeping.
A silence she can't yet hear. A mother in labor. A new life to give.
Loving your neighbor. Sinning to live.

A jester is joking. No one is laughing. A needle is poking.
A crazed man is laughing. A soul is on fire. No one in sight.
You, I admire. Love me, you might. An aged man has fallen.
He's helpless and afraid. No one will call him. His bed has been made.
Look here, I'm smiling. It's not easy to fool. Someone is dying.
Drowned in a "world" pool.

Lovers are gentle. Their touch is sweet. A kiss is sentimental.
No lips do I meet. Th' imagination is wild. Someone will notice.
The sleepwalking child. She will outgrow this. A wife is forgiving.
She's blind to the truth. A husband deceiving. He has a sweet tooth.
Mother is drinking. Last night's a blur. Father is sleeping.
Hiding from her.

A mystery lay hiding. Lost in the dark. Love is abiding.
Leaving its mark. Emotions are ripped. In pieces they lay.
Passion I sipped. In the glass it shall stay. Beauty is flawed.
No one will see. Perfection is odd. What shall we be?
Swallowed by fear. Haunting the mind. Holding the tear.
What will they find?
    It is a mystery of the mind.
Lindsay A. Wood

Searching

Call out to me as only you can.
I look around, I search with all your understanding
and yet I still ponder why are you not here with me?
I have longed to talk to you.
Longed to reach deep into your being and find you.
Are you there? Can you hear me?
I cry out.
I scream.
Are you available to me like a loved one is to a person in need?
Or do I continue to fall freely into this deep, dark abyss.
There is no sun here, no rays of light.
I fear there too may be no stars.
For you my love are the light of my waking,
the wonderful glow of starlight as dusk falls.
Come to me, be one with me my love.
For as the sun is sure to rise
and will also soon set,
my life will hang in the balance until the time comes
when our love will reign as one.
Lisa Marie Howard

Lost In A Maine Forest?

The cool blue sky above
Wisps of clouds scurry by
Filtering rays of pure light
Through a park primeval forest I walk
The leaves of autumn flutter to the matted ground
Soft moist earth upon my feet
Wet lichens upon ancient rock
Cool, gurgling, cascading water
Resounding echoes down stream
A lone raven cries out
Through the dense white pines
Am I lost?
No, in a sense I am found
Sometimes in life's turmoil
The light through the forest
Is hard to find
John Clark Shields

Hauntings

I am constantly reminded
of how sad it seemed I had been.
To live a life without knowing why
or to whom would I give offend;

A trying-times kind of growing
was endured but proven unfair.
A grand future, if any I thought,
was looked upon in despair.

My desire to remember great times
A host of, there must have been;
Are quickly somehow intercepted
By what could have and should have spins.

Tomorrow was sure to be better.
This new day was finally at end.
It was moments likely to ponder on
and gain strength from I would depend.

Although I am very happy now,
or seem to be it still remains,
Will ever this haunting leave me
or forever in mind be contained?

Charles Papillion

From My Heart

These tears that fall are of sorrow and pain.
I forgive you for all that has been done, it's time to forgive,
yet not forget them and move on. We have a future to fulfill
not to sit and dream on.
I am in love with you as you are me too, but how do I go about
showing you when you think I'm not true? Believin' in you
as you should me and hopefully one day you'll too see, that
I stand here right by your side and I promise deeply to
hold forever tight, show your pain for I can take it all
while building your confidence so you can swore over all.
Each day that goes by I think of you and at night I
pray for us too, asking the Lord to make our love strong
so we may unite. There will always be times that are rough,
but you can't allow your eyes to close giving everything up.
So you say I act a fool? It's only the proof that my
love is true to you. I guess you don't realize what
you've got until it's gone, then when you've realized
time has gone by you turn to witness,
regain, but slowly they slip away. As you wake
knowing of yet another hopeful love dream...

Julia I. Ianniciello

My Love

There is one that I know that has a heart of gold. He has a
strong, but loving exterior. He is steadfast and true, loyal
and courageous. He shows no fear to those who know him.

But I have seen a side of him that most do not see. I see the
fragile, frightened warrior who fights the battles for his
children. The one who loves deeply and hurts even deeper. I
see the pain from his past when I look into his eyes. I feel
the longing for his children in his touch. I long to reach out and
hold him, to protect him from these things, but realize I cannot.

Who a person is today greatly depends on their experiences
from the past. He has suffered tremendously and has walked
away from adversity a great and loving man.

He is a hero. With all that has been placed before him,
he has walked away a loving and compassionate man in
a society where compassion and love are rarely found.

We will find his happiness, his joy, his inner being once again.
For two hearts that know one love, one life, will always know
true joy. He is kind, compassionate, loving, sympathetic, good,
brave, courageous and fearless....He is My Love.

Jessica Sullivan

The Parasite's Polka

Amidst the dreaded webs we weave - the ones that only we dregs are
unable to perceive there lives a power, a source of strength -
an iniquitous surge of illegitimate earthquakes
that thrashes through our skulls till it blasts through the hulls of
our shattered heart's haven

Its eyes search for a lack of confidence - its nose snorts for fear
of insignificance
its tongue laps up any trace of innocence - its fangs inject an
insidious malevolence

Then it lays there, seething, sloshing its drool, cleansing its teeth
of the rancid gruel
crystallizing our dreams into razor-sharp jewels and then flushing
them down our soul's vestibules

They slash up our throats as we're forced to swallow our final hopes

Then they crash to our stomachs, they're melted by frustration
birthing gas of anger, irateness, indignation
the expulsion of everything that loneliness has revived from our
child-like imagination is disguised as
the savior that offers us alleviation

And once it's all over, we look for our pain to cease - in trusting
the rope to hang us in peace.

David Allen Gulajski

The Mailbox

I walk the dry and dusty road,
And feel the autumn breeze;
It softly rustles thru my hair,
And frolics in the trees.

The foolish forest, from each side,
Does try to guise my route,
But I go on undauntedly -
Of this path there's no doubt.

I hear the birds in carefree glee,
A sound I've so well known;
I could believe I'd never gone,
But with these friends had flown.

Rounding the bend, I cross the brook
Whose secrets filled young years.
I spy the mailbox down the road;
It whispers to my ears.

It's been too long since I've been here.
I've had my time to roam.
This mailbox beckons on to me;
It calls me back to home.

Natalie Denise Offringa

Paralysis

The lurking lion is about to pounce on its feast.
From whence I know not where.
Only knowing the feast is inevitable
And my tormentor is eternal.

Paralysis awaits as I sense his closeness.
His closeness brushes against me
Leaving its emotional, physical and mental effects.
Only to retreat and find its feast again.
In a terrifying game of cyclical repetition
Of haunted and hunter.

I lift up my being to its end and final death.
I await to lay in its ashes
And to rise up ever fresh and new.
Knowing safety is always mine to have
And to hold from this day forth...

Death has done its part.

Annie Wetterer

I Stand

As I wait, time lingers.
The disappearing day gives way
to the darkness of night.

I am alone
Sitting in a corner, confused, scared.
The house is silent, dark,
No signs of life within
I am forgotten.

Hearing the voices that are not here,
lonely,
I tremble.

Looking for some sign;
headlights pulling in,
people walking towards the house
That is no longer home.

I sigh, the walls echoing my emptiness.
I stand.
My knees buckle.
I straighten.
I am.

Andrea M. Harris

The Unbearable Lightness Of Being

Ah, ye journeyless Argonauts
Where are your dragons to be slain
Or will you guest to find your quest
Assuredly your quest is in vain
For you have no chance of fleeing
The Unbearable Lightness of being

Ah, ye warless Pattons
What is this disease that infests
You are in great danger
And still you yearn for a test
If only you had a chance of seeing
The Unbearable Lightness of Being

Ah, ye slaveless Lincolns
Who ache so sourly for a trial
Why not create your own?
By drinking the poison in this vial
But you have no chance of defeating
The Unbearable Lightness of Being

All ye content societies will soon be meeting
The Unbearable Lightness of Being

Timothy Lankau

Without You

When I feel alone
There is to one place I run,
So I can hide from this world of lies
Somewhere all things I believe in, stand.
And I know deep inside, the sun will shine
Once again, onto a brand new day

If I'm on my own
And don't seem to call it home,
I retreat to that familiar voice to bring me close.
It is my bridge to cross the river
When the waters deepen, enough to drown in
But that smile on the other side, ensures me it'll be all right

Now that I've gone this far
It wasn't all me when I look back,
A light of caring and understanding helped bring out
A will in myself I never knew.
Now anyone can see, what it means to me
I would lose it all...without you

David Marcelo

Rainbows

Rainbows are created
for us lonely souls
After the storms of life
It eases our hearts - so full of holes
Rainbows give meaning
A re-birth of life
When our existence is chaotic
Our hearts filled with strife
Rainbows bring hope
For the future and for now
Telling us we will survive
Someway - somehow
Rainbows bring smiles
Replacing our fears
A feeling of love
From the ones we hold dear
So after the next storm
Look for the rainbows in the deep blue sky
If it makes you feel warm and hopeful
Now you know why-

Shawn L. Rider

"I, Peasant That I Am"

I, peasant that I am,
  look toward the sky and am awed by the beauty of the clouds.

I, peasant that I am,
  smell the gentle fragrance of a flower and am filled with a sense of joy.

I, peasant that I am,
  watch a setting sun and am filled with a sense of wonder.

I, peasant that I am,
  breathe in the scent of a spring rain on a soft breeze and am
filled with peace and love.

Others, the movers and the shakers,
  look to fill their lives with materialism.

Others, the movers and the shakers,
  hunger for power and domination.

Others, the movers and the shakers,
  they thirst for financial wealth and control.

Alas, I peasant that I am,
  I fill my hunger and thirst with the beauties of nature that surround me.

And - I, peasant that I am,
  am richer by far than they!

Francine Corley Walton

withered

dedicated to: Leah Joanne Lefler
Your endless glow, never fading
all these severed dreams, lost and breaking
to think we'd never get any closer than this tears me all apart
like the skeletons of memories, scratching at my heart
just keep screaming, dreaming for a way out of the dark
these illusions live forever in a world of empty dreams
but then again, nothing's ever as sweet as it seems
lust is here again, spreading her disease
and i know no matter how hard i try i'll never be at ease
because You seem so far away
keep waiting fading in the shadow of the day
and how You stretch and yawn just before You're always gone
it just falls away inside
with nowhere left to hide
like the dreams of love that slowly wither and die
how i wish You'd never never say
good-bye.

Jonathan Lee

Through The Eyes Of A Child

Through the eyes of a child, fairies can fly.
You nose will grow if you tell a lie.
To step on a crack will break your Mom's back.
Tooth fairies come, soothing sore gums. Leaving money to buy what catches the eye.

Through the eyes of a child, to catch a Frog is the hardest of jobs, keepings it wet in the hopes for a pet, trying to hide it, so no one will find it. Alas letting it go, in the hopes it will grow.

Through the eyes of a child despite what you're told, you will never grow old. When kissing a toad you will most certainly wince. But this simplest effort might bring you a Prince.

Through the eyes of a child we are all beautiful. Pretending to be what we want for a moment. Wanting to beautiful, wanting to be handsome. Most of all wanting to grow up.

Through the eyes of a child. Despite what is probable anything's possible. Tomorrow will always be open for adventure, wiping away tears, going experience to try again.

Through the eyes of a child looking through a mirror all your flaws can disappear. By seeing yourself in the best possible light, projecting your inner beauty through the deepest darkest night.

Cathleen Murray

"Fantasy"

For who would bear the whips and scorns of time?
Angels and Ministers of grace defend us—
Against the pangs of despised love;
Avoid what is to come, repent what's past.

Bestial oblivion or some craven scruple,
Yet I have cause and will and strength and means;
Exposing what is mortal and unsure
In a dream of passion, to mine own conceit.

I am myself indifferent honest
Devoutly to be wished, perchance to dream.
I have in quick determination
Blasted with ecstasy, o woe is me!

For a dream itself is but a shadow
It came to pass, as most like it was
With all my love do I commend me to you,
To die, to sleep, must give us pause.

Native hue of resolution puzzles the will
And I will wear him in my heart's core
O heart, lose not thy nature
That for a fantasy, it is no more.

Michelle D. Bennett

Out Of Sight

I once painted a picture of Dorian Gray
The art I need for a display
I decided to change a few things around
By placing him in a room sitting down
The room I painted in a pale green
Placed drapes to the window in the colour of cream
Then I stopped for a moment and studied the scene.
A vase of flowers to make the room bright
Some red and yellow, orange and white
Colours to give it that touch of light
And the chair I painted as black as the night
I finished it and let it dried
Then I applied a fixative spray
I was anxious and full of pride
The showing was to be the next day
But when I unveiled my display
 I was surprised
For the picture I painted had faded away.

Jean C. Jabradally

I Am Happy

"I am happy," said my little son.
I looked at him and said,
"Run along, son. Go outside and play and run
for Daddy has no time for fun.
Daddy's work is not yet done."

"Hello, Dad, I'm having fun.
Will you come out with me and share my fun?"
"No, my son, Daddy's work is still not done."

The days go by, and when Dad's work is done
He looks up to see he has no son but a man
Who stands with a destiny, a child, and a wife
And a busy, busy life.

Jack Rosselli

Picture This

You can feel the sun upon your face
And just tell you are in the presence of God's grace,
You look up and find there isn't a cloud in the sky,
It is like a big bunch of blue cotton candy way up high,
You wander off and discover a beautiful lake,
And realize how much God really did make,
You fall asleep resting under a marvelous maple tree,
And dream about each day what all we see,
Then suddenly you are awakened,
By a chance for a drink a deer had taken,
On your way back you see the loveliest flowers,
It seems as though you can watch them for hours,
When you get back you take a deep breathe of fresh air,
And feel as though you don't have a care,
You go to sleep that night real late,
For the next day you just can not wait,
You thank the Lord for his wonderful day,
For it helped you in a wonderful way.

Jana Hess

Beauty Of Image

How beautiful is she?
Is her hair black and long?
Or is her face nice and round?
Does she have brown eyes
that twinkle when she smiles?
Is she skinny, fat, or plump inside?
I am the lady of beauty!
Graceful and Sweet am I.
The one with long black hair and huge brown eyes,
That twinkle when I smile.
The one who is skinny,
Pretty and Graceful am I.

Shea Monique Roane

My Burdens Are Lifted

Tears fall from my eyes like rain
I have a guilty conscience because of sin's stain
My burdens are heavy, and I can't seem to move on
I've struggled with these things, now my strength is gone
It seems every obstacle I face causes me to fall
Stopping my steady pace, to a slow and painful crawl
"When will the sun shine again," I pray
"When will these clouds begin to break away"

Tears fall from my eyes like rain
Salvation comes to me without restraint
My burdens are lifted, and Christ's blood washes my wrong
My doubt becomes trust, my faith becomes strong
Every obstacle I face, Jesus helps me overcome
Moving steadily when I look ahead, not where I came from
Now the night is overcome by day
Now these clouds begin to break away.

Nathan Ingle

Black Sense

Don't judge me by my color.
Listen to me an my mind.
I have green money, my skeleton is white
Red blood courses thru my veins
These things are similar to yours
Yet were not treated the same
I worship the same God.
Still my life's quite complex.
I awake every morning with prayer for change.
Sometimes the sun peeks thru.
But often it rains.
Tomorrow not promised.
That it won't be the same.
Things need to be improved.
Hopefully one day my ship will sail.
I'll have the Lord to thank.
They said prayer never fails.
Black is truly beautiful
A good education isn't free.
Maybe one day, you'll really love me.

Ella McBride

A Mother's Silent Cry

In Memory of Derrick C. West Sr.
"Listen"; Her song is sung loud,
  Yet filled with great sadness
"Look"; The eyes appear dry,
  But the tears flow like a river
"Touch"; The heart is beating strong,
  With so much love and pain.
Do you choose not to acknowledge her agony,
  Or are you too afraid to feel!
Life as she once knew it will never be the same
Her first born son, she'll never see again
Not because of drugs, gangs, crime or a disease
Some lost soul released a gun trigger on him with ease.
The gift of life was taken at the age of twenty-four
Now her only solitude is knowing,
  Her baby walked thru "Heaven Doors",
Shhh....Now listen closely, tell me what you hear
  That cry, that cry, that endless cry!
Yes it is my mothers strong silent cry.

Veronica West-Williams

On The Finger Tips Of Rose

Sitting on a limb
Dreaming in my head
Nothing's happening
Witness of hope
Cries in tattered rags
Nothing's happening
Chorus raises a voice up
Clergy praying of miracles
Nothing's happening
Budding so beautifully
Blossoming so easily
Something's happening
Children stop to smell it
Floral scents fill the air
Something's happening
A smile on the face of joy
Happiness on a town of friends
Hope nor miracle
Tear nor song
Might carry joy like a spring bed of roses

Biagio Scibetta

Starz

Like a stepping stone in someone else's dream, Watching the fire in someone else's eyes turn to steam, And all because something had gone wrong, Now all they are left with is a song, Seeing everyone shine then watching their flame as it dies, Staring into you, into the stars in your eyes, So bright so meaningful, still looking for the answer, While others seek the questions, Smile then frown, life is a mixed emotion, and with each day you live the devotion, Like a light bulb for your brother's working mind, You shall seek as you shall find, Maybe a cloud for someone else's thought, Or a victory for the battle they fought, Constantly sharing, frequently caring, for all that you hold dear, Hold on with might or what you fear may grab tight and what you want, what you need, could be all gone tonight, Tonight the glorious morn the promise was sworn, Your man and your woman united in trust, Your man and your woman united in lust. Problems and nightmares bond to attack your young head, And pride and respect fall with each tear you shed, To the ground with a hollow lonely sound, The world dies, each time a star falls from somebody's eyes...

Christina Smith

Dreams Do Come True

I listen to the stories of you as a boy...
And how the race car was your favorite toy.

This race-car, your toy...
Put a special spark into your eye.

You soon started racing on two wheels...
Your bike at full speed up and down hills.

A few years later you went another step, not too far...
You went and bought an R.C. car.

You still were not satisfied...
You wanted to be part of the ride.

So you went and bought a go-cart...
And this is where talk of a Sprint Car came to start.

The go-cart had so many limits...
So that's when you went and bought the Micro-Midget.

The midget still wasn't good enough...
It was too small and didn't go as fast or look as tuff.

You saved your money to complete your life dream...
To go and buy that black 360 machine.

Now you are racing your 360 Spring car...
I hope your dream lasts forever and takes you far.

Melissa Elaine Mossi

The Sea Of Souls

Cast out on a sea of souls
Adrift on the waters of lost hope
Drowning in a sea of despair
Started by one single tear
These waters run deep
So many silently weep
These waters are dark
And they run straight through your heart
So many people who are alive
Are withering inside
And these are the waters in which they swim
The light of love that once burned bright
Has now grown dim
Set adrift in a ship of my own making
Overwhelmed by the rate at which I am sinking

Andrew Anderson

For Eternity

For I was new and you were old,
We told those scary stories that you mostly told.

We rode on the bus Winter and Spring,
For all I knew you filled my dreams.

For my days were filled with grief and urge,
I wanted to tell you, I really liked you.

Time passed you started to like me, it seemed
like that to me.

I started to dislike you, was this true?
Were we still together because of me or you?

I made you a Valentine,
Which I still dread to this day.

Valentine's Day came, rumors spread,
I heard from someone who said.

He hates you, you like him, this is true?
Go away, go away, see you soon.

The story has been told
I shall never see you, you shall never see me
  For Eternity

Faye Des Aulnier

Essence

My Black Sister;
Oh, how magnificent you are!

Brilliant...Brave...Beautiful;
You are all the elements intended by God and many more.
My Brilliant Sister,
You have outsmarted those known as the smartest,
You have taught those who were thought incapable of learning,
You have taken your God-given intelligence and graced it upon many.
My Brave Sister,
You have led our people singlehandedly from bondage to freedom.
You have stood with our men and fought to claim our right to Life,
Liberty, and the Pursuit of perfect happiness.
You have used the strength given to you by God to ensure
  our people's emancipation.
My Beautiful Sister,
Your grace stands out from all others,
Your elegance is mimicked by women universal,
Your femininity and vibrance are envied by many.
You are all that a woman could ever be.
You are everything all women hope to ever become;
Brilliant...Brave...Beautiful.

Zakiyah L. A. DeVaughn

Time And Patience

Few will deposit a little time and patience
into a safe reserve within.
But these precious deposits
can ease life's vicious burdens.

When the deposits of time run short,
patience becomes an emotional balance
that keeps us focused on tomorrow's dreams.

So always remember that as time
moves on, patience becomes the
challenger today and again tomorrow,
and you must get up, ready to fight
the next round.

Mae B. Keyes

If I Could

If I could love you as much as you love me, I would,
But it's not possible.
To give that much of myself would leave me with no protection.
It breaks my heart not to be able to return your love with the depth
That you give me yours, but I can't.
I need my protection.
Emotional pain is a terrible thing to suffer.
But when you've experienced it, more than once,
It's difficult to forget.
You can forgive, but forgetting is harder to do.
So, you continue on, with a wall gradually building up
Around yourself
As more emotional pain happens in your life, the wall gets thicker.
Until one day you realize that you can no longer reach out and give
As much of yourself... to anyone.
I love you very much, as much as I can.
But not as much as you love me.
I know this is true, and I wish I could change it.
But I cannot.
If I could....

Floy Bodden

My Lamp-Lighted Room

Rain pours beyond these walls, now and then, thunder calls.
My vanity lamp shines in the corner of my room,
Casting dancing shadows that somehow cause me gloom.
I suddenly realize how lucky I may be, I looked around my room,
  and think about the things I see.
I see my big yellow chair, sitting between two windows of glass,
I see my withered blue balloon, I got at my first communion mass.
I see my basketball trophy, standing shiny and still.
I see my soft red satin ribbon, hanging by my window sill.
I see the pictures of my school friends, for which I have a lot of
  affection
I see my many paintings, with no need of correction.
I see my porcelain Irish doll, with hair of curly red.
Then I looked up at my big painting of a sun, and on it,
  this is what it says:
    You still have a long way to go, and many things to know.
    If your mind does not thrive now, your imagination will never show.
    Don't stop dodging the obstacles, don't give up now,
    Finish the performance, then take your bow.
The last drop of rain had its fall, and the last roll of thunder had
  its call.
The dancing shadows still did cause me gloom,
But I realize there is something different yet to show,
In my little lamp-lighted room.

Colleen Mulcrone

All Hallows Eve

Cool October breezes and blood red sunsets,
a Full moon pale against a blackened backdrop,
and a Nightmare to chill the bone.

From sundown to sun-up two worlds shall meet
where the trail crosses the stream
and down at the cross roads.

Wondrous sights seen and soulless bargains made,
this night will end...
  with the next Sun's rising.
  Someone's life, after all.
Too soon. All too soon.

William A. Lucas

Wake Up

They should be running merrily through the park; play all day long, but be home before dark. Love is what they should feel when they hear those remarks. Instead, life has dealt them a raw deal, their roaming the streets searchin' for their next meal. It breaks my heart to see a child astray. What happened at home to make them run away? Beggin' for money from everyone they meet, this is your wake-up call America our future's on the street.

They have no food to eat. The sidewalk is their bed, upon which they lay their heads. Some as young six, survive by turning Trixx. There's nothing they can do it's up to me and you. There's no time for play, it's gotta be a better way to help the children of the world today, lives filled with nothing but disgust and no one to trust.

A helping hand we'll lend, their li'l hearts we'll mend. It's time to take a stand, let's walk hand and hand. This urgent situation needs immediate facilitation. They rely on their will to survive, trying to stay alive. Age nor race matters not with them, without love and support, anyone can fall victim. Wake-up America, the alarm has sounded for years. Let's stand up, take control and wipe away their tears.

Tatia Lee

Our Children

You are my Motherhood awaken.
God imprints upon all souls an
Immeasurable yearning for fulfillment,
Serious girl too women dreaming; then
too wife dearly loved.
One day tender longing burst forth
Visible with swelling of body pregnant.
God loved - and then there was you.
Five times my hand in your dad's, fixed
Faith in Him above, like yesterday I
Remember; my fears, my hopes, yet beneath
All, the urgent tender yearning.
Years fly, I gaze into eyes of children
Belonging, and warm am I
A brilliant sun sweetly lowers a halo of
Motherhood upon me, now the sunset nears;
Thanks dear children for enriching our lives,
Cognizant am I that you are ours; yet
Initially and Eternally you are children of God.

Hazel M. Stanley

My Cry

Shadows like a raging ocean encompassed me.
Far in the distance a light gleams brightly.
The light beckons to me.
The light is so very far away.

A dimness falls around me.
Crimson stains my head.
My soul and body are weak and beaten.
The light is so very far away.

The inky black of starless night is everywhere.
Something clenches me.
It pierces my skin with its wicked hold.
The light is so very far away.

An eclipse covers me.
Striving toward the light I fall.
My blood drips from the evil hand that holds me tight.
The light is so very far away.

Light is everywhere.
I cried out and the light came to me.
The evil thing has lost its grip.
It is so bright here.

Luke Oetker

A Widows's Lament

He is gone. From my life has gone a light.
The chair stands empty, where he sat each night.

His voice is forever silenced. No longer will he call my name.
My heart fills up with loneliness, my life will never be the same.

I miss his gentle touch, his hand upon my head.
I can hardly bear to look at the empty pillow on my bed.

Never again will my lips know his kiss
His smile, his steps, now just memories exist

The pain and sadness cut through me like a knife,
They call me his widow, but I want to be his wife.

Can death be so final? All those years came to an end.
Have I really lost forever, my husband and my friend?

Arlene Sylvia Albin

Senses Of War

See people emaciated; babies orphaned;
   houses charred; animal scavengers.

Hear leaders commanding; weapons discharging;
   mothers wailing; rattle of death.

Smell crops rotting; building smoking;
   bodies decaying; stench impregnating.

Touch nothing clean; anything still whole;
   something alive; everything contaminated.

Taste sweet air; salty sweat;
   sour stomach; bitter medicine.

Know war's finality,
   irreversibility,
     totality,

War has no sense.

Gretchen M. Robison

Stolen Prince

The ocean's waves crash hard, hard against the silent shore;
a fragile sand castle has washed away to nothing more.

An orange fading sun disappears into the sea;
the same color of midnight eyes she holds in memory.

Lying in the soft sand, she stares into the darkening sky;
as night descends upon her, a tear falls from her eye.

Her broken heart is still as it bleeds deep inside;
she pretends to be okay, but the girl in her will hide.

She tries to understand as the sky begins to rain;
oblivious to everything, she only knows her pain.

Angry, sad and hurt, should she cry or should she swear?
She's quiet and does nothing, deciding the ocean doesn't care.

The tides took her castle, the beloved castle she once knew;
and they stole the boy who lived there with the eyes of midnight blue.

Danielle H. McBride

The Dance Of The Fairies

In the spring fairies are born,
Some get new wings that have never been worn.

From their glistening eggs they awake,
Dancing about on a shimmering lake.

Hidden in the shade of a willow tree
Hidden so that no one can see,

The dance of the fairies,
The dance of the fairies.

Emily Vince

I Weep

I weep
The trees weep
Raindrops dripping like tear drops off leaves
The earth is silent
The world cries
We have lost our loved one

The white dove walks about under the walnut tree.
She cries
Her soft and mournful cry
Teardrops drip from my eyes
Like the raindrops dripping off leaves
The trees weep
The dove weeps
I weep...

Ruth Rutherford Carque

The Devil

Have we ever thought as human beings where does the devil
come from?
Who he is? What is his job, his job is to rob, steal, and destroy
everything God has made good.
Especially the human race, with his lies, tricks, deceit,
with greed, envy, anger, jealousy, madness
with his charming ways and looks
he'll make you think that you're living a good life
when it is sinful in God's eyesight.
Some of his ways are slick, tricky, wicked, ugly, mean, nasty, hateful,
just to name a few.
He'll have you fooled when you're not up under the power
 of the Holy Spirit, and the word of God.
We need knowledge to get out from under his control,
Jesus can do the impossible in everyone's life if you can want him to.
Who will you believe in, the spirit or the flesh?
Let God's will be done in our lives not our will. Think.

Mildred McCann

Friendship

Friendship is the unbroken strand
A strong rope twined together,
rarely apart,
It never gets old with age,
The unbendable love of deep souls
    Spring—always blossoming,
        Willing for fresh starts
        Like the sea, full of
High tides, low tides, and smooth courses
It's charity—always supporting, lending
    the extended hand
Friendship is fragile;
    Like glass, one crack and it
    shatters
    Delicate as a spider's web
The chain of friends may be driven apart by age
    but reunited by time
Friendship is strong,
    Like the unbroken strand,
    which never frays.

Sherry Huang

Untitled

If children are judged on their parents' mold
And the parents' breath is still on hold
Then yours should be known before you're old
The job you've done should be awarded gold.

Here's your gold medal, Pop.
Happy Birthday!

Jeff Murphy

A Smile

A smile so far away, that I could only see,
I knew it was sent from heaven, though it was on a balcony,
As it approached a little closer, I felt a warmth inside,
Then my "life" suddenly started changing to what I can't describe,
My saddened days had ended, the world had a whole "New View"
A lifetime of anticipation, had suddenly "come true"
A dream was locked into my heart, that I could never "feel"
Then "You" came into my life and I knew that it was "real"
My knight in shining armour had finally found a "way"
To take me to my younger years and see a bright new day,
The wonder of his "magic touch" does set my heart on "fire"
With a never ending feeling of "love" and "desire"
"My life" "My Love" I give to him "forever" and a day,
A "smile" I'll always have for him, whether "near" or "faraway"
Please! Dear God I pray to you that he may feel the same too!

Carol Ann Berkin

My Place

I'd like to go to a faraway place, a place that's quiet and calm.
With a lake and a stream running from it and a breeze rustling
through the trees.
But who would I take? A child, a friend, a lover, a pet, myself,
God, who?
I am alone. I wish to take them all, for you see I need each of
them in my life.
A child to cuddle and dream with.
A man friend for support who will accept me for who I am,
not what I have.
A woman friend to share my feelings and know she will never tell,
to yell, to cry, to care, to share, always there.
A lover for romance, to hold me for endless hours while the breezes
rustle through trees.
A pet to cuddle, to walk while talking endlessly about whatever
while he tags along.
Myself to take time out of the day to gaze into the stream
and wonder what life really means.
And God, who is always there when no one else is.

Helen Raisch

More Fun

I watched a lamb play in a meadow,
    kicking up his heels.
I almost wished I were a lamb.
    there ought to be more lamb in man.

I watched a kitten run through the house,
    squealing from pure delight.
And I thought, "My, what a pity,
    man is not more like the kitty"!

I heard a bird sing from a tree
    when I awoke one morning.
Cheerful so early? How absurd!
    I wish I were a little more "bird".

I watched a man walk to his work,
    reluctantly trudging along.
Man is intelligent. Maybe some
    should be less smart and have more fun!

Geneva P. Taylor

The First Time

The first time I saw you I said "Oh My"
Because of the beauty on your face.
Your eyes were like diamonds in the sky,
Your hair as beautiful as golden lace.
Back then I had no guts to say,
That I will always love you in every way.
You tell me you love me I hope you do,
And I hope it lasts until it's time to say I do.

Arturo Gomez

To My Child

As I felt you grow in me
I knew that my love would always be,
Forever and ever, till the end of time
For in my eyes you will always shine.

As your journey begins with a crawl
I will be there when you fall,
To pick you up and try to show
That you will fall as you grow.

As you grow older you will see
That some of these falls just seem to be,
Too hard to get back up and try to stand
But your mommy will always reach out her hand

For my sweet child
You will always be,
That little baby
Inside of me.
Barbara A. Cummings

Watching David Grow

A, B, C's and 1, 2, 3's,
Juice boxes, Matchbox cars, and wounded knees,
Lullabies, teddy bears and Cheerios,
Oh, the joy of watching David grow.

Singing songs, long walks and telling rhymes,
Silly jokes, funny faces and story time,
Quiet talks, secrets and cuddling up together,
I wish these moments would last forever.

Mickey Mouse and playing house,
With Winnie the Pooh, there's so much to do,
Warm kisses, tight hugs and sweet good nights,
These are the things that matter in my life.

Dirty hands and smiling faces,
Train tracks and Matchbox races,
Bicycles, swing sets, games and clothes,
I don't have to wonder where the money goes.

Watching him learn and ask countless "why's,"
Evoking less often an answer than a sigh,
Hide and seek, and just watching him sleep,
These are the memories I will forever treasure and keep.

They say to give your children two lasting things,
One is roots and the other is wings.
For me the former is as easy as pie,
But the latter will be difficult, I cannot lie.
My heart belongs to David and I love to watch him grow,
But I don't think I will ever be ready to let him go.
Susan L. Betts

My Daddy's Piano

My heart overflowed with sadness,
when movers came to take it away.
I had a vision of him sitting there
playing a song I had asked him to play.

I could hear his music clearly,
as they rolled it out the door.
Realization made me shiver inside.
He won't be playing for me anymore.

Some say it was filled with magic,
but the magic was in his soul.
When he caressed the keys with his fingers,
he made that old piano roll.

God gave him this glorious talent
and to think he shared it with me,
brought tears of joy and sorrow,
as I remembered how it used to be.
Judith Nichols

On What It Means

On what it means to be in it,
and on how it is we lose it,
No soul has yet been able to tell.
Though many try,
As am I,
and on how it is heaven can turn to hell.

When everything is complete,
and the world has no end.
When lovers eyes meet,
and their souls slowly blend.
This thing called love that gives us life,
But when it's lost, one's soul takes flight.
And nothing is complete.
And the world seems to end.
To find an other, once love is lost,
You'd think would come at such a cost.
But love you'll find is free.
There is no expense.
Just wait...
and see.
Josh Parker

A Message

As darkness surrounds me like a shroud
and all light that once was, ceases to be
I send a message to you
carried on the night,
hidden in the soul,
seen in the eyes,
and heard only in the heart
It whispers I love you
A single tears slips down my cheek,
My lips part, and a single strangled cry escapes
your memories like ghosts, cloud my mind
and whispers of a past life
As the hope I hold so dear, slips from my grasp
I can only dream that I will see you
when the sun comes out again
I carry your love with me now,
and I will live again.
Melissa Hendrickson

Dear Mom

Dear Mom, the beginning of a letter, I can write, but never send.

I want to write about staying up till 3 a.m. just the two of us,
eating too much ice cream and talking the night away.
Shared secrets hopes and dreams inside jokes real connection love.

But that's not my letter. Those are someone else's memories.

I remember spankings with a hairbrush crying so hard I choked wishing
like hell your lousy alcoholic husband would come home from the club
so I could tell on you.

This lazy, spiteful brat wants you to know, I wasn't what you seemed
to believe, that was never really me.

I was conference coordinator of the youth group, chamber Singer, and
Class Actress destined for the bright lights of Broadway.
Trusted friend and amateur therapist for all the stragglers and strays.
Absorbing myself in their needs while studiously avoiding my own.

I always hoped you would understand the words I never said to you.
It's hard to confide in a mother who only listens to what
she wants to hear. Dear Mom.
The beginning of a letter to the one woman I truly wish I could Love.
Lisa Steele

For All the Things You Have Taught Me

For all the things you have taught me
and knowledge you've helped me gain
For all the comforting advice you gave
that chased away my pain

For all the feelings we have shared
the laughter and sadness, the smiles and tears
These are things I'll always remember
as I get older with the years

For all those little talks we've had
that have shown you understood
For all the times you have stood by me
like you always said you would.

For all the times I've caught you waiting up
to make sure I got home O.K.
For all the kisses you left on my forehead
before you left for work each day

So I guess this is as good a time as any
As I leave to seek my future endeavors
to tell you that I'll always love you
and you'll remain in my heart forever

Stephanie Tosca

Fairy King

I go to the meadow at 5 till 8
Find the mushrooms and then wait
The clock strikes and they start to glow
Then they appear, as quiet as snow
I watch in wonder then I jump through
Into the ring as the fairies do
The horses of our world can not compare
With the horned steed and the winged mare
I see a flower change from red to white
Then a dragon spreads its wings in flight
I spot a pixie in an odd old tree
He laughs and giggles as he looks at me
Though I want to stay I must go
It disappears at 9:00 you know.
On the way out I meet a Leprechaun
Tending to a little baby fawn
He gives to me a four leaf clover
And an invitation to "come back over."
Later I wake up and think it all was dreamed.
Then see the clover it was as real as it seemed.

Katina Ramer

Day-Care In Heaven

It was time to start the day like they always had
Time to learn and have fun and for that they were glad

As the children arrived they found it was time to play
But their time became short on that particular day

Soon a noise rang out and they all looked to see
Their world coming apart before they could flee

Then God reached down to take the hurt away
His hand held out for them to come play

So they travelled away and left their families behind
But in the comfort of God's arms they knew they were fine

And soon they were playing in the day-care above
As God watched over them with everlasting love

He oversees this day-care in a very special way
For the sign on the door says "angels at play"

Nancy A. Waters

Lost Connections

Dedicated to my uncle, who was a victim of the AIDS virus.
We were connected through family, though we were so far apart.
I didn't have the opportunity
to ask the questions I needed to ask.

We didn't get to have any small talks
to share our good and bad times
and our laughter and tears of pain.
There were no good-byes, no last words to keep as a memory.
Only sadness and tears.

I didn't get to tell you about high school
or about all the friends I've lost and gained.

I didn't get to tell you
about all that has caused my pain.

But now, this all seems insignificant.
None of it matters anymore and
none of it would make sense.

I could never blame you for any of this.
Your heart has been broken and so has a part of mine.

This is my good-bye to you.
I love you and will miss you.
May God heal your heart.

Stephanie Michelle Turner

Distant Love

If I were to live through a thousand deaths
My love for you will never die, but
be forever cherished.

If I were to see a hundred faces
No other would have your luscious features
or magnificent graces.

Though I made a vow long ago
never to love again,
But the moment we were introduced;
it was a feeling far more above
that I could not maintain.

It seemed as if we were brought
together by fate.
Like sacred candles burning
eternal flames.

And I could not tell if you felt
the same as I,
But I then knew the moment
I saw that smile and the
passion in your eyes.

Maria Galicia

The Wish

Through the hourglass, grains of sand crash down
  like boulders onto a mountain of time
In a tree the mockingbird sings, lifts his wings
  and flies away
Up in the sky, some distant light
A dream is born and takes to flight
The sound of silence
Piercing and loud
Even reaches the highest cloud
Running but still in place
The earth moves, keeping pace
Visiting absence, empty indeed
The captive caught, then is freed
The willow walks with the wind
As the wise whispers the wish of the willing
Thus we begin

Kerri Cummings

Killed Spirit

My spirit died
along with my enthusiasm.
Somewhere—
in my past—
a chain was put around my neck.
My future slashed me
with knives.
   Cutting
     deep.
Scars will soon diminish,
but the
  pain
Will still be there.
As I climb up life's ladder
I slip.
The rungs have been coated with my unseen future.
The chain pulls me down.
My spirit will die.
Take my hand.
Hold my heart.
   Jean Sneller

Shame

If ever there was a time to weep
Now is the time to let the tears fall
Our world has changed
Now all that is left is the tears
Mankind has fallen from grace
All that is left are the tears
As each of us takes our turn in the fires
All we can do is mourn for what was
As we continue to burn bridge after bridge
We will all feel a tear upon our cheek
Centuries go up in a single blue flame
And each of us falls to our knees to weep
Once we saw the trouble we disbelieved
And now we most relegate to tears
As we felt fate's cold breath upon our skin
We fell to pestilence rather than look for a cure
Too weak to change
And too proud to say we were wrong
   Dennis Flesch

My Epitaph

If it happens I do not see another sunset with you,
a twilight or a new moon;
I entreat you to remember,
all that I believed is true.
When you see a bright green star,
please think of me;
telling you that I was a martian,
but you just would not believe.
Think of who you are and who you might become.
In the days we had together,
there is a lesson to be learned.
Mine is in the offing,
in that great expanse of space,
with a grand Ottoman sultan
who just might put me in my place
I ask you to be happy,
and celebrate my death.
I am at peace with my creatress, who is putting me to rest.
I will sing a song, for you my friends,
full of rain and wine and arias.
   Rose Marie Varga

The Day That I Met Jesus

   The day that I met Jesus
was a wondrous day to me,
it was a day that I will never
forget you see.
   The pastor was praying,
the music was playing, the people were
singing, and my head was swinging.
   The pastor said the door of the
church is open. Somehow I was
out of my seat and up on my feet.
   I felt the spirit of Jesus.
I felt the touch of his hand leading me.
   It seemed like it was taking a
very long time but now I know
it was all in my mind.
   Everything lit up with a glow,
I could no longer see anything but
The smiling face of a loved one who
left us not long ago, holding the
hand of Jesus saying, "I told you so."
   Marion E. Gant

Martin Luther King, Jr.

M man of peace
A arranged freedom for blacks
R reversed evil to love
T the Nobel Peace Prize winner
I I admire you
N national leader for civil rights

L led many in the march for freedom
U used his soul to let peace ring
T taught us tolerance for mankind
H his message continues
E each of us chooses violence or peace
R right to liberty is for all

K killed in the year of 1968
I in Atlanta he is buried
N no more violence because of him
G go to Atlanta to see his grave: "Free at last, Free at last, Thank God Almighty, I'm free at last."
   Bradley W. Chick

The Dream Journal

I wanted him.
I still loved him,
He was my first love
And he had stopped loving me a long,
  long time ago.

He wanted my niece,
Two years younger than me,
Blonde and pretty in a bimbo sort of way.
But he didn't care.
He loved her the way I wanted him
  to love me.

She wanted my blessing to go out with him.
My desire for him was such that -
I lost all pride.
I went to him.
"I will tell her to go with you," I said,
"But you have to do something for me."
I tried to look seductive
But I only looked pitiful.
   Karen E. Pressley

Be Mindful

One day as I was walking, all lonely by the sea
I spied a weary old man, who reminded me of me

I am young and supple, he is old and bent
My life has only just begun, his is gone and spent

I said that he reminded, my own self of me
He showed me how, that one day, this too, could be me

So be mindful of the old ones, though bothers they may be
Be patient with their efforts, though it pains you sore to see

Be generous with helpful hands, love doesn't hurt to share
And listen to the old ones, then they will know you care

And 'though they may never thank you, with a kind word or a nod
You can be sure your kindnesses, are overseen by God

Kathy E. Krafft

Enchantment

The countryside is wrapped this morning,
In a blanket soft, cold and white.
The snow that began in the twilight,
Continued on through the night.

Falling in muffled silence.
It tucked in the sleeping earth
Now peacefully all nature will slumber,
'Til gentle spring kindles her rebirth.

Tracks in the snow tell a story,
Rabbits scurried o'er the yard in great bounds,
A raccoon left hand prints by the creek bed,
Stray hounds have been nosing around.

Birds queue up by the feeder,
Like nations, an order exits,
The small and weak wait in subjection,
Knowing how futile it would be to resist.

Spring rains pattering on the roof tops,
Summer sun warming the earth with its glow,
Autumn colors transforming the land with their beauty
Are less enchanting then winters white, gentle snow.

Alice McMurry

Memories

We walked alone on the beach hand in hand
Pausing just long enough to write our love in the sand
As time passed on we knew we couldn't stay
How sad, the tide had washed our love away
Now we have but fond memories that make us laugh and cry
But how I remember those beautiful times whenever I watch the seagulls fly
Today I walk those same beaches alone thinking beautiful memories, time and time again
Always wondering what life together might have been

Clint Moses

Paths

As I walked through the forest one day,
I came across a separation in the path,
I said to the dog at my heels,
"What path shall I wander today?"
Pondering the thought of what path to walk down,
I looked at them and studied the way they looked,
The one on the left is dark and gloomy,
As to where the one on the right is light
  and full of life,
I chose to take the right path,
The path of goodness and love

Kristen Grossklas

Astonished

The astonished were admonished
not to frolic in the rain.
These disheveled at once bevelled
looking glasses out of grain.

With these tools we'll sculpt our answers
though we know that we are wrong.
We are fools but we'll keep scratching
bedrock caves that sing no song.

For we were born with thoughts that wander
and where they go lead us on.
Orphans born with minds that wonder
and no recourse but ride along.

Brian Schuette

In Pari Materia

As you turn within your mother's womb,
My child, the world softly and silently turns
Around me. As you sleep amidst her coursing blood,
Cocooned within the softness of her flesh,
I am tossed among the neurons of His mind.
Neither of us can escape the humming,
Nor can we escape the constant whirling:
We rather spin with and are spun by.
An incessant force gathers to hurl us,
You through the door into the fallen garden,
I into the concluding passage, the destination.
As the earth when it was formless, vast, and void,
We await a sudden dissonance of light.

Mark S. Scheffer

Black

Darkness falls, my eyes are low,
here comes the crying of the crow.
From whence it came I know not where,
yet I feel the weight of his fiery stare.
He flies he is the eyes of night,
the judge, the juror, he makes wrongs right.
Darkness falls I hide below,
here comes the crying of the crow,
his eyes of justice which do not blink,
I hear my chains hiss clink...clink...clink.
Darkness falls I've nowhere to go,
for I hear the crying of the crow.
He comes for me, the servant of right,
to carry me off into the night.
He comes to claim my heart of black,
this is it, once and for all, his final attack.
Darkness falls the clock has tolled,
I am no more, my soul has been sold.

Christie Csonka

Queen Of Hearts

When the heart was created what was the plan?
For the heart is the place where one understands.
Though the heart was created for loving and caring,
Did the creator know that times would be daring?
Made to be filled with joy and laughter,
Because in the heart is where all life matters.
Hearts also known to experience sorrow,
Making the mind wonder of the next tomorrow.
In creating the heart, to know its true depth,
Experience displayed its part, the creator owned one Himself.
It's a high price to pay when considering the cost.
For when it is shared, reservations are lost.
One might believe he owns one whole heart
But a true owner is known for he gives all in parts!

Sylvia Halison

Growing Old

When as a child, stories were told,
About many people, and how they grew old.
I never knew just what it meant,
When it told about the many years "spent."

Years went by, high school done,
Worked my job and just had fun.
Forget those stories that were told,
It wasn't me who was growing old.

Family around me, their hair turning gray,
Will this happen to me some day?
What? Me get old? No! Never!
I'll be a blonde forever!!

Many years have gone by,
Things have happened to make me cry.
I look at the family all grown old,
And think of the children's stories told.

Now I know what the stories hold,
About all the people who grow old.
I know where they go when their years are "spent,"
They return to the Creator from whom they were sent.

Beverly J. Splan

Land Of The Free....

America...Wonderful land of the free!
So... Why do you always forget about me?
Teenager alone...Pushing drugs in the street....
Only because I have nothing to eat....
Not going to school...Staying up late....
I learn from the best....Sealing my fate...
People pass by and frown in my face
Thinking that I am a charity case...
Don't need any help... Haven't you heard?
My story is only the unspoken word
Of people everywhere....without anything...
And as for me...I am only the beginning...
The children cry out with innocent tears...
If they're lucky they'll live a few years...
Sometimes I just sit here...Wondering why....
Then I get up and run as a bullet flies by....
I wander aimlessly...I hope day to day...
Streets...Where I refuse to pass away....
Oh, America...Wonderful land of the free!
This is not the freedom we want it to be...

Alice Wills

Panther Pride

At 6:30 the student body fills the metal bleachers
There is harmony between students and teachers
We know our fate will soon be sealed
As we watch the teams enter the field
But this is no longer just a field, this is Panther territory
It feels like a dream, but it will soon be a story
The band's sound of harmony floats
We all stand in our Kelly Green coats
The national anthem is the last thing
Before the beginning of our game
This is what we have been waiting for
As we closely watch the climbing score
Through the uncomfortable bitter cold we stay
We are warmed by our pride; we can not miss the big play
The game is tied with a minute on the clock
To the field crowd begins to quickly flock
Together we stand by the field side
Chanting, "We have Panther Pride!"
It does not matter who lost and who won,
Because together, Panthers stand in the sun.

Carla Stull

Beauty Of Love

Because you love me I have found
You've picked me up off the ground.
You've brightened newer stars in my sky,
You gave me the wings so I could fly.
All your glories growing more and more,
I found new joys unknown before,
Because you love me, now I can rise,
Understanding your love has made me wise.
Soaring to the heights of fame and power,
Your knowledge I gain every minute and hour.
To look through your eyes and see,
Beyond all the beauty of eternity.

Beverly J. Taffee

Silver Bell

You stood apart from the rest,
Cast from a different mold.
Beautiful in your simplicity.

Your melodic sound made your presence known
And all paid heed —
Eager to do your bidding.

The years only enhanced your lustre.
Time could not diminish your radiance
Nor quell your need to help.

Yet, all things come to an end, as they must,
And finally assume their rightful place —
Stilled forever in deserving rest.

Matriarch, silver bell of my world,
I miss your calling.
Your silence is my constant reminder.

Josephine B. Chase-Jennings

This Land We Love

Our country has its rivers, its Gardens and its
  Isles. It also hast all mountains with
    green valleys for your eyes.

If you live in America the country
  where I live. I hope you think the way
I do as long as you may live.
  As long as you may live said I. For
America will never die.
  America will onward live long after in my grave I lie.

Armando D. Flores

An Appreciation For Inspiration

Confusion of the day's heat arises at night like a stolen
child from their mother's womb.
The threat of unknown desires and inspirations gone awry
swiftly spin and churn within your mind,
Reaching out for that one phenomenon which could prove to be
so quizzical to others yet so indispensable for yourself;
Yet do you yourself even realize what that one marvel may be
that could cease the constant funneling of ideals?
Stop! Suddenly it ends, your mind can't absorb any further
desire and your body has no more energy to search for the solvents.

The day's heat turns to the numbness of night just as your
energy turns to listless appreciation;
You watch the movements of others and look at their hollow
silhouettes;
Finally it happens, the realization that everyone is just as
confused as you strikes your stagnant reality.
The instability of life is much like the strength of the sun
and the restlessness of the night.

Amy Richardson

World Of Delusions

Loneliness and emptiness
That's what we feel
In a world of hatred
Where rage runs free
And happiness is killing
And living is sorrow
There is nothing to protect us from the pain.
In a world of delusions
Where only sobriety is real
And sleep is the only savior
Since it delivers us into dreams
Dreams of peace and bright blue skies
Instead of the reality of war
And bloodstained battlefields
And trenches full of dead bodies
Yet death is a blessing
Since we dispose of the harshness of life
And move to a brighter place
Where we can live together in harmony.

Martha Dodd

In My Dreams

In my dreams, there is no color in the human race,
There is no sorrow when I look at a child's face.
Pain can never be felt among this worked we live in,
Light a torch to create a nation full of love and we can put all this
Hatred to an end.
Hold each others hand and help one another find happiness,
All this violence brings our world into a state of sadness.
In my dreams, respect is powerful among us all,
With this, women and men can finally stand together, together
They can stand tall.
In my dreams, I can hear no words of despair,
Arms are out there to help you everywhere.
To reach the highest peak, we must help one another to reach the top
And not let the other one down,
To swim the deepest sea, we must not let one another drown.
In my dreams, I see equals among all of humanity,
But in my dreams, I see us all, not just you and me!

Sothea Kuy

Nature

I looked in the trees and saw the birds, singing and chanting those beautiful words. Their songs are so tender soft and sweet, that they slowly sweep me off my feet.
The deer in the grass lay soft in the ground, while the crickets in the meadow lurch around. The ants on the leaves plead for food, while the Buffalo herd slowly moves.
A happy couple come and see a beautiful sunset setting by the valley.
The stars pop out and the moon shines bright and soon they notice it is night. The couple leave to a far off place where hardly any animals grace. The city is where they're bound to be and not in nature here with me..
They live where the cars, trucks and buses go, is this too much for me to know? Tall buildings block the land, so animals trees and grass can't stand.
Nature is being torn part for everyone heart to heart. Ask yourself I insist, "Do you think nature still exist?"

Phoebe Bachofer

Painter Of The Soul

Lord Jesus, help me paint the canvas of my life, with the subtle colors of forgiveness, with the intricate details of excellence, with the thin threads of hope gently weaving through its fabric, with the shading of sweet humility, and the striking brilliancy of faith abounding. And most of all, oh gentle Savior, help me paint a picture that speaks so simple and free, of your love inside of me!

And Master of my heart, if you will, help me build a frame made from the grain of your grace, and beveled with the edge of prayer, joined in all corners with the glue of truth and stained with the richness of your word, polished to a shine by suffering!

Now best friend of men and a painter of souls, work together with me to finish it all. By the fruit of the Spirit we will take this frame and place my canvas into it, use the nails you bore to hold it all together and remind me always of what made it possible, secure it with wisdom wire made of gold tested by fire, then hang it on holiness leveled by your standard of righteousness. And lastly, Lord Jesus, display it on a wall of transparency for all to see, my gift to you is bringing your name all the glory.

Anonymous

School

In school you sit and learn all day
Can't wait to get home and play
But you know you have to do homework
You think your teacher's such a jerk
Math, Science, History, Spelling
You think they're hard you're just not telling
Outside you hear small children playing
And you just feel like saying,
Who invented dumb old school?
Then you think, I got a tool
I'll use my brain to read and write
Maybe, oh maybe, oh maybe just might
Go down to the corner store
get a job and maybe more
Oh boy, oh man, oh golly gee
See how much fun school can be!
Maybe if you just try,
You could do just like I.
Turn that T.V. off and run,
School can be really fun!

Ashley Lieb

Accepting Good-bye

There comes a time in a woman's life,
When she realizes that holding hands isn't security,
Kisses aren't considered contracts,
And presents aren't promises of forever.

When she realizes that some things,
Just aren't meant to be,
That life is about change,
And is willing to let go.

There comes a time when a woman accepts defeat,
Facing it with her head held high,
Instead of with a childish grievance,
And knows that she'll be ok.

When she begins to build her dreams on today,
Dealing with the past,
To make tomorrow a better day.

When she is able to pick up the pieces,
Of her seemingly shattered life,
And go on accepting good-bye.

Jill Shober

Come To Rest in a Place So Near

Come to rest in this place, so near
but, so far it's not clear. To be in
a so forgivingly, sincere atmosphere.
As the sun sets into nightfall and stars,
all large and small begin to call.
The lonely sounds of a crane calling good night.
The sounds of the frogs and crickets take place.
And the sounds of owls in the old pines,
make an occasional call, watching the bats
in flight, after the lightning bugs and all.
There is a dog in the distance howling
in rhythm with the sounds of a rolling
train, that has a gentle whistle as it passes by
as the darkened starry night, begins a
gentle rain, the airport tower lights, that
blink red, and rotate green and white.
Begin to fade, for the foggy, misty break through
of the morning sun, the birds and locusts
Begin to sing and the sounds of the day
A Buzz begin to ring.

Faustyn Sharee Toth

Undying Love

You used to be here in my thoughts,
  but now you're gone and my heart has dropped.
I thought about you everyday,
  and when you died, my mind went astray.
We were together through despair and fun,
  and I couldn't believe that death had won.
Our love was strong and grew everyday.
  but this wretched thing called cancer came and took you away.
In trouble sometimes I will think of you,
  because you'll give me faith and then I'll be right on cue.
In the hands of God, I know you're safe,
  for everyday I see your loving face.
I take that as a sign that you're always near,
  and that God has bestowed upon you, his most divine love and care.
I'd like to take a moment to say,
  what I couldn't, before you slipped away.
I'll accept your death and go on with life,
  even if I don't get over my pain and strife.
When I say these last words, I break down and cry,
  I love you so much, so why do I have to say goodbye?

Rebecca J. Lee

Soul Conviction

For you...
A man of convictions and dreams... a timeless soul
The endless beauty within your eyes
creates a space which has no boundaries
For you my feelings are timeless

The provocative simplicity of engulfing my hand in yours
not of past commitment simply present desires and
the love for ourselves lives in everything we touch
Touching you - that's beauty

Contradictions are real and imagined. Imagine... and they are
Believe in serenity and passion... they prevail
Through sharing true intentions, some inherited pains
we honor a new creation in which spirit knows truth
from varying dimensions while a hug is still a hug
A kiss a kiss...

   From a woman with convictions and dreams
      A timeless soul

Jill Mason

A Battered Woman's Cry

Here I lay
  bruised and tormented
    from a late night beating
      damn near starved from lack of eating
        haven't eaten all week
          can't even sleep
            crying constant tears of horrendous pain
              squeezing my pillow
                covered with teardrop stains
                  asking myself
                what did I do that was so terribly bad?
                  asking myself
                what had I said to make him get so mad?
                  wondering why
                he hits me so
                  thinking of leaving
                    but afraid to go

Bridget McFerren

Innocent Blood

Walking down the street the pavement beneath his feet
The young boy walks along singing a cheerful happy song
Suddenly without warning a fight broke out
The boy not sure what the noise was all about
Gunshots rang out through the crowd
The young boy standing all a proud
The boy lifeless just barely alive lying helpless about to die
So young so innocent he plays no more
Just sit and waits at heavens door
His mom stands so still as if she was paralyzed
She slowly lets out a painful sigh
My little son of only seven shall leave this world to be in heaven
She cry's and wonders silently why
her dear little one should have to die
The young boy just painfully replied
My dear mother cry no more for I am not afraid to die
For I have no worries for the Lord is on my side
And slowly he closed his eyes
To be in heaven by the saviors side

Toni Gray

True Happiness

   A simple hand, a mother's smile, a kindly
deed done in service. A simple chat with
those you love. All these things bring
happiness. But happiness comes from the
heart. We give it freely and sometimes
unknowingly. Even a simple hello is enough
to make a stranger's day brighter.
Many of us spend our whole lives
searching for a part of us that's missing.
Not even knowing that it was
with us all along. All we had to do
was to find it within us. As human beings,
we need to know that we belong somewhere,
someplace. We needed to tell ourselves that
we are loved no matter what we do or have done.
We are accepted for who we are inside not what
the world sees outside. And only we know
what is in our hearts. And what is in our hearts
is what truly makes us happy and that is being
loved for who we are.

Cheryl Osbourn

Let Me, Please

Please, let me into your heart
And I will love and care for it
Until, it shall stop beating...
Please, let me into your kind and loving soul
And I will admire and behold it
Until, it shall leave you...
Please, let me into your mind
And I will value and listen to it
Until, it shall fade away...
Please, let me into your body
And I will hold and respect it
Until, it shall weaken and grow limp...
Please, let me into your life
And I will honor and commit to you
Until, I shall live no more...
Let me...Please...

Aimee M. Seeley

Evergreen Convalescent Home

Walking down the bare-walled corridors
Of the Evergreen Convalescent Home,
I'm counting the white ceramic tiles
And breathing the medicinal scent
Of my grandmother's house from years ago.
The white bearded man with one arm
Who always sits in his leather-padded wheelchair
Looks at me in that way he has before
As though he knows that someday I'll be old
With wrinkled skin and gray hair,
And he knows that I will be waiting someday for someone,
Anyone, who will come to visit me,
Maybe even a frightened young girl with blond hair
Curious about the way the years diminish life
And how bodies become eaten away by old age.
I see myself jumping rope outside after school
And hear my mother calling me home,
And I wish to remain young forever.

Katie Heffernan

The Dove

In the middle of December, on a cold winter night,
There came a knock at my door, that filled me with such fright.
It was heard by me three times: knock, knock, knock.
And I sat just so still, as if made of solid rock.

I did not know what to do, nor where I should go,
So I tip-toed 'round the stairwell, so as not to show.
I peeked through the window, and to my surprise,
'Twas only a dove, staring back with dull, lonely eyes.

I had feelings for the creature, so I let him come inside,
And I was careful not to leave the door open wide.
We sat down by the fire, and I offered him a snack.
When it was time for him to leave, he promised to come back.

I've heard that knock many times since, and when I reach the door,
I find the front porch lonely and bare, just as it was before.
Four years have passed and still, the Dove has not returned,
And since that fateful visit, there are things that I have learned.

'Tis summer now, and things are going fine at this ol' house,
The Dove, of course, has not returned...I think he's traveled south.
Sometimes, when I sit thinking, and an outward glance I take,
I think I see his shadow, soaring o'er the lake.

Marin Brooke Hoplamazian

A Changed Man

You hear a ring and see a bullet come lunging towards you
You jolt backwards like lightning has just struck you
You feel stunned and paralyzed
The blood drains out your stomach
You fall backwards and close your eyes
Hoping that the pain will fade
You see a red light thinking it's the end
You wish so much that you had lead your life differently
But you didn't
But God was on your side this time
When you wake back up you're in a white room
You realize you're alive
And jump for joy
But a jolt of pain tears through your body
After weeks of pain and struggle you decide to change your life
And when you did you felt better
And when you died you saw white not red
And you knew that if it wasn't for the grace of God
You would have died and gone to Hell.

Michelle C. McDonald

Personification

Pouring rain filled the sky outside my window. When I looked out I saw little plants ducking under the blades of grass. The clouds dropped heavy marbles on my roof and let them topple over the side of the house. The rain felt like tiny bullets aiming to kill each and every blade of grass. Suddenly, the clouds felt sorry and dropped tiny dust balls instead of marbles. Slowly, everything became a little quieter. Tap... tap... tap. The rain stopped and every flower sprouted out of hiding. The sun reached up from beneath the trees and hugged the crying leaves.

Stephanie Gordon

Knock Knock

Let me visit a while in your head.
  Just inside for a while with your brain.
Let me watch you give birth to your thoughts.
  And just feel for a while your pain.

Give to me your understanding.
  Please, just show me this world from your eyes.
Open wide your heart before me;
  Clear away the facade and disguise.

Let me see what you hold so dearly.
  Just a peek at the treasures you hide.
Breathe me into your soul, I beg you.
  Let me in, let me visit inside.

Ruth Petty

Forbidden

I look out my window and I see him,
His face looks lost and confused from within.
He sits there alone waiting patiently,
As his hair blows in the wind like a swaying tree.
I see his face everywhere I turn,
His eyes so dark my heart starts to burn.
His hair so dark and his face so sweet,
I see it everywhere even in my sleep.
"I can't live without you", I say,
I want to be with you night and day!
"Where are you going?" "Wait for me!"
As he turns around I watch him flee.

Cecilia Ceresa

What May Become

One special night I wished upon a star and hoped someone would hear and come to me from afar.
I gazed into the black of night brightened only by a star's twinkling light.
There I lie in my bed a million thoughts rushing through my head,
wanting someone to call my own; someone to make sure that I will
never be alone... someone to trust in 'till they lay to the test...
someone to believe in me through the good times and the bad...
someone to remember with me all the joy we've had.

And now as I look upon that very star that has granted my wish
and brought you to me from afar, I tell you of my experience,
to use your wish with wisdom because whatever you wish for may someday become...

Robyn N. Heming

To My Daddy

I love you Daddy, but yet today you yelled and took my fun away.
I want to act like grownups do, so I copy their actions and yours Dad too.
I didn't know I was doing wrong, I was just having fun and playing along.
I feel so bad when you shout at me, I get angry and hurt deep inside,
I want to grow to be proud and strong so I can walk tall by your side.
I cannot always explain myself, and I really don't know who
Can tell you I didn't mean it and explain my point of view.
I have to learn how to kid around, and sometimes I might err,
I'm only three years old you see, and just learning to confer!
The other kids will teach me how to yell and hit and scream,
But you're the example I need in my life to build my self esteem.
When you're angry with me, my heart just sinks and I feel I'm no good and I've failed,
Please Daddy forgive me and help me to learn, I'm only a little child.
I love you Daddy, please love me too, and with gentleness show it in all that you do
To help me grow strong and gentle and good so I'll always treat others the way that I should.

Elspeth-Ann Kick

A Morning Is Forever!

The alarm startles my relaxed body.
Do I decide to roll over or press myself out of a peaceful and warm cocoon.
The sun beams allure me to arise and greet the day as the dawn lights up the room.
It's another silent morning in my quest to meet a genuine soul.
The sheets entrap me and warn me of the hostile world that will shortly await me.
The pillow is drenched to my satisfaction of last night's erotic sensual dream, but reality is now.
Pleasure of an overnight adventure slowly fades into oblivion
Do I take on the world, or does the world take on me?
A thousand images enlighten my mind, places too distant to remember,
faces overshadowed by time and space, suddenly blurred out of existence.
Visions of fantasy, wanting so desperate to happen this very moment.
A sudden taste for the pure ecstasy of life, but not knowing how to achieve such as desire tugs inside of me.
A voice deep within calls me to paradise.
I arouse myself to sheer enjoyment, touching my innermost being where no one can observe.
The security of my cozy bed engulfs me beyond my conscious and bedazzled imagination.
Am I now ready to accept the challenges that so vibrantly await my pathway this very morn,
or do I drift back into the serene and contentment of a genteel past?

Glenn Kephart

"Emotions"

No one can hurt me or has ever hurt me as much as you.
No one has made me as happy or unhappy, so complete or incomplete or made me laugh or cry as hard.
No one has ever made me want to live life more fully or succumb to the darkness of death more quickly than you.
No one has made me feel so good or so bad, as much pain or as much pleasure, or as much Love or Hate till you.
What magic do you possess that allows you to control my every thought even from hundreds miles away?
Can my weakness for you be used to measure the depth of my Love?
Why is it that what supposedly tastes so sweet is so bitter?
How can you make me feel like so much of a Woman and than make me regret being one?
How on Earth do you force me to exhibit great strength, when the force you use is my greatest weakness,
and please don't ask me to explain how it is that I crave to see your face in the morning
and regret the memory of it when I lay down at night.
Why is it with every heartbeat I live for you and curse your name with every breath?
The only thing that I know is, I want to feel you in my arms, here tonight,
to touch you and to possess that which you swore to be mine forever.

Mary Crossland-Huggar

The Bogeyman Is Dead

A telling of your soul makes mine leap, ache, want to offer shielding light,
ask forgiveness and blanket you in a healing Love complete and powerful.

Your offering of pain, stolen innocence, found-terror, fear and searching through countless
sleepless dusk to dawns; make my offering blank in the ever-expanding light you have shone.

The telling of your soul, as I read your heart-lines, words, soul-sadness echoing, drop me to
first-time, beseeching knees to pray for your soul, all souls, but especially, your soul.... YOU.

I pray your sorrow, unchildlike childhood pain, innocence stolen were not yours;
not anyone's, but especially, not yours.

Your soul-journey wanderings, mind-haunting voices and dedications to know who you are,
who you are not, keep you searching, always searching.......
for woman...mother...wife...sister...teacher...angel.. fellow adventurer...
Searching for YOU.

I know YOU.

I know your radiant smile, light, gentle Love beyond all measure; you went within,
deeper always deeper, to discover and grow self-being self-healing YOU.

The telling of your soul magnifies all Light, shines brightness into sister souls lost in same
peace-shattered dark whirlpools of self-doubt and stolen innocence.

I pray, while still on contrite earnest knees, you forgive betrayal,
eyes which could not see
truth, a heart, that until the telling of your soul, could not fathom your being......YOU.
    Deborah Preece

The Symbol Of Love

A rose is but a symbol of the love two people share,
a love that journeys through a lifetime and a love that's always there.
A love that reaches into the heart and fills the soul and mind
with the rich, sweet fragrance of dreams ahead and of memories left behind.
The stem is but the pathway into a future that's yet unknown,
that together two will travel and together will make a home.
The thorns are but the trials and hardships that along the way they'll bear,
but together, they'll rise above and conquer through the love that they both share.
These times are when they'll draw on the strength the other provides
and together trust in the faith of God to keep happiness in their lives.
And as their love becomes stronger, and through the years, blossoms
and grows, the petals of true love will softly open forever into the beauty of a rose.
Although the rain will always fall and in the wind, the petals blow,
the sun will always shine again and from the rain, the rose will grow.
So when two people who are in love are married and each other they
have chosen, they vow to always be the gardeners and care for their flower as it grows.
And when their fingers meet as they take vows of husband and wife,
their new world is just beginning and they become one for life.
Their thoughts are now of dreams ahead and their hearts now beat together.
The circle of love is now complete and the rose will live forever.
    Julie A. Kahler

Peace

The stoic barn shields its animals like the mother of a frightened child.
It sits by the seldom-used dirt road which never disappears.
Along this trusted road one can see the sheep softly grazing as they
intermittently baa-a-a in the comfort and serenity of their home, the placid pasture.
The pond softly stirs as young ducklings quietly glide across.
While the wind gently sways through the lustrous leaves looming over the tall spring grass,
The empty schoolhouse stands barren on this Saturday ever beside the graveyard,
The final home for those who have met their ultimate fate,
Comforted only by occasional flowers which faithfully reside among the soothing quiet
From which one may never escape.
    Kileen Cheng

Little Reflections

They bring us so much pleasure
They bring us so much love
These precious little treasures
From our wonderful God above

They watch our every reaction
Even copying one or two
Our own little reflections
so be careful of what you do

They learn from us the way to be
From happiness, anger and love
Reflections copy what they see
So choose to reflect God above

Look into the mirror before you
See the reflection that is shown
Remember it sees all you do
So make it one you're proud to own

Gwen Kelson

The Wonder Of A Child

Sticky little fingers
Chubby little toes
And how she reached that cookie jar,
Only heaven knows.
Now the dog's gone into hiding
All the plants fear for their lives
And I swear I saw the cat today,
Breaking out in hives.
I can handle tripping over toys
And watching kiddie shows
But I haven't figured out yet,
How she gets out of her clothes.
Oh, our child looks like an angel
It's deception at its best
'Cause when she's up and running,
She'd put the devil to the test.
She has a lot of things to learn
But so much more to give
And because two people found true love,
A child began to live.

Charlie Murphy

Pride

The dreams I wove so carefully,
 lined with golden thread
The failures remembered tearfully,
 swimming in my head
The love I held within,
 nurtured by my heart
The wistfulness of sins,
 my soul could not impart
The faith which burned for my success,
 was blown out by your wind
The sacrifices made in jest,
 left me hopeless and chagrined
Strongly and boldly I will forge on,
 with pride and hope again
I will fight until I have won,
 the flame of hope within

Nicole M. Clemens

Love

What is love? Can you make love?
Can you give love? Love is heart.
Love is life. You can't make it.
You can't give it, it just is. It just
happens. Families love, lovers love
and also most importantly friends love.

Sarah Riffenburg

My Grandpa

My grandpa was a sweet old man
he gave his love to everyone.
My grandpa raised me as a boy
he taught me how to live and love.
My grandpa taught me all he could
and this I admire him for.
Now we have to say goodbye
but there isn't enough time.
He left this world a year ago
like an angel in the sky
but yet he is still alive.

Anthony Leanza IV

Just Married

Romance is a budding bloom
Spreading, encompassing all

Happiness is a spring bubbling over
Refreshing our souls everyday

Joy is an early morning dew
Sparkling diamonds of ice

Love is an everlasting
Rose, pressed and preserved

Hearts joined as a ring
Without beginning or end

A vow is spoken
Marking an eternal promise.

Samantha Waters

The Door Closes

The door closes...
and all hope is lost
The door closes...
and all options are gone
The door closes...
and the communication is cut off
The door closes...
and the hate begins
Why do we close the doors?
Why do we shut it all out?
why don't we open the doors
and let love out?

Rachel Kelly

Canine Appreciation

There was this dog who saw
Modern Art, and wondered at
What it would impart.
He stared it long!
He stared it hard!
Upon which he bestowed
His calling card!

Jonathan Edsel Hughes

After Tragic News.....

If all my days and all my nights
End to end would lie
They could not, dear, sufficiently
Measure the depth of my love for thee

If all my thoughts and all my dreams
"Comforter" could be
How gladly would I send them out
To be with thee....to be with thee.

Betty Attema Gravott

Haikus Of Mexican Art

Diego Rivera
 Aztec God of mural art
 In New Museum.

German-Jew Kahlo
 Fathers Frida, nee Frieda
 Hirsute, illness prone.

Frida pursues Diego—
Loving...passion for painting
Necklace by little monkeys
Winsome Frida's self-portraits
A visual delight
But Diego's "Natasha"
Long-limbed luxuriant coiffeur
Like billboard tobacco ad.

 Diego, how could you?
 This Aztec God was mortal
 A celebrity.

Benjamin Siegel

"Shelter"

Shelter of the world
 a place where evil dwells

Lost and lonely, go for help
 only to find HELL!

Money by the millions given
 to the keepers.

Only produces, misery, despair
 and "Homeless Weepers"!

There is a shelter, where one may go
 It is above, and not below

Under the pinions of his wings,
Peace, prosperity He does bring.

He makes the "Way" to get you out
He turns your life round about

Go to "HIS" shelter
 The shelter of life

And not the world's
 shelter of strife!

Gloria Nicolelli

Memory Magic

Memory Lane is a wondrous place
Where passage of time cannot erase
The joy on day that we first met
And made a glow that lingers yet.

The pleasures from admiring glance
Remain as bright as first romance,
And kisses sweet I shared with you
Linger still as bright as new.

The triumph of some goals attained
That brought applause so unrestrained.

The ecstasies that came to me
With babies one, and two, and three
Their triumphs and disasters, too,
In memories rich remain as new.

So what of wrinkles on my face?
They're minor things that can't erase
The memory magic that I'm feeling
The constant joy it keeps revealing!

Moyne Jamison

Paper Pixie

What impish thing is this
Skipping down the street
Hopping, twirling, skimming low
On little fairy feet?

Can my eyes deceive me so?
What pert thing doth caper?
Why 'tis only a refuted scrap
Of crumpled, twisted paper!

It pauses for a rest-
No, a lull within the wind.
It turns as if to wink at me
And skips on off again!

Felicia Moore

How It Feels To Fly Like A Bird

I would like to fly like a bird
To be as free as can be
To go from place to place with
My two feather wings
To sore on the high mountain peak
Or above the water or ground
To feel the breeze passing by me
As quick as it sounds
To see the little doll people and
The little toy car
How wonderful it would be
To fly high above.

Elizabeth Del Carmen

Letting Go

Your life you gave
forever unselfishly
the needs of others
always first

Your unwavering strength
you've passed along
your lessons well learned
making us all strong

Your heart and soul
overflowing with love
his light shining down
beckoning from above

Weighted by pain
only wanting release
not truly leaving
just going in peace

A part of us
you'll always be
our souls joined
throughout eternity

Rose Marie Dube

"Our Flag"

I watch it floating.
On the breeze,
I think of not seeing it,
And freeze,
It represents country,
Freedom and love,
How I thrill,
Seeing it above,
This banner of red, white,
And blue,
That means security,
To me and you.

Mattie M. Stewart

"Our Life Together"

Our marriage has survived a lot
through the years. Through all
the ups and downs, and many tears.
You are there for me, through thick and thin.
I know there will never be an end. Our life
together has truly been blessed. For our
five children are the best.
Our love for each other grows stronger,
with each passing day may we always
find joy along the way.
For we never gave up on each other.
Deep down I knew there would never be
another.

Linda Perron

A Valentine's Poem

My heart
black as coal,
open to no one,
destined to cook
cajun.

Chicken fat
impenetrable gristle,
surrounds my aorta.

Opaque kryptonite tanning goggles
shield my vision.
I refuse to see Love.

A coffee grinder sits on Aisle 2,
grinding fine fresh beans into dust,
Grinding coffee grinding coffee...

No Swiss Mocha or French Roast for me.
My soul hangs frozen on a meat hook.

Michael Porter

A March Night

The bitter cold wind blows,
Across the pavement and,
Bites you through your clothes,
All alone you stand.

The shadow of the night,
Claims its defenseless prey.
The moon your only light.
Yearning for the day.

Against the icy wall,
Of stony brick you lean.
You are this nightmare's thrall,
Peace is still unseen.

Kate Ricke

Start Here

Which path to follow
A hard one to swallow
Everything is such a clutter
I must be in the gutter
grabbing the rope with all my might
off in flight
with everything to lose
I reach for the drugs and booze
Awakened by a scream
It must have been a dream
Lying in a field of clover
Tis time to start over
Start Here

Gary R. Drehmer

Conquer The Night

Many live each Day,
  Without love and hope!
They have no vision of tomorrow,
  They cannot cope!

Turning to illusions,
  Coating their minds with dope!
Some break their necks,
  With a wrangler's rope!

Smile show the world,
  God's love is bright!
You are a window,
  God is the light!

Shine, let them see,
  Take away their fright!
Show them God's love,
  Conquer the Night!

William R. Turner II

Untitled

The night is full of your radiance
Each star twinkles your name
The moon is your bouncing puppet
And my world is all aflame.
Janet, the wind keeps whispering
Janet, the crickets recite
Janet, Janet, Janet
Is all that I hear tonight.
Janet, what a lovely name for a story
I shall play the leading man.
Dragoons, legions and monsters
Shall flee before my hand.
I will rescue for the purpose of loving
Of getting one beautiful smile
And all along I know
That it will be a long, long while.

Jack A. Birkland

The Old Theatre

A graceful bird she floated
Across the stage worn bare
By years of lost confusion
And scuffling of bare white feet.
The green paint was chipped away,
The only beauty to be found
Was the rhythm of her feet
And flowing lines of her dance.
Her hair swung like a rope
Braided tight to stay from her eyes.
Her light complexion contrasted
With the darkness of the room.
Creating beauty was her strength
At this weaker stage of life.

Amanda Reynolds

When My Grandfather Died

I was always by his side.
We had lots of fun
Near the sun.
I was the moon,
He was like the butterfly
In his coon.
We always ran,
We were also football fans.
Once I lied,
He finally died.

Carolyn Williams

Immersed By Blue On A Red Sunset

Swimming in the ocean blue
catching a tide
pulled by moon
sunset going down red
my body descends
engulfed in blue
one final glimpse
beautiful red sunset
disappearing as I sink
into darkness.
Can anyone see I'm blue?

Jason Hunter

Destiny

Life is what we choose to make it
As many choices come our way
We do not always see them
For we hurry through our day

When a child, the days are long
The hours filled with learning
From a teenager we emerge
Adults, with goals of yearning

Will the success that we attain
Be the conquests of your dreams
Or does our destiny lie dormant
Lost in truth like muddy streams

Settling for the have to dos
Forgotten aims in memory's wing
Waiting visions to be discovered
Our hopes aside until the spring

We listen to the voice within
And learn the facts in quiet peace
To focus on our real desires
Before it's time for life to cease

Ellen F. Reedy

In My Eagle's Eye

In my eagle's eye
my bird can fly so
high into the sky
somewhere near but
not to far to leave me here.

He flies so high
into the sky he
disappears into
the mountains
into the clouds.

Even though I'll see
my eagle again I'll
never forget what we
did together when he was here.

So until we meet
again my friend live
well and free.

Shonna Lafferty

Reflection

I saw a stump while in the wood
Where once a mighty tree had stood.
A monument to ages past
Where once stood verdant forests vast
Stands silent, as in reverie,
A tribute to its majesty.

Kathleen V. Follette

A Small Bit O'Name

Show me some blue
  I shall call it the sky.
A large piece of green
  I shall call it the land.
Show me a planet
  I shall christen it "earth".

But show me somewhere I can say;
  "Hello, Sister Harmony",
Somewhere to forget Brother Trouble
  And I shall call it "heaven".

We are yet to be Angels, just men.

Deborah M. Connor

I'd Like To Feed You

I know you're hungry
I'd like to feed you
although sometimes
I don't want to see you
I see your sign
it's plain as day
will work for food
I look away
it's your face I can't bare to see
although you stare straight at me
I'd like to feed you,
but not like this
I'd like to feed you,
but not under this bridge
not on a corner with a sign
I'd like to feed you, but take the time
to hear you and understand
what brought you to this
my fellow man.

Kelley M. Hairgrove

September Dreams

The road not traveled is just
a couple of miles away
The tollman's rates are higher
now I can't afford to pay

I lose myself in the crowd
hiding out from old regrets
All my demons cover me
So unwilling to forget

Everything is hard to find
and yet so easy to lose
To trade my lifetime of used
for a minute of brand new

I would search that dirty road
where I left my soul behind
Oh, Angel of Yesterday,
share your precious gift of time!

Kelly Kennedy

I'm Special!

I like my hair,
I like my teeth,
But best of all,
It's my skin and beneath!

I like my hands,
I like my art,
But best of all,
It's my heart!

Eleanor Santo

Sunrise

This morning's sunrise offers
a weary looking turquoise sky
readying to weep,
as myriad cupped leaves
stretched for heaven's morsels.

Last evening's tall giants
now deeply bow to a strong wind,
while colorful bouquets
dance wildly throughout the forest.

Down spouts echo of life's nectar
as lightning momentarily highlights
a distant horizon filled with promises
made of last night's dreams.

George J. Ondish

Brotherly Love

Loving people and using things
Is what God had in mind
Because using people and loving things
Would certainly be unkind.

Dear Father show us the difference
Help us to love one another
Material things are nice to have
But only God can give a brother.

A loving brother or sister
To share our deepest thought
Material things just come and go
But a family cannot be bought.

Marjorie S. Siegel

The Square Of Nouveau Riche

It's the square of nouveau riche,
And they all eat lots of quiche,
And their houses are gross,
They are just de trop.
It's the square of nouveau riche.

They're a pretty sorry lot.
They buy everything they got.
They ain't got no class.
They will never last.
It's the square of nouveau riche.

And I pity them to death.
They just take away my breath.
They go up and down,
They go all around.
It's the square of nouveau riche

Well I'm finishing my song.
I just hate when things are wrong;
I'm a little snob,
It's a horrid job.
It's the square of nouveau riche.

Carolyn Levy

Silverware

In a window
I see my dad
Playing with me.
I wish that was true
But it isn't.
So I have fun in
The window.

Alex L. McDonald

It All Comes Down To

In a world of rush and crush of crowds,
It all comes down to this...
A tender word, a gentle touch,
A smile, a look, a kiss.
It all comes down to faith and trust,
It all comes down to whether
we're doing it alone or know
we're in this thing together.
In a world of hype and hurry,
In a world of push and shove,
It all comes down to you and me,
It all comes down to love.

Jason Johnson

Imagine It!

Snow tops the sharp-pointed mountains.
The bay is rippled with crashing waves.
The young mountains surround the bay.

Puffins, gulls and eagles soar.
The wind rushes by.
The gray waters churn.

Whales migrate through.
Salmon turn the waters black.
Sea otters romp in the kelp.

Timothy Michael Edward Fitzgerald

Time Hurtling

Each year I live another year
That's shorter than the last,
A smaller fraction of my whole
As measured by my past.

It seems I've gained velocity,
Proficiency, the knack
To process time more facilely,
Foreverly—*alack!*

I hurdle weeks and months and years
In my mad rush to Night,
While Time, in turn, impassively,
Hurtles past in flight.

O, Mother Fate, why must I race
So urgent to my Sleep?
Is it because the Universe
Has other trysts to keep?

Walter Oberer

I Used To Have

I used to have happiness
  and days full of love
Now I have nothing
  but a life of pain.

I used to have dreams
  of always being in love
Now my life is nothing
  but pointless reality.

I used to have sunshine
  and rainbows of joy
Now there is nothing
  but rain and gloomy days.

My life is so empty
  but I don't really care
The only thing I ever cry about
  or even think about
Is when I used to have.... you.

Helen M. Carr

"My Daddy Left A Year Ago"

My Daddy left a year ago
he had better things to do.
God needed him in Heaven
to start his life anew.

It's peaceful there where he's at
Not a problem can be found.
No wars, no aids, no drugs, no crime
Just pretty flowers all around.

I think he has a job there
moving furniture around.
And every time it thunders
I enjoy its every sound.

I know that he is happy
I see a smile on his face.
I'll remember when I think of him
That he's in a better place.

So I close my eyes and say my prayers
Just thanking God above
That he was kind enough to give to me
My Daddy that I loved.

Betty Ann Stoneburgh

Where Hath Love Gone?

Where hath love gone?
Love is like the wind
When it comes it
Touches everything in its path
It feels good
It makes life look nice
It makes life's heat bearable
It tosses our cares away;
But
Then when it leaves
Everything becomes still
Lifeless as though it may seem
There is a void
Love like the wind is gone,
And no one knows where it went
It cannot be found.

Jenny Justice

Painting

I paint
my body blue
and pray
for it to fly.
I taste you
for a moment:
sweet and smoky.
Sliding up my
thighs,
I invite you in,
name
carved on walls.
I drown in
  your body
  your breath
  your sex
Mixed with you
I dissolve -
my painting
is ruined.

Jennifer Tuzzeo

Holy Men

Cheers to my fears,
And my tears,
And my keeper.

All the holy men,
Are lined up in a row.
I want to,
Baptize all their sorrows,
Anoint them with my holy oil.
Sprinkle them with salt,
And let their holy water flow.

Christ come over
Buy me a drink.
I want to be your lover tonight.

I want to lay down,
In your heaven,
'Cause I believe in you.

Take me to the highest altar,
Tell me that you're lonely, too.

Jean Corley

I Hate Lies

Don't tell me that you love me
when you're making love to me
as you lie between my quivering thighs
shout and obscenities, anything,
but, don't tell me that you love me
I hate lies.

I'd rather hear you say that
my beauty is breath taking,
that my breasts are overwhelming,
that you're having a good time,
that my body is divine.

Shout out obscenities, anything,
but, don't tell me that you love me
I hate lies.

Regina Hopper

The Sacrifice Of A Non-Virgin

Once killed
Always a murderer,
But I am no saint.

I wait,
Dressed in paper,
To be brought to the sacrificial altar.

Cold hands,
So cold they freeze the memory
Of the warmth that once parted my thighs.

I hear the whirl as the mechanical python
Prepares to suck every drop of life
From my body.

As the ritual is performed I stare at the ceiling
Wondering how many women have counted
These same cracks.

The sacrifice is over.
The altar is prepared for the next victim.
I leave, the same as before.
Except for the baby I bled.

Susan C. Winsor

Touch

It is the press of singular atom against singular atom;
thumping one another like club-footed pachyderms dancing ballroom

Exposed by silken sandpaper kisses, the moment has become a
testament to her craftsmanship

The mineral glands are welling

Gravity's gray ooze changes my shape and numbness is born from
her frictionless expanse

The swelling cavity adjusts my limbs to corporeal non-existence

Moistening flesh crawls with salt glaze

I have become a c**k, a life-sized fleshy fruit stretching with new skin

Sputtering for breath

The last bits of placenta are hacked free
from my convulsing stomach

Hold me mommy!...
Joel Holder

Prisoners Of Private Wars

1 The white light behind my eyes

    burns into shades of autumn then Hell
    as I am told my place

2 Run along my children

    Don't crouch by the door to listen
    cold clap of palm to cheek
    Know that you did not cause tomorrow's headache and
    you are safe

3 It's rigid past my lips

    not the velvet touch
    but an incessant push
    Try to gasp, to breathe
    grip in my hair keeps me steady
    I think in rhythm to make pass
    "I am forced to receive
    but it is you who
    takes, takes, takes"
Joanne Sobieck-Lingg

Standing Naked In The Evening Rain

How I hate - am jealous of - that rain,
her Lover in a way I cannot be!

Sheathing her in sensuous, warm embrace;
her face, her eyes, her mouth, so gently kissed;
those jet-black tresses pregnant from its touch.

Gliding down her shoulders, arms and hands,
to briefly brush her slender fingertips,
then fall in frothy sheets along her back,
across and down her curving derriere.

Cascading over and between her breasts,
drops hanging fast upon each nipple's tip,
as being quite reluctant to depart;
then, down her hips and belly, to converge
in rivulets - on Eros' Temple site.

Continuing its flow along her thighs,
it follows curve of calf, and ankle's turn;
kissing them (its final act of love),
it comes to rest beneath her feet and toes.
Silently it pools around her form,
its Evening Journey delicately done.
Robert B. Godwin

Eventide

The sun descends into the sea, the moon the merest sliver
The ocean waves caress the sand and smooth the slightest wrinkle
She gazes out into the dusk, the breezes make her shiver
Her eyes relive a memory that makes them glow and twinkle:

    A night like this, not long ago, she learned about her passion
    Her lover and herself alone, inflamed with all desire
    Her luscious, golden honey skin aglow in likely fashion
    As water and horizon were with sunset's crimson fire

    All overcome with ardor's heat, her lips and hands confessing
    Her every lust, most sensual, and most erotic feeling
    As she lay naked in his arms, aroused by his caressing,
    All inhibition flowed away; excitement left her reeling

    She raised herself and straddled him and amorously mounted;
    Upon her gentle, willing steed she was an eager rider
    Her climax came repeatedly, too many to be counted
    She shared the heights of ecstasy that he had found inside her.

Enchanted by the waves again — their quiet ceaseless rushing
An echo of the endless sighs remembrance brought upon her -

Her lovely face and body bask in warm, nostalgic blushing
Reliving with her man tonight the memory they honor.
Robert Volk

Cocaine Blues

I trade my cocaine thighs
For your cocaine eyes.
You give me your death wish
For my death touch.
I mingle my snowy dreams
Into your snowy life.
You take ecstasy from my body,
Repay me with ecstasy from a spoon.
I blow you for the blow in me.
You bring me snowflakes
To transform my tears.
You bring me snowflakes
To pay for my time.
Terry Azamber

Oh Child

    oh child with eyes of blue and skin and snow
you ride your three wheeled vehicle and stop at my feet as i walk down
  the street you look up with your eyes into mine and as they meet
    from such angelic lips you spit the word n****r

n egro meaning dark flesh of evil
i ignit cause you are mommy said so and so it goes goes like
  the blink of an eye
gg geeee you black not cream like i
e is for the evil you breed black abyss of consciousness
r rough, rough hair rough features rough are the words you speak
why so rough? why so black? why mommy? The n****r is scaring me.

Why Child.
Oh Child
the air you breathe is so heavy it's thick
like mud the race racism you breathe. Why mommy you
teach your child hate not love and such power in such youth
  innocence.
so powerful the depth of those eyes
eyes of blue and skin of white white white.
Stacey Robinson

Untitled

Within these walls I sit there's an emptiness
There's a deviant mind giving in to their tests
Feelings build up with all the lies
Demons attracted like sh** to flies
In the darkest hole I sink beneath this feel
I fake this smile but the loneliness is real
In the everlasting black a soul is torn
In the darkest hole a killer is born
In the shade of night I stalk beneath the fear
The terror builds when I am near
Where there's a morbid thought there's a sickening will
A beautiful hate a compulsion to kill
I've suffered enough now it's your turn
You've kept me down now your world will burn

Talbert Cypress

Nature's Wonders

Nature is beautiful
flowers, trees, and animals are all part of nature.
Forests, gems, gold and silver are nature's finest.
The rain falls then, the rainbow shines
Mother Nature sings a song as the wind goes by.
The sun, the moon, and the stars are nature's wonders.
We wonder about nature,
but think nature wonders about us.

April Hiler

Lovestruck

'Tis nothing short of sheer pleasure
to rest mine eyes upon thy beauty:
to hold thy supple body nigh to mine own
makes me perceive there is no evil
can draw me within reach.

To gaze into thine eyes repeals all principle;
my thoughts become still,
as a ship anchored within a serene harbor,
having no particular destination....

Scott A. Mordja

Diode

Running toward oceans and running from tides,
faster than a wave of translucent spiders
galloping, like wild horses, into the sun.

Limbs splayed across contentment like
the rainbow on a bubble,
being the bubble;
I am the bubble
and the rainbow is my unborn lover,
trapped in embryonic innocence.

Mirrored by anticipation,
forgotten by a fate with no obligatory favors,
skipped and plunked into an abyss of yielding pain,
plopping softly like cat's-eye marbles would.

I am only one, yet all and none,
imprisoned in my hollowed nautilus-world,
climbing, climbing, dizzily up an endless, stepless staircase
and ignored by my false profundity.

And as my surface expands,
I must implode.

Karen DiBenedetto

For Lisa - My Unplanned Child

You came into my arms differently than the others.
It was a forced entry upon us both.

Never did I feel you kick from within; like I did with your sisters
   and brother.
Nor did I watch you take your first step or braid your hair.

You came into my arms differently than the others.
You were forced into my door and my heart.

Soon I found out I really cared.
Yet both of us were scared.

You came into my heart differently than the others.
Now you are my child that I cry and pray for.
One that I miss when you're gone for just a moment.
One who comes to me to wipe away your tears and your fears.

You make me smile and laugh;
Your long hair and sparkling eyes.
Your valiant spirit for the right.

You came into my soul differently than the others.
Through times of talks and hugs.

Now you comfort me and I you.
For now - I am your mother.

Katharine Woolley

Josh

When I think about the way it was,
The fights, the pain, the hurtful things,
I wonder why I stayed?
I had long ago, stopped loving you,
I believe I never did,
The memories, the pain you caused,
Still linger in my mind,
People wonder why,
I let you hit me,
Throw things at me,
Walk all over me,
No one understands my reason, no one except me,
Someday I'll forgive you, someday I'll let it all go,
But when people ask me, why I stayed,
I look at them, and I say,
My son is why,
I endured so much hell, so much pain,
If it weren't for that little man,
It would have been easy,
To just walk away, a long time ago.

Micke Wolf

Just Thinking

   As I walk down the street on a cloudy moonlit night,
I think about you, and dream about you, and holding you so tight.
   I'm waiting for the day, when all my dreams come true,
I'm waiting for the day to get oh so close to you.
   We've been together once or twice,
It's been heaven you might say, but each and
every time you've almost swept my heart away.
   It's hard to express my feelings, sometimes I act pretty shy,
but it's just because I like you and it's hard to tell you why.
   But deep inside my heart my feelings have yet to grow,
and there are still things about you, that I still need to know.
   Maybe one day we'll be as close as to saying I love you,
but baby just to let you know, I've been thinking about you.

Perry James Wilson

Untitled

You're in your twenties, I'm close to fifty
You tell me to leave him to get a divorce
You ask me, "How can you love him?"
I tell you, "You don't know what love is."
We've shared every emotion known to man
We've laughed together, we've cried
We've cursed each other and then...
When anger subsided, we held each other close
Wondering how we allowed ourselves to be swept away
Away by feelings that rip one's soul apart
Twenty some odd years from today
When you have shared your inner self
When you have given and taken
When you have stood by one man's side
Through every peril in life
Then I shall ask you, "What is Love?"
Perhaps then, you can tell me why I've stayed.

May Louise Shenod

The Familiar Friend

It's worn fabric was a map of the past;
It's essence unmistakable;
The ambiance ever-present.
It evoked a thousand instant memories;

Memories inseparably
Woven into the very soul of the fabric.
The creaks and squeaks were
Old acquaintances making pleasant conversation.

The touch and feel were the warm embrace
Of an intimate friend: Informal, yet all familiar;
Familiar enough to provide support and respite;
Informal enough to instantly put one at ease.

Stress seemed to melt away with the vanishing
Distant thoughts of the day gone by...
As I drifted away... in the perfect security of my
Old familiar friend: My favorite...comfortable chair.

Thomas J. Mason

Your Love

Your love feels like a gift from heaven.
God smiled on me when I met you.
I hope this gift will last forever,
Because this love feels so true.

You came to me in a time of pain,
You came to me when I was lost.
You smiled at me and every hurt was gone.
To keep your love, I'd pay any cost.

Please tell me all your secrets,
I'll tell you all of mine.
Please tell me all your dreams,
Like sleeping under the pines.

Your love feels like a gift from heaven.
God smiled on me when I met you.
I hope this love will last forever,
Because this love feels so true.

Leslie Bennett

Dreams

   The way to real growth
is not to become more powerful
or most famous, but to become tolerant.
With the faith of those who know
you and love you, with faith in yourself
to carry through, God will help you
climb till your dreams come true!

Sarah Coss

The Dream

As I drift slowly away
The long arms of the trees start to sway
Slowly and cautiously
I begin to dream
If I was a bird
Or maybe a stream
As free as the wind
As light as a feather
Flying through the sunny weather
So free and light
Even at night
Looking down far below
Coming back very slow
As the birds go weightlessly by
I wish that I was born to fly.

Lauren De Young

Untitled

Never did I choose a road
Instead - I chose a stream
Slowly traveling, seeing it all
In search of my life's dreams.

Lost - I got - but to be found
For just around the bend
A light shone through and carried me home
When I reached the inlet's end.

Tracy Lyn Howison

Love

Soft as silk in the warm summer sun,
with sparkling dew drops as the day's begun.
They gently sway along with the breeze,
One strong sniff and a sweet little sneeze.
One special bloom was taken from place,
and raised up to mach and equally pink face.
The breeze blew glittering strands of blond,
As two circles of sky looked so fond.
Pudgy and sweet,
She stretched toward her feet,
Lace bent over,
and found a four-leaf-clover.
With luck in the left and beauty in the right,
She giggled at the sunlight.
With two cheeks of rose framing a crescent moon of pearls,
Her face was embraced by hundreds of curls.
Rolling over the putting one end in the air,
She soon was standing quite well aware.
The warm summer sun soon began to slide,
and Love brought luck and beauty inside.

Teresa Anne Bailey

Course

There is an old river, back at home.
Winding its way to the sea.
I remember the sound of water on rocks
And the wind in the boughs of the trees.
To sit in cool shade by gentle pools
Or ride its raging torrent
To leap from a cliff and plunge to its depths
I was completely content
Laughing with friends, or sitting alone,
Strolling with that one so dear
My heart never is touched ever so much
Than when to that river I'm near
For in full truth in could be said
That there my mem'ries begin
My family, my friends, my life, my home
And I long for my river again.

Jerome Lucas Boettner

"The Night The Stars Cried"

As rays burst through
The cloud-filled skies,
I'm overwhelmed with gratitude
For God's blessings in my life —
A loving husband, friends who care,
A rewarding career.
I sense God's presence
As I feel the warmth of the sun —
And I am at peace.

But there are times when darkness comes
And painful memories surface —
A miscarriage, a wayward son,
The death of a beloved grandmother.
It is at night when I behold
The star-studded sky,
And watch the shimmering tears
Falling to earth.
It is then I also sense God's presence
And know he understands —
And I am at peace.

Dianne Bradfield

A Mother's Touch

Her warm embrace, her smiling face
the memories never left me.
The way she looked, the trips we took
the memories never left me.
How she talked, the way she walked
the memories never left me.
Her caring thoughts, the times we fought
the memories never left me.
Her long brown hair, the times we shared
the memories never left me.

And after she had passed away,
a long gray life was left to stay.
As I quietly sit down to cry
tears slowly trickle from my eye.
I lay back and wonder how
she had to die at least not now.
I say a prayer for her everyday
and slowly the pain drifts away.
But my memories of her stay in my heart
and truly we'll never be apart.

Ashley Wethey

Untitled

I watch as others pass me by
With straight bodies and limber legs
How I too was once so lucky.
But then I see others with
Canes and some with seeing eye dogs
And then I feel ashamed.
How lucky that I can walk -
Maybe not so steady, but can
Get from place to place - it just
Takes a little longer!
Please God make me feel for others
And offer to help in whatever way I can.
Even if it is just a smile or a
Few kind words that might make
One not so lucky, as me, smile back.
Life is a journey - long and hard
For some - but should not be
Accepted with long of face
But with courage and love for others.

Helen Morrison

Simple Rose

Simple roses at its corner
the house had stood for years.
Alone and empty, except for nature,
its owner shed their tears
one moonlit night the sky was brighter
and nature gone forever.
The only sight the following morn,
was a black and burnt out dorm.
The sparrow sought their treasured young,
the bees their faithful beam,
The juxtaposition of their home
was left them in a dream.
The owner, truly, sought the cause,
but mystery loves her game,
Move on my sparrows, move on my bees,
The gentle roses at the corner,
simply stayed the same.

Kim Gazzillo

Untitled

Shine your brightest smile upon my face.
May the whiteness of your teeth blind my eyes,
and the warmth of your happiness scorch my skin,
for that shall be the sweetest pain.

Fix your longest gaze into my mind.
May the blackness of your pupils pull apart the mazes of my thoughts,
and your soft blue iris open the confusing wad of grayness,
for that will be the most pleasing mutilation.

Smother me with your deepest love.
May this complicated emotion cut off my breath,
and each wave of care smash my lungs,
for that shall be the proudest death.

But if all these things are dreams and all we seem merely a fantasy,
each smile will create the most bitter pain,
each gaze unpleasant mutilation,
and each drop of love the most undignified death one could experience.

Crystal Thacker

My Life Is....

Life's running away from me and
all I can do is stare.
My life is my own personal hell, I
know this is not fair.
Get me out of this burning fire.
For my life has no needed desire.
My life is like a long, dark, dead end road.
Get the flames off my back, get me out of
this hell hole.
The life I once loved turned right around,
Went in the wrong direction and went
straight underground.
My life is like the deep, dark ocean,
Never in one straight piece, always in
a peculiar motion.
Get the burning off my face, lead me to the
soft, gentle light.
Get me out of this fire, get me out of here tonight.

Jen Whitehouse

Untitled

Take an example of Education.
As much as you give, it would never lessen.
Likewise the wealth, given to you by your Lord.
Bestow on me, it would never fall short.

E. Hyder

Night

Of course you have a family, those cold winter
nights. Hot cocoa and patchwork blankets
in a nest on the floor, yellow light flooding
out the window. Fields, fields long and flat
bedded in the moon light. Children look up
at the stars, clear and magical
in the sky. They rest their heads on their mother's
when they cough. How their dreams
float, ascending, ascending, swirling
and winding like steam pierced by beautiful
song, and finally disappearing pulled
home by the moonlight like a magnet,
slowly. When the wind flattens
the grass, and the crickets are silent, a tear
slips down her face as smoothly
as an orange sunset on the sea. The stars
are so bright that when the clouds
block their rays, the light dances
like rain in the sun
on the shingles of that cottage.

Ben Keating

True Love Awaits Thee

Don't be like me sweet thee.
Don't bury yourself in misery.
Don't look down, look up!
Pain, sorrow and despair is beneath thee.
Love, joy and happiness is thy key.

Open the door!
Open your eyes!
Open your heart!
Make a triumph stand.
The key to happiness is in your hand.

Passionate love is great to have if only you dare!
Sometimes the mates we choose aren't true.
Don't let feelings of love drift away like the dew.
Because true devotion it within you.

Take that key.
Open that door to happiness and devotion

Sigh no more.
Cry no more.
True love awaits thee!
Don't be afraid of that mystery!

Larry Canady

The Fifth of July

The fifth of July just another day
At least I used to think of it that way.
But since last year, it means so much more
That's when God opened a very special door.
I found out I had a brother, nephews and nieces
We've all been working together to fit all the pieces.
Could I really accept all this - I just didn't know
How should I proceed? Go fast? Go slow?
He looks so much like our father it almost gets eerie
Feelings of hurt and betrayal started getting rather weary.
I loved both he and his wife almost from the start
But their children and grandchildren really stole my heart.
What could've been - what should've been still cause me pain
All our lives have changed so much now nothing is the same.
Although we are separated by hundreds of miles
Long distance telephone calls always bring lots of smiles.
What the future holds in store none of us can guess
We'll just be family and love each other and not accept less.
May we be blessed with many years to love each other
It's really very special to finally have a big brother.

Marilyn J. Truppo

Untitled

On Valentines Day electricians expect kisses and hugs,
For who is more qualified to wire your lights and plugs.
But said California's Guv Pete Wilson,
Inventor of the counterclockwise Stillson,
Organized thugs, you're just loud "organized thugs".

On Valentines Day 1996, 15000 organized labor members,
friends, and families, marched to the California State
Capitol to voice their displeasure for the Governor's attack
against prevailing wage rates. During the subsequent rally
at the Capitol steps, Governor Pete Wilson spat the epithet:
"You're not organized labor, but organized thugs".

A. Neville Williams

Untitled

What is love at first sight?
I think of us and our unique beginning.
I remember the beautiful sunset, the walks along the beach,
The laughs, the jokes, the lengthy talks.

The time flies by when you're by my side.
I think not of work, nor that of play.
I think of you, your life, your happiness,
your love for me.

Be with me until I die.
We'll spend our lives together,
as husband and wife. With our house,
our children, our dogs, our debt.

Our path is one, please stay with me.
I'll not be your shadow, nor will I walk ahead.
I will stand by your side,
As your lover, your wife, your hopes, your dreams.

Look at the stars in the heavens above.
I see love on the horizon
As our two souls come together as one.
With our hopes, our dreams, our lives.

Cheryl A. Uyematsu

The Oak Tree

It rained last night and soaked the earth
My mind and all my wishes for you...
I thought something must be new
I came out of my house and looked at my yard
A little, tiny oak seed has come out
Of the wet and amused soil
With a pair of tired and curious leaves
I stopped and started
Watching the little tree to grow
Farther beyond my imagination

Alas! She was so shy,
She started watching me in her innocent eyes
Just a drop of water on those
Tiny leaves were her eyes
So clear, I could see through her
Bemused heart, waiting to grow
With such ecstatic desire
And I thought I should go
And let her grow...

Bhabani S. Das

Man To Remember

One who stands tall in his belief in justice
and fairness for all. For the principles of
a Nation which represent all Military men
and women. Gave of himself to protect this
Honor for all to follow, God Bless a man this
former Marine will miss! Rest in Peace you
have the respect of all! Sir.

Clara Gange

The Turning Point

Why do you stand so near when I push you far away?
Why do you take my hand when I run astray?
Why do you shield me from the wickedness I bring upon myself?
Why do you lift me up to hide me in your cleft?
Why do you bless me even though I do so wrong?
Why do you send me comfort for the days that seem so long?
Before I could not understand the precious things you do for me,
Until the weight became too heavy and I fell on bended knee.
That night I felt your presence, you kept me safe from harm.
I took that leap of faith and landed in your arms.
I have found the friend I lost, and Jesus is your name,
With you always by my side I will never hang my head in shame.
For now you hold me up to soar on the mighty wings of life,
Your arms descend from heaven, you hold me from the sky!

Crystal Christian

The Shadow Of My Mind

Somehow I always thought you would be there
All I would have to do is call you
And you would come to me
At my time
When I was ready
I left you to pursue my life
To follow it where it took me
But it took me away from you
Yet you were always there
In the shadow of my mind
Waiting for me to call you
Waiting for me to grow up
I called you yesterday
Your wife answered the phone
I could hear your daughter playing in the background
She sounds nice, your wife
I'll miss you
The warmness of your caring
I'll look for you
In the shadow of my mind

Nancy Luz

Freedom

Her ears and heart heard the last whistle blow
Loud scraping of metal against metal made her wince
Thud, thud, she heard the footsteps pounding
Echoing off the cold cement floor of the cave-like hallway
Her heart beat in unison with the footsteps
She inhaled the musty, uncirculated air
Footsteps echoed closer, more metal scraping against metal
Nervously, she stood on shaking jelly-like legs
Leaned against her cane for balance
Smoothed out invisible wrinkles in her skirt with a shaky hand
Unfamiliar voices spoke around her
She heard clicks and a chain rattling
Arms came around her in an embrace
Gleeful whispers in her ear of freedom
She smiled and breathed a sigh of relief
Everything was alright
Her prayers had been answered
Her boy was coming home

Inga Halvorson

The Death Of The Trees

On a soft, grassy meadow, she lay her head down
Bitter sweet memories in her mind wandered round.
She remembered the plants, and the forest, and trees
Of such spectacular beauty she'd fall to her knees.

But, those days where fair, when the people did care
About the life of the forest and all it could share.
Now in her heart there's no song. She knew the people were wrong.
For when they killed all of these. We all died with the trees.

Robert J. Mortenson

Time Travel

Adrift, in the sea of somber dreams
My voyage appears endless
Today, yesterday, tomorrow
as I search for the slightest prayer
To find my true ancestry

On course, I'm bound for some beginning
While lost moments, present and anew
Quickly rushes by
Spinning my wildest thoughts
Revealing captured glimpses of ancient worlds

Exposing man's worst nature and finest essence
From mind gripping accounts of strengths and weakness
In struggles of life and death
Since the first atom blew
And Adam sang

Witnessing one defeat after another
Until a finale of success appeared to flourish
like calm waters after a tropical storm
Centuries pass before my eyes until
I reached my destiny, mankind's first day of infancy.

Baffahagh Daamon

I Love You

As I sit here I think of you
The touch of your hand holding mine,
Tells me you'll be with me all the time.
Your gentle kiss touching my lips,
And your hands moving up and down my hips
The whisper of your voice in my ear,
I love you! Is what I hear.
The look of your eyes
Is just like the beauty of the skies.
Your smile warms my heart
And then it feels sad when we're apart.
The thought of your arms around me tight,
Makes me think that we will never fight.
I know the love we have is real,
Because it's you I always feel.
So please love me forever,
And that way, I know we will always be together.

Beth Ann Mitchell

My Friend

I once had a friend
I thought she'd be with me till the end
Then one day I got a call
It said "Hurry up and come to the mall
There's been an accident
The car's got a huge dent".

When I got there
She looks up at me and said
"I can't feel below my head
Please, won't you help me".

I leaned over and said "Trust in the Lord
He may not save your 'Honda Accord'
but He will protect His children
All you have to do is believe in Him".

That day she asked Him in
And I'm happy to say she walked again
She's alive still today
And she will probably always say
"Thank you for leading me down the right path
To my spiritual bath".

Michele Grubbs

Cross Trees

For a thousand miles you comforted, and then a thousand more.
You've seen the gentle creeks and bays, you heard the ocean roar.

You shaded burning comets, accentuated stars.
Adorned by baggywrinkle and silver shining spars.

For a thousand miles you comforted and then a half a score.
You've seen the dolphins whales and rays, you saw the shuttle soar.

You've stood beyond endurance, while sailing in the stream.
You stalled a bond ill fated, you've seen me live my dream.

For a thousand miles you comforted, and watched the sea folklore,
Experiencing Saint Elmo's Fire and barely missing war.

And then there came a stranger, with want to tear apart.
'Twas there my marriage ended and for you another start.

For a thousand hours you comforted, as we went from bay to bay.
Will we ever feel that ocean swell, as we live from day to day.

For a thousand hours you comforted, as we went from bay to shore.
Will we ever feel that ocean swell, will we ever live once more.

Deirdre T. Nye

"The Laughter"

What is laughter?
A brief expression of happiness.
Happiness short lived that is.
Can laughter be of fear, hate or confusion.
Is laughter a shield used by a child?
To hide pain and anguish chosen not to be revealed.
Is laughter the evil force behind satan's deed?
A toxin used to anesthetize a persons wants of vengeance and greed.
What happened to laughter being of love and need?
Can you hear the laughter as the evil hunts and feeds?

Terea Nanos

Screams Of Silence

I was stripped of every last ounce of innocence
For countless years I've bowed my head to shame

Violated by your sick, distasteful ideas of fun
I was toyed with nightly
for the payroll kept in the cookie jar
And then deceived by your tricks of evil
to believe that it was I who was the culprit of crime

Banished and suppressed into a world of silence
I was muted by your mastered manipulation

Now terminated from our place of life
your presence isn't much missed
And I can't help but wonder
Is this true justification from my Lord?

Had I only been the child of confidence you knew I wasn't
I would have screamed my silence to any who'd listen
But to my great misfortune,
I was only a naive, impressionable Baby
A baby left in your hands to be taken cared of
......Not to be Taken!

Yolanda Marie Perez

With Every Breath

In the wind
we all can see, what it is like to be free.
Free in heart and in soul, but in life we must pay the toll.
The toll of life which we call Death, grows a bit nearer
with every breath. The reason of life nobody knows,
yet it can be felt in the hearts of those,
who show respect to our mysterious creator,
whom we all shall meet
in the later.

Daniel I. Gordon

American Hopeful

oh say can you see by the dawn's early light
   i've come so far, always fighting the good fight
what so proudly we hailed at the twilight's last gleaming
   what if i'm a waste, no good, just another kid's naive scheming
whose broad stripes and bright stars, through the perilous fight
   i can't think like that, i'm a champion, i gotta keep going it's
my God given right
over the ramparts we watched were so gallantly streaming
   here i go, no turning back, everyone is watching;
everyone is screaming
and the rockets red glare
   I can feel my dad's stare
the bombs bursting in air
   and the jump-no fear
gave proof through the night that our flag was still there
   where did everyone go, it's only me I hear
oh say does that star-spangled banner yet wave
   I did it, it's done, I won, I didn't cave
for the land of the free, and the home of the brave

Chris Kurpiewski

My New World

The place I am you've been to, although you won't admit.
You visited so long ago, you can't recall a bit.

This country is a galaxy, a world all its own,
but someday soon I'll leave it, and you'll wish I hadn't grown.

As for now I'm there, in that mystery of a place,
and as for now it seems sometimes, things hit you in the face.

But that's the way it goes right now, while I'm in my new world,
but soon I'll find the answers, and my life will be unfurled.

I'm learning and I'm risking, experiencing and enjoying.
But sometimes I am edgy, and sometimes quite annoying.

My standards have been raised, and my guidelines have been thinning,
My journey isn't over, though, in fact, it's just beginning.

Ahead of me is wonder, behind me is the past.
Both of which will play a part, and harmonize at last.

But as for now I'm living in my galaxy of dreams,
the place I am you've been to, as crazy as it seems.

The world I'm in is old, yet new in many ways,
the place I am you've been to, it's your Adolescent Days.

Amy McFadden

Say Goodbye!

I see the black, I see it all,
The sky is starting to fall.

God, does that mean it's my turn to go?
Why must it happen so slow?

My body, it doesn't hurt,
Do you think I'll be buried in dirt?

Please don't leave me,
I can't believe so many people are here to see me.

My body, it feels so cold,
I wonder if heaven is made of gold.

I feel my soul drifting away,
I wish I could be alive just one more day.

Please don't cry,
Just think about me, love me, and
Say good-bye.

Amanda Marie De Soto

Spirit In The Wind

A soothingly divine spirit fell upon her knees
And looked into the wind and whispered with the breeze
Her golden hair flowing in the wind
Spoke of an angel who had fallen to sin
She wore the lace of a solemn whiteness
Which told of danger, devastating brightness
The body of the woman exposed itself to the sun
Which sparkled of the innocence which quickly had become
The words are expressed imposed not a sound
While beneath her the grass floundered to the ground
The wind swirled wildly turning the land
Asking everyone to listen to her demand
For the valley of which she had a rose
Sought unto her beautiful prose
To call the friends and animals unborne
That the sharpness of an expression burns like a thorn
Upon the majestic shores in the mist
It is here that this angel really exists
Next time you whisper with the breeze
Speak with a feeling and they will believe.

Stephanie Hiteshew

Grandmother You're So Special

Years ago God called you home,
To ease your pain and no more woe.
My heart aches for you even today,
For I miss and love you more each day.

Grandmother, thank you for all your care,
Sometimes the thoughts are more than I can bear.
Thank you for your love so pure,
You've given me the strength to endure.

You're still with me in the things I do,
I couldn't go on unless I was still with you.
You taught me valuable things in life,
You were a great mother, grandmother and wife.

You're missed more and more as the days go by,
But I feel your presence above me in the sky.
Yearning for your arms around me just one more time,
What a comfort, what a joy, you're still mine.

Someday I pray we'll meet in the sky,
You've gone through troubles and so have I.
Trusting in God's promises, I will abide,
Someday soon I'll be by your side.

Ann Simmons

The Beggar

With eyes of a sinner, the hands of a priest,
spread forth over the flock.
Grizzled white hair, leather face, quivering body,
transgressors home does he plead.
"Amazing Grace How Sweet the Sound",
overcomes the pastor's mournful wail.
Tears leak upon each person's face,
as the music fades away.

No false prophet under a shabby torn tent,
clearly a true son of God.
Only a harvester, a reaper of souls,
mining minerals more precious than gold.
Burden of eternity placed upon his heart,
Through laughs of scorn and hate,
he implores, trying to make us see.
Serving God as best he humanly can,
the life he leads wearing him thin.
All that are lost take away part of him,
leaving only a brittle man,
With the eyes of a sinner and the hands of a priest.

Mark C. Huffstetler

Glory Forever

A light beckons him at the end of time
   As it will for all of us

Moving slowly and silently
   It draws him closer to heaven

With each new step
   Yet another child will be born

He does not think about the pain and sorrow
   Or who he is leaving behind

It all does not play a part anymore
   No more a role in his dying life

Many things will become of him
   And of his findings, discoveries

The light shines brighter now
   For he is almost there

Many things are left undone
   For someone else to finish

The light is blinding now
   As he steps into the unknown

This is his moment of glory
   From now until forever...

Heather Fritzinger

"Oh Child Of Mine"

How can I help you, "Oh child of mine?"
How can I tell you that everything will be fine?

The children of today are mean and unkind;
Life is not easy for you and a friend is hard to find.
Continue with your life my child, be strong my little man,
Show then you are strong little man, I know that you can.
For on this hateful road on earth, our God has a plan,
Sorrow and grief makes it so hard to understand.

How can I help you, "Oh child of mine?"

This child they make fun of; he has a heart of gold,
And what lies within him, they will never know.
These children of today are heartless, still your story goes untold.
What have their parents taught them what have they done?
The way their children treat others, they would not wish
on their own son.

This pain and sorrow, I can not bare to see you go through,
For I am your mother with hopes and dreams for you.
Always remember to keep your heart strong,
For I will always love you all your life long.

How can I help you, "oh child of mine?"

Janet Robertson

Evening Walk

The winter sun has set some time ago
And from the cliff-top I can see below
The gentle waves glide softly 'cross the sand—
This peaceful marriage of the sea and land.

Where warmer water meets the colder air
The mists obscure the rocks protruding there.
And somewhere out among the fog and rock
A lonely boat calls, searching for the dock.

The North wind blew the winter storms away
But with them went the warmth we had today.
The stars shine with a chill and frosty light
As last of day turns into first of night.

Now all is cold and dark and getting late—
I turn toward home where warmth and laughter wait.

Richard L. Ott

A Day At The Office

Fossils of coffee cup rings embedded
in wood grain
paper clips entangle with elderly staples amidst
an eerie, grey jungle.
The sound of woodpeckers harmonically peck a tune
as paper lint clings to garments adorned.

It is time
bags crumple open while pop tops open in unison
chairs significantly scuffing the pale white tile.

Unfinished tasks are calling,
demanding attention promptly.
The black bean aroma is enveloping the air
calling to embrace with its warmth and sudden energetic power.

The number five becomes a sorcerer
turning calmness into chaos
toward the metal box

Sanity begins.

Michelle M. Cosmato

Happy Dreams

Dream a dream of kittens; dream of bunnies in their nests.
Dream a dream of robins with soft and smooth red breasts.
Dream a dream of turtles with funny little claws;
And dream a dream of squirrels with peanuts in their paws.

Dream a dream of puppies; dream of ponies you can ride.
Dream a dream of smooth white eggs with fuzzy chicks inside
Dream a dream of little elves, only one inch high;
And dream a dream of fluffy clouds way up in the sky.

Dream a dream of daisies with blossoms everywhere.
Dream a dream of lilacs making perfume in the air.
Dream a dream of little lambs, soft and furry white;
And dream a dream of Jesus who keeps us safe at night.

Peggy Hamm

Yesterday

I came back to see, if I could find something I lost a long time ago.
It all looked different, somehow strange, but yet some place I know.
I slipped back into yesterday, as a tear rolled down my face.
The memories that haunt a soul, from a different time and place.
In a field of seclusion, yet open for the world to see,
Stood the feelings, the woods, the old house and me.
Daring to remember, what long ago, should have been forgot.
Thinking back to the days before, lost in time and thought.
Now it's time to move on, and go straight ahead,
Making new memories, happy ones instead.

Dixie Darnell

Sea Breeze

My hopes, my dreams, my memories,
All gone by one quick breeze...
Sails from passing boats catch theses hopes and dreams...
But... they leave the memories behind...
My hopes and dreams sail around the world on a breeze...
Hoping this gives them time to grow...
But when the sails return with the last gust of wind
the hopes and dreams have died...
But you shouldn't feel so sad...
Because tomorrow is another day
And the memories were left behind
Besides I'll be more careful of where I place my hopes and dreams
So that they don't go drifting away.

Cynthia Swenson

Creatures

Are there creatures out in space?
What do they like? Do they have a "normal" face?
Have they acquired two eyes with eyelids so they can blink?
Do they have a complex education teaching them to think?
Have they knowledge of travel? Can they communicate with us?
Is their world all hustle and bustle and as much of a fuss?
What's their lifestyle? Where is their home base?
Will our civilizations ever meet? Can we hurdle the mysterious,
    forbidding space?
How advanced a civilization does this universe hold?
Will our society ever reach a peaceful time? Do our planets come from
the same mold? Do they possess wondrous ideas for others to learn?
Has their environment reached an ultimate, livable world? If so,
when is it Earth's turn?
Can there really be another creature writing the same thing as I?
Wondering these intriguing, endless questions as time flies by.
So many answers we do not yet know.
If we want to find out - then let's get up and go!!

Joshua I. Faden

I Have Come To The Conclusion (The Heart Of A Child)

I have come to the conclusion
You're not my father anymore.
I wish that you could love me
The way you did before.
Now mommy found a new love,
He takes good care of me.
He even took me to the doctor
When I fell and cut my knee.
You never were around for this,
You always were away.
You never even cared for me,
You'd never want to play.
But I have gotten over it,
And as the saying goes,
(I think that you should know it)
You reap just what you sow.
Now you've lost your daughter, and now my heart is torn.
But you'll always be in my blood, and I will be in yours.
And even though it's painful, even though it's sore,
I have come to the conclusion, you're not my father anymore.

Ronda Jefferson

Somewhere Between Day And New

As I was flipping through the channels one day
I stopped at Mr. Rogers Neighborhood.
I love Mr. Rogers.

His sneakers, the trolley, the way he feeds the fish.
It was the end of the show and he was taking off his sneakers
and putting on his shoes, singing his "I'll be back" song,
and somewhere between "day" and "new" he tossed his sneaker.

Now, it was classic Mr. Rogers sneaker tossing,
he was singing and smiling all the while, looking at the camera
tossing his sneaker, never looking at it, never watching it,
confident that it would reach the other hand,
but this time it didn't.

It sailed past his hand and bounced, twice, on the floor,
embarrassed, he grabbed for the sneaker and tossed it again.

This time he caught it,

And as he walked to his closet,
where he hangs his coats and sweaters,
I flicked the channel but a picture in my mind wouldn't leave
as I saw him toss the sneaker for the second time
and the memory of his eyes, as this time they never left it.

Jennifer Stipes

Breath Of Flame

She calls to me with a mouth of flame,
She wants me to embrace her,
I hold her close, I am too weak to resist
And I feel her power.
The temptation too much.
I embrace her, she is strong and controls me
My lips touch her.
The ecstasy, the state of bliss.
She holds me with a tight grip,
I hate myself for giving in,
Yet I squeeze her lovingly,
I want her, only her, no substitutes,
Only the breath of flame.
She fills my lungs, my soul.
But, she murders me slowly,
Quietly she kills me,
And I hold her, love her, want her.
I die for her.
But I am not the only one, she owns many.
I hold her knowing this.
Steven Glenn Tyndall

Untitled

The haunting moon glow guides the ancient pathway
Silver stars hide behind the tormented clouds
Dawn peeks behind the dark, soon becoming the light of day
Tormented souls fly with clipped angel wings drawn down
Forgive not the willing to be set free hate, for not, foreseen
Breed the soon becoming to be
Cast away to the universe's mighty seam
Child's cry howls through the cold days
Foam from the engulfing sea spits mighty rays
Set apart the worlds shall they become
Hollowed drones to thee almighty one
Show me the way from this tearing world
Cast upon me the only one to order
Show me the flying ones who love only one
Take me to the upper where there's only one sun
Rivers so freely run with children along them
Cities so bright, never losing their gleam
Happiness for once I shall feel
Josh Carver

A Cornfield Revisited

It was an evening of beauty.
Darkness had settled over the cornfield,
A darkness holding hands with a luminous moon
To cast artful shadows over the field.
The sky, a celestial chandelier of stars,
Close enough to touch.
And the hush of this night broken only
By solo songs of the cricket,
The fervent fiddler.

Suddenly, the sound of sobbing.
There, in panic and fright, was a little mouse
Running in circles, beating and thrashing
His panting heart against the stately stalks
Of the field, and whimpering,
"I am lost, I am lost".

No, little mouse, not lost,
Only needing to grow. I know,
For I have been in that cornfield.
Pearl Stockbarger

Hidden Secrets

From the brooks to the dawn
Can you hear it, hear the baby yawn
For my children shall cry, lie, and die
Therefore the mother is so quiet, so shy.

So we wonder about shy people
The secrets they keep from us.
It's hard to get into their soul,
But it can be done
As if you're talking to someone's daughter, someone's son.

Everyone dies, but for a purpose
A purpose to set something free
Their soul, their life, their spirit.
Once you're set free, nothing can stop you
From feeling what you want to feel,
For seeing what you want to see,
loving what you want to love.
Shall you be pushed or shoved?
We shall never know, maybe loved!
Brandon Durousseau

My Love!

What has happened to my love?
People say he has risen to the skies above, but
I believe he has fallen deeper into my heart.
No matter where he is we'll never be apart!
Every night I lay beside myself in dreams.
I know from what I had, I have found what the words true love
  really mean.

Where has my love went to?
He may not be near, but he's not gone.
People say that he is dead and
to the earth refed, but,
I believe he has not returned to earth, but
to the place where our love was given
birth, in the deepest part of my heart.
What has happened to my love?
Mendy Portell

Only To Dream

When he was a boy
He dreamt of slaying dragons, being a superhero, flying in the sky.
When he became older
He had dreams of being a movie star, a professional ballplayer,
winning olympic gold.
When he became a man
He dreamt of becoming a lawyer, a doctor, owning a business.
Now he is old
His face shows regret
He only dreamed — never tried.
So none of his dreams came true.
But, his dreams are now memories.
And memories are meant to fade.
Charles Park Jr.

Hold On To The Wind

I had the wind in my arms
but it inhaled me like the sea.

I trapped the wind within my lungs,
but it knew I had to breathe.

Each time a breeze flew across my path I would
take a sip, from wind, to breeze, to air, to
life, to breath diving from my lips.

The trees were laughing at me again.
Because I kept trying, I keep trying, to hold on
to the wind.
Jeremiah Mickens

The Barn Man

There is a man by the name of Grenko.
He takes pictures wherever he does go.

He takes them and draws them with his ink and pen.
He passes them out to his fans and his friends.

He takes pictures of barns and old gas station pumps;
Old worn out rice gates and swamp cypress stumps.

He takes pictures of old tractors and sugar cane grinders;
He autographs some for seekers and finders.

He takes pictures of slave quarters and tobacco sheds;
He draws the tombstones of those that have long been dead.

He's a preserver of heritage and remnants of the past;
And though his subjects will decay, his art will last.
   Jerri L. Smoak

"A Special Lady"

There is a lady, who makes me very proud
She is extremely beautiful and really stands out in a crowd

She is very bright and has a humorous side
And everything she does, is with great pride

She always has a big smile
Wherever she goes and even a hearty laugh every once in a while

She is very pleasant to be around
And extremely easy to have a conversation with
Her energy just seems to abound
And the stories she tells are certainly no myth

Very friendly and very warm
But when angered, can be like a violent storm

She is very artistic, that's for sure
And for any problem, she has a quick cure

She can paint a flower that will attract a bee
And all the birds would flock to her painted tree
If possible to spend the rest of my life with her
What a pleasure it would be

A long stemmed rose, sent to her one day
The written message didn't have to say
She knew the meaning the rose was meant to convey
My love for her would never stray
   Dwight Stewart

Conversation With Absurdity

Four days ago, the old man said
a woman walked her man.
He was down on all fours, with a leash on his neck,
but he didn't give a damn.
Absurdity, I then replied and cast
a cynical glance.
The old man then reminded me
he wasn't wearing pants.
I said, that's true my naked friend
I should've remembered that,
and since we're talking observation
what's underneath your hat.
Funny you should ask me that,
for here as you can see.
Removing the hat from my head
you'll see my tiny pea.
A pea? I wondered for a bit,
what's it doing there?
And he said, sarcastically,
it's conditioning for my head.
   Sean Felix

What Will It Take?

What will it take for all of them to finally join hands?
What will it take for all of them to reclaim their precious land?
I look at those whose sweat and toil to maintain the USA,
And watch with fear and sadness as their freedoms slip away.
Yet, it's hard to feel compassion for many who are wronged.
They do nothing to stop the madness, and often go along
With the boss on the job who just won't stop
   until they're on their knees,
And with laws that kill their livelihoods and destroy their families.
They allow those they empowered to slowly chip away
At rights and privileges others fought for only yesterday.
I'm often angered when I hear their apathetic views,
And I wonder if they realize how much they stand to lose.
Are they really unaware of all that's happened in the past?
Don't they realize, not long ago, there was no middle class?
The clock is turning backward and they just turn their heads.
They could really make a difference, but they choose instead
To spend their time complaining, always blaming someone else.
They never stop to think - the answers lie within themselves.
They have a million reasons why they don't participate.
Just what will it take to wake them up, and will tomorrow be too late?
   Charles Bush

Solitary Confessions

Things are not always as they seem
I have found on my way
Love it seems to be a dream
The one that fades away
Children will always turn old
That is safe to say
Will you always be alone I'm alone here to stay

Dreamers must have a dream mine left yesterday
Will my pain always hurt
I think so, I'm afraid
Day will always turn to night
And light will fade
The earth will crumble to dust
And the dust is blown away

Like people at a grand ball I live a masquerade
Like the loved ones I have lost
My decisions have been made
I try not to live in the past
But on my shoulders it lies
I still hope that love can last but who am I to say
   Robert D. Weems

A Wish

A wish is hope in the form of a dream
  when in sleep it comes into view.
And dreams are the windows of the soul
  beholding your heart sees thru.

While wishes wait for their end to come
  with joy as the expected reward.
Realities winds blow and blow
  and cut just like a sword.

Now you are a wish, a secret hope
  your smile makes the day more grand.
The sun shines warm and the breeze is sweet
  Tis a dream to hold your hand.

So the dreamers sit and dream their dreams
  and life goes on its way
And all the dreamers can only hope
  is to have their wish someday.
   Walter Baker Jr.

Eternally

He looks into her eyes in search of an answer
only to uncover something immense
and beyond the gracefulness of a dancer
effortlessly soaring and never tense,
finding himself enraptured within her golden brown portals
he discovers the world in which only they exist
savoring their lives as if they were immortals
and he comes across a mirror he cannot resist.
He sees her peering into his eyes
in awe of what she has located
a soul so pure it takes the prize
a heart so filled with love it is intoxicated.
They see within each other why they must not love externally
for they are two meant to be, eternally.

Elizabeth Pineiro

Road Duty

My task to uphold the vehicle above me gives gratification
   to being part of the team — each having a similar duty
   in our own section of the foundation.

In varying seasons, my job differs depending on conditions
   of the road. Usually I protrude to and fro as I'm told
   without incident.

On occasion, I skid and slide in all directions concerned
   that no one is in control. Cowardly feelings fail to
   escape me as I look for comfort among my brothers.

As calm again falls among us, I suddenly feel the sensation
   of white rain. I forge on leading fellow teammates over
   the snowpacked highway until tranquility succumbs us once more.

My duties remain the same until my tread runs bare.

Julie Trudeau Jones

A Mother's Cry

   Have you ever seen a mother cry in her son's arms?

   Have you ever seen a mother collapse from feeling pain in her heart?

   Have you ever seen a mother lose part of her heart when
a loved one fades away into thin air?

   It's the hardest feeling to take when you're the son.

   Knowing that for so long your mother was a fortress of
solitude and one day, just like that, the walls crumble down into
the roaring ocean which is ready to sweep it all away.

   How can someone survive this?

   I don't even know if a mother can survive such
travesty. I guess only a mother could be able to sustain the
strength and hope to survive, but I don't know.

   The reason why I don't know is because what hurts the
most is when I see, what I see and feel what I feel it makes me
wonder how a mother can survive. And what I see and what I feel
is the saddest part of a son's life.

   How can I stop from crying when I see and feel a mother's cry?

Alfredo A. Tauriello

Love Will Strike

Love will strike,
And love strikes true,
But I will never be with you,
For Cupid's arrow runs straight through,
The center of my heart.
Now I will miss you all the more,
For now my love my heart is sore,
The heart that through the arrow tore,
The heart that loves no one no more.

Brie Smith

The Eternal Question

Why am I here?
To see the beauty of a rainbow
To hear the soft music of summer rain fall
To kiss a tiny babe's silken cheek
To smell the fragrance of the rose by the wall
That's why I'm here.

Why am I here?
To love my children and now their children
To find adventure in meeting our needs
To make a neighbor's way seem brighter
To feel wonderful joy from all our deeds
That's why I'm here.

Jennifer Glaser

Within Separation

Inner screams
caused outward cries
An overwhelming sense of loss
made for a weakened smile.
The crush of reality
made the moment unforgiving.
A scene of two holding a bond
strong and fierce
everlasting in memory only.
Wet faces and hoarse voices
pain and fear strung up together.
Hurt and love combined
in the ultimate separation.
Thoughtful gestures and intertwined lives,
removed from grace and plunged into a ferocious darkness.
Light comes in a voice.
Sadness is heard from a line.
Pain is caused and touch is forbidden.
Tears come often while the belief is constant,
and the power of the mind holds together the mystical memory.

Lori M. Gabriel

An Unfading Love

Would my life be all complete if I don't have you;
Would my strong heart all turn weak if I don't have you;
I would turn all life's tables just to seek and to know;
That your love for me will never, ever fade nor grow old;

If I get lost in the dark should I lose my way to you;
Would you shed a beam of light where I could find my way to you;
I would climb the highest mountain to proclaim my love for you;
Just to know your love for me will never, ever fade nor grow old ;

Love knows no limits it can turn your life around;
Turn your rags into riches or leave you looking all around;

Could we withstand the test of time as we sail life's raging sea;
Would our heart still beat as one in perfect love and harmony;
I would trade all fame and fortune to spend eternity with you;
Just to know your love for me will never ever fade nor grown old ;

Love holds no limits it can turn your life a round;
Turn your rags into riches or leave you looking all around;

And when death shall do us part would I still be in your heart;
Should you fall for someone new would my memories linger too;
Would you cherish and remember the good and bad
   that we've been through;
And would your love for me will never, ever fade nor grow old;

Kenneth W. Rose

Today...

Now I'm older, in school and all,
Talking on the phone, going to the mall.
  Deep within me dreams are there,
That I can't fulfill each one of them is just not fair.
  Babysitting and thinking hard,
Do I really have to rake the yard?
  Once I get older, things will be fine,
No problems at all, I'll always be on time.
  "Is that statement true," I often thought,
"Will parenting be as easy as that or with jobs
  and disasters will I be caught?"

Brianna Miller

Voices Whisper

"Charles is dying", that's My Name!
Now I'll never know the fame
Of great accomplishment before I die.

I have waited too darn long
To compose that pretty song
And all those other things I had in mind.

How I did procrastinate
When they come to check the slate
There's nothing there to show that I went by.

I go to join the many
Who have passed without any
Mark upon the world they left behind.

Life on this earth has been good to me
But I cannot leave it a legacy
I've lived my life as do we all,
  And now must answer to the call.

Charles G. Baldwin

Dreaming

Something so genuine I thought we had
Is making my heart so lonely and sad

Special dreams that I believed would come true
Are now hateful wishes that only make me blue

Thoughts with you all of the time
Everyday wondering if you could ever be mine

My heart knowing that you do care
Your life, you still do not wish to share

Never regretting the times we had
But also never admitting that not having making me sad

Brandy M. Riley

Just Because I Loved You

I waited by the phone waiting for your call
Just because I loved you
I've stayed your friend thru it all
Just because I loved you
I prayed for God to bring you to me
Just because I loved you
I was beside you when you needed me
Just because I loved you.
The time finally came when
Everything felt right and we were together.
Just because I loved you.
You said no condom and I said okay
Just because I loved you
Now you're gone and I have aids.
Just because I loved you.

Eunice Kann

The Joker

"The Game has changed," the Joker said.
  "I've rearranged the cards.
You should know by now to use your head
  Instead of trusting your heart."

"You're all alone now," the Joker said.
  "He's left you for someone new.
And so tonight when you go to bed
  There'll be no one there but you."

"I've reshuffled the deck," the Joker said,
  "And I'm dealing out new cards.
For you, my lady, my heart has bled,
  For this game of life has been hard."

"Most cards are wild," the Joker said,
  "But don't let that be confusing.
Once you get the hang of it,
  The game of life is amusing."

"Pick up your cards," the Joker said,
  "The new game will soon start.
Remember to always use your head,
  And fiercely guard your heart."

Susan Moody Faria

Ode To Old

To all the folks, this means you and me
That have reached the age of maturity
Come on, get going, somebody cares
You have to get up, out of your chairs
Look around you, give life a try
Don't just sit there, waiting to die
There's a lot of love in this world
As you will see
And the nice part, it's all free
There are flowers to look at, music to hear
Get up, get going
God loves you, my dear.

Eva M. Wiebeck

Untitled

A man can never hold that truth - until he says ah God
with saintly clothes and sandals of peace - I am
poorly shod - I'm sure you know me
through and through, I ask you now in pain
if I should follow you the way - could my soul regain
My body too - I fear for it - respect I've
showed it none - and all the time I
thought those things were adding up to fun.
And now I'm at a turning point - I know
not what to say - except my God I
ask you to be with me both night and day.

Gary D. Maring

Love Is

As beautiful as the mountains high
As graceful as the eagles fly

Knowing all that Nostradamos knows
Ever deep as the ocean's flow

Reverent in its brilliance untold
Mysterious as how our lives unfold

Through time and space it knows no bounds
And though we can hear it, it has no sound

Imagine the cloud you wish to have ridden
And Eden so plentiful with the fruits forbidden

Like the petal of a rose, so hard to describe
Is the depth of one's soul or the love of your life!

Helen M. Frost

Morning Star

In the darkness there's a candle, that shines upon the night
With a fragrance so inviting, as the ever present Light

In the covert of the stars, there's a shield of power and might
With the dawning of the knowledge, comes the Star that shines
 so bright

The heavens are created, for those who own the stars
From the nations and the oceans, they are gathered from a far

Through sincerity of heart, and ever present faith
They travel through the world, sharing Love with those who wait

In the shadow of existence, lays an ever present Star
Whose beauty is elated, and illuminating far

Its purpose is to draw, to the One Who's made them Whole
To reward the ones who aid, in gathering the souls

The beauty of this splendour, and the wonder of it all
Comes from understanding, based on those who've heard their call

The majesty of knowledge, will beset the Ones above
And the power of His spirit, will strengthen them with Love...

Judith V. Wyzkiewicz

Narrow Path

We walked hand in hand down the narrow path,
Knowing that one day we would come that part of the path
Where it divides into two separates paths.
We didn't think of what lay ahead for us, though,
We just lived each day and made the best of it.

As we drew closer and closer to the two paths,
He stopped and turned to me and said, "Don't cry, but be happy.
Keep in me your heart always for we'll see each other again."
We continued walking and as we reached the two paths,
He let go of my hand and turned to me and said,
"Go live your life for I cannot live it for you,
 nor help you to live it."

I stood there at the path that I must take and looked toward
 the path that he was taking.
There was sadness in my heart, but I didn't cry.
I stood there and watched as he walked down the path where at the end
I saw Jesus waiting for him and I wished that I could go with him.
But I knew that I couldn't because I had yet to live my life.
As I started walking down the path alone, I said to myself,
 "I miss you Grandpa."

Helen R. Newport-Woodward

Untitled

Cool air filters through the window
Where there is a pale moon greenness beyond -
I lie in the wide angle of your thighs,
Speak your name quietly against the smooth
 feel of your skin,
And so softly that only you can hear.

Is there some corner in your mind
That cradles me gently as that place
 between your soft breasts
Where my head lies? In these slow hours
Before the dawn, leaves whisper outside,
A feeling of rain in the air -
 and questions unasked
Linger, though love's answer is plain.

Turn, and fall where my arms hold you,
How easily we fit with each other!
I could breathe against your shoulder all night,
Knowing that, content in this wide bed,
You will never turn away -
Nor ever give me less than love.

Leonora V. Rogers

Who Am I?

I serve every child in the community.
I empower, enlighten, embellish, extend the process of thought.
I am the culmination of all the combined:
 a policeman, a referee, a counselor, nurse,
 a psychiatrist, a mentor, a father, a mother.
I am underpaid, overworked, under appreciated,
and over stressed.
 I am the underdog that will not quit; who strives
 for the betterment of all and not just a few.
I am an ocean who is abundant with knowledge eager
to share it with others.
 I am a model in which in the right hands will become
 an extension of the master.
I am the instrument from which learning occurs.
 I am the catalyst that inspires thought, animation,
 and inspiration in all children.
I am the key to our children's future.
 Who Am I?

Dora Elva Gomez

Dear Lord Why?

I stand outside every now and then,
Looking toward the sky.
With a heavy heart
Dear Lord, I ask you why?
You chose to take our precious grandson away.
We all miss and love him each and every day.
He was such a happy boy and had so much fun.
But asthma kept him from breathing well,
when he tried to run.
It took his life over a year ago,
but there is one thing I know.
I'll see him again when it's my time to go.
So when I get sad, with a heavy heart
and don't know what to do.
I stand outside, look up toward the sky,
and ask you Dear Lord, why?

Joan Lynch

Ode To My Little Maple Tree

Although you've lost some limbs and leaves
with missing branches, too,
I still visualize your beauty in my minds eyes so clear and true.

Once adorned with foliage your limbs are now so sparse and bare,
unadorned for winter's dress of winds and storm and freezing cold
with snow scattered without care.

I love this little maple tree that changes with the seasons
whose charm emits from every pore,
where birds can nest, feel safe from harm,
rely on God's protective arms and more.

Many different trees there are, too numerous to name,
but I'll take my little maple tree who holds fond memories
within its folds, remember planted I the seedling from
whence it came.

Marolyn E. Baker

Quietly In The Night

 Quietly, in the night, I listen to the sound of your heart beating softly.
As I hear that sound, I know that I am safe and protected.
 For if one of our hearts were silenced, I know the other
would soon follow.
 For I believe that our hearts, have become one. And in so being
will live and laugh, cry and love together until silence comes to
each of us.
 And in that silence, we will be together again in a different
place, quietly, in the night.

Susan G. Scott

Life

You strive in life to maintain a standard.
Always look forward, never look back.
Always look up, never look down.
Always look inward, never look out.
Set goals and accomplish them,
never let life have too many owes,
follow your dreams, and never let go.
Stand firm and not weary your chances are near.
Be bold and don't hold on to life's past injury.
Hope for the best never regret.
Your life has a purpose to be fulfilled and met,
your highest extremes will always be met.
Believe in yourself and never forget.
Life is a challenge not easily met.

Christy Willoughby

One Special Papa

When I would go to Papa's house, the first thing I did was go in the kitchen to see what smelled so good. See, my Papa made the best chocolate pie and banana pudding I've ever tasted. What a great cook he was!

One day I was watching him as he fixed himself some ice-cream with vanilla wafers crumbled on top. My eyes got real big! He fussed over me a lot! I didn't know my Papa could make ice-cream taste so good.

Suddenly one day my Papa couldn't see anymore. He was getting old and losing his hearing and eyesight. Now I would just sit when I went to his house and talk to him. Boy, he was a talker and had lots of stories to tell me! Papa's health declined through the years.

Then one day it happened...the tears came in great drops, I can't explain the peace I felt. At last Papa had gotten his wings and could fly, he was an angel. He could see, hear, and was no longer in pain. At last, after all of these years he finally met Mama as the heavens opened for him to come home. As I look up to the sky I can see him waving good-bye to me, at the same time I can feel his presence.

Now heaven has the best cook there ever was. Papa can cook for all of the angels. It will be the best chocolate pie and banana pudding heavens ever had! I will always remember when we were together and the joy Papa brought into my life. He will always be one special Papa.

Gail Linstead

Darkness

Somewhere, there is a time of darkness for each of us
not when we expect it, but when it comes
nothing personal, just nature's way of saying
that living includes the sum total of life's ebb and flow

Darkness is fraught with terror and aloneness
like a small twig amid the redwoods of the soul
where a single ray of sunshine struggles to break
the canopy to reach the forest's floor below

At such moments,
life's abundance is inexplicably everywhere:
in each leaf of knowledge,
each spider's web of connection,
each bird's song of friendship,
each lily's hopeful presence on a glistening pond

These gifts are our solace for life's darkest moments,
our only security that we matter deeply
as we bathe in the nourishment and blessing
of being fully who we are.

Richard U. Rosenfield

The Darkness

Everything that is love, is everything that is darkness;
so blind we walk; like water we move with no eyes
Embellishing, we throw ourselves to its mercy:
the way that water crashes upon the sand
With hurt pride we recede.

So blind we crawl; like water we move without feet;
indulging, we float; not feeling of the rocks below
With enveloping souls we engulf.

Leaving our fears to drift, we wrap ourselves in the mercy of the darkness, with no certain direction and no defined bounds.

Christine M. Hatzipetro

Sea Love

I could not live in an in-land place
Where there is no sound of surf, nor smell of sea.
No gulls wheeling 'round with grace.
No sand to fill my shoes, or trickle
    slowly through my hand.
No fog creeping across the bay,
Or sound of buoys ringing through the mist.
No light swinging in an arc
Guiding those sailing in the dark
of rocks along the shore,
No, I could not live in an in-land
place where there is no sea.

Ruth H. Hunton

Alone

　She stands alone with leaves in her hair;
they're memories that have
dropped from trees that were her yesterdays.
　She watches as the winds of today sweep
them gently out of sight and she wonders,
she wonders will she see them again?
　Because she's looking for
and hoping for a break in the clouds.
For she want a star, needs a sun will
settle for a moon to warm her way
　But the sky is hid.
And so she slowly folds the night around
her like a cloak for she knows his
warmth will soon be gone for good.

　And as she draws the light that they
knew into her mind and soul, it will
guard her heart against the tears
she will shed - alone.

Kathryn Gonder

Never Long Enough

You left me before I got to know you
And you came and went through the years
But never long enough to remember you
Got the chance to sit and talk
Not enough to hear you speak of life, family, love, and me
You call now and then not because you want to
But never long enough to tell me you miss and love me
Got the chance to see your face
But not long enough to see if father like son
Finally got to do all I wanted to do, and say
But not long enough to see you before you died
Never seemed long enough, never enough time
Never able to say what I wanted and needed to say
Now only one thing separated us, ... Time
But in the back of my mind as I sit in my chair
With my son in my arms I always wonder
Will he have his chance to express himself to me
Will I ever have mine?

Stephen Ortiz

If This Were A Song

You ask me to write a poem, and to let it come out of me
   That I cannot do
The pen and paper will not let me write what I feel
They just let me write what you want to hear
   But what is it that you want to hear?
Is it the dull sound of words flowing from my lips
while I read you this poem?
   Or do you want to Hear what I feel?
Keys of ebony and ivory could tell you what I feel
   Without words
They would tell you of feeling of happiness and love
And also of feelings of anger and hate
   All this in a song
A few simple keys played, played the right way, at the right time
   They will tell you what you want to hear
     Now is this what you want to hear?
     Or do you care to hear at all?
That I do not know..... Then again, what do I know?

   If only this were a song...............

Jason Mathews

Widow's Journey

The path I've traveled since you've been gone
has never been an easy one,

Forever longing for your touch,
always missing you so much.

I need your guidance, advice, and love.
I pray you're watching from above.

I will make you proud that you left behind,
a strong-willed woman, yet, gentle and kind,

Who's determined to provide some stability
for our ever-growing family.

It makes me sad you're not by my side
to greet each grandchild's birth with pride;

To watch our children as they accomplish
each dream, each milestone, their every wish.

I will stand there alone as each day breaks
and help each child, whatever path he takes,

And when my task on earth is through,
I pray to spend eternity with you.

Nancy S. Hickey

The Demands Of Men

I am not his mother.
I am not his child.
I am not going to surrender to his endeavor.
I am not going to defend my position
To mend his convictions.
I am not going to prove my worth
For him to see if this works.
I am not going to live by what he recommends.
I can not solve this institution
Between man and woman.
I am not going to succumb to his pressures.
I am not going to wait
All night for him arrive.
I am not going to conform to his ideals.
I am going to stand and be a woman
Of my own ideals,
Of my own convictions,
Of my own definitions,
Of my own limitations,
Of my woman sensations, and contemplations.

Jenny L. DeGregorio

Regards To The Moon

I like to see by the moonlight,
nocturnal instincts
produce a large darkness
within your eyes...
and by the fullest purest white
the wolf howls where the lamb lies...
I address this shade
as the center of breeze,
bulls-eye of the streaking comet,
one half of rotation
and surly the more wise,
it takes my hope, it seems,
and floods it with allowance dreams
basic needs without the cream...
out my window flawless night
on my pillow, sleeping detoured insight,
the translucent moon
eye-sight of the rocket, and on

Brian Williams

And You And I

You came looking for me in my dreams last night/ and I, saw you there/ and you/ were searching around in the darkness for me/ with your desperate eyes/ and I/ watched you from the shadows/ and I/ was hidden from your view/ and you/ called out my name/ and your sweet yearning voice made me moan my location away/ and you/ found me with your out-stretched hands/ and I/ floated like a feather into your black waiting arms/ and you/ held me tight/ and you/ pressed closer to me/ and I/ felt your warm soft lips kissing for my face/ and you/ and I/ woke up/ damn/ I hate when that happens/ I hope you come looking for me in my dreams tonight/ because I will be watching you from the shadows/ and I /will be hidden from your view/ waiting for part two/ of you/ and I.

Janine P. Holmes

Sherre

My little girl with hair of snow
is growing up and I know,
that I must let her do her thing,
and grow independent from my apron strings,

But Lord, it hurts
to see her cry
when someone hurts her.

But the growing pains I feel with her
are pains of joy too.

She's turning into a beautiful rose,
so delicate, but strong.

I pray she'll serve you Lord,
and her life will be as pleasing to you
as it has to me.

Protect her and keep her safe I pray,
I love her so much it's hard to say.

She's given me so much joy and happiness,
and I thank you Lord,
I've really been blessed.

Loretta Aspinwall

The Sea Shell

Today, I tossed a sea shell into the lonely sea
and watched the little fellow dissolve so suddenly

It started out as child's play, and ended up to be
A familiar path of ponder that often captures the—

Oh! How my heart was like that sea shell, once lost and now set free

Cheryl P. Bitoun

My Son

At birth I counted your fingers and toes
Last night I counted the graduation rows

It took a joyful eighteen years
And I might add, a few little tears

But here we are, and you're finally done
You've made me so proud, that you're my son

In your past years you've learned a lot
How to stay out of trouble, or at least not get caught

Most came from within your heart
Like love and family, all of which I had a part

Remember these things as you go on your way
And in my heart you will always stay

Don't make trouble, but do stand strong
At times you'll be right, at times you'll be wrong

Keep laughter in your soul, and love in your heart
And from your family never part

Live life for all it's worth
And leave your mark upon this earth

I ask myself how did you come to me, you dear
Well God thought of me, and you were here

Jo Anne Griffin

Suicide

I think of killing my self, in dreams I have at night
I visualize and plot my dreams, of soon ending my life.
What is there to live for, why should I stay alive
The only thing I come up with, is to commit suicide.
People talk about me, they don't like me, there's no one ever around
I sometimes stare off a cliff, to see how far is down.
I'm scared to close my eyes, to know one day they won't open again
I want to talk to someone, but I'm alone I have no family,
 I have no friends.
I think back in time, when my life wasn't really so bad
When I use to smile and gather around, back then I wasn't so sad.
But times have changed, and my life has too
This life of mine has left me, with not much to do.
I have a little boy, he brings me joy, but no enough to want to stay
To know he'll be around, so much sadness, each and everyday.
There's no reason, why he should have to live, his life this way
So I will continue, to think about suicide, day after day.
Sometimes I think, if I was dead, no one would care if I was gone
No one would cry, or come to the funeral, they wouldn't even mourn.
So now I ask you, with the way I feel, would you want to stay alive?
I didn't think you would, that's why I feel like committing suicide.

Lashana Boneparte

Vision And Reality

The noise from the grasshoppers
caught on the thicket barbed wire
fence is hurting my ears. The sharp stones
in the high wet grass is cutting my tired
sore feet. Satan's blood hounds are snapping
close on my cracked heels! Even the breath
within my bosom is vexing me! I'm tired.
Sweat is dripping from my weary soul. I know
I'm concentrating to deeply on my bad times.
I'm longing for the sweet smell of the honey
suckle vines near by. It's coming to me now,
that the 4 o'clocks will always open in the
morning if I can just endure for the night.
I'm beginning to connect with my prayer partner and
nourish from my portion of daily bread. Wait a
minute! My good days do out weigh my bad days.
I can't complain. My soul cries out, Halle-lujah!
I thank you, Lord.

Lula M. Cannon

Your Special Day

Once in a while there comes a time
to find the right card you had in mind.
One that would say what you want it to say
In just a very special way.

But Happy Birthday is not quite enough
it needs that sorta special touch.
There are no words to express
my feelings for your happiness.

I wish you joy, I wish you health.
I wish you pleasure and even wealth.
I pray your rainbows will all come true
and that the sun will shine for you.

I think you know what I'd like to say
on this your very special day.
But since I can't make it clear
I'll just have to say Happy Birthday, Dear.

Lou Mitchell

Respect!!

If you give me respect you'll get respect from me!
That's just the way it should be!
No guns blazin' late at night!!
No more talk of another gang fight!!
No more wonderin' who we'll lose next?
Just sit back and open the text.
In this book you will find: Love, Happiness, and Peace of all kind.
No more talk of kids bein' strapped
That's all we need another friend capped!
Don't you worry about losing your head?
How would you like to see your friends dead?
I'm tired of wearing the solid black!
I'm tired of wishing my friends could come back!
They would still be here today, if the world wasn't this way!
Now the only place we meet is under the large maple tree.
Instead of looking them in the eyes, I stand above them and I cry!
Do you know what it's like not to get to say goodbye?
Instead of looking them in the face, I'm looking at their resting place!
Instead of hearing their voice, the laughing and the tone,
All I get to do is stare at their head stone!!

Stacey L. Bowler

Reflections On A Cloud

I saw a cloud today that reminded me of you.
As I sat on the ground under "our tree,"
I watched the cloud float across the sky as you
had floated through my summer all those years ago.

Like you, it seemed the cloud was content
to repose in the hazy sun,
and while away the afternoon
with the buzz of the bumblers and me.

So bright and sun-reflecting, like you
the cloud was only the thinnest mist,
fleeting and fickle
with the ambivalence of the wind.

All afternoon I watched it move across the sky,
until it tangled in the branches of our tree,
snared there as you had wished me to be
all those years ago.

As I rose to return to that world
of stifling stockings and toe-cramping heels,
the cloud broke
and rained itself out behind me.

Evelyn V. Hall

Nothing More, Nothing Less

When you thought you had it right,
You really had it wrong.
When you thought you were in the
Spotlight,
Your day seemed to be so long.
But once you fall in love,
All that begins to change.
You begin to thank the one up above,
Even at a very short range.
He's in your dreams about every night,
You think of him all the day.
He comes into your life like a shining light,
you wish him always to stay.
Nothing more, nothing less,
true love will never depart.
Just hope things turn to be the very best,
because he's made it into your heart.

Melissa Williams

Lifetime

The wind blowing against me,
Blowing me to writing land.
The wind blowing the grass north,
Taking me to that path.
The sky so peaceful.

Rain drops coming down,
Telling me their story each day.
The flowers like a piece,
And the sun taking a piece of pie,
And eating the piece.

When the wind blows against the trees,
And when it's blowing the leaves on the trees,
The leaves are like they're dancing.
The clouds like a piece of paper,
All wrinkled up.

The flowers opening up the truth.
When I am in nature
I feel freedom,
Coming inside of me.

Annette Hyla

New Feelings

We all have to feel our way
Sometimes much to our dismay

If we listen to the voice within
We have a chance to propel without sin

A new way is always there
And it gives us an opportunity to declare

In any event-we must hold our head high
It gives us pleasure if occasionally we deny

With every new chance we can employ
And forget about any decoy

With each new stroke
We have a chance to revoke

If we keep this in mind
That it's never good to be on the decline

Many things will help us in our quest
Hopefully, we can address

There is always help on its way
If we remember not to sway
Only we alone can betray
But it's up to us to save the day.

Edward T. Philpitt

Ole John Paul

John Paul can ya hear it coming?
John Paul can ya see the track?
Can ya hear the train a coming?
Spouting chugga out its stack!
Been waiting such a long time, to hear that chugga choo...
John Paul while you were waiting, what did you have to do?
With a smile upon his face, John Paul he had replied,
"I pretended I was in it, the conductor!" He had cried.
John Paul went on to tell us his events upon the rail;
and in the making of history, continued with his tale.
When suddenly! Within our sights!
The train! A chugga choo!
And all at once we cried out, "Chugga choo choo, wooo wooo!"
One thing I did remember from that day so long ago.
John Paul he had then vanished, to where we did not know!
The train its engine started.
Then "All aboard" we heard them call.
Last thing that I remember was the voice of Ole John Paul.
"I am the train conductor, my wish it had come true.
When wishing in the future, don't forget to chugga, choo!"

Donna Osterman

Alex

Alex...I'm gonna summarize up my love for you,
As your lover and as your best friend.
Well, I'm devoted to you with all my heart,
From the beginning to the end.

I feel so proud and very lucky,
To have you as my man,
And I want us to stay together,
For as long as we possibly can,

I love your sweet and sexy voice,
When we're romancing all alone,
I love your hair, I love your body,
And I love the smell of your Tommy cologne.

You treat me better than gold,
From the bottom to the top.
I know I'm very lucky to have you,
God, you're so charming and hot!

I've always dreamed about meeting Mr. Right,
I'm absolutely sure that it's you.
Well, the truth is, I wanna be with you forever,
And love you through and through.

Robin Tanzini

Agony And Sorrow

You have won the battle but not the war.
You have taken my heart and left it to rot.
And while my soul is being crushed
My lover stands in the shadows of darkness
behind the bars of our so called protectors,
and waits to be sentenced.
So I stand in my tears of loneliness
while it forms a pool around me.
And when I look into my lovers eyes
I feel his pain and wish to revive him

He is my love
And I shall
Cry for him

He is my heart and it shall break when
I can no longer hold him

He is my love
And I do and will love him.

Melissa Fielder

My Child My Child

How long it has been, waiting for thee
my thoughts were of you before you could ever be.

Three times you were almost only a dream
with death's claim near in life's mystic scheme.

Now all my prays have been answered:
My Child, my child: you are now here with me.

Through the years I will share your tears and fears,
And together we will grow older but wiser.
Never will we break this bond between us.

Though one day you will leave and go on
your own, our fond memories shall be as an
unmovable stone.

As the sands of time pass through life's hour glass,
God will call me to take my leave,
but always believe, that someday you will hear,
My Child: My Child:
You are now here with me, for all Eternity,

Harry E. Keller

Typical Workday

The alarm goes off
But you can't get out of bed
It's just too easy
To hit the 'Snooze' instead

You crawl from the tub
Put your face on while you weep
You may seem dressed and ready
But, you're body's still asleep

You finally arrive at the office
Luckily the shoes are a pair
Then you notice runs in your hose
Under the wrinkled clothes you wear

You don't want to hear negative
You need spirits up and up
So just keep grinning
And fill your coffee cup

You wouldn't be here if you didn't have to
So eight hours we must stay
Work away to forget the time
So you'll be closer to Friday!

Michelle O'Neal

The Thinking Spot

I was walking in the forest one morning,
when I sat down beside a tree.
I thought to myself, I wonder,
what would the world be like without me?

There would be no more of me to make fun of,
and no more of me to push around.
Where there once was a smile and laughter,
there will no longer be a sound.

I thought how life would be,
after I was gone.
And then I came to see,
how people's lives moved on.

Many loved ones now are gone,
and each had different views.
But I could only think of one,
that I could not bear to lose.

When times in my life went bad,
only one memory I could find.
Only one person could lift me up,
That's when I kept you in mind.

Chip Hutchcraft

"That Strange And Uplifting Wind"

The journeys of my soul began and are carried
By this "Friend", a mighty and strange uplifting wind."

It's past midnight when I awake, with fear I am
Gripped and know not why, as my last life breath,
Is breathed without,... my spiritual journey begins again.

My fears are quickly laid aside, as I am lifted
Into the high, with that friend, "That strange uplifting wind."

I have journeyed far and wide, and in my sight I
See that light, no fears abound, my soul is free,
I feel love and peace within me.

But fear arises once again, as I can feel that
Strange uplifting wind, that moves me onto journeys
yet unknown to worlds uncharted and that life of death once again.

Max M. Morgan

Broken Peace

Who woke me from my eternal sleep?
With a shocking sound it broke my peace,
And brought me here out of my rest;
To a place I would rather not be.
I was, till now, soft asleep,
In a land far away, that I wish I could stay;
In that most relaxing bliss.
Who woke me up and brought me to this doom?
My alarm clock has been flung across the room.

Curt Yowell

Peace, Love, Dove

They changed things forever,
the hippie-freak kind.
They restored your freedom,
though I hear you still whine.
They saved our young men,
from more political wars.
But I hear you call them,
Pot heads and whores.
Everyone was welcome
At the hippie-freak ball,
The lame and the homeless
made no difference at all.
Charles Manson and his like
was all you could see,
long hairs and coke heads and lapping up speed.
They stopped the war and political charade,
Things changed forever
but what a price they all paid
Crucify them now for sex and space drugs.
We all were not perfect, but most were white doves.

Robert Damron

Zebra

Sprinting through the spectacular Serengetti,
But being alert at all times.
Equivocating the lethal lion in his arch and playful ways.
He takes pride in his magnificent, beautiful coat,
with ebony stripes on an ivory background,
in all its glorious splendor.
It does not only shine with the radiance of beauty, but with the
security of camouflage as well.
Cloistering his body from his pernicious pursuers
who believe him to Mother Nature's majestic makings.
Though his ways of protection do not always prevail.
His rival must also survive
and have the zebra take his rightful place in the great circle of life.
Mischievous, splendid, exuberant and clever.
Those are the ways of the Zebra.

Ray Pacia

Untitled

Look outside and tell me
If the rain is coming near
Tell me what you see and feel
And I'll tell you what I hear
For the warmth of yesterday
By a fire teamed with laughter
Subsides in the autumn breeze
So the rain might come soon after
And with the ambers growing dim
Of the once proud pine and oak
You can feel the coming cold
And watch the far off chimneys smoke
But when the shadows vanish
And the night mist brings the gloom
Let the silence lend a thought to a night that's ending soon
And morning sounds whisper near with Aurora dressed in blue
There are wishes on your doorstep and fresh cut roses washed in dew
So look outside and tell me if the rain has come and gone
Tell me what you see and feel
And that you've been here all along

Brett Lassa

Hand Of An Angel

Reach a hand to earth and touch the dead,
do not fear the poison in their head,
they were ripped from our life and land,
and they can never understand.

Reach a hand to earth and touch their soul,
guide their lives you cannot take control
their memories erased when they were born,
you must not look on them with scorn.

Reach a hand to earth and touch their heart,
but be careful, they're easily to rip apart,
they are confused, they have much fear,
they mistake love and friendship when you are near.

Reach a hand to earth and touch their mind,
do not be afraid of what you'll find,
as the simple creatures are so insecure,
relishing in the touch of one so pure.

Joel Anderson

Two Lovers

   Then the green eyes
the dark forest green eyes,
looking like diamonds,
pretending now to be jewels,
now stars, now filled with
love looked at her.
While her gray eyes like a
rainy sky watched him.
She felt warm and smell of
cinnamon was all around
her and he grabbed her hand
so soft and so warm. Like a
blanket on a cold day.
Then suddenly it happened;
he pulled her close, close
so their lips would touch.
It was as if she were in a dream there
was nothing around them and the love
between them grew.
While the sunset and the night came alive.

Brandy Graves

Pain

Here I am, please take me away
Can't bear to stay, another day.
here I am, not much to be found.
Please put me in the ground, I won't make a sound.
Here I am, I had a heart of gold.
The heart that you stole, and then you sold.
Here I am, nothing left to gain.
Slowly going insane, I can't deal with the pain.
Here I am, standing in the flames.
I'll never be the same, it's you I blame.
Here I am, what are you waiting for.
Want to hurt me some more, I can't close the door.
Here I am, fighting all my dreams.
You want to hear me scream, feeling remain unseen.
Here I am, condemned to never fly.
I just want to die, only you know why.
Here I am, paying for your sin.
This should have never been, I guess I'll never win.
Here I am, learning how to hate
Your poison I ate, if you're sorry it's too late!

Patrick Latozas

A Father's Son

I watched as they walked in the distance across the field,
arms locked around each other walking, loving, laughing,
   building a shield.

I watched as from a generation unalike they each came,
a gap bridged from a single force of love just the same.

I watched as they worked to become one set of friends,
years of love and life shared through fads and trends.

I watched with a feeling of hurt and jealousy,
feeling left out of a moment in time for me.

I watched as they grew in life and love,
a gift that was given to me from above.

I watched as they became birds of a feather,
a love that would last forever and ever.

I watched as they grew to become one,
they're the loves of my life,
they are my father and my son.

James E. Cothran

Then I'm A Witch

As she bade the world adieu,
The wraithlike woman's last word
They say was "—Holt."
They speak of her delight
In herbs and tisanes.

Bats flew undisturbed into the blue
Above her house.
Neighbors say she watched,
Smiling, head held high.
They saw her many times
Remove struggling creatures from a trap.
Like the poet she felt pathos
For a mouse, trembling in its field.

I have a love affair with herbs.
I, just as she, can suffer pain
Of living things in steel traps.
Because my name is Holt,
The wraithlike woman's last word
In dying, must have called to me;
If so, — then I'm a witch.

Holt Carlton

The Encounter

As I strolled along the beach one day
On a misty, foggy morning
I could hear the ships pass in the bay
Their foghorns sounding warning
I met an old man along the way
Dressed in uniform of blue and grey
Captain of a freighter docked ahead
"Headed for the Indies," the old man said
His snowy beard fell to his chest
He grinned and shook hands giving his best
Upon his shoulder a parrot spat
"Ahoy Matey", interrupting our chat
Then up the gangplank the old man went
Looking quite eager and content
When I return from my walk
His ship was leaving the dock
The fog and mist suddenly cleared
Patches of clouds and blue skies appeared
I saw the old man at the rail
Waving goodbye as his ship set sail

Ann Whelan

Israel My Lost Love

In all this universe you were created
No other before beheld this life through your precious eyes
Which, they say, are the windows to your soul
As much as man is a tool for goodness and light
Or to spread his evil nature
You were the first, by far,
And even as my flesh knows
it has touched you for the last time
The memory of that touch will go on for eternity

Joanna Victor

The Death Of Wonderwoman

Look at the girl in the picture,
At that absurd Wonderwoman costume.
Remember her?
She once laughed,
But her laughter's been silenced.
She once played "soldiers"
Alongside the boys,
But the soldier has died
In the midst of a different battle.
She once hugged her daddy
And told him she loved him this much,
Stretching her arms as far as they would go,
But now there's no daddy to hug.
The little girl's gone.
Don't you miss her?
If only she could return,
But I know she can't.
What's gone is gone.
What's lost is lost
And we can never bring it back to life.

Marisa Jean Downs

To You

I never thought that I would ever meet a man,
    who is almost perfect,
Who to me would be so very special,
A man whom I adore.

I found that man,
The man is you.

You must have flaws,
You must have faults,
But I am just too blind to see them.

Edith Astrid Yeager

Time Being

I want to abandon my dreams and drown my soul,
    Fall from my pedestal and complete the toll.

I'm looking for me in the woods of hell
    As I whisper to myself, hoping no one can tell.

The tracks of a stranger keep filling my path
    As from the depths of the shadows I am only behalf.

A gentle rain falls, cleaning my mind
    As my thoughts await the next excursion of time.

I leap over the boundaries that my past has set apart
    And enter a world so very dark.

Facing the obstacles that so many call life
    I lace my thoughts with dreams of great height.

I carry my severed pride which contains no metal
    Trying to stay in the shadows; my humbleness I settle.

With no conception of my existence I search for myself
    Content with the fact that it is only the purpose I've felt.

Katherine Aumer

Summertime

The sun covers us in a layer of gold.
We are free like the wildflowers
beautiful and untouched
growing on the glistening crystal hills.
Our souls float upon the warm breath of summer.
Our spirits fly into the sky becoming
one as if we had never been born,
our lives vanish into a golden dream to be forgotten.
We are the sky, the flower, the earth
until the dawn of autumn comes and we scatter
back into our sacred houses.
Only to live the dream that we almost forgot.

Ramona Tania Chavez

Autumn Moon

I walked around; under the autumn moon.
The only sounds, soothed my aching ears.
The sounds of the wind.
My path was lit - only to no real destination;
As always: to the future; the light dimmed.
No fear embraced me on this cozy night.
For on this road; so many times,
My feet have trodden.
To the passersby: my joy unseen.
For my mind was bewildered
And heart; in a trance.
Yes, it happened to many; who have chosen this path.
You ask - what path can I follow?
The path that is "Lit by the Autumn moon?"
I hesitate no longer; to share with you,
My enchantment and wonder of this autumn moon.
It's this way, follow me; to the place where,
The wind-sings and the leaves dance along.
Onto the path of no end:
The path lit by the autumn moon.

Sylvia Polanski

What God Might Be

God might be as graceful as the dove.
He might be the colors of a rainbow.
He might be as swift as the rushing river.
He might smell as wonderful as the flowers.
He might be as red as a heart.
He might be as soft as a bear.
He might shine like the moon.
His love might be greater than the world.

Jaimie M. Lopez

Untitled

I ran fast and hard for as long as I could,
Then one day they judge me for not doing what I should.

This world is hard enough on young growing minds,
Corruption, disease and abuse, evil lurks among us,
Its shape takes many kinds.

I know not who or what I am; or why I'm even here,
Yet every time I think of a future all I see is a tear.

Live and let live, to each his own, no one the Lord shall judge.
I'm sorry if I am different, in feelings and in thought
But I must release this grudge.

So next time you scold someone for not doing what is right,
Bow your head and pray for them,
Eventually there will be some light.
Raymond Tuthill

Grey

Abstract
Someone else's teardrop smears an
Inkspot of the mind
Dance as the world passes
Its time to run in circles
Around the sunflower
Upside-down chess pawn reigns
Over the painted car window
A shoe box college shows the universe key.
Somersault into the smoke filled
Air filter
Maybe tomorrow I will forget today
But remember yesterday
Contradictive irony writes poetry
From the nose
Secret
Edward Nordan

Writing With Zen

A dead man falls into
A big room
And searches for a pen.

A girl, painting her toes, sits on a couch
And watches him.

"All of my true mishaps have been passionate ones;
All my true passions have been mishaps..."

The dead man writes with such passion
That he never notices her staring.
Tomas A. Beauchamp

The Stranger Within

You left for school to get away from me -
  But you're still here.
Who are you?
You joined the service to get away from home -
  But you're still here.
Who are you?
I no longer see you as my son,
You no longer respect me as your father.
You're trying to tear this family apart,
Bit by bit; but you'll fail at this tool
Because that's the only thing you know how
to do well. (You have no heart for anything else).
Why don't you just go away - and not
  Be here anymore.
Strangers come and go, they never stay.
  So why do you?
Elmo L. Herrera

The Road

We travel the same roads
Sun and moon cover us
Time and season push us
Events are a shared passenger
Together we journey to the same destination

We never see each other
Yet I know you are out there
Shadows of you cross my memory

You go where I've been
Always moving yet never meeting
The future is where we both are racing
There is where our perfection lies

Tomorrow holds the prize of hope
Love and joy await us
Somewhere along the road we both travel
Donna Lawson

Through His Eyes

As I sit here watching, so high above,
I'm keeping an eye on those that I love.
I see a young girl, in need of my care,
It seems that her sorrows are too much to bear.
I want to go down, and wipe the tears from her eyes.
I can feel her pain through her hurting sighs.
Her father has left and she misses him so.
They don't know where he is, or why he had to go.
So many questions run through their heads,
"Is he thinking of them? Could he possibly be dead?"
They get lots of support from family and friends,
But still they wonder, "Is this the end?"
If he does come back, can they forget,
The pain that he caused that put her whole family in fret?
Well, he came back, and he told his tale,
And after a lot of apologizing, and forgiveness,
Her soul, uplifted, had been unveiled.
Jessica Traw

Bird Cage

Alone I sit, perched for everyone to view.
Trapped in a binding cage I've made for myself, unconsciously.
The sinister expressions of onlookers, gawking, infuriates my soul.
I force a chirp, "peep," unheard.
Cowering slightly, anger and frustration once more envelop me.
Spreading my weak wings outward, I force the brass bars to bend.
Them letting out a screeching creak, soothing.
Astonished at my effective act of rebellion
the supposed "superior" onlookers scurry to safety,
never amounting to much.
I stand alone to wallow in my glory and freedom.
Jamie Gumieny

Certain Memories

Watching as the sun slips down beneath the shimmering
water stretching as far as the eye can see, the grounds
at camp are silent, except for the exceptional chirp of
the sweet song of the robin.
The stars are arranged in an array of designs and shapes.
The cool faint breeze whispers sweet nothings in my ears,
as the memories of the past week flow into thought.
I long to stay in Charlotte forever, yet my heart aches to go home.
The bright shimmering moonbeams shine down, and outline
my tears, as the whispering willows steal my secrets, and keep them.
These are the memories of a lifetime, memories of hope, fun,
laughter, love and tears.
These are the memories that are locked deep within my soul.
Cheri Collin

Tempest

The ground trembled intemperately
clouds burst awakening intoxicated sky
torrential rain plummeted
reverberating vehement savagery
stars and comets faded unheeded
deeming premature darkness encompass earth
overcome amidst illuminating bolted lightning
contriving tyrannical authority
winds roared assuming Zeus' thunderous infuriation
penitent anguished land rendered impotent
besieged by ocean waves unleashing rage
exhausted contracting mountains disparaged
birthing disintegrating dusting pebbles
dislodged trees hurled awry
embellished with
ribboned roots once anchoring them immovable
Hell's demonic gates beckoned
overseered by feverish-eyed Satan
Apocalypse interposed
God gathered-in the animals two-by-two
   Carole E. Richardson

After Life

In heaven there is a special place,
Where every soul is ridden of disgrace,
Every sin has been forgiven,
And everyone is grateful
For what they are given,
Yet deep below the angels feet roots,
A festering evil that is men in
Armani suits, their greed and lust overcomes the nation,
And good and trust is beyond contemplation,
This place is Earth,
And the people are different,
But only the good must die,
The pure souls will mourn them,
But you will never see,
A cold hearted person cry,
To live with the angels,
The grateful souls will go,
But when the greedy meet death
They will have nothing to show for the suffering they
  embarked on others.
   Jacqueline Marie Vollenboven

Reflections

Images,
Clear as night as though you have seen before.

Distorted pictures,
Twisted from their original frame of mind.

Obscure memories,
Dreams of what we wish it was like.

Hopeless fantasies,
Duplicating our thoughts and movements.

A point of view,
As seen from many different angles.

Artistic creations,
Scenes we can change and change again.

Shapes,
Smashed together to form an intricate puzzle.

Formations,
Showing the truth whether we like it or not.
   Matthew Tremblay

No One But Me

Life is a game, it's all the same.
Winners, losers, players, users.
There's nothing you can do
  against being used.
Many strategies I have tried,
  Many rivers I have cried,
  wishing then and there I could've died.
But, I hold my head high
  and walk with a strong stride.
Because, I realized there's no one to please.
  That is, no one but me.
   Katy Golecki

Where You Are

People continually go through the motions of everyday life.
However to give of oneself to help serve and guide others,
that in itself is the ultimate commitment.
To accomplish this commitment, one must remember the basic reasons
that brought you to this point,
and, to help keep you focused on what you strive to achieve.
Always remember, who and what you are.
Where you came from and why you chose to do what you are doing.
Try to put yourself into other's shoes.
Look at the situation from their prospective.
Always give credit where credit is due.
Remember your manners, no matter how hard it is to be civil.
A please and thank-you go a long, long way. Smile, genuinely.
People respond better to a friendly face and attitude.
Most of all, look upon life's ups and downs with a good sense
  of humor
You will be able to look back and reflect on a situation and learn
from your mistakes, as well as smile at your achievements.
Don't be afraid to stick your neck out.
That's one reason you are where you are today.
If your intentions and goals are pure, you will always have the
support and respect of those that put you where you are.
Peace be with you on your journey!
   Sheryl Barker

The Truth About You

Your secrets scream headline, your dramas inane
You leave me in anguish, you drive me insane,
Your nebulous lectures, pedantic in from
Your safe little life keeps you far from the storm.
Your one saving grace is having known Me
Your one pending bill: I'll send you my fee!
The truth is you're lacking in substance, my friend,
The truth is I'm sick of how much you pretend.
The vacuous look in your eyes says it all
The numerous lives that you've tried to enthrall.
There's no longer room left in my life for you
There's no longer doubt that you haven't a clue.
These words are quite harsh, yet I'm sure that you see
These words speak the truth we're no longer We.
   Nadine Hart

The Ignored

All alone in the midst of many;
  putting on a smiling facade,
    for my sadness is not worth showing.
Pushing my desperation back
  into the pit of my stomach,
    showing no pain to being ignored.
You get used to the pain,
  you don't let it ruin your mask,
    for who wants to see a loser's agony?
   Beverly Figueroa

Forsake Not Forget

I speak my native tongue
I dance my native dance
I eat my native food
I am a native...made in the USA

I speak their native tongue
I dance their native dance
I eat their native food
I am a native...made in the USA

I graduated from their school
I speak and teach their language
I teach in their school system
I understand their utterances...made in the USA

My husband is a native
he dances our native dance
he eats our native food
he is a native

  All is lost
  all is different now
  all does not matter anymore forsaken but not forgotten

  Why? Grace
Diana Faatai

Love At First Sight?

Back on that precious day, the day we met
I would never be the same I bet
To that party I'm glad I went
I never knew that hearts would mend.

That red skirt and shirt you wore
Grabbed my eyes and heart it stole
You were in my mind that New Year's Eve
Where we're at I could not believe.

I gave you flowers and gifts and all
I hope this relationships would never fall
Kissing you puts my heart on fire
Getting dizzy is not what I desire.

But I do desire being with you
I care about you infinity plus two.

Ruel Manuel

Be Strong

Be strong
Don't turn back
I hear a sad song
True love is what I lack

Be strong
Remember what mother said
"The right man will come along"
Look ahead

Be strong
Continue to explore
I hear a sad song
I don't cry for him anymore

Be strong
Remember what mother said
"The right man will come along"
Instead

Be strong
I have a choice
The right man has come along and whispers "you are strong"
Then I hear my mother's voice

Rosemary Pelle

My Sweetheart For Life

I can hardly believe how long it's been, since the day we said "I do".
The things we've seen, the dreams we've dreamed since 1982.

We've been through many difficult days, and learned to lean
  upon each other.
When we thought we wouldn't make it, we trusted the Lord together.

We've seen days when we didn't have jobs, and money became
  less and less.
That's when we learned the truth, that "money don't buy happiness."

There have been days when it seemed, we couldn't say
  anything right.
And everything we did just prompted us to fight.

But most days have been filled with love, laughter and pride.
And nights filled with pleasure with you there by my side.

You'll be my sweetheart and I'll be your wife.
In spite of the hardships and disagreements in life.

I'm so very proud of the man that I see.
Of the husband and daddy you've turned out to be.

Your love means more to me as each day slips away.
Your patience and caring, I could never repay.

Just know that I love you and I'm glad I'm your wife.
And you'll be my sweetheart for the rest of my life.

Tonya L. Ray

Silly Me - Silly You

Silly me, silly you, we did not know, what to do.
Funny me, funny you, whenever laughed, this much is true
Honest I, honest we, we couldn't talk, we couldn't see
Shame on us, shame on we, we never were, all we could be

Life's a drag, life's a joy, first a girl and then a boy
It got easy, it got hard, you so close, me so far
There is no answer, the answer's clear
What we did, we did through fear.
We got lazy, we got tough, though it seems we just gave up

Funky me, funky you, we sang a love song and trashed its tone
We so cute, we such clowns, smoked a peace pipe, blew up town
I've got an idea, I've got no clue, nothing's certain, oh what to do?
Let's climb this mountain, let's fall back down, it seems
To be we go round and round.

I'll ride the trolley, you ride the bus
You pick up Lindy, I'll pick up Gus
Let's move on now before we bust
Time's on our side, time's unjust
Tighten the bolts here, no let's unscrew
Silly me, silly you.

Matt Kurlowicz

Greetings

Thanksgiving has come and gone.
The turkey has all been ate.
We're sitting here, the day is done.
Time does fly, it's half-past eight.

Christmas is around the corner, we're having some.
We're all getting ready and it's late.

We've hung the holly down low.
We are in our easy chairs, waiting for snow.

People are like ships, they come and go.
But you're the true family and friends, we know.

Christmas is going to come, that's so.
Our family is all blessed, because of who we know.

Nelie Rinkel

The Dark

The shadow comes to me, again, in the night
Shivers, loneliness, the chill in my veins
I stand alone.
As cold dark waters bleed within;
Then I wait, I fear, I hide,
My pride, she'll come when it's right

The night carries lies; my eyes deceived what is real is not.
Reality damned; cut deep by sorrows sword
I stand alone.
Spirit near gone and strength weak
I wait, I listen, I cry, denied
Once I had believed

The heart is patient but must be strong
Night is fierce; the shadow comes,
It won't be long.
I see her; I open my eyes she's gone.

My peach; now a tree growing, growing
For all to see the wind changes I am now free
Darkness

Chris DeMaria

North

A memory brought again to flesh
A wayward glance and eyes that met
Does knowing dance inside your mind
Or am I just of lonesome kind

A breath of smoke upon a step
A unique bond and seldom slept
Resigned for now to days gone by
When more than roofs disguised our skies

Everclear
Those days remain
And shelter me
From endless pain

Geremy Hess

"Solitude-Woods"

Never have I ever seen such splendor bliss as this,
A pathway winding deeper and further as far as the abyss.
The solitude and calmness I feel around within,
do I dare go any further? It's drawing me ever in.
The minutes running by me will I ever see the clear?
at that moment I thought "why worry" it loves me being here.
I see a open area where there's a hint of real-soft-light,
is this where it wants me to sit, and think until the night?
It is, I'll sit awhile now and think about the day,
although I just can't really tell how long I'm going to stay.
I'm awfully glad I come here, my mind has wandered far,
I'd love to take it with me and put it in a jar.
Quietness and solitude I've found throughout this day,
the "woods" my mind needs often
As if I were to pray.

Linda Runchka

Thoughts On A Summer Afternoon

Let us consider the lark and the dove,
Are they free, or only lamenting what they might be.
The lark sings his delight but then fades away,
While the dove mourns about I know not what all day.
When the chick-a-dee twitters and hangs by his toes,
The wren sings so clearly and plucks at a rose.
The duck in his pond floats regal and proud,
And the robin wrests a worm from the ground,
The Lord in his heaven peers at all from a cloud.

Donna R. McGrew

First Love

First love are people you never forget,
Even if you try, you can't just yet.
The impression on your heart will last forever,
Even though you're not together.
Back through the memories, you travel through time,
Thinking about your love so divine.
Some made you laugh, some made you cry,
Then you remember your tearful goodbye.
You thought your love would never end,
But the truth is, it's a painstaking trend.
So often they come, and so often they go,
The pain and sorrow you don't want to show.
You'll move on thinking it's the right thing to do,
In your heart always knowing, the love you had first,
    will always be true.

Melissa Eichele

Rose Daughters Of Mother's Day

Once upon a time, long, long ago in a land far away.
There came the dawn in May of the first Mother's Day.
Each year after year we see this date arise again to be reborn,
As if faith has made this Mother's Day come as a soft radiant morn...

A mother's rose grew here once where all could see,
Embraced by her loving mother's caverns near by the sea,
Behold the rose's beauty grew as the days passed swiftly by,
Like a bird she spread her leaves out as to fly...

What is so special about this rose - for she is your daughter
    honesty to you,
Mother dear, she sends you a wish for a Happy Mother's Day that
    will not be blue...
For daughters be the ones who turn into mothers for the coming
    years of the Mother's Day,
Renewing faith with magical images of new roses becoming
    Mothers only in May...

Katherine S. Lofton

Earth

My plains bear the food that you eat.
My mountains soar to the sky they meet.
My trees give you the air that you breath.
The sky up above brings rain for your seed.
My rivers spawn the fish that swim upstream.
My lakes full of wondrous and curious things.
My oceans bring tides in which you play.
My sun rises and sets with every new day.
My moon at night fills me with light.
These things I give you are wondrous indeed.
For I wish you to see I am a living thing.
I need your help to keep me alive.
So please take care of me lest I should die.

Jana Flath

Come Summer's Sun

Comes Summer's sun to the sounds of the sparrows and robins,
    as the noise of the silence pierced the flow'r.

I watched the brightness of the dark cloud flash by,
    and Heaven's ray of hope breaks the hate of Earth.

As I follow the traces of love, the pretty birds sing with
    melodic magnificence.

Crickets and frogs in the Summer night air sing their songs
    and the flow'rs flavor that air with sweet fragrance.
    Lullaby

Comes Summer's sun to the sounds of the sparrows and robins...

Ralph P. Rescigno III

Am I My Brother's Keeper

Am I my brother's keeper?
Do you cause your brother to sin?
Are you a stumbling block to others,
And drive them into sin deeper and deeper?

God says I am my brother's keeper,
Do you pull him down in the miry clay?
Do you constantly berate him by words you say?
All of these things cause him to go into sin deeper.

We are to help our fellow man,
Help him the very best you can;
God's commandments to keep,
Help him to be upbeat.

Keep God's covenant to man,
Do the very best you can;
Jesus will gladly receive,
All who truly believe.

Jesus says, "all power is given to me in heaven and earth,
Go into all of the world;
and teach the gospel to every creature,
Baptizing them in the name of the Father and of the Son and of
   the Holy Ghost."

Clara C. Wellons

Life's Journey

Dreams, fantasy, and unknown reality
Floating on the winds of life
What should I do?
Where should I go?
Lost in a world of hate, denial, and depression
Looking for something to believe in
Something to strive for
But where is it?
It's not here
Every corner turned I walked into a dead end
Though finally I find my place, my dream
In friends, life, and beliefs
What else is to come but to finish this journey
Walking, talking, living my life
Fulfillment is coming near
Laughing at myself when I didn't know
Remembering all the heartaches and frustrations
Striving for better but not quite making it
Face down in a world of accomplishments
Finally with death I'm here!!!!!

Adam Edgar Davis

My Future

As the bus bumps down the rock-covered
road, my friend and I try to predict the
future. We place ourselves in a small
room with a tiny window, no door, and
algae green walls. Next, we put a blue
rug on the floor and I sit on that with
a typewriter, pad of paper, and my
trusty pen that will help me write the
first chapters of the plotless book we
so look forward to working on together.
She will be at her cheap oak desk typing
things to people she meets on the
internet. Then she will slowly turn to
me and say, "I hate them all," as she
does now, and then rotate around again
to type in a clever reply.
   This is what we imagine our future to
be like today. Tomorrow the color of the
walls will be black and we won't be sitting together writing a book
but in a meadow eating grapes and reading our brilliant work.

Stacey

Our Child's Baptismal Day

God has answered and blessed us this day
By giving us a soul so tiny and frail.
A little soul to share our life, our love
A gift truly from God above.

The road's been along, with many tears
But God has helped us through the years
To prepare ourselves for that wonderful day
When at last, he would bless us this way.

Our family consist of many souls, to laugh with you and cry with you.
To experience God's universe with you
As he helps us on our own path too.
Our happiness we share with family and friends
as one, we celebrate your coming.
Welcome dear little one, this glorious day
God's light shines upon us today.

Our lives, our hearts, our souls we share
He has blessed us with your soul to care.

Welcome little one. May your life be happy and peaceful
God's light shine upon you, little one
And on all of us gathered here as one.

Regina Fullenkamp

All In Due Time

Not a day goes past
That I don't yearn
For your smile

Not an hour goes past
That I don't need to hear
Your gentle voice

Not a minute stretches beyond
That I don't long to
Stroke my hands through your hair

Not a second can be captured
That I don't long to be within
Your attention span.

Not a moment can be seized
That I don't want to be by your side,
To kiss, hold and submerge in your subliminal caresses.

All in due time
You will come to understand
This goes beyond lust or infatuation.
All in due time
You too will succumb to the pleasures of total submission!

Erika-Tammeiko L. Felix

"Me At Four Years Old"

I remember the days of years gone by
Looking out of a window pane at the snow
The glass so thin, the window so old
With traces of snow on the sides

A stew boiling on the old black stove
The aroma filled our three-room cove
The old stove crackling and the burning of wood
Meant love and warmth we all understood

My father smoking his old worn pipe
Mom ironing our clothes, oh so bright
My brothers reading books from their class
And me at four, making figures on the glass

That moment stood still, and still caresses my mind
I don't ever want to forget it, not ever for a time
The love of my parents, the contentment of love
Still cradles my mind with that peace, and with that love.

Anne Sicola

Never Remembered

Falling into an eternal sleep, forgetting those I left behind
As the forgotten souls weep, they sing a song of day come to mind
Hearing the pain, crying and suffering, wondering how long this
  will last
Climbing into a daze come from the past, walking through
  my mind's reality
Not sure what it might show, twisted, broken, heart divine
Blood red snow, grabbing, gasping for something that's not there
Repenting for your sins, drowning fast in your own despair
Follow me to your last breath, no one else can take you there
Falling fast can't you see, once you hit its your final plea
As you burn the last sheep down, you'll soon wear your God's crown
Give your soul up, don't ignore the calling
Watch out for all mankind is falling, the last day will soon be here
You'll no longer care, for we'll all be tortured
and never remembered, yelling, screaming in pain it will always
sustain and now I cry 'cause I know my destiny
Help me for I'm the prodigal son
I'm not lying, you'll soon see
I'm telling the truth, you'll never remember me
  Mike Tedore

Sparkling Dreams

Look at the stars up above you...
Sparkling down from the heavens so high.
Sometimes they're bold - brightly shining
And other times painfully shy.

Now look once more at their presence
They illuminate all of the earth.
And choose the most beautiful one
Could you place an amount on its worth?

Now suppose that each star is a dream,
Or a goal that you have in your life.
God's constant reminder to you
of hope's struggles, heartaches and strife.

You can see that your dreams will not fail you,
Though for some, you must put up a fight.
But the star that you keep your eyes turned to,
Always shines to be your guiding light.

So when looking at stars up above you,
When they're sparkling from Heaven so high,
Will your dream be bold - brightly shining?
Or just a dim light in the sky?
  Michelle Montgomery

Dance Black Woman Dance

Dance black woman dance
Move your body over and under
Move your body just like thunder
Dance black woman dance

Just as rain falls from the sky
Move your body as a bird flying high
Dance black woman dance

Just as emotions stem from nowhere
Create unknown movements to show how you care

Care about your struggles, care about your race
Care enough to not be ashamed or afraid
To show your face
Dance black woman dance

And when you're tired, seeking to dance no more
Pick yourself up black woman, no need to stay down
Your grace and your dignity are undeserving of a frown

Dance black woman dance and continue to dance more
Dance black woman dance, you now own the floor
  Emily D. Heard

The Lean Years Remembered

Mortgage due, no money to pay,
Jack at seventeen, decides to save the day.

Good President Roosevelt, had a plan,
To meet the needs of every needy young man.

Throughout the country, he set up camps,
The chance to work, made us feel like champs.

The pay per month in dollars was thirty,
For your keep and this, you didn't mind getting dirty.

Twenty five, monthly of this, was sent home to fill a need,
To survive at home, this was the seed.

The program set up, known as C.C.C. For Civilian Conservation Corp.,
Was the solution for many poor boys, and not a bore.

The camps were set up throughout the land,
From the East Coast of rock, to the West Coast of sand.

Some camps were set up for rodent control,
Jack Rabbits on ranch lands were taking their toll.

Their forestry work, including the planting of trees,
Improved our Park Systems, creating vast revenues in fees.

To those who berate President Roosevelt, don't do it to me,
My answer is, Thank God for Roosevelt and the C.C.C.
  Jack E. Rininger

A Miracle From God

It starts inside as a tiny seed
Planted by God for a mother to feed.
Unbelievable how fast it goes
Them growing inside of you - a feeling only a mother knows.
The moment they are born - nothing can compare
To that feeling that surrounds you - that tiny touch of care.
A little person - on you they will depend
Many scraped knees and broken hearts to mend.
How we wish they would stay small
But God has his plan for one and all.
Mistakes will be made and there are lessons to learn
Feelings of fear and great concern.
But the best feeling of all, has to be the pride
Your heart just fills ad she stands by your side.
Think back on that special day, squeeze her hand, give her a nod
Always remind her she is a gift of love, a miracle from God.
  Teresa Goad

Summer On Sanibel

She comes each afternoon it seems, long - nailed to scratch
the swollen maw - the gulf recoils, then heaves again,
  hot cannon cracks the lowering cloud. Gray - black
  she hovers in - between the periwinkle sky, the beryl - jade sea.
Florida in stasis, barometers whirl
and dumb struck tide concedes
gravity.

   Still, my hands furrow the sands of lighthouse park
   for moon shell and whelk and shards of shark jaw,
   taut shoulders blistered in olive tattoo...
   O needled palmetto, I will not move.

Wroth wind courses diamonds down spine, electricity strikes
  the tower.
   I claw, I claw, amid driftwood and vine,
     the combed shore grass hisses displeasure...
   all is maternal upheaval
     and knows
I seek ancient catastrophes
   unsung as my own.
  Ronan McNamara

Memo on the Studio of John F. Peto

These articles — the mundane things he depicts —accessories
of an ordered existence: boxes, bottles, letters and books,
the things he chose to paint with such apparent care,
patience and precision we use each day, as if intent
that these objects should always be there — these tokens

of a civilized life he showed in disarray, become
the substance we hold onto, these trifles we cherish so;
in one painting a magnifying glass enlarges the newsprint beneath,
symbols and events all together, as though a great hand
you couldn't see could always hold these things together

for us somehow, from the despairing chaos to follow,
that followed as in Dali's famous portrayal, for example, of watches
bent so out of shape in a frenzied world out of time,
and how he hurried, we are told, to get these objects down
before they got away from him; on this brief visit here,

in this fine old house he lived in, some presence
brushes by my shoulder with a chill, and stirs the objects
there at his workplace: a muted wail laying some anarchic
past claim here. "Take care, friend!" it declares — hold it close,
before it <u>all</u> flies away!"

C. Samsel

The Laughing Necklace

The lush meadow awaits,
Square of juicy green that awaits our trompings,
I am so young and tiny
While Dadda is so strong,
he's He-man.
I latch myself around his neck with my hands clasping behind,
My arms the strands of his necklace.
I laugh as he turns about and I jostle around in front of him.
Then I am broken jewelry, and collapse on the ground as my Dadda
looks on in surprise.
He tries to fasten me back on, but my arms are limp, and will not
clasp again.
I giggle at his confused attempts,
Until he carries me to the jeweler's in the center of the grass
and he becomes the jeweler,
tickling me to repair.
Then all is well, and his necklace is returned to its rightful place,
only to play its game again,
loving to create trouble for him,
the amazing Dadda.

Katie Morein

Withering

My flowers hang limply, I reach for the sun
I look for kindness, but find none
I remember a time, not so long ago.
When I was young and beautiful, how I miss that so.

Many people came to smile and look at me.
They would water me, and clip my flower gently,
They talked of my beauty, and cared for me in every way.
Oh how I do miss those days.

Now no one cares for me, or clips my flower anymore,
I guess my puny flowers aren't worth getting through the thorns.
I still smile at them though, as they pass on by,
Maybe they can't see me, the weeds are getting awfully high.

I can't get much water, the earth is brittle and dry,
I'm afraid that sometime soon I will whither and die.
But maybe someday I'll find kindness, instead of none,
And whenever I reach up, I'll be greeted by the sun.

Michelle Terry

"Adagio"

Once we were strangers
Standing on distant shores
Our souls dancing alone
To the rhythm of separate lives

Then we met
The counterpoint of our souls merged
Becoming a melodic interpolation of a new song
Our song

Our dance
Swaying gracefully together
Your essence flowed through the prism of my mind
Refracting the light of simultaneous creation

Too soon
The echoes of earlier phrases and fragments of life
Diffused the harmony of momentary convergence
Now we stand again on distant shores
Waiting for the prescient call
To once more dance amoroso the Adagio

Marlyn Evers

The End

As the fluid of darkness fills the skies
The people fill with fear
The pupils enlarge in the human's eyes
Knowing that death is near
As a burst of light fills the skies with fires
And as stated in Revelations chapter sixty-seven
They will be the false prophets and liars
The ones forbidden from heaven
This will be the final war
Between divine being of good and the archenemy of evil hell
Good will cast away evil like wind blowing sand away at the shore
And to be destroyed by purity like birds pecking at a shell
The true believers don't make it by their fates
But allowed by God who is generous and nice
He then will open up heaven's gates
And all followers of Christ will see this paradise
But what happened to the false prophets and followers of the fake
Their king the one that speaks lies and slivers
The ones that follow that dishonest snake
They will suffer eternally in fiery rivers

Aaron Tunstall

Cycle Of The Word

<u>Words:</u>
define, store, purchase, whore
    pittering drops of life's lore

<u>Silent Words:</u>
secret, stream, whisper, gleam
    seedlings spent on moonbeam

<u>Nurturing Words:</u>
petals, flow, earth, grow
    greening span of meadow

<u>Important Words:</u>
you, me, he, she,
    witlessly wooden diplomacy

<u>Grand Words:</u>
reality, democracy, currency, society
    temporal palace of the bee

<u>Angry Words:</u>
racial, mire, faggot, liar
    shadowed fuel of the fire

<u>Words:</u>
    pittering drops of life's lore

m. dhaemers

Drinking of Friendship

Let the wine of friendship never die.
Never drink the bottle dry.

Roll it on the tongue, take time to savor.
Each friend has his own sweet flavor.

Drink it slowly, it warms the heart.
It never is dry, it never is tart.

I'll love you, if you'll love me.
Together we'll drink throughout eternity.

Jackie Oldfield

Man On The Move?

What good is a man when you're trying to move?
Really, he's just in the way!
There's boxes and packing and sorting and planning
He can't hear a word I say!

I want our of here and to get into there,
I've a time frame set in my mind.
But he's on the phone or watching T.V.
Do I need to draw him a sign?

Will you help lift this, or please move that,
Now, where has that man gone?
I call "dear" and I mumble "where?"
Why he's taking a nap on the lawn!

No pots or pans, the dishes are packed,
And now he want's to eat!
He tries to dress and starts to yell
He can't find the shoes for his feet!

Where are the aspirins? His head hurts now.
And oh the ache in his back.
I took care of my pain now he's out of sight
In the back of the truck in a sack!

Donna Dalrymple Barton

Moonscreen

Swimming in a lake of silver
Getting out makes you shiver
No one knows what's leaving
Don't know what you had
Till it's all gone.
It flies from the sky onto our earth
Moonlight guiding its way
Sunflowers strung around the world
Suddenly broken apart
Stars are falling from the sky
As we sit looking through the window
Don't know what it means
The sun will be next
Going from one color to the next
It's always changing
Consuming your heart, it's always different
You say, you walk right back
Never saying goodbye.

Lauren McAlister

Protector's Death

Before the pending charge, implements of battle await their doom
Their silver radiance will be brutally taken away
Stolen from them by man's aggression
They cherish their possession to the final hour
As the combatants race towards battle,
Mud stains the armor, showing no mercy
The bearer is struck,
Blood rages like a crazed beast breaking from captivity
The once brilliant glow is now a distant memory.

G. S.

The Loser

Beads of sweat drip down my swollen face.
I debate on the card; hope it's an ace.
Next of course, I roll my lucky dice.
They land on two sixes; how very nice.
I order myself another drink.
A genius always needs time to think.
The hour has come to start a war.
I'm moving across the ruby red floor.
To my favorite table in the whole place.
I stare at the dealer; what a handsome face.
He throws down two cards and looks at me.
I raise my bet; let's see, let's see.
Then I lost.

Eva Smolenski

Talented Teacher Touches Many Lives

You were so kind to bring flowers to welcome me
on the first day of my teaching career.

So on the last day of your teaching career, I have
brought them to say goodbye.

Although it may seem like a day to close a chapter
in your life, this chapter will remain open forever.

You were so generous to share your talents with me. Now,
I will be one of the ones to carry on your legacy.

The talent of teaching that you shared with so many, will in
turn be passed on to others.

So, this chapter will always remain open.
You are just handing the pen to a different author.
And in this case, you have handed it to many different authors.

Michelle Schmitz

Little Joe

His eyes were like shiny, blue stars,
His hair uncurled like golden threads,
His teeth, white pearls without mar,
His smile, a sunbeam amid the dreads,
His features small but masculine built,
His courage, no enemies strength could wilt.
So full of life, so free from care,
No task or feat he left a dare.
But in this nation's greatest strife,
My brother lost his carefree life.
Now far off with the heroes he lies,
His memories lingering in my eyes.

Martha M. Petty

Fall

Did you see how the wind blew today,
the light and gentle breeze?
Slowly drifting over the grass,
mountains, lakes, and trees?

The leaves have now changed their coats
of the wondrous color green,
now are red, yellow, golden brown
or perhaps just in between.

The temperature is now dropping,
no more summer days,
warm winds turn to cool
a season changes ways.

Can't you sense it all?
I do, it's the first day of Fall!

Heather Christine Kaiser

Outdoor

Sitting outside,
Hearing so many different noises,
Birds chirping,
Pigs burping,
Most sounds are relaxing and nice,
I vaguely hear little kids playing with dice,
It is so quiet that I can hear the beautiful
sound of swaying trees,
looking at the fascinating blue sky,
which is definitely no lie.
Brr a breeze,
I'm starting to freeze,
A car drives by,
As a cat suddenly starts to cry,
Slowly starting to get dark,
A weird and comes, maybe a worried dog,
looking at all of the gorgeous flowers,
My eyes then spot this great tower,
So many things are running through my mind,
But the great outdoors is helping me unwind.

Kristen Lerch

"Love Equilibrium"

How do I love the one who has so much love already? Do I have the love to exhale without being left unloved? Where does all the love go in order to no longer have any love, is it stored for another or is it just used up? Love should be balanced where no one would be left loveless. If you are one who has too much love you will be crushed from stealing the love from another. Why is love so hard to control and balance? One who has very little love may still be searching for love. If one cannot intake love, they will never be in love. There is enough love for everyone, it is just a matter of knowing where to look for it.

Michael L. McCorkle

"Guilt"

I feel so bad.
I am guilty in a court of my mind.
I have no place to go... I have no hope.
My life is a mess and will remain one until I die.
Why do I feel so bad?
I hope and deny that things will be all right.
This guilt can put me to my death.

The winds howl, my lips are dry and tears are coming out
from my insides.
I can't escape this demon in my mind until I'm forgiven and forgiven

I walk along every minute in thought and I can not stop.
I can't stop thinking of my wrong and, how I can solve it and live on.
Must I tell the truth? Alas, I don't know the whole truth.
I cannot tell it if I do not know it myself.

I'd like to wither away and die like a fall flower.
But, that flower has life and will come back someday in other forms.
It spreads its seeds and will continue to live on. So...must I.

I must scatter my guilt and pain to live again.
I will wither from my guilt; but I will grow again someday.
I could be free......

Charity Claire Boilesen

Friends of Mine

I know so many people,
And they say they are friends of mine.
Then why when I'm with them do I feel so alone
I found out the hard way that they weren't friends at all.
There are only a few that are true friends
Of mine, and I won't let them down.
For the rest of them they will find, that I don't
Care no more, for they are no more friend of mine
The few that are my friends, they know who they
Are, for they are the ones who kept my hopes up
When I had no hope at all.
A true friend should stand by your side,
Even if it means to die.
Everyone who knows me knows I would die
for the ones I care about.
The ones who are my friends know who they are.
If you feel you have to ask don't bother
It might be you that isn't a friend at all.

Robert Brissette

An Ode To Nell

The hour is late the night is dark.
When through the blackness there's a pistol's bark.
A man in black races through hyde park.
Grabbing his shoulder where the ball had hit its mark.

In his hand he holds a purse,
And under his breath he murmurs a curse.
He had vowed that he'd never get caught.
Yet it seems he'd received his lot.

He should have listened when they'd say,
Never enough is a highwayman's pay,
For in the end, death is the price,
And never again can you pay it twice.

From his horse he falls to the ground,
Never again to hear a sound.
Truth comes with death, is what they say,
Revealing the secret he'd kept at bay.

Beneath that coat stained crimson now,
Lays a girl whose beauty's renown.
I tell the story, for I knew her well,
She was my sister, my sister Nell.

Ami Isabell

Poetry

Poetry is a way of life for me,
a way to release my inner tensions,
to relieve the unbearable faults in my life,
to make me feel at peace with myself.

And in times of distress, I'll relay to myself
the most pleasant thoughts of all,
I've found my inner talent,
and to poetry I'll give my all.

Words and thoughts come easily,
unlike many things that don't,
And thanks to my inspiration,
I won't lose my motivations.

Allison Bryan

Last Moment's Embrace

Time doth not exist between us
Memories and future are held at bay
Mist covers the mystic path we've crossed enough
Yesterday and tomorrow are what we speak today
Cherish the thought thru this mist we find our way
In and out each other's lives we must leave, can't win
Only to find we're back in each other's arms again
So many years, so many fears yet elated joy
Catching you on the path, a travelled time like the boy
I loved with this memory first began in the mist
A path that has us seize this moment, like our first kiss
We do not look back nor forward for us to view
What becomes of each stolen moment between us two
Time mists over us our last moments embrace
Shall we meet again, my lover's trail to your boyish face?
Christine Alison Bennett

The Color Of The Vowels

A is blue like the never-ending ocean's wave
smacking the shore on a sunny day or as the high-flying
sky with airplanes, and clouds rolling along in it.

E is green like the rows of the trees in the
jungles of Brazil or the grass of a football
field on which legends are made.

I is pink like the sun setting into the ocean to retire
or my sister's dress ironed and ready to be worn for church.

O is purple like the violets in my neighbor's
garden soaking up the sunlight or the dark
night sky against the moon and the stars.

U is gold like my long soft hair waving
in the wind or the color of the land when the
sun is just waking up to a new day.
David Adling

Opportunities

When you're older you are supposed to have things that you regret
But I am too young to have feelings like that yet
There's things you think you want that will do no harm
Yet if you think about it differently, those are the things that
cause the greatest alarm
You try to please everyone, no one likes rejection, but then you
  realize that what you are giving out is the cheapest form of affection
It hurts to be deprived and to be the one doing the taking, but if
  I don't stop now, pretty soon there will be nothing left, and it will
  be my heart that's breaking
Why these decisions matter, I really don't know, but the best choice
  now is to take every move slow
Michelle Ward Hansen

Humanity's Offspring

An eternity can be so long and lonely a thing
to endure all alone. But from loneliness grows strength
and character. Through this we become cold as ice and
hard as nails, we grow apathy for those of whom have hearts
filled with fear and full of ignorance. We become that of which we
fear and that of which we respect; a voracious monstrosity, perfect
and yet...imperfect. Humanity's offspring. Where rules do not apply
as they should or things that should matter to you actually hold very
little relevance...But love is paramount for from its promise of
fulfillment... we become human
Carlye White

Remains

Tangled in heartbeats, playing blind, we fused,
    amusing the gods with our small vapors,
        our mortal graspings;
    so little on our mind, so undivine,
        racing bent time
            and the quick clouds of May's sunspilt days,
        your smooth touch shading our small secret from their stare.

Still adrift in morning wet the waking heart
    brushes spent dreams from its lap,
        lost moments rushing off through windstirred grass and leaves—
    but not your face, your slipped embrace,
        your eyes, your soft surprise,
            the lingering warmness of your hands becalmed,
        your hushed word, your lasting grace.

For now, for just this little now,
our hearts know something that the gods do not
    in our parting:
        the exquisite unravelling,
            the poignant stab of the untied knot.
Francis Connolly-Weinert

Our World, Our Problem, Our Guilt

It's a world, lit up by night,
Found on each corner, yet another fight.
Us, tourists, think it's a great place,
But only because, to some, made invisible
    is its other face.
The streets seem full of beauty,
But in reality, every cop has to be on duty.
It's actually a spot of horror and fear,
Made true by lots of drugs and beer.
"Bang," another shooting, someone's dead,
The president, a child, maybe a fed!
Us, tourists, ask who made this mess,
Trying to lie, so we don't have to confess!
Why are we killing, this world that's
    made for us,
Without minds, evilness, and the
    start of every bus.
Jollen Wagner

Choices

Life is full of choices we must make
Some we do well with
Others, we cause our hearts to break

Invariably the time comes when we will say
If I had done it like this...
I wouldn't be here today

But here, today is where we are
And we must remember to file our mistakes away
In a tight-lidded jar

If the time comes to open the lid
May it be only to reflect, briefly...
Just long enough to prevent us from doing what we did

Let this advice guide us in our day-to-day grind
So we can enjoy our well-chosen choices
And leave the others behind
Rose Gagliotti

The Nightmare

The mad thoughts jumped at me
like an Olympic runner leaping over his hurdles.
No objections were raised as I
transgressed into the muddy waters
of criminal behavior.
Her life was taken by me in a
vengeful desperate manner, for
I had no recourse, I had lost my dignity.
Now the legal system began
to roll over me grinding me
down until my eyes popped out of my head.
I awoke as beads of sweat rolled over my anguished body.
I looked up through a hazy cloud of uncertainty, but could
only see her naked eyes staring at me.
   Melton J. Guth

I'll Dream Of You

I feel you pulling away,
Away from me, away from you.
It tears my heart to think
That all the love I felt wasn't true.
I'll dream of you.

Life is empty and void,
The world meaningless and cruel.
Like shadows in a darkened room,
I hide from myself, a fool.
I still dream of you.

My dreams taunt me uncaringly,
Flashes and glimpses of a love that was new.
My mind jerks my body awake;
In the stillness I close my eyes to pursue...
The dream I'll dream of you.
   Jeff Waibel

My Family

As I sit here in my twilite years
  I ponder if t'was worth the tears -
The Lord saw fit to take my mate
  While I just sit and wait and wait
  Five sons made up my family
Who then added more to the family tree -
  I try to keep them loving each other.
But than, as you know, I'm only their mother
  Very soon, I know, that I will go
To join my mate of long ago
And as each son goes, his own way in life
  I know that it was worth the strife
   Rose M. Grignon

Untitled

The shimmering colors of what is not real
Shatters the images of what I feel
The brightening of the darkness,
and the darkening of the day
What I shall never feel, will still be felt today
We live with the ever changing weather,
of what we will never know
I hope the glory of the day will never lose its glow
Wanting to feel and wanting to be
Wanting nothing more than wanting to see
Words can never be what a touch can give
Death will be not of those who will live
   Heather Bennett

But You Didn't Communicate

I must be naive to let you walk all over me,
  I've given you the contentment of
  knowing you are free;

But you didn't communicate or really even
  try; I promised myself no pain, over
  no one would I cry;

But you didn't communicate, just preserved
  the lie; I thought you'd realize my
  sensitivity as time passed by.

But you didn't communicate, you'd watch
  me cry; With no remorse you'd move
  on and give no reason why.

I'm wrapped around your finger and I really
  don't know why; Am I being a fool
  living on a high — thinking that soon
  you'll communicate.
   Angela Faye Runyon Novak

Heaven

A beautiful place where innocent souls rest
Upon fluffy clouds of ivory mist
Up against clear blue skies
Not a trace of sorrow within their eyes
Trees of jade and streams of crystal,
Silver stones so fun to throw
Graceful swans white as snow
Floral meadows to skip upon
Golden stairways to climb along
Each one wears a satin gown
And plays the harp, such a magical sound
With tiny halos glittering upon their heads,
Not one tear a soul has ever shed
For diamond stars twinkle in the night,
And a big pearl moon gives them light
To sing their songs of peace and joy,
And tell the living down below,
Things every soul needs to know
Their words are whispered on wings of doves,
And one need not worry, for Heaven is love.
   Dena Silverman

Salubrious

They all have their little tests for me
I've got my own;
  I'm busy with my own
Their lives have their own turns, travelling away from me
They found something of interest to me
I recall it was the first glimpse of the future
I could hold it; I could suspend time in my mind
They all have opinions about it, I wish I could share mine
They said it so easily;
  that I'd guessed at something like that and I remained ...theirs
So what is it then?
I know something's going on
When I first suspected, they tried to destroy me
They had time to make me cheap
They had time not to understand, my problems so heavily within me
Thank God I am the way I am
Thank God you weren't there
Had you been, I would have killed you
Now that it's over they only wanted one thing
Thank God you weren't there
   Annielle Montjar

Credence

As the pyramid is burning,
Still remains the utter confidence
Of its wisdom

Surviving even death,
Through the purge of ages

Tempering rough edges of reality
With soothing, enduring, Time

Lucent threads of wisdom are bound,
Like figures entwined as One, woven into
Perplexing love

Ashes adrift on the solar wind.
  Lavonne Michaeli

"Missing You"

My mother and father broke up
my father moved out
I'm still just a little boy
what's this thing all about

I love my mommy and daddy
we should all be together
will my life be ruined for good
or is there still stormy weather

They taught me to love the family
never mind the bid
not they are doing the opposite
I'm confused right now, being and kid

Well parents knows best
like the winter knows chilly
I sometimes stop and wonder
Do parents know really

I'm a small fish, in a big pond
way out of my range I know parents adults
are unpredictably strange

But I love them!!!
  The Davis Boys

Night Air

As Night Air whirls around my room
  Goose bumps began frantically spreading about
    my neck in a most tantalizing way.

As the Night Air gets cooler and cooler yet
  the chills began running a race
    fearlessly through my deepening blue body.

As the Night Air starts to fall below freezing
  the once warm blood of a strong beating heart
    turns to slow moving chunks of ice within
      the frozen heart of mind.

As the Night Air began to get crisper and turn for the worse,
  the once light breaths became very heavy thick white clouds
    of smoke freezing my lungs at first then everything
      in sight of my eyes and soul.
  Ruben Z. Dominguez

Untitled

Red is the rose in springtime
  Delicate are its velvet petals
    that glow in morning light
Magical are its green sharp thorns
  Weaving tales of adventure and sorrow
    going into the ground in winter
To burrow and nestle the lonely soil
  Katie Adams-Besangon

Armageddon

Look at what you have done
The spell you unleashed can not be undone
The four horsemen have been released
Riding upon their savage beasts
Destroying all people from sweet to fool
Time began the destruction of the souls
filling them with age and envy of the younger
Pestilence only fed the hunger
Giving the soul the deadly anger
Famine destroyed any remaining hope and compassion
Death reaped the souls in a harsh fashion
The souls were sent to their final judgement
Some were sent away with resentment
While others were accepted into heaven
Where their sins were forgiven
Where would you go?
Only God shall know
  Jeffrey Esposito

This Rosy Youth

"Ah to be young," they cry, and yet
  There are some things the wise forget
The things that make the young grow old,
  That make the heat of youth grow cold.

It's true, young hearts are gay and free,
  Young backs are strong, young eyes can see
Beyond the clouds a rosy glow
  Youth loves hard, lives fast, yearns to grow.

A rose that's full is best to view;
  It uses well the early dew,
But innocent, and open wide,
  'Tis vulnerable, whate'er betide.

And yet it's better that it grows
  From seed, to bud, then to the rose
Lives fully, for when summer's gone
  That full-blown fragrance lingers on.

Perhaps the bloom is saved, and pressed,
  And they will say, "See, youth was best!"
And youth replies, "Agreed!" but knows
  A thorny stem supports each rose.
  Martha S. Kearney

Timber Days

Mother, chose where we were to live.
It was the love of our life.
Walking distance to our elementary school,
A gently flowing creek nearby to swim in,
and paddle our canoe.

Helping Mother, with chores, so we could all plan
and plant our summer garden.
The beautiful colors of the tall larkspur,
and Delphinium in the back ground,
Blending with Daffodils, tulips and narcissus,
also many other sweet flowers.
The soft gentle breezes, were a joy to beheld.

The younger sister decided it was time with
our baskets to pick from the fields luscious
strawberries and pretty white daises, to prepare
for our evening meal.
The dainty bouquet of daisies made a lovely display for our
dinner arrangement.
Dad, with his baton would then lead the evening Song.
"Happy Days are here again."
  Jane Blackburne Cox

Cries Of Night

When I hear the cries of night,
all the little cries from babies,
all I hear are cries from sad people.
Cries from babies,
cries from children,
cries from adults,
cries from China,
cries from Cuba,
cries from Mexico,
cries from United States.

These cries all over the world,
people from different places.

Every time you look out from a window,
you will heard a different cry each night.

Amber Thorning

In Daze of Old

Sometimes i wish I could have been born
Eighty years ago...
When life was so much easier and it seems
there was so much less to know.

When people took pride in things they had done
and the wisdom they had received,
from a god who was so ever present to men,
fore-fathers to societies bereaved.

A day when a man's word was his bond
it seems has long since past,
a plain white casket,
an unmarked grave,
one word 'dignity' the epitaph.

Strive for individuality
to batter down the loneliness...
Make the race technology
and hurdles of human ignorance...
Search for understanding.

Steven Trinca

Sunset

I watched the sun sink down below the horizon
An orange ball of flame
Filled with a magnetic radiance
Drawing all the troubles of the world to it
And lessening their pain
The symbol of life, closing another chapter
In that too short period of time
Before that date
When our troubles are forgotten forever
And our tired bodies sink into that final sleep
That is our fate

Robert Northrup

Dark Glasses

Dark glasses are the finest masquerade.
They keep my mood in safe eclipse from eyes
Too quick to sense the grief behind their shade.
With them in place I have a sure disguise.
Dark glasses hide the tears that do not halt
Although the usual mourning time has passed.
Unbidden, welling up, I taste their salt
And swallow hard, and blurt some jest too fast;
I pause to paint again the too-red lips
And smiling greet friends on the promenade.
Dark glasses keep my grief in safe eclipse—
Dark glasses are the finest masquerade.

Hazel Mori

Freedom?

Without any representation Taxes were set
By greedy kings across the sea.
The Colonists, working the land, were bled
With high Taxes. But now in order to be free
They knew blood had to be shed.

After years of oppression there came the day
The Colonists had it up to here.
In December, seventeen-seventy-three was the year
When disguised as Indians they stormed Boston Pier
And dumped Tea from China into the Bay.

At Valley Forge the nights were cold
When Washington and his men camped there.
In trying to free the country from England's hold
And to make living for everyone fair,
They braved the cold and despair.

After years of war the land was free
Of England. But would the Victors with George
Freeze their buns at Valley Forge
Had they known beforehand of the Taxation
We now have, but with mis-representation?

Irmgard Mokos

What Will You Do Today?

I watch you sleeping in your crib,
Your hair tossed all over your head.
I wonder what you'll do today;
When you awake, what will you play?

Will you play with you Teddy Bear and squeeze him so tight?
Will you hug him close to you with all of your might?
Will you play with your elephant, doggie and bunny . . .
Squealing with glee 'cause you think they look funny?

Will you play with your telephone, ring one number after another,
Who will you call? — Perhaps your Grandmother.
Will you say "Hello" then chatter away . . .
Telling Mom-mom what you'll do today?

Will you play with your ball — roll it on the floor . . .
Then crawl after it and roll it some more?
Will you look at your picture books with colors so gay?
I will play toys with you and we will have fun today.

For now I watch you sleeping in your crib,
Your hair tossed all over your head.
Your room is filled with sunshine — what a lovely day!
Wake up Baby Gennie, let's go and play.

Bonnie Lynn Fletcher

The Pale Horse

Death has arrived before me,
Riding upon his pale horse.
Laughing with an evil tinge,
He gently grasps my body;
Seizing my soul tenderly.

As my essence fades away,
The light and flame summon me.
Both tempting and full of lust.
My mind becomes a whirlwind,
Faced with good and evil thoughts.

Choice is an everlasting burden,
Both overwhelming and succumbing.
If the wrong decision is chosen,
Eternal punishment shall become my fate.
If right, a heavenly light shall flow downward.

As the wick, which is my life, shortens,
The flame in my heart burns out slowly.
Soon the path for my afterlife shall be paved,
And endless doom or timeless bliss shall come forth.

Cheryl Dotterer

Who?

Who is that girl?
That beautiful girl, the one that I'm staring at.
With beautiful hair that shouldn't be covered with a hat.
Whose body is slender and fair.

I'm lost in her eyes, in that deep, dark depth.
In which I see beauty, color, and emotion.
That beautiful face, which I can not resist.
Those irresistible lips, which I simply must kiss,
must be so very soft to the touch.

And as some people say, who is that girl? Who?
And I proudly say, my girlfriend, You.
Dane Chapman

The Gift Of Love

I know that love is not so simple, though we all wish
it could be. It is not your gifts that will be
remember, but the giving of yourself to me.

Will you laugh while I'm laughing and weep to see me morn?
Will you love me while I'm youthful and when I'm older love me more?
And will you calm me with your soothing eyes - although
your heart is torn?

Will you hold me in the darkness with a passion filled with love?
And will you hold me in that darkness when fate calls me up above?

I know that love should last through laughter and even
stronger through the tears - it should not come with
just one day, but love should last throughout the years.
Jivonne N. Prioleau-Green

Forever More

Imagine the wind blowing through your hair;
The sweet smell of a hot mint tea in the air.
Imagine the children laughing loud.
Feel a cool drop of rain from the faucet of a cloud.
See up in the trees
A web of cotton a spider weaves.
Hear the whisper of the dancing leaves.
Now imagine this:
You and me standing in this bliss.
The warm loving feeling that you bring
Gives my soul powerful wings.
High above the sky it soars.
Imagine this forever more.
Jennifer Tennille Michael

Little Children

Little children, laughing in the distance,
Little children, why don't they listen?
They don't understand, so they don't bother;
all they do is scream and holler.

They dream away their fiends, as they scheme,
On how to get the cookies out of the jar,
and cry about their daddy, locked behind bars;
On that dreary, gloomy day.

The mother tells them "hush", and gives them a toy bus,
for they must get away, to the bay,
with what they can handle once again,
before her husband gets out of the pen.
Rhonda DeLuney

Little Hands

Little hands so warm and trusting.
Little hands that grasp me with love.
I have such a responsibility
to those little hands.

Little hands outstretched,
show love, trust and delight.
Little hands withdrawn
mean rejection, hurt, and sadness.

Oh! For the joy to grasp
that dear, warm little hand.
It pulls my heart strings
and causes my tears to flow.

The little hands are grasping in trust
for protection, security, and love.
And are looking to me for guidance.

Dear Lord help me not forsake that trust
or lead them astray, or cause them to withdraw.
Please Lord, help me to be all that they see in me.

And thank you Dear Lord,
for those little hands.
Karen Joan Hoover

Death Of An Age

Our age is dying,
But our age is not old.
Our generation is falling,
While most others are rising.
We are intense and disturbed to the onlooking eye.
But we are cool and collected to an insider.
Young society has no supports,
But it won't collapse
We are not structure,
But we have strengths and weaknesses.
We are the future,
But we are not near the present.
Jennifer Cocanougher

The Truth

Horror stricken was her face,
and blood stained was the lace.
Frantically, all she did was cry.
Mumbling continuously the word, "why?"
Nothing that he said would give her peace,
her body he would not release.

She looked up at him with hurtful eyes,
and finally he regretted all the lies.
At last he whispered what was true,
"I love you."
And to his amazement she ceased to weep,
and in his arms she fell asleep.
Maria Sandell

Roses

Ruby Roses, ruby roses
Your velvet touch reigns
Throughout the midnight hours
Your elegant scent is inspiration for lovers
Longing for hopeless romantics
And fantasies come true for dreamers.
You may be plucked
Many times over
And yet your fire lives on,
Flowing through our own veins
Is the passion that drives you and
us to greatness.
Jessica Dishong

One Of Those People

Sometimes people come into your life
And they bring you feelings of joy and happiness.
Are you one of those people?
Sometimes people leave your life
And they leave with you feelings of loneliness and sadness.
Are you one of those people?
Of course there are people who come and leave your life
Without bringing or leaving you with anything.
Is it possible you could be
One of those people?

I believe you to be one of those people,
Yet, which one of those people are you?
The answer to this, you see, is quite simple for me.

You are one of those people
Who brought so much joy and happiness into my life
Yet I know when you leave, you'll be one of those people
Who will leave me feeling lonely, sad and blue.

However, it's nice to know, for you and me,
That you're not one of those people
Who came and left me with nothing at all.

Samantha Brewer

Jewels

Children are jewels; pure.
Sparkles, which no gems, or crystals compare.
They radiate True Love, the cure,
for mankind to see, and become aware.
To return that love, as it's given,
reflect the clarity, and brilliant light,
erase wrong for right.
Begin to live as they do.
See the chance begin, in me and you.
Dismiss colors, race and creed.
Build a new world, that we need.
Remove the barriers, to achieve brotherhood.
Make this a must, as we should.
Children know nothing worldly; when born.
What they learn, is what we teach.
Let's not keep man divided, and torn.
Universal Love, is not impossible to reach.
We need no more of man's duels.
Like children, we can all become "Jewels".

Ernest D. Carter

Time For The Power Within You

Come loose:
Pick-up the power within you.
Don't remain a closet poet:
Years of wasted time and sweat;
Mocking your creator.
Poems were made to savor
The greatest in you
While satisfying the reader,
Browsing them, too. Poet, poet,
Challenges thrust you, you bet,
More the capable. Shake loose the nable:
Flaunt books and tapes; Albums and plaques to thrust
Your wings into rainbow shapes.
Flowing - just glowing lines of Melody,
Drumming up my ears with sounds - so timely
Poet, you are though God is the giver
Playing you as a star to hand them full potential.
Just look at you, you are essential.
Come loose: What the use?
Just pick up the power within you.

Louise Brady

Trust

I trusted them and loved them so,
Kept their secrets so no one would know.
I was their confidant, their sounding board.
Yet they want me in a Nursing Home today Lord.
I'm not feeble, my back is straight,
I still get around with a slow shuffling gait.
My body still functions and I'm proud on my own,
But today my children say I can't stay alone.
Don't let them do this Lord, I'll be all right.
I can still enjoy my programs with my fading eyesight.
Don't let them take out my money and cash.
Don't let them put all my stuff in the trash.
I may be 80, but I'm still on my own.
I love my home and my telephone.
How could they trick me to sign unknown,
all that is mine to be carted away.
My kids are putting me in a Nursing Home today.

Norma Burnham

Clueless

Her skin was cold to the touch
but she was warm inside
they took her for someone she wasn't
all she could do was hide
in a field of dreams she thought everyday
wishing there was a place like that
and for eternity she'd stay
to others her dreams made no sense
so they became lost in the restless blue sea
she just figured that was how life was suppose to be
where nobody could understand
where everyone was clueless in some
giant land.

Sarah Brennan

A Cookie's View

I have fallen into a pit of dark salivation.
I feel so used.
When life began, the perfect mixture came
    together, forming a perfect creation.
A touch of extract, a pinch of salt, a pile of
    flour and butter, etc...me,
    so I thought.
What ultimate corrupt deception!
When the chips were down, spread across the
    counter tops, I SAW THE TRUTH!
All my ingredients were purchased from the H.E.B. Generic aisle!
I was, and am, a cheap tool for human use.
Without even considering my feelings,
    they swallowed my pride.
    I didn't have to,
(But who cares.)
I came out again later.

Christina R. Plahetka

Live Without Regret

The wind blowing through your hair
The bees humming
The birds singing
Perfect peace
If you let the sequoia grow and the animals dwell
You will let all nature grow eternity but
If you destroy nature you will regret what you have done because
No longer will you be able to walk through the forest
With the music of the birds of the wind through the leaves
Or the wind through your hair
No longer will there be peace only noise mad people running
Around trying to get things done.

Maegann April Reed

Your Hair Ain't Nappy For Nothing

A dying species is what he is called by some
The descendent of nobles, he was forced to run
He had pride and dignity, he knew no shame
A fierce man, yet known to be mild and tame
Stripped of heritage abuse broke his spirit
This once proud man, now a source to be pitied

Drugs and its violence is claiming him today
He is ashamed to say "help me; show me the way"
His self respect is gone, a quality that is lacking
The young ones need morals and guidance for backing
The gift of education was not given freely
To ignore its benefits, the future suffers clearly

Power dominates those who can neither read nor write
Suppressed people left ignorant, lose the will to fight
Stand and feel worthy, for you have nothing to hide
There is no shame to be "Black", say it with pride
Give respect to the women who have borne your pain
Take responsibility for choices and find self respect is gained

You are men;...a gender determined by your birth
The love of self and others is how you prove your worth
   Minnie R. Owens

Future Plan

I have only one dream that leads me to my future job,
Join the military, earn money and give my parents love
It's the only job I can think of,
To pay them both for the support and love.
I hope I will pass my military test,
It's the only job I love the best.
Just when I enter the military,
I'll just turn around and surprise you mommy and daddy.
I close my eyes and open again,
Dreaming about military servers good men.
I haven't figured out when to finish my career,
Hey, who knows what's coming near.
Now I'm off with my dream,
I hope everything I've dreamed of, is what military means.
   Violet Effie Eseroma

The Dancing Leaves

The dancing leaves how high do they go?
When you hear the wind blow
They swirl here and there
Flying to the ground everywhere

The grass waves them along
They don't need music or a song
The flowers nod their heads now and then
When the wind stops blowing
All this fascinating motion will end
   Vivian A. Acker

Thunderstorms

Thunderstorms are a collection of feelings,
Tears, and a collection of memories.
Feelings are represented by the thunder,
They all come back at once with a "Boom!"
Tears are represented by the raindrops,
Once they start they don't stop until it's all over.
Memories are represented by the lightning,
As long as you have feelings and tears,
You'll have memories to go with them -
And as long as there is thunder and rain,
There will be lightning to go with it.
You can't stop feelings; tears, and memories
At all from reappearing in your life.
   Tracie Scott

Untitled

In my dream I hear you calling
We go down by the river
into the night
Around the edges of your voice
I hear your pain

The moon, hanging just above the trees,
almost within reach
drops its light upon your face
You let me glimpse
the shadows of your soul

We sit on a hollow log
my hand reaches out to you
We speak softly-
our words, like ghostly moths
drift up into the leaves.

The quiet scent of the night air
surrounds and protects us
Together, as one, we walk on,
listening to the river
whisper to itself.
   Rosemary Schoene-Harshbarger

Memories

Like ripples on a quiet sea
Thoughts of long ago come back to me.
Days from my childhood years.
Times of happiness and a few tears.

Sometimes when I day dream
I can see Mother and Dad
They sunny days
And the fun we had.

They will stay with me a long time,
Sometimes bring tears to these eyes of mine
I will always treasures those days
And sometimes wish for one more.

But time can't turn back
And memories live on.
So great to have
In this heart of mine.
   Ora W. Griffin

Summer Sampler

For a Sunday stroll, please accompany me -
   Allow your spirit to be free.
Tranquil trails temptingly beckon
   Extending enticin' timeless welcome.
A summer breeze accompanies the stroll,
   Caressing body, comforting soul.
We join God's creatures, large and small,
   In celebration of life for all!
Smell the wild roses of delicate pink
   As we walk along and think?
Come, sit on a log beside the stream -
   Listen to the songbird and dream.
And feast upon bountiful blackberries sweet,
   Nature's tantalizingly tasty treat!
This delightful day we create and store
   Summer memories to later explore.
Marvelous memories for later recall
   As we watch whimsical winter snow fall.
   Dorothy A. Wallace

Rage

And the rain that washes over my body
as I lay naked in the mud
feels like the embrace of a demon.
The lightning that rips open the sky
looks like pain from many broken hearts
And the thunder sounds like it is trying to remember
something long ago lost in nightmare.
The wind howls like a woman in bed,
the orgasm making her body shudder.
And I lay here dying,
In a pool of hot blood
And the devil mourns for me
As do the black clouds of death above.

Sarah Bannister

Escape

A lifetime has gone by, in dread and fear
Amidst a host of painful memories here
Let's away from this valley of the shadow of death
Ere darkness close my eyes, and holds my breath

Away, away from these sights and sounds
Where the scepter of Death stalks, and fear surrounds
Where the shades of the past, stand and leer
Where the chords of sounds are silent in fear

The mirrors have cracked in shock and horror
At the sight of those faceless images there
The eyes have turned to stone ages ago
Watching the dance of Life and Death in sorrow.

Why should I stand and watch the emptiness around
The reflections and illusions that sometimes about
And sometimes in total darkness disappear
The host of painful memories which continue to hound

Come, let us take leave of these scents and smells
A lifetime have I spent in these valleys and dells
Come, let us go far, far away from here
Where the lands is bright, and the sky is clear

Zahida Asghar

A Day

It was dark, complete darkness
All was still, quiet, and no one existed
Then venus became visible in the eastern sky
As the baby cried for the first time

The sky became clear, bright and blue
As the child played happily
Later, the sun moved to the zenith position
As the man danced about

Then from the lower western sky the reddish sun
peeped to the east
just as the old man was being eulogized

Tomas Franklin Moore

There Is No Change In Love

Everything changes;
people change, things change, situations change,
dreams change, feelings change, seasons change,
relationships change.
The one thing that doesn't change is love;
it never fails, love is the heart of caring, the
heart of sharing, the heart of understanding, the
heart of everything we do and say.
It is the most important thing in
this world. We desire it, we need it, we
require it, and most importantly, we deserve it.

Kristina M. Meldrum

"Field Of View"

They parlance I have a strong way of thinking.
I always considered myself kind of weak.
I'm my own best friend I found out,
through life as the memories I seek.
You got to think strong to be strong,
And make your self adjust and belong.
I'm hankering to let my guns down and just cry.
Knowing I can only make myself get by.
With high affluence that nothing will go wrong.
Abandoning my soul to the only town I'll ever belong.
I raise my glass to my confidants
whom I am honored to know.
And disconnect my heart to the guy who
stole it from me long ago!

Maria M. Interrante

A Familiar Stranger

I was instantly drawn to his loping gait
which to me is a most endearing trait.
He was a curious figure, who on account to fate,
wandered into my life, one August date.

As he swaggered by with appreciable grace,
I caught a glimpse of his handsome face.
He looked young but wise and vulnerable yet strong
as he crunched his face in the morning sun.

Although he dressed in suit and tie,
he resembled a cowboy as he ambled by.
So I dared to linger just a little while
as would an eager and zealous child.

Ultimately, I would meet "my stranger" Ray
For Liz, my good friend, became his colleague that day.
He is animated, entertaining, and at times even wild,
and adorably resembles a mischievous child.

I had so many feelings buried deep inside of me,
such as fears and past hurts, which he has helped me to see.
I now feel so wonderfully soothed talking so openly and free
and I am grateful to Ray for he let's me truly be me.

Katherine Hochberg

An Ocean Apart

Rambling tide softly lay,
    Wash me to the scenic bay.
Float me to a hidden port,
    Where all of my fears I shall abort.
Take me out to sea again,
    Where the cycles of life anew begin.
Anchor me to a sturdy rock,
    Where birds up above circle in flock.
Render me to freely flow,
    The way the exotic breeze blow.
Though storm clouds may gather up above,
    Secure me with your constant love.
When the time cometh to say goodbye,
    Do not let me see you cry.
Do not even shed a tear,
    For death is not a time to fear.
On that sad and dismal day,
    Kindly let me sink away.
For all is well as my soul breaks free,
    Forever able to roam the sea.

Andrew Thomas Fetcho

Grandpa, We Love You

We are filled with deep regret,
The day, the month, we will never forget.

With aching hearts and tears unseen,
We wish your absence was but a dream.

Facing life without you is very hard to bear,
Losing you the way we did seems so unfair.

Your passing was so sudden, we often ask why,
The hardest part of all is that we never said, "Good-bye."

Time will never heal our wounds, our grief,
Our love for you is much too deep.

Today, tomorrow, our whole life through,
We will always love and remember you.

Chad Lee Daly

I Loved You When

I loved you when you held my hand,
When you lifted my hopes when they could not stand

I loved you when you gazed into my eyes,
When you said, "Everything will be alright"

I loved you then but it's not over yet,
I love you now, please don't forget

You were there for me, now I'm here for you,
You've made all my dreams come true.

I love you.

Brandy Lowery

"Merry Christmas"

All is covered with snow of white,
For it is that special night.
The cookies and milk are by the tree,
I hear bells, Can it be!
The man in red, with a white beard,
Came down the chimney and suddenly appeared.
His bag was full of wonderful toys,
For all the special girls and boys.
What magic and special cheer,
This great man brings from year to year.
There is only one, who deserves applause,
It's the great Santa Clause!

Teresa Cope

Paradox

I was never a soldier!
Even when I wore a uniform, I was never a soldier.
Parades, passing in review,
Damn lot of nonsense for adult adolescents!

Still . . . when the war drums sound.
My heart flutters, the pulse quickens, the adrenaline flows
and somewhere in my being a dark need burns.
Some part of me aches for . . . what?

They tell you that anyone can fight and win!
Truth is, only the skillful and lucky survive.
I'm not trained in combat, I'd quickly die.
My body is too soft.

This is foolish!
Humankind is outgrowing war,
And besides only a fool wants to fight.
Right?

But still I wonder,
Is the softness of my body
My mind's attempt to control
A need which cannot be reasoned with?

Raymond L. Burgess

I Remember

I remember way back when things were so simple.
We always had things to see and places to go.
But that all seems so long ago.
Please tell me it isn't so.
Cause now you never seem to have the time for me.
I just can't believe this has to be.
All the plans we used to make.
What the heck happened for goodness sake.
　Your friends are always there when you're
Out to have some fun.
But when it comes to being serious, you really
Can't find anyone.
I remember how it used to be, when you always
Found time for me.
But now all I ever hear is we'll see, we'll see,
We'll see.

Lisa Rivera

Different Shades Of Gray

Do you wander through this life as I do
only seeing black and white
with your eyes closed most of the time
ignoring the violence,
turning your back on the death,
never seeing the shades of gray that make this world what it is
never experiencing laughter, pain, sorrow, or happiness
forever following the path of black or white
do you do this as I do

Bobbie Williamson

The Fratillary Butterfly

I caught a trophy butterfly
She took my breath away.
With glistening silver markings set
She sparkled in her bright array.

I grasped her gently by a wing
With love I held her fast,
Then locked her in a Mason Jar
My treasure surely mine at last.

But through the night I heard her plead,
As she beat wings against the side.
When morning came I let her go,
For she would surely soon have died.

She fluttered up into the air
A helpless struggle I could see.
She'd left too many silver feathers
In the lonely jar with me.

P. Thomas Manchester

Wouldn't It Be Great If...

There was no violence all around
And peace on earth was surely found.
If there were no such things as drugs, guns, or knives,
and the world wasn't full of harsh, bitter lies.
If we didn't have to have alarms on our cars,
or on our windows, the bars.
If when we turned on the news there weren't killings or abuses,
But seems that the kindness the whole world refuses.
I ask myself "Is this the way it was meant to be,
Did God intend for us to be enemies?"
Then to myself, I answer my question,
God did not intend for us this repression.
So in our hearts, let's light a flame,
that builds a spark for peace in his name!

Tiffany Newsom

Tears Are Like Rain

Tears are like rain,
They flow down when you are in pain.
Glittering in the shine of light,
They fall freely at night.
They don't show often for me.
I must be in pain you can really see.
I don't like tears.
They show your weakness and your fears.
Tears are an expression of a broken heart.
You see them when your world falls apart.
A drop of water down your cheek,
Shown when harsh words doth speak.
Tears of joy sometimes there,
When someone is fact does care.
But many tears that follow
Are wasted on those too hollow
To understand the pain,
That cause the tears to fall like rain.

Belen Romero

Dear Ma's Pride

Mama declared she'd drive that beast,
   When it chugged up the lane from out of the east.
Across the barnyard it charged with a snort,
   They called it a "T" model just for short.

Pa set the throttle and adjusted the spark,
   We kids climbed aboard like Noah's Ark.
Behind the wheel she was so con-fi-dent,
   Pa spun the crank and away we all went.

It shimmied and shook and boy it did rattle,
   Spooked the horse and stampeded the cattle.
Pa jumped aside and lost his hat,
   Chickens and geese went this way and that.

Ma aimed it for the wide open gate,
   But her turn of the wheel was a bit too late.
We kids were laughing and shouting with glee,
   'Til we were stopped cold by a big oak tree.

The men folk chuckled and began to tease,
   We 'younguns' crawled out all weak in the knees.
But when the dust settled and the engine died,
   Nothin' was hurt but dear Ma's pride.

Robert L. Anderson

Night

Drop your heavy breathing,
time for heavy sleeping,
time to keep on going,
not knowing, knowing, knowing.

Here you are in transit,
locked away tight,
kept closed with something called night.

Dream as you lay helpless in bed,
the world spins without you,
not a single thought in your head.

Think of the days that have passed,
and to come.
Wishing, wishing on a single star

Till your thoughts are interrupted,
you get a terrible chill.
As you listen outside your window and lay still.

A movement from above,
and a sound from below,
a moan from you as you wonder what to do.

Lie still in bed, until night has passed over,
and the dark angel will be with you when day is over.

Nicole Satkofsky

The Whispering Of The Wind

Swushh, the sound is making, as it gently flows on by
Sshhh, rattle the leaves of trees, while they tower in the sky

The flowers, they begin to shake
The grass gives a gentle bend

A mystery of the ages
The whispering of wind

The birds restart their calling, as they fly from here to there
When suddenly from no where, there's magic in the air

The cat, he stops his prowling
The squirrel stands on his limb

Our mystery's returning
The whispering of the wind

A man leans on his fence post, as the sweat runs down his brow
He's waiting for a miracle, relief hat must come now

The children hear it coming
This time it's a God send

A mystery, a miracle
The whispering of the wind

Randy McDonald

Untitled

You've loved, you've laughed, you've
shed some tears, you've stayed together
throughout 60 years.

You've raised 3 children, who
now have kids of their own, but
your love is strong, and you
know you'll never be alone.

You've stuck together through thick
and thin, if there was a contest
for love, you'd surely win.

You live in the hands of the Lord above.
There is something stronger
than the ocean; your love.

We've all got together, to celebrate this
day, the 60th anniversary of Bea and Ray.

There's no more gush and no more
goo, we're just here to say that we love you.

Bernice Grish

Thank You

Oh! What is this I see? A letter of reply?
Could it be a reminder to me,
that my mom is so special, one I can depend on,
when it would seem that there is no one.
She is always there for any favor,
a good listener, when arcs pull me down.
She is always there for good positive advice,
night or day, she brightens my hopes.
She would never ignore me or my dreams,
or shame them to the ground.
She chooses to struggle with me and my troubles,
instead of moving on.
She is proudly supportive of my talents
I have personally focused to improve.
She never laughs at the wrong moments
yet she happily smiles at the correct ones.
I don't expect her to be proud of what I have
put her through in return.
I'm just happy she's my mom
and that's a candle which will always burn, I love you mom.

Jame Earl Dunham

The Mallard Duck

The weeds rustle as the Mallard glides by
A bird sings to her mate for
The crisp air means
She must leave her nest and join the leaving flock
The alarmed Mallard cocks his head
He too must soon leave for winter is soon to come
The golden pond flows so nicely and yet is still calm
Though he dreaded leaving this beautiful place
He had to
This was the seventh sunset since summer had ended
If he didn't leave now he would never see this place again
The Mallard gazed around
Then quicker than a blink he disappeared into the evening sky.
Carrie Ferguson

Real Life, Not A Dream

The pain, the suffering, the heartaches,
All the wrong decisions, all the wrong mistakes.
Our carelessness, our jealousy,
Have chosen and given us heartbreaks.

The crimes, the lies, the scandals,
The changes in our souls.
We make a choice without thinking,
We have all taken our tolls.

The paybacks, drawbacks, and setbacks,
The reasons for finding out the facts,
Have told us the truth DOES hurt,
It's left us in its dust, it's left us in the dirt.

But sooner or later, we get on with our lives.
We forget about our pains, we forget about our dives.
Being left alone is the worst possible feeling.
We want a "near" perfect life,
And not get stuck with just dreaming.
Angie Coughlan

"We Made Each Other Strong"

My friend, I don't wish for you to go,
But life will not wait for us, I know
Don't look back and see the tears streaking down my face,
In my heart you'll never be replaced.
Hold tight to today and it will be take you to tomorrow.
Hold your head high and you will see that the sorrow,
will soon fade with a dream that yet is borrowed
We're going to be the best of all, just you wait and see.
Take me with you when you go.
I'll stay forever in your heart.
That way we can always say, "we were never apart.
You're just a part of me, I can't let go
Thank God you're a friend I'll always know
So thank you for growing up with me my friend.
   "We made each other strong."
Starla Rosenberg

Strength Is What I See

Looking into the faces that tell the story
Of a past of strength, and hope, and glory,
Feeling the smiles and wisdom filled eyes
Leaving an impression that never dies.

This is what I see now and have always known
My respect for them has forever grown.
Looking at their lives, strength is what I see
Of people who have always been a part of me.

Love, pride, and admiration...that is what I feel
For people whose influence is so living and real.
There are special strength-filled people that everyone knows.
For me, they're my grandparents, Carmel, Tony, Fred, and Rose.
Elizabeth Mongillo

The Powers

When I was born, I was born with special powers,
the power of imagination.

When I walk down an alley,
I grow fur and a tail.
I am an alley cat.

When I swim in the ocean,
I grow fins and gills.
I am a tropical fish.

When I come out of the ocean and onto the beach,
I grow four short stubby legs and shell.

I slowly walk to the jungle
where I became a white Bangal tiger.

I'd prowl until the mountains show.
I step on the foot of it and bam!
I let out a fierce cry and my family of mountain lions call back.

With a rustle of yellowish fur, I make my way back to
my building where I become human.

See, anyone who is everyone can do just the same if
they use their powers of imagination.
Deana Chausse

Color Me Clear

I believe I saw the future today
Sitting in the park watching children play
All running all laughing all playing as one
From opposite directions Mom's came fast
Shaking a finger and kicking up grass
Pulled the children apart
Screaming do as you have been taught
Play only with your own kind
One child crying ran away
Into mom arms and I heard her say
Hush hush my baby you will be ok
A little head tilt forward my way
With two little eyes shining
Through a constant flow of tears
Beyond the quarreling came the words
That I will all ways hear so clear
Mommy you taught me all children are the same
Red blood on the inside all children of God
Mommy I cry for the children cause their mom just now forgot.
Margaret L. C. Glass

We're All Looking For A Love

We're all looking for a love,
sometimes it's a task.

We're all looking for a love,
have they already crossed our path?

We're all looking for a love
someone to share with and laugh.

We're all looking for a love,
we'll cherish them and express it
they won't have to ask.

We're all looking for a love
they don't have to have been perfect
because we all come with a past.

We're all looking for a love
that when found through sharing, caring,
and giving in Jesus Christ's name,
will last.
Reginald Joyce

"The Dynamism Of Contemplation"

On a night so still and starry,
My heart soured up to heaven
Where infinity lay awaiting,
And love became a leaven.

When love affixed its claim on me,
And touching earth, fair deity,
Pursued me like the "Hound of Heaven",
Caressed me like fond "Mother Hen".

"With great longing have I awaited thee,
With tender care, I prepared a place for thee,
While on earth, yet still, you chance to be
Through my loving 'providential decree'.

"Rise up now, and you will see
Unforgettable, celestial congeniality,
My bride, my beloved, come,
You are home, though on earth, you are home"!

Anne M. Miller

Untitled

Late arrived; the final parting
Hinted at for long enow
And always smoothly slipped around us
Off behind us
Harsh truth too piercing to allow

I cannot think yet; through my numbness
Though faint relief is offered now
Still my tears are held in deadlock
Behind my heart's lock
Straining still at cherished vows

Words rise up slowly; wanting solace
Beyond my spirit's yen to fly
While here inside grave blackness gnaws
With mirthless jaws
Whose hopeful dreams their teeth belie

Step me now unto the daylight; haste, more haste on new leaves turn
Wherein this pain will pass and die
Which blankets now from light of sun
How dear to me, how near to be mine
Were you when suddenly - we said goodbye

Samson Orion

"Decision Time"

No love in my life, no smile on my face.
The night winds around me, a dark and cold embrace.

A gentle breeze is blowing, it feels good upon my skin.
But I must end my painful sorrow, I must burn for all my sins.

The crack of a gun, another statistic, this is no way to die.
But the pain is now gone, the torture is over, a selfish waste of life.

I wake up quite confused in a dark, mysterious space.
Black angels float around me in this strange, chaotic place.

People lie here shackled, they're all in so much pain.
They strive so hard to free themselves, but their tries are only in vain.

I hope that I am in Heaven, though I'm sure that I am in Hell.
But through the darkness and confusion, I really cannot tell.

So in a rush of terror, I drop to my knees and pray.
The angels only laugh, I'll never see the light of day.

Then my God speaks down to me in a deep and thunderous voice.
"Spend eternity here or come with me, this is your final choice."

Heaven or Hell: That's no decision, there's only one way to win.
But I choose to stay here where I am, I must burn for all my sins.

Lucas Miller

Ole Tree

The "Ole Tree" stood bare and brown
He was lonesome without his leaves around.

He watched his foliage that windy day,
The yellow, brown and red - flit around so gay.

They rolled along the road - then flew into the air
And swirled and danced without a care.

They flew against the window and through the door.
As if to say, "Hello - we're free - not prisoners anymore".

But "Ole Tree" was wise and strong.
He knew their dancing wouldn't last long.

He had seen it happen time after time.
The birth of his beauty so green and fine.

At first, his leaves would be happy and content
To sway on his branches without lament.

But as fall neared, he knew they would leave
To roam around until the winter freeze.

Then shrivel and rot and turn back to the earth.
And "Ole Tree" just stands and waits for new birth.

Helen Rose Bohman

The Beauty Of My Mom

As I look at the beauty around me, which God has created,
I think of the inward beauty he has created in you.

God has created in you the beauty of sensitivity:
You know when to speak and when to be silent —
Allowing me to experience my own choices.

He has created in you the beauty of compassion:
You're very aware of my feelings and emotions.
Not only are you willing to share in my happiness,
But my pain as well — no matter how painful it may be.

God has created in you the beauty of unconditional love:
You love me for who I am — not for what I do.
And not only do you love me, but you like me, too.

He has created in you the beauty of affection:
You're always ready to give that special touch or hug that says,
"I love you and I care."

Thank you, mom, for allowing God to create in you all of these
Beautiful characteristics, that portray the love a mother
Can give her daughter: A love you have given to me!

I love you very much and I thank God I have the
Special blessing of being your daughter.

Kim M. Olson

Interlude

Resting on a hilltop where strong
gusts of wind swirl, I willingly yield
to forces lifting - twisting me
till I am freed from earth. Green fields
below forgotten as I rise
to greater heights than eagles soar...
higher still piercing sun - shot clouds
into quiet where winds rush no more.
At last I view the vast unknown -
surely, this concealed life must be
more real than all imagining...
not mine to touch but mine to see
are beckoning worlds beyond my reach
and huge clusters of stars in sleep -
only mortal - I waken - look
heavenward unfulfilled and weep.

Jorian

Beautiful

There I saw her, plain as day.
Her hair was lighted by the sun's ray.
Her hair was beautiful as a dove in
Flight, that gleamed in the day as
Well as the night.

Yes, she's beautiful, this I know, as a
Snow bunny with a pearl white
Glow. Yes I know here, this is true,
Now I know my thoughts are few.
It is as if I knew her in another life.
Maybe she was someone, maybe my wife.

So I take my game, and I go on over,
With the luck of a four leaf clover.
Now she is mine, and yes I'm doing fine.

And she loves me this I know, we
Both share that same glow.
I love my wife so much more, of this love,
I will never bore.
Michael Ewing

Power

The power of the truth is too hard to say;
when someone betrays that power it blows your day.
You know they are sorry, but how can you believe
the power that was broken through you and me.
Me and myself sit here in shame,
you think that this power is just a game.
Take it seriously or you'll be sad
you took our friendship away 'cause you were mad.
You're sitting there all alone
wondering if you should call me at home.
You know you can't 'cause what will you say?
"I'm sorry, and I'm ashamed I blew your day."
You lost the wonder to this power;
maybe you'll have a better time next hour.
If you're listening to me you'll understand
how valuable it is to have a trusting friend.
So if your friendship went up in fire,
you'll know that one of you is a liar.
Delia Baker

My Granddad

This tree we have is not an ordinary Christmas tree.
George Haskell Cockrum was not an ordinary man.

This tree's trunk is now tall and strong; its roots have long since burrowed into the soil.

Just as this tree's trunk is its strength, George Cockrum was the backbone of our family.

Although this tree is healthy and alive, it has needed much care, attention, support, and love.

Just as this tree required several necessities for its growth, George Cockrum unselfishly gave each one of us encouragement, praise, nurturance, and values so that we could grow to be decent human beings.

This tree has silently and firmly managed to survive several journeys to and fro.

Just as this tree has survived its travels, in various words and deeds, George Cockrum, helped each one of us along our life journeys.

This tree's branches have grown one layer each of the past six years.

Just as a new layer has been added to this tree, each year a new addition has been added to our family.

This tree we have is not an ordinary Christmas tree.
George Haskell Cockrum was not an ordinary man.
Holly Jean Croak

Blue Dolphins

Beautiful blue dolphins swimming in the sea
They play tag while jumping into a summer's breeze
Down in the water the babies take their
naps they yawn and drool but when
they wake up they cry real loud that's a fact
Back at school the dolphins learn to draw
and write to know what's wrong and right
The blue dolphins go to work on their
horse power sea dragons
Stuck in traffic and late for work but
the excuses don't ever work
This is what the dolphins do everything for
me and you they keep the sea nice and clean
Sweeping and swoop making it as
clean as it could be!
Ashley Pangilinan

A Lost Soul

I'm Rufus, the disabled.
Yet in front of women,
    I'm capable.
'Cause I was born a man, the chivalrous,
    by whom anything is possible.

My body may be beaten up.
But I can walk
    to have my nightly brewer's cup.
That satisfies my cravings
    and keeps me in the hub.

While the world is so wide.
And all men can sing and ride.
But only the wise ones
    can have a lady by his side.
To hold and to chide
    unto yonder and beside.
Earl E. Tan

East, West, Coast To Coast

They arrive hand in hand
Whispering sweet good-byes
Remembering days gone by
Passionate kisses in the sand

They feel a strong true love
Thinking only of the other
Wanting to be together
What a beautiful skies above

They part feeling detached
Knowing they'll meet again,...eventually
Hoping the time will prove solidity
The gate is now unlatched

She moves away, afraid to depart
Staring into his amazing green eyes
Singing herself a winsome lullaby
Tears in her eyes, love in her heart

He grabs at her, afraid to let go
Holding on for dear life
Knowing the days ahead are full of strife
Their time is up, they both know

They go to their separate posts
She is his, he is hers.
People pass in pale blurs
East, west coast to coast.
Astelle Dona Sandford

His Name Is Alex

Looking out the kitchen window into
the back yard, we could see him running and playing.
Eleven years old with his whole life ahead of him.
You could not ask for a better little boy.
We were very lucky, that was one year ago.

Then the doctor discovered the tumor on his leg.
He only had a few months to live.
We were very angry, that was one year ago.

When he lost the use of his leg, he did not let that stop him.
His spirit and courage were endless.
We were angry because his life was going to be cut short, but
he showed us how to cherish the life we had remaining together.
We were very lucky, that was one year ago.

On the day we put him into the hands of the Lord,
his little brother introduced him in a prayer, he said;
"His Name is Alex."
We were very lucky, that was one year ago.

Mark Taylor

The Story

Look at me, now I'm so lonely
I don't know what to do, I don't know what to say
I can't just live without you, missing your every way
The mind can bring you back, even though you're not with me
How can I react to this pain and grief?
I guess you chose her, there is no doubt
I can beg to differ, but you'd shut me out
Those words, said by certain people
Thought we could last, all the way to the steeple
So many things, but I'll do all I can
Anything, everything, to get my man
But wait! He's running back
Should it be him I take, or is it just a selfish act
This could only happen in my dreams, this can't be for real
He's calling out to me, yet I found myself turning, him stumbling
  on my heels
What about me now you say? I have wandered on my way
Sometimes things are hard to see, but something deep inside of me
Had a special victory
Only my heart knew,
The whole story....

Heather Seymore

Val

My very special pal.
It would be difficult to disguise,
The adoring look in his eyes.
The faith that he has in me he shows,
With a gentle nudge by a cool wet nose.
He is happy with praise and a pat on the head,
To him that is his life's bread.
He is the joy of my day,
And is never one to demand pay.
He is always faithful and ever so true,
All that he asks in return is a kind word or two.
Of his wonderful temperament I love to brag,
For everyone he has a friendly wag.
His heart is as big as the open sky,
No matter what of him you ask he will try.
As his years begin to take their toll and show,
He never seems to lose his beautiful glow.
When his time arrives, and he loses life's race,
I pray that he finds a very special resting place!

Norma H. Dieter

The One In Everything
Dedicated to the I am

To Be or not to Be, That is the question.
To be in Manifestation, or to be formless.
But here I Am, in full disguise,
With a head, a nose and two eyes.
I have come to take the test
Of the Spirit in the flesh.
But there's one thing I know,
And that is that I Am the One,
And I came to have some fun:
To be good, to be bad,
To be happy, to be sad,
To have fame, to have shame,
To win, to lose
To live or to die,
My, My, to live or to die.
But how could you kill the one I Am,
The One in everything.
For I Am the puppet,
I Am the string,
I Am the one in everything.

John K. Hajjar

Flight 800

Flight 800 went down and no one knows why it had to be,
was it caused by surface to air missile, was it a bomb, or
will it remain a political mystery;
Flight 800 went down only minutes after take-off into the cold,
rough, waters of the Atlantic, it was just an inbound flight
from Athens, Greece outbound to Paris, France. Some will argue
that it was a remake of the Titantic;
Flight 800 with all its passenger and crew, will forever remind us
of our vulnerability, and how little power we really have when it
comes a time that there's nothing we can really do;
Flight 800 and its obituary list, has all of our condolences
and sympathy for the families of whom they will truly be missed,
although you all are gone you will never be forgotten, as in this case
I personally believe that in Denmark something was surely rotten;
Flight 800 I know you all went with God's grace, but you
certainly made the 96 Olympics in Atlanta come in 2nd place;
As we head toward the twenty-first century, may God help us
all, and let us pray for a more civilized society.

John H. Perry

As I Look

As I look into your eyes,
I see the beauty of a sunrise.
Making the skies colorful as a rainbow,
The purples, oranges, and blues,
Are wonderful, brightly, colored hues!

As I look into your eyes,
I see the beauty of a sunrise.
The warmth of a brand new day,
Is somewhat like your smile, I'd say.
Blossoming of a flower,
Such perfection! Staring at them hour after hour.

As I look into your eyes,
I see the beauty of a sunrise.
A gentle breeze, that flows through trees,
Making treetops sway with ease!

As I look into your eyes,
I see the beauty of a sunrise.
And to my surprise!
I am deeply hypnotized...

Patricia D. Winrow

Myriad Of Colors

Have you ever watched the sights of Spring
when snowflakes dust the ground -
The birds down South form in colorful flight
and the sun shines all around?

Where the lazy cocoon with caterpillar
suspends in silence before your eyes -
And bursts open with a sudden gust of fury
to send butterflies that rainbow the skies?

Where the flowers bloom in their radiant hue
and dance to songs on the subtle breeze -
Or seen a small child squeal in pure delight
as the wonders of God he sees?

Have you ever played with dandelions
and blown the seeds up into the air -
Watching the wind take them in flight
and deposit them everywhere?

Oh! The colors of spring beat all you have seen
in the seasons throughout the years -
The myriad of colors sway beneath the sky
and bow in the dew of God's tears!

Katie Tinch

A Never Ending Love

All good things come to an end so they say
That is why this day I pray
That this good thing we have will never go away
I dream that three magical words
To each other we will always say
I hope that with me you will forever stay
No matter what the price I am willing to pay
For I love you more
than words could ever express
I hold you close to my heart
From there I know you will never part
God gave you to me
For it is you that I will always cherish
I will love you every way that I can
I will not stop till that day that I perish
I love you very much and with all my heart
So please don't ever leave me
May our love never end

Gabe F. Lake

Heart Broken

Star light
Star bright
I look into your eyes
Thinking of the other guys

Should I dare to tell you
Maybe you should wait
Tell me it's not true
I don't want this love to turn to hate

The time has come
I must not run
I have to tell you
The love I had is gone

I don't want this to end
I need time to think
You have to know
It's time to go

My love for you was like a stone
It would not move or groan
I just want you to know
You were my first kiss and that's all for now.

Maria Quiles

Untitled

My life was so boring, more excitement there must be.
The party loving girl, that should have been me.

So much stress and so many worries, a way out there must be.
The girl that drank away her problems, that should have been me.

I tried that solution and addicted I became, but hey no
  problems or worries ever got me.
The irresponsible drinker, that became me.

The dropping school grades and lost friendships, the family
falling apart because I wanted to be free.
The person who caused so much sorrow, that couldn't possibly be me!

My life is nothing now, I will go nowhere, oh now it's so easy to see.
The girl that always said "No", that should have been me!

Courtney Ross

Meditation Of The Heart

Oh seek ye meditation
Find the Lord of all creation,
For in the stillness of your heart
Where words of mind shall play no part,
Is the Rubaiyat of Omar,
The peacefulness of "No More"
It is the everlasting and eternal now.
No longer hug your grief in vain despair
But in this unjust world be true and fair.
The real substance of this world is faith
We rest our hopes on its free will and grace.
In pure silence alone, all our sins atone.
We peel away each defect after fault,
Until understanding pours into the vault.
Asking for his help to see our plight.
He gives us wings to flee the dark of night.
Gives us ears to hear the phoney words:
Of media, of temptress, and nerds.
For we may only help our brother
When we can feel with the heart of another.

Delora Jean Porter

Your Son's Love

After a day of dark clouds rolling in
There always seem to be a ray of light free of sin
It adds to our faith that better things are to come
And also to show that God has not forgotten
He gives us tests to prove our faith and power
But never will he leave us in our hardest hour
Sometimes it seems it will never get better
So just think of the good things that hold us together
For if you believe in the love that we share
Never will you worry because the cupboard of love will never be bare
So whenever you think you are in doubt or despair
Look up in the trees and hear the blue bird singing you a prayer
He sends a message of love and happiness for your sake
To show that for your son's love you will never have to wait.

Edwin W. Green II

The Color Of The River

Every river has a certain, color, 'a personality'.
Its blue waves lap playfully on the bank when happy,
and the gray waves pound the sand in anger.
Very few can understand it.
But those who can, have a sweet, everlasting peace.
Their need is to live by water.
Some say they have strange powers.
What is it they have, that we don't?
No one knows for sure,
not you, nor I.
Only the river knows.

Kayla M. Anderson

Joy Of Life

I feel the morn's first light gently persuade my still-closed eyes to open.
"Thank-you, Great Spirit, for another day."
As I stand in the dew wet grass, I breathe deeply;
The sweetness of the fresh, spring air is my fuel for the day.
The birds are as full of joy as I,
As they sing their individual songs; blending to create a symphony of sweetness unequaled by man.

It is spring and All things are celebrating.
The high trill of the peeper is an aria of their Own birth.
All the small wood's creatures scamper in play, knowing food is again abundant.
The birds, as all the wild creatures, celebrate life by re-creating,
As they sing their most beautiful songs,
And dance their most beautiful dance,
To attract their mate.

Me—I feel inadequate in expressing my joy.
I cannot equal the beauty of the Wild Things.

I celebrate silently,
As my heart is so full of joy, it wells up and spills from my eyes.
    Judith Doughty

Reflections

It just doesn't make it anymore, my feeble attempts fall short.
I feel sadness and guilt.

We're two strangers sharing a home, sharing a bed.
Afraid to really admit it is over. I pull away and he draws closer.
My heart breaks for his pain. I'm numb, so numb. Is it wrong not to want to make it work?

Is it right to stay and yet not care?

Will I ever find love?

Why do I feel so intensely. Each feeling as though it were death.
The pain is too intense to bear. The pleasure always with guilt.
Does everyone feel this way? Or just pretend such disaffection.
It must be nice to live without feeling. To live each day for yourself.
What a cold world we would become.

But a much simpler one.

It's a deep, dark void. You enter into it with trepidation.

No one really understands. It becomes too deep, too dark.

But still you go on.

You put on your mask. And live out each moment. The light finally appears.
A glow at the end of the tunnel. You reach for it as if for a lifeline. And pull yourself back into the human race.

The happiness breaks forth like the sun through the clouds. And yet, the guilt is still there.

Why, Father, must I feel this way? As though true happiness is only for others.

Is it so bad? Must I always feel guilt? Can there not be pure happiness?
    Sammie Sparks

Slow Down

Slow down and know that I am God.
Slow down and talk to me, I am God, I will listen to you my child.
Slow down and spend more time with me.
Slow down and know that I am preparing you for every change that is coming your way.

Slow down and know that there is none other that cares for you as much as I do.
Slow down and listen to what I am saying to you my child.
Slow down and know that whatever you ask in my name you shall receive.
Slow down; keep the faith.
Slow down and know that I will be with you until the end.
Slow down and know that there is no one else but me, God, that can take you to new horizons.
Slow down and know that I am God and there is none other.
Slow down and follow me. I am alpha and omega.
Slow down.
    Rita Marks

I Am

I am strong but not fearless.
I wonder what heaven is like.
I hear God telling me to love all creatures.
I see so many people who don't care.
I want to have the courage to pursue all dreams.
I am strong but not fearless.

I pretend that I'm the best.
I feel sad for people without homes.
I can wish for a better life for all of us.
I worry that we may never see world peace.
I cry when I'm upset.
I am strong but not fearless.

I understand that I'm not always right.
I say anything is possible if you believe.
I dream of a life without crimes.
I try to make the best of my life.
I hope for the best education I can get.
I am strong but not fearless.

Mary Scott

To Dream A Dream

To dream a dream of being in love with you.
Yet not really.
Knowing you yet not knowing you.
Seeing your face and eyes.
Yet, not seeing you.
To dream a dream of wanting you.
But, not really wanting you.
Longing for you but not enough.
Thinking of you yet not thinking.
Wishing to be near you
But can do with out you.
To dream a dream of holding you.
But not holding you.
To dream a dream of wishing you were here.
But you are not.
To dream a dream of being near you.
Yet so far away.
To dream a dream is to really dream a dream.

Cynthia Moreno Watler

A Broad And Wide Place

A broad and wide place did He set us in, for His hand is upon us to go out and wind the souls He has in mind to call on His Name; those of His kind - His mercy reigns.

A land did He tell us to go and possess. His spoken Word, His promise, His caress. And though our knees would tremble and shake, His sovereign hand does still the quake.

For he has brought us in through an open door. In a time and a season when He is needed more. As darkness seeks to claim the land, He did set us as his watchmen. Into a place, a house of prayer, has He brought a people to dwell in His care.

A people to build the walls once again. Firm and set, a foundation in Him. A vision before us as big as the skies. Yet with each small step, we are delight in His eyes. For it is our faith He sees, as we take him at his word. He's told us to stand, stand tall and sure. Though the enemy tries to steal and destroy, the almighty, He reigns, and His strength is our joy.

So whenever He calls us to build Him an altar; to worship and praise and bring what we offer, there is shall be - His will, a perfect plan. And we're God's people, yet in His hand.

Frances Beauchamps

Out Of The Darkness

I have been crawling through the darkness
On shards of broken glass
My heart has been starving
For the love I dared not ask
I was locked in a room without windows
So I could not see life passing me by
Then one day through the cracks in my armor
I saw a break in the clouds
Your light pierced me straight to my very core
And crawled inside my heart
You got down on your knees, and helped me gather
The cracked pieces of my soul
I know your heart touches mine in ways hard to understand
I am wishing and hoping that this happiness won't end
I never thought I could know the wonder
And the emotions that I feel
Will I ever stop the wondering...
Is it truly real?...

Deborah Dominici

Am I But A Muse

Am I but a muse, a master('s) inspiration,
With a talent to infuse, a light to light the way?
And am I none but fodder for the blank sheet on the blotter,
A gift for every thief who smiles gladly as I pay.

Morning's grayish sky holds uncanny consolation,
And so I've sold my soul to every knave...
When kissed along the midway, it seems the poet *did* say,
"You are none but Goddess, and I, devout, your slave".

Oh, was I but a muse for any sycophant so smarmy
He'd steal my pearls, disarm me, and then go off to dance?
And was I mere diversion for every dashing jingo
Who never won at Bingo but always took the cash.

Mourning's darker sky lays claim to thorny revelation;
"Awake, and fie! There never *was* a poet, silly girl!"
As I, alas, remove Deception's mist and bow to Truth — I wonder,
How I make a poet of a churl...

Am I but a muse, a comic('s) inspiration,
With a talent to approve the perfect beat of Time?
Merely a confection seen oddly as Perfection;
And so disposed when the show has closed — left to amuse myself.

Debra Greenfield

Eternity

I dip down in the bowl of life
and find there's no more days of strife.
There's not another day of sun,
for now I find my life is done.

I cannot live another day.
I've used them up along the way.
There's no more days for me to see
For I am in eternity.

I come to you with one more prayer,
that I would be with you up there.
I know you died on Calvary.
Yes, this is what you did for me.

And I would use this final plea
To have my family there with me.
For you must know I love them too
And want them all to be with you.

My friends I've had down here on earth
and some I've had almost since birth.
I ask that they be there with me
while I am in eternity.

Francis M. Richardson

Dawn To Midnight

Vanilla flavored race cars zoom by,
turn into balloons, which rise and turn
into dragons, who turn into pirate ships,
which in turn capture my eyes.

I saw my childhood on a milk carton—but
no reward was offered.

I've been a spy, astronaut and doctor, all
in five years. And I wasn't old enough to drive.

I know my childhood like a book—but I can't
find the exact page.

I've jumped off swings and landed in oceans
wonder if there are dolphins in here? Maybe sharks!

The balloons return to my hands, wilted, beyond saving.
No race cars, no dragons, no pirate ships. Just a balloon.
No more spying, no space travel, no house calls.

I looked in the mirror and I didn't recognize my childhood.

Shawn Taylor

Two Sided

   My parents I resent not,
Their love sees no color, yet my peers do.
To dark depths of depression I've been brought,
When it comes to color, cannot they see through?
   God! The stares for pointing pierce!
The prejudice I've received, is it deserved?
Oh, the pain! The enemy is too fierce!
Yet Oddly different cultures I've observed.
   I'm proud of my mother's side,
African Americans, the suffering they've endured!
Her countenance is filled pride.
I'm no disease, I need not be cured!
   My father's side is powerful
Intelligent and sometimes cruel,
I ponder these things, making my hours full.
One conclusion, my heritage is a jewel.
   I bear the understanding of two races,
I'll rise above the prejudice and remain mild!
So here I stand, let it ring to all places!
Of this fact I am so proud: I'm a two-sided child.

Rachel Bowers

A Tribute To Tami

I'm in love with a beautiful woman;
This young lady has stolen my heart,
I feel such pain and sorrow;
Whenever we are apart.
She possess such stunning beauty;
It causes my body to shudder.
And just the thought of her lovely face;
Makes my heart go all a flutter.
Now I know it's not just infatuation;
When I look into her eyes.
She has so much love to give;
That sometimes it makes me cry.
She's not only smart, charming and witty;
She's the envy of every man's eye.
I have promised to pledge my life to her;
Until the day I die.
And I hope that she will accept me;
Just for who I am.
One very lonely and sincere but caring gentleman.

Robert J. Gebauer

"Wine And Heather"

An old New England summer haunt
Wraps itself 'round my brain
Smoke, dust, and fog
...are all that remain
A day of wine, a scent of heather
...things the mind forgets
...the heart remembers
Fields of grass littered with sunflowers
Give way to images lost
How disillusioned one becomes
When the line
Between love and hate is crossed
Visions old and grand
Flash like lightning before my eyes
In a world where vengeance rules
...there is no reaching a compromise
Like a day of wine
Like a scent of heather
When reality escapes from within
Sometimes, madness is all you remember.

Richard Scott

A Piece Of Stone

I wish I were a piece of stone
the kind that has no heart,
So I would not feel the need to love
and tear my life apart.
How much sorrow can I bear
upon my weary soul,
When I see my dreams walk by
reality feels so cold.
If I were a solid rock
embedded on a mountain side,
There would be no sadness, tears or fears,
No emotional waves to ride.
As I live throughout my life
I will keep wishing I were stone.
Until my heart beats no more
and my flesh turns into bone.

Edna C. Proo

Untitled

You tell me that you love me
I believe it to be true
It's just that I'm scared
And so very confused

So you put your arms
Around me, and tell me
To relax, but then all
I can think about is
What's to come next

So I relax in your big arms
I feel so safe, and warm
Then I let you guide me
Through the worst of
This emotional storm

I'm all pinned up inside
Ready to be released
Then I come to understand
That you were sent to me
Maybe by a higher grace that I can't understand
But I know you're here to help me, and maybe love again

Christina Wagasky

Christmas

My favorite time of
The year is Christmas
When the snow is falling
And the trees are so white,
they're just like
Pretty
Feathers
Falling
Falling
From the sky.
When we give and receive
When we love and care
When you catch the snow with your tongue.
And smell the fresh air
I see the beauty in the sky.

Brittany Baird

The Lord Is My Friend

   The Lord is my friend as we walks and talks
to me each day. I know he's near because the air we breathe.

   He's the one I can turn to and he'd listen and show the way
I should go. He created the beauty that surrounds us the signs
of his wonder the stars, moon, sun in the heavenly sky.

   A friend is someone you can wake up to, look out
the window and see the blue sky with the shining sun
to say a heavenly prayer to start the day.

   The Lord can be your friend if you are willing to
let him come into your heart. He is waiting with open
arms. He's here for eternity. No friend can be compared to him.

   The Lord is my friend and he can too be your friend
if you only let him be placed in your heart as he has for you.

Tonya R. Olivas

My G.I.

I know a G.I., who is a swell guy.
Write to me he does, why? Oh just because.
Maybe he feels blue, like he knows I do.
So with paper pen and ink, we write what we think
I could hardly wait, for the mailman at the gate
I know he will write, that's why I sit tight.

Far away he had to go, and I miss him so.
Many things come back to me, and will always in me be.
No words can express, the feeling I caress.
Forget him I never will, my thoughts of him I'll fill.
And each day I pray, that he may always stay.
So happy and healthy and some day be wealthy.
With things in his heart, that he had to part
Soon better days will be, you just wait and see.

Bernice Scata

Fate

From the pit of my belly my baby
  is born, dies, gets buried.

Beneath a surgeon's knife a cry
  for life, a soul flies.

A son dies splattered, red upon
  a field of guts and blood.

A man in a wheelchair once was whole
  walking proud and straight.

Where is life's grace to ease the pain,
  the sorrow and the hurt?

The question is the answer.
  We each decide our fate.

Sheila Carolyn Taft

Who Am I

A traveler, wanderer, seeker of dreams,
Never fully understanding all I've done and all I've seen,
Lost, confused, a stranger in my own eyes,
Help me come forward, help me take off the disguise.

I have seen the world's beauty and experienced the awful misery,
Somewhere between the two lies my inevitable destiny,
Nothing seems real, I often wonder if my life is based on a lie,
Always turning to others for judgment, asking who am I.

Am I one filled with eternal dread or one who brings others joy,
Have I graduated to manhood or am I still an innocent boy,
Am I one who will help others in their time of dying need,
Or am I one consumed by materialistic value or selfish greed.

Am I one who will offer his unconditional love,
Am I one who lives his life with the guidance give from up above,
Will I answer this question before I die,
The question is simple, who am I?

Eric Barker

Forever Yours

Dear Anita and Tom,
This is a glorious day for both of you
With the promise of a bright future, and many fun things left to do
It's interesting to see how our lives unfold
So many ups and downs-then it suddenly turns to gold
The very day we meet that special person to love
It is a gift made in heaven by our dear Lord above
Today you celebrate 25, but oh, so quickly, 50 will arrive
Because you are God's children, you are held very dear
And with his continuous blessing, your love will grow year by year
How comforting to have your chosen mate by your side
To share problems, joys, successes - a truly triumphant ride!
Continue to love one another with all your heart
Because then, and only then, can you truly re-affirm
  "'till death do us part".

Frances A. Hines

A Mother's Love

There is nothing like the love of a mother.
Someone to be there to kiss the pain away; someone
  to play games with on a rainy day.
Someone to laugh with and cry with, too; a
  mother is always there, no matter what you do.
A mother's love is irreplaceable and she tries to understand...
the trials of growing up in today's crazy land.
She is there for guidance, support, and to see her children through;
A mother tries to do the best she can do.
A mother has to be strong for there comes the day;
when her children spread their wings and fly away.
To reach for their dreams and to fulfill their souls.
A mother's love never dies, not even as she grows old.
She has done her best to make her children feel;
that "love" was her foundation and her love was very real.
That no matter how young or how old you are;
everyone needs a little love to open their hearts.

Yvonne M. Lee

Laying Awake

I often lay awake
At night
And cannot sleep.
I often say a prayer
If I'm sad,
I often think about
Things I want to do.
After thinking or praying
Or listening to music
I fall asleep.

Erin Carney

We will carry on
To carry them
The pilgrim's path in christian war
Where other saints and moralists depart
Where rain glows sun behind the door
Leslie-Claire Dion

Ode To Sunflower

I am yellow. I am brown.
I bring joy to those around.
Smiles are what I like to see.
Please be very kind to me.
I am green. I am black.
I have bees on my back.
I chase away mean old black cats.
Please thank me for my tasks.
I make honey. I bring laughs.
I can sing a nice tune of Valse.
Please handle me with care.
I am the guardian of what is fair.
I am the power of your mind.
I am the sunshine of the land.
Katherine Lee

Your Eyes Show A Tenderness

Your eyes show a tenderness.
That I've never seen before.
Growing to know you.
Just makes me want you more.
Noticing things in you,
That other people don't see.
Makes me feel glad that I'm me
Loving you, in the way that I do.
(As time passes on)
I don't want to lose you.
Lisa Jahner

our shines full moon -
messes come alive!

Mountain behind Pueblo
where world spirit dwells
draws her blanket
all is well.
Jerry M. Fireshaker

The Apple Pie

I'm sending you this apple pie
With love from deep within
And I want you to share this poem
When you give something to a friend.

The message in this poem is true
I promise that you'll see
That what you pass along to others
Will come right back to thee.

The love that I share with you
Comes from Christ the King
And if you do not know Him
Just ask Him to come in.

And if you do know Christ the Lord
Then you'll understand
Why you'll want to pass this poem
To another friend.

Please enjoy this apple pie
As it is blessed by Him
And it is shared with all the love
From another from way down deep within.
Nellie Mae Johnston

Sonic Youth

Heavenly flickered light
dulled through bassful tunnels
dark with glistening teeth.

Beer fountains running wild foam
down pointed chins.

Smoking green hazes hovering
over stained glass eyes.

Xers sitting Indian-style
passing cigarettes, choking poverty
over pierced tongues.

Watered down eight dollar vomit
emanating from wide open
restroom doors.
Michael Mercer

Paradox 75

The Grey lady is pensive gray
An idol no longer, she finds
Channels rare for her pent passion.

Her lover pursues other dreams
Not feminine, but quite green
Achieving his yearned hole in one.

While Grey lady is still ardent
Fickle nature, cunning, deceives.
Men grow handsome! But Women Age!
Barbara Enid Grosvenor

Mom, I Pray

As I sit here
   day by day,
I watch mom's life
   slippin' away.

And though I'm too young
   to understand,
I wish my mom,
   could have her life
Back again.

Mom; I love you,
   And I want you to know,
I pray God makes you happy
   When it's time for you to go.
Rebecca E. Mullennix

Remembering Loved Ones

The beauty of the light
   And the stars just shining bright.
What a beautiful sight.
Why did you have to go;
   And leave us all below?
And you never said goodbye.
   Oh! Please tell me why?
We all miss you and prayed for you to stay;
   But now you've gone away.
I begged it to be a dream
   But it's just like a stream...
You flow inside our hearts,
   Almost like we're torn apart.
But our love is everlasting,
   You'll never be passing by me,
Because I'm a person who's ongoing
   Still I'm knowing the right way to go
AND I'LL SOON BE WITH YOU!

Love,
Danielle Marie Hodo

Thou Shall Not Fear

As I walk through the valley of the shadow of death
I fear no evil
The mind of an Evangelist transforms me to an omen
I fear no evil
Demonic sources come in large ranks
I fear no evil
But my angelic forces are greater than they
I fear no evil
The Foremost one tells me
I fear no evil
Extolling this one and through Him
I fear no evil
My mind, my heart, my soul is all I have to give
I fear no evil
Living to die, dying to live
I fear no evil

Thomas J. Scurry

Noah's Ark

Old Noah was a Godly man,
His family were the only good people in a wicked land.

God told Noah to build a big ship called an ark,
And gather animals two by two, even the meadow lark.

Noah did as he was told and built the huge boat,
The ark was so big, Noah wondered if it would float.

Noah gathered every animal in the world into his boat zoo,
The wicked people mocked him and called him a fool.

Noah didn't collect the behemoth dinosaurs,
Because he considered them pesty sores.

Soon thick dark clouds covered the sky,
And a big raindrop hit Noah in the eye.

Then the rain began to pour,
Noah gathered his family into the ark and closed the door.

The ark soon began to rise,
While the family sat at the table and ate Mrs. Noah's pies.

It rained 40 days and 40 nights and the ark was tossed about,
All the evil people in the world drowned without a doubt.

It stopped raining and the ark landed on a mountain top,
Noah and his family praised the Lord that the rain had stopped.

Terry Pieszchala

Untitled

Have you ever seen the sunshine from a lonesome prison cell,
  Or heard a train whistle blow, like a monster out of hell?

Have you ever seen the mailman greet a hundred other men,
When the letter you have longed for has failed to come again?

People say that they miss you and wish that you were there,
  But deep down inside it seems that they really do not care.

  They try to make you happy, by telling you all those lies,
  But all it does is hurt you, by getting your hopes up high.

When I get out on the streets again, and make my stand in town,
  How should I treat those so called friends, the ones that let me down?

Should I act like it does not matter, when it really mean so much?
  All I've asked, after all, is for them to keep in touch!

Lonely Inmate
Charles D. Curtis

Prisoner Of Love

Here I sit a prisoner of love,
without this love I would be lost and lonely.
  I found my love and I intend to keep
this love forever and a day.
  This love has kept me strong and
made me weak, but don't cry for me
for this love is sweet.
  As a prisoner of love I surrender
for it has made my heart so tender.
  Do not despair for love is in the
air for all to share!
  If you are also a prisoner of love
you know how I feel, for this feeling
of love is for real.
  So find your love soon under a moon
or maybe at high noon but find it soon.
  Join our team and dream of
being a prisoner of love!

Salvador Savala

My World

My world is full of hopes and dreams, in the hidden corners
of my mind, I pull it out sometimes,
To watch the way it works, this world of mine,

It has no fears or violence, no battles and no wars,
Just quiet disagreements settled in corridors,

Nature is respected there, animals are as equals, the forests are
    not cleared,
Humans live peacefully with each other too,
They believe in God, and that they are all the same,
Regardless of their sex or race or fame,

A place were dolphins swim and eagles fly,
A place were you can see the sunset rise,
Were wild animals play and horses run untethered,
Were everything is respected whether haired, leaved skinned, or
feathered,

So you see in the hidden recesses of my mind,
There's really something wonderful,
There's really something fine.

I hope one day this world can be just as great as mine,
And even if it isn't, I hope that you, can find a small unused
corner of your mind,
And have your own world too.

Jarié Hamilton-Graves

New Beginnings

I like to think of birthdays
As life's extra innings.
A time of setting priorities and concrete goals -
Asserting new beginnings.
It only happens once-a-year, but
Continues the whole year through...
Wether or not you set new sights
Is entirely up to you.
Opportunity and chance are often stolen
Obstacles causes one to get off track.
But birthdays, as sure as the rising sun,
Come and give it all back.
Don't let the number get you down 'cause
When added up it's only between zero and nine
You see, "age" is our primitive means of recording
Something we refer to as "time."
So happy happy birthday salutations
Are being sent to you
How lucky you are for another opportunity
To begin Life's journey anew!!

Annett Lalor

To Be A Child

Oh, to be child...
  For life to be so simple and free
  and not have a care or responsibility,
  to still hopeful, naive, and innocent
  and not fastened down by obligation or commitment,
  to perceive others with eyes colorblind
  a heart pure and clear, and, unabashed, speak your mind,
  to inspire another with your uncanny insight
  and eagerly approach each day with wonder and delight,
  to genuinely appreciate each friend, flower, and freedom
  to truly enjoy life and find His Kingdom,
Is it possible to be a child again?
    Gerarda Shields

For My Mom

Just like a shiny, little pearl that begins as a grain of sand
A mommy's love is too deep for her children to understand.

How does the sand and salt and sea create a beautiful pearl?
How does a mommy feel so much for her little boy or girl?

She watches quietly as they sleep and feels her love grow strong
To watch them play and learn and laugh - to her they do no wrong.

But sometimes a pearl forms not so nice - with blemishes and spots
Often children do things that makes mommy hurt a lot.

But still the shell will snuggle in its precious little gem
And mommy's love will still grow deep as she hugs her kids again.

Until her kids have their own kids they do not really know
Despite the trials and the fights how mom still loves them so.

So now I know - you've loved me much since I was your little girl
And my love for you grows even more, my mom, my precious pearl.
    Jennifer L. Stokes

The Hurting Soul

Her life has been torn apart by
  the evils of this world. She used
  to have so much faith that things
  would be well again.
But over the years her faith kept
  diminishing. Once it was lost all
  that remained was a hurting soul.
A hurting soul is so much more
  painful than any evil that must be
  faced in this world. Once she realizes
  this, the hurting soul will be
  mended once again, and she will be
  able to face these evils with all
  the faith in her soul with out
  discouragement.
    Courtney Harris

Blizzard

I seek; and so I leave
  but always my face turns to home
And if just once
  I lose my way
  will you come find me?
It is dark; the winds surround me
  I cannot see
    The road disappears beneath my feet,
    and all my fault
  I just want to stop, and sleep,
    and let the cold envelop me
    but my feet keep moving
    and I will keep walking
      until I find you again
      or until I forget
    Beth Tracy

Looking At You

Remember the old days, just you and me
Life was so happy, so carefree
And then one day, you went away
To leave me hurting, feeling all alone.

That's why: Looking at you, I see the sunshine,
I hear the cold rain and without you I feel
The lonely empty pain.

When you close your eyes tonight can you
Make it right or has my memory faded away,
Into the night.

Sometimes I still see you in my dreams,
The memories, but now my life is nothing
But "used to be's" so I'll let it go,
And you'll never know of what could have
Been shared if you had cared.

So: Looking at you I know the thunder,
Looking at you, there always will be
The wonder of a love left dying
Blown in the wind.
    David J. Mitchell

I'll Forget You

Tho' you have said, "Forget Me": Tho' you have said, "Good Bye":
You taught me love's deep meaning and love can never die.

Still in my dreams it always seems we'll meet when clouds roll by.
I'll forget you when I can live without the sunshine I cry.

I'll forget you when I can live without the rain,
When summer roses forget their fragrance and the song bird his sweet refrain.

I'll forget you when all the silver of the Moonlight fades forever and ne'er will bring love's dream again,
When Heaven's gladness has turned to sadness:
  I'll try to forget you in vain.

From all the world I chose you, Heart of my Heart to be,
Now you have left me sighing, tossing on love's great sea.

I pray love's star that gleams afar may guide you back to me.
    Brenda S. Fears

Bitter Truth

I am flawed as white cotton dipped in dye. My innocence gone from me, I am left without purity. From conception unto birth, my fathers have prepared for me all the lands of the earth. Through their many conquests, history portrays, their enemies forced to work night and day. Always fattening my father's purse, while for them life got worse. They left me legacies of which I now share, along with other privileges only I can draw near. I am adorned with a mask of superiority, born and bred to hate to define civility. I am flawed as white snow stained with blood. Paying tributes to my forefathers, whom in mine eyes have done no wrong. This trend I will follow, preserving only those of the same color. I have surrender my sister's neck to the restraints of the chain and have forced her to kneel before me in the dust. My eldest sister to whom my mother has given the world to entrust. Ripping her children from her bosom, to become their master, their Lord, their God. To destroy her sons with an inferior song, not allowing them to ever grow strong. My sons alone must decide the faith of man. I am flawed as white silk dipped in dye, constantly living life a bitter lie. Someday, one day they will see, that under my mask reveals inferiority. Someday, they will see concealed under my mask of superiority, the ugliness of hatred and despair. Naked and unmasked the bitter truth will appear, underneath reveals a boy in fear.
    Raul O. King

Untitled

Look into my eyes and you'll see forever — innocence is lost
  days long gone . . .
When we were young, dreaming endless — the light was found   *(it's too late)*
  days long gone . . .

My old friend, I see yourself in me — like a faded memory
  remember when . . .
A reflection of you, in infinite daze — deteriorated with old ways   *(can't see, come back)*
  remember when . . .

My anger burns like hellbent rage — loneliness inundated
  forget you not . . .
Self-absorbed, but in the master's restraint — solitary games   *(don't go)*
  forget you not . . .

I hear myself, deliberation exposed — mindless enigma
  betrayal is delusive . . .
I detest you not, please forgive your foolish friend — my love is immortal   *(love you, love me)*
  betrayal is delusive . . .

Teri Rittmann

People Love With Peace Being An Understanding (Peace Is Our Goal)

Luv's discovering peace within yourself, because love is not harming anyone. Love is to be brought to understand and share. Love by us has meaning of joy to love, share, and cared with peace not war to tear apart the feelings of love with sadness. The joy of peace is to share and care everywhere...Luv is love...4u and I...It's beautiful and bold; Love-Forever-Always. Peace is love; love is peace. A peace of mind is a mind of peace, which brings forgiveness of thoughts in the war of minds (have no hate in war). Peacefulness must be understood for we are to believe in the peace of love we have. Love and peace is the peace in love we have to share. The peace of love we have is the peace of love we share.
The luv'n peace is givin' ur luv'n share 2 peace my friend of work to do is spellt "Peace" friend. The goal of our love is to better the peace we have because it is not hate. The happiness of peace brings me to say "Ask What You Can Do For Peace" This brings a very happy love within you. The piece of happiness brings peace to war, peace not war, happiness of peace, love, peace not war, love not hate, no sorrow in sadness which brings no love into everything. Why can't People Love....With Peace And Understanding, mysterious - mysteries 'n love, luv's here 4 ever so kiss Peace with a lot 'uh' luv'n understanding (Peace is our goal). Bring our luv'n share together (share peace). Remember with love and understanding it only takes a piece of mind.

Danny L. German

Biographies of Poets

ABERNATHY, SHELIA
[b.] January 8, 1965, Fort Payne, AL; [p.] Robert Keef and Bessie Gilbert; [m.] Billy Abernaty, June 17, 1983; [ch.] Johnathan and Amanda; [ed.] Plainview High School; [occ.] Farm; [oth. writ.] "Amanda's Angels", "Time" and several others; [pers.] I thank God for the talent to write and my family and friends for believing in me.; [a.] Collinsville, AL

ABSHERE JR., NORMAN LEE
[b.] July 9, 1974, Nederland, TX; [p.] Ramona Gonzales and Norman L. Abshere Sr.; [ed.] Port Neches - Groves High School, Panola College, (Carthage, TX) Arkansas, Monticello, East Texas Baptist, University, (Marshall, TX), Lamar, Beaumont; [occ.] A Stocker at Market Basket Grocery Store; [memb.] First Baptist Church of Carthage, Texas; [hon.] Texas High School all - State Baseball Player 1992, most valuable Freshman Baseball Player, Panola College 1993, Customer Service Award Winner for the Month of April 1996, at Market Basket; [oth. writ.] I am in the process of copywriting a group of songs I began writing in 1992. What use to be a hobby is becoming a dream.; [pers.] It's never easy to lose a friend. Dawn was taken from us very unexpectedly. Sometimes, it's hard to deal with a friend being gone, so I wrote this song (poem) to keep the memories of Dawn alive.; [a.] Port Neches, TX

ADIN, MARIAH P.
[b.] May 31, 1978, Evansville, IN; [p.] Mary F. Adin, Richard H. Adin; [ed.] Currently an undergraduate at Arizona State University studying Technical Theater.; [occ.] College Student, Assistant Manager, Galvin Box Office; [memb.] World Wildlife Federation, National Arbor Day Foundation; [hon.] National Honor Society, ASU Honors College Member, Who's Who of American High School Students; [oth. writ.] Several plays, monologues, poems published in various contests/school papers.; [pers.] My poetry is centered around emotion because I believe there is no higher truth. Where words fail us our raw emotion prevails.; [a.] Tempe, AZ

AGUIRRE, HOLLY
[b.] July 16, 1982; [ed.] K-8th Grade - currently a freshman in High School.; [memb.] USTA member (United States Tennis Association); [hon.] Honor roll in 7th grade - high honors in 8th grade - athletic award for tennis; [pers.] I always try to find the good in everyone. That's why I wrote "I can not tell a lie". I hate racism and discrimination. And I will do stop it.; [a.] Milton, WI

AHMED, MISS JIMMIE
[b.] November 26, 1946, Memphis, TN; [p.] Cora Sias Stockley, George Stockley; [ch.] Michael, Donald, Eric; [ed.] B.S. State Univ. of N.Y. Empire State College, Registered Professional Nurse Certified in Infection Control; [occ.] Administrator of Infection Control - Catholic Med Cts, NY; [memb.] American Lung Association of Queens, A.P.I.C., O.E.S., NCA and T Alumni Assoc., NYSNA TB Committee, MYSAAC; [hon.] Who's Who Among Nursing, Health and Human Svcs, World Wide Business Leaders, Females in the East; [oth. writ.] Abstracts and Manuscripts in the Field of Infection Control Published in (AJIC) American Journal of Infection Control; [pers.] My philosophy is simple, start with God, stay with God, succeed with God. My idol is Dr. Maya Angelou.; [a.] Springfield Gardens, NY

AILER, JACOB
[b.] January 6, 1962, Ashland, OH; [p.] Alpha and Ruthie Ailer; [m.] Rebecca Ailer (Kissiar), June 14, 1986; [ch.] Tiffany Carwile, Alex and Megan Ailer; [occ.] Realtor; [memb.] American Legion; [a.] Lexington, OH

ALEXANDER, KATIA-MARIE
[pen.] Kat; [b.] March 21, 1984, Los Angeles, CA; [p.] Margaret Katherine Alexander, Steven Thorsen; [ed.] I am currently in the 7th grade at South Charlotte Middle School in North Carolina; [hon.] President's Education Awards for Outstanding Academics of June '96; [oth. writ.] Graduation, What is Purple, Poetry, Friends; [pers.] Poetry has enlighten me tremendously, and it has also opened a new world full of meaning for me. I find great pleasure unexpressing my feelings in poetry. I hope that when you reach my works you can venture with me into the beautiful abstracts life.; [a.] Charlotte, NC

ALEXANDER III, FRANK
[b.] January 29, 1981, Lompoc, CA; [p.] Frank Alexander Jr. and Belinda Wheatley; [occ.] High School Student; [memb.] Health Occupation Student of America, Computer Science Club; [pers.] My writings often reflect balances (Life/Death, Good/Evil). I aspire to one day become a novelist later in life. I enjoy studying religions, especially the eastern ones, and philosophy; [a.] Pearland, TX

ALEXIN, MALLORY P.
[b.] May 8, 1987, Troy, IL; [p.] Barry and Sara Alexin; [ed.] Currently in fourth grade at Oakview Elementary School; [occ.] Student; [memb.] Girl Scouts, Bell Choir; [hon.] Honor student, Second Place Ashland City Schools Literature Reflections Contest; [pers.] This is the first time I've been published. I hope to make writing my career.; [a.] Ashland, KY

ALLEN, DEBORAH KAY
[pen.] Kay Montgomery; [b.] October 22, 1972, Tuscola, IL; [p.] Gail K. Conner; [m.] Michael W. Allen, October 16, 1992; [ch.] Deanna Kay Allen; [ed.] Tuscola High School, Parkland College; [memb.] Certified Domestic Violence Advocate for Woman, After School Reading Program Volunteer; [hon.] 1987 and 1989 Gold Key Awards-Scholastic Aart Awards, 1990 Senior Edition Tuscola Review - front cover, also 1994 Edition, 1990 Senior Art Work chosen for permanent display in High School Art Gallery; [oth. writ.] Many writings yet unpublished; [pers.] I believe that through love and education we can strive together to make our world a safe place for our children. It is my hope that my writing will touch and teach.; [a.] Tuscola, IL

ALVARADO, BEVERLY ANN
[pen.] Bev Alvarado; [b.] June 25, 1963, Los Angeles; [p.] Eloy Sandoval, Maria J. Sandoval; [m.] Sergio Alvarado, June 11, 1983; [ch.] Steven Christopher, David Anthony; [ed.] Saint Joseph High School Lakewood California; [occ.] Hr Payroll Specialist, Implamentation Specialist; [memb.] Early grad, 1981, St. Joseph's. Crowned Queen, Knights of Columbus, Rancho San Antonio.; [oth. writ.] Eighty other poems written, near completion, a full length novel.; [pers.] One must first love the "Art" of writing, before any inspiration's can become true masterpieces. "Write from your heart... Do what you know... Follow your dreams... Achieves what you will..."; [a.] Buena Park, CA

ALVAREZ-MANILLA, CLARE MARIE
[b.] May 8, 1963, Milwaukee, WI; [m.] Joseph Dubon Alvarez-Manilla, July 30, 1983; [pers.] My writings are not a reflection of great intellectual achievement or technique but a bit of who I am. It flows from the inner most part of my soul. I write for myself, for my need of expression but if others read and find joy then I am gifted.; [a.] Milwaukee, WI

ALVEY, EVELYN L.
[pen.] Evelyn L. Alvey; [b.] October 2, 1941, Naples, FL; [p.] Lee Roy Allen, Grace Allen; [m.] Jerry Lee Alvey, July 13, 1985; [ch.] Steven, Cathy, Scott, Jerrit; [ed.] Naples High School; [occ.] Retired - United States Postal Service; [memb.] Florala Church of God, Writer and Composer for BMI (Broadcasting Music Inc.); [oth. writ.] Two songs, lyrics and music recorded by gospel singer Clint Butler published and copyrighted (1982) 45 RPM; several unpublished gospel songs, lyrics and music, a book of poetry (unpublished).; [pers.] My desire is to reflect the goodness and the majesty of God in all my writings and music. Since retirement, my goal is to persevere in having my writing published.; [a.] Florala, AL

AMENDOLARA, NICOLE D.
[b.] January 12, 1977, Brooklyn, NY; [p.] Dr. Lorraine P. Amendolara and Nicholas Amendolara; [m.] (Fiance) Joseph F. Gergis; [ed.] St. Joseph Hill Academy High School, (currently) State University of New York at Stony Brook; [occ.] Student; [memb.] Stony Brook Computing Society, The Science Fiction Forum; [oth.writ.] All currently unpublished; [pers.] To all those who supported me, I thank you with a hug and again. Special respectful thanks to Isaac Asimov, Peter David, and Douglas Adams, who have unknowingly influenced me. "It is better to die in honor than live in dishonor, though a throne be served up as temptation." M.T."; [a.] Long Island, NY

AMES, KIRK LEON
[b.] July 14, 1962, Anchorage, AK; [p.] Alonzo and Sylvia Ames; [ch.] Kirk Leon Jr. and Kirtis Lee Ames; [ed.] Aviano Italy (High School) Graduated (Burkburnett High) Burkburnett TX; [occ.] Auto Sales consultant Bledsoe Dodge, Arlington, TX; [pers.] As a result of travelling and meeting people worldwide, my writings reflect that matters of the heart (Love, loneliness joy and sorrow) touch us all, in some way everyday.; [a.] Fort Worth, TX

ANDERSON, ANDREW
[b.] September 17, 1965, Dallas, TX; [m.] Cynthia Anderson, January 3, 1985; [ch.] Sean Steven, Samuel Scott; [occ.] Paint and Body Tech.; [a.] Loudon, TN

ANDERSON, ROBERT
[b.] July 18, 1980, Phoenix, AZ; [p.] Rirchard and Cindy Anderson; [ed.] Junior at Issaquah High School, Class of 1998; [occ.] Full time student, part time McDonald's crew worker; [memb.] Cadet in Issaquah/Liberty Naval Junior Reserve Officer Training Corps; [pers.] I write what I see and hope it makes people think.; [a.] Issaquah, WA

ANDERSON, ROBERT L.
[b.] May 7, 1927, Mount Vernon, IL; [p.] Opal Everett and Stella F. Anderson; [m.] Janell Burdick, August 28, 1948; [ch.] Ronell Rae, Karolyn Kae, Lucinda Lee, Steven Robert and James William; [ed.] University of Illinois (No Degree) Southwestern Baptist Theological Seminary (Associate Degree); [occ.] Retired Minister - working as Bank Courier; [memb.] Have been member of several Baptist churches in Ill., Texas, and Ohio. Including three in Ill. that I led in organizing; [hon.] "Tree Topper Award" - Independent Order of Foresters, "Salesman of the Year" Apple Creek Realty, First President of Baptist Student Union at Uni. of Ill., Moderator (President) of Maumee Valley Association of Baptists (Ohio), Written up in Ill. bell. Tele. News on two different occasions.; [oth. writ.] "Ode to Orvella", my sister on her death (not published), wrote a song on prayer based on II Chron. 7:14 (not published) I am presently working at compiling our family history.; [pers.] All I am, or have, or hope to be is because of the goodness and greatness of God, his Holy Spirit, and his son Jesus Christ, my Lord Saviour.; [a.] Holland, OH

ANDERSON, SHARIA
[b.] April 27, 1971, Fairfax, CO; [p.] Robert and Sheri Cheek; [m.] Terry Anderson (Deceased) January 21, 1993; [ch.] Shante Lakia and Bianca Terry; [ed.] Halifax Co., Sr. High 2 years at VCU; [occ.] Ward Secretary in ICU at Halifax Regional Hospital.; [oth. writ.] Several poems unpublished; [pers.] I love to write poems from the heart for everyone to enjoy.; [a.] Halifax, VA

ANDRUS, STACEY D.
[b.] September 22, 1965, Beaumont, TX; [m.] John D. Andrus, March 8, 1992; [ch.] Karl Keith; [ed.] Elsen Hower High School (Lawton, Oklahoma) Delta Career College, Certified Nurses Aide (Beaumont Texas); [oth. writ.] I've written other poems that I do hope to have published one day, but until then, I keep writing these poems because its a "Labor of Love".; [pers.] My writing comes from personal experiences that I've had, and I hope hat anyone who sees. My poems are able to enjoy reading them as much as I've enjoyed writing them.; [a.] Beaumont, TX

ANKROM, HOLLY S.
[b.] December 11, 1979, Portland, IN; [p.] Steve Ankrom and Linda Ankrom; [ed.] D.H. Conley High School (Junior); [memb.] DECA, and Association of Marketing Students; [hon.] National Junior Honors Society, competed in Rotary Club Ortorical Contest; [pers.] My writings are purely the feelings I am experiencing. They are raw, uncut, and therefore very realistic.; [a.] Greenville, NC

ANN, TONI SALINETRO
[b.] November 10, 1923, Manhattan, NY; [m.] Divorce, after 28 years of marriage; [ed.] High School and studied for a while at the Institute of Children's Picture, many years ago - but not Connecticut.; [occ.] Have been retired now - but not fully.; [hon.] "The Four Seasons"; [oth. writ.] I have written the story of my life and people now that I am stabled back to Florida, hopefully - I will finish my book; [pers.] My most important job was..., first - to raise my 5 children to the best of my knowledge - I was very successful. I started to write in 1972, I've always wanted to be a writer and etc.; [a.] Fort Lauderdale, FL

ANNINO, PAULA
[b.] September 11, 1947, Dallas, TX; [p.] William Rosson, Marjorie Espe Rosson Hallowell; [m.] Divorced; [ch.] James Scott, Kristine Yvonne; [ed.] Unity High School, Dental Technician class "A" school, Wayne School of Dental (Assisting), Practical Nurse Education Program, Middletown, Ct.; [oth. writ.] LPN/Podiatric Assistant; [memb.] American Legion, Waves National, VFW Women's Auxiliary, Field Representative WIMSA (Woman in Military Service to America); [hon.] High School National Honor Society, Honorable Discharge as DT2(E-5), US Navy Waves (Viet Name Era); [pers.] Most of my 20 years of nursing have been in the field of Geriatrics, and my poem is a tribute to the elderly that I have been privileged to have known.; [a.] Tolono, IL

ANTOINE, DELORES DAVIS
[b.] April 11, 1935, Newark, NV; [p.] Robert and Viola Davis; [m.] Henry Lawrence Antoine, August 4, 1953; [ch.] Kathy Antoine Smith, Veda Antoine Theodore, Marcia Antoine, Bailey-Henry L. Antoine Jr; [ed.] Barringer High School, Kean College BA - MA Early Childhood Kindergarten Teacher Rand School, Montclair, NJ; [occ.] K. Teacher; [memb.] (1) U.S. Holocaust Museum, (2) NAACP, (3) Friends of The Children; [hon.] (1) N.J. Governor's Teacher Recognition Program, (2) Judy and John Weston Award For Excellence, (3) Eve Marchiony Award; [oth. writ.] Play all in rhyme Phoebe Fraunce - American, Heroine, Anne Frank Revisited, The American; [pers.] Those who dare to teach must never cease to get to know as much about the various children whose lives they touch.; [a.] Montclair, NJ

ARIETANO, MICHAEL D.
[b.] November 19, 1923, Italy; [p.] Domenico and Coronata Arietano; [m.] Frances, April 24, 1949; [ch.] Michael, Michele, Denise; [ed.] Emerson High School, Edison Elementary - Union City, NJ; [occ.] Retired - Former Branch Vice President - Lindenmeyr Paper Corporation; [pers.] I have enjoyed the intellectual stimulation found in the works of truly great writers. If I have grown wiser as I have grown older it is because I learned to read!; [a.] Gaithersburg, MD

ARNOLD, JENNIFER M. BAUBLITZ
[b.] March 2, 1972, York, PA; [p.] Catherine Ream/Thomas Baublitz; [m.] Jerry S. Arnold, May 14, 1994; [ed.] 1990 York County Area, Vocational/Technical High School Graduate; [occ.] Computer Room Specialist at Stewart Connector Systems, Glen Rock, PA; [memb.] Colonial Williamsburg Society; [hon.] Won a love poetry contest for WPOC 93.1, Baltimore, MD; [oth. writ.] Class poem for graduating class of 1990 at York Vo-Tech; [pers.] My writings reflect personal experiences from my life. I thank T-Bone for believing. Emily Dickenson and Helen Steiner Rice are my inspirations.; [a.] Shrewsbury, PA

ARNOLD, KEN
[b.] June 27, 1949, Providence, RI; [p.] George and Dorothy Arnold; [m.] Patricia A. Arnold, May, 1970; [ch.] Stephanie Lynn; [ed.] St. Petersburg High, St. Pete Junior College, Univ. of South Florida; [occ.] Residential Loan Officer; [memb.] Cathedral of St. Peter's Oratorio Choir of St. Peter's (Bass), Second Time Arounders' Marching Band (Percussionist); [hon.] None associated with my artistic endeavors; [oth. writ.] Published my first poem at 14 via an English class and mirror Lake Jr. High School - have written a short story and some music but have not had them published.; [pers.] I strive to incorporate realism and mental images into a central theme that transcends the human spirit into the realm of future possibilities.; [a.] Saint Petersburg, FL

ARRICK, XENIA
[pen.] Tiffany (pre-baptismal name); [b.] May 26, 1972, Fort Worth, TX; [p.] David and Betty Barfield; [m.] Basil Arrick, September 22, 1991; [ch.] Aaron Arrick (May 9, 1995); [ed.] Richland High, Tarrant Co., Junior College, Institute of Children's Literature (partial course); [occ.] Artist, writer, housewife/mother, editor of "Homestead.org" (on line magazine); [memb.] Russian Orthodox Church, Outside of Russian (R.O.C.O.R.), Ferret Lover's Club of TX; [hon.] Have won awards in several art contests in high school, college and fairs, but no poetry awards as of yet.; [oth. writ.] "The Albatross" published in college poem/prose anthology; it and most of my other poems can be viewed at "www.homestead.org/my poems.htm."; [pers.] As an Orthodox Christian attempting a simpler, more natural and pious way of life in preparation for life eternal, I hope my poems reveal the harmony, joy and necessity of such living, as well as the glory and grace of God in all His Creation.; [a.] North Richland Hills, TX

AUMER, KATHERINE
[b.] January 8, 1981, Cedar Rapids, IA; [p.] Gary and Ellen Aumer; [ed.] Jefferson Senior High School; [memb.] Jefferson, Thespian, Grant Wood AEA "Tech" team: Teen's educating the community.; [hon.] "Right Stuff", Leadership in Astronomy Team Exercises - presented by Space Academy; Modern Woodmen of America third place essay, President's Education Awards Program; [oth. writ.] Publishing in Playwrights, Adventure, a design-an-ad contest for students, many publishing in the Gazette, Anthology of Poetry by Young Americans, and contest winnings in I Love America Because....; [pers.] Through life I've experienced many triumphs and several failures, but I realize that as long as I do my best and continue to work hard, I will always come out on top.; [a.] Cedar Rapids, IA

AUTEN, JOHN WILLIAM
[b.] May 15, 1915, Charlotte, NC; [p.] William D. and Maggie Pearl Auten; [ed.] High School Graduate; [occ.] Farming; [hon.] Song Melancholy Memories at karoke recieved much applause; [oth. writ.] Book "Properly Finished," The Old Man Last, Christmas At Home (submitted not published).; [a.] Charlotte, NC

AYERS, JEFFREY GLENN
[b.] July 19, 1974, Pontiac, MI; [p.] Lewis Ayers and Nancy Ayers; [hon.] Editor's Choice Award for "Remember", elected into The International Poetry Hall of Fame, October 1, 1996; [oth. writ.] Previous published in Of Sunshine and Daydreams, Memories of Tomorrow, The Colors of Thought, Into the Unknown, and Whispers at Dusk; [pers.] I wrote this poem for and about a very special and very important person whose love and friendship saw me through the darkest days of my life: Bobby Phelps, this one's for you.

BAGWELL, MARY JANE
[pen.] M. J. Bagwell; [b.] March 7, 1942, Clarksburgh, WV; [p.] William ReBrook, Mary Jane ReBrook; [ch.] Ann Kristina Corbett, John Joseph Bagwell; [ed.] Victory High School, P.G. Community College, Bowie State University; [occ.] Asst. Mgr., Senior Citizen Hsg., Arlington, VA; [hon.] Slogan award for clean environment, Bowie, MD, Honors Student, P.G. Com. College, Magna Cum Laude, Bowie State Univ., Bowie, MD; [oth. writ.] Editor of "Family News and Ties," former writer for "Renters' Corner," for home owners' ass'n., poetry written for pleasure and for work; [pers.] Writing poetry, and writing in general liberates my thoughts, and produces a type of catharsis for me. Walt Whitman, Shakespeare, et. al. have been inspirational to me.; [a.] Alexandria, VA

BAIA, CHRISTOPHER
[b.] November 1, 1974, New Haven, CT; [p.] Anthony Baia, Carl Baia; [ed.] Lyman Hall High, Middlesex Comm. College; [oth. writ.] Numerous poems such as Windswept - Beach Comer - 1946 - Green - etc. non-published.; [pers.] Christopher Michael Baia, ended his life January '96. He was sensitive and talented - gifted - among his accomplishments were the violin, guitar, piano, art, and poetry. He is greatly missed by all who knew and loved him.

BAILEY, TRENTON C.
[b.] September 6, 1979, Wooster, OH; [p.] Jeff and Sandra Bailey; [ed.] I am now a senior in High School.; [occ.] Student; [oth. writ.] Hundreds of other poems and essays, but none published.; [pers.] Most of my poetry tends to reflect my past frustrations with love, while others were inspired by something as simple as a shadow. I idolize Poe's and Ono No Yoshiki's works.; [a.] Liberty, KY

BAKER, AUDRA
[b.] June 3, 1983, Springfield, MA; [p.] Ernest Baker, Kristin Baker; [ed.] Murrayfield Elementary School, Gateway Regional Middle School; [occ.] Student; [memb.] 4-H Rabbit Club First Congregational Church of Chester; [pers.] Dragons, Unicorns, and Trolls, the Stuff that separates my dreams from my reality.; [a.] Huntington, MA

BAKER, DELIA M.
[pen.] Delia Baker; [b.] July 13, 1984, Portage, MI; [p.] John Baker and Linda Baker; [ed.] I'm a 7th grade Student at Portage Central Middle School; [occ.] Student; [memb.] I'm in Girl Scouts, been in it all my life.; [hon.] Last year I received an Award for getting a 3.75 grade point average. Also many others.; [oth. writ.] I love writing poetry. I've written many others, although I've never had one published before. This is the first time I've ever had anything published.; [pers.] I really only write about how I feel, what has happened to me, or what has happened to one of my friends.; [a.] Portage, MI

BAKER, LORRAINE
[b.] December 25, 1944, Bronx, NY; [p.] Cleveland Cusack, N.Y.C.; [ch.] Three; [ed.] Bachelor's of Health Science, Physician Assistant Studies, University of Kentucky, Lexington, KY; [occ.] Pharmaceutical Sales Representative; [hon.] Scholastic Recognition; [pers.] Writing is a wonderful avenue which allows me to ventilate my feelings, perceptions of nature, world events and life experiences. Events that touch my heart I can best translate in the form of poetry.; [a.] Lexington, KY

BAKHRU, SARITA
[b.] January 8, 1983, Columbus, OH; [p.] Prakash and Mary Bakhru; [ed.] 8th Grader at Lake Jackson Intermediate School; [occ.] Student; [pers.] A mind is like a computer and unfortunately some people don't know how to turn it on. Don't forget to read the manual.; [a.] Lake Jackson, TX

BALUCH, SHAANA MICHELLE
[b.] January 19, 1977, Inglewood, CA; [p.] Geraldine and Akram Baluch; [ed.] Currently attending UCLA, majoring in Psychology; [occ.] Student; [oth. writ.] "My Pet", an article published in a local newspaper when I was 11 years old, and many works of poetry in progress.; [pers.] I'm sure many adolescents will identify with the aura created by my style. Sometimes knowing others have experienced the same turbulent emotions provides a sense of security in one's heart.; [a.] Rancho Palos Verdes, CA

BANNISTER, SARAH M.
[b.] March 14, 1979, London, ON; [p.] David and Anne Bannister; [pers.] I write poetry and short stories for personal reasons - so I can record my thoughts and feelings. Most of my poetry is written as a reflection of my life.; [a.] Exeter, Ontario, Canada

BARD, MARY
[b.] April 10, 1945, Solon, OH; [p.] Theodore and Marcella Bard; [m.] Gordon Selfridge, January 15, 1982; [ch.] Kelly and Lynn; [ed.] Solon High, Miami University Oxford Ohio, San Jose State University; [occ.] Resource Specialist - Special Education; [memb.] International Reading Association, California Reading Association, National Association of Bilingual Educators; [pers.] I enjoy reading good literature. From this and my personal experiences I obtain tremendous pleasure in expressing myself on paper.; [a.] Hollister, CA

BARDESSONO, DAVID
[b.] February 17, 1954, Prosser, WA; [p.] Joseph Bardessono, Joyce Bardessono; [m.] Sherilyn Bardessono, May 31, 1972; [ch.] David Jr., Jennifer, William; [ed.] Prosser High; [pers.] I write my poems through the eyes of my boyhood, always wishing I could go back, and always knowing I can't return. I hope from my words others will reflect and learn.; [a.] Prosser, WA

BARRON, ELIZABETH
[b.] May 14, 1950, Sharon, PA; [p.] Mary and Joseph Barron; [ed.] Reynolds High School, New Castle Business College, Southern Ohio College; [occ.] Sales; [hon.] Graduated Summa Cum Laude from Southern Ohio College; [pers.] Be honest with yourself about what's important to you, and then don't let anyone convince you to settle for less.; [a.] Streetsboro, OH

BARTHOLOMEW, FERN B.
[b.] September 1, 1909, Canada; [p.] Otis L. Bradley (Father), Hasseltine Durham (Mother); [ch.] I have two sons.; [ed.] Masters and other college; [occ.] Retired; [oth. writ.] Only journal on family.

BARTUCH, JEANNIE
[pen.] Jeannie Bartuch; [b.] February 27, 1980, Chicago, IL; [p.] Hui Bartuch and Bill Bartuch; [ed.] High School; [occ.] Cashier; [pers.] I love to write and get lots of ideas from the world around me. I believe good poetry should reflect a point the author is trying to make in his/her mind.; [a.] Sealy, TX

BASS, CORA DOUGLAS
[b.] February 27, 1943, Jellico, TN; [p.] Herbert Douglas, Florence Hackler Douglas; [m.] Robert Bass, July 11, 1962; [ch.] Shelia Marie Price, Lisa Denise; [ed.] ADN Troy State University, BSN University of New York; [occ.] Registered Nurse, VA Medical Center; [memb.] Maupin Ave, Presbyterian Church - Friends for Youth, Order Eastern Star, IRR US Army Corp.; [hon.] Lieutenant US Army 1992; [oth. writ.] Several unpublished poems and personal reflections.; [pers.] My goal is to be a servant to others by sharing their pain, grief and disappointment in life and help them reach a state of inner peace and spiritual growth.; [a.] Salisbury, NC

BAUMGART, KIMBERLY
[b.] August 31, 1983, Monterey, CA; [ed.] T.C. Walker Elementary School, Page Middle School Gloucester, Virginia; [occ.] Middle School Student; [hon.] A Honor Rolls; [pers.] I hope to be a well-known author throughout my life.; [a.] Gloucester, VA

BAUSLEY, ALICE
[b.] April 17, 1935, Helena, AR; [ed.] John C. Fremont High, Los Angeles Business College, and Philips J. College; [occ.] Part time Sales Associate at Sears; [hon.] Retired from previous job, Defense Investigative Service as Industrial Security Asst. - Typing; [oth. writ.] Special occasion for family friends and on the job, such as birthdays, promotions, departure, retirement and bereavement: all were personal, none were published.; [pers.] The late Rev. Clayton Russle of the Church of Divine Guidance encouraged me to write my true feelings of expression to others: I enjoy it.; [a.] Compton, CA

BEAUCHAMP, TOMAS A.
[pen.] Tom E. Llama; [b.] March 11, 1959, Princeton, NJ; [p.] William and Mary Beauchamp; [m.] Anna I. Alexandrova-Beauchamp, May 22, 1995; [ch.] Dasha Alexandra, Andrea; [ed.] As Commercial and Industrial Photography, BS English/BioPhysics, Masters Public Affairs; [occ.] Sustainable Development of Emerging Market Countries; [memb.] Integrated Systems Institute; [hon.] Various Scholastic and Professional; [oth. writ.] Currently writing a (duet or trilogy) novel about the "Heroic Journey" of a midwestern youth; [pers.] My writings are what I bring back from my thoughts and experiences. I share them in order to reveal a new dimension of our common experience.; [a.] Bloomington, IN

BEAUCHAMPS, FRANCES
[b.] March 22, 1961, Bronx, NY; [p.] Palmiro and Ivelina Figueroa; [m.] Alex Beauchamps, July 26, 1981; [ch.] James Alexander, Paul Alexander; [ed.] The Baldwin School, NYC; [occ.] Homemaker/Writer/Poet; [memb.] Member of Everlasting Covenant Christian Ekklesia (ECCE); [hon.] Honorary Commendations in English; [oth. writ.] Unpublished manuscripts: "As He Leads The Way," and "Days Along The Way".; [pers.] This poem is one of many inspired by and given in glory of my Lord and Savior, Jesus Christ, and speaks especially of the family of God at ECCE in New York as we press toward our destiny in Him.; [a.] Jersey City, NJ

BEDFORD, LAURA
[b.] November 8, 1962, Dallas, TX; [m.] Bruce Boyer, August 17, 1996; [ch.] Raine, Jefferey, Alyssa; [pers.] To my three children, the very lights of my life. May God be with you always.; [a.] Hockley, TX

BELIVEAU, MATTHEW
[pen.] Mateo; [b.] April 24, 1973, Pomona, CA; [p.] Robert and Elaine; [ed.] Social Science Degree at Concordia University at Irvine, Bishop Amat High School; [occ.] Soccer Coach and Trainer; [memb.] California Youth Soccer Ass. (CYSA), U.S. Soccer Federation (U.S.S.F.); [pers.] I strive to reveal reality through a deep thought.; [a.] Claremont, CA

BELTRAN, RONALD B.
[pen.] Ron Beltran, Nartleb; [b.] July 4, 1966, Caloocan City, Philippines; [p.] Eduardo Q. Beltran, Gloria B. Beltran; [m.] Flor Geronimo Beltran, December 18, 1993; [ch.] Patrick Geronimo Beltran; [ed.] Marilao Central School, Meycauayan College, Technological Institute of the Philippines, (B.S. in Electrical Engineering); [occ.] Systems Consultant; [oth. writ.] Several unpublished poems.; [pers.] Hope for the best, expect the worst.

BENN, JANNIE
[b.] February 14, 1932, Akron, AL; [p.] James and Thelma Rice; [m.] Henry H. Benn, March 5, 1949; [ch.] Betty, Lorcena, Taylor, Mary, Doris, Jacqueline, Michelle; [ed.] G.E.D. 1979, Detroit, Mich. Community College for quality Control, San Diego, Calif.; [occ.] Retired; [pers.] To have peace is to be honest with yourself.; [a.] Las Vegas, NV

BENNETT, HEATHER
[b.] January 21, 1981, Norwalk, OH; [p.] Robert and Althea Bennett; [ed.] South Central High; [memb.] SADD, HS Softball Team, HS Band; [hon.] United States Achievement Academy, Presidential Academic Fitness Award; [oth. writ.] Several unpublished poems.; [pers.] "We only get what we will settle for..." - Noel Gallagher of Oasis, lyrics from "Fade Away."; [a.] Willard, OH

BENNETT, MICHELLE
[b.] May 17, 1980, West Covina, CA; [p.] Cynthia Bennett; [ed.] Aliso Niguel High School, Junior Year, Graduate in 1998; [occ.] Student; [hon.] 3 Time GSACS Debate Champion (1st prize), Volleyball All-League (PCAL); [pers.] "I find that my inner feelings are best expressed in my writing. All of my work is dedicated to my Savior, Jesus Christ. Luke 1:37 KJV".; [a.] Laguna Niguel, CA

BENSON SR., KIRK L.
[b.] May 2, 1953, Wilmington, DE; [p.] Robert L. and Flora E. Benson; [ch.] Kirk Jr, Aaron, Dom Kirk and Sharmell; [ed.] High School, Howam High; [occ.] HVAC; [oth. writ.] Other poems unpublished that I keep at home.; [pers.] God is faithful.; [a.] Wilmington, DE

BERKIN, CAROL
[b.] September 29, 1948, Brooklyn, NY; [p.] Eleanor and Herbert Kaufmann; [m.] Mel Berkin (Deceased, May 5, 1995), April 26, 1968; [ch.]

Elizabeth, Dawn Marie, Lorraine; [ed.] Grover Cleveland HS, Queens Beauty Institute; [occ.] Hair Stylist, Pres. Midtown Tank and Selter; [hon.] None written "Just Verbal" 1) Great wife 27 yrs, 2) Great mother 26 yrs, 3) Creative talented hairstylist, 4) Writes great "Love" letters; [oth. writ.] I am currently working on a book of poems about "Love," "Life," and "Death" from my own personal experiences (I've certainly had lots of them).; [pers.] "If" I can leave a valuable contribution to this world someday to help others (with my writings) from my many challenges of learning to cope with death and struggling to survive at a very early age 10, then I will consider my life to be great.; [a.] Massapequa, NY

BEST, BONNYE
[b.] November 2, 1944, Baltimore, MD; [p.] Wm. and Mollie Rosen; [m.] Michael Best; [ch.] Melinda, David, Jeffery; [ed.] Sinai Hospital School of Nursing; [occ.] Registered Nurse; [memb.] Sinai Alumni; [hon.] Honorable Mention for poem submitted to World of Poetry in 1990 "You Were Once A Child"; [oth. writ.] "You Were Once A Child," many other poems and prose never submitted.; [pers.] I dedicate my poem to my parents who gave me life, my children who bring joy to my life and my husband who brought love into my life.; [a.] Owings Mills, MD

BETZOLD, IRENE M.
[pen.] The Betz; [b.] August 16, 1960, Crystal Lake, IL; [p.] Dolores and Edward Betzold; [m.] Gary Reed; [ch.] Robbie Burcharty; [ed.] GED - Al Collins Graphic Design School, Temple Ariz. - Production Art and Desk Top Publishing; [occ.] Cashier and Freelance Artist (starving artist); [memb.] Iowa Artists' Association; [hon.] 2nd Place Poetry Contest. Al Collins Completion Award. Honorable Mention for a painting submitted to Iowa Artists' Annual Competition; [oth. writ.] 2nd Grade National Contest Catholic Schools: 2nd Place with "His Word." Wrote a children's book never sent out: still have it and it is a sell. Don't know the next step.; [pers.] I'm a born artist. I have always painted and written poems and stories since I can remember. I feel my potential is endless. I lack the education on who and where the interested parties would be - and the legal end.; [a.] Osceola, IA

BICKERSTAFF, WILLIAM D.
[pen.] Bick; [b.] December 24, 1955, Parkersburg, WV; [p.] William E. Bickerstaff, Thermal L. Bickerstaff; [m.] Victoriana Pangalay, February 16, 1982; [ch.] Digna Evarola, Jacqueline Denice, William John, Janette Lynn, Anna Lee; [ed.] Parkersburg South High, Parkersburg Community College; [occ.] Unemployed; [pers.] I write for my children in an attempt to make them think about choices they will make and how their choices could affect their futures.; [a.] Gulfport, MS

BILLINGS, MONIQUE
[b.] November 16, 1973, Bronx, NY; [p.] Jerome Billings, Miriam Serrano; [ed.] Morris H. S. Monroe College; [oth. writ.] Several unpublished poems and songs.; [pers.] I sometimes cannot express myself out loud. I write what I feel, and what is in my heart. Good or bad!; [a.] Bronx, NY

BILLINGS, TRACIE
[b.] October 18, 1971, Monterey, CA; [p.] Dexter and Shirley Billings; [ed.] Will attend Wichita State University to work on Bachelor's degree in Journalism; [occ.] Bank teller; [memb.] SCA (Society for Creative Anachronism); [hon.] Who's Who in American Students, Honor Roll, Dean's List; [oth. writ.] I have been, up till now, writing for myself, family and friends but I would love to have some of my work published.; [pers.] I love poetry because I do think that it is the window to the soul. I love to play with words and give them more meaning than being letters on a paper.; [a.] Wichita, KS

BINNS, JAIME
[b.] October 4, 1985, Kingsha, Jamaica, WI; [p.] Maria Cole and James Binns; [ed.] Currently in Grade 6; [oth. Writ.] Life And Its Effects.

BIRKLAND, JACK
[b.] May 15, 1919, Spokane, WA; [p.] Albert and Bertine Birkland; [ed.] ALB - JD; [occ.] Retired; [pers.] It's a beautiful world.

BLAGOJEVIC, BOJANA
[b.] July 15, 1976, Gorazde (Ex - Yugoslavia), Bosnia; [p.] Andro and Stojanka Blagojevic; [occ.] College student in New Jersey; [oth. writ.] Poems published in local newspapers in Bosnia and Serbia (Ex - Yugoslavia), in the magazine, "Avenue De La Paix" (Switzerland), and "Courier-News" (USA); a collection of poems in Serbian ("Heaven of Lost Birds") published in 1995.; [pers.] I write poetry in Serbian, English, and sometimes in French. I am trying to publish a collection of my poems written in English, during the war in Bosnia ("Story of One Heart)". Those poems were made in the hope of reaching the hearts of people who have been living in peace.; [a.] North Plainfield, NJ

BLAKENEY, PATRICIA
[b.] December 12, 1956, Crossett, AK; [p.] Aubrey Chadwick, Mary Chadwick; [m.] Ray H. Blakeney Jr., September 6, 1974; [ch.] Russ, Todd, Kristen; [ed.] Taylorsville High School; [occ.] Day Care - owner and operator of Puak's Day Care; [memb.] St. Jude's Childrens Hospital; [oth. writ.] Heaven's Rainbow, Life is a Journey, Our Mother, Living Your Life, Touched By an Angel, My Children; [pers.] As my hand starts to write, two other hands from above write with me. One hand belongs to the Lord, and the other hand belongs to my mother.; [a.] Taylorsville, MS

BLAND, CYNTHIA L.
[b.] March 13, 1961, Washington, DC; [p.] Donald and Veronica Mitchell; [m.] Frank Wilson (as of), May 10, 1997 (will be married); [ch.] Donald Mitchell Bland; [occ.] Telecommunications Network Analyst; [oth. writ.] Poetry published in Treasure the Moment. Also I've been writing poetry for friends, family and myself for the past 20 years.; [pers.] My personal favorite writing is about anything I have experienced in life, closeness with family, friends, great loves or closeness to God and writing about the triumph of the human spirit.; [a.] Manassas, VA

BLANTON, SHARON ELIZABETH
[b.] May 14, 1969, Portsmouth, VA; [p.] Larry and Sue Bennett; [m.] Paul Russell Blanton, November 26, 1993; [ch.] Laura Elizabeth, Cera Ashlei; [ed.] Redan High School, Georgia, Jacksonville State University, Alabama; [occ.] Apartment Manager, Gables Residential, Atlanta, Georgia; [memb.] Gamma Sigma Sigma, ROC Kaydettes, Sigma Tau Delta (English Honor Society), The Society of Professional Journalists, Sigma Delta Chi; [hon.] Finalist in Arrive Alive Essay Contest, Finalist in Alabama Associated Press Broadcasters' Association for work as Discjockey, Newsreporter; [oth. writ.] Wrote for college and high school yearbooks and newspaper.; [pers.] My words are inspired by my two special angels, Laura and Cera. Life's most beautiful treasures.... children.; [a.] Snellville, GA

BLINDENHOFER, JOAN F.
[b.] August 5, 1947, Flushing, NY; [p.] James F. and Irma J. Blindenhofer; [ed.] BS Chemistry Daemen College; [occ.] Research Chemist; [hon.] National Science Foundation Research Grant NYS Regent's College Scholarship; [oth. writ.] Several published letters to the local newspapers.; [pers.] Poetry is food for the soul and is essential for modern day cultures to become more humane.; [a.] Norwich, NY

BLOCK, MYRA
[b.] June 19, 1942, Millston, KY; [m.] David Block, June 3, 1995; [ch.] Five adult children, seven grandchildren; [ed.] Happy Camp High, Josephine County Community College, Oregon College of Art; [occ.] Home-based Business Owner and Artist; [memb.] Church of Religious Science, Unity Church, Jr. Chamber of Commerce, Several Artist's Associations; [hon.] Many Blue Ribbons and Honors for art work; [oth. writ.] 1956, Yreka, CA. Local Newspaper published my school paper about the fires and floods in our valley. I was fourteen. Currently working on a new age story, "Is Anna There?" Poems and articles in local church publications.; [pers.] I write what I hear in my mind and feel in my heart. "The Eagle" screamed...I wrote, then cried.; [a.] Santa Rosa, CA

BLOSSOM, GABRIELLE
[b.] June 11, 1985, Evanston, IL; [p.] Gwen and Steve Blossom; [occ.] 6th grade student at Highcrest Middle School; [oth. writ.] My Name (poem), Conversation, 1998 (poem) (pending publication); [pers.] I'm an active tap dancer, enjoy reading, like singing, and was in a community theater production. My writing is really who I am through my writing; [a.] Wilmette, IL

BLOYDER, JOSEPH
[b.] December 3, 1939, Bayonne, NJ; [p.] Joseph and Estelle Bloyder; [m.] Linda, January 13, 1962; [ch.] Jessica and Jeb; [ed.] St. Peter's Prep, Parks College of St. Louis Univ.; [occ.] Pilot, Delta Airlines; [memb.] SETP (Society of Experimental Test Pilots), International Society of Poets; [oth. writ.] "Serendipity," "Rapture," "Perennial," and "Diurnal" published in National Library of Poetry anthologies and other personal through reflections decades past; [pers.] Poetry is the music of prose.; [a.] Conway, AR

BOATRIGHT JR., DEAN D.
[m.] Jean M. Boatright, September 11, 1944; [ch.] Dean III, Darby, Pam; [ed.] Wisconsin Inst. of Teach. U.S.C. grad captain U.S.M.C.

BOETTCHER, ROBERT B.
[b.] August 30, 1928, Norwood, MA; [p.] Walter and Hazel Boettcher; [m.] Marion E. Boettcher, June 15, 1974; [ch.] Raina D. Boettcher; [ed.] Voorheesville High School, Voorheesville, NY; [occ.] Retired; [pers.] Reading and writing poetry has brought inner peace to my life. I have been influenced and inspired by my mother.; [a.] Delmar, NY

BOISVERT, ERIN
[b.] January 16, 1984, Waterbury, CT; [p.] George and Maureen Boisvert; [ed.] 7th Grade Barnard School; Currently in West Side Middle School; [occ.] Student; [memb.] Focus (Gifted Program), Ct. Pre-Engineering Program, Softball Team (Town Plot), Basketball Team, W.S.M.S.; [hon.] President's Award for Academics, High Honors 7 grades, 2nd place City Essay Competition, 1st place State Maglev Competition 1996; [pers.] Preserving nature is our ultimate goal.; [a.] Waterbury, CT

BONEPARTE, LASHANA
[pen.] Bone; [b.] April 26, 1975, Manhattan; [p.] LaVurne Berry, James Boneparte; [m.] Raliek B. Allah, August 17, 1995; [ch.] Rashawn Raliek Bey Allah; [ed.] Walton H.S., Bronx College; [occ.] Cashier/Cook; [hon.] Merit Roll in High School; [oth. writ.] Several poems in high school papers.; [pers.] I haven't gone a long way, but I feel my

writings will take me there. My husband and son have been all the influence that I need to make it as a true poet.; [a.] Norfolk, VA

BORDEN, CYNTHIA J.
[pen.] C. J. Brant; [b.] February 20, 1961, Buffalo, NY; [p.] Denise and James Brant Sr.; [m.] Richard P. Borden, August 31, 1991; [ch.] Nathan (15), Samantha and Sean (Twins), James (9 yrs old); [ed.] 1 yr College J.C.C., Elementary, High; [occ.] Mom, Crafter and I work at the Cravingshop in Arkrun, NY; [memb.] Cub Scout Leader, Alden Latter Day Saints Church; [oth. writ.] Still working on it; [pers.] I am the great granddaughter of Joseph Brant, a famous, Indian Chief (Mohawk).; [a.] Akron, NY

BORES, JEFF
[b.] December 21, 1971, Georgia County; [p.] Robert and Linda Bores; [ed.] High School, Newbury, OH; [occ.] System Sales Consultant Kinetico Inc., Ohio; [hon.] Artist of The Year 1991; [oth. writ.] Several unpublished short stories and poems.; [pers.] It's odd how depression can bring out wonderful creativity and at the same time destroy your self confidence.; [a.] Newbury, OH

BOWERS, RACHEL
[pen.] Rachel Bowers; [b.] September 23, 1983, FL; [p.] Author (Lee) and Teri Bowers; [ed.] 7th Grade; [hon.] Considering my age, all I have is a D.A.R.E. essay that won in Putnam County, FL; [oth. writ.] None that I have been bold enough to get published.; [pers.] My mind matured before I did, and I see the wrongs of my peers and it hurts to see it. I want to bring these to the light and help people see their wrongs and change.; [a.] Chauncey, GA

BOWIE, EDMUND C.
[b.] Washington, DC; [m.] Margaret S. Bowie; [ch.] Edmund C., Bowie Jr., Ellen M. Bowie; [occ.] Retired; [memb.] Bars of District Court of U.S., D.C., U.S. Court of Appeals, U.S. Supreme Court; [hon.] Ninth Generation Marylander, Captain U.S. Army, World War II, Retired U.S. Army Reserve Major, Former Legal Analyst, Legal Examiner, and Attorney Advisor, U.S. Government; [pers.] May peace prevail, and happiness fill all hearts.; [a.] Temple Hills, MD

BOYEA, KELLY
[b.] January 18, 1983, Albany, NY; [occ.] Diane and Robert Boyea; [ed.] Bethlehem Central Middle School, currently in 8th grade, High Honor Roll Student; [occ.] Student; [memb.] Girl Scouts for 8 years; [pers.] Horses have played a big part in my life as well as in my writing. Besides being a journalist after I attend college, I hope to own my own horse farm and many horses. I really want to thank my grandmother for encouraging me in all my writing.; [a.] Delmar, NY

BRADBURN, JAIMI
[pen.] Jaimi Bradburn; [b.] February 25, 1981, Herdson, KY; [p.] Pat Wes Bradburn; [ed.] I am attending Union County High School, I am a sophomore, and I am 15.; [memb.] I am a member of the drama club; [hon.] I have several trophies in softball, and bicycling; [oth. writ.] Beyond a Sunset's Horizon, Angels, Under The Sea, Two Special People, A Dad Prayer, Mom I Love You so Very Much, Dad I love You So Very Much; [pers.] Try, try again, just because you didn't win one contest doesn't mean, you can't win others, everyone has talent, weather its written or singing.; [a.] Sturgis, KY

BRADFIELD, DIANNE V.
[b.] August 14, 1945, Long Beach, CA; [p.] Donald and Dorothy Kessinger; [m.] Barry Bradfield, October 20, 1967; [ch.] Eric Michael and Ryan Scott; [ed.] B.A. Degree (Calif. State Univ. of Long Beach); [occ.] Librarian (Marshall Middle School); [memb.] National Education Association, California School Library Association, International Reading Association, Delta Kappa Gamma; [hon.] Golden Apple Award (Teacher's Assoc. of Long Beach); [oth. writ.] Several articles published in local newspapers, article published in Today's Christian Woman.; [a.] Lakewood, CA

BRADY, KED
[b.] November 29, 1916, Roann, IN; [p.] Clinton and Jennie May Brady; [m.] Divorced; [ch.] Two grandsons, two greatgrandsons, 3 great granddaughters, two daughters, four granddaughters; [ed.] B.S. Degree in Mechanical Engineering; [occ.] Retired from Bottle Design Engineering Glass Plant; [memb.] Minnetrista Associates Who Provide Lifelong Learning Opportunities; [oth. writ.] Written poems for birthdays, Christmas gifts and Pastor's appreciation days.; [pers.] My grandfather, T. W. C. Anderson, published a book of poems he had written entitled "Under the Skies" (nature poems); he has always been my inspiration for my poetry writing.; [a.] Wabash, IN

BRANCH, BONNY
[b.] November 13, 1955, South Boston, VA; [p.] Smith and Agnes Murray; [m.] Michael Dale Branch, March 17, 1995; [ed.] A.A.S. in Respiratory (Degree) Therapy; [occ.] Registered Respiratory Therapist; [memb.] National Board for Respiratory Care, American Heart Association; [hon.] Winfred Isom Scholarship, Phi Theta Kappa; [pers.] I believe that all individuals are divinely gifted, and I hope to inspire and encourage others through mine.; [a.] Richmond, VA

BRANDON, RUTHIE L.
[b.] February 14, 1957, Shreveport, LA; [p.] Nellie Willis; [m.] Wallace Brandon, September 26, 1993; [ch.] Cedric Allen Willis (Deceased); [ed.] Lewis and Clark Jr. High School, Spokane Washington; [occ.] Certified Nurse Tech.; [oth. writ.] Several other poems, I have in collection; [pers.] My goal is to inspire people, and to encourage people to express themselves to release the pressure.; [a.] Murfreesboro, TN

BRANTLEY, VERA
[b.] July 2, 1925, Perth, West Australia; [p.] Hannah Grenville and William Carstairs; [m.] Roy William Brantley (Deceased), May 30, 1955; [ch.] John Arnold Rekow; [ed.] 2 Years West Aust RLN Missionary College (WAMC) Carmel, Western Australia, Australia; [occ.] Retired Retail Manager; [memb.] St. Francis Episcopal Church, Fair Oaks Calif.; [pers.] I am an active member of the Friendly Family of St. Francis. I enjoy gardening in the golden California sunshine and bird watching.; [a.] Fair Oaks, CA

BRASWELL, JOSEPH C.
[b.] March 4, 1973; [p.] Joseph H. Braswell Jr., Virginia Braswell; [ed.] Central High School, University of Memphis; [occ.] Student; [hon.] 1st Place District Level, Young Tennessee Writer's Contest, Who's Who of American High School Students; [a.] Chattanooga, TN

BREWER, DAVID ALLEN
[b.] February 7, 1970, Fairborn, OH; [p.] Jack L. and Margaret E. Brewer; [ed.] Fairborn Baker High School; [oth. writ.] This is the first poem I shared with the public but I have many others that I hope to have published one day.; [pers.] I write directly from the heart pertaining to personal past experiences.; [a.] Fairborn, OH

BREWER, SAMANTHA L.
[pen.] Sammie B.; [b.] May 8, 1972, Cape May Court House, NJ; [p.] Joan and Samuel Brewer; [ed.] Middle Twp. H.S. Wesley College, B.A. Liberal Arts; [occ.] Clerk Typist - Welfare Dept.; [memb.] Delta Phi Epsilon National Sorority; [pers.] I wrote this poem for a friend that lived with me for a short time in that short time, he helped me to experience life. For that, I dedicate this poem to him, Joe Graisbery. He really is "One of Those People".; [a.] Cape May Court House, NJ

BRIGUGLIO, ANTHONY E.
[pen.] Tony B.; [b.] March 5, 1962, Bronx, NY; [p.] Ernest Briguglio, Jennie Briguglio; [m.] Denise Briguglio, July 22, 1987; [ch.] Anthony Michael Briguglio; [ed.] Hicksville High School, Community Colleges; [occ.] Run the daily operation of a Toyota Dealership; [oth. writ.] Several poems and stories I keep for my our personal achievement.; [pers.] I'm not trying to change the world with my writing. I'm just trying to let people know who I am and what I feel about my life experiences. (I have been greatly influenced by life); [a.] Farmingville, NY

BRISCO, KENNETH
[pen.] K. Alexander; [b.] January 12, 1971; [p.] Charles Brisco, Lela Brisco; [ed.] Howard University; [a.] Capitol Heights, MD

BRITTON, MARY BOATWRIGHT
[pen.] Mary Boatwright Britton; [b.] January 8, 1948, Walterboro, SC; [p.] Mr. and Mrs. Sampson Boatwright; [m.] Abraham Britton (Deceased), June 16, 1976; [ch.] Tammi A. Britton; [ed.] Graduated Bonds-Wilson High School, currently attending Limestone College; [occ.] Travel Assistant Naval Hospital, Charleston, SC; [memb.] Toastmasters International EEO Committee; [oth. writ.] Several unpublished poems, one poem published in high school paper.; [pers.] Poem was written for and is dedicated to my daughter Tammi A. Britton.; [a.] Charleston, SC

BROCKINGTON, LENORA M.
[pen.] Lenora Brockington; [b.] September 17, 1928, Okahumpka, FL; [p.] Mose C. and Claudia Lee Brockington; [m.] Deceased; [ch.] Fredricka Howard, Wm. F. Dabney; [ed.] B.S. Degree, A&T Univ. Greensboro, NC; Graduate Study at Pittsbury Univ. and Atlanta Univ.; [occ.] Retired from the State of Florida with 32 yrs.; [memb.] Iota Phi Lamba Sorority, New Bethel Ame Church; [oth. writ.] Copyright poem "Say That You Love Me"; [a.] Okahumpka, FL

BROOKS, TRAVIS
[b.] August 16, 1984, Statesboro; [p.] Mr. and Mrs. Brooks Henry and Karol; [ed.] Copeland Elementary, Langford and Glenn Hills Middle School; [memb.] Glenn Hills Middle School Chorus, Glenn Hills Middle School Student council alternate, Science ecology club, and member of prosperity Holiness Church; [hon.] Spelling Bee 1st runner up, Honor roll, and 2nd place in a singing contest; [pers.] Keep trying. Do your best. Read the last 2 lines of my poem and remember it forever.; [a.] Augusta, GA

BROWN, AMY
[b.] December 9, 1977, Fremont, MI; [p.] Steve and Terry Brown; [ed.] Newaygo High School, and the Newaygo County Career Tech Center; [occ.] Student; [memb.] Students Against Drunk Driving, Vocational Industrial Clubs of America; [hon.] Scholastic Awards, and various ribbons and medals for art.; [oth. writ.] Several other personal poems; [pers.] I firmly believe that poetry is the most emotionally expressive form of literature. When I'm writing I not only try to stir up emotions within myself, but in other people as well.; [a.] Newaygo, MI

BROWN, CYNTHIA
[pen.] C. Brown; [b.] July 11, 1950, Bar Harbor, ME; [p.] Charlene Burton; [m.] Gary Brown, February 14, 1989; [ch.] Dawn, Lynn, Steven; [ed.] Pemetic High School, Southwest Harbor, Maine; Tremont Elementary, Tremont, Maine; [occ.] Apt. Manager; [memb.] Assoc. Hud Managing, Agent's Institute Real Estate Management; [oth. writ.] I have a portfolio of 40 poems; none have been published. This is my first!; [pers.] Poetry writing gives me a sense of self satisfaction and is a wonderful way of relieving stress from today's influences. I did not realize my talent until I composed my first poem for my granddaughter.; [a.] Bakersfield, CA

BROWN, CYNTHIA ANN
[pen.] Cindy Brown; [b.] April 16, 1960, El Dorado, AR; [p.] Kay Francis White and Billy Mack Ford; [m.] John Harvey Brown, October 23, 1993; [ch.] Brian Ford, Justin and April Hodges; [ed.] Graduated High School at Haltom High in Haltom City, TX in 1978; [occ.] Mail clerk for Radio Shack mailroom; [pers.] I've been writing poems for a while as an unknown. After my co-worker's continuous advice to enter a contest, or something to display my talent, I finally did.; [a.] Watauga, TX

BROWN, KENNETH RAYMOND
[b.] July 24, 1909, Lemoore, CA; [p.] Luther S. Brown and Edith A. McDonald; [m.] Matilda Carmen Puerta, June 17, 1938; [ch.] Carolyn L., Kathleen R., Pamela M.; [ed.] High School, Fresno Public Schools, A.B. Fresno State College, 1931, M.A., Stanford University, 1937, Ed.D., Stanford University, 1947; [occ.] Retired Classroom Teacher; [memb.] Nat'l Educ. Assoc. Life; Calif. Teachers Assoc., Life; Fresno Teachers Assoc., Life; Phi Delta Kappa, since 1934; Retired Military Officers' Assoc., Calif.; Retired Teachers' Assoc., since 1971; Oakmont Community Church, Santa Rosa, CA; [hon.] Served as historical officer to 316th Bombardment Wing, Eight Air Force, on Okinawa, 1947-48; [oth. writ.] Conditions of Work for Quality Teaching, NEA Dept Classroom Teachers, 1959.; [pers.] Sonnets were written to Matilda Puerta during engagement.; [a.] Santa Rosa, CA

BROWNE, SYLVIA HATCHER
[b.] July 15, 1932, Portsmouth, VA; [p.] John (Deceased) and Sophia Hatcher; [m.] Thos. L. Browne, September 4, 1951; [ch.] Endia, Thos. Jr., Ronald; [ed.] Associate degree - Norfolk Div. of VA State College and attending VA State College (Petersburg, VA) 1950-1953; [occ.] Substitute Teacher; [pers.] This poem is dedicated to my husband, who has been hospitalized 3 1/2 yrs.

BROWNLEE, WENDY
[pen.] Betty Brown; [b.] August 29, 1966, Detroit, MI; [p.] Willie Sr., Jeannette; [ed.] Osborn High, University of Alaska, University of South Carolina; [occ.] Computer Operator; [memb.] N.A.A.C.P., AFRKAN American Association; [pers.] All praises to Him which gives me life. And much respect to those who have influenced me to write (ie. Donald Goines, Maya Angelou, Jamaica Kincaid, Patricia Gaines, Nathaniel McCall, Nikki Giovanni, Osman Waberi etc).; [a.] Detroit, MI

BRUDNOK, MARGARET
[pen.] "Maggie"; [b.] October 29, 1930, Pittsburgh, PA; [p.] Margaret and Fred Stein; [m.] Raymond J., February 15, 1952; [ch.] Peggy, Jeffrey, Ray C., Barbara, Elizabeth; [ed.] Master Education, Lindfield College BA - Cum Laude; [occ.] Owner - Educational Medical Training Service or EMTS; [memb.] Master Trainer for EMP America, Instructor Trainer American Heart Assoc., EMTI State of Oregon (I stands for Intermediate); [hon.] Correspondent of the Year Award from Statesman Newspaper, Certificate of Award from Board on Police Standards and Training for Communications Personnel Certificate from Oregon Trail Chapter, Roll of Honor for over 40 yrs. of Service Certificate of Appreciation from the National Oregon Sheriff Assoc. for Services; [oth. writ.] Articles in Statesman Newspaper and Sheridan Sun Newspaper (now poetry); [pers.] With God as #1 - my family and I can do anything - without Him we would have nothing and could do nothing. God is our comfort, our love and our guide - sometimes he says no, but that's ok, he doesn't close one door before he opens the next one.; [a.] Sheridan, OR

BRUNER, ERIC
[b.] July 28, 1969, Pittsburgh, PA; [p.] Edward Bruner, Carrie Bruner; [occ.] Teller, Bell Federal Savings and Loan Association; [pers.] Dreams can become reality if you never forget them.; [a.] Whitaker, PA

BRYANT JR., HERBERT MCCOY
[pen.] Herbie DeLaney; [b.] August 8, 1943, Sebring, FL; [p.] Edgar H. and Evelyn DeLaney; [ed.] Avon Park High School, Univ. of S. FL; [occ.] Statistical Programmer/Analyst, SW Fla. Water Mgt. District, Tampa, FL; [memb.] American Statistical Association, Amnesty Int'l, Common Cause, Unitarian Universalist Church of Tampa; [hon.] 1996 Edition of Marquis Who's Who in America; [oth. writ.] Many (100+) unpublished short poems; [pers.] I write poems by describing images which evoke feelings. I wish to experience. My favorite poet is Robinson Jeffers.; [a.] Tampa, FL

BUCK, KELVY
[pen.] I; [b.] June 1954, Clairborne County; [p.] Willie and Lorriane; [ed.] Graduated Port Gibson High 1972 and Alcorn State Univ. 1987; [occ.] Educational Clerk - Education Department - MCCF; [hon.] Honorable Mention for poems entered in an earlier poetry contest; [oth. writ.] Two poems - A Poem and Etiquette in Profile - respectively.; [pers.] Inspiration is a most valuable asset, with it - God moves humanity to bitterness. I hope to inspire humanity through my poetry.; [a.] Port Gibson, MS

BURIAN, JEANA
[b.] November 20, 1983, Petersburg, VA; [p.] Vi Beem and Honk Burian; [ed.] I am currently in the 8th grade at West End Christian School; [occ.] Student; [memb.] I am a member of River's Edge Bible Church. I also participate in Chess Club, Karate and am a dancer and gymnast at Traylor Dance Academy.; [hon.] I have won my class Spelling Bee and participated in the Regionals since 1st grade and have also been in Gifted and Talented for that long. I am also an Honor Roll student; [pers.] Although I am only 12 years old, I love to express my feelings in poetry form. It never occurred to me that I would have any of my poems published.; [a.] Hopewell, VA

BURKE, MARTHA L.
[pen.] Martee; [b.] December 20, 1968, Apple Valley, CA; [p.] Mr. and Mrs. Del D. Dutcher; [m.] Mark T. Burke, July 29, 1989; [ed.] Barstow High School, Barstow Junior College; [occ.] Manager - Terrible Herbst AM/PM #135; [pers.] This poem was written when my dad was in the hospital. He was to undergo open heart surgery. This was the first of 4 poems I wrote during this trying time. Thank God he's fine now!; [a.] Barstow, CA

BURKE, MELBA J.
[pen.] Melba Burke; [b.] April 19, 1932, Cullman Co, AL; [p.] Jessie G. and Eva L. Hill; [m.] James Rainey, December 15, 1953, Billy Ray Burke, February 7, 1980; [ch.] Cynthia Buckelew; [ed.] Tarrant High, Gadsden State College; [occ.] Retired; [memb.] Barnabus Club; [oth. writ.] Magazine, short stories, Yesterday's Memories; [a.] Boaz, AL

BURLEIGH, RAY
[b.] May 22, 1939, Syracuse, NY; [p.] Robert and Francis Burleigh; [m.] Divorced; [ch.] Ray Jr. (35), Robert (34), Yvonne (33), Colleen (30); [ed.] High School Graduate - 1958, Virgil Central School, Virgil, N.Y.; [occ.] Resident Manager of 3 apt. complexes in Phoenix; [memb.] Baldwinsville Moose Lodge #644, Sam's Club, Handyman Club of America; [hon.] Won Dekalb Award in High School; [oth. writ.] Wrote 10 songs - have been recorded in Nashville, TN: American Puppy Dogs, She Had To Roam, Recipe of Love, Lawn Rod, Thank You, Father, Greedy Breed, Cop Teaser, Joking, Thank You Fans, Buck Fever; [pers.] Love antique autos - have 247 models - car calendars from 1957 - own 1948 Dodge Pu to be used to make street rod - I have been very enthused with my writings.; [a.] Phoenix, NY

BURNHAM, JENNIFER
[b.] November 10, 1984; [p.] Thomas Hart (Stepdad), Laura Wolf (Mom); [ed.] 7th Grader - East Shore Middle School; [occ.] Student; [memb.] Drama Club, Foran High Colorguard; [hon.] 3 Merits for my good behavior and helping when help's needed. Numerous merit badges in Girl Scouts; [oth. Writ.] The Cat, The Furry Little Rabbit, and Who am I? (not published); [pers.] Writing makes me feel better. It helps me get all my feelings out. I feel good when people read one of my poems, and really enjoy reading it.; [a.] Milford, Ct

BYERS, ELAINE
[pen.] J. T. Royce; [b.] February 20, 1959, Easley, SC; [p.] B. F. and Stella Byers; [oth. writ.] Reflections of Anger, published in the book Amidst the Splendor.; [a.] Easley, SC

CAILEY, EVELYN M.
[pen.] Bending of Twigs; [b.] September 15, 1937, Cincinnati, OH; [p.] Edna Heidenreich and Bruce Anderson; [m.] Leroy Delbert Cailey, May 12, 1979; [ch.] Michael V. and Timothy W. Theus; [ed.] College Credits in Psychology from Univ. of Cinti (Batavia). Bachelor of Theology-Trinity College Master of Arts Counseling-Trinity Sem.; [occ.] Retired Housewife; [memb.] Trinity Alumni Assoc.; [hon.] Trinity Theological Seminary Master of Arts-graduated Summa Cum Laude. Two Editor's Choice Awards for 1996 - "Nosey Mosey" and "Tears" poems - Nat'l Library of Poetry; [oth. writ.] Local church newsletters. Two published poems for the Nat'l Library of Poetry 1996.; [pers.] I strive to reflect back to friends, family and my little animals all of the love and joy that I receive from them.; [a.] Cincinnati, OH

CALDWELL, CLIVE
[b.] November 28, 1947, Washington, DC; [p.] Douglas W. Caldwell, Edith B. Caldwell; [ed.] Churchland High School, Portsmouth, VA Attended VA Tech and Old Dominion Univ.; [occ.] Fields System Engineer, Goddard Space Flight Center, Greenbelt, MD; [memb.] Aircraft Owners and Pilot Assoc. (AOPA); [oth. writ.] Poem published in local newspaper; [a.] Waldorf, MD

CALLAHAN, MICHAEL R.
[b.] August 22, 1956, Long Beach, CA; [p.] Ray and Ruth Callahan; [ed.] Claute County Community College Nevada, University of Nevada, Las Vegas; [occ.] Gardener, Canyon Gate Country Club, LU, NV; [memb.] International Sculpture Center, Smithsonian Institution, American Legion; [pers.] Serious art, whether it is literary or visual, must go beyond the obvious in our world, to reach out to a level where humankind can grow on a spiritual or

philosophical plane by reflecting truth.; [a.] Las Vegas, NV

CAMPBELL, LUCILE M.
[pen.] Lucile M. Campbell; [b.] September 15, 1906, Halcyondale, GA; [p.] Thomas Alonzo McGregor, Annie Laurie McGregor; [m.] John Thomas Campbell (Deceased); [ch.] Charles Thomas Campbell (Deceased); [ed.] Georgia State Women's College, B.A. - Scarriett College, Masters - Auburn University; [occ.] Retired School Teacher and Writer; [oth. writ.] Junaluska Lyrics, To God Be The Glory, Bright and Morning Star, On Wings of Power.

CANTRELL, LAVONNE O.
[b.] December 27, 1935, Pontiac, MI; [p.] Archie and Pearl Warden; [m.] Willis W. Cantrell, September 11, 1979; [ed.] Pontiac High - Univ. of Mich., Glendale Community College (Calif) [occ.] Retired Military and Law Enforcement; [memb.] American Legion - American Legion Auxiliary - Life Member of Law Enforcement Alliance of America; [hon.] Dean's List - Honor Grad-Alpha Gamma Sigma (Calif State Honor Society); [oth. writ.] Poems published in local newspapers - articles in church newsletter; [pers.] I found few poems of interest to me so I wrote my own - I write animal stories, based on true life experiences, for children of all ages. Each story exhibits achievement or triumph over tragedy.; [a.] Kendalia, TX

CANTU, JOHN ANTHONY
[pen.] Gordo; [b.] November 27, 1978, San Antonio, TX; [p.] Juan and Ernestna Cantu; [ch.] Adrianna Nicole Cantu; [ed.] Johnston High School 10th grade; [occ.] Student; [hon.] Got my diploma from "Victory School of the Bible"; [pers.] An expression for a love that will last through all time - giving of myself and loving unconditionally - just as God has taught us all to do.; [a.] New Brauntels, TX

CAPEDER, RACHEL
[b.] August 7, 1985, Saint Paul, MN; [p.] Vincent and Sandra Capeder; [ed.] Bayport Elementary currently in 6th grade - Bayport, MN; [memb.] Girl Scouts of America, Stillwater Swim Club, Valley Athletic Association; [oth. writ.] Bayport Elementary MAJ newsletter; [a.] Stillwater, MN

CAPERTON, BRIGITTE CHRISTINE
[b.] October 20, 1966, Munich, Germany; [p.] Friedrich and Judith Aschberger; [m.] Samuel Caperton, June 2, 1986; [ed.] B.S. in Mathematics, 1990, University of North Texas; [occ.] Support Analyst, Moore Business Forms, Denton, TX; [pers.] Hobbies: martial arts, horseback riding, reading, Ain't life grand?; [a.] Sanger, TX

CARDENAS, LAMBERTO DIAZ
[b.] September 17, 1934, Mexico; [ed.] Diploma I.C.S. (Mechanist); [occ.] Journeyman Welder, N.A.T. Rockwell Milpitas CA; [memb.] Mechanist Union #504; [hon.] Diploma I.C.S.; [oth. writ.] In process; [pers.] Touch someone and soul heart.; [a.] San Jose, CA

CARFI, J.
[b.] August 6, 1964, Sewickley, PA; [p.] Donald and Patricia Martin; [m.] Marc S. Carfi, August 5, 1995; [ch.] David Harvey Gibson; [ed.] Moon High, Parkway West Technical School, Bradford School of Business, Courses at Robert Morris College; [occ.] Accounting Manager/Systems Administrator; [oth. writ.] Many poems written for wedding and anniversary programs, newsletters and church bulletins.; [pers.] I have been greatly influenced by the poets Alfred Tennyson and Lydia Baxter, but my relationships with my family and friends and the special love we share has been the true inspiration for my writing.; [a.] Peekskill, NY

CARLE, EMILY ELIZA
[pen.] Emmie E. Carle; [b.] November 14, 1983, Portland, ME; [p.] Maggie and Steve Carle; [ed.] Student, grade 7; [occ.] Student; [hon.] Honor Roll Student, DARE Speaker (Award)/Essay; [oth. writ.] Written other poems, and writing a novel, "A Friend for Life," about a light house; [pers.] Never just focus on the clouds blocking the sunshine, but look over that cloud and find a shining sun filled with light of goodness.; [a.] Woolwich, ME

CARLISE, CHUCK
[b.] June 14, 1977, Akron, OH; [p.] Charles and Catherine Carlise; [ed.] Canton Central Catholic H.S., Wittenberg University; [occ.] Student; [memb.] Beta Theta Pi Fraternity, WUSO - Radio (DJ), Varsity Track, with Indoor and Outdoor; [hon.] CCHS Education Foundation Scholarship, Witt Slum Association Scholarship, Hattie Gilmore Memorial Scholarship, Best New Member - Wit. Greek System; [oth. writ.] Various poems published in high school literary magazine.; [pers.] More than anything else, I try to find emotions people can relate to, then portray it in writing. The poetry of the last halt-century has been most influential on me.; [a.] Canton, OH

CARLISLE, VON ALLAN
[pen.] Von Allan Carlisle; [b.] June 19, 1911, Van Buren, AR; [p.] John and Alice Carlisle (Deceased); [m.] Elizabeth Carlisle, January 18, 1981; [ch.] Four, one Deceased; [ed.] A.B. '35, J.D. '38 I have parctised law since 1938, the last 10 years of which I served as a Federal Administrative Law Judge in Illinois (Chicago) and, lastly, in Missouri; [occ.] Retired; [hon.] President of my senior class in high school (Kansas City), Coach of debate and director of forensics at the university where I received my law degree, from 1935-38; [oth. writ.] I have had poems published in the "Missouri Student", Univ. of MO., the St. Louis Post Dispatch and the Kansas City Star. They were submitted by me voluntarily; I was not paid.; [pers.] My poem, written after my first born, a daughter, reflects my sorrow at not having been a better father to her. She died June 21 of this year.; [a.] Biloxi, MS

CARLSON, OLA M.
[pen.] Ola Margaret James; [b.] July 23, 1917, Wilburton, OK; [p.] John Baird James Sr. and Ada L. Redume James; [m.] Carol Elmer Olinghouse, May 17, 1942; [ch.] John Edward, Carolyn L. and Mary Margaret; [ed.] Milburton High School, Polytechnic Beauty College; [occ.] Retired Beautician; [memb.] Eastern Star Chapter 204, Rebekah Lodge #54, Poetry Society of Oklahoma, Twin Cities Garden Club; [hon.] "Oh Winds My Voice," Golden Plaque Poetry Society of Oklahoma 1975., Lyric Poem. "San Francisco", Oklahoma Teacher 1936, poems in "Latimer County News Democrat" "A Farmer Father Rembers," and "Progressive Farmer 1940," "Lullaby for a Country Club," farm and ranch 1939.; [oth. writ.] "High on the Hilltop," grade school news. Local articles on Garden Club, and Rebekah Lodge; [pers.] I strive to write good nostalgic and Christian poetry, to uplift, and encourage others.; [a.] Hartshorne, OK

CAROSELLO, MARK ANTHONY
[pen.] Mark Anthony Carosello; [b.] January 7, 1957, Saint Louis, MO; [p.] Tony and Ruth Carosello; [m.] Sharyn Marie Carosello, (2nd) November 10, 1992; [ch.] (From 1st marriage) Anthony - 19, Nichole - 18, Alicia - 17; [ed.] Graduated from Riverview Gardens High School in 1975, attended the University of Missouri - Saint Louis, 1976; [occ.] Poet; [oth. writ.] Have written a great number of poems in the categories of: children's poetry, contemporary and American Civil War poetry. Yet to be published.; [pers.] My poetry deals with several topics. I especially enjoy writing poetry for children. I wish for my children's poetry to cause children to smile and laugh. I have a keen interest in the American Civil War. I wish to honor those who played a role in the war with my poetry.; [a.] Saint Louis, MO

CARPENTER, CHARLES RAYMOND
[pen.] Skip; [b.] August 21, 1952, L.A., CA; [p.] Charles Lavern Carpenter and Mary Elizabeth Chrildress; [m.] Elizabeth Christine Ziegler; [ch.] Theresa JoAnne and Mary Elizabeth; [ed.] North Central High School; [occ.] River Bottom Impound and Storage; [hon.] Charles Raymond Carpenter was baptized in the name of the Father and the Son and of the Holy Spirit on the 10th day as of November 1996, at Grace Community Church, Tempe, Arizona by Pastor, Larry Finch (602)-894-2201; [pers.] Always remember no matter how big or how small, keeping God in your heart will be a blessing for us all!; [a.] Tempe, AZ

CARPENTER, CHARLIE HENRY
[pen.] Angel Colon; [b.] October 7, 1964, East Meadow, NY; [p.] Edna May Carpenter, Charlie D. Carpenter; [m.] Mariluz Claudio Carpenter, February 29, 1992; [ch.] Kevin-James, Araceli-May, Anna-Maria-Lynn, Edna-Lee-Anna; [ed.] Bellport High School, Canisius College, St. Joseph's College; [occ.] Student St. Joseph' College; [hon.] Dean's List, Associate of Arts, Cum Laude graduate, Tutor training; [oth. writ.] Short stories, poems, children's books (none published to date); [pers.] To those who had faith in my abilities and supported me through very hard times: I could not have done it without you. Thank you for believing in me. I love you all!; [a.] East Patchogue, NY

CARR, MELISSA J.
[b.] September 14, 1964, Connellsville, PA; [p.] Richard Fisher, Martha Fisher; [m.] Frankie D. Carr Jr., May 6, 1995; [ch.] Jessica Marie; [ed.] Mary Fuller Frazier Memorial High School, Perryopolis, PA; [occ.] Sales, Advance Auto Parts, Jefferson City, TN; [memb.] First Christian Church, Perryopolis, PA; [pers.] I feel every day should be looked on as a gift. The poem I wrote was written from the heart for my favorite person.

CARRUTH, MICHELLE RENEE
[b.] October 30, 1970, Washington; [pers.] I'm influenced to write by life experiences, goals, achievements and dreams.

CARSON, CARL G.
[b.] September 1, 1954, Baton Rouge, LA; [p.] Herbert V. Carson and Marie Graham Carson; [ch.] John, Chris, Ann Marie; [ed.] Texas Military Institute, University of Texas at San Antonio; [occ.] Computer Consultant; [pers.] I strive to view life as an adventure to be treasured and enjoyed, but most of all shared with family and friends. Using the gifts God has given me and the things I have learned, I try to make life a little easier, a little brighter and encourage others to do the same.; [a.] Houston, TX

CARTER, AMANDA LYNN
[pen.] Melody Steel; [b.] January 30, 1983, Newport News, VA; [p.] Kathleen Pusey and David Carter; [ed.] K-4 Parklawn Elem. Farfax VA, 5-6 Centreville Elem., Centreville VA, 7 Rocky Run Middle School Chantilly VA, Current 8, Selbyville Middle School Selbyville, DE; [occ.] Student; [hon.] I have gotten at least 5 awards for my singing ability and about 3 for poetry from my schools.; [oth. writ.] Hurt, Questions, Forever My Love, Set Free, Lines, To My Love, Forever Your Girl, All Over Again, Broken Heart, I Always Fall, If He Loved Me, One Night; [pers.] Anything I have to say can be read in my poems.; [a.] Dagsboro, DE

CARTIER, RUTH E.
[b.] September 30, 1915, Danvers, MA; [p.] Mr. and Mrs. Arthur Salomon; [m.] Raymond F. Roger Sr. (Deceased) April 11, 1934, James F. Cartier (Deceased) September 20, 1975; [ch.] Raymond Jr., Elizabeth Marion; [ed.] High School Grad., Danvers, Mass; [occ.] Retired; [memb.] Hampton Falls Grange United Trinity Church, Seabrook, NH; [hon.] Happy and honored that my poem was selected; [oth. writ.] Several poems and limericks.; [pers.] Have always loved poetry and started writing in the 70's.

CASSEDAY, RUBY D.
[pen.] Christian Wise; [b.] November 12, 1941, Greene Township, PA; [p.] Goldie T. and Burns W. Wise (The Late); [m.] Blaine A. Casseday, September 8, 1962; [ch.] Raymond, Damon and Hope; [ed.] High School Diploma; [occ.] Student; [memb.] First Baptist Church of Greensboro, Dorcas Society, Dunkard Grange, Mountaineer Parent's Club; [hon.] PA Game Commision's Sports Ethics Award; [pers.] By following the teachings of the Bible, I strive to reflect goodness and friendship so that others can see Christ living in me.; [a.] Greensboro, PA

CASTIGLIONE, DOMINICK
[b.] September 3, 1944, Brooklyn, NY; [p.] James and Josephine; [ed.] BA, MA, City University of New York - Economics; [occ.] Freelance Writer; [hon.] Economics Fellowship, City University of New York; [oth. writ.] Beyond right and wrong - novel a balanced ph diet - essay. Pettifogger's pickle - poem 3rd prize National Library of Poetry 1996 Drive 65, essay on raising state speed limit, Newsday; [pers.] If you can't believe it - don't!; [a.] Aquebogue, NY

CASTRO, GAIL
[b.] December 22, 1948, Okeechobee, FL; [p.] Allen Hancock, Pearl Hancock; [m.] Greg Castro, May 25, 1990; [ch.] Billy, Jeff, Tina Kloosterman; [ed.] Okeechobee High; [occ.] Housewife; [memb.] American Museum of Natural History, National Home Gardening Club; [pers.] I write what I feel in my heart, what I feel others need to hear. My mother and my husband have been great influences in my writing. I have also been inspired by Helen Steiner-Rice.

CAUFFIEL, SEAN
[pers.] I would like to thank some very special friends that have supported me in what I write, even when they don't agree with it: Julia Baker, NyQ Bonaventura, Man-d Bonaventura, Sarah Teutschm Tori Turner, Amy Orr, Divergent Point - I hope you're big someday, Mrs. Julie Smith, and everyone who has ever encouraged and supported me. Thank you for everything. I love you all.

CAVERLY, NANCY I.
[b.] March 15, 1955, Santa Cruz, CA; [p.] Jack F. Blakesley, Frances Blakesley; [m.] Joseph Caverly, June 15, 1974; [ch.] Wayne Eugene, Diana Victoria; [ed.] Edison High, Cypress College, Richard's Beauty College; [occ.] Student, Cypress College of Mortuary Science; [memb.] Eastern Star, Hunt, Bch.; [oth. writ.] Several poems used in speeches for non-profit organizations.; [pers.] I often enjoy writing about the beauty of nature or about my father, who was an inspiration in my life.; [a.] Huntington Beach, CA

CAVINESS, CHRIS
[b.] November 19, 1969, Chicago, IL; [p.] Everett Caviness, Susan Keith; [m.] Caryn Caviness, August 31, 1991; [ch.] Alixandria Paige, Jessica Leigh; [ed.] General Education Diploma; [occ.] Security Alarm Installer, Security Link from Ameritech; [pers.] At times I see the world in a different light. I try to convey the various inner thoughts and feelings of mankind.; [a.] Bensenville, IL

CHAMP, PAT E.
[b.] June 10, 1941, Cincinnati, OH; [p.] Arthur and Lucille Neudigate; [m.] Divorced; [ch.] Tony, Terri, Tim, Ted; [ed.] Center Vocational H.S. Southern Ohio College; [occ.] Nurse - Office Manager for Stacey Greenert MD, Inc.; [hon.] Dean's List x3; [pers.] My words reflect my feelings; [a.] Cincinnati, OH

CHEN, AILEEN
[pen.] Aileen Chen; [b.] February 27, 1984, China; [p.] Xia Hong and Qinyun Chen; [ed.] 7th Grade JH; [occ.] Student; [hon.] Piscataway Sidewalk Drawing Competition 1st 1991, Central Jersey Chinese Speeches, 1992 1st, 1994 1st, 1995 1st; Home News Mother's Day Drawing Competition 1st 1994; [oth. writ.] Chinese essay, "What It Takes To Be The Person I Want To Be When I Grow Up" 2nd 1995. Westlake School "Essay of the Month" award twice; [pers.] I've always loved to read and write. One of my dreams is to become famous, so I entered a lot of drawing, writing, and speech competitions. The greatest influence in life is my mom, Xia Hong, and my dad, Qingyon Chen.; [a.] Indianapolis, IN

CHEN, MELISSA
[b.] September 18, 1982, Shanghai, China; [p.] Rusan Chen, Meiping Feng; [hon.] The National Junior Honor Society; [pers.] When you do something, do it well or why bother?; [a.] Saint Louis, MO

CHIPMAN, CYNTHIA
[b.] October 1, 1957, Milledgeville, GA; [m.] Kent Chipman; [ch.] Travis Chipman; [ed.] Attended Georgia College, Graduated High School, GMC; [occ.] Director, Children's Ministries First United Methodist Church, Milledgeville, GA 31061; [memb.] Member, First United Methodist Church; [hon.] Lay Speaker for the Augusta District Methodist Church; [oth. writ.] Numerous unpublished poems; [a.] Milledgeville, GA

CHRISTIAN, CRYSTAL
[b.] April 5, 1975, Watauga Hospital; [p.] James and Willa Wall; [m.] Richard D. Christian Jr., May 26, 1995; [ch.] Thomas Clayton; [ed.] I attended Watauga High School through my tenth grade year; [occ.] I am a Mother and Housewife; [pers.] I want to thank God first and foremost for being my inspiration. Throughout the rough times of my life, He has been my rock. He is the light, the truth, and the way.; [a.] West Jefferson, NC

CIOCCO, TIM
[pen.] "T.C."; [b.] January 28, 1958, Latrobe, PA; [p.] Nicholas and Catherine Ciocco; [occ.] Waiter/Lyricist; [oth. writ.] I began writing poems in 1975, needing a credit in High School. I have since accumulated in the area of two-thousand song/lyrics. Each one is, in some small way, a part of me.; [pers.] "Don't within" mean what it once did" is a tribute to a man I hardly knew, my father, who passed on 33 years ago. It is an attempt to express the love I have for him, something a six-years old boy could not come to terms within.; [a.] Latrobe, PA

CLARK, HEIDI
[b.] May 12, 1981, Iowa City, IA; [p.] Jeff Clark and Kaye Hennessey; [ed.] I am a Sophomore at Jefferson High School in Cedar Rapids, IA; [occ.] Student; [hon.] I am a devoted student and have therefore been awarded for excellence in academics; [oth. writ.] This is my first published writing.; [pers.] I try to write in a way to which many other kids my age can relate. I hope that I can influence at least one person through my writing.; [a.] Cedar Rapids, IA

CLARK, JOHN J.
[b.] April 10, 1950, Burlington, VT; [ed.] An I.Q. test in the 6th grade, designed to place me in a less demanding environment. It backfired but left me to continue my self education; [occ.] Daydreaming for a fertile member of the species; [memb.] The last thing I would want to do, unless it is one of those great husband and wife things great biographies are written about.; [hon.] A couple in writing here, a couple in photography there.; [oth. writ.] The Delian Quest, prep work for a radically different approach to logic using Euclidean geometric figures for mediations on principles which were released in electronic format but very out of date. An end to the mystic religion of logic is in sight.; [pers.] My greatest wisdom is my deepest silence. And lucid-dreaming is not a free-for-all fantasy state. Poem inspired by Laurie Lange.; [a.] White Lake, MI

CLARK, SHANNON
[b.] June 13, 1970, Bellflower, CA; [p.] Donald Clark, Claire Clark; [m.] Billy Martinez, November 22, 1996; [ed.] Interlochen Arts Academy, various community colleges; [occ.] Administrative Assistant, The Chela Institute Corp., Dana Point, CA; [hon.] National Jr. Honor Society; [oth. writ.] None published; [pers.] Thank you to my friends at the Chela for letting me be courageous enough to let others see my heart. Knowledge may be the key to empowerment, but only action opens the door.; [a.] Dana Point, CA

CLEVELAND, LOIS ANN
[pen.] San; [b.] March 7, 1971, Phoenix, AZ; [p.] Richard and Karen Cleveland; [m.] Jeremy, December 5; [ch.] 5 Birth 1 Foster - Sandie, Sasheen, Charles, Jonathan, Tristan and Atrea; [occ.] U.P.S. Processor; [hon.] Editor's Choice Award Nat'l Library of Poetry; [oth. writ.] Currently 85 poems; [pers.] I hope that through my writing I can speak out for people who may not have the strength to speak out for themselves.; [a.] Apache Junction, AZ

CLEVENGER, JONELL
[b.] September 29, 1980, Arizona; [p.] Keith and Linda Clevenger; [occ.] Currently finishing high school.; [pers.] I use my poetry like a mirror. Through it I try to reflect life and all its powerful emotions. When the reader grasps these emotions and claims them as their own, it's the greatest gift ever given to me.; [a.] West Palm Beach, FL

COBILLAS, JESSICA
[b.] December 30, 1982, Los Gatos, CA; [p.] Joe and Linda Cobillas; [ed.] Freshman at Westmont High School, Campbell, CA; [occ.] Student; [hon.] Honor Roll, Scholarship Award, 1st recipient of Leadership Award, Rolling Hills Middle School, Los Gatos, CA; [pers.] I have always been interested in Abraham Lincoln, the Civil War period, and generally, the American Revolution. Lincoln played a huge role in Gettysburg, and that is what inspired my poem.; [a.] Campbell, CA

COCO, DOREEN
[pen.] Doreen Coco; [b.] June 9, 1924, Wabash, IN; [p.] Cletis and Estelle Smith; [m.] Paul H. Marks Jr., December 23, 1945; [ch.] Cheryl Ann, Daniel Wayne; [ed.] Wabash High, Indiana Central College; [occ.] Dry Cleaner, Phoenix, Arizona; [memb.] Midtowner's Business and Professional Women's Club, Prestigious Past President's Club; [hon.] Woman of the Year, Midtowner's BPW Club, 1965; [oth. writ.] Poems published in publications for Dry Cleaners, The Arizona Republic, The Sun City Independent, Senior Magazine, other local publications.; [pers.] Humor in rhyme - gives me quality time - to share with those that I love - e'er I'm taken above.; [a.] Sun City, AZ

COKER, TONI WILSON
[pen.] Toni Shew; [b.] August 20, 1961, Birmingham, AL; [p.] Walter Shew, and Doris Jenkins; [m.]

Rick Coker, July 27, 1996; [ch.] Paul Brian, Christopher Jerrell (step-children); [ed.] Graduated from Gardendale High, Jefferson State College; [occ.] Homemaker, Caregiver; [memb.] Lee's Chapel Baptist Church; [hon.] Beta Club (National Honor Society), Dean's List; [oth. writ.] Several poems including, "My Yellow Rose"; [pers.] I admire Helen Steiner Rice for her spirituality in her poetry, now faith is being sure of what we hope for and certain of what we do not see. Hebrews 11:1.; [a.] Pell City, AL

COLE, HELEN
[b.] April 27, 1918, Ford City, PA; [p.] Mr. and Mrs. Dan Yanoff (Both Deceased); [m.] Wm. Edward Cole (Deceased), October 14, 1943; [ed.] 12 Years - Grade and High School Ford City, PA; [occ.] Now retired from Wood Pkg. for School Youngstown Lunches; [memb.] Retired of Youngstown Schools - I worked for 20 years; [hon.] Only for Poetry - one poem ("My Mother's Smile") and now ("How Nice"); [pers.] I enjoyed my two poems they are "My Mother's Smile") came to me thru her last days - and "How Nice" was a thank you to school and work friends who had a surprise party for my 65th Birthday.; [a.] Youngstown, OH

COLEMAN JR., MICHAEL I.
[pen.] Baffahagh Daamon; [b.] September 14, 1954, Harlem, NY; [p.] Theodoria and Isaac Coleman; [m.] Jeanette Adams (Divorced), November 22, 1974; [ch.] Damien Coleman; [ed.] One year of college at University of South Carolina, English Major; [occ.] Auto Technician; [memb.] Masonic Order, Ornamental Iron Workers' Union, Amway Distributor; [hon.] Military awards in training; [oth. writ.] Passion Falls, Time, Broken, Feeling Sorry; [pers.] Learn to live and live life fully and all it has to offer and do it again and again and again.

COLEY, APRIL SMITH
[pen.] April Smith Coley; [b.] April 1, 1965, Buffalo, NY; [p.] Cottie B. Williams, Melvin L. Smith; [m.] Duane O. Coley, June 25, 1994; [ed.] B.S. Business Administration from NCA&T State University in Greensboro, North Carolina; [occ.] Claims Manager, Freelance Writing; [oth. writ.] I recently completed my first manuscript. "Young Scholar" is a fiction novel about growing up and moving on during college life.; [pers.] The Lord said, "come unto me, watch with me." He has made all things possible for me. I am inspired by the works of Maya Angelou.; [a.] Charlotte, NC

COLGAN, BRIAN
[b.] July 19, 1955, Hanover, PA; [p.] Daniel Colgan, Regina Colgan; [m.] Christina Smith Colgan, September 2, 1995; [ed.] Delone Catholic High School, York College of PA.; [occ.] Musician and Music Teacher (Private); [memb.] ASCAP The Colgan Brothers Band; [oth. writ.] Several songs released since 1980 on a local level and some have gotten regional, state and out of state air play (radio); [pers.] In recent years started writing other forms of poetry other than lyrical to find other means of expression through words, much like instrumental music uses solely music, besides romantic and Victorian poetry, love e.e cummings Ogden Nash, Carl Sandberg.; [a.] McSherrystown, PA

COLLIER, KASEY V.
[b.] May 27, 1983, Conroe, TX; [p.] Thomas M. Collier and Marly Shawne Barnes Collier; [ed.] Currently in 8th grade Lynn Lucas Middle School, Willis, TX., '96-'96; [occ.] Student - Reach Program, Symphonic Band - Trombone; [memb.] Unifield Tae-Kwon-Do-Black Belt at 10 years old (3/94), Honor Roll Student, Kindergarten through 7th grade; [hon.] 1996 - First places for UIL Impromptu Speaking, UIL Trombone Solo, UIL Trombone Trio. Also participated in UIL Theatrical Arts. First Place National Crayola Coloring Contest at age 5; [oth. writ.] This "Body Bag" written 5/96 at the age of 12.; [pers.] Military Enthusiast. "Man makes lies to explain what he doesn't understand or fears. I choose not to worry about what I don't understand, and yet, it still makes me wonder."; [a.] Willis, TX

COLLINS, W. LOUVORN
[pen.] El Poeto Lobrego; [b.] October 1, 1947, Lamar City, GA; [p.] James E. F. and Betty J. Louvorn; [m.] Widower; [pers.] I find nothing so sad in life as looking back upon the days I have wasted.; [a.] Arvada, CO

CONNELLY, MARY LOU
[b.] July 8, 1960, Boston, MA; [p.] Robert A. Connelly and Barbara H. Connelly; [ed.] Bachelor of Arts from Boston College, Chestnut Hill, MA; [hon.] Summa Cum Laude, Alpha Sigma Nu National Honor Society, The Morgan Award for General Excellence; [oth. writ.] Various poems and short stories.; [pers.] Love and truth are the shield and the sword our children need in a world without conscience. To Jimmy, my angel, you will live on in my heart forever.; [a.] Brighton, MA

CONNOLLY-WEINERT, FRANCIS
[b.] September 27, 1941, Philadelphia; [p.] Philip Weinert, Mary McGuigan; [ch.] James Bernard; [ed.] St. Joseph's University Phila., Fordham University, NY; [occ.] College Profession, St. John's University, NY; [memb.] American Academy of Religion, Society of Biblical Literature, Catholic Biblical Association, American Association of University Professors, National Physics Honor Society, National Society for Religions Shades and Theology; [hon.] Danforth Associate Professor, NEH Summer Grant, The Alpha Kappa Leader of the year (1995), St. John's University Teacher of the Year (1996); [oth. writ.] Biblical Theology Bulletin, Catholic Biblical Quarterly, poetry published in The Bible Today; [pers.] I look to connect with that moment of human courage when hope reassess itself in the midst of pain and opaqueness.; [a.] Jamaica, NY

CONRAD, BETTE A.
[pen.] Kit Kester/Bette Conrad; [b.] Chester, PA; [m.] Michael A. Conrad; [ed.] Juris Doctor; [occ.] Attorney/Transpersonal Counselor/Singer/Songwriter/Author

CONRAD, NATHAN
[pen.] Too-Tall, Nate; [b.] June 13, 1982; [p.] D. Scott and Peggy McNamara; [ed.] Hughes Road, Silbernagel, and Fisher Elemetaries, Park View Intermediate, Pearland High School; [occ.] Freshman in high school; [hon.] The Scholastic Art and Writing Awards of 1996 - Silver Key and Certificate; [oth. writ.] Several unpublished poems, essays, and short stories.; [pers.] I strive to touch the heart.; [a.] Pearland, TX

CONTE, LIZANNE J.
[pen.] Lizanne J. Conte; [b.] August 24, New York; [ed.] High School Grad., Business Grad., 2 yrs. college courses; [occ.] Leisure; [memb.] Too many; [hon.] Private; [oth. writ.] Personal

COOPER, GERARD G.
[b.] September 3, 1927, Santa Ana, CA; [p.] Fran and Harold Cooper; [m.] Shirley Juiner Cooper, September 10, 1949; [ch.] Steven, Suzanne and Marylou; [ed.] BA - Geology - UCLA '51; [occ.] Retired Exploration Geologist - Oil and Gas Industry; [oth. writ.] Unpublished poems to parents, wife, children and grandchildren on anniversaries, birthdays, etc.; [pers.] In the poem God points out the difference in my life between recognition for a few minor discoveries over the years and the continuing influence of my loving wife.; [a.] Lakeway, TX

COOPER, HEATHER YOUNG
[b.] August 6, 1972, Grand Rapids, MI; [p.] Roiw Young, Barbara J. Young; [m.] Matt Cooper, October 12, 1996; [ed.] High School - Lafayette High School, Ellisville, MO, Received a Bachelor of Arts Degree from Arizona State University.; [occ.] I am currently working on my masters in Education at Michigan State University.; [memb.] International Readers Association, National Assoc. for the Education of Young Children; [hon.] Dean's List; [pers.] Through my writing, I hope to touch those people who are close to me and to those whom I have never met.; [a.] Brighton, MI

COOPER, MARY
[pen.] Maria Lenie; [b.] November 14, 1942, Lavonia, GA; [p.] Robert and Oualene Highland (Deceased); [m.] James Cooper, August 6, 1965; [ch.] Esther, Oualene/Angela Jean/Timothy Dale/Richard Herschel/Virginia Jane; [ed.] O'Keefe - Smith Hughes HS, Dekalb Technical College; [occ.] Retired Bell south, Telecommunications Co.; [memb.] Telephone Pioneers of America Brookwood Hospital Volunteer Auxiliary; [oth. writ.] I have written several hundred poems, and currently writing a romantic novel. I have never tried to publish any of my world and would like to publish my poems, and book in the future; [pers.] Married at the age of 13, divorced, re-married, my two son's died within 3 mo. in 1991, and recently my 6 year old granddaughter has Leukemia. I have 9 grand children, and 3 great-grandchildren. In the first months after my son's death friends of family encouraged me to write and publish my work, and through the years writings has been an outlets for my emotions my desire for the next year is to complete the romantic novel and search for a publisher. If I should win this contest the money will be used for expenses for my granddaughter "Kellis" fight with leukemia.; [a.] Birmingham, AL

CORBETT, MONA VIRGINIA
[b.] June 5, 1972, Brooklyn, NY; [p.] Edward Kolenda and Gerda Kolenda; [m.] John Corbett, June 29, 1996; [ed.] St. Joseph's College B.A., Brooklyn College M.S.; [occ.] Special Education Preschool Teacher; [hon.] Delta Epsilon Sigma, Kappa Gamma Pi, Sigma Iota Chi, B.A. with General Honors and Departmental Honors, M.S. with Honors; [pers.] The speck in the eye of one person, may be the world to another.; [a.] Brooklyn, NY

CORBETT, RICHARD
[b.] July 26, 1969, Boston, MA; [p.] Roberta and Zielinski; [m.] Marlene DaRosa, March 7, 1992; [ed.] East Boston High School - Graduated 1987, attended Bunkerhill Community College; [hon.] Youth Leadership Award, 1985; [pers.] Believe in your dreams and believe in yourself.

COREY, DAVID P.
[b.] August 5, 1931, Pittsburgh, PA; [p.] David and Ann Corey; [m.] Jeanne, May 5, 1965; [ch.] David, Kelly and Jill; [ed.] High School; [occ.] Retired; [oth. writ.] Many poems.

CORLETT, MICHELLE
[b.] December 16, 1980, Pueblo, CO; [p.] Robert and Donna Corlett; [ed.] Sophomore at Pueblo South High School; [memb.] J.R.O.T.C., Commander of Color Gaurd, Drill Team, South J.R.O.T.C., Helping Hands; [hon.] Ranking Commander, Color Gaurd and Drill Team Awards; [oth. writ.] Many unpublished poems and short stories.; [pers.] If a reader can feel the emotion behind your words, then and only then, are you a good writer.; [a.] Pueblo, CO

CORNWELL, BENJAMIN THOMAS
[b.] April 30, 1978, Huntington, WV; [p.] Thomas and Susan Cornwell; [ed.] Anderson High School, attending University of Cincinnati; [occ.] Writer of poetry and short stories; [oth. writ.] Several poems published in high school creative writing publication. Multiple articles published in the News Record; [pers.] The trees that grow decrepit in the far pits of my mind shall soon cease to grow balloons.; [a.] Cincinnati, OH

CORRIDON, JONELLE
[b.] November 2, Trinidad, WI; [p.] Joan Corridon; [ed.] John Bowne H.S., York College Queens NY; [occ.] Computer Programmer; [hon.] Silver Medal Winner for Poetry and Architecture Contest in NAACP ACT-SO Competition for the NY State; [pers.] As I reflected on the life of Christ as it relates to my experience, I was inspired to write this poem. It occurred to me that Christ is none other than the greatest hero of all time. We should teach children about Christ as a hero.; [a.] Corona, NY

COSMATO, MICHELLE MYERS
[b.] November 6, 1964, Saint Augustine, FL; [p.] George and Mae Myers; [m.] Jeffrey M. Cosmato, May 28, 1988; [ch.] Cara and Christopher Cosmato - (twins age 7); [ed.] High School Graduate - attended Junior College 2 years, St. Augustine High School, Florida Junior College; [occ.] Asst. Supervisor-Traffic Division - St. Augustine Courthouse; [memb.] Anastasia Baptist Church, P.T.A.O.; [hon.] Graduate of Denise Carol Modeling School; [pers.] I enjoy getting a reaction from people. If my poetry can make a person smile or if it can touch their inner being than I feel I have succeeded as a writer.; [a.] Saint Augustine, FL

COSS, SARAH ANN
[b.] July 9, 1982, Elkhorn, WI; [p.] Barbara and Rick Coss; [occ.] Student; [memb.] Lisa Frank Club; [hon.] Brookwood School Choir Award; [a.] Genoa City, WI

COTHRAN, JAMES E.
[b.] January 24, 1954, Denver, CO; [p.] Bruce and Mildred Cothran; [m.] Alice Quintanar Cothran, October 21, 1972; [ch.] Paul James and Crystal Ann; [ed.] West High School - Denver, Colorado; [occ.] Disabled; [hon.] Outstanding volunteer for Headstart program for 20 years.; [oth. writ.] Personal writings on birthday cards and christmas cards.; [pers.] I like to write personal notes about special occasions.; [a.] Denver, CO

COUCH, PETER S.
[pen.] P. Svensson Couch; [b.] April 18, 1964, Watertown, NY; [p.] George and Lis Couch; [ed.] '82 Hotchkiss School, '87 Colgate University, B.A., '92 Syracuse College of Law, J.D.; [occ.] Writer and Fred Hutchinson Cancer Research Center; [memb.] Multiple Sclerosis Society, Duck's Unlimited, Lambda Chi Alpha; [oth. writ.] Hotchkiss Record, Colgate Maroon News, Syracuse Law Docket, poems: Pickle Factory, Canal Lines, Settle Times (Letter to the Editor); [pers.] My interest in poetry began in Lakeville. I'm, thankful to the mentors and peers discovered.; [a.] Seattle, WA

COUGHLAN, ANGELINA
[pen.] Angie Coughlan; [b.] Chicago, IL; [p.] Alice and Eugene Coughlan; [ed.] Most Precious Blood School; [occ.] Student at most precious blood; [memb.] Student Council, Stretch, Youth Group; [hon.] Honor Rolls, 4th and 5th place achievement in Academic Olympics, 3rd place Award for team competition in Rosatti-Kain Math Competition 2nd place in Science fair ('95); [oth. writ.] Anthology of poetry by young Americans ('96 edition); [pers.] I love to write and I hope that my success will continue, and it can let people enjoy my works; [a.] Saint Louis, MO

CRANDDENT, YANDHI T.
[pen.] Yandhi T. Cranddent; [b.] November 20, 1964, Copen Hagen, Denmark; [p.] Former Diplomat; [ed.] Visha/Arts/Commercial and Business Management (1986), Study at Algonquin College, Ottawa, Ont. Canada; [occ.] Full Time Clerk; [memb.] U.F.C.W./ Canada Local 175, P.R.O. Canada - Socan; [hon.] "Editor's Choice Award," High School Honor Diploma; [oth. writ.] Wrote songs, available trough PRO/Canada for copies or music sheets. Wrote many poems, many have been published and one is included in "Beneath the harvest Moon" book.; [pers.] Always believe in your dream, your craft. Be yourself, don't try to be something or someone you're not! Hard work and determination, and most of all have a lot of love to share!; [a.] Ottawa, Ontario, Canada

CREWS, HELEN L.
[b.] September 18, 1919, New York City, NY; [p.] Hannah and Spiros Livathares; [m.] James Q. Crews (Deceased), March 6, 1945; [ch.] Evanne Louise, Mary Ellen, Robert S. Corrine Mae; [ed.] H.S. Graduate, 2 Semester College; [occ.] Retired; [memb.] Pierce County Democratic Club, (Precinct Committee Officer), Washington State retired Public Employees Club (Adopted as member since I retired from a similar organization in Florida. Graham Senior Citizen's Club.; [hon.] Several awards for supervisory management from State Board of Health in Jacksonville, Florida. This Board was later transferred to State Capitol in 1976 during reorganization at which time I was transferred to Social Services in the sad area of Child Abuse.; [oth. writ.] Short Story, Other Poems, a one-act play written for the Cub Scouts; [pers.] I was a member of the Savoy Opera Guild for three years, where we appeared doing Gilbert and Sullivan Operettas at the famous Cherry Lane Theater in the Village in New York City. The Guild subsequently disbanded, but I understand it has recently been reactivated.; [a.] Tacoma, WA

CRIGLER, P. LUCILLE
[pen.] Poet Crigler; [b.] July 18, 1926, Kingswood, WV; [p.] Olgia and Bertha Hartman; [m.] Richard L. Crigler, June 28, 1945; [ch.] Nancy - 50, Nancy - 48, Rick - 45; [ed.] 11 1/2 years; [occ.] Homemaker; [memb.] Sylvan Nook Church of Christ; [hon.] Being married over 51 years. Having 10 grandchildren, 17 greatgrandchildren, expecting one part of 1997.; [oth. writ.] "Think," "Grandma," "My Dream," and I have several others.; [pers.] Usually, I write about people very close to me and events that actually happen in my life.; [a.] Richmond, IN

CRISMON, JACOB P.
[b.] December 22, 1982, Waynesville, MO; [p.] Paul B. Crismon, Tammy E. Crismon; [ed.] 8th Grade Lewis and Clark Middle School, Jefferson City, MO; [hon.] MO State Show me Games Cold Medal Winner - Archery MBH Indoor State Championship 1st Place Team Shoot; [oth. writ.] Poems and short stories on hunting published through Lewis and Clark Middle School; [pers.] I strive to reflect how much I enjoy hunting.; [a.] Jefferson City, MO

CRONIN, JAMES ROBERT
[b.] October 15, 1966, Melrose, MA; [p.] Dennis J. Cronin, Kathleen E. Cunningham; [m.] Nancy C. Cronin, September 24, 1995; [ch.] Beautiful baby on the way; [ed.] Timberlane High School, U.S. Army Engineer School; [occ.] Flooring Contractor, Protective Coatings Plus; [memb.] 100 Beers Club; [oth. writ.] Solitude, Echoes of Yesterday, and still writing; [pers.] To my brother Keith who found so much of himself and others on his Epic Journey along the Appalachian Trail. I'm proud of you Kip. Love, Jim.; [a.] East Hampstead, NH

CROSS, ALLISON C.
[b.] June 11, 1976, New Orleans, LA; [p.] Charles Cross, Melinda Mullis; [ed.] Parkwood High School, University of North Carolina at Charlotte; [occ.] Construction Scheduling and Estimating (Commercial) Pic. Tec; [memb.] Mecklenburgh Hounds, Inc. (Foxhunting Club); [hon.] National Honor Society; [oth. writ.] 1994 Parkwood High Yearbook contains several articles I wrote about national and international events.; [pers.] No matter where you are, something beautiful is there. Notice and remember it.; [a.] Monroe, NC

CRUZ, CHRISTOPHER PATRICK
[b.] November 14, 1987, Brooklyn, NY; [p.] Patricia and William; [ed.] PS52, 4th grade, Eagle Program; [occ.] Student; [memb.] BSA, King's Bay Little League, St. Mark's Basketball Association; [hon.] "My Smile" Poster Contest Award - '96; [pers.] "I will always try my best".; [a.] Brooklyn, NY

CULLINS, MARGARET
[b.] May 27, 1961, Winston-Salem, NC; [p.] Richard Carter and Anne Carter; [m.] Larry Cullins, June 8, 1991; [ed.] North Carolina Agricultural and Technical State University (B.S. - Banking and Finance), Piedmont Bible College - attended 2 yrs; [occ.] Customer Service Representative USAir (Frequent Traveler Program); [pers.] My goal in writing poetry is to convey the love of God, salvation to all mankind through. Jesus Christ, and inspiration for successful daily Christian living. I am influenced by my personal saviour, The Lord Jesus Christ that gives me these inspirational promptings writings for this Glory and Honor. These inspirational promptings and writings for his Glory and Honor.; [a.] Winston-Salem, NC

CURRY, AMY
[b.] July 4, Ft. Wayne, IN; [p.] Denny and Linn Farmer, Sarah and Ralph Hilker; [m.] Donald Curry, August 13, 1983; [ch.] Jeremy Curry, Laura Curry and Katie Curry; [ed.] Wawasee High School.; [occ.] Sales Coordinator, Star Craft Automotive; [memb.] Jaycees, St. Martin de Porres Choir; [hon.] Employee of the Math Star Craft; [oth. writ.] Several poems that have not been published and have wrote over the years and are compiled in my won book.; [pers.] My poems are written directly from my heart and are put on paper. I have written poems to express my feelings about life, love and family, because life is so special and short.; [a.] Syracuse, IN

CURTO, SUSAN LEE
[pen.] Susan King; [b.] February 9, 1966, Baltimore, MD; [p.] Victoria Moffitt and Leo King; [m.] Michael Curto, May 20, 1995; [ed.] Overlea Sr. High; [occ.] Computer Help Desk Analyst; [hon.] Gifted and Talented throughout school years, Honor students; [pers.] This poem is a true story. My grandfather, Lee Roy Warren (Big-Pop), was lost at sea October 24, 1980. He was the captain of a cargo carrier the Poet! He and 33 other crew members are presumed dead. As of today, 1995, the ship has never been found. It was lost in a storm, headed for Egypt. He may be lost, never forgotten.; [a.] Felton, PA

DAIGLE, ANN
[b.] April 8, 1949, Falls Church, VA; [p.] Carolyn Calderwood (Mother), Lewellyn Clifford Daigle (Father); [ed.] B.A. degree in Art, (Ceramics) from University of California (Davis); [occ.] Administrative Assistant to National Senior Vice President; [memb.] Westminster Presbyterian Church, Sacramento Zoological Society; [hon.] Alpha Gamma Sigma Honor Society; [pers.] "I can do all

things through Christ who strengheneth me."; [a.] Sacramento, CA

DALY, CHAD LEE
[pen.] Chad Lee Blowers, "Zorro"; [b.] June 14, 1977, Minot, ND; [p.] Lester and Veronica Daly; [ed.] Rancho High School (Las Vegas, NV), John Jay High School (San Antonio TX), University of Texas at San Antonio; [occ.] Sears Tele-Service Consultant; [memb.] Air Force Reserve Officer's Training Corp; [hon.] U.T.S.A. Program for Young Scholars (Summer '94), U.T.S.A. Alumni Association Scholarship ('95), General Henry H. Arnold Education Grant ('95); [oth. writ.] No previous published writings; [pers.] Write what you feel and you will be a success.; [a.] San Antonio, TX

DALY, MEGHAN
[b.] March 23, 1985, Cherry Hill, NJ; [p.] Pat and Paul Daly; [ed.] 6th Grade; [occ.] Student in 6th grade at Stockton Elementary, Cherry Hill, NJ; [memb.] Wexford Leas. Swim Team, Cherry Hill Girls Softball, Jazz Unlimited Dance Studio; [a.] Cherry Hill, NJ

DAMRON SR., ROBERT CLAY
[pen.] Robert Clay Damron Sr.; [b.] Virgie, KY; [ch.] Aaron Mike and Rob; [occ.] Writer; [oth. writ.] Am writing novels - Angels Burning, and have finished a book of verse - Arrow Star.; [pers.] My philosophy is to have no philosophy, for we are each so different. Just be kind. Remember, even an insect has its own right to life.; [a.] Dayton, OH

DARDINI, ANGELA
[b.] May 18, 1968, Columbus, OH; [p.] Charles Elderson, Hilda Stanek; [m.] James Dardini, March 4, 1995; [ch.] Brandon Dardini; [ed.] Lakeview High; [a.] Saint Petersburg, FL

DAUGHTRY, GRACE W.
[b.] November 22, 1924, Snow Hill, NC; [p.] Deceased; [m.] Thomas L. Daughtry, Jr., June 11, 1950; [ch.] One son and one daughter; [ed.] Finished high school and one year of business school; [occ.] Retired, now 70 years of age, worked many years as a bookkeeper; [hon.] One that I have kept was High School Class Poet.; [oth. writ.] Did most of my writing while in school - was only a hobby. I wrote one play that was given at my church. Wrote poems for those who didn't have any part in church or school programs.; [pers.] Most things I have written were done on demand in helping in school or church programs. Most I never saved or kept.; [a.] Goldboro, NC

DAVIS, ADAM EDGAR
[pen.] Ocs or Edgar Perigo; [b.] May 7, 1978, Dallas, TX; [p.] Jim and Cindy Davis; [ed.] Bed Oak High School, Senior; [occ.] Full-time student; [oth. writ.] Several short stories and poems have been published in the '95-'96 perceptions an Ellis County High School Literary Magazine; [pers.] Poetry is my release. It is how I get rid of my anger, express happiness, and communicate my feelings to others. Though I think most of my poems show the influence of my favorite poet Edgar Allen Poe.; [a.] Oak Leaf, TX

DAVIS, BRIAN L.
[b.] November 13, 1972, Vandenberg AFB, CA; [p.] Carolyn Davis, Terry Davis; [ed.] Jefferson Davis High School; [occ.] Student, Auburn University Montgomery; [oth. writ.] None published (yet); [a.] Montgomery, AL

DAVIS III, JESSE J.
[b.] January 31, 1977, Stamford, CT; [p.] Jesse J. Davis Jr. and Carolyn Davis; [ed.] Westhill High School, University of Connecticut; [occ.] Student; [pers.] I believe that house in God is the only way to be a success. I express the emotions and human tendencies in my writing. I have been influenced by Langston Hughes and Maya Angelou.; [a.] Stamford, UT

DEAL, GAYE FOLLMER
[pen.] Gaye Follmer; [b.] October 22, 1924, Omaha, NE; [p.] Crawford Follmer and Gladys Follmer; [m.] Deceased, April 22, 1944; [ch.] Rebecca Crawford, Ph.D., Peter Crawford, Stuard Deal, B.S. Sarah Deal, Katrhyn Deal, M.A.; [ed.] B.A. University of Chicago (social science - psychology), M.A. University of California at Northridge, Certificate Teaching English as second language, U.C.L.A. Life Teaching Credential; [occ.] Retired Teacher; [memb.] UCLA Alumni Assoc., AARP, American Association of University Women, Violada Gamba Society, Southern California Early Music Society, Neo-Renaissance Singers; [hon.] Second prize, AAUW Writer's Project, Honorable Mention Esquire-Bantam Short Story Contest; [oth. writ.] "The Second Best Bed," published by Adelphi Press 1995. 3 unpublished novels; [pers.] I am also a cellist and play a lot of chamber music. Artistic expression is very important to me.; [a.] Santa Monica, CA

DEGRAVE, TRISHA
[pen.] Princess; [b.] October 6, 1982, Green Bay; [p.] Joan and Randy DeGrave; [ed.] Basic Schooling; [occ.] Schooling; [pers.] "This is dedicated to my friends and family".; [a.] Green Bay, WI

DEGUISE, CHRISTOPHER TODD
[pen.] Chris Deguise; [b.] January 31, 1969, Rochester, MN; [p.] Jake and Wendy Deguise; [ed.] Riverland Technical College Rochester, MN; [occ.] Area Supervisor, Casey's General Stores in MN, Karaoke Disc Jockey; [hon.] Student Senate President at RTC; [oth. writ.] Personal enjoyment writings for myself.; [pers.] All of my writings come straight from the heart. All of my poems are based on my own experiences and influences.; [a.] Rochester, MN

DEL CARMEN, ELIZABETH
[b.] October 27, 1983, Manhattan, NY; [p.] Nelida and Francisco Del Carmen; [ed.] P.S. #98 Elementary School, P.S. #8 Elementary, Junior High School; [occ.] Student; [memb.] School Photographer, School Safety Patrol; [hon.] Reading awards, effort awards, Social Studies, Science, Citizenship, Merit (outstanding student), Merit (math), Merit (choir), Honor Roll, Safety Patrol awards; [oth. writ.] One poem published in school newspaper; [pers.] At the moment of writing this poem, I felt an inspiration of freedom. I have been influenced by many poets as well as family members. Thanks to God; he gave me the talent to express my feelings.; [a.] Paterson, NJ

DELANEY, EVELYN L.
[pen.] Robbie DeLaney; [b.] Bobson Park, FL; [p.] Robert M. and Glennie Smith; [m.] Edgar A. DeLaney Jr.; [ch.] Herbert, Delton and Kris; [occ.] Retired Medical Assistant, Orchid Collecting in Rain Forests of Central and So. America. Licensed Pilot; [oth. writ.] "A Kumquat Morning," "Night Breezes," and other short articles and poems. Favorite author: Kahlil Gibran; [pers.] We each are necessary to the orchestration and harmony of this earth and universe. Each pulsates with a rhythm of a song to sing, whether calm and tranquil, or complex and chaotic.; [a.] Avon Park, FL

DELA SOTA PALOMO, MARIA CHRISTINA
[pen.] Maria Dela Sota; [b.] July 24, 1968, Mexico; [p.] Elena Palomo and Juan Dela Sota; [m.] Donald E. Johnson; [ch.] Donald, Jose and Donna; [ed.] Edison Computech High School, Colorado High; [occ.] Janitor for Yorkshire Dried Fruits and Nuts; [oth. writ.] Had poem published in high school newspaper; [a.] Fresno, CA

DELOATCH, MARTHA HALL
[b.] September 5, 1962, Greensboro, NC; [p.] James and Doris Hall; [m.] Jimmie Lee Deloatch, August 1, 1991; [ch.] Sandra, Crystal and Jerry; [ed.] I graduated from Smith High School in Greensboro in 1980.; [occ.] Security Officer; [oth. writ.] Nothing else published yet but currently working on other writing projects.; [pers.] If at first I don't succeed, I shall try again and again, for if a fear of failure prevents me from trying at all, then I will never achieve success.; [a.] Greensboro, NC

DELOS REYES, MARIA EVANGELINA LEVISTE
[pen.] Maria Leviste; [b.] December 27, 1944, Malvar, Batangas, Philippines; [p.] Maria Leviste and Francisco Delos Reyes; [m.] March 1959, (Separated since 1963); [ch.] Bernardita, Marivelle, Maria and Marco Antonio; [ed.] High School - 1959 Graduate Lyceum University, Bachelor of Arts, Major in Industrial Psychology - (Undergraduate) Holy Angel University; [occ.] Employee (Cashier) I worked as Reutilization Specialist for the U.S. Defense Logistic Agency at DRMO Clark for 17 years; [memb.] In high school, I was a staff member of the school organ, the "Lycean"; [hon.] Dean's List; [oth. writ.] Unpublished poems: From Color to Color, Desert Rose, Windows, Patria, Ecology; [pers.] My son and I arrived here in the United States of America last May 21st on a special immigrant visa granted by the U.S. Embassy in Manila, Philippines. Special immigrant visas are issued to deserving employees who have served the U.S. Armed Forces in the Philippines as civilians. The bases closed in 1991 and 1992. At 17, I decided to be a single parent. My three daughters, all married now, have given me ten wonderful grandchildren. Bernardita, the eldest, who has a BSC Degree majored in Accounting, Marivelle is a CPA (Certified Public Accountant) and Maria is an artist, a singer and a painter. Marco is now 18 years old - love child of mine. All the blessings I thank God for and I am now in that stage of life where one wishes to be of service to his fellow men in whatever little way he can, wherever he is in this planet. I just want to be an inspiration to young and single mothers, to widows and abandoned wives who are burdened with raising and caring for their children. May God show me the way!; [a.] Las Vegas, NV

DELSID-AVERY, EBONY
[b.] December 16, 1984, San Francisco; [p.] Andrea Delsid Carrington; [ed.] 6th Grade; [occ.] Student; [hon.] I was honored at my school with a grand prize award for creating a poster to encourage recycling and preserving our earth.; [pers.] I have been influenced by my dog Nila, because she has a lot of love in her heart.; [a.] Alameda, CA

DEMASE, RACHEL
[pen.] Red; [b.] January 6, 1982, Pittsburgh, PA; [p.] Marsha and Steve Demase; [ed.] Student at North Allegheny; [occ.] Student; [memb.] North Allegheny Strolling Strings/Orchestra, Act One Theater School; [oth. writ.] Many at home, but want to get published in a book when older.; [pers.] I wish for people to understand the truth of a pure person's heart. I was influenced by a very special friend to find my heart.; [a.] Bradford Woods, PA

DEMBRO, PATRICIA
[p.] Richard and Marguerite Dembro; [ed.] Dante Alighieri School Gove Street East Boston MA, Grade 5

DENUTO, LISA MARIE
[b.] August 29, 1966, Elmhurst Queens; [p.] Julio and Theresa Lopez; [ch.] Teresa Caraballo, Steven Caraballo, Eric Caraballo, Amanda DeNuto; [ed.] Long Island University; [occ.] Sales/Management; [oth. writ.] This poem was published in the Greenpoint Gazette in Brooklyn in June of 1987.; [pers.] I give special thanks to my mother who has inspired me throughout my life. She has helped a great deal. I love you mom.; [a.] Glendale Queens, NY

DEPARTO, JUDITH A.
[b.] August 7, 1945, Englewood, NJ; [p.] Rose DeParto, George DeParto; [ed.] North Bergen High, Berkeley Business School, Bergen Community College; [occ.] Administrative Ass't., Office Manager; [oth. writ.] "Gold And Silver," "The Omega Warrior," (Books unpublished) "I Was Worried You Wouldn't Find Me."; [pers.] My mother is my greatest inspiration and my biggest fan. She is 85 years old and in bad health - As care giver, my writing keeps me anchored to reality as well as helping me to escape when necessary.; [a.] Fairview, NJ

DEPT, RUTH C.
[b.] Cadiz, OH; [p.] Rebecca Golsby; [m.] Arthur Dept, 1980; [ch.] Susan, Cary, Timothy, Sherri; [ed.] Dunbar School, Cadiz High, GED 1969; [occ.] Ret. Nurse; [memb.] Saint James AME Church, VFWA Uxiliary; [hon.] A Poet Award in 1996 at the International Society of Poets; [oth. writ.] Poems in local paper also in mist enchantment sunshine and day dreams.; [pers.] I am leaving for my children and grandchildren to follow. It is never to make a dream come true.; [a.] Cadiz, OH

DERLETH, BRYON
[b.] October 20, 1977, Saint Louis, MO; [p.] Teresa Conley, Kenneth Derleth Jr.; [ed.] Northwest High; [pers.] May favorite saying and words I live by "I have had my up and downs in stouts my share of bad breaks but now that it has all been said and done I raise my bear and swear to God it's been fun.; [a.] Saint Louis, MO

DETHROW, JEFFERY R.
[b.] June 28, 1961, Union City, TN; [p.] Albert Dethrow, Verline Dethrow; [occ.] United States Army, Signal Corps.; [hon.] Southwest Asia Service Medal, Bronze Service Star, Kuwait Liberation Medal, Army Commendation Medal, Army Achievement Medal; [pers.] Reflections of our former actions enable us to choose between redemption and destruction.; [a.] Tupelo, MS

DEUTSCH, HENRY
[b.] August 17, 1948; [ch.] Andrew, Katharina, Susan-Mary; [ed.] Monterey Peninsula College, Monterey, Calif.; [occ.] Business Consultant; [hon.] "Soka" Award for excellence in Education" (International) Team Captain, US Chess Team; [oth. writ.] Monthly Columnist for Magazine, Nationally published articles on food, chess, and Management Theory, Internationally Published (4 Languages) Motivational Articles. Short stories and poetry in Regional Publications; [pers.] Communication is the means to building trust, which is the critical element for humanity's survival in the next century; [a.] Lake Oswego, OR

DEVER, CHARLES T.
[b.] April 20, 1960, Staunton, VA; [p.] Garland S. and Lillian S. Dever; [m.] Rebecca S. Dever, November 1, 1986; [ch.] Chritos Monika LaTese, Victoria Morgan; [ed.] Highland High, US Army; [occ.] Electrician and Plumber; [memb.] Seybert Chapel United Methodist; [oth. writ.] Several poems; [pers.] This poem was written of my father in law for whom I had great respect and love. With God's gift and with deep sorrow for our loss, this poem was written. The poems I write reflect my feelings and what I see at the time.; [a.] Monterey, VA

DIAZ, JODI S.
[b.] April 26, 1966, Cleveland, OH; [p.] Don and Sandy Kaufman; [m.] Danny Diaz, September 10, 1995; [ed.] N.M.B. Senior High,(BCC) Brownd Community College, Florida State University (FSU); [occ.] Special Education, Teacher or Special Educator; [hon.] Dean's List; [oth. writ.] Poems published in "Listen With Your Heart" and "Down Peaceful Paths." I have been a writer since 1981.; [pers.] Writing is a passion of mine. It allows me to express my innermost thoughts and emotions. I hope to one day published a book of my own personal collection!; [a.] North Miami, FL

DIETER, NORMA H.
[b.] April 8, 1931, Crystal City, TX; [m.] Cyril F. Dieter Jr., July 8, 1954; [ed.] Crystal City High, Texas A and I University, Baptist Mem. Hospital School Medical Technology of San Antonio; [memb.] American Society of Clinical Pathology, Weimaraner Club of America; [oth. writ.] A number of other poems hopefully to be published at a later date.; [pers.] I believe that our animal friends deserve our respect for their devotion and loyalty. Their welfare is our concern, and they should be shown our kindness as well as our unconditional love.; [a.] Cibolo, TX

DIONNE, JENNIFER
[b.] October 28, 1981, Rhode Island; [p.] Sandra and George Dionne; [ed.] High School Sophomore at St. Mary's Academy, Bay View; [occ.] Student; [memb.] S.E.T.I, The Planetary Society, People to People Ambassadorship International, USFSA, USGF; [hon.] Science and Math Awards, gymnastic and ice-skating titles, Honor Society; [pers.] "Love is but a treasure to be found by searching through the journeys of life."; [a.] Warwick, RI

DIPROSPERO, BETTY
[b.] November 23, 1927, Hazelhurst, PA; [p.] Dyer Lamb, Jennie Dippo Lamb; [m.] Peter DiProspero, December 29, 1945; [ch.] Betty Lachowski, Rita Lindell, Peter J. DiProspero, Susan Case, James DiProspero; [ed.] Hamlin Township High Hazelhurst, PA; [occ.] Free Lance Writer; [oth. writ.] Numerous articles published in Woodall's publications, also newspaper articles.; [pers.] Through discernment and knowledge I endeavor to provide a deep insight in my writing. Impressed by early in my writing: Joyce (Alfred) Kilmer, Henry Wadsworth Longfellow.; [a.] Ocala, FL

DITSCH, RICHARD C.
[b.] Louisville, KY; [p.] Sarah and Richard E. Ditsch; [ed.] G.E.D., B.A. Pastoral Min./Psych., M.A.R. Theology/Religion Assoc., Pastor' Degree 1985, Member of U.S.C.F. (Life), Certification Christian Counseling; [occ.] Minister; [memb.] Certification Family Counseling, Clinical Hypnotherapy, Notary; [hon.] (1996) Editor's Choice Award, (1996) Poetry Hall of Fame, Appeared on Channel 41 as pianist. Appeared on channel 18 Louisville Poetry Guild; [oth. writ.] The Bewitching Hour, The Bewitching, The Book Mausoleum, The Princess and the Toad, Child of RA, Winter Idyll, (1996 Editor's Choice Award) (1996) Poetry Hall of Fame; [pers.] I have been influenced by the works of Lucullus Dante, Shakespere, Milton, Longfellow, Poe, Ovid, Stevenson, Melville, Dickens, Hemingway, Conrad, Keats, Spenser, and Goethe. I admire authors who write about life in the raw, not just about the good.; [a.] Louisville, KY

DOBSON, JEFFERY J.
[pen.] Jason Jefferies; [b.] December 19, 1968, Ary, KY; [p.] Clyde and Melda White; [m.] Missala Ann Dobson, March 20, 1994; [ch.] Brent A. and Angie M.; [ed.] Associate Degree, various Technical and Personal Training, Military; [hon.] Two honorable discharges, U.S. Army, Various Awards during my youth, boy Scouts. Various Awards during Military Service.; [oth. writ.] Many poems, stories (finished and "In The Works") and song lyrics.; [pers.] Being true to ones own convictions and feelings is the only beginning to respect of others feelings and convictions.

DOLLEMAN, JONATHAN
[b.] July 20, 1977, Garland, TX; [p.] Cyndy and Mike Phone; [ed.] Rockwall High School; [occ.] Waiter, Chandlers Landing Yacht and Tennis Club, Gymnast; [oth. writ.] Several books of poems unreleased to the public; [pers.] I write exactly what I feel at that moment of time, normally a sharp emotion. I credit my writing to God and Shirley Shoquist.; [a.] Rockwall, TX

DOMINGUEZ, JENNA
[pen.] Jenna Dominguez; [b.] June 15, 1984, Las Cruces, NM; [p.] Shirley Dominguez and Joel Grieshaber (step-father); [ed.] Los Lunas Middle School, Los Lunas New Mexico; [occ.] Student; [hon.] Honor Roll, Honor Student, Cheerleading (gold, silver, superior), Science Fair 2nd District 3rd; [pers.] Poetry is a fun and easy past time!; [a.] Los Lunas, NM

DOMINGUEZ, RUBEN Z.
[pen.] Mexican and Fake Mexican; [b.] July 16, 1975, Madrid, Spain; [p.] Arturo and Pauline Dominguez; [ed.] Marian High School; [occ.] Military Police, Correctional Specialist; [memb.] BOSS (Better Opportunity for Single Soldier); [hon.] Recognition during prison disturbance at the USDB March 3, 1996. Awardee Army Achievement Medal For performance; [oth. writ.] Poems for friends and girls.; [pers.] In an encouraging or futile attempt to achieve acceptance, one must remember to be true to his or her self and everything will be alright.; [a.] San Antonio, TX

DOMINICI, DEBORAH R.
[pen.] Deborah R. Dominici; [b.] March 7, 1963, Pensacola, FL; [p.] Robert Owen Reilly and Shirley Mary Reilly; [m.] Divorced; [ch.] Rheanna Nicole and Michael David Dominici, Asia Martin Dominici (Stepdaughter); [ed.] Aiea High School 1981, Certificate Of Achievement In Practical Nursing Kapiolani Community College 1986, Associate Degree In Nursing Kapiolani Community College 1994; [occ.] Registered Nurse, Certified Perinatal Nurse, Perinatal Loss Counselor; [memb.] Awohnn; [hon.] Deans List Kapiolani Community College, "Po Hana No Ka Oi" Award Kahu Malama Nurses, October 1994, Commanders Coin Of Excellence Tripler Army Medical Center 1995, Department Of Nursing Award for Excellence Tripler Army Medical Center 1995 and 1996; [oth. writ.] Several other unpublished poems; [pers.] "Stand for something, or you'll fall for anything", Thank you Eric for helping me to stand once again.; [a.] Ewa Beach, HI

DONOHOE, VINCENT P.
[pen.] Vincent Donohoe; [b.] December 2, 1947, Rochford, England; [p.] William and Mary; [ed.] In England to college level; [occ.] Airline Reservations Sales and Services Representative; [memb.] The Humane Society of the United States; [hon.] Appeared on several episodes of B.B.C. Television series 'Dad's Army' with British actors, Arthur Lowe and Clive Dunn (Comedy about WW II); [oth. writ.] 'Girl So Pretty,' 'Guilty As Charged,' 'Soda Bread,' 'Dar-Lyn Ellen,' 'Toots,' 'Not A

Patch On Toots,' 'I Really Love You,' plus many more. Determined to have girl so pretty.; [pers.] A hit song world wide. 'Greatest influence on my writing comes from England's greatest 'Poets,' John Lennon and Paul McCartney. I also greatly admire the genius of American 'Poet' song writer Paul Williams; [a.] San Jose, CA

DONOHUE, MADELINE
[b.] June 19, 1960, New York City; [m.] Chris Donohue, May 27, 1988; [ch.] Dennis and Arlene Donohue; [ed.] Eastern District H.S. La Guardia Community College; [oth. writ.] "Ardent Love"; [pers.] To my dear friend Anthony Muscat whose work of art inspired me to write "The Artist."; [a.] Brooklyn, NY

DORNBUSCH, NICOLE
[b.] July 13, 1987, Florida; [p.] Jaime and Karen Dornbusch; [ed.] 4th Grade Student; [hon.] Dean's List, Choir, Academic Excellence 3rd Grade; [pers.] I enjoy reading and writing. My goal is to be a gifted writer.; [a.] Miami, FL

DOTY, MATISSA L.
[pen.] Matissa Whitefeather and Shillelagh Setterwind; [b.] January 28, 1968, Eire, Ireland; [ed.] Lake W.A. High School and Bellevue Community College; [occ.] Retail - Lamonts - Totem Lake in Kirland, WA; [oth. writ.] Anthology - Wind In The Night Sky - Paper Life. Family Treasury of Great Poems - Hamlet's Song of Love and short story entitled - Visions of a Haunting in magazine - Night Cry.; [pers.] I would like to dedicate this poem to two very special people - John Eagleday and Rossi Norris - who have taught me to reach for all I'm worth.; [a.] Bellevue, WA

DOWNS, MARTHA
[b.] May 24, 1948, Lufkin, TX; [p.] Hulan Hoyle, Mary Hoyle; [m.] Divorced; [ch.] Dennis William; [ed.] Marshall High School; [occ.] Kiddie Kare and Pre-school Worker; [memb.] Olivet Free Will Baptist Church, Leader in Pioneer Club Girls (Christian Scouting); [hon.] Editor's Choice Award 1995 (The National Library of Poetry); [oth. writ.] Other unpublished poems. Programs for Ladies Auxiliary church. Poem published in book, " A Moment in Times". Past contributor to the National Library of Poetry; [pers.] If it wasn't for a special aunt, my poems would still be in my drawer hidden away. The poem "God's Gift" is in memory of my son (age 12 1/2 years) Faith knowing God truly cares gets us through Valleys, and we can be victorious in all situations. Then we are more able to help others; [a.] Marshall, MO

DOYLE, DOLORES
[pen.] De De Gibison; [b.] June 7, 1933, Bellivue, IL; [p.] Herb and Nona Gibison; [m.] LaVerne Doyle, October 25, 1994; [ch.] Donald, Ricci, Kristi; [ed.] East High School, IBM School of Accounting; [occ.] Retired, Poet, Writer, Grandmother; [hon.] I'm honored with my children and awarded by my 7 grandchildren.; [oth. writ.] Them There Eyes (1990), Just As I Am (1989), Morning Thoughts My Gentle Son (1996) Maybe, One Day Soon (1996) (none published); [pers.] I have found my childhood sweetheart of 61, after 25 years of searching. We married 2 yrs. ago and he is my inspiration. We were engaged in 1948.; [a.] Janesville, WI

DOYLE, MICHAEL K.
[b.] June 26, 1972, Boston, MA; [p.] Tim Doyle, Bonnie Doyle; [ed.] Bakersfield High, Bakersfield College; [occ.] Independent Rep. with Excel Telecommunications; [hon.] Medal of Merit on 1-20-87 awarded by Boy Scouts of America upon recommendation of the National Court of Honor. (Saved Mother's life); [pers.] Do not rush through life. Pause and enjoy it. I see my life go drifting like a river from change to change.; [a.] Bakersfield, CA

DRISCOLL, BEATRICE ELIZ
[pen.] Betty Driscoll; [b.] October 8, 1921, Detroit, MI; [p.] Ernest and Christine Miller; [m.] Elmer H. Driscoll, November 24, 1956; [ch.] Lorel Beth Driscoll Brady; [ed.] Left Emerson High, age 16 to help mother support 3 siblings; [occ.] Homemaker; [memb.] Former Patchogue, Doll Fanciers Club of L.I., United Fed. Doll Clubs Inc.; [hon.] 1st Place Hand Made Dolls and Hand Dressed - Suf. City Fed Bank of L.I.: Floats (among 50) received 1st Place for costumes (in local newspapers) including "1976 Bicentenial" and "1977 Showboat" designed and made by Betty Driscoll; [oth. writ.] "From the "Thoughts" of Betty Driscoll" published in "Doll News," United Fed. of Doll Clubs Inc., Fall 1977; [pers.] The accomplishments I've achieved show my love for artistry because my heart is in every finished product.; [a.] Raleigh, NC

DRUMRIGHT, GINA R.
[b.] February 3, 1969, Denver, CO; [p.] Gerald and Cheryl Drumright; [ed.] Frederick High, Front Range College; [occ.] Safety/Project Manager; [pers.] My soul is my inspiration for writing. May it touch the ones who read it just as deeply.; [a.] Platteville, CO

DUBE, ROSE MARIE
[pen.] Rose Marie Bailey; [b.] October 3, 1946, Amesbury, MA; [p.] Bernard Bailey, Rose Bailey; [m.] Divorced; [ch.] Lisa, Mike, Toni, Chris and Tina; [pers.] The Purity of Love is the Essence of Life - I wrote this poem for my Mother, 5 weeks before she died of cancer.; [a.] Gardena, CA

DUNLAVY, CAROL
[b.] March 14, 1960, Davis County, IA; [p.] Richard and Violet Dunlavy; [ch.] Stephanie and Makayla; [ed.] Graduated from high school 1978, attended Indian Hill Comm. College. Attumwa, have Associate Degree Nursing; [occ.] Registered Nurse., VA Hospital, Knoxville, Iowa; [pers.] My poem was written in honor of Cindy and Sue Ann whose loss made me treasure my girls.; [a.] Knoxville, IA

DUPERT, THELMA M.
[b.] May 16, 1922, Gypsum, OH; [p.] Mr. and Mrs. George Witter; [m.] Clive Dupert, remarried; [ch.] Five; [ed.] 8th Grade; [occ.] Homemaker; [memb.] I have belonged to Lakemore Ladies Joycies - Crimes Prevention Help in my Community anywhere, I can.; [hon.] Was Outstanding Choir Woman, Lakemore Ladies Jaycees 1978-79-82. Leadership 78-80, Akron Summit Community Action Agency for Volunteer services. Have belonged to crime prevention; [oth. writ.] I have wrote about 90 other I am a Christian I would love to send my poems to shut in Hospital nursing home hoping my poems could cheer them up.; [pers.] If any of my poems could be published it would please me, if only I can touch the hearts of others to help us anyway here or two more.; [a.] Lakemore, OH

DUREN, JERRY L.
[b.] September 18, 1943, Brownwood, TX; [p.] Norman and Coleta Duren (Deceased); [m.] Linda K. Duren, December 24, 1994; [ch.] Pam Kay, Kevin Lynn, Cyndis, Kim Marie; [ed.] Goldthwaite High, B.S. Texas A and M Univ. Med - Texas A and M Univ.; [occ.] Science Teacher - Zephyr ISD; [pers.] I have never published, though I have been writing for many years. I am influenced by the harmony that exists in God's creation and the love that results from striving to further the harmony and prevent the chaos resulting from going against it.; [a.] Mullin, TX

DUSSEN, BRANDY VANDER
[pen.] B. M. Jacobus; [b.] January 13, 1978, Long Beach, CA; [p.] Jim and Sandra Vander Dussen; [ed.] Ripon Christian School, currently enrolled in Pacific Union College majoring in Dental Hygiene; [pers.] I wish to thank my parents for all their sacrifices to give me a better life. "He who does not love does not know God, for God is love." I John 4:8; [a.] Escalon, CA

DYER, SUSAN
[b.] September 15, 1978, Monticello, UT; [p.] Thomas and Janis Dyer; [ed.] Albert R. Lyman Elementary School, Blanding Elementary School, Albert R. Lyman Middle School, San Juan High School, College of Eastern Utah; [memb.] National Honor Society; [hon.] Column writer for local paper San Juan Record, News Editor of school paper Rattler, Head Editor of school literary magazine, Edge of the Blues, poetry and short stories published in anthologies, won several writing contests; [oth. writ.] short story "Great Grandma's Box", poems: "Beauty," "The Painting Of Life," "Heritage," "Small Town American in Retrospect: Their Ignorance or our Innocence," "The Land of Red Sandstone Cliffs, Bluff City, Utah," poem: "The Beauty Of Life".; [pers.] Writing is reflection of our innerself, as a writer, I try to capture the reality of what humans really are. Mankind's emotion is something that will remain an influence of philosophy to writers.; [a.] Blanding, UT

EARL, NORMA B.
[b.] July 23, 1931, Granger, UT; [p.] John Henery and Kate Warr Bawden; [m.] (1st) Floyd Rushton (Deceased, 1966), (2nd) Harold L. Earl, August 31, 1968; [ch.] Steven, Bert, Debra and Jill Ann; [ed.] Cyprus High School, Utah Technical College; [occ.] Retired - Granite School District; [memb.] Church of Jesus Christ of Later Day Saints, Daughters of the Utah Pioneers; [oth. writ.] Poems: "The Shadows Of Her Mind" about my sister who had Alzheimers, "Memories Of My Childhood," "Just A Little Humble Man" about my Father-in-law.; [pers.] I have always loved poetry. My poems come from my heart and soul about the people I have known and loved.; [a.] West Valley City, UT

EARNSHAW, JIM
[b.] June 2, 1948, Wheeling, WV; [p.] Jim and Mary Jo Earnshaw; [m.] Vicki, March 3, 1988; [ch.] Terra and Ryan Kleshinski (Step-children); [ed.] Ohio University Graduate 1970, BS Journalism, Sigma Alpha Epsilon Fraternity; [occ.] Sales Representative for Norandex; [memb.] Sports Car Club of America, Porsche Club of America, Volkswagen Club of America, Central Ohio Vintage Volkswagen Club; [hon.] Have received several award for photographic work - Primary of Landscape; [a.] Mansfield, OH

EASTON, PAMELA M.
[b.] March 22, 1957, Brooklyn, NY; [p.] Edward and Leola Hawkins; [m.] Edmond D. Easton Sr., May 24, 1980; [ch.] Tiffany Jade and Edmond Jr.; [ed.] Graduate of Brooklyn Tech. High School, attended Borough of Manhattan Community College; [occ.] Housewife, P.T.A. President; [memb.] P.T.A. (PS. 72), New Hope Baptist Church - Trustee and Usher Board, School Volunteer Program; [hon.] Recipient of the American Legion Award for Citizenship, Volunteer Community Service Award; [oth. writ.] Wrote and produced an unpublished play entitled "Reading Writing and Remembering" for sixth grade assembly - P.S. 72 district 19, Brooklyn, N.Y. Wrote a unpublished short story "Why Can't I Be Jewish"; [pers.] Silence is Golden, but the truth will shatter the glass ceilings, let our voices be heard!; [a.] Brooklyn, NY

EDWARDS, JAY HAROLD
[b.] January 26, 1963, Conroe, TX; [p.] Margie Edwards and Harry Edwards; [m.] Julie Edwards, April 7, 1997; [ch.] Brianna Jaye and Joshua Lee; [pers.] Always keep your heart and mind open because you never know when inspiration will hit you. My main inspiration came from my children and my new wife.; [a.] Jones Creek, TX

EIDEM, MARY ANN
[pen.] Katarina Keller; [b.] February 20, 1962, Chicago, IL; [p.] Alois and MaryBeth Helfenberger; [m.] John (Jack) H. Eidem, August 24, 1985; [ch.] Steven, Emily, Laura, Michael; [ed.] Necedah Area High School, Western Wisconsin Technical Institute (Associate Degree-Nursing); [occ.] Homemaker; [pers.] Two of my most admired people are Mother Theresa, who has so little but is rich in love and generosity, and Helen Keller, who was blind and deaf, yet could see and listen so keenly with her heart.; [a.] Horicon, WI

EKSEVICS, MARITA
[b.] December 25, 1967, Seattle, WA; [p.] Imants Eksevics (Deceased) and Velta Eksevics; [ch.] William Eksevics; [ed.] Graduated from Roosevelt High School - 1986, currently enrolled in Institute of Children's Literature; [occ.] Full time single mother; [pers.] Thank you to all that have believed in me and my writing. If you don't take chances, you will never know the outcome.; [a.] Seattle, WA

EL-AAYI, HEBA
[pen.] Heba El-Aayi; [b.] September 4, 1985, San Jose, CA; [p.] Abdul and Waltraud El-Aayi; [ed.] Currently enrolled in sixth grade; [occ.] Student; [a.] Aurora, CO

ELAM, DIXIE J.
[b.] November 22, 1937, Ripley, MS; [p.] William and Mettie Yates; [m.] James E. Elam, June 23, 1961; [ch.] Robert and Laura; [occ.] Director of Christian Education; [a.] Livonia, MI

ELLISON, SHANNON SHANTIL
[b.] October 23, 1980, Dallas, TX; [p.] Rick and Hilda Ellison; [ed.] Sophomore Rains High School; [occ.] Student; [memb.] Elm Baptist Church Fellowship of Christian Athletics Student Council Member FFA Member; [hon.] All American Scholar Award, Sophomore Class President, FFA Secretary, President's Educational, Excellence Award, National Honor Roll Award, Who's Who Among American High School students, R-Awards in Biology I; [pers.] I strive to express my true feelings about people and things which have affected me throughout my life.; [a.] Emory, TX

ELSASSER, MELISSA
[b.] July 16, 1978, Ridgeway; [p.] Harry and Deb Elsasser; [ed.] Ridgemont High School, Ohio State University; [memb.] Ohio Murray Grey Association, Faith Baptist Church; [oth. writ.] A couple of poems published in school newspaper.; [pers.] I write to write, whenever I feel like it. I write to please myself, to express my feelings, and sometimes, to let people know how much they mean to me.; [a.] Ridgeway, OH

ENEBAK, RICHARD
[pen.] Dick Enebak; [b.] December 18, 1931, Clarks Grove, MN; [p.] Mr. Oscar Inez More and Mrs. Oscar Enebak; [m.] Lilly Adeline Enebak (1992 Deceased), August 13, 1952; [ch.] Donald, David, Debbie, Danette; [ed.] High School Graduate, Harding High, St. Pauline, MN, Electronic Technician Training I.C.S. Graduate in Electronics, Computer Programing.; [occ.] Self Employed - owner of "Valley View Electronics"; [memb.] Veterans of Foreign (VFW) Wars. National Geographic Society, AARP; [hon.] Honorable Discharge, USN with The Following Medals, Korean Combat W/2 Battle Stars., Chinese Service Medal, United Nations Medal, National Defense Medal; [oth. writ.] "A Fleeting Moment", "My Kitten", "Trucking Northward To Alaska", poem; [a.] Eagan, MN

EPOLITO, CALEIGH
[b.] March 30, 1984, McK. Hospital; [p.] Tari Epolito and Tony Epolito; [ed.] I'm in 7th grade at Saint Angela Merici School in White Oak Pennsylvania.; [oth. writ.] 'Friends' - 1994, 'The Key' - 1994, 'The Tree' - 1996, 'The Rainforests' - 1995; [pers.] In my poetry, I look to everyday things for inspiration, and turn it into writing. All my poems reflect on the wonderful things that surround me.; [a.] McKeesport, PA

ERAMO
[b.] Age-Less Aquarian; [m.] Katie; [ed.] Self-Taught Un-Learning; [occ.] Being myself; [oth. writ.] I combine my poetic writing, purposeful abstract painting, self-photo, and recorded natural voice with listenable experimental music into a unified package; [pers.] I'm not Dwelling, Telling, or Story-Selling. My Style is Timeless, Tasteful, Direct, and Anti-Stereotypical to inspire people to respect their Own individuality.; [a.] Reclusive, AZ

ESEROMA, VIOLET EFFIE
[pen.] Florence Yanglimau; [b.] April 5, 1980, American Samoa; [p.] Lefanoga and Jeanne Hunkin Eseroma; [ed.] Graduated from Leone Midkiff Elementary, now attending Leone High School (Home of the Lions); [memb.] Leone High School Cheerleading Squad, Soccer Team, Drill Team, Softball; [hon.] Honor Roll List from Freshman to Junior Year in Leone High School, Captain of JROTC Organization; [oth. writ.] "What is a Friend?" and "JROTC" published in our school newspaper.; [pers.] I love writing poems so I could express my feelings and thoughts on a piece of paper.; [a.] Pago Pago, AS

ESPOSITO, JEFFREY
[b.] April 10, 1981, Jersey City, NJ; [p.] William and Patricia Stefan; [ed.] Saddle Brook High School; [occ.] Student; [memb.] USA Wrestling Association, Iota Eta Pi; [hon.] Honor Roll, Wrestler of the Year, Most Improved Wrestler; [oth. writ.] Poem book for school English. News paper article, The Record.; [a.] Saddle Brook, NJ

ESSINGER, MELISSA RENEE
[b.] May 9, 1985, Hayward, CA; [p.] Cathlene and Raymond Essinger; [occ.] 6th grade student, Del Rey School, San Lorenzo, CA; [memb.] Girl Scouts, G.A.T.E., Student Council - Del Rey School; [hon.] Scholarship student; [pers.] I was encouraged to write poems by my Grandma, Renee Weber. She especially liked my poem, "Roof top". She encouraged me to enter this poetry contest. I love her and I miss her.; [a.] San Lorenzo, CA

ETHERIDGE, H. STEVE
[b.] November 28, 1949, Rockingham, NC; [p.] Howard Etheridge, Betty Y. Etheridge; [ch.] Alan Clifford, Robert James, John Richard; [ed.] Rockingham, NC High School, United States Military Academy, West Point, NY; [occ.] Environmental Engineer; [memb.] National Association of Environmental Professionals; [oth. writ.] Environmental Management System for Waste management '97 Symposium. Case Study: Savannah River Site Environmental Management System; [a.] Aiken, SC

EUBANKS, TONI MICHELLE
[b.] December 13, 1982, Jonesboro, AR; [p.] Tony and Lisa Eubanks; [ed.] Delaplaine Grade School, now attending Delaplaine Jr. High School; [hon.] 7th grade Geography and Home Economics Award 6th grade Salutatorian; [oth. writ.] Some poems in local newspaper one in school paper; [pers.] When I write I try to reflect what teens are feeling and what goes in some of our lives. I was greatly influenced in 7th grade by my English Teacher Mrs. Martha Rodriguez.; [a.] Delaplaine, AR

EVANS, RACHEL
[b.] April 17, 1980, New York City; [p.] Mel and Elaine Evans; [ed.] Attend Mamaroneck High School. Honor student is Junior Year; [memb.] Active on track teams S.A.D.D. and performing Arts thru dance and theater presentations; [pers.] Goal is to be in performing arts in combination with Law.; [a.] Larchmont, NY

EVANS, SHAWNEY
[pen.] Shawney Rae; [b.] January 16, 1964, Fleetwood, PA; [p.] Buddy Rauenzahn, Miriam Rauenzahn; [m.] Roger Evans, October 3, 1981; [ch.] Joseph Lee, Christopher Allen, Meghann Marie; [ed.] Liberal Arts Student at Reading Area Community College; [occ.] Dental Office Assistant Kutztown, PA; [pers.] It is with the glory of words that I view the expressions of life.; [a.] Fleetwood, PA

EVANS JR., JOHN R.
[b.] April 29, 1924, Philadelphia, PA; [p.] Dr. and Mrs. John C. Evans; [m.] Helen Lorenzo (Deceased), April 3, 1955; [ch.] Kim C. Evans, John R. Evans Jr.; [occ.] Retired - all my life, I was Technical Writer - Editor, Spec. Writer Editor; [memb.] Amer. Legion, CSI - Allentown, PA Chapter, ANA. West Chester Coin Club, Albright Alumni Assoc.; [hon.] J. Bennett Nolan Prize for History 1949. "Reading Artillerists" published in October issues 1949 in Berks Co. Historical Society magazine, (condense version of 3,000 word those that won the J.B. Nolan prize for History - 1949). Poem "First Love" written on Troop Train heading from PA to Texas in February 1943.; [oth. writ.] Poem written when I was a young, impressionable kid.; [pers.] I love life - "Every Golden Minute of it."; [a.] Pottstown, PA

EVERETT, BEVERLY L.
[b.] July 9, 1966, Rushville, IN; [m.] Andrew Everett, May 14, 1994; [ed.] East High, Columbus, IN, Academy of Health Sciences, Fort Sam Houston, TX; [occ.] Surgical Technologist Certified; [oth. writ.] All other writings yet to be exposed to the public eye.; [pers.] There are at least three occasions on which I am compelled to attempt poetry. Those times being, when love touches my heart, when mother nature renews my spirit, and when God enlightens my mind.; [a.] Franklin, IN

EVERETT, DARLA
[pen.] Darla Everett; [b.] September 16, 1959, Garden City, KS; [p.] Rachel and Delbert Allenbaugh; [m.] Daniel Everett; [ch.] Steven Elsen; [ed.] Garden City High School, DeVry Institute of Technology; [occ.] Accountant; [hon.] National Dean's List, Dean's List, Summa Cum Laude; [oth. writ.] Poem published in local trucking magazines.; [pers.] I have been influenced by my family who has given me unconditional love and support as I have strived to become a writer.; [a.] Freeman, MO

EVERETT, JENNIFER
[b.] November 27, 1971, Dallas, TX; [p.] Rachel and Charles Everett; [ed.] Wills Point High School, special training in Emergency Child Care (for children in crisis); [oth. writ.] Currently working on my own book of poetry, and/or life story; [pers.] Seek first to understand, seek second to be understood. Through this, we will all achieve universal understanding. Thanks to my family. Thanks to the teachers that believed in me and even those who didn't.; [a.] Minnesota, TX

EWELL, LINDA
[pen.] Sam L. Thomas; [b.] December 5, 1960, Flint, MI; [p.] J. T. and LaVera Thomas; [m.] Ryan Ewell, August 14, 1982; [ch.] Karrie Ewell; [ed.] Montrose Hill McCloy High School, Baker Junior College of Business, Flint, Michigan; [occ.] Head Cashier and Photo Department Manager; [memb.] Flint Writer's Association, Flint Michigan; [oth. writ.] Children's stories and poems, eulogies for family members and friends. I have submitted several poems in the local newspaper.; [pers.] Whenever you feel depressed, hurt or happy writing is the best therapy for everybody.; [a.] Montrose, MI

EWERSEA, VIRGINIA
[pen.] Virginia Pease Ewersea; [b.] June 7, 1922, Van Wert Co., OH; [p.] Elza and Pearlie Peare; [m.] Herbert Ewersea (Deceased), October 18, 1942; [ch.] Dale and Carol Ewersea; [ed.] Hoaglin Jackson High School, BS in Education, Bowling Green State University, Graduate Hudier, University of Toled., Ohio State University; [occ.] Retired Reading Coordinator Teacher, Port Clinton, OH City Schools, Poet; [memb.] Kappa Delta Pi's, International Reading Ass'n, Human's Society of the United States; [hon.] IRA Literary Award, "Who's Who in American Education," "Who's Who in American Child Development Professionals," "Who's Who in the Midwest," being published and recorded by the National Library of Poetry; [oth. writ.] "From Hyperactive to Happy - Active" (Activity Card, are help for learning disabled children, articles reading and learning in local newspaper, Chapter/Handbook, poetry published in "Poems Across America."; [pers.] In all my life's endeavors, I strive for excellence, with a cheerful heart. My favorite saying: "A merry heart does good like a medicine." (The Bible).; [a.] Port Clinton, OH

EXLINE, BILLY
[b.] November 15, 1982, Alexandria, LA; [p.] Brenda and Bill Exline; [ed.] Alexandria Jr. High 8th; [occ.] Student; [memb.] 1st Church of the Nazarene Quiz team.; [hon.] Spelling Been winner; [oth. writ.] I haven't had any published but I have some others. Including: "Remember when", "Those Last Few Words", and "One Chance at Forever".; [pers.] I think everyone should strive for their best no matter what. I'm poetry it's not always a contest, poetry is something you can do for fun.; [a.] Alexandria, LA

EZEJIOFOR, CHUKWUEMEKA
[b.] August 15, 1971, Isulo; [p.] Benard Ezejiofor, Lucy Ezejiofor; [ed.] Primary School Isulo, Aguata High School Aguata, Compu Data International LTD, University of Lagos, Nigeria, Prince Georges Community College, Largo, MD; [occ.] Habilatation Specialist; [memb.] Science Students, Student Union Government, Computer Science Students, Anambra State Student Union, University of Lagos, Isulo Student Union; [hon.] House Prefect; [oth. writ.] Several poems published is school magazines and several poems unpublished.; [pers.] I believe in God, ancestors, and a strong family unit, all of which result in a higher striving for mankind. I have been greatly influenced by ancestor poets, ideology, beliefs and philosophy.; [a.] Hyattsville, MD

FAATAI, DIANA
[pen.] Diana Tulatoa Faatai; [b.] June 2, 1966, Torrance, CA; [p.] Tulatoa Faanati and Fofoa Mapuoletuli; [m.] Tuvai Selafi Faatai, June 4, 1994; [ed.] Carson High School, UC University, Christ College Irvine (Concordia Univ., Irvine); [occ.] English Teacher, Carson Sr. High School; [memb.] Calvary Chapel South Bay Women's Ministry, Asian Pacific Island Educators; [oth. writ.] Unpublished; [pers.] I bring hope, truth and life to all who read my work. Thanks to my true and personal friend, Jesus. To him be the glory forever!; [a.] Long Beach, CA

FAROH, SHAUNA
[b.] October 30, 1981, Lorain, OH; [p.] Mr. and Mrs. Faroh; [ed.] I go to Lake Ridge Academy, I've been going there since Kindergarten; I'm currently in 9th grade; [occ.] Sometimes I work at my parents' candy store (Faroh's Finest); [memb.] I'm in the Oberin Choristers. I've been in the group for 3 yrs. This is my fourth. I can only be in it for another year after this one. I hope I'll move on to a bigger choir.; [hon.] I've been on the honors and high honors since 6th grade. Our principal and headmasters hand out special pins. I hope to get many more.; [a.] Avon Lake, OH

FARVOUR, GARY W.
[b.] June 24, 1947, Milwaukee, WI; [p.] Buelah Farvour and Edgar Farvour (Deceased); [m.] Carol Farvour, February 20, 1976; [ch.] Nathan and Seth Farvour; [ed.] Predominantly life; [pers.] I write what I see, feel and remember. Everyone at some juncture in life should be heard.; [a.] Hayward, WI

FEHMER, CRYSTAL
[b.] November 10, 1979, Oklahoma City, OK; [p.] Anita Lang, Carl Lang; [oth. writ.] This poem was written for grandpa's funeral. It went on the funeral card.; [pers.] This poem was written for the greatest man I ever knew, it is also dedicated to him, may he rest in peace. Bill Fehmer (my grandpa).; [a.] Minco, OK

FELDBRUEGGE, JAMES
[b.] August 6, 1952, Dorchester, WI; [p.] Frank Feldbruegge, Mary Feldbruegge; [ed.] Colby High School Graduate; [occ.] Factory Worker; [pers.] Society must realize the terrible effects of violence, only then can the "Message of Love" be understood.; [a.] Medford, WI

FELIX, SEAN F.
[b.] June 23, 1975, Washington, DC; [p.] June A. Felix and Derrick Felix; [ed.] Gonzaga College High School, Georgetown University; [occ.] Starbuck's Barista, Freelance Writer; [oth. writ.] Koan - an anthology of short stories and poems that I assisted in writing, editing, and proofreading. Yet to be published.; [pers.] Freedom and constancy of thought are the keys to universal understanding.; [a.] Hyattsville, MD

FELMET, RACHELLE L.
[pen.] Rae; [b.] July 22, 1936, Savannah, GA; [p.] Cecil and Rose Woodcock; [m.] Marion Wayne Felmet, November 6, 1970; [ch.] Marsha Louise, Steven G., Michael W.; [ed.] GED and Massey Business College, Civil Service; [occ.] Independent Contractor for various large companies, and writing; [memb.] National Author's Registry, Past: Woodland Acres Community Church, Singing Ministry of the Youth, and Church Secretary. Fiction Writer's Connection. Republican Presidential Legion of Merit; [hon.] Republican Presidential Honor Roll, Republican Presidential Legion of Merit Medal of Honor; [oth. writ.] Several poems soon to be published. Song, "He'll Still Be Your Friend" just finished the recording by Dodie Frost.; [pers.] God has blessed me with a very caring and supportive husband. Each poem is an inspiration from God, and it is my hope that they will encourage, lift and help someone along life's way. I cannot express my personal joy, and gratitude at having this opportunity. God bless.; [a.] Atlantic Beach, FL

FERGUSON, CARRIE ANNE
[b.] May 31, 1986, Denville, NJ; [p.] John Ferguson, Julia Ferguson; [oth. writ.] Poems published in: A Celebration of Pennsylvania's Young Poets and the Anthology of Poetry by Young Americans; [a.] Stroudsburg, PA

FETCHO, ANDREW THOMAS
[b.] December 17, 1972, Scranton, PA; [p.] Andrew Fetcho Sr., Jean Homentosky Fetcho; [ed.] Bishop O'Hara High School, Dunmore, PA, Marywood College, Scranton, PA; [oth. writ.] "Through Depression, Life, and Love" Volume I Poetry, fictional novel to be completed in 1997.; [pers.] I wrote the poem "An Ocean Apart" in honor of the 230 people who lost their lives on TWA flight 800 over the Atlantic Ocean on July 17, 1996.; [a.] Eynon, PA

FETZ, HAZEL S.
[b.] August 26, 1953, Pittsburgh, PA; [p.] Walter Miller Jr., Violet R. Brittner; [m.] Divorced; [ch.] Gregory Steven Fetz; [ed.] Carrick High, Greene Co. Vo-Tech College, IVY Tech State College, Terry Middleton's Karate, Boxing, Kick Boxing School; [occ.] Nurse, Neuroscience and Spine Center of Norton Hospital, Louisville, KY; [memb.] Phi Theta Kappa, Dean's List, Instructor of Martial Arts, Alliant Health and Fitness Center, Self-Defense Instructor; [hon.] Recognized for volunteer work by the State of Florida for AIDS Educator. Phi Theta Kappa Honor Society. Certificate of Excellence in Martial Arts. Black Belt Status in Karate. Twenty two years of nursing experience; [oth. writ.] Unleashing The Woman Within Life's Riches, Introduction To Karate, For The Love of A Horse.; [pers.] I love to write for impression. I want the reader to feel the sinking feeling in the pit of their stomach, or the exuberant feeling of winning, or the tears of losing something forever. I have a dream of writing a suspense novel.; [a.] Clarksville, IN

FIGUEIREDO, KELLIE M.
[b.] November 20, 1965, Modesto, CA; [p.] H. C. House and Alice Jeanne House; [m.] Victor Manuel Figueiredo, August 29, 1992; [ed.] Columbia Christian College, Foothill Sr. High School; [memb.] Phi Alpha Sigma; [hon.] Dean's List, Who's Who in American High School Students, Society of Distinguished American High School Students; [a.] Santa Clara, CA

FILLIE, DONNA E.
[b.] April 26, 1950, Torrington, CT; [p.] Stanley Randall, Alice Randall; [m.] Robert L. Fillie Sr., October 17, 1970; [ch.] Michelle Lynn, Robert Louis; [ed.] Torrington High, Northwestern Connecticut Community Tech. College, A.S. - in Art; [occ.] Owner of small business; [hon.] National Arts Program Graphic Art Div. Award, Dean's List, High Honors all semesters; [pers.] Through my writings, I strive to place the reader into a thought provoking situation, of visual images that cannot quite be real.; [a.] Torrington, CT

FINCHER, JOSEPH W.
[b.] May 2, 1978, Mt. Vernon, TX; [p.] Roy and Wanda Fincher; [occ.] I am a sailor in the US Navy; [pers.] Those who follow the path of righteousness in Christ will receive great rewards in his kingdom.; [a.] Mount Vernon, TX

FINESTEAD, BETHALENE
[b.] July 11, 1938, Chariton, IA; [p.] Waldo Crandall and Eva Ellen Crandall; [m.] L. Alan Finestead, December 27, 1959; [ch.] Ramona Rae, Ellen Dawnene, Arlan Lee and Tonya Doreen; [ed.] Chariton High, Iowa State Teacher's, Cedar Falls, IA. Drake University, Des Moines, IA; [occ.] Retired Lower Elementary Teacher; [memb.] Mercy Auxiliary of Central Iowa. Cee Do Cee Square Dance Club. Central Iowa Caller Association, Waukee Christian Church (Disciples); [pers.] My writings come from the depths of my "inner

being," which I believe are generated by God, our creator.; [a.] Granger, IA

FIRESHAKER, JERRY ANN
[b.] March 19, 1923, Muskogee, OK; [p.] Grace and Ben Marshall; [m.] Franklin Fireshaker, April 27, 1942; [ch.] Ouannah Karvar and Alana Rushton; [ed.] Bacone College/Krotona Ins. Psychology, Adelle Davis-Nutrition/Micronesian Studies, Guam; [occ.] Sec. Companion, Staff, Mgr. Employer, Randolph Hearst; [memb.] I am a member of the Creek tribe Muskogee Nation, my spouse is a member of the Ponca Tribe; [hon.] Balfour Trophy - Bacone College, Bacone, Okla; [oth. writ.] Translator of unpublished legends, songs, and historical events in American Indian languages for explanation and a compliment to painting by T. Fireshaker for Museum - Gallery; [pers.] Many Native Amer. Indians have not changed basically in their innermost hearts and souls. Their abode, their adornment, language and transportation are contemporary, but the ancient appreciation for nature, family, children and ceremony are still strong within our racial memories. My poems are whispers of what was and is.; [a.] Ojai, CA

FISCHER, KATRINA
[b.] August 3, 1965, San Bernardino, CA; [p.] Mary Adams; [m.] Leo A. Fischer, October 10, 1992; [ch.] Kelly Lynn, Jason Andrew, Tylor Anthony; [ed.] Gary High School, Chaffey Community College; [occ.] Finance Manager, Bell Road Lexux, Phoenix, AZ; [oth. writ.] Several poems published in newsletter.; [pers.] My poetry reflects feelings from within, and helps me to help others.; [a.] Glendale, AZ

FISHER, LINDSEY
[b.] February 4, 1983, Appleton, WI; [p.] Charlie and Joyce Fisher; [ed.] 8th Grader at St. Joseph's Middle School, Appleton, Wisc; [occ.] Student at St. Joseph's Middle School - Appleton, Wisc; [hon.] Academic Honor Roll, Paper Arts Festival Picture Finalist

FISHER, TWYLA DAWN
[pen.] Twyla Dawn Fisher; [b.] March 13, 1928, Tiffin, OH; [p.] James and Bessie Turner; [m.] William Earl Fisher, August 12, 1986; [ch.] Bonnie Dawn, Brenda, Becky Ann and Charles Brisbin; [ed.] Graduated from Columbian High School, Tiffin, OH, 1946; [occ.] Domestic Engineer; [memb.] United Methodist Church, Daughter's of America, VFW; [hon.] Ran for a while in 1985, came in first in my age group 50, 2 miles. Since I came in first, couldn't go any higher, so I hung up my shoes.; [oth. writ.] September 22, 1987, my article appeared in Woman's World, Precious Moments.; [pers.] When I write, it gets rid of my pent up energy.

FITZGERALD, ANNE CURRIE
[b.] March 13, 1970, Detroit, MI; [ed.] Wayne State University, John's Hopkins University; [occ.] Graduate student studying English/Education; [memb.] National Council for Teachers of English; [hon.] National Honor Society, Wayne State University Outstanding Academic Achievement Award, Wayne State University French Poetry Award; [pers.] My writing tends to examine the spiritual relationship between humankind and the natural environmental. I have been inspired by writers such as, James Joyce, Toni Morrison, Dillon Thomas, and Seamus Heaney.

FLANNERY, MARIAN WAUFLE
[b.] August 3, 1925, Hornell, NY; [p.] Mr. and Mrs. Harry Waufle, (Belva Porter Waufle); [ch.] John Michael Flannery and Daniel Patrick Flannery; [ed.] Hornell High School, Hornell, N.Y. Mt. St. Joseph Teachers College, Buffalo, NY, Radio - Television Production, poetry under Poet Laureate and Advance Poetry Florida at Barry University, Vivian Laramore Rader, short story and article writing; [occ.] Retired; [memb.] Academy of American Poets, Florida Public Relations Assoc., Dade County Juvenile Council, Miami Shores Presbyterian Church; [hon.] Phrase written by Mrs. Flannery and chosen for youth theme by the Dade Juvenile Council of Miami County "Huff and puff the devil out, and breathe in the love of God" which helped to reduce the crime rate; [oth. writ.] Poem - "Maranne, The Mermaid"; [pers.] Miami Shores moved to Florida from Buffalo, New York with two young sons in 1954.; [a.] Miami Shores, FL

FLATH, JANA
[b.] November 26, 1963, Washington; [p.] Ken Thain, Myra Hacker (Deceased); [m.] Robert Flath, April 10, 1982; [occ.] Disability Processing Underwriter with The Guardian Life Insurance Co.; [a.] Spokane, WA

FLICK, ETHAN
[b.] March 9, 1981, Pittsburgh, PA; [p.] David and Gloria Flick; [pers.] Read for the content, not the author. Always remain honorable in everything you do. Chivalry lives in us all.; [a.] Pittsburgh, PA

FLORES, ARMANDO
[b.] September 17, 1921, Mission, Texas; [p.] Braulio G. Flores - Preciliana Flores; [m.] Maria Luisa V. Flores, September 27, 1947, Corpus Christi, Texas; [ch.] Four: Armando, Thelma, Richard, And Rose Mary; [ed.] High School - Business College - Southwest Texas State College (Legal Training); [occ.] Retired - Justice of the Peace - Nueces County, Texas; [memb.] Life Member D.A.V., Life & Charter Member Amer. G.I. Forum, Life Member J.P. & Constable Assoc. (Tex.), Texas 1st Families - 1846-1996 - Texas State Genealogical Society; [hon.] Hall of Fame - Roy Miller High School (1941 Graduate), Hall of Fame - Local Bowling Chapter; [oth. writ.] Poets - Songwriters - 1947 Haven Press; Letters to Editor - Opinions - Local newspaper; [pers.] Two principal languages - two great cultures - The Americas, North - Central and South America - Together and United under Democracy. We must set the course for the world to follow.; [a.] Corpus Christi, Texas

FOLLETTE, KATHLEEN V.
[b.] Monroe, WA; [p.] Robert E. and Verle Mosier Casey; [m.] Walter L. Follette, December 27, 1951; [ch.] David, Barbara, and Robert, 6 grandchildren; [ed.] Sultan Union High School Everett Senior College; [occ.] Homemaker Retired R.N. Pianist; [a.] Snohomish, WA

FRANKLIN, DAVID
[pen.] Zlus; [b.] October 9, 1962, Plaquemine, LA; [p.] Mr. and Mrs. Jack Franklin; [m.] Vanessa Franklin, November 14, 1992; [ch.] Mary Lu Franklin; [ed.] St. John High School, Plaquemine, LA; [occ.] O.S. Dow Chemical, LA Div.; [oth. writ.] Private Collection; [pers.] Trust in the Lord.; [a.] Baton Rouge, LA

FRANKLIN, ESTHER
[pen.] Star Peace; [pers.] March 22, 1981, Waynesville, NC; [p.] Mike Howell, Martha Howell; [ed.] Home Schooler, 10th grade student; [occ.] Travelling and singing, Evangelistic Team; [memb.] Singing group "The Prophetsyers," Christian Forward School Reading Club, Teen for the Homeless; [hon.] 1993 3rd place for reading the most books, 1995 1st place reading award, North Carolina 4 Good Citizen Awards, 9th grade honor student award; [oth. writ.] Other poems and short stories; [pers.] I wrote this poem for my friends and loved ones I leave behind when I travel, to sing for the glory of the Lord, and my sister Tammy.; [a.] Waynesville, NC

FRASE, DOUGLAS C.
[b.] May 10, 1979, Maryland; [p.] Diane Keys, Daniel E. Frase (Deceased); [ed.] Senior in High School; [occ.] Student at Colonel Richardson High School; [memb.] Spanish Club, Soccer, Immanuel Luther Church youth group, Talbot Bible Church Youth Group; [oth. writ.] A couple of unpublished; [pers.] I've been influenced by Gothic, Transcendentalist and a mixture of Ancient and Modern Writers, Song Writers and Poets.; [a.] Preston, MD

FRASER, SARAH
[b.] November 27, 1973, Tempe, AZ; [p.] Linda Fraser, Alexander Fraser; [ed.] Photography major at the University of Arizona, BFA in Photography, degree received in Spring '97; [occ.] Photo Lab Technician; [hon.] Received 2nd place awards in the City of Temple Amateur Photography Contest in 1992 and 1993.; [a.] Tucson, AZ

FREDA, CAROLYN
[b.] November 16, 1942, Brooklyn, NY; [p.] William Sweeney and Augusta; [m.] Richard Freda, April 18, 1970; [ch.] Debra, Billy, Richard Jr.; [ed.] Maxwell High, The Institute of Children's Literature; [memb.] St. David's Lutheran Church; [pers.] I hope to publish many more articles, stories and poems.

FREDRICKSON, ALICIA L.
[pen.] Lee Austin; [b.] February 4, 1946, Chicago, IL; [p.] Arthur and Sylvia Austin; [m.] Charles R. Fredrickson, May 1, 1970; [ch.] Sylvia and Arthur Wilkerson; [ed.] Lowell High, Lowell, Indiana; [occ.] Retired; [hon.] The MDA Bronze Award, Indiana State 4-H Key Award; [pers.] This poem was inspired by Brian and Michelle Yandell in loving memory of great grandma Eva Yandell and grandma Nana Austin.; [a.] Harrisburg, AR

FREEMAN, NICOLE
[b.] February 11, 1980, Durham, NC; [p.] Tony and Debra Freeman; [ed.] Southern High School Junior; [memb.] National Honor Society, Mu Alpha Theta, Varsity Cheerleading Squad, Spartansong Show Choir, Durham Public Schools Curriculum Committee; [pers.] The inspiration for my poetry is my love, Marcos Scott Ostria.; [a.] Durham, NC

FREI, THERELANDRUS
[b.] August 3, 1942, Idaho Falls, ID; [p.] S. Reed and Melba B. Andrus; [m.] A. Merlin Frei, April 21, 1961; [ch.] Doug W. and Greg M. Frei; [ed.] Graduated from Bonneville High School, I.F., ID, Colleges attended: Rick College - Rexburg, ID, B.Y.U. - Provo, UT, Tulsa University - Tulsa, OK; [occ.] Private organ and piano Music Teacher; [memb.] Latter-Day Saint (Mormon) Church - Stake Organist, Idaho Falls Music Club, American Guild of Organists (AGO); [hon.] Outstanding Citizenship - awarded by Civitan Club of Idaho Falls, ID, High Honors high school graduate, "Search for Pearls" poem voted first place in "Lines and Stanzas" paper - Ricks College - Rexburg, ID, a published composer of 3 hymn arrangements, "Sweet is the Work" - piano arrangement - 3rd place - L.O.S. Church Music Contest; [oth. writ.] "Illusions" published in "Eda-How Gems," received Honorable Mention; [pers.] "The windows of the soul are reflected in one's works. Therefore, let one's works EDIFY." "May my talents always be worthy of Edification."; [a.] Idaho Falls, ID

FRIBERG, ERIKA A.
[b.] December 28, 1977, Milwaukee, OR; [p.] Lonny and Beverly Friberg; [ed.] Scappoose High School, Portland Community College; [occ.] Bank Teller, US National Bank of Oregon; [memb.] Metro Washington Park Zoo's "Friends of the

Zoo" member 1996-1997, Wolf Education and Research Center Member (1996, life member); [pers.] I want to move people with my writing, make them think. I strive to enlighten people about the beauty of all living things, to remind them to respect mother nature and all her creatures.; [a.] Scappoose, OR

FRIMER, LAURA
[b.] January 60, 1950, Brooklyn, NY; [p.] Olga and Baer Frimer; [ed.] BA, Queens College, MS, American University; [occ.] National Account Manager, Xerox Corporation; [pers.] Contemporary poetry influenced by today's sociological challenges and relationships.; [a.] Saint Petersburg, FL

FRITCH, JOYCE RIVERS
[pen.] Joyce Rivers Fritch; [b.] July 9, 1942, Butler, PA; [p.] John and Elsie Rivers; [m.] John R. Fritch, May 27, 1989; [ch.] Victoria and Shawn Burns; [ed.] Butler High School BS Education, English/Communication, Slippery Rock, Master of Arts English-Slippery Rock, Phd Rhetoric and Linguistics-Indiana University of PA; [occ.] Writing Instructure at Penn State, Altoona Campus; [memb.] Saltsburg Presbyterian Church, Deacon, NCTE, CCC, PACCA; [hon.] Sigma Tha Delta President Kappa Delta Pi, Cum Laude/Bachelor Degree Marshall/Masters Degree; [oth. writ.] University and local paper publication of poetry/articles; [pers.] My writing reflects my love of God, family and nature the forever processes.; [a.] Saltsburg, PA

FROST, GAYLE
[pen.] Gayle Carreker Frost; [b.] January 31, 1965, Atlanta, GA; [p.] Samual and Jean Carreker; [ch.] Michael David, Kevin William; [oth. writ.] For the Love of Kevin/Being Inside, Looking Out/Wild, Young and Free; [pers.] I thank God for all of my personal experiences. For they have changed me into the person I am today. Through every challenge, God has strengthen me. My inspiration to write are my beautiful children Kevin and Michael.

FRYAR, DAVID
[b.] October 25, 1967, Arlington, TX; [p.] Judy and Glyn Fryar; [ed.] Covington I.S.D., Hill College, McLennan Community College, East Texas State University; [occ.] Teacher; [memb.] Johnson County Song Writers' Association, JSCA; [hon.] Music Scholarship, H.C. 1987, Certificate of Merit for Outstanding Accomplishment in Music, H.C. 1989, Most Memorable Song, MCC, 1991; [oth. writ.] Instrumental music and songs, unpublished.; [a.] Rio Vista, TX

FRYER, JEFF
[pen.] Jeff Fryer; [b.] March 5, 1977, Galesburg; [p.] Daniel Fryer, Alvah Fryer; [ed.] Galesburg High School, Western Illinois University; [occ.] Student; [memb.] Phi Mu Alpha Sinfonia Music Business Association - WIU Central Illinois Jazz Society; [hon.] Illinois Young Author - 1991, Who's Who Among American High School Students '91 - '95, The National Dean's List 1995; [oth. writ.] Poems published in student newspaper; [pers.] Many of my writings are very introspective. My pride comes from expressing through pen what my life is on paper.; [a.] Macomb, IL

FUDGE, L. GLADYS
[b.] November 15, 1911, Summer County, WV; [p.] Mr. and Mrs. C. H. Ballard; [m.] Billy M. Fudge Sr., October 25, 1932; [ch.] Carroll Faye, Virginia Lee, Billy Marshall; [ed.] Princeton High, (Concord State Normal Athens, West Virginia); [occ.] Retired, from Montgomery County Board of Education, School Food Service (23 years); [memb.] Order Easter Star, Joppa Lodge Chapter #27; [pers.] I have always been interested in poetry. I have collected an album of poetry that I deem important and interesting.; [a.] Bethesda, MD

FULGHUM, EMILY
[b.] November 19, 1983, Memphis, TN; [p.] Shelia and Jimmy Endress; [ed.] Presently a 7th grade student at Colonial Middle School for the Performing Arts; [occ.] Student; [memb.] Junior National Beta Club; [hon.] Best Science Student, Most Outstanding Student, Presidential Award in Excellence 3 times, Science Fair Winner; [oth. writ.] "The Winner Is," "Glory," "Pasturelands"; [pers.] You might not always be the best but don't give up and you'll be a winner!

FULTON, MATT
[pen.] Matteo Di Vicenza, Teo Fulton; [b.] December 31, 1959, Vicenza, Italy; [m.] Michelle Javid Fulton, June 8, 1985; [ch.] Two; [ed.] BS E USAF Academy 1982, MBA Kensington University 1991; [occ.] Manager Jabil Cirevit, Inc., Auburn Hills, MI; [oth. writ.] Journalist 1975-78, with Fairfield Daily Republic, advanced MFG seminar NWC China Lake "Expert System for Wave Soldier" 1987, Various poems in magazines; [pers.] Goal: To contribute to an improving quality of life for family and friends by both word and deed. Romantic and classical literature influence my writing.; [a.] Auburn Hills, MI

GAINER, MICHAEL E.
[pen.] Michael E. Gainer; [b.] August 24, 1956, East Chicago, IN; [p.] Dorothy and James Gainer; [ed.] Obtained G.E.D. and went to Paralegal School; [occ.] Legal Assistant, Writer; [hon.] None, at this present time.; [oth. writ.] Other writings include, Route Seven (1994), Pink Rose (1994), The Big Wheel (1995), Jet Flight Of Love (1980), Ignorance and Racism (1995), The Chains Of Poverty (1995), Dan the Klan (1996) (all these writings have not yet been published.); [pers.] In my poetry, I glorify the God of Heaven, and speak out at injustice that so many people encounter, simply because they do not have the money or, because they are the wrong color.; [a.] Mesa, AZ

GALINDO, JOSHUA
[b.] February 19, 1981, Adrian, MI; [p.] James Galindo, Kimberly Galindo; [ed.] Currently a Sophomore at Apache Junction High School; [pers.] It is said that art imitates life. I just hope that someday, people will accept each other for who they are on the inside, and not judge each other by the way they look on the outside.; [a.] Apache Junction, AZ

GALTON, CHAVELLE
[pen.] Chevy; [b.] October 24, 1983, Honolulu, HI; [p.] Beatrice Galton; [oth. writ.] 6th grade graduation poem, citizenship poem.

GALUSKA, JOHN D.
[pen.] Johnny Oboe; [b.] July 12, 1971, Elmwood Park, IL; [p.] Richard and Joy Galuska; [m.] Alice Ann Dobie-Galuska, June 26, 1993; [ed.] Beloit College Beloit WI, Indiana University, Bloomington IN, University of Technology, Kingston, Jamaica; [occ.] Folklore/Ethnomusicology Graduate Student; [memb.] Poetry Society of Jamaica, American Folklore Society, Ethnomusicology Student's Association; [hon.] Phi Beta Kappa, Indiana University International Enhancement Scholar, Beloit College Presidential Scholar; [oth. writ.] Poetry published in: Alternative Arts and Literature (1995), Byron Poetry Works (1994), Avatar (1993), The Round Table (1992); [pers.] I thank all my friends in Jamaica for the poem vibes we have shared and experienced together...peace, Johnny Oboe.; [a.] Bloomington, IN

GARCIA, ADRIANA
[pen.] Nana; [b.] September 9, 1984, Falfurrias, TX; [p.] Mr. and Mrs. Adriana and Olga Garcia; [ed.] 6th grade Honor Roll student at Immaculate Conception Catholic School in Rio Grande City, TX; [occ.] Full time 6th grade student; [memb.] 4-H, Safety Patrol Club, Band, Little Miss Star, Altar Server, Little Miss Texas, Little Miss Roma, CIL, UIL; [hon.] (A&B) Honor Roll, Safety Patrol Service, Perfect Attendance, Citizenship, Effort, 2nd place Speech Contest in Dallas, TX., Altar Server Award, CIL 1st District Place, Relay Races, Softball, First Communion; [oth. writ.] Poem contest by the Anthology of Poetry by Young Americans (Asheboro, NC), BIC (1997) Essay Contest (Fairfield, Conn.); [pers.] My first priority is education. My achievements and accomplishments are a reflection of the goodness instilled and influenced by my parents. I may not grow up to be a famous poet, but I'm a winner just simply by pursuing my goals.; [a.] Rio Grande, TX

GARCIA, EDDIE CHRISTOPHER
[b.] August 1, 1965, Los Angeles, CA; [p.] Paul Garcia, Maria Garcia; [m.] Cindy Garcia, September 18, 1994; [ed.] John Rowland High, Mount San Antonio Jr. College; [occ.] Warehouseman, Medtronic Cardiopulmonary; [oth. writ.] Several other poems not published or entered.; [pers.] I enjoy writing what I feel, expressing myself from deep inside. I've always been one to be quiet with a heart of feelings and expressions to write.; [a.] Fullerton, CA

GARRICK, AMY ROBYN
[b.] August 5, 1986, Rockville, MD; [p.] Michael and Laura Garrick; [ed.] In 5th grade at Heim Middle School, Williamsville, New York; [occ.] Student; [hon.] President's Education Gold Award; [pers.] I love to read, and that influenced me to write. Also my cousin Jane Yolen is a writer and meeting her made me want to write more.; [a.] Getzville, NY

GARRISON, RENEE
[b.] December 22, 1965, Hill City, KS; [p.] Verline (Red) and Virginia Pfeifer; [m.] Scott Garrison, June 22, 1985; [ch.] Zeb (7), Abby (5), and Jaden (2); [occ.] YMCA Kid Zone, Staff Co Owner with spouse of Garrison Concrete Constr.

GARROW, JOYCE
[pen.] Gertrude Joyce; [b.] August 11, 1950, Albany, NY; [p.] Gino Francisconi and Carmella Bassotti; [m.] Donald W. Garrow, August 7, 1968; [ch.] James R. and Donald G. Garrow; [ed.] High School (RCS); [occ.] Receptionist (Douberley Insurance, Zephyrhills, FL); [memb.] Poet Group at River Branch Library, Zephyrhills, FL; [oth. writ.] Currently working on a novella: Walks Near Water. It's about a little girl lost in the wilds of Niagara County, New York in the late 1700s who is befriended by a Seneca Native American Boy on his dream fast.; [pers.] I believe that you must try and never to say you can't!; [a.] Zephyrhills, FL

GASPER, DAVID R. L.
[pen.] Fuzzy; [b.] September 4, 1974, Twin Falls, ID; [p.] Danny Lee and Gabrielle Marie Gasper; [ed.] Palm Desert High School, College of the Desert, Jefferson Davis Community College, Boise State University; [occ.] Full-time student, BSU, Boise, ID; [memb.] Sons of the American Legion, Destiny Telecomm. International, Inc.; [hon.] 1st place Mixed Media in National Date Festival, Honorable Scholarship Shadow Mt. Pallette Club; [oth. writ.] Your eyes, dead thoughts, innocence, the boxers, manifest destiny and Nightmare are all poems I've written in reflection of my art.; [pers.] I thought to acknowledge Shakespeare and Rembrandt as the two greatest influences in my poetry, but the credit goes to all Truth, found in the

Book of Mormon and the Bible. Read daily from them, for God truly speaks from their pages.; [a.] Waveland, MS

GAYMON, MICHELE
[pen.] Michele Gaymon; [b.] May 23, 1970, Belleville, NJ; [p.] Robert and Luis Gaymon; [ed.] Rutgers University, Rutgers School of Business, New Brunswick, NJ; [occ.] Plan Administrator, Merrill Lynch, Somerset, NJ; [memb.] Second Baptist Church, Rahway, NJ; [oth. writ.] Several poems published in college newspapers.; [pers.] With God's help, I reach into my heart, release all of the love, and let it radiate through my poetry.; [a.] Colonia, NJ

GAZZILLO, KIM
[b.] September 15, 1959, Princeton, NJ; [p.] William and Roberta Wutke; [m.] John Gazzillo Jr., December 17, 1978; [ch.] John III and Sara; [ed.] Hunterdon Central High School, Flemington, NJ; [occ.] Hair Dresser; [memb.] Lynn Methodist Church, National Wildlife Fed., National Arbor Foundation; [oth. writ.] Poems, short stories, children's stories - never published.; [pers.] I greatly admire writers, though poets I hold dear. Emily Dickinson I find myself most drawn to; her writing is fascinating, as was her life.; [a.] Meshoppen, PA

GEISER, PAULA C.
[b.] June 30, 1953, Wilmington, DE; [p.] Mildred Cocco; [m.] David E. J. Geiser Sr., June 27, 1988; [ch.] Eddie and Jimmy; [ed.] A. I. DuPort High School Wilmington, Delaware; [occ.] Housewife and Full time mother and Indian Jewelry Crafter; [oth. writ.] A poem in high school - called I have a little dog.; [pers.] In my life time I would like to see a better, peaceful world for my boys and all the other children of the world, love is what the children need; [a.] Plains, PA

GEORGE, MICHAEL T.
[pen.] Tommy George; [b.] September 9, 1982, Mobile, AL; [p.] Thomas and Kerry George; [ed.] St. Vincent De Paul, K-8th Grade, currently attending Theodore High School; [occ.] Student

GERHARDT, HOLLY MARIE
[b.] July 29, 1976, Topeka, KS; [p.] Edward and Kathleen Gerhardt; [ed.] High School graduate of Highland Park High School, Johnson County Community College; [occ.] Full-time College student; [memb.] NKHA (Equestrian Show jumping, Northeast Kansas Hunter Assoc.), American Heart Association, Sadha (Dental Hygiene Student's Association); [hon.] Who's Who of America's High School Students, top 5% of graduating class.; [oth. writ.] Several poems, none published.; [pers.] In our minds the words are always there. Poetry is the art of collecting and arranging the words to create a vivid and wonderful image for all who may take a moment to reflect.; [a.] Topeka, KS

GIANOULIS, TARA
[b.] July 15, 1981, Staten Island, NY; [p.] John Gianoulis, Gloria Gianoulis; [ed.] New Dorp Christian Academy, Staten Island Technical High School; [occ.] Student; [memb.] Borough President's High School Advisory Council, Staten Island Ballet Academy, National Honor Society, Manhattan Theatre Club; [hon.] NYCATE Essay Contest; [oth. writ.] (Poem) Someone Special, (essay) Simply Explanatory; [pers.] "Render unto Caesar that which is Caesar's" Mark 12:17.; [a.] Staten Island, NY

GIBB, RUTH L.
[pen.] Ruth Roy (Musician); [b.] September 18, 1936, Coral Gables, FL; [p.] Anthony J. and Gloria O. Daino; [m.] Joseph P. Gibb, February 22, 1987; [ch.] Stephen J. Pachan, Mark E. Pachan; [ed.] Miami Sr. High, Sharron-Williams Commercial College; [occ.] Forec L. Processor/Legal Sec'y., Prof. Musician, Cartoonist, Real Est. Sales Person; [memb.] American Legion, Disabled American Veterans, Auxiliaries, Ladies of the Moose; [hon.] Nat'l. recognition for completion of "Speed writing" course in 12 days 1956, Dava State Dept., FL Musician 1983-84; [oth. writ.] Published cartoon character named "Osbald," and yet unpublished children's stories and poems fully illustrated.; [pers.] If you look at the world through children's eyes, you will see only the beauty and humor in everything.; [a.] Alpharetta, GA

GIBSON-MUELLER, ELISABETH
[b.] February 9, 1985, Boston, MA; [p.] Rick and Karon Gibson-Mueller; [ed.] I am currently a student at Whipple Middle School in Ipswich, MA; [occ.] Student; [memb.] St. Pauls Episcopal Church Malden, MA; [oth. writ.] Student News and Literary publications.; [pers.] I'm influenced by my surroundings.; [a.] Ipswich, MA

GILBLAIR, CAROL
[b.] March 21, 1959, Rumford, ME; [p.] Cealand Burgess Jr., Virginia Gordon; [m.] Arthur Gilblair, September 7, 1985; [ch.] Sarah Elizabeth, Benjamin William; [ed.] Windham High School, Portland Regional Vocational Technical Center, Fisher Junior College; [occ.] Teacher, The Growings Years Day Care; [hon.] Honor Roll, Dean's List; [pers.] I have always had a special love for children. My love for all children was what my inspiration was to write this poem. All children should be loved.

GILMER, WILLIAM D.
[pen.] Bill Gilmer; [b.] May 19, 1917, Kansas City, MO; [p.] Dresel Gilmer and Mary Roberts; [m.] Rosemary (Deceased), March 5, 1942; [ch.] Lawrence; [ed.] Grade school, high school, Kansas University, Law Enforcement courses; [occ.] Retired from Law Enforcement (45 years); [memb.] Various Law Enforcement organizations, church, volunteering in piano and organ presentation.; [hon.] Numerous certificates and awards; [oth. writ.] Articles in local newspapers, poetic presentations as religious services, and funerals; [pers.] Excepting mental illness, I attempt to place in perspective positive aspects of unusual persons.; [a.] Raymore, MO

GIROUX, MARC
[b.] New Hampshire; [m.] Patricia; [ch.] Jason, Zenobia, Kellen and Alex; [a.] Lexington, SC

GLANTON, THOMAS P.
[pen.] Pettis; [b.] February 21, 1940, Newman, GA; [p.] Thomas A. and Judy Glanton; [m.] Divorced, January 30, 1959; [ch.] E. Wynn Grisham, Thomas M. Glanton; [ed.] B.S. in Business - Auburn University, M.S. in Management - Georgia Tech.; [occ.] Marketing Representative; [memb.] Dunwoody United Methodist Church Stephen Minister; [hon.] Phi Kappa Phi Scholastic Society 1962, Leadership Georgia 1977, Georgia General Assembly 1975-78; [pers.] "The Past is But Prologue" means you can always begin again where you are now.; [a.] Atlanta, GA

GOAD, TERESA M.
[b.] March 9, 1964, Roanoke, VA; [p.] Bruce and Jo Musgrove; [m.] Jimmy L. Goad, December 7, 1991; [ch.] Kaylee Rae Goad; [ed.] Cave Spring High School, Roanoke College; [occ.] Kindergarten Teacher; [hon.] Distinguished Teacher Award, 1988; Great Expectations Award, 1991; [pers.] Thank you to my daughter Kaylee for being my inspiration - I Love You!; [a.] Roanoke, VA

GODFREY, DAVID ASHLEY
[b.] January 6, 1969, Brenham, TX; [p.] Gerry and Camilla Godfrey; [m.] LaNette Godfrey, June 6, 1992; [ch.] Kate Ashley; [ed.] Sam Houston State University; [occ.] 4th Grade Teacher, New Caney Elementary, New Caney, TX; [pers.] Some people believe song is poetry set to music. I disagree. Poetry stands alone and need not be accompanied by music.; [a.] Huntsville, TX

GODWIN, ROBERT B.
[b.] June 14, 1933, Minneapolis, MN; [p.] Bruce and Norma V. Godwin; [m.] Divorced, December 16, 1962; [ch.] David Michael, Theodore Elliott, Ry; [ed.] BA (Sociology), UCLA, 1963; [occ.] Computer Analyst Programer, Washington State; [oth. writ.] Sonnets on the Preamble to the Constitution, 1977, and poems on Mt. St. Helen, 1981; [a.] Olympia, WA

GOI, JAMES J.
[pen.] James J. Goi; [b.] December 22, 1939, North Arlington, NJ; [p.] Mr. and Mrs. Joseph P. Goi; [m.] Gail Goi, May 9, 1987; [ed.] High school graduate and several college credits; [occ.] County Correction Officer; [memb.] Fraternal Order of Police; [oth. writ.] Other writings include short stories and poems (all unpublished) that were written as a personal enjoyment.; [pers.] For many years, writing has been my passion. I will continue to write because words are forever.; [a.] Belleville, NJ

GOLECKI, KATY
[b.] December 2, 1978, Hammond, IN; [p.] Cindy and Leonard Golecki; [ed.] Bishop Noll Institute; [occ.] Cashier; [hon.] Junior National Honor Society, National Honor Society; [pers.] I live by three sayings I have been told: Listen to yourself, you might learn something new; the more you know, the more you realize you don't know; and (one my mom told me) go for happiness and love, not money and loneliness.; [a.] Calumet, IL

GOMEZ, DORA ELVA
[b.] May 30, 1963, Uvalde, TX; [p.] Herminia Guedea Gomez and Hector Luis Gomez; [ed.] Batesville Middle School, Batesville, TX, Uvalde High School - Uvalde, TX, Southwest Texas Jr. College Uvalde, TX, Southwest Texas State University - San Marcos, TX; [occ.] English Teacher of the 6th and 7th grade at Crystal City I.S.D. in Crystal City, TX.; [memb.] American Federation of Teachers; [hon.] Valedictorian of Batesville Middle School '76. English Honor Society '79-'80, National Honor Society '80. Nance Garner Memorial Scholarship '81-'82. Lulac Scholarship at Southwest Texas State University. Won a Teacher of the Year Contest (local). I am in the Who's Who Among American Teachers; [oth. writ.] I am bearly starting but I am in the process of writing as we speak.; [pers.] I want to reflect truths in my writing with which everyone can relate and associate. Poetry, just like a song, is a universal language that will never die.; [a.] Batesville, TX

GONDER, KATHRYN
[b.] December 27, 1952, Phillipsburg, KS; [p.] Averill and Eleanor Gonder; [ed.] Bachelor Music of Education (Cum Laude), 20 hrs of graduate school (4.0); [hon.] Voted most talented on campus two years in a row, first place in talent contest - piano composition first place in talent contest for guitar solo - both original compositions; [pers.] All my writings have stemmed from musical compositions for which I also wrote the lyrics, writing the music first - words second.; [a.] Mankato, KS

GONZALES, EMILIO
[pen.] E. Abriel Gonzales; [b.] January 28, 1975, Tucson, AZ; [p.] Helen R. Powell; [ed.] Berea High School, Severe Behavioral Handicap Program; [occ.] U.S. Marine, Camp Pendleton, CA; [hon.] The love and support of Molly S. Mendyka; [oth.

writ.] None yet published, but looking for direction.; [pers.] Longing is experienced by all. Believe in, and thank your higher power, and one day your needs will be fulfilled.; [a.] Berea, OH

GONZALES, SHEILA DAWN
[b.] December 7, 1965, Fremont; [p.] Beverly Wade; [ch.] Raymond, Kathleen, Joshua; [ed.] Irvington High School; [occ.] Mother

GOOD, LINDSAY
[pen.] Lindsay Good; [b.] January 2, 1983, Philadelphia; [p.] Janice and Allen Good; [ed.] Presently in 18th Grade; [occ.] Student; [hon.] Art and Literature; [oth. writ.] Poetry short stories; [a.] Chesterfield, MO

GOODE, LORETTA
[ed.] Master of Arts - Legal and Ethical Studies; [memb.] MD. Paralegal Assoc. Notary Public; [hon.] Dean's List - Who's Who; [oth. writ.] Several other poems unpublished; [pers.] This poem is dedicated to my son, with love Mom.; [a.] Baltimore, MD

GOODING, DONALD P.
[b.] July 22, 1919, Bellingham, WA; [p.] Jewell and Paul Gooding; [m.] Barbara B. Gooding, October 23, 1955; [ch.] Paula, Tracey, Alison, Lynn, Kelly; [ed.] Graduate Western Wash. College of Education, Bellingham, Wash.; [occ.] Retired; [memb.] Wash. State Environmental Council, U.S. Navy Correspondent, WWII Pacific Theatre, assigned to Desron '54; [hon.] Seattle Press Photographer Journalism Award of Excellence for Magazine Editing, American Society of Travel Agents Award for Magazine Editing - 1976 newspaper writer for - Bellingham Herald - Seattle Post Intelligence; [pers.] My life has rotated around an ability to use the English language in a variety of ways and journalistic assignments. This interest and ability was largely drawn from my father who was an early enviornmentalist, news writer based on his wide range of exploration. My own travel and writing continue the family tradition.; [a.] Olympia, WA

GORMAN, DOROTHY J.
[b.] June 23, 1916, Lakewood, OH; [m.] Carried away 42 yrs ago; [ch.] I am a great Grandmother of 3; [ed.] Graduated Lakewood High School June 1933, 2 yrs of Psychology and the old Cleveland College; [occ.] I call myself a Domestic Engineer; [oth. writ.] More poem, short story about my dog; [a.] Cleveland, OH

GOSLIN, AUDREY
[b.] June 30, 1926, California; [p.] Olive Bloye and Fredrick Goslin; [ch.] Bonnie McLachlan and Heather McLachlan; [ed.] Grade 8; [occ.] Retired; [memb.] AA 32 years; [hon.] Walter Thorton Model GGJ Jeweller, (Grandchildren) Lee-Ann Bryan - Laurie Preston Isac McGuire, (great grandchildren) Jimmy, Bryan, Keven, Kenny, Cody; [oth. writ.] Many poems of nature and birds (not published); [pers.] Even without an extensive education and at a late age (70) you can achieve a dream. I feel deeply about nature and it's beauty, and would love to publish my poems for schools throughout the states.; [a.] Cleveland, OH

GRADICK, NATALIA G.
[pen.] Glynne; [b.] April 27, 1977, Dallas, TX; [p.] Danny and Susie Gradick; [ed.] Eisenhower High School; [memb.] Thespian Society, Future Homemakers of America; [hon.] Outstanding Drama Student for the years of '95 and '96; [oth. writ.] Unpublished works: Distant Lies, Time, Our Love, You and I, Paper Heart and many more.; [pers.] I believe you create your own happiness. You have to be positive about any given situation for anything good to become of it. I was raised to believe you have to make the best of a bad situation.; [a.] Houston, TX

GRAHAM, LEAH C.
[b.] August 19, 1976, Stanford, CA; [p.] Robert and Doreen Graham; [ed.] High School, some military, freshman in college; [occ.] 911 operator; [hon.] Mosaic Award for Poetry - "Don't Blink" senior year in high school; [pers.] I would like to thank my parents for all the influence and inspiration they've given me. And to my Uncle Wayne - God Bless you: I love you as much in death as I did when you were alive.; [a.] Powder Springs, GA

GRAMS, KATHERINE
[b.] September 2, 1980, Trenton, MI; [p.] Violet R. and Gary W. Grams; [ed.] Currently a junior at Dundee High School, Dundee, MI; [occ.] Student; [memb.] French Club, Spanish Club, SADD, National Young Leader's Conference Alumnus, Yearbook Staff, Member of Who's Who Among American High School Students; [hon.] 4.00 Cumulative grade point average, two time academic letter achiever, Co-editor of yearbook; [oth. writ.] "All Apologies", "The Way of Fate"; [pers.] "The deepest cuts are healed by fate, time heals all wounds. Just when you think you can't go on one moment longer, someone always finds a way to restore your hope. Never lose the faith."; [a.] Dundee, MI

GRANADO, MONICA DARLENE
[b.] July 26, 1967, Orange County; [p.] Elena Granado; [ch.] Samson and Steven; [oth. writ.] Poems; [pers.] Never give up hope. And always believe no matter how hard it may seem you can always change or improve your life if you want it bad enough; [a.] Riverside, CA

GRANGER, JAMES RICHARD
[b.] February 21, 1970, Findlay, OH; [m.] Beverly Merkle, August 14, 1993; [ch.] Nathan Alexander Granger

GRANT, TIFFANY SHAWN
[pen.] Tiff G.; [b.] November 21, 1970, Knoxville, TN; [p.] Mrs. Judith Grant and Mr. Osceola Grant Sr.; [ed.] Tennessee State University Majoring in AIT (Aeronautical and Industrial Tech.) Senior; [occ.] Crystal Springs Bottled Water Com.; [memb.] Vice Pres. NAIT (National Association of Industrial Technology) and I am also a Member of AHP (Alpha Eta Rho); [pers.] In my poem I expressed the pain and emptiness I felt with the death of my oldest sister Renee.; [a.] Nashville, TN

GRASS, LINDA C.
[pen.] Linda Christena; [b.] January 11, 1951, Kansas City, MO; [p.] Christena (Koval) Crowder and Otha F. Stephens; [ch.] Stephanie Lynn (Elfrink) Keeling, Heidi Lorraine Elfrink; [ed.] Dublin High School - Dublin, Ohio, Glendale Community College, AAS Business, University of Phoenix - current student; [occ.] Procurement Administrator, Palo Verde Nuclear Generating Station; [memb.] National Association of Purchasing Management AZ (NAPM), Chapel of the Sunflower, Family History Society of AZ, AZ Genealogical Computer Interest Group (A.G.C.I.G.); [oth. writ.] 'Retirement Ode To Stu' to be published in Treasured Poems of America in the summer of 1997.; [pers.] I enjoy writing poems for friends during special occasions and all of them are from the heart. I especially like humor. This poem was written in June 1975.; [a.] Phoenix, AZ

GRAY, BARBARA
[b.] May 25, 1952, Richmond, WV; [p.] Ivajean Riley and Fred Gray; [ed.] GED 1973; [occ.] Work for a printing company for past 5 yrs; [oth. writ.] Other poems hopefully will be published in the future.; [pers.] I would like to dedicate this poem to Monzella Madison for her confidence in me.

GRAY, TONI JEANNETTE
[pen.] Toni Gray; [b.] October 25, 1976, Jasper, AL; [p.] Robert and Evonne Gray; [ed.] Curry High School in Walker County, Alabama, WCCT Vocational School, Walker County, Alabama; [hon.] WCCT Class President. 2 years Graphic Arts course at Walker County Center of Tech. (WCCT); [pers.] To me, poetry isn't words which someone writes. It's not rhyme. It is worth much more than the paper on which it is set. It is priceless, it is the happiness, sadness, horror, laughter; the feeling of emotion you feel as you read it. It has to real, emotional and from the heart and soul.; [a.] Jasper, AL

GREEN, CRYSTAL
[pen.] Chris, Kiko, Crete; [b.] December 23, 1983, Hondo; [p.] William and Lorraine Green; [ed.] Meyer Elementary, McDowell Jr. High; [memb.] Spanish Club, Herman Sons Dance, Project Challenge (gifted and talented); [hon.] Three yrs. of Presidential Physical Patch Award, A&B Honor Rolls, 1st Runner-up Miss Pageant; [a.] Hondo, TX

GREEN, JIVONNE N. PRIOLEAU
[b.] April 20, 1973, Charleston, SC; [p.] William Prioleau, Melvenia Prioleau; [m.] Clyde V. Green II, December 29, 1994; [ed.] James Island High, Weist - Barron - Ryan of New York Acting School; [occ.] U.S. Coast Guard; [oth. writ.] Unpublished book "Back in Time," unpublished lyrics titled "Alone."; [pers.] My mom once told me that I was the one who's going to carry out all of her dreams. I was a young child then and I didn't know exactly what she meant until now.; [a.] Villas, NJ

GREGORY, SCOTT
[b.] January 16, 1975, Paducah, KY; [p.] James and Marlene Gregory; [ed.] Livingston Central High, Paducah Community College, University of Toledo, Murray State University; [occ.] Carpenter/Painter at Bob Morris Builders, West, KY; [oth. writ.] Although this is my first publication, many of my past teachers have told me I should have tried publishing other works of my own.; [pers.] I am most often inspired by the "angel" you read about in my poem. I may have lost my best friend, but I can always put my memories of her on paper.; [a.] Calvert City, KY

GRIBBLE, DORIS LEE
[pen.] Doris Lee Gribble; [b.] April 27, 1934, Valley Bend, WV; [p.] John McElwee, Greta McElwee; [m.] James Gribble (Deceased), November 7, 1952; [ch.] Deborah Lynn, David Lee, Jeffrey Wayne; [ed.] Tygart Valley High School; [occ.] Administrative Secretary recently retired; [memb.] The Church of Christ; [hon.] "My three granddaughters and one grandson" under the age of eight!; [oth. writ.] 1st publication; [pers.] I wish to always recognize the reality of God as he shows me that He, family and friends are a priority for happiness. Thanks to each of my children and friends who encourage me to write to share with others.; [a.] Chesapeake, VA

GRIESMEYER, ROGER J.
[b.] November 15, 1976, Syosset, NY; [p.] Roger J. and Patricia E. Griesmeyer; [ed.] Massapequa High School, Dartmouth College; [occ.] Student; [memb.] U.S. Tae Kwon Do Union, Chi Gamma Epsilon, Massapequa Reformed Church, Granite of New Hampshire Investments (Founding Member, Chief Financial Officer); [hon.] 1993-94 2 on 2 Mock Trial Champion in NY State, National Merit Scholarship Finalist, Meenam Oil Top Scholarship Winner, A.P. Scholar, Black Belt, Tae Kwon Do,

NY All-State Soloist (Vocals); [oth. writ.] Articles printed in "The Beacon" (Dartmouth campus weely newspaper); [a.] Massapequa, NY

GRIFFITH, MILDRED PAULINE
[pen.] June Griffith; [b.] November 24, 1958, Clarksville, AR; [p.] Richard and Pauline Lease; [m.] Robert Griffith, January 14, 1995; [ch.] Russell, Shane and Mize; [ed.] DeValls Bluff High, The Institute of Children's Literature; [occ.] Package Operator, Sara Lee Hosiery, Clarksville, AR; [memb.] Trinity Chapel Pentecostal Church of God, Trinity Chapel Choir; [oth. writ.] A few poems and songs, "Lord Should I Give My Heart" written for our wedding.; [pers.] I long to reflect Godly truth and possibilities. I draw inspiration from Christian music, the Bible and all the beauty of God's creations.; [a.] Lamar, AR

GRIGNON, ROSE M.
[b.] December 24, 1910, New York City; [p.] Thomas and Theresa Ostuni; [m.] Gilbert P. Grignon, June 1, 1930; [ch.] Gilbert, Richard, John, Robert, Michael; [ed.] Graduate of Northport H.S.; [occ.] Was a Homemaker; [memb.] 60 yr. Membership of the Catholic Daughters; [hon.] Two time Grand Region Catholic Daughters, Miss Crab Meadow Beach, Northport, NY, 1928; [pers.] She used to always say "May God Bless you and watch over you always."; [a.] Northport, NY

GRIMES, ANNE ELISABETH
[b.] September 28, 1948, Oakland, CA; [p.] John and Winifred Gerth; [m.] L. Michael Grimes, August 15, 1969; [ch.] Damon Matthew, Shaleen Joy, Amy Christine; [ed.] Hillsdale High School (San Mateo, CA) College of San Mateo (Associate in Arts); [occ.] Homemaker/Writer; [memb.] Road Squires Car Club, Epsilon Delta Sorority, Women's Lobby, Focus on the Family, Republican National Committee, Christian Coalition.; [hon.] "Best Speaker" conference on incest and rape.; [oth. writ.] Several poems published locally and on National radio shows, book in progress, church newsletter, pre-school newsletter editor; [pers.] I write to encourage others in their struggles and to look to God for their strength. I am, also a child advocate and much of my work is aimed at encouraging survivors of abuse.; [a.] Roseville, CA

GRONER, DANIEL JOSHUA
[b.] March 11, 1979, Poughkeepsie, NY; [p.] Himdy Groner and Lou Groner; [ed.] High School Senior; [occ.] Weekend Warrior; [memb.] USHA, USIHA; [hon.] John Jay Ice Hockey MVP; [oth. writ.] Too personal to release, yet I'm young, plenty of time to write more.; [pers.] I never had a model to write from. It all comes from my experiences and from my heart.; [a.] East Fishkill, NY

GROSS, JOAN
[pen.] Joan Gross; [b.] February 16, 1946, Peoria, IL; [p.] Hollis Lance and Lillian Lance; [m.] Divorced; [ch.] Gregory, Michael, Dale, Valerie, Jennifer; [ed.] G.E.D. - Kankakee Community College; [occ.] Peer Counselor for AFL-CIO; [memb.] A.S.Q.C. - Quality Member Clifton Baptist Church; [hon.] Honorable Mention - The National Library of Poetry Poem - "I Want"; [oth. writ.] Several poems published in church news. Article in Kankakee Daily Journal.; [pers.] Most of my poems come from personal reflections or muses of my children.; [a.] Clifton, IL

GROVE, DEBORAH K.
[b.] August 1, 1952, Alexandria, LA; [ch.] Kindrah Marie, Shea Ryan; [ed.] (1973) BS, Penn State University, (1982) MA, University of Iowa; [occ.] Elementary School Teacher; [memb.] National Education Association, Pi Lambda Theta; [oth. writ.] Unpublished children's stories; [pers.] This poem is special to me, because the love that inspired it so precious to me.; [a.] Marion, IA

GUARDADO, MARTHA
[b.] August 16, 1945, El Salvador; [p.] Andres Leonor and Leonor Merino; [m.] Luis Guardado, October 24, 1996; [ch.] Katherine; [ed.] 11 yrs.; [occ.] Office Clerk; [oth. writ.] Poems; [pers.] My inspiration, the endless treasures of Mother Nature.; [a.] San Francisco, CA

GULAJSKI, DAVID A.
[pers.] Many pains have I felt in life, so far all have been relieved by Christ.; [a.] Akron, OH

GURLLY JR., ARTHUR
[b.] April 4, 1950, St. Louis, MO; [p.] Mr. Arthur Gurlly, Ms. Hasby Brown; [ed.] Abraham Lincoln High School, San Diego, CA, City College of San Francisco, San Francisco, CA; [occ.] Purchasing Agent, MSCPAC, Naval Supply Ctr., Oakland, CA; [hon.] On my job as a purchasing agent I have received several achievement awards and promotions. I also have received awards for lyric writing in songwriting competitions.; [oth. writ.] For the past 20 years, I have been having my skills as a lyricist and poet. I've never had anything published but I have received awards as I stated before in competition.; [pers.] This world in which we live provides us with a lot of food for thought. It's from this life that I draw on to reflect my most deep and honest feelings. With that in mind, I hope my work will inspire a need in all of us to make a better world.; [a.] Oakland, CA

GUTIERREZ, MONICA
[b.] August 24, 1959, Santa Monica, CA; [p.] Jean Taylor and Felix Castro; [m.] Michael David Gutierrez, May 5, 1985; [ch.] Michael Paul Gutierrez; [ed.] Venice High School and Santa Monica College; [occ.] Mother, Housewife; [oth. writ.] I have many other writings.; [pers.] All honor should be directed to Jehovah God. Much love to Bono Vox, a light and inspiration in a dark world.; [a.] Burbank, CA

GUZA, JOSEPH
[b.] April 14, 1980, Riverhead, NY; [p.] Vernon Guza, Concetta Guza; [ed.] William Floyd High School; [occ.] High School Student; [oth. writ.] A growing collection (50+) of poetry, none of which, except for "Sweet Salvation," have been published.; [pers.] The poem, `Sweet Salvation,' was written for, inspired by, and is about Jessica Casamassa, my one and only love. `For you my love is infinite!'; [a.] Mastic, NY

HACKL, NORBERT FRANK
[pen.] The Wanderer; [b.] May 5, 1953, Stevens Point, WI; [p.] Frank and Alvinia Hackl; [ed.] U.W. Steven Point, Avis Mid State Tech. College, North Central Technical College, Wausau, WI.; [occ.] Union Carpenter, and Electromechanical Student Astrologer; [oth. writ.] The Wonderer, Seeker of Old; [pers.] I have been greatly influenced by the tales of myths, legends, and the concepts of Astrology. I have seen loves come and go. But my love of Louise (Lowie) inspired such a love in life I must go. Forever Wanderer.; [a.] Curter, WI

HAGAN, SHAWN ANN
[b.] January 16, 1963, Coshocton, OH; [p.] Bill Stewart, Shirley Stewart; [m.] Richard A. Hagan, May 21, 1994; [ch.] Kelly A. Hagan; [ed.] River View High, Prairie High, Ohio State University, Surry Community College; [occ.] Mother, wife. I am an Army Master Trainer for Army Family Team Building; [memb.] American Red Cross, Phi Beta Kappa Business Fraternity; [hon.] Government Employees of the Year Award; [oth. writ.] A poem published in "The National Anthology of High School Poetry," poems published in school papers and church publications.; [pers.] The more I read, the better I write, and the better I write, the more deeply I understand.; [a.] Hillsville, VA

HAIRGROVE, KELLEY M.
[b.] May 29, 1971, Beaumont, TX; [p.] Roy A. Simmons and Francis Daniher; [ed.] None other than required; [occ.] Massage Therapist; [oth. writ.] The Glory; [pers.] I believe to relate to one another we must see the connection that we hold as human beings, and to evolve through the awareness for which we all search.; [a.] Houston, TX

HAJJAR, JOHN K.
[b.] July 1, 1943, Lawrence, MA; [p.] Mr. and Mrs. Kareem W. Hajjar; [pers.] The "One" who is looking out of my eyes. Is the "One" who is looking out of your eyes. It's the "One In Everything," "One Spirit" many forms - many names.; [a.] Andover, MA

HALISON, SYLVIA L.
[pen.] Ms. S. B.; [b.] September 6, 1958, Portsmouth, VA; [p.] Bessie B. and Frank Halison Jr.; [ch.] Six nieces, six nephews, two great niece; [ed.] I.C. Norcom High Ports VA, Norfolk State University Norfolk VA, Dean's List 1977-1978; [occ.] Stenter Assistant Operator, ICI Americans Inc. Hopewell, VA; [memb.] Richmond Christian Center Richmond, VA (Church Home); [oth. writ.] Several poems in personal possession; [pers.] To live to be a blessing and being strong in the Lord and in the power of His might.; [a.] Richmond, VA

HAMILTON, APRYL CAMERON
[pen.] Bo Cameron; [b.] April 26, 1952, Canada; [p.] Glen and Geniel Cameron; [m.] Rob Hamilton, June 15, 1974; [ch.] Barbara, Jeff-Ray, Ryan, Scot; [ed.] Ricks College, Maynard A. Travis Vocational College; [occ.] Property Management Accntg., Architectural Designer - Draftsman; [hon.] Numerous Music Awards for Vocal Performances; [oth. writ.] Several poems published in newspapers and college papers; [pers.] Writing has always been my "Therapy." It has helped me through the rough spots and many joyous as well.; [a.] West Jordan, UT

HAMILTON, PATRICIA
[pen.] Patricia Hamilton; [b.] January 21, 1973, Motherwell, Scotland; [p.] Frederick and Ann Hamilton; [ed.] St. Aldans RC High Waverly Drive, Wishaw (Home Town); [occ.] Nanny; [hon.] Robert Burns Certificate for poetry reciting; [oth. writ.] None, this is my 1st attempt.; [pers.] Live and let live as life is too short.; [a.] Saint Louis, MO

HANDIS, ALEX ELY
[pen.] Alex Handis; [b.] September 19, 1926, Manhattan, NY; [p.] Isidore Handis, Rose Handis; [m.] Namie Handis, September 15, 1957; [ed.] P.S. 11, P.S. 64 J.H.S. Seward Park H.S., New York University, School of Education, B.S. 1951, M.A. 1954, A-12 Astrp, Spring 1944 Cornell University, Basic Engineering. Teacher Math and English and Accounting NYC High Schools 1955 - 1956; [occ.] Retired from cash control and International Auditing Dept. Position, in Amalgamated Ins. Fund Amalgamated Life Ins. Co., Inc., AC and T. with Union, USA.; [memb.] Jewish War Veterans, U.S.A, AARP Flatbush Chapter #2172, JASA Luna Park Senior Center, Quentin Rd., E. 10 St. Council Center Brooklyn, NY. For Senior Citizens, National Museum of American Jewish military History, Shore Front Inter -Agency Council on Aging, Inc.; [hon.] BNAI Brith Award, Volunteer Service Award School volunteer service New York City, Jewish war veterans Award Post #50 Community Service Award, 60th PCT. Police Community

Council Award, Fort Hamilton Va Hospital Volunteers Service Award, Jasa Senior Center Luna Park Volunteer Service Award, literary group leader, coney Island Community Council Service Award; [oth. writ.] Have written articles and poems published in p.s. 64 in Junior High School, newspaper, in "Seward World", seward park high school - newspapers, in school of education, NYU, newspaper, "The Ed Sun", in Luna Park co-op newspaper, "Luna Spark", and amalgamated life insurance co., inc., newspaper, "Amalgamated Life," and local newspapers.; [pers.] I have always believed in the concept of, "the little people," meaning ordinary citizens, all working together in peace and harmony, in 2 democratic society, to better themselves, 2nd create 2 better world for themselves and all people greatly influenced by Carl Sandberg, Walt Whitman and Eugene O'Neill; [a.] New York City, NY

HAO, LANCE KANOA
[b.] September 29, 1963, Tipton, IN; [p.] Lawrence Kaholo Hao and Ramona Newton Hao; [ed.] Kamehameha High School, Indiana University - Kokomo, IN, Indiana U./Purdue U. at Fort Wayne, IN; [occ.] Self-employed; [oth. writ.] 1st submission; [pers.] Thanks to family.; [a.] Kailua, HI

HARDEN, ROVENNA
[pen.] Rovenna Harden; [b.] May 30, 1943, Gainesville, FL; [p.] Roosevelt Harden, Gertrude Harden; [ed.] Rochester Business Institute, Rochester, NY, Evergreen Valley College, San Jose, CA, San Jose State University, San Jose, CA; [occ.] Library Assist. Emory University, Atlanta, GA; [hon.] "Distinguished Service Award" for Exec. Board Member of the Evelyn T. Robinson Scholarship Committee; [pers.] My works mostly reflect the human interaction with each other. I try to express the importance of being sensitive and compassionate to those around us. Mark Twain and Maya Angelou are two of my favorite authors.; [a.] Atlanta, GA

HARLEY, KAYYEN C.
[b.] August 11, 1972, Saint Thomas, VI; [p.] Denfield Harley and Jadine Batchelor; [ch.] Quiannah C. Williams; [ed.] Ivanna Eudora Kean High, Central TX College, Director of Kay's Day Care Center; [occ.] Full time Mom and Avon Representative; [memb.] Veteran of U.S. Army, NAACP; [oth. writ.] Over 80 poems unpublished. I only write for fun.; [pers.] I did not expect to come this far with my poem, but it has made be believe in myself even more now. I have always loved poetry, but I only started 2 years ago. Thanks for the insights.; [a.] Killeen, TX

HARNDEN, RAYMOND
[pen.] Raymond Harnden; [b.] January 15, 1922, El Paso, TX; [p.] Richard M. and Mattie; [m.] Sylvia, May 6, 1945; [ch.] Four girls, two boys; [ed.] High School, El Paso High School, El Paso, Texas; [occ.] Carpenter for 45 years.; [hon.] Lay Minister; [oth. writ.] Have several others, none published to now; [pers.] Married 51 years May 6, 1997, all living, 6 children, 9 grandchildren, and 4 great grandchildren. Children are precious and should be treated as such.; [a.] Whittier, CA

HARPER, GRACIA A.
[pen.] Gracia A. Harper; [b.] November 14, 1918, Elgin, IL; [p.] Daniel Green and Mabel Webber Green; [m.] Col. James H. Harper (Deceased), January 8, 1942; [ch.] Judith Ann and Melissa Kay; [ed.] B.S. Degree U of Wis. Stoot, Menomonie, WI; [occ.] Retired Teacher; [memb.] San Diego Crones, "Women of Ancient Wisdom"; [oth. writ.] Prize winning article published in the reader, San Diego, CA. Poems published in College paper and community newspapers.; [pers.] I try to write about events happening to me or loved ones.; [a.] San Diego, CA

HARRELL, FELICIA A.
[b.] June 24, 1966, Wadena, MN; [p.] Joe Sr. Harrell and Anna E. Harrell; [ch.] Jyshon J. Harrell (10), Levi W. Harrell (6); [ed.] Montville High, Mohegan College Computer Processing Institute, Asst. Choir Director; [memb.] St. John's Christian Church Asst. Choir Director, Sunday School Teacher Member of Usher Board, Clean up Committee; [oth. writ.] I write poems often to express, present or past situation and feelings.; [pers.] For the vision is yet for an appointed time, but at the end it shall speak, and not lie: Though it Tarry, wait for it, because it will surely come, it will not Tarry.; [a.] Norwich, CT

HARRIGER, EVELYN
[b.] March 3, 1953, Marysville, CA; [p.] George Harriger Sr. and Shirley Harriger; [ed.] Marysville High, Yuba Community College; [occ.] Clerk-Typist, PG and E (Pacific Gas and Electric Co.) Auburn, CA; [memb.] Much Vocal and Choral Expression: Church, School, Rating Festivals, Musicals, Community Groups, Weddings, etc.; [hon.] Member CMEA (CA Music Educator's Association) 1973 All-State College Honor Choir, Gregg Smith, Director, Member 1974 Honor Choir for Music Association of CA Community Colleges, Paul Salamunovich, Director; [oth. writ.] None professionally. People seem to enjoy my writing style in personal communications.; [pers.] I consider music and similar artistic endeavors necessities (not luxuries), for personal enjoyment/renewal and the elevation of humankind. Family tops everything in life's celebrations and priorities.; [a.] Marysville, CA

HARRIS, JOAN
[b.] February 8, 1947, Richmond, IN; [p.] Howard and Geraldine Bennett; [m.] Ronald Harris, September 10, 1965; [ch.] Dawn Davis, Ronnie Harris; [pers.] I would like to dedicate "Your New Home" to Mary and Burgess Chasteen, my loving mother and father-in-law. May God richly bless the two of you.; [a.] Richmond, IN

HART, JEANNE
[b.] June 12, 1954, Borger, TX; [p.] Richard Watts (Deceased), Louada Watts; [m.] Cecil Hart, May 18, 1996; [ed.] Altus (Okla.) High School, Altus Junior College (Assoc. Degree), Wayland Baptist Univ. (Bachelor's Degree), Univ. of North Texas (M.S. Degree); [occ.] Civil Service, Instructor, Sheppard AFB, Texas; [memb.] Colonial Baptist Church, Wayland Baptist University Alumni Association, Univ. of North Texas Alumni Association; [hon.] Sheppard AFB Volunteer of the Year (1991), 3750 Air Base Group Civilian of the Year (1988), Outstanding Administrator of the Year (1985 and 1987), 20 years Federal Service Certificate (1994); [oth. writ.] (None published) The poems describing the courtship of my husband and myself, our wedding, and our honeymoon, also, a few other poems.; [pers.] I read about the poetry contest just a few hours after sharing a poem about a mission trip, stating that I wanted my poems to minister to people. I knew God wanted me to write this poem.; [a.] Wichita Falls, TX

HARVIE, BRIAN W.
[b.] May 9, 1964, Wauwatosa, WI; [p.] Caryl and David Harvie; [ed.] James Madison High School - Milw., WI., Rose-Hulman Institute of Technology - Terre Haute, IN - BS in Mechanical Engineering; [occ.] Manager of Engineering Systems for Madison Cable Corp.; [memb.] American Society of Mechanical Engineers; [pers.] "The rainbow is more beautiful than the pot at the end of it, because the rainbow is now. And the pot never turns out to be quite what I expected." Hugh Prather.; [a.] Greensboro, NC

HAYES, EILEEN ANN
[b.] April 12, 1956, Huntington, NY; [m.] Patrick B. Hayes, January 22, 1982; [ch.] Two daughters; [ed.] Texas A and M University, Texas Chiropractic College; [occ.] Mother, Quiltmaker and Writer; [memb.] American Quilter's Society, Friends of Garden City Ballet, Hellgate Writers; [hon.] Who's Who Among Students in American Colleges and Universities (1992), Montana State University Advisory Council, Special Recognition Award for Efforts to Eliminate Hunger in Montana (1994); [pers.] It is a personal choice to extract the positive lessons from difficult times in life. Parents are entrusted with an innocent soul in the life of their child - may we strive to be worthy of this gift.; [a.] Missoula, MT

HAYES, KAREN T.
[b.] September 30, 1970, Charlotte, NC; [p.] Phillip and Shirley Hayes; [ed.] Currently attending Tennessee Technology Center; [occ.] Student; [memb.] Member of the House of Prayer in Pleasant Hill. Also a Member of the World Outreach for Christ Evangelistic Ministry as a drummer/back-up vocalist; [oth. writ.] Several poems published in religious magazines; [pers.] I enjoy observing and writing about the mysteries nature reveals about God, relationships, and life.; [a.] Pleasant Hill, TN

HAYNES, NATALIE
[pen.] Natalie Haynes; [b.] October 20, 1981, Russellville, AR; [p.] Linda and Larry Newell; [pers.] This poem is dedicated to Jed. For all the times you've suffered and all the times you've hurt, I've also felt your pain.

HAYWARD-RILEY, GLORIA
[pen.] Lady G.; [b.] June 6, 1955, Jacksonville; [ch.] Four - 2 Boys, 2 Girls; [ed.] Stanton High, Florida Community College, Career Concorde; [occ.] Writer, Manager and Producer; [memb.] NAACP, Cathedral of Faith Adult Choir; [hon.] Outstanding Nursing Assistant, Appreciation of Contribution to Cancer Ass.; [oth. writ.] My life story; [pers.] Success comes in all ages, colors and sizes, don't give up your dream.; [a.] Jacksonville, FL

HEARD, EMILY D.
[b.] March 13, 1967, Chattanooga; [p.] Howard and Emily Heard; [ed.] Kirkman Technical High School, Middle Tennessee State University; [occ.] Participant Service Rep, BT Services, Tennessee; [oth. writ.] Many poems have been written but none published.; [pers.] My writing is very important to me and I try to write with meaning. If my writing can touch someone's heart, then my work has been done. My talent comes from God, and for this I am truly blessed.; [a.] Antioch, TN

HEARD, SARA GAIL
[b.] February 24, 1951, Atlanta, GA; [p.] Sara Hyde Heard and Junior Heard; [ch.] Stanley Wayne Heard; [ed.] Milton High School; [occ.] Day Care Provider; [oth. writ.] Several but none published before now.; [pers.] They say you have to suffer to perfect your art, so I must be on my way. All my work expresses my feelings at the time of writing.; [a.] Alpharetta, GA

HECKMAN, SHEILA A.
[b.] August 24, 1968, Florida; [p.] James and Fern Heckman (In-laws); [m.] David Heckman Sr., April 3, 1988; [ch.] David Scott, Sarah Mae; [ed.] Dauphin County Technical School; [occ.] Homemaker; [memb.] PTA, Hummerlstown United Chruch of Christ; [oth. writ.] "Someone to Cherish," "My Mother-in-law/My Friend," "Grandmother," "Fern" written for family members unpublished.; [pers.] Writing is something I have always enjoyed. My greatest accomplishment is to

know that I've touched the lives of the people who have read something I've written.; [a.] Harrisburg, PA

HEINZE, GEORGE-ALICEA
[pen.] D. H. Boyd; [b.] Santa Monica, CA; [ed.] Studied art at Otis Art Ins., Art Center L.A., Lipson School of Design, Priv. piano lessons, sculpture, attended writing groups, also studied dramics with Josphene Dillion; [occ.] Retired as Creative Artist Designer; [hon.] Awards for Photography, Tech. Art, writing, 40 years as artist for Northrop Adv. Sys., 7 years Commissioner Northrop Art Club, played in small theater, some WWII shows, TV comm's, several awards (job related); [oth. writ.] I love writing mysteries, children's fairy tales, poems and stories, especially poetry. Paint in water colors, oils, pastels, portraits, and landscapes.; [pers.] My work is dedicated to father, mother, brother and his wife and to dearest friends, Roy and Mezzie Holes. I believe all the arts are intertwined. Each sparks a light in our lives bringing beauty, engeries at the beginning, and ending of each day. With love and faith, believing is how we can and must survive with all God's creatures, ourselves, one and all. Love is food and strength and in my work I try to create both fantasy and reality as I see it and pray others will enjoy what I've done.; [a.] Thousand Oaks, CA

HELMINIAK, NICOLE
[pen.] Nicole Helminiak; [b.] August 14, Baltimore, MD; [p.] Cheryl and Michael Helminiak; [ed.] I have been through elementary and middle school, and I'm in my first year of high school (Overlea); [occ.] Nothing; [memb.] Chesaro United Methodist Church Health Club at Overlea; [hon.] Won a poetry (PTA) contest in 8th grade June '96; [oth. writ.] Nothing published; [pers.] I write what I think or feel. I try to do all the good I can for all the people I can for as long as I can. I am what I am today because of my parents.; [a.] Rosedale, MD

HEMKEN, BEBBY GENE
[b.] October 24, 1981, Wichita, KS; [p.] Edwin C. Hemken Jr., Diana L. Hemken; [ed.] Currently Derby High School Student; [occ.] Student; [memb.] Pleasentview Baptist Church; [oth. writ.] For own enjoyment poems, etc.; [a.] Derby, KS

HENDRICKSON, KENNETH
[b.] November 12, 1912, North Roby, TX; [p.] Walker and Azzie Hendrickson; [m.] Rosemary Wallick (Deceased), August 27, 1946; [ch.] One son, two daughters; [ed.] High School; [occ.] Retired; [memb.] Primitive Baptist Church Boy Scouts of America; [occ.] None, except several other poems and started brief history of my life.; [a.] Fresno, CA

HESLEP, STEVE
[b.] July 4, 1948, Mansfield, OH; [p.] Dorothy (Fisher) Heslep, Chester Heslep; [ch.] Angela Christine, Dawn Marie; [ed.] Assoc. Deg. Electronic Eng.; [occ.] Telephone Operator; [oth. writ.] Many poems; [pers.] Most of my poetry has been written for family, friends, and my own pleasure. I would love to write for a living.; [a.] Mansfield, OH

HESS, JANA
[pen.] MeMe; [b.] January 10, 1983, Greenville, IL; [p.] Larry Hess, Jan Dodson; [ed.] Breese/Beckemeyer Elem. Dist. #12, IL; [occ.] 8th grade student, Beckemeyer, IL; [pers.] I enjoy writing and using the talents God has given me.; [a.] Pocahontas, IL

HEUANGSAVATH, PHONESAVANH
[pen.] Phonzy Heuang; [b.] July 29, 1981; [p.] Sipheauk and Somvang; [ed.] Attending Central High (Student); [hon.] Rhode Island Hospital: Volunteer and Representatives; [pers.] I like to dedicate this poem to a very special person, who's always beside my side: Rethana Huy.

HIGBE, SAUNDRA TONEY
[b.] June 30, 1941, Columbia, SC; [p.] Horace W. and Ruby Turnipseed Toney; [m.] Lloyd W. Higbe, September 2, 1960; [ch.] Scott, Stacee, Toney; [ed.] Dreher High, Columbia, SC, University of SC, Columbia, SC; [occ.] Co-owner Living Vine Bookstore; [memb.] (1) Lexington County Children Shelter (Board of Directors), (2) Bailey Manor Retirement Center (Ex-Officio Board Member), (3) Scholarship Committee - Palmetto Presbytery Women in the Church - Presbyterian Church in America, (4) Christian Bookseller's Association; [hon.] 5 State Regional Winner - 1996 Christian Bookstore of the Year (named by Christian Retailing) '95 and '96 Top 100 Bookstores in US (Independent); [oth. writ.] Bookstore Journal Magazine - various articles, Christian Retailing various articles, Women's Aglow fellowship magazine, community newspaper (St. Andrews News), various articles on neighborhood news; [pers.] I write from personal expression of life experiences and reflection of the Christian faith.; [a.] Columbia, SC

HILL, LORI
[b.] June 6, 1962, Bloomsburg; [p.] James Millard, Wanda Millard; [ch.] Tanya Hill; [ed.] GED 1991, currently attending Bloomsburg University; [pers.] I've been writing since I was thirteen and have compiled about 75 poems and short stories. Life is like a rollercoaster ride, you've got your ups and downs, twists and turns, and a heck of a jolt at the end.; [a.] Bloomsburg, PA

HILLMAN, DR. CAROLE D.
[b.] November 24, Chicago, IL; [p.] Thomas James and Dorothy M. Hillman; [ed.] B.Ed, M.Ed, Ed.D and Post Doctoral Work; [occ.] Asst. Prof of Education Elmhurst College, Elmhurst IL; [memb.] Kappa Delta Pi, Phi Delta Kappa, ASCD; [hon.] Tri-lakes Literacy Award, Media Awards, Honorary Awards, Outstanding Learning Center in the Nation; [oth. writ.] Bold Beginnings in Early Childhood, the Learning Center, Finger Plays for Children, Collegial Networking (Column) plus more; [pers.] I agree that life long learning involves a quest for self-expression and the ability to deal with change.; [a.] Downers Grove, IL

HINSHAW, GEORGE
[b.] March 18, 1921, Wakeeney, KS; [p.] Ren and Grace Hinshaw; [m.] Maxine Clopine, July 28, 1946; [ch.] Ren, Melody, Candy; [ed.] Trego Community HS, Wakeeney, KS, BA Hastings (Neb.) College, MA University of Southern Calif., Ph.D. University of Nebraska; [occ.] Retired, Emeritus Faculty, Northwest Mo. State University, Maryville; [memb.] Speech Communication Association, Kiwanis Club, American Legion; [oth. writ.] Poetry and short stories published in local newspaper, Ph.D. Dissertation: A Rhetorical Analysis of The Speeches of Frederick Douglass during and after the Civil War; [pers.] I try to find the humor in situations to highlight insights.; [a.] Maryville, MO

HOBBS, BARBARA DELL
[b.] October 27, 1943, Hubbard, TX; [p.] Mr. and Mrs. Ellie Hobbs (Mother Deceased); [ch.] Dexter L. Hall (US Coast Guard); [ed.] Dunbar High, A.A. Degree, LA Metropolitan College, BA Degree, California State University, Dominguez Hills; [occ.] Administrative Secretary, Los Angeles City College; [memb.] West Angeles Church of God in Christ (Member), West Angeles Literacy Team (Member); [hon.] Editor's Choice Award for poem "A Gift They Can't Take," Across the Universe, 1996 anthology. Received an expression of thanks from President Bill Clinton for the "Atlanta 1996 Olympic's poem".; [oth. writ.] Poems, "A Gift They Can't Take," "Givers and Takers," published by the National Library of Poetry. Former staff writer for university newspaper, current editor in chief for an employee's publication.; [pers.] I am usually inspired to write poetry that will send a spiritual message to society in general, especially to young people.; [a.] Gardena, CA

HOBBS, CHERIE L.
[b.] May 11, 1967, Marshall, MI; [p.] Okey Sturgell, Linda Holloway; [m.] Scott B. Hobbs, August 20, 1994; [ch.] Cody and Alicia Hamrick, Ryan and Kyle Hobbs; [hon.] Civilian Commendation: Albion, Michigan, Department of Public Safety, for facilitating the escape of residents from a burning structure.; [a.] Homer, MI

HOCH, JEAN
[b.] March 16, 1933, Wampsville, NY; [p.] William and Hazel (Fellows Deceased); [m.] Melvin Hoch, May 30, 1953; [ch.] Three children, one living, Bonnie Jenkins and Diane Roache, Ronald (Deceased); [ed.] North Broad Street One'da High; [occ.] Babysitter; [memb.] Bowling team at Beach Bowl at Sylvan Beach; [oth. writ.] I wrote many poems for people for birthdays and anniversaries and births; [pers.] I wrote for years because it gives me pleasure to make people happy.; [a.] Canastota, NY

HODGE, RICHARD LYNN
[pen.] Ricky; [b.] October 20, 1958, Nashville, TN; [p.] Leonard and Mary Hodge; [m.] Patsy Juanita Hodge, February 14, 1991; [ch.] Ricky, James, Chriss, Anthoney and Anita Hodge; [ed.] Goodlitsville High School. Always studied History and been inspired by it; [occ.] Singer and Song Writer; [memb.] Member of Co-Operative Housing of Smyrna, TN; [oth. writ.] A book I am currently writing, called from the "Hearts of Many Countries" and gospel songs and many other poems as well such as (A poet).; [pers.] My personal experience of writing has given me understanding in the beauty of all forms of life, no matter how small or insignificant they may seem.; [a.] Nasville, TN

HODGES, GINA
[b.] March 27, 1967, Arvada, CO; [p.] Mike Hodges, Susan Canestre; [ed.] North Salinas High, Hartnell College; [occ.] Eligibility Supervisor, Monterey County DSS, Salinas, CA; [pers.] I enjoy capturing life experiences with poetry; for me it is a reflection of my emotions.; [a.] Salinas, CA

HOEK, CORTNEY
[b.] August 2, 1983, Modesto, CA; [p.] Brian and Genell Hoek; [ed.] Dent Elementary, El Portal Middle School; [occ.] Student; [memb.] Club Live; [hon.] Presidential Physical Fitness Award (2 Consecutive years) and State Champion Physical Fitness Award; [oth. writ.] Many poems written, but not published or read by public.; [pers.] I get my inspiration for my writing from surroundings and knowledge from my teachers.; [a.] Escalon, CA

HOFFMAN, JOE
[b.] January 17, 1980, Youngstown, OH; [p.] Mary Jo and Cyril Deley; [ed.] High School Sophomore (currently); [occ.] Student; [pers.] Love is like a road, if you take the wrong mate, it could lead you in the wrong direction, just like a wrong turn. Some say you have to wait for true love, and in time you'll find the right one.; [a.] Youngstown, OH

HOLLEY, COLETTE HAWKINS
[b.] March 29, 1969, Del Rio, TX; [p.] Tim Hawkins Sr. and Bette Hawkins; [m.] Ernest Holley, October 3, 1995; [ch.] Taylor Blair and Trevor

Leigh; [ed.] Tiry High School Kerrville, TX. Care Nurse Aid Course; [occ.] Care Nurse Aid; [oth. writ.] Several poems written but still in my closet. One short novel written. Just got up the nerve to send it to a publishing house.; [pers.] For a long time I was a single mother. Now I'm in an international marriage. I write a lot about both of those situations because I lived through it or am living through it and loving every minute of it.; [a.] Amarillo, TX

HOLT, WYTONA DORETHA
[b.] October 27, 1972, Detroit, MI; [p.] Frances E. Holt, Homer C. Holt; [ch.] Jordan Cymone Posey; [ed.] Bishop Borgess High School, Eastern Michigan University, Henry Ford Community College; [occ.] Leasing Consultant, Management Systems, Detroit, MI; [pers.] My writings reflect my emotions, desires and experiences. My greatest influences have always been my family and close personal friends.; [a.] Detroit, MI

HOPPE, SHANNON D.
[b.] December 2, 1981, Milwaukee, WI; [p.] Patrick and Lind Hoppe, Rosey Hoppe and Mike Vickers (Step-parents); [ed.] I am a freshman, attending Mukwanago High School. I also attended Hackhand North and Horade Mann Middle School; [occ.] I'm in High School, hope to be a cosmetologist; [memb.] St. Rita's Catholic Church volunteering as a clown in local Holiday Parades with my mom; [hon.] I've won 2 first place ribbon's in our forensic contest. Competing in cheer leading this winter.; [oth. writ.] This is my first published writing and ever! I've never even had anything published in a school paper. I've always thought of my poetry as a secret inspiration.; [pers.] I have 3 great brothers, Mike, Joe, and Nick. I've also have 2 wonderful sisters, Stacey, and Dolly. I'm a J.V. Cheerleader. I've been writing since I was 11 years old. Thank you Jamie for encouraging.; [a.] Big Bend, WI

HORNER, PATRICIA GALE
[pen.] Gale; [b.] September 10, 1950, Atlanta, GA; [p.] Mary Langston, Howard Sherriff; [m.] Sammy K. Horner, March 11, 1971; [ch.] Three sons, two daughters; [ed.] 10th grade; [occ.] Housewife and Mother; [oth. writ.] I have some other poems that I would like to have published someday.; [pers.] This poems came to me one day as I was going down the road. I had lost my oldest son in a very tragic car accident. I didn't know how or where I would get the strength to carry on. I feel that the Lord gave me this poem. This gift.; [a.] Fairburn, GA

HORTON, KENNETH J.
[b.] December 4, 1954, Denver, CO; [p.] Ellen Horton and Everett Horton; [ch.] Marlin Everett and Dustin Robert; [ed.] Santa Fe High, Santa Fe, New Mexico, New Mexico State University, University of New Mexico, NorthWestern and LaSalle University; [occ.] Police Captain, Los Alamos County Police Department; [memb.] International Assoc. Of Chiefs of Police, Los Alamos Little League Board of Direct., New Mexico Bass Federation, B.A.S.S., Boy Scouts of America; [pers.] For the young, instill honesty and respect for others, if you fail to instill any other values.; [a.] Los Alamos, NM

HOSIER, CHARLES
[b.] January 10, 1970, New Jersey; [ed.] Never ending; [occ.] Pharmacy Technician; [oth. writ.] Collection of poems called, Drowning in a Fountain of Youth. Unpublished.; [pers.] Read Bukowski.; [a.] Marlton, NJ

HOUSER, LARENNA
[b.] July 30, 1963, Sacramento, CA; [p.] Carolyn and Charles Headley; [m.] Lonnie Houser Jr., July 16, 1982; [ch.] Lonnie III, Carolyn, Melissa, Richard; [ed.] Graduated from Daylor School in 1982; [occ.] Mother and housewife; [oth. writ.] I have a number of poems not yet published.; [pers.] If you or a loved one has problems with drugs, please get help. Life is worth it. We have to set an example for the children of our future, and theirs. There are people out there who care.; [a.] Citrus Heights, CA

HOWARD, CHRISTINE ANN
[b.] May 31, 1974; [ed.] Ponaganset High School, Rhode Island College; [occ.] Student Teacher, I am going to be an Elementary/Special Education Teacher; [hon.] Dean's List; [oth. writ.] I have written several poems that are unpublished.; [pers.] It is only those people with open minds who really see the world.; [a.] North Scituate, RI

HOWISON, TRACY LYN
[b.] February 2, 1973, Charlotte, NC; [p.] Jack and Linda Howison; [ed.] North Mecklenburg High, Mitchell Community College, Montreat College; [occ.] Customer Service/Student; [a.] Cornelius, NC

HOWZE, KATHLEEN R.
[b.] February 2, 1967, Jacksonville, FL; [p.] Patricia Chitwood; [ed.] Orange Park High, Florida Community College of Jacksonville; [occ.] Accountant II, Barnett Banks, Inc.; [memb.] Barnett People for Better Government; [hon.] Dean's List, President's List; [oth. writ.] Several editorials published in local newspapers.; [pers.] Anyone can succeed in life, all one must do is try.; [a.] Jacksonville, FL

HUANG, SHERRY
[b.] March 7, 1982, Taiwan; [p.] Eddy and Jessica Huang; [ed.] Barnum Woods Elementary School, Woodland Middle School, East Meadow High School; [memb.] Key Club (East Meadow High); [hon.] 3rd Prize in the Chase Manhattan Bank's Create a Season's Greetings Card Contest, 'Highest Academic Achievement' plaque in French, National Junior Honor Society, Finalist in the PTA Reflections Competition "Imagine That," Nyssma: Certificate of Achievement in Visual Arts, etc.; [oth. writ.] "The Missing Clock" - short story mystery (for PTA Reflections Competition), "If The World was once 3 Colors" - children's book, and various other short stories/articles for school projects.; [pers.] First of all, I would like to thank God for all my major accomplishments, along with all of my past teachers, but especially Mrs. Lynn Levy - who was my first great friend and tutor when I first came to America.; [a.] East Meadow, NY

HUBBARD, EDNA
[b.] July 18, 1919, Jefferson, WI; [p.] John and Eva Kranz; [m.] Benjamin Hubbard, November 23, 1940; [ch.] Three daughters; [ed.] High School, Vocational School; [occ.] Retired from family owned business; [a.] Jefferson, WI

HUDGINS, MICHAEL P.
[pen.] Steven Michael; [b.] November 30, 1954, Wyandotte, MI; [p.] Homer and Virginia Hudgins; [m.] Debra, November 23, 1994; [ch.] Hallie, David, Chris; [ed.] Huron High School, J.A.C. Technical School (4 years) Detroit; [occ.] Construction Superintendent, Peter R. Brown Construction, Inc., Clearwater, Florida; [oth. writ.] A Warrior's Legacy, Touch The Sun, Who's In The Mirror, Lost Courage, A Son's Farewell; [pers.] Seek strength, not to be superior to your brother, but to fight your greatest enemy, yourself.; [a.] Saint Petersburg, FL

HUDSON, LINDA
[pen.] Linda Hudson; [b.] September 8, 1956, Independence, MI; [p.] William K. Brownfield, Peggy J. Stockton; [m.] Linn E. Hudson, September 6, 1988; [ed.] September 1992, graduate of: Long Ridge Writer's Group, May 1978 graduate of: State Fair Community College; [occ.] Partnership of: White Wolverine Trading Post; [hon.] Dean's List; [oth. writ.] My poem, Loving Memories is my first published writing.; [pers.] I wrote Loving Memories to honor the memory of my aunt, who passed away January 1996 of cancer, and in my heart, I will always love her as my sister.; [a.] Sedalia, MO

HUGGINS, PENNY J.
[b.] August 28, 1952, Harlingen, TX; [p.] Donald and Lorana Huggins; [ch.] Shaw, Chucky, Wayne and Jerry; [ed.] Foothill High School, attended Sac City College; [occ.] Courier; [oth writ I Miss You Little Beggar, "Cherish The Son", "The Girl In The Class", "At Last I've Found Her"; [pers.] "The thief in the night rapes and pillages secret thoughts from my mind. I awoke, feeling refreshed with all the pretty and sometimes not so pretty words in a row"

HUGHES, JONATHAN EDSEL
[b.] February 15, Orange, NJ; [p.] Edsel and Sherry Hughes; [ed.] Santa Rosa Junior College; [occ.] Student; [memb.] I formerly raced with the Peugeot Racing Team (bicycle); [oth. writ.] I am compiling a book of 'one liners', as I enjoy doing a 'play on words.' My goal is to be a stand-up comedian. I am a vocalist, and my objective is to even out-perform Danny Kaye! (I am a realistic artist.); [pers.] I am heavily into physical fitness and nutrition, hence my favorite old proverb states: "There is no such thing as disease - only various forms of malnutrition." To me, bigotry is 'a big dead tree,' wherein there is no lire, you see!; [a.] Monte Rio, CA

HUMMER, NANCY J.
[b.] February 9, 1931, Cleveland, OH; [p.] Helen and Harvey Ryan; [m.] Ronald G. Hummer, January 5, 1950; [ch.] Cheryl, Mark, Dave, John, 13 grandchildren; [ed.] Graduate of Cleveland Heights High School; [occ.] Housewife; [memb.] Divine Word Church, International Organization of Couples for Christ; [hon.] Scholarship from Euclid General Hosp. for LPN School. Chosen to write composition for "Touch of Class" for Lakeland Community College English Comp. Class, Bedford Books, St. Martin's Press; [oth. writ.] Five poems published in National Library of Poetry Books: finished top 3%, and one poem in top 2%.; [pers.] I wish to convey a deep, uplifting message to mankind. I thank the good Lord for showing me in these later years, that I could write.; [a.] Willoughby Hills, OH

HUNTER, JASON
[b.] January 12, 1973, Edmond, OK; [p.] Cynthia and Stewart Hunter; [ed.] I am a senior at the University of South Florida at Sarasota. I am a Creative Writing major.; [occ.] Student; [oth. writ.] I have written an unpublished volume of poetry called "A So Journer's Tale" containing 50 poems.; [pers.] I am a quiet and shy person. Poetry for the most part is the only outlet I have for expressing my feelings. My favorite poet is Donald Justice, and I strive to emulate him.; [a.] Rotonda West, FL

HURT, JASON
[b.] April 21, 1977, Lexington, KY; [p.] Alvin Hurt, Stephanie Marie Gooden; [ed.] Graduated Barren County High Class of '95; [occ.] Machinist - Part time Musician; [pers.] If you believe in a lie, does that make you a fool armed with the truth?; [a.] Glasgow, KY

HYDER, EHTIRAMUDDIN
[pen.] Hyder; [b.] April 27, 1907, Sheiklupur Badaun UP, India; [p.] K. B. Moliuddin and Mayat Fatima; [m.] Alima Hyder, April 28, 1944; [ch.] Four; [ed.] Graduate of Aligarh University (India);

[occ.] Retired Life; [hon.] Reward of Maritious Service during regim (copy enclosed); [oth. writ.] Mostly in Urdu poetry; [pers.] Special Magistrate and Chairman Education. D.I.S.T. Board Budaun U.P. India.; [a.] Houston, TX

IANNICIELLO, JULIA MARIE
[b.] September 24, 1971; [p.] Sue and Joe Ianniciello Jr.; [ed.] Cleveland High, South Community College, Majors - Sociology, Law, Writing, Artist and Real Estate; [hon.] "Create Writing" in school. "CDA" in child care and Track athlete.; [oth. writ.] A lot of miscellaneous poems.; [pers.] I write of my inner thoughts and feelings that revolve around me which inspire my creativity. I give recognition to my mom for always encouraging my talents. Dedicated to: Michael (MB).; [a.] Seattle, WA

IDO, ALLISON
[pen.] Dorian Gray, Deceit; [b.] March 4, 1982, Watertown, NY; [p.] Christine and Douglas Ido; [ed.] I am currently in the 9th grade; [hon.] National Junior Honor Society, Class President, Student Council Representative; [pers.] In my poems, I try to reflect reality and truth, no matter how harsh or cruel it may be.; [a.] Franklin, NY

ISAACS, HERBERT A.
[b.] March 7, 1939, Detroit, MI; [p.] Herbert D. Isaacs and Ruth Isaacs; [m.] Carole L. Isaacs, June 6, 1959; [ch.] Cynthia and Lisa; [ed.] Algonac High, St. Clair Co. Comm. College, American Institute Hypnotherapy, Ph.D - BS, Jerome School of Photography, Other-related training Certificates; [occ.] Professional Hypnotherapist (HYPNOTIC ONE), Teacher and Trainer of Holistic Health - (INNER QUEST DYNAMICS); [memb.] American Hypnosis Institute, American Council of Hypnotist Examiners, National Society of Hypnotherapists, Michigan Society of Hypnotherapists, Michigan Metaphysical Society, Seekers Metaphysical Group, Edgar Cayce Soc., Past Vice President - Pearl Beach Lions Club; [hon.] Various speaking documents from clubs, organizations and charity events; [oth. writ.] "Holistic Health News Letters", Articles - in local newspapers; [pers.] My poems generate from the Heart and Soul. They form deep within the Subconscious flow.; [a.] Algonac, MI

ISLER, SHERRI FLOWERS
[pen.] Eve; [b.] June 28, 1968, Santa Rosa, CA; [p.] Paul John and Mickey Louisa Flowers; [m.] Jack Morgan Isler (Fiancee); [ch.] Breanna Lynn; [ed.] H.S. Diploma - partical (3/4) College for Legal Asst. had to drop/due to finances head of the family responsibilities.; [occ.] Mother-PH Printers Aid, all aspects of printing bus.; [memb.] PTA - my daughter Breanna Lynn, who is in the 1st grade 6 1/2 (December 28, 1989); [hon.] Actually I'm very much at a loss for words, this is the greatest honor one of in my life, since my "MVP" in soccer when I was 13 (played for) (9 yrs. all together). This honor to be (published) rates right up there by my greatest honors ever which are, the honor of being one of Gods chosen few (you know) who are blessed, by being "Able" to experience all the wonderful things that God has created "My Ideal Way of sing it all is with all that is me, through "Love"! and in the same breath of "Love", my "Dearest", "Best Friend", "Whom Fills Every Depth of Me", "My Adam", (for he named me Eve).; [oth. writ.] Special Friendship - Far Away Thoughts - Never Fragile - lots more but never shown to anyone like this before.; [pers.] Love and live for today happily, for life is too short to have been miserable and not have tried for the greatest gift ever "Love"!; [a.] Fresno, CA

JACKSIC, MICHAEL J.
[b.] October 26, 1965, Cleveland, OH; [p.] Mike and Doris Jacksic; [occ.] Charge Nurse; [pers.] I dedicate this poem to all I have loved that have hurt me. For if it wasn't for the pain I would have never picked up my pen to create.

JACKSON, AARON HUMDY
[b.] April 14, 1947, San Diego, CA; [p.] Florence Jackson and Clyde Humdy; [m.] Bengeline Jackson; [ed.] San Diego High School; [occ.] Electrician, Dallas Water Utilities; [oth. writ.] Publications - none. I find myself writing to myself when I felt the need.; [pers.] My writings are reflections of feelings.; [a.] Dallas, TX

JACKSON, BARBARA BENICE MILES
[pen.] B. Miles Jackson; [b.] June 24, 1948, Forth Worth, TX; [p.] C. B. Miles and Maybelle Dugan Miles; [m.] Divorced; [ch.] Tracy D. Jackson; [ed.] I.M. Terrell Class of '66; [occ.] Head Start Day Care of Ancient County of Ft. Worth; [memb.] Carter Metropolitan, CME Church; [hon.] State Employee of the year 1990, Usher of the Year for Usher's of Cater Metropolitan Church; [oth. writ.] Poetry - Atmospheric Condition Renewal, Go You Way, Ancient Of Days, Silent Voice, A Sign, Void Of Times, Be Sure, Answer, Keep Times, Changing Times, The Void Of Times, Be Sure, Answer; [a.] Arlington, TX

JACKSON, CHARMEIKA D.
[b.] December 3, 1977, Savannah, GA; [p.] Wesley and Georgette Jackson; [ed.] Attending Georgia Southern University Major: Journalism, A.E. Beach High School; [pers.] I have been greatly influenced by authors (poets) such as: Maya Angelou and Nikki Giovanni.; [a.] Savannah, GA

JACOVINO, MICHELLE L.
[b.] July 28, 1988, Waterbury, CT; [p.] James and Lynn Jacovino; [ed.] 3rd grade student - St. Lucy School; [occ.] Student; [memb.] Brownie Waterbury Girls Club; [hon.] 1st prize winner in the Silas Bronson Library Poetry Contest for 2nd Grades City-wide 1996, all schools; [pers.] Avid reader, loves dancing, Gymnastics, T-Ball.; [a.] Waterbury, CT

JAMERSON, DIANN MICHELE NEWCOME
[pen.] Michele Newcome; [b.] March 4, 1970, Galion, OH; [p.] Paul and Dee Ora Newcome; [m.] Steven W. Jamerson, September 8, 1990; [ch.] Leigha Louise and Emily Marie; [ed.] Associate Degree in Accounting from North Central Tech. College; [occ.] Book keeper; [oth. writ.] "Letting Go" in On the Threshold of a Dream. "A Teardrop" in of Diamonds and Rust.; [pers.] My dad once told me, "Look for the good things in life for the bad find us without much trouble."; [a.] Plymouth, OH

JAMES, ALANDA
[pen.] Landa James; [b.] December 30, 1978, Northside; [p.] Magalene and Frank James; [ed.] Senior in High School "The Rayer School"; [occ.] I work at McDonald's.; [hon.] Student of the Week Youngstown Area Goodwill Industries Award, Cultural Arts Youngstown PTA Council, Music Intermediate (1990 1st place); [oth. writ.] A Broken Heart, Remember, When I Met You; [pers.] Based upon various situations, some things are better expressed on paper. If you don't hurry and write it down, it's gone in a vapor.; [a.] Youngstown, OH

JAMISON, BARRY
[b.] March 9, 1958, Johnstown, PA; [p.] Nick Jamison, Norma Brooken-Jamison; [ch.] Joseph Bruce Jamison; [ed.] United High School Graduate class of 1976; [oth. writ.] This was the first I ever submitted but have notebooks full of other poems and short stories.; [pers.] I hope to use my talent to make people more aware of the importance on conservation and taking better care of our Mother Earth! (Before it's to late!); [a.] Indiana, PA

JANSSEN, AUGUST
[b.] Santpoort, Holland; [p.] Peter W. Janssen, Henriette J. Cremer; [m.] Betty King Janssen, September 1956; [ch.] Herbert August and Henriette Juliana; [ed.] B.A. in Human Relations Principia College, Elsah Ill., M.A. Sociology University of Colorado, M.A. Secondary Education, University of CO; [occ.] Professor of Anthropology Amway Distributor, Pikes Peak Comm. College Primitive Painter, Publisher Author; [memb.] Elected Trustee of the Town of Elizabeth, CO; [hon.] Faculty Member of the Year, 1988-89 Community College of Aurora, Colorado Founder Multi Cultural Exchange Program Between Pikes Peak Community College of Colorado Springs and Preppa Fransisco Villa, Casas Grandes Nuevo, Chihuahua, Mexico; [oth. writ.] Pee Wee The Fly, Apple Pie and I geared to Elementary and Second graders. Mixed Blood, historical novel Not Guilty non fiction, Second World War teenager in Japanese Concentration Camps Escape from Java, Destination Australia Border Crossings and how to write, bind and publish your own books and the mexican election; [pers.] 1) We have our own, individual path, and must travel it., 2) Recognize a power greater than one's own., 3) Realize that you always have a choice, then choose!, 4) Be an optimists expect good things to come you way, 5) Live in the present, 6) Be grateful for the positive things you've got, 7) Be yourself, 8) Share!, 9) Be of service!, 10) Experiment, dare!, and dare to make mistakes! In his travels through Japanese concentration caups, Universities, Marriage, Janssen Janssen round the above pints extremely useful.; [a.] Elizabeth, CO

JARRETT, POET
[b.] January 31, 1983; [p.] Yvonne Jarrett, Carlton Jarrett; [m.] none; [ch.] none; [ed.] Junior High School; [occ.] Student; [hon.] International Art Award, NGPT Piano Award; [oth. writ.] Dreams; [pers.] Never stop dreaming. It heals the soul.; [a.] New York, New York

JEBB, THOMAS G.
[b.] April 30, 1960, Grand Rapids, MI; [p.] Gordon Jebb, Mary Jebb; [ch.] Emily Anne, Gordon Kingsley; [ed.] Rogers High; [occ.] Restaurant Management; [memb.] Westminster Preshyterian Church, (PCA), Trauma Intervention Program; [pers.] The only person that needs to be afraid of the truth is the person who does not embrace the truth.; [a.] Fort Walton Beach, FL

JENNINGS, MEGHAN
[pen.] A. Meghan Jennings; [b.] October 17, 1978, Montrose, PA; [p.] Linda and Keith Jennings; [ed.] Still Attending Blue Ridge High School; [occ.] Student; [pers.] I believe good writing comes from the heart.; [a.] New Milford, PA

JOANNOU, RENEE MICHELLE
[pen.] Renee Joannou; [b.] December 16, 1981, Sydney, Australia; [p.] John andn Diana Joannou; [occ.] Student

JOHNSON, ALFRED LEE
[b.] October 30, 1928, Hamilton, MT; [p.] Bernadetta L. and Irven T. Johnson; [m.] Edith R. Johnson, November 15, 1980; [ch.] Elaine and Vernon, Beverly, Marcia and Lance Johnson; [ed.] Cody, Wy. H.S., Mt, SAC; [occ.] Retired; [memb.] Sacred Heart Catholic Church; [oth. writ.] Have written poetry and song poems for 40 years, but only for friends and family.; [pers.] I try to obey the "Golden Rule."; [a.] Fort Washakie, WY

JOHNSON, CAROLYN L.
[b.] October 15, 1946, Oakland, CA; [p.] Chuck and Dolly Dyer; [m.] Mark E. Johnson, December 3, 1966; [ch.] Mark, Brett, Brian, (Granddaughter) Natalee, Brook; [ed.] San Diego State University,

Ophthalmic Medical Assistant - American Academy of Ophthalmology; [occ.] Ophthalmic Assistant to Retinal Specialist; [memb.] Joint Commission of Allied Health Professionals in Ophthalmology; [hon.] Kaiser Permanente's First Low Vision Coordinator - Founder's Award; [pers.] To communicate an emotion with passion and expression of one's inner feelings is a gift from God, a gift to be shared with the world.; [a.] Poway, CA

JOHNSON, CHARLES E.
[b.] November 14, 1950, Dayton, OH; [p.] Edward and Betty Johnson; [m.] Cheryl E. Johnson; [ch.] Brett L. Johnson; [ed.] Miami Carol City Sr High School, Graduate Class of 1970; [occ.] Night Dispatcher for Courier Company; [hon.] Editor's Choice Award for Outstanding Achievement in Poetry 1996; [oth. writ.] Someone to Share Help Us to Pray Lord, The History of Rock and Roll, The Enchanted Stallion, The Sweetest Music, The Quarterback, When the Wind Blows; [pers.] Sometimes when I might write a poem based on just one line. I would make the story up in my head as I go along. I have to feel it first in order to write it. An example of this is a parent's prayer, I wrote this poem for my son, Brett.; [a.] Boca Raton, FL

JOHNSON, DEANA
[pen.] De Anna Johnson; [b.] April 19, 1966, Louisville, KY; [p.] John and Kathy Hutson; [m.] Dennis Johnson, December 29, 1995; [ch.] John IV and Denise; [ed.] (2) yrs Commercial Art. Sociology, Deans List; [occ.] Air Handler, Homemaker; [oth. writ.] Several writings that have not yet been disclosed; [pers.] Laugh for yesterday, love for today, live for tomorrow.; [a.] Louisville, KY

JOHNSON, KATHY PAULEY
[b.] July 18, 1957, Lynchburg, VA; [m.] Ronald L. Johnson, June 6, 1975; [ch.] Ronnie, Tania, Dion; [ed.] High School Grad., Rustburg High School, 1974; [occ.] Housewife; [a.] Lynchburg, VA

JOHNSON, KAY E.
[b.] August 13, 1935, Chewelah, WA; [p.] Wm. Johnson (Deceased), Martha Johnson; [ed.] MSW, University of Washington; [occ.] Retired Flight Attendant and Social Worker; [pers.] I try to make the "Get Level" feelings and conflicts to which people can universally relate. I have been largely influenced by my experiences as a social worker.; [a.] Spokane, WA

JOHNSON, LINDA
[b.] August 11, 1953, Green Bay, WI; [ed.] West Senior High School, Northeast Wisconsin Technical Institute; [pers.] Writing is a way for me to escape - lyrics to music are really poems - the Lennon/McCartney team was the best.

JOHNSON, SIGNE M. RAMSEH
[b.] March 19, 1912, Merrill, WI; [p.] Rev. Ivar Ramseth and Bertha Mason Ramseth.; [m.] S. Lyle Johnson (Deceased), May 24, 1941; [ch.] Ingrid Christine, Juliana Ruth; [ed.] Waseca Minnesota High School, St. Olaf College, U. of Minnesota; [occ.] Music Instructor at N.I.A.C.C. (North Iowa Community College. Retired.); [memb.] ACDA, NATS, ISEA, AARP; [hon.] High School Valedictorian.; [oth. writ.] Published by world of poetry.; [pers.] Life is too short to be wasted on ugly, in consequential and worthless things, I love the beautiful and the best in music and all the arts.; [a.] Mason City, IA

JOHNSON IV, KEROS
[b.] January 17, 1970, Cheyenne, WY; [p.] Sheldon and Mary Jean Johnson; [ed.] Overland High School, University of Arizona '93; [occ.] Ground Skeeper, Castle Pines Golf Club, Castle Rock, CO; [pers.] I believe that music and laughter set the soul free. That's why I love a good groove and love to make others smile with my pen. I hope to one day write for Saturday Night Live.; [a.] Parker, CO

JOHNSTON, NELLIE
[b.] August 4, 1952, Bartlesville, OK; [p.] George R. and Flora Ann Moland; [m.] Tommy L. Johnston, January 30, 1972; [ch.] Tommy, Jr. and Margie Ann; [ed.] Bartlesville College, High, Rogers State College, Current Student at Northeastern State University.; [occ.] Pursuing BA Degree in Spec. Ed, L.D.; [memb.] Seventh-day Adventist Church, Student Oklahoma Education Association, Salvation Army Home League; [pers.] All of my poetry is inspired by God.; [a.] Bartlesville, OK

JONES, BOB
[b.] January 11, 1975; [p.] Susan Goodrich, Steve Goodrich; [ed.] Flushing High School; [occ.] Parts Driver for Prestige Chevy, Buick; [pers.] Every now and then, go out on a limb, and take a chance. We oftentimes can find inspiration in the must unlikely of places.; [a.] Flushing, MI

JONES, CHRISTINE M.
[pen.] Chris Jones; [b.] December 25, 1929, Navasota, TX; [p.] Solomon Miller Jr. and Cornelia A. Miller; [m.] Robert E. Jones Sr., June 1, 1958; [ch.] One Son; [ed.] Bachelor's and Post Graduate Study; [occ.] Retired/School Teacher, Retired/Md. State Legislator; [memb.] Delta Sigma Theta Sorority, Phi Delta Kappa Sorority, Prince George's Mental Health Assoc., John Hanson's Women's Club, Oxon Hill Democratic Club, MSTA and NEA, Bethlehem Baptist Church Lay Leader; [hon.] Maryland State Teacher's, Prince George's County Educator's Assoc., Women of Achievement, National/Hook Up of Black Women, Delta Sigma Theta Service Award, Alumni of the Year from Huston Tillotson College; [oth. writ.] Two children's books in progress and a book of poetry.; [pers.] I strive to give pleasure to the enjoyment of humankind by awakening the soul to the magic of words.; [a.] Temple Hills, MD

JONES, ISOLYN
[pen.] Isolyn Wallace - Jones; [b.] February 2, 1964, Jamaica, WI; [p.] Gerslam and Alma Wallace; [m.] Charles E. Jones Jr., June 15, 1991; [ed.] St. Catherine High School, Jamaica WI, Norwalk Community College, Norwalk CT; [occ.] Disable/Housewife; [memb.] New Bethel Church of God in Christ; [oth. writ.] Unpublished novel and poetry, a little slice of heaven to be published by Carlton Press.; [pers.] My spiritual writings are inspired by a life and death situation, which involved my life before and after lung transplantation. Through the help of God and my writing, I was able to comfort a disease which tried to control my mind.; [a.] Hampton, VA

JONES, MURLESS
[pers.] I am a Christian who truly loves the Lord who also believe we all have a spirits that live in us that keeps us strong when we are weak.; [a.] Dayton, OH

JONES, PHYLLIS H.
[b.] August 5, 1909, Perham, ME; [p.] Anna and Richard Hallowell; [m.] Vernor T. Jones (Deceased), July 27, 1943; [ch.] Two daughters; [ed.] B.S. Gerham Maine Normal School, Master of Eod., University of Maine; [occ.] Retired after 38 yrs. of teaching, mostly English in Preaque Isle, Sanford, Auburn, Brewer, Mae; [memb.] Mid-Coast Presbyterian Church, Delta Kappa Gamma; [oth. writ.] Some poetry, article in Echoes, a Northern Maine Journal "Picking in the 20's"; [pers.] As you will see, I am just an amateur but I have always enjoyed writing. "After the Storm" was written after the worst winter storm I have ever experienced.; [a.] Topsham, ME

JONES, WILLIAMS HENRY
[pen.] William Henry Jones, Captain J., Bill Jones, W. H. Jones; [b.] April 1, 1924, Black Diamond, WA; [p.] Helenor Jones (Father Deceased); [m.] Barbara A. Jones, May 17, 1960; [ch.] Robert Jeffery Jones, Denise Lynn Williams; [ed.] B.A. San Diego State, Naval School of Hospital Administration; [occ.] Captain, U.S. Navy (Ret); [memb.] Federal Health Care Executives, Fleet Reserve Association, Distinguished Member, International Society of Poets; [hon.] Legion of Merit (Navy), numerous service medals and awards, graduated with honors 5 Military Schools, advanced from Apprentice Seaman to Captain during Naval Career. Editor's Choice Awards (11), The International Poetry Hall of Fame; [oth. writ.] Endless Thought - Treasured Poems of America April 1996, In His Wisdom We Must Trust - Poetic Voices of America June 1996, Symphony of the Night - Treasured Poems of America August 1996, A Humble Apology - Poetic Voices of America October 1996, The Window of His Soul - Treasured Poems of America December 1996, How Sad Memorial Day - Poetic Voices of America February 1997, Shared Dreams - Treasured Poems of America April 1997, Just Deserts - Poetic Voices of America June 1997; [pers.] I believe in personal achievement, inspiring others to fulfill their dreams, at peace with self and others, all with a sense of humor, dedication and perspective.; [a.] Lake San Marcos, CA

JORDAN, SYLVIE
[pen.] Sylvie Jordan; [b.] April 26, 1958, Miami, FL; [m.] Andrew C. Jordan, July 9, 1996; [ed.] Coral Gable High School, Miami Dade Community College; [occ.] Paralegal; [oth. writ.] I am in the process of completing a book of poems, as well as a novel.; [pers.] I have many passions, but none has moved me more than words. In my writing I find truth, then I share it!; [a.] Miami, FL

JOYCE, REGINALD BRETT
[b.] April 25, 1964, Detroit, MI; [p.] Bernard Joyce, Gertrude Joyce; [ed.] Mumford High; [memb.] Member of the YMCA, Member of Indiana P.C. Black Club, Member of the Bagley Community Council; [oth. writ.] Several other poems and currently writing 2 children's stories.; [pers.] I truly believe that poetry writing can't be taught, but that it comes naturally from the soul.

JUSTICE, JENNY
[b.] June 28, 1978, Houston; [p.] Diane Justice; [ed.] High School, graduate from college for Law Enforcement and Criminal Justice; [occ.] Ticket Operator at Tenneco Energy; [pers.] I like to write to express my feelings at that time. It helps me vent out in ways I cannot in spoken words, and then later I can reflect back and realize no matter good or bad, everything will pass.; [a.] Houston, TX

JUSTYNA, JOEL
[pen.] Fred Justyna; [b.] August 14, 1975, Columbus, NE; [p.] Ig Justyna and Mary Justyna; [ed.] Mary Carroll High/Eastwood High; [occ.] Receiving Supervisor, Barnes and Noble Booksellers, C.C., TX; [hon.] National Honor Society (H.S.); [oth. writ.] None published; [pers.] My writing is a reflection of me. However distorted it my seem, the words describe my feelings. A major influence in my life and writing is Metallica; their music shines the light that leads me through darkness.; [a.] Corpus Christi, TX

KADY, MARTHA L.
[pen.] Lynn B. Kadimar; [b.] February 22, 1932, Seattle, WA; [p.] Hazel V. and William Bevens; [m.] Ernest R. Kady, September 12, 1968; [ch.] Mark A. Kady; [ed.] Franklin High, class in writing, U of W Secretary, Chem. Dept. U of W - intro to

computers; [occ.] Retired from University of Washington Chemistry Department, Seattle, WA; [oth. writ.] Amer. Poetry Anth. Vol II, 3/4 Poetic Voices, Su, 1990 Amer. Fairy, Ode to Cimo, Prologue to Margon's Poetry Ant. IX4 Quiet Moments 1990 Quest, Return to my Home Land; [pers.] My writing is very broad based and represents trying to improve their lives; [a.] Lynnwood, WA

KAHLER, JULIE A.
[b.] April 22, 1968, Portland, ME; [p.] Aiden E. LaSalle and Mildred A. LaSalle; [m.] Robert M. Kahler, October 20, 1990; [ch.] One on the way; [ed.] Westbrook High School, University of Southern Maine - BS Elementary Education; [occ.] Secretary, Falmouth, ME.; [hon.] Cum Laude, Dean's List; [oth. writ.] Numerous poems written over years for enjoyment and personal gifts for friends and family - no poems previously submitted for publication; [pers.] I believe poetry reflects a very personal part of a poet as with any other type of art, poetry is created through personal experience and emotion. I can only write about something if I can truly believe in it and truly feel it inside. To me, it is almost a type of diary. It becomes interesting to others when they can transfer their own experience and emotions into it. I have always greatly admired and been influenced by the poetry of Helen Steiner Rice.; [a.] Westbrook, ME

KAISER, HEATHER CHRISTINE
[b.] December 12, 1983, Eglin AFB, FL; [p.] Gerald and Theresa Kaiser; [ed.] 7th grade student at San Felipe Middle School, Del Rio, TX; [occ.] Student; [memb.] Alter Services - Base Chapel Laughlin AFB, TX ARC Babysitters; [hon.] 1st Place PTA Reflections Contest 1992 for Art and Poetry Divisions. 2 year Altar Server Recognition Award. American Red Cross Volunteer to Pool Cardiac Rehab Program; [oth. writ.] Musical compositions for piano; [pers.] I am 12 years old. I enjoy playing piano (playing piano for 5 years) and gymnastics (7 years) (competitive). I also play cello. I enjoy sports, especially basketball, reading, traveling, drawing, and doing crafts.; [a.] Del Rio, TX

KAMLET, LAUREN
[b.] August 9, 1978, Sandy Spring, MD; [p.] Kenneth and Francine Kamlet; [m.] William Rhea; [ed.] Sherwood H.S., Currently attending Frostbursg State University; [occ.] Full-time college student; [memb.] Psychology Club; [hon.] Superintendent's Writing Award; [pers.] I enjoy being creative. I write poetry for fun!

KASPRACK, KIMBERLY A.
[b.] February 11, 1971, Jersey City, NJ; [p.] Claire and William Smith; [m.] Michael Kasprack, June 18, 1994; [ch.] Joseph Christopher; [ed.] Secaucus High School, Douglass College, Rutgers University, BA Psychology; [occ.] Homemaker, CCD Teacher, St. Jude's Parish; [hon.] High School Valedictorian (1989), Best of Show - Photography (Jr. yr.), graduated vollege, with honors 1993; [pers.] I delivered my son by myself. It was a great and wonderful experience that reminded me of life's joy and beauty and God's greatness and love.; [a.] Clementon, NJ

KASUBA, MICHAEL S.
[pen.] Michael S. Kasuba; [b.] November 16, 1974, Rutland, VT; [p.] Edward and Carlene Kasuba; [ed.] Poultney High School; [occ.] Chef; [oth. writ.] Writings published in local newspaper. Several unpublished works of poetry; [pers.] This poem is dedicated to my parents for pushing me to go for it and supporting me along the way. And to Sue for standing by me through all good and bad. I love you with all my heart.; [a.] Poultney, VT

KELLEY, TIFFANY CATHERINE
[pen.] Tiffany Kelley; [b.] November 21, 1980, Harrison, AR; [p.] John and Patricia Kelley; [ed.] Currently enrolled in Jasper High School; [pers.] Writing has always been one of my favorite pastimes. Through my poems, I strive to express great emotion and get people to view something from a totally new perspective.; [a.] Parthenon, AR

KELLY, RACHEL
[b.] May 8, 1981, Cincinnati, OH; [p.] Barbara and Brian Kelly; [ed.] Dickson County High School, Sophomore; [occ.] Student; [memb.] National Art Honors Society, Dickson County Chorus, World Wildlife Federation; [hon.] Several math and science competition teams, Most Outstanding Student in Math Award; [oth. writ.] "Head Or Heart," "Revenge Took Her Well," "We Stronger Than She"; [pers.] My mother has always taught me to be strong because the strongest will survive in life.; [a.] Dickson, TN

KELSO, ANN K.
[pen.] Baba; [b.] June 12, 1944, Prosser, WA; [p.] Mr. and Mrs. James A. Kelso; [m.] Chooses to remain hidden, July 1992; [ch.] Too many to count; [occ.] Private Investigator; [memb.] L.A.D.I. Pres.; [hon.] Watching chicks leave the nest and make it on their own. Survival-of-the-Clans.; [oth. writ.] Everyday living and doing it with a left brain. I write Soap Operas and What Ifs. Are really antiquated as I've written them all in journals. Some are quite funny...; [pers.] They call me Baha, and I teach love, understanding and never give up. If you use the word "Can't" we all show you "you can".; [a.] Zillah, WA

KELSO, COURTNEY LAURA
[b.] October 27, 1985, Orange, CA; [p.] Debra A. Kelso and Brian L. Kelso and Matthew Chang; [ed.] Just entered 5th grade; [occ.] Student; [memb.] The Responsibility Club at school.; [hon.] This is my first writing recognition.; [oth. writ.] Other poems and stories; [pers.] I get my ideas from some of my dreams. I enjoy writing. Thanks to my Meadowpark teachers, who taught me so well. I dedicate this poem to my friends and family.; [a.] Irvine, CA

KELSON, GWEN
[pen.] Gwen Kelson; [b.] July 21, 1962, Atmore, AL; [p.] Norman and Brenda Steele; [m.] Kenneth L. Kelson, April 3, 1993; [ch.] Casey Whitley, Kendra Kelson; [ed.] Tate High School; [occ.] Public Defenders Office State of Florida; [memb.] Olive Baptist Church; [oth. writ.] In the process of putting my poems together for a book.; [pers.] I try to give inspiration trough my poems for others that feel lost. My husband has been my dearest fan and my children my inspiration. They are my life.; [a.] Pensacola, FL

KENION, JANET L.
[b.] February 29, 1928, Asheboro, NC; [p.] Grant Lugher and Lucy Luther; [m.] Clyde C. Kenion Jr., December 18, 1955; [ch.] Beth Andrea, Gina Brent and Clyde Joseph; [ed.] Asheboro High School, Forsythe Memorial Hosp. School of Nursing, Montgomery Jr. College, Takoma Pk. Md., St Joseph's College (EMT program), Maine; [occ.] Registered Professional Nurse (Retired); [memb.] Strait Gate Christian Center, American Nurse's Association, Founder of Area Children's Book Club; [hon.] Honors for "Special Act" in Nursing (1982), Dean's List, Commendation for Excellence in the Nursing Service Profession; [oth. writ.] Many other poems being made ready for possible publication, also narratives.; [pers.] As a writer, I feel compelled to bring to the surface in poetic and narrative form, the virtual pulsating essence of the human spirit. I have great admiration for Maya Angelou's writings and poetry.; [a.] Cary, NC

KENNETT, BERNARD J.
[pen.] Bernard of Bath; [b.] June 22, 1914, Rochester, NY; [p.] Herbert and Mary Kennett; [m.] Genevie Cole, June 24, 1939; [ch.] Jeannine, Nancy, Marte and Pamela; [ed.] High School Grad. I had a private reading course, following high school; [occ.] Presently retired but worked 40 yrs. for Corning, Inc.; [memb.] Many churches. Both Writers Giving and Homells Poet Theater; [hon.] Last X'mas I was the Features reader for the Bath Peace and Justices group, many open readings and I scheduled my own reading; [oth. writ.] I have written about 100 poems, which I'm hoping publish even if I have to do it myself; [pers.] I enjoy people - must communicate. I believe a poet helps others enjoy this beautiful world and point out what is going on.; [a.] Barton, NY

KEPHART, GLENN ALAN
[pen.] Glenn Alexander; [b.] February 11, 1950, Philadelphia, PA; [p.] George Albert and Edna Marie Kephart; [ed.] Neshaminy Senior High, Bucks Co. Technical, Letourneau University Dallas Bible College, El Centro College American Banking Institute; [occ.] First U.S.A. Bank - Collections Dept., and Lighting, special effects Monier Enterprises; [memb.] Prime Timers - Dallas Branch, Affirmation of Dallas; [oth. writ.] Local newspaper and regional publication; [pers.] To write inspirational poetry and prose of mankind dealing with the body, soul and mind and spirit. I have been influenced by Robert Frost, T. S. Eliot, and Walt Whitman; [a.] Dallas, TX

KESSLER, CHRISTINA I.
[pen.] Christina I. Kessler; [b.] January 2, 1976, Sandusky, OH; [p.] Mr. and Mrs. Robert B. Kessler; [ed.] Sandusky High 1995, one semester Mount Vernon, Nazarene College, Music; [occ.] Zed Key Holder Kichen Collection, Sandusky, OH; [memb.] First Church of Nazareth Church, Sandusky; [hon.] Honor Orch., First and 2nd contest in Solo and Ensemble, band awards, orch awards, choir awards, and student aid award; [pers.] I hope my poetry can help others and stop and make people think about what I write from down deep inside.; [a.] Sandusky, OH

KESSLER, JOHN G.
[b.] July 25, 1954, Omaha, NE; [p.] Henry and Jennie; [m.] Kimberly, June 22, 1981; [ch.] Tawnya and Amanda; [ed.] I have only a fifth grade Education, but I believe that anyone can accomplish their goals. If they just work at it.; [occ.] Janitor at Nebraska City High School; [oth. writ.] I wrote some children's stories. And I am still trying to get them published.; [pers.] I write stories and poetry for and about children, because I believe that our children need to be recognized. God bless our children.; [a.] Nebraska City, NE

KETTER, KATHY BUTLER
[pen.] "Trahanna"; [b.] June 10, 1957, Topeka, KS; [p.] Kenneth and Ramona Butler; [m.] Howard Ketter, December 14, 1984; [ch.] Staci D., Brent M.; [ed.] HS Grad. various other Educational Training; [occ.] Director, Emergency Services, Let's Help, Inc. Topeka; [oth. writ.] Two poems published in Local Newspaper, Co-partner Wild Heart Productions, Songwriter in Partnership with David Butler; [pers.] A positive outlook in life will take you anywhere you want to go! Live! Love! And Learn!; [a.] Topeka, KS

KETTLEWELL, LISA
[b.] September 12, 1970, Salt Lake City; [p.] Ray and Rinda Christensen; [m.] Christopher Kettlewell, June 1990; [ch.] Mark, Lisa, Clay, Crystal and Benjamin; [ed.] Graduated from Orem

High School in Orem, Utah; [occ.] Mother; [memb.] LDS Church, President of PTA Hanthorn Elem. Independence, MO; [pers.] I have always written to find peace within myself. My poem is a piece of my soul shared with you.; [a.] Independence, MO

KHAIRA, INVDEEP
[b.] August 22, 1983, Punjab, India; [p.] Gurpreet Khaira and Charantjit Khaira; [ed.] Elementary school, Bowers Middle School - Peterson; [hon.] Always make the Honor Roll at Peterson Middle School. My grades are A'S and B'S. My goal is to be a veterinarian (Animal Doctor) just like my dad.; [pers.] First of all I wouldn't have had this chance if it weren't for my sister 'Jyoti' because she told me about the contest. This poem was written just for fun. And for an assignment in Mr. Cramer's class.; [a.] Sunnyvale, CA

KHLOK, KETHSHARA
[pen.] Kethshara Khlok; [b.] September 15, 1955, Siem-Reap, Cambodia; [p.] Sann Khlok, Chhim Loan Khong; [ed.] High School Competition in Cambodia, presently attending NVCC for Associate's Degree in Liberal Arts. I am a part-time student who studies at my own pace for self-improvement and seeking further knowledge in the field of English writings; [occ.] Clerk-Typist, Smithsonian Institution, OHR, Washington, DC; [memb.] The Smithsonian Associates; [pers.] English is my favorite international language, it serves as an important key to my interest in the field of writing. With further study, I hope to become a real writer in the future.; [a.] Arlington, VA

KILBOURN, FORREST
[b.] March 29, 1919, Flint, MI; [p.] Hazel and Guy Kilbourn; [m.] Helen Kilbourn, November 10, 1979; [ch.] One son, one daughter and three grandsons; [ed.] High School - graduate Flint, MI, 20 years Navy Retired, (Chief War Off.) USN Pay Clerk; [occ.] Retired; [memb.] Bahia Shrine (Garden City Masonic City Lodge 537 Past Master), Osceol Shrine Club - Past Pres. and Secretary; [oth. writ.] Between Two Points.

KILBY, FLORENCE A.
[b.] November 19, 1954, Dover, DE; [p.] Frances and Samuel Lamb; [m.] James Kilby Sr.; [ch.] Randall Scott, James Kilby Jr. and Frances Kilby; [occ.] Owner of Florence's Ultimate Image Hair Design; [memb.] Mt. Zion Ame Church; [oth. writ.] "Poem For Thought and Inspiration"; [pers.] God has given us all special gifts and talents to help each other and to survive in this world. To help others gives me a feeling of inner peace and satisfaction.; [a.] Dover, DE

KIM, JEHAE E.
[b.] May 21, 1982, Elkins Park, PA; [p.] Hoon and Jeong H. Kim; [ed.] Immaculate Heart of Mary School 8th grade; [occ.] Student; [memb.] N.J.H.S. (National Junior Honor Society); [oth. writ.] Poem: Garden of Peace; [pers.] Most of my poems are sad, and reflect what I happen to feel at the moment, I wrote my very first poem when I was 7 years old.; [a.] Decatur, GA

KINCAID, SARAH
[b.] January 11, 1984, Bloomington, IN; [p.] Don and Jane Kincaid; [ed.] Jefferson Middle School and St. Charles West High School; [memb.] I attend the Salvation Army Church in O'Fallon, MO; [hon.] I won first place in a solo competition (singing); [a.] Saint Charles, MO

KING, GLENA M. JESSEE
[b.] March 21, 1948, Scott Co., VA; [p.] Hop and Emily Jessee; [m.] Ronald King, September 5, 1967; [ch.] Greg and Rev. Mark King; [ed.] High school, 3+ years College, working on degree in Bittical Studies; [occ.] Minister, Creative Writer, Artist (drawing and painting), Singer; [memb.] "The King Singers," "Elliston Church of God"; [hon.] Golden Poet Laureate with "Whispering Wind" poem presented 15 and plays; [oth. writ.] Written and presensed over 15 plays. Novel just completed Against All Odds: A true story of Appalachia. Poems: "Only Yesterday, But Forever Gone," "Three Christmas Miracles," "Whispering Wind." Short stories: "The Price of Silence," "Moonlight Murders": based on a true incident; written and presented over 15 plays.; [pers.] I am in the process of obtaining publisher for newly completed novel Against All Odds: A true story of Appalachia. I write faith building stories and plays reflecting the ability to overcome and survive because of deep-rooted faith in God, and respect for people and one's self.; [a.] Elliston, VA

KING, KC
[b.] November 20, 1944, Phoenix, AZ; [p.] Leonora Mary Robertson; [ch.] Troy Corriere, Cristopher Mastin; [oth. writ.] Poems: Thoughts Of A Wooden Snowman, My Dearest Son. Stories: Story in my pocket "Nettie and Me", Timothy the Rainbow Trout, and "At Last I'm Here To Take You Home".; [pers.] I believe we all, as children, are filled to the brim with seeds of courage. But we must remember, these seeds grow best in the rich soil of self-confidence.; [a.] Monterey, CA

KINN, ELIZABETH MARIE
[pen.] Elizabeth Marie Kinn; [b.] June 15, 1969, Angola, NY; [p.] Robert Allen Kinn, Doris Karin Gelencser; [ed.] Buffalo State College, Buffalo, NY, Eckerd College, St. Petersburg, FL, Manatee Community College; [occ.] Retail sales; [memb.] Phi Theta Kappa, NU Zeta; [hon.] Deans List (M.C.C.); [pers.] "Sometimes you are the fly, sometimes you are the windshield." Author unknown; [a.] Sarasota, FL

KIRBY, MARSHA K.
[pen.] Rachel Rose; [b.] August 28, 1950, Anderson, IN; [p.] Kermit Kirby and Alice Kirby; [ed.] Frankton High School, (Valedictorian); [occ.] Publishing Coordinator, PAB Publishing, Real Estate Agent, and Medical Transcriber; [memb.] Board of Realtors; [hon.] Valedictorian; [oth. writ.] Three children's stories and many poems, as well as starting a novel; [pers.] After putting God first and foremost in my life, his word is reflected in much of my writing. Many poems were inspired in the stillness of nights when my thoughts turned to God.; [a.] Frankton, IN

KIRTH, PATRICIA A.
[b.] September 4, 1947, Gracemont, OK; [p.] Orb and Mary Lee; [ch.] Sandra Kirth - (Melanie Bernard); [ed.] Lookeba - Sickles Schools Okla. Porterville High - Calif; [occ.] Alteration Seamstress; [memb.] Joice of Praise Penecostal Church El Reno, OK. Ministry in song to various nursing homes; [oth. writ.] Numerous poems and songs of life and religious subjects; [pers.] My songs and poems depict the love of God, growth in my own life and understanding of the human life, heart and soul.; [a.] El Reno, OK

KIRTLEY, SCOTT M.
[b.] January 25, 1966, Towsen, MA; [p.] Michael Kirtley, Bonnie Kirtley; [ed.] Autodidact; [occ.] Carpenter; [hon.] Life; [pers.] I have found that poetry is a unique tool for channelling the innate common awareness among all of us.; [a.] McDonough, GA

KLEISTER, HEIDI LEIGH
[pen.] Edel Weiss; [b.] October 26, 1985, Goshen, NY; [p.] Richard and Donna Kleister; [ed.] Monticello Middle School - grade 6; [occ.] Student; [memb.] Middle School Talent, Community Church of Wurtsboro Junior Choir, Monticello Middle School String Orchestra, Monticello Middle School Peer Mediator; [hon.] Monticello Middle School Honor Roll, Student of the North for English, President's Award for Educational Excellence.; [oth. writ.] "What Lies Beneath Winter", Morning Song, several unpublished poems and stories; [pers.] Writing gives me a feeling of fulfillment. I am pleased to be able to share my writings with other people.; [a.] Wurtsboro, NY

KNIGHT, BRENDA L.
[p.] John and Grace Hiller; [m.] Jeffrey B. Knight; [ch.] Carrie, Jacci, Katie; [occ.] Wife, Mother; [pers.] "To God be the glory, great things He has done."

KOHL, KATRINA
[pen.] Brimstone; [b.] August 27, 1977, Pekin; [p.] Erwin and Theresa Kohl; [ed.] 2nd year of college; [occ.] Student; [a.] Pekin, IL

KOLCZ, STEPHANIE
[b.] November 6, 1984, Fort Lauderdale, FL; [p.] Ed and Gail Kolcz; [ed.] Quiet Waters Elementary, Rickards Middle School (Gem Program); [occ.] Student; [memb.] St. Andrew's Church Choir; [hon.] AB and A Honor Roll, Duke University Talent Identification Program (MAP), Outstanding Fitness Award, reading awards; [oth. writ.] No others published; [pers.] I love to read and write, and I hope to write (and publish) many more poems, stories, and illustrations.; [a.] Deerfield Beach, FL

KOSACK, ALICIA JOYELLE
[b.] February 6, 1975, Buffalo, NY; [p.] Denis and Jeanette Kosack; [ed.] Lancaster High School, HARID Conservatory of Music; [occ.] Student/Musician (Flutist); [memb.] National Flute Association, Niagara Frontier Flute Association; [hon.] Director's List (HARID), National Society of Arts and Letters (NSAL), (Boca Raton Chapter) Career Advancement Grant, Niagara Frontier Flute Association Scholarship, Full Tuition Scholarship to the HARID Conservatory; [a.] Lancaster, NY

KOZLOWSKI, JAMES E.
[b.] November 29, 1942, Webster, MA; [p.] Edward L. and Cecile Kozlowski; [m.] Susan Kozlowski, April 4, 1964; [ch.] Michael and Debra Kozlowski; [ed.] Bartlett High School Class of 1961; [occ.] Meat Manager, Shaw's Supermarkets; [memb.] Coached baseball: Little League through American Legion, coached Youth Football.; [pers.] My greatest achievements in life are my children, my best friend is my wife.; [a.] Webster, MA

KRAAI, JACK
[pen.] E.J.; [b.] May 4, 1943, Grand Haven, MI; [p.] Henry and Katie Kraai; [occ.] Retired; [hon.] U.S. President Hon. Bill Clinton's Presidential Letter for Adult Smokers' Rights. Granted Full Royal (Noble Status) - HRH Prince Leonard Australia; [oth. writ.] "A Grand River Vale Winter Ballad No. 1 in C Major" 1st organ musical ballad - unpublished poem dedicated to: Dell Shannon Rock and Roll Star Coopersville, MI; [pers.] "Always strive to do your best, even when others believe you're doing your worst." Poem dedicated to: family and friends.; [a.] Allendale, MI

KRAFT, WILBUR-REUBEN ARTHUR
[pen.] Reuben Kraft; [b.] February 24, 1974, Ocala, FL; [p.] Edward D. Kraft, Susana Noyes Lehew; [ed.] Vaguard High School, Ocala, Florida; [occ.] Cashier; [oth. writ.] Poems published in Vanguard High School's "Knight's Legend" and in the Oneida Community Journal; [pers.] Through my poetry,

I bare a part of my soul. By sharing it, I hope it encourage thought and perhaps, some insight into the human condition.; [a.] Ocala, FL

KRATZER, PAMELA NYCZ
[pen.] Pamela Nycz Kratzer; [b.] February 15, 1956, Elizabeth, NJ; [p.] John and Virginia Nycz; [m.] James Kratzer, September 20, 1980; [ch.] Amanda and Samantha; [ed.] Grad. of Linden High School; [occ.] Self employed with husband Jim at Ashley Phosphate Auto and Truck Repair and Kratzer's Towing; [oth. writ.] Publish "Tea Time News," a small newsletter distributed to family and friends, (in its second year).; [pers.] Be happy - stay happy!; [a.] Summerville, SC

KRAUS, KATRINA MARIE
[b.] December 22, 1983, California; [p.] Chonni Elizabeth Kraus; [ed.] LaPresa Elementary, Rolando Park Elementary, Spring Valley Middle; [memb.] First Baptist of College Grove; [hon.] President's Academic Award, Academic Achievement Award, Dare Awareness Award; [pers.] Follow your dreams because if you keep on trying, you'll get where you want to be. Remember to stay happy and enjoy life.; [a.] Spring Valley, CA

KROEZE, JEFFREY SCOTT
[pen.] J. S. Kroeze; [b.] May 11, 1966, Pomona, CA; [p.] Robert D. Kroeze, Marcia A. Kroeze; [ed.] Corona High, Riverside Community College, California State University at San Bernardino; [occ.] Computer Programmer with Parker Systems, Ontario California; [memb.] US Army Veteran; [hon.] Honorable Discharge, Good Conduct Medal, Army Achievement Award 4th Oak Leaf Cluster, A.S. Degree in Computer Information Systems, Dean's List; [pers.] Treasure your vision and health. Live each day like it is your last...because tomorrow never knows. Special thanks to James Douglas Morrison, U2, Stephen King, and De Niro for piquing my interest in poetry, music, literature, and movies.; [a.] Corona, CA

KUNICKI, FLORENCE J.
[b.] May 19, 1912, Erie, PA; [p.] Max and Martha Kaminski; [m.] Bennett W. Kunicki, August 22, 1942; [ch.] Raymond G., Thomas J., Joseph A. and Mark X.; [ed.] Edinboro State U. - B.S. Ed., Kent State U. - M.S. Ed.; [occ.] Retired Biology Teacher, Memorial H.S., Campbell, Ohio; [hon.] Grad. - Magna Cum Laude; [pers.] Love of music and beauty of words.; [a.] Campbell, OH

KUNOW, PATRINA
[b.] March 8, 1967, East Stroudsburg; [p.] Mr. and Mrs. Chester Miller Jr.; [ch.] Alexander and Alia; [ed.] Pocono Mt. High School graduate, continuing education at North Hampton Community College; [occ.] Mother and Student; [oth. writ.] "Exaustion," "My Aggravation," "Our Children," "Who Am I?"; [pers.] Everyone has a future, take every day for what it's worth! Thanks, to my high school English teacher: you made a difference.; [a.] Stroudsburg, PA

KURLOWICZ, MATT
[b.] May 23, 1953, Brooklyn, NY; [p.] Helen and Philip; [m.] Susan, August 19, 1979; [ch.] Kalynda and Matty; [ed.] Associate Degree - North Country CC, Bachelors Degree - Fredonia State University; [occ.] Singer, Songwriter, Poet; [memb.] Aero Force One (Aerosmith Fan Club); [oth. writ.] Currently working on a solo recording project and a band recording project. The name of the band is Matty's Deli.; [pers.] I choose to write with as much ambiguous reference as possible so my readers can personalize my writings.; [a.] Bethpage, NY

KURPIEWSKI, CHRIS
[b.] December 27, 1979, Trenton, NJ; [p.] Joseph Kurpiewski, Margaret Johnson Kurpiewski; [ed.] Notre Dame High School; [occ.] Student, NDHS, Lawrenceville, NJ; [memb.] National Honor Society, National Latin Honor Society, Amnesty International, West End Soccer Association, St. Francis RC Church; [hon.] Honor Roll of Distinction, Academic Excellence Award, VFW Essay Scholarship Award (1996); [oth. writ.] Several pieces of currently unpublished prose, historical essays and poetry.; [pers.] This work models my favorite poetic technique. The opposing trains of thought perfectly summarize the human condition. And as for myself, I try all, excel at what I love, and know there is no excuse for hypocrisy. Thanks Mom.; [a.] Trenton, NJ

KUSHNER, KRISTEN
[b.] July 1, 1985, Annapolis; [p.] Jeff and Peggy Kushner; [ed.] Elementary; [occ.] Student; [memb.] Girl Scouts, Peer Helpers; [hon.] Science Fair, straight As, book reading; [oth. writ.] Science reports, school stories, poems; [pers.] "Always take that little step to do something."; [a.] Severna Park, MD

LABBATE, PATRICIA ANN
[b.] April 11, 1954, Richmond, VA; [p.] Virginia E. Payne; [m.] Richard A. Labbate, May 4, 1991; [ch.] Joshua Graham Cathey and Samuel Quinn Labbate; [ed.] Highland Springs High School, Virginia Commonwealth University; [occ.] Research Specialist, Massey Cancer Center.

LABRIE, JOAN A.
[b.] December 29, 1960, Manchester, NH; [p.] Mr. and Mrs. Leon H. Rice; [m.] Paul A. Labrie, July 22, 1984; [ch.] Courtney and Sarah; [ed.] Graduated from West High School. Went to Bay Path Junior College in Longmeadow, Mass., also attended New Hampshire College; [occ.] Catering for Castle Caterers; [memb.] Daughters of the Revolution - Molly Stark Chapter; [hon.] Graduated from Barbizon School (modeling school in Boston); [oth. writ.] I wrote an article about Courtney's Aide - which was published in the Parent Times - a local newspaper. I wrote essays for contests - one of which was published in a local newspaper.; [pers.] My daughter Courtney, who is diagnosed with autism and cystic fibrosis, inspired me to write this poem.; [a.] Manchester, NH

LAFFERTY, SHONNA MARGARET
[b.] February 27, 1984, Burlington, NC; [p.] Juley and Robert Kelly; [ed.] I go to Horace Mann Middle School. Since I'm only 12 Years old, I'm in 7th grade, but plan to finish School and go on to College.; [occ.] Student; [a.] Burlington, IA

LANDIS, JOHN W.
[b.] October 1917, Kutztown, PA; [p.] Edwin C. Landis, Estella B. Landis; [m.] Muriel T. S. Landis, July 5, 1941; [ch.] Maureen L. Landis, Marcia L. Dent; [ed.] Phillipsburg (NJ) High School, Lafayette College (Summa Cum Laude), B.S. and Sc.D.; [occ.] Retired Industrial Executive; [memb.] Director - Harvard Center for Blood Research, International Association of Macro Engineering Societies, several professional organizations, Chairman/Member - Numerous government advisory committees; [hon.] Total of 26, including - Smyth Nuclear Statesman Award, Churchill Medal of Wisdom, Eisenhower Award of Honor, George Washington Kidd Award, Phi Beta Kappa, Tau Beta Pi, Sigma Xi, Omicron Delta Kappa, Pi Delta Epsilon; [oth. writ.] Contributing author - 8 books. Over 160 technical and management papers.; [pers.] Writing poetry challenges mind, heart and soul.; [a.] Weston, MA

LANFEAR, SUZANNE M.
[b.] December 16, 1974, Columbus, OH; [p.] James and Phyllis Lanfear; [ed.] Senior at Ohio University degree: Communications in Human Services, Emphasis English, Minor in Theatre; [occ.] Student; [memb.] Ohio University Forensics Team, Etha United Methodist Church, National Council of Teachers in English; [hon.] Dean's List, Forensics Talent Award, Ohio Valley Summer Theatre Scholarship Recipient, Teaching Leadership Scholarship; [oth. writ.] Several poems written but, they are hiding in my desk - just as this poem had done.; [pers.] I look forward to graduation and eventually completing my master's degree in Elementary Education. I hope to make a difference in a child's life and open up their eyes to the world of writing.; [a.] Baltimore, OH

LANGIEWICZ, CHERYL
[pen.] C. Langiewicz; [b.] July 7, 1954, Morris, MN; [p.] LaVonne and Raymond Waldron; [m.] Douglas J. Langiewicz, May 25, 1974; [ch.] Toby and Douglas Jr.; [occ.] Veterinary Tech. and Receptionist, Wife, Mother and Grandmother; [memb.] Honorary Member of the Animal Rights Coalition; [hon.] Protection of Domestic Animals (Animal Rights Collation); [oth. writ.] Unpublished: "Grandchild," "A Child's Prayer" - "Becoming Parents," "Another Little Miracle," "A Lesson In Life," "With Love Dad"; [pers.] For me, poetry is an unselfish act, of self- expression.; [a.] Spring Lake Park, MN

LANGILLE, LOUISE
[pen.] Louise Langille; [b.] May 6, 1906, Cape Coal, MA; [p.] Ella and Daniel Lee; [m.] Elma Langille, November 28, 1923; [ch.] Evon, Leonard and Clair; [ed.] Bourne, Mass. High; [occ.] LPN; [memb.] Tewsbury Mass. Methodist Church; [oth. writ.] Promise, Done With Earthly Closes, Mother, To My Husband, Their Dad, (these are all the poems she wrote); [pers.] My Grandmother wrote either when she felt pain from a love or she had something to celebrate. I loved her very much and I would love to see her poems published.

LAPP, SUSAN M.
[b.] December 26, 1960, Buffalo, NY; [p.] Patricia Meiller, George Meiller Jr.; [m.] Clifford Lapp Sr., March 7, 1986; [ch.] Muriel, Gabrielle, Beau, Clifford Jr.; [ed.] Bennett High School; [occ.] Receptionist, St. Paul's R.C. Church Kenmore, NY; [oth. writ.] Several poems written but not published.; [pers.] I hope people will find comfort in this poem. It was dedicated to Laura Lapp when she passed away April 12, 1994 at the age of 24. Daughter of Dianne and Bill Lapp.; [a.] Grand Island, NY

LARIONOVA, NINA
[b.] November 18, 1984, Leningrad, Russia; [p.] Natasha Kouprina and Vladimir Larionov; [ed.] Finished 5th grade Estes Elementary School, Chapel Hill, NC, 27514; [hon.] Music awards, poem award; [a.] Chapel Hill, NC

LARSON, CLIFF
[pen.] C.J.; [b.] September 14, 1985, Morristown, NJ; [p.] Debbie Larson; [ed.] Fifth in St. Peter's The Apostle School, Parssipany; [occ.] Attendant St. Peter's The Apostle School

LASSA, BRETT
[b.] November 27, 1963, Gainesville, FL; [p.] Walter and Dolores Lassa; [m.] Kimberly Lassa, December 30, 1995; [ed.] Bachelor of Science in Electrical Engineering, University of Florida; [occ.] Engineering Specialist at Lockheed Martin Tactical Aircraft Systems; [memb.] 1853 Society University of Florida, International Kenpo Karate Association; [hon.] Extraordinary Achievement in Engineering (1987), Extraordinary Achievement in Engineering (1991); [oth. writ.] Many unpublished poems and songs, several short sto-

ries.; [pers.] I have an overwhelming passion for the Florida Gators and for my beautiful wife.; [a.] Fort Worth, TX

LAVAN, KAREN F.
[b.] November 25, 1960, San Diego, CA; [p.] Ted and Dorothy Fallgren; [m.] Joseph N. Lavan III, December 21, 1985; [ed.] Christian High, BA, MA, SDSU; [occ.] Small business owner, JKL Enterprises, Daging Co.; [memb.] The Writing Center, Hospitals and Institutions Committee; [oth. writ.] Articles for local and international recovery journals, poetry and inspirational, spiritual.; [pers.] My writing emphasizes the bondage of addiction and the freedom of recovery through Jesus Christ. (Romans 7); [a.] La Mesa, San Diego, CA

LEADER-PICONE, WHITNEY
[b.] August 20, 1983, Berkeley, CA; [p.] Malcolm and Linda Leader-Picone; [ed.] Thousand Oaks Elementary School, Franklin Intermediate School, Martin Luther King Jr. Middle School; [occ.] Student; [memb.] Berkeley City Ballet; [hon.] Martin Luther King, Jr. Middle School Honor Roll, Martin Luther King Award, School Honor for performance in Shakespeare's *MacBeth*, chosen to read poem "Women" at dedication of San Francisco Women's Building Mural, September 25, 1994; [oth. writ.] "Life" to be published in *Best Poems of the 90's*.; [pers.] My friend Edythe Boone, Muralist, asked me to write a poem to celebrate the dedication of the "Maestrapiece" mural which decorates the San Francisco Women's Building. My poems are from my heart but they aren't always fiction. Sometimes my poems state my opinions on issues.; [a.] Berkeley, CA

LEANZA IV, ANTHONY
[b.] May 3, 1984, Mayfield Heights, OH; [p.] Anthony Leanza III, Teresa S. Goodin; [memb.] Nashville Soccer Assoc., Boy Scouts of America, Dupont Tyler Math Team; [hon.] Honor Roll; [pers.] This poem was written after the passing of my grandfather who was also my best friend.

LEE, BELITA A.
[pen.] Belita A. Lee; [b.] May 1, 1986, Mather Air Force Base; [p.] Brian and Beverly Lee; [ed.] 5th Grade; [hon.] Yes; [oth. writ.] Other poems in my collection.; [pers.] I like to write about my dreams.; [a.] Lodi, CA

LEE, BRENT
[b.] February 3, 1969, Houston, TX; [p.] Harold and Noma Joyce Lee; [m.] Lisa Flenniken Lee, September 6, 1997; [ed.] Bay Area Christian School, University of Houston - Conrad Hilton School of Hotel and Restaurant Management; [occ.] Accountant; [memb.] Active Member of Houston Second Baptist Church and their music ministry; [pers.] I dedicate my poetry to the love of my life, Lisa, who has taught me to laugh more freely, live more fully, and love more deeply, and to God who has given me the ability to express my emotions on paper and has inspired me to write from the heart.; [a.] Houston, TX

LEE, HOR-MING
[pen.] Hor-Ming Lee; [b.] November 29, 1972, Jiangmen, Xinhui, Guangdond, China; [p.] Yi-Quin Lee, Zhong-Shi Lee; [m.] Min-Ya Liu Lee, December 25, 1964; [ch.] David Yao Lee (MD), (Nephew) Kenneth W. F. Lee; [ed.] Hui Tong High, Taiwan Chung Hsing University, M.A. Program of Asian Studies in Seton Hall University; [occ.] Prof. of Directed Reading on Traditional Chinese Medicine, Director and Vice President College of TCM; [oth. writ.] Translation Works, Chinese Masso-Therapy, Symptoms and Treatment of Menses and Leukorrhea. Articles on: Psoriasis, Alopecia, etc. Song poems translated, medical articles for Victoria Chinatown magazine; [pers.] I would endeavor to attempt to bring the world into a big family by way of poetry, and at living through the mutual cooperation of East-West medicine. I have been greatly influenced by ancient Chinese odes, Tang and Song poems.; [a.] Vancouver, British Columbia, Canada

LEE, JONATHAN
[pen.] JV; [b.] October 26, 1977, Fairfax, VA; [p.] Taik Jane; [ed.] I'm a senior in High School; [occ.] Clerk at Tower Records, Fairfax, VA; [hon.] (?) Class President at my High School Cedar Lane Center, Vienna Virginia; [pers.] "Withered" is dedicated to Leah Joanne Lefler; [a.] Herndon, VA

LEE, KATHERINE Y.
[b.] June 10, 1976, Seoul, Korea; [p.] Eun Soo Lee and In Sook Lee; [ed.] Attended Tustin High School - currently attending University of California, Irvine as a Classics Major (Latin Major) - 3rd (Junior) year; [occ.] Student at UCI; [memb.] E and Q; [hon.] E and Q (Eta Sigma Phi) Classical Honor Society; [oth. writ.] Several poems and short stories published in Tustin High School Literary Publications.; [pers.] There are many roads, but one destination. Happiness comes from within and how satisfied you are of yourself and your decisions.; [a.] Tustin, CA

LEE, TATIA
[b.] May 14, 1970, Los Angeles, CA; [p.] Mary and James Bryant; [ed.] George Washington High, Professional Development Systems; [occ.] Administrative Assistant, Cedars-Sinai Medical Center, Los Angeles, CA; [memb.] Peace Apostolic Church of God in Christ; [oth. writ.] Other writings not published; [pers.] My inspiration for writing derives from pleasant and harsh realities of life. I believe God is using me as a vehicle to disseminate information. In hopes of providing a positive outcome.; [a.] Los Angeles, CA

LEGOWIK, RISA MARIE ELIZABETH
[pen.] Risa Marie Goodwin; [b.] October 28, 1935, Brunswick, GA; [p.] Lora And Clayton Goodwin; [m.] Ronald S. Legowik, February 3, 1984; [ch.] Randy, Keith, Britt, Veronica and Ron Jr.; [ed.] Twelth grade - Brunswick GA, Glynn Academy, "Life" and observance of people's reactions living it; [occ.] Retired Bartender now Housewife; [memb.] Bible Baptist Church, Brunswick, GA - Collecting for Heart Association yearly. And counseling as well as helping the many members of my family.; [hon.] I have not, up until this time, pursued anything - except satisfaction in writing things down, that touched my heart.; [oth. writ.] My children have been my "Sounding Board" thus far, and " I Theirs.".; [pers.] Having traveled some during my life, and resolving problems encountered along the way, I've become a "People Watcher". As such, an empathy for them has evolved. The happy things, as well as sad. Grief for loved ones that burden our very souls. And joy - for "their" joy when a thing happens after all hope seemed gone. This is why I write! To try and express the unpressable.; [a.] Jacksonville, FL

LEICHLITER, DANIELLE
[pen.] Constantine; [b.] December 31, 1983, Sandy, UT; [p.] Jeffery and Jody; [ed.] ALPS Program (Accelerated Learning Program) since 1st grade, currently in 7th grade; [occ.] Student; [memb.] UNSS (Utah Nature Study Society), UOVA (Utah Outdoor Volleyball Association), USA Volleyball Association, Utah Museum of Natural History; [hon.] Competed in District for Debate, Scholarship for U of U Volleyball Camp, UNSS full Scholarship to Camp: Animals, Animals, Animals, Honor Roll 1st-6th grade, competed in District for Creative Pursuits; [oth. writ.] Poetry: The Stranger Within, This Time, The Silent Weakness, (none published); [pers.] Poetry is art. It takes time, patience, and effort. Never limit yourself. I never thought I would win this honor, since I'm so young. But I kept on trying, and that is all that matters.; [a.] Sandy, UT

LEIGHTON, WENDY LEANN
[b.] March 26, 1967, Reno, NV; [p.] Marion E. and Shirley M. Andrews; [m.] Scott Ray Leighton, June 1, 1985; [ch.] Blake (11), Cody (6) and Samantha (4); [ed.] High School Graduate (GED), Certified Nurse's Aide (College Course); [occ.] Housewife, mother; [hon.] Honorable mention for poem submitted in a contest approx. 6 years ago; [oth. writ.] "My Father, The Man" submitted in a contest previously. Many other poems that have not been seen publicly or by anyone other than myself and close friends and family.; [pers.] Through my writing I try to relate the feelings of normal people who are unable to put their thoughts into words. Honesty and compassion are your greatest assets.; [a.] Auburn, WA

LESSICK, MELISSA S.
[b.] March 17, 1974; [p.] Raymond E. Lessick, Mary Ann Lessick; [ed.] Carmichaels Area High School, California University of Pennsylvania; [memb.] PSEA/NEA, National Council of Teachers of English, Western PA Council of Teachers of English, Alliance of C.U.P. and Western PA English Teachers, and Council for Exceptional Children.; [oth. writ.] "Writing in the Fully Inclusive Classroom: Listening to All the Voices" in the ACUWPET Journal, "The Ironic Dialogue of Hills Like White Elephants" in the anthology, A Piece of Our Minds.; [pers.] In my work, I strive to point out the truth in society, as well as that which occurs in everyday life. If one can read my poem and see the truth and reality of it, then my objective has been achieved.; [a.] Carmichaels, PA

LETTERLE, LISA J.
[b.] December 3, 1961, Cleveland, OH; [p.] Samuel and Caroline Gumbish; [m.] Nicholas W. Letterle, October 25, 1985; [ch.] Christopher and Nichole; [ed.] Jane Addams Business Career Center High School; [occ.] Housewife; [hon.] Editor's Choice Awards for a friend; [oth. writ.] A Friend; [pers.] I write because it help me understand life and to give hope to other. I express what I'm feeling inside.; [a.] Cleveland, OH

LEWIS, COLLEEN JOANN
[pen.] Moon; [b.] February 13, 1980, Lafayette, LA; [p.] Cynthia and Edward L. Lewis; [oth. writ.] Lavender, Summer Splendor, Mr. Borealis; [a.] Abita Springs, LA

LEWIS, REBA
[b.] November 8, 1970, Phoenix, AZ; [p.] James and Daxlene Lewis; [ed.] Independence High School, Phoenix Community College; [occ.] School Bus Attendant; [oth. writ.] Although I have no other writings published, I have written several poems which have been enjoyed by family and friends.; [a.] Phoenix, AZ

LIDDELL, DANIEL W.
[p.] Rev. T. T. Liddell, Mrs. Adele Liddell; [ed.] Master of Music, plus additional hours beyond the M.M.; [occ.] Retired - formerly: Univ. Teacher, Public School Teacher, Interior Design Business; [memb.] NATS, MENC, Who's Who in Interior Design, Chairman of Illinois Choral Directors Assn.; [hon.] Who's Who in Interior Design; [pers.] My whole life has been dedicated to God, church, teaching and love of fine arts and humanity.; [a.] Kankakee, IL

LIEB, ASHLEY
[b.] July 16, 1984, Pittsburgh; [p.] Harry and Betsy Lieb; [ed.] Attends Shaler Area School District; [occ.] Student; [memb.] Girl Scouts; [hon.] Honor

student at Shaler Area Middle School, many awards in Girl Scouting; [oth. writ.] This is first publication; [pers.] Writing has always been one of my favorite past times. I enjoy poetry, romance novels and fictional biographies.; [a.] Pittsburgh, PA

LIGOURI, MARY C.
[pen.] Catherine (Fedro) Ligouri; [b.] June 12, 1955, Des Moines, IA; [p.] Calvin and Catherine (Kate) Fedro; [m.] Louie M. Ligouri, November 24, 1973; [ch.] Adonia, Angelo, Lynsey; [ed.] Attending college, Peru State University; [occ.] Student; [pers.] Greatest feat a person can perform - grant the world a part of your self to make it a better place. Children are our future and our gifts to that future - grant them our knowledge and our love.; [a.] Auburn, NE

LILAVOIS, KETTLY
[pen.] Ketty; [b.] October 14, 1951, Port-Au-Prince Haiti, WI; [p.] Carmelle and Andre Lilavois; [ed.] Special Degree in Fashion from Parsons School of Fashion design NY, A Division of the New School in New York; [occ.] Quality Controller for a Fashion Pattern Publishing Co.; [oth. writ.] I wrote a few poems such as: Friendship - Door - Goodtime but they have never been published; in fact "People" was my first poem and I decided to present it to the contest.; [pers.] "People" reflect my own experience in life, and I know anyone who reads it, in one line or two may have to say "oh yes" this is so true, it happened to me.; [a.] Uniondale, NY

LINARES, ALEXANDRA
[pen.] Alexandra Linares; [b.] July 11, 1981, Paterson, NJ; [p.] Carmen Linares, Humberto Linares; [ed.] Waldwick Seventh - Day Adventist School; [hon.] Spiritual Gift of Understanding; [pers.] With God all things are possible. Don't let circumstances control your life and get in the way of your dreams. Dreams do come true.; [a.] Paterson, NJ

LINDSEY, CARMONEDA
[pen.] C. J. Lindsey; [b.] June 1, 1984, South Eastern Methodist, Dallas; [p.] Robert and Jackie Lindsey; [ed.] Mabank Middle School; [occ.] Mabank Middle School, 7th grade; [memb.] Beta Club; [hon.] School Honor Roll; [oth. writ.] Sweet dreams smile, not published; [pers.] It is an honor to have my first poem published for the first time and to do something that was merely a dream yesterday.; [a.] Gun Barrel, TX

LINN, JENNIE JOANA
[b.] June 16, 1967, Laguna Beach, CA; [p.] Marilyn Bean; [ed.] Grad. from Poly High School 1985 - grade point average 4.0 grad with honors; [occ.] Checker trainer at Top VAIU Market AKA (Kumartco); [hon.] Outstanding Service in High School Office, as an Aide, Outstanding Service in Roosevelt Elementary as teacher's aide. Won many awards for employee of the month through present and past jobs; [oth. writ.] The poem was published in a school (Poly High) creative writing magazine "Acacia 84" for outstanding student writing (was in the 11th grade at the time.); [pers.] There are three kinds of people: 1 - Those who make things happen, 2 - Those who watch things happen, 3 - Those who wonder what happened. I believe anything can happen if you put your mind to it. Life is what you make of it.

LINSTEAD, GAIL
[pen.] Gail Atwood; [b.] June 12, 1964, Jackson, MS; [p.] Rhue Atwood and Mary Atwood; [m.] Bryan Linstead, May 28, 1994; [ed.] The Education Center and Phillips Junior College; [occ.] Executive Secretary; [memb.] North Shore Animal League; [hon.] 1st Runner-up in Imperial MS Mississippi Pageant, Queen Photogenic in IMperial mississippi and graduated from Barbizon School of Modeling; [oth. writ.] Poem published in christian single magazine; [pers.] My inspiration to write begins with myself. I put my feelings into words and those words make my poems always grasp tomorrow with faith, for each other day carries a different color rainbow.; [a.] Phoenix, AZ

LIPINSKI, EDWARD R.
[b.] November 2, Jersey City, NJ; [p.] Joseph and Margaret Lipinski; [ed.] Graduate of Wilkes College in Wilkes - Barre PA. and School of Visual Arts in NYC; [occ.] Writer and Illustrator; [oth. writ.] Write and illustrate the weekly home clinic in the New York Times. Author and illustrator of the children's book: "Pucasso, the cat who wanted to be an artist"; [pers.] "Life is more interesting if you don't take it too seriously".

LIPSCOMB, HARRIET
[pen.] Sister Woman; [b.] September 28, 1941, Laurel, MS; [p.] Joe and Ruth May; [m.] Divorced, Widowed; [ch.] Eddie, Cynthia, Marlon, Charlotte, Thomas, Sheri, Tiana; [ed.] Gary Roosevelt High School, Indiana University Northwest, Associates Degree in Allied Health; [occ.] Respiratory Therapist; [memb.] God's Grace Church, Choir Member, Church Nurse, Sunday School Teacher; [oth. writ.] Special occasions, holidays, weddings, poems on greeting cards, mostly in my church home, God's Grace Church of the Apostolic Faith Gary, IN; [pers.] I've always loved rhyme. And now I find great joy praising and giving thanks to the Lord, for His goodness and for His wonderful works unto the children of men.; [a.] Gary, IN

LISTER, KATRINA
[b.] August 29, 1947, Huntsville, AL; [p.] James S. Cantrell, Florence Cagle; [ch.] Timothy Allen, William Michael; [ed.] Butler High School, Bartons School of Hair Design, Continuous Education in Chid Care; [occ.] Child Care Provider, owner of Happy Time Day Care; [memb.] Auxilliary member of the Legion of Mary at Holy Spirit Church, Vice President of Home Child Care Ass; [oth. writ.] Several poems published in HCCA Newsletters and church publications, poems published by The National Library of Poetry.; [pers.] I thank God for the talent he has given me. I wish to touch the hearts and souls of others through my writing.; [a.] Huntville, AL

LOFTON, KATHERINE S.
[pen.] Kitty Lofton; [b.] June 24, 1954, Micro, NC; [p.] Clyde Vern Starling, Mary Bruce Starling; [m.] Aaron Lewis Lofton, November 14, 1991; [ch.] Stephen Ray Bradshaw, Donnie Wayne Bradshaw; [ed.] Charles B. Aycock High School (10 grade 1971), Wayne Community College (GED - 12/08/81, Executive Secretary - incompleted, Nursing School 1981-1986), Johnson Technical College (Chemistry - 1985), Wilson County Technical College (Nursing - incompleted due to disiocated right arm 1985-1987); [occ.] Health Care Technician 1990-1991, totally disabled due to accident at work 1991; [memb.] Ray of Hope PFWB Church; [hon.] Volunteer 1987 (Meals on Wheels in Fremont NC), Phi Beta Lambda Business Club 1981 at Wayne Community College, and Boy Scout Den Mother (1986-1989), and Dean's List twice; [oth. writ.] None, but I did do the typing for Goldminds at Wilson Technical College in Spring 1986 as Katherine Bradshow. Also, I always do little poems on cards to family members or friends at special events like birthday cards and holidays cards.; [pers.] I was one of twelve children, fourth from the baby and two half brothers and one half sister. Broken home, mother raised all twelve of us by herself, all married and left home, mother still living (74) but dad died in 1971, pick cotten by hand, put in tobacco by hand, first marriage lasted 19 1/2 years, with two boys, and will be married for 5 years November 14, 1996 and had back operation 3/13/92. I always believe that if you could smile, laugh, or hold your head high that you can do anything that your heart desires to make something out of yourself.; [a.] Goldsboro, NC

LOPEZ, LINDA MAE
[b.] January 3, 1953, Lehighton, PA; [p.] Marlene Lee Jackson; [ch.] Belinda Elise Lopez - October 16, 1979, Shaun Christopher Lopez - December 29, 1981, Michael Anthony Lopez - July 7, 1986; [ed.] Redlands High School (1991), Cal State S.B. Univ. BA (1979) MA (1990), Multiple Subjects Cred. Univ. of Redlands, severely Handicapped Cred. Cal State S.B. Univ.; [occ.] Special Educ. Teacher, S.B. Co. Supt. of School; [memb.] Executive Board Member (V.P.) Calif. Teachers Assoc. S.B., CTA/NEA Women's Caucus; [hon.] 1996 Teacher of the Year - East Valley S.B. Co. Supt. Schools, Dean's List Cal State Univ. of S.B.; [oth. writ.] "Remembrance Of A Lost Love" published in Song On The Wind, The National Library of Poetry; [pers.] My poetry reflects my journey through life. As in life my poetry displays many emotional tones.; [a.] Yucaipa, CA

LOPEZ-LAVALLE, MARCELLA
[pen.] Marcy R. C.; [b.] July 22, 1970, Harbor City; [p.] Absalon and Lilly Lopez-Lavalle; [ed.] A.A. Degree in Word Processing Specialist in 1992. B.S. degree expected in 1998 in Business Administration; [occ.] I am a Receptionist for Rolling in Hills Covenant Church; [memb.] I am a Member of the Elks Club; [hon.] I was qualified to be among Who's Who Among American High School Students during my 10th and 11th grade years. I received all three years in High School. I received an Award for the study of piano.; [oth. writ.] I have written over 100 songs and ten of them have a copyright date.; [pers.] At the age of 10, I had the potential of writing poems. As I grew older my poems turned into writing songs. I have written over 100 songs and I have been labeled the lyric queen. I have recorded 10 songs and now I have my first album.; [a.] Carson, CA

LOTHIAN, WALTER SCOTT
[b.] December 27, 1976, Paramount, CA; [p.] Walter and Silvia Lothian; [ed.] 4 Years Loyola High, currently Sophomore At USC; [occ.] Student; [hon.] Dean's Scholarship at USC and Leadership Scholarship; [pers.] My work is a journal of sorts, which I use as a source of memories and reflection.; [a.] Huntington Park, CA

LOVEKAMP, GREGORY
[b.] April 26, 1971, Shoughtgard West, Germany; [p.] Regan Lovekamp; [m.] Janine Anne Lovekamp, March 18, 1995; [ed.] Commonwealth College Thomas Nelson Community College Graduate of New Kent High School; [occ.] Assistant Manager; [memb.] Hampton Christian Church; [hon.] Award certificate to become and Nursing Assistant, awarded certificate to become a Laboratory Assistant.; [oth. writ.] Daddy, Good Did, Help, Here I Am, Leaving, Silent Cup, Tarnish Angel, Tears, The Walk, Where Are You, I Am Here, Dreams!; [pers.] If God walks with you, you are never alone; [a.] New Port News, VA

LUCANIA, ALEXANDER M.
[b.] September 13, 1986, Hayward, CA; [p.] Penelope Smith and Salvatore Lucania; [ed.] Presently a 4th Grader in private school; [occ.] Being a kid; [memb.] Jamie's Dance Co., Pleasanton, CA; [pers.] Listen to your children, you might just learn something.; [a.] Danville, CA

LUCAS, LEEROY
[b.] November 11, 1978, Lake Village, AR; [p.] Nora and Leevell Lucas; [ed.] Job Corp (Duachlta) Royal, AR; [pers.] I have been influenced by Maya

Angelou. Because she strived for everything she had in life. I give thanks to my friends in Job Corp.; [a.] Lake Village, AR

LUJAN, AGGIE
[b.] January 22, 1950, Albuquerque, NM; [ch.] Three children (1st child and 2nd child separated by 22 years.); [occ.] Registered Nurse; [pers.] The greatest influence in my life have been my children.

LUSTER, DIANE K.
[pen.] Di Luster; [b.] March 3, 1948, Salina, KS; [p.] Mr. and Mrs. W. R. Appleby; [m.] Roland C. Luster Jr., August 20, 1982; [ch.] Catherine and J. Eric Riley; [ed.] B.S. in Elementary Education from the College of Charleston in Charleston, South Carolina; [occ.] Housewife; [memb.] Lladro' Society; [oth. writ.] I have published an article for Michael Plumb's Horse Journal.; [pers.] I strive to touch the "soul" in my writing. I'm greatly influenced by the people I've encountered in my life and the animals I care for on my farm.; [a.] Brooksville, FL

LUTINI, PAUL
[pen.] Palee; [b.] June 23, 1976, Springfield; [p.] Ann and Sam; [ed.] St Mary's Elementary, St Mary's High Holyoke Community College, EMT Certificate Student of Ed Parkers Kerpo Under Steven Serwecki, Skip Hawkin, Bran Hawkin; [occ.] Assistant Manager of Clear Blue Pools and Spa; [memb.] (UKS) United Kerpo Systems St Mary's Church; [hon.] I need no awards to know what I have done.; [oth. writ.] All but one are in my head.; [pers.] Everyone should take time to feel the electron and protons that make up their cells then feel the individual organ and muscles and the motion and energy then realize there is no difference between themselves and their lover or a tree or a car or a spirit.; [a.] Westfield, MA

LYNN, CLEVELAND PATRICK CONRAD
[b.] March 17, 1950, New York City; [p.] Arnold E. Lynn, Joanna V. Lynn; [m.] Celeste Maxine Lynn, October 17, 1984; [ch.] Sean Patrick, Christopher Stephan, Kevin Tirrell; [ed.] Springfield Gardens High School Nassau Community College Howard University; [occ.] Former: Prof. Tennis Instructor, M.H. Counselor, Behaviouralist, Rec. C.T.R.A., Activity Therapist, P.E. Teacher; [memb.] Nat'l Council for Therapeutic Recreation Certification, MD State Dept. of M.H. and Hygiene, Wash. Area Patrons Tennis Foundation; [hon.] Best Teacher-D.C. Special Olympics, Coach of the Year-H.S. Tennis, Dev. Pilot Special Needs Programs for the Handicapped/Disabled Population, Dean's List. Capt./1st Singles and Doubles of H.S. and College Tennis Teams, All Extracurricular; [pers.] Viewing the world through childrens eyes. Value judgement: Remembering to wish "Christ" a happy birthday!; [a.] Takoma Park, MD

LYSETSKA, ALENA MARY
[b.] October 19, 1980, Ukraine; [p.] Maria Lysetska; [ed.] Right now I'm going to St. George Academy. It's in New York City. I love my school because it's in the village.; [oth. writ.] I have written a poem in Ukrainian which was published in a Ukrainian newspaper.; [pers.] Basically, I write poems to express my feelings and to show up's and downs of life. Also, if someone want to get to know me better all they have to do is read one of my poems.; [a.] Brooklyn, NY

MACH, MANDY
[pen.] Mandy Kay; [b.] June 26, 1980, Concordia, KS; [p.] Randy and Deanna Mach; [ed.] High School (Belleville High); [occ.] Lifeguard; [memb.] Red Cross, American Heart Association; [hon.] Honor Roll, Honor Choir; [oth. writ.] Other poems and short stories, songs for local music groups; [pers.] My love and inspiration derives from my fiance Ryan. He has shown me so much and I appreciate his honesty. I'll always love him dearly!; [a.] Belleville, KS

MAGSIG, SHILA CHANTEL
[pen.] Shi; [b.] May 18, 1981, Orange County, CA; [p.] Belinda Porrini; [ed.] I'm in the 10th grade at Notre Dame High School in Riverside, CA; [hon.] School awards, and beauty pageants; [oth. writ.] This is my first writing.; [a.] Riverside, CA

MAGUDER, TIM
[pen.] Timothy D. Maguder; [b.] May 6, 1981, CT; [p.] Theodore and Liz Maguder; [ed.] High School 10th Grade at time of now, but I wrote the poem in 9th Grade.; [occ.] Student; [memb.] Hard to explain; [oth. writ.] "Power," "Little," "Thoughts," "Mistakes," "Learning"; [pers.] I just write about what I feel. I try to help a little too.; [a.] Windsor, CT

MAI, JIMMY
[pen.] Jimmy Mai; [b.] November 9, 1985, Anaheim, CA; [p.] Yhank and Yrang Mai; [ed.] 6th grade; [pers.] All my life I have been doing arts, crafts, and literature. I started when I was three years old. I lived with two caring parents and two lovable brothers. I love doing all kinds of sports like basketball and karate.; [a.] Garden Grove, CA

MAKIUD, LA MEEK
[pen.] Montez; [b.] December 20, 1976, Greenville; [p.] Corethia Allen; [ed.] Greenville High, attending Art Instruction School; [a.] Greenville, SC

MALAMIS, MARINA
[b.] October 28, 1978, Moscow, Russia; [p.] Natalie Lepsky, Alexander Malamis; [ed.] LV Berkner High School, now a Freshman at University of North Texas; [pers.] Sadness and depression intensify my feelings, and that is when I write the best.; [a.] Dallas, TX

MALITO, VINCENT A.
[b.] August 9, 1937, New York, NY; [m.] Widowed; [ch.] Two; [ed.] Regis High School, N.Y., NY, St. Peter's Coll., Jersey City, NJ, Fordham Law School, N.Y., NY; [occ.] Attorney; [memb.] President, Suffolk County Bar Association, 1997-98; [pers.] The poem "Patricia" is for the woman I love; [a.] Lindenhurst, NY

MALONE, GEORGE
[b.] October 5, 1940, Baltimore, MD; [m.] Betty, June 25, 1960; [ch.] David, Lisa, Michelle; [occ.] Teacher; [memb.] First Lutheran Church of Gray Manor, several hunting and fishing clubs; [hon.] Teacher of the Year MVA; [oth. writ.] Several poems in my personal collection (unpublished).; [pers.] There are times when my heart seems to put words in my head and I feel obligated to put them on paper.; [a.] Baltimore, MD

MANNING, BENJAMIN J.
[b.] June 7, 1974, Cleveland, OH; [p.] Edward T. Manning Jr. and Charlene V. Manning (1938-1994); [ed.] Bay Village High School, Cleveland State University; [occ.] Sales; [hon.] Eagle Scout; [pers.] Everyone should be more like Winnie the Pooh, because the world needs more people who can just be.; [a.] Bay Village, OH

MANUEL, RUEL
[b.] October 8, 1977, Manila, Philippines; [p.] Rolando A. Manuel, Eugenia H. Manuel; [ed.] Watkins Mill High, University of Maryland at College Park; [pers.] Poetry is one of the ways I like to express myself.; [a.] Gaithersburg, MD

MARCANO, CRUZ
[b.] April 29, Santurce, PR; [p.] Ramon and Olga Marcano; [ed.] PS 38, PS 80, JHS 45, Julia Richman High School, College of New Rochelle and Teachers College - Columbia University; [occ.] Teacher of the Deaf (Hearing Education Services) at PS 79/90, PS 90, PS 58, PS 128, PS 148138, PS 165 and JHS 54; [memb.] Member of Latin American Pentecostal Church "La Sinagoga," Teacher Committee (Sunday School Teacher); [hon.] The Council on Education of the Deaf Professional Certificate for Teaching the Hearing Impaired, Certificate of Achievement Teachers College Columbia University Teacher Opportunity Corps Project, Winner of 1986-87 and 1987-88 Empire States Teachers Fellowship Awards, 1996 Plaque for Teacher of the Year (La Sinagoga - children dept.); [oth. writ.] Wrote a song, but it's not published (in Spanish and one in English). Wrote a poem for my graduate students in 1990.; [pers.] Born hearing impaired and being able to do many things in this world influenced me to write about the deaf, hard-of-hearing, blind, etc. When I write, I write with feeling, love, experience and knowledge.; [a.] New York, NY

MARCHAL, SCOTT F.
[b.] May 28, 1963, Erie, PA; [pers.] Stories of deep courage inspire me.; [a.] Indianapolis, IN

MARICLE-FITZPATRICK, TALETHA MARIE
[b.] July 28, 1979, Aurora, CO; [p.] Kelly M-Fitzpatrick, Stanley F.; [ed.] Attending George Washington High School, Denver; [pers.] My insanity is all that can escape.; [a.] Denver, CO

MARING, GARY DEAN
[b.] November 9, 1940, Newark, OH; [p.] Leo S. and Betty C. Maring; [m.] Divorced, November 16, 1963; [ch.] Christian D. and Kimberly S.; [ed.] High school graduate, Newark Senior High School 1959, Newark, OH, additional studies; [occ.] Disabled; [memb.] St. Francis de Sales Roman Catholic Church, Newark, Ohio - Knights of Columbus - American Legion, Dept. of Ohio Former Member 82nd ABN. Div.; [oth. writ.] "A Treatise of the Lord,"(Copyright-Library of Congress); [pers.] "Truth is the Ability of Man To Accept It."; [a.] Newark, OH

MARKS, RITA
[b.] May 31, 1953, San Mateo, CA; [p.] Joseph and Sarah Marks; [ch.] Lazet Howard and Tanesha Howard; [ed.] Canada College, Redwood City, CA - AA Degree, College of Notre Dame, Belmont, CA, expect Computer Science Degree in 1998; [occ.] Sr. Admin., Asst./Purchasing Agent at Sun Microsystems, Inc., in Mountain View, CA; [memb.] Member of Fremont Bible Fellowship Church in Fremont, CA; [hon.] Dean's List - Twice, American Business Women's Scholarship - Three times, Redwood City Citizen's Scholarship, Canaca College Scholarship, Bay Area Urban League Scholarship; [oth. writ.] Self, Rare Bird, Who Was That? The Love, Life, I Want You, Education, To God, The Joy You Bring, The Miracle, and Slow Down; [pers.] All the honor, praises, thankfulness, glory, and my blessings go to God for providing me with the talent to write poetry and to share with others to enjoy and encourage. I thank my daughters for their love.; [a.] East Palo Alto, CA

MARLOWE, DONNA J.
[b.] March 16, 1931, Dearborn, MI; [p.] Dale Wilder, Marguerite Wilder; [m.] Orval Marlowe, August 5, 1950; [ch.] Ruth Colleen, Larry Dale, James Orval; [ed.] Clarkston High School; [occ.] Owner of Whoopee Bowl, Inc. Michigan's most unusual discount surplus store. Co-Owner-Marlowe's Building and Developing.; [memb.] Davisburg P.T.A., Oakland County 4-H, United Way, Women of the Church of God; [hon.] This poem was written as a legacy to my beloved children and grandchildren to remind them that

they are a "Child of a King"; [oth. writ.] I have written poetry all my life and have shared with my family and friends. This is my first attempt to publish and I was overwhelmed with joy and excitement when the letter came from The National Library of Poetry telling me I was a semi-finalist for my poem "A Mother's Prayer."; [pers.] "A Mother's Prayer" was written years ago. I was 35 years old and had just given my heart to the Lord and accepted Jesus Christ as my personal Savior. When I put the words on paper my heart was so full of love, compassion and emotion I knew my sweet Jesus was right beside me helping me to phrase each word.; [a.] Clarkston, MI

MARSHALL, ALETHEA ST. BERNARD
[b.] December 11, 1963, Trinidad, WI; [p.] Randolph and Daphne St. Bernard; [m.] David Marshall, November 15, 1986; [ch.] Makeda, Aaliya and Nandi; [ed.] City College NY BA, Adelphi Univer. MA; [occ.] Speech Clinician NYC Public School and EI Speech Provider; [memb.] Brooklyn Truth Center, M.U.C.H. Club, Daughters of Africa Alumni, Golden Key Honor Society; [hon.] Louis Shapiro Award CCNY, City Women Award Dean's List, Prof. Weisman Speech Award CCNY Black Faculty and Staff Leadership Award; [oth. writ.] Poetry and plays performed by student and members of MUCH club (Mothers Uplifting Children Horizons) and Local drama class.; [pers.] I believe that all dreams and goals are reachable, and the only thing that can prevent your success in life is your mind.; [a.] Brooklyn, NY

MARSHALL, GEORGE K.
[b.] August 13, 1912, Millville, MA; [p.] Hilton A., Annie G. Marshall; [m.] Emelie P. Potvin, Woonsocket RI, October 5, 1935 (Woonsocket); [ch.] George K. (1938), Michael P. (1955); [ed.] Millville, Uxbridge High, USNA '33, Annapolis; [occ.] Retired, formerly Exec, G.E. and Chrysler, Markt'g, Engr'g,; [memb.] USNA Alumni, Athletic, Association and Local, HAM, AMA, Red Wing Senior Golf Assoc.; [hon.] One of G. E. Team which gave us the heat pump. Made many presentations, media, in error, tabbed me as inventor. Lord Kelvin discovered it, 1700's; [oth. writ.] 3 novels (1 published), 4 plays and poems to offer ideas to save our nation, last chance for our world. Scared we are in awful trouble, - terminal, - and must correct 3 vital areas.; [pers.] Re-elections dominate minds of legislators. Must have Single Ten Year Terms of Senate, House, Pres and VP. Rotate Academicians to Capitol area to counteract lobbies. Improve Participation of public.; [a.] Virginia Beach, VA

MARSHALL HEATH, ANN
[pen.] Ann Marshall Heath; [b.] January 21, 1942, Hillsville, VA; [p.] Vinson & Bertie Marshall; [ch.] Johanna & William Roy "Billy"; [ed.] Cedar Lee High, Bealeton, VA; [occ.] Retired; [memb.] Sunset Baptist Church, Communications Workers of America, Telephone Pioneers of America; [oth. writ.] Several poems published in Bell Atlantic office paper; [pers.] My goal is to have others enjoy what I see through my eyes. To leave something for coming generations, so they may know I passed this way.; [a.] Catlett, VA

MARSTON, CASEY LEE
[b.] May 26, 1984, Portland, ME; [p.] Greg E., Mary J. Marston; [ed.] Dyer Elementary Memorial Middle School; [occ.] Student; [hon.] Soccer trophies, Softball trophies, National Fitness Award; [pers.] Treat everybody kindly and care for others; [a.] South Portland, ME

MARTIN, EDNA J.
[b.] August 8, 1941, Lawton, OK; [ch.] Two daughter and four sons; [ed.] 1 year MTI Business College, 2 years American River Jr. College Grant High, Del Paso Jr High, North Ave. Elem.; [occ.] Manage Home for the Elderly; [memb.] A.A.R.P., William Memorial C.O.G.I.C.; [oth. writ.] Several poems, and a book in progress (my autobiography); [pers.] I enjoy playing the piano and writing lyrics to my personal styles. Rhythm and blues jazz and gospel; [a.] Sacramento, CA

MARTIN, ERIC ALLEN
[b.] October 11, 1974, Davenport, IA; [p.] Phillip and Ellen Martin; [ed.] High School Diploma at Davenport North High School, Davenport, IA; [occ.] I am in the United States Navy working as a Gunner's Mate; [hon.] None Poetical; [pers.] My personal belief is that apathy and procrastination are the thieves of creativity, so don't put off writing down what's on your mind or it may be stolen and never returned.; [a.] Pearl Harbor, HI

MARTINEZ, BOB G.
[b.] June 7, 1949, New Mexico; [p.] Mrs. Mary Jane Martinez; [m.] Annette E. Martinez, February 10, 1973; [ch.] Lita - 19; [ed.] North High School in '68; [occ.] Security Guard at The Denver Merchandise Mart; [memb.] Distinguished Member of National Library of Poetry, Mile High Poetry Society, Columbine Poets of Colo., National Federation of Poets; [hon.] Honored to be published in over 25 National Anthologies, currently: 14 Editor's Choice Awards; [oth. writ.] "My time To Rhyme" a journey through my life from 1949 to 1994 (302 pgs) in an unbroken single poem...also "Side tracks," a compilation of 45 of my poems.; [pers.] With lines upon lines on every aspect breed words of our pines ...moments to reflect.; [a.] Denver, CO

MARTINO JR., R. J.
[pen.] R. J. Martino Jr.; [b.] April 17, 1966, Long Island, NY; [p.] R. J. Martino Sr. and Carol Ann Venezia; [m.] Robin Lee Martino, October 22, 1993; [ch.] Jacqueline Rose, Nicholas Paul; [ed.] Commack H/S South, Community College of the Air Force; [occ.] Federal Gov. - Civil Service; [memb.] NY Air Guard - 274th Combat Comm Sq.; [hon.] Operation Desert Storm Service Medal; [pers.] Since the beginning of time, mankind has been conquered and divided over religious convictions but in the end we'll be united by common spirituality and belief in one God. -R.J.; [a.] Selden, Long Island, NY

MARVEL, QUERITA
[b.] September 28, 1935, Hartman, AR; [p.] John William and Jessie Jane Scott; [m.] W. S. Marvel; [ch.] Joseph and Patricia; [ed.] Gray Ridge High and Nursing Training; [occ.] Retired. Before retiring I did nursing and trained aides; [hon.] My honors are knowing God and worshiping Him. My awards are the many blessings He has bestowed upon me.; [oth. writ.] Several poems published in newspapers. A play for our church and little readings for children to read in church.; [pers.] My goal is to try to help put a stop to child abuse and help people to turn to God instead of abusing their children; to help them see that a child is a precious gift from God.; [a.] Gray Ridge, MO

MASON, CAROLYN CAIVANO
[b.] May 13, 1952, Astoria, NY; [p.] Marie and Samuel Caivano; [m.] Joseph Mason; [ch.] Dustin, Samara, Joseph Jr.; [ed.] BA: St. Joseph's College, MA: Suny at Stony Brook; [occ.] Teacher, Oxhead Rd. Elementary School, Centereach, NY; [pers.] "We can do not great things, only small things with great love."

MASON, LARRY M.
[b.] September 23, 1977, Winchester, VA; [p.] Lester and Helen Mason; [ed.] John Handley High School, Lord Fairfax Community College; [hon.] Honorable Mention in the Regional Science Fair; [oth. writ.] Three Births, published in the school's magazine Images, currently writing a novel entitled Felis.; [pers.] The answer is the question and the question is the answer.; [a.] Winchester, VA

MASON, THOMAS JEFFERY
[pen.] Jeff Mason; [b.] October 23, 1961, Springfield, TN; [m.] Renee Evans Mason, July 25, 1987; [ch.] Hunter Evan (Sept '94), Trevor Allen (Oct '96); [ed.] A.S. Degree in Business Data Processing, Nashville Tech '85, Suma Cum Laude, pursuing B.S. at MTSU; [occ.] Computer System Mgr., Willis Corroon Corp. Nashville, TN; [hon.] Nominated to 1977 USA - Today all USA Academic Team for Outstanding Academic Excellence; [oth. writ.] Technical Articles in "Network World"; [pers.] Passion Inspires.; [a.] Mount Juliet, TN

MASTERSON, JACK NEIL
[b.] December 31, 1951, Tell City, IN; [p.] D. J. Masterson and Lorena L. (Snyder) Masterson; [m.] Barbara Jean (Batie) Masterson, July 28, 1973; [ch.] John Amos, Derikalee, Breanna Dey; [ed.] Tell City High, Lockyear Business College; [occ.] Correctional Officer, Indiana Department of Corrections; [oth. writ.] Several poems and contemporary Christmas songs.; [pers.] I believe that the youth are the future of our world but they need guidance. Most of all love and strong family atmosphere.; [a.] Tell City, IN

MATHUS, MINDI
[b.] May 5, 1983, Peoria, IL; [p.] Pam Mathus, and the late Robert Mathus; [ed.] Pleasant Hill Grade School; [occ.] Student; [a.] Peoria, IL

MATTHEW, VIRGINIA
[pen.] Vickie Matthew; [b.] February 27, 1926, Chicago; [p.] Harry and Mildred Davis; [m.] Robert G. Matthew, July 6, 1963; [ch.] James P. Reilly (From 1st marriage); [ed.] Grammar School; [occ.] Retired; [memb.] WOTM - "Women of The Moose" #325; [oth. writ.] Just poems now and then, when they come to me, so far; [pers.] I like to listen to my tapes and draw, I like making a lot of seasonal cards and I try to do the poetry in them, but I have to be in the mood, it has to flow.; [a.] Berwyn, IL

MATTHEWS, DONNA
[b.] July 4, 1965, Laconia, NH; [p.] Linda Matthews, Edward Matthews III; [m.] Divorced 1993; [ch.] Jennifer Amy, Christopher Thomas; [ed.] Belmont High School, Hesser College Manchester; [occ.] Nursing; [oth. writ.] Several poems never been published personal collection for friends and family; [pers.] My writings reflect a lot of my personality I write from experiences in my life, often about past romances. Many of my writings are to people close to me, a personal statement of how I feel.; [a.] Belmont, NH

MAZUR, GLORIA DEE
[b.] April 15, 1965, Winfield, KS; [p.] Claude and Rose Giddens; [m.] Walter Mazur; [ch.] Edwin Kurt, Andrew Gage, Thomas Kyle; [pers.] I have no degrees or special writing skills. I write what I feel in my heart, people have to reflect on the past memories and remember, so they can pass on memories to the future generation.; [a.] Wellington, KS

MCALARY, DEBRA
[b.] May 3, 1979, Englewood, NJ; [p.] Anne McAlary; [ed.] Holy Family Academy; [occ.] A Senior in High School; [oth. writ.] A collection of unpublished poems.; [pers.] My writings are expressions of personal feelings and emotions.; [a.] Bayonne, NJ

MCALPINE, PEGGY
[pen.] Peg; [b.] June 20, 1962, Millinocket, ME; [p.] Alton Russell Jones, Evelyn Lenora Jones;

[m.] Douglas Green, December 30, 1995; [ch.] Shelly Lenora, Robert Dewayne, Cad Everette; [pers.] I dedicate this poem in the memory of my father, Alton Russell Jones. There's so many things I could say about him. He was the kindest man I ever know and a wonderful father. I never had the chance to tell him how proud I was to be his daughter. This poems says everything he meant to me. I want to thank him for helping me put my feelings into words. I thank the heavens above for making him my father. I love you Dad.; [a.] Bristol, NH

MCBRIDE, DANIELLE H.
[b.] March 10, 1975, Woodbury, NJ; [pers.] A reflection of my emotions is what has always influenced my writing. I thank God for blessing me with the ability to effectively put my thoughts and feelings into words. I especially thank Him for guiding me to a truly special person, the one who most inspires me, Gary Edward Kramer Jr.; [a.] Blackwood, NJ

MCBRIDE, LUCIA
[pen.] Lucy McBride; [ed.] B.S., Graduate Work; [memb.] National League of American Pen Woman, Recipient of several Merit Awards; [oth. writ.] Yes

MCCANN, MILDRED
[b.] March 8, 1959, Hartford; [p.] Dennis McCann, Inez Arthur; [ch.] Takima, Dyron, Akia McCann; [ed.] 1977 Graduated from Little Arsenal School, Junior High Lewis Fox Middle School Hartford High School, Hartford High, Annex Public High School; [occ.] Work at Boston, Market Restaurant; [hon.] I made Honor Roll at Hartford Public High School the three years I was there finishing High School. I went to Trinity College upward bound school during the summers of 1975-1977.; [oth. writ.] Am I My Brother's Keeper; [pers.] There is something on the back side; please read it put it first with my notes there are things that are unknown to mankind that only with the word of God and the holy spirit can we know about life it's all in the spirit within all of us. Confession is good for your soul.; [a.] Hartford, CT

MCCARTHY, EDWARD J.
[pen.] Budd Mack; [b.] February 16, 1926, New York; [ed.] B.A. (Psych) Univ. of Wyoming 1963, one year graduate study in Social Work at Suny, Albany, NY; [occ.] Retired; [memb.] Southern Poetry Assoc., V.F.W., D.A.V. and Am. Legion; [hon.] Army Medals for Staying Alive in WW II; [oth. writ.] A novel, Undaunted Spirits, by Budd Mack - out of print.; [pers.] I try to transform words into images in the mind like lead into gold.; [a.] Lake City, FL

MCCARTHY, MICHAEL MAURICE
[pen.] Michaias Bonus; [b.] March 27, 1946, Akron, OH; [p.] Booker T. McCarthy, Ella Mae N. McCarthy; [m.] Lula Francis McCarthy, July 11, 1969; [ch.] Denise, Michael, Christina, Emmanuel; [ed.] Barberton High, Tillmook Conservation Center,: International Data Center, Mansfield Business College, NRI McGraw-Hill School of Photography, ICS School of Law Enforcement, Hickok Technical Drafting.; [occ.] Wild-life Photographer, Wild-life Conservation; [memb.] Disabled American Veterans, Veterans of Foreign Wars, Vietnam Veterans of America, American Legion, National Rifle Association,: North American Hunting Club, Smithsonian Associates,; [hon.] Booker T. McCarthy, Ella Mae McCarthy. Anglo Lambo, and Michelle Lambo, Dan Gookin, Michael Eugene Batties, NRI Achievement Award, International Freelance Photographers Organization, Ambassador Bible College Certificate, Certificate of Membership-National Press Card Association; [oth. writ.] Three is no other writing's, send in just this one poem of understanding ones own self within space and time.; [pers.] My love for God's law so I try to have understanding with myself and with my follow-man. I believe that God so love all of us as that he bless us all with understanding of all things. So that we as a human-kind may learn to love each other. With kindness and full understanding of his law's for us all. My prayer are for one an all of the human-kind.; [a.] Akron, OH

MCCAULEY, CARLISA
[b.] October 9, 1966, Evarts, KY; [p.] Frances Shirley, Bill King; [m.] Joseph McCauley; [ch.] Trenton James, Chanlin Jubill; [oth. writ.] I have various other writings, although none has been published.; [pers.] I strive on emotions in all of my poetic writings.; [a.] Scottsburg, IN

MCCLELLAN, BIRDIE B.
[b.] October 30, 1918, Marshall, TX; [p.] Claude and Della Price; [m.] David McClellan, December 20, 1936; [ed.] B.S. Degree Wiley College Marshall, TX. Med ETU Commerce, Texas, Additional study USC Los Angeles, CA; [occ.] Retired Educator Program. Coordinator 1st CME Church; [memb.] First Christian Methodist Evangelist Church Sigma Gamma Rho Sorority Inc. - Girl Scouts of America NABSA - National Assoc. Black Ed.; [hon.] Teacher of the year. Science Fair Winner 1st Prize (1st Grade) class; [oth. writ.] Growing up in Texas. "The Christmas Story." The legend of the Christmas Candle litany of dedication to pastor at first CME church.; [pers.] My writing reflects my feelings and interest in my profession, especially teaching and training young minds, to become worth while citizens of the world.; [a.] Dallas, TX

MCCLUDE, SHAWN
[pen.] 187; [b.] January 19, 1976, Israel; [p.] Lynne and Pat McClude; [ed.] High School; [occ.] Writer; [oth. writ.] Short stories and many many poems.; [pers.] I never learned or was taught how to write poetry. I write what I feel and what I think a lot of other people feel. This is my form of expression.; [a.] Tempe, AZ

MCCLUNG, CARRIE
[b.] December 31, 1979, Sacramento, CA; [ed.] Richard King High School, Corpus Christi Texas; [occ.] Student; [oth. writ.] Poems in a literary magazine for school; [pers.] My poems are from the innermost part of my soul.; [a.] Corpus Christi, TX

MCCOBB, CHARLOTTE L.
[pen.] Charlotte Lee; [p.] Mary and Jack Lee; [ch.] Jason McCobb; [oth. writ.] Work in progress: inspirational article and book on Traumatic Brain Injury Recovery.; [pers.] Star is dedicated to Henry Paul of Black Hawk, a country music group. He is a great artist and friend who has inspired and brought out the lost writer within me. I am grateful.; [a.] Sarasota, FL

MCCONNELL, BELINDA GAYLE
[b.] June 8, 1958; [pers.] This poem is dedicated to my sister "Gigi". We were separated for 17 years, using S.S. # she was able to locate me. She wrote me a letter when in front of the mailbox she was undecided whether this was a good idea to try and get in touch with me. An elderly gentleman walked up and could not help but notice the concerned and confused look on her face - well, he inquired and she told him the story of our separation and her fear of rejection. Upon hearing this he asked, "May I see the letter" she handed it to him, he turned dropped it in the mailbox and stated, "There, it's done," smiled and walked away... thank God for this gentleman...Three days later I received the letter. The same day I called my long lost little sister - one month later I met her at the airport - 4 months later she moved to Maryland - 700 miles she moved with no hesitation - looking forward to making up for those 17 years we lost. We went from children to adults, "Caterpillars to Butterflies". I'd like to give a special thanks to "The Gentleman" who supported Gigi, and my good friend "Lori" who supported me!; [a.] Glen Burnie, MD

MCCOY, SHIRLEY
[b.] January 24, 1951, Nashville, TN; [p.] Mary Dotson, Leslie Dotson; [m.] Carl Edward McCoy, May 11, 1991; [ch.] Kelly Marie Harris, (Stepsons) Michael Jess McCoy, Carl Edward McCoy II, (Grandson) Vincent Lennon Carter Harris; [ed.] North High, Draughons College; [occ.] Financial Representative with "The Associates"; [memb.] National MS Society; [oth. writ.] Several poems in the works; [pers.] This poem was written through the eyes of a six years old child. I enjoy the works of the Romantic Poets.; [a.] Hendersonville, TN

MCCRAY, DIANE E.
[b.] July 16, 1956, Jacksonville, FL; [p.] Donella and Arthur McCray; [ch.] Latisia and Patreace McCray; [ed.] Masters degree in Educational Leadership; [occ.] Elementary Teacher; [memb.] Coalition against Literacy, Teachers of America, Student Enhancement committee.; [hon.] President's List, Valedictorian, graduated Summa Cumlaude at the top of class; [pers.] My desire is to continue to express and convert the negativeness of life into positiveness through poetry.; [a.] Jacksonville, FL

MCDONALD, ALEXANDER L.
[pen.] Alex McDonald; [b.] October 16, 1986, Wilmington, DE; [p.] John S. McDonald, Patti P. McDonald; [ed.] Tower Hill School, Wilmington, DE Baltz Elementary Elsmere, DE; [occ.] Ten years old, 4th grade student, Musician (drums allochanter), Artist; [memb.] Spanish Club; [hon.] Student of the week Achievements in Math, Achievements in Social Studies; [oth. writ.] "My Best Friend", "Harry Had A Harry Horse"; [a.] Wilmington, DE

MCDONALD, MICHELLE
[pen.] Michelle McDonald; [b.] June 27, 1983, Good Samaritan Hospital in San Jose, CA; [p.] Robert and Mary McDonald; [ed.] Evergreen Elementary, Chaboya Middle School; [occ.] Babysitter; [hon.] W.A.C. Writing Award, block letter in sports, 4th place award for discus in a county track meet, honor society for three years (5, 6, 7); [oth. writ.] Writing across the curriculum award (W.A.C., one of 7 out of whole school) and I am writing a poetry book.; [pers.] My writing is based on real life situations that have or will happen in this devastating world we live in. And I hope I can spread the message to teenagers like me.; [a.] San Jose, CA

MCDONALD, WENDY
[b.] July 16, 1981, New Orleans, LA; [p.] John and Jeanne McDonald; [ed.] Tomball High School; [occ.] Student; [memb.] Houston Repertoire Ballet Company; [oth. writ.] Several poems published, one short story, in local newspapers and literary magazines.; [a.] Houston, TX

MCDONNELL, KELLY
[b.] April 7, 1969, Philadelphia; [p.] Brian and Donna McDonnell; [ed.] St. Basil Academy, Allentown College of St. Francis De Sales; [occ.] Owner, Creature Comforts Pet Sitting Service; [hon.] Honorable Mention Scholarship Writing Awards (Junior Poetry); [a.] Coral Springs, FL

MCFALL, BENNIE RUTH
[pen.] Bennie Ruth; [b.] August 9, 1947, Houston, TX; [p.] Stella Deque Saugia and Clint Savaya; [m.] William Curtis McFall, January 19, 1976; [occ.] Housekeeping Supervisor at a small resort in Vero Beach, FL; [hon.] I've had a small article written

about me in a magazine called, Vacation Ownership World. The interest was drawn because of the way I've set up and operate my department at work; [oth. writ.] I have penned my thoughts quite often in small spiral tablets, because at any given time the thoughts start to flow, and they tend to bring a smile to my face, and I pray, to the face to others.; [pers.] After meeting myself, and searching though my thoughts, my beliefs, my successes, my failures, I can relate to the imperfections of my fellowman, and find some beauty in all that I see.

MCGUINNESS, MIKE
[pen.] Lorcan D. McGuinness; [b.] July 7, 1948, Dublin, Ireland; [p.] Ellen, James; [m.] Valerie Ann, April 14, 1979; [ch.] Kristen, Michelle, Lorraine, Lisa, David; [ed.] North Strand Technical College, Dublin, Ireland; [occ.] Electric Train Repairman; [pers.] Interest - NFL Denver Broncos Fan - Country Music - writing.

MCNULTY, JOSEPHINE M.
[pen.] Jo Bowler; [b.] October 9, 1939, Chester, PA; [p.] Margaret E. and Patrick T. Bowler; [m.] Divorced, October 7, 1967; [ch.] Four (two of each); [ed.] Graduate with Masters in Ed. 1996 from Cambridge College; [occ.] Transcriber; [memb.] Affiliated with Amherst Writers and Artists - Amherst, MA, Sligo, Ireland; [pers.] To improve writing style and technique, to try as many forms of stories, in perfecting craft. Also, striving to teach writing as a healing therapy, which I'd like to teach to various groups.; [a.] Springfield, MA

MEADE, MRS. JERRY
[pen.] Jerry; [b.] May 26, 1925, Louisiana; [p.] Leslie and Alice McClure; [m.] John Meade (Deceased), August 18, 1944; [ch.] Donna Millsaps and Bonita Altoveros; [ed.] High School; [occ.] Homemaker; [memb.] Associate U.M.W.A. Ocean View Assembly of God; [hon.] Being a Mother, Grandmother and Great Grandmother; [oth. writ.] Unpublished folder containing poems titled A Village Of Verse. Sections, Dreams In Flight, Pages Of Praise, Leaves Of Love, A Treasure Of Thoughts, Flowers Of Fun; [pers.] Today is it the golden tomorrow of yesterday, or will be the forgotten yesterday of tomorrow.; [a.] Norfolk, VA

MECKES, FAITH LYNN
[b.] January 26, 1954, Ethiopia; [p.] Rev. Theodore and Florence Meckes; [ed.] Elementary School - Papua/New Guinea, High School - Melbourne, Australia; Nursing 17 yrs., throughout Australia, Travel Sales Manger - Pacific Islands; [occ.] International Trader; [pers.] To take the challenges of life head on, and to achieve each one to the best of my ability.; [a.] Blakeslee, PA

MELE, AMANDA LEIGH MARIE
[b.] November 23, 1977, Patchogue, NY; [p.] Linda and James Mele; [ed.] Patchogue - Medford High School, St. Joseph's College; [occ.] College Student; [memb.] Thelma N. Temple Chapter of The National Honor Society of Secondary Schools; [pers.] There are two things that I never forget to remember: the soul has no rainbow if the heart has no tears, and if you don't get it from yourself, where are you gonna get it from?; [a.] Patchogue, NY

MELTON, VIRGINIA
[b.] December 24, 1949, North Carolina; [p.] Lewis and Louise; [m.] Divorced; [ch.] Kimberlee - Daughter; [ed.] Paisley Jr.-Sr. High School, Winston-Salem, NC; Harlem Hospital School of Nursing, New York, NY; Borough of Manhattan Community College, NY; Ultrasound Diagnostic School, White Plains, NY; [occ.] Registered Nurse - Ultrasound Technologist; [oth. writ.] Poems, personal writings - non-published; [pers.] I believe there is good in every living being, and in every situation there is something good, and if we all have faith and trust in the highest "Power" good will overcome evil.; [a.] Louisville, KY

MESSINA, GILDA
[b.] February 17, 1920, Italy; [p.] Both Deceased; [m.] Deceased; [ch.] One son, two daughters; [ed.] Graduated Nursing College Prep., LPN Graduate - R.N. Graduate; [occ.] Retired; [pers.] Always interested in poetry. Teachers graded poetry I wrote with excellent words.; [a.] Bradenton, FL

MEYER, TRESSIE R.
[b.] October 10, 1981, Sedalia, MO; [p.] Ricky Meyer and Teresa D. Watts; [ed.] Camdenton High School, now in 9th grade, looking forward to college; [occ.] Student, Volunteer at local nursing home; [memb.] Spanish Club, National Junior Honor Society, Young American Bowling Alliance, Fellowship of Christian Athletes; [hon.] Language Arts Award (School Award); [pers.] Kelly Dawn is a poem about my sister who died when she was nine days old. She was like an angel to me. This is my first year in high school and I enjoy writing and drawing.; [a.] Belton, MO

MICK, MARILYN
[b.] January 21, 1947, Beloit, KS; [p.] Leo Mick, Dorothy Hoffer; [m.] Jim Palmer; [ch.] Chris Potter; [ed.] Marymount College of Kansas, Kansas State University; [occ.] Integral Educator for Dreamwork; [hon.] Dean's List; [oth. writ.] Many unpublished poems, "Sophia" is presently being published in the anthology, "Ariel," by Mile High Poetry Society.; [pers.] I am dedicated to the task of bringing the creative feminine principle to consciousness on this planet. I have been greatly influenced by Jungian Psychology; [a.] Lincoln, NE

MICKENS, CHARLES
[pen.] Jeremiah Mickens; [b.] August 11, 1971, Baltimore; [p.] Charles Mickens Jr., Deborah Corckett; [m.] Azzure Mickens; [ch.] K'tresha and Kshana Mickens; [cd.] Harbor City, Baltimore City Community College; [occ.] Substitute School Teacher, Actor, Writer and Father, and Husband; [memb.] SAG, Actors Center, People Rising, Baltimore Writers Alliance, Thespians Club Troup 2311; [hon.] 1st Place five hundred dollars cash for poem performed monologue style at Arena Player L.A.B. 7th Annual Talent Competition; [oth. writ.] Book entitled Feel Me and Char Girls should be in book stores and libraries at the end of '97, beginning of '98.; [pers.] I believe my poetry to be inspirational, motivational, entertaining and educational. With poetry you can wipe tears or dry eyes, and in a poem for someone somewhere something special lies.; [a.] Baltimore, MD

MIDDLETON, CHARLES F.
[b.] March 16, 1917, Chester, PA; [p.] Charles F. Middleton Sr. and Mary Bengiser; [m.] Dolores Hill Middleton, September 12, 1942; [ch.] Linda Ann, Charles F. Middleton and James H.; [ed.] M.S. Education, Administration University of Pennsylvania; [occ.] Retired (Public School Teacher); [memb.] NEA (life member) Holy Trinity Lutheran Church, American Red Cross (Vol.), Brandywine Conservancy, Oxford Senior Center, Delaware Co. Institute of Science, Friends of the Caleb Pusey House; [hon.] (VICA) Vocational Industrial Club of America; [oth. writ.] Several poems (unpublished); [pers.] I strive to focus on the gifts of God as manifested in nature, by observation of examples that are so commonplace that we often overlook their true beauty, and their existence.; [a.] Oxford, PA

MIKELEVICIUS, VITA
[b.] April 6, 1973, Chicago, IL; [p.] Stase Mikelevicius and Anthony Mikelevicius; [ed.] Maria High School, Northern Illinois University; [occ.] Job Coach; [hon.] University Honors, English Honors, Golden Key National Honor Society; [pers.] Art is a dog we put on a leash, and when we catch it we're dragged, running behind, trying to keep up with it.; [a.] Hometown, IL

MILLER, ANNE
[b.] September 1924, Saint Louis, MO; [p.] Henry and Gertrude Miller; [ed.] Ursuline Academy, B.S. Physical Ed. Fontbonne College, Clayton, MO, M.A.T. Religion Studies - Webster Univ. Webster Groves, MO, Masters Plus - Theology - St. Louis University, St. Louis, MO; [occ.] Retired - part time substitute teacher, parochial schools; [memb.] Fontbonne Alumnae Ass'n. Margaret Mary Alacoque Spirituality Committee, Webster Univ. Alumnae Ass'n; [hon.] Poem published in "Contemplative Outreach," newsletter, Skit performed at Fontbonne at Eden Theological Seminary as class project between Socrates, Christ, Bonhoeffer and Jesse Jackson, N.D.E.A. Gov't. Grant, Alverno College, Milwaukee, Wis.; [oth. writ.] "And On The Way" ("And On The Way..."), "I Look A Search," "Incomparable Love," "A Psalm for Today," "Now Lifted Up"; [pers.] I have been strongly influenced by the writings of John of the Cross, Theresa of Avila, Cardinal Newman and Francis Thompson. I wish to bring others closer to their true self and their God.; [a.] Saint Louis, MO

MILLER, HEIDI L.
[b.] February 7, 1975, Edmonds, WA; [p.] Kathleen A. Miller and Richard Miller (Divorced Parents); [ed.] Graduated High School 1993, currently attending CC; [occ.] Clerk's Helper at Grocery Store; [pers.] It goes to show that after a hard time you've been through the sky is still blue.; [a.] Santa Ana, CA

MILLER, JOLYN
[b.] June 19, 1964, Berwyn, IL; [p.] Dolores Coyle; [m.] Kurt Miller, February 18, 1989; [ed.] Lakeland College Sheboygan, WI; [oth. writ.] Short stories, poems, songs; [a.] Wheaton, IL

MILLER, KATHLEEN A.
[b.] February 23, 1945, Seattle, WA; [p.] Eileen and Leslie Nelson (Mother Deceased); [ch.] Three daughters, four grandsons, one granddaughter; [ed.] Graduated High School 1963; [occ.] Administrative Officer for the Federal Government (U.S. Small Bus. Administration); [memb.] In my youth I was a member of Blue Birds, Campfire Girls, Job's Daughters; [oth. writ.] Personal Collection only - have not submitted any others for publication; [pers.] All credit and glory to be given to God who inspired the writing. May all those who read it be able to relate and go beyond.; [a.] Santa Ana, CA

MILLER, KWAN
[b.] March 17, 1973, Washington, DC; [p.] Dennis Pender, Annie Miller; [ed.] Howard D. Woodson High, Virginia State University, University of the District of Columbia; [occ.] Library Technician, The Library of Congress, Wash., DC; [memb.] Founders of the Brazilian Institute, Wash., DC, True Deliverance Church of God, Forestville, Maryland; [hon.] Mayor Kelly's Summerworks Monitoring Unit Program, 1994 Virginia State University ROTC, 1992. Intergenerational Conference on Infant Mortality "We Will Make A Difference," 1991 Computational Number Theory Workshop, 1991 H.D. Woodson Chapter Alpha Omega Young Men Association, 1991 Street Law- Student Trial Case Competition, 1991, Baritonist, 1990-1991, Woodson High School Fair, 1990, Tenor, Choir Member, 1985-1990, Certificate of Achievement in Chemistry, Algebra I, Business

and Finance Attendance, Dress Award, 1989-1990, Membership in the national Junior Honor Society, 1988, national History Fair, 1988, Presidential Academic Fitness Award, 1985, Phi Beta Sigma Education Workshop; [oth. Writ.] "Prayer Tower Rescue" - A U.S. Sayings Bond Contest, 1996 "Revelation: My life," My personal journal compositions, 1995-1996. Several poems in the "Phoenix," 1994-1995 "The Flash" a newsletter of the Mayor's Youth Institute, 1989; [pers.] Education is a artistic, cultural, and valuable tool that must be invested within citizens in order to preserve peace, justice, and freedom in modern society.; [a.] Washington, DC

MILLS, DICIE LOUISE
[b.] February 15, 1937, Cleveland, Bradley County; [p.] Ruby and Frank Crumbley; [m.] James Robert Mills, February 27, 1954; [ch.] Keith and Karen Mills; [ed.] Elementary 1-8 at Blythe and Prospect Schools, High School 9-12 (GED) Bradley High School however more school, attended Cleveland State Community College...took office skills.; [occ.] Retired; [oth. writ.] Have written many poems, have written 8 children's books, have written one long manuscript (none of my writings have been published).; [pers.] Most of the poems I have written were personal poems which were written to reflect good in those I wrote about.; [a.] Cleveland, TN

MILLS, ELNORA
[pen.] "Sunshine Girl"; [b.] January 26, 1927, Jess Co., KY; [p.] Luther and Rose Corman; [ch.] Rollie Gene, Edna, Terry and Phyllis; [ed.] Bethel Elementary, Nicholasville High, Wilmore High, Dayton Bible College; [occ.] Retired; [memb.] "Boys Town," Cystic Fibrosis Foundation, National Arbor Day Foundation, Paralyzed Veteran and V.F. Wars Foundation; [hon.] My 3 children and one adopted one are "My Honors and my Awards," plus my friends and God above to guide me.; [oth. writ.] Several writings in local newspaper. Article in "The Message of the Open Bible Churches." And several were read in churches and on the radio.; [pers.] I write my poems and stories as God gives them to me. I stood in a prayer live and prayed that God would help me to say what I wanted too, and I give him all the praise. These I would like to leave as my legacy.; [a.] Nicholasville, KY

MINCH, JUANITA
[pen.] Juanita Minch; [b.] May 16, 1947, Marion, IN; [p.] Mr. and Mrs. Jacob L. Minch; [ed.] Mississinewa High School; [occ.] VA Medical Hospital - Merion Indiana, Nurse's Assistant; [memb.] Holy Family Altar Rosary Society, St. Mary Study Club Holy Family Choir, Spiritual Growth Community #8 at John XXIII Retreat Center; [oth. writ.] Poems, songs, and short stories which I write when attending silent retreats at The John XXIII Center, and also written at my work of a nurse's assistant at the VA Hospital.; [pers.] The poem I submitted, I wrote while listening to a suicidal person. They seemed to be trying to get off an endless road to despair, calling for help.

MITCHELL, BELVA JEAN
[pen.] Bj; [b.] July 29, 1945, Astoria, OR; [p.] Loras and Ann Mitchell; [ed.] St. James High School; [occ.] Assistant Manager - Apartment Complex, Maple Shade, NJ; [memb.] Arm, NJ, Notary Public State of NJ; [hon.] Silva Mind Control Health, NJ; [oth. writ.] Poem - published in local newspaper in the midwest. Soon to be published in the midwest - a book of poems.; [pers.] My writings are based largely on personal experiences. I hope to convey to others with similar experiences that they are not alone, it does get better and life is worth living.; [a.] Maple Shade, NJ

MITCHELL, BETH ANN
[b.] April 7, 1964, Hazel Crest, IL; [p.] Buford Winsett and The Late Beverly Winsett; [m.] Spencer Mitchell, November 26, 1982; [ed.] Cornersville High School; [occ.] Customer Relations Representative; [oth. writ.] I have written several poems, none of which have ever been published.; [pers.] My poems reflect on my feelings and memories. I have on different things that have happened or will happen in my life. My family and friends have influenced me and encouraged me to continue writing.; [a.] Cornersville, TN

MIXON, JACKIE K.
[b.] January 14, 1948, Columbus, MS; [p.] Doyle and Alice Knight; [m.] William P. Mixon, December 23, 1973; [ch.] Jane; [ed.] Northwest Jr. College Phil Campbell, Ala; [occ.] Homemaker and Keeper; [pers.] The poem Bill, Sam and Joe show how divided our country was on Vietnam. People of all walks of life found ways not to go, while others went and gave their all. I pray if war comes again, we will go as a united nation or we will all stay home.; [a.] Sulligent, AL

MODICA, ANTOINE E.
[pen.] Antoine E. Modica; [b.] June 25, 1968, Oakland, CA; [p.] Robert and Leatrice Banks; [m.] Dori Estrella-Modica, January 1998; [ch.] Antoine II, Jalen Maurice, Kayla Yasmine; [ed.] Healdsburgh High, Santa Rosa Jr. College; [occ.] Retail Sales; [memb.] San Francisco Folk Musicians Association; [oth. writ.] Several unpublished songs and poems; [pers.] I believe that all men are equal.; [a.] Santa Rosa, CA

MONTAGUE, RAE E.
[b.] August 9, 1911, Washington, DC; [p.] Walter and Maude Hyson; [m.] Divorced; [ch.] Tow children; [ed.] Dunbar High School, Miner Teachers College, University of the District of Columbia, Wash. DC; [occ.] Retired, Formerly Elementary Teacher, Warrenton, VA, Voucher Clerk, Federal Gov't, DC Sub-Teacher, DC; [memb.] National Association of Negro Business and Professional Women's Clubs, Inc. (Century Club Unit Senior Member); [hon.] United Methodist Women's Appreciation Award, 1993; [oth. writ.] I wrote a poem for each employee when he/she retired from our Federal Agency Unit.; [pers.] Poetry is an expression of beauty you see in persons, places and things. I've been composing poems since I was twelve years old.; [a.] Washington, DC

MONTGOMERY, SUSAN
[b.] September 12, 1954, Chicago, IL; [p.] Alice and Arthur Jones; [m.] Michael Montgomery; [ch.] Jessica Christine; [occ.] Vice President, Finance Hilman Inc. New Jersey

MOONEY, KEVIN P.
[b.] June 15, 1960, Dorchester, MA; [p.] Led Mooney, Katherine Mooney; [ed.] Wentworth Institute of Technology; [occ.] Associate Civil Engineer; [hon.] American Society of Civil Engineers Home Walker Award, Magna Cum Laude, Dean List

MOORE, ANDRE ALVIN
[pen.] Mr. Poet; [b.] July 28, 1954, Chicago, IL; [p.] Vernell Perkins Moore, William Bridson; [ed.] B.A. Sociology; [occ.] 1st and 2nd grade School Teacher, at Moore Christian Academy; [oth. writ.] Author of the soon to be released children's book "Little Tree" Published by Common Wealth Publications - Edmonton, Alberta, Canada.; [pers.] I believe if you put something out in life you must at some point in time get something back, which completes the circle of life.; [a.] Lancaster, CA

MOORE, ANNA MARIE J.
[b.] December 8, 1982, Atlanta, GA; [p.] Matthew and Pauline Moore; [ed.] 8th Grade 1996-97; [occ.] Student; [hon.] Honor student; [pers.] I would like to dedicate this poem to my grandfather Richard A. Moore.; [a.] Jasper, GA

MOORE, ERRILL
[b.] December 11, 1945, Los Angeles; [oth. writ.] None, my first poem; [pers.] Emotionally motivated to write as a Eulogy for Ercell Mathews my foster mother. Hoping this will touch the hearts of those who read it, and give enlightenment to those who believe "blood is always thicker than water."; [a.] Los Angeles, CA

MOREIN, KATE
[pen.] Kate Morein; [b.] May 2, 1980, Orange, CA; [p.] Danett and Ron Morein; [ed.] 11th Grade; [occ.] Student; [hon.] Science and Math Awards in School; [oth. writ.] Journaling, personal poetry, magic - adventure stories, twister-novel version, yosemite novel and in progress - nothing published as of yet.; [pers.] Writing is really important to me, if I don't write, I'll go insane. My loved ones are my whole life, and I love my home and family. I'm a homebody. I like to have as much fun as I possibly can.; [a.] Long Beach, CA

MORENO, ANDREA
[b.] June 6, 1975, San Jose, CA; [p.] Camelia and David Moreno; [ed.] Independence High School, Evegreen Valley College; [memb.] Enlace Program; [oth. writ.] This is the first poem I've ever written which was certified as a semi-finalist.; [pers.] In my opinion poetry is a writing of creative thoughts. Express yourself on paper.; [a.] San Jose, CA

MORI, HAZEL W.
[b.] May 9, 1909, Erie, PA; [p.] Claude Austin Weed and Myrtle Salmon Weed; [m.] Prudencio P. Mori (Deceased, 1991), 1945; [ch.] Preble and Paul; [ed.] BA Genever College 1928 advanced study - Edinboro U. (Math) am Lit (U. of Pittsburgh at Erie, PA. Econ and History - U. of Washington, Seattle; [occ.] Retired, area director for ILWU - PMA Benefit Funds. Poets of the Vineyard, Santa Rosa, CA, Baha'i Faith; [memb.] Phi Alpha Theta (History Honorary) U of Washington Chapter, (Seattle) second prize Traditional Poetry Sonuma County Fair 1996; [oth. writ.] Books, prickles and plums 1989 (poetry) a slice of the loaf, 1990 (prose - biographical) Life has never been too grim for me to chuckle, raise my chin, and puckle in to harvest laughter.; [pers.] First publication poetry at age 10, college A.B. 19, high school taught for four years (included coaching basketball and drama) secretary to Marine Survey or for Norwegian vessels repaired in Seattle, Area Director for 20 years for health and pension benefits in the longshore industry, manager for 20 years of morisel Enterprison, while resident in the Philippines when my Filipino husband died in 1991 I returned to U.S.; [a.] Santa Rosa, CA

MORRIS, CAROL LYNN
[b.] October 13, 1949, Minneapolis, MN; [p.] Pauline and Carlon Morris; [ed.] High School Valley, Santa Anna College - CA Professional College 1973; [occ.] Back Office Surgical Nurse M.A.; [hon.] 4.0 G.P.A; [oth. writ.] Poem, "Of Dreams of Wonder" in book - fields of gold...poem "Through Ageless Time" in book...morning song; [pers.] I dedicate this poem to my loving mother, Mrs. Pauline N. Morris of Santa Ana, CA whose Christian faith reflected and inspired my writing, and my life. "In Memory"...1915-1996 (July) "Until We Meet Again Mom..."; [a.] Newport Beach, CA

MORRIS, DONNA M.
[pen.] Donna Constantine; [b.] March 12, 1961, Mobile, AL; [p.] Audrey Constantine, Harold Constantine; [ch.] Christopher Brian Morris; [ed.] Ben C. Rain High School, Bishop State Community

College; [occ.] Monitor Technician, Mobile Infirmary Medical Center; [pers.] I have been greatly influenced by Tobie Day and Carol Kyser. Thank you both for letting me be me.; [a.] Mobile, AL

MOSBY, TYRAH K.
[pen.] Tyrah Khalaji (ha-lay-ye); [b.] March 25, 1981, Oskaloosa, IA; [p.] Wayne and Denise Mosby; [ed.] Ben Franklin prep - Elementary School, St. Margaret Mary, Hbg., Middle School, John Harris, Hbg High School; [memb.] Vice President of International club, band front, track; [oth. writ.] Are kept privately in my poem book.; [pers.] All my writings are based on my life. Events that happened to me. I hope people could related to my writings and understand where I'm coming from.; [a.] Harrisburg, PA

MOSS, ELIZABETH OVERTON
[b.] November 2, 1927, Sumner, CO; [p.] Lee and Nellie Overton; [m.] Benjamin J. Moss, November 30, 1947; [ch.] Four Sons - Mike, Don, David and Bill Moss; [ed.] Graduate of Gallatin High School, plus 12 yrs private study of music; [occ.] Home Maker, Retired Piano Teacher; [memb.] Chairperson of Benevolent Program in Gallatin Church of Christ for 18 yrs.; [oth. writ.] I have written several poems of human interest such as Sunday Morning, Going Home at Christmas, Our Soldier, etc. I also have written inspirational poems such as, His Beauty, Unworthy, Lord.; [pers.] I strive to convey to my four sons, and their families, the need to live a Godly life and show compassion for those less fortunate than they.; [a.] Gallatin, TN

MOSZISIK, ALLA
[b.] July 11, 1982, Fortlauderdale; [p.] Diana Moszisik, Ben Guzman; [ed.] Forest Lake Educational Center, 7-day Adventist, Private; [occ.] Student, 8th grade; [oth. writ.] Other poems and short stories.; [pers.] Do your best, don't set limits, and reach for your dreams!; [a.] Longwood, FL

MOUNT, DIANNA
[pen.] Dee Wynne; [b.] April 15, 1945, Napa, CA; [p.] Darvin Mount, Joyce Mount; [m.] Divorced; [ch.] Kelly, Danny, Eliz, April, Deanna; [occ.] Special Packs Co-ordinator (22 yrs.) Robert Mondavi Winery - Napa, CA; [memb.] Napa-Solano WIBC (Bowling) Calif. State 600 Club (Bowling), National 600 Club (Bowling); [oth. writ.] Unpublished verses, children's story poems.; [pers.] I enjoy writing, and do so whenever the spirit moves me. I also do my own Birthday and Special Occasion cards for family and friends, and have a passion for reading. My favorite authors are M.H. Clark, J. Daily, R. Cook among others too numerous to mention.

MRAZ, MELISSA KAY
[pen.] (Missy); [b.] August 29, 1974, Gallup, NM; [p.] Frank and Lavern Mraz; [ed.] Gallup High, Eastern NM College; [occ.] Rancher, New Mexico and Arizona

MULLENNIX, REBECCA E.
[b.] August 2, 1951, Alabama; [p.] Joyce Thomas Harris/Step Dad Ewel L. Harris; [m.] William Robert Mullennix, June 24, 1972; [ch.] Victoria, Dawn and Amber Grandchildren Ben and Katie Stubbs; [ed.] Lithonia High School and Transferred to Stone Mountain High; [occ.] Housewife and Mother Disabled with Muscular Dystrophy and (Disease); [hon.] Golden Poet Award 1990 and 1991 for my poem "Tubular Pain", Library of poetry; [oth. writ.] Other poem's in several Anthologies. Poem "Silence" to come out in beginnings. Poem "Tubular Pain" came out in Mists of Enchantment. Poem "I'm Afraid" to come out in A Delicate Balance. And others I would like to publish before my death for my children.; [pers.] Never say forever, cuz' forever never last.....; [a.] Smyrna, GA

MUNDELL, GROVE
[b.] July 1, 1964, Kansas; [ed.] Business BA WTSU; [occ.] Marketing Director, Livenote Inc; [oth. writ.] WWW. Mediacity. Com/Grover; [pers.] I strive to be a big tipper.; [a.] Philadelphia, PA

MUNGRO, MURRAY EUGENE
[pen.] JR; [b.] June 14, 1957, Maiden, NC; [p.] Bishop C. D. Mungro and the late Emma Mae Mungro; [m.] Linda Gail Mungro, November 23, 1990; [ch.] Mario Ikard, Candice Ikard, Shaun Ikard and Marcus Ikard; [ed.] Newton Conover High School; [occ.] Ethan Allen Maiden, NC; [memb.] Grace Temple Holiness Church; [hon.] Deacon, and the only Award I've ever received was from God, Freedom; [oth. writ.] My little family, home church poems write other poems for people.; [pers.] I look at the world today, at young kids. I wish there was something we all could do to help. And there is: pray for a change to come before Jesus comes. I feel and cry for the world.; [a.] Lincolnton, NC

MUNSELL, DOROTHEA
[b.] February 14, 1923, Coblenz, Germany; [p.] George and Gertrude Wagstrom; [m.] William O. Munsell, October 14, 1944; [ch.] Claudia and Eric; [ed.] Advanced studies in History, Literature and Philosophy; [occ.] Retired Computer Operator; [pers.] I strive to state concisely and tersely attitudes toward current social situations. I am influenced by Taoist E. and other mystical philosophies.; [a.] Austin Town, OH

MUNSEY, SYLVIA
[b.] July 10, 1939, Brunswick, ME; [p.] Alice and Linwood Kaler; [m.] Clarence Munsey, March 16, 1967; [ch.] Danny, Randy, Shari, Chucky and Billy; [ed.] Brunswick High; [occ.] At home; [memb.] Maine Country Music, Midcoast Hospital Aux, DECMA Country Music, East Brunswick Baptist Church; [hon.] 1989-1994 Song Writer for Maine Personal Letter from President George Bush have won several Song Writers Contests throughout Maine; [oth. writ.] Sylvia's songs and poems have been in newspaper and are still being sung by country music singers such as Hee Haw's Lulu Roman and Grand Ole Opry's Jack Greene.; [pers.] I am very impressed by good poems that relate to the gospel.

MURCHISON, SANDI
[b.] August 29, 1938, Kewanee, IL; [p.] Dave and Jane Murchison; [ed.] B.S. in Educ. - Illinois State University, M.S. in Educ. Univ. of Colorado (Boulder), 50+ hours above M.S. - Various Univ.; [occ.] Retired Teacher - VISTA (Domestic Peace Corps) in Literacy in Correctional Facilities (Youth); [memb.] American Assoc. of Univ. Women, N.O.W., Beta Sigma Phi, Episcopal Church, Certified Literacy Volunteer of America, Retired Teachers of America; [hon.] Woman of the Year (Beta Sigma Phi), three Awards for work in Literacy; [oth. writ.] Newspaper (press releases, essays); [pers.] The poem, "David," was inspired by a wonderful man! He just happens to have the same name as my dad! He is my "muse!"; [a.] Aurora, IL

NAGLE, PHYLLIS M.
[b.] May 31, 1932, Lockport, NY; [p.] Walter and Ethel Goldberg; [m.] Franklin C. Nagle (Deceased), April 3, 1981; [ed.] High School; [occ.] Retired; [memb.] Various Wildlife Organizations; [oth. writ.] Book called "Land of Enchantment." Not published because I did not know how to accomplish it. The book is on my 5 week Safari to Africa in 1968. My poem was at the end.; [pers.] The wild beauty of Africa is breathtaking the vast Serengeti plains to Mt. Kilimanjaro to small game reserves. Once you have been there - you leave a part of yourself there. It is always with you.; [a.] Largo, FL

NAIRN, THOMAS F.
[b.] March 25, 1937, Washington, DC; [p.] Walter Nairn and Margaret Nairn; [m.] Jo Ann F. Serowick (Nairn), February 15, 1958; [ch.] Thomas Jr., James and Susan, Grandchildren: TJ, Kevin and Christine; [ed.] Anacostia High, Ben Franklin University, International Correspondence School; [occ.] Lead Cost Analyst, Potomac Electric Power Co.; [oth. writ.] Several poems not published.; [pers.] I have had two heart transplants and with the help of my family and friends I have led a fairly normal life. My inspiration to write poetry comes from my family and friends.; [a.] Huntingtown, MD

NANCE, JANE
[m.] Dean Nance; [ch.] 3 - Steve, Craig (Deceased), and Darrell; [ed.] High School; [occ.] Retired - Housewife; [memb.] American Baptist, Women Ministries, First Baptist Church of Chrisman, IL, The Enhancers Club, purpose is to keep, improve, and beautify the city. We are in limbo at present we put Flower Barrells around the Square; [hon.] Two Blue Ribbons for Watercolor Paintings and 1 for an Oil Painting; [oth. writ.] Making my own Christmas Cards with my original poems inside. Writing poems for the church. Two poems for the schools honoring the teachers.; [pers.] My talent for writing poetry is a gift from the Lord and I just want to use it according to His will.; [a.] Chrisman, IL

NAVIN, KEVIN M.
[pen.] Kevin Michael Navin; [b.] September 24, 1968, Richmond, VA; [ed.] BGS from Virginia Commonwealth University in Scandinavian and European Studies, graduate work at the University of Karlstad in Sweden; [occ.] Working on a 2nd BS in Political Science at VCH; [memb.] Alumni at Virginia Commonwealth University, Student Union boards at Follo Folkenhogskole in Norway and the International People's College in Denmark; [hon.] Will be attending the University of Copenhagen in Denmark as an individual guest studies student in 1997; [oth. writ.] Have completed a book of poetry and prose entitled - Friends, Lovers and Other Mistakes - and currently looking for a publishers. I would say it is very 90's.; [pers.] Pessimist one who, when he has the choice of two evils, chooses both.; [a.] Richmond, VA

NEGRI, JOHN F.
[b.] June 11, 1952, Manhattan, NY; [p.] John A. and Ann Negri; [ch.] Deanne, Jason and Sean; [ed.] Associate - Metallurgy, Community College of the Air Force, Bachelor's - Work Force Education, Southern Illinois University; [occ.] Welder; [hon.] National Dean's List, Scholastic Honors; [oth. writ.] Several poems on various subjects, Articles for Air Force newspapers, speeches for awards and graduation ceremonies, Air Force Histories, Lesson plans.; [pers.] I want my readers to feel life, through their own experience, while they read mine. My poems are pure emotions to be felt not just read.; [a.] Hempstead, NY

NELIS, AMANDA KATHLEEN
[b.] June 4, 1985, Atlanta, GA; [p.] Tom Nelis and Kathy King; [ed.] King Springs Elementary, Griffin Middle; [occ.] Sixth Grade Student; [hon.] President's Academic Award. Also, Amanda is in the "Gifted Students" program.; [pers.] I live by one statement: Time will heal. Whenever I feel really bad, I know that in the future I will feel better.; [a.] Smyrna, GA

NELSON, APRIL L.
[pen.] Lynn; [b.] April 15, 1982, Hannibal, MO; [p.] Kurt and Christina Nelson; [ed.] Graduated

Valedictorian of my 8th grade class. Currently a Freshman at Palmyra High School.; [occ.] Full time student; [memb.] 4-H, Palmyra Marching Band, FHA, Zion Lutheran Church; [hon.] American Legion School Award; [oth. writ.] Short stories and many other poems all for personal and family enjoyment, none of which have ever been published.; [pers.] Follow the dreams of your heart and let God be your guide. Thank you to all those who have made this possible.; [a.] Palmyra, MO

NEWMAN, PHYLLIS B.
[b.] June 1, 1957, New Hyde Park, NY; [ed.] BS Accounting from Suny Binghamton, CPA since 1992; [occ.] Internal Revenue Service 15 years - Large Case Manager; [pers.] I continually observe and digest the details of life, through poetry, as well as photography, I'm able to express not just what I see, but how I see it.; [a.] Brooklyn, NY

NEWSOM, TIFFANY
[pen.] Tiffany Newsom; [b.] June 3, 1983, Odessa, TX; [p.] John and Jan Newsom; [ed.] 8th grader at Hood Jr. High School; [memb.] Student Council, Choir; [hon.] Member of all city choir for 2 years, Gifted and Talented Program, A Honor Roll Student, Choir Officer, Rating I in solo and Ensemble.; [oth. writ.] Unpublished poetry selections.; [pers.] Poetry is a very good way to express many different feelings.; [a.] Odessa, TX

NEWTON, JUNE
[pen.] June Newton; [b.] September 7, 1927, Illinois; [p.] Mr. and Mrs. G. Lance; [m.] Warren W. Newton; [ch.] One daughter, Michelle; [ed.] High School; [occ.] Housewife; [memb.] Mt. Vernon Church of Christ; [oth. writ.] Published in Mt. Vernon Newspapers; [pers.] I have deep personal morals, I try to live a Christian life. In most of my work I try to convey these sentiments, perhaps I can teach someone by doing so.; [a.] Mount Vernon, IN

NEWTON, KENNETH W.
[pen.] Ken; [b.] August 13, 1949, Atlanta, GA; [p.] Wm. Paul Newton Sr. and Mary Grace Arnsdorff Newton; [m.] Jacquelyn G. Manning, June 7, 1996; [ch.] Kelsey Marie Newton; [ed.] Valley Forge Military Academy, Sandhills Community College - AA Psychology, Appalachian State University - BS Criminal Justice; [occ.] Officer-Dekalb County Sheriffs Dept. - Atlanta, GA/Instructor-Criminal Justice, Physical Training; [memb.] Southern Criminal Justice Association, North Carolina Criminal Justice Association, U.S. Law Enforcement Coordinating Committee, Vice-Chairman- Lee County, American Red Cross.; [hon.] Who's Who Among America's Teachers - 1994, most outstanding instructor of the year - 1992, James B. Merritt Award for Distinguished Service in the Criminal Justice Field - 1989, Director Basic Law Enforcement Training, Black Belt/Martial Arts - Shotokan; [oth. writ.] I have written poems and philosophical treatness since young adulthood. I have also been strongly influenced by the writings of Ernest Hemingway, Kahlil Gibran, Classical Literature and Philosophy; [pers.] I believe in the highest ideals of service to mankind, love, honor and commitment. The greatest loves of my life are my high school sweetheart, who is also my wife, beautiful daughter, Kelsey, my wonderful family, and my beloved mother, whose beautiful spirit and memory have shaped course of my life.; [a.] Atlanta, GA

NGUYEN, SARA THAO HA
[pen.] Phlower; [b.] May 28, 1982, Richmond, VA; [p.] My loving parents Lapha and Lau Thanh Nguyen; [ed.] An eight grader at Swift Creels Middle School; [occ.] Cheerleading; [memb.] Volunteer Vietnamese Cultural Dances; [oth. writ.] Awakening (poem) as well as several stories that are unpublished.; [pers.] If you've gone and done it's in the past. Life goes on and that is that.; [a.] Midlothian, VA

NICHOLS, JUDITH
[pen.] Judith Nichols; [b.] April 6, 1949, Charlotte, NC; [p.] Hazel and Hazeline Hudson; [ch.] Dale Nichols and Jeffrey Nichols; [ed.] West Mecklenbury H.S. Currently Enrolled at Central Piedmont Community College, Working Toward and Business Administration Degree; [occ.] First Union National Bank - Human Resources, Employee Relations; [pers.] Writing is very enjoyable and relaxing, for me. I hope the readers of my poems find them entertaining.

NICHOLS, PHYLLIS D'AMBROSIO
[b.] December 8, 1956, Bronx, NY; [p.] James and Rose D'Ambrosio; [ed.] Walter Panas H.S. Peekskill NY, Grad. 1974, Courses at Pace University and Golden West College; [occ.] Vice President, Office Manger - Manufacture's Repfirm; [memb.] Soroptimists International Huntington Beach, Huntington Beach Chamber Of Commerce, Richard III Historical Society, National Geographic Society, Electronic Rep. Assoc.; [hon.] National Honor Society, Gregg Shortland Awards; [oth. writ.] Nothing Published. I am currently working on an Elizabethan Historical Novel.; [pers.] Reading has always allowed me to travel to places and times that I love, such as England, and I'd love to give some of that back to others who love to read as I do!; [a.] Huntington Beach, CA

NICHOLSON, LOREE
[pen.] Lenai Stevens; [b.] April 24, 1963, Stettler, Alberta, Canada; [p.] Raymond Fix, Janette Miller; [ch.] Theo, Triston, Ausha; [ed.] Viscount Bennett Center (Upgrading); [occ.] Business Administrator; [pers.] We as people should united together under one love of neighbors, and all mankind; [a.] Calgary, AB, Canada

NICKLE, GIDGET R.
[b.] November 3, 1974, Salt Lake City, UT; [p.] Robin Ekker and Dwight Nickle; [m.] Engaged to Paul Curtis; [ch.] Toni Curtis; [ed.] Hunter High School; [oth. writ.] I have a journal of other poems and songs.; [pers.] I inherited my talent from my father, whom I love dearly. In my writing, I express my feelings. My mother encourages me and stands by me.; [a.] West Valley City, UT

NIMS, ROSALIND
[pen.] Roz Nims; [b.] February 27, 1951, Tallahassee; [p.] Mr. and Mrs. Paul Myles; [m.] Divorced; [ch.] Al Nims Jr.; [ed.] B.S. Degree Florida A and M University; [occ.] English Teacher; [memb.] Alpha Kappa Alpha Sorority Bethel A.M.E. Church; [hon.] Who's Who Among American's Teacher; [pers.] Poetry serves as an echo of my inner feelings and it soothes the soul and warms the heart.; [a.] Tallahassee, FL

NOBLET, THURMAN
[b.] July 20, 1923, Detroit, MI; [p.] Dean Noblet & Shirley Ackley Noblet; [m.] Sylvia Poast Noblet, May 26, 1946; [ch.] Eric, Stephen, Joe and Scott; [ed.] Washington Elementary school, Marion, OH; Washington Twp. High School, Ibena, OH; Muskingum College, New Concord, OH; Ohio Northern Univ., BS in Ed.; Ohio State Univ., MA; [occ.] (retired) Teacher, Coach, Ridgemont H.S.; guidance Counselor, Col. Crawford H.S.; [memb.] Clerbrook Men's Golf League; [oth. writ.] none; [pers.] I believe close-knit families are the answer to our nation's problems.; [a.] Bucyrus, OH

NOEL, BARBARA J.
[b.] January 6, 1942, Greensburg, PA; [p.] Earl and Bessie Hite; [m.] Francis "Bud," December 23, 1960; [ch.] Tracy, Tanice, Terry; [ed.] Hempfield Area Sr. High School, W.C.C.C. Community College; [occ.] Retired 22 years from Beneficial Finance, Part-time Bookkeeper and Real Estate Agent-Century 21 Warren Real Estate; [memb.] American Legion Post 515 Ladies; [oth. writ.] I wrote a poem for my daughter's wedding and had music written for it and have copyrights called "A Mother's Love."; [pers.] I have always written poems for my family and friends and am inspired by the love that I see in each of them.; [a.] Latrobe, PA

NORMAN, ALICE
[pen.] June West; [b.] March 16, 1920, Nadeau Twp.; [p.] Bennardt and Nettie Norman; [ed.] 8th grade Demolish Harris High Intermediate Class 1935; [occ.] Retired; [hon.] School Health, Confirmation News Writer, School Typist, Church Language Tribal. Monetary Names; [oth. writ.] Many; [a.] Conway, MI

NORRIS, ANNABELLA S.
[b.] June 19, 1944, Catanzaro, Italy; [p.] Caterina and Dante Siclari; [m.] William B. Norris, January 29, 1972; [ch.] Denise and Sean; [ed.] "L. Siciliani" Scientific Lyc Fum, High, Italy, Kee's Business College, Norfolk, VA, ODU, Norfolk, VA; [occ.] Medical Clerk, Norfolk, VA; [hon.] Civilian of the Quarter 1995, Up for Civilian of the Year, 1995-1996.; [oth. writ.] This is the one and only poem of my life. The inspiration and composition of "Kites" came to me as an urge to express my feelings of excitement in watching and making kites flying, in a cold, windy afternoon on the beach.; [pers.] Enjoy simple things in life: This is where the beauty is.; [a.] Virginia Beach, VA

NORRIS, PHIL
[pen.] J. P. Norris; [b.] September 4, 1964, Newport, AR; [p.] Joe Lampton, Kathleen Lampton; [m.] Nadine Norris, November 24, 1989; [ch.] Melina Norris; [ed.] Associate in General Studies Degree, Barton County Community College; [occ.] MIAI Abrams Tank Commander, US Army; [memb.] Association of the United States Army; [hon.] Arcom Medal, AAM Medal - 5th Oak Leaf Cluster; [oth. writ.] Several unpublished poems.; [pers.] True life is through God and family. True death is having neither.; [a.] Fort Riley, KS

NORRIS, SHEILA D.
[b.] June 1, 1955, Georgia; [p.] Walter and Lora Wolfe; [m.] Tony A. Norris, December 1, 1989; [ch.] Jason C. Wolfe; [ed.] Rockmart High; [occ.] Homemaker; [memb.] American Cancer Society, American Heart Asso., Disabled Veterans; [oth. writ.] Poems published in local newspaper. Poems and songs written for special friends.; [pers.] I try to put words on paper that God gives me through his love. I long for others to see and feel the things I feel. Made possible by my Lord Jesus Christ.; [a.] Rockmart, GA

NOVAK, ANGELA FAYE
[pen.] Angela F. Runyon; [b.] January 6, 1966, Berea, OH; [p.] Gladys Ernest Runyon; [m.] Dennis Frank Novak, October 27, 1996; [ch.] Celeste Paige and Steven Michelle; [ed.] Berea High School Polaris Vocational Center; [occ.] Proprietor of Angel Faire Products; [memb.] Earth Renaissance; [hon.] Honor Roll in High School Certified Commercial Advertiser; [oth. writ.] Published in Carvings in Store " You Lost" and also in The Best Poems of the 90's" You Never Noticed".; [pers.] My poems are dedicated to my daughter Celeste, may you follow your dreams and enjoy life to its fullest potential Harming none along the way.; [a.] Lakewood, OH

NUNEZ, DAVID MARCELO
[pen.] David Marcelo; [b.] August 20, 1972, Buenos Aires, Argentina; [ed.] Forest Hills High, E-4 U.S.

Marine Corps.; [pers.] I dedicate this poem to Jennifer...and to all that's meant to be. Although I failed you, may these simple words remind you, my thoughts and love for you never will. Hope to see you again. June 4, 1995 is forever. Wuv you.; [a.] Hollis, NY

O'BRYAN, HEATHER
[b.] February 7, 1970; [p.] Audrey and Gary O'Bryan, (Step-Dad) David O'Bryan; [ed.] I am a Senior in High School, New Franklin, MO; [hon.] 9th grade - Mathematics Metal, and Business Metal; [oth. writ.] I have over 40 poems. Some are Too Hard To Heal, Flown Away, Did You Know?, The Love That Was Taken Away, Thank You God, Friends, Dear Friends, Someone Special, etc.; [pers.] I get my poems from within. I write whatever I am feeling inside.; [a.] New Franklin, MO

O'GORMAN, JEFF
[b.] July 31, 1961, Cold Spring, NY; [p.] Tom and Jean O'Gorman; [m.] Annette O'Gorman, May 2, 1992; [ch.] John; [ed.] MBA - University of Baltimore, BS - Suny College of Environmental Science and Forestry, AAS - Paul Smith's College; [occ.] Engineering Consultant (part time), Stay at home Dad (full time); [memb.] American Water Works Assn., Water Environmental Federation, Registered Professional Engineer; [hon.] Alpha Xi Sigma, Dean's List; [oth. writ.] Marylad Public Health Assn. Newsletter, other poems short stories of life, love, friendship and nature (unpublished).; [pers.] I write about life's experiences. I'm influenced by my faith, family, friends and my own slightly sarcastic and cynical nature.; [a.] Waukesha, WI

O'LEARY, ALAN C.
[b.] October 6, 1969, Cork City, Ireland; [p.] Con O'Leary, Katherine O'Leary; [pers.] Poetry is a written description of an individual's soul's perception of a physical world, a world where perception is limited and possibilities are endless.; [a.] Washington, DC

O'NEIL, JOHN KENNETH
[b.] January 12, 1978, Glenwood Springs, CO; [p.] John and Christine O'Neil; [ed.] Graduated 1996 Ft. Collius High School, Ft. Collius, CO., currently attending Colo State University, Ft. Collins Co.; [occ.] Student; [pers.] "Search as though you will live forever, live as though you would die tomorrow" Viking Creed; [a.] Fort Collius, CO

ODOM, ANITA HUTCHINS
[pen.] Paul, Pauline; [b.] September 9, 1951, Greenville, SC; [p.] Anita Greer and Samuel Harper Hutchins; [m.] Charles Howard Odom, December 26, 1985; [ch.] Charles Benson Odom, II and Annie Anita Greer Odom; [ed.] Clemson University - 2 years Greenville Tech.; [occ.] Licensed Practical Nurse; [oth. writ.] I have written over one hundred poems and am planning to publish all of them in a book of my own in the near future.; [pers.] Through God's love, I have always been giving and understanding. My writing is "His gift" to share.; [a.] Greenville, SC

OETKER, LUKE
[pen.] Metthew Salt; [b.] July 25, 1979, Poplar Bluff, MO; [p.] Norman and Mary Oetker; [ed.] CSU Fresno; [occ.] Student, CSU Fresno; [memb.] Light Amidst the Mong; [hon.] N.E.M.A. - National English Merrit Award; [pers.] I try to reflect God's love for us in my work. I want others to read about what God means to me. I give him all the credit.; [a.] Fresno, CA

OLIVER, LAKE
[b.] August 25, 1975, Beuford, SC; [p.] Sandra Wakeford and Harry Oliver; [ed.] Ponaganset High; [occ.] Supervisor at Churchhill and Banks Inc.; [pers.] I write on my spare time to express my feelings. Thanks to Tammy, my true love, forever.; [a.] North Scituate, RI

OLIVER, VICKIE J.
[b.] March 20, 1954, Forth Smith, AK; [p.] Fay Hoshell, Clyde McGee; [ch.] Wynter Joye, Marla Janel; [ed.] Mumford, Wayne State U., Howard U.; [occ.] Buyer, PBS, Alexandria, VA; [oth. writ.] Kalyn's Life Adventures, Not Even In A Book, published 1991.; [pers.] My writings: Just everyday thoughts about life and living.; [a.] Alexandria, VA

ORTIZ, AUREA E.
[b.] September 6, 1960, Arroyo, PR; [p.] Clotilde Solis, Carmelo De Jesus; [m.] Josue Ortiz, August 30, 1986; [ch.] Josue and Luis Ortiz; [ed.] 3 years course work in Secretarial Science and Business Adm. Graduated Hospitality Supervision Course. Worked as banquet Manager and Group Service Coordinator for Hotels; [occ.] In training for Customer Consultant - Bell Atlantic; [memb.] Previous memberships included P.R. Hotel Association, Tourism Habit at for Humanity - (Volunteer), Volunteer - Millersville University Migrant Education, Parents Board. Special ED Bible Teacher; [hon.] Certificate - Short Story, Writing Contest - University of P.R. when I was 18 years old. This was a prerequisite to pass the class (1980) "Conversational English". 1991 Top Hearts Winner - Sales Dept. Conda Do Plaza Hotel. Best Service Person in Sales; [oth. writ.] I have written many poems and short stories, but never I have presented them in a contest. Just one page story to pass my class writing contest in 1980. "Rob The Robot Plays Ball".; [pers.] I believe that every living thing give us the inspiration to write. I see life hurdles as a painter would see a beautiful sunset or a bright smile. I take people's suffering and convert it in hope.; [a.] Allentown, PA

ORTIZ, STEPHEN ANTHONY
[b.] September 14, 1981, Wylie, TX; [p.] Virginia Pecina and David Pecina; [ed.] Freshman at Wylie Middle School; [a.] Wylie, TX

OSBORNE, JAMES R.
[pen.] James R. Osborne; [b.] January 31, 1943, Lenior, NC; [p.] Ray and Opal Osborne; [m.] Janet L. Osborne, May 25, 1973; [ch.] James Wayne (Deceased), Sherry Osborne Burns; [ed.] Happy Valley High School Lenior N.C., Ohio Peace Officer School Toledo OH, Certified Associate in Bereavement Support and Education; [occ.] Disabled; [memb.] The National Library of Poets, The Association of Death Counselors and Educators, The Remember Me Support Group and Co Thunder of Group; [hon.] Father of the Year from Remember Me Support Group for hours of Counseling and Education dealing with bereaved parents; [oth. writ.] Several poems published in articles of Bereavement magazine and the Forum, Bittersweet... Hello Goodbye (book) P.S. Magazine, Tomorrows dream and of Moonlight and Wishes.; [pers.] My poems reflect feelings of grief, sorrow, memories and recovery of neonatal grief associated with pregnancy and infant death. My message continues: You were wanted, you were loved, you are remembered.; [a.] Oregon, OH

OTA, CARLA LEE
[b.] November 12, 1954, Portsmouth, OH; [p.] Norman Adkins, Sylvia Adkins; [m.] Edward Isamu Ota, October 10, 1987; [ch.] Derrik E. Farmer, Chris A. Ota; [ed.] John Glenn High School, Cerritos Jr. College; [occ.] Word Processor in LA Mirada, CA; [memb.] Parent Teachers Association; [pers.] My writings are inspired by love and written from the heart!; [a.] La Mirada, CA

OTT, JOANNE
[pen.] Joanne Ott; [b.] April 9, 1934, San Jose, CA; [p.] Eugenia and Warren Berry; [m.] Max Ott; [ch.] Cheryl Sommer, Jill Pollara and Stephen Pollara (Deceased); [pers.] Poem is in memory of my son.; [a.] Pollock Pines, CA

OWEN, MARYBELLE
[b.] March 3, 1906, Centerville, KS; [p.] Elta Huffman, Estella Huffman; [m.] Avalo E. Owen (Deceased), September 12, 1944; [ch.] Elvvyn E. Owen, Dina Schwaltz; [ed.] Enterprises Academy, Kansas Union College, Nebraska; [occ.] Retiree have been an English Teacher; [memb.] Seventh-day Adventist Church; [oth. writ.] Have edited various school papers and written stories.; [pers.] "I don't know what the future holds but I know who holds the future." The Lord has led me these 9 years. My son is a missionary in Brazil where I I wrote this poem.; [a.] Loveland, CO

OWENS, ANDREA
[pen.] 'Drea; [b.] January 11, 1982, Palos, IL; [p.] Rochelle L. Owens and John E. Owens II; [ed.] Pre School - Freshman writing poetry of Lake highlands Jr. High influenced to enter contest by Susan Goldsberry; [memb.] I am currently in band, Spanish class, and poetry club; [hon.] I received honors for band, student council, and other poetry work.; [oth. writ.] What I want in a man, Black Young Teen National Anthem, Why I Feel The Way I Do, and My Summer Love; [pers.] I began to write when I was 10 years old. The first poem I wrote was called broken hearted because my friend's boyfriend broke up with her and I wrote it to cheer her up. I only write with influence. I have to feel or live what I write.; [a.] Richardson, TX

OWENS, JEROMY
[b.] September 24, 1976, Henderson, KY; [p.] Wanda Owens; [ed.] Graduated High School, 3 yrs of Welding; [occ.] Work on Water Tanks and Radio Tower (Repair); [oth. writ.] Several poems but never once thought about publishing; [pers.] Most of my poems our personal thoughts, they reflect my past and my feelings.; [a.] Henderson, KY

OWENS, MINNIE R.
[b.] January 23, 1954, Belton, SC; [p.] Robert Arnold (Deceased), Ruby Arnold; [m.] Divorced; [ch.] James Edward, Janese Evonne, Justin Everett; [ed.] John Adams High School, Cuyahoga Community College, Institute of Children's Literature; [occ.] Coordinator Accounts Payable; [pers.] A friend gave me a poem on a wall hanging. The author is unknown but I find the words inspirational. It simply says: If You Can Imagine It, You Can Achieve It. If You Can Dream It, You can Become It.; [a.] Shaker Heights, OH

OZENGHAR, DENNIS D.
[pen.] Dennis DuPaul; [b.] July 20, 1972, Tucson, AZ; [p.] Linda Ohswaldt, Dennis Ozenghar; [ed.] March Mountain High School; [occ.] Customer Service Representative; [oth. writ.] Comic books (S-Comics) 1994. Several songs, poems and ideals still in the old box.; [pers.] Soul Mates, is my very first poem. I've kept it buried for three years, I never thought it was publishable...I would like to thank a very special friend for bringing out the writer in me (Charmain Kay). "Love has many faces, just be glad when your smiled upon."; [a.] Tucson, AZ

PACHOLKE, KATHLEEN M.
[b.] December 28, 1941, Saginaw, MI; [p.] Helen and Ralph Pietrzak; [m.] Alfred P. Pacholke, November 3, 1962; [ch.] Brian James, Tracy Lynn; [ed.] Holy Rosary High School; [occ.] Homemaker; [memb.] Mary Martha Society, Altar Guild at St. Peter Lutheran Church Hemlock, MI

PACIA, JR, RAY
[b.] March 27, 1946, Providence, RI; [p.] Ray & Shalla Pacia; [ed.] Moses Brown School, Gordon School, St. Augustine School; [occ.] Student; [hon.\ High honors - St Augustine 6th Grade; [oth. writ.] Wrote anthology of 5 poems, poems have been published in local newspapers.; [pers.] In poetry, I believe one must not only know the elements of it, but the confidence that you are made up of, the ingredients it takes to make a poet.; [a.] Providence, RI

PALMER, JANICE DAVIS
[pen.] Janice D. Palmer; [b.] July 10, 1956, Mobile, AL; [p.] Albert Davis Sr. (Deceased) and Sadie Q. Davis; [m.] Costroe F. Palmer Sr., May 27, 1977; [ch.] Costroe Jr. and Vincent; [ed.] Davidson High School, B.S. Accounting - The University of Alabama Graduate Studies in Human Resources The University of Alabama; [occ.] Human Resources Representative/Training Specialist - The University of Alabama, Tuscaloosa, Alabama; [memb.] Society of Human Resource Management, Alabama Society of HRM State Council Tuscaloosa Human Resource Professionals, National Association of Female Executives, West Alabama Chamber of Commerce The University of Alabama Commerce Executive Society; [hon.] Outstanding Young Woman of America - 1978, 1984, Outstanding Citizen of the Year - Northport Kappa Alpha Psi, Accounting Honors Board, Outstanding Minority Graduate of Colleges and Universities, Who's Who Among Students in Colleges and Universities; [oth. writ.] Tribute to Teachers, Retirement, Especially for You, Sisterhood, Twas the Week Before Christmas, Tribute to Grandmother Delta, OH Delta - Sorority Song, Ode to A Co-Worker; [pers.] My motto is "Others." I strive to reflect others in my work and how they impact my life. My work reflects a deep desire and commitment to help people their hearts and experience the unity of humankind.; [a.] Tuscaloosa, AL

PALMER II, ROBERT S.
[b.] February 22, 1945, NYC; [p.] Robert Palmer, Frances Steenbeke; [m.] Michele Wargo, February 1981, May 1987; [ch.] Robert III, Kevin; [ed.] Putney School, VT, UNH, Foothill C, CA, USF; [occ.] Int'l Agency Sales/ Northwest Airlines (int) Ecology, Native America supporter /Wounded Knee '73/Longest Walk,'78, Union Activist/ Hughes Airwest Board Member/Remember Kid's in Divorce Settlements, Children's Right Council, D.C., Struggled w/Mpls Inner City Rental 88-95, 1st MN PCB well cleanup; [hon.] Printer Emeritus/ Social action printing/Mid-Penisula Free Univer, Palo Alto, CA '68, NW plague/Offline Document Recovery Project '96; [oth. writ.] Co-author Pelican Trip, East Village other '66, Guest Storyteller/ Gurney Norman class/Foothill C, Hughes Airwest Printshop chemicals and Exposures of Products to Employees, Photo in Chem Textbook; [pers.] W/ sons/Mpls "Heart Of the Beast? May Day Parade/ Theatre, Rainbow Family MN '90, Imagine a healthy earth. Help the mellow flow. Farmington, MN.

PAMPERIN, CARLA SUE
[pen.] Scarlet Carla; [b.] October 30, 1963, Rome, NY; [p.] Beverly Harms and Robert Gump; [m.] James Alan Pamperin, April 17, 1995; [ch.] Brandon Louis Pamperin (age 14), Terry James Pamperin (age 12); [ed.] Kindergarten in Sioux City, IA, 1st through 6th Clarion, IA 50525, 7th through 9th Clarion Jr. High, 10th through 11th Clarion Senior High. G.E.D. in April of 1989 in ICC in Eagle Grove. 1 year of college, majoring in Secretarial at ICC in Eagle Grove, IA 50533.; [occ.] I'm working towards a Journalism career! And writing short stories, and children's books and poems.; [memb.] Church of the Nazerine, The Eagle Grove Fitness Center; [hon.] Through my school years, I won an art scholarship and all the physical fitness awards; [oth. writ.] Poem titles: Impressions, A Mother's Request, What's Love, Dreams Will Conquer, The Night We Met, Twin Sister, Who Am I, Guess What I Am, No Time is My Time, The Day Never Ends; [pers.] All of my poems I've written from my heart, living the moment. I express myself through writing, when I have time! My dream is to be a journalist!; [a.] Eagle Grove, IA

PANGILINAN, ASHLEY
[pen.] Ashley V.; [b.] December 2, 1986; [p.] Joselito and Bea Pangilinan; [p.] JoJo Pangilinan; [ed.] 11th grade; [occ.] Student at Polser Elementary; [memb.] Choir Member, Dance Member; [hon.] First Honors 1st Grade To 3rd grade; [pers.] To be the best.; [a.] Carrollton, TX

PAQUET, JUDITH B.
[pen.] Elizabeth McGowan; [b.] March 19, 1944, Wilmington, NC; [ch.] Daniel; [ed.] RN, BS (Communication/PR); [occ.] Director, Program Development, for a Medical Education Company; [memb.] Author's Guild, Humor and Heath Institute, Health Care Marketing Council, Toast Masters International; [hon.] Who's Who in American Nursing, 1994-95 and 1996-97; [oth. writ.] Have published game book, multiple (15 years worth) trade and professional articles and one poem "Octogenarian" published in Journal of General Internal Medicine. Editor of I am National Nursing Journal.; [pers.] Laughter, honesty, allegiance - all necessary to survival and to growth in learning. Love and hugs are essential to life.

PARAMO, RAUL
[pen.] Roy Paramo; [b.] May 11, 1947, Houston, TX; [p.] Ramon and Catarina Paramo; [m.] Gricelda Elvia Paramo, March 18, 1994; [ch.] Eugene, Carolyn, Victoria; [pers.] Speakers, writers, lecturers...bring verbal representation to our feelings. When ideal words are found, they serve those who cannot convey those feelings readily. "Hey! That describes exactly how I feel!" "That's what I wanted to say".; [a.] Houston, TX

PARK, MARION E.
[b.] November 10, 1961, Ft. Riley, KS; [m.] James David Enright; [ch.] Cedric, Emmeline, Elizabeth, Richard, James II; [ed.] Junction City Public Schools, Cloud County Community College; [occ.] Mother; [memb.] Abilene and Smoky Valley Rail Road Association; [pers.] I thank my beloved James for putting in inspiration back into my heart where it had been missing for so long. He is a poem in making.; [a.] Abilene, KS

PARKER, BONNIE
[pen.] Bonnie; [b.] August 8, 1949, Mountain Lake, MN; [p.] Aron and Ethel Harder; [m.] Divorced; [ch.] Toni Lynn; [ed.] Mountain Lake, High; [occ.] Hewlett packard, Colorado Springs Division; [oth. writ.] I've been writing poems for quite a few years now, but this is the first one I've ever attempted to have published.; [pers.] I love to write poetry to my family members and to people I care about. It's amazing how a simple little poem can boost a person's spirits and brighten up their day!; [a.] Colorado Springs, CO

PARKER, JOSHUA M.
[b.] February 14, 1977, Ann Arbor, MI; [p.] Sherman C. Parker Jr., Mercedes R. Parker; [ed.] Green Hills High School, Albion College; [occ.] Student; [memb.] Tau Kappa Epsilon, Phi Mu Alpha Sinfonia, Theta Alpha Phi, Albion College Players, order of DeMolay; [oth. writ.] Numerous poems and short stories WWW Albion Student/ JParker; [pers.] "When trying to assess self worth, don't judge by what one can or cannot do. Judge by what one if. Keep in mind that some of world's most prized treasures don't do anything at all. They just are, and so are you, and them and me"; [a.] Ann Arbor, MI

PARKER, ROBERT F.
[b.] August 8, 1926, Chicago, IL; [p.] Jerome Palecek, Christine Palecek; [m.] Jean Parker, November 28, 1970; [ch.] Sergio Parker, Lisa Parker; [ed.] Batavia High, Carnegie Mellon Univ (C.I.T.); [occ.] Retired; [memb.] Apache Junction Society for the Arts (board Member), Mesa East Valley Rose Society; [oth. writ.] Several poems published in local papers.; [pers.] My poetry is influenced by emotional reaction to distressful situations. I try to find the good therein.; [a.] Apache Junction, AZ

PASCIUTO, GINNY
[b.] September 30, 1980, Portsmouth, VA; [p.] Robert Pasciuto and Patricia Pasciuto; [ed.] In High School (Andrew Jackson Senior High School - Medical Magnet Program). A Sophomore.; [oth. writ.] Never before published, but I hope to be soon.; [pers.] Smiles are free so give them away!; [a.] Jacksonville, FL

PATRICK, MICHELLE WILLIAMSON
[b.] August 2, 1966, Vidalia, GA; [ch.] Four children; [occ.] Medical Assistant; [pers.] Writing is a way to make peace with myself.; [a.] Sacramento, CA

PATRICK, SHARON
[pen.] Sharon Norman; [b.] May 8, 1947, Mount Vernon, NY; [p.] Norvella Norman Fuller/Edward Fuller; [m.] Jimmy R. Patrick, June 20, 1970; [ch.] Jewel Angeline Patrick; [ed.] Mount Vernon High School, and attended Monroe Business Institute for key punch, and computer sciences.; [occ.] Teacher's Assistant - 6th Grade, at Longfellow Elementary School, Mt. Vernon, NY, and Special Education, Pennington-Grimes School, Mt. Vernon NY. In addition, Lincoln Elementary School - Special Education, Mount Vernon, NY; [memb.] Mt. Vernon Teachers F.C.U. New York State United Teachers, Pastoral Care Volunteer at Mount Vernon Hospital, The Rose YM-YWHA of Southern Westchester, and choir directress-First Pentecostal Church, Mt. Vernon.; [hon.] Willing Worker's Certificate, Recognition from Shalom Nursing Home, and the Seabury-Wilson Retirement Home for volunteer services.; [oth. writ.] Several poems and lyrics for songs (non-published) used in church bulletins, and special program features.; [pers.] Striving to encourage others through writing, or by song, lifting their spirits higher and the day brighter. Never settling for less, but seeing the true accomplishments of all individuals. Being yourself, and always taking pride in whatever you do because, it will reflect, you!; [a.] Mount Vernon, NY

PATTEN, LORI
[b.] April 13, 1973, Iowa; [p.] Tommy and Janice Patten; [ch.] Anthoni Patten (January 5, 1995); [ed.] Currently attending American Institute of Commerce for Business Management; [occ.] Full time Student and Mother; [hon.] Dean's List past Three Semesters; [oth. writ.] "Rivers" in Across the Universe; [pers.] My poetry is how I express my feelings, the best on any topic.; [a.] Morrison, IL

PATTERSON, SHERRY
[b.] June 14, 1954, Henderson, KY; [p.] W. E. Householder and Almeta; [m.] James Arter, October 21, 1972; [ch.] James Arter V, Emily Lorene;

[ed.] Henderson County High School graduate 1972; [occ.] Accounting; [oth. writ.] Unpublished; [pers.] There is always hope, never stop believing.; [a.] Crete, IL

PATTON, DEBORAH
[b.] March 17, 1954, Raleigh; [ch.] One Daughter - Angel Patton; [ed.] Currently finishing my under graduate degree at Queens College, Charlotte, NC my degree will be in Music Therapy; [occ.] Salon owner/hair stylist; [hon.] Recipient of New Dimension at Queens College and The Wings Scholarship Sponsored by the Women Executives; [pers.] I journal and write poetry for my personal edification. It is a marvelous way to explore and release my thoughts and feelings.; [a.] Charlotte, NC

PAWLOWSKI, JASON
[b.] April 7, 1971, Philadelphia, PA; [p.] Stan and Marianne Pawlowski; [ed.] Paul VI High School, Fairfax, VA, B.A. Gannon University, May 1994; [occ.] Customer Sales Representative, U.S. Electrical Motors; [a.] Haymarket, VA

PELLE, ROSEMARY
[b.] October 10, 1972, St. Marys Hosp., Hoboken, NJ; [p.] Giulio and Nancy; [ed.] St. Aloysius Academy Englewood Hospital School of Nsg R.N. diploma program. Jersey City State College; [occ.] Nurse; [pers.] Live, Love and Learn; [a.] Jersey City, NJ

PENN, NANCY
[pen.] Nancy Penn; [b.] November 6, 1939, Wiggins, MS; [p.] Aubrey Barnett, Bobbye Barnett; [m.] Dr. B. Rivers Penn, September 1, 1972; [ch.] The Rev. Melissa Hollerith and Ms. Elizabeth Forman Zuber; [ed.] Millsaps College; [occ.] Church and Community volunteer; [memb.] St. James Episcopal Church, East Baton Rouge Medical Society Auxiliary, B. R. Food Bank Board, Prison Chapel Foundation, Colonial Dames of the XVII Cent.; [hon.] Excalibur Club, Unsung Heroes, Mayor's Proclamation Nancy B. Penn Day; [oth. writ.] The Advocate, Churchwork, The Mediscene, Episcopal Diocese of Louisiana Hunger Notebook.; [pers.] My writings spring from the awareness of, and reflection on, God's grace and activity in my life.; [a.] Baton Rouge, LA

PENNYPACKER, JASON L.
[b.] April 28, 1996, Reading, PA; [p.] Marjorie A. Pennypacker, Gregory C. Pennypacker; [ed.] Schuylkill Valley High School, Shippensburgs University; [hon.] Phi Sigma Pi, Beta Beta Beta, Dean's List; [pers.] This poem was written for my beautiful and loving girlfriend, Jenna Keil. Thank you sweetheart for inspiring me to express my feelings for you in this poem and many others.; [a.] Leesport, PA

PEPKOWSKI, RUTH
[b.] January 28, 1974, Miami, FL; [p.] William Alewis and Mena Lewis; [ch.] Frances Pepkowski; [memb.] St. David's Catholic Church, Civil Air Patrol West Braward Composite Squadron.; [pers.] I write mostly about things I see in day to day life. I use a great deal of symbolism in my poetry which reflects how I feel about that poem.; [a.] Miramar, FL

PERIANDI, ADRIENNE
[b.] February 5, 1958, Reading, PA; [occ.] Licensed Practical Nurse; [pers.] I live life as though it were a romantic movie with only happy endings. I only want to care for and love you. I was inspired by a man who believed in me and loved me for who I am and what I believe in. Not for what others expect me to be. He gave me self confidence. I will always I love him.; [a.] Reading, PA

PERRIGAN, JASON
[b.] April 3, 1981, Lorain, OH; [p.] Sandra and Kurby Perrigan; [ed.] Sophomore at Southview High School in Lorain C/O 99; [memb.] I am a member of the Southview Chess Club; [oth. writ.] I was healed of cancer when I was 12. It inspired me to write this poem.; [pers.] Remember, God is always there, He is with you, and He watches over you always.; [a.] Lorain, OH

PERRON, LINDA FAULKNER
[b.] February 23, 1948, Crystal Springs, MS; [p.] Mr. and Mrs. Joe Faulkner; [m.] Dalbert Perron, December 17, 1966; [ch.] Five; [occ.] Homemaker; [oth. writ.] My first entry.; [pers.] My strong faith in the Lord. Strong family ties.; [a.] Chalmette, LA

PETERS, ANGELA
[b.] January 19, 1981, Latrobe, PA; [p.] Thomas Peters, Brenda Peters; [ed.] Greensburg - Salem High School; [occ.] Student, Greensburg Salem Senior High School, Greensburg, PA; [hon.] Honor student; [oth. writ.] Poem published in 9th grade high school yearbook; [pers.] I strived to fulfill my dream. I didn't let anything stand in my way. I believed in myself, and I succeeded.; [a.] Greensburg, PA

PETERS, NANCY
[pen.] Gari Johnson; [b.] March 6, 1953, Bronx, NY; [p.] Robert and Vivienne Peters; [ch.] Jason Danner; [ed.] B.A. Psychology - S.U. N.Y. at Stony Brook; [occ.] Business Account Associate for AT&T Communications; [oth. writ.] Children's Short Stories; [pers.] My poetry is a reflection of my life. Its joys, sorrows and the gift of just breathing.; [a.] Pacoima, CA

PETTIT, GLADYS B.
[pen.] Gladie Pettit; [b.] October 22, 1929, Salem, NJ; [p.] Mary A. Kline, Eugene R. Brown; [m.] Joseph C. Pettit Jr., September 2, 1949; [ch.] Beverly Jane Eileen Ann, Larry Joseph; [ed.] Woodstown High School - 1947; [occ.] Enjoy Community Volunteer work, retired; [pers.] I have always enjoyed rhyme in both song and verse, I have recently begun to express my love for both family and friends through poetry.; [a.] Pilesgrove, NJ

PEZZELL, CINDENE
[b.] April 22, 1977, Michigan; [p.] Ron and Jean Pezzell; [ed.] Armada High School, currently a student at Central Michigan University; [occ.] Resident assistant, Saxe Hall, Central Michigan University; [memb.] Phi Sigma Pi National Honor Fraternity, CMU Marching Chippewas Alumni; [hon.] Dean's List, Louis Armstrong Jazz Award, John Phillip Sonsa Award, English Department Award - Armada High School; [pers.] You may need to go beyond the staff and scale to find the song that is yours.; [a.] Armada, MI

PIERCE, JUDY MAE
[b.] December 30, 1943, Knox, IN; [p.] Lawrence and Mary Bell Mills; [m.] Glendel Dean Pierce, June 17, 1982; [ch.] Six by previous marriage; [ed.] Knox High School, Art Institute of Minneapolis, Grace Baptist College of Michigan; [occ.] Industrial Sewing Machine Operator until stroke in 1993, which took me to a disabled status; [memb.] Five Star Music of Nashville; [hon.] Honorable Mention 1983, Golden Poet Awards 1984, 1985, 1986, Honorable Mention 1986, Merit Certificate 1989, all of which were received from World of Poetry; [oth. writ.] My poem, "Oh My God," was published in 1987 in the World Poetry Anthology, edited by John Campbell (found on page 418); [pers.] Most of my work comes from real life happenings I have observed and from my feelings as a mother.; [a.] Marion, NC

PINEIRO, ELIZABETH
[b.] September 26, 1979, Bronx, NY; [p.] Nectali Pineiro, Iris Pineiro; [ed.] The Loomis Chaffee School, Windsor, CT, Class of 1997; [occ.] High School student (Senior Boarder); [memb.] School extra-curriculars: Prefect, Community Life Group, Disciplinary Committee member, Tour Guide, Prism (Multicultural Org.), Varsity Volleyball, Big Sister/Little Sister Program/Prep. for prep student (NY based program); [pers.] Through my writing I express that which I cannot through spoken words. I do not try to "come up" with something. I only write down what my heart wants to reveal.; [a.] Bronx, NY

PIORNACK, BARRY
[b.] December 28, 1959, Mount Clemens, MI; [p.] Tillie and Wilbur; [m.] Karen Lee, August 14, 1982; [ch.] Jenna Danielle; [ed.] Macomb Comm. College - (Bus.); [occ.] Account Executive - Best Block Co. - Warren, MI; [hon.] Dean's List; [occ.] Mostly for hobby - passed along to friends and family; I aspire to write music with lyrics.; [pers.] I seek to truly understand the essence of existence and connection between lives both past and present. I thank Fr. Graham (Notre Dame High) for the teachings of Thoreau, Emerson, Dickinson, etc. I thank my father for his wisdom.; [a.] Warren, MI

PIPINICH, JOHN
[b.] October 19, 1961, Missoula, MT; [p.] Robert and Luella Pipinich; [m.] Heather Claire Pipinich, October 26, 1986; [ch.] David and Marie; [ed.] High School Graduate 1979 Anaconda Senior High; [occ.] I am a House Husband, I take care of our two children ages 5 and 1; [hon.] Four Years in the United States Air Force. Several Letters of Commudation and Appreciation; [pers.] Most all my writing is from the heart and from my memories. Some good, some not so. But all toll a good life so far. I hope to portray that in my writings.; [a.] Loveland, CO

PITTMAN, LILLIAN
[b.] June 25, 1979, Los Alomitas; [ed.] Etiwanda High School; [pers.] Inspired by the ever changing days, I write what I feel in my heart. "Hespera" is about me, and my love for the night, the moon, the darkness.; [a.] Rancho Cucamonga, CA

PLAHETKA, CHRISTINA R.
[b.] November 19, 1974, Fort Bragg, NC; [p.] Bonita E. Plahetka and the late John S. Plahetka; [ed.] Graduate of John Jay High School, Associate of Arts Degree Fr. San Antonio College; [occ.] Human Resources Assistant for Healing Hands Home Care, Inc.; [oth. writ.] Take great pleasure in creating birthday card messages for our patients and staff, also thank you cards, sympathy cards, and appreciation cards for clients and associates of healing hands.; [pers.] Whether expressing through words your thoughts, your feelings, your imagination, or your fantasies, the pleasure of writing should be one's personal satisfaction.; [a.] San Antonio, TX

PLYMAN, HOLLY J.
[b.] June 17, 1971, Lawrenceburg, IN; [p.] Roy Bessler and Kathy Hayes; [m.] Gregg Plyman, August 27, 1994; [ed.] University of Cincinnati and Art Academy of Cincinnati; [occ.] Finance Manager, CNAC, Finance Co.; [pers.] There is no greater gift than understanding the one you love.; [a.] Aurora, IN

POLICARE, RONALD T.
[b.] June 1, 1941, New York, NY; [p.] Peg and Dom Policare; [m.] Bernadette, November 11, 1983; [ch.] Daughter - Christie, son - Ronnie; [ed.] St. Sebastians Elementary St. John's Prep (H.S.) St. John's Univ. Master of Arts - John Jay College (CUNY) Bachelor of Arts (Magna Cum laude) - Jonh Jay Associate of Arts - Jonh Jay College (CUNY); [occ.] N.Y.C.P.D. Supervisor of Detectives (Ret.); [memb.] Honor Legion of N.C.C.P.D.

American Academy of Professional Law Enforcement Honor Society Of The Crim. Justice Assoc. N.Y.C. Mayors Commission on Child Abuse (1986) Board of Directors East Atlantic Beach Tax Assoc. 1990-1993; [hon.] Numerous Award, Medals and Letters of Commendation Chief of Det. Award (2), NYC Educ. Achiev. Award (3), Except. Merit (1), Commendation (2), Merit. Police Duty (2), Excell. Police Duty (6), Liberty Medal (1). First Decoy to receive National Attention (1965); [oth. writ.] Lectured for NYCPD Detective Bureau, Wrote Training Material re Rape, and other Sex Crimes in the Detective Bureau Process of writing two books at this time, Concerning Various Police Topics.; [pers.] Evil thrives when good men do nothing!; [a.] New York, NY

PONS, EDWIN OTTO ALCANTARA
[pen.] Edwin Alcantara; [b.] December 31, 1920, Guatemala; [p.] Adrian Alcantara, Adriana Pons; [m.] Alicia Sibaja, December 23, 1944; [ch.] Mayra, Juliet, Augusto; [ed.] Ph.D. in Economics, Harvard 1996, Licen Economia, Univ of San Carlos, Guatemala, C.A. 1954, Maestro de Edocasion Primaria, Escuela Normal, Guatemala 1939; [occ.] Retired; [memb.] Mizpah-Faith Lodge, A.F. and A.M., 38 Spring St, Somerville, Ma., "Americans for Change", Presidential Task Force, American Assn. of Retired Persons, Colegio de Economistos de Guatemala; [hon.] Financed my eduction mainly by means of scholarship awarded on competitive basis by public institutions - Bank of Guatemala and (O.A.S.) Organization of American States, Washington, DC; [oth. writ.] Other than a few insignificant articles on economic studies published in Sundry Journals and Newspapers in Guatemala, I have not contributed to the inextricable jungle of contradictions of modern civilizations.; [pers.] The future of the Western Hemisphere depends on agreeing on a modicum of basic principles, values and social attitudes - culturalization - through democratic and peaceful means, and on the gradual unification of the economies through liberalization and adequate compensatory measures.; [a.] Orange, TX

PONSKY, BARBARA J.
[b.] June 4, 1984; [p.] Mary and Jerry Ponsky; [occ.] 6th Grade Student at St. Joan of Arc School; [hon.] Leading Roles in several School Productions, Linus in "Charlie Brown's Christmas," The Queen of Hearts in "Alice in Wonderland," and Mrs. Miller in "Bye Bye Birdie," and others; [a.] Bainbridge, OH

POP, MAGDALENA
[b.] May 15, 1954, Bucharest, Romania; [ed.] University of Bucharest, Romania; [occ.] Teacher - Los Angeles Unified School District, LA, CA; [oth. writ.] "Hourglasses" - booklet of poems in Romanian language, published in 1990, Bucharest, Romania; [pers.] I believe in the healing power of the arts. Poetry is an endless journey into the depths of our inner self and the inner beauty of the world ruled by harmony.; [a.] Los Angeles, CA

PORTER, DELORA JEAN WADE
[pen.] Hedlund, Delora; [b.] March 22, 1932, Portland, OR; [p.] Ernie and Helen Hedlund; [m.] Robt W. Wade, June 18, 1950; [ch.] Sue Ellen and Jennie; [ed.] Southern Oregon State College Ashland, Oregon 1954 B.S. degree in Elementary Education, Un. of Eugene, Oregon '76 Counseling Education; [occ.] Retired and part-time Substitute Teacher K-8 Mesa, AZ; [memb.] SOSU Alumni Assoc., A.A.U.W., A.A.R.P, O.E.A. and N.E.A. (Life member), St. Timothy's Catholic Church, Mesa, AZ; [hon.] 4 years College Scholarship from Oregon Congress of Parents and Teachers Sabattical leave '76 from Coos Bay Education Assoc. '94 Cibecue Teacher of the Year, Apache Indian Reservation White Mountains, Arizona; [oth. writ.] "My Kitty Dear" published in the Oregon Journal Newspaper 1941 various poems for Journalism class Klamath Krator Newspaper '46-49 K. Falls, Oregon "All Grown Up and 21" poem for daughter Jennie's Birthday in 1979. Tears On The Roses '89; [pers.] My philosophical statement as seen in this poem and as shown by teaching primary kids these 42 years is: In order to be "creative" in the classroom one also needs an equal, quiet, meditation time.; [a.] Chandler, AZ

PORTER, MICHAEL
[b.] August 9, 1970, Kansas City, MO; [p.] James H. and Molly Porter; [ed.] B.S. - Kansas State University, M. Ed. - University of South Carolina; [occ.] University Student Life Administration; [memb.] St. John's Episcopal Church, National Assoc. of Student Personnel administrators; [hon.] Outstanding Residence Hall Director, U of S Carolina 1994/95, Member of the Year: Univ. of S. Carolina, Student Personnel Association; [oth. writ.] Only writing; [pers.] Special thanks to: Mambo King Jasper (aka Casey Pruett).; [a.] Stockton, CA

PORTER, RICKY LEE
[pen.] Rick; [b.] February 20, 1955, Dallas, TX; [p.] Bill Porter and Cleva Joyce Porter; [m.] Ellen Thompson, July 31, 1992; [ch.] Candace, Ashely, Brandon; [ed.] High School; [occ.] Orlin Saleman; [oth. writ.] 1) Jimi Hendrix Highs or Lows, 2) Its My Life; [pers.] Want to dedicate this to my best friend, Ellen Thompson who is my source of inspiration.; [a.] Lewisville, TX

POUNDS, JENNY MAE
[b.] February 12, 1963, Odessa, TX; [p.] Ben and Dorothy Wheeler; [m.] Randall L. Pounds, October 23, 1990; [ch.] Timothy, Wesley, Misty, Brandi; [ed.] Cisco Junior College (Nursing School); [occ.] Home Health Nurse (LVN), Concepts of Care in Wichita Falls TX; [pers.] I have my own guardian angel, everything I write comes from personal experience, the heart and most certainly from above!; [a.] Wichita Falls, TX

POWER, MARK
[b.] August 14, 1960, Havana, IL; [p.] James W. Power, Laura L. Power; [m.] Reta K. Power, May 17, 1980; [ch.] Johnny Dale, Jacque Lyn, Jaymi Erin; [ed.] Lincoln College, Sangamon State University; [occ.] Self Employed; [hon.] Phi Theta Kappa National Honor Society, Florence Molen Award for English (LC), Marcia Stuart Brooks Award for Creative Writing (LC)), Dean's List, National Dean's List, Undergraduate Marshall - Literature Program (SSU), Board of Regents Scholar (SSU); [oth. writ.] No previously published material but currently working on a variety of poetry, short fiction, and non-fiction essays.; [pers.] Poetry inarguably validates the transcendent nature of humanity. By writing about the ordinary, the poet achieves the extraordinary when the reader is compelled beyond self into reflections on the human condition in general. Poetry, then, is the looking glass through which we view our being.; [a.] Easton, IL

POWER, PEGGY LYNNE
[b.] September 4, 1959, Norfolk, VA; [p.] Anthony Phillip Yannotti, Mary Ellen Yannotti; [m.] Daniel James Power Sr., March 23, 1979; [ch.] Christopher John, Daniel James II; [ed.] Grandby High School, Polaris Career Center, Ohio State Department of Education/Driver Training; [occ.] Bus Driver, Berea City Schools; [memb.] International Cake Exploration Society, North Coast Sugar Artists; [oth. writ.] High School English Lit. Magazine; [pers.] Love, family, and friendship are the greatest blessings in life.; [a.] Brook Park, OH

POWERS, MICHELLE L.
[b.] March 5, 1971, Grand Island, NE; [p.] Leonard and Gail Powers; [ed.] Centura High, Chadron State College; [occ.] Child Care Provider; [memb.] First Baptist Church of Dennebrog, Inter Varsity, Christian Fellowship; [hon.] Dean's List, Cum Laude, Who's Who Among Students in American Universities and Colleges; [pers.] This poem is dedicated to my mother who died on June 4, 1995, and to God for his faithful watch over me.; [a.] San Diego, CA

POWERS, NATHAN
[b.] November 29, 1981, Sewanee, TN; [p.] Don and Jeannie Powers; [ed.] Grade School, middle School, first year of high school (presently 9th grade) (I was in eight grade of the time of writing "A Midnight Bewitching"); [occ.] Student; [hon.] Georgia Young Authors Poetry Award - May 28, 1996; [oth. writ.] "Man Might Understand", "In the Cradle of Dreams", "The Essence of Morality", Truth defies lies and until this is accepted, true morality will remain undiscovered.; [pers.] What reigns in thought is represented by action. The verbal poison is spoken, natures hold on her own is broken, by this, see the world weaken.; [a.] Thomasville, GA

PRENTICE, PAULINE D.
[pen.] Pauline Kincaid Prentice; [b.] September 20, 1915, Edgerton, KS; [p.] Paul and Agnes Kincaid; [m.] October 1, 1940; [ch.] Lyndel R. Prentice; [a.] Arlington, TX

PRERA, AILEEN MARIE
[b.] July 7, 1973, Guatemala City, Guatemala; [ed.] Ulysses S. Grant High, L.A. Valley College, Otis College of Art and Design; [pers.] One circle, the momentum of life in a flashing minute with only enough time to question: Is it real? Mira La Luna...; [a.] Sun Valley, CA

PRESLEY, ELVIS
[b.] December 8, 1958, Bakersfield, CA; [p.] Floyd and Mary Presley; [ch.] Five kids all over USA on going. Thank God above; [occ.] Painter; [memb.] I have my own band C&W R&R; [hon.] Working on it always Boxing 20&0 first in art; [oth. writ.] Book of song's and poem's by Elvis Presley; [pers.] The world is a great place and it needs all our love hopes and dreams.; [a.] Bakersfield, CA

PRESSLEY, CHARLES
[b.] April 13, 1942, Fox, OK; [p.] Charles and Lola Pressley; [ed.] Everett A. Rae High Costa Mesa, Calif; [occ.] Janitor; [oth. writ.] I've had a song "Life Is An Uphill Journey" copyrighted in 1994!; [pers.] Writing poetry, to me is like an Artist composing a seen for the moment on a certain subject!; [a.] Vancouver, WA

PRITCHARD, DAVID ALAN
[b.] January 12, 1971, Richmond, TX; [m.] Lorena Pritchard, April 17, 1995; [ch.] Mercedes Yvette Pritchard; [ed.] Waco High School; [oth. writ.] I write all my poems for my beautiful wife.; [pers.] I write my poems because it's my way of expressing my deepest love to my wife in so many ways...also I've always loved poems that have love in them for family...; [a.] Waco, TX

PROO, EDNA CECILIA
[b.] March 10, 1970, San Antonio, TX; [p.] Abelino C. Proo, Hilda B. Proo; [m.] Ramon Corona Jr., June 29, 1991; [ed.] Harlandale High, Graduate of St. Philips College; [occ.] Licensed Vocational Nurse; [oth. writ.] I've written several other poems, not published, that I keep in my own personal journal, others I give away as gifts.; [pers.] Laughter may be the greatest medicine to cure a broken heart, but poetry is the song of the heart. In my poems, I just let my heart sing and my feelings flow as I write.; [a.] San Antonio, TX

PRUCNAL, ALLISON E.
[b.] June 3, 1990; [p.] Duane D. Prucnal, Kathleen A. Prucnal; [occ.] Student

PULVER, SEYMOUR
[b.] October 28, 1929, New York City; [ed.] Lafayette High School, 3 Semesters Brooklyn College Brooklyn, NY; [oth. writ.] A number of personal poems - nothing published.; [pers.] A rose opens its petalled heart and reveals beauty, a tree, in the fall, sheds a sunset of leaves, a field of snow smooths out the wrinkles of a troubled brain - that which gladdens the heart - brings meanings to life.; [a.] Brooklyn, NY

QUINTIN, LIDIA R.
[pen.] Lidia R. Quintin; [b.] August 4, 1969, San Jose, CA; [p.] Joseph C. Newman, Norma J. Borbon; [m.] Robert Quintin, July 29, 1995; [ed.] Soquel H.S., DeAnza College; [occ.] Truck Driver; [pers.] This is my first poem published, I have been writing for many years, and my poems are based on my personal experiences, always coming from my heart; [a.] Lake Ozark, MO

QUITORIANO, JOSEFINA SARE
[pen.] Josie; [b.] November 19, 1936, Manila, Philippines; [p.] Fermin C. Sare and Teresa C. Sare; [m.] Mike D. Quitoriano, August 23, 1963; [ch.] Marilyn Janelle Q. Smith, Alphonso M. Quitariano, Michelle Q. Robinson, Mike Joe Allen; [ed.] Bachelor of Arts and Sciences, Univ. of Sto. Thomas, Bachelor of Psychology Medical Technological California License.; [occ.] Med. Technologist Lic #12363 (1965) retiree from Valley Med. Center. Fresno, CA (1989); [memb.] Anchor Lodge #626 Fresno, CA, Philippine Women's Association; [hon.] Best Hand-Writing 1954 High School 1956, mother of the year 1983, Scramble Word Award.; [oth. writ.] United Methodist Church Papu "Bamboo" article El Shaddai Article Phils' Magazine 1952, Filipino Poem.; [pers.] I dedicate the poem "I believe" to my husband who is suffering from stroke. I was inspired writing "El Shaddai" and "I Believe" for I am suffering on my throat tremor and had suffered cancer. I'm inspired by love and God in my willingness.

RAISCH, HELEN
[b.] June 22, 1961, Cincinnati, OH; [p.] Dora Mae Goley and Hershel Abbott; [m.] Divorced; [ch.] Jacob Raisch; [ed.] Ross High, D. Russell Lee Vocational; [occ.] Volunteer at Children's Hospital and Breyer School with Handicapped Children; [hon.] Athletic Award for Preschool Gym Volunteer and Certificate for Participation in Head Start at Breyer School. Certificate of Recognition for 4 Years in 4-H; [oth. writ.] "Friends Always," "Through The Years," "Doctor," "Our World," "Nature," "Falling World," "The One I Cannot Have," "Candy," "Life," "The Joy Of My Heart"; [pers.] I like to write poems about the people I love and things that matter to me.; [a.] Cincinnati, OH

RALEY, BONNIE J.
[b.] October 12, 1940, Fresno, CA; [p.] Myron and Goldie Wyatt; [m.] L. J. Raley, June 7, 1976; [ch.] Seven - three boys and 3 girls (six living); [ed.] 8th Orange Center Fresno, CA; [occ.] I am taking care of my Mother and Father; [a.] Fresno, CA

RAMADASS, ELIZABETH
[pen.] Chandra Chatterji; [b.] July 12, 1942, Hanover, PA; [p.] Robert Schiebel, Mary Schiebel; [m.] V. Ramadass (Divorced, 1984), April 18, 1964; [ed.] Northwestern High, PA State University; [occ.] Fair Housing Specialist; [memb.] NAACP, Nat'l Assn. of Human Rights Workers, Image, Lake Arbor Civic Assn.; [oth. writ.] Northwestern Alma Mater, Articles for Journal of Intergroup Relations and NAHRW News; [pers.] Life is a process of constant adjustment and every day is a new beginning.; [a.] Mitchellville, MD

RAMIREZ, LAURA D.
[b.] March 3, 1980, Lima, Peru; [p.] Alfredo and Kety Ramirez; [ed.] Currently a student at Stephen F. Austin High School; [pers.] This poem is dedicated to my family. My parents have always been supportive and loving. My brother, Paul, also deserves a lot of credit for helping me with this poem.; [a.] Houston, TX

RAMIREZ, VALERIE
[b.] July 18, 1975, Elizabeth, NJ; [p.] Lucy and Jerry Gosselink; [ed.] Currently enrolled at Florida State University. I am a senior in the BFA Acting program and will graduate Fall '97; [occ.] Student; [memb.] American Fitness Assoc. of America (AFAA). Intl. Thespian Society.; [hon.] FSU Dean's List '94 and '95; [oth. writ.] Several poems published locally.; [pers.] My goal for both my acting and writing is to move people, whether it be to laughter, tears, on thought then I've done something amazing and beautiful.; [a.] Tallahassee, FL

RAMNAUTH, KAMALDAI
[b.] January 26, 1983, Guyana; [p.] Nymoon Ramnauth and Lalman R.; [ed.] Halsey Junior High, J.H.S. 157 Q Haisey; [memb.] Police Athletic, League Inc., New York City; [hon.] Presidents Award for Educational Improvement, Award Certificate the United Federation of Teachers, (4) Student of the Month, Award of Merit School Safety Patrol; [oth. writ.] A Diamond Water Is Crystal Clear, It Dazzles Like A Piece Of Diamond; [pers.] I believe if people work hard they will get any thing they want. I also believe that every one should respect each other.; [a.] Rego Park, NY

RANDALL, JACOB LEE
[b.] January 1, 1979, Grand Rapids, MI; [p.] Mary Conley and Starl Randall; [ed.] Belding Area High School; [occ.] Cook, The Grattan Bar and Restaurant, Grattan, MI; [a.] Sheridan, MI

RAPISURA, SUSAN
[b.] September 12, 1945, Warren, OH; [p.] Elwin and Dorothy Spears; [m.] Don Rapisura, August 24, 1963; [ch.] Cliff, Craig, Todd; [ed.] Graduated San Juan High School - 1963 Citrus Height, CA, currently taking writing Class at Sierra College, Rocklin, California (20 miles above Sacramento); [occ.] Homemaker; [oth. writ.] I write short stories, last semester, one of mine - "A Lonely Place TO Be" - was published in "The Sierra Journal" - a literary magazine of Sierra College. (Spring '96); [a.] Loomis, CA

RASKIN, MIKE
[b.] December 1977, New York City; [p.] Gary and Fran Raskin; [ed.] Student at Queens College; [occ.] Student at Queens College; [pers.] "If you had a million years to do it in, you couldn't rub out even half the `Fuck you' signs in the world. It's impossible." Now I ain't no W. Axl Rose but that's just a `whole lotta rosie' to me.; [a.] Nyew York, NY

RATHERT, JAMIE
[b.] November 1, 1982, Clark Co., IN; [p.] Tom and Belinda Rathert; [ed.] 8th grade Wm H. English Middle School; [pers.] 1st published poem; [a.] Scottsburg, IN

RAYN, SALLY
[b.] September 9, 1963, Alexandria, VA; [p.] Rand and Judy Tuttle; [ch.] Oren Rigel and Sienna Grace Beckman; [ed.] Miraleste High School, Rancho Palos Verdes, CA, B.A. 1985 Stanford University, attended Die Freie University "at" Berlin; [occ.] Artist and Art Teacher; [memb.] Board of Directors, La Honda Educational Foundation, Green Party; [hon.] Community Service Award, La Honda Pescadero Unified School District; [oth. writ.] Cole Street Refrigerator Poetry, (Work in Progress), special Features in views from the Coast Newspaper; [pers.] I am primarily a visual artist interested in creating a depth of symbolic imagery. I love to create visions by linking words and layering meanings. I find alliteration an alluring accent to the synthesis of sight and sound.; [a.] San Francisco, CA

READY, MARGARET A.
[pen.] Margaret Ready; [b.] March 31, 1965, Atlanta, GA; [p.] Margie A. Swaney (Mother); [m.] Terry M. Ready, November 3, 1994; [ed.] Forest Park High; [occ.] Housewife and Homemaker; [hon.] My 7th grade teacher keep my poems and share them with her other students throughout the years; [oth. writ.] I have written several other poems, only to my husband.; [pers.] I just want to thank my husband for believing in me.; [a.] Smyrna, GA

RECK, KATHLEEN
[b.] July 26, 1967, Pittsburgh, PA; [p.] John and Joan McCluskey; [m.] Joel Mason Reck, May 6, 1995; [ch.] Two cats - Tibris and Stoli; [ed.] Plum Senior High; [occ.] Bartender; [memb.] Humane Society of the United States, People for the Ethical Treatment of Animals; [oth. writ.] Currently working on children's poem book and a compilation of my other poems.; [pers.] I live my life with the philosophy "do unto others..."; [a.] Pittsburgh, PA

REDWINE, FAITH SHAR'RON
[b.] May 1974, Detroit, MI; [ed.] Currently a College student at Oakland University in Rochester Michigan; [oth. writ.] A wide collection of essays, short stories, articles, poems and journals that have been written over a period of time.; [pers.] Leave all eyes on God and continue to focus on the prize!

REED, MAEGANN
[b.] April 23, 1984, Modesto, CA; [p.] Raymond Reed and Hope Reed; [occ.] Jr. High Student; [hon.] 1st Place 4H Hog, 7th Grade Volleyball Championship, Gold Metal 4H Speech; [a.] Turlock, CA

REED, MARGARET
[b.] November 13, 1930, Waco, TX; [p.] N. M. and Ruby Lee (Jarrard) Calfee; [m.] Alvin Morris Reed, May 27, 1950; [ed.] Mosheim High School (1948), Mary Hardin Baylor College ('48-'49), Texas A and I College 1961 and 1962, Clifton Jr. College (1949); [occ.] Housewife; [memb.] "Playhouse of Design Art Organization since 1981 (Kingsville, TX); [hon.] I was Validectorian of my senior graduating class, Mosheim High School in 1948, Mosheim, Texas; [oth. writ.] Poems published in "The American Poetry Assn." of Santa Cruz, Anthologies: (1985 - "Hearts on Fire: A Treasury of Poems on Love" - Vol II (1 - poem), (1986 Vol III (3 poems), Vol IV (1 - Poem) (1986 - Anthology: Best Poets of 1986, 1 - poem (1987 - Anthology: Words of Praise: A Treasury of Religions and Inspirational Poetry - Vol III (3 poems); [pers.] Poetry is a verbal expression arising from the stimulation of our hearts and souls from the people we meet and know, events we are caught up in, and our reactions to the beauty of God's pale in nature. There is a great satisfaction in expressing these feelings.; [a.] Riviera, TX

REEVES, MIKE
[b.] October 2, 1949, Owensboro, KY; [p.] Fred and Pauline Reeves; [m.] Kim, June 3, 1989; [ch.] David and Daniel; [ed.] B.A. Kentucky Wesleyan 1971, M.A.T. U of Louisville 1974; [occ.] History Teacher and Girl's Basketball Coach; [memb.] Phi Alpha Theta, Right to Life, Fellowship of Chris-

tian Athletes; [hon.] Outstanding Young Man 1985, Who's Who for Teachers 1996-97, Coach of th Year for Fellowship of Christian Athletes 1994; [oth. writ.] Unpublished poems and short articles; [pers.] The greatest influence on my life is Jesus Christ.; [a.] Calhoun, KY

REEVES III, SEABREN PATRICK
[b.] September 17, 1982, Vicenta, Italy; [p.] Seabren Reeves Jr. (Deceased), Brenda Reeves Sturgis and Gary Arthur Sturgis (Stepfather); [m.] Brother: Stephen David Reeves, Sister: Stephanie Elizabeth Reeves; [ed.] Student at Sacoppee High School in 8th grade Cornish Maine; [occ.] Student 14 years old; [hon.] Play baseball, soccer, basketball; [a.] Cornish, ME

REMISHOFSKY, MARIANNE BILICKI
[b.] December 26, 1945, Bayonne, NJ; [p.] Stephen and Stephanie Bilicki; [m.] Edward Remishofsky, June 19, 1966; [ch.] Mederith Anne; [ed.] Bayonne High School (Class of 93) Notre Dame College of Staten Island (Attended Rutgers University (Bachelor of Arts 1967), Jersey City State College Graduate School; [occ.] Teacher of French, English and Russian; [memb.] Rutgers Alumni Association, NEA, NJEA, WTEA, CMS PTO; [hon.] Bayonne High School Language Award 2963, Auxilium Latinum Recognition of Merit awards, Dean's List RU, merit awards and Silver Award - World of Poetry; [oth. writ.] Poems published in Poetry Parade, World of Poetry, and Overview Ltd.; [pers.] I believe that life is a dream driven in a definite direction by decisive determination. My wish for humanity is that all dreams come true and that nightmares be few; [a.] Colonia, NJ

RESCIGNO III, RALPH P.
[pen.] Rapheal; [b.] April 26, 1948, Yonkers, NY; [p.] Ralph and Marie; [ed.] Gorton H.S., New York Tech., Manhattan Teach. Inst.; [occ.] Draftsman - Telecommunication Company (N.Y. Tel.); [memb.] Professional Rodeo Cowboys Association, P.B.S. (tr); [oth. writ.] Several poem (unpub.) three short stories (unpub - as yet)

RETTIG, DANA ELIZABETH
[b.] July 5, 1984, Chicago, IL; [ed.] I attend Andrew Carnegie Elementary on the Southside of Chicago and I'm in the 7th grade.; [occ.] Inspiring poet and songwriter.; [memb.] Jonathan T. Thomas Fan Club Zachary Tye Bryant Fan Club Girl Scouts of America; [hon.] Honor Roll, Citizenship, 2nd place Spelling Bee Champ and B+ student average.; [pers.] Live life to the fullest!

REYNOLDS, AUDREY K.
[pen.] Aud; [b.] October 17, 1983, Brooklyn, NY; [p.] Arthur and Margaret Reynolds; [m.] Edward J. Enright (Dec/Div), April 12, 1952; [ch.] Edw., Joseph, Dorothy, Patricia and John; [ed.] High School - Richmond Hill and some College, no Degree; [occ.] Retired (Writing); [memb.] Legion of Mary at my Church Colombiettes of S. Ozone Park, Rosarians also at my Church Secretary to both Organizations at Church - St. Anthony of Padua; [hon.] In High School for Excellent Art Work; [oth. writ.] Three - songs copyright "1977" - Many short stories and poetry. Now working on two manuscripts.; [pers.] My mother wrote poetry and songs, also played piano. I had a brother that was an artist, and an Uncle that also was an artist. I believe that if there is anything in life that you want to do then you should go for it. I always wanted to be a writer and yet never tried hard enough to pursue that dream. I am now going to do so. My mentor for writing was my Mom.; [a.] South Ozone Park, NY

REYNOLDS, CHRISTOPHER
[b.] March 31, 1980, Oakland, CA; [p.] Sheila Foster, John Reynolds; [ed.] Bishop O' Dowd High School; [occ.] Student; [memb.] California Scholastic Federation, Black Student Union, Methodist Youth Fellowship; [hon.] Scholar Athlete, Honor Roll; [oth. writ.] Poem published in anthology of poetry by Young American's.; [pers.] Do your best, God will do the rest.; [a.] Oakland, CA

REYNOLDS, LORENA APRIL
[b.] April 3, 1981, Newport Beach, CA; [p.] John Reynolds, Mary Reynolds; [ed.] Yosemite High School, Oakhurts, CA; [occ.] 10th Grade student, Yosemite High School; [memb.] Yosemite High School Year book (Student Life Editor), Spanish Club, CSF California Scholastic Federation, Yosemite High School Varsity Volleyball; [hon.] Honor Roll Student, "International Poet of Merit", Award medallion (1996), Varsity Volleyball Most Improved Player Award.; [oth. writ.] Friends, published in Beneath The Harvest Moon, Emotions, published in The Best Poems of the '90's; [pers.] New experiences in life feeds a poet's imagination.; [a.] Coarsegold, CA

REYNOSO, LORAINE S.
[pen.] Lori; [b.] January 15, 1958, Mobile, AL; [p.] Wanda and Bud Spillers; [ch.] Seve Tomas Reynoso; [ed.] Currently, Doctoral Candidate at the Univ. of Maryland at College Park. in Recreation. M.S. - Univ. of South Alabama, B.S. Univ. of South, AL- Both in Recreation. Murphy High School, Mobile, Alabama; [occ.] National Recreation and Parks Assoc., Society of Park and Recreation Educators, National Trust for Historic Preservation, Natural Resources Defense Council; [pers.] Recreation is human action and lived experience in the fullest, mightiest sense. I quote Friedrich Nietzche in emphasis of this point. "One must not commit a blunder at any price (in) the choice of one's own bind of recreation" (1908, in Ecco Homo).; [a.] Mobile, AL

RHODES, JENNIFER L.
[pen.] Jennifer Leigh Rhodes; [b.] December 12, 1979, Henderson, NC; [p.] Norma E. Rhodes; [ed.] Currently Attending Louisburg High School in Louisburg, NC I am in my Junior Year; [occ.] Pie Maker/Order taker at Domino's Pizza in Louisburg; [hon.] Junior Beta Club; [oth. writ.] None published; [pers.] My writings are a form of feelings provided to persuade people not to take life or death of granted. The death of my cousins has greatly influenced myself as well as my writing.; [a.] Louisburg, NC

RICCI, ROSE ANN
[pen.] Rose Ann Ricci; [b.] June 4, 1925, Cleveland; [p.] Ralph and Margaret Viccarona; [m.] Daniel (Deceased), February 23, 1946; [ch.] Five; [ed.] West High Baldin Wallace; [occ.] Retired; [memb.] Manor Bonner Staff I am currently in a Nursing Home - St. Augustine; [hon.] Blue Ribbon for a water color of an Indian girl; [oth. writ.] Many - and still writing.; [pers.] Keep your chin up even when your neck is dirty - (Keep your hopes up).; [a.] Cleveland, OH

RICE, PAUL MARSH
[b.] December 30, 1946, Haverhill, MA; [p.] Hollis and Alice Rice; [m.] Mieko Rice, October 2, 1967; [ch.] Aaron and Sarah Rice; [ed.] Some College at U. Mass, Amherst MA; [occ.] Postal Clerk; [memb.] Knight Templar, A.F. and A.M., Randolph Mountain Club, 4000 Footer Club, A.M.C., National Wood Carvers Association National Rifle Association; [pers.] The creation of beauty is the most noble effort of mankind.; [a.] Georgetown, MA

RICHARDS, MARLENE S.
[pen.] Marlene Stemple, M.S. Richards, T. Elliott Masterson; [b.] July 6, 1945, Dayton, OH; [p.] Worley Stemple and Violet Stemple; [m.] Deceased, November 20, 1965; [ch.] Matthew and Rebecca, grandchildren: Danielle, Cassondra, Alexander; [ed.] Graduated from Patterson Cooperative High, attended Belmont and Beavercreek Schools, Sinclair and Front Range Colleges; [occ.] Production Assistant for Society for Range Management; [memb.] AARP, Independent Order of Foresters, various others; [hon.] Alternate Commencement Speaker at Patterson Coop., Victim Advocacy, Children's World Learning Center; [oth. writ.] Forests of So Long Ago, I Am But A Child, The White Rose, published in various newspapers and magazines. Some in progress.; [pers.] "Entranced" is dedicated to my dear friend, Rodney Saeguling, for whom it was written, because he inspired my resurrection. Also, to my lifelong friend, Leigh Zavakos, and my loving family. "I believe all things are possible and that all things work toward good for those who know Love."; [a.] Federal Heights, CO

RICHARDSON, AMY MICHELE
[b.] September 1, 1976, Englewood, NJ; [p.] Kathleen Richardson, Joseph Richardson Jr.; [ed.] Pt. Pleasant Beach High School, Elizabethtown College; [occ.] Student; [memb.] Central Pennsylvania Blood Bank, Elizabethtown College's Annual Fund Association; [oth. writ.] High School Literary Magazines, 'The Etownien' (Elizabeth College Newspapers); [pers.] To all those who have molded me and in turn have become my inspiration: Never let the light in your eyes or the fire in your hearts be darkened by the reality of the world.; [a.] Brick Township, NJ

RICHARDSON, CAROLE E.
[b.] New York; [m.] Deceased; [ch.] Chaye Conwell, Alexis Castelle, Scott Richardson; [ed.] E. Rutherford H. S., New Jersey attended College - not degreed; [occ.] Playwright, freelance writer, public speaker; [memb.] Quill and Scroll Literary Society (Smithsonian Institute) - Detroit Institute of Arts Zoological Society Detroit Repertory Theatre- Mayor of Detroit's Speakers Bureau; [hon.] 1989 and 1990 "Who's Who in Poetry", U.S. Government Certificate of Accomplishment - (Public Speaking) Oscar Graves Lifetime Achievement Award - Resident Poet on 1400 AM Detroit Radio - Poem "Black Moses" presented to Nelson Mandela while visiting in Detroit; [oth. writ.] Self published Kaleidoscope - currently working on "Echoes Whispers and Soul Food" - both poetry collections; [pers.] No writer should feel that their work is diminished nor unworthy simply because it has not yet been published.; [a.] Detroit, MI

RICHARDSON, EDWIN ANTHONY
[pen.] Eddie; [b.] January 26, 1968, Pinehurst, NC; [p.] Edwin and Margaret Richardson; [ed.] HS Graduate Associate Degree Education; [occ.] Sheet Metal Mechanic Ostrich Farmer - Part Time; [hon.] Eagle Scout - 1986 Boy Scouts of America; [oth. writ.] Lots of poems written not published; [a.] Ellerbe, NC

RICHARDSON, FRANCIS M.
[pen.] Francis M. Richardson; [b.] December 19, 1917, Indianapolis; [p.] Francis and Florence; [m.] Bonnie, May 30, 1941; [ch.] Karen; [ed.] High School and Trade School Millwright - Ford Motor Co Indianapolis; [occ.] Retired; [memb.] V.F.W. Beech Grove Ind. Navy 1942 - 1945; [hon.] Oldest man to graduate from Automotive apprenticeship; [oth. writ.] I have about 225 poems which I have written in less than 1 yr; [pers.] I often enjoy hearing from any of my friends in Indianapolis or Navy friends or V.F.W. friends.; [a.] Apache Junction, AZ

RICHARDSON, WILMA
[pen.] Wilma Richardson; [b.] August 5, 1940, Tulare, CA; [p.] Raymond Morris and Naomi Morris; [m.] Jack C. Richardson, January 7, 1963;

[ch.] Six and grandchildren (11); [ed.] Chula Vista High, Chula Vista, Calif.; [occ.] Housewife; [oth. writ.] None published 5 others put away (too long); [pers.] Wrote poems after children (small at the time) went to bed and truck driver husband was out on the road. Lived in Kansas when I wrote "Ranse Pollution"; [a.] San Antonio, TX

RICHMOND, AMELIA E.
[pen.] Featherchild (given Indian name); [b.] January 1, 1964, Harrisburg; [p.] Ruth and Harry Smith; [ch.] Three; [ed.] H.S. Grad., 2 yrs. College for Human Services, 1 1/2 yrs. Art School Philadelphia, 1 yr. Cosmetology School - HBG; [occ.] Heavy Duty Cook at Alice's Rest. in Towanda; [memb.] New Albany Baptist Church; [hon.] Long Hair Design Award. State Champ 3rd Place in Nails. Flood Writings for Sullivan Review Town Newspaper, Victim Services; [oth. writ.] The Conflict (play), To Wish Upon A Star, Distinct Friend, Good Angel, Song of Love, Remember the Rhythm, Motionless, Cloudscape Sky, Endings, More Time, Dreams to Come, So I Dream Yet Another Dream, But a Dream, Someone To Care, Just Another Unhappy, Lonely Day, I Could Use a Friend, Beauty of Life, Strategies of Destruction (contract on children), Eyes to See, New Birth, Love Foretold, My Last Goodbye, The Unborn, Today, Dream Land, Future of the Human Race, Concerto Rains, His Words, Ocean Without Shores, Little Voice, Summers Night, It's You I Found, Sands of White, Promise of Love, nothing more; [pers.] I believe life is what you make it out to be. Sometimes life is like a Roller coaster - yet you need to enjoy the ride.; [a.] Dushore, PA

RILEY, BRANDY
[pen.] Brandy Riley; [b.] July 12, 1980, Chapil Hill, NC; [p.] Joyce K. Riley, Marvin Walker; [ed.] Currently a Junior at Orange High School. Plans to go to a North Carolina University.; [occ.] Sports Endeavors, Hillsborough, NC, 27278; [memb.] Who's Who Among Americas High School Students, MSEN for University Chapil Hill, Law Enforcement Explores, writing club, Key Club, History Club, Drama Club, Literary Magazine Staff.; [hon.] Honors Classes. Biology, English, Algebra II, Honors Play Productions; [oth. writ.] 101 poems plus short stories.; [pers.] Dreams are great to treasure but real memories will last forever.; [a.] Hillsborough, NC

RININGER, JACK
[pen.] Jack Rininger; [b.] January 19, 1920, Cleves, Ohio; [p.] Harry and Lura Rininger; [m.] Jacqueline Hughe Rininger, October 12, 1945; [ch.] Two boys, Michael and Jack Jr.; [ed.] High School Diploma, Courses in finger printing and police investigations. Numerous other courses in my duties as a Police Chief, Retired as a Small Town Police Chief from Cleves, OH.; [occ.] Serving my fifth four year term in an elective office as Miami Township Trustee in a Township of 12,000 people.; [memb.] Member of the Pearl Harbor Survivors Association, V.F.W., American Legion Fleet Reserve Association, Masonic Lodge, Scottish Rite, Shriners plus others. Retired from the Naval Reserve as a Senior Chief Petty Officer.; [hon.] American Defense Medal, Asiatic South Pacific Campaign Medal, Naval Reserve Meritorious Service Medal, World War II victory medal, etc.; [pers.] As a survivor of the Pearl Harbor attack I am called upon to speak on Memorial Day, etc. My theme is our precious freedoms don't come without a price. We must be prepared to pay that price when called upon.; [a.] North Bend, Ohio

RIORDAN, DIANE MACDONALD BILLINGSLEY
[pen.] Kara Billingsley-Riordan; [b.] July 30, 1937, San Francisco, CA; [p.] Muriel Clayton and Walter A. MacDonald; [m.] Dennis Riordan, April 28, 1979; [ch.] Roxanne Locher, Christopher Locher; [ed.] B.A. Antheropology - S.T. State Univ., Elementary Education - St State Univ, Elementary Education U. of Hawaii; [occ.] Coffee Farm Owner, Substitute Teacher - KONA; [memb.] West Hawaii Writers, West Hawaii Art Guild, Good and Water, Kona Coalition to stop food Irradiation; [hon.] K.K.O.N. Radio - Community Person of the Month U. Hawaii at Hilo - Featured Poet Reception - Book Opening Merit of Excellence - Poetry in Paradise Anthology 5th place Sparrowgrass Poetry Forum; [oth. writ.] Short stories and poetry, and viewpoint articles on food irradiation in local newspapers. W.W. II childhood memories published, "Children Of The Storm", London U. Hawaii Arts and Literary magazines. "Kona Gold" Anthology.; [pers.] My poetry originates from an island that has "lost half of it's native flora and fauna." My words reflect my love and concern for a paradise lost, and a hope, that with proper care, Hawaii can once again be paradise found.; [a.] Captain Cook, HI

RIOS, JACQUELINE L.
[b.] April 15, 1951, Grayson County, TX; [p.] Jack Masters and Clara Gilstrap Henderson; [m.] Julian E. Rios, March 27, 1994; [ch.] Angela D. Bourgeois and Anthony D. DeLuca; [ed.] Los Gatos High Los Gatos, California University of San Francisco, San Francisco, California; [occ.] Business Administration Manager; [memb.] Partnership in Education, Special Olympics Volunteer (multi-year), Community Services Volunteer, United Way Campaign coordinator through Applied Signal Technology, Inc.; [hon.] United Way Communications Awards; [oth. writ.] Many, none of which are published; [pers.] "Focus daily on becoming childlike for children only see in primary colors." To my grandsons Louke A. Bourgeois and Blake A. DeLuca thank you for keeping me focused!; [a.] Sunnyvale, CA

RIOS, JOAN LALONDE
[b.] October 11, 1952, New Jersey; [p.] Margaret and Donald Lalonde; [m.] Blass Rios, May 19, 1996; [ch.] Jeffrey Lalonde and Donald Lalonde; [ed.] High School Miami Carol City, Miami, FL - Tax. School - Tallasshee, FL Banking School - Computer/School; [occ.] Homemaker, Poet, Notary Public; [hon.] Talent Publication of F.B.I. February 1972; [oth. writ.] Have composed a song from poem hope to have on market someday.; [pers.] I try to live the basis of my poem. I want to be remembered by all touch as my poem states.; [a.] Coral Springs, FL

RITCHEY, DAVID LEE
[b.] July 11, 1963, Joplin, MO; [p.] Terry and Gwew Ritchey; [ch.] David Jordan Ritchey; [ed.] Grand Prairie High, Hawds-on-Therapy School of Massage, Eastfield College; [occ.] Massage Therapist, Electronic Inspector; [pers.] I love to write Poetry and Coah Pee Wee Foot Ball, Most of my writings are from a personal relationship with my Lord Jesus Christ.; [a.] Grand Prairie, TX

ROANE, SHEA MONIQUE
[b.] April 14, 1984, Richmond, VA; [p.] Clint and Deborah Roane; [ed.] Stonewall Jackson Middle School 7th Grade; [memb.] Unity of Faith Fellowship Church, SJMS Drama Club, Mechanicsville Youth Football League-Junior Cheerleader; [hon.] Honor Roll Student, Rapme-Summer Engineering Institute 1996, YWCL "Miss Royal 1996", Presidential Citizenship Awards, Citizenship Awards, P.E. Writing Award 1992, "Super Kid" Essay Winner 1991.; [oth. writ.] Several poems/stories published in elementary school newspaper, essay contest winner in elementary school; [pers.] My poems and stories reflect how I feel inside. The Lord inspires me to write from my heart my feelings and how other people may feel inside.; [a.] Mechanicsville, VA

ROBERSON, MARY T. LONGO
[b.] July 12, 1959, Wyckoff, NJ; [p.] Dot and Jim Comis and John W. Longo; [m.] Michael W. Roberson, April 24, 1995; [ed.] Southern Regional H.S. Atlantic County Community College; [occ.] Distribution Supervisor Service Merchandise Co.; [oth. writ.] Numerous poems during the course of my life which reflect the many emotions we all encounter; [pers.] I've enjoyed writing since a very young age. When inspired by life I tend to release these emotions in my poetry. When other people can relate with that I've written I find it very rewarding.; [a.] Las Vegas, NV

ROBERTS, NANCY
[pen.] Tobi Roberts; [b.] October 13, 1932, Natick, MA; [p.] Gladys MacKenzie Hines, Joseph Hines; [m.] Widow; [ch.] Steve Kuzil, Rannah Ryan, Chris Williams, Leah Blinoff; [ed.] Melrose High School, Univ. of North Carolina; [occ.] Freelance Writer; [memb.] St. Andrew's Society, Irish Amer. Club, American Legion, Cursillo; [hon.] Service Medal (U.S. Army), Dean's List, Volunteer Award N.C. Dept. Human Services; [oth. writ.] newspaper articles, investigative reports for political newsletters, write, direct, and produce children's plays.; [pers.] I strive to capture the joy and wonder of life in my writing. My favorite poets are Carl Sandburg and Emily Dickinson.; [a.] Windsor, ME

ROBERTSON, HEATHER
[pen.] Sunflower; [b.] July 31, 1981, San Antonio, TX; [p.] Robert and Melodie Robertson; [ed.] Radford High School; [occ.] Student at Radford High School; [memb.] National Junior Honors Society, Varsity Cross Country, Junior Varsity Track, Female Wrestling, VICA, Nazarene Youth International; [hon.] Who's Who Among American's High School Students; [pers.] Reflection: When I was younger, all I wanted was to grow up. Now that I'm older, all I want is to be young again.; [a.] Pearl City, HI

ROBINETT, SEAN CHRISTOPHER
[pen.] Sean C.; [b.] October 16, 1978, Fresno, CA; [p.] Robert Robinett and Kimberly Seale; [ed.] Senior at Centennial High School, after graduating in '97, plan to study Psychology at Southern California College; [occ.] Rapping, singing, and writing; [memb.] Family Of God In A World Of Hip Hop; [hon.] Nothing tangible; [oth. writ.] Songs for my group, One Way Crew, who perform the art of rhythmical rhyme and a personal notebooks of poems entitled, True Reflections; [pers.] I strive to artfully let everyone know the knowledge of saving grace given by God, through His Son, Jesus Christ. I have been influenced by the modern, underground, West Coast poet, Redbonz. I have been even more influenced by living experience and perfect love; [a.] Bakersfield, CA

ROBINSON, ANNE MARIE
[b.] February 16, 1941, Springfield, MA; [p.] Edward and Earline Mansfield; [ch.] Melisa and Charles (Lisa and Chuck); [ed.] Sacred Heart (Elementary), Buckingham Junior High, High School of Commerce, Western New England College; [occ.] Bookkeeper; [memb.] Clapp Memorial Library Adult, Book Discussion Group; [pers.] "Between Two World's" was written in 1969.; [a.] Belchertown, MA

ROBINSON, DR. HARRIET MARIE
[b.] April 17, 1933, Baltimore, MD; [p.] Edward and Emma Madden; [m.] Divorced; [ch.] Three plus three (one deceased); [ed.] Ph.D. - Pastoral Counselling; [occ.] Musician for 2 Churches, Retired School Teacher and Pastor; [memb.] National Women Ministers Assoc. - Founder/President, Full Gospel Baptist Fellowship: Ministerial Alliance; [hon.] Numerous Certificates and Plaques;

[oth. writ.] "Reflections: Worship thru Church Music, Doctoral Thesis: "Crisis Intervention - It's Impact on Improving the Fulfillment of Woman Minister," 12 more Insp. Poems; [pers.] As a singer, musician and minister, I have recorded 4 albums. Most of all I have overcome several obstacles 8 heart attacks, 8 by-passes (2 sep. open heart surgeries) and at 63, I still go roller skating weekly.; [a.] Flint, MI

ROBINSON, FRED M.
[b.] December 10, 1933, Stockholm, ME; [p.] Charles and Pauline Robinson; [m.] Betty A. Robinson, August 29, 1959; [ch.] Susan, Fred Jr., Kelly; [ed.] 1 1/2 yrs College Business Management; [occ.] Retired - Workshops on Notary Law in Maine, Teach Notary Public Law Adult Evening; [memb.] I.O.U.F. Masoras, Disabled American Veterans, AmVets, Inform of Notaries of Maine, Volunteer Fire Fighter American Cancer Society; [hon.] Diabled Veterans, D. of the year (volunteer); [oth. writ.] Please Don't Take My Life Away (recorded into song), Childhood Sweetheart, To The One I Love, Thank You God, Give Me A Hand, Do It Your Way, Dad Is Home, Do You Love Me For What I Am, My Love, Lourane, Granddaughter; [pers.] Try each day to make at least one person smile!!

ROBISON, GRETCHEN M.
[b.] May 21, 1947, Altoona, PA; [p.] Henry and Helen Evangelista; [m.] Thomas L. Robison, August 12, 1978; [ch.] Jennifer Jo, Thomas Lee Jr., Stefanie Lyn; [ed.] Bishop Guilfoyle High School, Lock Haven University, Indiana University of Pennsylvania; [occ.] Teacher; [oth. writ.] Several poems published in anthologies, poems placed in 2 local contests.; [pers.] All I am comes from God - and an exceptional bloodline!; [a.] Altoona, PA

ROCKEFELLER, JOSEPH
[b.] December 24, 1954, Los Angeles; [ed.] University of the Pacific, Rexford High School of Beverly Hills: GPA 3.8, #2 Class Standing; [occ.] Office Work; [hon.] Salutatorian Award, Honors in Biological Science; [pers.] I want to publish my autobiography entitled: "The Little Book of Hot Water" and I'm crazy about Barbara Streisand.; [a.] Los Angeles, CA

RODRIGUEZ, OSCAR
[b.] June 16, 1977, Miami, FL; [p.] Antonio and Eloisa Rodriguez; [ed.] Christopher Columbus High School, Florida International University; [occ.] Student at Florida International University; [pers.] Simplicity of life grants freedom of strife.; [a.] Miami, FL

RODRIGUEZ, TRINA
[b.] February 17, 1978, Sacramento, CA; [p.] Don and Diane Rodriguez; [ed.] Folsom High School; [occ.] High School Student, class of 1997.; [memb.] Senior Womens Club; [hon.] Perfect Attendance Award, ROP/Comp. office, Softball Trophy Award, I love to read award ribbons.; [oth. writ.] My Angel, My Friend; [a.] Folsom, CA

ROGERS, DANIEL
[pen.] Daniel Rogers; [b.] July 7, 1962, Fresno, CA; [p.] JoAnn and Charles Rogers; [m.] Laurina Elizabeth Rogers, June 17, 1995; [ed.] Associate Arts Degree in Liberal Arts Fresno City College; [memb.] Yosemite Association; [oth. writ.] Poem "Remembrance" in National Library of Poetry book entitled Whispers At Dusk; [pers.] God's creations inspired me to write reflections. I am thrilled to have my writing published in a moment to reflect. I hope reflections will remind the people who read it, of the beauty around them.; [a.] Fresno, CA

ROLF, AUDRA K.
[b.] June 20, Lawrenceburg, IN; [p.] Aaron and Delores Rolf; [ed.] Bachelor of Arts in Economics and Philosophy, Double-degree from Indiana University, Bloomington, 1990, Masters of Science in Radio/TV, Butler University, Indianapolis, 1994; [occ.] Manager of Retail store, On-Air-Talent for WEBN, 102.7 FM, Cincinnati, OH; [oth. writ.] A multitude of poems, many published in local newspapers, magazines etc., Several short stories and, to date, I'm at work on my 3rd novel. Also, I've writer a great variety of songs, my favorite, "Man Above Love" is a hit waiting to be!; [pers.] As an author, my main goal is to convey the feeling and emotion behind the writing. "Remember Me" is about eternal life and was inspired by my grandfather, Edward H. Schmidt. Words are only words until they're put together to create the feelings which define life.; [a.] Lawrenceburg, IN

ROMAN, NICHOLAS
[b.] December 18, 1921, Youngstown, OH; [p.] George and Anna Roman; [m.] Alice Bernice, August 13, 1949; [ch.] Nick E., John T. and Alice Bernadette; [ed.] High School - 1 year College; [occ.] Retired; [memb.] Anvets Post 35, Youngstown Symphony Chorus; [pers.] U.S. Army - 1942-1945 Honorable Discharge as Staff Sergeant - I try to remember "It's nice to be important, but more important to be nice".; [a.] Youngstown, OH

ROSCA, IRINA
[b.] March 16, 1955, Romania; [ch.] Daniel, Dalia, Romana Lucian-David, Gabriella; [ed.] 4 years of College in U.S.A.-Ca. Also B/S pr. SBI - Manager and MA, BO and FO; [occ.] Leasing Agent Manager and Medical Ass.; [memb.] First Evangelical Church and Damascus Romanian Church; [hon.] USA Rosston School - Gold Medal and Poetry; [pers.] I'm a poet for 3 years I did a performance of 3 - 6 poetry everyday in Romanian, language I reflect in my poetry naivety, romance, description etc.; [a.] Fullerton, CA

ROSE, ADAM HARRY
[b.] April 12, 1974, Worcester, MA; [p.] Howard and Kathleen Rose; [ed.] Choate Rosemary Hall, College of Wooster - BA in English; [hon.] Honorable Mention at Annual Writing Prize at College of Wooster; [pers.] Reality intermingled with "Entertainment" we have all been subject to via television, film, music etc. - this is what I try to express through my poetry.; [a.] Sudbury, MA

ROSE, ANGELA DEE
[b.] September 9, 1978, Wheat Ridge, CO; [p.] Bruce and Barbara Rose; [ed.] Graduated from Parma Senior High School in June of 1996, attending College to create a more successful future; [pers.] Creating poetry is a form of expression as well as personal escape route from reality into fantasy!; [a.] Parma, OH

ROSE, RUBY PAULINE
[b.] November 4, 1922, Knox Co., TN; [p.] Arthur E. Weaver, Hollie Chesney Weaver; [m.] William Carl Rose, October 8, 1945; [ch.] Gary Carl Rose, Sherry Jean Chambers, and Mary Kay Emge; [ed.] High School - Gibbs High School; [occ.] Housewife formerly worked in Clothing Factory; [pers.] I put my sorrow into words, then put words on paper. God's way of giving me comfort after Carl's death. He was 84 yrs. old. I am 73. We were married 50 years and 7 months.; [a.] Knoxville, TN

ROSENBERG, STARLA
[b.] December 12, 1969, The Dalles, OR; [p.] Saron Wise and Nikki Wise; [m.] Kurt Rosenberg, March 29, 1996; [ch.] Kile Rosenberg; [a.] Athena, OR

ROSENTHALER, MS. BARBARA
[b.] November 19, 1924, Detroit, MI; [p.] Mr. and Mrs. Marx Rosenthaler; [ed.] Miss Newman's School (High), Detroit, MI, Marjorie Webster Junior College, Washington, DC, University of Michigan, Alpena Community College (Associate of Art Degree); [occ.] Senior Companion; [memb.] Northeast Michigan Community Service Agency, Inc.

ROSSELLI, JACK B.
[pen.] Jack B. Rosselli; [b.] August 31, 1940, San Jose, CA; [ch.] Michael and James Rosselli; [ed.] 2 San Francisco Bay area colleges Shasta College, Redding, CA; [occ.] Entrepreneur-owner since 1971 of Rosselli Art Gallery, Redding, CA, former owner of an import co., junior size women's clothing stores former cabinet maker, contractor, reserve deputy game warden for state of California—7 years; [hon.] (Other achievements) accomplished artist—wildlife and portraits, art restoration, keyboard and piano compositions; [pers.] Reflected through my writing is a mere recollection of brief moments in time.; [a.] Redding, CA

ROUNTREE, ANNIE R.
[pen.] Annie; [b.] Burke County; [p.] Mr. and Mrs. Wilson Rountree; [ed.] High School - Tech. School; [occ.] Shipping Clerk, Samson's Mtg. Waynesboro, GA; [hon.] None as of yet, however I am working on it.; [oth. writ.] I have many that I have written over the years. It is just now in this stage of my life I would like to see me of my work in print.; [pers.] Poetry has always kept my senses keen, my emotions high, and my thoughts beyond ordinary thinking.; [a.] Louisville, GA

ROURK, MARGARET A.
[b.] June 17, 1913, Oconto, WI; [p.] Emma and Frank Trepanier; [m.] Dalton V. Rourk, August 24, 1940; [ch.] Frank, Patrick, Constance; [ed.] Marquette University B.A. '37 St. Mary's College M.A. '65; [occ.] Retired; [hon.] Special Award form U.S. Veterans Hospitals for Volunteer Works from 1936 - 1973; [oth. writ.] Wrote for personal enjoyment - not publication.; [pers.] I believe in helping wherever I can to make life easier for others and give comfort and support when needed.; [a.] Concord, CA

ROUSE, MARCY
[b.] February 16, 1981, Louisville; [p.] Dale and Debbie Rouse; [ed.] South Oldham High School; [occ.] Student; [hon.] Honorable Mention in the Reflections Program at South Oldham Middle School; [oth. writ.] Short stories and other poems.; [a.] Pewee Valley, KY

RUDD, KARIN
[b.] March 21, 1963, Trinidad, WI; [p.] Herman Rudd and Joan Rudd; [ed.] Attended Marquette University, Milwaukee, Wisconsin currently attending the University of Maryland; [occ.] Configuration Management Assistant; [hon.] Vocalist Duet 1st Place and 2nd Place - National Competition. Local TV show called "Teen Talent" Soloist Category - played the Guitar and Sang - 1st place. During the Finals Danced and Song.; [oth. writ.] This is my first piece of work published. I have over 30 poems that are non-published.; [pers.] I am inspired to write words that strive to uplift the consciousness of mankind.; [a.] Gaithersburg, MD

RUDLOFF, MARY F.
[b.] September 13, 1976, Miami, FL; [p.] F. Dale Rudloff, Marilyn K. Rudloff; [ed.] Gainesville High School, Art Instruction School, Central Missouri State University, Joseph Baldwin Academy; [occ.] General Manager, F.D.R. Marketing Inc.; [memb.] National Thespian Society; [hon.] High School Recognition Award and Alumni Scholarship - CMSU, Junior Achievement Excellence Award-Oratory; [oth. writ.] Several poems and short stories published in local journals.; [pers.] To affect just one

person with my words, is a job well done.; [a.] Gainesville, FL

RUDYK, ARLENE JUNE
[b.] March 5, 1934, Buffalo; [p.] E. K. Stormes, Alice Stormes; [m.] Alfred Rudyk, June 29, 1957; [ch.] June, Joyce, Jill; [ed.] Sacred Heart Academy, Buffalo State (Teachers) College; [occ.] Retired (1996) Elementary School Teacher; [memb.] Fourteen Holy Helpers Church Eucharistic Minister, West Seneca Historical Society, Buffalo State College Alumni Association; [hon.] Religious Educator of the Year 1989, Who's Who Among America's Teachers, 1994; [oth. writ.] Poems read in church and school, poems written for class use and for class use and for a school Newsletter, for family and friends.; [pers.] With its beautiful cadence, poetry uplifts and inspires. It can describe, relate, entertain or humor. How enjoyable it is to read or write a poem!; [a.] West Seneca, NY

RUECKERT, LYLE
[b.] April 2, 1954, Lansing, MI; [ch.] Three girls - Chris, Holly, Katie; [hon.] Semi-finalist in the North American Open Poetry Contest for 1996; [oth. writ.] Putting together a collection of poems hopefully for publication sometime in 1997; [pers.] Everyone in the world is a genius, but not everyone has the time.; [a.] Saranac, MI

RUIZ-CASTANEDA, CARMEN
[b.] September 7, 1981, Miami; [p.] Norman Ruiz-Castaneda, Carmen Ruiz-Castaneda; [ed.] Epiphany School, Our Lady of Lourdes Academy; [occ.] Student; [memb.] Epiphany Alumni Association; [hon.] Duke University, Talent Identification Program; [a.] Miami, FL

RULLA, PAUL
[b.] July 16, 1970, Lincoln, NE; [p.] Donna and John Rulla; [m.] Katie Rulla, April 14, 1996; [ed.] Aurora Central High, University of Colorado at Denver; [occ.] Senior Maintenance Technician and Police Officer; [oth. writ.] Several other non-published poems for family and friends.; [pers.] All the poems I write are true and from the heart directly to and for the people I write about.; [a.] Aurora, CO

RUNCHKA, LINDA JOYCE
[pen.] Linda Lou; [b.] March 26, 1953, Chester County; [p.] Conley Forrester - Jane Forrester; [ch.] Angela Swavely - Maia Swavely; [ed.] Downingtown High School, Downington, PA, VO - Tech GED 1994; [occ.] Nursing attendant; [hon.] Place of Employment Employee of the Month.; [oth. writ.] "Fallen From A Clouds", I wrote this one when I was a teenager. Did not publish it.; [pers.] I want to thank my mother and father for my "good upbringing". Also with the world being in so much stress these days, no one takes the time anymore to notice nature. Writing about nature and getting out in the middle of it is like a sedative to me.; [a.] Honeybrook, PA

RUNNE, SASHA
[b.] April 13, 1983, Lake Worth, FL; [p.] Eugene and Imara Runne; [ed.] 8th grade; [occ.] Student; [hon.] Honor Student; [pers.] My philosophy in writing leads me to do the best in power to express the value of every human being, to teach self respect, and the beauty of uniqueness in everybody.; [a.] Maryville, TN

RUSSELL, NILE
[b.] July 20, 1982, Baltimore, MD; [p.] Sharon Russell Pinchback, Charles Pinchback; [m.] Charles Pinchback; [ed.] Leithwalk Elementary, Chinquapin Middle School, McDonogh; [occ.] Student; [hon.] Academic Achievement Award, Excellence in Spelling Award, Athletic Award, Appreciation Award for Early Intervention Program, Academic Achievement Award for Drama, Presidential Physical Fitness Award; [oth. writ.] Poem. "What Is Love," and story. "The Haunted House"; [pers.] Each day of a person's life is to be treasured forever.; [a.] Baltimore, MD

RYAN, APRIL
[b.] August 23, 1981, Pecos, TX; [p.] Lee and Wanda Ryan; [ed.] I'm a Sophomore at Pecos, High School; [occ.] Student; [memb.] I've been in band for 5 yrs, a member of the Youth Advisory Committee National Honor Society, was a Park Baptist Church; [hon.] In 6th and 7th grade I was asked to be in a National ride Honor Society book, for grades, voted most likely to succeed in 6th grade. I also have a twin brother named Christopher.; [oth. writ.] Various poems; [pers.] Always keep your confidence and believe in your self.; [a.] Pecos, TX

RYAN, IONA ROSEMARIE
[pen.] Rose; [b.] October 8, 1956, Cinti., OH; [p.] Charles and Rachel Glacking; [m.] Andre Ryan, October 19, 1991; [ch.] 3 Rachelle, Christina, Alexandrea; [ed.] Westark Comm: College 2 yrs Secretarial Science; [occ.] Lead Educator Northwest Coordinator A.P.P.L.E.; [memb.] (Associate of Parents to Prevent Lead Exposure), and Mother Church (Church of Jesus Christ of Laterday Saints) L.D.S.; [hon.] As a Freshman in St. Louis two of my other works were published in the personal of the graduating Art Students. "Quick Sand" and "Playing"; [oth. writ.] "Tomorrows Child", "Quick Sand", "Solitary Stroll", "Playing" many others; [pers.] I am simply a mother to my children, a child of "God". I strive to be whole, in spirit. My favorite poet is "Helen Stigner Rice"

RYDER, MICHELLE
[b.] December 9, 1969, Vincennes, Indiana; [p.] JoAnn Ryder & Richard Ryder; [m.] none; [ch.] none; [ed.] Bachelors Degree in Criminal Justice; Currently taking Graduate courses in Public Management; [occ.] Casemanager/Counselor at Volunteers of America; [memb.] Indiana Correctional Association; [hon.] Employee of the Year; [pers.] Always follow your heart.; [a.] Indianapolis, IN

RYSZEWSKI, DAVE
[b.] March 8, 1978, Grosse Pointe Farms, MI; [p.] Joan and Randy Ryszewski; [ed.] High School graduate, currently Freshman at Western Michigan University; [hon.] Received an award senior year from Western Michigan University. A poetry contest was taking place and I entered a poem of mine and won; [oth. writ.] I have many varieties of writings such as plays and sattires to poem's and movies.; [pers.] I have always been able to notice things in life that shock other people. I have a life long dream of being a movie script writer or the youngest poet alive. IU find my writing very unique and people who read it are very drawn in.; [a.] Grosse Pointewoods, MI

SABA, ELIAS MICHEL
[b.] January 1, 1982, Syracuse; [p.] Michel and Vivianne Saba; [ed.] Holy Cross Elementary, Moses Dewitt Elementary, Jamesville Dewitt Middle School; [occ.] Student; [pers.] For a strong poem I think you should have: A powerful beginning to catch their attention, good flow (them) and most of all have it come from the heart/from experience.; [a.] Dewitt, NY

SAMARRIPPAS, ORLANDO
[b.] June 5, 1928, Edinburg; [p.] Petra Espinoza - Pedro Samarrippas Sr.; [ed.] 1996 Graduate of Immokalee High School, Immokalee Florida; [occ.] Enlisted in United States Army; [memb.] Member of US Chess Federation; [hon.] Received medal from American Veterans of Foreign Wars

SANCHEZ, DIALID
[b.] August 8, 1969, Puerto Rico; [p.] Julio Sanchez and Blanca I. Medina; [m.] Ralph Rodriguez Jr. (significant other); [ch.] Julio Enrique and Arielle Shareese; [ed.] Holyoke High School, Holyoke Community College; [occ.] Communication Asst, Macfadden Assoc - Holyoke, MA; [pers.] Poetry should not alienate but enmesh the run-of-the-mill individual. This is my aim for writing poetry.; [a.] Springfield, MA

SANDERS, CAROLYN ANN
[pen.] Carol; [b.] August 31, 1943, Beaumont, TX; [p.] Wade and Lilian Sisk; [ch.] Brenda A. Sanders and Billy Jr.; [ed.] 1 through 12th grade at Liberty Texas, Bussiness Adm. at Western Wyo College, Laramie, WY; [occ.] Fabrics and Crafts, Walmart, Food Server, Lottie's Restaurant; [oth. writ.] "Come Little Sparrow," "A Friend or Lover," "As the Eagle Flies," "You Cannot Have My Soul," "Set Me Free," "Under the Bed I Wait"; [pers.] I am greatly influenced by my past, being given away at birth and never feeling like I belong to anyone. Very unhappy childhood. "I love Children."; [a.] Evanston, NY

SANDERS, SARA
[b.] January 16, 1980; [p.] Bill and Libby Sanders; [ed.] Chesterton High School and currently Valparaiso High School; [hon.] Reserve Grand Champion for a Story I rote for 4-H: 'The Dog Really Has Nothing To Do With The Story'; [oth. writ.] I have been "Published" in school created magazines, I write when I have something to say.; [pers.] I don't believe in writers, per se, I believe in people that can write, that anyone that has a mind or a point of view can out it down on paper. Go ahead, do not be afraid, say it.; [a.] Valparaiso, IN

SANFORD, TERI LYNN
[b.] September 3, 1976, Spartanburg, SC; [p.] Colleen Sanford; [ed.] None yet but I want to become a chef, and I would continue to write poems in my spare time. And hope they get published.; [hon.] I got awards in high school, and I got an Award for taking care of the Handicapped.; [oth. writ.] I write poems a lot. I have twelve poems and I keep them in my Poetry Folder. I have been writing poems since I was twelve years old.; [pers.] My name is Teri Sanford I was born in SC. I am 20 years old. And writing poetry has always been my hobby. And I like to read other poetry. And in the future I would like to have my own Poetry book.; [a.] Orlando, FL

SARKIES, JOSEPH P.
[b.] May 19, 1956, New Iberia, LA; [p.] John and Ina Sarkies; [m.] Susan H. Sarkies; [ch.] Rachel and Victoria Sarkies; [pers.] I dedicate my poem to my father, John Sarkies who taught me to both enjoy and respect my natural surroundings.

SAWDEN, ERIN ELAINE
[b.] September 16, 1983, Spokane, WA; [p.] Dale Sawden (Deceased), Guardian Elaine England (Mother of Dale Sawden); [ch.] Cassandra Sawden (Twin Sister); [ed.] 7th Grade, Honor Roll; [occ.] Student; [hon.] Awards in Writing from Elementary and on published Poetry in School Books The Buzz, Two poems etc; [pers.] I admire the writings of Shel Silverstine and R. L. Stein in my poems Compassion and Surprise.

SAWICKI, ERIC JAMES
[b.] June 18, 1975, Buffalo, NY; [p.] Bonnie and James Sawicki; [ed.] Northeastern Clinton Central School, Springfield College, Green Mountain College; [occ.] Student at Green Mountain College,

VT; [memb.] Boy Scouts of America Troop 42, Adirondack Council, Americorps - Plattsburgh, NY; [hon.] Eagle Scout - BSA, Vigil Honor - BSA, Leadership Scholarship - Green Mountain College; [pers.] "Direct your eye right inward, and you'll find a thousand regions in your mind. Travel them and be expert in home-cosmography". Thoreau; [a.] Rouses Point, NY

SAXTON, JASMINE DESIREE MARIAH
[b.] January 7, 1989, Westwood, NJ; [p.] Brandy Mariah, Jeff Saxton; [ed.] 2nd grade Slocum Skewes School, Ridgefield, NJ, 3 years piano lesson at Yamaha Music School Ridgefield NJ, 2 years Martial Arts Academy NJ,; [occ.] Red Belt in Tae Kwon Do, Ridgefield Park NJ; [oth. writ.] Poem published in the record (Newspaper - Hackonsack NJ); [pers.] I want to write poems and story's for children so I can teach them to be fair, and that life is funny.; [a.] Ridgefield, NJ

SCARCHELLO, DOMINICK
[b.] September 26, 1970, Hagerstown, MD; [p.] Barry and Margaret; [ed.] B.A. Philosophy, Univ. of Maryland; [occ.] English Tutor; [pers.] The totality of experience is encompassed differently in every individual.

SCATA, BERNICE
[b.] June 4, 1919, Middletown, CT; [p.] Mary and Joseph Lewkowicz; [m.] Tony Scata Sr., Feb. 3; [ch.] Four; [ed.] Elementary; [occ.] Retired - Housewife

SCHAFER, MATTHEW
[p.] Gerald and Patricia Schafer; [memb.] National Wildlife Federation, The Humane Society, World Wildlife Fund, Animal Rescue League, ASPCA, Environmental Defense Fund, Siera Club; [hon.] Two Presidential Academic Achievement Awards, High School Honor Roll.

SCHAFFNER, FRANIC
[b.] May 22, 1953, Canton, OH; [p.] Richard and Harriet; [ed.] Kent State Univ. City Colleges of Chicago, Central Texas College, Army Medical Corp.; [occ.] Self-employed; [memb.] North Shore Animal League, Greenpeace, WWF, Arbor Day Foundation, National Parks Conservation Ass. National Resources Defense Council, Defenders of Wildlife ASPCA, The Nature Conservancy, Clean Water Action; [hon.] 1 Salesmman 1995, 1994; [oth. writ.] Poetry book called Pass The Roles Our Nerves Are Getting Cold; [pers.] Life's a never-ending philosophy class. We study mirrored images of toy soldiers and dolls. While some scale the mountains, some scale the walls.; [a.] Wampum, PA

SCHOFIELD, DAVID JAYSON
[pen.] Roy Teauge; [b.] April 30, 1977, Providence, RI; [p.] Joan Mary Schofield; [ed.] North Providence High School, University of Rhode Island; [memb.] Speak Easy Sexuality Peer Educators of URI; [hon.] Dean's List; [oth. writ.] Several poems and short stories; [pers.] Inspiration can come from anywhere at anytime. Thank you to those who continually inspire me. Then you, Mom, for supporting and putting up with me. Love all around!; [a.] North Providence, RI

SCHOONOVER, TIM
[b.] April 12, 1948, Waterloo, IA; [p.] Wm. and Arlene Schoonover; [m.] Divorced - 1994, 1982; [ch.] Ryan (13), Mike (11), Kyle (5); [ed.] Dysart High School, Dysart Iowa 114 Hrs. Completed at Memphis State 132 Required for Degree; [occ.] A&D Counselor, Jobs Development Counselor; [memb.] AA - GA, Galloway Methodist Church (18 years without a drink), 2 years without a bet; [hon.] Vietnam Veteran (1968-69), (USMC 0 1967-1971), Honorably Discharged; [oth. writ.] Several non-fiction articles twenty years ago in local media - contributing writer for local publications (Ongoing).; [pers.] For years I numbered my feeling with any behavior available. I am now healing through recovery, only because I opened up and let God in.; [a.] Memphis, TN

SCHUSTER, DENISE MARIE
[b.] June 17, 1973, New London, NH; [p.] Pio and Linda Shampney; [m.] Jeffrey K. Schuster, April 24, 1993; [ch.] Amber and Jeff Schuster; [ed.] Andover Elem Andover NH, Mitchell Jr. High CA, Cordova Sr. High CA; [occ.] Private Nurse; [memb.] Good News Committee; [hon.] Poetry Awards in 8th grade Customer Service in Working with People; [oth. writ.] I have over 200 poem I have written including "Dreams Of My Heart," "I Thought Of You," "Alone," "Strangers," "Death On The Horizon" etc...; [pers.] I never let anyone read my poetry before this with the exception of 8th grade contest. I am very happy that someone really likes it.; [a.] Andover, NH

SCHUTZ, BOBBIE A.
[pen.] Bobbie A. Schutz; [b.] October 26, 1953, Evansville, IN; [p.] Robert and Najla Grotius; [m.] Daryl E. Schutz, September 17, 1977; [ch.] Paul James - 14, Craig Robert - 9; [ed.] Sacred Heart Grade School, Mater Dei High School, Ivy Tech College, Technical Writing, and Typing. (Courses at Ivy Tech), ICS International Correspondence School; [occ.] Part time teacher's aid and after school day care worker.; [memb.] Holy Redeemer PTO, served two yeas as President of the PTO. Right to life.; [oth. writ.] I have written many poems and would soon like to write a children's book. Also my hobby is to rewrite new lyrics to old songs. I have sung some of these songs in front of the student body in my children's elementary school.; [pers.] In the poems that I have written I found inspiration through the beauty of nature, and God's gifts of friendship, family and the works of Erma Bombeck.; [a.] Evansville, IN

SCOTT, JESSIE A.
[b.] October 11, 1934, Lawrence, KS; [ch.] Andrea; [ed.] High School 1 year at University of Arkansas; [occ.] Clerk, District Attorney Contra Costa, California; [pers.] I am surprised and pleased that two of my poems are being published. I hope whoever reads them will enjoy them as much as I did writing them.; [a.] Martinez, CA

SCUDDER, ALLEN L.
[pen.] Wicked; [b.] May 29, 1971, Richmond, CA; [p.] Marcia and Allen Scudder; [m.] Jana Scudder, March 8, 1995; [ch.] Marissa Scudder; [ed.] Graduated High School at Pinole Valley High School in Pinole, CA; [occ.] Cook; [memb.] Was a member of a band I formed in 1993 called "Wicked"; [oth. writ.] Endangered, Confusion Meant To Be, Within, The Wind Will Blow, and a whole lot more...; [pers.] Influenced by reality, all writings come from personal experiences I have encountered in life....thanks to mom, and dad, and my Lorrie chuck combs...; [a.] Kokomo, IN

SEAMAN, SARAH KATHLEEN
[pen.] Ana Lisle Murray, Ariana Spenser; [b.] July 21, 1982, Chicago, IL; [p.] Kim Seaman and Paul Gerlach; [ed.] In the 9th grade at West Hall High School, in Oakwood, GA; [memb.] Jr. Civitan and Avid Actress for the Spartan players; [hon.] Minor School Awards and honors through Clubs.; [oth. writ.] One other poem published in "Childlife" magazine at age 11, many unpublished short story's, poems, and one unfinished novel.; [pers.] I never thought my writing would have gotten me so far at 14, and now I find I have had a least one small dream fulfilled. To all those dreams that are so small - keep some hope.; [a.] Flowery Branch, GA

SEGRETI, MARY
[b.] June 18, 1981, Poughkeepsie, NY; [p.] Marylou and Albert Segreti; [ed.] Sophomore at Sarasota, Christian High School; [pers.] I hope that through my writing people will come to appreciate all the beautiful "poems" God gives us everyday that we often take for granted.; [a.] Sarasota, FL

SEILER, MICAH
[b.] February 9, 1984, Dansville, PA; [p.] Jack and Jane Seiler; [ed.] 6th Grade; [occ.] Student; [memb.] Pleasant Valley Baptist Church, Overcomers Bible Club, Brotherly Love Club; [hon.] Name written in the Lamb's Book of Life; [oth. writ.] The Fabric of life; [pers.] I try to reflect my feelings about the wonders of God in my writing. I have been greatly influenced by God's word.; [a.] Gowanda, NY

SEITZ, GENE
[b.] December 4, 1980, Smithtown, IL; [p.] Kevin and Barbara Seitz; [ed.] Centereach High School, Dawnwood Middle School, Oxhead Elementary; [occ.] Sophomore at Centereach High; [memb.] Junior Varsity Football Team of Centereach High; [hon.] Played for the Central Suffolk Junior Football Travel Team, Won Nassau - Suffolk Championship and Lineman of the year Award; [oth. writ.] Poems and stories I write I usually keep to myself.; [pers.] I try to write of the beauty of things that most people take for granted, such as things that are made by men and women, and the environment.; [a.] Centereach, NY

SELIGO, VIOLA Q.
[b.] January 25, 1903, Cherryville, NC; [p.] Sherman and Joanne P. Quien; [m.] Eric Seligo, June 1932; [ch.] Joan and Fred; [ed.] BA Winthrop College Rock Hill SC, Grad. Study NY Univ. Long Island Univ,, Dean's List; [occ.] Retired; [memb.] Sierra Club, W.W. Haiku Soc. U.F.T. - N.E.A., AARP; [hon.] Haiku Prizes; [oth. writ.] Various poetry anthologies Haiku Magazines. I try to write humorous, tolerant, liberal, democratic poetry.; [pers.] Understanding, tolerant, caring.

SELLECK JR., WILLIAM
[b.] June 24, 1977, Bay Shore, NY; [p.] William and Barbara; [ed.] West Islip High School, Penn State University; [occ.] Student - Sophomore at PSU, Biochemistry Major; [memb.] Penn State Marching Blue Band; [hon.] High School All State Band; [a.] University Park, PA

SEYMORE, HEATHER
[b.] March 16, 1981, Kingsport, TN; [p.] Doug and Rena Seymore; [ed.] Cherokee High School; [occ.] Student; [oth. writ.] Some of my other poetry has been in the school newspapers or magazines.; [pers.] I don't really know what inspires me to write poetry. I find it to be a great honor if someone reads one of my poems and likes it. My poetry gives others a chance to see the world through my eyes.; [a.] Rogersville, TN

SHADE, BRIAN KEITH
[b.] October 7, 1961, Oakland, CA; [p.] Dale Edward, Patricia Maureen Shade; [m.] Divorced; [ch.] Tyler (11), Trevor (5); [ed.] H. S. Graduate some College Richard Jr. College; [occ.] Postal Letter Carrier; [memb.] Collin County Historical Society, Custer Road First United Methodist Church; [hon.] No writing awards. I have the honor of being a proud father though.; [oth. writ.] No other material has been published at this time. I do however, journal on a daily basis. I am currently enrolled in a writing course for children's stories.; [pers.] Life is relationships. I believe that the only way to measure true success is by way to measure true success is by what kind of human being a person is. Live with uncertainty. It's the only place where real, sustained growth is taking place.; [a.] McKinney, TX

SHAH, SEEMA
[b.] August 15, 1984; [p.] Bharat and Falguni Shah; [ed.] Vandenberg Elementary, Thompson Middle School; [occ.] Student 7th Grade; [memb.] Student Council, Forensics, Young Astronauts Club, Orchestra; [hon.] Presidential Academic Achievement Certificate; [pers.] If you believe in yourself you can achieve your goal.; [a.] Southfield, MI

SHAPIRO, BEAU
[b.] August 18, 1983, Los Angeles; [p.] Willa, William; [occ.] Student; [oth. Writ.] "The View Of An Owl," "From My Eyes"; [pers.] "We must learn in order to teach, we must teach in order to learn."; [a.] Santa Barbara, CA

SHARIK I, MICHAEL E.
[pen.] Eddie S.; [b.] September 14, 1953, McKeesport; [p.] Bernard and Ann Sharik; [m.] Cindy Sharik, June 21, 1974; [ch.] Laura, Heather, Mike II; [memb.] VFW American Legion Moose; [oth. writ.] Bandit, Uncle Dan, The Lord Is Their; [pers.] "My Son" is a poem written for my son who was hit by a car at 8 yrs old and is still in a semi-coma at 17.; [a.] West Mifflin, PA

SHAW, CORY
[pen.] Cory Shaw; [b.] November 29, 1985, Cambridge, MA; [p.] Roberta and John Shaw; [ed.] I go to Lt. Job Lane School in Bedford MA; [occ.] Student; [pers.] My 4th grade teacher Mr. K. Schmitt inspired this poem and liked it very much; [a.] Bedford, MA

SHAW JR., ODESSA
[pen.] O. Shaw, Jr.; [b.] September 8, 1953, Durham, NC; [p.] Mr. and Mrs. Odessa Shaw Jr; [m.] Mrs. D. Davis-Shaw, July 14, 1984; [ch.] Gillian E. Shaw; [ed.] Shaw University, Durham Public Schools; [occ.] T.V. Director, WNCN Raleigh, NC; [memb.] Trustee and Decon Board Fisher Memorial U.H.C.; [oth. writ.] Currently working on a book of fiction. Wrote a Christmas Musical, adapting songs from Handel's Messiah.; [pers.] I feel that words are the best way to convey a point or idea, to not only entertain but to make one think and contemplate.; [a.] Durham, NC

SHEPARD, MELISSA L.
[pen.] Missy Shepard; [b.] June 14, 1967, Fond du Lac, WI; [p.] Dirk and Jean Williamson Sr.; [m.] Mark Shepard, July 16, 1994; [ch.] Beau Daniel; [ed.] Horace Mann High School; [occ.] Supervisor, Hardee's Family Restaurant, Horicon, WI; [memb.] Church of Peace, Fond du Lac, WI; [a.] Horicon, WI

SHERLOCK, LORI JEAN
[pen.] Jenifer Rand, Jenae Shelton; [b.] August 1, 1964, Anaheim, CA; [p.] William Lang and Jean Lang; [m.] Daniel Sherlock, May 24, 1986; [ch.] Elizsabeth Dawn; [ed.] B.A. - Psychology and M.A. - Behavioral Science from California State University Dominguez Hills; [occ.] Desktop Publishing; [hon.] Silver Poet, Golden Poet, Distinguished Scholarship; [oth. writ.] Several poems published in World of Poetry Press, Newsletter, Pioneer Press.; [a.] Fullerton, CA

SHERMAN, HILARIE A.
[b.] March 27, 1977; [p.] Wayne and Linda Sherman; [ed.] Oak Hill High, North Western Connecticut Community Technical College; [occ.] Interpreter - Sign Language; [memb.] National Grange, State and Local Grange Member, Wales Presbyterian Church, NWDC; [pers.] I've always tried to write from my own personal and educational experiences. I think it brings a greater depth to a persons writing if a price of the person is with it. Thanks to my family and all my friends.; [a.] Wales, ME

SHERROD, MARY LOUISE LAMM
[b.] July 27, 1947, Johnston Co., NC; [p.] Bernice and Monz Hinnont Lamm; [m.] Daniel Willie Sherrod, March 29, 1973; [ch.] Sandra, Jennette and Daniel; [ed.] Degree in Nursing; [occ.] Licensed Practical Nurse; [a.] Micro, NC

SHIELDS, JOHN CLARK
[b.] October 5, 1953, Miami, FL; [p.] Eileen and James Shields; [ed.] Miami Dade Community College, AA Degree (1973), University of Florida, BA Degree in Landscape Architecture with Honors, (1977); [occ.] Self Employed Landscape Architect, Own a Design/Build Landscape Firm.; [memb.] American Society of Landscape Archetict's (ASLA), Florida Nursery Man and Growers Assoc. (FNGA), Miami Design Preservation League, Fair child Tropical Garden Nature Conservancy, Center for the Fine Arts, Sierra Club, Fla Native Plant Society; [hon.] Coral Gables Beautification Award (1986), Sesco lightning Award (1986), Florida Asla Award of Excellence (1986), Florida ASLA Award of Excellence (1986) FNGA Landscape Awards of Excellence (1986) (1987), Basf Fame Award (1987) Alca National Environmental Merit Award (1987), Dade County Presidential Award (1991); [oth. writ.] None published, took literature and creative writing in early College. Enjoy writing poetry as a pass time.; [pers.] To create the power of the pen to inspire mankind.; [a.] Miami, FL

SHIFFLETT, DEBRA K.
[b.] August 25, 1965, Alexandria, VA; [p.] Curtis and Mary Nobles; [m.] John M. Shifflett, September 3, 1993; [ch.] Amanda, Johnny, Joey, Johnny Jr., Kenny and Dillon; [ed.] James W. Robinson High School, Burke, VA; [occ.] Mother and Housewife; [oth. writ.] Several poems and editorials for local newspapers.; [pers.] This poem is dedicated to my step children, John Jr., Kenny and Dillon Shifflett. The majority of my poems are written from my own personal experiences.; [a.] Lucama, NC

SHOCKLEY, JASON LEE MITCHEL
[b.] November 2, 1984; [ed.] Junior High; [hon.] D.A.R.E. Essay (Class Winner); [oth. writ.] I've written other things that have won awards when I was in Elementary nothing serious.; [pers.] As young as I am, it goes to show that children like me have the ability to express their feelings through writings.; [a.] Lebanon, TN

SHOOK, YVONNE
[b.] May 30, 1948, Middletown, MD; [p.] Deceased; [m.] Richard A. Shook, July 17, 1982; [ch.] Two sons and two grandchildren and one stepson; [ed.] High School graduate, Heme Study - Cornell University - Human Resources; [occ.] Cashier-Office Assistant for large grocery chain - P and C.; [memb.] Local One Union (UFCW); [oth. writ.] A few dozen pieces of work none published as yet - I am just beginning! Have not shared and of my work as yet for publication.; [pers.] I am inspired by nature. Although extremely shy about sharing my work and letting others see our world through my eyes.; [a.] Youngsville, PA

SHORT, JUSTIN D.
[b.] March 27, 1982, Shelby, NC; [p.] Dale Short/Angie Short; [ed.] Currently-will graduate Shelby High School, Class of 2000; [memb.] Beta Club, Latin Club, Soccer Team; [hon.] First Chair Viola, All-state Repertory Orchestra 9th Grader; [a.] Shelby, NC

SHORT, KENDRA
[b.] March 21, 1982, Idaho Falls, ID; [p.] Neil Tener Short and Debby Short; [ed.] Freshman at Centennial High School; [memb.] National Junior Honor Society, Art Club, band, Centennial Theatre Company; [hon.] Honor Roll, First place poetry contest, Winner for Oasis Middle School 1994 and 1995; [a.] Peoria, AZ

SHOWERMAN, DIANE L.
[b.] May 31, 1943, Amsterdam, NY; [p.] Philip and Angie Lapi; [m.] Sometime in July 1970; [ch.] Four children, four grandchildren; [ed.] Grad. High School; [occ.] Beech-nut Baby Foods Labor; [pers.] My love of children, and granddaughters "Angie."; [a.] Fort Plain, NY

SHUMPERT, EDWARD
[b.] April 22, 1976, Columbia, SC; [p.] Larry E. and Ramona Shumpert; [ed.] Grad. High School, Airport High School; [occ.] Sales Person Shumpert Garden Shop; [oth. writ.] I have never been published till now, however I have a lot of other poems that I wish to published one day, either in collections of my own or collections with other poets.; [pers.] Well I just want to say that poetry for me is a way to release emotional feelings. Poetry has helped me out a great deal through my band in Songs, and I have also learned a lot about myself.; [a.] Lexington, SC

SICILIA, VITALIANO
[b.] October 10, 1973, New Jersey; [ed.] Elmwood Park Memorial High School, National Education Center-rets Campus; [occ.] Copier Technician, McsKanon New York, NY and a student of life; [memb.] I am a member of a Toller Hockey Team and I also help coach another; [oth. writ.] I have written many poems on many different topics, none have been published before and only few have been read.; [pers.] Anything I have ever written reflects something emotional I am feeling at the moment. Even though I am only 23, I am very old-fashioned and a true romantic at heart.; [a.] Elmwood Park, NJ

SIELA, TIMOTHY E.
[b.] April 9, 1963, Kansas City, MO; [p.] Robert, Eileen; [ch.] Chantell; [ed.] Utah St. University; [occ.] Rancher; [memb.] George Washington Boyhood Home Foundation, Earth Watch, the Nature Conservancy, The Wilderness Society, Rainforest Rescue, National Wildlife Federation, National Park Association, Environmental Defence Fund. Father Flanagans Boy's Home, Rare Breed Conservancy, National Arbor Day Foundation Noyers Children's Home, Green Peace, Sierra Club, National Audubon Society, American Livestock Bread Conservancy, American Ayrshire Association. American Holstein Association, American Guernsey Association, Illinois Ayrshire Club; [pers.] My writing's are lonely and sad due to my outrage of the deforestation of the rainforest, my sadness of all the hungry children in the world, and my broken heart by a girl named Angie.; [a.] Easton, MO

SIGNORE, MICHAEL J.
[b.] June 14, 1960, Pittsburgh, PA; [p.] Charlie Signore, Grace Signore; [ch.] Tonia Signore; [ed.] Gateway Senior High School; [occ.] Carpenter; [memb.] Sobermen, Motorcycle Club, Greensburg, PA; [hon.] Two Years Clean and Sober as of 9-15-94; [oth. writ.] Many songs and poems from the heart; [pers.] My goal is to write songs and poems to be used by great musicians.; [a.] Monroeville, PA

SILVERMAN, DENA
[pen.] J. L. Sarandon; [b.] October 19, 1974, Hollywood, FL; [p.] Cheryl and Jack Appel; [m.] Richard Silverman, May 10, 1996; [ed.] A.S. Degree Dental Hygiene; [pers.] "Heaven" Dedicated in memory of Robert L. Dean.

SIMMONS, ANN
[b.] August 21, 1947, Warren, CO; [p.] Edward M. and Ruth F. Clark; [m.] Richard C. Simmons, Februrary 20, 1984; [ch.] Richie Eastham and Edie Falls; [ed.] Rappahannock Co. High School; [occ.] Self-employed with mountain starter and alternation bookkeeper and sales; [memb.] Washington Baptist Church; [oth. writ.] Several (not published)

personal; [pers.] This poem "Grandmother You're So Special" is truly a reflection of love, care, honesty, respect, honor and guidance that my grandmother gave to me. I miss her so much. This poem is dedicated to Sarah Alice Frazier, my light, that today carries me though all my days - I love her and I miss her more as each day passes.; [a.] Washington, VA

SIMMS, ELSIE L. B.
[b.] November 10, 1912, Atlantic City; [p.] Viola and Samuel Brotten; [m.] Wallace Simms (Deceased U.S. Navy), June 1, 1932; [ch.] Shirley, Darlene; [ed.] Prille H.S. 1931; [occ.] Deceased; [memb.] IBPOE of W; [oth. writ.] Book of poems not published.

SIMON, JACK W.
[b.] August 12, 1936, West Newton, PA; [p.] John and Mary Simon; [m.] Mary Kay Simon, April 18, 1960; [ch.] Kelly, Chris, Gina, Michele; [ed.] University of Pittsburgh 1958, Speech Major, English and Journalism Minor; [occ.] Director of Communications NEETC Inc., Indiana, PA; [memb.] National Fire Protection Association, Greensburg Volunteer Fire Department, International Society of Fire; [hon.] National Professional Qualifications Certified Firefighter III, Who's Who - Business Leader 1994, W.W. Kellog Foundation "Fellow," retired Pennsylvania State Fire Commissioner; [oth. writ.] "Commissioners Comments published monthly 1990-1995 in the Pennsylvania Fireman. Published 12 articles for National and State Fire Service Organizations.; [pers.] "Doing it right the first time is easier than doing it over again."; [a.] Greensburg, PA

SIMONS, TYLER LLOYD
[b.] December 17, 1984, Saltlake, UT; [p.] Darren and Tamra Simons; [ed.] Fillmore Elementary and I'm presently going to Fillmore Middle School. I'm in the 5th grade; [oth. writ.] None, this is my first and only poem that I've written, and that has ever been noticed by anyone other than my close family; [pers.] I'm a very personable person I was adopted at eleven which was almost a year ago and have greatly been influenced by my parents Darren and Tamra Simons for their insight in reading and writing.; [a.] Fillmore, UT

SIMPSON, LORRICE
[pen.] Micki Brigham; [b.] April 27, 1949, Clifford, MI; [p.] Edward and Lorrie Lester; [ch.] Gary, Dana, Byran, Juri, Deanna; [ed.] 9th grade Caro Community received a GED in 1984; [occ.] Retail Sale manager at wal-mort in Cornelia, GA; [memb.] Life time Membership in Clover Book of Verse; [hon.] Danae Award from Clover Book of Verse, Platinum Award from Arkansas Poetry Association, Recognition Award from Anne Cole and other Various Awards; [oth. writ.] I've been writing poetry since the age of 9. I have so many poems they are too numerous to count.; [pers.] I lost my father when I was very young, I withdrew from family and friends and turned to writing, reading and writing became my outlet and gradually my Comrade.; [a.] Cleveland, GA

SIPHO, EILEEN RUTH AGUILAR
[pen.] Eileen Sipho; [b.] August 16, 1935, San Diego, CA; [p.] Tomas Aguilar, Willie Anna Aguilar Grace; [m.] Ollie Sipho Sr., May 16, 1953; [ch.] Michael Ollie Jr., Gary, Briggitte, Lilo, Derrick; [ed.] GED (Equivalency Test); [occ.] Homemaker; [oth. writ.] Not yet published.; [pers.] I write what I feel and what comes from my heart and deep down in my very soul - and I know that I can reach out and touch someone, whether it be funny, sad, or mysterious. I strive for that perfection.; [a.] Spring Valley, CA

SKOLNICK, PHIL
[b.] October 7, 1942, Brooklyn, NY; [p.] William and Dorothy Skolnick; [m.] Linda Nosseh, May 1, 1964; [ch.] Cyd, Charese and Sean; [ed.] Master's degree in Social studies Teaching, from Brooklyn College, June 1966, G.P.A. 3.37; [occ.] Teacher; [memb.] "Golden Key' National Honor Society at Brooklyn College for the top 30% of the class. Brooklyn chapter of the "United Karaoke Singers of America"; [hon.] Past president of the Sea-Gate/Coney Island "Little League": Founder of the "United Youth Baseball League of Brooklyn". Dean's List Kingsborough Community College; [oth. writ.] Poems and essays in local newspaper. Writer of song lyrics some used in 1950's Rock 'n roll music.; [pers.] Every person must find his/her own worth and then has a moral and civil obligation to share it with the rest of Society. "He who heals himself, heals the rest of the world".; [a.] Brooklyn, NY

SLAUSON, ANTHONY
[b.] May 4, 1961, Buffalo, NY; [oth. writ.] "Dead Trees" book of short stories, essays, poems etc. (unreleased), '99 semi-great poems (unreleased).; [pers.] After 25 years of writing, I am finally putting my fear of artistic criticism to rest.; [a.] Russell, KY

SMITH, BRIE AVERY
[b.] September 8, 1984, Keezletown, VA; [p.] Clendy Pleasants-Smith and Randy Smith; [ed.] Home Schooled; [occ.] Home School Student; [memb.] Broad Street Mennonite Church, Paulington Geographic Society; [pers.] Mostly my poetry is inspired by human emotions, nature, and my spirituality. Writing poetry has come naturally since I was 4 years old. The encouragement of my parents and older brother has been a very big part of my poetry.; [a.] Keezletown, VA

SMITH, DANNIE M.
[b.] February 6, 1979, Dalton, GA; [ed.] 11th enrolled in Lafayette High School; [oth. writ.] "Life" in of moonlight and wishes. An unpublished book of poetry, "Looking Through my Immortal Soul."; [pers.] "Everybody in my world knows insanity, disorder, and chaos. Everyone outside my world knows sanity, and calm serenity. The people in between know nothing but what is told to them".; [a.] LaFayette, GA

SMITH, JENNY
[pen.] Jenny Smith; [b.] September 2, 1982, Lancaster, OH; [p.] Jim Smith, Patsy Smith; [ed.] Logan-Hocking High School (still attending) I'm a Freshman (9th); [oth. writ.] First one published, I haven't published any others.; [pers.] I am greatly influenced by my family and nature. I also enjoy writing deep, dark, and mysterious poems.; [a.] Logan, OH

SMITH, PAUL E.
[pen.] Paul E. Smith; [b.] March 3, 1930, Noble County, IN; [p.] Frank and Fairy Smith; [m.] Mary L. Smith, March 12, 1950; [ch.] Connie, Kenneth, Kevin, Wallace; [ed.] High School; [occ.] Retired Pt. Time Res. Mgr. Glencroft Ret. Comm.; [memb.] Missionary Church; [hon.] School Member 12 years; [oth. writ.] Three poems in anthologies of the National Library of Poetry; [pers.] I like to write about nature and wildlife especially as it pertains to God. I also enjoy writing about God's love for His people.; [a.] Glendale, AZ

SMITH, SANDRA G.
[b.] June 23, 1967, Ithaca, NY; [p.] Dr. Robert E. Smith and Mr. and Mrs. Guiendolyn C. Smith; [ed.] B.A. Psychology from Angelo State University, San Angelo, TX; [occ.] United States Postal Service Clerk; [pers.] Most of my poetry has been inspired by both the joys and sorrows of love. Peter McWilliams said it best, "It is a risk to love. What if it doesn't work out? Ah, but what if it does."; [a.] Midland, TX

SMITH, SARAH
[b.] September 15, 1978; [p.] Tom and Ann Crabb, Rex Smith; [ed.] Hillside, Academy, Oak Woods Intermediate, Granbury Middle, Granbury High School; [occ.] Waitress, Pizza Inn, Bank Teller, Community Bank; [memb.] Mentor Program, Key Club; [hon.] National Honor Society, National Merit Scholar, Who's Who Among American, High School Students; [a.] Granbury, TX

SMITH, VERONICA E.
[b.] December 5, 1962, Evansville, IN; [p.] Mattie Terry, James Terry; [m.] Mark Allen Smith, February 27, 1991; [ch.] Nathaniel Thomas Allen Smith, Ashley Summer Smith; [ed.] Boonville High, CST Fashion Academy; [occ.] Machine Operator, Mead Johnson Bristol - Myers Squibb Evansville, IN; [hon.] Simplicity, sewing award and metal; [pers.] Circumstances can cause one to force energies, into areas of hidden talents, only to surface when the reality becomes uncertain, and unchanged. Influenced by God.; [a.] Evansville, IN

SMOAK, JERRI L.
[b.] July 27, 1975, Hampton, SC; [p.] Jerry and Toni Smoak; [ed.] Wade Hampton High, USC - Salkehatchie -2 yrs., USC - Aiken - 2 yrs.; [occ.] Receptionist for Oral Surgeon; [memb.] Huggin Oak Church of God SIFE; [hon.] Gamma Beta Phi, Invitation to Omicron Delta Kappa, Dean's List, President's List, D.L. Scurry Scholarship; [pers.] It is easy to get inspired when surrounded by colorful people!; [a.] Varnville, SC

SNIVELY, ELAINE D.
[b.] December 24, 1939, Detroit, MI; [p.] Wes and Helen Hanson; [m.] John A. Snively, June 12, 1976; [ch.] Jennifer; [ed.] BS Eastern Michigan University, 1961; [occ.] Elementary Librarian; [memb.] Ohio Education Library Media Association, Ohio Reading Council, OEA-NEA Central Presbyterian Church; [hon.] Northwestern Teacher of the year, 1988; [oth. writ.] Published in local newspapers, Drummond Island Digest, Loon Echoes (Michigan Audubon Soc.) 2 Anthologies and Lines from Lois (Peaceable Kingdom); [pers.] I encourage students to write poetry by holding "Poet Corner" during recess and by conducting special poetry sessions in classrooms.; [a.] Massillon, OH

SNODGRASS, AMANDA
[b.] Texas; [p.] Tom and Beverly Snodgrass; [occ.] Student; [hon.] Numerous Academic including science, writing and geography; [oth. writ.] Poetry and short stories but working on a novel for teens.; [a.] New Mexico

SNOW, MICHAEL L.
[b.] January 29, 1973, Hobart, OK; [p.] Mike and Lisa Snow - Dennis and Shirley Goulden; [m.] Judi Snow, April 12, 1996; [ch.] Zavry Michael Snow; [pers.] I credit my family for my inspiration. My brothers Quincy Goulden, Casey and Conn Snow. As well as my wife and son. And a very special thank you to my parents who never let me give up.; [a.] Newton, KS

SNYDER, DANIEL L.
[pen.] Daniel Snyder; [b.] December 22, 1959, Toledo, OH; [p.] James Snyder, Wanda Quinn; [m.] Sarah, July 23, 1983; [ch.] David Grand Douglas, Darren Curtis; [ed.] Springfield High; [occ.] U.S. Navy; [oth. writ.] Several unpublished works. This is my first; [pers.] Some people command respect. Others demand respect which are you?; [a.] Jacksonville, FL

SOCASH, CAROL A.
[pen.] Kathryn Sokac; [b.] December 23, 1952, Atlantic City, NJ; [p.] Alfred E. Pierce, Tillie M. Schmincke; [m.] Dennis J. Socash, November 17, 1995; [ch.] (From previous marriage) Michelle, Jonathan and Brian; [ed.] Atlantic City High School; [occ.] Administrative Assistant, Johnston, Nelson and Shimmel, CPA's; [memb.] St. Agnes Roman Catholic Church; [oth. writ.] Several poems and lyrics, children's story "Santa's Gift," all currently unpublished; [pers.] I desire to utilize my God talent to bring joy to others.; [a.] Winburne, PA

SOTHEN, KATHY
[b.] October 15, 1965, Columbus, OH; [p.] Bobby J. and Vivle G. Orsborn, Bill Conley; [m.] Ronald Sothen, June 1, 1985; [ch.] Melinda Sothen, Elizabeth Sothen, Jayla Adams; [ed.] Newton Elementary, Utica High; [occ.] Homemaker, Housewife; [pers.] I enjoy writing down things I have experienced in my life time.; [a.] Newark, OH

SOUCY, NICOLE
[b.] October 29, 1985, Manchester, CT; [p.] Daniel Soucy, Mary Soucy; [ed.] Saint Mary School, Simsbury, CT; [memb.] Girls Leadership Club; [oth. writ.] 1995 Anthology of poetry by young American's, 1996 Anthology of poetry be young Americans. I had poems published in both years.; [pers.] I love to write and want to be a writer when I grow up. I have written hundreds of stories and poems. I also hope to become a teacher.; [a.] Simsbury, CT

SPARKS, RICHARD
[pen.] Richard Sparks; [b.] May 9, 1974, San Antonio, TX; [pers.] To everything that goes astray, there will always be one that will never leave your heart.; [a.] Great Lakes, IL

SPENCER, BILL
[b.] August 21, 1967, Nashville, TN; [p.] Walter and Georgia Ann Spencer; [ed.] Page High School, David Lipscomb University, University of Memphis; [occ.] Graduate Student (Univ. of Memphis), Customer Relations—FANB; [hon.] Phi Alpha Theta, Cum Laude, Dean's List; [oth. writ.] Articles for High School and University newspaper and yearbook, free-lance, non-published poems.; [pers.] My goal is to connect with people emotionally. I take life's experiences and translate them into poetry—poetry that hopefully creates an impact on the reader.; [a.] Memphis, TN

SPINNER, RANSOM
[pen.] Ransom Hyde Spinner; [b.] April 27, 1961, Malone, NY; [p.] Mr. and Mrs. R. Venne; [ed.] Graduate of Northern Adirondack Central School; [occ.] Writer and Janitor; [hon.] Literacy Volunteer Student of The Year; [oth. writ.] Poetry published in ARC and DDSO newsletters; [pers.] Believe in your dreams. Why walk when you can fly?; [a.] Plattsburgh, NY

SPOTSWOOD, STEPHEN K.
[b.] November 27, 1977, North East, MD; [p.] Paul Spotswood, Margie Spotswood; [ed.] North East High, Washington College; [occ.] Student of Washington College, Chestertown, MD; [memb.] Writers Union, Riverside Players, Writer's Theatre; [hon.] Dean's List, 1993 International Media Festival, 1995 International Media Festival; [oth. writ.] Forthcoming; [pers.] I am greatly influenced by the brilliance and suffering of others, and by the continuously lush absurdity of ever other day life.; [a.] North East, MD

STACKHOUSE, DEVYNNE
[b.] November 1, 1980, Waukegan, IL; [p.] Michael and Debbie Stackhouse; [ed.] I am a Junior at Zion, Benton High School in Zion, IL; [occ.] I have no job right now, I'm concentrating on volley ball and grades; [hon.] I never entered my poems in any contests.; [oth. writ.] A man named Albert Einstein, Greed, no love at all, the wall, spring.; [pers.] I live my life every day to it's fullest because I know "I can do all things through Christ who strengthens me."; [a.] Zion, IL

STANLEY, ISABELL E.
[pen.] Lebasi, Gail; [pers.] I believe that will power is a combination of two things. Your will to resist and God's power to assist. My inspiration to write comes from personal and real life trials, experiences, etc.; [a.] Atlanta, GA

STEELE, LINDSEY
[pen.] Lindsey Steele; [b.] April 23, 1983, Mission Viejo, CA; [ed.] I'm in eight grade at Newhart Middle School in Mission Viejo, CA; [pers.] I'd like to be a children or young adult book author. I also enjoy writing poetry, because I believe it expresses the way people truly feel.; [a.] Aliso Viejo, CA

STEGENGA, D. A. DAWN
[pen.] Dawn Stegenga/D. A. Stegenga; [b.] December 17, 1940, Michigan; [p.] Alvah and Ivah Stegenga; [m.] Divorced; [ch.] Jennifer; [ed.] M.A. Univ. of Michigan, B.A. - Eastern Mich. University; [occ.] Ret. from Penn State and on disability; [memb.] U. Of Mich. Alumni Assoc., Phila. Museum of Art, Balch Inst. Ethnic Studies, the Y, AARP, Neth - Am Assoc., N.O.W.; [hon.] Poetry publications in Mich. and Nat'l Library of Poetry, oil painting exhibits in PA, Scholarships in Mich.; [oth. writ.] Classified ads foe sports magazines; [pers.] The Lord is 1st always. And I am to be who the Lord wants me to be. When I was about seven my father taught me how to write poetry.; [a.] Media, PA

STEGER, NICKY
[pen.] Nicky Steger; [b.] March 3, 1982, Saint Louis, MO; [p.] Cynthia Steger and John Steger; [ed.] St. George grade school, Notre Dame High School; [occ.] Student; [memb.] Notre Dame High School Tesserae Club; [hon.] President's Education Awards Program (1996); [oth. writ.] I write poems frequently, but those will be my first published poem.; [pers.] I write my thoughts to help express myself. Many of my poems have wordplay and a deeper level of meaning. My poems may be confusing towards many readers, but very special and very meaningful to myself. I also hope many readers fully understand and appreciate my thoughts and writings.; [a.] Saint Louis, MO

STENGER, ALMA G.
[pen.] Alma; [b.] October 27, 1925, Nowata, OK; [p.] Thomas May, G. May; [m.] Bruce Stenger (Deceased); [ch.] Four; [ed.] San Pedro, CA High School - Graduate of Los Angeles Harbor College, 3 yrs. of field and Clinical Studies (Psy/Soc. studies); [occ.] Ret. writer; [memb.] Many past; [hon.] Blue Ribbons in track and field back in Junior and Senior High Schools, Girl's Basketball and Softball, Coaching trophies; [oth. writ.] First novel just published "Tears On The Wind". A childrens' book in the works, plus a book of poetry. Earlier articles and poems in local newspapers, human interest articles for mfg monthly mags.; [pers.] As a spiritual person, my writings usually reflect how I feel and what I've experienced. It has been a long life for me, and I wish to reach out to others with understanding and words of encouragement.; [a.] Mansfield, AR

STEPHENSON, MARY
[b.] November 8, 1923, Pocatello, ID; [ch.] Three (now adults); [ed.] Graduate of Idaho State University; [occ.] Retired; [a.] Chubbuck, ID

STEUBER, JODI
[b.] November 14, 1966, Chadron, NE; [p.] Harry and Minnie Leithead; [m.] John F. K. Steuber, July 11, 1992; [ch.] Jared James and Justin James; [ed.] Lingle-Ft Laramie High, Eastern Wyoming College; [occ.] Administrative Assistant for family business; [pers.] I had made this poem for Mom and Dad's 50th anniversary memory book because they are two special people. They not only affect their families lives but people who they have contact with. As a child and parent, I can't thank them enough for what they've done.; [a.] Fountain Hills, AZ

STEVENSON, TAMMY
[pen.] Tammy Stevenson; [b.] February 24, 1964, Burlington, VT; [p.] Clarence and Carol Hutchins; [m.] Kevin Stevenson, June 9, 1990; [ch.] Nathan (5), Ashley (4), David (2); [ed.] Champlain Valley Union High School, Hinesburg, VT, Maranatha Baptist Bible College, Watertown, WI; [occ.] Secretary, Faith Memorial Baptist Church, Richmond VA; [oth. writ.] Several poems unpublished, two unpublished plays, one workbook/study guide for children - unpublished.; [pers.] I seek to write material that has a direct impact on the heart!; [a.] Richmond, VA

STIFFLER, BRYLIE
[b.] October 22, 1982, Iola, KS; [p.] Lyndall Stockebrand; [ed.] 1996-97 8th Grade; [occ.] Student; [memb.] Common Threads Quilt Guild; [hon.] 1st Place - North Central Texas College Poetry Contest, People to people student ambassador to New Zealand and Australia, Academic Recognition from the State of Texas.; [a.] Gainesville, TX

STILLWELL, KATIE USHER
[b.] Senior, San Antonio, TX; [p.] Deceased; [m.] Deceased; [ch.] Cheryl, Wilbert, Susie, Mike and Mark; [ed.] High School, College Training T.S.U. University (Journalism); [occ.] Retired Housewife; [hon.] Small Cash Prize, Klein Writing Contest, Newspaper Institute of America, N.Y. (N.I.A.) September 1971 Diploma, December 5, 1988, The Institute of Children's Literature, Redding Ridge, Ct. Certified to write for Children's Magazine; [oth. writ.] Articles for local newspapers "Case of Amnesia" Dr. Christian writing contest for Radio - 1951; [pers.] My interest in little children inspires me to put together a book of verse exclusively for them. Among my collection of poetry, I have written many poems about the little ones.; [a.] Houston, TX

STOCKBARGER, PEARL
[b.] April 8, 1920, Harvey, IL; [m.] Dan M. Stockbarger (Deceased, June 4, 1992), August 2, 1947; [ch.] Danise E. Krueger, Sally J. De Liberato; [ed.] Illinois State University, University of Illinois; [occ.] Retired Widow; [oth. writ.] Tributes, eulogies, whimsical letters "To The Editor" and letters of comfort and entertainment - a few essays - local paper.; [pers.] I try always, in my writing, to use words as musical notes: To please, to soothe, to fill the empty parts within each of us with harmony.; [a.] Western Springs, IL

STOKES, HEATHER
[pen.] Rae; [b.] May 30, 1980, Indianapolis; [p.] Roseann Stokes; [ed.] Attended Arlington Elem. #2, for pre-School thru 6th Grade School #72 for 7th Grade, School #99 and Our Lady of Lourdes for 8th Grade, now attending Broad Ripple H.S.; [occ.] I'm a Junior at Broad Ripple H.S.; [memb.] Member of the world's first miniature golf country club, Indianapolis Marion County Public Library Card Holder.; [hon.] Music Awards, Spelling Bee Winner 5th Gr., was in Science Fairs, Horsemanship Awards (Whispering Meadows), Award for superior Research paper (8th Gr.) Principals Award (8th) Award for Alice in Wonderland Performance (8th), 1st and 2nd place winner in Rodeo; [oth. writ.] Done many research papers, mostly for school, a

lot more poems have been written in spare time.; [pers.] If you're going to do something and you want it done right, do it. Your self and do it the very best that you know how. And always remember: "Good things come to those who wait"!; [a.] Indianapolis, IN

STRICKLAND, SUMMER
[pen.] Summer Strickland; [b.] April 24, 1983, Pineville, LA; [p.] Chris Strickland and Camilla Aultman; [ed.] Caldwell Parish Junior High; [occ.] Student; [memb.] Performing Choir; [pers.] I have been influenced by poets like Edgar Allen Poe and play writers such as William Shakespeare.; [a.] Kelly, LA

STROLE, KAREN
[b.] April 10, 1960, Denver, CO; [p.] Norma and George Strole; [m.] David Klosowski; [ed.] UNC, UTD - Business Management and Marketing; [occ.] Sales Management and Marketing - Professional Salon Industry; [pers.] Words on paper is how I cry and suffer, laugh and hope.; [a.] Albuquerque, NM

STRUIJK, HENDRICUS
[b.] October 9, 1947, Rotterdam, Netherlands; [p.] Hendricus Struijk, Cathrina De Waal; [ed.] Redford High School, Wayne State University; [occ.] Elementary Teacher; [memb.] John F. Kennedy Library, Democratic National Committee, Audubon Society, AIDS Project Los Angeles; [oth. writ.] Screenplay "Anderson Affair," writer "Entertainment Tonight," novel "Senseless Deceivings"; [pers.] I have always tried to live my life like the philosophy of my fellow country man - Anne Frank - that in spite of everything people are really good of heart.; [a.] Long Beach, CA

STUBBLEFIELD, KURTIS
[b.] October 15, 1960, Fort Worth, TX; [p.] Joe Stubblefield and D. J. Stubblefield; [ed.] Aledo High School, Texas Tech. University; [occ.] Asst. Service Mgr., Larry North Fitness; [pers.] I seek redemption in the journey writing represents, not in the destination found in each completed work. My debt lies with T. S. Eliot and Dylan Thomas.; [a.] Poolville, TX

STUKEY, KAREN
[b.] April 30, 1971, Lakeland, FL; [p.] Joseph J. and Minnie M. Stukey; [m.] Todd Houck (soon to be), March 1, 1997; [ed.] Evangel Christian School, Polk Community College, University of South Florida; [occ.] Treasury Management Analyst, Suntrust Bank; [hon.] American Legion Award, Phi Theta Kappa; [pers.] My goal is to live my life in a way that will bring glory to God and joy to the lives of others. I hope that I accomplish this in some small way through my writing.; [a.] Lakeland, FL

STURTEVANT, TENORZELLE
[b.] February 13, 1963, Newark, NJ; [p.] Shirley and John Harris; [ch.] Ebont Dominique Wells; [ed.] Graduated Reid Ross High School, 1981 attended N.C. State; [occ.] Military Pay Clerk; [oth. writ.] The Lesson, Destiny; [pers.] You will never know life if the risks you take are small and meaningless.; [a.] Lenwood, CA

SUH, RA YOUNG
[pen.] Elizabeth Lee; [b.] February 20, 1983, Seoul, South Korea; [p.] Jeong Suh, Pyong Suh; [ed.] Jackson Middle School; [pers.] I love to reflect my feelings to people and write it down into a poem. Poems are such lovely things.; [a.] Jackson, MN

SUMMERS, DOLORES
[b.] May 25, 1931, Schenectady, NY; [p.] Philip McEller, Clara McEller; [ch.] Patricia Ann, Julie Anne; [a.] Knoxville, TN

SUTTON, CYNTHIA
[b.] November 15, 1961, Boulder, CO; [p.] Charles and Twila Crismon; [m.] Vincent Sutton, September 18, 1992; [ch.] Kyle Alan and Amanda Ann-Marie; [ed.] Boulder High and Fairview High, Front Range Community College; [occ.] Independent Avon, Representative, Newspaper Carrier; [oth. writ.] None at this time; [pers.] I always try to find the good in people and like them for who they are. Poetry has been a hobby since Jr. high english, thanks to my teachers.; [a.] Lafayette, CO

SWAIN, SHARON K.
[pen.] Babe; [b.] January 27, 1947, Johnstown, PA; [p.] Fern (Gardner) George and Glen F. George; [m.] David L. Swain, Valentine's Day, 1975; [ed.] Johnstown High 2 years of writing classes at V.P.J. (Pittsburgh) at Johnstown and travel; [occ.] Handicap Activist also taking care of parents; [memb.] None, I have my own thoughts and want to keep my freedom to change or build on those thoughts; [hon.] Dean's List, From the Public, and life gave me a loving mother and a challenge (Celebral Palsy) do not take life for granted but as an award.; [oth. writ.] A poem in a local flyer on John Lennon's death "Lennon's Profile"; [pers.] I have always looked into my expressions and thoughts with a twist. Everyday my senses observe and at night I put those thoughts down.; [a.] Johnstown, PA

SWANBY, MEGAN N.
[b.] September 2, 1984, Anchorage, AK; [p.] Richard Swanby and Eleen Rossman; [ed.] Academy of St. Joseph; [a.] Oakdale, NY

SWANSON, RICHARD HENRY
[pen.] Richard Henry Swanson; [b.] September 14, 1918, South Haven, MN; [p.] August and Tina Swanson; [m.] Betty V. Swanson, July 27, 1946; [ch.] Raymond, Virginia, Marilyn, Richard Jr.; [ed.] Grammar, School Cheryl Burns High School (Lake View Chicago), 4 months Greer College 1937; [occ.] Retired from Floor Covering Industry; [memb.] First Assembly Church Orlando Florida - 2740 - E. Michigan; [hon.] Quarter Century Award, Installation Specialist Magazine April 5-1972; [oth. writ.] 2nd Grade Story South Haven News - 2-3 Songs (1940) Poems 1943; [pers.] Regardless of Man's limited knowledge there stands an awesome accountability to divine law and order. It is accepted by few. The vast majority become aware at times, through warnings of scripture, heeding "our hairs of head being numbered," and "fall of a sparrow"!!; [a.] Orlando, FL

SWENSON, CYNTHIA
[b.] October 20, 1960, Framingham, MA; [p.] Yoshie Suzuki Murey, Kenneth Arlen Murey Sr.; [ch.] William Bernard Swenson, Ashlee Alexandra Cruz, Jamie Lee Mirah Cruz; [ed.] Milford High School, Roger Williams College, Quinsigamond Community College; [occ.] Manager, Nynek; [pers.] I take from nature and personal feelings. Experiences I symbolize by putting my emtrans into the world around me; [a.] Nebster, MA

SWIHART, AMIN B.
[b.] July 16, 1972, Trinidad and Tobago; [p.] Don Swihart, Linda Parc; [ed.] Hesperia High, Santa Barbara City College; [occ.] Teacher and Professional Storyteller; [memb.] National Story telling Association, National Association for the Education of Young Children; [pers.] It is partly through the bond of the written word: Poetry, tale fable, myth, that we create on experience that defines us as uniquely human.; [a.] Santa Barbara, CA

SWINEY, SAMANTHA
[pen.] Sammy; [b.] December 11, 1981, Big Stone Gap, VA; [p.] Steven and Mary Swiney; [ed.] Currently in 9th Grade 1996 at Powell Valley High; [occ.] (FBLA, FCA) Future Business Leaders America, Fellowship Christian Athletes New Testament Baptist Church; [oth. writ.] Lots but none published.; [pers.] Growing up with the Lord is all that matters. If you do something with God on your mind you shall always succeed.; [a.] Appalachia, VA

TAFT, SHEILA CAROLYN
[pen.] Sheila Carolyn; [b.] March 25, 1941, Brooklyn, NY; [p.] Oscar and Beatrice Mescon; [m.] Charles Arthur Taft, March 23, 1996; [ch.] Eric Joshua Hoffman, Sarah Aviva, Yaffa Mizrachi and Lisa Valerie; [ed.] Abraham Lincoln H.S, Brooklyn College, Pratt Institute (NY), Metaphysical Studies - various courses; [occ.] Legal Secty, Full-time, Psychic and Astrologer - Part-time; [memb.] Civic League of Miami Beach, FL., Press Club member, high school, make-up artist for plays; [hon.] Certified of Appreciation for raising money for victims of scud Missile War in Israel, Certificate of Appreciation for assistance during Hurricane Andrew; [oth. writ.] "Lady Child" published in Across The Universe, (National Library of Poetry), "If I never" published in "Poems Across America (a new magazine published by Gloria Jean Hill).; [pers.] I have written about 75 poems. Although they are personal statement of my life, heart and soul others who have read them have similar feelings. Thank you to my lovely daughter, Sarah Aviva Mizrachi, for encouraging and pushing me to do something about and with any poetry.; [a.] Miami Beach, FL

TAN, EARL E.
[pen.] Earl E. Tan; [b.] March 2, 1932, Malaysia; [p.] A. Tan and H. E. W. Tan; [m.] Kim L. Tan, July 19, 1968; [ch.] Peggy P. Tan and Michael Tan; [ed.] National Taiwan University - B.S., M.D., College of William and Mary - M.S.; [occ.] Physician (Retired); [memb.] Not active, Malaysian-Singaporean Associate, National Taiwan University, Alumni Association; [hon.] Fukien Provincial Government Scholarship, Fishery Biology Scholarship, Research Associate ships; [oth. writ.] Many short stories and travelog published in local newspapers and monthly several scientific papers in various journals.; [pers.] I was influenced by many English, Chinese, and Russian authors and poets. After seeing peoples of many walks of lives, with different ideas and many live dramas in years of medical practice, I like to put some of these in writings to entertain and to share with people having literary interest in my retirement years.; [a.] Missouri City, TX

TANKSLEY, SANDRA LYNN
[b.] November 3, 1965, Philadelphia, PA; [p.] Edna and James Tanksley; [ed.] Martin Luther King High School, Temple Univ. undergraduate studies, Widener Univ. - BSN; [occ.] R. N. HIV/AIDS Clinical Research - UTSWMC; [hon.] National Honor Society - 1983; [oth. writ.] Nursing is, submitted poem National Nurse's Week Graduate Hosp. (1993) several writings to be published; [pers.] My reality to write I believe is a God given talent. A gift to express words of life, love, encouragement and peace. May you be blessed as you need the words which how from his heart of love.; [a.] Dallas, TX

TANZINI, ROBIN ELIZABETH
[b.] August 25, 1981, Trenton, NJ; [p.] Pete and Susan Tanzini; [ed.] 10th grade student at Northern Burlington Regional High School; [occ.] Student and Model; [memb.] The National Arbor Day Foundation, the Interact Club, and Operation Smile; [hon.] Addie Fuller Award Columbus NJ, Essay Contest, MADD Poster Contest; [a.] Columbus, NJ

TARWACKI, HEIDI
[pen.] Chrystal Porter; [b.] April 6, 1973, Idaho Falls, ID; [p.] Patrick and Penny Tarwacki; [ch.] Christopher Thomas Moleski; [occ.] Pricing Coordinator - AFL (Alcoa Fujikora Ltd); [memb.] American Red Cross - Monthly Domer, Make - A Wish Foundation; [oth. writ.] Several unpublished poem and short stories.; [pers.] Strive for your definition follow it - you never know what you might achieve.; [a.] Woodhaven, MI

TAURIELLO, ALFREDO A.
[b.] November 15, 1972, Jersey City, NJ; [p.] Alfredo Tauriello, Irma Tauriello; [ed.] Emerson High School, Hudson County Community College, Jersey City State College; [occ.] Shipping/Receiving Clerk Part-time Student; [pers.] I want to dedicate this poem to my mother. To my fiance who pushed me into believing in my writing skills.; [a.] Union City, NJ

TAYLOR, AMY M.
[pen.] Amy M. Taylor; [b.] May 31, 1970, Beckley, WV; [p.] Dorinda and Rodney Taylor; [ed.] Marshall University Huntington, WV; [occ.] US Navy; [a.] Mililani, HI

TAYLOR, PATRICIA ANN
[pen.] Tris, Tisha; [b.] June 18, 1948, Pike County, AL; [p.] Aaron and Euritha Leatherwood; [m.] Larry A. Taylor, January 1, 1980; [ch.] Ronald and James Bryan, Alan and Angel Taylor; [ed.] Graduated Central High School - 1966 in Phoenix City, Al. Completed Career Training Institute in IBM - 1967 in Columbus, Ga.; [occ.] Housewife; [memb.] Trinity Temple Assembly of God Church. Word Warriors Sunday School Class; [hon.] Two poems I submitted in a local contest won honorable mention - "Struggles" and "Bitterness" They are published in book titled, Alabama Poet's Reunion - 1988 by Star Publishing; [oth. writ.] "Waves of Loneliness" and "Strength" Poems also published in Alabama Poets Reunion - 1988 by Star Publishing.; [pers.] Live peaceably with everyone. Love God, love others and love yourself. It is a winning combination.; [a.] Phoenix City, AL

TELFER, LORRAINE
[b.] September 12, 1962, Huntsville, AL; [p.] Thomas and Janet Telfer; [ed.] Richland High, Tennessee Valley College, University of Alabama in Huntsville; [occ.] General Electric Decatur Alabama; [pers.] Up until now I have always written for myself and my writing is based on my feelings. My writing is spontaneous and not planned.; [a.] Somerville, AL

TEMPLAR, JO ANNE
[b.] July 2, 1959, Montour Falls, NY; [p.] William and Joanna Taft; [m.] Glen Templar, October 28, 1978; [ch.] Jason and Jill; [ed.] Corning Community College; [occ.] Registered Professional Nurse; [hon.] DAR, P.E.G (Positive Energy Group of Steuben County), Who's Who in American Nursing, Honorary Membership The National Honor Society; [pers.] I currently work at Steuben County Community Mental Health Center as a Children and youth Nurse.; [a.] Beaver Dams, NY

TEMPLET, LONNETTE M.
[b.] January 26, 1952, McComb, MS; [p.] Carl and Clarice Gerald; [m.] Darryl Bruce Templet, August 21, 1972; [ch.] Angela; [ed.] Central High; [occ.] Pizza Clerk; [pers.] My inspiration comes from my family and real life experiences that I have had; Gerald's tree is a true story. My father planted the oak tree. When he passed away in 1995 the tree died the same year.; [a.] Baton Rouge, LA

THOMAS, PAMELA HATHCOX
[b.] May 25, 1959, Birmingham, AL; [p.] James and Patsy Hathcox; [m.] Allen R. Thomas, March 5, 1988; [ch.] Alaina Noel Thomas; [ed.] Gardendale High School, Jefferson State College; [occ.] Physician Assistant Multi-Tech; [hon.] Dean's List, Jefferson State College 1984; [oth. writ.] Several articles published by Good Shepherd Lutheran Church. Poem used by the Old Belmont Baptist Church as Basis for Christmas Program. Several unpublished Children's Stories.; [pers.] I enjoy writing about simple, basic subjects that are close to my heart.; [a.] Birmingham, AL

THOMASON, MARY LEE
[b.] April 6, 1949, Dade City, FL; [p.] Cop and Ethel McKendree; [ch.] Melissa and Barbara; [occ.] Secretary; [pers.] I have always been a romanticist deep down!; [a.] Dade City, FL

THOMPSON, CHAUNIQUEWUAH
[pen.] "Myma"; [b.] November 6, 1982, Luling, TX; [p.] Ms. Cynthia L. Thompson; [ed.] Thirteen years old eighth grade Honor Student at Carlos Houck Middle School, in Salem, Oregon; [occ.] Baby Sitter; [memb.] Yearbook Committee at Carlos Houck Middle School; [hon.] 1988-1996 Honor Roll, Math Gold Cup Award, 1994 Citizens of the Month Award, 1995 Artistic Talent Award, 1994-1996 Super Student Award, 1996 Outstanding Husky Award, March 22, 1996; [oth. writ.] 1988 Mother's Day Award (writing) 1989-1993 Portland Trail Blazers write-on segmant essay award. 1993, 1996 Art Show Award. 1996 exemplary writing award. Prizes were three large encyclopedias.; [pers.] Do it right the first time, and you won't have to do it again.; [a.] Salem, OR

THOMPSON, JOSEPH ADAM
[pen.] Alizar; [b.] February 25, 1981; [p.] Terry Joe Thompson and Peggy Sue Thompson; [pers.] "Goddess of Fire" was my first poem, I would like to thank the fiery headed goddess who inspired it, and the author who helped me start writing. Thanks Rani and thanks piers Anthony.; [a.] McMinnville, TN

THORNBURG, SHELA
[pers.] I am looking for the magic and mystery in life.; [a.] Dexter, MO

THORNDIKE, TIMOTHY P.
[b.] June 3, 1955, Warren, OH; [p.] Paul and Mary Lee Thorndike; [m.] Beverly M. Bartlett, June 22, 1980; [ed.] Chalker High (Southington, OH) BA. - Michigan State University - Theatre, Small Business Studies - College of Marin Graduate Christian Science Nurse - Arden Wood Benevolent Association Sanitarium, San Francisco; [occ.] Christian Science Nurse, Overlook House, Cleveland, OH, Small Bus. owner; [memb.] First Church of Christ, Scientist, Cleveland; [hon.] Chalker Academic Awards in American Gov't and Business Law, Outstanding Performance in a Minor Role, Kent State Univ., Asher Student Foundation Activity and Service Achievement Awards, Michigan State Univ. Distinguished Service, Award for Excellence in Technical Theatrical Production, Dean's List; [oth. writ.] Poem published in in-house company publication.; [a.] Cleveland Heights, OH

THURSTON, BARBARA R.
[b.] April 11, 1941, Charlotte, NC; [m.] Donald E. Thurston, September 30, 1978; [ch.] Mark, Mike, Scott, Randy, Christy (Deceased); [ed.] 12th Grade; [occ.] (Office) Major Trucking Co. (Estes Express Lines); [memb.] Bowling, Campground Membership National Arbor Assoc.; [oth. writ.] Too numerous to mention. None ever published.; [pers.] I have loved writing poetry since I was very young. This is the first time I have ever entered my work in any contest. I write poems for friends and family for their special occasions. Writing is a form of entertainment for me.; [a.] Charlotte, NC

TILLERY, ALGIE
[b.] November 15, 1949, Sharpsburg, NC; [p.] Dorothy and Johnnie Battle; [m.] Horace Tillery, November 1, 1968; [ch.] Brandon and D'Anthony; [ed.] Frederick Douglass High, Central Piedmont College; [occ.] Senior Analyst for a leading Insurance Company; [memb.] Nations Ford Baptist Church; [oth. writ.] Several other poems and other articles written, but this is the first published.; [pers.] This poem was written to bring comfort to those who are struggling with the loss of a loved one.; [a.] Charlotte, NC

TOAVS, BONNY S.
[b.] March 20, 1941, Austin, MN; [p.] Robert L. and Blanche B. Greiner; [m.] Warren V. Toavs, July 9, 1960; [ch.] Jodi L. Feller, Jeff W. Toavs, Jolene L. Toavs; [ed.] Graduated from Lyle Public High School 1959 and attended St. Paul Bible College, and earned my CMA (Certified Medical Assistant) degree 1996; [occ.] Home maker of Business Partner with my husband in advanced Air Heating and Cooling Inc.; [memb.] Faith Evangelical Church - Montana Associates of CMA's Active in Local and State Pro-Life Grandma of 8, 6 boys, 2 girls!; [hon.] Systemic Lupus Foundation Member having a loving hubby, children, grandchildren, friends and knowing that one day, I too will join my savior and my precious father. Faith is the victory!; [oth. writ.] Am currently working on my life's story. A victim of Systemic Lupus Ereathemosis, Breast cancer survivor and have survived two surgeries, and have many funny, sad, and interesting things to tell.; [pers.] I am deeply religious and believe in the Lord Jesus Christ. He truly is the King of Kings and he holds my hands and my heart thro all of life's trials and struggles and success. My favorite saying is: "Let Go and Let God." My twin sister Betty L. Grinstead who was published by your company in 1995 wrote "Ode to Galicer." We were born on our deceased father's 25th birthday and we had a large party to celebrate his 75th b-day and our 50th just 20 days before he was transported to Jesus's arms in a vehicle accident.; [a.] Billings, MT

TOMMASO, DEBORAH C.
[pen.] Catharina Hoetmer; [b.] December 29, 1961, Netherlands; [p.] Klaas and Dirkje Hoetmer; [m.] Joseph R. Tommaso, February 6, 1984; [ch.] Nicholas, Kirsten, Matthew, Joseph; [ed.] Connetquot H.S., Nassau Community College, C.W. Post; [occ.] Mother - Future Elem. Teacher graduating C.W. Post '97; [memb.] Marine Corps. League; [hon.] Meritorious Mast in U.S.M.C., Magna Cum Laude at N.C.C.C., Dean's List at C.W. Post; [pers.] Poetry has been a part of me since my youth. I'm able to express myself through my words while the words reflect the ebb and flow of the tapestry of life.; [a.] Carle Place, NY

TORZEWSKI, KONRAD
[b.] August 8, 1980, Warsaw, Poland; [p.] Bozena Torzewski, Andrzej Torzewski; [ed.] St. Bartolomew Grade School, currently in St. Patrick High School; [occ.] High School Student at Patrick High School; [hon.] Best Student of St. Bart's, Honor Roll for 3 years in St. Pat's High School; [oth. writ.] Several unpublished poems a novel which I'm trying to publish. This is actually my first publication.; [pers.] Writing means a lot to me. It's a good way to express yourself and your true feelings. My two favorite writers are Shakespeare and Edgar A. Poe. I had help in inspiration from my Aunt Grazyna Klepacka and my mother Olga.; [a.] Harwood Heights, IL

TOSCA, STEPHANIE
[b.] September 12, 1978, Philadelphia, PA; [p.] Joseph Tosca, Dolores Tosca; [ed.] Pleasant Valley High School; [occ.] Computer Hardware Temp at Cornet Internl. Stroudsburg, PA; [hon.] Honor

Roll student; [pers.] Poetry allows me to express my feelings freely, they are no limitations. True poetry comes from deep within your heart and soul.; [a.] Effort, PA

TOULOUMES, LYNN
[ed.] Institut Esthedern; [occ.] Esthetician; [memb.] Greek Orthodox Church; [oth. writ.] Nothing published; [pers.] I am deeply concerned for the needs of our children, they are our future. We should invest in them. We as adults have to protect them and stop abuse. I was inspired to write this poem after hearing the story of an abused child in our area.; [a.] Harrisburg, PA

TRACY, MARJORIE CARLISLE
[pen.] Margie C. Tracy; [b.] December 12, 1946, Savannah, GA; [p.] Margaret Taylor Tuten, John Claussen Tuten Jr; [m.] May 21, 1967; [ch.] Michael John, Jennifer Michelle; [pers.] I write about people, places, or events that fill my life with incredible love.; [a.] Savannah, GA

TRAN, TUAN A.
[pen.] Mac Tran Lan; [b.] December 17, 1954, Phu Yen, Vietnam; [p.] Quy Tran, Chinh Thi Ta; [m.] Lang-Chi Nguyen, June 15, 1991; [ch.] Mai Chi Monica Tran, Anh Duy Anthony Tran; [ed.] A.A. in Math and A. S. in Electronic Computer Technology Mission College, Santa Clara CA; [occ.] Lead, Repair Technician, Lam Research Crop., Fremont, CA; [hon.] Mission College, Dean's List; [oth. writ.] Several poems published in Vietnamese Newspaper such as Hon Viet Magazine, Hoa Binh, Dan Chu, Tien Phong and Lang Van Magazine in Canada; [pers.] In 1979, I was walk people, lived in Sikew Camp, Thailand and Galang Camp, Indonesia. I came to the U.S. in 1981.; [a.] San Jose, CA

TRAVISS, JASON D.
[b.] May 10, 1970, Cadillac, MI; [p.] Dan Traviss, Sue Traviss; [m.] Robin Traviss, May 20, 1995; [ed.] Cadillac High School, Grand Rapids Junior College, Western Michigan University; [hon.] Dean's List at Western Michigan University; [pers.] I find creative power within the dynamics of my family, the strength of my lineage, and my coexistence with the earth. I respect and admire the writings of many contemporary writers, particularly Jim Harrison, Rick Bass and Stephen Dobyns.; [a.] Cadillac, MI

TREIBLEY, CAROLYN
[b.] June 8, 1981, Richmond, VA; [p.] Robert Treibley and Joyce Treibley; [ed.] Currently attending Monacan High School as a Sophomore; [occ.] Tenth grader at Monacan High School; [hon.] Distinguished Honor Roll Student; [pers.] For me, writing is a way to delineate feelings and emotions I would not otherwise be able to express.; [a.] Richmond, VA

TREMAIN, MARIJA
[b.] February 1, 1978, Seattle; [p.] Diane Marie and Tremain Richner; [ed.] Bowlake Elementary, Chinook Middle School, Tyee High School - Graduated June 1996; [occ.] Gas Station Cashier; [oth. writ.] My Little Angel, Adrian, Beauty - poems from my heart; [pers.] I look forward to tomorrow, to what might or might not happen. I look forward to the challenges life will throw my way, they will make me stronger and wiser. I know I will be somebody someday. My life has only just begun.; [a.] Seattle, WA

TREMBLAY, MATTHEW
[b.] January 19, 1981, Buffalo, NY; [p.] Robert Tremblay, Katherine Tremblay; [ed.] Tenth Grader at Saint Francis High School; [occ.] Student; [memb.] School and Church activities, Boy Scouts of America; [hon.] Honor Student, American Legion Essay Award.; [oth. writ.] Poems published in magazines, and a publication of a poem the book anthology of poetry by young Americans. (1994 Edition); [pers.] I feel that when life is very demanding and stressful, poetry can help anyone relax and unwind, while allowing you to express your emotions in a way that will give you self-esteem and life.; [a.] Orchard Park, NY

TUCKER, CARRIE
[b.] March 14, 1972, Texas; [p.] Robert and Alicia; [ed.] Sherwood High School, Towson State University; [occ.] Community Relations Coordinator; [hon.] Dean's List; [oth. writ.] Songs and other musical pieces.; [pers.] I am greatly inspired by the beauty of nature and humankind.; [a.] Fairfax, VA

TUNC, MURAT
[b.] March 21, 1968, Ankara, Turkey; [p.] Ali Tunc and Ismet Deniz Tunc; [ed.] Ankara Fen Lisesi, Ankara University Faculty of Medicine, Turkey; [occ.] Medical Doctor; [memb.] Turkish Medical Association, Turkish Ophthalmic Society; [oth. writ.] Turkish language books for elementary school. Several poems and short stories.; [pers.] Writing is like cooking. You should mix the correct amount of life-love-reality and dream with your imagination.; [a.] San Francisco, CA

TURNER, STEPHANIE M.
[b.] May 16, 1980, Toledo, OH; [p.] Martin Turner, Ellen Turner; [ed.] Notre Dame Academy High School; [occ.] High School Student and a part-time Receptionist at the Sisters of Notre Dame; [memb.] Flower Hospital/Toledo Hospital Medical Careers Explorer Program, NDA Spanish Club, North Coast Junior Olympic Diving Team; [hon.] Member of Who's Who Among American High School Students, Honor Roll (Commended), Nominated to be a Student Ambassador for the Youth Science Exchange, Ohio State Diving Finalist, all Ohio Interscholastic Team, all District/Northwest District Team, Damon's Athlete of the Week; [pers.] I feel the best way to express one's inner most thoughts is through writing. I believe that hard work and perseverance is the key to success.; [a.] Toledo, OH

TUZZEO, JENNIFER
[b.] February 7, 1979, Dallas, TX; [p.] Theresa Libonati, Michael Tuzzeo; [ed.] Nazareth Academy High School; [oth. writ.] Several poems published in small national newspaper; [pers.] The need for self-expression leads us to explode forth with the cry, "We are human."; [a.] Hamlin, NY

ULERY, MYRNA L.
[b.] June 26, 1938, Winner, SD; [p.] Gaylord and Estella Boerner; [m.] Norman Ulery, June 19, 1965; [ch.] Karen Kaye, Bradley Duane; [ed.] Winner, SD High, Central Bus. Col., Denver, Co.; [occ.] Child Care Provider; [memb.] Emmanuel Meth. Church; [oth. writ.] "What is truth," the Episcopalian.; [pers.] God has a plan for our lives, but we decide whether to use that plan.; [a.] Abilene, KS

UMHOEFER JR., LEONARD J.
[pen.] Leonard J. Umhoefer Jr.; [b.] October 3, 1959, Clifton, NJ; [p.] Leonard J. and Lois M.; [ed.] Working Toward BA English, South Plantation High School; [occ.] Photographer, Student; [memb.] National Wildlife Federation, Natural Resources Defense Council, Downtown Rescue Mission, American Cancer Society, Florida Wildlife, March of Dimes, Habitat for Humanity Int'l.; [hon.] Honorable Discharge U.S. Army, 82nd Airborne Infantry, For Bragg, NC. Sgt E-5; [oth. writ.] President, Editor "The Beach Bulletin 1991"; [pers.] We are here to give, to teach, to learn. My father is my greatest source of inspiration. He was killed in a fire in May, 1994. He taught me to do things right the 1st time, to have empathy and compassion, and to love my fellow man, nature and my God.; [a.] Port Richey, FL

UNGER, TOM
[pen.] Tom; [b.] March 17, 1950, Reading, PA; [p.] Walter R. Unger and Grace A. Unger; [m.] Bonnie M. Unger, April 24, 1973; [ch.] Joy Lynn Petrie; [ed.] Vo-Tech 12th Grade; [occ.] Estimator, Maint. Mech.; [memb.] Penna. Federation of Injured Workers; [oth. writ.] My Grandchild, My Feelings Go On, My Daughter's New Life, My Silver Years; [pers.] I try to write what would interest people other than myself, also whatever feels right for me.; [a.] Mohrsville, PA

VACCARO, CHRISTINA
[pen.] Chuddy Varasco; [b.] February 14, 1980, Reading; [p.] Debra and Joseph; [ed.] 12th and Marion Elementary (Grades 2-5), 13th and Union Elem. (PK-1) Northeast Middle (6-8) Reading High (9-?); [occ.] Student (Junior), Video Store Clerk; [memb.] Reading High French Club, Who's who among American Students, Vocational Industrial Clubs of America.; [hon.] Who's Who among American Students.; [oth. writ.] I have my own poem book, but nothing's been published yet.; [pers.] "If you have the moon, forget the stars" meaning if you're in love, forget about all the other people around you. Like another person who will make you unhappy.; [a.] Reading, PA

VAGO, DAVID
[b.] April 6, 1975, The Hague, Netherlands; [ed.] Twenty-one years of Input, Integration, and Awareness (Incl. four years and the University of Rochester), BA in Brain and Cognitive Sciences; [oth. writ.] Many; [pers.] One must learn to release the social constructs which encompass the mind, having done so, life simply becomes a good story to tell.

VALDEZ, BRITTANY R.
[b.] May 24, 1986, Fontana, CA; [p.] Marty and Becky Valdez; [ed.] Cottonwood Elementary, also attending the G.A.T.E. Program for gifted and talented students.; [oth. writ.] Wrote an article on the internet for my schools Tortoise Reserve; [pers.] I was inspired to write "The Country Life" when sitting on my grandparents Porch Swing in the Mark Twain Forest.; [a.] Hesperia, CA

VALENCIA, BLANCA INES
[pen.] Shorty Rock or Ines; [b.] August 27, 1982, New York; [p.] William and Amanda Valencia; [ed.] Gone through Pre-school, Elementary Junior H.S. (I.S. 125) and High School in Astoria; [occ.] 9th grade in Long Island City High School; [memb.] Movie Membership; [hon.] 32 Awards in all. From Pre-School to Junior H.S. (Pre-School Awards and Diplomas, Commendation Card, Certificate of Participation 4 of them), Certificate of Completion 2 Merit Awards, Hand Writing Award, Science Fair Participation, Certification at Appreciation, Certificate of Earth Award, 2 Reading Achieve Art. 3 Certificate of Achievements, Citizenship Certificate, Music Achievement, Service Award, Elementary Diploma of Grad, National Free Enterprise Award, Certificate of Recognition Spelling Achievement Certificate, Language Arts Achievement Award, Science Achievement Certificate Award for excellence, in S.P.E.C.D.A., 2 Honor Roll Certificate, and Diploma of Junior High School.; [oth. writ.] Poems: Water Falls, Loneliness, Love Is A Symbol; [pers.] I'm delighted for knowing that I've accomplished one of my wishes which came true, to have one of my writings in an anthology. Knowing that I strived through the good and bad times with my family by my side. I'll never forget these beautiful feelings, a moment to reflect and to remember 4 ever.; [a.] New York City, NY

VALLEJOS, CANAAN LEE GRANO
[b.] January 31, 1987, Raton, NM; [p.] Walter and Louise Vallejos; [ed.] Heritage Elementary School, Pueblo, Colorado; [mem.] Class Representative; [hon.] Reading Certificates; [oth. writ.] Poems: "The Dragon and the King" God's Right "Gangs" Short stories: The Mammoth who Found a Friend Nicky Visits Grandma The Legend of the Great Fisherman The Great Spring; [pers.] The poem "God's right" was written for my family. When my uncle passed away it was hard for everyone to understand why. I thought about it and remembered my parents telling me God has a reason for everything. I hope this poem will help ease the pain of everyone who reads it, that has lost someone they love.; [a.] Pueblo, CO

VAN CAMP, MELBA E.
[b.] July 31, 1917, Kansas; [p.] Peter and Lidia Scalfi; [m.] Robert Ball Van Camp (Deceased), December 20, 1941; [ch.] Robert Bruce; [ed.] High School; [occ.] Retired; [oth. writ.] "A Forlorn Remembrance" quite long, is about an old forgotten Cemetery in Lone Pine California. Another about my deceased mother.

VAN DYKE, A. H.
[b.] October 30, 1938, Beaumont, TX; [p.] Mary E. and Peter Van Dyke; [m.] Darlene, July 1992; [ch.] Sonya Van Dyke; [occ.] Postal Worker

VAN HOOZER, LOWRY
[pen.] Logan Carlson; [b.] June 25, 1947, Bethany, MO; [p.] Vern Van Hoozer, Marlan Van Hoozer; [ch.] Jeff Van Hoozer; [ed.] Trenton High School, Trenton Jr. College, University of Missouri; [occ.] Farmer; [oth. writ.] Other poems not published; [pers.] To lead a happy productive life you need humility, perseverance and to know that God has a purpose for us all.; [a.] Trenton, MO

VANDERGAAG, ALEXIS
[pen.] Alexis Vandergaag; [b.] Netherlands; [p.] Alexander and Sylvia Vandergaag; [ed.] Miami Dade Community College - Drama Major Music Minor, Broadcasting School in Boston; [occ.] Entertainment Industry; [oth. writ.] "Physical," flannel and teens, "Uneasy Glance," "Rock," "Switzerland by Flight," "Guitar Man," "Vulnerable Child"; [pers.] Whenever life served me a challenge my pen practically wrote by itself. If a child or animal is abused and or mistreated the pain that they endure motivates me not only to act but to write about their plight.; [a.] Miami, FL

VASS, LEAH L.
[b.] August 1968, Denver, CO; [ed.] Oakland Special Education School, Telluride High School; [occ.] Architect Student; [hon.] Video Communications TCTV, Telluride Co; [oth. writ.] 7 years of journals; [pers.] Life can be difficult; it's important that you find the high note in everything. Be happy.; [a.] AZ

VAUGHN, DARLENE GARDNER
[b.] January 3, 1959, Philadelphia, PA; [p.] Herbert and Dorothy Gardner; [m.] Clarence R. Vaughn, June 23, 1984; [ch.] Christina Gardner, Jeannine Vaughn, and Danette Vaughn; [ed.] Great Valley High School York College of Pennsylvania; [occ.] Self-Employed Certified Day Care Provider, Hugs in Care Montclair, NJ; [oth. writ.] The tucker wood adventures series is a collection of children stories I have dedicated to my own children although unpublished, this book will be a family heirloom.; [pers.] I dedicate this poem to my beloved daughter Jeannine.; [a.] Montclair, NJ

VAZQUETELLES, GLORIANN
[pen.] Gloriann Vazquetelles; [b.] November 20, 1981, Bronx, NY; [p.] Lilian Rodriguez and Kelvin Vazquetelles; [ed.] 10th grade High School Student; [hon.] Received Poetry Award in Junior High School Name "What a Strong Mother"; [oth. writ.] "Daddy", "Times Are Changing", My Guardian "Angel"; [pers.] This poem is Dedicated to my strong Mother Lillian Rodriguez. The poem is based on the events which occurred in my family.; [a.] Bronx, NY

VERDIN, EARLINE SIMS
[p.] Mr. Leroy Sims and Mrs. Earline Sims; [m.] Alvin J. Verdin, October 29, 1994; [ed.] Assumption High School, Nicholls University; [occ.] Secretary; [pers.] I enjoy expressing my feelings through my writing. It gives me great pleasure to be able to touch others with the words I write.; [a.] Gray, LA

VETTER, MARRIE
[b.] October 26, 1983, Wellsboro, PA; [p.] Sharon and Mark Vetter; [ed.] From 1-7th Grade at Troy Schools; [memb.] A Girl Scout in Troop 955, A Band Member and Choirs Member at Troy Middle School; [hon.] Last Year in 6th Grade a Perfect Attendance Award; [oth. writ.] I have only written in English Class and for fun.; [pers.] I just want to have fun with my best friends: Casie Brewer, Amy Wagner, and Samantha Tice. Love ya bye-bye!; [a.] Troy, PA

VICIDOMINI, LAUREN N.
[b.] February 10, 1977, Belleville, NJ; [p.] Anthony and June Vicidomini; [ed.] Mater Dei High School graduate, Momouth University Attendee; [occ.] Exec. Sec. in Real Estate Office, Bartender, Rosegirl; [memb.] Phi Sigma Sigma, Who's Who Among American High School Students, National Honor Society; [hon.] Partial Scholarship to Monmouth University, Honors for 4 years, President's Education Award, Momouth County Guidance Directors Caring Award, SADD, Word Process, Eucharistic Minister; [pers.] You and only you can make the dreams you want happen.; [a.] Middletown, NJ

VILLA, NICOLE C.
[pen.] Niki C. Villa; [b.] June 20, 1979, Amsterdam, NY; [p.] Dominick Villa and Katherine McGillin; [ed.] Amsterdam High School, Amsterdam, NY, (GASD) Greater Amsterdam School District (currently 11th grade); [occ.] Student; [memb.] Basketball CYO, Softball/City; [hon.] Physical Fitness, President's Awards; [oth. writ.] Personal logs.; [pers.] Since I'm just 17, I've had a few wishes one was to achieve and by making it this far it's definitely a dream come true.; [a.] Fort Johnson, NY

VILLELLA, MICHAEL R.
[b.] August 23, 1977, Eglin AFB, FL; [p.] Ralph J. Villella Jr.; [ed.] High School graduate of Parkway High School, Bossier City, Louisiana, currently undergraduate at Louisiana Tech. University Majoring in Psychology; [occ.] Student; [memb.] Louisiana Tech. Band Member; [oth. writ.] Passion's Anthem (unpublished) several articles for the Cardinal Flyer (1993-1994); [pers.] Love is the highest virtue of mankind, so sacred that only in truth is it gained and through long suffering maintained.; [a.] Ruston, LA

VINSON, JENNIFER RENEE
[pen.] Little Pup or Renee; [b.] May 30, 1985, Brooklyn, NY; [p.] Mr. and Mrs. James and Patricia Vinson; [ed.] I attend the John T. Lambert Intermediate School. I am in the 6th Grade; [hon.] I Won Second Prize in a Talent Contest for Singing because I wish to be a Singer when I grow up. I won $75.00; [oth. writ.] Actually this is basically my first poem that I intended to write.; [pers.] The poem that I wrote was just something that came to my mind. What I'm trying to say is that anybody can do what they want to do if they try.; [a.] Bushkill, PA

VITUCCI, DUSTIN M.
[b.] September 13, 1984, Fresno, CA; [p.] Ronald and Lynda Vitucci; [occ.] Student 7th grade; [memb.] USA Free style Wrestling Assc. CVAL Pop Warner Football; [hon.] Principals Honor Roll, Second place Calif State Championships for Wrestling, Second place Western Regional Finals for Wrestling; [pers.] I strive to do well in my sports such as wrestling, football, and soccer to get a scholarship and go to North Carolina State and fulfill a writing career.; [a.] Clovis, CA

VIVEIROS, HORACIO RAY
[b.] June 11, 1972, Bridgeport, CT; [p.] Horacio and Valdemira Viveiros; [ed.] Central "Magnet" High School, Housatonic Community College, Tunxis Community - Technical College; [hon.] Dean's List; [oth. writ.] "As I Look Into Your Eyes"; [a.] Bridgeport, CT

VOGLER, RICK
[pen.] Richard Michael Vogler; [b.] June 2, 1975, Phoenix, AZ; [ed.] Currently pursuing a B.A. in Geography at Central Washington University: Ellensburg, Washington; [occ.] Full-time student; [memb.] National Geographic Society; [hon.] Central Washington University, Alumni Association Scholarship, Dean's List, Naches Valley High School Salutatorian; [oth. writ.] A few other poems published in my high school newspaper, yearbook, and company newsletter; [pers.] I use my creative writing as a means of expressing inner thoughts, ideas, or feelings on paper, which I otherwise would not so tactfully say aloud.; [a.] Naches, WA

VOHRA, ASHISH
[b.] June 15, India, Bombay; [ed.] St. Vincent's High School, Pune India, S.P. College Pune India (H.S.C. with Electronics) worked for Tailor Industries Inc. (plastics technology); [occ.] Student, Computer Science, Northern Illinois University (NIU); [hon.] Informatics Computer Institute, India, Pune (Scholarship Awarded towards Computer Studies); [pers.] "Love to be Loved."; [a.] Chicago, IL

VOLK, ROBERT
[b.] May 28, 1968; [ed.] B.A. Media Studies, University of Buffalo; [oth. writ.] Short plays and screenplays, short and medium-length poems and stories.; [pers.] Write what you feel and feel what you write.; [a.] North Babylon, NY

WADE, ANGELA CHRISTINE
[b.] May 14, 1980, Roanoke, VA; [p.] William J. and Barbara J. Wade; [ed.] Northside High School (Class of 1998); [occ.] Student (Junior); [memb.] National Honor Society, "Pride of Northside" Marching Band, Northside German Club (Treasurer), Girl Scout of America (10 years), Ex-Red Cross Clown "Pookie"; [hon.] Honor Role Student, Prudential Spirit of Community, Student of the Month (NHS), Girl Scout Silver and Gold Leadership Awards; [oth. writ.] Published poem! "No More War" Kids World (1992); [pers.] Listen to your heart, it knows you best.; [a.] Roanoke, VA

WAGNER, JOLLEEN
[b.] June 4, 1982, Troy, NJ; [p.] Janet DuBray and Charles Wagner Jr.; [ed.] Now in ninth grade; [occ.] High School Student; [memb.] Peer Leadership, S.A.A.D., Spanish Club, Drama Club, Basketball, Softball, Soccer; [hon.] Honor Roll, Merit Roll etc.; [oth. writ.] None published; [pers.] I look at my writing as a friend, a way to let out my feelings.; [a.] Green Island, NY

WALLACE, CAROLINE H.
[pen.] Caroline H. Wallace; [b.] November 30, 1943, Portland, ME; [p.] Gordon Braun, Helen Wallace Braun; [ed.] Westbrook College, Port-

land, Maine Integral Hatha Yoga Teacher Training, the Ashram, Belmont, MA, Yoga for Cardiac Disease Patients, Preventative Medicine Research Institute (PMRI), Sausalito, CA.; [occ.] Yoga/Stress Management Consultant for Beth Israel Hospital (Boston, MA) Dr. Dean Ornish Cardiac Disease Reversal Program; [memb.] Integral Yoga Teachers Ass'n - Satchi Denanda Ashram, Buckingham, VA, Seacoast Choral Society, Durham, NH, Board member - Mill pond Center for performing Arts, Durham, NH.; [hon.] "Blue Stocking" Literary contest - 1st Place Westbrook College, Honorary Mention - Beta Sigma Phi International Sorority poetry contest, "Fields Of Earth" poetry contest, Newmarket Town library.; [oth. writ.] Editor for a local seacoast newspaper for 4 years, with various articles published.; [a.] Newmarket, NH

WALLACE, DOROTHY A.
[b.] September 11, 1942, Wright County, MO; [p.] Stephen Foster Dudley, Lois Breman Dudley; [ch.] Michael Huckaby, David Wallace; [ed.] Mansfield High School, Mansfield, MO, Drury College and Southwest Missouri State University, Springfield, MO; [occ.] Special Services Director Mansfield Schools, Mansfield, MO; [memb.] International Society of Poets, American Salers Association, Council of Administrators of Special Education, Missouri State Teachers Association; [oth. writ.] Several poems published, family histories for county history books, newspaper articles.; [a.] Mansfield, MO

WALSH, NITA A.
[b.] November 3, 1966, Richmond, VA; [p.] Sylvia Southworth Walsh, Alvin Walsh; [ed.] Patrick Henry High, Brigham Young University; [occ.] Writer; [oth. writ.] Several poems published in anthologies.; [pers.] I try to write from my soul and hope others listen with theirs.; [a.] Richmond, VA

WALTER, WILLIAM J.
[b.] August 3, 1974, Saint Louis, MO; [ed.] Meremac Community College - Student; [occ.] Gas Station Attendant; [pers.] If a point has to be made, it's not worth making. This is in regards to negative peer pressure.; [a.] Saint Louis, MO

WALTERS, DORTHEA JOYCE
[pen.] Joyce Wener Walters; [b.] November 26, 1927, Mansfield, OH; [p.] Allan M. Weber and Mabel Scott Weber (Both Deceased); [m.] T. Doyle Walters (Deceased), November 18, 1950; [ch.] Douglas (Deceased), Susan Dean; [ed.] High School Grad., Mansfield Business College, Seminars, Ohio State Univ.; [occ.] Retired from Human Resources Position Local Mfg. Kent Work part time at a motel - Audit and Desk Clerk.; [memb.] Attend Butler Methodist Church but I'm not a "joiner" in any clubs or organizations; [hon.] President of Butler Alumni Assoc. 1976-1996; [oth. writ.] None ever submitted for publishing.; [pers.] Live by the "Golden Rule". Interested in Traveling and History (Been to Europe 9 times).; [a.] Bellville, OH

WALTON, JAMES E.
[b.] January 8, 1960, Salem, NJ; [p.] Edith and Richard Kent, James and Roberta Walton; [ed.] Conestoga High School, Dickinson College, American Graduate School of International Management, California Family Study Center, Pacifica Graduate Institute, Doctoral Candidate in Clinical Psychology; [occ.] Licensed Psychotherapist, Studio City; [memb.] California Association of Marriage and Family Therapists, C.G. Juis, Library of Los Angeles; [hon.] Omicron, Delta Epsilon Honor Society in Economics, DAR Good Citizenship Award; [a.] Los Angeles, CA

WAMBSGANSS, WILLIAM F.
[b.] November 22, 1928, Kendallville, IN; [p.] Ila Mae (Lytle) Wambsganss, Ernest Wambsganss; [m.] Mary Jane (Hagen), July 16, 1952; [ch.] William F. II, Rebeccah K., Michael Charles and Caroline Marie; [ed.] Kendallville HS, Ind., Valparaiso University, Ind, of Recog. Famous Writers School May 1970, many post grad. courses Univ. of Calif. State U. San Bernardino, Valley Coll. San Bernardino; [occ.] Retired - primary occupation Social Services Supervisor (County) Program Director for Private Foundation, experience in Federal Govt. and Industry; [memb.] Current, has to do with senior programs, Oldtimers Foundation, Highland Senior Center; [hon.] Recognition from Fed. Govt. for promoting Voluntarism.; [oth. writ.] At age 16, while attending H.S. in morning, I was full time news reporter for a small town daily. Edited/wrote 6 page newsletter monthly for private foundation, circulation 2000, wrote column (humorous vein) for, (at that time) daily paper, Fontana Herald News for about two years. Etc. Etc.; [pers.] Nothing can give more pleasure or release, with the most infinite variety, than the written word.; [a.] Rialto, CA

WANG, JANET
[b.] August 8, 1980, Midland, MI; [p.] Hsiu-Kuei Wang, Pen-Chung Wang; [ed.] Currently a Junior at Stratford Senior High - Houston, TX; [occ.] Student; [hon.] Stratford Senior High English Honor Award (1995), Houston Region Orchestra, Texas All-State Solo Winner (Violin); [oth. writ.] Publications in "Poetry Works: The Second Stanza", "We are Writers, Too," and "Thumbprints" magazines; [a.] Houston, TX

WANTLAND, JEFFERY K.
[pen.] Tober, Trigger; [b.] December 18, 1975, Augsberg, Germany; [p.] Robert S. Wantland and Cheryl Wantland; [pers.] Life is like a window, ultimately you're looking on through to see what is ahead of you, yet at a glance you can reflect on the things behind you.; [a.] Saint Louis, MO

WARD, ELIZABETH
[pen.] Elizabeth McCarthy Ward, Elizabeth Shanahan; [b.] Co Limerick, Ireland; [p.] John Shanahan, Mary Shanahan; [m.] Peter Ward; [ed.] Raised and Educated in England St. Mary's High School and Chesterfield College, Derbyshire, England; [hon.] Royal Society for the Encouragement of Arts, London, England Distinction - English Literature and English Language; [pers.] My writings have mainly been gifts for family and friends in the form of short stories. In the past twelve months, poetry and rhyme entered my life as an expression of emotion on paper to different happening in the world. This is my first publication of poetry.; [a.] Stamford, CT

WARD, JOHN L.
[b.] November 4, 1931, Sommitt, NJ; [m.] Joan G., August 31, 1956; [ch.] Marie, Mary, John, Jerry; [ed.] High School; [occ.] None - currently a full-time Grandfather; [pers.] I enjoy the time I am able to spend with my grandchildren and feel very fortunate to be a significant person in their lives. My four year old granddaughter Sarah Jean was my inspiration to write "Grandfather's Time."

WARD, PAULA
[pen.] Paula Ward; [b.] December 21, 1977, Kansas City, KS; [p.] Larry Ward, Melba Ward; [ed.] Leavenworth Senior High School; [occ.] A sales associate; [memb.] Students Against Drunk Driving (SADD); [hon.] Perfect Attendance Pleasant Ridge High School; [oth. writ.] One of my poem was published in the literary magazine at Pleasant Ridge High School.; [pers.] I hope to go further with other poems and achieve more in life with my talent.; [a.] Lawrence, KS

WARREN, BARBARA B.
[b.] January 25, 1921, Washington, DC; [m.] John A. Larson, February 1, 1986; [ch.] Three from first marriage; [ed.] Masters of Education and Supervision, American University; [occ.] Retired School Teacher and Administrator; [memb.] Montgomery County Public School System Montgomery County, MD; [oth. writ.] Many poems - not published (yet)!; [pers.] Life is full of surprises some wonderful and some horrible! Rejoice in the positive and overcome the negative.; [a.] Silver Spring, MD

WARREN, BRIANA
[pen.] Julie J. and Tiny and Pooh Bear; [b.] October 17, 1981, Goshen, NY; [p.] Harold and Sharon Cushing; [ed.] Full time Student Valley Central High School; [occ.] School and part time baby sitter; [memb.] Multi Culture Club, Step Dance Team; [hon.] 4 Olympic Trophies Braeside Camp 1994, MS Photogenic Galaxy Modeling Co., 1st Runner Up Beauty Pageant, 2 Trophies Galaxy Modeling Co.; [oth. writ.] "The Night I Met You" in books Ebbing Tide and Rippling Waters; [pers.] My poems are basically about the things on my life, boy troubles, and things I believe strongly in.; [a.] Walden, NY

WARWICK, TERESA
[b.] May 8, 1962, Helena, MT; [p.] Tom and Kaye Miskovich; [pers.] I search my mind and soul and even beyond, to unveil a truth or emotion, be it love or fear or something even stronger we don't yet comprehend. I go to that place deep inside myself left unexplored, due to anxiety or uncertainty to reveal a ray of hope or a dark secret. The discovery can free you to a new knowledge of what is possible. It will awaken your senses to reality and the insanity in which we live and love. P.S. Edgar Allen Poe is definitely an inspiration.; [a.] Peoria, AZ

WATERMAN, SANDRA
[pen.] Nikki; [b.] November 27, 1978; [p.] Carol Waterman; [ed.] 9th Grade; [occ.] Student; [pers.] I write poetry about life and how me as and individual see's it. Being in programs helped me understand my feelings better, they gave me a dream no need, to be a poet.; [a.] Boston, MA

WATERS, ERIN MICHELLE
[b.] May 14, 1982, Anchorage, AK; [p.] Alfred and Jacqueline Waters; [pers.] This is the first poem I have ever submitted to a contest, and it is an honor to have it published.; [a.] Macomb, IL

WATERS, KERRYNN
[b.] June 8, 1978, Maryville, TN; [p.] Conni Trent (Mother), Steve Trent (Step-father), Tony Waters (Father), Tami Waters (Step-mother); [ed.] William Blount High, Pellissippi State College; [hon.] Tennessee Honors Diploma; [pers.] I dedicate my poem to Brian Birchfield, my loving boyfriend. Always believe in your hopes and dreams and they can come true.; [a.] Maryville, TN

WATERS, NANCY A.
[pen.] NAW; [b.] April 22, 1945, Trenton, NJ; [p.] Raymond and Katherine; [ed.] Stienert High School, IBM Business Machine School; [occ.] Technical Assistant II, with State of New Jersey Treasury; [memb.] American Legion Post 31 NJ; [hon.] Several different Honors and Awards for many of my poems; [oth. writ.] Poems The Real Me, My Make Believe Friends, Seasonal Visitors, Little Baby Mine Memories in The Attic of My Mind, all have been published in different anthologies, plus many more poems on the topic of child abuse.; [pers.] Also many of the above have been published in newspapers put out by associations that help sexually abused people. If my words through poetry can touch people in a positive way. Then

I will know God gave me this talent for a very special reason.; [a.] Mercerville, NJ

WATERS, SAMANTHA E.
[b.] July 20, 1975, Perry, FL; [p.] Buddy Ellison and Gail Walsh; [m.] Edward F. Waters, September 3, 1994; [ed.] Edward H. White High School; [occ.] Assistant Manager Oak Plantation Apartment Community Kissimmee, FL; [pers.] This poem is dedicated to my husband. Edward, you are my inspiration and hope. I love you.; [a.] Kissimmee, FL

WATKINS, CUNTIS
[pen.] Malcolm D. Watson; [b.] September 9, 1917, Decoy, KY; [p.] Jasper and Cora Watkins; [m.] May 24, 1968; [ch.] Joan, Olga and Reggie; [ed.] High School and AB, ThB at Andersion V. at Anderson, Ind.; [occ.] Clergy; [memb.] Order of St. Luke, Cheplon Kit OMK, Wheeling, WV; [hon.] Social Recognition for Promotions of the Joni - Film - for Billy Graham, Enam. Assoc.; [oth. writ.] I have written a book, titled, "A Toad From Golden Road." I must retype it and make some changes.; [pers.] I believe in practicing Also - I want to live a pure life.; [a.] Dorcas, WV

WATSON, YASMEEN
[pen.] Yaz; [b.] July 27, 1982, Anchorage, Alaska; [p.] John and Beatrice Watson; [ed.] I am currently 14 and am in the 9th grade. I plan to attend Howard University and receive a Bachelors degree in Communications.; [occ.] Journalist with Ingenius Communications Network; [memb.] YWCA, Kwanza Club; [hon.] Kids Radio Air Force, Lit. Miss Hemisphere, Senaca Valley Track Awards, Looks Talent Agency Public Speaking Award; [oth. writ.] If Only They Knew, Moving, Alone, The Way It Use To Be, Would You, Snow; [pers.] I know that I can't change the world with my words. However, I feel that if I can impact just one person's life for the better, my job is done.; [a.] Cranberry Twp., PA

WATT, MALCOLM R.
[pen.] "Victor Voyer"; [b.] December 12, 1927, Pineville, KY; [p.] Robert and Elizabeth; [m.] Annalyn, June 8, 1952; [ch.] Malana and John; [ed.] College, U. of AZ, B.F.A. Degree; [occ.] retirement: Doing what comes naturally; [memb.] Screen Actors Guild American Federation of Television and Radio Artists; [hon.] For Fine Arts in Drawing and Painting, Acting, Calligraphy, Storytelling, Entertaining, and Non-fiction, as well as Poetry; [oth. writ.] A book of Witticisms a volume of poetry "Angela's Memorable Month" (Fiction, Comedy); [pers.] "Art" is a word for the experience which occurs when human souls meet, touch, and recognize each other.; [a.] Tucson, AZ

WEBB, MARIE ANNETTE HAMILTON
[b.] September 11, 1960, Kannapolis, NC; [p.] Grace Gainey Hamilton and Larry G. Hamilton; [m.] Jeffrey Scott Webb, December 16, 1988; [ch.] Nathaniel Scott Webb - 5, Jeffrey Thomas Webb - 2 1/2; [ed.] Graduated from AL Brown High 1978 - started working on a Commercial Art degree in 1990 at Gaston College in Gastonia, NC, I'm hopeful that it be completed soon.; [occ.] Homemaker; [hon.] Submitted a song to an International Song Writers Contest in 1984 and was honored for being listed as one of the a chosen contestants worldwide to enter as a finalist.; [oth. writ.] I have written many songs, since the age of 12., but none have ever been published I have also written many poems through - as music and english have always been my favorite subjects of attention.; [pers.] I pay chose attention to the people around me and their situation. My greatest sources of inspiration comes from just the inevitable trial of life one must face, including my self. I hope the people who have inspired me will be touched by their simple truth. My dream is to "Music Literature become a composer, author and illustrator of children's books.";
[a.] Stanley, NC

WEFERLING, OLIVER
[b.] October 11, 1972, Schluchtern, Germany; [p.] Erhard and Angelika; [m.] Felicia Weferling, September 14, 1993 (Denmark); [ed.] Nigesens, Mariengmna-Sium Jever, 1. San Bh. 11 Leer (all Germany), Life itself has been my Constant Teacher; [occ.] Entrepreneur; [oth. writ.] Over the past five years I have written about two hundred poems and lyrics for my own collection, none have ever been published anywhere.; [pers.] Captured forever are my thoughts, a wisdom based on pains and past. Read between my lines. You will discover a hidden truth based on life, love and emotion, and you will understand...; [a.] Winston-Salem, NC

WELCH, JOHNNY
[pen.] J. W.; [b.] March 19, 1951, Stewart County, Richland, GA; [p.] Walter and Margaret Welch; [m.] Divorced; [ch.] John Walter Welch III; [ed.] High School advanced, Musical Training (25 years); [occ.] Q.C. Manager, Kings Custom Builder's/ Ellaville, GA, Modurar Office Buildings; [memb.] Church Hill Baptist Church, BAD - Habit Country and Rock Band, King's Custom Prayer Group; [hon.] John Philip Sousa, (Band Award); [oth. writ.] Song's/poem's To Be Soon (Copy written) Southern Rock, Country and Gospel; [pers.] I've learned to be patient and pray to have peace of mind, from my father, I've dreamed to never give up quitter's never win and winner's never quit from my mother. And a good friend is better than a $100.00 bill any day!; [a.] Buena Vista, GA

WELLS, KATHLEEN
[b.] January 28, 1944, New York City, NY; [p.] Ernest and Margaret Fiore; [m.] Frank Wells, April 30, 1960; [ch.] Henry and Howard; [ed.] Memorial High School; [occ.] Homemaker; [memb.] Right to life movement St. Francis of Assisi Prayer group; [oth. writ.] I had a poem published in my local newspaper as well as in the Memphis, TN paper and several local radio stations played one of my songs on the air.; [pers.] Life and the times we live in are the direct source of my inspiration for my poems and songs. I enjoy reading poetry about nature. My favorite poem is "Trees" by Joyce Kilmer.; [a.] Vineland, NJ

WELLS, TIMOTHY ALLEN
[pen.] Wulfgar Saint John; [b.] February 20, 1963, Modesto; [p.] Carolyn Deanda; [m.] Kathleen Cara Wells, July 4, 1988; [ed.] Apollo High; [occ.] California State Prison; [hon.] None as yet, but still striving.; [oth. writ.] Several non-published writings.; [pers.] There is a great key for the door to the future. The keeper of the key is the children - guide our children.; [a.] Blythe, CA

WENGER, JERRY R.
[pen.] Jerry R. Wenger; [b.] September 18, 1952, Harrisonberg; [p.] Joseph Wenger Sr., Mildred Wenger; [m.] Linda Wenger, November 17, 1973; [ch.] Christopher, Jerry, Nocholas, Melinda, Belinda; [ed.] Brandon High School, Ruder Technical Ing., Ridge Vocational Technical; [occ.] Area Mechanic (Walt Disney World); [memb.] Dundee Baptist Church; [hon.] Ordained Minister in the Christian Faith; [oth. writ.] Writing a book now; [pers.] Without my Lord I am nothing.; [a.] Dundee, FL

WERKALL, EVELYN R.
[b.] June 11, 1945, Biloxi, MS; [p.] Malsby and Elvina Raley; [m.] John Russell, July 7, 1963; [ch.] Kelly Russell, Karlene Renee; [ed.] Biloxi Senior High; [occ.] Home Furnishing Sales; [memb.] Sacred Heart Catholic Church; [pers.] Life and love is a gift from God to each of us. Let us strive to live our lives with love for all, and show that love to all. For tomorrow is not promised.; [a.] Biloxi, MS

WERNER, SARAH
[pen.] Sarah; [b.] July 25, 1984, Trenton, NJ; [ed.] I am currently going to Seaford Middle School, I am in the 7th grade; [hon.] I have been included on the Honor Role since I started school; [oth. writ.] I have written many poems, stories, and essays mostly for my own enjoyment.; [pers.] I enjoy writing casual poems about fictional characters and their feelings about life. I am encouraged by my parents to keep on writing. Poets like Shel Silverstien have greatly influenced me.;
[a.] Seaford, DE

WESSEL, PATRICIA A.
[pen.] Patricia Fanning Avery Bawcum Wessel; [b.] May 11, 1942, Weehawken, NJ; [p.] James J. and Elizabeth C. Fanning Sr.; [m.] James R. Wessel, March 1989; [ch.] Deborah K. Avery O'Mara (daughter), Jayson K. Bawcum (son); [ed.] Graduated from St. Mary's High School in 1960 in Albuquerque, New Mexico Attended the University of New Mexico, Attended Albuquerque Technical Vocational Institute; [occ.] Housewife, Retired Administrative Secretary; [memb.] National Authors Registry, The International Society of Poets, International Society of Authors and Artists Songwriters Club of America; [hon.] Fourth place in Captured Moments, several Honorable Mentions in Iliad Press Anthologies, Accomplishment of Merit Award from Creative Arts and Sciences, Ent. Editors Choice Awards from The National Library of Poetry, World Artist Award from World Art Publishing; [oth. writ.] Numerous poems in the National Library of Poetry anthologies Creative Arts and Science, Ent. anthology Captured Moments, and Between the Quotes, Best New poems of 1995 and 1996, Sparrowgrass Poetry Forum, Inc. several anthologies, Quill Books the Amherst Society, JMW Publishing Rhyme or Reason, World Art Publishing Enduring Harmony, Who's Who in New Poets 1996, The Poetry Guild, Iliad Press several anthologies; [pers.] A close loving family is a blessing. My son, Jayson Keith Bawcum, the first person to encourage me to try my hand at writing. It has turned out to be the most enjoyable hobby for me and a wonderful outlet. My song writing has also. My daughter, Deborah K. Avery O'Mara also encouraged me to try my hand at various forms of writing. I was a single parent for a long period of time as my children were growing up. They were the joy of my life!; [a.] Albuquerque, NM

WEST, JO ANN
[b.] November 6, 1942, Atascadero, CA; [p.] James Arthur and Nell West; [m.] Divorced; [ch.] Bradley Charles, Michael John, Jody Allen, Aaron Eugene; [ed.] Gresham High School, Portland State College (OR), Ohlone College (CA), Diablo Valley College (CA), Martinez Adult School (CA), Subjects: literature, photography, art, music (singing); [occ.] Secretary; [memb.] Church of Jesus Christ of Latter Day Saints (Mormon); [hon.] Scholarship, Brigham Young University; [oth. writ.] A book of poems which is currently using my own water colors and photographs for the backgrounds of the pages.; [pers.] I write from my heart about life as I have known and lived it. I reflect often on God's gifts to us and the love we should show for each other.; [a.] Pleasant Hill, CA

WEST, PAULA FOSTER
[pen.] Paula Foster West; [b.] April 8, 1954, De Quincy, LA; [p.] Robert and Lillian Foster; [m.] Dennis A. West, June 24, 1972; [ch.] Benjamin A. West; [ed.] Port Neches Groves High School; [occ.] Floral Designer, and Mortuary Cosmetol-

ogy; [memb.] Local Community and Civic Organizations.; [oth. writ.] Various poetic forms, Music and Lyrics in Gospel and Country; [pers.] I draw on life's experiences to put down on paper, what I feel. I think emotion, whether mine or another's, has a great influence on my writings.; [a.] Port Neches, TX

WHELAN, ANN
[pen.] Anka; [b.] May 11, 1931, Johnstown, PA; [p.] Amelia Mervos, Stojan Dudukovich; [m.] Clinton D. Whelan Jr., February 22, 1969; [ch.] Mary Ann Madigan (Deceased) Michael V. Madigan, Kevin P. Madigan, James S. Madigan, Brian Madigan, Alice Grommett; [ed.] Johnstown Central High School, Irvine Valley College, U.S. Air Force. Fifteen years of vocal training and study; [occ.] Retired - was Clerical Supervisor at Farmers Insurance. Currently a vocal teacher, Writer, Poet; [memb.] International Society of Poets, National Assoc of Teachers of Singing, L.A., Chapter and National. Past President of V.F.W. Post 2122. Irvine Valley Chorale, St Steven's Cathedral choir, Alhambra, Ca. Hospitality Chairman for L.A. chapter of N.A.T.s; [oth. writ.] Published in Serb Word Magazine Poem Kosovo Peonies, Story "Remembering Christmas Past", "Memories of Johnstown Flood of 1936" several stories, poems and articles published in newspaper "Srbobran".; [pers.] I believe that God gave us our talents to be cultivated and shared with our fellow man.; [a.] La Habra, CA

WHITAKER, SEPRENIA
[b.] January 22, 1966, Huntington, NY; [p.] Mary and Amos Coleman; [m.] Richard M. Whitaker, August 31, 1991; [ch.] Victor, Alexander, Vincent, Arron; [ed.] B.A. Liberal Art, Penn State; [occ.] Disabled, Writer; [hon.] Mary McLeod Bethune Leadership, NAACP Outstanding Leadership, Who's Who in the East, NCBS (National Caucus of Black Students), Creative Writing, OCSA (Outstanding College Students of America), Presidential Physical Fitness, OAU (Organization of African Unity), Ms. ACESO beauty Pageant; [oth. writ.] S.O.S. (Sisters of Struggle). Play, "Losing Our Babies", poem, "The I'll Wind". Poems, P.S. I luv U. screenplay, no mere stroke of luck but a blessing, book manuscript; [pers.] Jesus wept then too shall I.; [a.] Cheltenham, MD

WHITE, CHERYL L.
[pen.] Cheri White; [b.] August 24, 1964, Bourne, MA; [p.] Ronald and Nancy Cassell; [m.] David F., September 4, 1988; [ch.] Stephen Allan, Jeffrey David and Drew Ronald; [ed.] Holmdel High School; [oth. writ.] Several poems for special family members and friends.; [pers.] Thank you for your inspiration - grand parents Makowka, Thompson and especially Donald Pelton for whom "His Eulogy" was written.; [a.] Rome, NY

WIEDEMAN, CHERYL
[b.] February 11, 1961, West Covina, CA; [p.] Richard Caty, Irene Caty; [m.] Jeff Wiedeman, March 5, 1984; [ch.] Michael Richard, Kyle Lewis; [ed.] Glendora High, Citrus College; [occ.] Accounting Assistant, Caltech; [pers.] Someone once told me that I have alot to give to others so I wanted to share my poem with who have alot to give.; [a.] Mira Loma, CA

WIGINGTON III, JOHN H.
[pen.] Caesar Rex; [b.] April 20, 1961, Wooster, OH; [ed.] The University of Akron; [occ.] Clerk; [oth. writ.] Poetry, a journal; [pers.] Knowledge is power, power is discourage.; [a.] Akron, OH

WILCOX JR., FRANK
[pen.] Frank Wilcox; [b.] October 25, 1942, Battle Creek, MI; [p.] Frank Sr. and Mabel Wilcox; [m.] Martha June Wilcox, January 23, 1977; [ch.] Paula Sue, Frank Paul, Melissa Lynn and Harold Wayne; [ed.] Grad. Union City High School 1960, attended the University of Mich. Master of Sci. in Financial Services, The American College, Bryn Mawr, PA; [occ.] Insurance Brokerage and Financial Planning; [memb.] Christ's Community Church, Fishers in the American Legion, Murat Temple Shrine of Indianapolis, Int'l Assn. of Financial Planners, Fishers Indiana Chamber of Commerce, and many others; [hon.] Several H.S. Awards, Elected to Calhoun County, MI, Board of Commissions 1975 thru '78. Served as its Chairman '75 and '76. Chairman Calhoun County Democratic Party '79 and '80. Several Insurance Industry Awards; [oth. writ.] The Frog On A Log (a children's story), and other varied poetry.; [pers.] When I am blue or in a reflective mood and I pray for God's guidance, I often end up writing something. It is a wonderfully refreshing way to release pent up emotions, and to recharge my batteries.; [a.] Fishers, IN

WILDES, DEBORAH L.
[b.] July 8, 1963, Hillsboro, WI; [p.] LeRoy W. Wildes, Mary H. Tadder; [ed.] Royall High, Elroy, WI, A.S. - UWC - Richland, B.S. - UW - LaCrosse, I have learned from life experiences.; [oth. writ.] Poems published, story started about my parents.; [pers.] Much thanks to my beloved parents who have told me over and over about many things, you can do it!!! I praise and thank my Savior Jesus Christ!!!; [a.] Kendall, WI

WILKERSON, RICHARD L.
[pen.] Itsa Lulu; [b.] December 6, 1938, Brown County, IN; [pers.] I try to imitate the antics of my friends in my writing.; [a.] Columbus, IN

WILLAMAN, DARRYL G.
[b.] October 27, 1960, Canton, OH; [p.] Frank J. Willaman, Phyllis Willaman; [m.] Suzanne M. Willaman, October 23, 1993; [ed.] Timken Senior High, Stark Technical College; [occ.] Accounting Clerk; [pers.] I seek to touch the reader's heart whether it be through great joy or great sadness. I am a fan of, and been inspired by, the words of Edgar Allan Poe.; [a.] Cincinnati, OH

WILLIAMS, A. NEVILLE
[pen.] Tony Williams; [b.] July 16, 1945, Virginia; [p.] Peyton Williams, Doris Orr; [m.] Carole V. Dorsey; [ch.] Carl, Edward, Carrie; [ed.] Wilberforce University; [occ.] Electrician; [memb.] L.U. 595; [a.] Oakland, CA

WILLIAMS, BEATRICE
[b.] December 23, 1961, Saint Louis; [p.] John and Flora Williams; [ch.] Crystal and Barry Williams; [ed.] Vashon High School; [pers.] I wrote this poem End Of The Road to my fiancee Ernest because he was having a hard time in the Navy.; [a.] Saint Louis, MO

WILLIAMS, CARL
[b.] December 29, 1981, Saint Louis, MO; [p.] Jesse Hall, Vickey Hall; [ed.] Middle School Student; [occ.] 8th grade student Hancock (1987-1996) Cross Keys (1996); [memb.] Jr. Honor Society; [hon.] Jr. Honor Society, Honor Roll, Perfect Attendance, Fight Free Honors; [a.] Saint Louis, MO

WILLIAMS, CAROLYN
[b.] July 5, 1985, Norfolk, VA; [p.] Frances and Dennis G. Williams; [ed.] 6th grade student at Bayside 6th grade campus, Evie Mansfield Modeling School graduate; [memb.] Drama club, all - city chorus (1995), St. Nicholas Greek Orthodox Church Choir; [hon.] Football and Cheerleading trophies, Honor Roll, Principal's List; [oth. writ.] Colorado's Beauties, Pretty Leaves, The Color Blue; [pers.] I write as a hobby, through writing I express my feelings and share part of myself with others.; [a.] Norfolk, VA

WILLIAMS, CLARA M.
[pen.] Shuba; [b.] February 26, 1929, Ridgely, TN; [p.] Thilbert and Myrene Young; [m.] Luther Williams, January 27, 1955; [ch.] Sabrina Moore, Myrene Williams; [ed.] Summer High; [occ.] Retired; [memb.] West End Baptist Church; [pers.] A career has its rewards but for a woman with a family, rewards are everlasting. I was inspired by Helen Steiner Rice.; [a.] East Saint Louis, IL

WILLIAMS, EDNA
[b.] January 10, 1924, Champaign, IL; [p.] Mr. and Mrs. A. W. McLintock; [m.] Luther H. Williams; [ch.] Karen, Eddie, Bruce, Lance

WILLIAMS, JENNIFER
[b.] September 26, 1983, Madison, WI; [p.] Kathleen and Kenneth Williams; [ed.] Currently a seventh grader at Rose Hill Middle School. I will graduate in 2002; [occ.] Student; [memb.] Voice Lessons, Girl Scouts, 4-H Cheerleading; [hon.] Principle's Honor Roll, Student of the Week; [oth. writ.] I have done a lot of writing, once I made a booklet for a school project named "Heaven and Earth" with two poems of mine, "Why" and "Life". It also had a story in it.; [pers.] I believe all people should make the world a better place and in doing so, we may all prosper. Poets help by getting people to the state of realization.; [a.] Rose Hill, KS

WILLIAMS, MELISSA
[pen.] Melissa; [b.] March 7, 1979, Rome, GA; [p.] Tommy and Joyce Williams; [ed.] Senior in High School, Temple, GA; [occ.] Student, part-time work at Target Dept. Store.; [memb.] Band Member, Annual Staff; [oth. writ.] Short Stories in Middle School - Honorable Mention; [pers.] I strive to put my deepest feelings into my writing to touch someone who may need it, when they read my poems and stories.; [a.] Powder Springs, GA

WILLIAMS JR., BENTLEY N.
[pen.] Willie B. (Army); [b.] April 23, 1970, Kingston, Jamaica; [p.] Mr. and Mrs. Bentley H. Williams; [ed.] Plantation High, Plantation, FL. Broward Community College, current McFatter Vocational Technical School, Studying Nursing; [occ.] Customer Service/Sales at Luria's US Army Reservist; [memb.] Christian Life Center, Church, International Club, Veteran of Operation Desert Shield/Storm; [hon.] Army Achievement Medal, Army Commendation Medal, Meritorious Service During Operation Desert Shield/Storm; [oth. writ.] A Soldier's Eyes, End of An Era. Published in P'an Ku, The Literary Magazine at Broward Community College enclosed is a copy of A Soldier's Eyes for your reading pleasure; [pers.] Life is a paradox and its answers intriguing, yet among the many pathways to choose, one stands out. It's plain and rugged, but its end is fulfilling, and the rewards worth the journey. There's an invisible hand in all things, and its source in obvious, something beyond ourselves, our emotions, feelings, intellect, philosophies or religions. It's the hand of love, in the face of colors, cultures, and all things, it's the hand of God and there's but one.; [a.] Lauderhill, FL

WILLIAMSON, BOBBIE
[pen.] BLR; [b.] June 20, 1980, Winslow, AZ; [p.] Mike and Lennie Stewart; [occ.] High School Student; [pers.] Thank you Crystal Lynn. I couldn't help but to continue writing with you constantly remembering me.; [a.] Colorado Springs, CO

WILLINGHAM, JANE BENNETT
[b.] April 2, 1930, Brooklyn, NY; [p.] Margaret Grof Bennett, Fred Bennett; [m.] Calder B. Willingham Jr. (Deceased), September 15, 1953; [ch.] Fred, Sara, Mark, Pamela, Christopher; [ed.] Berkeley Institute, Brookly, Wellesley College, Plymouth State College; [occ.] Retired English

Teacher and Administrator; [memb.] New Hampton Community Church, Trustees Gordon-Nas'h Library, Pemigewasser Choral Society; [hon.] Cum Laude, Senior Teacher Award; [oth. writ.] Newsletters and other communications of local organization; [pers.] I guess I consider poetry a "divine" inspiration, a little individual moment of grace - the result is not always beautiful, but it is as true as I can make it.; [a.] New Hampton, NH

WILLOUGHBY, CHRISTY J.
[b.] November 11, 1966, Fairfax, VA; [p.] Robert and Reatha Willoughby; [ed.] Osbourn High School, Northern Virginia, Community College; [occ.] Sales Associate Shaw's Jewelers, Roller Skating Professional/Ins. Coach; [memb.] SRSTA - Rolling Skating Teacher's Association, RS/USAC, National Association for Coach's; [hon.] SE/USAC Coach's Award, for Coaching National Champion, Six Time Gold Regional Medalist Southeastern Region 1989-1991 - Ranked 4th Nationally 1989-1990 U.S. Olympic Sports, Festival Competitor (only top 6 in Nation); [oth. writ.] I have written several poems, however this was my first opportunity to have my poetry critiqued by literary experts.; [pers.] My poems are influenced by issues in my life. They are inspired by emotions and relationships that are common to the development of maturity in life.; [a.] Manassas, VA

WILLSIE, LINLEY J.
[b.] November 24, 1963, New Zealand; [p.] Bruce and Glenis Robertson; [m.] Brian Willsie; [ed.] Lincoln University (NZ) University of Maryland - (European Division); [occ.] Horticulturist; [hon.] Dean's List (University of Maryland); [oth. writ.] Personal poems for family and friends, nothing published.; [pers.] I believe it's all about love, too much is not humanly possible and too little creates all the ills that destroy us from within and without. So let's come down to earth, back to reality and still love it all.; [a.] Gulfport, MS

WILSON, CARLOS DEVAUGHN
[b.] September 15, 1974, Oklahoma; [p.] Gladys Wilson; [m.] Ressa Wilson, March 25, 1995; [ch.] La Vaughn De Vonte, Elijah D'Andre; [ed.] Star Spencer High School; [memb.] Black Historical Re-Educational Alliance (BHRA), Children of the Future in Christ (CPTFIC); [oth. writ.] Soon to be published "Shattered Diamonds: A Tragic Tale of Child Abuse." Includes a poem entitled "Diamonds."; [pers.] A simple life is only for a simple man without a goal. Carlos Wilson 10/28/96 inspired by Stephen King and Edgar Allen Poe.; [a.] Midwest City, OK

WILSON, MICHAEL LEO
[b.] May 21, 1974, Indianapolis; [p.] Paul and Beverly Burns; [ed.] I attended Tates Creek High and Graduated in 1993; [occ.] Pizza Delivery/my Career goal is to John the fire Department; [pers.] I hope that others will see life through my work and come to appreciate life and see the true gift we have been given by God and know we can accomplish anything in life; [a.] Lexington, KY

WILSON, REBECCA JEAN
[b.] September 19, 1972, Pontiac, MI; [p.] Mr. and Mrs. Ted Colassey; [m.] Steve Jay Wilson, January 8, 1994; [ch.] Samantha Marie Wilson; [ed.] High School Graduate; [occ.] Homemaker; [memb.] Fitness USA; [hon.] Elementary School Awards. Numerous Awards in Math and Spelling. And also in Junior High School.; [pers.] I started writing poems when I was 13 years old. My parents have been telling me all these years I should try to get my poems published. I finally listened to them and I'm glad I did.; [a.] Orion Township, MI

WILSON, SHIRLEY LOUISE
[b.] July 22, 1959, Lake City, FL; [p.] Enondos and Iris Parker; [m.] Trennis Marvin Wilson, December 25, 1994; [ch.] Iris LaSonya Parker; [ed.] Pre-K - 13 Grade, S.P. Lingston (Elementary), Technical High (Graduate); [occ.] Teacher's Assistant working with babies 2 wks. to 6 mos.; [memb.] God Ark of Society Family Worship Center - I'm a witness for the Lord; [pers.] I love living and doing for God, if it had not been for him I wouldn't be here today. My life with God is like the sun and the moon only God makes me shine!; [a.] Jacksonville, FL

WINTERS, TOMMY PATRICK
[pen.] Raven; [b.] August 22, 1981, Millington, IN; [p.] Tommy Winters Jr. and Patricia Ann Winters; [ed.] Kirby High School; [occ.] Student in 10th grade at Kirby High School; [memb.] Member of the Chest Club, Football Team, Computer Club, Boys To Men; [oth. writ.] Nights In Many Ways, Everyday Is Mother's Day, Love, Someone, Life To The End; [pers.] When you believe in God all things are possible!; [a.] Memphis, TN

WISE, SABRINA
[pen.] Sabby; [b.] March 6, 1984, Miami, FL; [p.] Patricia Ledford, Earnest Ledford; [ed.] I'm in 7th grade at South Forsyth Middle School. My favorite subjects are Art, Social Studies, Language Arts; [memb.] Young Astronauts, Spelling Bee (School and County) Chorus, and 4-H.; [hon.] Spelling Bee 1st place at School and 2nd at County. Highest average in Social Studies. Always in Summer Reading Club.; [oth. writ.] Short Story: A Mysterious secret of 3 generations, spook House, Spook House Triple the Thrill. About 35 poems and 4 songs.; [pers.] Everyone has a dream and is given a chance. This is the first of many dreams of mine to come true. I always believe in kindness of people.; [a.] Cumming, GA

WONG, KRISTEN
[b.] December 29, 1980, Hawaii; [p.] Eric Wong and Eloise Yoshino; [ed.] St. Andrew's Priory School for Girls since Kindergarten; [occ.] Still attending High School; [memb.] Writer's Club (School), International Club (School); [hon.] Head Master's List at School; [pers.] When I write, I try to make sure it's my own words, and no one else's.; [a.] Kaneohe, HI

WOOD, WILMA L.
[pen.] Wilma Spaur Wood; [b.] February 26, 1933, Exchange, WV; [p.] Perry H. and Gertrude Spaur; [m.] Earl P. Wood (Deceased, January 4, 1996), June 21, 1952; [ch.] Jeffrey Lee, Stephen P., Jayne Wood Harris; [ed.] Sutton High School, Mountain State Business College; [occ.] Retired - WV Dept. of Health and Human Resources; [memb.] Gassaway Baptist Church, Adult Choir, Treasurer; [hon.] White Ribbon on Poem - Braxton Co., Arts and Crafts; [oth. writ.] Currently writing book on my Grandmother and Mother's life. 1892-1990, Just starting to write more after retiring.; [pers.] To reflect Christ and Hope for Mankind. Encourage.; [a.] Gassaway, WV

WOOLFROM, TARA
[b.] April 5, 1979, Massillon, OH; [p.] Dale Woolfrom; [m.] Karen Starr, December 11, 1971; [ed.] Tuslaw High School; [occ.] Student; [pers.] Life is like poetry, it can mean anything, or it can mean nothing. Don't throw your life away. Make it mean something. You are the author of your life. Make people remember it, make it good.; [a.] North Lawrence, OH

WORKMAN, FLORA MUNFORD CHRISTENSEN
[b.] September 17, 1933, Cedar City, UT; [p.] Robert C. and Jane S. Munford; [m.] M. J. Christensen (Deceased), Bill R. Workman; [ch.] Five Children; [ed.] High School - Some Col worked as Color Artist in Photography for years "Living"; [occ.] Housewife Grandmother - Mother; [hon.] Never have entered any poem or writing contests; [oth. writ.] Love to write; have many poems.; [pers.] Writing has been a way for me to express the feelings. Of love I have to our heavenly father for this wonderful world, so full of ever beautiful exciting things I love Robert Frost.; [a.] Hurricane, UT

WORRELL, ANNIE
[pen.] Annie Worrell; [b.] July 14, 1922, Macon, TN; [p.] Dr. and Mrs. P. M. Bishop; [m.] Joe D. Worrell (Deceased), June 1, 1939; [ch.] David Worrell, John Worrell; [ed.] D.Ed.; [occ.] Retired; [memb.] N.S.D.A.R., N.S. Magna Charta Dames; [hon.] B.A. Cum Laude; [a.] Bolivar, TN

WORTMAN, MICHAEL
[b.] December 29, 1967; [p.] Dave and Vi Wortman; [m.] Sherrie Wortman; [memb.] United States Parachute Association; [pers.] Poetry is not from the heart of the heart. I thank God for giving me the opportunity to express myself in so many ways, from vast artistic talents to sky diving. Thanks also, to my reason to strive for success. You've been Loyal, Honest, and a true friend. Thanks, Andy - 818.; [a.] Murfreesboro, TN

WRIGHT, MARGARET S.
[pen.] Penny Wright; [b.] October 5, 1946, East Orange, NJ; [p.] Harry Ambler Wright, Content Smith Wright; [m.] Annulled, September 1972; [ch.] Muriel C. and Connie Wagner; [ed.] Overbrook School for the Blind and Ursinus College; [occ.] Metaphysician; [memb.] Alumni Assocs. International Society of Poets, Poets Guild, North Shore Animals League, Episc. Church; [hon.] Academic, Craft, Singing and Speaking Awards, D.A.R. and Amern. Legion Medals of Good Citizenship; [oth. writ.] Poems and school papers and 'Ideals' magazine, essays for "The Secret Place". Two privately done books of verse.; [pers.] From the first to the last all we really have to give of is ourselves. Every dear thought, every gentle gesture, every act of kindness springs from and creates love.; [a.] Upper Darby, PA

WRIGHT, PHYLLIS
[b.] September 6, 1964, Covington, KY; [p.] Robert Iseral, Wilma Iseral; [m.] Anthony Wright, October 15, 1983; [ch.] Jacob Andrew, Keisha Rachelle; [ed.] Grant County High

WYNN, CANDICE M.
[pen.] Candi Mathews, Candi S. M. Doe Zemol; [b.] October 11, 1972, Corydon, IN; [p.] Halleck III and Diana Mathews; [m.] Brian Wynn, December 31; [ch.] Leon Steven and Justin Andrew Halleck; [ed.] Corydon Central H.S., Faulkner State; [occ.] Mother and volunteer Sunshine Club, Puppet Director (3rd, 4th and 5th graders); [memb.] Daphne United Methodist; [hon.] Many in my childhood and teenage years - none recent; [oth. writ.] A few poems published in local newspapers.; [pers.] In my life I do not believe in looking for the end of the tunnel. I find a way to light it!; [a.] Fairhope, AL

WYNTER, ANDREA A.
[pen.] Andrea Wynter, Lady Angie; [p.] Mr. I. McGibbon; [ed.] Howard University, Psychology Degree, Business School, Computer School; [occ.] Teacher; [memb.] Howard Univ. Alumni Church Groups; [hon.] Honor Roll student Award, Who's Who Among High School Students Award President of International Club Award (High School); [oth. writ.] I'm in love with your ways.; [pers.] I like to write about human nature. As a member of our society, I strive to see how we can better work together, in love and peace by the help of our Almighty God.; [a.] Washington, DC

XELOURES, CHANDRA LEIGH
[b.] September 5, 1982, Canton, OH; [ed.] I'm an eight grade student and attend Jackson Memorial

Middle School; [occ.] Student; [hon.] Honor Roll, Student of the Week, and Certificates for Writing Achievement; [a.] North Canton, OH

YANCEY, PAMELA FAYE
[pen.] Charisse Marcell; [b.] April 11, 1963, Joliet, IL; [p.] Simon Jones, Mary Jones; [m.] Henry Yancey Jr., June 14, 1986; [ch.] Adrienne Marcel; [ed.] Joliet West High, Paul Quinn College; [occ.] Poet; [memb.] Alpha Kappa Alpha Sorority, Brown Chapel A.M.E. Church, Youth Coordinator; [hon.] Community Service Award, Magna Cum Laude College Graduate, Distributive Education Award of Excellence, 12 Year Perfect Attendance School Award, Dean's List; [oth. writ.] Several poems published in local newspapers, poems printed in several obituaries, chairperson for poetry readings at social gatherings.; [pers.] I hope that sharing my life experiences with touch someone in need of compassion. Through God, all things are possible.; [a.] Raleigh, NC

YANTISS, ALVIN C.
[b.] January 15, 1921, Jerusalem, Palestine; [p.] Jesse and Anita (Baldwin) Yantiss; [m.] Gladys (Linscott) Yantiss, April 6, 1946; [ch.] Robert Allan, Ronald Alvin; [ed.] English and German Schools in Jerusalem, German School, Haifa, Palestine, American Community, Beirut, Lebanon, Greensboro Senior High School, NC. University of North Caroline - class of 1943; [occ.] Retired; [memb.] UNC Alumni Association - Fitzwilliam Historical Society; [oth. writ.] "The Tale of a Kite", "Now Hear This", "The Cattapooh Letters"; [a.] Fitzwilliam, NH

YAZAR, ARZU
[b.] July 16, 1971, Istanbul, Turkey; [p.] (Mother) Sukran Aki and Cenap Aki (Father); [m.] Sabit Yazar, July 16, 1996; [ed.] High School graduated (Literature Section), Pasakapisi Ilkokulu (5 years), Burhan Felek Lisesi Ortakisim (3 years), Burhan Felek Live Kismi (4 years); [occ.] McDonald's, Trainee for Swing Mng.; [oth. writ.] My Flower, Faith, People, World, Children; [a.] Cupertino, CA

YOUNG, EDWARD
[b.] May 5, 1952, Pittsburgh, PA; [ed.] Current Student Florida Atlantic University - English Literature Major; [occ.] Registered Respiratory Therapist; [oth. writ.] Vietnam Trilogy and God Died too - CAT Publication 1988. Poems published in Recovery News Letters. Co-Author on a Study of Aerosolized Pentamidine in Medical Journal Chest 1990.; [pers.] "To be" and my other works try to reflect not just the pain or "Darkness" of abuse but the growth and strength that can be obtained thru the experience when shared.; [a.] Hollywood, FL

YOUNG, JOHN S.
[b.] May 5, 1959, Aurora, IL; [p.] Gale Young and Durella Young; [m.] Barb E. Young, November 25, 1990; [ch.] Amber M. Young, G. Kendall Young; [ed.] Fairfield Community High School - Wayne County, IL "Jr year", GED in Pontiac, IL in Nov. 83"; [occ.] Cook, Painter, Councilor of Young adult's; [memb.] Salem Evangelistic Midnight Church, American Cancer Association, American Vetrian's Disability Association, Save the Whale's and Water National Animal Foundation; [hon.] Award for Vallor "1990"; [oth. writ.] Other poems written have assisted in helping songs written and musically, Song and sound adjustments and in soft rock and new country artists "only 3"; [pers.] I've always been a realist idealist. I write only of true happenings in life also get spiritually inspired from prayer and receive to me the best artist and expectionist is God Philosophy "stay positive".; [a.] Flanagan, IL

ZAWOL, CHAD
[b.] March 20, 1979, Flint, MI; [p.] Dennis Zawol and Rita Koehler; [ed.] I am in my senior year of High School at Kearsley High School in Flint, MI; [occ.] I work on a horse farm called Rookers tending to the horses.; [memb.] Davison Racquet and Fitness Club, National Honor Society, Kearsley H.S. Track, Kearsley H.S. Cross Country; [hon.] Cross Country Academic All - State, varsity letters in track and cross country; [oth. writ.] Several poems, a few short prose pieces, some humorous essays, and a list of original quotes.; [pers.] Believing that humans are the supreme beings in the universe is the least pondered and most conceded belief in existence. There is a God.; [a.] Davison, MI

ZEIDERMAN, MARLA A.
[b.] February 12, 1980, Omaha, NE; [p.] Abraham and Hollie Zeiderman; [ed.] Eaglecrest High School; [occ.] Student (11th Grade); [memb.] National Honor Society, Spanish National Honor Society, B'nai Brith Youth Organization, BMH-BJ Congregation Synagogue; [hon.] Academic Awards, Language Arts Awards, Synagogue Monetary Award; [pers.] I believe we all have a path we take throughout life, this path helps us look ahead toward the future, while always remembering the past.; [a.] Aurora, CO

ZUNIGA, SARA ANN
[b.] December 6, 1985, Minneapolis, MN; [p.] Oscar Zuniga and Patricia Zuniga; [ed.] Moreland Elementary School; [occ.] Student 5th Grade; [memb.] Moreland Student Council and Choir; [hon.] Reading Tutor; [oth. writ.] Presently pursuing to get once of my short stories published.; [pers.] Education is unlimited. You can never stop learning.; [a.] West Saint Paul, MN

Index of Poets

Index

A

Abboud, Sarah 153
Abdullah, Cheryl 257
Abernathy, Shelia 328
Abner, TaulBee 180
Abraham, Jennifer J. 353
Abrams, Susan 3
Abshere, Norman L. Jr. 234
Acker, Vivian A. 496
Adams, Andrea J. 21
Adams, Gennie 413
Adams, Joy M. 289
Adams, Kathleen 13
Adams, Pat 340
Adams, Rosalie 125
Adams-Besangon, Katie 492
Addy, Sue 101
Adin, Mariah P. 229
Adkins, Bradley 411
Adling, David 490
Adolf, Kari 155
Adolphs, Sandy 405
Aguilera, Teresa 373
Aguirre, Holly 428
Ahdel, Erinn Denaix 96
Ahmed, Jimmie 167
Ailer, Jacob 188
Alana, Christine 275
Alanis, Frank 101
Alarcon, Larissa J. 221
Albert, Daniel Volk 111
Albert, Sophie M. 160
Albin, Arlene Sylvia 444
Alcantar, Heidi 260
Alcantara, Edwin 437
Aldrich, Nicole M. 57
Aldridge, Jeremy W. 15
Alexander, Frank 374
Alexander, Katia-Marie 436
Alexin, Mallory P. 385
Allen, Cassie 335
Allen, Donna B. 408
Allen, George 71
Allen, Lisa Gayle 350
Almonte, Maria R. 370
Alston, John A. 357
Altman, John M. Sr. 340
Altyr, A. B. 397
Alvarado, Beverly 85
Alvarado, Sara 173
Alvarado, Wendi 116
Alvarez-Manilla, Clare 92
Alvey, Evelyn L. 249
Amendolara, Nicole D. 146
Ames, Kirk L. 305
Anderer, James 302
Andersen, Margaret M. 306
Anderson, Andrea C. 422
Anderson, Andrew 442
Anderson, Anne B. 94
Anderson, Ashley 211
Anderson, Beverly 342
Anderson, Christy 228
Anderson, Jeffery 393
Anderson, Joel 479
Anderson, Kayla M. 504
Anderson, Keith F. 131
Anderson, Robert 54, 114
Anderson, Robert L. 499
Anderson, Shavia 357
Andrus, Stacey D. 64
Anguiano, Maria Luz 40
Ankrom, Debbie 22
Ankrom, Holly 361
Ann, Jo West 283
Annadale, Laura 42
Annin, Paul 242
Annino, Paula L. 17
Anthony, Brian 437
Anthony, Tamatha A. 222
Antoine, Delores 37
Apel, Amber 236
Arbelaez, Northon Jr. 223
Arbuckle, Edna 382
Arellano, James S. 251
Arietano, Michael D. 223
Ark, Margaret G. 14
Armes, Christopher S. 261
Armstrong, Shannon 109
Armstrong, Tiffany 127
Arnold, Emily 13
Arnold, Jennifer M. 187
Arnold, Ken 50
Arnold, Robert III 95
Arrick, Xenia 109
Arthur, Brian 402
Asay, Grant 97
Asghar, Zahida 497
Asheraft, Sarah 284
Ashley, C. J. Jr. 219
Ashman, Nanci-Ann 228
Askeland, Angela 425
Aspinwall, Loretta 475
Ates, Giselle 202
Atkielski, Laura 234
Auger, Sue 111
Ault, Sarah Kay 396
Aumer, Katherine 480
Austin, Melanie 268
Austin, Sharon Jean 380
Austin, Steve 195
Auten, John William 26
Auton, Andrew 221
Avery, Ryan 255
Awalt, Scott 250
Axxemanne, W. 198
Aycock, Laura 173
Ayers, Jeffrey Glenn 325
Azamber, Terry 460

B

Babb, Shauna 76
Babcock, Charles S. 346
Bachelor, Phyllis 205
Bachofer, Phoebe 451
Bacon, Allison 87
Baer, Shelly 92
Bagley, Debbie 438
Bagwell, Flora C. 109
Bagwell, Mary Jane 275
Baia, Christopher 345
Bailey, Jerry N. 98
Bailey, Teresa Anne 462
Bailey, Trenton 160
Baines, Kathryn Kyker 131
Baird, Brittany 508
Baker, Agnes P. 397
Baker, Ardith M. 329
Baker, Audra 214
Baker, Christy 127
Baker, Delia 502
Baker, Lorraine 142
Baker, Marolyn E. 473
Baker, Tommy 151
Baker, Walter Jr. 470
Bakhru, Sarita S. 352
Balderas, MariSol 61
Baldridge, John Richard 317
Baldwin, Charles G. 472
Ball, Kim 414
Ballantyne, Sarah I. 189
Balonis, Marie 73
Baluch, Shaana 349
Bambenek, John A. 122
Bangle, Donald 311
Banks, A. R. Jack 338
Bannister, Sarah 497
Bant, Jason 215
Banta, Eva J. 323
Baran, Andrew Daniel 105
Barbe, Andrew T. 365
Barbee, Jessica Nicole 99
Barber, Josiah 110
Bard, Mary P. 81
Bardessono, David 358
Barger, Dawn Marie 170
Barker, Charles B. 407
Barker, Eric 508
Barker, Sheryl 482
Barlow, Thomas 340
Barnett, Patricia 213
Barra, John 181
Barron, Elizabeth 101
Barron, Tawnya 17
Barsky, Michelle Ann 96
Barthlein, Jimmy Dan 364
Barthlein, Sandra M. 60
Bartholomew, Fern B. 106
Bartlett, Robert 329
Barton, Donna Dalrymple 488
Bartuch, Jeannie 389
Bass, Cora Douglas 19
Bass, Reed 181
Basu, Poonam 337
Bates, Elisia 356
Baty, Jackie Leigh 139
Baughman, Rhonda K. 232
Baum, Trudy 196
Baumgart, Kimberly 185
Bausley, Alice M. 68
Bazzle, Timothy E. 128
Beach, William E. 226
Beale, Crystal 359
Beaty, Nellie 331
Beauchamp, Tomas A. 481
Beauchamps, Frances 506
Beaudry, Laurice 196
Beck, Kristin 77
Beck-Hathcock, Marsha 310
Bedford, Laura 272
Bedore, Robert 52
Begley, Sommer Michelle 158
Behrmann, Marlene 95
Beighe, Christina L. 201
Bela, Akhtar Banu 303
Belanger, Jamie 272
Beliveau, Matthew 382
Bell, Christopher 24
Bell, Leslie 400
Bell, Marquita 275
Bell, Nadine 212
Bellissimo, Michelle 273
Beltran, Ron 85
Benn, Jannie L. 100
Benner, Cindy 39
Bennett, Amber 65
Bennett, Casey 29
Bennett, Christine Alison 490
Bennett, Heather 491
Bennett, Leslie 462
Bennett, Michelle D. 441
Benson, Kirk L. 65
Benton, Shauna 46
Benyola, Jereme 317
Beran, Mary 226
Bergen, Kamila 393
Berkin, Carol Ann 445
Bernosky, Justin 44
Berry, Vicki Taylor 396
Berumen, Amelia 198
Berzoza, Anthony 398
Best, Bonnye 325
Bethea, Nathan 266
Betterman, Melissa 102
Betts, Robert 355
Betts, Susan L. 446
Betzold, Irene 141
Bevacqua, Wilhelmina 274
Bhargava, Geetika 376
Biby, Shannon M. 111
Bickers, Amber Lee 411
Bickerstaff, William D. 330
Bickerton, Charlotte 436
Bieber, Thomas S. 165
Bieri, Karen 54
Bigge, Pam 405
Billings, Jordyn 24
Billings, Monique 359
Billings, Rebecca 4
Billings, Tracie 186
Billingsley-Riordan, Kara 332
Bills, Gail C. 175
Bilyeu, Esther 307
Bindas, Melinda R. 106
Bingham, Jack 90
Bingham, Lila 335
Binns, Jaime 254
Biondo, Gina 86
Birkland, Jack A. 457
Bitoun, Cheryl P. 475
Bjerk, Daniel R. 141
Bjorndahl, Heather 341
Blacker, Andrew A. 221
Blagojevic, Bojana 430
Blake, Christy 52
Blake, Dexter B. 204
Blakeney, Patricia 85
Blanco, Ashley 398
Bland, Cynthia 104
Bland, Krista 78
Blankenship, Carole Lee 51
Blanton, Sharon E. 121
Blattner, Peggy 355
Blaylock, Sarah 239
Blevins, Jane 353
Blindenhofer, Joan F. 100

Blinn, Gary Donald 407
Blinson, Kelly 107
Bliss, Dan 58
Block, Myra J. 215
Bloom, Gregory Steven 253
Blossom, Gabrielle 331
Bloyder, Joseph J. 264
Bludworth 240
Boatright, Dean D. Jr. 34
Boatwright-Britton, Mary 384
Bob, V. 269
Bodden, Floy 443
Boettcher, Robert B. 261
Boettner, Jerome Lucas 462
Boggs, Teresa C. 164
Bohman, Helen Rose 501
Boilesen, Charity Claire 489
Boisse, Amber Fawn 60
Boisvert, Erin 427
Bolle, April J. 175
Bolliger, Chelsea 113
Bolling, Sheryl N. 247
Boneparte, Lashana 476
Bonn, Bridgett 304
Bonneville, Karen Lee 352
Boone, Frank A. 15
Boone, Virginia L. 372
Boos, Wendy 146
Borden, Cynthia J. 127
Bores, Jeff 185
Borja, A. J. 426
Borrowman, Karen 113
Borst, Anthony R. 4
Bosworth, Todd W. 28
Bouchard, Mark R. 322
Boudreau, Charles M. 6
Bouler, Heather 201
Bowen, Leslie 90
Bowerman, H. C. 183
Bowers, Florence 324
Bowers, Kathryn N. 257
Bowers, Rachel 507
Bowers, Shelley 224
Bowie, Edmund C. 9
Bowler, Stacey L. 476
Bowley, Randy 182
Bowman, Misty 118
Bowman, Nancy Jane 345
Box, Daniel 433
Boyd, J. K. 197
Boyea, Kelly 431
Boyer, Daniel Jr. 140
Boyington, Edwyna E. 356
Boyle, Kalei Lynn 211
Boynton, Melissa J. 269
Bradburn, Jaimi 95
Bradfield, Dianne 463
Brady, Ked 58
Brady, Louise 495
Branch, Bonny 364
Brandimore, Patrick A. Jr. 333
Brandon, J. Smith 367
Brandon, Ruth 360
Brant, Wilson E. 318
Brantley, Vera 224
Braswell, Joseph Carlyle 84
Braxton, Susan 435
Breckenkamp, Christina 381
Breland, Nancy Elizabeth 206
Brennan, Jeanie 371
Brennan, Sarah 495

Bresnitz, Darin 137
Brewer, David 143
Brewer, Elizabeth A. 139
Brewer, Samantha 495
Brick, Stephen Lance 74
Brickman, Todd 115
Bridges, Nannie K. 201
Briguglio, Anthony E. 204
Brimmer, Tasha D. 191
Brings, Christine 68
Brinkman, Dee Dee 239
Brisco, Kenneth Alexander 387
Brissette, Debbie 395
Brissette, Robert 489
Brockington, Lenora 308
Brockman, Heather 219
Brodeur, Sarah 409
Brogdon, Lynette 170
Brooks, Janice 295
Brooks, John 124
Brooks, Sheila 32
Brooks, Sue Ellen 346
Brooks, Travis 397
Broussard, Nicole 249
Brown, Amy 296
Brown, Arnold 146
Brown, Autumn 183
Brown, Belinda 235
Brown, Cindy 421
Brown, Cynthia G. 301
Brown, Eleanor 111
Brown, Ellenor 286
Brown, Emma 315
Brown, Joyce M. 177
Brown, Kenneth R. 120
Brown, Kirsten S. 369
Brown, Lindsay-Ann 336
Brown, Mary Cathleen 89
Brown, Richard 411
Brown, Runa Delisser 139
Brown, Sandra E. 194
Brown, Shaye 18
Brown, Susan E. 177
Brown, Tenia E. 295
Brown, Tony Douglas 189
Browne, Noreen P. 292
Browne, Sylvia 45
Brownlee, Lenora A. 349
Brownlee, Wendy 19
Bruce, Sarah V. 88
Brudnok, Maggie 165
Bruner, Eric 319
Bryan, Allison 489
Bryan, Kristi 144
Bryant, Euris M. 148
Bryant, Herbert M. Jr. 298
Buck, Kelvy 128
Budzinski, Carol E. 38
Bueneman, Heather 100
Buetemeister, David J. 76
Bulaich, Tracy Lynn 84
Bullock, Pharistina 71
Bulzomi, Danielle 220
Burch, Lenie D. 306
Burgess, Jodi 129
Burgess, Raymond L. 498
Burgess, Sharonjeanne 315
Burgess, Susan 65
Burgin, Tracey Sean 196
Burian, Jeana 25
Burke, Chris 114

Burke, Martee L. 107
Burke, Melba J. 158
Burkley, C. R. 58
Burkum, Brian 414
Burleigh, Ray 25
Burnham, Jennifer 103
Burnham, Norma 495
Burnham, Susan 344
Burns, Jen 72
Burns, Jennifer Marie 313
Burns, Madeleine 99
Burns, Rebekah L. 368
Burr, Melanie A. 412
Burrell, Andrea L. 105
Burroughs, Richard Kenneth 204
Busch, Elizabeth 353
Bush, Charles 470
Bush, Vivian 104
Butler, Eva 259
Butler, Nancy 328
Butler, Tamira 56
Buttice, Gary 361
Buttle, Lindsay 406
Buttonow, Patrick 153
Bye, Carol Johnson 225
Byers, Elaine 344
Bymers, Kara 404
Bynum, Patrice K. 291
Byrd, John P. Jr. 247
Byrd, Leslie 242
Byron, Andrea 418

C

Cabral, Jheri 72
Cailey, Evelyn 289
Caldwell, Clive 178
Caldwell, Robbie 171
Callahan, Michael R. 167
Callahan, Tracy 388
Cameron, Melissa 266
Camona, Rolando 152
Camp, Stefanie 344
Campbell, Gloria 11
Campbell, Karen C. 269
Campbell, Lucile M. 392
Campbell, Michelle 257
Canady, Larry 464
Cannon, Lula M. 476
Cantreil, LaVonne O. 78
Cantrell, JoAnn Dena 405
Capeder, Rachel 509
Caperton, Brigitte Christine 221
Cardenas, Lamberto Diaz 237
Carella, Moriah 65
Carey, Brittany 345
Carey-Foster, Maryanne 138
Carfi, Jacqueline M. 271
Carl, Shanna 322
Carle, Emily 278
Carlise, Chuck 386
Carlisle, Von Allan 345
Carlstedt, Joanne 36
Carlstrom, Katie 436
Carlton, Holt 479
Carlton, Jamie 166
Carney, Dorothy Louise 327
Carney, Erin 508
Carosello, Mark Anthony 156
Carpenter, Charles Raymond 249
Carpenter, Charlie M. 252

Carque, Ruth Rutherford 445
Carr, Helen M. 459
Carr, Jackie 314
Carr, Melissa J. 166
Carreth, Michelle 209
Carroll, Janie B. 193
Carroll, Laura 98
Carroll, Tony 68
Carson, Carl G. 156
Carter, Amanda L. 167
Carter, Dana 332
Carter, Ernest D. 495
Carter, Frederick Lee Jr. 343
Carter, Jerré 72
Carter, Kristie 187
Carter, Sharon K. 23
Cartier, Ruth E. 145
Caruloff, Denise M. 86
Caruso, Mary 224
Carver, Josh 469
Casseday, Ruby D. 280
Cassidy, Brianna 144
Castiglione, Dominick 422
Casto, Joy 3
Castro, Gail 362
Castro, Jose M. 407
Catanzaro, Mabel 10
Cathcart-Palmer, Christine A. G. 184
Caudill, Stefanie 52
Caudle, Della 169
Cauffiel, Sean 107
Caverly, Nancy I. 126
Caviness, Chris 125
Cedervall, Stephanie 55
Ceresa, Cecilia 453
Cetee, P. J. 404
Chace, Laura E. 383
Chacon, Esequiel 425
Chamberlain, Ross 397
Chambers, Jenny 397
Champ, Pat 243
Champoli, John 106
Chaney, Pamela Marie 300
Chapman, Dane 494
Charvet, Mary 134
Chase, Elizabeth 340
Chase, Jennifer Marie 78
Chase-Jennings, Josephine B. 450
Chaudhary, Zikiria 204
Chausse, Deana 500
Chavez, Ramona Tania 480
Chavez, Xavier E. 225
Chavier, Beatrice M. 49
Chavira, Adrean 51
Chen, Aileen 131
Chen, Melissa 331
Cheng, Kileen 455
Cheshek, Frances D. 332
Chester, Laura 56
Chetterton, Mick 223
Chi, Maria 235
Chiarello, Lorraine 267
Chick, Bradley W. 448
Chickering, Jessica 318
Childers, Orvan W. 414
Childs, Charlotte 363
Chipman, Cynthia 141
Chokreff, Shaun M. 178
Chorpening, Kathy 429
Choudhury, Anjan 12
Chouinard, Jill 116

Christensen, Jason 323
Christian, Crystal 465
Christopherson, Amy L. 277
Christy, Sarah 395
Church, Thomas S. 424
Chute, Hillary L. 98
Cintron, Charlene 405
Ciocco, Tim 53
Clark, Andrea 339
Clark, Deborah 325
Clark, Frederick D. 185
Clark, Heidie 105
Clark, Helen J. 95
Clark, John J. 296
Clark, Shannon C. 396
Clark, Yolanda N. 32
Clarke, Karen R. 119
Clarke, Thomas W. 186
Clawson, Laura Jean 418
Clayton, Julia 160
Clayton, Martha 17
Cleary, Ryan 228
Clemens, Nicole M. 456
Clenard, Lulah 368
Cleveland, Lois Ann 360
Clevenger, Jonell 389
Clinton, Dorothy Randle 228
Clippard, Erik 61
Cobden, Lynda 233
Cobillas, Jessica 218
Cocanougher, Jennifer 494
Coco, Doreen 267
Coffee, Jane 299
Coffman, Judy 281
Coffman, Margaret Helen 378
Cohen, Shana R. 10
Cohn, Michelle 86
Coimbra, Lorgio 151
Coker, Toni Shew 281
Cole, Helen 297
Coleman, David M. 242
Coleman, Kary 329
Coley, April Smith 231
Colgan, Brian 48
College, Laura 369
Collier, Kasey V. 408
Collin, Cheri 481
Collins, W. Lovvorn 303
Colmus, F. E. 115
Coln, Barbara 154
Comeau, Patricia 412
Commarota, Laura 321
Coning, Stephanie A. 156
Conley, Linda Derrick 346
Conley, Shannon 399
Connelly, Mary Lou 434
Connelly, Nicole 399
Connolly-Weinert, Francis 490
Connor, Deborah M. 458
Connor, Michael James 298
Conrad, Bette A. 12
Conrad, Nathan 43
Conrad, Stephanie 124
Conte, Lizanne 402
Cook, Helen A. 393
Coolbaugh, Christine 77
Coolidge, Marie G. 218
Coombs, Aimee L. 92
Cooper, Daniel J. 420
Cooper, F. M. 313
Cooper, Gerald G. 290

Cooper, Gladys 279
Cooper, Heather Young 44
Cooper, Jeanne 218
Cooper, Margery 157
Cooper, Shirley Ann 83
Cope, Teresa 498
Copley, William 39
Corbell, Stephen 351
Corbett, Mona V. 147
Corbett, Richard 358
Corey, David P. 64
Corlett, Michelle 111
Corley, Asta 382
Corley, Janet 174
Corley, Jean 459
Cornell, Keri 12
Cornell, Sherry Lynn 143
Cornwell, Benjamin 131
Coronel, Susanna 402
Corridon, Jonelle M. 400
Corrigan, Thomas G. 355
Corum, Jennifer 171
Cosmato, Michelle M. 468
Coss, Sarah 462
Costen, Derek 407
Cothran, James E. 479
Couch, P. Svensson 345
Coughlan, Angie 500
Coutorie Jr., John Marcel 377
Covington, Caroline 201
Cox, Jacquelyn Lee 281
Cox, Jane Blackburne 492
Cox, Lottie 401
Crabtree, Kimberly Burton 116
Craft, Jesse T. 221
Cranddent, Yandhi T. 285
Cranford, Julia 44
Creary, Herman J. 404
Cremo, Allison 330
Crespin, Candice 339
Crews, Helen 218
Crigler, P. Lucille 315
Crimmins, Amanda 22
Crismon, Jacob 404
Crist, Gerald 421
Croak, Holly Jean 502
Crockett, Charles 402
Crone, Nanci 35
Cronin, James Robert 210
Crosby, Michael J. 152
Crose, Darrel F. 84
Cross, Allison C. 27
Crossland-Huggar, Mary 454
Crotti, Thomas S. Jr. 381
Crouch, Megan 260
Crowe, Mary Anne 327
Crowe, Shirley M. 20
Crum, Ethel M. 350
Cruz, Christopher 314
Crystal, Eileen J. 347
Csonka, Christie 449
Cullins, Margaret C. 204
Cummings, Barbara A. 446
Cummings, Kerri 447
Cunningham, Jennifer 113
Curry, Amy 248
Curtis, Charles D. 510
Curtis, Marilyn H. 29
Curtis, Rachel 96
Cushman, Jeanne 380
Cushman, Kate 183

Cypress, Talbert 461

D

Daamon, Baffahagh 465
Dahlberg, Janet 211
Daigle, Ann 333
Dalton, Diana E. 316
Daly, Chad Lee 498
Daly, Meghan 69
Daly, Tracey 414
D'Amico, Krista J. 398
Damron, Robert 478
D'Angelo, Francesca 17
Daniel, Ernest W. 394
Daniel, Grace 125
Daniels, Marilyn 64
Dantzig, Christopher 214
Dara, Helen Ann 107
Dardini, Angela 227
Darensburg, Byron 135
Dargan, Shirley 247
Darnell, Dixie 468
Das, Bhabani S. 464
Dauphinee, Dorothy 99
Davenport, Marissa 348
David, Carrie 106
David, Meta 39
Davis, Adam Edgar 485
Davis, Besthines Maria 16
Davis Boys, The 492
Davis, Brian L. 215
Davis, Catherine 146
Davis, Cindy Ann 217
Davis, David L. 322
Davis, Elizabeth 352
Davis, Jesse J. III 383
Davis, Jana 326
Davis, Jean Beckham 114
Davis, Jennifer Lynn 385
Davis, Jonathan C. 4
Davis, Lesley 84
Davis, Lori K. 416
Davis, Pamela 102
Davis, Phyllis J. 352
Davis, Rocky 26
Dawson, Laura 144
Day, Martha 250
Dayhoff, Betty J. 398
De Berry, Marjorie 451
De, Maria C. La Sota 227
De Nuto, Lisa 145
De Soto, Amanda Marie 466
De Veny, Peg 291
De Young, Jack 256
De Young, Lauren 462
Deal, Gaye Follmer 295
Dean, Blanche 142
Dean, Callie 395
Dean, Grant 28
Decker, Margaret 391
DeGarmo, Erica 216
DeGrave, Trisha 174
DeGregorio, Jenny L. 475
DeGuise, Chris 310
DeHart, Laura 338
DeHaven, Carrie 335
Del Carmen, Elizabeth 457
Delaet, Christine 388
DeLaney, Robbie 103
Delaughter, Kevin 117

Delehanty, Marilyn G. 220
Deleo-Hendry, Veronica 406
Dellapenta, Karen L. 364
Deloatch, Martha 154
delos Reyes,
    Maria Evangelina Leviste 60
Delsid-Avery, Ebony 176
DeLuna, Patty 408
DeLuney, Rhonda 494
DeMaria, Chris 484
Demase, Rachel 77
DeMasi, Ann L. 394
Dembro, Patricia 221
Dement, Laura Elizabeth 360
Deming, Melissa L. 16
Denmon, Jonie 435
Denton, Kelly 371
Departo, Judith A. 311
Dept, Ruth C. 253
Derleth, Bryon 402
Derrick, Janel Lee 179
Des, Faye Aulnier 443
Desautel, Philip Jr. 362
Desjardins, Michelle 326
Desrochers, Sara Lynn 132
Dethrow, Jeffery R. 148
Deutsch, Henry 158
DeVaughn, Zakiyah L. A. 443
Deveau, Paul 312
Dever, Charles T. 263
Devorak, Stephanie 253
Dewberry, Jesse 258
Dhaemers, M. 487
Dias, Albert J. 321
Diaz, Hector Luis 388
Diaz, Jodi S. 143
Diaz, Richard 155
Dibble, Dorothy J. 429
DiBenedetto, Karen 461
Dieter, Norma H. 503
Dietz, Sue Myers 263
DiGerolamo, Kate 212
DiLucia, Francine 331
DiLuglio, Maryann 246
DiMaio, Anthony 206
Dingle, Scott 213
Dion, Leslie-Claire 509
Dionne, Jennifer Anne 69
DiProspero, Betty 287
Dirks, Quinn 238
Dishong, Jessica 494
Dispensa, Talia 395
DiSpigna, Lilian 148
Ditsch, Richard C. 299
Dittmar, Guenter H. 409
Diven, Jessica 286
Divenuto, Marianne 103
Dixon, Kimberly Brannan 315
Dixon, William 256
Doan, Lamman T. 413
Dobbins, Richard A. 141
Dobson, Jeff 217
Dodd, Aaron 101
Dodd, Martha 451
Dodge, Veronica L. 192
Doig, Myrna 225
Doll, Nancy J. 80
Dolleman, Jonathan Michael 419
Domeika, Ruta 199
Dominguez, Jenna 149
Dominguez, Ruben Z. 492

Dominiak, Mary Ann 392
Dominici, Deborah 506
Domondon, Cornelia Brown 226
Donaldson, Stacy 108
Doner, Haylie 238
Donner, CarolAnn 287
Donohoe, Vincent 187
Donohue, Madeline 326
Dopler, Jack A. 410
Dorer, Thomas H. 300
Dornbusch, Nicole 272
Dorrel, Charles A. 422
Dorsey, John J. 206
Dosier, Dorothy 293
Dotterer, Cheryl 493
Doty, Meagan E. 362
Doughty, Judith 505
Douglass, Danielle A. 41
Dowling, Dorothy 63
Downing, Kristina 122
Downs, Marisa Jean 480
Downs, Martha Sue 289
Doyle, Dolores 217
Doyle, Fawn Marie 409
Doyle, Michael 390
Dragone, Linda 271
Drallos, Julie Ann 23
Drapeau, Aline J. 66
Dreblow, Scott 99
Drehmer, Gary R. 457
Dressler, Joyce 69
Dreyer Graziani, Nancy E. 351
Driscoll, Beatrice 290
Droste, Susan L. 33
Drumright, Gina R. 8
Dube, Rose Marie 457
Dube-Gold, Melanie M. 214
Duby, Kelly 129
Duffield, Stephanie A. 293
Duffy, Carla J. 434
Duffy, Jan Everts 343
Duffy, Lynn P. 116
Duggins, Michaela 330
Dunagin, Brian C. 265
Dunaway, Maggie 134
Dunford, Fred 353
Dungan, Amanda 373
Dunham, Jame Earl 499
Dunkel, Carol A. 230
Dunlap, Eliana Capri 110
Dunlavy, Carol 279
Dunn, Beulah G. 392
Dunn, Diane 86
Dupert, Thelma 269
Duren, Jerry L. 51
Durnell, Nancy 269
Durousseau, Brandon 469
Dust, Adrienne S. 143
Dutro, Alison J. 106
Duvall, Dalace-Skye 190
Dyer, Susan 103
Dyke, Amy 238

E

Eagleson, Joshua 398
Earl, Norma B. 403
Early, Terry W. 245
Earnshaw, Jim 157
Easley, Amy 63
Easterling, Felicia A. 392
Eastes, Amber 80
Easton, Pamela M. 83
Eaton, Melanie 94
Eaton, Shirley 210
Ebenger, Ryan 90
Eckhoff, Lydia 10
Edgar, Robert A. Jr. 19
Edgerley, Carolyn L. 401
Edwards, Deon 59
Edwards, Jay Harold 413
Edwards, Lewis W. 88
Eichele, Melissa 484
Eichler, Bonnie L. 110
Eidem, Mary Ann 6
Eksevics, Marita 395
El-Aayi, Heba 164
Elam, Dixie J. 135
Eldred, Kim 254
Eldridge, Marika 167
Elford, Karen 399
Elizabeth, Helen Williamson 317
Elko, Heather 218
Ellis, Aubrey 155
Ellis, Chris 9
Ellis, Glenda 226
Ellison, Shantil 140
Elmerick, Eleanor Grace 323
Elsasser, Melissa 258
Elslager, Tyler 10
Emery, Gerry 308
Emily 366
Emmerich, Charlene 313
Enders, William T. 11
Enebak, Richard 318
Epolito, Caleigh 341
ERAMO 270
Erose, Saint 254
Escoto, Jeniece 432
Eseroma, Violet Effie 496
Esparza, Valerie 356
Espinet-Borges, Emelina 99
Esposito, Jeffrey 492
Essenburg, Loren D. 211
Essinger, Melissa Renee 136
Etheridge, Steve 122
Etherington, Christina 402
Eubanks, Joshua Carl 346
Eubanks, Toni Michelle 393
Eugene, Gregoire 163
Evans, Irene L. 403
Evans, Jessica 116
Evans, John R. Sr. 98
Evans, Rachel 136
Evans, Shawney 199
Everett, Beverly 385
Everett, Darla 170
Everett, Jenifer L. 392
Evers, Marlyn 487
Ewell, Linda Lee 310
Ewell, Pamela E. 97
Ewersen, Virginia Pease 188
Ewing, Michael 502
Exline, Billy 213
Ezejiofor, Chukwuemeka 43

F

Faatai, Diana 483
Fabela, Candyce 338
Faden, Joshua I. 468
Fain, Teresa 408
Fair, Jenna 167
Famiglietti, Lauren 50
Fancher, Anita 347
Faria, Susan Moody 472
Farley, Wilbur 138
Farmer, Nichole L. 323
Farnquist, Gary 214
Farnum, Lana 120
Faroh, Shauna 97
Farr, Patrick 382
Farrior, Lee Ann 369
Farvour, Gary W. 219
Fason, Elizabeth M. 291
Faulk, Abigail 110
Favre, Jo Ann 172
Fearon, Lisa A. 32
Fears, Brenda S. 511
Fehmer, Crystal 67
Feldbruegge, James 172
Felix, Erika-Tammeiko L. 485
Felix, Michael 169
Felix, Sean 470
Felmet, Rachelle L. 159
Felton, Phyllis A. 298
Femenella, Steven J. 190
Ferguson, Carrie 500
Ferrara, Laura 211
Ferrell, Jennifer 391
Ferrier, Graham 300
Ferris, Jessica 358
Fetcho, Andrew Thomas 497
Fetterman, Melissa D. 169
Fetz, Hazel S. 80
Feuerbach, Jennifer 62
Fielder, Melissa 477
Fields, Amanda 118
Fields, June 333
Figel, Tiffany 25
Figueiredo, Kellie M. 225
Figueroa, Beverly 482
Fillie, Donna 105
Fillit, Marielle Damara 129
Fincher, Joseph W. 120
Finestead, Bethalene 407
Finholm, Faith 271
Finke, Janelle R. 225
Finn, Angela 252
Fiora, Blanche H. 57
Fireshaker, Jerry M. 509
Fischer, Eric A. 57
Fischer, Katrina L. 140
Fischer, Martha Cummins 406
Fischer, Melissa 236
Fisher, Burt 129
Fisher, Catherine 342
Fisher, Frank W. Jr. 273
Fisher, Fred F. 82
Fisher, Kevin 303
Fisher, Lindsey 401
Fisher, Melissa 327
Fisher, Ramona F. 59
Fisher, Twyla Dawn 98
Fiske, Ashlee 417
Fissel, Taylor 409
Fitzgerald, Anne Currie 318
Fitzgerald, Timothy Michael Edward 459
Fitzpatrick, Erik 22
Fitzpatrick, Mary 297
Fitzsimmons, Catherine 359
Flagler, Norris 174

Flanagan, Jennifer 235
Flanigan, Joseph 318
Flannery, Marian Waufle 242
Flaschka, Monika J. 207
Flath, Jana 484
Flesch, Dennis 448
Fletcher, Bonnie Lynn 493
Fletcher, Karen 38
Flick, Ethan 320
Flinspach, Mack L. III 383
Flint, Rita V. 146
Flood, Ariell 155
Flores, Armando D. 450
Flores, Jennifer 415
Flowers, Sherri 380
Flynn, Kerry K. 430
Flynn, Virginia Ann 375
Foard, Katherine A. 173
Foley, Renee Lynne-Cochran 181
Follette, Kathleen V. 458
Followell, Marina 430
Fontaine, Christina 115
Forbes, Elizabeth Anne 375
Ford, Brian A. 337
Ford, Crystal L. 376
Ford, Keith 82
Fore, JoAnn 305
Foss, Amanda Jeanette 372
Fountaine, Katherine 117
Fowler, Richard L. 406
Fox, Helen 343
Fox, Jackie 215
Fox, Lisa J. 248
Fox, Sarah 61
Francies, Gerise 396
Francis-Dunn, M. 157
Franklin, David Bryan 374
Franklin, Esther 325
Franks, Anne 325
Frase, Doug 209
Fraser, Sarah D. 356
Frazier, Mindy 294
Frear, Brenda 101
Freda, Carolyn 115
Frederick, Joan C. 276
Frederick, Matthew P. 95
Fredrickson, Alicia L. 404
Freeman, Beulah 281
Freeman, Cathy, age 10 256
Freeman, Nicole 174
Frei, Therel A. 190
Freitag, Tracy D. 21
Friberg, Erika A. 101
Fridas, Kristina 110
Friesen, Scot D. 44
Frimer, Laura 416
Fritz, Lori L. 215
Fritz, Melissa 173
Fritz, Susan C. 178
Fritzinger, Heather 467
Frommer, Barnet 255
Frost, Gayle 17
Frost, Helen M. 472
Fruehe, Matt 89
Fruge, J. Aldon 397
Fry, Sarah C. 284
Fryar, David 398
Fryer, Jeff 359
Fudge, L. Gladys 297
Fukino, David Jr. 373
Fulghum, Emily Ann 280

Fullenkamp, Regina 485
Fuller, Clay 434
Fuller, Harold B. 233
Fuller, Jessie 255
Fuller, Lisa 108
Fulton, Cynthia R. 256
Fulton, Deborah E. 273
Fulton, Matt 359

G

Gabhart, Natalie 219
Gabriel, Lori M. 471
Gabrielson, Tania 431
Gagliotti, Rose 490
Gail, Sara 58
Gainer, Michael E. 15
Gaines, Cynthia L. 105
Gale-Howell, Janice 141
Galente, Mary Jo 324
Gales, Jacqueline 79
Galey, Lesa 107
Galgano, Michael 155
Galicia, Maria 447
Galindo, Joshua 272
Galton, Chavelle Tihati 388
Galuska, John D. 5
Gamble, Kristi 331
Gammicchia, Fran 333
Gange, Clara 464
Gant, Marion E. 448
Garcia, Adriana 88
Garcia, Carlos 373
Garcia, Eddie 384
Gardner, Jeanne 190
Garrett, Hollie 113
Garrick, Amy 396
Garrison, Renee S. 371
Garrison, Violet 234
Garrott, Kristen 324
Garrow, Joyce 138
Garza, Ongela Nitra 237
Gasper, David R. 150
Gatewood, Jane E. 106
Gatschet, Andrea 389
Gaymon, Michele 317
Gayton, Deborah 399
Gazzillo, Kim 463
Gebauer, Robert J. 507
Gee, Debra S. 27
Geerdes, Stephen 243
Gehring, Yvonne V. 354
Gehringer, Lou 330
Geiger, Brandy E. 197
Geiser, Melissa 142
Geiser, Paula 185
Gename, Shanna 143
Gendon, Mandy 251
George, Marie 145
George, Tommy 342
Gerchak, Steve 227
Gerhardt, Holly 106
German, Danny L. 512
Germany, Amber Dawn M. 188
Geston, Anita Morales 185
Geyer, Charlotte H. 19
Ghirardi, Jeanne 373
Giancristofaro, Camille 378
Gianoulis, Tara 66
Gibb, Ruth L. 44
Gibson, Jack 132

Gibson, Joanna 410
Gibson, Lisa 285
Gibson-Mueller, Elisabeth 345
Giglitto, Tasha 208
Gilblair, Carol L. 194
Gilmer, Bill 368
Gilmore, Adrienne Butler 210
Gilmore, James T. 311
Ginetti, Christine 357
Gironda, Erin 400
Giroux, Marc 238
Gizzi, Joe 219
Glanton, Thomas P. 163
Glaser, Jennifer 471
Glass, Margaret L. C. 500
Glassford, Alma Therese 435
Glisson, Ozzie B. 11
Glover, Henrietta 121
Goad, Teresa 486
Godbee, Chris 399
Godfrey, David Ashley 261
Godin, Barry 5
Godshall, Kelli 164
Godwin, Robert B. 460
Goetz, Janice M. 224
Goi, James J. 280
Golden, Cydnee 370
Golecki, Katy 482
Golson, Ruth 37
Golson, Thomas Bret 370
Gomez, Arturo 445
Gomez, Dora Elva 473
Gomez, Jamie 342
Gonder, Kathryn 474
Gone, Esteban 311
Gonzales, Debra Joy 233
Gonzales, E. Abriel 319
Gonzales, Sheila 6
Gonzalez, Bianca I. 312
Good, Linda Kay 429
Good, Lindsay E. 254
Goode, Loretta 270
Goodell, Lucy Bair 180
Gooding, Donald P. 191
Goodmanson, Mark J. 214
Goodwin, Melvin 205
Goodwin, Risa Marie 125
Gordon, Daniel I. 466
Gordon, Stephanie 453
Gordon, Tiya 151
Gorman, Dorothy J. 58
Goslin, Audrey 213
Gossett, Theresa 59
Gotts, Jennifer 15
Goughnour, Kelsey 112
Gouldsbrough, Narrissa 39
Gradick, Natalia G. 171
Graham, Amy 13
Graham, Brian 356
Graham, Leah C. 67
Graham, William H. 405
Graham, Zachary 47
Grams, Katherine 217
Granado, Monica O. 339
Granger, James R. 21
Grant, Bryon J. 422
Grant, Tiffany S. 391
Grantham, Hannelore 115
Grass, Linda C. 220
Graves, Brandy 479
Graves, Tammy L. 25

Gravott, Betty Attema 456
Gray, Barbara 222
Gray, John E. 227
Gray, Toni 452
Greaves, Shakyra 98
Greek, Jacqueline L. 350
Green, Barbara A. 406
Green, Crystal 110
Green, Edwin W. II 504
Green, Marcus A. M. 106
Green, Sandy 412
Greenberg, Anna R. 109
Greenfield, Debra 506
Greenfield, Michael 429
Greenwald, Steven 112
Greenwood, Courtney 97
Greer-Meadows, Kerrie 408
Gregory, Scott 437
Gregory, Victoria 199
Gribble, Doris Lee 428
Griesmeyer, Roger J. 164
Griffin, Jo Anne 476
Griffin, Ora W. 496
Griffin, Rayna M. 159
Griffith, June 176
Grignon, Rose M. 491
Grigsby, Amanda 334
Grimenstein, Gabriele 290
Grimes, Anne Elisabeth 278
Grish, Bernice 499
Griswold, Marguerite P. 98
Grogan, Christine 109
Gronemeyer, Kimberly 307
Groner, Danny 308
Grootenboer, Shannon 431
Groseclose, Barbara 270
Gross, Joan 243
Gross, Marie 374
Grossklas, Kristen 449
Grosvenor, Barbara Enid 509
Grove, Deborah K. 265
Grove, Rachel 259
Grubbs, Michele 465
Gschwend, Pat 369
Guardado, Martha 408
Guarneri, Elia 377
Guarracino, Danielle 70
Gudlin, Kimberly A. 70
Guerette, William M. 388
Guile, Yolanda A. M. 348
Guilliams, Ladeana 49
Gulajski, David Allen 439
Gumb, Kelly Marie 388
Gumieny, Jamie 481
Gunderson, Laura 371
Gunter, Kimberly 388
Gurlly, Arthur Jr 339
Guskie, Pam 234
Gustafson, Mara 267
Guterman, Jennifer 216
Guth, Melton J. 491
Gutierrez, Carlos 16
Gutierrez, Lori 164
Gutierrez, Monica 159
Gutierrez, Ricardo 399
Guyot, Sally F. 326
Guza, Joseph 351

H

Habegger, Nikki 380

Hablewitz, David 167
Hackl, Norbert F. 370
Hadden, Georg 211
Hagan, Shawn A. 199
Hagen, Nanci L. 322
Hagood, Jennifer I. 240
Hahn, Marie 279
Hahn, Tracy 180
Haines, Stacie Diane 111
Hair, Helen Reneé 294
Hairgrove, Kelley M. 458
Hajjar, John K. 503
Hale, Katie 423
Halenar, Joseph A. 40
Halison, Sylvia 449
Hall, Ann 251
Hall, Evelyn V. 476
Hall, Norma J. 120
Hall, Richard F. 400
Halley, Deatrice 227
Hallman, William R. 225
Halloway, Brian 31
Halvorson, Inga 465
Hamer, Julie 125
Hamilton, Apryl Cameron 84
Hamilton, Dawn 90
Hamilton, Olga Harvey 143
Hamilton, Patricia 138
Hamilton, Renee 149
Hamilton, Sharon 210
Hamilton-Graves, Jarié 510
Hamilton-May, Donna 212
Hamm, Caroline Sharone 41
Hamm, David 411
Hamm, Peggy 468
Hamm, Russel 40
Hammond, Arnaz 352
Handis, Alex Ely 378
Handy, Jessica 220
Hannibal, Taunya 389
Hannon, Joyce J. 75
Hansen, Michelle Ward 490
Hansen, Virginia H. 264
Hanslip, Wynter 509
Hanson, Emma J. 95
Hanson, Mark 316
Hanson, Sharron 271
Hao, Lance Kanoa 165
Harbison, Bessie Denise 218
Harden, Rovenna 268
Harding, Mindy 259
Hardister, William L. 287
Hardy, Tovah 108
Harley, Kayyon C. 102
Harlow, Helen Elodora 224
Harm, William D. 169
Harman, Stacy 116
Harmon, Jennifer 168
Harnden, Raymond G. 314
Harper, Cammy 28
Harper, Gracia 262
Harper, Ruth D. 258
Harrell, Felicia A. 186
Harriger, Evelyn I. 60
Harris, Andrea M. 440
Harris, Bobbie Lee 118
Harris, Courtney 511
Harris, Curtis 405
Harris, Joan 239
Harris, John F. 252
Harrison, Melonee 390

Hart, Jeanne 121
Hart, Nadine 482
Hart, Richard 322
Hartman, Nelda 90
Hartman, Sharon 24
Hartmann, Beth A. 431
Hartwick, Emmy L. 61
Harvie, Brian W. 394
Harwood, Kortney K. 316
Hasbrouck, John F. 75
Hassert, Derrick L. 398
Hasslinger, Jennifer 391
Hatfield, Naomi L. 220
Hathaway, Laura 115
Hatzipetro, Christine M. 474
Hause, Tamera 225
Havan, Sara 77
Haworth, Brian 389
Hayden, Jhone 316
Hayes, Eileen A. 245
Hayes, Karen 284
Hayes, Kenneth R. 114
Haynes, Natalie 395
Haynes, Pamula Monique 324
Haynes-McCall, Sheila 288
Haynie, Ron 35
Hayward, Gloria 119
Hazen, Pamela L. 209
Healy, Julie 130
Heard, Emily D. 486
Heard, Sandra L. 304
Heater, Clarence 103
Hecker, Susan M. 213
Heckinger, Yvonne 131
Heckman, Sheila A. 196
Heffernan, Katie 453
Hegwood, Kimberly Faye 338
Heider, Elizabeth 117
Heim, Maria L. 83
Heiry, Melissa 248
Helminiak, Nicole 47
Helms, Gina 340
Helms, Valerie 147
Heming, Robyn N. 454
Hemken, Bobby 433
Hendley, Essie Kirkland 108
Hendrickson, Kenneth 13
Hendrickson, Melissa 446
Hendrickson, Rick 208
Hendrix, Lolita 162
Hendron, Crystal 299
Henkoff, Carole 11
Hennerberg, Cheri L. 394
Hennessy, Elizabeth 326
Henrie, Laura 74
Henry, Mary Gardner 409
Hensley, Elizabeth 401
Henson, Mary L. 358
Henson, Tracy 24
Hepp, Helen E. 189
Herbert, Mitchell Vernon 327
Herbst, Kelly 421
Herlinger, Shenoa 5
Hernandez, Peter 235
Herrera, Elmo L. 481
Herweh, Sherryl 183
Heslep, Steve 36
Hess, Geremy 484
Hess, Jana 441
Heuangsavath, Phonsy 236
Hickey, Nancy S. 475

Hicks, Linda J. 191
Hicks, Pauline 166
Hicks, Tanya 38
Hieber, Laura A. 44
Higbe, Saundra T. 59
Higgins, Alberta E. 260
Hight, Ronald E. 191
Hightower, Sharon 372
Hilbert, Phillip C. Sr. 74
Hildreth, William IV 232
Hiler, April 461
Hilgeford, Eric 432
Hill, Danell L. 293
Hill, Jack R. 288
Hill, Janet R. 282
Hill, Lori A. 151
Hill, Mark 352
Hill, Paula Marie Bryant 27
Hill, Stephanie A. 194
Hillman, Carole D. 380
Hillman, Dale J. 348
Hillman, Michelle 115
Hilpert, Morgan 41
Hines, Frances A. 508
Hinshaw, George 147
Hiteshew, Stephanie 467
Hixson, Shirley 366
Hobbs, Barbara Dell 212
Hobbs, Cherie 244
Hoch, Jean 97
Hochberg, Katherine 497
Hodge, Richard Lynn 291
Hodge, Rox Ann 419
Hodges, Antonio 427
Hodges, Courtney M. 304
Hodges, Gina 358
Hodo, Danielle Marie 509
Hodson, Ernest 431
Hoek, Cortney M. 353
Hoeksema, Jeff 370
Hoffman, Joe 20
Hoffman, Kristian 221
Hoffman, Malvino Jose III 409
Hofmann, Kelly 374
Hogan, Joseph L. 246
Hoggatt, Kim 366
Hoke, Jessica A. 395
Holda, Samantha 324
Holden, Elisa 234
Holder, Joel 460
Holder, Lindsey 58
Holguin, Melissa Cerrissa 7
Holland, Charlene L. 335
Hollen, Heather 237
Holley, Colette Hawkins 69
Holmes, Janine P. 475
Holmes, Sarah A. 359
Holt, Alice J. 310
Holt, Dorothy June 433
Holt, Wytona D. 172
Holtmeier, Tiffini 340
Homady, Christina 79
Homan, Diane Y. 308
Honan, Catherine 337
Hooker, MerryJo 386
Hooks, Frances L. 142
Hoover, Eunice Yordy 401
Hoover, Karen Joan 494
Hoover, Sandra 65
Hoplamazian, Marin Brooke 453
Hoppe, Shannon 104

Hopper, Regina 459
Horent, Alissa 343
Horgan, Christine Marie 52
Horne, Angel 59
Horne, E. M. 34
Horner, Gale 400
Horton, Kenneth J. 304
Horton, Minnie 102
Horton, Robbie L. 49
Hosier, Charles 113
House, Leslie 405
Houser, Larenna 222
Hovanec, John 175
Howard, Christine A. 140
Howard, Lisa Marie 438
Howard, Nicole 129
Howard, Sarah 178
Howe, Robert C. 47
Howison, Tracy Lyn 462
Howlett, Dria 406
Howze, Kathleen R. 29
Hoyt, Deborah D. 235
Huang, David 23
Huang, Sherry 445
Hubbard, Edna 257
Hubbard, James 127
Huber, Bess 402
Hubler, Tom 157
Huddleston, Nell 214
Hudgins, Michael P. 358
Hudson, Linda 365
Hudspeth, Mary Louise 396
Huffman, June Doris 244
Huffman, Mindy 422
Huffman, Tabitha Jean 361
Huffstetler, Mark C. 467
Huggins, Penny J. 415
Hughes, Jonathan Edsel 456
Hughs, Myrlene 74
Hulett, Mathew 84
Hull, Jessica 344
Hummer, Nancy 177
Humphrey, Robert 172
Humphreys, Anita Culloon 193
Hunsaker, Arundel 406
Hunt, Martin 146
Hunt, Meghan 337
Hunt, Thelma 9
Hunter, Jason 458
Hunter, Patricia 226
Huntley, Emily N. 238
Huntley, Nancy A. 155
Hunton, Ruth H. 474
Hurt, Jason 207
Hutchcraft, Chip 478
Hutcherson, Julie 357
Hutchinson, Carol 288
Hutto, Ami 327
Huynh, Alexandria 339
Huynh, Melissa 313
Hyatt, William E. III 211
Hyde, Karen 233
Hyder, E. 463
Hyla, Annette 477
Hyres, Jennifer A. 109
Hyten, Barbara 333

I

Ianniciello, Julia I. 439
Ido, Allison 277

Ingle, Nathan 441
Ingold, Jaelithe 134
Insdorf, Nikki 348
Interrante, Maria M. 497
Isaacs, Herbert A. 54
Isabell, Ami 489
Islam, Jasmin 215
Ivey, Amanda 399

J

Jabradally, Jean C. 441
Jacksic, Michael J. 250
Jackson, Aaron 207
Jackson, Barbara Benice Miles 31
Jackson, Charmeika Denise 285
Jackson, Jackie 368
Jackson, Lemuel 271
Jackson, Rose Marie 333
Jackson, Shannon 216
Jackson, Sharron T. 274
Jacobs, Rachel Ann 408
Jacovino, Michelle L. 394
Jahner, Lisa 509
Jaimeson, Jo 278
James, Dianna 316
James, Landa 83
James, Lawrence 215
James, Leondra 285
James, Ola Margaret 184
Jamison, Barry 262
Jamison, Moyne 456
Janik, Brian L. 112
Janis, Florence Carpenter 293
Janssen, August 186
Jantzen, Robert J. 55
Jaramillo, Jennie B. 296
Jarrett, K. 424
Jebb, Thomas G. 427
Jefferson, Ronda 468
Jeffrey, Margie 421
Jenkins, Bobbie Jo 100
Jennings, Meghan 330
Jenot, C. L. 37
Jessee King, Glena M. 432
Jeter, Paul 218
Jewell, Richard C. 265
Jimenez, Cindy 116
Jimenez, Eddie 215
Joannou, Renee 125
Johns, Toni 263
Johnson, Alfred Lee 157
Johnson, Amanda E. 152
Johnson, Anna L. 70
Johnson, Brett T. 112
Johnson, Carolyn L. 42
Johnson, Carrie E. 208
Johnson, Catrina L. 330
Johnson, Charles E. 28
Johnson, Daniel C. 275
Johnson, Danielle 174
Johnson, DeAnna 247
Johnson, Eleanor L. 412
Johnson, Jackie 377
Johnson, Jason 459
Johnson, Jim 279
Johnson, Jimmy 278
Johnson, Kathy P. 116
Johnson, Kay E. 388
Johnson, Keros IV 214
Johnson, Kristen 26

Johnson, Linda Diane 227
Johnson, M. R. 241
Johnson, Patti A. 7
Johnson, Rosa C. 328
Johnson, Sheri 353
Johnston, Jamie 335
Johnston, Nellie Mae 509
Jollie, Sean Barry 212
Jones, Anna C. 289
Jones, Bob 72
Jones, Charity 362
Jones, Christine M. 389
Jones, Courtney Anderson 49
Jones, Coywinna 401
Jones, Gregory S. 296
Jones, Isolyn 386
Jones, Jessica Ann 8
Jones, Julie Trudeau 471
Jones, Kay 73
Jones, Larry L. 50
Jones, Lisa Norris 312
Jones, Murless 154
Jones, Phyllis H. 310
Jones, Richard E. 20
Jones, Robert 147
Jones, Samantha 106
Jones, Shailah McEvilley 317
Jones, Steven A. 136
Jones, Susan 72
Jones, Sylvia 409
Jones, William Henry 63
Jordan, Adriana 209
Jordan, Sylvie G. 327
Jorian 501
Joseph, Becky 341
Joyce, Reginald 500
Joyner, Henry F. 100
Julien, Kristie 4
Julsen, Sue 330
Jung, Ressie 258
Jurica, Kevin 26
Justesen, Dorothy 105
Justice, Jenny 459
Justice, Orion 79
Justyna, Joel 216
Juszkiewicz, Carol A. 199

K

Kaderli, Cindi 235
Kady, Martha L. 417
Kahler, Julie A. 455
Kahn, Lillian 333
Kaiser, Heather Christine 488
Kamber, Deirdre J. 150
Kamberger, Deanna M. 137
Kamenova, Dariana 97
Kamlet, Lauren 250
Kamps, Jennifer 212
Kampstra, Katie 82
Kane, Delores Jane 280
Kann, Eunice 472
Kanne, Ida F. 85
Kasprack, Kimberly A. 5
Kasuba, Michael S. 181
Katranis, Evangeline 181
Kaul, Sandra 130
Kawato, Anne 348
Kearney, Martha S. 492
Keating, Ben 464
Keever, Joan F. 255

Keitch, Kevin 41
Keith, Rachel 232
Keith, Venus M. 277
Keithley, Richard 336
Kelemen, Steven 147
Kell, Sandi M. 65
Keller, Florence 229
Keller, Harry E. 478
Keller, Jaime 386
Kelley, Tiffany Catherine 283
Kelliher, Mary Ellen 213
Kelly, Colleen 437
Kelly, Jennifer 253
Kelly, Larry 57
Kelly, Rachel 456
Kelly, Teresa Marie 297
Kelso, Ann K. 240
Kelso, Courtney 226
Kelson, Gwen 456
Kendall, Dorothy Steinbomer 179
Kenerson, Dave 257
Kenion, Janet L. 30
Kennedy, Amanda 220
Kennedy, Jena 56
Kennedy, Joseph 102
Kennedy, Kelly 458
Kennedy, Ronda L. 309
Kennett, Bernard J. 106
Kentch, Gavin 52
Kenyon, Lawrence R. 62
Kephart, Glenn 454
Kerchner, John William Earl III 98
Kerecz, Helen M. 226
Kersey, Drew 363
Kershaw, Sonja 86
Kessler, Christina I. 326
Kessler, John 47
Kessler, Karen 297
Ketchersid, Jennifer 151
Ketcherside, Sean 276
Ketter, Kathy 25
Kettlewell, Lisa 295
Keyes, Mae B. 443
Khaira, Nvdeep 80
Khan, Saman 378
Khlok, Kethshara 428
Khoury, Matt 62
Kick, Elspeth-Ann 454
Kick, Rachel 243
Kiel, Jessica 392
Kight, Carolyn 228
Kilbourn, Forrest 306
Kilby, Florence A. 268
Killebrew, Rachel 251
Kim, Jehae 220
Kimble, Everett D. 43
Kimbler, Mildred 215
Kincaid, Sarah 86
Kincaid, Terri L. 184
Kinealy, Terrence P. 369
King, Candyce 308
King, Dorothy 376
King, Heather 229
King, Jeanette 170
King, Jeff 190
King, K. C. 327
King, Raul O. 511
King, Susan 87, 111
King, Walter 163
Kingsley, Carol 114
Kinkel, Karin 29

Kinn, Elizabeth M. 192
Kinsey, Jodi E. 266
Kirby, Marsha K. 424
Kirkpatrick, Michelle 435
Kirth, Patricia A. 410
Kirtley, Jackie 323
Kirtley, Scott M. 337
Kittelson, Cindy L. 223
Klamerus, Brenda L. 156
Klee, Betty 148
Klein, Joshua Herschel 281
Klein, Vicki 396
Kleister, Heidi 12
Kline, Marshall 224
Klingenstein, Diane 313
Klose, Joanna 341
Kloth, Alex 151
Knetter, April Lynn 336
Knight, Brenda 41
Knight, David E. 235
Knight, E. J. 161
Knight, Laura 120
Knispel, Paul 259
Knoeppel, Shawnna 142
Knott, Frances E. 299
Knudson, Troy 255
Kocourek, Matthew 33
Kohl, Katrina 393
Kolarits, Andrea 168
Kolcz, Stephanie, 393
Kosack, Alicia J. 105
Koshuta, Nelson A. 401
Kostopoulos, Carmela 403
Kouril, Karen 424
Kozlowski, James 338
Kraai, Jack E. 303
Krafft, Kathy E. 449
Kraft, Reuben 202
Kramer, Alicia 104
Kratzer, Pamela Nycz 270
Kraus, Katrina 166
Kreuter, Matthew 47
Kreutzer, Anna 308
Kreutzer, Dee Ann 111
Kring, James A. 94
Krisher, Lindsay A. 184
Kroeze, J. Scott 301
Kroll, Jill 409
Kroll, Joseph M. 385
Krueger, Stephanie 138
Krug, Kelly 364
Krystosek, Pat 298
Kuhlman, Shelley 211
Kukowski, Kimberly 205
Kunicki, Florence J. 377
Kunow, Patrina 95
Kuper Bushman, Evelyn Lather 335
Kurlowicz, Matt 483
Kurpiewski, Chris 466
Kurten, Joan 376
Kushner, Kristen 390
Kuy, Sothea 451
Kuzmkowski, Autumn Rae 249
Kythail, Elizabeth 413

L

La Prade, Jim 182
Labbate, Patricia Ann 392
Labrie, Joan 290
Lacy, Micah D. 424

Lademan, Julie 207
Lafferty, Shonna 458
Lagattolla, Maria Teresa 189
Lagrange, Wendy Hope 187
Laguna, Gabriel R. 390
Lake, Gabe F. 504
LaLonde, JoAnn M. 348
Lalor, Annett 510
Lampron, Tanya 277
Landis, John W. 68
Landon, Agatha 363
Landrum, Makenzi Sims 347
Laney, Rick 306
Lanfear, Suzanne M. 192
Langiewicz, Cheryl 102
Langille, Louise 110
Lankau, Timothy 440
Laporte, Margot 69
Lapp, Susan 395
Larionova, Nina 186
Larsen, Catherine M. 397
Larsen, Marie 68
Larson, Cliff 105
Larson, Meredith 396
Lascoe, Matti 5
Lassa, Brett 479
Latham, Shanna 268
Latozas, Patrick 479
Lavan, Karen 372
LaVante, Gennifer 315
Lawless, Benjamin Daniel 27
Lawson, Donna 481
Lawson, Rachael 96
Lawton, Erika D. 388
Leader-Picone, Whitney 280
Leahy, Johanna 276
Leamy, Kit 70
Leanza, Anthony IV 456
Ledford, Judy 275
Ledoux, Dana 422
Lee, Azzie Stroble 282
Lee, Belita A. 59
Lee, Belma 292
Lee, Brent 417
Lee, Charlene S. 417
Lee, Coreen 36
Lee, Hor-ming 334
Lee, James 356
Lee, Jeanne Marie 250
Lee, Jennifer 232
Lee, Jonathan 440
Lee, Katherine 509
Lee, Kristin 354
Lee, Michelle 128
Lee, Morgan 371
Lee, Rebecca J. 452
Lee, Tatia 444
Lee, Yvonne M. 508
Leedy, Michelle 119
Legge, Darren 368
Leichliter, Danielle 407
Leighton, Wendy L. 334
Lekan, Amy Sondra 159
Lemond, Christopher J. 430
Lemons, Joseph 366
Lenie, Maria 72
Lentini, Paul D. 286
Lentini, Sara 152
Leonard, Ashley 426
Leonard, J. C. 370
Leone, Kati 20

Lepien, Stephanie 430
Lerch, Kristen 489
Lescalleet, Alice I. 290
Leser, Paul 186
Lesica, Francis 126
Leslie, Cheryl J. 324
Lessick, Melissa S. 37
Lester, Alice 371
Lett, Emprise S. 119
Letterle, Lisa J. 210, 279
Levasseur, Tina 220
Levinstone, A. Winfred 286
Levy, Carolyn 458
Lewis, Colleen 81
Lewis, Elizabeth 144
Lewis, Karen 86
Lewis, Patricia 405
Lewis, Reba 357
Lewis, Stephen M. 366
Lewis, Willie E. 376
Lewis, Zella Mann 130
Lewis-Pavlock, Rosemarie 66
Leybovich, Galina 13
Liddell, Danny 46
Lieb, Ashley 451
Lifeset, Ty S. 55
Ligouri, Catherine 74
Lilavois, Kettly 318
Linares, Alexandra 303
Lincicum, David 91
Lincoln, Jessie 108
Lincoln, Kelli M. 138
Lincoln, Robert 403
Lindsay, Louise 324
Lindsey, Carmoneda J. 391
Linman, Trista 73
Linn, Jennie Joana 393
Linstead, Gail 474
Lipinski, Edward R. 276
Lipscomb, Harriet 31
Lisa, Patrick C. 302
Lister, Katrina 8
Lister, Marie Christine 223
Little, Kathleen A. 292
Livingston, Gilbert S. 150
Lobo, Lynette 266
Locke, Sarah 332
Lockenour, Lynn L. 127
Lockhart, Raffael N. 99
Loder, Makesha 356
Loeffler, Chris 16
Lofton, Katherine S. 484
Logan, Sandra Dragt 195
London, Cathy 111
Long, Dave 334
Long, Virgil A. 121
Longenecker, Shannon 219
Longfellow, Richard Earl 80
Longo-Roberson, Mary 216
Longobardi, John C. 425
Longtine, Dana 344
Lopez, Gina 381
Lopez, Jaimie M. 480
Lopez, Laura 389
Lopez, Linda Mae 133
Lopez, Peter Twist 332
Lopez-Lavalle, Marcella 58
Lord, Vivian I. 70
Lorditch, Renee M. 320
Loria, Joe 104
Lorkowski, James 229

Lothian, Walter Scott 202
Loughlin, Terri 209
Lovekamp, Greg 177
Lovett, Genevieve 168
Low, Janette 329
Low, Jennifer L. 133
Lowe, John 365
Lowe, Kellie 415
Lowery, Brandy 498
Lowther, Roger L. Jr. 104
Lucania, Alexander M. 410
Lucas, LeeRoy 223
Lucas, William A. 443
Luciani, Stacy L. 107
Ludmi 352
Lui, Berachah 312
Luisi, Loredana 222
Lujan, Aggie 20
Lumbra, Maynard 365
Luna, Eileen Dennis 423
Lund, Mandi 349
Lunsford, Patricia R. 200
Luster, Diane K. 289
Luttman, J. 113
Luz, Nancy 465
Lynch, Joan 473
Lynch, Nicole 201
Lynn, Cleveland P. C. 278
Lysetska, Alena 76

M

MacGermany, Caleb 434
Mach, Mandy K. 172
MacKenzie, Dorothy J. 210
MacKenzie, Zach 34
Macklin, Lisa 368
MacWilliam, LeeAnn 313
Madden, Kevin 177
Madigan, TJ 193
Madsen, Linda E. 357
Mae, Shelby 222
Maeby, Marsha 27
Magana, Antonio 200
Magsig, Shila 219
Maguder, Tim 29
Maher, Agnes 307
Mai, Jimmy 294
Maiden, Lisa Ellen 324
Mair, Virginia 251
Majercak, Sarah A. 99
Makins, LaMuk 246
Malamis, Marina 410
Maldonado, Evelyn Janet 243
Malito, Vincent A. 341
Mallory, Ben 328
Malo, Albert 292
Malone, George D. 237
Malone, Marian L. 50
Manchester, P. Thomas 498
Manes, Helen 132
Manger, Melissa 403
Mangin, Cheryl 338
Manney, Kathy 89
Manning, Benjamin J. 52
Manning, Joseph 263
Manno, Bruno V. 93
Manns, Sieglinde 400
Mantello, Alexandrea 210
Manuel, Ruel 483
Marc, David J. 71

Marcano, Cruz 300
Marcelo, David 440
Marchal, Scott 203
Marcon, Alison 188
Maricle-Fitzpatrick, Taletha 67
Maring, Gary D. 472
Mark, George E. 250
Marks, Rita 505
Markwood, Dexter 336
Marling, Brittany 4
Marlowe, Donna 323
Marquart, Jeni 295
Marra, Andrew P. 271
Marsh, Carol Ann 377
Marshall, George K. 123
Marshall Heath, Ann 187
Marsten, Erin K. 331
Marston, Casey 23
Marter, Diana 14
Martin, Amanda Leann 148
Martin, Connie 100
Martin, Edna J. 36
Martin, Eric Allen 56
Martin, Joseph D. 427
Martin, Marilyn A. 115
Martin, Rose 392
Martin, Scott 425
Martinez, Bob G. 118
Martinez, Sarah 325
Martino, R. J. Jr. 231
Martucci, Peggy 229
Marvel, Mary 393
Marvel, Querita 120
Mason, Carolyn Caivano 103
Mason, Jill 452
Mason, Larry 344
Mason, Thomas J. 462
Massey, William L. 288
Masters, Jack 135
Masterson, Jack N. 157
Matayoshi, Sara 398
Matessino, Cory 144
Mathews, Candi 224
Mathews, Jason 475
Mathieus, Kim E. 13
Mathus, Mindi 255
Matroni, Harold J. 423
Matteson, Korrinna 328
Matthew, Virginia C. 72
Matthews, Allison 144
Matthews, Donna 193
Matthews, Georgianne E. 193
Matthews, Keeshawn C. 219
Matthews, Larry F. 323
Mayes, Gabriele 265
Mayol, Ashley 105
Mazur, Gloria Dee 369
Mazur, Steve M. 221
McAlary, Debra Lynnanne 209
McAlexander, Tom 300
McAlister, Lauren 488
McAlpine, Peggy 305
McAnally, Erica 221
McBeath, Loretta 280
McBride, Danielle H. 444
McBride, Ella 442
McBride, Jean L. 3
McBride, Lucia 123
McCafferty, Trudy 67
McCambridge, Ken 306
McCann, Mildred 445

McCann, Sharon E. 226
McCarthy, Edward J. 14
McCarthy, Melissa 263
McCarty, Michael Maurice 93
McCauley, Carlisa J. 230
McCaw, Jane 87
McClellan, Birdie B. 51
McClintock, Pam 102
McClung, Carrie M. 251
McClung, Stephanie 197
McClure, Shawn Michael 351
McCobb, Charlotte Lee 428
McColligan, Shannon 145
McConnell, Belinda G. 307
McCorkle, Carol M. 438
McCorkle,
    Gertrude LaTanya Jones 49
McCorkle, Michael L. 489
McCormack, Joseph 208
McCoy, Becky 95
McCoy, Shirley 80
McCray, Diane 387
McCray, Jennifer 286
McCreight, Kelly A. 6
McCulloh, Evelyn B. 301
McCullough, Angela 133
McCutchen, Margaret Sawyer 132
McDaniel, Larry Jr. 8
McDavid, Anthony 346
McDonald, Alex L. 458
McDonald, David D. 174
McDonald, Jane 27
McDonald, Michelle C. 453
McDonald, Randy 499
McDonald, Wendy 388
McDonnell, Kelly 421
McEllistrim, Don 7
McFadden, Amy 466
McFall, Bennie Ruth 314
McFall, Rhonda 241
McFerren, Angela 151
McFerren, Bridget 452
McGee, Ashley 217
McGilloway, Eric L. 334
McGowan, Amy S. 195
McGrady, Sarah Marie 368
McGregor, Donna B. 136
McGrew, Donna R. 484
McGuinness, Mike 109
McIntosh, Marie 326
McKeen, Kristen L. 322
McKelvey, Peggy 370
McKenna, Cora 343
McKinney, Diane S. 237
McLain, Christopher K. 71
McLendon, Patti Jean 322
McMahon, Tracy J. 309
McManus, Denis A. 367
McMurry, Alice 449
McNamara, Ronan 486
McNeel, Laird 133
McNulty, Donna 95
McNulty, Josephine M. 403
McNulty, Timothy 227
McPherson, Dawn 334
McRae, Danita Q. 202
McTaggart, Stacy 117
McWilliams, Natalie 319
MDR 432
Meade, Jerry 426
Meadows, Patricia A. 412

Means, Willie Earl   140
Meckes, Faith   113
Medford, B. C.   362
Medley, Selina   409
Medrano, Mamie L.   35
Meily, P.   46
Meldrum, Kristina M.   497
Mele, Amanda Leigh Marie   121
Melendez, Elisa Mercedes   35
Mellas, Michael J.   19
Melton, Virginia D.   31
Memari, Kristina   403
Mena, Philo   409
Meranda, Christine   162
Mercado, Lillian D.   196
Mercer   436
Mercer, Michael   509
Mercs, Cheryl A.   422
Merina, Hilary   245
Merritt, Fran G.   246
Messina, Gilda   22
Metcalf, Carolyn C.   328
Metzgar, Ray A.   29
Meyer, Tressie   375
Meyer, Trice   146
Meyer, Virginia Martin   8
Michael, Jennifer Tennille   494
Michael, Linda M.   242
Michaeli, Lavonne   492
Michaud, Albert E. L.   101
Michaud, Randy   220
Mick, Marilyn   333
Mickens, Jeremiah   469
Mickey, Angela   408
Middleton, Charles F.   199
Mikelevicius, Vita   287
Mikowychok, Ellen   115
Miles, Carlita J.   9
Miles, James Thomas   248
Miles, Pamela R.   325
Milkey, Frances   394
Miller, Amanda   95
Miller, Anne M.   501
Miller, Brianna   472
Miller, Franklyn Lee   150
Miller, Heidi L.   214
Miller, Jessica   79
Miller, Jolyn   335
Miller, Julie M.   98
Miller, Kathleen A.   222
Miller, Kwan D.   254
Miller, Larry   81
Miller, Laura   10
Miller, Lucas   501
Miller, Madeline   302
Miller, Marilyn S.   392
Miller, Rodney C.   200
Mills, Elnora   206
Mills, Louise   87
Milne, Samantha L.   391
Mims, Antonette   53
Minch, Juanita   254
Minear, Allyson   10
Minietta, Kristi   338
Minniefield, Shereada   65
Minor, Tamara NaCole   436
Minshall, Michele   90
Miracle, Tracey   241
Mishaan, Salha E.   305
Misner, Peggy   205
Mitchell, B. J.   337

Mitchell, Beth Ann   465
Mitchell, Clifford   97
Mitchell, David J.   511
Mitchell, Janette   22
Mitchell, Lou   476
Mitchell, Norma L.   400
Mitchell, Rebecca Ann   238
Mitchell, Thresea   239
Mitchell, Universal D.   194
Mitchiner, Ronald   96
Mixon, Jackie   25
Modellas, Jennifer   129
Modenbach, Kathleen K.   417
Modica, Antoine E.   224
Mohammed, Nedra   415
Mojica, Michele   206
Mojzisik, Alia   104
Mokos, Irmgard   493
Moll, Crissy L.   341
Molleur, Shelley   393
Molnar, Stephanie   253
Monger, Steven   51
Mongillo, Elizabeth   500
Monk, Crystal R.   388
Monroe, Jennifer   252
Montague, Rae E.   200
Montgomery, Danessa   322
Montgomery, Kay   276
Montgomery, Michelle   486
Montgomery, Susan   242
Montjar, Annielle   491
Moody, Joy   32
Mooney, Kevin P.   233
Moore, Alice G.   353
Moore, Andre Alvin   38
Moore, Anna Marie Jane   214
Moore, Daisy L.   164
Moore, Errill   89
Moore, Felicia   457
Moore, Forest   340
Moore, Natasha L.   130
Moore, Tomas Franklin   497
Morales, Evelina C.   188
Moran, Rose O.   418
Moravec, Andrea   175
Mordja, Scott A.   461
More, James W.   79
Morehart, Nathan S.   137
Morein, Katie   487
Moreno, Andrea   402
Morgan, Ardis M.   402
Morgan, Linda   49
Morgan, Max M.   478
Morgan, Tracey   150
Morgello, Nicole   209
Mori, Hazel   493
Morris, Allan   153
Morris, Carol Lynn   81
Morris, Donna M.   348
Morris, James M.   292
Morrison, Helen   463
Morrissey, Beverly   314
Morrow, Amber   103
Morrow, Patty   251
Morscher, Jeanette   274
Morse, Georgette   385
Mortenson, Robert J.   465
Mortenson, Thomas G.   368
Morton, Muriel   17
Mosby, Tyrah K.   95
Moses, Clint   449

Moss, Elizabeth O.   73
Mossaad, John Cross   354
Mossi, Melissa Elaine   442
Moulton, Debbie   421
Mounsey, Jenney   112
Mount, Dianna   35
Mouton, Dwaine   30
Mraz, Missy K.   225
Mueller, Linda   166
Mulberry, Josh   331
Mulcrone, Colleen   443
Mulder, Kevin   162
Mulkey, Latricia   125
Mullennix, Rebecca E.   509
Mullins, Cathy   404
Mundell, Grover   109
Mungro, Murray   66
Munro, Susan C.   428
Munsell, Dorothea   123
Munsey, Sylvia A.   43
Munsinger, Crystal   409
Munyer, George   410
Murchison, Sandi   35
Murphy, Charlie   456
Murphy, Jeff   445
Murphy, Jim   289
Murphy, Maria   318
Murray, Cathleen   441
Murray, Colleen   261
Murray, John   314
Mustafa, Emily   337
Myers, Barbara M.   135
Myers, Dennis A.   39
Myers, Margie M.   366
Myers, Wade T.   158

N

Nadeau, Cheryl   97
NaDell, Joanna J.   371
Nagle, Lara   217
Nagle, Phyllis M.   381
Nahalka, Joy   290
Nairn, Thomas F.   203
Nance, Jane   339
Nanos, Terea   466
Narkievich, Larry   355
Nason, Melissa   288
Nau, Kirsten   282
Navarro, Silvana K.   56
Navin, Kevin Michael   46
Neal, Edith M.   290
Nearon, Adam   213
Neeley, Victoria Ann   425
Negri, John F.   336
Nelis, Amanda   392
Nell, Harold D.   343
Nellis, Virginia   299
Nelson, April L.   213
Nelson, Denise   257
Nelson, Mike   377
Nelson, Steven J. Sr.   37
Nemovicher, C. Kerry   272
Nero, James   23
Nesbitt, Felicia   205
Netters, Tyrone H.   133
Neuschafer, Terry J.   218
Neuteboom, Robert K.   103
Newberger, John F.   391
Newbill, Christina   364
Newcome, Michele   311

Newman, Phyllis B.   215
Newport, Melissa Sue   367
Newport-Woodward, Helen R.   473
Newsom, Tiffany   498
Newsom, William Allen   390
Newton, Alice Spohn   337
Newton, Frost   298
Newton, June   426
Newton, Kenneth W.   23
Newton, Wayne E.   330
Nichols, Austin   398
Nichols, Brandy   266
Nichols, Helen Trowbridge   380
Nichols, Jane S.   334
Nichols, Judith   446
Nichols, Phyllis D'Ambrosio   228
Nicholson, Edward A.   40
Nicholson, Loree   105
Nickle, Gidget   336
Nicolelli, Gloria   456
Nielsen, Erma E.   229
Nigo, Margo M.   411
Nikias, Nick   296
Nikkhou, Sina   262
Nikoley, Teresa   383
Nill, Karen   351
Nims, Jack Vernon   401
Nims, Rosalind   319
Nipper, Tammy LeAnn   343
Nivens, Billy J.   240
Noblet, Thurman D.   30
Nocera, Maria   408
Nodo, Patricia   71
Noel, Barbara J.   246
Nolan, Carol A.   361
Nonnenmocher, Kerry W.   243
Noonan, Stephen J.   165
Nordan, Edward   481
Norman, Alice B.   329
Norris, Annabella   8
Norris, Phil   188
Norris, Sheila D.   367
Northrup, Robert   493
Norton, Kelley   382
Norwood, Peggy   63
Nowak, Jennifer Lynne   409
Nunez, Teresa   225
Nuoffer, Brooke L.   175
Nye, Deirdre T.   466

O

Oatts, Courtnay   285
Oberer, Walter   459
Oberg, Maria M.   312
Oberkircher, Grace E.   10
O'Bryan, Heather   305
O'Connor, LaVern   81
O'Connor, Mab   402
O'Connor, Thomas   426
Odom, Anita H.   432
O'Donnell, Dawn   428
Oehler, Carol   385
Oenbrink, Paul   198
Oetker, Luke   444
Offringa, Natalie Denise   439
Ofori, Doris Oforiwah   200
O'Gorman, Jeffrey D.   100
Ogunbiyi, Joseph Adeola   418
Okonkwo, Michael Nnaemeka   192
O'Lanahan, Charles Gavan   88

Olander, Herbert 169
Oldfield, Jackie 488
O'Leary, Alan C. 394
O'Leary, Thomas J. 104
Olivas, Tonya R. 508
Oliver, Lake 309
Oliver, Vickie J. 397
Olney, Stacy 216
Olson, Kim M. 501
Olson, Kristen 182
O'Marra, Eileen 242
Ondish, George J. 458
O'Neal, Michelle 478
O'Neil, John Kenneth 378
O'Neill, Mary 241
O'Neill, Patricia 107
O'Neill, William C. 278
Onest, Maria 32
Opferman, Samantha 112
Opher, Valerie D. 248
O'Quin, Brenda 47
O'Quinn, Brittany 224
Orion, Samson 501
Orlando, Marie 421
O'Rourke, Michael K. 103
Orr, James Ross 328
Ortiz, Aurea E. 346
Ortiz, Stephen 474
Orum, Shana Marie 203
Osborne, Crystal 427
Osborne, James R. 70
Osbourn, Cheryl 452
Osterman, Donna 477
Ota, Carla Lee 108
Ott, Joanne 13
Ott, Richard L. 467
Ours, Tressie 364
Ovens, Jeromy 53
Overton, Robert 407
Overy, Kevin M. 332
Owen, Marybelle 54
Owen, Traci 420
Owens, Andrea 396
Owens, Chris 305
Owens, Jason 396
Owens, Minnie R. 496
Owens, Richard Todd 9
Oxidine, Gregory L. 402
Ozenghar, Dennis DuPaul 382

P

Pace, Jeri 142
Pace, Jodie 179
Pacholke, Kathleen M. 246
Pacia, Ray 478
Pacilli, Jason 12
Pack, Juliet 143
Page, George C. 388
Pai, Anisha 296
Paizis, John 84
Palecki, Charlene 384
Palermo, Antoinette 244
Paliani, Fred 415
Palka, Mary Jo 7
Palmer, David 228
Palmer, Dorothy C. 108
Palmer, Harvest 189
Palmer, Janice Davis 68
Palmer, Robert 423
Palmisano, Frank 331
Pampain, Carla S. 222
Pancio, Kristen 398
Pangilinan, Ashley 502
Pankhurst, Corrie 209
Pantaleon, Ocherie 127
Pao, Roger 117
Papaeliou, Junerwanda 395
Papillion, Charles 439
Paquet, Judith B. 53
Paramo, Raul 24
Parekh, Roshani 188
Pargoff, Angelina Marie 30
Park, Amy Elizabeth 399
Park, Charles Jr. 469
Park, James R. Sr. 374
Park, Marion E. 87
Park, Sy 114
Parker, Bonnie 34
Parker, Claire Elise 46
Parker, Josh 446
Parker, Robert F. 14
Parkin, Louie 325
Parks, Louise A. 97
Parras, Reagan 161
Parsley, Chad 288
Parsons, Grace L. 199
Parsons, Jimmie H. 344
Pasciuto, Ginny 96
Pascoe, Kinsey 255
Patrick, Michelle 395
Patrick, Sharon N. 372
Patten, Lori 194
Patterson, Kirsten Maria 325
Patterson, Sherry 123
Patton, Deborah 184
Paty, Michael F. 264
Pavlik, Michele M. 118
Pawlowski, Jason 168
Payàn-Agudelo, Carlos-Andres 51
Payne, Katrina 312
Pearl, Rachel 221
Peda, Andrea 63
Peeples, Donald H. Sr. 128
Pelle, Rosemary 483
Pellettier, Michael James 85
Pena, Marisol 270
Pendleton, Deborah 381
Pendola, Joy Nicole 220
Penn, Nancy 291
Pennybaker, Paige L. 113
Pennypacker, Jason L. 14
Pepkowski, Ruth 372
Perdue, Jim 207
Perez, Tracy 20
Perez, Yolanda Marie 466
Periandi, Adrienne 34
Pernigotti, Marci 169
Perotti, Kelly 130
Perrigan, Jason 53
Perron, Linda 457
Perrone, Kristin 314
Perry, John H. 503
Pershing, Alan J. 207
Pesin, Laura 11
Peter, Michael 245
Peters, Angela 330
Peters, Gracie C. 420
Peters, Nancy L. 201
Petersen, Renee 42
Peterson, Doris 376
Peterson, Harvey Jr. 18
Peterson, Jan 383
Peterson, Rachele Lynn 342
Pettit, Gladie B. 183
Petty, Martha M. 488
Petty, Ruth 453
Pezzell, Cindene 334
Phifer, Hoyte Jr. 283
Phillips, Brian 292
Phillips, Ellen 216
Phillips, Roberta 384
Philpitt, Edward T. 477
Pickard, Desmond 82
Pickering, Brian 107
Pierce, Betty Jean 45
Pierce, Jean C. 102
Pierce, Judy 128
Pierre-Pierre, Jean-Rene 51
Pierson, June E. 331
Pieszchala, Terry 510
Pietrykowski, Aaron Wayne 104
Pike, Kenneth 394
Pineiro, Elizabeth 471
Pinner, Lindsey 358
Piornack, Barry 180
Pipinich, John 367
Pittman, Lillian 229
Pittmon, Beth Leighanne 145
Pitts, Ima Jean 340
Plahetka, Christina R. 495
Plisis, Stacy 378
Ploof, Sandi 349
Plunkett, Harry L. Jr. 283
Plyman, Holly 107
Pogirnicki, Todd 430
Polanski, Sylvia 480
Policare, Ronald T. 175
Pollard, Gladys M. 329
Polon, Eduardo Alejandro 311
Polovina, Julie D. 397
Ponsky, Barbara 184
Pop, Magdalena 397
Pope, Gary 244
Portell, Mendy 469
Porter, Audrey B. 149
Porter, Delora Jean 504
Porter, Michael 457
Porter, Ricky L. 90
Portivent, Justin 433
Potts, Elizabeth C. 16
Potts, Luke 134
Potts, Sheila I. 88, 230
Pounders, Jill G. 394
Pounds, Jenny M. 350
Power, Dena 8
Power, Jenny 205
Power, Mark 259
Power, Peggy Lynne 323
Powers, Michelle 149
Powers, Nathan 415
Prange, Debra Crawford 176
Prasad, Neenu 435
Preece, Deborah 455
Preheim, Sheena 392
Prentice, Pauline Kincaid 75
Prera, Aileen M. 112
Prescott, Jesse Lee 174
Presley, Elvis Dwayne 239
Pressley, Charles Don 3
Pressley, Karen E. 448
Prestriedge, Linda 109
Pretekin, Jane Ellen 197
Price, Brandy L. 329
Price, Darlene A. 326
Price, Madonna Hartman 90
Priestley, Hilda N. 414
Prim, Randy L. 383
Prince, Frances Anne 369
Prince, Paul D. 430
Prioleau-Green, Jivonne N. 494
Prioreschi, Brandon 5
Pritchard, David Alan 54
Pritts, Lindsay 329
Proo, Edna C. 507
Prucnal, Allison E. 362
Pruett, Tally 262
Puckett, Arnold A. 342
Puglia, Dublin M. 182
Puleo, Bryan 99
Pulver, Seymour 341
Puppel, Don Jr. 298
Putt, Geoffrey 260

Q

Quigley, Elizabeth 344
Quiles, Maria 504
Quintin, Lidia 33
Quitoriano, Josefina S. 48
Quitt, Tina M. 139

R

Rachal, Erma Lee 406
Rader, Larry D. 16
Radford, Jack 238
Rafferty, Jim 363
Raisch, Helen 445
Raiti, Ashly 246
Raley, Bonnie 396
Ramadass, Elizabeth 97
Ramer, Katina 447
Ramey, Peggy A. 139
Ramirez, Angelina 340
Ramirez, Courtney Anne 301
Ramirez, Laura 131
Ramirez, Valerie 108
Ramnauth, Kamaldai 404
Rampton, Kathleen 199
Ramsey, Dena L. 109
Ramsey, Kitty 117
Ramsey, Lesa Lynette 419
Rapisura, Susan 133
Rathert, Jamie 370
Ray, Paul 396
Ray, Tonya L. 483
Rayn, Sally 208
Ready, Margaret Ann 222
Reck, Kathy 100
Rector, Lord Laurence E. 316
Redwine, Faith S. 236
Reed, Dana 178
Reed, Maegann April 495
Reed, Margaret E. 60
Reed, Mimi 33
Reedy, Annabelle 66
Reedy, Ellen F. 458
Reese, Deirdre 354
Reeves, Mike 150
Reeves, Seabren Patrick 320
Rehmer, Heidi B. 210
Rehs, Pamela G. 322
Reid, Jeff 12

Reid, Mary J. 115
Reid, Sherrie 80
Reid, Zeailer 147
Reil, Jason 361
Reilly, M. Eileen 114
Reiter, Brad 420
Remishofsky, Marianne Bilicki 114
Reno, Ron 124
Renzoni, Melissa 60
Rescigno, Ralph P. III 484
Rettig, Dana 408
Revels, Kerrie 106
Reynolds, Amanda 457
Reynolds, Audrey 57
Reynolds, Chance 5
Reynolds, Christopher 89
Reynolds, Elizabeth Ashley 272
Reynolds, Frances 195
Reynolds, Jackie 359
Reynolds, Katie Jo 334
Reynolds, Lorena April 316
Reynoso, Loraine S. 122
Rhea, Kerri 178
Rhian, Jason E. 48
Rhinehart, Apryl 341
Rhoades, Jo 152
Rhodes, Christopher Lee 75
Rhodes, Frances Ruth 119
Rhodes, Jennifer Leigh 126
Ribeiro, Virginia Maria rebello 156
Ricci, Rose Ann 399
Rice, Amy 406
Rice, Billie L. 107
Rice, Mary Ellen 116
Rice, Paul Marsh 218
Richards, Marlene S. 28
Richardson, Amy 450
Richardson, Anne 375
Richardson, Carole E. 482
Richardson, Desserie 7
Richardson, Edwin Anthony 289
Richardson, Francis M. 506
Richardson, Sandra B. 194
Richardson, Wilma 208
Richert, Diane 96
Richmond, Amelia E. 46
Ricke, Kate 457
Riddle, Matthew 326
Rider, Shawn L. 440
Riedel, Donna M. 232
Riffenburg, Sarah 456
Rigatoni, Diz 333
Riley, Barbara 404
Riley, Brandy M. 472
Riley, Julie 286
Ringer, Shannon M. 164
Rininger, Jack E. 486
Rinkel, Char'i 404
Rinkel, Chari Lynn 260
Rinkel, Nelie 483
Rinkel, Nellie 360
Rintz, Gary 141
Riordan, Christina 14
Rios, Jacqueline L. 65
Rios, Michael A. 187
Rister, Becky 170
Ritchey, David 375
Rittmann, Teri 512
Rivas, Bambi 240
Rivera, Debra K. 198
Rivera, Linda 229
Rivera, Lisa 498
Rivera, Renee 154
Rivers-Fritch, Joyce 363
Roane, Shea Monique 441
Robb, Sara Kay 408
Robbins, Beulah P. 333
Robbins, George 83
Robbins, Leslie 325
Robert, Joanna 389
Roberts, Andrew B. 217
Roberts, Gayle 228
Roberts, Mike 38
Roberts, Penny E. 48
Roberts, Robyn M. 209
Roberts, Tobi 225
Roberts, William J. 411
Robertson, Heather 31
Robertson, Janet 467
Robichaud, Mary Louise 249
Robinett, Sean C. 420
Robinette, Diane 55
Robinson, Anne M. 182
Robinson, Carolyn 264
Robinson, Dionna 112
Robinson, Doris 350
Robinson, Fred W. 7
Robinson, Harriet Marie 276
Robinson, Kelly 310
Robinson, Matthew 263
Robinson, Nina S. 243
Robinson, Shawnta 289
Robinson, Stacey 460
Robison, Gretchen M. 444
Robledo, Dean 179
Rockefeller, Alfred G. 117
Rockefeller, Joseph 50
Rockwell, Donald Jr. 126
Rodgers, Margaret 35
Rodgers, Natalie 283
Rodriguez, Frank L. 161
Rodriguez, Oscar 214
Rodriguez, Sonya 73
Rodriguez, Trina 125
Roebuck, Sonnie Wade 124
Roehling, Paul 424
Rogers, Christopher P. 309
Rogers, Daniel 300
Rogers, Leonora V. 473
Rogers, Lois 236
Rogers, Pat 320
Rohrbach, Carolyn 352
Rolf, Audra K. 82
Rollin, Marty 77
Roman, Nicholas 115
Romano, Joseph 354
Romanowsky, Sarah 132
Romero, Belen 499
Rominger, Ryan Yung 55
Rondorf, Marolyn M. 303
Roop, Marjorie Helen 202
Root, Todd James 398
Rosario, Debra 36
Rosca, Irina 40
Rose, Adam Harry 331
Rose, Angela D. 11
Rose, Kenneth W. 471
Rose, Ruby P. 154
Rose, Steve 256
Rosenberg, Darryl 218
Rosenberg, Starla 500
Rosenfield, Richard U. 474
Rosenthal, Judy K. 67
Rosenthaler, Barbara 343
Roser, Amanda 332
Roskowinski, Erika 198
Roslund, Rachel Miriah 270
Ross, Courtney 504
Ross, Stan 342
Ross, Trevor H. 105
Rosselli, Jack 441
Rothfuss, Virginia 210
Rotola, Katherine 234
Rountree, Annie R. 365
Rourk, Margaret Ann 213
Rouse, Marcy 89
Rowan, Shawn M. 191
Rowe, Beverly 246
Rowe-Bultinck, Courtney 296
Rowlette, Gretchen G. 300
Roy, Lisa 335
Rubal, Autymn 381
Rudd, Karin 321
Rudela, Jelena 400
Rudloff, Mary F. 221
Rudyk, Arlene 41
Rueckert, Lyle 338
Ruff, Frances N. 336
Ruiter, Emma 21
Ruiz, Jason 264
Ruiz-Castaneda, Carmen 334
Rulla, Paul 49
Runchka, Linda 484
Runne, Sasha 311
Runner, Kimberly L. 244
Runyon Novak, Angela Faye 491
Rupert, Alisa D. 282
Ruppert, Barbara S. 228
Rush, Christina 433
Rusk, Donna 148
Russell, Nile H. 252
Russo, Linda Adele 279
Rutter, Danielle 315
Ryan, April 394
Ryan, Patrick 74
Ryan, Rose 177
Rychlik, Christopher 115
Rydeen, Matthew 175
Ryder, Michelle L. 78
Ryszewski, David R. 45

S

Saba, Elias 364
Sager, Kathleen 18
Salas, Richard G. 245
Salie, Kerin Celeste 294
Salinetro, Toni 411
Salmon, Karen 326
Salnave, Valerie 423
Salter, Carla J. 62
Salvatore, Rick 123
Samarrippas, Orlando 69
Samatowic, Amanda 195
Samms, L. 53
Samsel, C. 487
Samuelson, Candace 264
Samuelson, Honey L. 234
San Jose, Elizabeth 414
Sancaster, Julie 323
Sanchez, Angelina O. 403
Sanchez, Dialid 414
Sanchez, Monet 179
Sanchez, Ruby 426
Sanda, Mildred 308
Sandell, Maria 494
Sanders, Aimee 212
Sanders, Carolyn A. 192
Sanders, Sara A. 209
Sandford, Astelle Dona 502
Sanford, Teri 218
Santa, Isabel 160
Santo, Eleanor 458
Sapp, Dinah 176
Sapp, Lena 78
Saric, Sara 323
Sarinana, Joe H. Jr. 379
Sarkies, Joe 223
Satkofsky, Nicole 499
Sauve, Rebecca A. 117
Savage, Stephanie 12
Savala, Salvador 510
Sawden, Erin Elaine 79
Sawicki, Eric 380
Sawyer, Beverly H. 259
Saxton-Mariah, Jasmine 280
Scandrick, Mary 171
Scarchello, Dominick 101
Scarfone, Joseph M. 385
Scata, Bernice 508
Scelsi, Emmy 338
Schaefer, Forrest 236
Schaefer, Phillip 180
Schafer, Matthew 50
Schaffert, Margaret 55
Schaffner, Frank 287
Schalk, Wayne 102
Scheetz, Jessica 102
Scheffer, Mark S. 449
Schell, Travis Neil 283
Schermerhorn, Sarah J. 76
Scheuffele, Justin 208
Schmeling, Virginia 204
Schmidt, Al 347
Schmidt, Rosemary C. 417
Schmitz, Michelle 488
Schmoe, Martha 304
Schneider, Barbara Mantell 91
Schneider, E. M. 176
Schoene-Harshbarger, Rosemary 496
Schofield, D. Jayson 74
Scholes, Joyce Hope 211
Schooley, Jennifer N. 307
Schoonover, Tim 407
Schram, Betty L. 87
Schryer, Dianne 328
Schuette, Brian 449
Schultski, Edward L. 420
Schultz, Tina 327
Schurg, Kristene Elaine 171
Schuschke, Kali 6
Schuster, Denise M. 179
Schuster, Don 265
Schutz, Bobbie A. 260
Schuweiler, Andrea 200
Schwall, Terry 109
Schwarz, Sara 15
Schwemmer, Kyle 438
Schwiger, A. P. 263
Scibetta, Biagio 442
Sciotto, Jacqueline E. 384
Scire, Sarah 398
Scorzo, Katherine 256
Scott, Jessie A. 61

Scott, Mary 506
Scott, Richard 507
Scott, Susan G. 473
Scott, Tracie 496
Scrogin, Melissa 105
Scudder, Allen L. 40
Scurry, Thomas J. 510
Seaman, Sarah Kathleen 62
Search, John 326
Seasock, Keri 63
Seel, Selina M. 281
Seeley, Aimee M. 453
Segreti, Mary 213
Seiler, Micah 349
Seitz, Gene 488
Seligo, Viola Q. 240
Sell, Edward 18
Selleck, William Jr. 183
Semler, Donald Stanley 153
Sentz, Melanie 327
Serebrennik, Flora 428
Serr, Amy 82
Serwan, Thomas J. 343
Seymore, Heather 503
Shade, Brian K. 345
Shafer, Mary J. 390
Shah, Seema 109
Shamp, Jennifer 274
Shapiro, Beaumont 299
Shapiro, Ian 28
Sharik, Michael I 341
Sharman, Rebecca 206
Sharp, Heather L. 329
Sharp, Vicki 360
Sharpe, Michael 77
Shaw, Cory Rae 137
Shaw, Eloise King 229
Shaw, James E. 429
Shaw, Keith M. 329
Shaw, Odessa Jr. 145
Shears, Micah L. 54
Sheets, Jessica 408
Shell, Gail Lebowitz 239
Shenkle, Laura P. 354
Shenod, May Louise 462
Shepard, Melissa L. 249
Shepherdson, Stephanie M. 126
Sherlock, Lori Jean 207
Sherman, Hilarie 14
Sherrard, Ronda 156
Shields, Gerarda 511
Shields, John Clark 438
Shifflett, Debbie 243
Shober, Jill 451
Shockley, Jason Lee Mitchel 262
Shook, Yvonne 121
Short, Justin D. 436
Short, Kendra 339
Short, Lavinia M. 433
Shouse, Lora 268
Showerman, Diane 117
Shropshire, Pamela 350
Shultz, Gretchen L. 231
Shumpert, Edward 79
Shura, Julie 56
Sicilia, Vitaliano 277
Sickle, Marianne J. 306
Sicola, Anne 485
Siegel, Benjamin 456
Siegel, Marjorie S. 458
Siela, Tim 168

Siewiorek, Nora 391
Signore, Michael J. 18
Silano, Josephine 22
Silva, Marina 223
Silva, Patricia 379
Silverman, Dena 491
Simmons, Aaron 258
Simmons, Ann 467
Simms, Elsie 341
Simon, Jack W. 303
Simon, Lani Yvonne 50
Simons, Michael J. 317
Simons, Tyler L. 153
Simpson, Beverly A. 282
Simpson, Micki 127
Simpson, Tara 214
Sims, Jamie 341
Sims Verdin, Earline M. 216
Singarella, Sabrina A. 423
Singer, Cami 96
Sipho, Eileen R. 384
Six, Christine E. 249
Skinner, Vernetta M. 140
Skolnick, Phil 144
Slauson, Anthony 42
Smeltzer, Susan 253
Smidl, Elaine 197
Smith, Amy 68
Smith, Andrew H. 71
Smith, Brie 471
Smith, Carrie 302
Smith, Cheryl A. 60
Smith, Christina 442
Smith, D. Sank 165
Smith, Dannie 350
Smith, Gail 378
Smith, Jane Dreifus 57
Smith, Jenny 397
Smith, Jolieta Constantine 189
Smith, Josette A. 256
Smith, Karry L. 211
Smith, Kathy G. 219
Smith, Lee B. 93
Smith, Leigh 253
Smith, Paul E. 136
Smith, Raven 96
Smith, Ronald E. Jr. 123
Smith, Sandra G. 337
Smith, Sarah 149
Smith, Tiffany 68
Smith, Tommy J. 327
Smith, Veronica Elaine 117
Smithey, Carol 367
Smoak, Jerri L. 470
Smolenski, Eva 488
Smothers, Jerry 176
Snead, Kerri 283
Sneller, Jean 448
Snively, Elaine D. 342
Snodgrass, Amanda 327
Snow, Michael L. 36
Snyder, Daniel L. 275
Snyder, Doris 245
Snyder, Marian 266
Snyder, Marion B. 331
Sobieck-Lingg, Joanne 460
Socash, Carol A. 124
Soden, Amy Marie 284
Soderstrom, Elizabeth D. 391
Sorensen, Ruth 145
Sorrell, Angela 289

Sothen, Kathy 332
Soto, Jessica DeAnn 43
Soucy, Nicole P. 178
Southam, Pearl A. 67
Southerland, Vanda 343
Souza, Rebecca 362
Sowers, Anita G. 344
Spahn, James Michael 427
Spangher, Leonard 373
Sparks, Amber 107
Sparks, Howard 434
Sparks, Sammie 505
Sparrow, Aimee T. 279
Spaulding, Cheri Marie 412
Speiglman, Mollie 212
Speir, Andrea 401
Spellman, Jeanne 237
Spencer, Bill 42
Spinner, Ransom Hyde 172
Spinosi, Dotty 189
Splan, Beverly J. 450
Spoerl, Anne Ehlen 185
Sposato, Patty 340
Spotswood, Stephen K. 190
Spratlin, Billie L. 130
Springer, Kari 223
Sprouse, Patricia A. 20
Srivastava, Siddharth 101
St. Bernard-Marshall, Alethea 227
Stace, Brandon W. 287
Stacey 485
Stack, Kerry Anne 197
Stackhouse, Devynne 164
Staczewicz, Teresa Maria 3
Stanley, Donnie E. Jr. 15
Stanley, Hazel M. 444
Stanley, Isabel 64
Stansbury, Gerald 137
Stanton, Christopher 250
Stanzione, Dawn 301
Stapler, Sandra A. 335
Stapleton, S. 259
Stark, Michelle 431
Starks, LaRobin 325
Statler, Sarah 100
Steavenson, Kera 102
Stech, Audrey 153
Stecyk, Oleksander A. 209
Steed, Nanci Elise 302
Steele, Lindsey 127
Steele, Lisa 446
Steelman, Kathy 33
Stegenga, D. A. Lawn 261
Steger, Nicky 295
Stein, Michael 218
Steinbach, Gabriel 176
Steiner, Lance 154
Stenger, Alma G. 24
Stephens, Bradley A. 336
Stephens, Jan 390
Stephens, Sandy 238
Stephens, Tad G. 392
Stephenson, Mary 96
Sterner, Carl S. 413
Steuber, Jodi 294
Stevens, Amanda 100
Stevens, Bruce 281
Stevens, Caitlin Elin 147
Stevenson, Tammy 345
Stewart, Dwight 470
Stewart, Mattie M. 457

Stewart, Melvin 360
Stewart, Stephanie 430
Stiffler, Brylie 191
Stillwell, Diane Jeane 157
Stillwell, Katie Marie 182
Stipes, Jennifer 468
Stockbarger, Pearl 469
Stokes, Heather 254
Stokes, Jennifer L. 511
Stoltmann, Randy 226
Stoneburgh, Betty Ann 459
Stout, Rita A. 295
Stover, Summer 347
Stoyer, Adam 191
Strable, Mary K. 324
Strickland, Summer 405
Stringer, Amber 429
Strohm, Jaime D. 96
Strole, Karen 136
Strong, Kathryn 10
Strong, Mike II 222
Stroud, Sara 293
Struijk, Hendricus 75
Stubblefield, Kurtis Joe 379
Stucki, S. 106
Stukey, Karen R. 166
Stull, Carla 450
Stump, Jeanette B. 389
Sturtevant, Tenorzelle 400
Stylos, Pota L. 265
Sueiras, Maria R. 291
Suh, RaYoung 202
Suhr, Maureen 404
Suits, Shirley M. 168
Sullivan, Jessica 439
Summerall, Lilly 322
Summers, Dolores 310
Suttles, Jenny 400
Sutton, Cynthia 181
Swailes, Douglas 284
Swain, Sharon 110
Swallow, Amanda S. 76
Swanby, Megan Nicole 14
Swaney, Julie 37
Swanson, Richard H. 193
Swart, K. C. 216
Swatkowski, Ed III 44
Sweeney, Robert Terry 118
Sweigart, David A. 419
Swenson, Crystal 152
Swenson, Cynthia 468
Swerkstrom, Annie M. 208
Swiderski, Nikki 408
Swihart, Amin B. 419
Swiney, Samantha 269
Switzer, Lois Jean 229
Swope, Joseph B. Jr. 273
Swords, Gabriel 333
Syce, Joyce 410
Sylvester, Jo Cheryl 114
Szerlag, Lottie M. 307
Szilagyi, Claudia 150
Szukala, Shannon 96

T

T.C.'s Silent Heart 272
Taaffe, John J. Jr. 79
Tabbara, Deema 331
Tabor, John 325
Tack, Sonja R. 139

Taffee, Beverly J. 450
Taft, Sheila Carolyn 508
Takamatsu, Faye 117
Tamarkin, Pat 45
Tan, Earl E. 502
Tankersley, James D. 176
Tanksley, Sandra Lynn 377
Tanner, Jody 222
Tanya, Voitik 61
Tanzini, Robin 477
Tarango, Rachel 190
Targowski, Francis A. 301
Tarver, Shirley T. 64
Tarwacki, Heidi J. 43
Tat, Chau 285
Tauriello, Alfredo A. 471
Taylor, Amy Michelle 402
Taylor, Carolyn 45
Taylor, Geneva P. 445
Taylor, Mark 503
Taylor, Maxine 404
Taylor, Michael J. 325
Taylor, Michelle 201
Taylor, Patricia Ann 15
Taylor, Rebecca M. 304
Taylor, Shawn 507
Taylor, Thadd 400
Tedore, Mike 486
Tefft, Heather L. 120
Telfer, Lorraine 247
Templar, Jo Anne 239
Templet, Lonnette M. 80
Teoli, Melissa 26
Terry, Alyson 342
Terry, Michelle 487
Tetirick, Jennifer 116
Thacker, Crystal 463
Thacker, Lisa M. 329
Thames, Heidianne L. 395
Thatcher, Charles M. 280
Thomas, Don E. 78
Thomas, Dorshire 242
Thomas, Fannie 85
Thomas, Hannah 247
Thomas, Leigh 30
Thomas, Leon R. 5
Thomas, Nadine V. L. 339
Thomas, Pam 220
Thomas, S. L. 103
Thomas, Wayne 113
Thomason, Marie Lee 34
Thompson, April 214
Thompson, Chauniquewvah 400
Thompson, Eva 66
Thompson, Janice 281
Thompson, Jennifer 323
Thompson, John David 36
Thompson, Joseph 82
Thompson, K. DeLaine 385
Thompson, Misty M. 222
Thompson, T. J. 319
Thornburg, Shela 48
Thorndike, Timothy Paul 379
Thorning, Amber 493
Thrash, Tina 194
Threat, John E. III 363
Thue, James 30
Thurston, Barbara R. 338
Thut, Lois J. 342
Tillery, Algie 114
Tilley, John 173

Tilley, Ryan 24
Tillman, Deborah Lindsay 134
Tillotson, Martha S. 130
Tinch, Katie 504
Tindula, Jeanette 241
Tingle, Shannon 416
Tisher, Lloyd 25
Titchnell, Eileen M. 64
Toalston, Phil 416
Toavs, Bonny S. 135
Tolbert, Stephanie 208
Tommaso, Debby 319
Tommasulo, Anthony F. 267
Torzewski, Konrad 97
Tosca, Stephanie 447
Toth, Faustyn Sharee 452
Totten, Patricia A. 114
Touloumes, Lynn 173
Tracy, Beth 511
Tracy, Margie C. 62
Trammel, James 299
Tran, Tuan 324
Travis, Edward M. 159
Travis, Sheila 173
Traviss, Jason D. 418
Traw, Jessica 481
Treadway, Dolores A. 192
Treibley, Carolyn V. 81
Tremain, Marya 153
Tremblay, Matthew 482
Trina, Lloyd R. 387
Trinca, Steven 493
Troccia, Tara M. 232
Trotter, Betty B. 434
Truong, Tuyetmai 134
Truppo, Marilyn J. 464
Tucker, Beverly L. 363
Tucker, Carrie Denise 160
Tucker, Jeff Truett 330
Tuckey, Denver L. 108
Tugwell, Stephanie 252
Tunc, Murat 100
Tunison, Garett 211
Tunstall, Aaron 487
Turner, Clarence D. 203
Turner, Dawn M. 349
Turner, Stephanie Michelle 447
Turner, William R. II 457
Tuthill, Raymond 481
Tuttle, Rhonda J. 391
Tuzzeo, Jennifer 459
Twitchell, Ilene E. 322
Tyndall, Steven Glenn 469

U

Ufford, Dorothy Anne 389
Uhrich, Steven M. 418
Ulery, Myrna 111
Umhoefer, Leonard J. Jr. 97
Unger, Thomas W. 431
Unzueta, Leslie 357
Uyematsu, Cheryl A. 464

V

Vaccaro, Christina 134
Vago, Dave 178
Valdeabella, Hendrix 110
Valdez, Brittany R. 158
Valencia, Blanca Ines 58

Valeska, Dorothy 39
Vallejos, Canaan Lee 393
Valvo, Amy L. 399
Van Camp, Melba E. 41
Van Gundy, Valerie 339
Van Hoozer, Lowry 86
Van Houten, Ryan 261
Van Sise, Melanie 142
Van Vuuren, Andre 143
Van Wynen, K. G. 307
Vander Dussen, Brandy 360
Vander Velde, Katie 351
Vandergaag, Alexis L. F. 232
VanDyke, A. H. 212
Varga, Rose Marie 448
Varma, Priya 96
Varner, Earl 415
Vass, Leah L. 99
Vaughn, Darlene Gardner 232
Vaught, Margaret Peach 332
Vazquetelles, Gloriann 350
Ventura, Sandra 437
Vera, Joseph G. 56
Vernon, Misty 229
Vesovski, Marjorie 196
Vetter, Marrie 380
Vicidomini, Lauren N. 223
Victor, Joanna 480
Vieira, Cordelia 336
Vigna, Anna A. 367
Villa, Nicole Catherine 319
Villa, Vanessa 374
Villanueva, Rachel P. 6
Villella, Michael R. 298
Vince, Emily 444
Vincent, Jennifer Marie 260
Vines, Clara 245
Vinson, Jennifer 398
Vitale, Nicki M. 334
Vitucci, Dustin 132
Viveiros, Ray 3
Vogel, Cheryl 203
Vogel, Steven 123
Vogler, R. Michael 21
Vohra, Ashish 297
Voit, Lisa 75
Volk, Robert 460
Vollenboven, Jacqueline Marie 482
Votruba, Larry Jr. 118
Vukas, Daniel J. 165
Vyborny, Praxedes 83

W

Wachowiak, Christian 326
Wade, Angela C. 170
Wade, T. C. 407
Wagasky, Christina 507
Wagenknecht, Sara 180
Wagner, Jason 329
Wagner, Jollen 490
Wagner, Margaret Bunt 294
Wagner, Melanie 136
Wahi, Raj 9
Waibel, Jeff 491
Walag, Edward S. 131
Walbrecht, D. L. 328
Waldkirch, Brie 367
Walker, Donna M. 221
Walker, Ellen Nicholson 437
Walker, Mary C. 316

Wall, Diana 348
Wall, Martha 343
Wallace, Brian 351
Wallace, Caroline 328
Wallace, Dorothy A. 496
Wallenta, Eileen M. 233
Wallis, Grace Ellen 128
Walsh, Nita 284
Walston, Grace Daughtry 365
Walter, Brittany 98
Walter, William J. 267
Walters, Joyce Weber 431
Walters, Thomas M. 23
Waltke, Agnes 108
Waltman, Teresa 419
Walton, Francine Corley 440
Walton, James E. Jr. 307
Wambsganss, William F. 391
Wanamaker, Jennifer 309
Wang, Janet 54
Wantland, Jeff K. 416
Ward, Cara C. 323
Ward, Celeste 424
Ward, Cheryl 107
Ward, Cynthia 189
Ward, Elizabeth McCarthy 126
Ward, Eric 340
Ward, John L. 311
Ward, Paula 217
Ward, Terena 141
Ware, Shannon 435
Warren, Barbara B. 63
Warren, Briana Michelle 361
Warwick, Teresa 48
Washington, Angela 365
Washington, Denquia 17
Washington, Marcel 38
Waterhouse, Peter C. 182
Waterman, Sandra 383
Waters, Erin 73
Waters, Jeffrey S. 84
Waters, Kerrynn 337
Waters, Nancy A. 447
Waters, Samantha 456
Watkins, Curtis D. 302
Watkins, Natalie 268
Watkins, Rebekah Leah 201
Watler, Cynthia Moreno 506
Watson, Fawna 183
Watson, Matthew T. 122
Watson, Yasmeen 349
Watt, Malcolm R. 205
Watz, Barbara J. 117
Weatherby, Kristal 194
Webb, Kurtis R. 76
Webb, Marie H. 258
Webster, Brenda 397
Weeks, Shawn 13
Weems, Robert D. 470
Weferling, Oliver 509
Wegner, Carl E. 219
Wehrman, Rebecca 208
Weiser, Ami E. 216
Welch, Johnny 122
Wellons, Clara C. 485
Wells, Christopher 130
Wells, Douglas T. 198
Wells, Elvis D. 301
Wells, Kathleen 165
Wells, Nicole Marie 209
Wells, Tammy M. 179

Wells, Tim 274
Wells, Uldean T. 19
Wendling, Rich 177
Wenger, Jerry 91
Werkau, Evelyn R. 391
Werner, Sarah E. 149
Wessel, Patricia A. 361
West, Edward 407
West, Joshua J. 19
West, Paula Foster 128
West-Williams, Veronica 442
Westin, Emma Lynn 21
Westover, Toni 413
Westrup, April A. 62
Wethey, Ashley 463
Wetterer, Annie 439
Wheeler, Richard 364
Whelan, Ann 480
Whetzel, Jeanne B. 343
Whitaker, Seprenia 32
White, Carlye 490
White, Cheri 344
White, Cynthia 99
White, David 184
White, Elaine 420
White, Joyce M. 167
White, Mary 339
White, Maryann 30
White, Ronda Louise 269
White, Sonya Jill 347
Whitefeather, Matissa 403
Whitehead, Robert Jr. 124
Whitehouse, Jen 463
Whiteside, Matthew 417
Whitley, Tammy S. 203
Whitten, Jennifer 379
Whitten, Ryan 168
Whittenburg, Elizabeth Penn 389
Wick, Jessica 406
Wickre, Jon 360
Widener, Kelly 15
Wiebeck, Eva M. 472
Wieczorek, Jessica 62
Wiedeman, Cheryl 376
Wiener, Florence K. 402
Wieschowski, Anna 339
Wietrzykowski, Kerry 102
Wightman, Mary-Alice 6
Wigington, John H. III 435
Wilcher, Carole Ann 202
Wilcox, Frank P. Jr. 355
Wilcox, Roberta M. 267
Wildes, Deborah L. 224
Wileman, Elaine 412
Wilkerson, Richard 16
Wilkins, Julia 101
Wilkinson, Terry L. 217
Willaman, Darryl G. 411
Williams, A. Neville 464
Williams, Andrea 247
Williams, Annette J. 375
Williams, Beatrice 55
Williams, Bentley N. Jr. 104
Williams, Brian 475
Williams, Bryan M. I 110
Williams, Carl 45
Williams, Carolyn 457
Williams, Clara 291
Williams, Debbie 287
Williams, Edna M. 116
Williams, Jennifer 274

Williams, Johnnie S. 138
Williams, Joseph Ralph 42
Williams, Katherine 372
Williams, Lori 227
Williams, Lorraine 94
Williams, Lynda 255
Williams, Melissa 477
Williams, Melvin C. 268
Williams, Pat 222
Williams, Ruth 195
Williams, Shelly F. 211
Williams, Stephanie H. 219
Williamson, Bobbie 498
Williamson, Jessica N. 354
Willingham, Jane B. 406
Willms, Donna 288
Willoughby, Christy 474
Wills, Alice 450
Willsie, Linley J. 355
Wilson, Bruce 254
Wilson, Candy 278
Wilson, Carlos 425
Wilson, Hazel 37
Wilson, John 100
Wilson, Johnny T. 149
Wilson, Lois 261
Wilson, Michael Leo 390
Wilson, Patricia 81
Wilson, Perry James 461
Wilson, Rebecca 158
Wilson, Sharon Y. 395
Wilson, Shirley 390
Wilson, Tiffany Marie 103
Wilson, Virginia 378
Windsor, Linda L. 262
Wing, Dawn 88
Winrow, Patricia D. 503
Winsor, Susan C. 459
Winters, Mona 366
Winters, Tommy P. 273
Wise, Sabrina 332
Wise, Pamela S. 33
Wise, Rhonda 241
Witherspoon, Gertie 52
Witt, Gilbert 412
Wolf, John E. 171
Wolf, Micke 461
Wolterman, Tami Lynne 432
Wong, Kristen 260
Wood, Aimee Rose 335
Wood, Jeff 416
Wood, Lindsay A. 438
Wood, Mardell 73
Wood, Roberta A. 373
Wood, Wilma L. 24
Woodcock, Linda 294
Woodruff, Mindy 137
Woolfrom, Tara 98
Woolley, Katharine 461
Wooten, Martha D. 287
Wootten, Patricia E. 27
Workman, Flora M. 33
Worrell, Annie Laura 135
Worthington, Dean 422
Wortman, Michael D. 212
Wrede, Sarah 429
Wrenn, Virginia W. 337
Wright, Dennis 333
Wright, Jeanette 293
Wright, June 116
Wright, Margaret S. 119

Wright, Nicole 112
Wright, Paul K. 4
Wright, Phyllis 76
Wright-Baswell, Lena 339
Wrye, Shannon Hale 379
Wyant, Stacy 390
Wynder, Jennifer N. 210
Wynter, Andrea 218
Wysocki, Susan M. 402
Wyzkiewicz, Judith V. 473

X

Xeloures, Chandra 33

Y

Yadon, Chris M. 26
Yakawiak, A. 273
Yancey, Pamela Faye 381
Yang, Eunice 217
Yang, Xin 393
Yantiss, Alvin C. 159
Yarborough, Pamela 212
Yarger, Robin 213
Yates, Claud D. 108
Yates, Rhonda 144
Yazar, Arzu 18
Yeager, Edith Astrid 480
Yelek, Cheryl 31
Yelton, Amy Michelle 277
Yelton, J. L. 160
Yen, Irene 222
Yocus, Tillie L. 22
Young, Edward 248
Young, John S. 141
Young, Laura 210
Younger, Harold 229
Yourish, C. 224
Yowell, Curt 478

Z

Zakusylo, Susan 399
Zambonis, Helena R. 208
Zatarski, Catherine 244
Zawol, Chad 70
Zeiderman, Marla 160
Zenkus, Jody 390
Ziegenfuss, Brynn 286
Ziegler, Amy 384
Zilko, Mary Ann 282
Zimmer, Ilene 228
Zink, Rebecca 309
Zollchian, Maytal 210
Zuber, Margaret R. 342
Zuniga, Sara 344